Microsoft®
Access 2000 Bible, Gold Edition

Microsoft®
Access 2000 Bible,
Gold Edition

**Cary N. Prague and Michael R. Irwin
with Jennifer Reardon**

IDG Books Worldwide, Inc.
An International Data Group Company

Foster City, CA ✦ Chicago, IL ✦ Indianapolis, IN ✦ New York, NY

Microsoft® Access 2000 Bible, Gold Edition

Published by

IDG Books Worldwide, Inc.

An International Data Group Company

919 E. Hillsdale Blvd., Suite 400

Foster City, CA 94404

www.idgbooks.com (IDG Books Worldwide Web site)

Copyright © 1999 IDG Books Worldwide, Inc. All rights reserved. No part of this book, including interior design, cover design, and icons, may be reproduced or transmitted in any form, by any means (electronic, photocopying, recording, or otherwise) without the prior written permission of the publisher.

ISBN: 0-7645-3404-1

Printed in the United States of America

10 9 8 7 6 5 4 3 2 1

1B/RZ/QY/ZZ/FC

Distributed in the United States by IDG Books Worldwide, Inc.

Distributed by CDG Books Canada Inc. for Canada; by Transworld Publishers Limited in the United Kingdom; by IDG Norge Books for Norway; by IDG Sweden Books for Sweden; by IDG Books Australia Publishing Corporation Pty. Ltd. for Australia and New Zealand; by TransQuest Publishers Pte Ltd. for Singapore, Malaysia, Thailand, Indonesia, and Hong Kong; by Gotop Information Inc. for Taiwan; by ICG Muse, Inc. for Japan; by Norma Comunicaciones S.A. for Colombia; by Intersoft for South Africa; by Eyrolles for France; by International Thomson Publishing for Germany, Austria and Switzerland; by Distribuidora Cuspide for Argentina; by LR International for Brazil; by Galileo Libros for Chile; by Ediciones ZETA S.C.R. Ltda. for Peru; by WS Computer Publishing Corporation, Inc., for the Philippines; by Contemporanea de Ediciones for Venezuela; by Express Computer Distributors for the Caribbean and West Indies; by Micronesia Media Distributor, Inc. for Micronesia; by Grupo Editorial Norma S.A. for Guatemala; by Chips Computadoras S.A. de C.V. for Mexico; by Editorial Norma de Panama S.A. for Panama; by American Bookshops for Finland. Authorized Sales Agent: Anthony Rudkin Associates for the Middle East and North Africa.

For general information on IDG Books Worldwide's books in the U.S., please call our Consumer Customer Service department at 800-762-2974. For reseller information, including discounts and premium sales, please call our Reseller Customer Service department at 800-434-3422.

For information on where to purchase IDG Books Worldwide's books outside the U.S., please contact our International Sales department at 317-596-5530 or fax 317-596-5692.

For consumer information on foreign language translations, please contact our Customer Service department at 800-434-3422, fax 317-596-5692, or e-mail rights@idgbooks.com.

For information on licensing foreign or domestic rights, please phone +1-650-655-3109.

For sales inquiries and special prices for bulk quantities, please contact our Sales department at 650-655-3200 or write to the address above.

For information on using IDG Books Worldwide's books in the classroom or for ordering examination copies, please contact our Educational Sales department at 800-434-2086 or fax 317-596-5499.

For press review copies, author interviews, or other publicity information, please contact our Public Relations department at 650-655-3000 or fax 650-655-3299.

For authorization to photocopy items for corporate, personal, or educational use, please contact Copyright Clearance Center, 222 Rosewood Drive, Danvers, MA 01923, or fax 978-750-4470.

Library of Congress Cataloging-in-Publication Data

Prague, Cary N.
  Microsoft Access 2000 Bible / Cary N. Prague and Michael R. irwin, with Jennifer Reardon. – Gold ed.
    p. cm.
  ISBN 0-7645-3404-1 (alk. paper)
  1. Microsoft Access. 2. Database management. I. Irwin, Michael R. II. Reardon, Jennifer. III. Title. IV. Title: Microsoft Access two thousand Bible
QA76.9.D3P7268 1999
005.75'65–dc21   98-38068
                                                        CIP

ABOUT IDG BOOKS WORLDWIDE

Welcome to the world of IDG Books Worldwide.

IDG Books Worldwide, Inc., is a subsidiary of International Data Group, the world's largest publisher of computer-related information and the leading global provider of information services on information technology. IDG was founded more than 30 years ago by Patrick J. McGovern and now employs more than 9,000 people worldwide. IDG publishes more than 290 computer publications in over 75 countries. More than 90 million people read one or more IDG publications each month.

Launched in 1990, IDG Books Worldwide is today the #1 publisher of best-selling computer books in the United States. We are proud to have received eight awards from the Computer Press Association in recognition of editorial excellence and three from Computer Currents' First Annual Readers' Choice Awards. Our best-selling ...For Dummies® series has more than 50 million copies in print with translations in 31 languages. IDG Books Worldwide, through a joint venture with IDG's Hi-Tech Beijing, became the first U.S. publisher to publish a computer book in the People's Republic of China. In record time, IDG Books Worldwide has become the first choice for millions of readers around the world who want to learn how to better manage their businesses.

Our mission is simple: Every one of our books is designed to bring extra value and skill-building instructions to the reader. Our books are written by experts who understand and care about our readers. The knowledge base of our editorial staff comes from years of experience in publishing, education, and journalism — experience we use to produce books to carry us into the new millennium. In short, we care about books, so we attract the best people. We devote special attention to details such as audience, interior design, use of icons, and illustrations. And because we use an efficient process of authoring, editing, and desktop publishing our books electronically, we can spend more time ensuring superior content and less time on the technicalities of making books.

You can count on our commitment to deliver high-quality books at competitive prices on topics you want to read about. At IDG Books Worldwide, we continue in the IDG tradition of delivering quality for more than 30 years. You'll find no better book on a subject than one from IDG Books Worldwide.

John Kilcullen
Chairman and CEO
IDG Books Worldwide, Inc.

Steven Berkowitz
President and Publisher
IDG Books Worldwide, Inc.

Eighth Annual Computer Press Awards ≥1992

Ninth Annual Computer Press Awards ≥1993

Tenth Annual Computer Press Awards ≥1994

Eleventh Annual Computer Press Awards ≥1995

Credits

Acquisitions Editor
Andy Cummings

Development Editors
Janet Andrews
Sara Salzmann

Technical Editor
Dennis R. Cohen

Copy Editors
Marti Paul
Ami Knox

Production
IDG Books Worldwide Production

Proofreading and Indexing
York Production Services

Cover Design
Murder By Design

About the Authors

Cary N. Prague is an internationally known best-selling author and lecturer in the database industry. He is the president of Database Creations, Inc., the world's largest Microsoft Access add-on company. This direct-mail company creates and markets add-on software, books, and video training for personal computer databases.

Under Cary's leadership, Database Creations has developed and marketed many add-on software products for Microsoft Access, including Yes! I Can Run My Business, a business sales and accounting program and winner of the 1998 Access Advisor Magazine Readers Choice award for best accounting application; Check Writer financial software, winner of the Microsoft Network award for best Access Application; the EZ Access line of developer products; the Access Business Forms Library distributed by Microsoft with Access 2.0 upgrades; TabMaster Pro Wizard; User Interface Construction Kit, winner of the 1996 Access Advisor Readers Choice award; the Calendar Construction Kit; the Picture Builder Add-On Picture Pack; and the Command Bar Image Editor and Image Pack. Their Web site address is www.databasecreations.com.

Cary also manages a successful consulting company, a Microsoft Certified Solution Provider specializing in Microsoft Access applications. His local and national clients include many Fortune 500 software companies, manufacturers, defense contractors, and insurance industry companies. His client list includes Microsoft, Borland International, ABB-Combustion Engineering, Smith & Wesson Firearms, Office Max, Continental Airlines, Pratt and Whitney Aircraft, Otis Elevator, State of Connecticut, United Healthcare, Travelers Insurance, Omar Coffee, Rockwell International, and SNET telephone company.

Formerly Cary held numerous management positions in corporate information systems, including Director of Managed Care Reporting for MetraHealth, Director of Software Productivity at Travelers Insurance where he was responsible for software support and training for 35,000 end users, Director in Corporate Finance where he was responsible for the selection and installation of Fixed Asset and Payroll Systems and Manager of Information Centers for Northeast Utilities.

He is one of the best-selling authors in the computer database management market (with sales of nearly one million), having written over thirty-five books on software, including Microsoft Access, Borland's dBASE IV, Paradox, R:Base, and Framework. Cary's books include *PC World's Microsoft Access Bible*, recently number 1 on the Ingram Best-Selling Database Titles list and on several top national best-seller lists, including amazon.com; *Access 95 Secrets*; *dBASE for Windows Handbook*; *dBASE IV Programming*, winner of the Computer Press Association's Book of the Year award for Best Software Specific Book; and *Everyman's Database Primer Featuring dBASE IV*. He is currently writing several new Access 2000 books.

Cary is certified in Access as a Microsoft Certified Professional and has passed the MOUS test in end-user subjects in Access and Word. He is a frequent speaker at seminars and conferences around the country, and he has been voted the best speaker by the attendees of several national conferences. Recently he was a speaker for Microsoft sponsored conferences in Hawaii, Phoenix, Chicago, Toronto, Palm Springs, Boston, and Orlando. He has also spoken at Borland's Database Conference, Digital Consulting's Database World, Microsoft's Developer Days, Computerland's Technomics Conference, COMDEX, and COMPAQ Computer's Innovate. He was a contributing editor to *Access Advisor* magazine and continues to write for them.

Cary holds a master's degree in computer science from Rensselaer Polytechnic Institute, and an M.B.A and Bachelor of Accounting from the University of Connecticut. He is also a Certified Data Processor.

Michael R. Irwin is considered one of the leading authorities on automated database and Internet management systems. He is a noted worldwide lecturer, a winner of national and international awards, best-selling author, and developer of client/server, Internet, Intranet, and PC-based database management systems. His expertise includes database processing in and between mainframe, minicomputer, and PC-based database systems; he is a leading authority on PC-based databases.

Michael has extensive database knowledge gained by working with the Metropolitan Police Department in Washington, D.C. as a developer and analyst for the Information Systems Division for over 20 years. Since retiring in June 1992, he runs his own consulting firm, named Database Integrators, specializing in Internet database integration and emphasizing client/server and net solutions. With consulting offices in Cincinnati, Ohio and Manila, Philippines, his company does training and development of Internet and database applications. His local, national, and international clients include many software companies, manufacturers, government agencies, and international companies.

He has authored numerous database books, with several of them consistently on the best-sellers lists. His most recent works include *The OOPs Primer* (Borland Press), *dBASE 5.5 for Windows Programming* (Prentice Hall), *The Access Bible 97*, and *Working with the Internet*. He has also written a book on the customs and cultures of Asia (to be released in 1999). Two of his books have won international acclaim. His books are published in over 24 languages worldwide.

Michael has developed and markets several add-on software products for the Internet and productivity-related applications. Many of his productivity applications can be obtained from several of his Internet sites or on many common download sites. His productivity tools include The Universal Calendar and Scheduling program, the Telephone Contact System, Password Keeper, and several others. All of these systems are distributed as freeware and careware. He has also developed and distributes several development tools and add-ins for a wide range of developer applications.

Jennifer Reardon is considered a leading developer of custom database applications. She has over ten years' experience developing client/server and PC-based applications. She has accumulated much of her application development experience working as lead developer for Database Creations. She has partnered with Cary Prague developing applications for many Fortune 500 companies.

Her most significant projects include a spare parts inventory control system for Pratt & Whitney's F22 program, an engineering specifications system for ABB-Combustion Engineering, and an emergency event tracking system for the State of Connecticut. She was also the lead developer of many of the Database Creations add-on software products including Yes! I Can Run My Business, Check Writer, and the User Interface Construction Kit.

Ms. Reardon owns her own consulting firm, Advanced Software Concepts, providing custom applications to both the public and private sectors. She specializes in developing client information systems for state-managed and privately-held healthcare organizations. She has also developed a job costing and project management system for an international construction company. Her corporate experience includes seven years with The Travelers where she was an Associate Software Engineer serving on numerous mission-critical client/server software development projects using Easel, C, SQL Server, and DB2.

Jennifer has contributed several chapters for books on dBase and Microsoft Access. Her contributions to this book include the chapters on Data Access Pages, the Microsoft Database Engine, the VBA programming environment, creating help systems, and using Microsoft Office 2000 Developer. She has also authored chapters in *Microsoft Access 97 Bible* and *Access 97 Secrets,* published by IDG Books.

Jennifer holds a Bachelor of Science degree from the University of Massachusetts.

This book is dedicated to my golfing and racing buddy, Vic Plagge. Thanks for getting our tee times each week and forcing me to get away from work. Thanks for introducing me to NASCAR racing where I have been having so much fun. It's been a blast collecting Mark Martin memorabilia, sponsoring the #82 car of Mike Christopher at Stafford Motor Speedway, and going to all the Winston Cup races around the country. Viva Las Vegas!

CNP

This book is dedicated to several people that have helped me over the past year. First Darrell Woolley, partner of the Bourbon Street restaurant and hotel (Bangkok, Thailand) for his friendship. He has just found Access (Version 97) and has already built several applications — this from a bean counter! Peter J. Roberts, owner of the Pan Pacific Koi Farms in Thailand, who has become as close a friend as a person can become — I am honored to have you as a friend. F. Michael Kist, my oldest friend, who is always there when I need to talk. Attorney Delfin Gonzalez, a neighbor in Manila, Philippines for his friendship and guidance. Finally, Don Ross, fellow world traveler, who has offered his friendship without reservation.

MRI

This book is dedicated to my husband, Jeff, who always encourages me to grasp every opportunity, and to my mother for her 70th birthday, who taught me at an early age the importance of good reading ad writing skills.

JR

Preface

Welcome to the *Microsoft Access 2000 Bible, Gold Edition* — your personal guide to a powerful, easy-to-use database management system.

This book examines Microsoft Access 2000 with more examples than any other Access book ever written. We think that Microsoft Access is an excellent database manager and the best Windows database on the market today. Our goal with this book is to share what we know about Access and, in the process, to help make your work and your life easier.

This book contains everything you need in order to learn Microsoft Access to a basic advanced level. You'll find that the book starts off with the fundamentals and builds, chapter by chapter, on topics previously covered. In places where it is essential that you understand previously covered topics, we present the concepts again and review how to perform specific tasks before moving on. Although each chapter is an integral part of the book as a whole, each chapter can also stand on its own. You can read the book in any order you want, skipping from chapter to chapter and from topic to topic. (Note that this book's index is particularly thorough; you can refer to the index to find the location of the specific topic you're interested in.)

The examples in this book have been well thought out to simulate the types of tables, queries, forms, and reports most people need to create when performing common business activities. There are many notes, tips, and techniques (and even a few secrets) to help you better understand the product.

This book can easily substitute for the manuals included with Access. In fact, many users do not get manuals today, often relying on just the online help. This book will guide you through each task you might want to do in Access. We even created appendixes to be used as reference manuals for common Access specifications. This book follows a much more structured approach than the Microsoft Access manuals — going into more depth on almost every topic and showing many different types of examples.

Is This Book for You?

We wrote this book for beginning, intermediate, and even advanced users of Microsoft Access 2000. With any product, most users start at the beginning. If, however, you've already read through the Microsoft Access manuals and worked with the Northwinds sample files, you may want to start with the later parts of this book. Note, however, that starting at the beginning of a book is usually a good idea so you don't miss out on the secrets and tips in the early chapters.

We think this book covers Microsoft Access in detail better than any other book currently on the market. We hope you will find this book helpful while working with Access, and that you enjoy the innovative style of an IDG book.

Yes — If you have no database experience

If you're new to the world of database management, this book has everything you need to get started with Microsoft Access. It then offers advanced topics for reference and learning.

Yes — If you've used other database managers like dBASE or Paradox

If you're abandoning another database (such as dBASE, Paradox, Approach, R:Base, or Alpha Four) or even upgrading from Access 2.0 or Access 95 or 97, this book is for you. You'll have a head start because you're already familiar with database managers and how to use them. With Microsoft Access, you will be able to do all the tasks you've always performed with character-based databases — without programming or getting lost. This book will take you through each subject step by step.

Yes — If you want to learn the basics of Visual Basic Applications Edition (VBA) programming

VBA has replaced the Access Basic language. We know that an entire book is needed to properly cover VBA, but we took the time to put together several introductory chapters that build on what you learn in the macros chapters of this book. The VBA programming chapters use the same examples you will be familiar with by the end of the book.

How This Book Is Organized

This book contains 42 chapters divided into six main parts. In addition, the book contains five appendixes.

Part I: First Things First

Part I consists of the first five chapters of the book. In Chapter 1, you receive background information on Microsoft Access and an overview of its features. Chapter 2 covers installation — what you need in terms of hardware and software, as well as how to get Access running properly. You also learn how to start and stop Access, plus several techniques for moving between Access and other applications. Chapter 3 provides an explanation of database concepts for new users of a database product. Chapter 4 is a hands-on test drive of Access, provided to give you a quick look at some of its features. Chapter 5 is a case study of the up-front design that is necessary to properly implement a database system; otherwise, you must go through many false starts and redesigns when creating an application. You will design on paper the tables, forms, queries, reports, and menus necessary for creating the application.

Part II: Basic Database Usage

The next six chapters make up Part II. You learn how to create a database table in Chapter 6, and you also examine how to change a database table, including moving and renaming fields without losing data. You also learn about the new internet data types in Access 2000. In Chapter 7, you learn how to enter, display, change, and delete data. Chapter 8 teaches the basics of creating data-entry forms and using Wizards to simplify the creation process; using data-entry forms is also discussed. In Chapter 9, you examine the concept of queries; then you create several queries to examine how data can be rearranged and displayed. Chapter 10 covers the basics of report creation and printing. In Chapter 11, you create the many tables used in the case study, and then learn how to relate multiple tables.

Part III: Using Access in Your Work

Part III contains 11 chapters that go into more depth on creating and using forms, queries, and reports. In Chapter 12, you take a look at how to create the expressions and built-in functions that are so important in forms and reports. In Chapter 13, you learn how to create relations and joins in queries. Chapter 14 discusses basic selection queries, using many examples and pictures. In Chapter 15, you examine the concepts of controls and properties, and then learn how to manipulate controls in a form. Chapter 16 examines in detail how to create and use data-entry forms. Chapter 17 covers how to use visual effects to create great-looking forms and reports that catch the eye and increase productivity. In Chapter 18, you learn how to add complex data validation to tables and data-entry forms. Chapter 19 explains the use of pictures, graphs, sound, video, and other OLE objects. Chapters 20–22 cover reports — from simple controls to complex calculations, summaries, printing, and desktop publishing.

Part IV: Advanced Database Features

This part contains six chapters that present advanced topics on each of the basic tasks of Access. Chapter 23 examines how to import, export, and attach external files, and how to copy Access objects to other Access databases. Chapter 24 discusses advanced select query topics, including total, cross-tabulation, top-value, and union queries. Chapter 25 covers action queries, which change data rather than simply displaying records. Chapter 26 is a compendium of advanced query topics that will leave you amazed at the power of Access. Creating forms and subforms from multiple tables is the subject of Chapter 27; this chapter examines how to create the one-to-many relationships found in many database systems. Part IV ends with Chapter 28, which offers a look at additional types of reports not previously covered, including mail-merge reports and mailing labels.

Part V: Applications in Access

This part looks at Access as an application environment. Chapter 29 covers the concept of event-driven software and how Access uses macros to automate manual processes. This chapter also examines what a macro is, how macros are created, and how to debug them. Chapter 30 explains data manipulation, including posting totals and filling in data-entry fields. In Chapter 31, you learn how to create button menus known as switchboards, as well as traditional pull-down menus, custom toolbars, and dialog boxes using the new Access 2000 tab control. In Access 2000, you will also learn about the new command bars used to build menus and toolbars. Chapter 32 covers the new Data Access Pages used for creating live data links to intranet web pages and the other incredible Web capabilities of Access 2000. In chapter 33, you will learn about client/server topics including installing, starting, connecting to, and building Access Data Projects using the new Microsoft Database Engine. This is a personal edition of SQL Server 7.0. Chapter 34 is an introduction to modules using VBA, which teaches you how to create a basic module and debug a program. Chapter 35 builds on the discussion of modules, teaching you logical constructs, error processing, DAO, the newer ADO, and recordset processing.

Part VI: Advanced Access Topics

This final part presents seven distinct, seldom-covered topics that teach advanced use of Microsoft Access. Chapter 36 offers important tips and techniques for making Access faster and gives you proper workarounds for some of the software's perceived limitations (there are none). Chapter 37 delves into permissions, creating workgroups, and how to extend the Access security model to tables and even lock out people from seeing or changing any design screens or VBA code. Chapter 38 shows you how to program the cute (or annoying) Office Assistant and how to add real help systems to Access applications. Chapter 39 introduces the Office Developers Edition, which creates standalone applications using the Access runtime and great installations using the Access Setup Wizard. In Chapter 40, we explain how to integrate Access data with other Office applications, including Word and Excel. The most difficult components of replication are discussed in Chapter 41, while creating add-ins and wizards and using external libraries end the book in Chapter 42.

Appendixes and Reference Material

This book contains five appendixes. Appendix A presents a series of tables listing Access specifications, including maximum and minimum sizes of many of the program's controls. Appendix B displays a database diagram of the many database tables used in this book so you can create your own system. Appendix C describes the CD-ROM. Appendixes D and E are a complete cross-reference to all of the examples used in the book, listed by both object (table, query, form, etc.) and chapter.

Conventions Used in This Book

The following conventions are used in this book:

+ When you are instructed to press a *key combination* (press and hold down one key while pressing another), the key combination is separated by a plus sign. Ctrl+Esc, for example, indicates that you must hold down the Ctrl key and press the Esc key; then release both keys.

+ *Point the mouse* refers to moving the mouse so that the mouse pointer is on a specific item. *Click* refers to pressing the left mouse button once and releasing it. *Double-click* refers to pressing the left mouse button twice in rapid succession and then releasing it. *Right-click* refers to pressing the right mouse button once and releasing it. *Drag* refers to pressing and holding down the left mouse button while moving the mouse.

+ When you are instructed to *select* a menu, you can use the keyboard or the mouse. To use the keyboard, press and hold down the Alt key (to activate the menu bar) and then press the underlined letter of the menu name; press Alt+E to select the Edit menu, for example. Or you can use the mouse to click the word Edit on-screen. Then, from the menu that drops down, you can press the underlined letter of the command you want (or click the command name) to select it.

+ When you are instructed to select a command from a menu, you will often see the menu and command separated by an arrow symbol. Edit ⇨ Paste, for example, indicates that you need to select the Edit menu and then choose the Paste command from the menu.

+ *Italic* type is used for new terms and for emphasis.

+ **Bold** type is used for material you need to type directly into the computer.

+ A special typeface is used for information you see on-screen — error messages, expressions, and formulas, for example.

Icons and Alerts

You'll notice special graphic symbols, or *icons*, used in the margins throughout this book. These icons are intended to alert you to points that are particularly important or noteworthy. The following icons are used in this book:

Note This icon highlights a special point of interest about the topic under discussion.

Tip This icon points to a useful hint that may save you time or trouble.

Caution This icon alerts you that the operation being described can cause problems if you're not careful.

Cross-Reference This icon points to a more complete discussion in another chapter of the book.

On the CD-ROM This icon highlights information for readers who are following the examples and using the sample files included on the disk accompanying this book.

New Feature This icon calls attention to new features of Access 2000.

Sidebars

In addition to noticing the icons used throughout this book, you will also notice material placed in shaded boxes. This material offers background information, an expanded discussion, or a deeper insight about the topic under discussion. Some sidebars offer nuts-and-bolts technical explanations, and others provide useful anecdotal material.

Acknowledgments

When we first saw Access in July 1992, we were instantly sold on this new-generation database management and access tool. We've both spent the last six years using Access daily. In fact, we eat, breathe, live, and sleep Access!

Now we've rewritten this book to incorporate all the incredible new features in Access 2000. We cover every new function, and we've added a programming and Internet section. Over 250,000 copies of our Access Bibles have been sold for all versions of Microsoft Access; for this we thank all of our loyal readers.

We've also written countless systems, designed and brought to market many add-on products for Access, and created the largest Access add-on software company in the world. We've served nearly 100,000 customers, our staff has answered thousands of technical-support questions, and we've received critical acclaim from readers and reviewers alike. Our first acknowledgment is to all the users of Access who have profited and benefited beyond everyone's wildest dreams.

Many people assisted us in writing this book. We'd like to recognize each of them.

To Diana Reid, who wrote the original introductory chapters (2, 3, and 5) and was the technical editor for the last four versions of this book, we offer a special thank you. Thanks also to Mary Lynn Maurice for her assistance in writing Chapters 4 and 6 so very long ago. Thanks to Jennifer Reardon, for working on many of the chapters. She wrote or updated Chapters 32, 33, 34, 35, 38, and 39. She is one of the best Access developers we know, and she is loved by all of our Fortune 500 clients. Thanks to Amy Johnson, now at Price Waterhouse, for her updating of Chapters 1-20, when I couldn't start the book as early as IDG needed me to. You took over 500 screen shots and I only had to redo three. You are the best. To John S. Dranchak, for designing the reports in Chapters 21 and 23 and creating the logo for Mountain Animal Hospital.

To the people who really made this gold edition possible. To IDG Books Worldwide's Andy Cummings, who conceived this idea one day while harassing me about my Access 2000 book. Andy challenges me every day with some impossible task ("I don't care if the power is out and the software doesn't work yet — write the book anyway! Use your imagination!"). I'll bet his great-great-great-grandfather walked into a blacksmith's shop in 1850 and asked the owner to build a jet aircraft! To James Foxall, my favorite work-in-progress. James is a young Bill Gates (or Warren Buffet living in Omaha) who I corralled at COMDEX one fall; he's responsible for Chapters 36, 37, 38, 39, and 40. He had never written one word of a book in 1995, and now has five to his name, including some of the best Visual Basic books on the market, the second-best Access business product ever written, and several silent works (we call 'em ghosts!). To Bill Amo, for writing Chapters 41 and 42. He's now in the Transact-SQL world (what is that, anyway?).

To the people of Database Creations, where I hang my hat every day (actually, I don't wear one). To Diana Reid, for running my business when I'm not there and when I am there. To Larry Kasevich, who helped me buy that IBM PC back in 1983 instead of that Apple thing. (He now runs our development company and creates the EZ Access line of products.) To Phuc Phan, our technical-support specialist and one of my favorite people in the world. Phuc helped take many of the screen shots you see in this book; without him, this book would not have been produced on time. To Amy Johnson, who works on all my special projects. To Ryan Novak, developer extraordinaire, for solving my two-hour fights with Access in two minutes. To Julie (snydercow) Frattarolli, who secretly makes the company work each day without letting anyone know how she does it. To Debbie Schindler, Sarah Andrews, Kim Cote, and Andrea Momnie, for getting it all done.

To my family: Karen, David, Jeffrey, Alex, and, of course, Snowflake and Magellan.

To Ken Getz, the world's greatest Access mind, for always answering my strange questions.

To the best literary agents in the business, Matt Wagner and Bill Gladstone, and all the folks at Waterside Productions.

To the pilgrims at IDG Books: To Walter Bruce, who never calls to say hello but always comes up with the reasonably fair contract. To Greg Croy, my favorite pilgrim. To our old editors and friends Pat O'Brien and Erik Dafforn — those were the days. To our new acquisitions editor, Andy Cummings (who only calls when there are real problems). And a special thanks to the editors of this book — Ken Brown, Janet Andrews, and Marti Paul — for the incredible job you did managing the project.

Cary N. Prague

Contents at a Glance

Contents

Chapter 7: Entering, Changing, Deleting, and Displaying Data 145

Part III: Using Access in Your Work   293

Chapter 19: Using OLE Objects, Graphs, and ActiveX Custom Controls 501

Part V: Applications in Access   859

Part VI: Advanced Access Topics   1149

Chapter 36: Optimizing Performance 1151

First Things First

What Is Access 2000?

Before you begin to use a software product, it is important to understand its capabilities and the types of tasks it is designed to perform. Microsoft Access 2000 (Access) is a multifaceted product whose use is bounded only by your imagination.

Access Is . . .

Essentially, Access is a *database management system* (DBMS). Like other products in this category, Access stores and retrieves data, presents information, and automates repetitive tasks (such as maintaining accounts payable, performing inventory control, and scheduling). With Access you can develop easy-to-use input forms similar to the one shown in Figure 1-1. You can process your data and run powerful reports.

Access is also a powerful Windows application — probably the best end-user/developer product ever written. Microsoft Access brings the productivity of database management to the usability and consistency of Microsoft Windows. Because both Windows and Access are from Microsoft, the two products work very well together. Access runs on the Windows 95, Windows 98, or Windows NT platform, so all the advantages of Windows are available in Access. You can cut, copy, and paste data from any Windows application to and from Access. You can create a form design in Access and paste it into the report designer.

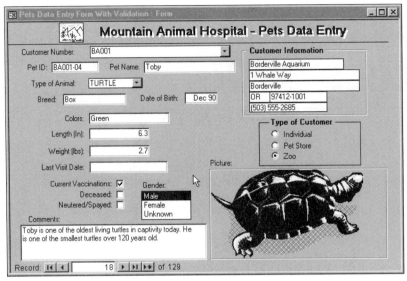

Figure 1-1: A typical Access data-entry form.

Using *OLE* (Object Linking and Embedding) objects in Windows and Microsoft Office 2000 products (Excel, Word, PowerPoint, and Outlook), you can extend Access into a true database operating environment by integrating it with these products. With the new Internet extensions, you can create forms that interact with data directly from the World Wide Web and translate your forms directly into data access pages for corporate intranets that work directly with your Internet browser.

Note   The new Data Access Pages feature, which creates live forms on a corporate intranet, only works with Microsoft Internet Explorer 5.0. It does not work with Netscape Navigator, a competing Internet browser from Netscape Corporation or with previous versions of Internet Explorer.

Even so, Access is more than just a database manager. As a *relational* database manager, it provides access to all types of data and allows the use of more than one database table at a time. It can reduce the complexity of your data and make it easier to get your job done. You can link an Access table with mainframe or server data or use a table created in dBASE or Excel. You can take the results of the link and combine the data with an Excel worksheet quickly and easily. If you use Microsoft Office 2000, there is complete interoperability between Access and Word, Excel, Outlook, and PowerPoint.

Figure 1-2 shows the original Microsoft marketing concept for Access. This simple figure conveys the message that Access is usable at all levels. Beginning at the lowest level of the hierarchy and moving upward, you see *Objects* listed first; these give the end user the capability of creating tables, queries, forms, and reports easily. You can perform simple processing by using *expressions*, also known as functions, to validate data, enforce a business rule, or display a number with a currency symbol. *Macros* allow for automation without programming, whereas VBA (Visual Basic for Applications) code lets the user program complex processes. Finally, by using Windows API (Application Programming Interface) calls to functions or DLLs (Dynamic Link Libraries) written in other languages such as C, Java, or Visual Basic, a programmer can write interfaces to other programs and data sources.

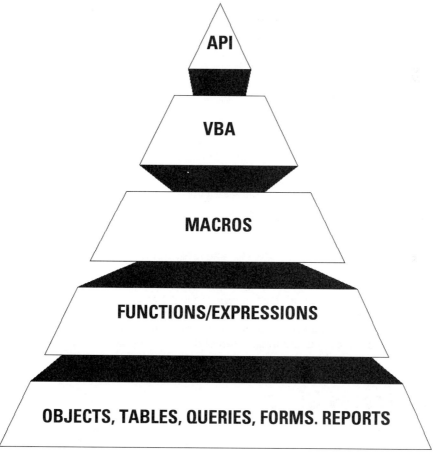

Figure 1-2: The Access usability hierarchy.

Access is a set of tools for end-user database management. Access has a table creator, a form designer, a query manager, a data access page creator, and a report writer. Access is also an environment for developing applications. Using macros or modules to automate tasks, you can create user-oriented applications as powerful as those created with programming languages — complete with the buttons, menus, and dialog boxes shown in Figure 1-3. By programming in Visual Basic for Applications (known as VBA), you can create programs as powerful as Access itself. In fact, many of the tools in Access (such as Wizards and Builders) are written in VBA.

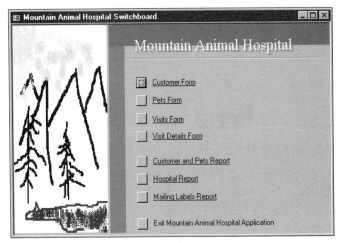

Figure 1-3: A macro switchboard.

The power and usability of Access make it, by far, the best database management software on the market. Simply telling you about what Access can do, however, doesn't begin to cover the material in this book. In the first 600 pages, you learn to use Access from an end user's point of view. In the next 600 pages, you learn Access from the power user's point of view. Finally, you learn the basics of VBA, the Internet, and the Client/Server, and you examine many topics in a depth your reference manuals can only begin to touch.

What Access Offers

The following paragraphs briefly describe some of Access's key features and prepare you for some of the subjects covered in this book.

True relational database management

Access provides true *relational database management*. Access includes definitions for primary and foreign keys and has full referential integrity at the database engine level itself (which prevents inconsistent updates or deletions). In addition, tables in Access have data-validation rules to prevent inaccurate data regardless of how data is entered, and every field in a table has format and default definitions for more productive data entry. Access supports all the necessary field types, including Text, Number, AutoNumber (counter), Currency, Date/Time, Memo, Yes/No, Hyperlink, and OLE objects. When values are missing in special processing, Access provides full support for null values.

The relational processing in Access fills many needs with its flexible architecture. It can be used as a stand-alone database management system, in a file-server configuration, or as a front-end client to products such as a SQL server. In addition, Access features ODBC (Open DataBase Connectivity), which permits connection to many external formats, such as SQL/Server, Oracle, Sybase, or mainframe IBM DB/2.

The program provides complete support for transaction processing, ensuring the integrity of transactions. In addition, user-level security provides control over assigning user and group permissions to view and modify database objects.

Context-sensitive help and the Office Assistant

The Microsoft Help feature is still the industry's best for beginners and experienced users alike. Access provides context-sensitive Help; pressing the F1 key whenever you're stuck brings up help information about the item you're working on instantly. Access also has an easy-to-use table of contents, a search facility, a history log, and bookmarks.

In Access 2000, Microsoft goes a few steps further by introducing the Office Assistant and Screen Tips. As Figure 1-4 shows, the *Office Assistant* responds in plain English when you ask for help. *Screen Tips* (also known as What's This?) give you short, onscreen explanations of what something is. The assistants are cute at first, and you can choose from a gallery of ten different assistants. You can also turn them off at any time if they become annoying.

Ease-of-use Wizards

A *Wizard* can turn hours of work into minutes. Wizards ask questions about content, style, and format, and then they build the object automatically. Access features nearly 100 Wizards to design databases, applications, tables, forms, reports, graphs, mailing labels, controls, and properties. Figure 1-5 shows a Form Wizard screen. Wizards are customizable for use in a variety of tasks.

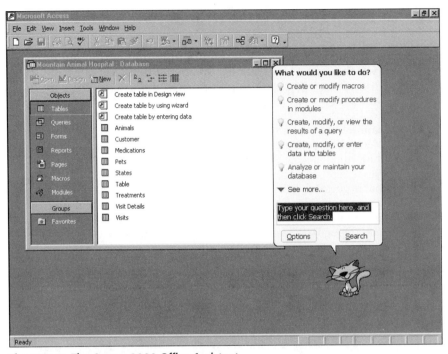

Figure 1-4: The Access 2000 Office Assistant.

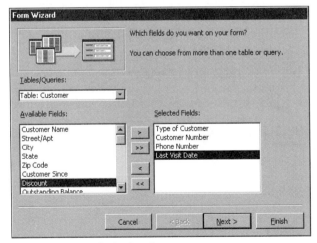

Figure 1-5: A typical Wizard screen.

Importing, exporting, and linking external files

Access lets you import from or export to many common formats, including dBASE, FoxPro, Excel, SQL Server, Oracle, Btrieve, many ASCII text formats (including fixed width and delimited), as well as data in HTML format. Importing creates an Access table; exporting an Access table creates a file in the native file format you are exporting to.

Linking (formally known as *attaching*) means that external data can be used without creating an Access table. You can link to dBASE, FoxPro, Excel, ASCII, and SQL data. Linking to external tables and then relating them to other tables is a powerful capability; you can link to Access, FoxPro, dBASE, and SQL server.

Note   Some import or export types require purchasing a license from their respective vendors while some are available from Microsoft's Web site as a free download. Today, the Web is a valuable source of free software, such as import and export engines, along with valuable tips and techniques.

WYSIWYG forms and reports

The Form and Report Design windows share a common interface and power. Your form or report is designed in a WYSIWYG (What You See Is What You Get) environment. As you add each control, you see the form take shape.

You can add labels, text data fields, option buttons, tab controls, checkboxes, lines, boxes, colors, shading — even pictures, graphs, subforms, or subreports — to your forms and reports. In addition, you have complete control over the style and presentation of data in a form or report, as shown in Figure 1-6. Forms can have multiple pages; reports can have many levels of groupings and totals.

You can view your form or report in *page preview* mode, zooming out to get a bird's-eye view. You can also view your report with sample data when you're in design mode so that you don't waste valuable time waiting for a large data file to be processed.

Most important, the Report Writer is very powerful. It allows up to ten levels of aggregation and sorting. The Report Writer performs two passes on the data; you can create reports that show the row percentage of a group total, which can be done only by having a calculation based on a calculation that requires two passes through the data. You can create many types of reports that include mailing labels and mail-merge reports.

Mountain Animal Hospital Pets and Owners Directory

All Creatures	○ Individual
21 Grace St.	◉ Pet Store
Tall Pines WA 98746-2541	○ Zoo
(206) 555-6622	

General Information

Pet ID: AC001-01
Type Of Animal: RABBIT
Breed: Long Ear
Date Of Birth: Apr 92
Last Visit: 7/1/95

Bobo

Physical Attributes

Length	Weight	Colors
20.0	3.1	Brown/Black/White

Status
☑ Neutered/Spayed ☑ Current Vaccinations Deceased

Gender
◉ Male
○ Female
○ Unknown

BoBo is a great looking rabbit. Bobo was originally owned by a nature center and was given to the Pet store for sale to a loving family. Bobo was in good health when he arrived and was returned to the pet store for sale.

General Information

Pet ID: AC001-02
Type Of Animal: LIZARD
Breed: Chameleon
Date Of Birth: May 92
Last Visit: 11/26/93

Presto Chango

Physical Attributes

Length	Weight	Colors
36.4	35.0	Green

Status
☐ Neutered/Spayed ☐ Current Vaccinations Deceased

Gender
○ Male
◉ Female
○ Unknown

The lizard was not readily changing color when brought in. It only changed color when it was warm. This is not abnormal for a chameleon. However, the species which is believed to originate in northern Australia usually manifests this problem in warm weather only. It is very unusual to see a chameleon not change color when cold.

General Information

Pet ID: AC001-03
Type Of Animal: SKUNK
Breed:
Date Of Birth: Aug 91
Last Visit: 5/11/93

Stinky

Physical Attributes

Length	Weight	Colors
29.8	22.0	Black/White

Status
☐ Neutered/Spayed ☐ Current Vaccinations Deceased

Gender
◉ Male
○ Female
○ Unknown

The skunk was descented and was in perfect condition when it left Mountain Animal Hospital.

General Information

Pet ID: AC001-04
Type Of Animal: DOG
Breed: German Shepherd
Date Of Birth: Jun 90
Last Visit: 11/5/93

Fido

Physical Attributes

Length	Weight	Colors
42.7	56.9	Brown

Status
☑ Neutered/Spayed ☐ Current Vaccinations Deceased

Gender
◉ Male
○ Female
○ Unknown

Figure 1-6: A database-published report.

Multiple-table queries and relationships

One of the most powerful features in Access is also the most important. As Figure 1-7 shows, the relationship lets you link your tables graphically. You can even link tables of different file types (such as an Access table and a dBASE table); when linked, your tables act as a single entity you can query about your data. You can select specific fields, define sorting orders, create calculated expressions, and enter criteria to select desired records. The results of a query can be displayed in a datasheet, form, or report. You do not have to set relationships in advance. Rather than set your relationships permanently, you can use a query window to set them when you need to for a specific purpose, such as a report.

Tip   If you are working in an environment where people are using several different versions of Access (2000, 97, 95, and 2) you can attach to .MDB files of different versions and update data without any problems. This way, the people who only have Access 2 or Access 97 can continue to use that version and those who have upgraded to Access 2000 can use their data for reporting.

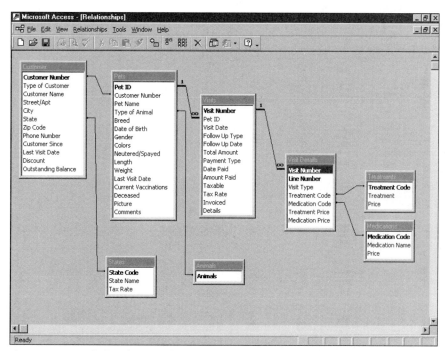

Figure 1-7: A relationship window.

Queries have other uses as well. You can create queries that calculate totals, display cross-tabulations, and then make new tables from the results. You can even use a query to update data in tables, delete records, or append one table to another.

Business graphs and charts

You will find the same graph application found in Microsoft Word, Excel, PowerPoint, and Project built into Access. You can create hundreds of types of business graphs and customize the display to meet your every business need. You can create bar charts, column charts, line charts, pie charts, area charts, and high-low-close charts — in two and three dimensions. You can add free-form text, change the gridlines, adjust the color and pattern in a bar, display data values on a bar or pie slice, and rotate the viewing angle of a chart from within the Access Graph program.

In addition, you can link your graph with a form to get a powerful graphic data display that changes from record to record in the table. Figure 1-8 is an example of linking a graph to a form.

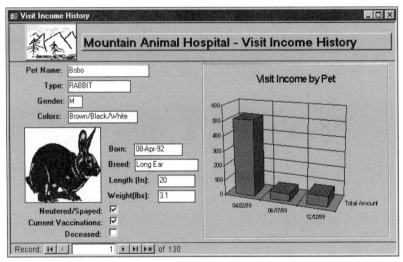

Figure 1-8: A typical form linked to a graph.

DDE and OLE capabilities

Through the capabilities of DDE (Dynamic Data Exchange) and OLE (Object Linking and Embedding), exciting new objects can be added to Access forms and reports. The objects that can be added include sound, pictures, graphs, and video clips. You can embed OLE objects (such as a bitmap picture) or documents from word processors (such as Word or WordPerfect), or link to a range of cells in an Excel spreadsheet. By linking these objects to records in your tables, you can create dynamic database forms and reports and share information between Windows applications.

The Internet is now accessible

Access is now full of features that allow you to easily make your applications Internet/intranet ready. With just a click of the mouse, you can save tables, queries, reports, and form datasheets as HTML (HyperText Markup Language). A new feature known as Data Access Pages lets you create complex forms for a corporate intranet that link with live data on your network. Even a novice can create live data pages on the Web. Hyperlinks allow you and others to access your published data (and others' published data) as hypertext links, directly from your Access forms.

Many people feel that the process of publishing data to the Web is something to be left to a Webmaster. Access 2000 definitely turns this idea into a myth. Data Access Pages walk you through the steps of creating the form and linking to your data for selected database objects and of placing the generated HTML on your Web site. As Figure 1-9 shows, using the Wizard you can create dynamic forms!

Figure 1-9: Creating a Data Access Page.

True Client-Server for Everyone

In previous versions of Microsoft Access, true client-server was very difficult. You first had to have a copy of SQL Server. This required owning a high-end computer capable of running Windows NT Server and a high-priced consultant to install and maintain it. Now, Access 2000 comes with the Microsoft Database Engine, also known as the SQL Server 7.0 desktop edition. This allows you to create true client-server based applications on your desktop and then upsize them to the more robust SQL Server 7.0 Enterprise Edition when you are ready.

Access 2000 like its predecessors, also comes with Jet. This is known as the Access or Jet Database Engine. It is what handles creating and storing your tables and running your queries. Though not as powerful or as fast as SQL Server, it is quite satisfactory for most smaller applications of 10 or less workstations and up to about 10MB of data. Unless you have hundreds of thousands of data records, Jet is satisfactory.

Built-in functions

Access contains more than 200 *functions* (small built-in programs that return a value) that perform tasks in a wide variety of categories. Access includes database, mathematics, business, financial, date, time, and string functions. You can use them to create calculated expressions in your forms, reports, and queries.

Macros: programming without programming

For nonprogrammers (or power users who simply don't want to program), there are *macros*. Macros let you perform common tasks without user intervention. Nearly 50 macro actions let you manipulate data, create menus and dialog boxes, open forms and reports, and basically automate any task that you can imagine. Macros can probably solve 75 percent of your processing problems.

Modules: Visual Basic for Applications – database programming

Access is a serious development environment with a full-featured programming language. The Visual Basic Application edition (VBA, for short, and formerly known as Access Basic) features an event-driven programming model that lets you do more things than you can do with just forms and reports. VBA is a powerful structured programming language; it is also fully extensible, featuring API call routines in any dynamic link library (DLL) for the Windows 95, Windows 98, and Windows NT operating systems.

A full-featured development environment allows multiple windows for color-coded editing and debugging, automatic syntax checking, watchpoints, breakpoints, single-step execution, and even syntax help that displays each possible commands option as you type.

Information for Database Users

If you're already a database user, chances are that you're ready to jump right in and start using Access. A word of warning: *This is not your father's database.* You may be an expert in relational database management software such as dBASE, FoxPro, or Paradox, but you may never have used a database under Windows.

You should be familiar with Windows software before you jump into a database package. Play with Windows Paint; experiment with Word or Excel. Learn how to use the mouse to click, double-click, select, drag, and drop. Create a graph in Excel, use a Wizard, and try the Help system. All these tasks will make your learning experience much faster when you use Access.

You also need to get used to some new terminology. Table 1-1 lists the Access terminology and its dBASE/FoxPro and Paradox equivalents.

Table 1-1
Access, dBASE/FoxPro, and Paradox Terminology

Microsoft Access	dBASE/FoxPro	Paradox
Database	Catalog	Directory of related files
Table	Database file	Table
Datasheet	BROWSE command	View command
Table Design	MODIFY STRUCTURE	Modify Restructure
Text data type	Character data type	Alphanumeric data type
Primary key	Unique Index	Key field
Index	Index	Tools QuerySpeed
Validation rule	PICTURE/VALID Clause	ValChecks
Query	Query, QBE, View	Query
Form	Screen	Forms
Subform	Multiple File Screen	Multiple-record selection
Open a form	SET FORMAT TO, EDIT	Image PickForm
Find command	LOCATE AND SEEK	Zoom
Data entry command	APPEND	Modify DataEntry
List box, combo box	Pick list	Lookup
Exclusive/shared access	SET EXCLUSIVE ON/OFF	Edit/Coedit mode
Module	Program file	Script

Information for Spreadsheet Users

If you are an Excel expert, you'll find that many things about Access are similar to Excel. Both programs are Windows products, so you should already have experience using the Windows-specific conventions used in Access. Access has a spreadsheet view of the data in a table or query that is known as a *datasheet*. You can resize the rows and columns in much the same way as within Excel worksheets. In fact, Access 2000 has a data-entry mode exactly like that of Excel. You simply enter data and define column headings; Access creates a table automatically (see Figure 1-10).

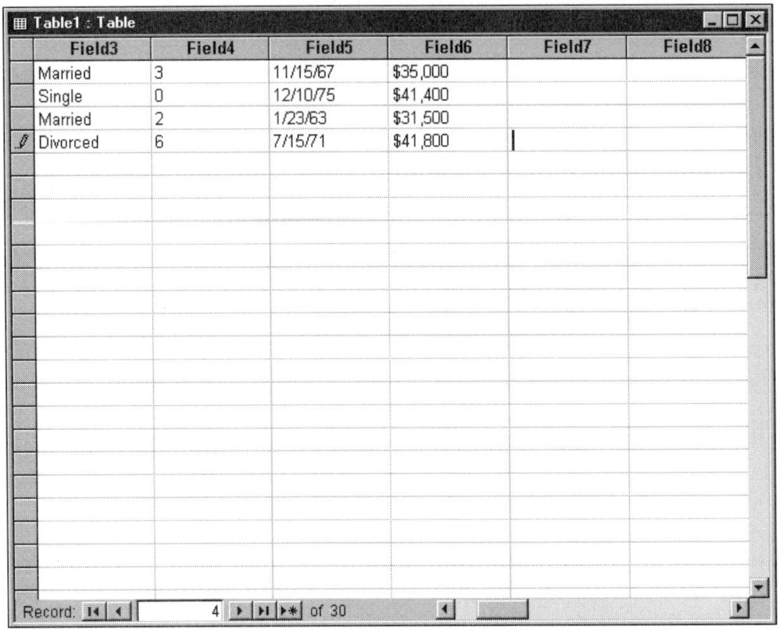

Field3	Field4	Field5	Field6	Field7	Field8
Married	3	11/15/67	$35,000		
Single	0	12/10/75	$41,400		
Married	2	1/23/63	$31,500		
Divorced	6	7/15/71	$41,800		

Record: I◄ ◄ | 4 | ► ►I ►* | of 30

Figure 1-10: Creating a new table using an Access datasheet.

Access has a WYSIWYG drawing capability similar to that of Excel, and it shares the same graph application. Thus, you can create the same types of graphs in both programs and annotate the graphs in the same way. Also, Access uses graph Wizards that you might have used in Excel.

Access 2000 contains a Pivot Table Wizard just like Excel's; in fact, it can create Excel pivot tables. You can also drag and drop information from an Access database to an

Excel spreadsheet and link Access databases to Excel spreadsheets. You can query and sort data in both products as well, using a common query interface. (If you've used the Excel menu options for queries and sorting, you already are familiar with these concepts.) Access 2000 is interoperable with all Microsoft Office 2000 products.

Summary

In this chapter, you learned about Access's capabilities and some of the types of tasks Access can accomplish. These points were discussed:

✦ Access is a database management system (DBMS).

✦ Access can be used to store and retrieve data, present information, and automate repetitive tasks.

✦ Using Access allows development of easy-to-use input forms, data processing, and running of powerful reports.

✦ Access 2000 has a powerful new feature known as Data Access Pages to publish Access forms to intranet sites. Also, the Microsoft Database Engine brings the power of client/server through the SQL Server 7.0 Desktop Edition to Access 2000 users.

✦ By using Access macros, you can create applications without programming.

✦ If you already are a database user, you should learn the differences in terminology between Access and the product you are familiar with.

✦ Spreadsheet and database users are already familiar with many of the key concepts used in Access.

In the next chapter, you learn to install Access and to start it.

✦　　✦　　✦

Installing and Running Access 2000

Access 2000 must be installed on your computer before you can use it. Since the majority of copies of Microsoft Access today are purchased through the Microsoft Office suite, it will be used to install the Access 2000 programs on your computer. Whether you install one of the Microsoft Office 2000 Suites that include Access (the Professional, Premium, and Developer Editions), or the stand-alone version of Access 2000, after you get to the portion of the setup routine that lets you select the Access 2000 options, both installation routines are the same.

Access 2000 is installed in a manner similar to Windows 95, 98, or NT software products. If your company has a special person or team designated to install and troubleshoot software, you may want to have this person or department install Access for you so that your system will be installed like the other systems in your company.

If you are installing an upgrade or competitive version of Access or Office 2000, the older program must already be installed on your machine. New installations of Access 2000 do not require a previous version to be already installed on your machine.

Determining What You Need

Access 2000 requires specific hardware and software to run. Before you install Access, check to see that your computer meets the minimum requirements needed to run it.

Hardware requirements

To use Access 2000 successfully, you'll realistically need an IBM (or compatible) personal computer with a Pentium 75 or higher processor and 32MB of RAM. To get really good performance from Access 2000, we recommend a Pentium II 233 computer with at least 64MB of RAM. With more memory and a faster processor, you'll be able to run more applications simultaneously, and overall performance will be increased. A fast video card is also recommended to display pictures and graphs.

You will also need between 200MB and 400MB of hard disk space for a typical installation of Microsoft Office 2000. If you are installing only Access 2000, you will still need about 100MB because many of the Office shared files are used by Access and are loaded in the stand-alone version. Keep in mind that you will need additional space to store your database files when you create them.

If space is a problem, there are some options new to Office 2000. This includes the ability to run various options from the CD such as Clipart or various large size templates. You can also automatically be prompted by each Office application to install a feature on first use. This way, if you or one of your users never needs a certain feature like Wordperfect support, it will never be loaded. Using the custom installation, you can decide what features are installed and even choose to exclude individual features or entire applications. You can perform a partial installation, or you can delete unwanted files from your hard disk to free up space needed for the installation. Access needs a VGA monitor as a minimum requirement, but we recommend an SVGA (or better) display. This configuration allows you to view more information at one time and to get a sharper resolution.

A mouse or some other compatible pointing device (trackballs and pens will work) is mandatory for you to use Access 2000.

If you're planning to print from Access, you need a printer. Any printer that is supported by Windows 98, 95 or Windows NT works.

Software requirements

Access requires that Microsoft Windows 2000 (formerly named Windows NT), 98, 95 or Windows NT be installed on your computer. Windows does not come with Access; it must be purchased separately. If Windows 2000, 98, 95 or Windows NT is not installed on your computer, install it before you install Access or Office 2000. Microsoft Office 2000 does not run on OS/2 or Windows 3.1.

Upgrading to Access 2000 from Access 2.0, 95, or 97

If you are upgrading to Access 2000 from earlier versions of Access, you should consider a few things. Earlier versions of Access databases must be converted to Access 2000 format before they are usable. After an Access 2.0 or Access 95 database is converted to Access 2000 format, it cannot be converted back; it's unusable by Access 2.0, 95, or 97. You can however, save an Access 2000 database in Access 97 format. As an Access 2000 user, you can open and work with Access 2.0, 95, or 97 data by attaching to them as external databases, but you cannot modify any of the objects (forms, reports, queries, and so on) you find in them.

If you are sharing data files with people who use older versions of Access, think about leaving the older version of Access on your machine. Then you can create files in Access 2000 but still use Access 2.0, 95, or 97 to work with files that are shared with others.

Installing Access 2000 or Office 2000

You can now install Office 2000 or Access 2000. Insert your CD-ROM into your CD-ROM drive. A startup screen for the install should automatically be displayed. If not, then select Run from the Windows Start menus. Windows will display the Run dialog box. In the Open box, type D:\SETUP (or use whatever letter corresponds to the drive containing your installation CD-ROM), as shown in Figure 2-1. Click on OK to begin the installation. This procedure works for both new installations and upgrades to Access 2000.

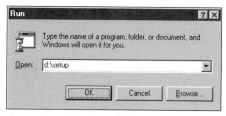

Figure 2-1: The Run dialog box.

Because some Windows programs interfere with the Setup program, Access or Office may warn you to shut down any applications currently running. You can simply click on the Continue button to continue the setup, or you can click on the

Exit Setup button to cancel the installation and shut down your applications (you then can run Setup later). The program then welcomes you, as shown in Figure 2-2.

The Setup program now requires some information from you. The welcome screen contains entry areas for your name, initials, company, and the Office 2000 license key from your CD. If you have previously installed any Microsoft Office component, you will see your name, initials, and company from your previous installation. Microsoft Office stores these entries in the Windows registry for use by all Office components.

Tip   You can always find your product ID, the software version number in any Microsoft product by selecting the About option on the Help menu. You can also find technical support options and help on the web from the Help menu as well.

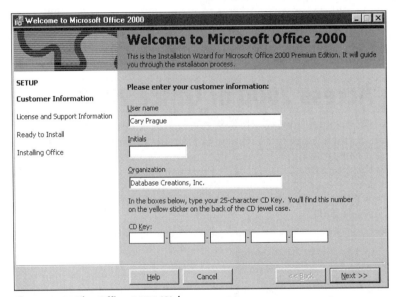

Figure 2-2: The Office 2000 Welcome screen.

After you enter your license key information, you have to agree to Microsoft's licensing. As you can see in Figure 2-3, this is a very intimidating screen. You can read all of the text, or have your lawyer read it for you. Basically, you have no choice but to select *I accept the terms in the license agreement.* Though this will obligate you to give all the money you ever make to Microsoft, you should still accept the terms of the agreement. OK, not all your money, just the amount left over after the IRS takes it all.

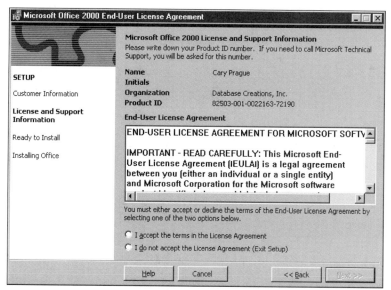

Figure 2-3: The Office 2000 License Agreement screen.

Next, Setup gives you two choices as to how you want to install Microsoft Office or Access. As you can see in Figure 2-4, the choices depend on whether you are a first time user of Access or Office in any version or you are upgrading from a previous version of Microsoft Office or Access:

Typical (New Users)
: For new users, this option installs each Office product with a most used set of options. It makes all the choices for you including the location of the Office files which will all be installed in C:\Program Files\Microsoft Office.

Upgrade Now (Existing Users)
: If you have any version of an Office product on your computer, this option will automatically remove older versions of Office.

Customize
: This lets you decide how Office is installed including where files are placed, what specific product features, options, shared Office components, sample files, and even help systems are installed. You can also decide what older products in the Office family you want to remove or keep.

New Feature   Regardless of the option you choose, new technology in Microsoft Office 2000 will prompt you to insert your Office CD if you need to use a feature that was not installed. Though this may be annoying for the first few weeks you use Office, it may save you a lot of hard disk space and registry entries you might otherwise never need.

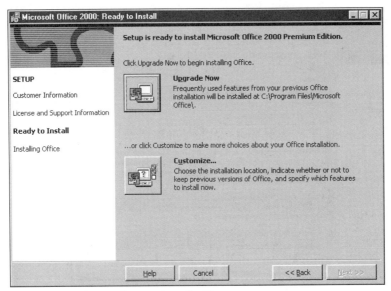

Figure 2-4: Selecting how to install Office 2000.

In this example, you will see a custom installation. Figure 2-5 shows the screen where Office asks you where you want to install the files. The installer also checks your hard drive for space and reports how much space is initially needed. As you choose to not install certain options, this number may later change.

The default location is C:\Program Files\Microsoft Office if you have Microsoft Office Professional or Premium. If this location is satisfactory, click OK to continue with the installation. If you want to change the location, type the new drive and folder name. For example, to have Access installed in a folder called Access located on drive E, you type **E:\ACCESS**. If you type the name of a folder that does not exist, one is created for you. Some shared Office components must reside on Drive C: (or the hard drive where Windows or the System Registry is installed).

Once you have determined where to install Office 2000, the installer checks to see what previous version of Office components you have installed. As you can see in Figure 2-6, this author's computer has a lot of previous versions. For each version, you can select each one to keep or delete. You can also check the *Keep these programs* check box to keep all of the older versions.

Note   Microsoft Office 2000 products can co-exist with almost no problems with Office 97 versions or even Access 2.0.

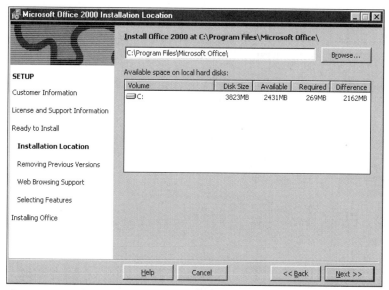

Figure 2-5: Selecting the location for Office 2000 components.

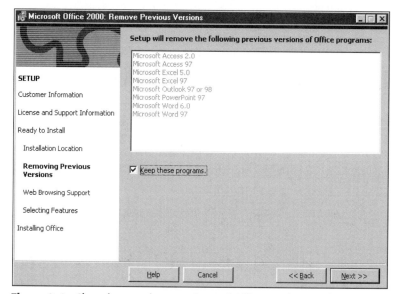

Figure 2-6: Choosing previous versions of Office products to keep.

The next screen shown in Figure 2-7 is perhaps the most important. This screen lets you choose which Office products to install and how each of them will run. As you can see in Figure 2-7, a tree view of all the products is shown on this screen. Each product is listed with a + sign next to the product name. Clicking the + sign will expand the offering into more and more levels. While most icons are white, indicating the options will be installed, some icons are gray, meaning that there are still options that have not been selected to install yet.

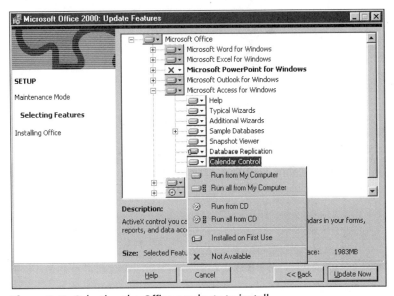

Figure 2-7: Selecting the Office products to install.

In this figure, you can see that Microsoft Access for Windows has been expanded and that the Sample Databases option could be expanded even further. You can see several different icons in the figure. Each of the icons represent a different option. These options include:

Run from My Computer/Run all from My Computer	Install on the local or server hard disk previously specified
Run from CD/Run all from CD	Whenever you use the product, the Microsoft Office CD must be in your CD drive. This will cause Office to run much slower than installing it on your hard drive
Installed on First Use	Install it on your computer the first time you try to use the feature or product
Not Available	You cannot use the feature or product without rerunning the Office setup program

In Figure 2-7 you can see that Microsoft PowerPoint will not be available, the Database Replication feature will be available on first use and the Office Tools (the text is hidden in the figure) will be run from the CD, the rest of the products will be installed on your hard drive.

When you have chosen all the items you need, press the Install Now button. Setup next determines which disks and files to copy. The installation proceeds. This process will take some time — approximately 20 to 120 minutes for a complete installation, depending on your processor speed, CD-ROM drive speed, and hard disk speed.

As the installation continues, a series of pictures appears on-screen. These provide some basic information about various features of Office and Access and how you can use them.

After the installation is complete, you are returned to wherever you were when the installation began. If you installed the stand-alone version of Access, a new program named Microsoft Access will be on your Start menu. If you installed the entire Office suite, you will see an entry for each Office product. You can run Access by either choosing Microsoft Access from the Start menu or locating the Microsoft Access folder on the desktop or in Windows Explorer and then finding the Access icon and double-clicking on it. If the Office 2000 shortcut bar is present, you can start Access by pressing the Access (key) icon.

Converting Access 1.x, 2.0, and 95 Files

Access 2000 can convert and read databases created in older versions of Access; you can add, change, and delete data. You can run Access 2.0, 95, and 97 queries, forms, reports, macros, and even Access BASIC or VBA modules. Even so, you cannot change any objects (tables, queries, forms, reports, macros, or modules). To redesign an Access 2.0, 95, or 97 object, you must either use Access 2.0, 95, or 97 itself or convert the object to Access 2000.

If you attempt to open a database created in a previous version of Microsoft Access, you will be given the option to convert it or open it in read-only mode, as shown in Figure 2-8.

Note   You can also convert older Access databases by selecting Tools ⇨ Database Utilities ⇨ Convert Database ⇨ To Current Access Database Version in the Access Database window. It is just as easy to open them and let Access ask you, as you can see in Figure 2-8. No database can be open if you want to see the Convert Database menu option.

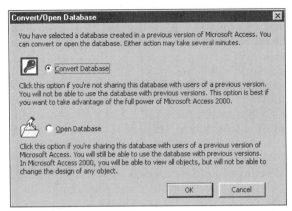

Figure 2-8: Converting an Access database.

A standard Windows file-selector dialog box appears. You select the database to be converted and give it a new name. The database is then converted.

Note If the database is already in Access 2000 format, Access tells you and the database is not converted.

If you use Microsoft Access security, you must own the database or be a member of the Admins group that was in effect when the database was created.

Caution If you try to convert the database and save it to the same path and name, you get an error message; the conversion does not take place.

Troubleshooting

If you run into problems while installing Office or Access, Setup displays a message telling you what the problem may be. Some common problems include lack of disk space and problems reading the CD-ROM.

If you receive a message saying that an error has occurred during Setup, you may have run out of disk space. You need to delete some files before proceeding with the installation. You can delete files from the Windows or NT 4.0 Explorer. Remember to be careful not to delete important files. If you find that you have plenty of available disk space, something else has failed in the installation; you should contact Microsoft Product Support for help.

If your CD-ROM or floppy disk drive has problems reading the installation disks, there may be a problem with your drive. You may want to contact someone in your company's MIS or tech-support department to check the drive for you. Then, if you still receive this message and cannot find the problem, call Microsoft Product Support for help in troubleshooting the problem.

Getting Started with Access 2000

After you've installed Access successfully, you are ready to learn the various ways to start the Access database program.

You can start Access in several ways:

✦ From the Windows Start menu

✦ From an Access shortcut icon

✦ From the Access icon in a folder

✦ From the Windows Explorer

Starting from the Windows Start menu

When you use Windows to install Access 2000, Windows adds Access to the Start menu's Programs selection automatically. A simple way to start Access 2000 is to click on the Start menu, select the Programs submenu, and then select Microsoft Access. This will start Microsoft Access and display the initial Access screen.

Starting from an Access shortcut icon

If you've gotten the hang of Windows, you've probably learned how valuable a *shortcut* can be. Figure 2-9 shows the Windows desktop belonging to one of the authors. The top part of the screen shows the Office 2000 toolbar along with shortcut buttons to all of the Office 2000 Premium edition programs. The programs on the Office Programs toolbar are (in left to right order):

Access, Word, Excel, PowerPoint, Outlook, MapPoint, PhotoDraw, Publisher, MS-DOS, Office Binder, Internet Explorer, and FrontPage.

Also note that there is a copy of the Access 2000 icon; dragging it to the Windows desktop from the Office 2000 folder creates a shortcut. You can start Access 2000 quickly by clicking on this icon.

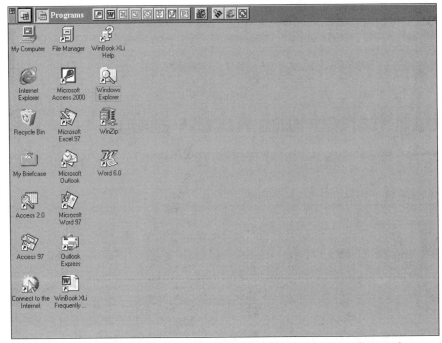

Figure 2-9: The Windows desktop, showing the Office Program toolbar and a shortcut to Access.

Starting from an Access icon

If you purchased Access as part of Microsoft Office, then one of your folders in Windows is probably the MSOFFICE folder (or, as shown in Figure 2-10, C:\Program Files\Microsoft Office 2000\Office). Inside that folder you should find a shortcut icon to launch Access 2000 and each Office 2000 product. You will also find a file, perhaps in a folder named Office or ACCESS, that contains the file MSACCESS.EXE, which is the actual icon for launching Access 2000. You can start Access by double-clicking on either one of these icons.

Starting from Windows Explorer

You can also start Access from the Windows Explorer (which has kind of replaced Program Manager and File Manager) by selecting the .MDB database file you want to load. When you find the database file you want to load, double-click on the filename. Windows then start the version of Access you have last installed and defined in the System Registry and opens the database you selected. If this is not the correct version of Access, the database file may not run or you may be asked to convert it to the current version of Access.

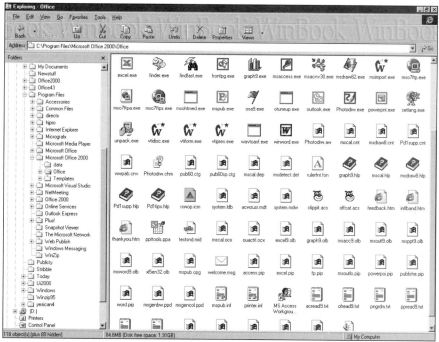

Figure 2-10: The Office 2000 folders.

If you are unsure of which file you should choose, check to see that it has a proper file extension. Microsoft Access database files normally have the file extension MDB. Because Microsoft Access is a registered application in Windows, you will launch Access whenever you select a file with the .MDB extension. You may also find files with an .MDA or .MDE file extension. These will also launch Access. MDA files are library files typically containing add-ins or wizards. MDE files are Access databases that contain preprogrammed applications but in which all the module source code has been removed. You can run the application, but you cannot see any of the modules.

Note

If you already have Access running and you double-click on a file in the Windows Explorer, another copy of Access will start, which will load the file you selected. You may want to do this if you want more than one database open at a time. (Access does not let you open more than one database at a time if you are running only one occurrence of Access.)

Options for starting Access

You can customize how Access starts by adding options to the MSACCESS command line from the properties of a shortcut icon. For example, you can have Access open a database, execute a macro, or supply a user name or password — automatically. Table 2-1 identifies the options available for starting Access.

Table 2-1 Command-Line Options for Starting Access	
Option	**Effect**
<database>	Opens the specified database. Include a path if necessary.
/Excl	Opens the specified database for exclusive access. To open the database for shared access in a multiuser environment, omit this option.
/RO	Opens the specified database for read-only access.
/User <user name>	Starts Microsoft Access using the specified user name.
/Pwd <password>	Starts Microsoft Access using the specified password.
/Profile <user profile>	Starts Microsoft Access using the options in the specified user profile instead of the standard Windows Registry settings (created when you installed Microsoft Access). This replaces the /ini option used in previous versions of Microsoft Access to specify an initialization file. However, the /ini option will still work for user-defined .INI files from earlier versions of Microsoft Access.
/Compact <target database>	Compacts the database specified before the /Compact option and then closes Microsoft Access. If you omit a target database name following the /Compact option, Access compacts the database using the original database name. To compact to a different name, specify a target database.
/Repair	Repairs the specified database and then closes Microsoft Access.
/Convert <target database>	Converts a database in an earlier version (2.0, 95, pr 97) to a Microsoft Access 2000database with a new name and then closes Microsoft Access. Specify the source database before using the /Convert option.
/X <macro>	Starts Microsoft Access and runs the specified macro. Another way to run a macro when you open a database is to use an AutoExec macro or the Database Startup properties.

Option	Effect
/Cmd	Specifies that what follows on the command line is the value that will be returned by the Command function. This option must be the last option on the command line. You can use a semicolon (;) as an alternative to /Cmd.
/Nostartup	Starts Microsoft Access without displaying the Startup dialog box (the second dialog box you see when you start Microsoft Access).

Tip   To run a VBA procedure when you open a database, use the RunCode action in a command-line macro or the AutoExec macro, or use the Access 2000 Startup dialog box. You can also run a VBA procedure when you open a database by creating a form with a VBA procedure defined for its OnOpen event. Designate this as the startup form by using the right mouse button to click in the database window, click on Startup, and then enter that form in the Display Form box.

For example, to have Access automatically execute a macro called MYMACRO, you enter the following parameter in the Shortcut Properties section of an Access shortcut. (You may find the command MSACCESS.EXE preceded by its path.)

```
MSACCESS.EXE /X MYMACRO
```

You can also use a special option that Access runs automatically when you first open a Microsoft Access database (you will learn more about this in Part V). This is the *Startup form.* You can use it to open certain tables or forms every time you enter a database or to perform complex processing, change the menus, change the title bar, hide the database window, or do just about anything you can think of.

Note   In Access 2.0, you created a macro named Autoexec to do this. In Access 2000, the startup form is an easier way to run a program automatically when you open a database.

Tip   To prevent a startup form from running automatically, hold down the Shift key as you open the database.

Exiting Access

When you are finished using Access (or any application), you should always exit gracefully. It bears repeating: Simply turning off your system is not a good method and can cause problems. Windows and your applications use many files while they are running, some of which you may not be aware of. Turning off your system can cause these files not to be closed properly, which can result in hard disk problems in the future.

Another reason for exiting gracefully is to ensure that all your data is saved before you exit the application. If you have spent quite a bit of time entering data and then you turn off your system, accidentally forgetting to save this work, all this unsaved data will be lost! Save yourself time and grief by exiting your applications the correct way.

You can exit Access in several safe ways:

✦ Click the Close button on the Title bar.

✦ Double-click on the Control icon on the Access title bar.

✦ From the Access menu, select File ➪ Exit.

✦ Press Alt+F4.

✦ Display the taskbar and select Microsoft Access. Then right-click and select Close. You can use this method to close Access from within another application.

When you exit Access with one of these methods, you may see a message displayed on-screen that prompts you to save any changes you may have made. You can select Yes to save the changes and exit Access. Selecting No will exit Access without saving the changes you made. Cancel stops Access from closing, and you are returned to Access. You can also choose Help for more information on exiting Access.

Getting Help

Now that you have learned how to start Access, you may need some help in learning how to use the software. After you have started Access, you can choose from any of the Help options that are available. Some of these include:

✦ Office Assistant

✦ Standard Windows Help (Contents, Index, and Find tabs)

✦ Screen Tips (What's This?)

✦ Web-based resources on the Microsoft Web site

✦ Northwinds database

✦ Solutions database

Office Assistant

When you first press F1 to request help, Access displays the friendly new Office Assistant. The default assistant is Clippit, your guide to help. Figure 2-11 shows Links the Cat. As you can see in the figure, the Office Assistant provides you with a list of options. You can type a request in standard English (or whatever language you use), get helpful tips and hints, or select options to change the Office Assistant character. There are several to choose from, including Clippit, Dot, the Office Logo, the Genius Albert Einstein, Power Pup, Rocky the Dog, or even Mother Nature.

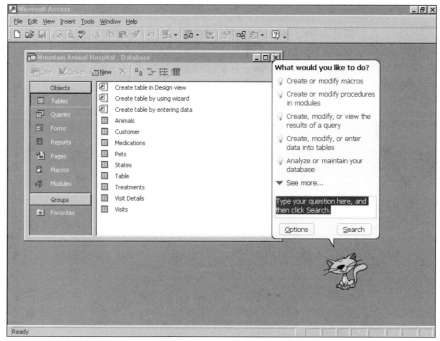

Figure 2-11: The Office Assistant.

Tip

Right-click on the Assistant and select Animate. You will be treated to an amazing show. Each character comes with between 10 and 30 different shows.

If you have access to the Microsoft Web site, you can use a variety of other characters in the Office pages.

Standard Help

When you choose Help on the menu bar and select Contents, Access presents you with a tabbed dialog box (as shown in Figure 2-12). This dialog box provides several ways to help you get started using Access. You have three options to choose from:

Contents	As shown in Figure 2-12, the Table of Contents lists major topics grouped by task. When you select a topic, a menu of subtopics appears and leads you to various Help screens.
Answer Wizard	Lets you type a question in to an area and then evaluates the words you type and displays a list of matching help topics. This is similar to using the Office Assistant but not as annoying.
Index	This displays an alphabetical list of Help topics. You can type the first few letters of the Help topic you are searching for or scroll through the list.

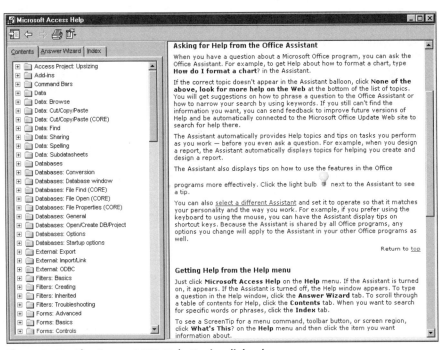

Figure 2-12: The Access 2000 Help Topics dialog box.

Help in Access is always a keystroke away. There are many easy ways to get help:

✦ Press the F1 key to get the Assistant and then ask a question or select a help suggestion.

✦ Click on the Help button that resembles a cursor arrow and a question mark (on the Access toolbar), and then click on the desired item to get Screen Tip help. You can also press Shift+F1 to display the question-mark cursor or select What's This from the Help menu. More on Screen Tips later.

✦ Select Help from the Access pull-down menu and then choose Contents, Answer Wizard, and Index.

You can get help at any time in Access, no matter what you are doing. Help is available for every aspect of Access — commands, menus, macros, Access terms and concepts, and even programming topics.

Note   Help is a separate program from Access and has its own window. Therefore, you can move, size, minimize, or close the Help window.

Screen Tips (What's This?)

Screen Tips are a new type of help found in all Microsoft Office products. They give you short explanations of tasks in the various products. They are text only, generally displayed in a small rectangle. Although standard toolbar ToolTips display only a word or two, Screen Tips display a paragraph. When you select the Help icon on the toolbar, the mouse pointer changes to an arrow with a question mark. You can then click on various parts of an Access 2000 screen and receive a short explanation of the task or function you clicked on. You can also press Shift+F1 for the same effect. For example, if you press Shift+F1 and then click on the Tables tab in the Database window, you will see a Screen Tip explaining what you can do with a table, as shown in Figure 2-13.

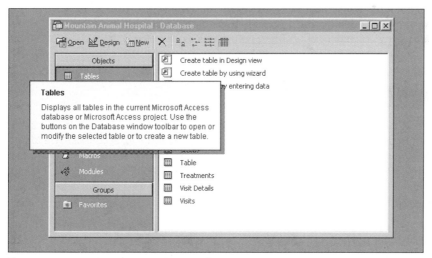

Figure 2-13: An Access 2000 Screen Tip.

Tip   You can create your own Screen Tips in your applications, using the same techniques that create standard Access 2000 Help.

Web-based resources on the Microsoft Web site

On the Access 2000 Help menu is a group of options to give you access to the Microsoft Web site and a plethora of free resources to help you use any Microsoft product. All the options launch the Microsoft Internet Explorer Web browser and take you right to the appropriate page on the Microsoft Web site. This page includes Free Stuff, Product News, the Access Developer Forum, FAQs (Frequently Asked Questions), and Online Support. The bottom most options also let you go directly to the Office Home Page, send Feedback to Microsoft, go to a list of the best Web sites, search the Web, take a tutorial about using the Web, and go to the general Microsoft Home Page.

Sample databases

You should be aware of one more place you can get help. The Office Samples directory contains several special databases: Northwind.MDB (the Northwinds Example file used throughout the Access documentation), ORDERS.MDB (a sample order-entry program also used in the Access programmer's documentation), and SOLUTIONS.MDB (a teaching database).

When you open SOLUTIONS.MDB, a Help-like interface appears. You can select a global topic in the top list box and then choose from a set of specific subtopics in the lower list box. When you double-click on a subtopic, a working example from Northwinds is displayed along with instructional Help. This allows you to work with a real example while learning some of the more complex topics. Unlike the visual introduction, which explains concepts, the Solutions database is used to show you how to solve a particular problem using Access.

Summary

In this chapter, you learned about the equipment you need to install Access, how to install Access, and how to convert Access 2.0, 95, and 97 databases. You also learned various ways to start Access and how to exit the program. In addition, you learned about the many ways to use the Access Help system.

The chapter covered the following points:

✦ You need to have Microsoft Windows 98, 95, or NT (Windows 2000) installed on your system before you can install Access.

✦ At least 100MB of free hard disk space is needed to fully install Access 2000, and 400MB for installing Office 2000.

✦ If available hard disk space is a problem, you can select Customize or Run from CD-ROM installation to limit the options that are installed. (You can install the omitted options at a later time by rerunning Setup.)

✦ You must convert older Access databases to use with Access 2000.

✦ You can start Access in various ways; the easiest and most common method is using the Start menu or double-clicking on an Access shortcut icon.

✦ You can add options to the Access command line that can automatically open a database, execute a macro, or set a user name or password.

✦ You should use one of the suggested ways to exit Access. If you exit by simply turning off your system, the result can be loss of data or a damaged hard disk.

✦ Using the Office Assistant, you can ask questions in plain language and see various Help topics that match your question.

✦ Many types of Help are available in Access. Help can provide step-by-step instructions for learning Access; it can walk you through the setups needed to create your own database objects.

✦ You can press F1 to activate the Help feature, which gives information on how to use Access or defines various concepts used in Access.

✦ Microsoft provides direct access to its Web site for free software and many free resources to help you get started and to be productive.

✦ Help appears in a window of its own that can be minimized or resized; you can keep it open as you work on your database.

✦ The Access Introduction will teach you the fundamental concepts of working with databases using Microsoft Access 2000.

✦ Three sample databases will help you get started: Northwind, Orders, and Solutions.

In the next chapter, you review basic database concepts as you begin the journey to understanding database management with Access.

✦   ✦   ✦

A Review of Database Concepts

✦ ✦ ✦ ✦

In This Chapter

Understanding what a database is

Examining the differences between databases, tables, records, fields, and values

Learning why multiple tables are used in a database

Looking at database objects

✦ ✦ ✦ ✦

Before you begin to use a database software package, you must understand several basic concepts. The most important concept is that the data is stored in a "black box" known as a *table* and that by using the tools of the database, you can retrieve, display, and report the data in any format you want.

What Is a Database?

Database is a computer term for a collection of information concerning a certain topic or business application. Databases help you organize this related information in a logical fashion for easy access and retrieval.

Figure 3-1 is a conceptual view of a typical manual filing system that consists of people, papers, and filing cabinets. This lighthearted view of a manual database makes the point that paper is the key to a manual database system. In a real manual database system, you probably have in/out baskets and some type of formal filing method. Information is accessed manually by opening a file cabinet, taking out a file folder, and finding the correct piece of paper. Paper forms are used for input, perhaps with a typewriter. Information is found by sorting the papers manually or by copying desired information from many papers to another piece of paper (or even into a computer spreadsheet). A calculator or a computer spreadsheet might be used to analyze the data further or to report it.

Figure 3-1: A typical manual filing system.

A computer database is nothing more than an automated version of the filing and retrieval functions of a manual paper filing system. Computer databases store information in a structured format that you define. They can store data in a variety of forms, from simple lines of text (such as name and address) to complex data structures that include pictures, sounds, or video images. Storing data in a precise, known format enables a database management system (DBMS) to turn the data into useful information through many types of output, such as queries, and reports.

Figure 3-2 is a conceptual view of an automated database management system such as Access. The person uses a computer to access the data stored in tables — entering data in the tables through data-entry forms and retrieving it by using a query. Queries retrieve only the desired data from the tables. Then a report outputs the data to the screen or a printer. Macros and modules allow the user to automate this process and to create new menus and dialog boxes.

A *relational* database management system (RDBMS) such as Access stores data in many related tables. The user can ask complex questions from one or more of these related tables, with the answers returning as forms and reports.

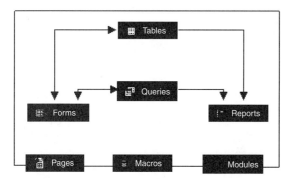

Figure 3-2: A computer database system.

Databases, Tables, Records, Fields, and Values

Microsoft Access follows traditional database terminology. The terms *database*, *table*, *record*, *field*, and *value* indicate a hierarchy from largest to smallest.

Databases

In Access, a *database* is the overall container for the data and associated objects. Database *objects* include tables, queries, forms, reports, macros, and modules, as shown in Figure 3-2. In some computer software products, the database is the object that holds the actual data; in Access, this is called a *table*.

Access can work with only one database at a time. Within a single Access database, however, you can have hundreds of tables, forms, queries, reports, pages, macros, and modules — all stored in a single file with the file extension .MDB (multiple database) or .ADP if you are using SQL Server (more about that later).

Tables

A table is a container for raw data. When data is entered in Access, a table stores it in logical groupings of similar data (the Pets table, for example, contains data about pets) and the table's design organizes the information into rows and columns. Figure 3-3 is a typical Access table design; its *datasheet* (also known as a *browse table* or *table view*) displays multiple lines of data in neat rows and columns.

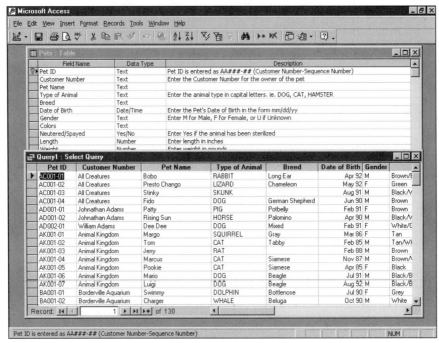

Figure 3-3: A Database table design and datasheet.

Records and fields

As shown in Figure 3-3, the datasheet is divided into rows called *records* and columns called *fields*. The data shown in the table has columns of similar information, such as Pet Name, Customer Number, Breed, or Date of Birth; these columns of data items are fields. Each field is identified as a certain type of data (Text, Number, Date, and so on) and has a specified length. Each field has a name that identifies its category of information.

The rows of data within a table are its records. Each row of information is considered a separate entity that can be accessed or sequenced as desired. All the fields of information concerning a certain pet are contained within a specific record.

Values

At the intersection of a row (record) and a column (field) is a *value*—the actual data element. For example, Bobo, the Pet Name of the first record, is one data value. (How do you identify the first record? It's the record with the rabbit. But what if there is more than one rabbit?) Whereas fields are known by the field name, records are usually known by some unique characteristic of the record. In the Pets table, one field is the Pet ID; Pet Name is not unique because there could be two pets named Fido in the table.

Sometimes it takes more than one field to find a unique value. Customer Number and Pet Name could be used, but it's possible for one customer to have two pets with the same name. You could use the fields Customer Number, Pet Name, and Type of Animal. Again, theoretically, you could have a customer come in and say, "Hi, my name's Larry — this is my pet snake Darryl, and this is my other pet snake Darryl." Creating a unique identifier (such as Pet ID) helps distinguish one record from another without having to look through all the values.

Why Use More Than One Table?

A database contains one or more tables (that is, logical groupings of similar data). Most applications that are developed in Access have several related tables to present the information efficiently. An application that uses multiple tables can usually manipulate data more efficiently than it could with one large table.

Multiple tables simplify data entry and reporting by decreasing the input of redundant data. By defining two tables for an application that uses customer information, for example, you don't need to store the customer's name and address every time the customer purchases an item.

Figure 3-4 shows a typical table relation: the Customer table related to the Pets table. If there were only one table, the customer name and address would have to be repeated for each pet record. Two tables let the user look up information in the Customer table for each pet by using the common field Customer Number. This way, when a customer changes address (for example), it changes only in one record in the Customer table; when the pet information is onscreen, the correct customer address is always visible.

Separating data into multiple tables within a database makes the system easier to maintain because all records of a given type are within the same table. There is a significant reduction in design and work time by taking the time to segment data properly into multiple tables.

Tip   It is also a good idea to create a separate database for just your tables. By separating your design objects (queries, forms, reports, pages, macros, and modules) and the tables into two different databases, it is easier to maintain your application.

Later in this book you have the opportunity to work through a case study for the Mountain Animal Hospital that consists of eight tables and learn to use the Access 2000 Application Splitter to separate the tables from the design objects.

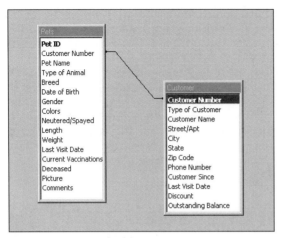

Figure 3-4: Related tables.

Database Objects and Views

If you are new to databases (or are even an experienced database user), before starting to use Access you need to understand some key Access concepts. The Access database contains seven objects, which consist of the data and tools you need to use Access:

Table	Holds the actual data (uses a datasheet to display the raw data)
Query	Lets you search, sort, and retrieve specific data
Form	Lets you enter and display data in a customized format
Report	Lets you display and print formatted data, including calculations and totals
Pages	Lets you publish live forms to a corporate intranet
Macro	Gives you easy-to-use commands to automate tasks without programming
Module	Program written in VBA

Datasheets

Datasheets are one of the many ways by which data can be viewed. Although not a database object, a datasheet displays a list of records from a table in a format commonly known as a browse screen or *table view*. A datasheet displays data as a series of rows and columns (comparable to a spreadsheet), as shown in Figure 3-5. A datasheet simply displays the information from a table in its raw form. This spreadsheet format is the default mode for displaying all fields for all records.

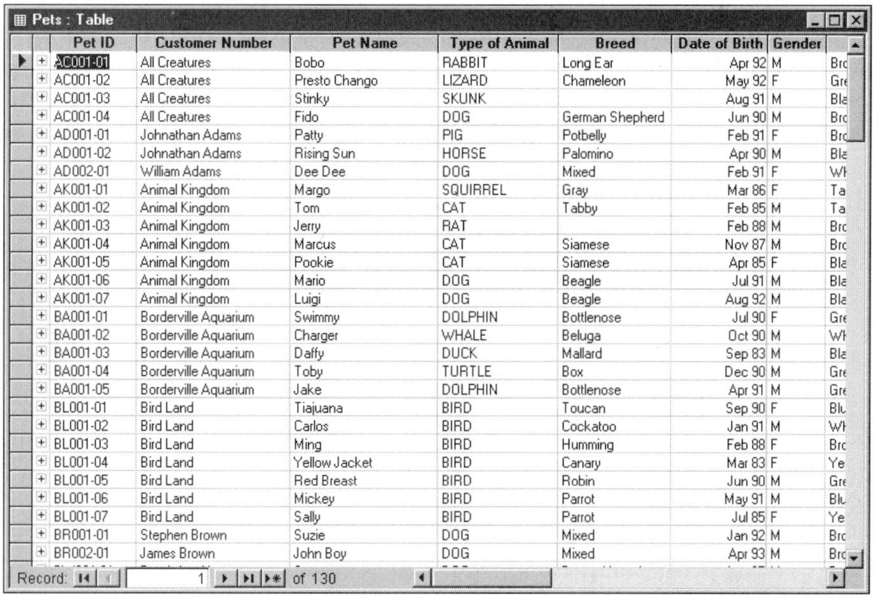

Pet ID	Customer Number	Pet Name	Type of Animal	Breed	Date of Birth	Gender	
AC001-01	All Creatures	Bobo	RABBIT	Long Ear	Apr 92	M	Brc
AC001-02	All Creatures	Presto Chango	LIZARD	Chameleon	May 92	F	Gre
AC001-03	All Creatures	Stinky	SKUNK		Aug 91	M	Bla
AC001-04	All Creatures	Fido	DOG	German Shepherd	Jun 90	M	Brc
AD001-01	Johnathan Adams	Patty	PIG	Potbelly	Feb 91	F	Brc
AD001-02	Johnathan Adams	Rising Sun	HORSE	Palomino	Apr 90	M	Bla
AD002-01	William Adams	Dee Dee	DOG	Mixed	Feb 91	F	Wh
AK001-01	Animal Kingdom	Margo	SQUIRREL	Gray	Mar 86	F	Ta
AK001-02	Animal Kingdom	Tom	CAT	Tabby	Feb 85	M	Ta
AK001-03	Animal Kingdom	Jerry	RAT		Feb 88	M	Brc
AK001-04	Animal Kingdom	Marcus	CAT	Siamese	Nov 87	M	Brc
AK001-05	Animal Kingdom	Pookie	CAT	Siamese	Apr 85	F	Bla
AK001-06	Animal Kingdom	Mario	DOG	Beagle	Jul 91	M	Bla
AK001-07	Animal Kingdom	Luigi	DOG	Beagle	Aug 92	M	Bla
BA001-01	Borderville Aquarium	Swimmy	DOLPHIN	Bottlenose	Jul 90	F	Gre
BA001-02	Borderville Aquarium	Charger	WHALE	Beluga	Oct 90	M	Wh
BA001-03	Borderville Aquarium	Daffy	DUCK	Mallard	Sep 83	M	Bla
BA001-04	Borderville Aquarium	Toby	TURTLE	Box	Dec 90	M	Gre
BA001-05	Borderville Aquarium	Jake	DOLPHIN	Bottlenose	Apr 91	M	Gre
BL001-01	Bird Land	Tiajuana	BIRD	Toucan	Sep 90	F	Blu
BL001-02	Bird Land	Carlos	BIRD	Cockatoo	Jan 91	M	Wh
BL001-03	Bird Land	Ming	BIRD	Humming	Feb 88	F	Gre
BL001-04	Bird Land	Yellow Jacket	BIRD	Canary	Mar 83	F	Ye
BL001-05	Bird Land	Red Breast	BIRD	Robin	Jun 90	M	Gre
BL001-06	Bird Land	Mickey	BIRD	Parrot	May 91	M	Blu
BL001-07	Bird Land	Sally	BIRD	Parrot	Jul 85	F	Ye
BR001-01	Stephen Brown	Suzie	DOG	Mixed	Jan 92	M	Brc
BR002-01	James Brown	John Boy	DOG	Mixed	Apr 93	M	Brc

Record: 1 of 130

Figure 3-5: A typical datasheet.

You can scroll through the datasheet using the directional keys on your keyboard. You can also display related records in other tables while in a datasheet. In addition, you can make changes to the displayed data. Use caution when making any changes or allowing a user to make any modifications in this format. When a datasheet record is changed, it is the data in the underlying table that is actually changing.

Queries and dynasets

A *query* is used to extract information from a database. A query can select and define a group of records that fulfill a certain condition. You can use queries before printing a report so that only the desired data is printed. Forms can also use a query so that only certain records (that meet the desired criteria) appear onscreen. Queries can be used within procedures that change, add, or delete database records.

An example of a query is when a doctor at Mountain Animal Hospital says, "Show me which of the pets that we treat are dogs or cats and located in Idaho. Show them to me sorted by customer name and then by pet name." Instead of asking the question in actual English, the doctor would use a method known as *QBE*, which stands for Query by Example. Figure 3-6 is a typical query screen that asks the doctor's question.

When you enter instructions into the QBE window, the query translates the instructions and retrieves the desired data. In this example, the query first combines data from both the Customer and Pets tables, using the related field Customer Number (the common link between the tables). Then it retrieves the fields Customer Name, Pet Name, Type of Animal, and State. Access then filters the records, selecting only those in which the value of State is ID and the value of Type of Animal is dog or cat. It sorts the resulting records first by customer name and then by pet name within the customer names that are alike. Finally, the records appear onscreen in a datasheet.

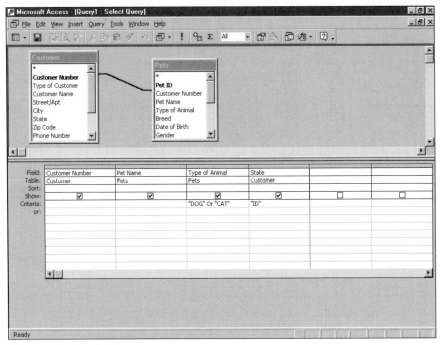

Figure 3-6: A typical query.

These selected records are known as a *dynaset* — a *dynamic set* of data that can change according to the raw data in the original tables.

After you run a query, the resulting dynaset can be used in a form that can be displayed onscreen in a specified format or print on a report. In this way, user access can be limited to the data that meets the criteria in the dynaset.

Data-entry and display forms

Data-entry forms help users get information into a database table in a quick, easy, and accurate manner. Data-entry and display forms provide a more structured view of the data than does a datasheet. From this structured view, database records can be viewed, added, changed, or deleted. Entering data through the data-entry forms is the most common way to get the data into the database table. Figure 3-7 is a typical form.

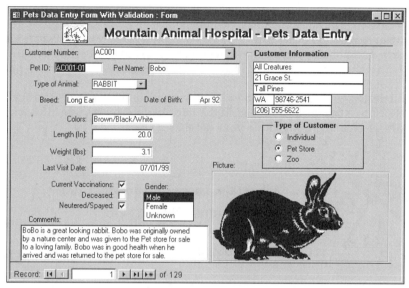

Figure 3-7: A typical data-entry form.

Data-entry forms can be used to restrict access to certain fields within the table. You can also use these forms to check the validity of your data before you accept it into the database table.

Most users prefer to enter information into data-entry forms rather than datasheet tables; data-entry forms can be made to resemble familiar paper documents. Forms make data entry self-explanatory by guiding the user through the fields of the table being updated.

Display-only screens and forms are solely for inquiry purposes. These forms allow for the selective display of certain fields within a given table. Displaying some fields and not others means that you can limit a user's access to sensitive data while allowing inquiry into other fields.

Reports

Reports present your data in printed format. You can create several different types of reports within a database management system. For example, your report can list all records in a given table, such as a customer table. You can also create a report that lists only the customers who meet a given criterion, such as all those who live in the state of Washington. You do this by incorporating a query into your report design. The query creates a dynaset consisting of the records that contain the state code WA.

Your reports can combine multiple tables to present complex relationships among different sets of data. An example is printing an invoice. You access the customer table to obtain the customer's name and address (and other pertinent data) and the sales table to print the individual line-item information for the products ordered. You can then have Access calculate the totals and print them (in a specific format) on the form. Additionally, you can have Access output records into an *invoice report*, a table that summarizes the invoice. Figure 3-8 is a typical invoice report.

When you design your database tables, keep in mind all the types of information you want printed. Doing so ensures that the information you require in your various reports is available from within your database tables.

Mountain Animal Hospital
2414 Mountain Road South
Redmond, WA 06761
206-555-9999

Report Date: 8/25/95

William Primen
1234 Main St
Mountain View,WA 98401-1011
(206) 555-1230

Visit Date
7/7/95

Pet Name: Brutus

Type of Visit	Treatments		Medication		Total
	Description	Price	Description	Price	
INJURY	Cast affected area	$120.00	Byactocaine - 4 oz	$11.00	$131.00
INJURY	Repair complex fracture	$230.00	Nyostatine - 2 oz	$20.00	$250.00
				Brutus Subtotal	$381.00

Pet Name: Little Bit

Type of Visit	Treatments		Medication		Total
	Description	Price	Description	Price	
ILLNESS	Internal Examination	$55.00		$0.00	$55.00
ILLNESS	Lab Work - Blood	$50.00		$0.00	$50.00
ILLNESS	Lab Work - Cerology	$75.00		$0.00	$75.00
ILLNESS	Lab Work - Electrolytes	$75.00	Dual Antibiotic - 8 oz	$8.00	$83.00
ILLNESS	Lab Work - Misc	$35.00	Xaritain Glyconol - 2 oz	$34.50	$69.50
				Little Bit Subtotal	$332.50

Total Invoice:	$713.50
Discount (0%):	$0.00
Subtotal:	$713.50
Washington Sales Tax (4%):	$28.54
Amount Due:	$742.04

Figure 3-8: A typical invoice report.

Summary

You can find more new concepts (and thorough discussions of them) throughout this book. Chapter 11, for example, provides an in-depth discussion of database concepts when working with multiple tables as well as primary and foreign keys, referential integrity, and relationships. This chapter covered these points:

✦ Database is a computer term for a collection of information related to a certain topic or business application.

✦ Databases let you organize this related information in a logical fashion for easy access and retrieval.

✦ An Access database is a single file with an MDB or ADP file extension; it holds all the database objects used in Access.

✦ Database objects include tables, queries, forms, reports, pages, macros, and modules.

✦ A table holds the raw data in fields and contains a definition for every field.

✦ A record is a row in the table, identified by some unique value.

✦ A field is a column in the table, identified by a field name.

✦ The value is an element of data found at the intersection of a record and a field.

✦ Relational database management systems use more than one table to simplify database reporting and eliminate redundant data.

✦ A datasheet (also called a browse table or table view) is a spreadsheet-type view of your data. The datasheet lets you view raw data in a table.

✦ A query lets you ask questions of your data; you use the Query by Example (QBE) screen to select fields, sort the data, and select only specific records by specified criteria. The result of a query is a dynaset. This dynamic set of data can be used with a datasheet, form, or report.

✦ Forms let you view your data in a more structured format. Data can be entered into a form or the form can be read-only.

✦ Reports are used mainly for calculating and summarizing data and are frequently printed.

The next chapter gives a guided tour through Access and shows how some of these objects are used.

✦   ✦   ✦

A Hands-on Tour of Access 2000

Throughout this book are many Access windows and shortcut dialog boxes, and many specific terms are used. It's a good idea to become familiar with these terms. If you used another database software package before Access, you need to translate the terms you already know into the words Microsoft Access uses to refer to the same task or action.

A Tour of the Access Window

The first stop on our tour of Access is a look at the major windows in Access and how to navigate to them using the mouse and the keyboard.

Using the mouse and the keyboard

You can navigate the Access screen by using the mouse, the keyboard, or a combination of both. The best way to get around in Access is by using a mouse or another pointing device. The keyboard is useful for entering data and for moving around the various data-entry areas. It is unproductive, however, to use only the keyboard when designing new forms, queries, or reports. In this book, you learn to complete tasks by using both the keyboard and the mouse. In most cases, using the mouse is preferable.

The Access window

The *Access window* is the center of activity for everything that is done in Access. From this window, many windows can be open simultaneously, each of which displays a different view of your data. Figure 4-1 shows the Access window with a Database window open inside it.

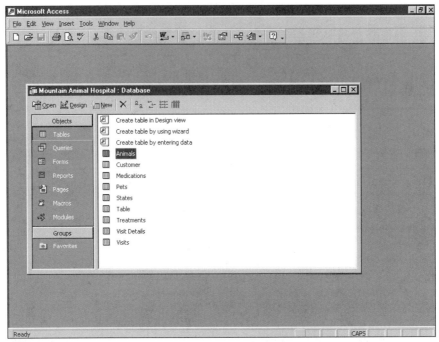

Figure 4-1: The Microsoft Access window.

Options That Change How Access Looks

You may notice when following along in the book that some screens may look slightly different than the screen pictures in the book. Microsoft Access lets you or your company decide how Access works and how the screens look. You can display or hide various toolbars by right clicking on any of the toolbars or the toolbar area and then checking or unchecking the toolbar you want to view or hide.

You may also notice in the main database window the New Object shortcuts. These appear before the other database objects such as Table, Form, or Report names. New Object shortcuts will appear with an Access gold key icon in front of them and decriptive text such as Create table as shown in Figure 4-1. You can turn off this feature by using the Tools ➪ Options menu selection.

Some Access window features that you should be familiar with are:

Title bar   You know what program is currently active by the
                                 name of the program you see displayed on the title
                                 bar. The title bar always displays the program name

Microsoft Access, the Control-menu, Minimize, Restore/Maximize, and Close buttons. The title bar displays the text Microsoft Access by default. When you are viewing a table, form, or other object, it also displays the name of the object in brackets and the object type if the window is maximized. For example, `Microsoft Access - [Pets : Table]`.

Tip   If you are writing a custom application, you may not want the user to see the text Microsoft Access. You can change the title bar display by entering a different application title in the Startup dialog box, which you can display by right-clicking in the gray area of the database container and selecting Startup.

Control-menu button	This button is found in the upper-left corner of the title bar. When this button is clicked once, a menu appears that lets you do certain tasks, including move, size, minimize, or close the current application window. When you double-click on the Control button, the application is exited automatically.
Minimize button	Clicking this button reduces Access to an icon on the Windows taskbar. Access is still running and can be redisplayed by clicking the icon on the taskbar.
Restore/Maximize button	You can use this middle button (displayed only when the Access window is maximized) to restore the window to its previous size. The Maximize button (a square with a dark top border) resizes the Access window to a full-screen view. The Maximize button does not appear in Figure 4-1 because Access is already maximized.
Close button	This button has an X on it and closes Access when clicked.
Menu bar	The menu bar contains commands. When you click a name, a list drops down, offering a selection of commands. Depending on what you are working on, the items on the menu bar and the choices found on each menu vary in Access. The pictures on the menus correspond to pictures on the toolbar. In Access 2000, you can completely customize the menu bars and toolbars.
Toolbar	The toolbar is a group of picture buttons just below the menu bar; it provides shortcuts for running commands. The buttons on the toolbar vary, depending on what you are working on. The toolbar can be resized and moved by clicking between buttons and moving it around the screen. You can also select

	View ➪ Toolbars to show, hide, define new, or customize different toolbars; the same command can be used to select large or small buttons, turn off tooltips, and even display monochrome buttons.
Status bar	The left side of the status bar, at the bottom of the window, displays helpful information about what you are doing at the time. In Figure 4-1, the status line simply says Ready. The right side of the status line tells you whether certain keyboard settings are active. For example, if you have the Caps Lock feature turned on, the word CAPS appears on the status line. In Figure 4-1, you can see NUM, indicating that the Num Lock key is down.
Database window	This window appears whenever a database is open; it is the control center of your database. You use the Database window to open the objects contained within a database, including tables, queries, forms, reports, macros, and modules.

Tip You can change the display on the title bar by changing the Database Startup form. You can display this by selecting Tools ➪ startup ➪ Application Title from the Database window.

The Database window

The name of the open database always displays on the Database window's title bar. In Figure 4-1, for example, you see the *Mountain Animal Hospital: Database* on the title bar. The Mountain Animal Hospital database is on the CD-ROM that comes with this book; it contains all the tables, forms, and other objects demonstrated in this book.

New Feature The *Database window* has three basic parts to it: a set of seven object buttons in a vertical row on the left side, a set of eight toolbar buttons along the top of the window, and a list of files in the right pane.

Object buttons	These buttons are located in a vertical row along the left side of the Database window. Using these buttons, you can select the type of object you want to work with. For example, selecting the Form button displays a list of forms created for that database. Selecting this button also lets you create a new form or redesign an existing one.
Toolbar buttons	The toolbar buttons that are located along the top of the Database window are used to place a database object in a different window or view. These buttons let

you create, open, or design a database object, and view certain details about those database objects.

Object list | This list displays existing files for the database object you select. You can choose a name from the list to display or redesign the object. You can also select what type of view you want for these objects. For example, you can view the *details* about your database objects such as description, date modified, date created, and the type of database object that it is.

You can change the view of the objects in the object list by selecting View from the Database window menu bar, or by using the buttons on top of the database window. There are four choices:

Large Icons | Displays a large icon with the type of object and the object name

Small Icons | Displays a small icon with the type of object and the object name

List | The default view, as shown in Figure 4-1

Details | Lists the object name, date created, and date last modified (see Figure 4-2)

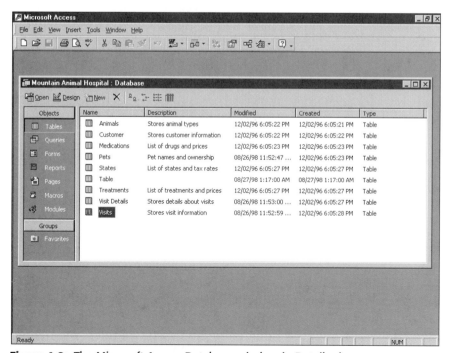

Figure 4-2: The Microsoft Access Database window in Details view.

As Figure 4-2 shows, Details view displays more information about each object. Most important is the date last modified. If you are trying to maintain different versions of a database, this is a great way to see which database contains your latest version. Of course, you can also use the Briefcase replication features in Access 2000 to keep multiple databases synchronized.

You can click on the column headers in the Database window and re-sort the data by the value in the column. Each time you click on a column, you change the order of the sort. For example, clicking on the Name column sorts the data by Name in ascending order. Click on the Name column again, and the data is re-sorted by descending name. The details of the Database window objects can be sorted by any of the columns. A column's width can be changed by placing your mouse pointer on the divider between column names and then dragging to the right to make a column wider or to the left to make it narrower.

Tip A description for an object can be entered by right-clicking on the object name and selecting Properties. You can enter a long description for the object as well as hide the object if you want.

Design windows

The Database window is just one of several windows that you use in Access. Several other commonly used windows are the *object design windows*, which let you design such objects as tables, queries, forms, reports, pages, macros, and modules, and the windows that let you view or edit your data in datasheets, forms, and report previews.

Figure 4-3 shows the Database window, along with the Form Design window and several other windows that assist in the design of forms and reports. These are generally known as *design windows*. The Form window is shown with several fields displayed. The form you see in the figure, Animals, can be used for displaying information about each pet in the Pets table.

The most common design windows are displayed in Figure 4-3: the toolbox, foreground color window, field list, special effect window, borders window, and property window. Because the Form window is active, the toolbar is different.

Access 2000 features tear-off windows on the design toolbar. After a window is displayed from the toolbar, it can be dragged anywhere on the desktop and resized.

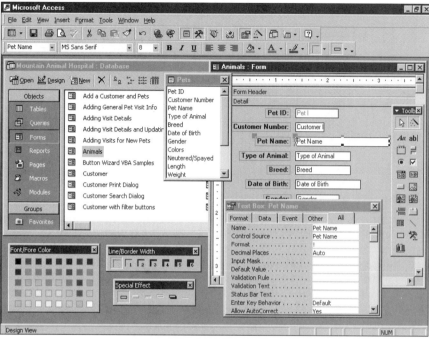

Figure 4-3: Microsoft Access design windows.

The Toolbox

Figure 4-3 displays the *Toolbox* in the right portion of the screen. The Toolbox is used to design a form or report. The Toolbox is similar to a toolbar, but the Toolbox is initially arranged vertically and can be moved around. The Toolbox shown in the Figure 4-3 contains toggle buttons that you can select to add objects to a form or report, such as labels, text boxes, option group boxes, and so on. You can move the Toolbox or close it when you don't need it. You can also resize it by clicking and dragging the its border. It can be anchored as another toolbar by dragging it to an edge of the screen.

Color, Special Effect, and Border windows

The *Font/Fore Color window* is shown at the bottom-left of the screen in Figure 4-3. There is also a background color window and a border color window. Also in the figure are the *Special Effect and Line/Border Width windows*. These windows are used to change the colors of objects, such as text (foreground), lines, rectangles, background, and borders of a control. The Special Effect window is used to give the objects a three-dimensional look (sunken or raised, for example), add a shadow, or add the Windows chiseled look. As with the Toolbox, the palette is resizable. The

Border Width window lets you change the thickness of lines, rectangles, and control borders.

The Field List window

The *Field List* window displays a list of fields from the currently open table or query dynaset. Field List windows are used in Query Design, Form Design, and Report Design windows. You select fields from this window by double-clicking them, and you can drag the fields onto a query, form, or report. If you first select a control type in the Toolbox and then drag a field from the Field List, a control is created (using the selected control type) that is automatically bound to the data field in the Field List.

The Property window

In a form or report, each field (called a *control* in Access) has *properties* that further define the characteristics of the control. The form or report itself and sections of the form or report also have properties. In Figure 4-3, in the lower-center area, you see a Property window displaying some of the properties for a form. Usually, a Property window displays only a portion of the properties available for a specific control, so a tabbed dialog box and a vertical scrollbar in the window let you scroll through the complete list. You can also resize a Property window and even move it around the screen.

Having many windows open at once and resizing and rearranging them onscreen helps you use information productively as you create such objects as forms and reports and use Access's features. Each of the windows is described in detail in the appropriate chapters in this book.

A Simple Access Session

Now that you are familiar with the two main Access windows, you can go through a simple Access session even before you know much about Access. Before proceeding, make sure that you are ready to follow along on your own computer. Your computer should be on, and Access should be installed.

Cross-Reference   Chapter 2 discussed installing and starting Access. You can refer to that chapter for details.

If you have not done so already, perform these steps to get ready for this session:

1. Start your computer and Windows or Windows NT.

2. Start Access 2000 from the Programs menu or find the Access 2000 icon or shortcut and double-click on the icon with the left mouse button. See Chapter 2 if you need more help starting Access.

3. Remove the Microsoft Access dialog box that asks you to Create a New Database or Open an Existing Database by pressing the Cancel button (for now). The Access window without opening or creating a database will display.

4. Maximize the Access window. If the Restore/Maximize button in the title bar shows two rectangles, Access is already maximized; you can go on to the next section. If there is only one square, click on the button to maximize the Access screen. Your screen should now look like that in Figure 4-4.

Figure 4-4: The initial Access window.

You are now ready to move on. Your goal for this session is to open a database and then perform such simple steps as opening a table, displaying a form, and creating a query using the Mountain Animal Hospital database that came with this book (Mountain Animal Hospital.MDB).

The CD-ROM at the Back of the Book

At the back of this book is a CD-ROM that contains several database files that you use throughout this book as well as some other files that are used for practicing importing other file types (Chapter 23) and a variety of other goodies. To use this CD-ROM, follow the directions at the back of the book on the pages opposite the CD-ROM envelope. The two main database files used in this book are:

Mountain Animal Hospital.MDB: A database that contains all the tables, queries, forms, reports, and macros used in this book.

Mountain Start.MDB: A file that contains only tables.

Beginning with Chapter 7, you can use the Mountain Start database file to create your own queries, forms, and reports. You can use the Mountain Animal Hospital database file to see how the final application is created and used.

If you haven't yet used the book's CD-ROM, now is a good time to take it out and run the Setup routine to copy the files to the Access folder or another folder (perhaps named Bible2000) on your hard disk. Updates to this CD will be posted on the Official Access 2000 Bible Web site run by Cary Prague's at www.databasecreations.com/ accessbible2000. This site will be maintained with any known bugs or reader suggestions and will contain news about Microsoft Access and many free goodies to download.

Opening a database

The first thing to do is to open the Mountain Animal Hospital database. When you first start Access, you can open an existing database or create a new database. When you press the Cancel button, you see a blank screen, as shown in Figure 4-4. To open the database, follow these steps:

1. Select File ➪ Open.

2. Navigate to the folder where you placed the files for the book.

   A dialog box similar to the one in Figure 4-5 appears, listing all the databases available in the current folder. If you don't see the Mountain Animal Hospital database listed, you may have to change the folder Access is looking in. To do so, select the drive and folder in which you stored this database. After you tell Access where to find the database, the name should appear in the File List window of the dialog box.

3. Click the name Mountain Animal Hospital.mdb and click Open.

Access opens the database. You should find the name Mountain Animal Hospital at the top of the Database window.

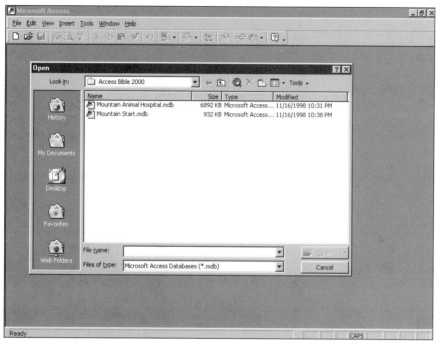

Figure 4-5: The Open dialog box.

Opening a table

With the database open, open the Pets table so that you can view some of the data stored in the Mountain Animal Hospital database. This *table* contains information about the various pets that are treated at the hospital, including the pet and customer identifications, type of animal, pet name, breed, gender, height, weight, and so on. Follow these steps to open the Pets table:

1. Click the Tables button in the Database window if it is not already selected.

2. Select the table called Pets.

3. Select the Open toolbar button in the top part of the Database window. You can Open a table and see the data, Design a table and change the design, or create a New table using the database container buttons.

4. Maximize the window by clicking the Maximize button in the title bar at the top-right of the window.

Access opened the Pets table and your screen should look like Figure 4-6.

| Microsoft Access - [Pets : Table] |

File Edit View Insert Format Records Tools Window Help

Pet ID	Customer Number	Pet Name	Type of Animal	Breed	Date of Birth	Gender	Color
AC001-01	All Creatures	Bobo	RABBIT	Long Ear	Apr 92	M	Brown/Black/Whi
AC001-02	All Creatures	Presto Chango	LIZARD	Chameleon	May 92	F	Green
AC001-03	All Creatures	Stinky	SKUNK		Aug 91	M	Black/White
AC001-04	All Creatures	Fido	DOG	German Shepherd	Jun 90	M	Brown
AD001-01	Johnathan Adams	Patty	PIG	Potbelly	Feb 91	F	Brown
AD001-02	Johnathan Adams	Rising Sun	HORSE	Palomino	Apr 90	M	Black/White
AD002-01	William Adams	Dee Dee	DOG	Mixed	Feb 91	F	White/Grey/Brown
AK001-01	Animal Kingdom	Margo	SQUIRREL	Gray	Mar 86	F	Tan
AK001-02	Animal Kingdom	Tom	CAT	Tabby	Feb 85	M	Tan/White
AK001-03	Animal Kingdom	Jerry	RAT		Feb 88	M	Brown
AK001-04	Animal Kingdom	Marcus	CAT	Siamese	Nov 87	M	Brown/White
AK001-05	Animal Kingdom	Pookie	CAT	Siamese	Apr 85	F	Black
AK001-06	Animal Kingdom	Mario	DOG	Beagle	Jul 91	M	Black/Brown/Whi
AK001-07	Animal Kingdom	Luigi	DOG	Beagle	Aug 92	M	Black/Brown/Whi
BA001-01	Borderville Aquarium	Swimmy	DOLPHIN	Bottlenose	Jul 90	F	Grey
BA001-02	Borderville Aquarium	Charger	WHALE	Beluga	Oct 90	M	White
BA001-03	Borderville Aquarium	Daffy	DUCK	Mallard	Sep 83	M	Black
BA001-04	Borderville Aquarium	Toby	TURTLE	Box	Dec 90	M	Green
BA001-05	Borderville Aquarium	Jake	DOLPHIN	Bottlenose	Apr 91	M	Grey
BL001-01	Bird Land	Tiajuana	BIRD	Toucan	Sep 90	F	Blue/Green
BL001-02	Bird Land	Carlos	BIRD	Cockatoo	Jan 91	M	White
BL001-03	Bird Land	Ming	BIRD	Humming	Feb 88	F	Brown
BL001-04	Bird Land	Yellow Jacket	BIRD	Canary	Mar 83	M	Yellow
BL001-05	Bird Land	Red Breast	BIRD	Robin	Jun 90	M	Green
BL001-06	Bird Land	Mickey	BIRD	Parrot	May 91	M	Blue/Green/Yellow
BL001-07	Bird Land	Sally	BIRD	Parrot	Jul 85	F	Yellow/Green
BR001-01	Stephen Brown	Suzie	DOG	Mixed	Jan 92	M	Brown
BR002-01	James Brown	John Boy	DOG	Mixed	Apr 93	M	Brown/Grey
BW001-01	Bow Wow House	Spot	DOG	Basset Hound	Aug 85	M	Brown
BW001-02	Bow Wow House	Sweety	DOG	Terrier	Sep 82	F	Tan/White
BW001-03	Bow Wow House	Quintin	DOG	Boxer	May 85	M	Black/White
CH001-01	Cat House Pets	Punkin	CAT	Tabby	Aug 84	F	Orange/White

Record: ◄ ◄   1   ► ►◄ ►* of 130

Pet ID is entered as AA###-## (Customer Number-Sequence Number)   NUM

Figure 4-6: The Pets table opened.

Tip   A table can also be opened by double-clicking the table name in the Database window or by clicking the right mouse button while the table name is highlighted. The latter choice displays a shortcut menu, and clicking Open opens the table.

Displaying a datasheet

When the Pets table is opened, a *datasheet* that contains all the data stored in the Pets table is displayed. The data is displayed in a column-and-row format. You can move around the datasheet to view the different types of data stored here. Table 4-1 lists the keyboard commands used to move around the Table window. You can also use the mouse to navigate throughout the table. Simply click on any cell with the left mouse button to move the cursor to that cell. You can also use the mouse to move the scroll bars to navigate around the table.

You can also move through the table with the mouse by using the navigation buttons found in the bottom-left corner of the Datasheet window. (These are sometimes called *VCR buttons.*) The arrows located at the left and right ends with a vertical line next to them move you to the first or last record of the table. The two arrows to the inside of the outer two arrows move you to the preceding or the next record. The right-pointing arrow with the asterisk goes to a new record.

Table 4-1
Keyboard Techniques for Moving Around the Window

Keyboard Keys	Where It Moves
Left(←)- and right-arrow(→)	Left or right one column at a time
Up(↑)- and down-arrow(↓)	Up or down one row at a time
PgUp and PgDn	Up or down one screen at a time
Ctrl+PgUp and Ctrl+PgDn	Left or right one screen at a time
Home	To the first column of the row the insertion point is in
End	To the last column of the row the insertion point is in
Tab	Right one column at a time
Shift+Tab	Left one column at a time
Ctrl+Home	To the first column of the first record in the table
Ctrl+End	To the last column of the last record in the table

Between these arrows is a rectangle that displays the current record number. The total number of records displays to the right of the arrows. If you know which record you want to move to, you can get there quickly by clicking the mouse on the record number (or by pressing F5), typing the number of the record you want to move to, and pressing Enter.

Tip   You can also use the GoTo command (found on the Edit menu) to go to the First, Last, Next, Previous, or New record.

Viewing a table design

Now that you've seen what kind of information is contained in the Pets table and how to navigate around the datasheet, you can look at the table's design in Design view.

To get to Design view, click the Design button on the toolbar; it is the first button on the Access toolbar and shows a triangle, ruler, and pencil, and has an arrow next to it. When you press the arrow, two icons are revealed that represent a set of choices (which include the possible views of the data, such as Design and Datasheet). When you click on the Design icon, the Design window for the Pets table replaces the Pets datasheet. Figure 4-7 displays the Pets Design window.

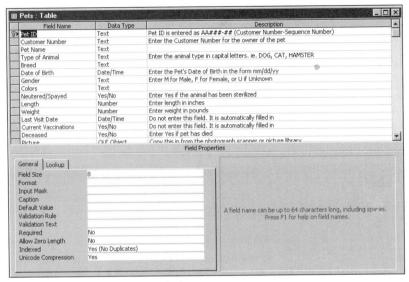

Figure 4-7: The Pets Design window.

Design view shows how the fields for the Pets table were set up. Depending on the type of information to be entered in each field, a specific data type is given to each field. Some of the data types you can choose are Text, Currency, Date/Time, and Memo. A field is also provided for a description of the type of data the field will contain.

The Design window has two parts. In Figure 4-7, the top half of the window lists the field names, field types, and descriptions for each field of the Pets table. Moving around this window is similar to moving around the Pets datasheet.

The bottom half of the Pets Design window displays the field properties for the currently selected field. Different properties can be defined for each field in the table. You can use the mouse or the F6 key to move between the top and bottom panes of the Design window.

The next object to display is a form. Close the Design window by clicking File ➪ Close, which closes the Table Design window and returns you to the Database window.

Displaying a form

The steps for displaying a form are similar to the steps for opening a table. You are just opening a different type of database object. Follow these steps to open the form called Pets:

1. Click the Forms button in the Database window.

2. Select the form named `Pets Data Entry Form`.

3. Click the Open toolbar button at the top of the Database window to open the form.

Tip   You can also double-click any name to open a form.

The Pets Data Entry Form should look like the one in Figure 4-8.

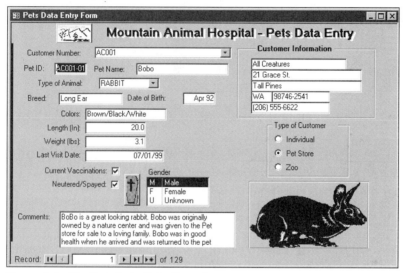

Figure 4-8: The Pets Data Entry Form form.

A *form* provides another way of displaying or changing data. The Pets form is an example of a simple form. You enter information in each text box just as you would enter information in a table. There are many advantages to using a form instead of a datasheet; in a form, you can view more fields onscreen at once, and you can use many data-entry and validation shortcuts. You can also view the picture of each animal on a form and the contents of the Comments Memo field. A datasheet cannot display the picture of each animal or the contents of the Comments Memo field.

To see how the Pets form was created, click the Design button located on the Access toolbar (the first button on the left with the triangle, ruler, and pencil). Your form should look like Figure 4-9.

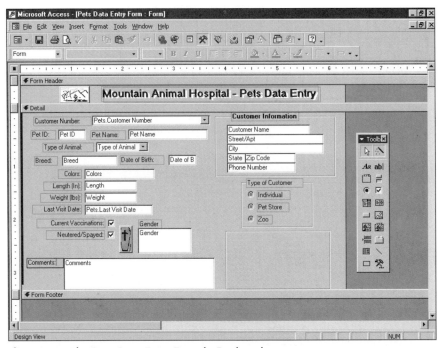

Figure 4-9: The Pets Data Entry Form in Design view.

In Figure 4-9, on the right side of the form is a long, rectangular box that contains several buttons. This is the Form Toolbox. You can move the Toolbox anywhere onscreen. The Toolbox lets you add controls to the form. A *control* is a graphical object, such as a label, text box, checkbox, or command button such as the ones on this form, that is used to display data from a field or enhance the look of the form.

Now that you've seen two different methods of entering data — datasheets and forms — you may have some questions about the data stored in the Pets table. You can find the answers to your questions through queries. Before creating a query, you should close the form by selecting File ➪ Close. This selection closes both the form and the Form Toolbox and returns you to the Database window. If you made any changes to the form, Access prompts you to save your changes before closing the form.

Creating a query

A *query* lets you ask questions about the data stored in your database. The data produced by the query can be saved in its own table for future use or printed as a report. Next, you learn to create a simple query by using the Pets table.

Suppose that you want to see only the records in the Pets table in which the type of animal is a dog and that you only want to see the pet name, type of animal, and breed. The first step is to create the query and add only the Pets table to it. You can add as many tables as you want to a query, but for this example you add only the Pets table. To create the query and add the Pets table, follow these steps:

1. Select the Queries button from the Database window.

2. Click New to create a new query. Access displays a list of all available Query Wizards. Design View should be highlighted.

3. Click the OK button. The Show Table tabbed window appears showing tables, queries, or both.

4. Select Pets by clicking the table name in the Show Table dialog box.

5. Click Add.

6. Click Close.

You should now see an empty Query window.

The query form consists of two panes. The top pane contains a Field List window of the Pets table fields. You use the Field List window to choose which fields are to appear in the query datasheet. The bottom part of the Query screen contains a series of rows and columns. In this pane, you ask questions about the fields in your tables. To view the fields Pet Name, Type of Animal, and Breed, and to select only the records where the value of Type of Animal is DOG, follow these steps:

1. Double-click the Pet Name field from the Field List window to add the field to the query.

2. Add the Type of Animal field to the query.

3. Use the scrollbar to display more fields and add the Breed field to the query.

4. Press F6 to move to the lower pane and place the insertion point on the Criteria: row of the Type of Animal column of the query.

5. Type **DOG** in the cell and move off of the field.

Your query should now look like Figure 4-10. You added the three fields that you want to see in your results to the query. In addition, you want to see only the dogs. Placing DOG in the criteria range tells Access to find only records where the value of Type of Animal is DOG.

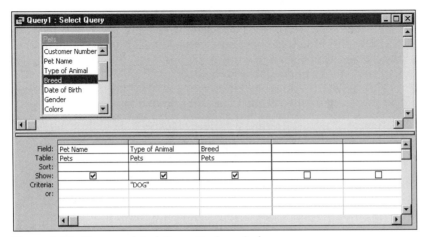

Figure 4-10: The completed Query Design window.

To run the query, click the Run button on the toolbar. It is the button that looks like an exclamation point. After you click the Run button, Access processes your query and produces the results in what is called a *dynaset*. Your dynaset should look like the one in Figure 4-11. The dynaset displays the pet name, type of animal, and breed for each pet that is a dog.

Pet Name	Type of Animal	Breed
Spot	DOG	Basset Hound
Thunder	DOG	Bassett Hound
Mario	DOG	Beagle
Luigi	DOG	Beagle
Pluto	DOG	Beagle
Sandy	DOG	Beagle
Quintin	DOG	Boxer
Rex	DOG	Boxer
Ceasar	DOG	Boxer
Fido	DOG	German Shepherd
Samson	DOG	German Shepherd
Brutus	DOG	German Shepherd
Cleo	DOG	German Shepherd
Dee Dee	DOG	Mixed
Suzie	DOG	Mixed
John Boy	DOG	Mixed
Chili	DOG	Pit Bull
Fi Fi	DOG	Poodle
Sylvester	DOG	Poodle

Record: 1 of 27

Figure 4-11: The Query dynaset.

The results from a query can be saved and used for creating a report that you can view or print. The next section explains how to display a report. Select File ➪ Close to close the query. Click No because you don't want to save the query.

Displaying a report

Queries or tables can be formatted and placed in a *report* for output to a printer. To view and print an already created report of all the pets in the Pets table, follow these steps:

1. Click the Reports button in the Database window.

2. Select Pet Directory from the File List.

3. Select the Preview button (or double-click the report name).

    The report is displayed in the zoomed preview mode. You can display the entire page by clicking the mouse pointer anywhere onscreen (the pointer is currently shaped like a magnifying glass).

4. Click anywhere onscreen again to redisplay the entire page.

5. Click the two-page icon on the toolbar to display two pages.

The report should look like Figure 4-12.

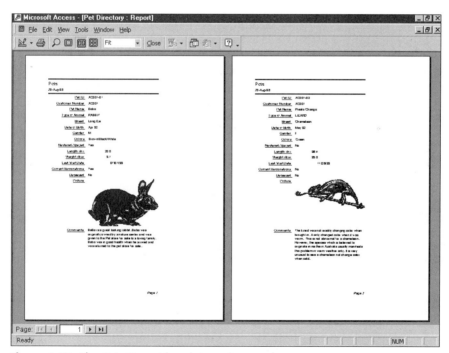

Figure 4-12: The Pets Report in print preview mode.

Tip   You can see as many as six pages at a time by clicking on the four-page icon located to the right of the two-page icon. You can then select any combination up to 2 × 3 pages.

The Pets Report shows all the fields from the first two records of the Pets table. You can use the PgDn key or the navigation buttons in the bottom-left corner of the window to see other pages of the report. The report can also be sent to a printer that has been setup in Windows, or you can return to the Design window to enhance the report.

Click the Close button to return to the Database window.

Ready for More?

You now have experienced many of Access's capabilities. If you had problems with this chapter, you should start again from the beginning. Make sure that you follow the directions exactly and don't move on to the next steps until you understand what you were supposed to do. Hopefully, this quick overview of Access makes you eager to learn to use Access in detail. Don't be afraid to experiment. You can always reload the files from the CD-ROM at the back of this book. You can't hurt Access or your computer.

Now that you have a basic understanding of the various database objects in Access, you are ready to create your own tables, forms, queries, and reports. Before moving on to Part II however, you need to understand how to design a database system. In Chapter 5, you learn how some of the tables, forms, queries, reports, and macros are designed. This design is implemented throughout the book.

Summary

In this chapter, you took a quick tour through Access to learn about the windows you can use. You learned some basic terms that you need to know as you progress through this book, and you now have some hands-on experience in creating and using forms, reports, and queries. The following points were covered:

✦ You can navigate through Access by using the mouse or the keyboard.

✦ The Access Database window contains several menus and toolbars.

✦ When you open a database, all the database objects that comprise the database are displayed in the Database window.

✦ When you open a database table, you see the information stored in the table as a datasheet.

✦ You can make your data entry easier by creating a form from an existing table.

✦ You can ask questions about data in a table by assembling a query and creating a view known as a dynaset.

✦ You can save a query to a report for output to a printer.

In the next chapter, you learn how to design a database.

✦   ✦   ✦

A Case Study in Database Design

The most important lesson to learn as you create a database is good design. Without a good design, you constantly rework your tables, and you may not be able to extract the information you want from your database. Throughout this book, you learn how to use queries, forms, and reports, and how to design each of these objects before you create one. The Mountain Animal Hospital case study provides fictitious examples, but the concepts are not.

This chapter is not easy to understand; some of its concepts and ideas are complex. If your goal is to get right into Access, you may want to read this chapter later. If you are fairly familiar with Access but new to designing and creating tables, you may want to read this chapter before starting the table-creation process.

You learn to design forms and reports that range from simple to complex beginning with simple forms and reports that have just a few fields from a single table, progressing to multiple-page forms and reports that use multiple tables. Eventually the forms and reports will use advanced controls (option buttons, list boxes, combo boxes, and checkboxes) and use one-to-many relationships displayed as subforms and subreports. Finally, you learn to design customer mailing labels and mail-merge reports. Most importantly, you use the tables in the Mountain Animal Hospital application to learn how to do data design.

The Seven-Step Design Method

To create database objects such as tables, forms, and reports, you first complete a series of tasks known as *design*. The better your design, the better your application. The more you think through your design, the faster you can complete any system. Design is not some necessary evil, nor is its intent to produce voluminous amounts of documentation. The sole intent of design is to produce a clear-cut path to follow as you implement it.

Figure 5-1 is a version of the design method that is modified especially for Access.

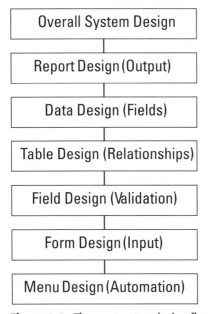

Figure 5-1: The seven-step design flowchart.

These seven design steps, along with the database system illustrated by the examples in this book, teach a great deal about Access and provide a great foundation for creating database applications, including databases, tables, queries, forms, data pages, reports, macros, and simple VBA (Visual Basic for Applications) modules.

As you read through each step of the design process, look at the design in terms of outputs and inputs. Although you see actual components of the system (customers, pets, visits, and visit details), remember that the focus of this chapter is how to design each step. As you watch the Mountain Animal Hospital system being designed, pay attention to the design process, not the actual system.

Step 1: The Overall Design — From Concept to Reality

All software developers and end users face similar problems. The first set of problems is in determining what will meet the needs of the end user (typically your client, your coworker, or yourself). It is important to understand the overall needs the system must meet before you begin to zero in on the details.

The seven-step design method shown in Figure 5-1 helps you create the system you need, at a price (measured in time or dollars) you can afford. The Mountain Animal Hospital, for example, is a medium-sized animal hospital that services individuals, pet stores, and zoos across three states. Mountain Animal Hospital needs to automate several tasks:

- ✦ Entering customer information — name, address, and financial history

- ✦ Entering pet information — pet name, type, breed, length, weight, picture, and comments

- ✦ Entering visit information — details of treatments performed and medications dispensed

- ✦ Asking all types of questions about the information in the database

- ✦ Producing a current Pets and Owners directory

- ✦ Producing a monthly invoice report

- ✦ Producing mailing labels and mail-merge reports

The design process is an *iterative* procedure; as you finish each step, you need to look at all the previous steps again to make sure that nothing in the basic design has changed. If (for example) you are creating a data-entry rule and decide that you need another field (not already in the table) to validate a field you've already defined, you have to go back and follow each previous step needed to add the field. You have to be sure to add the new field to each report in which you want to see it. You also have to make sure that the new field is on an input form that uses the table the field is in. Only then can you use this new field in your system.

Now that you've defined Mountain Animal Hospital's overall systems in terms of what must be accomplished, you can begin the next step of report design.

Step 2: Report Design – Placing Your Fields

Design work should be broken into the smallest level of detail you know at the time. Start each new step by reviewing the overall design objectives. In the case of Mountain Animal Hospital, your objectives are to track customers, track pets, keep a record of visits and treatments, produce invoices, create a directory of pets and owners, and produce mailing labels.

Laying out fields in the report

When you look at the reports you create in this section, you may wonder, "What comes first—the duck or the egg?" Does the report layout come first, or do you first determine the data items and text that make up the report? Actually, these items are conceived together.

It is not important how you lay out the fields in this conception of a report. The more time you take now, however, the easier it will be when you actually create the report. Some people go so far as to place gridlines on the report so that they will know the exact location they want each field to occupy. In this example, you can just do it visually.

The Pets and Owners Directory

Mountain Animal Hospital begins with the task of tracking customers and pets. The first report to be developed is to show important information about pets and their owners and is to be sorted by customer number. Each customer's name and address is to appear with a listing of the pets that the customer has brought into the Mountain Animal Hospital.

The hospital staff has already decided on some of the fields for the customer file. First, of course, is the customer's name (individual or company), followed by address (the customer's street, city, state, and ZIP code) and phone number.

The last visit date is another field that the hospital wants to maintain on file and use on the report. This field will let Mountain Animal Hospital know when it's time to remove a pet from the Pets table; a pet is to be removed if it hasn't been in for a visit in the last three years. The plan is to purge the Pets table each year; recording the last visit is the way to find this information. This field will also alert Mountain Animal Hospital when an animal is due for its yearly checkup so that the staff can send out reminder notices.

With that information in mind, the Mountain Animal Hospital people create the report form design shown in Figure 5-2.

Cross-Reference If you want to learn to implement this report, see Chapter 20. If you want to learn to complete this report with advanced database-publishing enhancements, see Chapter 21.

Mountain Animal Hospital Pets and Owners Directory

[Customer Name]
[Street/Apt]
[City][State][Zip Code]   Type of Customer: [Type of Customer]
[Phone Number]

	General Information	Physical Attributes
Picture	PetID: [Pet ID]	Length Weight Colors Gender
of	Type of Animal: [Type of Animal]	[Length] [Weight] [Colors] [Gender]
Animal	Breed: [Breed]	Status
	Date of Birth: [Date of Birth]	Neutered/Spayed Current Vaccinations Deceased
[Pet Name]	Last Visit: [Last Visit Date]	[Neutered/Spayed] [Current Vaccinations] [Deceased]
[Comments]		

Figure 5-2: The Pets and Owners Directory report design.

Figure 5-3 shows the final hard-copy printout of this report; it also illustrates the capabilities of Access.

The Monthly Invoice Report

Whereas the Pets and Owners Directory concentrates on information about customers and pets, the Monthly Invoice Report displays information about the individual visits of specific customers and pets. Mountain Animal Hospital needs to produce a monthly report that lists all the daily visits by each customer and the customer's pets. Figure 5-4 shows the design of this report.

The design of this report shows customer information at the top and data about each visit in the middle. The middle block appears as many times as each customer had visits on the same date. If a customer brings three pets to the hospital on the same day, the report shows the middle block of data three times — once for each pet. The prices are totaled for each line; the sum of these line totals appears at the bottom of the block.

Mountain Animal Hospital Pets and Owners Directory

All Creatures
21 Grace St.
Tall Pines   WA   98746-2541
(206) 555-6622

○ Individual
⦿ Pet Store
○ Zoo

General Information

Pet ID:	AC001-01
Type Of Animal:	RABBIT
Breed:	Long Ear
Date Of Birth:	Apr 92
Last Visit:	7/1/95

Bobo

Physical Attributes

Length	Weight	Colors
20.0	3.1	Brown/Black/White

Status
☑ Neutered/Spayed   ☑ Current Vaccinations   Deceased

Gender
⦿ Male
○ Female
○ Unknown

Bobo is a great looking rabbit. He was originally owned by a nature center and was given to the Pet store for sale to a loving family. Bobo was in good health when he arrived and was returned to the pet store for sale.

General Information

Pet ID:	AC001-02
Type Of Animal:	LIZARD
Breed:	Chameleon
Date Of Birth:	May 92
Last Visit:	11/26/93

Presto Chango

Physical Attributes

Length	Weight	Colors
36.4	35.0	Green

Status
☐ Neutered/Spayed   ☐ Current Vaccinations   Deceased

Gender
○ Male
⦿ Female
○ Unknown

The lizard was not readily changing color when brought in. It only changed color when it was warm. This is not abnormal for a chameleon. However, the species which is believed to originate in northern Australia usually manifests this problem in warm weather only. It is very unusual to see a chameleon not change color when cold.

General Information

Pet ID:	AC001-03
Type Of Animal:	SKUNK
Breed:	
Date Of Birth:	Aug 91
Last Visit:	5/11/93

Stinky

Physical Attributes

Length	Weight	Colors
29.8	22.0	Black/White

Status
☐ Neutered/Spayed   ☐ Current Vaccinations   Deceased

Gender
⦿ Male
○ Female
○ Unknown

The skunk was descented and was in perfect condition when it left Mountain Animal Hospital.

General Information

Pet ID:	AC001-04
Type Of Animal:	DOG
Breed:	German Shepherd
Date Of Birth:	Jun 90
Last Visit:	11/5/93

Fido

Physical Attributes

Length	Weight	Colors
42.7	56.9	Brown

Status
☑ Neutered/Spayed   ☐ Current Vaccinations   Deceased

Gender
⦿ Male
○ Female
○ Unknown

Figure 5-3: The completed Pets and Owners Directory report.

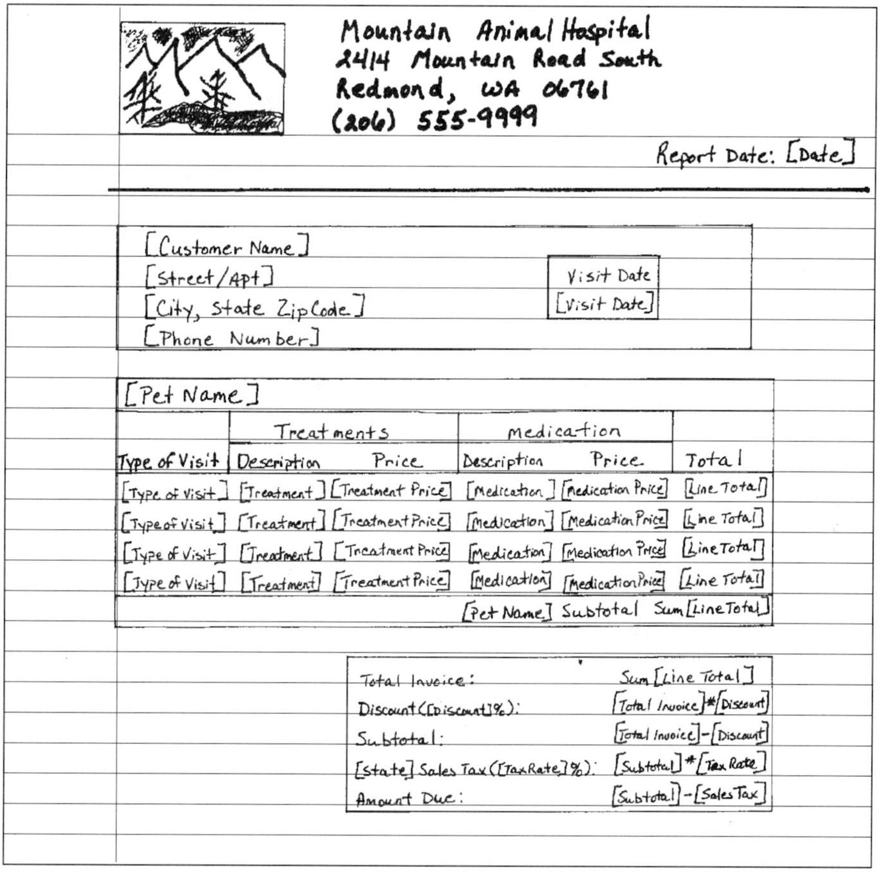

Figure 5-4: The design for the Monthly Invoice Report.

All the data items in the bottom block are summarized and calculated fields. (Because these fields can be calculated whenever necessary, they are not stored in a table.) After subtracting the discount from the subtotal, the report shows a taxable amount. If the customer's visit is subject to tax, the report calculates it at the current tax rate and shows it. Adding the tax to the taxable amount gives the total for the invoice; the customer pays this amount. Figure 5-5 shows the final report (created in Chapter 22).

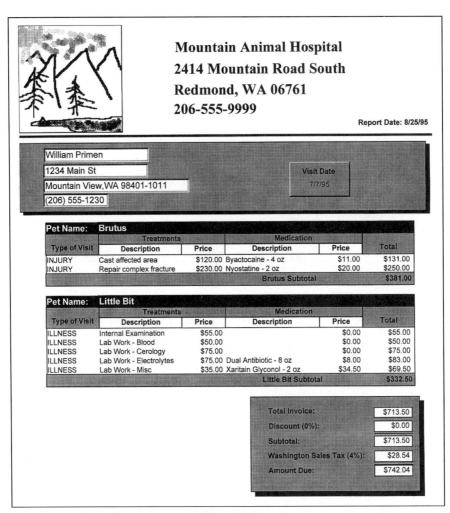

Mountain Animal Hospital
2414 Mountain Road South
Redmond, WA 06761
206-555-9999

Report Date: 8/25/95

William Primen
1234 Main St
Mountain View,WA 98401-1011
(206) 555-1230

Visit Date
7/7/95

Pet Name: Brutus

| Type of Visit | Treatments | | Medication | | Total |
	Description	Price	Description	Price	
INJURY	Cast affected area	$120.00	Byactocaine - 4 oz	$11.00	$131.00
INJURY	Repair complex fracture	$230.00	Nyostatine - 2 oz	$20.00	$250.00
			Brutus Subtotal		$381.00

Pet Name: Little Bit

| Type of Visit | Treatments | | Medication | | Total |
	Description	Price	Description	Price	
ILLNESS	Internal Examination	$55.00		$0.00	$55.00
ILLNESS	Lab Work - Blood	$50.00		$0.00	$50.00
ILLNESS	Lab Work - Cerology	$75.00		$0.00	$75.00
ILLNESS	Lab Work - Electrolytes	$75.00	Dual Antibiotic - 8 oz	$8.00	$83.00
ILLNESS	Lab Work - Misc	$35.00	Xaritain Glyconol - 2 oz	$34.50	$69.50
			Little Bit Subtotal		$332.50

Total Invoice:	$713.50
Discount (0%):	$0.00
Subtotal:	$713.50
Washington Sales Tax (4%):	$28.54
Amount Due:	$742.04

Figure 5-5: The final Mountain Animal Hospital Invoice Report.

In reality, you would design many more reports. In the interest of time and pages, however, the preceding two report designs suffice.

Step 3: Data Design — What Fields Do You Have?

Now that you've decided what you want for output, it's time to think about how to organize your data into a system to make it available for the reports you've already defined (as well as for any ad hoc queries). The next step in the design phase is to take an inventory of all the data fields you need to accomplish the output. One of the best methods is to list the data items in each report. As you do so, take careful note of items that are in more than one report. Make sure that the name for a data item in one report that is the same as a data item in another report is really the same item.

Another step is to see whether you can separate the data items into some logical arrangement. Later, these data items are grouped into logical table structures and then mapped on data-entry screens that make sense. You should enter customer data, for example, as part of a customer table process — not as part of a visit entry.

Determining customer information

First, look at each report. For the Mountain Animal Hospital customer reports, start with the customer data and list the data items, as shown in Table 5-1.

Table 5-1	
Customer-Related Data Items Found in the Customer Reports	
Pets and Owners Directory	*Monthly Invoice Report*
Customer Name	Customer Name
Street	Street
City	City
State	State
ZIP Code	ZIP Code
Phone Number	Phone Number
Type of Customer	Discount
Last Visit Date	

As you can see, most of the data fields pertaining to the customer are found in both reports. The table shows only the fields that are used. Fields appearing on both reports appear on the same lines in the table, which allows you to see more easily which items are in which reports. You can look across a row instead of looking for the same names in both reports. Because the related row and the field names are the same, it's easy to make sure that you have all the data items. Although locating items easily is not critical for this small database, it becomes very important when you have to deal with large tables.

Determining pet information

After extracting the customer data, you can move on to the pet data. Again, you need to analyze the two reports for data items specific to the pets. Table 5-2 lists the fields in the two reports that contain information about the animals. Notice that only one field in the Monthly Invoice Report contains pet information.

Table 5-2	
Pet Data Items Found in the Reports	
Pets and Owners Directory	*Monthly Invoice Report*
Pet ID	
Pet Name	Pet Name
Type of Animal	
Breed	
Date of Birth	
Last Visit Date	
Length	
Weight	
Colors	
Gender	
Neutered/Spayed	
Current Vaccinations	
Deceased	
Picture	
Comments	

Determining visit information

Finally, you need to extract information about the visits from the Monthly Invoice Report, as shown in Table 5-3. You use only this report because the Pets and Owners Directory report does not deal with visit information.

Table 5-3
Extracting Visit Information

Visit Data Items
Visit Date
Type of Visit
Treatment
Treatment Price
Medication
Discount
Tax Rate
Total Amount
Medication Price
Line Total

The table does not list some of the calculated fields, but you can re-create them easily in the report. Unless a field needs to be specifically stored in a table, you simply recalculate it when you run the report.

Combining the data

Now for the difficult part. You must determine the fields that are needed to create the tables that make up the reports. When you examine the multitude of fields and calculations that make up the many documents you have, you begin to see which fields actually belong to the different tables. (You already did some preliminary work by arranging the fields into logical groups.) For now, include every field you extracted. You will need to add others later (for various reasons), though certain fields will not appear in any table.

After you have used each report to display all the data, it is time to consolidate the data by function — and then compare the data across functions. To do this step, first you look at the customer information and combine all its different fields to create one set of data items. Then you do the same thing for the pet information and the visit information. Table 5-4 compares data items from these three groups of information.

| Table 5-4 |
| Comparing the Data Items from the Three Groups | | |
Customer Data Items	*Pet Data Items*	*Visit Data Items*
Customer Name	Pet ID	Visit Date
Street	Pet Name	Type of Visit
City	Type of Animal	Treatment
State	Breed	Treatment Price
ZIP Code	Date of Birth	Medication
Phone Number	Last Visit Date	Medication Price
Type of Customer	Length	Discount
Last Visit Date	Weight	Tax Rate
Discount	Colors	Total Amount
	Gender	
	Neutered/Spayed	
	Current Vaccinations	
	Deceased	
	Picture	
	Comments	

This is a good way to start creating the table definitions for Mountain Animal Hospital, but there is much more to do. First, as you learn more about how to perform a data design, you also learn that the information in the Visits column must be split into two columns. Some of these items are used only once for the visit; other items are used for each detail line in the visit. This is the part of the design process called *normalization*. One customer (for example) has one pet, which has one visit with many visit details. The customer and pet data items each represent one customer or one pet, but a visit may require multiple detail lines.

Table 5-5 divides the Visits column into two columns. The visit date is no longer a unique field for the second table, which contains multiple items for each visit. You have to add another field (which is shown in Table 5-6).

When you look at Table 5-5, you may wonder how to link these two files together so that Access knows which visit-detail information goes with which visit. A *unique field* (often an identification number or code) can do this job. By adding the same field to each group of information, you can keep like information together. You can create a field called *Visit Number*, for example, and use a consistent methodology to assign it. If you use a numeric sequence of year, the day number of the year, and a sequence number, then the third pet to visit on January 12, 1997, becomes 1997012-03. The first four digits record the year, the next three digits tell you the number of days since January 1, and a hyphen separates the date from a sequence number. After you have added this field to both columns for the Visits and Visit Details tables, you can tie the two files together.

Table 5-5 **Dividing the Visits Information**	
Visits	**Visit Details**
Visit Date	Visit Date
Discount	Type of Visit
Tax Rate	Treatment
Total Amount	Treatment Price
	Medication
	Medication Price

There is one more identification number to assign. The Visit Details table does not have a unique identifier, though it does have a *partially* unique identifier. The Visit Number identifier is unique for an individual visit, but not for a visit that has multiple detail lines. A common practice is to assign a sequential number (such as 001, 002, 003, and so on) for each visit detail.

Cross-Reference Commonly, in a one-to-many type of relationship, you need more than one field to make a record unique. See Chapter 11 for a complete discussion of keys and relationships.

Table 5-6 lists the original data items and the reworked items for the Visits and Visit Details tables. The identification fields are shown in bold italics to set them apart.

Table 5-6 A Final Design of Data Items			
Customer	*Pets*	*Visits*	*Visit Details*
Customer Number	Pet ID	Visit Number	Visit Number
Customer Name	Pet Name	Visit Date	Line Number
Street	Type of Animal	Discount	Type of Visit
City	Breed	Tax Rate	Treatment
State	Date of Birth	Total Amount	Treatment Price
ZIP Code	Last Visit Date		Medication
Phone Number	Length		Medication Price
Type of Customer	Weight		
Last Visit Date	Colors		
Discount	Gender		
	Neutered/Spayed		
	Current Vaccinations		
	Deceased		
	Picture		
	Comments		

These are not the final fields that are to be used in the Mountain Animal Hospital database. Many more changes will be made as the design is examined and enhanced.

Step 4: Table Design and Relationships

After you complete the data design, the next step is the final organization of the data into tables. Figure 5-6 shows the final design for the four tables; it's a database diagram that is found in Microsoft Access.

Tip   Creating the final set of tables is easy if you have lots of experience. If you don't, that's all right too, because Access lets you change a table definition after you've created it — without losing any data. In Chapter 6, you create a table in Access.

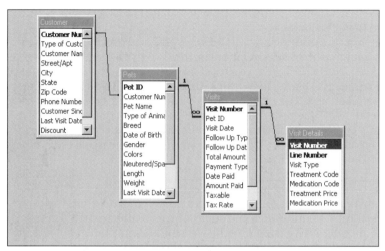

Figure 5-6: The final design, separating the data by function.

Figure 5-6 shows the relationships that join one table to another. Notice the relationship between customers and pets, which is created by adding the Customer Number field to the Pets table. Each pet has a link to its owner, the customer. The same method can be used to establish a relationship between pets and visits. When you add the Pet ID field to the Visits table, each visit itself involves a pet in the Pets table. The Visit Number field establishes a similar relationship between Visits and Visit Details.

Cross-Reference In Chapter 11, you learn all about using multiple tables and how to set relations in Access. For now, a brief discussion of this topic shows how to design the relations between the various tables you've identified.

Tables are related to each other so that information in one table is accessible to another. Usually, in systems designed with Access, there are several tables that are all related to one another. You establish these *relations* by having fields in the various tables that share a common value. The field names in these tables need not be the same; only the values have to match. In the Pets table, for example, you have the customer number. By relating the customer number in the Pets table to the customer number in the Customer table, you can retrieve all there is to know about the customer.

This saves you from having to store the data in two places, and it is the first reason to have a relation — for a *table lookup*. A field in one table can look up data in another table. Another example: You can use the Pet ID field to create a table-lookup relation from the Visits table to the Pets table. Then, as you enter each item, Access passes data about the item (such as pet name, type of animal, breed, and date of birth) from the Pets table to the Visits table.

There is a second reason to set a relation, however. As you decide how to relate the tables you have already designed, you must also decide how to handle multiple occurrences of data. In this system design, there can be multiple occurrences of visit details for each visit. For example, each treatment or medication is entered on a separate detail line. When this happens, you should split the table into two tables. In this design, you need to place the visit number of the visit in a separate table from the single-occurrence visit. This new Visit Details table is related by the Visit Number field found in the Visits table.

The Visits and Visit Details tables are the central focus of the system. The Visits table needs to be related not only to the Pets table but also to the Customer table so that you can retrieve information from it for the invoice report. Even so, you don't have to link the Visits table directly to the Customer table; you can go through the Pets table to get there. Figure 5-6 shows these *chain link* relationships graphically in an actual Access screen (the Query window), where you can set relations between tables.

In the course of a visit, the Pet ID field would be entered, linking the pet information to the Visits table. The Pets table uses the Customer Number field to retrieve the customer information (such as name and address) from the Customer table. Although the name and address are not stored in the Visits table itself, this information is needed to confirm that a pet in for a visit belongs to a particular customer.

Step 5: Field Design Data-Entry Rules and Validation

The next step is to define your fields and tables in greater detail. You also need to determine data-validation rules for each field and to define some new tables to help with data validation.

Designing field names, types, and sizes

First, you must name each field. The name should be easy to remember as well as descriptive so that you recognize the function of the field by its name. It should be just long enough to describe the field but not so short that it becomes cryptic. Access allows up to 64 characters (including spaces) for a field name.

You must also decide what type of data each of your fields will hold. In Access, you can choose any of several data types (as shown in Table 5-7).

Table 5-7
Data Types in Access

Data Type	Type of Data Stored
Text	Alphanumeric characters; up to 255 characters
Memo	Alphanumeric characters; long strings up to 64,000 characters
Number	Numeric values of many types and formats
Date/Time	Date and time data
Currency	Monetary data
AutoNumber	Automatically incremented numeric counter
Yes/No	Logical values, Yes/No, True/False
OLE object	Pictures, graphs, sound, video, word processing, and spreadsheet files

The *Lookup Wizard* is not actually a data type but is, instead, a way of storing a field one way and displaying a related value in another table. Generally, these are text fields, but they can also be numeric. For example, you could store 1, 2, or 3 for the Type of Customer and then look up and display the values Individual, Pet Store, and Zoo instead.

The AutoNumber data type was called Counter in Access 2.0.

One of these data types must be assigned to each of your fields (Part II explains data types in more detail). You also must specify the length of the text fields.

Designing data-entry rules

The last major design decision concerns *data validation*, which becomes important when data is entered. You want to make sure that only *good* data gets into your system — data that passes certain defined tests. There are several types of data validation. You can test for *known individual items*, stipulating (for example) that the Gender field can accept only the values Male, Female, or Unknown. You can test for *ranges* (specifying, for example, that the value of Weight must be between 0 and 1,500 pounds). Finally, you can test for *compound conditions*, such as whether the Type of Customer field indicates an individual (in which case the discount is 0 percent), a pet store (the discount field must show 20 percent), or a zoo (the discount is 50 percent). In the next chapter, you learn where you can enter conditions to perform data validation.

Designing lookup tables

Sometimes you need to design entire tables to perform data validation or just to make it easier to create your system; these are called *lookup tables*. For example, because Mountain Animal Hospital needs a field to determine the customer's tax rate, you decide to use a lookup table that contains the state code, state name, and state tax rate. This also allows you to enter no more than a two-digit state code in the Customer table and then look up the state name or tax rate when necessary. The state code then becomes the field that relates the tables. Because the tax rate can change, Access looks up the current tax rate whenever a visit record is created. The tax-rate value is stored in the Visits table to capture the tax rate for each visit since it is time-dependent data.

Tip   This is the perfect time to use a Lookup Wizard in the Customer table — to look up and display the state instead of the state code.

Although you can create a field on a data-entry form that limits the entry of valid genders to Male, Female, and Unknown, there are too many allowable animal types to create a field for animal type in a form. Instead, you create a table with only one field — Type of Animal — and use the Type of Animal field in the Pets table to link to this field in the Animals lookup table.

Tip   You create a lookup table in exactly the same way as you create any other table, and it behaves in the same way. The only difference is in the way the table is used.

In Figure 5-7, four lookup tables are added to the design. The States lookup table is necessary for determining an individual's tax rate. The Animals lookup table is added to ensure that standard animal types are entered into the Pets table (for the sake of consistency). The Animals lookup table is designed as an alphabetized listing of valid animal types.

The two tables on the far right, Treatments and Medications, are added for several reasons. The last thing you want is to require that doctors enter a long name to complete the Treatment or Medication fields after an animal's visit. Doctors should be able to choose from a list or enter a simple code. Then the code can be used to look up and retrieve the name of the treatment or medication along with its current price. The price that the doctor looks up must be stored in the Visit Details table because prices can change between the time of the visit and the time the invoice is sent out. The Treatments lookup table is added to store a list of treatments and their associated prices. Similarly, a Medications table is added for keeping a list of available medications and their associated prices.

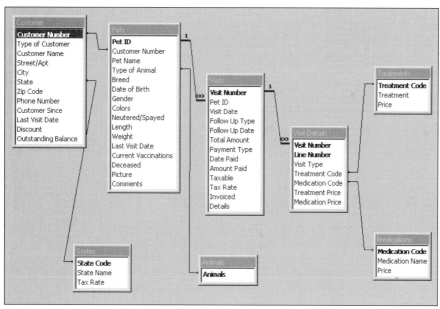

Figure 5-7: The final database diagram, with lookup tables added.

Creating test data

After you define your data-entry rules and how the database should look, it's time to create *test data*. You should prepare this data scientifically (in order to test many possible conditions), and it should serve various purposes. It should let you test the process of data entry: Do all the conditions you created generate the proper acceptance or error messages? In addition, it may lead you to some conditions that you should test for that you hadn't considered. What happens (for example) when someone enters a blank into a field? How about numbers in a character field? Access automatically traps such things as bad dates or characters in Date and Numeric fields, but you must take care of the rest yourself.

The first type of test data to create is simply data that allows you to *populate*, or fill, the databases with meaningful data. This is the initial *good* data that should end up in the database and then be used to test output. Output will consist mainly of your reports. The second type of test data to create is for testing data entry. This includes designing data with errors that display every one of your error conditions, along with good data that can test some of your acceptable conditions.

Test data should let you test routine items of the type you normally find in your data. You should also test for *limits*. Enter data that is only one character long for some fields, and use every field. Create several records that use every position in the database (and thereby every position in the data-entry screen and in the reports).

Create some "bad" test data. Enter data that tests every condition. Try to enter a customer number that already exists. Try to change a customer number that's not in the file. These are a few examples of what to consider when testing your system. Testing your system begins, of course, with the test data.

Step 6: Form Design — Input

After you've created the data and established table relationships, it is time to design your forms. *Forms* are made up of the fields that can be entered or viewed in edit mode. If at all possible, your screens should look much like the forms you would use in a manual system. This setup makes for the user-friendliest system.

Designing data-entry screens

When you're designing forms, you will need to place three types of objects onscreen:

✦ Labels and text box data-entry fields

✦ Special controls (multiple-line text boxes, option buttons, list boxes, check-boxes, business graphs, and pictures)

✦ Graphic enhancements (color, lines, rectangles, and three-dimensional effects)

Place your data fields just where you want them on the form. Although the insertion point normally moves from top to bottom and from left to right when you enter data, you can specify the movement from one field to another. You can also specify any size entry you want. As you place the fields, be sure to leave as much space around them as is needed. A calculated field, such as a total that would be used only for data display, can also be part of a data-entry form.

You can use *labels* to display messages, titles, or captions. *Text boxes* provide an area where you can type or display text or numbers contained in your database. *Checkboxes* indicate a condition and are either unchecked or checked (selected). Other types of controls available with Access include list boxes, combo boxes, option buttons, toggle buttons, and option groups.

Chapter 15 covers the various types of controls available in Access. Access also provides a tool called Microsoft Graph that can be used to create a wide variety of graphs. Pictures can also be displayed using an OLE (Object Linking and Embedding) object stored in a database table, as you learn in Chapter 19.

In this book, you create several basic data-entry forms:

✦ Customer

✦ Pets

✦ Visits general information

✦ Visit Details

The Customer form

The Customer Data Entry Form shown in Figure 5-8 is the simplest of the data-entry forms you create in this book. It is straightforward, simply listing the field descriptions on the left and the fields themselves on the right. The unique *key field* is Customer Number. At the top of the form is the main header, a title that identifies this data-entry form by type: the Customer Data Entry Form.

You can create this simple form by using a Form Wizard. See Chapter 8 for details.

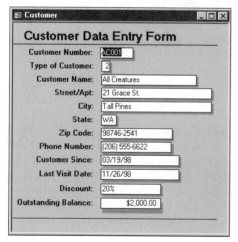

Figure 5-8: The Customer Data Entry Form.

The Pets form

The Pets Data Entry form is more complex. It contains several types of controls, including option buttons, a list box, several combo boxes, check boxes, a picture, and a memo field. As shown in Figure 5-9, the form contains two sections; one section contains pet information, while the other contains customer information.

Cross-Reference   You learn how to create this form in Chapter 16 and to modify it in Chapters 17, 18, and 19.

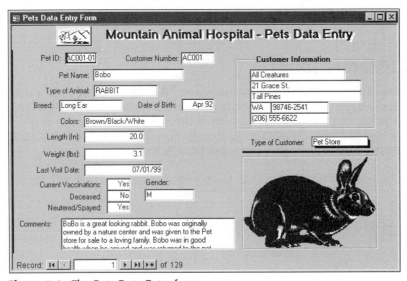

Figure 5-9: The Pets Data Entry form.

The General Visits form

As shown in Figure 5-10, the next data-entry form combines data from several tables to provide general information about visits. This form contains information about customers, pets, and visits; its primary purpose is to allow a user to enter such information into the database. Visit Number is the key field for this form.

The Visit Details form

The final form in this book (shown in Figure 5-11) is for adding the details of individual visits. (You create this form in Chapter 27.) This form contains a *subform* so that many visit details can be seen at once. Many types of subforms can be linked to a form; you can even have a graph as a subform, as you discover in Chapter 19.

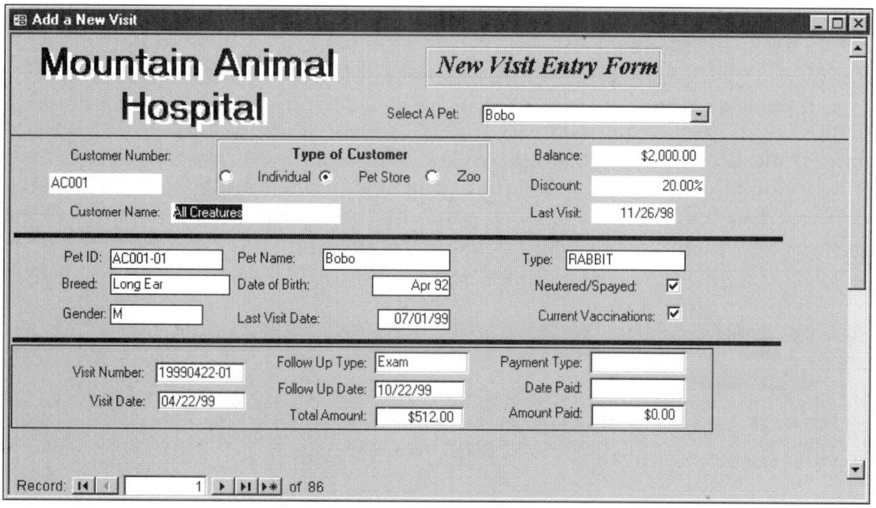

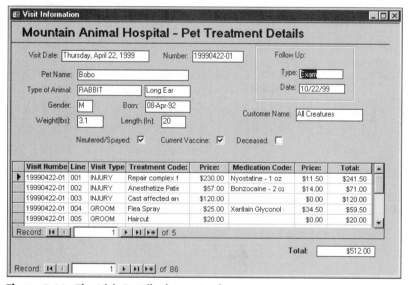

Figure 5-10: The general Visits data-entry form.

Figure 5-11: The Visit Details data-entry form.

Step 7: Automation Design – Menus

After you've created your data, designed your reports, and created your forms, it's time to tie them all together using *switchboards* and *menus*. Figure 5-12 is a switchboard form that also contains a custom menu bar. Switchboards are graphical menus in the center of a form that is usually built with command buttons with text or pictures on them. Menus refer to the lists of commands at the top of a window.

Menus are the key to a good system. A user must be able to follow the system to understand how to move from place to place. Usually each form or report is also a choice on a menu. This means that your design must include decisions on how to group the commands. When you examine the overall design and look at all your systems, you begin to see a distinct set of combinations.

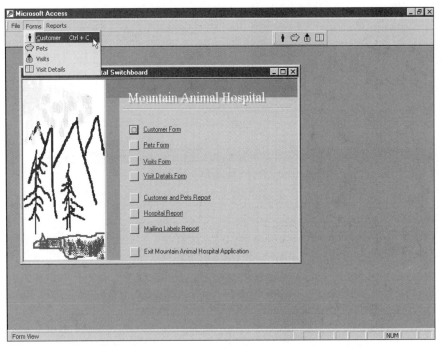

Figure 5-12: A switchboard and menu for Mountain Animal Hospital.

Access macros can be used to create a menu on the top menu bar of the switchboard. This menu gives the user the choice of using pull-down menus or switchboard buttons. You create this switchboard, along with the menus and a complicated dialog box, in Chapter 32.

Summary

In this chapter, you learned how to design reports properly and how to extract data items. You learned how to determine relations, and you saw the design process for the forms and menus that serve as examples in this book. You became acquainted with the Mountain Animal Hospital, a fictitious entity that is used to illustrate database processing. Mountain Animal Hospital is a medium-size veterinary hospital serving individuals, pet stores, and zoos in three states. This chapter explained these points

- ✦ The seven-step method for design includes overall system design, report design, data design, table design, field design, form design, and menu design.

- ✦ The overall design phase helps you think through your system from concept to reality before you touch the keyboard. This makes implementation much more efficient.

- ✦ Report design lets you plan for the output necessary to provide information from your system.

- ✦ In data design, you extract fields from your report to group them logically.

- ✦ After you can group your fields logically, you can create tables in which to store your data. You can then define relationships between related tables.

- ✦ During field design, you define the data types of each field and their sizes. You also define data-entry rules to allow only valid data into your system.

- ✦ You can design forms by using the Access Form Design window, which gives you a WYSIWYG view of your data; designing onscreen forms to resemble printed-out forms is the most user-friendly approach.

- ✦ In Access, you can create switchboards and menus to help you navigate through a system.

This chapter completes the first part of this book. In the next part, you learn to create a table, enter and display data in datasheets, and create simple data-entry forms, queries, and reports. Finally, you learn how to use multiple files.

✦   ✦   ✦

Basic Database Usage

◆ ◆ ◆ ◆

In This Part

Chapter 6
Creating Database
Tables

Chapter 7
Entering, Changing,
Deleting, and
Displaying Data

Chapter 8
Creating and Using
Simple Data-Entry
Forms

Chapter 9
Understanding and
Using Simple Queries

Chapter 10
Creating and Printing
Simple Reports

Chapter 11
Setting Relationships
Between Tables

◆ ◆ ◆ ◆

Creating Database Tables

In this chapter, you learn to start the process of database and table creation. You create a database container to hold the tables, queries, forms, reports, and macros that you create as you learn Access. You also create the Pets database table, which stores data about the pets treated by the Mountain Animal Hospital.

Creating the Pets Table

The Pets table is one of the best examples in the Mountain Animal Hospital database because it illustrates the major field types used by Access. In most tables, the majority of fields are *text fields*. Most data in the world is either numbers or text. The Pets table contains many text fields to fully describe each animal, but it also contains several *numeric fields* to give the animal's length and weight. Another common field type is *date and time*; the Pets table uses a date/time field to record the date of birth. The Pets table also contains several *yes/no fields* for making a single choice. Examples of this field are Neutered or Current Vaccination. Large amounts of text are stored in a *memo field* to record notes about the animal, such as special customer preferences or known allergies. Another field type is the *OLE field*, which is used for storing sound, pictures, or video. In the Pets example, this field will store a picture of the animal.

Before you can create a table, however, you must first create the overall database container.

Creating a Database

The Database window displays all the various object files from your database that you may create while using Access. Actually, a database is a single file. As you create new *object files*, they are stored within the database file. They are not DOS files in themselves; instead, they are stored objects. The database file starts at about 96,000 bytes and grows as you create new objects — tables, queries, forms, reports, macros, and modules. Adding data to an Access database increases the size of the file.

There are many ways to create a new database. When you start Microsoft Access 2000 you will see the new database window as shown in Figure 6-1. You can also display this window by selecting File ➪ New... from the main Access menu, or by clicking on the New icon (the first icon in the toolbar). It looks like a sheet of paper with the right top corner bent down.

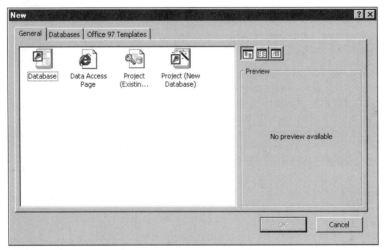

Figure 6-1: Different ways of creating a Microsoft Access database and data file.

The New Database Window has three tabs. These are:

General	Create new Access databases, data access pages, or Access databases connected to SQL Server projects.
Databases	Lets you use the Database Wizard to create a simple ready to run database created for Access 2000 including Asset Tracking, Contact Management, Event Management, Expenses, Inventory Control, Ledger, Order Entry, Resource Scheduling, Service Call Management, and Time and Billing. Figure 6-2 shows these selections.

Office 97 Templates This tab will be displayed if you previously had Access 97 installed on your system. This contains the ready to run databases that were available in Access 97. There are some different examples in this tab.

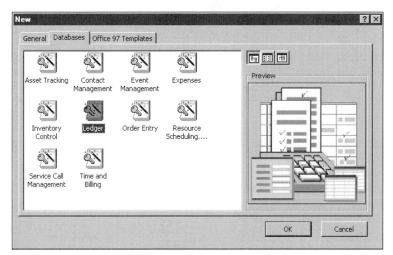

Figure 6-2: The Database window showing the database wizards.

Cross-Reference Chapter 34 shows you how to use the Database Wizard to create the templates you see in the New database form.

Create a new database now by clicking the first toolbar icon.

The New database window appears, as previously shown in Figure 6-1.

The first tab (General) is used to create new empty databases.

Database	Creates a new Access .MDB file to let you create tables, queries, forms, reports, macros, and modules.
Data Access Pages	Creates a web (Intranet) based form with live links to an Access or SQL database.
Project (Existing Database)	Creates a new SQL Server project (.ADP file) to hold the table data using the Microsoft Database Engine but uses an existing Access .MDB file as the front-end.
Project (New Database)	Creates both a new .Access database (.MDB) and a new SQL Server project (.ADP) to hold the data tables.

New Feature *Data Access Pages* are new in Access 2000 and are essentially live data forms that you publish to a corporate intranet. All the users on the intranet can update the data in the form, which updates a data table in an Access database. This requires that you have an intranet set up in your company (an intranet is a network incorporating Web technology such as Microsoft's Internet Information Server (IIS)). It also requires that you use Microsoft Internet Explorer 5.0. Data Access Pages will not work with previous versions of Internet Explorer or with any version of Netscape Navigator. These are discussed in Chapter 33.

Project (Existing Database) creates a new SQL Server project using either SQL Server 6.5, SQL Server 7.0 Enterprise Edition, or the new Microsoft Database Engine. The Microsoft Database Engine is also known as SQL Server 7.0 Desktop Edition that ships with Access 2000. You will attach to that database (more about attaching later) instead of using the tables in your existing .MDB data file. The Microsoft Database Engine is a single user desktop version of Microsoft's more powerful client server SQL Server 7.0 and is used in place of the .MDB file for storing data tables and queries. When you use an .MDB file this is known as using the Jet database engine. When you create a project, you are creating a database file with an .ADP extension that only contains tables and queries. You must also have an Access .MDB data file to contain your user interface objects (forms, reports, macros, and modules).

Understanding How Access Works with Data

There are many ways that Microsoft Access 2000 works with data. For simplicity, you will see the data stored in local tables in the examples of this book. A local table is a table stored within the Access .MDB file This is how you have seen examples so far.

In professionally developed Microsoft Access applications, the program and data are always separate files. The reason for this is maintainability. While you are using the system, data is being changed in the tables. If you find a problem with the forms or reports, how would you deliver a new copy if you are working on the program file while someone else is changing data? The solution is to always separate your tables from the rest of the application.

Figure 6-3 shows some of the ways you can do this. While you may want to first develop your application with the tables within the .MDB database, later you can use the Database Splitter wizard to automatically move the tables in your .MDB file to a separate Access .MDB file and then attach the tables.

You can also attach your tables to the Microsoft Database Engine or the larger SQL Server database. You can also attach to non-Microsoft servers such as Oracle, Informix, or Sybase.

 Cross-Reference You will learn more about file attaching in Chapters 12 (Setting Relationships Between Tables) and 23 (Working with External Data).

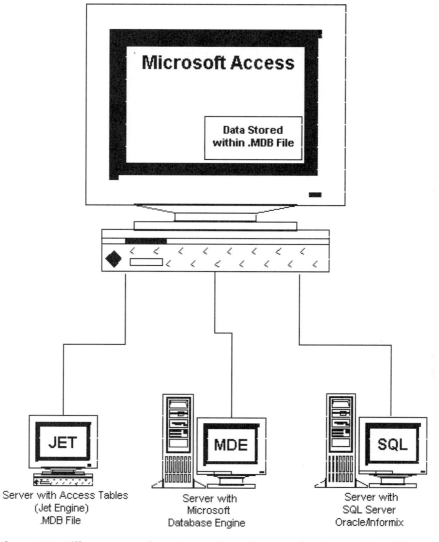

Figure 6-3: Different ways of creating a Microsoft Access database and data file.

After you start the creation process, you must type a name for the database. Figure 6-4 shows a standard Windows 95/98/NT file box with added features, which has several areas, including a combo box and a file list. A default name *db1.mdb* appears in the File name combo box. You can simply type the name you want over the default name. Adding the .MDB file extension is optional; Access adds it automatically when you create the file container. Because the database is a standard Windows 95/98/NT file, its filename can be any valid Windows 95/98/NT long filename. You can also see the existing .MDB files in the file list part of the window. Although the Save in combo box may be set to the My Documents folder initially, you can change this setting to any folder you have. In this example, that folder is C:\Bible2000.

For a shortcut to your History, My Documents, Desktop, Favorites, or Web Folders folder, you can click on the appropriate icons found on the vertical bar at the left side of the File New Database window. Clicking on these icons opens the corresponding folder. For a shortcut to your desktop, click on the desktop icon on the vertical bar.

Caution   An Access 2000 database cannot be used by previous versions of Access.

Tip   You can save an Access 2000 Database in Access 97 format by selecting Tools ⇨Database Utilities ⇨Convert Database ⇨To Prior Access Database Version.

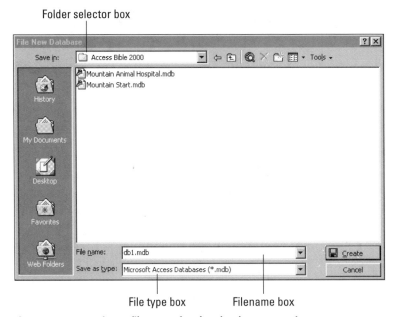

Figure 6-4: Entering a filename for the database container.

Caution   Type **My Mountain Animal Hospital.mdb** in place of `db1.mdb` as the name for your database. Click the Create button to save and open the new database.

If you enter a file extension other than MDB, Access saves the database file but does not display it when you open the database later. By default, Access searches for and displays only those files with an MDB file extension.

The File Selector box displays a list of Access databases in the current subfolder. The list is for reference only; you use it to see what databases already exist. All the database filenames appear *grayed out*; they are not selectable. You can switch to a different subfolder or drive to save the new database container by clicking the second icon with the yellow folder and arrow on it to the right of the Save in box and selecting a new folder or drive from the list.

If you are following the examples in this book, note that we have chosen the name *My Mountain Animal Hospital* for the name of the database you create as you complete the chapters. This database is for our hypothetical business, the Mountain Animal Hospital. After you enter the filename, Access creates the empty database. The CD-ROM that comes with your book contains two database files named *Mountain Animal Hospital Start* (only the database tables), and *Mountain Animal Hospital* (the completed application, including tables, forms, queries, reports, macros, and modules).

The Database Window

The Database window is shown in Figure 6-5. The window has an Object menu on the left, a pane to show the list of objects for the one selected, and a toolbar at the top.

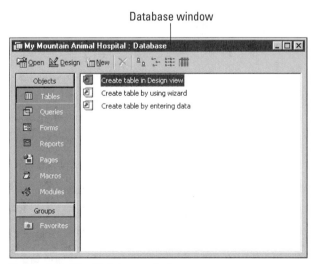

Figure 6-5: The Database window.

Object types

The Database window contains seven buttons on the vertical object menu bar; using them, you can quickly select any of these seven objects that are available in Access:

- ✦ Tables
- ✦ Queries
- ✦ Forms
- ✦ Reports
- ✦ Pages
- ✦ Macros
- ✦ Modules

As you create new objects, the names of the files appear in the Database window. You see only the files for the particular type of object selected. You can select an object type by clicking one of the object buttons.

New Feature   Inside the window are three icons and their labels. These can help you get started and are provided for each type of object. You can turn off this new feature by clicking Tools ➪ Options and selecting New object shortcuts.

The new icons are:

- ✦ Create table in design view
- ✦ Create table by using wizard
- ✦ Create table by entering data

You can see details about the object files in the database window by clicking the last icon on the top of the Database window, or by clicking View from your Access menu bar then Details. This shows information such as the Date Modified, Date Created, and Type.

Groups

Groups can be used to store different database objects in one place.

New Feature   When you place your database objects into a group, this creates a shortcut to that object. For example, assume you are working with a fairly large database with several hundred objects but that you are currently working with only three of those objects. Instead of switching between the seven database objects and browsing for the individual object names, you can store all the objects you use in a group you create. There is a default group setup named Favorites. As shown in Figure 6-6, there is one table, one query, one macro, and one form showing in the Favorites Group.

Note The object must already have been created to add it to a group. This figure uses objects that you create later and are not yet in this database.

Figure 6-6: The Animals table, Customer Names query, OpenCust macro, and Pets Data Entry Form are located in the same group, which is named Favorites.

To create a new group, right click on the Favorites group and select New Group. This will display a dialog box to type in a group name. Once you have typed in the group name, click OK and the group is created.

To display different database objects in your different groups, click and drag the object into the desired group. The same toolbar buttons appear for the different objects as they normally do. The only command you can't perform when you are in a group is to create a new object (Table, Query, Form, Report, Pages, Macro, or Module). The toolbar buttons are described in next section.

The Database window toolbar buttons

The toolbar buttons in the Database window enable you to create a New object or Open an existing object. You can also open an existing object for changes by selecting Design mode. When a button is selected, the appropriate action is taken. Before selecting Open or Design, you should select a filename. When you select New, the type of the new object depends on the object type that you have currently selected. If you chose the Tables type, a new table is created. When you select some of the other object types, the toolbar buttons change. When you select the Reports type, for example, the three available toolbar buttons are Preview, Design, and New. When you select a Pages object, the button choice becomes only New, and the other two buttons are grayed out. When you select a macro or module object, the button choices become Run, Design, and New.

The Access window toolbar

The toolbar shown in Figure 6-7 enables you to perform tasks quickly without using the menus. (Tools that are not available appear in light gray.)

If you place the cursor on an icon without clicking, a Help prompt known as a *tool tip* appears just below the icon, as shown in Figure 6-7 (the Spelling tip). If you want even more help, press Shift+F1, then move the cursor to the object you want more information about and click it. You will see *What's This* help: a small rectangle with a paragraph explaining the use of the selected object. Another method is to select the Office Assistant icon at the far right of the toolbar (it has a question mark inside a bubble), and then type a question in the Office Assistant box.

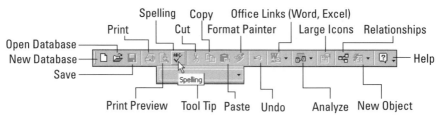

Figure 6-7: The Database window toolbar.

Creating a New Table

After you design your table on paper, you need to create the table design in Access. Although you can create the table interactively without any forethought, carefully planning a database system is a good idea. You can make any changes later, but doing so wastes time; generally the result is a system that is harder to maintain than one that is well planned from the beginning. Before you get started, you should understand the table design process.

The table design process

Creating a table design is a multistep process. By following the steps in order, your table design can be created readily and with minimal effort:

1. Create a new table.

2. Enter each field name, data type, and description.

3. Enter properties for each defined field.

4. Set a primary key.

5. Create indexes for necessary fields.

6. Save the design.

You can use any of these four methods to create a new table design:

✦ Click the New toolbar button in the Database window

✦ Select Insert ➪ Table from the menus

✦ Select New Table from the New Object icon in the Access toolbar

✦ Select Create table in Design view if the New object shortcuts option is turned on

Tip   If you create a new table by clicking the New command button in the Database window, make sure that the Table object is selected first.

Select the New command button in the Database window to begin creating a new table.

The New Table dialog box

Figure 6-8 is the New Table dialog box as Access displays it.

Figure 6-8: The New Table dialog box.

Use this dialog box to select one of these five ways to create a new table:

Datasheet View   Enter data into a spreadsheet

Design View   Create a table design

Table Wizard   Select a prebuilt table that is complete with generic field
                    definitions

Import Table   Import external data formats into a new Access table

Link Table   Link to an existing external data source

Access 2000 provides several ways to create a new table. You can design the structure of the table (such as field names, data types, and size) first, and then add data. Another method is to use the Table Wizard to choose from a list of predefined table designs. Access 2000 also gives you three new ways to create a new table easily. First, you can enter the data into a spreadsheet-like form known as Datasheet view; Access will create the table for you automatically. Second, you can use the Import Table Wizard to select an external data source and create a new table containing a copy of the data found in that source; the Wizard takes you through the import process. Third, you can use the Link Table Wizard, which is similar to the Import Table Wizard except the data stays in the original location and Access links to it from the new table.

To create your first table, the Datasheet view is a great method for getting started; then you can use the table's Design view to make any final changes and adjustments.

Cross-Reference   The Import Table and Link Table are covered in Chapter 23.

Using the Table Wizard

When you create a new table, you can type in every field name, data type, size, and other table property information, or you can use the Table Wizard (as shown in Figure 6-9) to select from a long list of predefined tables and fields. Unlike the Database Wizard (which creates a complete application), the Table Wizard creates only a table and a simple form.

Wizards can save you a lot of work; they are meant to save you time and make complex tasks easier. Wizards work by taking you through a series of screens that ask what you want. You answer these questions by clicking on buttons, selecting fields, entering text, and making yes/no decisions.

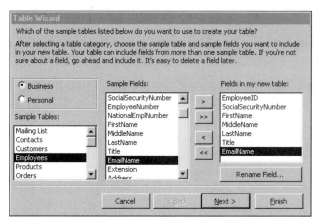

Figure 6-9: A Table Wizard screen.

In the Table Wizard, first you choose between the lists of Business or Personal tables. Some of the Business tables are Mailing List, Contacts, Employees, Products, Orders, Suppliers, Payments, Invoices, Assets, and Students. The Personal list includes Guests, Recipes, Exercise Log, Plants, Wine List, Photographs, Video Collection, and more.

When you select a table, a list appears and shows you all the fields that you might want in the table. Select only the fields you want. Although they are all predefined for data type and size, you can rename a field once it's selected. Once you've chosen your fields, another screen uses input from you to create a primary key automatically. Other screens help you to automatically link the primary key to another table and establish relationships. Finally, the Wizard can display the table, let you enter records into a datasheet, or even create an automatic form for you. The entire process of creating a simple table and form can take less than one minute! Whenever you need to create a table for an application on the Wizard's list, you can save a lot of time by using the Wizard.

Select Datasheet View and click on the OK button to display a blank datasheet with which you can create a new table.

Creating a new table with a Datasheet view

The empty datasheet appears, ready for you to enter data and create a new table whenever you create a new database. You begin by entering a few records into the datasheet. Each column is a field. Each row will become a record in the table. You will learn more about these terms later in this chapter. For now, all you have to do is add data. The more records you add, the more accurately Access can tell what type of data you want for each field, and the approximate size of each data item.

When you first see the datasheet, it's empty. The column headers that will become field names for the table are labeled *Field1*, *Field2*, *Field3*, and so on. You can change the column header names if you want; they become the field names for the table design. You can always change the field names after you have finished creating the table. The table datasheet is initially named *Table* followed by a number. If there are no other tables named Table with a number, Access uses the name *Table1*; the next table is named Table2, and so forth. You can always change this name when you save the table.

Add the five records as shown in Figure 6-10, and change the column headers to the names shown.

Note   You can change a column name by double-clicking the column name and editing the value. When you're done, press Enter to save the new column header. If you enter a column header name that is wider than the default column width, adjust the column width by placing the cursor on the line between the column names and dragging the line to the right to make it wider or to the left to make it narrower.

Pet Name	Type of Animal	Date of Birth	Value	Weight	Deceased
Bobo	RABBIT	4/8/97	$200.00	3.1	No
Presto Chango	LIZARD	5/1/95	$45.00	35	No
Margo	SQUIRREL	3/1/97	$15.00	22	No
Tom	CAT	2/1/94	$275.00	30.8	Yes
Jerry	RAT	2/1/95	$0.00	3.1	No

Record: 14 ◀ 5 ▶ ▶I ▶* of 30

Figure 6-10: A partially completed Datasheet view of the data.

Tip   The Access 2000 and Microsoft Excel spreadsheet Datasheet windows work similarly. Many techniques are the same for both products; even many menus and toolbar icons are the same.

Once you have finished entering the data, save the table and give it a name. To close the table and save the data entered, either choose Close from the File menu or click the Close button in the upper-right corner of the Table window (the button with the X on it). You can also click the Save icon on the toolbar, but this only saves the table; you still have to close it.

Click the Close button in the window to close the table and save the data entry. A dialog box appears, asking whether you want to save changes to Table1. Select Yes to save the table and give it a name, No to forget everything, or Cancel to return to the table to enter more data.

Select Yes to continue the process to save the table. Another dialog box appears because the table is unnamed (it has the default table name).

Enter **Pets** and click OK to continue to save the table. Yet another dialog box appears, asking whether you want to create a primary key—a unique identifier for each record, which you learn about later in the chapter. For now, just select No.

Access saves the table and returns you to the Database window. Notice that the table name `Pets` now appears in the table object list. If you did everything correctly, you have successfully created a table named Pets that has five fields and five records. The next step is to edit the table design and create the final table design you saw in Chapter 5.

To display the Table Design window, select the Pets table and click the Design button. Figure 6-11 shows the Pets Table Design window with the design that was automatically created by the data you entered in the Datasheet view. Notice the field names that you created. Also notice the data types that were automatically assigned by the data you entered. In the next part of this chapter, you learn about these field types.

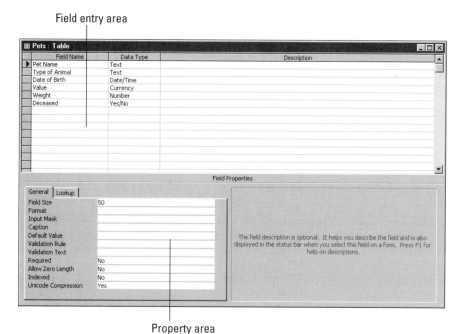

Figure 6-11: The Table Design window.

The Table Design Window

The Table Design window consists of two areas:

✦ The field entry area

✦ The field properties area

The *field entry area* is for entering each field's name and data type; you can also enter an optional description. The *property area* is for entering more options, called *properties,* for each field. These properties include field size, format, input mask, alternate caption for forms, default value, validation rules, validation text, required, zero length for null checking, index specifications, and unicode compression. You learn more about these properties later in the book.

Tip   You can switch between areas (also referred to as *panes*) by clicking the mouse when the pointer is in the desired pane or by pressing F6.

Using the Table window toolbar

The Table design window toolbar, shown in Figure 6-12, contains many icons that assist in creating a new table definition.

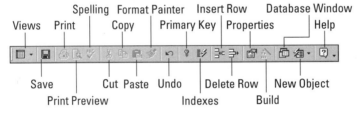

Figure 6-12: The Table Design window toolbar.

Working with fields

Fields are created by entering a *field name* and a *field data type* in each row of the field entry area of the Table window. The *field description* is an option to identify the field's purpose; it appears in the status bar during data entry. After you enter each field's name and data type, you can further specify how each field is used by entering properties in the property area. Before you enter any properties, however, you should enter all your field names and data types for this example. You have already created some of the fields you will need.

Naming a field

A *field name* identifies the field both to you and to Access. Field names should be long enough to identify the purpose of the field, but not overly long. (Later, as you enter validation rules or use the field name in a calculation, you'll want to save yourself from typing long field names.)

To enter a field name, position the pointer in the first row of the Table window under the Field Name column. Then type a valid field name, observing these rules:

✦ Field names can be from 1 to 64 characters.

✦ Field names can include letters, numbers, and many special characters.

✦ Field names cannot include a period (.), exclamation point (!), brackets ([ ]), or accent grave (`).

✦ You cannot use low-order ASCII characters, for example Ctrl-J or Ctrl-L (ASCII values 0 to 31).

✦ You cannot start with a blank space.

You can enter field names in upper, lower, or mixed case. If you make a mistake while typing the field name, position the pointer where you want to make a correction and type the change. You can change a field name at any time — even if it's in a table and the field contains data — for any reason.

Caution   Once your table is saved, however, if you change a field name that is also used in queries, forms, or reports, you have to change it in those objects as well.

Specifying a data type

After you name a field, you must decide what type of data the field will hold. Before you begin entering data, you should have a good grasp of the data types that your system will use. Ten basic types of data are shown in Table 6-1; some data types (such as numbers) have several options.

Table 6-1
Data Types Available in Microsoft Access

Data Type	Type of Data Stored	Storage Size
Text	Alphanumeric characters	0–255 characters
Memo	Alphanumeric characters	0–64,000 characters
Number	Numeric values	1, 2, 4, or 8 bytes
Date/Time	Date and time data	8 bytes

Continued

Table 6-1 *(continued)*		
Data Type	**Type of Data Stored**	**Storage Size**
Currency	Monetary data	8 bytes
AutoNumber	Automatic number increments	4 bytes
Yes/No	Logical values: Yes/No, True/False	1 bit (0 or −1)
OLE Object	Pictures, graphs, sound, video	Up to 1GB
HyperLink	Link to an Internet resource	0–6,144 characters
Lookup Wizard	Displays data from another table	Generally 4 bytes

Figure 6-13 shows the Data Type menu. When you move the pointer into the Data Type column, a down arrow(↓) appears in the text-entry box. To open this menu, move the cursor into the Data Type column and click on the down arrow(↓).

Figure 6-13: The Data Type menu.

Text data is any type of data that is simply characters. Names, addresses, and descriptions are all text data—as are numeric data that are not used in a calculation (such as telephone numbers, Social Security numbers, and ZIP codes). Although you specify the size of each text field in the property area, you can enter no more than 255 characters of data in any text field. Access uses variable length fields to store its data. If you designate a field to be 25 characters wide and you only use 5 characters for each record, then that is all the space you will actually use in your database container. You will find that the .MDB database file can get large quickly but text fields are not the cause. However, rather than allow Access to create every text field with the default 50 characters or the maximum 255 characters, it is good practice to limit text field widths to the maximum you believe they will be used for. Names are tricky because some cultures have long names. However, it is a safe bet that a postal code might be less than 12 characters wide while U.S. a state abbreviation is always 2 characters wide. By limiting the size of the text width, you also limit the number of characters the user can type when the field is used in a form.

The *Memo* data type holds a variable amount of data, from 0 to 64,000 characters for each record. Therefore, if one record uses 100 characters, another requires only 10, and yet another needs 3,000, you only use as much space as each record requires.

The *Number* data type enables you to enter *numeric* data; that is, numbers that will be used in mathematical calculations. (If you have data that will be used in monetary calculations, you should use the *Currency* data type, which enables you to specify many different currency types.)

The *Date/Time* data type can store dates, times, or both types of data at once. Thus, you can enter a date, a time, or a date/time combination. You can specify many types of formats in the property entry area, and then display date and time data as you prefer.

The *AutoNumber* data type stores an integer that Access increments (adds to) automatically as you add new records. You can use the AutoNumber data type as a unique record identification for tables having no other unique value. If, for example, you have no unique identifier for a list of names, you can use an AutoNumber field to identify one John Smith from another.

The *Yes/No* data type holds data that has one of two values and that can, therefore, be expressed as a binary state. Data is actually stored as –1 for yes and 0 for no. You can, however, adjust the format setting to display Yes/No, True/False, or On/Off. When you use a Yes/No data type, you can use many of the form controls that are especially designed for it.

The *OLE Object* data type provides access for data that can be linked to an OLE server. This type of data includes bitmaps (such as Windows 95 Paint files), audio files (such as WAV files), business graphics (such as those found in Access and Excel), and even full-motion video files. Of course, you can play the video files only if you have the hardware and necessary OLE server software.

The *Hyperlink* data type field holds combinations of text and numbers stored as text and used as a hyperlink address. It can have up to three parts: (1) the visual text that appears in a field (usually underlined); (2) the Internet address — the path to a file (UNC, or Universal Naming Convention, path) or page (URL or Uniform Resource Locator); and (3) any subaddress within the file or page. An example of a subaddress is the name of an Access 2000 form or report. Each part is separated by the pound symbol (#).

The *Lookup Wizard* data type creates a field that lets you use a combo box to choose a value from another table or from a list of values. This is especially useful when you are storing key fields from another table in order to link to data from that table. Choosing this option in the Data Type list starts the Lookup Wizard, with which you define the data type and perform the link to another table. You learn more about this field type later.

Entering a field description

The *field description* is completely optional; you use it only to help you remember a field's uses or to let another user know its purpose. Often you don't use the description column at all, or you use it only for fields whose purpose is not readily recognizable. If you enter a field description, it appears in the status bar whenever you use that field in Access. The field description can help clarify a field whose purpose is ambiguous, or give the user a fuller explanation of the values valid for the field during data entry.

Completing the Pets Table

Table 6-2 shows the completed field entries for the Pets table. If you are following the examples, you should modify the table design now for these additional fields. Enter the field names and data types exactly as shown. You also need to rearrange some of the fields and delete the Value field you created. You may want to study the next few pages to understand how to change existing fields (which includes rearranging the field order, changing a field name, and deleting a field).

Table 6-2 Structure of the Pets Table		
Field Name	**Data Type**	**Description**
Pet ID	Text	Pet ID is entered as AA###-## (Customer # Sequence).
Customer Number	Text	Enter the Customer Number for the owner of the pet.
Pet Name	Text	
Type of Animal	Text	Enter the animal type in capital letters, for example, DOG, CAT.
Breed	Text	
Date of Birth	Date/Time	Enter the Pet's Date of Birth in the form mm/dd/yy.
Gender	Text	Enter M for Male, F for Female, or U if Unknown.
Colors	Text	
Neutered/Spayed	Yes/No	Enter Yes if the animal has been sterilized.
Length	Number	Enter length in inches.

Field Name	Data Type	Description
Weight	Number	Enter weight in pounds.
Last Visit Date	Date/Time	Do not enter this field. It is automatically filled in.
Current Vaccinations	Yes/No	Do not enter this field. It is automatically filled in.
Deceased	Yes/No	Enter Yes if pet has died.
Picture	OLE Object	Copy this in from the photograph scanner or picture library.
Comments	Memo	

The steps for adding fields to a table structure are:

1. Place the pointer in the Field Name column in the row where you want the field to appear.

2. Enter the field name and press Enter or Tab.

3. In the Data Type column, click the down arrow and select the data type.

4. Place the pointer in the Description column and type a description (optional).

Repeat each of these steps to complete the Pets data entry for all fields. You can press the down-arrow (↓) key to move between rows, or simply use the mouse and click on any row.

 Tip You can also type in the name of the data type or the first unique letters. The type is validated automatically to make sure it's on the drop-down list. A warning message appears for an invalid type.

Changing a Table Design

As you create your table, you should be following a well-planned design. Yet, changes are sometimes necessary, even with a plan. You may find that you want to add another field, remove a field, change a field name or data type, or simply rearrange the order of the field names. You can make these changes to your table at any time. After you enter data into your table, however, things get a little more complicated. You have to make sure that any changes made don't affect the data entered previously.

In Access 2.0, changes to the table design could be made only in the Table Design window. In Access 97 and 2000, you can make changes to the table design in a datasheet, including adding fields, deleting fields, and changing field names.

New Feature In previous versions of Access, changing a field name usually meant that any queries, forms, reports, macros, or modules that referenced that field name would no longer work and had to be manually found and changed. Access 2000 automatically seeks out most occurrences of the name and changes it for you.

Inserting a new field

To insert a new field, place your cursor on an existing field and select Insert ⇨ Row or click on the Insert Row icon in the toolbar. A new row is added to the table, and any existing fields are pushed down. You can then enter a new field definition. Inserting a field does not disturb other fields or existing data. If you have queries, forms, or reports that use the table, you may need to add the field to those objects as well.

Deleting a field

There are three ways to delete a field:

✦ Select the field by clicking the row selector and pressing Delete.

✦ Select the field and choose Edit ⇨ Delete Row.

✦ Select the field and click the Delete Row icon in the toolbar.

When you delete a field containing data, a warning that you will lose any data in the table for this field displays. If the table is empty, you won't care. If your table contains data, however, make sure that you want to eliminate the data for that field (column). You will also have to delete the same field from queries, forms, and reports that use the field name.

Tip When you delete a field, you can immediately select the Undo button and return the field to the table. But you must do this step *before* you save the changed table's definition.

If you delete a field, you must also delete all references to that field throughout Access. Because you can use a field name in forms, queries, reports, and even table-data validation, you must examine your system carefully to find any instances where you may have used the specific field name.

Changing a field location

One of the easiest changes to make is to move a field's location. The order of your fields, as entered, determines the initial display sequence in the datasheet that displays your data. If you decide that your fields should be rearranged, click on a field selector twice and drag the field to a new location.

Changing a field name

You can change a field name by selecting an existing field name in the Table Design screen and entering a new name; Access updates the table design automatically. As long as you are creating a new table, this process is easy.

Caution If you used the field name in any forms, queries, or reports, however, you must also change it in them. (Remember that you can also use a field name in valida-tion rules and calculated fields in queries, as well as in macros and module expressions — all of which must be changed.) As you can see, it's a good idea not to change a field name; it creates more work.

Changing a field size

Making a field size larger is simple in a table design. However, only text and number fields can be increased in size. You simply increase the Field Size property for text fields or specify a different field size for number fields. You must pay attention to the decimal-point property in number fields to make sure that you don't select a new size that supports fewer decimal places than you currently have.

When you want to make a field size smaller, make sure that none of the data in the table is larger than the new field width. (If it is, the existing data will be truncated.) Text data types should be made as small as possible to take up less storage space.

Tip Remember that each text field uses only the number of characters actually entered in the field. You should still try to make your fields only as large as the largest value so that Access can stop someone from entering a value that may not fit on a form or report.

Changing a field data type

You must be very careful when changing a field's data type if you want to preserve your existing data. Such a change is rare; most data types limit (by definition) what kind of data you can input. Normally, for example, you cannot input a letter into a Numeric field or a Date/Time field.

Some data types do, however, convert readily to others. For example, a Numeric field can be converted to a Text data type, but you lose the understanding of mathematics in the value because you can no longer perform mathematical calculations with the values. Sometimes you might accidentally create a phone number or ZIP code as a Numeric and want to redefine the data type correctly as Text. Of course, you also have to remember the other places where you've used the field name (for example, queries, forms, or reports).

Caution   The OLE data type cannot be converted to any other format.

You need to understand four basic conversion types as you change from one data type to another. The paragraphs that follow describe each of these types.

To Text from other data types

Converting to Text is easiest; you can convert practically any other data type to Text with no problems. Number or Currency data can be converted with no special formatting (dollar signs or commas) if you use the General Number format; the decimal point remains intact. Yes/No data converts as is; Date/Time data also converts as is if you use the General Date format (mm/dd/yy hh:mm:ss AM/PM). Hyperlink data easily converts to Text. The displayed text loses its underline but the remaining Internet resource link information is visible.

From Text to Number, Currency, Date/Time, Yes/No, or Hyperlink

Only data stored as numeric characters (0, 1, 2, 3, 4, 5, 6, 7, 8, 9) or as periods, commas, and dollar signs can be converted to Number or Currency data from the Text data type. You must also make sure that the maximum length of the text string is not larger than the field size for the type of number or currency field you use in the conversion.

Text data being converted to Date data types must be in a correct date or time format. You can use any legal date or time format (such as 10/12/95, 12-Oct-95, or October 95), or any of the other date/time formats.

You can convert text fields to either a Yes or No value, depending on the specification in the field. Access recognizes Yes, True, or On as Yes values, and No, False, or Off as No values.

Tip   Access can also convert Number data types to Yes/No values. Access interprets Null values or 0 as No, and any nonzero value as Yes.

A text field that contains correctly formatted hyperlink text converts directly to hyperlink format — displaying text and address.

From Currency to Number

You can convert data from Currency to Number data types as long as the receiving field can handle the size and number of decimal places. Remember that the Field Size property in numeric fields determines the size (in bytes) of the storage space and the maximum number of decimal places. Anything can be converted to Double, which holds 8 bytes and 15 decimals, whereas Single holds only 4 bytes and 7 decimal places. (For more information, refer to "Entering Field-Size Properties" later in this chapter and to Table 6-2.)

From Text to Memo

You can always convert from Text to Memo data types because the maximum length of a text field is 255 characters, whereas a memo field can hold 64,000 characters. You can convert from Memo to Text, however, only if every value in the memo fields is less than the text field size — that is, no more than 255 characters. Values longer than the field size are truncated.

Understanding Field Properties

After you enter the field names, data types, and field descriptions, you may want to go back and further define each field. Every field has properties, and these are different for each data type. In the Pets table, you must enter properties for several data types. Figure 6-14 shows the property area for the field named Length; ten options are available.

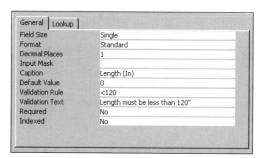

Figure 6-14: Property area for the Length Numeric field.

Pressing F6 switches between the field entry area and the property area. You can also move between panes by clicking the desired pane. Some properties display a list of possible values, along with a downward-pointing arrow, when you move the pointer into the field. When you click the arrow, the values appear in a drop-down list.

Here is a list of all the general properties (note that they may not all be displayed, depending on which data type you chose):

Field Size	Text: limits size of the field to the specified number of characters (1–255); default is 50
Numeric	Allows specification of numeric type
Format	Changes the way data appears after you enter it (uppercase, dates, and so on)

Input Mask	Used for data entry into a predefined and validated format (Phone Numbers, ZIP Codes, Social Security Numbers, Dates, Custom IDs)
Decimal Places	Specifies number of decimal places (Numeric/Currency only)
Caption	Optional label for form and report fields (replacing the field name)
Default Value	The value filled in automatically for new data entry into the field
Validation Rule	Validates data based on rules created through expressions or macros
Validation Text	Displays a message when data fails validation
Required	Specifies whether you must enter a value into a field
Allow Zero Length	Determines whether you may enter the value " " into a text field type to distinguish it from a null value
Indexed	Speeds up data access and (if desired) limits data to unique values
Unicode Compression	Used for multi-language applications. Requires about twice the data storage but allows Office documents including Access reports to be displayed correctly no matter what language or symbols are used.

Entering field-size properties

Field size has two purposes. For text fields, it simply specifies the storage and display size. For example, the field size for the Pet ID field is eight bytes. You should enter the size for each field with a Text data type. If you don't change the default field size, Access will use a 50-byte size for each text field in every record. You should limit the size to the value equal to the largest number of characters.

For Numeric data types, the field size enables you to further define the type of number, which in turn determines the storage size. Figure 6-14 shows the property area for the Length numeric field. There are seven possible settings in the Numeric Field Size property, as described in Table 6-3.

You should make the field size the smallest one possible; Access runs faster with smaller field sizes. Note that the first three settings don't use decimal points, but allow increasingly larger positive or negative numbers. Single and Double permit even larger numbers: Single gives you 7 decimal places, and Double allows 15. Use the Double setting when you need many decimal places or very large numbers.

	Table 6-3		
	Numeric Field Settings		
Field Size Setting	*Range*	*Decimal Places*	*Storage Size*
Byte	0 to 255	None	1 byte
Integer	−32,768 to 32,767	None	2 bytes
Long Integer	-2,147,483,648 to 2,147,483,647	None	4 bytes
Double	-1.797 x 10^{308} to 1.797 x 10^{308}	15	8 bytes
Single	-3.4 x 10^{38} to 3.4 x 10^{38}	7	4 bytes
Replication ID	N/A	N/A	16 bytes

Tip   Use the Currency data type to define data that stores monetary amounts.

Using formats

Formats allow you to display your data in a form that differs from the actual keystrokes used to enter the data originally. Formats vary, depending on the data type you use. Some data types have predefined formats, others have only user-defined formats, and some data types have both. Formats affect only the way your data appears, not how it is actually stored in the table or how it should be entered.

Text and Memo data-type formats

Access uses four user-defined format symbols in Text and Memo data types:

@   Required text character (character or space)

&   Text character not required

<   Forces all characters to lowercase

>   Forces all characters to uppercase

The symbols @ and & work with individual characters that you input, but the < and > characters affect the whole entry. If you want to make sure that a name is always displayed as uppercase, for example, you enter > in the Format property. If you want to enter a phone number and allow entry of only the numbers, yet display the data with parentheses and a dash, you enter the following into the Format property: **(@@@)@@@-@@@@**. You can then enter **2035551234** and have the data displayed as (203)555-1234.

Number and Currency data type formats

You can choose from six predefined formats for Numeric or Currency formats, and many symbols for creating your own custom formats. The predefined formats are as shown in Table 6-4, along with a column that shows how to define custom formats.

Table 6-4 Numeric Format Examples			
Format Type	**Number As Entered**	**Number As Displayed**	**Format Defined**
General	987654.321	987654.321	######.###
Currency	987654.321	$987,654.32	$###,##0.00
Fixed	987654.321	987654.321	######.###
Standard	987654.321	987,654.321	###,###.###
Percent	.987	98.7%	###.##%
Scientific	987654.321	9.87654321E+05	#.####E+00

Date/Time data-type formats

The Date/Time data formats are the most extensive of all, providing these seven predefined options:

General Date — (Default) Display depends on the value entered; entering only a date will display only a date; entering only time will result in no date displayed; standard format for date and time is 2/10/99 10:32 PM

Long Date — Taken from Windows Regional Settings Section Long Date setting; example: Wednesday, February 10, 1999

Medium Date — Example: 10-Feb-99

Short Date — Taken from Windows Regional Settings Section Short Date setting; example: 2/10/99

Tip   For the best Year 2000 compliancy, define all of your dates as Short Dates. When the Windows Regional Settings are changed to display four digit years, so will all of your date fields.

Note   Office 2000 automatically treats all two digit dates before 30 as 2000–2029. Other dates are treated as 1930–1999.

Long Time	Taken from Windows Regional Settings Section Time setting; example: 10:32:15 PM
Medium Time	Example: 10:32 PM
Short Time	Example: 22:32

You can also use a multitude of user-defined date and time settings, including:

: (colon)	Time separator; taken from Windows Regional Settings Section Separator setting
/	Date separator
c	Same as General Date format
d, dd	Day of the month — 1 or 2 numerical digits (1–31)
ddd	First three letters of the weekday (Sun–Sat)
dddd	Full name of the weekday (Sunday–Saturday)
ddddd	Same as Short Date format
dddddd	Same as Long Date format
w	Day of the week (1–7)
ww	Week of the year (1–53)
m, mm	Month of the year — 1 or 2 digits (1 – 12)
mmm	First three letters of the month (Jan–Dec)
mmmm	Full name of the month (January–December)
q	Date displayed as quarter of the year (1–4)
y	Number of the day of the year (1–366)
yy	Last two digits of the year (01–99)
yyyy	Full year (0100–9999)
h, hh	Hour — 1 or 2 digits (0–23)
n, nn	Minute — 1 or 2 digits (0–59)
s, ss	Seconds — 1 or 2 digits (0–59)
ttttt	Same as Long Time format
AM/PM or A/P	Twelve-hour clock with AM/PM in uppercase as appropriate
am/pm or a/p	Twelve-hour clock with am/pm in lowercase as appropriate
AMPM	Twelve-hour clock with forenoon/afternoon designator, as defined in the Windows Regional Settings Section forenoon/afternoon setting

Yes/No data-type formats

Access stores Yes/No data in a manner different from what you might expect. The Yes data is stored as a –1, whereas No data is stored as a 0. You'd expect it to be stored as a 0 for No and 1 for Yes, but this isn't the case. Without a format setting, you must enter –1 or 0, and it will be stored and displayed that way. With formats, you can store Yes/No data types in a more recognizable manner. The three predefined format settings for Yes/No data types are:

Yes/No	(Default) Displays –1 as Yes, 0 as No
True/False	Stores –1 as True, 0 as False
On/Off	Stores –1 as On, 0 as Off

You can also enter user-defined formats. User-defined Yes/No formats have two or three sections. The first section is always a semicolon (;). Use the second section for the –1 (Yes) values, and the last section for the 0 (No) values. If, for example, you want to use the values *Neutered* for Yes and *Fertile* for No, you enter **";Neutered;Fertile"**. You can also specify a color to display different values. To display the Neutered value in red and the Fertile value in green, you enter **";Neutered[Red];Fertile[Green]"**.

Hyperlink data-type format

Access displays and stores Hyperlink data in a manner different than what you would expect. The format of this type is composed of up to three parts:

Display Text	The visual text that is displayed in the field or control
Address	The path to a file (UNC) or page (URL) on the Internet
Sub-Address	A specific location within a file or page

The parts are separated by pound signs. The Display Text is visible in the field or control, while the address and sub-address are hidden. For example, **Microsoft Net Home Page#http://www.msn.com**.

Entering formats

The Pets table uses several formats. Several of the text fields have a > in the Format property to display the data entry in uppercase. The Date of Birth field has an *mmm yy* display of the date of birth as the short month name, a space, and a two-digit year (Feb 99).

Numeric custom formats can vary, based on the value. You can enter a four-part format into the Format property. The first part is for positive numbers, the second for negatives, the third if the value is 0, and the last if the value is null — for example, **#,##0; (#,##0);"- -";"None"**.

Table 6-5 shows several formats.

Table 6-5
Format Examples

Format Specified	Data As Entered	Formatted Data As Displayed
>	Adam Smith	ADAM SMITH
#,##0;(#,##0);"-0-";"None"	15 -15 0 No Data	15 (15) -0- None
Currency	12345.67	$12,345.67
"Acct No." 0000	3271	Acct No. 3271
mmm yy	9/11/99	Sep 99
Long Date	9/11/99	Friday, September 11, 1999

Entering input masks

Input masks allow you to have more control over data entry by defining data-validation placeholders for each character that you enter into a field. For example, if you set the property to **(999)000-0000**, parentheses and hyphens appear as shown, and an underscore (_) appears in place of each 9 or 0 of this phone number template. You would see (_) in your data entry field. Access will automatically add a \ character before each placeholder; for example, **\(999\)000\-0000**. You can also enter a multipart input mask, such as **(999)000-0000!;0;" "**. The input mask can contain up to three parts separated by semicolons.

The first part of a multipart mask specifies the input mask itself (for example, (999)000-0000!). The ! is used to fill the input mask from right to left when optional characters are on the left side. The second part specifies whether Microsoft Access stores the literal display characters in the table when you enter data. If you use 0 for this part, all literal display characters (for example, the parentheses and hyphen) are stored with the value; if you enter 1 or leave this part blank, only characters typed into the text box are stored. The third part specifies the character that Microsoft Access displays for spaces in the input mask. You can use any character; the default is an underscore. If you want to display a space, use a space enclosed in quotation marks (" ").

Note When you have defined an input mask and set the Format property for the same data, the Format property takes precedence when Access displays the data. This means that even if you've saved an input mask with data, it is ignored when data is formatted.

Some of the characters that can be used are shown in Table 6-6.

Table 6-6
Input Mask Characters

Character	Description
0	Digit (0–9; entry required; plus [+] and minus [–] signs not allowed)
9	Digit or space (entry not required; [+] and [–] not allowed)
#	Digit or space (entry not required; blanks converted to spaces; [+] and [-] allowed)
L	Letter (A–Z, entry required)
?	Letter (A–Z, entry optional)
A	Letter or digit (entry required)
a	Letter or digit (entry optional)
&	Any character or a space (entry required)
C	Any character or a space (entry optional)
<	Converts all characters that follow to lowercase
>	Converts all characters that follow to uppercase
!	Causes input mask to fill from right to left, rather than from left to right, when characters on the left side of the input mask are optional. You can include the exclamation point anywhere in the input mask.
\	Displays the character that follows as the literal character (for example, appears as just A)
.,:;-/	Decimal placeholder, thousands, and date time separator determined by Regional Settings section of the Control Panel

Tip   Setting the Input Mask property to the word **Password** creates a password entry text box. Any character typed in the text box is stored as the character, but appears as an asterisk (*).

The Input Mask Wizard

If you are creating a common input mask, use the Input Mask Wizard instead of setting the property to create the mask. When you click the Input Mask property, the builder button (three periods) appears. You can click the Build button to start the Wizard.

Figure 6-15 shows the first screen of the Input Mask Wizard. The Wizard shows not only the name of each predefined input mask, but also an example for each name.

You can choose from the list of predefined masks; click the Try It text box to see how data entry will look. Once you choose an input mask, the next Wizard screen lets you customize it and determine the placeholder symbol. Another Wizard screen lets you decide whether to store any special characters with the data. When you complete the Wizard, Access places the actual input mask characters in the property sheet.

Figure 6-15: The Input Mask Wizard.

You can enter as many custom masks as you need. You can also determine the international settings so that you can work with multiple country masks.

Entering decimal places

Decimal places are valid only for Numeric or Currency data. The number of decimal places can be from 0 to 15, depending on the field size of the numeric or currency field. If the field size is Byte, Integer, or Long Integer, you can have 0 decimal places. If the field size is Single, you can enter from 0 to 7 for the Decimal Places property. If the field size is Double, you can enter from 0 to 15 for the Decimal Places property. If you define a field as Currency (or use one of the predefined formats, such as General, Fixed, or Standard), Access sets the number of decimal places to 2 automatically. You can override this setting by entering a different value into the Decimal Places property.

Creating a caption

You use *captions* when you want to display an alternative to the field name on forms and reports. Normally, the label used to describe a field in a form or a report is the field name. Sometimes, however, you want to call the field name one thing while displaying a more (or less) descriptive label. You should keep field names as short as possible to make them easier to use in calculations. You may then want a longer name to be used for a label in forms or reports. For example, you may use the field name Length but want the label *Length (in)* on all forms.

Setting a default value

A *default value* is the value Access displays automatically for the field when you add a new record to the table. This value can be any value that matches the data type of the field. A default is no more than an initial value; you can change it during data entry. To enter a default value, simply enter the desired value into the Default Value property setting. A default value can be an expression, as well as a number or a text string. Chapter 13 explains how to create expressions.

Note   Numeric and Currency data types are set automatically to 0 when you add a new record.

Understanding data validation

Data validation enables you to limit the values that are accepted in a field. Validation may be automatic, such as the checking of a numeric field for text or a valid date. Validation can also be user-defined. User-defined validation can be as simple as a range of values (such as those found in the Length or Weight fields), or it can be an expression like the one found in the Gender field.

Figure 6-14 (shown earlier) displays the property area for the Length field. Notice the validation options for the Length field. The Validation Rule <120 specifies that the number entered must be less than 120. The Validation Text Length must be less than 120" appears in a warning dialog box (see Figure 6-16) if a user tries to enter a length greater than 120.

Figure 6-16: A data-validation warning box.

You can also use Date values with Date/Time data types in range validation. Dates are surrounded, or *delimited*, by pound signs when used in data-validation expressions. If you want to limit the Date of Birth data entry to dates between January 1, 1980, and December 31, 1999, you enter **Between #1/1/80# and #12/31/99#**.

If you want to limit the upper end to the current date, you can enter a different set of dates, such as **Between #1/1/80# and Date( )**.

The Gender field contains a validation rule based on an expression. The Gender field validation rule limits the data entry to three values: M for Male, F for Female, and U for Unknown. The validation rule for this is InStr("MFU",[Gender])>0. The expression InStr means Access must validate that the entry is in the string specified.

Following the design displayed in Figure 6-17, you can now complete all the property areas in the Pets database. You can also find this database (and the others in this book) in the Mountain Animal Start and Mountain Animal Hospital files on the CD-ROM that accompanies this book.

Pets Table Properties

Field Name	Field Size	Format	Input Mask	Caption	Default Value	Validation Rule	Validation Text	Required	Allow Zero Length	Index
Pet ID	8		LL000-00;0					Yes		Yes
Customer Number	10							Yes		No
Pet Name	35									No
Type of Animal	20									No
Breed	20									No
Date of Birth		mmm yy				#1/1/70 - DATE()	Date of Birth is Invalid	Yes		No
Gender	7	>@				M, F, U	Value must be M, F, or U			No
Colors	50									No
Neutered Spayed					No					No
Length	Single	Standard 1 decimal		Length(In)	0	< 120	Length must be less than 120"			No
Weight	Single	Standard 1 decimal		Weigth(lbs)	0	0 - 1500	Weight must be less than 1500lbs			No
Last Visit Date										No
Current Vaccinations										No
Deceased										No
Picture										No
Comments										No

Figure 6-17: Properties for the Pets table.

Understanding the Lookup Property window

Figure 6-18 is the Lookup Property window for a Yes/No field. Display Control is the only property. This property has three choices: Text Box, Check Box, and Combo Box. Choosing one of these determines the default control type when a particular field appears on a form. Generally, all controls are created as text boxes except Yes/No fields, which are created as a checkbox. For Yes/No data types, however, use the default Check Box setting. If you know a certain text field can only be one of a few combinations, use a combo box. When you select the combo-box control type as a default, the properties change so that you can define a combo box.

Cross-Reference   You learn about combo boxes in Chapter 18.

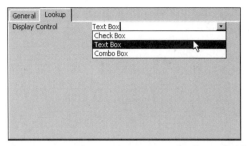

Figure 6-18: The Lookup properties for a field.

Note   The properties for a Lookup field are different for each data type. The Yes/No data type fields, differ from date/time fields or numeric fields. Because a Lookup field is really a combo box (you learn more about these later), the standard properties for a combo box are displayed when you select a Lookup field data type.

Determining the Primary Key

Every table should have a *primary key*—one or more fields that make a record unique. (This principle is called *entity integrity* in the world of database management.) In the Pets table, the Pet ID field is the primary key. Each pet has a different Pet ID field so that you can tell one from another. If you don't specify a unique value, Access creates one for you.

Creating a unique key

Without the Pet ID field, you'd have to rely on another field for uniqueness. You couldn't use the Pet Name field because two customers could have pets with the same name. You could use the Customer Number and Pet Name fields as a multiple-field key, but theoretically it's possible a customer could have two pets, each with the exact same name and even some of the same characteristics (such as Type of Animal and Breed).

Cross-Reference   Multiple-field primary keys are discussed in Chapter 11.

If you don't designate a field as a primary key, Access creates an AutoNumber field and adds it to the beginning of the table. This field contains a unique number for each record in the table, and Access maintains it automatically. For several reasons, however, you may want to create and maintain your own primary key:

✦ A primary key is an index.

✦ Indexes maintain a presorted order of one or more fields that greatly speeds up queries, searches, and sort requests.

✦ When you add new records to your table, Access checks for duplicate data and doesn't allow any duplicates for the primary key field.

✦ Access displays your data in the order of the primary key.

By designating a field such as Pet ID as the unique primary key, you can see your data in an understandable order. In our example, the Pet ID field is composed of the owner's customer number followed by a dash and a two-digit sequence number. If the Adams family, for example, is the first customer on the list of those whose last name begins with AD, their customer number is AD001. If they have three pets, their Pet IDs are designated AD001-01, AD001-02, and AD001-03. This way, the Pet ID field shows the data in the alphabetical order of customers by using the first two letters of their last name as a customer number.

Creating the primary key

The primary key can be created in any of four ways:

✦ Select the field to be used as the primary key and choose Edit ➪ Primary Key.

✦ Select the field to be used as the primary key and select the Primary Key button (the key icon) in the toolbar.

✦ Right-click the mouse to display the shortcut menu and select Primary Key.

✦ Save the table without creating a primary key and Access automatically creates an AutoNumber field.

Before you click the key icon or select the menu choice, you must click the gray area in the far left side of the field that you want as the primary key. A right-pointing triangle appears. After you select the primary key, a key appears in the gray area to indicate that the primary key has been created.

The Indexes window

A primary key is really an *index*. The key icon in the Pet ID column indicates that this is the primary key for the table. You can also see the primary key by looking at the Indexes window. (Figure 6-19 shows a primary key entered into the Indexes window.) You can display or hide this sheet by toggling the Indexes button on the toolbar.

You can determine whether an index is a primary key, whether or not it is unique, and whether null values should be ignored.

Figure 6-19: Working with indexes and primary keys.

The Table Properties window

Just as each field has a property area, the overall table has one, too. Right-clicking the design area and choosing *Properties* or clicking the Properties icon (hand with a piece of paper) on the Table Design toolbar displays it.

Cross-Reference

Figure 6-20 shows the Table Properties window. Here you can enter the validation rule and message that are to be applied when you save a record. You can set up a default sorting order (other than by primary key), and even a default filter to only show a subset of the data. This is also where you can setup your subdatasheets, which are discussed in detail in Chapter 12.

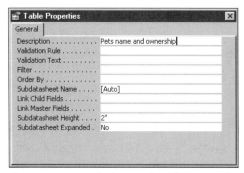

Figure 6-20: Setting general Table properties.

Printing a Table Design

You can print a table design by using Tools ➪ Analyze ➪ Documenter. The *Database Documenter* is an Access 2000 tool that makes it easy to explore your database objects. When you select this menu item, Access shows you a form that lets you select objects to analyze. In Figure 6-21, there is only one object, the Pets table.

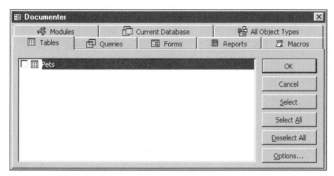

Figure 6-21: The Access Documenter form.

You can also set the various options for printing. When you click on the Options button, a dialog box appears that lets you select what information from the Table Design to print. You can print the various field names, all their properties, the indexes, and even network permissions.

Once you select which data you want to view, Access generates a report; you can view it in a Print Preview window or send the output to a printer.

Tip   The Database Documenter creates a table of all the objects and object properties you specify. You can use this utility to document such database objects as forms, queries, reports, macros, and modules.

Saving the Completed Table

You can save the completed table design by choosing File ⇨ Save or by clicking the Save icon in the toolbar. If you are saving the table for the first time, Access asks for the name of the table; enter it and click OK. Table names can be up to 64 characters long and follow standard Access field-naming conventions. If you have saved this table before and want to save it with a different name, choose File ⇨ Save As and enter a different table name. This creates a new table design and leaves the original table with its original name untouched. If you want to delete the old table, select it in the Database window and press Delete. You can also save the table when you close it.

Manipulating Tables in a Database Window

As you create many tables in your database, you may want to use them in other databases or copy them for use as a history file. You may want to copy only the table structure. You can perform many operations on tables in the Database window, including:

✦ Renaming tables

✦ Deleting tables

✦ Copying tables in a database

✦ Copying a table from another database

You can perform these tasks by direct manipulation or by using menu items.

Renaming tables

You can rename a table with these steps:

1. Select the table name in the Database window.

2. Click once on the table name.

3. Type the name of the new table and press Enter.

You can also rename the table by selecting Edit ➪ Rename or by right-clicking a table and selecting Rename from the shortcut menu. After you change the table name, it appears in the Tables list, which re-sorts the tables in alphabetical order.

Caution   If you rename a table, you must change the table name in any objects where it was previously referenced, including queries, forms, and reports.

Deleting tables

You can delete a table by selecting the table name and pressing the Delete key. Another method is to select the table name and select Edit ➪ Delete or by right-clicking a table and selecting Delete from the shortcut menu. Like most delete operations, you have to confirm the delete by selecting Yes in a Delete Table dialog box.

Copying tables in a database

By using the Copy and Paste options from the Edit menu or the toolbar icons, you can copy any table in the database. When you paste the table back into the database, you can choose from three option buttons:

✦ Structure Only

✦ Structure and Data

✦ Append Data to Existing Table

Selecting the Structure Only button creates a new table design with no data. This allows you to create an empty table with all the same field names and properties as the original table. This option is typically used to create a temporary table or a history structure to which you can copy old records.

When you select Structure and Data, a complete copy of the table design and all its data is created.

Selecting the button Append Data to Existing Table adds the data of one table to the bottom of another. This option is useful for combining tables, as when you want to add data from a monthly transaction table to a yearly history table.

Follow these steps to copy a table:

1. Select the table name in the Database window.

2. Select Edit ➪ Copy.

3. Select Edit ➪ Paste.

4. Type the name of the new table

5. Choose one of the Paste Options.

6. Click OK to complete the operation.

Figure 6-22 shows the Paste Table As dialog box, where you make these decisions. To paste the data, you have to select the type of paste operation and type the name of the new table. When you are appending data to an existing table, you must type the name of an existing table.

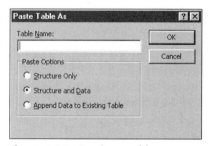

Figure 6-22: Pasting a table.

Copying a table to another database

Just as you can copy a table within a database, you can copy a table to another database. There are many reasons why you may want to do this. Possibly you share a common table among multiple systems, or you may need to create a backup copy of your important tables within the system.

When you copy tables to another database, the relationships between tables are not copied; Access copies only the table design and the data. The method for copying a table to another database is essentially the same as for copying a table within a database. To copy a table to another database, follow these steps:

1. Select the table name in the Database window.

2. Select Edit ➪ Copy.

3. Open another database.

4. Select Edit ➪ Paste.

5. Type the name of the new table.

6. Choose one of the Paste Options.

Click OK to complete the operation.

Summary

This chapter taught you to create database tables by creating a database window and then examining the types of fields and properties you are likely to use in a table. These points were covered:

✦ Databases contain objects, such as tables, queries, forms, reports, pages, macros, and modules.

✦ You can create a table by using a Datasheet View, Design View, Table Wizard, Import Table Wizard, or Link Table Wizard.

✦ Table designs consist of field names, data types, and descriptions.

✦ You can choose from ten basic data types: Text, Number, Currency, AutoNumber, Date/Time, Yes/No, Memo, OLE, Hyperlink, and Lookup Wizard.

✦ Each field has properties: Field Size, Format, Caption, Default Value, Validation Rule, Validation Text, Indexed, and unicode compression.

✦ Each table has a primary key field, which is an index that must contain a unique value for each record.

✦ When a table design is complete, you can still rearrange, insert, delete, and rename fields.

✦ You can rename, delete, or copy and paste tables in the Database window.

The next step is to input data into your table, which you can do in a variety of ways. In the next chapter, you learn to use a datasheet to input your data.

✦   ✦   ✦

Entering, Changing, Deleting, and Displaying Data

CHAPTER

7

In this chapter, you use a datasheet to put data into a Microsoft Access table. This method enables you to see many records at once, as well as many of your fields. Using the Pets table created in the preceding chapter, you learn to add, change, and delete data, and you learn about features for displaying data in a datasheet.

Understanding Datasheets

Using a datasheet is one of the many ways data can be viewed in Access. Datasheets display a list of records in a format commonly known as a browse screen in dBASE, a table view in Paradox, and a spreadsheet in Excel or Lotus 1-2-3. A datasheet is like a table or spreadsheet in that data is displayed as a series of rows and columns. Figure 7-1 is a typical datasheet view of data. Like a table or spreadsheet, a datasheet displays data as a series of rows and columns. By scrolling the datasheet up or down, you can see records that don't fit onscreen at that moment, and by scrolling left or right, you can see more columns.

Datasheets are completely customizable, so you can look at your data in many ways. By changing the font size, you can see more or less of your table onscreen. The order of the records or the fields can be rearranged. You can hide columns, change the displayed column width or row height, and lock several columns in position so that they continue to be displayed as you scroll around other parts of your datasheet.

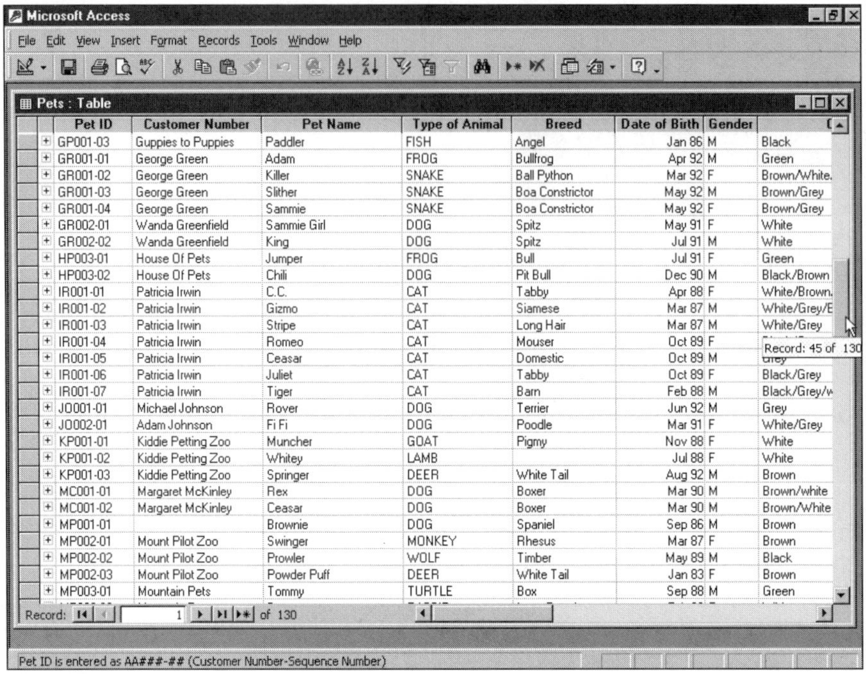

Pet ID	Customer Number	Pet Name	Type of Animal	Breed	Date of Birth	Gender	C
GP001-03	Guppies to Puppies	Paddler	FISH	Angel	Jan 86	M	Black
GR001-01	George Green	Adam	FROG	Bullfrog	Apr 92	M	Green
GR001-02	George Green	Killer	SNAKE	Ball Python	Mar 92	F	Brown/White.
GR001-03	George Green	Slither	SNAKE	Boa Constrictor	May 92	M	Brown/Grey
GR001-04	George Green	Sammie	SNAKE	Boa Constrictor	May 92	F	Brown/Grey
GR002-01	Wanda Greenfield	Sammie Girl	DOG	Spitz	May 91	F	White
GR002-02	Wanda Greenfield	King	DOG	Spitz	Jul 91	M	White
HP003-01	House Of Pets	Jumper	FROG	Bull	Jul 91	F	Green
HP003-02	House Of Pets	Chili	DOG	Pit Bull	Dec 90	M	Black/Brown
IR001-01	Patricia Irwin	C.C.	CAT	Tabby	Apr 88	F	White/Brown.
IR001-02	Patricia Irwin	Gizmo	CAT	Siamese	Mar 87	M	White/Grey/E
IR001-03	Patricia Irwin	Stripe	CAT	Long Hair	Mar 87	M	White/Grey
IR001-04	Patricia Irwin	Romeo	CAT	Mouser	Oct 89	F	
IR001-05	Patricia Irwin	Ceasar	CAT	Domestic	Oct 89	M	Grey
IR001-06	Patricia Irwin	Juliet	CAT	Tabby	Oct 89	F	Black/Grey
IR001-07	Patricia Irwin	Tiger	CAT	Barn	Feb 88	M	Black/Grey/W
JO001-01	Michael Johnson	Rover	DOG	Terrier	Jun 92	M	Grey
JO002-01	Adam Johnson	Fi Fi	DOG	Poodle	Mar 91	F	White/Grey
KP001-01	Kiddie Petting Zoo	Muncher	GOAT	Pigmy	Nov 88	F	White
KP001-02	Kiddie Petting Zoo	Whitey	LAMB		Jul 88	F	White
KP001-03	Kiddie Petting Zoo	Springer	DEER	White Tail	Aug 92	M	Brown
MC001-01	Margaret McKinley	Rex	DOG	Boxer	Mar 90	M	Brown/white
MC001-02	Margaret McKinley	Ceasar	DOG	Boxer	Mar 90	M	Brown/White
MP001-01		Brownie	DOG	Spaniel	Sep 86	M	Brown
MP002-01	Mount Pilot Zoo	Swinger	MONKEY	Rhesus	Mar 87	F	Brown
MP002-02	Mount Pilot Zoo	Prowler	WOLF	Timber	May 89	M	Black
MP002-03	Mount Pilot Zoo	Powder Puff	DEER	White Tail	Jan 83	F	Brown
MP003-01	Mountain Pets	Tommy	TURTLE	Box	Sep 88	M	Green

Figure 7-1: A typical datasheet view of data.

You can sort the datasheet quickly into any order using one toolbar button. The datasheet can be filtered for specific records, making other records invisible. You can also import records directly to the datasheet, or export formatted records from the datasheet directly to Word, Excel, or other applications that support OLE (Object Linking and Embedding) 2.0.

The Datasheet Window

The Datasheet window is similar to other object windows in Access. At the top of the screen, are the title bar, menu bar, and toolbars. The center of the screen displays the data in rows and columns. Each record occupies one row; each column, headed by a field name, contains that field's values. The display arranges the records initially by primary key, and the fields by the order of their creation in the table design.

The right side of the window contains a scrollbar for moving quickly between records. As you scroll between records, a Scroll Tip (shown in Figure 7-1) tells you precisely where the scrollbar will take you. In Access 2000, the size of the scrollbar *thumb* gives you a proportional look at how many of the total number of records are being displayed. In Figure 7-1, the scrollbar thumb takes about 15 percent of the scroll area, and 20 of 130 records are shown onscreen. There is also a proportional scrollbar at the bottom of the screen for moving among fields.

The last line at the bottom of the screen contains a *status bar*. The status bar displays the Field Description that you entered for each field in the table design. If there is no Field Description for a specific field, Access displays the words Datasheet View. Generally, error messages and warnings appear in dialog boxes in the center of the screen rather than in the status bar. If you need help understanding the meaning of a button in the toolbar, move the mouse over the button and a *tooltip* appears with a one- or two-word explanation, while the status bar displays a more comprehensive explanation.

Navigation inside a datasheet

You can move easily in the Datasheet window by using the mouse pointer to indicate where you want to change or add to your data: just click a field and record location. In addition, the menus, toolbars, scrollbars, and navigation buttons make it easy to move among fields and records. You can think of a datasheet as a spreadsheet without the row numbers and column letters. Instead, your columns have field names, and your rows are unique records that have identifiable values in each cell.

Table 7-1 lists the navigational keys used for moving within a datasheet.

Table 7-1 Navigating in a Datasheet	
Navigational Direction	*Keystrokes*
Next field	Tab
Previous field	Shift+Tab
First field of current record	Home
Last field of current record	End
Next record	Down arrow (↓)
Previous record	Up arrow (↑)
First field of first record	Ctrl+Home
Last field of last record	Ctrl+End
Scroll up one page	PgUp
Scroll down one page	PgDn
Go to record number box	F5

The navigation buttons

The *navigation buttons* (shown in Figure 7-2) are six controls that are used to move between records. You click these buttons to move to the desired record. The two leftmost controls move you to the first record or the previous record in the datasheet (table). The three rightmost controls position you on the next record, last record, or new record in the datasheet (table). If you know the *record number* (the row number of a specific record), you can click the record number box, enter a record number, and press Enter.

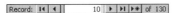

Figure 7-2: Navigation buttons.

> **Note**　If you enter a record number greater than the number of records in the table, an error message appears stating that you can't go to the specified record.

The Datasheet toolbar

The Datasheet toolbar (shown in Figure 7-3) provides another way to navigate the datasheet. The toolbar has many familiar objects on it, as well as some new ones.

Figure 7-3: The Datasheet toolbar.

The first icon lets you switch between the Table Design and the Datasheet views. Clicking the Table Design icon permits you to make changes to the design of your table. You can then click the Datasheet icon to return to the datasheet.

> **Note**　If you originally displayed a data-entry form, this icon will have three choices: Table Design, Datasheet, and Form.

The next icon, Save, saves any layout changes to the datasheet.

> **Caution**　Save does not allow you to roll back changes to the data. As you move from record to record, the data is forever changed.

The next set of three icons includes Print (which looks like a printer and sends your datasheet values to your printer) and Print Preview (which looks like a printed-page-with-magnifying-glass and shows onscreen how your datasheet will look printed). The third icon lets you spell-check your data using the standard Microsoft Office spell-checking feature.

The objects that can be pasted include a single value, datasheet row, column, or range of values. Objects can be copied and pasted to and from other programs (such as Microsoft Word or Excel), but the Format Painter is not available in a datasheet.

The next icon lets you Undo a change to a record or (more globally) undo formatting.

The next icon is the Internet icon that lets you insert a hyperlink.

The next two icons are the QuickSort icons. You can select one or more columns and click on one of these buttons to sort the data instantly, in ascending or descending order, using the selected columns as the sorting criteria.

The next three icons in this toolbar look like funnels. They let you determine and display only selected records. The first icon, Filter by Selection, lets you filter records to match a specific highlighted value. Each time you highlight a value, you add the selection to the filter. This additive process continues until the filter is cleared. (See the detailed discussion of this filter later in this chapter.) The second icon, Filter by Form, turns each column of data into a *combo box* where you can select a single value from the datasheet and filter for matching records. The last icon in the group turns any filters on or off.

The Find Specified Text icon is a pair of binoculars; clicking it displays a dialog box that lets you search for a specific value in a specific field.

The next two icons allow you to add a new record or delete an existing record. To create a new record, click the icon with the arrow-and-star and a new record row is added at the bottom of the datasheet. To delete an existing record, click anywhere in the record row that you want to delete and click the icon with the arrow-and-x. A message is displayed warning you that you will delete a record and that you won't be able to undo your change; select Yes to continue or No to save the record.

The next icon is the Database Window icon that displays the Database window. The New Object icons give you pull-down menus so that you can create new objects such as tables, queries, forms, reports, macros, and modules.

The last icon is the Help icon. When you click it, either Small Card Help or Office Assistant appears.

Opening a Datasheet

To open a datasheet from the Database window, follow these steps:

1. Click the Table button in the vertical menu bar.
2. Click the table name that you want to open. (In this example, it is `Pets`.)
3. Click Open.

An alternative method for opening the datasheet is to double-click on the `Pets` table name.

Tip   If you are in any of the design windows, you can click on the Datasheet button and view your data in a datasheet.

Entering New Data

When you open a datasheet, all the records in your table are visible; if you just created your table design, there isn't any data in the new datasheet yet. Figure 7-4 is an empty datasheet. When the datasheet is empty, the record pointer on the first record is displayed as a right-pointing triangle.

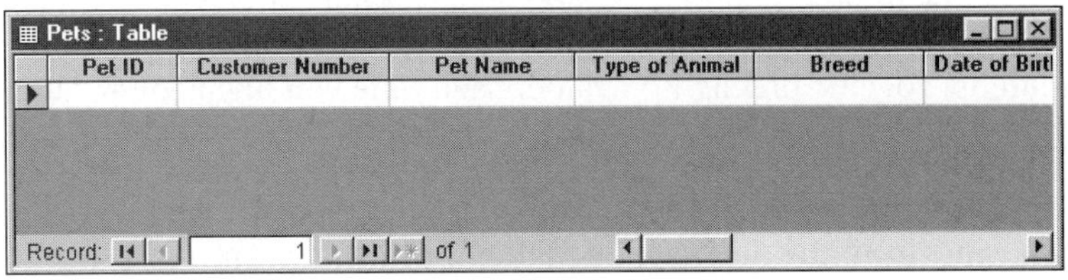

Figure 7-4: An empty datasheet.

You can enter a record into a datasheet field by moving the cursor to the field and typing the value. As you begin to edit the record, the record pointer turns into a pencil, indicating that the record is being edited. A second row also appears as you begin to enter the record; this row contains an asterisk in the record-pointer position, which indicates a new record. The new-record pointer always appears in the last line of the datasheet; after you enter a record, all new records appear there as well.

The cursor generally starts in the first field of the table for data entry.

If you performed the steps in Chapter 6, you already have five partial records. If not, you have an empty datasheet. To enter or edit the first record in the Pets table, follow the steps below. (A portion of the record is shown in Figure 6-10.) Figure 7-5 is an example of a record being entered into the datasheet.

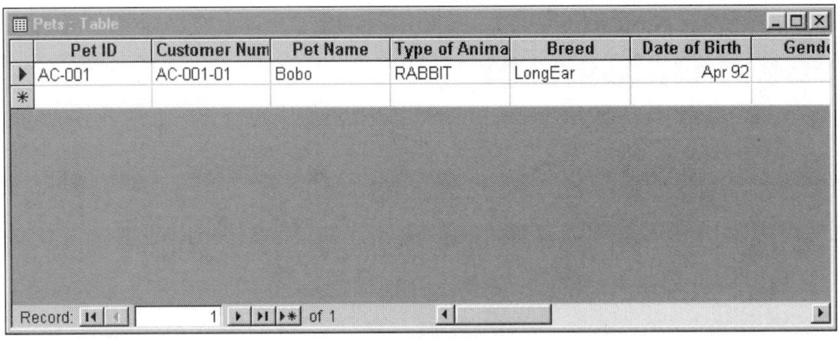

Figure 7-5: Entering a record into the datasheet.

1. Position the cursor in the Pet ID field.

2. Type **AC-001** and press Tab to move to the Customer Number field.

3. Type **AC001-01** and press Tab to move to the Pet Name field.

4. Type **Bobo** and press Tab to move to the Type of Animal field.

5. Type **RABBIT** and press Tab to move to the Breed field.

6. Type **Long Ear** and press Tab to move to the Date of Birth field.

7. Type **4/8/92** and press Tab to move to the Gender field.

8. Press **M** and press Tab to move to the Colors field.

9. Type **Brown/Black/White** and press Tab to move to the Neutered/Spayed field.

10. Press Tab to move to the Length field (because the default No is acceptable).

11. Type **20.0** and press Tab to move to the Weight field.

12. Type **3.1** and press Tab twice to move to the Current Vaccination field.

13. Type **Yes** (over the default No) and press Tab three times to move to the Comments field.

14. Once in the Comments field, press Shift+F2 to open the Zoom window.

15. While in the Zoom window, type **Bobo is a great looking rabbit. He was originally owned by a nature center and was given to the pet store for sale to a loving family. Bobo was in good health when he arrived and was returned to the pet store for sale**.

16. Press Enter to move to the Pet ID field of the second record.

While adding or editing records, you may see four different record pointers:

✦ Current record

✦ Record being edited

✦ Record is locked (multiuser systems)

✦ New record

Saving the record

After entering all the values in the record, normally you move to the next record. This action saves the record. Any time you move to a different record or close the table, the last record you worked with is written to the database and the record pointer changes from a pencil to a right-pointing triangle.

To save a record, you must enter a valid value into the primary key field. The primary key is validated for data type, uniqueness, and any validation rules that you had entered into the Validation Rule property.

Tip The Undo Current Field/Record icon in the toolbar will undo changes to only the current record. After you move to the next record, you must use the regular Undo icon. After you change a second record, you cannot undo the first record.

Tip You can save the record to disk without leaving the record by selecting Records ⇨ Save Record or by pressing Shift+Enter.

Now that you've entered a record, you understand what happens as you enter the first record. Next you learn how Access validates your data as you make entries into the fields.

Understanding automatic data-type validation

Access validates certain types of data automatically. You don't have to enter any data-validation rules for these when you specify table properties. Data types that Access validates automatically include:

✦ Number/Currency

✦ Date/Time

✦ Yes/No

Number or Currency fields allow only valid numbers to be entered into the field. Initially, Access lets you enter a letter into a Number field. When you move off the field, however, a dialog box appears with the message `The value you entered isn't valid for this field`. The same is true of any other inappropriate characters. If you try to enter more than one decimal point, you get the same message. If you enter a number too large for a certain Number data type, you also get this message.

Date and Time fields are validated for valid date or time values. If you try to enter a date such as 14/45/90, a time such as 37:39:12, or a single letter in a Date/Time field, a dialog box will show you the error message *The value you entered isn't valid for this field*.

Yes/No fields require that you enter one of these defined values: Yes, True, 1, or a number other than 0 for Yes; or No, False, Off, or 0 for No. Of course, you can also define your own acceptable values in the Format property for the field, but generally these are the only acceptable values. If you try to enter an invalid value, the dialog box appears with the usual message to indicate an inappropriate value.

Using various data-entry techniques

Because field types vary, you use different data-entry techniques for each type. You already learned that some data-type validation is automatic. Designing the Pets table, however, meant entering certain user-defined format and data-validation rules. The following sections examine the types of data entry.

Standard text data entry

The first five fields you entered in the Pets table were Text fields. You simply entered each value and moved on. The Pet ID field used an *input mask* for data entry. There wasn't any special formatting for the other fields. If you enter a value in lowercase, it is displayed in uppercase. Text can be validated for specific values, and it can be displayed with format properties.

Tip　Sometimes you want to enter a Text field on multiple lines. You can press Ctrl+Enter to add a new line. This is useful (for example) in large text strings for formatting a multiple-line address field. It is also useful in Memo fields for formatting multiple-line entries.

Date/Time data entry

The Date of Birth field is a Date/Time data type, formatted using the *mmm yy* format. Thus, even though you typed **4/8/96**, Access displays the value *Apr 96* when you leave the field. The value 4/8/96 is really stored in the table; you can display it whenever the cursor is in the Date of Birth field. Alternatively, you can enter the value in the format specified; that is, you can enter **Apr 96** in the field and the value *Apr 96* will be stored in the table.

Date of Birth also has the validation rule `Between #1/1/70# And Date()`, which means that you can enter Date of Birth values only between January 1, 1970, and the current date.

Tip　Formats affect only the display of the data. They do not change storage of data in the table.

Text data entry with data validation

The Gender field of the Pets table has a data-validation rule entered for it in the Validation Rule property. This rule limits valid entries to M, F, or U. If you try to enter a value other than M, F, or U into the Gender field, a dialog box appears with the message *Value must be M, F, or U*, as shown in Figure 7-6. The message comes from the Validation Text property that was entered into the Pets table Gender field.

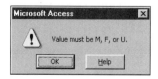

Figure 7-6: Dialog box for a data-validation message.

Numeric data entry with data validation

The Length and Weight fields both have validation rules. The Length field has a Validation Rule property to limit the size of the animal to a realistic length below 10 feet. The Weight field has a Validation Rule property to limit the weight of the animal to below 1,500 pounds. If either of the rules is violated, a dialog box appears with the validation text entered for the field. If an animal arrives that weighs more than 1,500 pounds or is more than 10 feet long, the validation rule can simply be changed in the table design.

OLE object data entry

The OLE (Object Linking and Embedding) data-type field named Picture can be entered into a datasheet, even though you don't see the picture of the animal. An OLE field can be many different items, including:

✦ Bitmap pictures

✦ Sound files

✦ Business graphs

✦ Word or Excel files

✦ Web Page or Hyperlink

Any object that an OLE server supports can be stored in an Access OLE field. OLE objects are generally entered into a form so you can see, hear, or use the value. When OLE objects appear in datasheets, you see text that tells what the object is (for example, you might see *Paintbrush Picture* in the OLE field). You can enter OLE objects into a field in two ways:

✦ Pasting from the Clipboard

✦ Inserting into the field from the Insert ➪ Object menu dialog box

Cross-Reference　For thorough coverage of using and displaying OLE objects, see Chapter 19.

Memo field data entry

The last field in the table is Comments, which is a Memo data type. This type of field allows up to 64,000 characters of text for each field. Recall that you entered a long string (about 160 characters) into the Memo field. As you entered the string, however, you saw only a few characters at a time. The rest of the string scrolled out of sight. By pressing Shift+F2, you can display a *Zoom box* with a scrollbar (see Figure 7-7) that lets you see about 1,000 characters at a time.

Note　When you first display text in a zoomed window, all the text is selected and highlighted in reverse video. You can unselect the text by pressing the Home key.

New Feature　In the zoom box, there is a font button at the bottom. When this button is pressed the dialog box in Figure 7-8 is displayed.

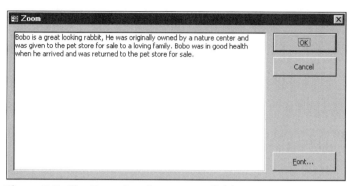

Figure 7-7: The Zoom box for a memo field.

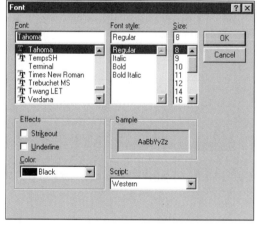

Figure 7-8: Change the font Type, Style, and Size, and add Effects such as Strikeout and Script for the memo field from this dialog box.

Note   When you change the font for the text in a memo field, all of the text is affected. You cannot change a single word or sentence.

Navigating Records in a Datasheet

On the CD-ROM   If you are following the examples, you may want to use the Mountain Start database file now. For the remainder of this section, you work with the data in the Pets table.

It isn't unusual to want to make changes to records after entering them. You may want to change records for several reasons:

✦ You receive new information that changes existing values.

✦ You discover errors that change existing values.

✦ You need to add new records.

When you decide to edit data in a table, the first step is to open the table, if it is not already open. From the Database window, open the Pets datasheet by double-clicking Pets in the list of tables.

Note   If you are in any of the Design windows, you can click the Datasheet button to make changes to the information within the table.

When you open a datasheet in Access 2000, if there are related tables, a column with a plus sign (+) is added to access the related records, or subdatasheets, and is displayed as the first column. Subdatasheets are discussed thoroughly in Chapter 11.

Moving between records

You can move to any record by scrolling through the records and positioning your cursor on the desired record. When your table is large, however, you want to get to a specific record as quickly as possible.

You can use the vertical scrollbar to move between records. The scrollbar arrows, however, move the record pointer only one record at a time. To move through many records at a time, you must use the scrollbar elevator (known as a scroll box in Windows 95/98/NT) or click the area between the scrollbar elevator and the scrollbar arrows.

The Edit ➪ GoTo menu, shown open in Figure 7-9, has several choices to help you quickly move around the worksheet.

The five navigation buttons, located along the bottom of the Datasheet window (also shown in Figure 7-9), can also be used for moving between records. You simply click these buttons to move to the desired record. If you know the record number (row number of a specific record), you can click on the record number box, enter a record number, and press Enter. You can also press F5 to move to the record number box.

Tip   TipWatch the Scroll Tips when you use scrollbars to move to another area of the datasheet. Access does not update the record number box until you click on a field.

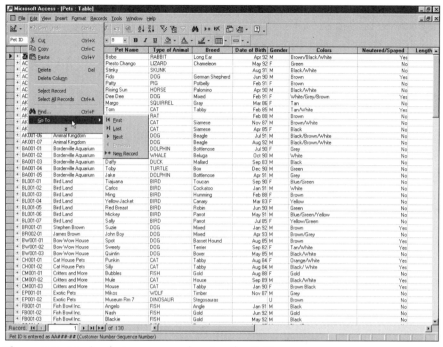

Figure 7-9: Moving between records using the GoTo menu.

Finding a specific value

Although you can move to a specific record (if you know the record number) or to a specific field in the current record, usually what you really want to find is a certain value in a record. There are three methods for locating a value in a field:

- ✦ Select Edit ➪ Find
- ✦ Select the Find Specified Text button in the toolbar (a pair of binoculars)
- ✦ Press Ctrl+F

Choosing any of these methods displays the Find and Replace dialog box (shown in Figure 7-10). To limit the search to a specific field, make sure your cursor is on the field that you want to use in the search before you open the dialog box. You can also choose to search the entire table for the specified record by clicking on the Look In combo box and selecting the table.

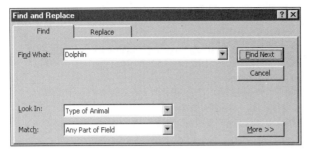

Figure 7-10: The Find and Replace dialog box.

To view the search options shown in Figure 7-11, click the button labeled More. When you are done viewing or changing the search options, click the button labeled Less to no longer display these options.

Tip   If you highlight the entire record by clicking on the record selector (the small gray box next to the record), Access 2000 automatically searches through all fields.

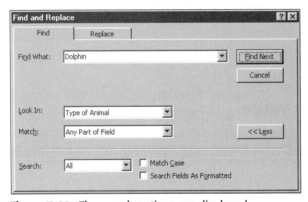

Figure 7-11: The search options are displayed.

The Find and Replace dialog box lets you control many aspects of the search. In the Find What text box, you enter the value to be searched for. You can also display and choose from a list of items that you have previously searched for in this database. You can enter the value just as it appears in the field, or you can use three types of wildcards:

* Any number of characters

? Any one character

Any one number

To look at how these wildcards work, first suppose that you want to find any value beginning with AB; for this, you enter **AB***. Then suppose that you want to search for values ending with 001, so you search for ***001**. To search for any value that begins with AB, ends with 001, and contains any two characters in between, you enter **AB??001**. If you want to search for any street number that ends in th, you can enter **#th** to find 5th or 8th. To find 5th or 125th, you can use ***th**.

The Match drop-down list contains three choices:

✦ Any Part of Field

✦ Whole Field

✦ Start of Field

The default is Whole Field. This option finds only the whole value you enter. For example, it finds the value SMITH only if the value in the field being searched is exactly SMITH. If you select Any Part of Field, Access searches to see whether the value is contained anywhere in the field; this search finds the value SMITH in the field values SMITHSON, HAVERSMITH, and ASMITHE. A search for SMITH using the Start of Field option searches from the beginning of the field, returning only values like SMITHSON or SMITHVILLE. You can click one or more of three choices (Up, Down, All) in the Search combo box.

When you have the search options displayed (displayed by clicking the More button), there are two options listed. Match Case determines whether the search is case-sensitive. The default is not case-sensitive. A search for SMITH finds smith, SMITH, or Smith. If you check the Match Case checkbox, you must then enter the search string in the exact case of the field value. (The data types Number, Currency, and Date/Time do not have any case attributes.) If you have checked Match Case, Access does not use the value Search Fields as Formatted, which limits the search to the actual values displayed in the table. (If you format a field for display in the datasheet, you should check the box.) In the Date of Birth field, for example, you can accomplish a search for an animal born in April 1992 by checking the box and entering **Apr 92**. Without this entry, you must search for the exact date of birth, which may be 4/8/92.

Caution   Using Search Fields as Formatted may slow the search process.

When you click the Find First or Find Next button, the search begins. If Access finds the value, the cursor highlights it in the datasheet. To find the next occurrence of the value, you must click the Find Next command button on the right side of the dialog box. You can also select Find First to find the first occurrence. The dialog box remains open so that you can find multiple occurrences. When you find the value you want, select the Close command button to close the dialog box.

Changing Values in a Datasheet

Usually, you change values by moving to the value that you want to change or edit and making the change. You edit a value for several reasons:

✦ Adding a new value

✦ Replacing an existing value

✦ Changing an existing value

If the field you are in has no value, you can type a new value into the field. When you enter new values into a field, follow the same rules as for a new-record entry.

Replacing an existing value manually

Generally, you enter a field with either no characters selected or the entire value selected. If you use the keyboard to enter a field, normally you select the entire value. (You know that the entire value is selected when it is displayed in reverse video.) You can erase a selected entire value by pressing any key, which replaces the value with that of the pressed key. Pressing Delete simply deletes the value without replacing it. Pressing the Spacebar erases the value and replaces it with a space.

To select the entire value with the mouse, use any of these methods:

✦ Click just to the left of the value when the cursor is shown as a large plus sign.

✦ Select any part of the value and double-click the mouse button. (This usually works unless there is a space in the text).

✦ Click to the left of the value, hold down the left mouse button, and drag the mouse to select the whole value.

✦ Select any part of the value and press F2.

Tip You may want to replace an existing value with the default from the Default Value table property. To do so, select the value and press Ctrl+Alt+Spacebar. If you want to replace an existing value with that of the same field from the preceding record, you can press Ctrl+' (single quote mark). You can press Ctrl+; (semicolon) to place the current date in a field as well.

Caution Pressing Ctrl+– (hyphen) deletes the current record.

Changing an existing value

If you want to change an existing value instead of replacing the entire value, you can use the mouse and click in front of any character in the field. When you position the mouse pointer in front of an individual character, you activate Insert mode; the existing value moves to the right as you type the new value. If you press Insert, your entry changes to Overstrike mode; you replace one character at a time as you type. You can use the arrow keys to move between characters without disturbing them. Erase characters to the left by pressing Backspace, or to the right of the cursor by pressing Delete.

Table 7-2 lists editing techniques.

Table 7-2 Editing Techniques	
Editing Operation	**Keystrokes**
Move the insertion point within a field	Press the right($\rightarrow$)- and left-arrow($\leftarrow$) keys
Insert a value within a field	Select the insertion point and type new data
Select the entire field	Press F2 or double-click the mouse button
Replace an existing value with a new value	Select the entire field and type a new value
Replace a value with the value of the previous field	Press Ctrl+' (single quote mark)
Replace the current value with the default value	Press Ctrl+Alt+Spacebar
Insert a line break in a Text or Memo field	Press Ctrl+Enter
Save the current record	Press Shift+Enter or move to another record
Insert the current date	Ctrl+; (semicolon)
Insert the current time	Ctrl+: (colon)
Add a new record	Ctrl++ (plus sign)
Delete the current record	Ctrl+– (minus sign)
Toggle values in a check box or option button	Spacebar
Undo a change to the current record	Press Esc or click the Undo button

Fields that you can't edit

Some fields cannot be edited, such as:

AutoNumber fields

Access maintains AutoNumber fields automatically, calculating the values as you create each new record. AutoNumber fields can be used as the primary key.

Calculated fields	Access creates calculated fields in forms or queries; these values are not actually stored in your table.
Locked or disabled fields	You can set certain properties in a form to disallow entry for a specific field. You can lock or disable a field when you designate Form properties.
Fields in multiuser locked records	If another user locks the record, you can't edit any fields in that record.

Using the Undo Feature

The Undo button is often dimmed in Access so that it can't be used. As soon as you begin editing a record, however, you can use this button to undo the typing in the current field. You can also undo a change with the Esc key; pressing Esc cancels either a changed value or the previously changed field. Pressing Esc twice undoes changes to the entire current record.

Several Undo menu commands and variations are available to undo your work. The following lists how your work can be undone at various stages of completion:

Edit ⇨ Can't Undo	Undo is not available
Edit ⇨ Undo Typing	Cancels the most recent change to your data
Edit ⇨ Undo Current Field/Record	Cancels the most recent change to the current field. Cancels all changes to the current record
Edit ⇨ Undo Saved Record	Cancels all changes to last saved record

As you type a value into a field, you can select Edit ⇨ Undo or use the toolbar undo buttons to undo changes to that value. After you move to another field, you can undo the change to the preceding field's value by selecting Edit ⇨ Undo Current Field/Record or by using the Undo button. You can also undo all the changes to an unsaved current record by selecting Edit ⇨ Undo Current Field/Record. After a record is saved, you can still undo the changes by selecting Edit ⇨ Undo Saved Record. However, after the next record is edited, changes are permanent.

Copying and Pasting Values

Copying or cutting data to the Clipboard is a Microsoft Windows task; it is not actually a specific function of Access. After you cut or copy a value, it can be pasted into another field or record using Edit ⇨ Paste or the Paste button in the toolbar. Data can be cut, copied, or pasted from any Windows application or from one task to another in Access. Using this technique, entire records can be copied between tables or databases, and datasheet values can be copied to and from Microsoft Word and Excel.

Replacing Values

To replace an existing value in a field, you can manually find the record to update or you can use the Find and Replace dialog box. There are four ways to display the Find and Replace dialog:

✦ Select Edit ➪ Find

✦ Select the Find Specified Text button in the toolbar (a pair of binoculars)

✦ Press Ctrl+F

✦ Select Edit ➪ Replace

This dialog box allows you to do a find and replace in the current field or in the entire datasheet. You can find a certain value and replace it with a new value in every place in the table that you are in.

Type in the value that you want to find in the Find tab, as shown in Figure 7-10. Once you have selected all of your search options, click on the Replace tab, and it is displayed as shown in Figure 7-12.

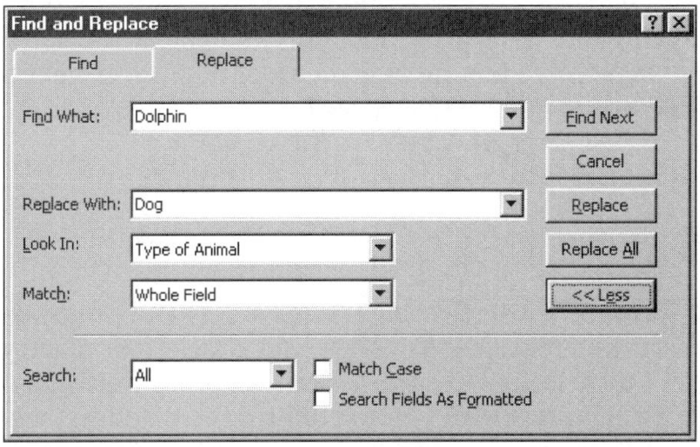

Figure 7-12: Find and Replace dialog box with the Replace tab showing.

You can select your search options in the Replace tab. Enter what you want to replace the existing value with. Once you have completed the dialog with all the correct information, select one of the command buttons on the side.

Find Next	Finds the next field that contains the value in the Find What field.
Cancel	Closes the form and performs no find and replace.
Replace	Must use the Find Next button first. When you click on Replace it replaces the value in the current field only.
Replace All	Finds all the fields with the Find What value and automatically replaces them with the Replace with value.
More/Less	Displays the search options/Hides the search options.

Tip   Use the Find Next and Replace commands if you aren't sure about changing all the fields with the Find What value. When you use this command it allows you to pick the fields that you want to replace and the fields that you want to leave with the same value.

Adding New Records

Records are added to the datasheet by positioning the cursor on the datasheet's last line (where the record pointer is an asterisk) and entering the new record. There are many ways to go to a new record. You can also select Insert ⇨ New Record or you can go directly to a new record by using the new-record button in the toolbar, the navigation button area, or the menu selection Edit ⇨ GoTo ⇨ New. Another way to move quickly to the new record is to go to the last record and press the down-arrow(↓) key.

Sometimes you want to add several new records and make all existing records temporarily invisible. The menu item Records ⇨ Data Entry will clear the screen temporarily of all records while you are editing new records. When you want to restore all records, select Records ⇨ Remove Filter/Sort.

Deleting Records

You can delete any number of records by selecting the record(s) and pressing the Delete key. You can also select the records and choose Edit ⇨ Delete or place your cursor in a record and select Edit ⇨ Delete Record. When you press Delete or choose the menu selection, a dialog box asks you to confirm the deletion (see Figure 7-13). If you select Yes, the records are deleted. If you select Cancel, no changes are made.

Caution   The Default value for this dialog box is Yes. Pressing the Enter key automatically deletes the records. If you accidentally erase records using this method, the action cannot be reversed.

Figure 7-13: The Delete Record dialog box.

You can select multiple contiguous records. To do so, click the record selector of the first record you want to select and drag the record-pointer icon (right-pointing arrow) to the last record you want to select.

Adding, Changing, and Deleting Columns

A very dangerous feature in Access 2000 is the capability to add, delete, and rename columns in a datasheet. This feature actually changes the data design. When you go to the Table Design screen and make changes, you know that you are changing the underlying structure of the data because you see yourself do it. Within a datasheet, however, you may not realize the consequences of the changes that you are making. Any field name that is changed may cause any query, form, report, macro, or module that uses that name to no longer function. If you are creating applications for others, you should not allow users to use a datasheet to make the changes described in this part of the book.

Deleting a column from a datasheet

Columns can be deleted from a datasheet by selecting one column at a time and selecting Edit ➪ Delete Column. When you take this action, a dialog box warns that you will be deleting all the data in this column, as well as the field itself, from the table design. More importantly, if you have used this field in a data-entry form or a report, you will get an error the next time you use any object that references this field name. You cannot delete more than one column at a time.

Adding a column to a datasheet

New columns can be added to a datasheet by selecting Insert ➪ Column, which creates a new column to the left of the column your insertion point was in. The new column is labeled *Field1*. You can then add data to the records for the column.

Adding a new column also adds the field to the table design. When you save the datasheet, Access writes the field into the table design, using the characteristics of the data for the field properties.

Changing a field name (column header)

When adding a new field, you will want to change the column name before you save the datasheet. You can change a column header by double-clicking the column header and editing the text in the column header. When you save the datasheet, this column header text is used as a field name for the table design.

Caution   When you change a column header, you are changing the field name in the table. If you have used this field name in forms, reports, queries, macros, or modules, they will no longer work until you change them in the other objects. This is a dangerous way to change a field name; only experienced users should use it.

Displaying Records

A number of mouse techniques and menu items can greatly increase your productivity when you're adding or changing records. Either by selecting from the Format menu or by using the mouse, you can change the field order, hide and freeze columns, change row height or column width, change display fonts, and change the display or remove gridlines.

Changing the field order

By default, Access displays the fields in a datasheet in the same order they would follow in a table or query. Sometimes, however, you need to see certain fields next to each other in order to analyze your data better. To rearrange your fields, select a column (as shown in Figure 7-14) and drag the column to its new location.

Pet ID	Customer Number	Pet Name	Type of Animal	Breed	Date of Birth	Ge
AC001-01	All Creatures	Bobo	RABBIT	Long Ear	Apr 92	M
AC001-02	All Creatures	Presto Chango	LIZARD	Chameleon	May 92	F
AC001-03	All Creatures	Stinky	SKUNK		Aug 91	M
AC001-04	All Creatures	Fido	DOG	German Shepherd	Jun 90	M
AD001-01	Johnathan Adams	Patty	PIG	Potbelly	Feb 91	F
AD001-02	Johnathan Adams	Rising Sun	HORSE	Palomino	Apr 90	M
AD002-01	William Adams	Dee Dee	DOG	Mixed	Feb 91	F
AK001-01	Animal Kingdom	Margo	SQUIRREL	Gray	Mar 86	F
AK001-02	Animal Kingdom	Tom	CAT	Tabby	Feb 85	M
AK001-03	Animal Kingdom	Jerry	RAT		Feb 88	M
AK001-04	Animal Kingdom	Marcus	CAT	Siamese	Nov 87	M
AK001-05	Animal Kingdom	Pookie	CAT	Siamese	Apr 85	F
AK001-06	Animal Kingdom	Mario	DOG	Beagle	Jul 91	M
AK001-07	Animal Kingdom	Luigi	DOG	Beagle	Aug 92	M
BA001-01	Borderville Aquarium	Swimmy	DOLPHIN	Bottlenose	Jul 90	F
BA001-02	Borderville Aquarium	Charger	WHALE	Beluga	Oct 90	M
BA001-03	Borderville Aquarium	Daffy	DUCK	Mallard	Sep 83	M
BA001-04	Borderville Aquarium	Toby	TURTLE	Box	Dec 90	M

Record: 1 of 130

Figure 7-14: Selecting a column to change the field order.

You can select and drag columns one at a time, or you can select multiple columns to drag. Say that you want the fields Pet Name and Type of Animal to appear first in the datasheet. The following steps make this change:

1. Position the cursor on the Pet Name field (column) name. The cursor changes to a down arrow.

2. Click to select the column and hold down the mouse button. The entire Pet Name column is now highlighted.

3. Drag the mouse to the right to highlight the Type of Animal column.

4. Release the mouse button; the two columns should now be highlighted.

5. Click the mouse button again; the pointer changes to an arrow with a box under it.

6. Drag the two columns to the left edge of the datasheet.

7. Release the mouse button; the two columns now move to the beginning of the datasheet.

With this method, you can move any individual field or contiguous field selection. You can move the fields left or right or past the right or left boundary of the window.

Note   Moving fields in a datasheet does not affect the field order in the table design.

Changing the field display width

You can change the *field display width* (column width) either by specifying the width in a dialog box (in number of characters) or by dragging the column gridline. When you drag a column gridline, the cursor changes to the double-arrow symbol.

To widen a column or to make it narrower, follow these two steps:

1. Place the insertion point between two column names on the field separator line.

2. Drag the column border to the left to make the column smaller or to the right to make it bigger.

Tip   You can resize a column instantly to the best fit (based on the longest data value) by double-clicking on the right column border.

Note   Resizing the column will not change the number of characters allowable in the table's field size. You are simply changing the amount of viewing space for the data contained in the column.

Alternatively, you can resize a column by choosing Format ⇨ Column Width or right-clicking the mouse and selecting Column Width from the menu. When you click the Column width icon, the dialog box in Figure 7-15, in which you enter column width in number of characters, displays. You can also return the column to its default size by checking the Standard Width check box.

An icon can be created on your toolbar for Column Width. To do this, click the down arrow next to the help button and select Add or Remove Buttons. Select the Column Width button. This button will now become the last button on that toolbar. To remove it, just repeat the process.

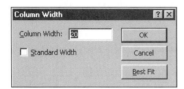

Figure 7-15: The Column Width dialog box.

Caution   If you drag a column gridline to the gridline of the next column to the left, the column hides. This also happens if you set the column width to 0 in the Column Width dialog box. If you do this, you must use Format ⇨ Unhide Columns to redisplay the columns.

Changing the record display height

You can change the record (that is, row) height of all rows. Drag a row's gridline to make the row height larger or smaller, or select Format ⇨ Row Height. Sometimes you may need to raise the row height to accommodate larger fonts or text data displays of multiple lines.

You can also create an icon on your toolbar for Row Height. To do this, click the down arrow next to the Help button and select Add or Remove Buttons. Select the Row Height button. This button will become the last button on that toolbar. To remove it, just repeat the process.

When you drag a record's gridline, the cursor changes to the vertical two-headed arrow you see at the left edge of Figure 7-16.

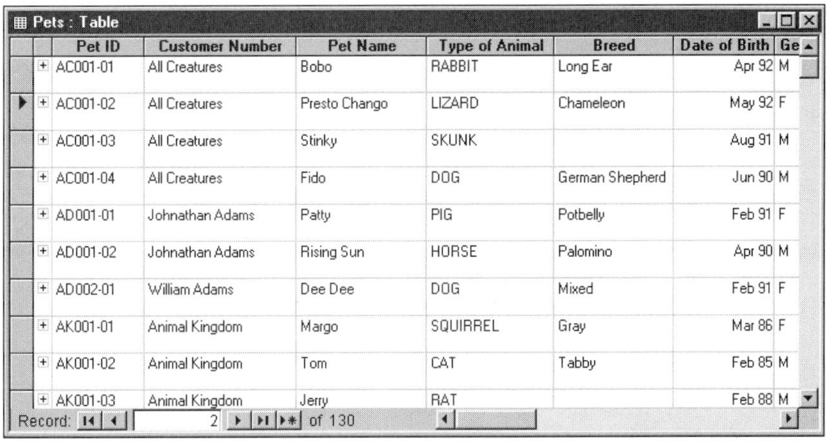

Pets : Table

Pet ID	Customer Number	Pet Name	Type of Animal	Breed	Date of Birth	Ge
AC001-01	All Creatures	Bobo	RABBIT	Long Ear	Apr 92	M
AC001-02	All Creatures	Presto Chango	LIZARD	Chameleon	May 92	F
AC001-03	All Creatures	Stinky	SKUNK		Aug 91	M
AC001-04	All Creatures	Fido	DOG	German Shepherd	Jun 90	M
AD001-01	Johnathan Adams	Patty	PIG	Potbelly	Feb 91	F
AD001-02	Johnathan Adams	Rising Sun	HORSE	Palomino	Apr 90	M
AD002-01	William Adams	Dee Dee	DOG	Mixed	Feb 91	F
AK001-01	Animal Kingdom	Margo	SQUIRREL	Gray	Mar 86	F
AK001-02	Animal Kingdom	Tom	CAT	Tabby	Feb 85	M
AK001-03	Animal Kingdom	Jerry	RAT		Feb 88	M

Record: 2 of 130

Figure 7-16: Changing a row's height.

To raise or lower a row's height, follow these steps:

1. Place the cursor between two rows on the record separator line.
2. Drag the row border upward to shrink all row heights. Drag the border downward to increase all row heights.

Note The procedure for changing row height changes the row size for all rows in the datasheet.

You can also resize rows by choosing Format ➪ Row Height. A dialog box appears so that you can enter the row height in point size. You can also return the rows to their default point size by checking the Standard Height checkbox.

Caution If you drag a record's gridline up to meet the gridline immediately above it in the previous record, all rows are hidden. This also occurs if you set the row height close to 0 (for example, a height of 0.1) in the Row Height dialog box. In that case, you must select Format ➪ Row Height and reset the row height to a larger number to redisplay the rows.

Displaying cell gridlines

Normally gridlines appear between fields (columns) and between records (rows). By selecting Format ➪ Datasheet, you can determine whether to display gridlines and how they will look. Figure 7-17 shows the Cells Effects dialog box you would use.

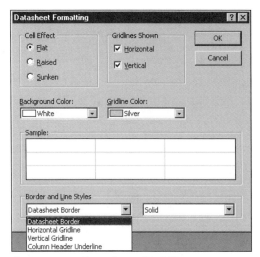

Figure 7-17: Changing cell gridlines.

The Datasheet Formatting dialog box gives you complete control over gridlines. Using the Gridlines Shown checkboxes, you can eliminate both Horizontal and Vertical gridlines. If you choose to keep the gridlines, you can change both the Gridline Color and the Background Color. A sample shows you what the effect you have chosen will look like. You can also determine whether the gridlines are Flat (default white background with silver gridlines), Raised (default silver background with gray gridlines), or Sunken (default silver background with white gridlines).

New Feature   You can also determine the border and line styles for each of the different data sheet borders. You can determine a different border for the Datasheet Border, Horizontal Gridline, Vertical Gridline, and Column Header Underline. To select a different border style for each border in the datasheet, first select the Border that you want to update from the left combo box and then the Line Style from the combo box on the right. Repeat the process for each border. Each border in Figure 7-18 has a different line style.

The different line styles that you can use for the different datasheet borders are:

Transparent Border	Short Dashes	Dash-Dot
Solid	Dots	Dash-Dot-Dot
Dashes	Sparse Dots	Double Solid

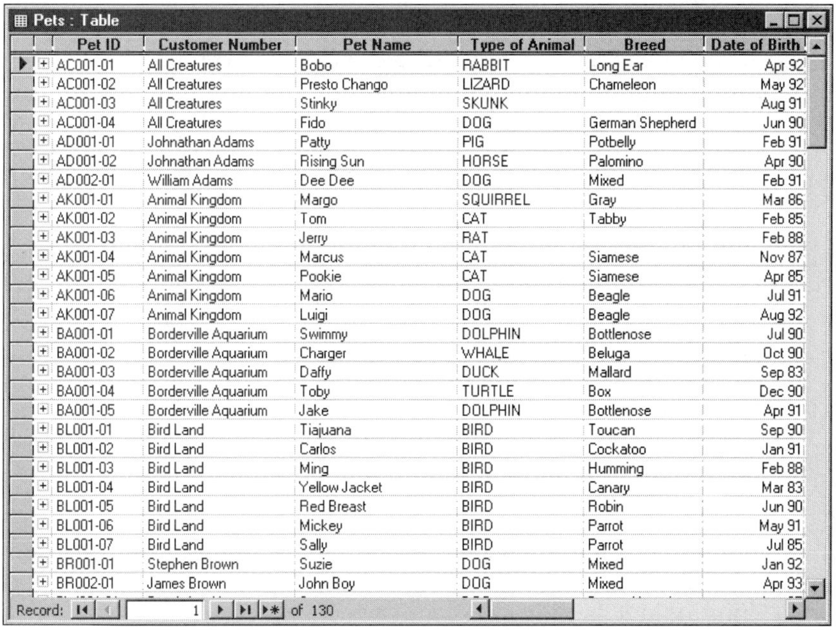

Pets : Table

Pet ID	Customer Number	Pet Name	Type of Animal	Breed	Date of Birth
AC001-01	All Creatures	Bobo	RABBIT	Long Ear	Apr 92
AC001-02	All Creatures	Presto Chango	LIZARD	Chameleon	May 92
AC001-03	All Creatures	Stinky	SKUNK		Aug 91
AC001-04	All Creatures	Fido	DOG	German Shepherd	Jun 90
AD001-01	Johnathan Adams	Patty	PIG	Potbelly	Feb 91
AD001-02	Johnathan Adams	Rising Sun	HORSE	Palomino	Apr 90
AD002-01	William Adams	Dee Dee	DOG	Mixed	Feb 91
AK001-01	Animal Kingdom	Margo	SQUIRREL	Gray	Mar 86
AK001-02	Animal Kingdom	Tom	CAT	Tabby	Feb 85
AK001-03	Animal Kingdom	Jerry	RAT		Feb 88
AK001-04	Animal Kingdom	Marcus	CAT	Siamese	Nov 87
AK001-05	Animal Kingdom	Pookie	CAT	Siamese	Apr 85
AK001-06	Animal Kingdom	Mario	DOG	Beagle	Jul 91
AK001-07	Animal Kingdom	Luigi	DOG	Beagle	Aug 92
BA001-01	Borderville Aquarium	Swimmy	DOLPHIN	Bottlenose	Jul 90
BA001-02	Borderville Aquarium	Charger	WHALE	Beluga	Oct 90
BA001-03	Borderville Aquarium	Daffy	DUCK	Mallard	Sep 83
BA001-04	Borderville Aquarium	Toby	TURTLE	Box	Dec 90
BA001-05	Borderville Aquarium	Jake	DOLPHIN	Bottlenose	Apr 91
BL001-01	Bird Land	Tiajuana	BIRD	Toucan	Sep 90
BL001-02	Bird Land	Carlos	BIRD	Cockatoo	Jan 91
BL001-03	Bird Land	Ming	BIRD	Humming	Feb 88
BL001-04	Bird Land	Yellow Jacket	BIRD	Canary	Mar 83
BL001-05	Bird Land	Red Breast	BIRD	Robin	Jun 90
BL001-06	Bird Land	Mickey	BIRD	Parrot	May 91
BL001-07	Bird Land	Sally	BIRD	Parrot	Jul 85
BR001-01	Stephen Brown	Suzie	DOG	Mixed	Jan 92
BR002-01	James Brown	John Boy	DOG	Mixed	Apr 93

Record: 1 of 130

Figure 7-18: Different line styles are used for the different borders in the datasheet.

Changing display fonts

You can resize the row height and column width automatically by changing the *display font.* By default, Access displays all data in the datasheet in the MS Sans Serif 8-point Regular font. You may find this font does not print correctly because MS Sans Serif is only a screen font. Arial 8-point Regular is a good match. Select Format ➪ Font to change the font type style, size, and style.

Setting the font display affects the entire datasheet. If you want to see more data on the screen, you can use a very small font. You can also switch to a higher-resolution display size if you have the necessary hardware. If you want to see larger characters, you can increase the font size.

To change the font to Arial 10-point bold, follow these steps:

1. Select Format ➪ Font. A dialog box appears.
2. Select Arial from the Font combo box, as shown in Figure 7-19.
3. Select Bold from the Font style combo box.
4. Enter 10 into the text box area of the Size combo box.
5. Click OK.

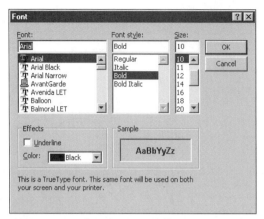

Figure 7-19: Changing to a different font and font size in the datasheet.

As you change font attributes, a sample appears in the Sample area. This way, you can see what changes you are making before you make them. You can also change the font color if you want.

Hiding and unhiding columns

You can hide columns by dragging the column gridline to the preceding field or by setting the column size to 0. You can also use the Hide Columns dialog box to hide one or more columns. To hide a single column, follow these steps:

1. Position the cursor anywhere within the column you want to hide.

2. Select Format ➪ Hide Columns. The column disappears. Actually, the column width is simply set to 0. You can hide multiple columns by first selecting them and selecting Format ➪ Hide Columns.

After a column is hidden, you can redisplay it by selecting Format ➪ Unhide Columns. This action displays a dialog box that lets you hide or unhide columns selectively by checking off the desired status of each field. When you are finished, click Close; the datasheet appears, showing the desired fields.

Freezing columns

When you want to scroll among many fields but want to keep certain fields from scrolling out of view, you can use Format ➪ Freeze Columns. With this selection, for example, you can keep the Pet ID and Pet Name fields visible while you scroll through the datasheet to find the animals' lengths and weights. The columns that you want to keep visible remain frozen on the far-left side of the datasheet; other fields scroll out of sight horizontally. The fields must be contiguous if you want to select more than one at a time to freeze. (Of course, you can first move your fields to place them next to each other.) When you're ready to unfreeze the datasheet columns, simply select Format ⇨ Unfreeze All Columns.

Saving the changed layout

When you close the datasheet, you save all your data changes, but you lose all your layout changes. As you make all these display changes to your datasheet, you probably won't want to make them again the next time you open the same datasheet. By default, however, Access does not save the datasheet's layout changes. If you want your datasheet to look the same way the next time you open it, you can select File ⇨ Save; this command saves your layout changes with the datasheet. You can also click the Save icon on your toolbar (the icon with the disk on it).

If you are following the example, do not save the changes to the Pets table.

Saving a record

As you move off a record, Access saves it. You can press Shift+Enter to save a record without moving off it. A third way to save a record is to close the table. Yet another way to save a record is to select Records ⇨ Save.

Sorting and Filtering Records in a Datasheet

Finding a value lets you display a specific record and work with that record. If you have multiple records that meet a find criteria, however, you may want to display just that specific set of records. Using the Filter and Sort toolbar icons (or the Records menu option Sort), you can display just the set of records you want to work with. You can also sort selected records instantly into any order you want: use the two QuickSort buttons to sort the entire table, or use the three filter buttons to select only certain records.

Using the QuickSort feature

There may be times when you simply want to sort your records into a desired order. The QuickSort buttons on the toolbar let you sort selected columns into either ascending or descending order. There is a different button on the toolbar for each order. Before you can click on either the Ascending (A-Z) or Descending (Z-A) QuickSort buttons, you must select the fields that you want to use for the sort.

You select a field to use in the sort by placing your cursor on the field in any record. Once the cursor is in the column you want to use in the sort, click the QuickSort button. The data redisplays instantly in the sorted order.

If you want to sort your data on the basis of values in multiple fields, you can highlight more than one column: highlight a column (as previously discussed), hold down the Shift key, and drag the cursor to the right. These steps select multiple contiguous fields. When you select one of the QuickSort buttons, Access sorts the records into major order (by the first highlighted field) and then into orders within orders (based on subsequent fields). If you need to select multiple columns that aren't contiguous (next to each other), you can move them next to each other, as discussed earlier in this chapter.

Tip   If you want to redisplay your records in their original order, use Records ⇨ Remove Filter/Sort.

Cross-Reference   You learn more about sorting in Chapter 9.

Using Filter by Selection

Filter by Selection is a technology within Access 2000 that lets you select records instantly on the basis of the current value you selected. For example, suppose you move your cursor to the Type of Animal column and click the Sort Ascending button. Access sorts the data by type of animal. Now highlight any of the records that contain DOG. When you press the Filter by Selection button, Access selects only the records where the Type of Animal is DOG. In the Pets table, there are 130 records. Once you have selected DOG and pressed the Filter by Selection button, only 27 records are shown and all have the value DOG in the Type of Animal field.

The navigation button area tells you whether the database is currently filtered; in addition, the Apply Filter/Remove Filter icon (third filter icon that looks like a large funnel) is depressed, indicating that a filter is in use. When you toggle this button, it removes all filters or sorts. The filter specification does not go away; it is simply turned off.

Filter by Selection is additive. You can continue to select values, each time pressing the Filter by Selection button. If (for example) you place your cursor in the Gender column in a record where the value of Gender is M and press the Filter by Selection button, only 21 records are displayed — the male dogs. If you then place your cursor in the Colors column in a record where the value of Colors is Brown and press the Filter by Selection button, only six records are displayed — the brown male dogs.

If you want to specify a selection and then see everything that doesn't match the selection, right-click on the datasheet and select Filter Excluding Selection. For example, when filtering by selection, move the cursor to the Breed column and select one of the German Shepherd fields and right mouse click to select Filter Excluding Selection. You will be left with four records. This selects everything *but* the two selected German Shepherd records (an *inverse* selection).

Imagine using this technique to review sales by salespeople for specific time periods or products. Filter by Selection provides incredible opportunities for drill-down into successive layers of data. As you add to Filter by Selection, it continues to add to its own internal query manager (known as Query by Example). Even when you click the Remove Filter icon to redisplay all the records, Access still stores the query specification in memory. If you click the icon again (now called Apply Filter), only the six records return. Figure 7-20 shows this Filter by Selection screen in a Datasheet.

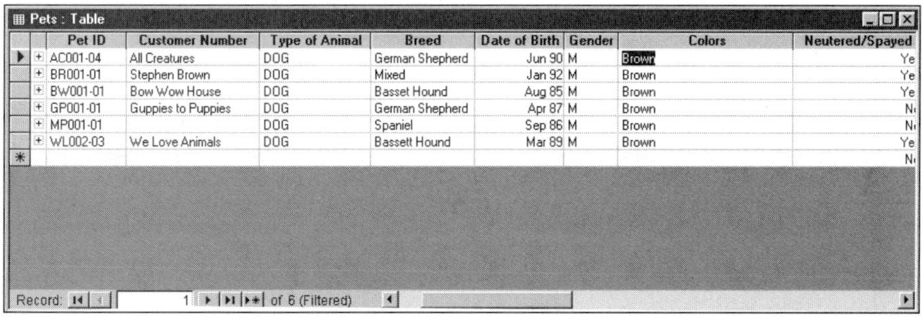

Pet ID	Customer Number	Type of Animal	Breed	Date of Birth	Gender	Colors	Neutered/Spayed
AC001-04	All Creatures	DOG	German Shepherd	Jun 90	M	Brown	Ye
BR001-01	Stephen Brown	DOG	Mixed	Jan 92	M	Brown	Ye
BW001-01	Bow Wow House	DOG	Basset Hound	Aug 85	M	Brown	Ye
GP001-01	Guppies to Puppies	DOG	German Shepherd	Apr 87	M	Brown	N
MP001-01		DOG	Spaniel	Sep 86	M	Brown	N
WL002-03	We Love Animals	DOG	Bassett Hound	Mar 89	M	Brown	Ye
*							N

Figure 7-20: Using Filter by Selection.

Filter by Selection has some limitations. Most importantly, all of the choices are *anded* together (i.e., DOG *and* Male *and* Brown). This means that the only operation you can perform is a search for records that meet all of the specified conditions. Another option, Filter by Form, lets you create more complex analyses.

If you want to use the Filter by Selection but cannot find the selection that you want to use but you know the value, right click on the field that you want to apply the filter to and select Filter For. This option allows you to type in the selection to filter for.

Using Filter by Form

Filter by Selection is just one way to filter data in Access 2000. Another way is Filter by Form. Selecting the second filter icon changes the datasheet to a single record; every field becomes a combo box that enables you to select from a list of all values for that field. As Figure 7-21 shows, the bottom of the form lets you specify the `OR` conditions for each group of values you specify.

In Figure 7-21, you can see the three conditions created in the Filter by Selection example (described previously) in the single line of the Filter by Form screen. If you click the Or tab, you can enter a second set of conditions. Suppose you want to see brown male dogs or any male ducks. You already have the specification for brown male dogs. You would click on the Or tab and then select DUCK from the now-empty Type of Animal combo box and M from the Gender column. When you click on the Apply Filter button (the large funnel), seven records would display.

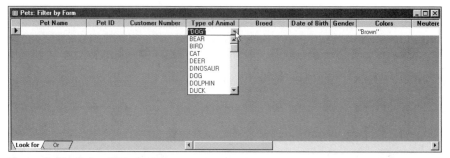

Figure 7-21: Using Filter by Form.

You can have as many conditions as you need. If you need even more advanced manipulation of your selections, you can choose Records ➪ Filter ➪ Advanced Filter/Sort and get an actual QBE (Query by Example) screen used to enter more complex queries.

Cross-Reference Later chapters explain more advanced concepts of queries.

Printing Records

You can print all the records in your datasheet in a simple row-and-column layout. Later you learn to produce formatted reports. For now, the simplest way to print is to select File ➪ Print or use the Print icon in the toolbar. This selection displays the dialog box shown in Figure 7-22.

Figure 7-22: The Print dialog box.

Assuming you set up a printer in Microsoft Windows, you can select OK to print your datasheet in the font you selected for display (or the nearest printer equivalent). The printout reflects all layout options that are in effect when the datasheet is printed. Hidden columns do not print. Gridlines print only if the cell gridline properties are on. The printout also reflects the specified row height and column width.

Only so many columns and rows can fit on a page; the printout will take up as many pages as required to print all the data. Access breaks up the printout as necessary to fit on each page. As an example, the Pets table printout is four pages. Two pages across are needed to print all the fields; the records require two pages in length.

Printing the datasheet

You can also control printing from the Print dialog box, selecting from several options:

Print Range	Prints the entire datasheet or only selected pages or records.
Copies	Determines the number of copies to be printed.
Collate	Determines whether multiple copies are collated.

You can also click on the Properties button and set options for the selected printer or select the printer itself to change the type of printer. The Setup button allows you to set margins and print headings.

Using the Print Preview window

Although you may have all the information in the datasheet ready to print, you may be unsure of whether to change the width or height of the columns or rows or whether to adjust the fonts to improve your printed output. For that matter, you might not want to print out the entire datasheet; you may need printed records from only pages 3 and 4. Before making such adjustments to the datasheet properties, you should view the report onscreen.

To preview your print job, either click the Print Preview button on the toolbar (a sheet of paper with a magnifying glass) or select File ➪ Print Preview. The Print Preview window appears (see Figure 7-23).

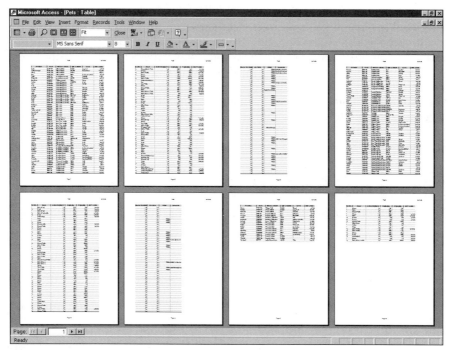

Figure 7-23: Print preview of a datasheet.

After you select the Print Preview button, the screen changes to *print preview mode*. You see a representation of your first printed page; a set of icons appears on the toolbar.

You can use the navigation buttons (located in the lower-left section of the Print Preview window) to move between pages, just as you use them to move between records in a datasheet.

The toolbar buttons provide quick access to printing tasks:

Close Window	Returns to Datasheet view
Print	Displays the Print dialog box, which is accessible when you select File ⇨ Print from the menu bar
One Page	Toggles in and out to make the Print Preview show a single page
Two Pages	Shows two pages in the Print Preview
Zoom Control	Zooms in and out of the Print Preview screen to show more or less detail

Tip   You can view more than two pages by selecting View ➪ Pages and selecting 1, 2, 4, 8, or 12.

If you are satisfied with the datasheet after examining the preview, select the Print button on the toolbar to print the datasheet. If you are not satisfied, select the Close button to return to datasheet mode to make further changes to your data or layout.

Summary

In this chapter, you learned to enter data into a datasheet, to navigate within the datasheet and change the data, and to reposition and resize rows and columns. Then you learned to preview and print the datasheet. The chapter covered these points:

✦ A datasheet displays data from a table in rows (records) and columns (fields).

✦ Using scrollbars, cursor keys, menu options, and the navigation buttons, you can move quickly in the datasheet and position the cursor on any record or field.

✦ You can open a datasheet from any Design window by clicking on the Datasheet button (or, from the Database window, by choosing Open with a table selected).

✦ Data is entered into a datasheet at the new-record indicator.

✦ Access performs automatic data validation for these data types: Number, Currency, Date/Time, and Yes/No fields. You can add your own custom data validation at the table or form level.

✦ You can paste or insert OLE objects (such as sound, pictures, graphs, Word documents, or video) into OLE fields with Insert ➪ Object.

✦ The navigation buttons enable you to move quickly between records.

✦ You can find or replace specific values by using Edit ➪ Find or Edit ➪ Replace.

✦ You can press Ctrl+Alt+Spacebar to insert the default value into a field or press Ctrl+' to insert the preceding record's value into a field.

✦ Some types of fields can't be edited. These include AutoNumber, calculated, locked, disabled, and record-locked fields, as well as fields from certain types of queries.

✦ The Undo feature can undo typing, a field value, the current record, or a saved record.

✦ You can delete a record by selecting it and pressing Delete or by selecting Edit ➪ Delete.

✦ You can change the display of your datasheet by rearranging fields, changing the field display's width or row height, or changing display fonts.

✦ You can hide or reshow columns, freeze or unfreeze columns, and remove or show gridlines.

✦ You can save any layout changes by using File ➪ Save.

✦ Using the QuickSort buttons, you can instantly change the order in which the records are displayed.

✦ Using Filter by Selection or Filter by Form, you can specify sort orders or filters to limit the record display of a datasheet. This is a limited version of QBE (Query by Example).

✦ File ➪ Print prints your datasheet; File ➪ Print Preview previews the pages on the screen.

In the next chapter, you learn to create a form and to use a form for data entry.

✦   ✦   ✦

Creating and Using Simple Data-Entry Forms

Forms provide the most flexible way for viewing, adding, editing, and deleting your data. In this chapter, you learn to use Form Wizards as the starting point for your form. You learn how forms work and the types of forms that you can create with Access.

Understanding Data-Entry Forms

Although you can view your data in many ways, a form provides the most flexibility for viewing and entering data. A form lets you view one or more records at a time while viewing all of the fields. A datasheet also lets you view several records at once, but you can see only a limited number of fields. When you use a form, you can see all your fields at once, or at least as many as you can fit on a screen. By rearranging your fields in a form, you can easily get 20, 50, or even 100 fields on one screen. You can also use forms to create multipage screens for each record. Forms are useful for viewing data in a formatted display, as well as for entering, changing, or deleting data. You can also print forms with the visual effects you created.

What are the basic types of forms?

There are six basic types of forms:

- ✦ Columnar (also known as full-screen) forms
- ✦ Tabular forms
- ✦ Datasheets
- ✦ Main/subforms
- ✦ Pivot table forms
- ✦ Graphs

Figure 8-1 is a *columnar form*; the fields are arranged as columns onscreen. The form can occupy one or more screen pages. Generally, this type of form is used to simulate the hard-copy entry of data; the fields can be arranged any way that you want. Most standard Windows controls are available with Access forms and make data entry more productive and understandable. Lines, boxes, colors, and special effects (such as shadows or three-dimensional looks) enable you to make great-looking, easy-to-use forms.

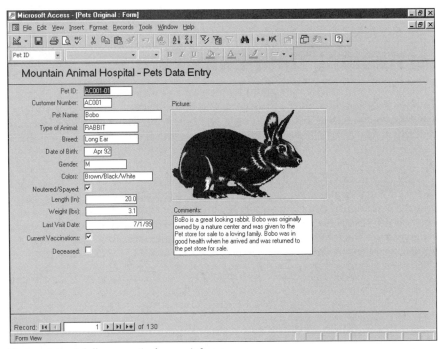

Figure 8-1: A full-screen (columnar) form.

Figure 8-2 is a tabular form that allows you to see several records at one time. You can format any part of a tabular form; your column headers can span multiple lines and be formatted separately from the records (unlike datasheets, which do not allow you to customize the column headers). Tabular forms can also have multiple lines per record, and you can add special effects (such as shadows or three-dimensional effects) to the fields. Field controls can also be option buttons or command buttons.

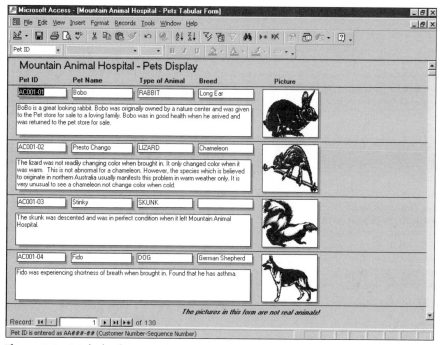

Figure 8-2: A tabular form.

A main/subform, which is shown in Figure 8-3, is commonly used to display one-to-many relationships. The main form displays the main table; the subform is frequently a datasheet or tabular form that displays the many portion of the relationship. For example, each pet's visit information appears once, while the subform shows many visit detail records. This type of form combines all the benefits of a form and a datasheet. A subform can show just one record or several records, each on multiple lines.

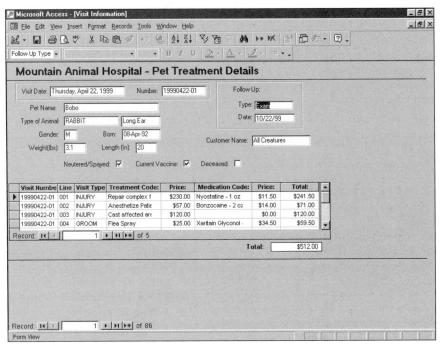

Figure 8-3: A main/subform.

How do forms differ from datasheets?

With a datasheet, you have very little control over the display of data. Although you can change the type and size of the display font, and rearrange, resize, or hide columns, you cannot significantly alter the appearance of the data. By using forms, you can place each field in an exact specified location, add color or shading to each field, and add text controls to make data entry more efficient.

A form has more flexibility in data entry than a datasheet. You can add calculated fields as well as enhanced data-validation and editing controls (such as option buttons, checkboxes, and pop-up list boxes) to a form. Adding lines, boxes, colors, and static bitmaps enhances the look of your data, makes your form easier to use, and improves productivity.

In addition, OLE objects (such as pictures or graphs) are visible *only* in a form or report. Additionally, although you can increase a datasheet's row size to see more of a Memo field, using a form makes it easier to display large amounts of text in a scrollable text box.

Tip   Once you create a form with editing controls or enhanced data validation, you can switch into *datasheet mode*, which lets you use data-validation rules and controls, such as pop-up lists.

Creating a form with AutoForm

From the Table or Query object in the Database window, a datasheet, or nearly any design screen in Access, you can create a form instantly by clicking the New button in the toolbar (a form with a lightning bolt through it) and choosing one of the AutoForm icons. Another method is to use Insert ➪ Form and select one of the AutoForm choices from the dialog box that appears. When you use the AutoForm button, the form appears instantly with no additional work. You can create columnar, tabular, or datasheets with AutoForm. To create a columnar AutoForm using the Pets table, follow these steps:

1. From the Mountain Animal Hospital Database window, click the Table object button.

2. Select Pets.

3. Click the New button in the toolbar.

4. Select AutoForm.

The form instantly appears, as shown in Figure 8-4.

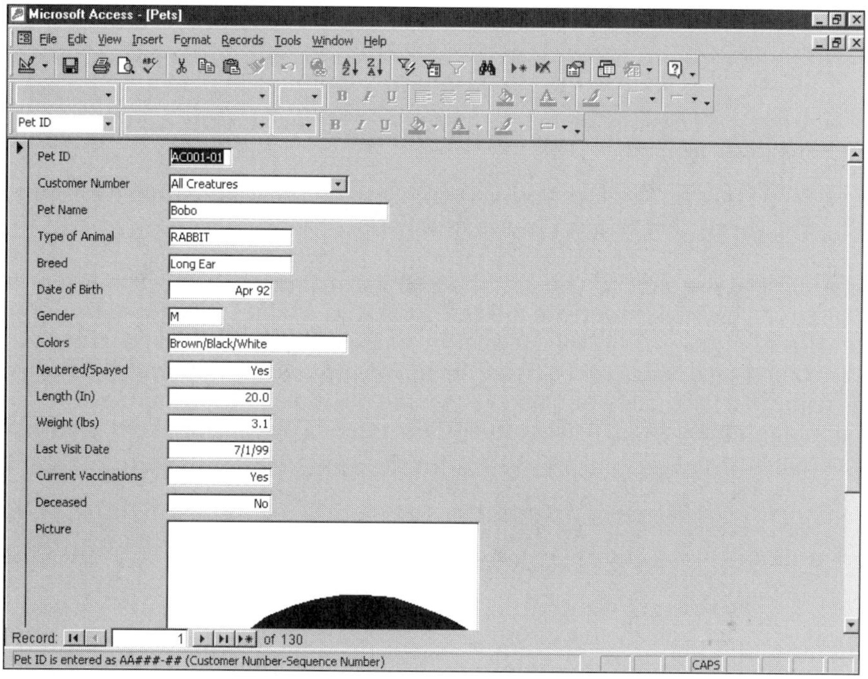

Figure 8-4: The AutoForm form.

Some values are not properly displayed in different areas of the form. For example, if you scroll down and look at the picture of the rabbit (yes, it's the hindquarter of a rabbit) in the first record, you see only a portion of the rabbit. Later you learn how to fix this, as well as how to customize the form.

AutoForm is the quickest way to create a form. Generally, however, you want more control over your form creation. Other Form Wizards can help you create a more customized form from the outset.

Creating a Form with Form Wizards

Form Wizards simplify the layout process for your fields. A Form Wizard visually steps you through a series of questions about the form you want to create and then creates it for you automatically. In this chapter, you learn to create single-column forms with a Form Wizard, using the columnar form as a starting point for creating a full-screen form.

Creating a new form

There are three methods available to create a new form:

✦ Select Insert ➪ Form from the Database window menu.

✦ Select the Form object button and select the New toolbar button from the Database window.

✦ Select the New toolbar button from the Database window, the datasheet, or the Query toolbar, and choose New Form.

Regardless of the method you use, the New Form dialog boxshown in Figure 8-5 appears. If you began to create the new form with a table highlighted (or from a datasheet or query), the table or query you are using appears in the text box labeled *Choose the table or query where the object's data comes from.* You can enter the name of a valid table or query (if you are not already using one) before continuing; choose from a list of tables and queries by clicking the combo box's selection arrow.

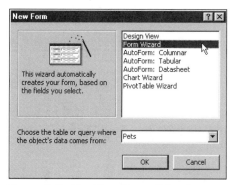

Figure 8-5: The New Form dialog box.

Selecting the New Form type and data source

The New Form dialog box has seven choices for creating a form:

Design View	Displays a completely blank form to start with in Form design
Form Wizard	Creates a form with one of four default layouts: columnar, tabular, datasheet, or justified using data fields that you specify in a step-by-step process that lets you customize the form creation process
AutoForm: Columnar	Instantly creates a columnar form
AutoForm: Tabular	Instantly creates a tabular form
AutoForm: Datasheet	Instantly creates a datasheet form
Chart Wizard	Creates a form with a business graph
PivotTable Wizard	Creates an Excel Pivot Table

As you make selections in a Wizard form, notice how the bitmap picture at the left of the Wizard form changes to show you your selection before you make it.

For this example, choose the Form Wizard option.

Choosing the fields

After selecting Form Wizard, the field-selection box shown in Figure 8-6 appears. The field-selection dialog box has three work areas. The first area lets you choose multiple tables or queries; you can create many types of forms, including those with subforms. As you select each table or query, the Available Fields list will change.

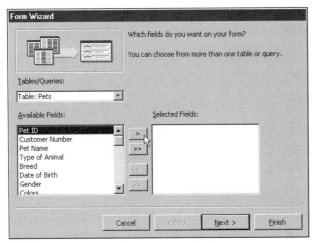

Figure 8-6: Choosing the fields for the form.

Note   If you are an experienced Access 2.0 user, you will find this process very different in Access 2000. There is no longer a separate subform Wizard. Instead, Access 2000 figures out when you have selected data related in a one-to-many relationship and adds extra screens to create a subform.

The field-selection area consists of two list boxes and four buttons. The Available Fields: list box on the left displays all fields from the selected table/query used to create the form. The Selected Fields: list box on the right displays the fields you have selected for this form. You can select one field, all the fields, or any combination of fields. The order in which you add the fields to the list box on the right is the order in which the fields will appear in the form. You can use the buttons to place or remove fields in the Selected Fields: box. Here is a description of these buttons:

> Add selected field

> Add all fields

< Remove selected field

<< Remove all fields

When you highlight a field in the Available Fields: list box and click >, the field name appears in the Selected Fields: list box. You can add each field you want to the list box. If you add a field by mistake, you can select the field in the Selected Fields: list box and click < to remove it from the selection. If you decide to change the order in which your fields are to appear in the form, you must remove any fields that are out of order and reselect them in the proper order.

Note   You can double-click any field in the Available Fields: list box to add it to the Selected Fields: list box.

At the bottom of the form is a series of buttons that are used when field selection is completed. The types of buttons available here are common to most Wizard dialog boxes.

Cancel	Cancel form creation and return to the starting point
< Back	Return to the preceding dialog box
Next >	Go to the next dialog box
Finish	Go to the last dialog box (usually the form title)

Note   If you click Next > or Finish without selecting any fields, Access tells you that you must select fields for the form before you continue.

Choosing the form layout

Once you have chosen the fields, you have to choose the type of layout. As Figure 8-7 shows, there are four types of layouts:

✦ Columnar

✦ Tabular

✦ Datasheet

✦ Justified

On the CD-ROM   Select all of the fields by clicking the > button. When you are finished, click the Next > button to display the dialog box from which to choose a form layout.

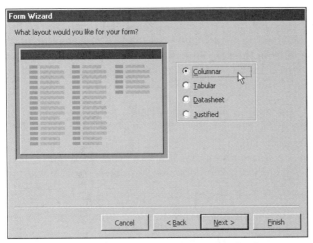

Figure 8-7: Choosing the type of layout for the form.

As you click the option button choices, the display changes to show how the form will look.

On the CD-ROM

Select the Columnar layout. Once you choose the type of layout, you can click the Next > button to display the style of the form.

Choosing the style of the form

After you select the form layout, you can choose the style for the form's look from the dialog box shown in Figure 8-8.

There are many choices, which are accessed by clicking the desired name in the list box. When you select a style, the display on the left changes to illustrate the special effect used to create the look.

As Figure 8-8 shows, the default look uses blends in the background. The Standard selection is a more traditional look, with a dark gray background and sunken controls. Select Expedition for the first form you create in this chapter. Once the form's style is selected, you are ready to create a title and view the form.

The style you select is used as the default the next time you use the Wizard.

Tip

You can customize the style by changing a form and then using the AutoFormat function in the Form design screen.

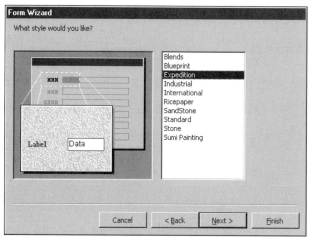

Figure 8-8: Choosing the style of your form.

Creating a form title

The form title dialog box is usually the last dialog box in a Form Wizard. It always has a checkered flag that lets you know that you are at the finish line. By default, the text box for the form title contains the name of the table or query used for the form's data. You can accept the entry for the form title, enter your own, or erase it and have no title. The title in Figure 8-9 is Pets, the name of the table.

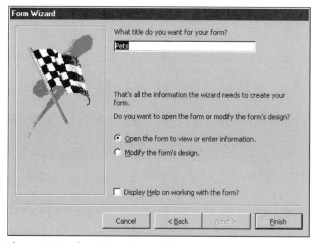

Figure 8-9: Choosing a form title.

Completing the form

After you complete all the steps to design your form, you open the new form by selecting one of these two options:

✦ Open the form to view or enter information

✦ Modify the form's design

In this example, select the former and then click the Finish button. Once you click the Finish button, the form appears in the Form View window (as shown in Figure 8-10).

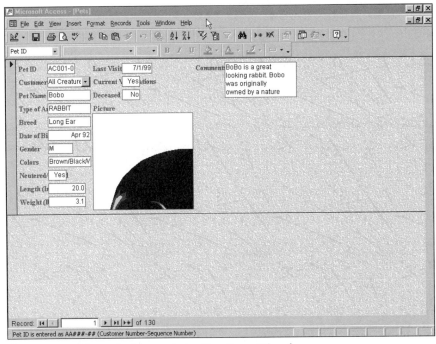

Figure 8-10: A form design created with a Form Wizard.

Changing the Design

To show how easy it is to manipulate the field controls, change the way the Picture field appears. Figure 8-10 has a lovely view of the hind part of the rabbit going over the fence; it would be nicer to see the whole rabbit. To fix this, follow these steps:

1. Click the Design button to open the form in the Form Design window.

2. Click the Picture field (the large, empty rectangle under the Picture label).

3. Click the Property icon in the toolbar (picture of a hand and a sheet of paper, the fifth icon from the right).

4. Click the Size Mode property and change it from Clip to Stretch (as shown in Figure 8-11).

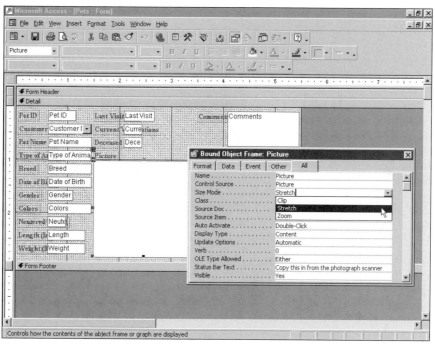

Figure 8-11: Changing a control property.

Tip

If you do not like having the Grid or Ruler displayed (as in Figure 8-11), they can be turned off by selecting View ➪ Ruler and/or View ➪ Grid.

After you complete the move, click the Form button to redisplay the form. The whole rabbit, as shown in Figure 8-12, is displayed.

Cross-Reference

Chapters 15–19 teach how to completely customize a form. In those chapters, you learn how to use all the controls in the toolbox, add special effects to forms, create forms with graphs and calculated fields, and add complex data validation to your forms.

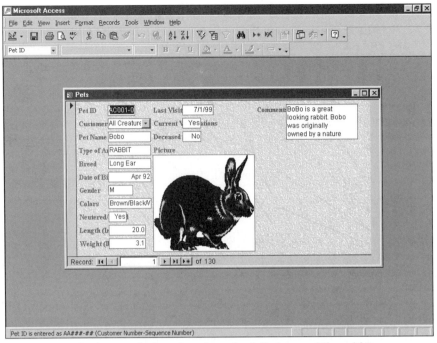

Figure 8-12: The form redisplayed to show the full picture of the rabbit.

Using the Form Window

The window shown in Figure 8-12 is very similar to the Datasheet window. At the top of the screen are the title bar, menu bar, and toolbar. The center of the screen displays your data, one record at a time, in the form window (unless you have the form window maximized). If the form contains more fields than fit onscreen at one time, Access 2000 automatically displays a horizontal and/or vertical scrollbar that can be used to see the remainder of the record. You can also see the rest of the record by pressing the PgDn key. The last line at the bottom of the screen contains a status bar. The status bar displays the Field Description you entered into the table design for each field. If there is no Field Description for a specific field, Access displays the words Form View. Generally, error messages and warnings appear in dialog boxes in the center of the screen (rather than in the status bar). The navigation buttons are found at the bottom of the screen. This feature lets you move quickly from record to record.

The Form toolbar

The Form toolbar, shown in Figure 8-12, is almost identical to the Datasheet toolbar. The only difference is that the first icon contains three selections: Form View, Design View, and Datasheet View.

Navigating between fields

Navigating a form is nearly identical to navigating a datasheet. You move around the Form window easily by clicking the field you want and making changes or additions to your data. Because the Form window displays only as many fields as will fit onscreen, you need to use various navigational aids to move within your form or between records.

Table 8-1 displays the navigational keys used to move between fields within a form.

Table 8-1 Navigating in a Form	
Navigational Direction	**Keystrokes**
Next field	Tab, right-arrow(→) or down-arrow(↓) key, or Enter
Previous field	Shift+Tab, left-arrow(←), or up-arrow(↑)
First field of current record	Home or Ctrl+Home
Last field of current record	End or Ctrl+End
Next page	PgDn or Next Record
Previous page	PgUp or Previous Record

If you have a form with more than one page, a vertical scrollbar displays. You can use the scrollbar to move to different pages on the form. You can also use the PgUp and PgDn keys to move between form pages. You can move up or down one field at a time by clicking the scrollbar arrows. With the scrollbar button, you can move past many fields at once.

Moving between records in a form

Although you generally use a form to display one record at a time, you still need to move between records. The easiest way to do this is to use the navigation buttons.

The navigation buttons offer the same five controls at the bottom of the screen that you saw in the datasheet. You can click these buttons to move to the desired record.

Pressing F5 moves you instantly to the record number box.

You can also press Ctrl+PgDn to move to the current field in the next record, or Ctrl+PgUp to move to the current field in the preceding record.

Displaying Your Data with a Form

In Chapter 7, you learned techniques to add, change, and delete data within a datasheet. The techniques you learned there are the same ones you use within a form. Table 8-2 summarizes these techniques.

<table>
<tr><td colspan="2" align="center">Table 8-2
Editing Techniques</td></tr>
<tr><td>*Editing Technique*</td><td>*Keystrokes*</td></tr>
<tr><td>Move insertion point within a field</td><td>Press the right(→)- and left-arrow(←) keys</td></tr>
<tr><td>Insert a value within a field</td><td>Move the insertion point and type the new data</td></tr>
<tr><td>Select the entire field</td><td>Press F2 or double-click the mouse button</td></tr>
<tr><td>Replace an existing value with a new value</td><td>Select the entire field and type a new value</td></tr>
<tr><td>Replace value with value of preceding field</td><td>Press Ctrl+' (single quote mark)</td></tr>
<tr><td>Replace current value with default value</td><td>Press Ctrl+Alt+Spacebar</td></tr>
<tr><td>Insert current date into a field</td><td>Press Ctrl+; (semicolon)</td></tr>
<tr><td>Insert current time into a field</td><td>Press Ctrl+: (colon)</td></tr>
<tr><td>Insert a line break in a Text or Memo field</td><td>Press Ctrl+Enter</td></tr>
<tr><td>Insert new record</td><td>Press Ctrl++ (plus sign)</td></tr>
<tr><td>Delete current record</td><td>Press Ctrl+– (minus sign)</td></tr>
<tr><td>Save current record</td><td>Press Shift+Enter or move to another record</td></tr>
<tr><td>Undo a change to the current record</td><td>Press Esc or click on the Undo button</td></tr>
</table>

Working with pictures and OLE objects

In a datasheet, you cannot view a picture or any OLE object without accessing the OLE server. In a form, however, you can size the OLE control area large enough to display a picture, business graph, or visual OLE object. You can also size the Memo controls on forms so that you can see the data within the field — you don't have to zoom in on the value, as you do with a datasheet field. Figure 8-12 displays both the picture and the Memo data displayed in the form. Each of these controls can be resized.

Recall from Chapter 7 that any object supported by an OLE server can be stored in an Access OLE field. OLE objects are entered into a form so that you can see, hear, or use the value. As with a datasheet, you have two ways to enter OLE fields into a form:

✦ Paste them in from the Clipboard from the Edit menu.

✦ Insert them into the field from the Insert ➪ Object menu.

Cross-Reference

Chapter 19 covers using and displaying OLE objects in forms in more detail.

Memo field data entry

Comments:, the last field in the form shown in Figure 8-12 (the rightmost column), is a Memo data type. This type of field allows up to 64,000 bytes of text for each field. You can see the first two sentences of data in the Memo field. When you move the cursor (also known as the insertion point) into the Memo field, a vertical scrollbar appears (see Figure 8-13). Using this scrollbar, you can view the rest of the data in the field. You can resize the Memo control in the Form Design window if you want to make it larger. You can also press Shift+F2 and display a Zoom dialog box in the center of the screen, which lets you view about 12 lines at a time.

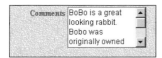

Figure 8-13: A vertical scrollbar appears in a Memo field when the text cursor is in it.

Switching to a datasheet

While in the form, you can display a Datasheet view of your data using one of two methods:

✦ Click the Datasheet button in the toolbar.

✦ Select View ➪ Datasheet View.

The datasheet is displayed with the cursor on the same field and record it occupied in the form. If you move to another record and field and then redisplay the form, the form now appears with the cursor on the field and record it last occupied in the datasheet.

To return to the form from a datasheet, you can use either of these two methods:

✦ Click the Form button in the toolbar.

✦ Select View ⇨ Form View.

Sorting and filtering form records

You use the same techniques to manipulate records in a form as you do in a datasheet. The only difference is that instead of positioning on a specific record, you display a single record.

Cross-Reference If you need to review the techniques for finding and replacing data or filtering and sorting your records, see the appropriate sections in Chapter 7.

Saving a Record and the Form

As you move off each record, Access automatically saves any changes to the record. You can also press Shift+Enter to save a record without moving off it. The final way to save a record is to save the form. You can save any changes to a form design by selecting Records ⇨ Save. This saves any changes and keeps the form open. When you are ready to close a form and return to the Database window (or to your query or datasheet), you can select File ⇨ Close. If you made any changes to the form design, you are asked whether you want to save the design.

Printing a Form

You can print one or more records in your form exactly as they look on the screen. (You learn how to produce formatted reports later in the book.) The simplest way to print is to use the File ⇨ Print selection or the Print toolbar button. Selecting File ⇨ Print displays the Print dialog box.

Assuming that you have set up a printer in Microsoft Windows, you can select OK to print your form. Access then prints your form, using the font you selected for display or using the nearest printer equivalent. The printout contains any formatting that you specified in the form (including lines, boxes, and shading), and converts colors to grayscale if you are using a monochrome printer.

The printout prints as many pages as necessary to print all the data. If your form is wider than a single printer page, you will need multiple pages to print your form. Access breaks up the printout as necessary to fit on each page.

Using the Print Preview Window

You may find that you have all the information in your form, but you aren't sure whether that information will print on multiple pages or fit on one printed page. Maybe you want to see whether the fonts need adjustment, or you need only the printed records from pages 3 and 4. In such cases, view the report onscreen before printing to make these adjustments to the form design.

To preview your printout, you either click the Print Preview button on the toolbar (a sheet of paper with a magnifying glass on top) or select File ➪ Print Preview. Figure 8-14 shows the Print Preview window; it works exactly like the datasheet Print Preview window you learned about in Chapter 7.

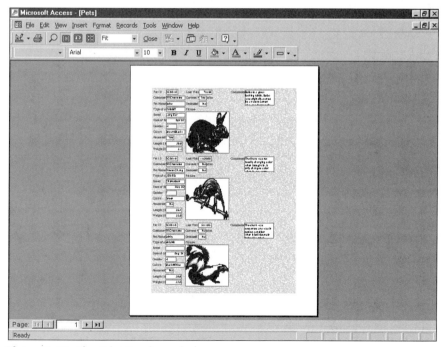

Figure 8-14: The Print Preview window.

If after examining the preview you are satisfied with the form, select the Print button on the toolbar to print the form. If you are not satisfied, click the Close button to return to the form to make changes to the data or design.

Summary

This chapter examined Form Wizards and the types of forms you can create with Access. You can use forms created by Wizards as the starting point for your form. You also learned how forms work. These points were covered:

✦ Data-entry forms provide the most flexible format for viewing your data; you can arrange your fields in any order you want.

✦ Whereas datasheets generally let you view many records at a time, you would use a form to view one record at a time.

✦ AutoForm instantly creates a form for you with just one keystroke.

✦ Form Wizards simplify form creation by giving you a starting point for form design and stepping you through the process.

✦ There are five basic types of forms: full-screen (columnar), tabular, main/subforms, pivot tables, and graphs.

✦ A Form Wizard lets you specify the type of form, the fields to be used, the type of look you want, and a title.

✦ You can specify one or more fields in a Form Wizard.

✦ A Form Wizard lets you choose from several types of styles.

✦ A form lets you enter data into Picture and Memo fields and displays the fields as well.

✦ You can switch to a datasheet view from a form view by selecting the Datasheet button.

✦ You can print a form with all its formatting, or you can preview it on the screen before printing.

In the next chapter, you learn about simple queries.

✦   ✦   ✦

Understanding and Using Simple Queries

I n this chapter, you learn what a query is and about the process of creating queries. Using the Pets table, you create several types of queries for the Mountain Animal Hospital database.

Understanding Queries

A database's primary purpose is to store and extract information. Information can be obtained from a database immediately after you enter the data or years later. Of course, obtaining information requires knowledge of how the database is set up.

For example, reports may be filed manually in a cabinet, arranged first by order of year and then by a *sequence number* that indicates when the report was written. To obtain a specific report, you must know its year and sequence number. In a good manual system, you may have a cross-reference book to help you find a specific report. This book may have all reports categorized alphabetically by type of report (rather than topic). Such a book can be helpful, but if you know only the report's topic and approximate date, you still may have to search through all sections of the book to find out where to obtain the report.

Unlike manual databases, computer-automated databases have a distinct advantage; with their tools, you can easily obtain information to meet virtually any criteria you specify.

This is the real power of a database—the capacity to examine the data any way *you* want to look at it. Queries, by definition, ask questions about the data stored in the database. After you create a query, you can use its data for reports, forms, and graphs.

What is a query?

The word *query* is from the Latin word *quærere*, which means to ask or inquire. Over the years, the word "query" has become synonymous with quiz, challenge, inquire, or question. Therefore, you can think of a query as a question or inquiry posed to the database about information found in its tables.

A Microsoft Access query is a question that you ask about the information stored in your Access tables. The way you ask questions about this information is by using the query *tools*. Your query can be a simple question about information stored in a single table, or it can be a complex question about information stored in several tables. After you ask the question, Microsoft Access returns only the information you requested.

Using queries this way, you can query the Pets database to show you only the dogs that are named within it. To see the dogs' names, you need to retrieve information from the Pets table. Figure 9-1 is a typical Query Design window.

After you create and run a query, Microsoft Access can return and display the set of records you asked for in a datasheet. This set of records is called a *dynaset*, which is the set of records selected by a query. As you've seen, a datasheet looks just like a spreadsheet, with its rows of records and columns of fields. The datasheet can display many records simultaneously.

You can query information from a single table. Many database queries, however, require information from several tables.

Suppose, for example, that you want to send a reminder to anyone living in a certain city that their dog or cat is due for an annual vaccination. This type of query requires getting information from two tables: Customer and Pets.

Cross-Reference   You may want Access to show you a single datasheet of all customers and their pets that meet your specified criteria. Access can retrieve customer names and cities from the Customer table and then pet names, animal type, and current vaccination status from the Pets table. Access then takes the information that's common to your criteria, combines it, and displays all the information in a single datasheet. This datasheet is the result of a query that draws from both the Customer and Pets tables. The database query performed the work of assembling all the information for you.

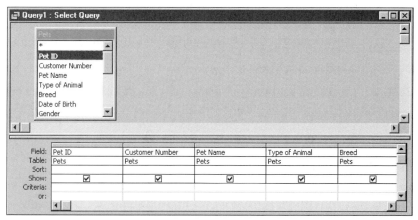

Figure 9-1: A typical select query.

Cross-
Reference

In this chapter, you work with only the Pets table; Part III covers multiple tables.

Types of queries

Access supports many different types of queries. They can be grouped into six basic categories:

Select These are the most common. As its name implies, the select query selects information from one or more tables (based on specific criteria), and displays the information in a dynaset that you can use to view and analyze specific data; you can make changes to your data in the underlying tables.

Total These are special versions of select queries. Total queries provide the capability to sum or produce totals (such as count) in a select query. When you select this type of query, Access adds a Total row in the QBE (Query by Example) pane.

Action These queries let you create new tables (Make Tables) or change data (delete, update, and append) in existing tables. When you make changes to records in a select query, the changes must be made one record at a time. In action queries, changes can be made to many records during a single operation.

Crosstab These queries can display summary data in *cross-tabular* form like a spreadsheet, with the row and column headings based on fields in the table. By definition, the individual cells of the resultant dynaset are tabular — that is, computed or calculated.

SQL	There are three SQL (Structured Query Language) query types — *Union*, *Pass-Through*, and *Data Definition* — which are used for advanced SQL database manipulation (for example, working with client/server SQL databases). You can create these queries only by writing specific SQL commands.
Top(n)	You can use this *query limiter* only in conjunction with the other five types of queries. It lets you specify a number or percentage of the top records you want to see in any type of query.

Query capabilities

Queries are flexible. They provide the capability of looking at your data in virtually any way you can think of. Most database systems are continually evolving, developing more powerful and necessary tools. The original purpose they are designed for changes over time. You may decide that you want to look at the information stored in the database in a different way. Because information is stored in a database, you should be able to look at it in this new way. Looking at data in a way that's different from its intended manner is known as performing *ad hoc* queries. Querying tools are among the most powerful and flexible features of your Access database. Here is a sampling of what you can do:

Choose tables	You can obtain information from a single table or from many tables that are related by some common data. Suppose you're interested in seeing the customer name along with the type of animals each customer owns. This sample task takes information from the Customer and Pets tables. When using several tables, Access returns the data in a combined single datasheet.
Choose fields	You can specify which fields from each table you want to see in the resultant dynaset. For example, you can look at the customer name, customer ZIP code, animal name, and animal type separated from all the other fields in the Customer or Pets table.
Choose records	You can select the records to display in the dynaset by specifying criteria. For example, you may want to see records for dogs only.
Sort records	You may want to see the dynaset information sorted in a specific order. You may need, for example, to see customers in order by last name and first name.

Perform calculations	You can use queries to perform calculations on your data. You may be interested in performing such calculations as averaging, totaling, or simply counting the fields.
Create tables	You may need another database table formed from the combined data resulting from a query. The query can create this new table based on the dynaset.
Create forms and reports based on a query	The dynaset you create from a query may have just the right fields and data that you need for a report or form. When you base your form or report on a query, every time you print the report or open the form, your query will retrieve the most current information from your tables.
Create graphs based on queries	You can create graphs from the data in a query, which you can then use in a form or report.
Use a query as a source of data for other queries (subquery)	You can create additional queries based on a set of records that you selected in a previous query. This is very useful for performing ad hoc queries, where you may repeatedly make small changes to the criteria. The secondary query can be used to change the criteria while the primary query and its data remain intact.
Make changes to tables	Access queries can obtain information from a wide range of sources. You can ask questions about data stored in dBASE, Paradox, Btrieve, and Microsoft SQL Server databases.

How dynasets work

Access takes the records that result from a query and displays them in a datasheet, in which the actual records are called a dynaset. Physically a dynaset looks like a table; in fact, it is not a table. The dynaset is a *dynamic* (or virtual) set of records. *This dynamic set of records is not stored in the database.*

Note   When you close a query, the query dynaset is gone; it no longer exists. Even though the dynaset itself no longer exists, the data that formed the dynaset remains stored in the underlying tables.

When you run a query, Access places the resultant records in the dynaset. When you save the query, the information is not saved; only the structure of the query is saved — the tables, fields, sort order, record limitations, query type, and so forth. Consider these benefits of *not* saving the dynaset to a physical table:

✦ A smaller amount of space on a storage device (usually a hard disk) is needed.

✦ The query can use updated versions of any records changed since the query was last run.

Every time the query is executed, it goes out to the underlying tables and recreates the dynaset. Because dynasets themselves are not stored, a query automatically reflects any changes to the underlying tables made since the last time the query was executed — even in a real-time, multiuser environment.

Creating a Query

After you create your tables and place data in them, you are ready to work with queries. To begin a query, follow these steps:

1. From the Database window, click the Queries object button.

2. Click the New button.

   The New Query dialog box appears, as shown in Figure 9-2. You select from the five choices. The first choice displays the Query Design window.

3. Select Design View and click the OK button.

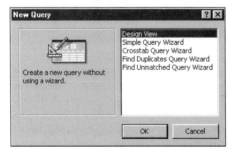

Figure 9-2: The New Query dialog box.

On the
CD-ROM

If you select the new query without first selecting a table, Access opens a window and a dialog box. Figure 9-3 shows both windows. The underlying window is the Query Design window. The accompanying Show Table dialog box is *nonmodal*, which means that you must do something in the dialog box before continuing with the query. Before you continue, you should add tables for the query to work with.

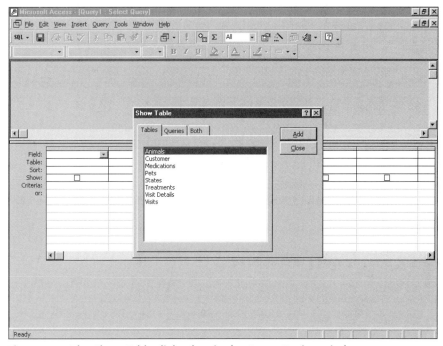

Figure 9-3: The Show Table dialog box in the Query Design window.

Selecting a table

The Show Table dialog box displays all tables and queries in your database. If you are following the examples, you should see one table named Pets. If you are using the Mountain Animal Hospital or Mountain Animal Start databases, you should see all the tables in the Mountain Animal Hospital database. You can add the Pets table to the query design with these steps:

1. Select the Pets table.

2. Click on the Add button to add the Pets table to the Query Design window.

3. Click on the Close button.

Tip
Another method of adding the Pets table to the Query Design window is by double-clicking the Pets table.

You can begin a new query by clicking the New Query button on the toolbar, or you can select Insert ➪ Query from the main Access menu. If you select a table or query before you start a new query, Access will load the selected table or query automatically.

You can activate the Show Table dialog box to add more tables at any time; select Query ➪ Show Table or click on the Show Table button (picture of table with plus sign).

Tip You can also add tables by moving the mouse to any empty place in the top-half of the window (the Table/Query Pane) and clicking the *right* mouse button. Right-click to activate the shortcut menu and then select Show Table.

When you want to delete a table from the Table/Query pane, click the table name in the query/table entry pane (see Figure 9-4) and either press Delete or select Query ➪ Remove Table.

Tip You also can add a table to the Query/Table Pane by selecting the Database window and dragging and dropping a table name from the Table window into the Query window.

Using the Query window

The Query window has two modes, the *design mode* and the *datasheet mode*. The difference between them is self-explanatory: The design mode is where you create the query, and the datasheet mode is where you display the query's dynaset.

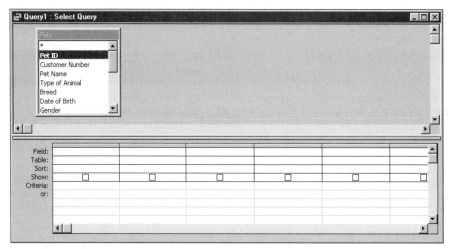

Figure 9-4: The Query Design window with the Pets table displayed.

The Query Design window should now look like Figure 9-4, with the Pets table displayed in the top half of the Query Design window.

The Query Design window is currently in the design mode; it consists of two panes:

✦ The table/query entry pane

✦ The Query by Example (QBE) design pane (also called the *QBE grid*)

The *table/query entry pane* is where tables and/or queries and their design structures are displayed. The visual representation of the table lists each field. The *Query by Example (QBE) pane* is used for the fields and criteria that the query will display in the dynaset. Each column in the QBE design pane contains information about a single field from a table or query in the upper pane.

Navigating the Query Design window

The *title bar* at the top of the Query Design window bears information about a particular window, the type of query, and the query name. Any new query is named Query1. Note that the title bar in Figure 9-4 displays the query type and name as *Query1 : Select Query*.

The two window panes are separated horizontally by a *pane resizing bar*. This bar is used to resize the panes: to enlarge the upper pane, click the bar and drag it down; drag the bar up to enlarge the lower pane.

You switch between the upper and lower panes either by clicking the desired pane or by pressing F6 to move to the other pane. Each pane has scrollbars to help you move around.

Tip   If you resize the Pets design structure vertically, you can see more fields at one time. With horizontal resizing, you can see more field names. To see more fields, first resize the top pane to size the Pets structure vertically.

You can design a query by dragging fields from the upper pane to the lower pane of the Query window. After placing fields on the QBE pane (lower pane), you can set their display order by dragging a field from its current position to a new position in the pane.

Using the Query Design toolbar

The toolbar in the Query Design window contains several buttons specific to building and working with queries, as shown in Figure 9-5.

Figure 9-5: The Query Design toolbar.

Using the QBE pane of the Query Design window

Figure 9-4 displays an empty Query Design pane (QBE grid), which has six named rows:

Field	This is where field names are entered or added.
Table	This is the table the field is from (useful in queries with multiple tables).
Sort	This choice lets you enter sort directives for the query.
Show	This checkbox determines whether to display the field in the resulting dynaset.
Criteria	This is where you enter the first line of criteria to limit the record selection.
or	This is the first of a number of lines to which you can add multiple values to be used in criteria selection.

You learn more about these rows as you create queries in this chapter.

Selecting Fields

There are several ways to add fields to a query. You can add fields one at a time, select multiple fields, or select all fields. You can use your keyboard or mouse to add the fields.

Adding a single field

You can add a single field in several ways. One method is to double-click on the field name; the field name then appears in the next available column in the Query Design pane. You can also add a field graphically to the Query Design pane by following these steps:

1. Highlight the field name in the table/query entry area.

2. Click the desired field and drag the Field icon, which appears as you move the mouse.

3. Drop the Field icon in the desired column of the QBE Design pane.

The Field icon looks like a small rectangle when it is inside the Pets table. As the mouse is dragged outside the Pets table, the icon changes to a circle-with-slash (the international symbol for "no"), which means that you cannot drop the Field icon in that location. When this icon enters any column in the QBE column, the field name appears in the Field: row. If you drop the Field icon between two other fields, it appears between those fields and pushes all existing fields to the right.

Tip   If you select a field accidentally, you can deselect it by releasing the mouse button while the icon is the No symbol.

To run the query, click the Datasheet button on the toolbar (the first icon from the left). When you are finished, click the Design button on the toolbar (the first one on the left) to return to design mode. You can also run the query by clicking on the icon on your toolbar with the exclamation point on it, or by selecting Query ➪ Run. To return to the design, click on the Design button on your toolbar (the first icon from the left).

Another way to add fields to the QBE Design pane is to click the empty Field: cell in the QBE Design pane and then type the field name in the field cell. Another method is to select the field you want from the drop-down list that appears (see Figure 9-6).

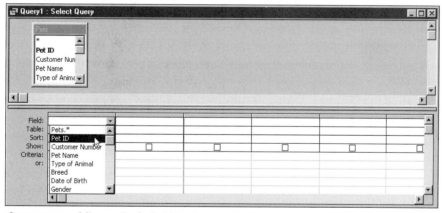

Figure 9-6: Adding a single field in the QBE Design pane (grid).

Adding multiple fields

You can add more than one field at a time by selecting the fields and then dragging the selection to the query pane. To add multiple fields from a table simultaneously, the selected fields do not have to be contiguous (one after the other). Figure 9-7 illustrates the process of adding multiple fields.

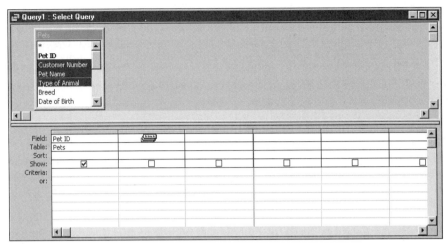

Figure 9-7: Selecting several fields graphically to move to the QBE Design pane.

To add multiple contiguous fields, follow these steps:

1. Remove any existing fields in the QBE pane by selecting Edit ➪ Clear Grid from the menu.

2. Highlight in the table/query entry area the first field name that you want to add.

3. Hold the Shift key down and click on the last field that you want to select. (All the fields in-between will be selected as well.)

4. Click the selected fields and drag the Multiple Field icon, which appears as you move the mouse. The icon appears as a group of three field icons.

5. Drop the Multiple Field icon in the desired column of the QBE Design pane.

To add multiple noncontiguous fields to the query, follow these steps:

1. Remove any existing fields in the QBE pane by selecting Edit ➪ Clear Grid from the menu.

2. Highlight in the table/query entry area the first field name that you want to add.

3. Hold the Ctrl key down and click on each field that you want to select. (Only the fields you select are highlighted.)

4. Click the selected fields and drag the Multiple Field icon, which appears as you move the mouse. The icon appears as a group of three field icons.

5. Drop the Multiple Field icon in the desired column of the QBE Design pane.

Adding all table fields

In addition to adding fields (either in groups or individually), you can move all the fields to the QBE pane at once. Access gives you two methods for choosing all fields: dragging all fields as a group or selecting the *all-field reference tag*—the asterisk (*).

Dragging all fields as a group

To select all the fields of a table, perform these steps:

1. Remove any existing fields in the QBE pane by selecting Edit ⇨ Clear Grid from the menu.

2. Double-click the title bar of the table to select all the fields.

3. Point to any of the selected fields with the mouse.

4. Drag the Multiple Field icon to the QBE pane.

This method fills in each column of the QBE pane automatically. All the fields are added to the QBE pane from left to right, based on their field order in the Pets table. By default, Access displays only the fields that can fit in the window. You can change the column width of each field to display more or fewer columns.

Selecting the all-field reference tag

The first object in the Pets table is an asterisk, which appears at the top of the field list. When you select all fields by using the asterisk, you don't see all the fields moved to the QBE Design pane. You see only that *Pets.* * is displayed in the Field: row, which indicates that all fields from the table named Pets are now selected. (This example assumes that the QBE Design pane is empty when you drag the asterisk from the Pets table to the QBE Design pane.)

The asterisk places the fields in a single Field: cell. When you dragged multiple fields with the first technique, you dragged actual table field names to the Query Design window, thus placing each field in a separate Field: cell across the QBE pane. If you change the design of the table later, you must also change the design of the query. The advantage of using the asterisk for selecting all fields is that you won't have to change the query later if you add, delete, or rename fields in the underlying table or query. (Access automatically adds or removes any field that changes in the underlying table or query.)

On the CD-ROM

If you are following the examples, you need to delete all fields from the query by selecting Edit ⇨ Clear Grid from the Query Design menu. When you've cleared all the fields, you can select the first nine fields in the Pets table (Pet ID through Neutered/Spayed, inclusively) and move them to the QBE Design pane.

To add the all-fields reference tag to the Query Design pane, follow these steps:

1. Click on the asterisk (*) in the Pets table to select this field.
2. Click on the selected field and drag the Field icon to the first cell in the QBE Design pane.

You now have the all-fields reference tag in the QBE pane. When you run this query, all the fields from Pets will be displayed.

Displaying the Dynaset

With multiple fields selected, it is time to display the resultant dynaset. Selecting either View ➪ Datasheet or the Datasheet button on the toolbar switches to the datasheet. The datasheet should now look like Figure 9-8. You can also display the dynaset by clicking the icon with the explanation point on it, or by selecting Query ➪ Run from your Access menu.

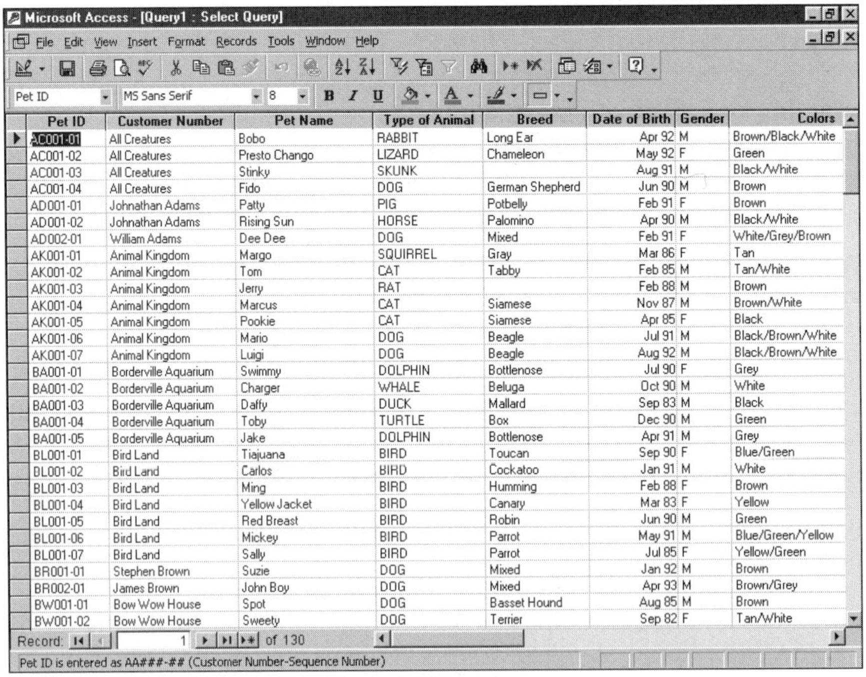

Pet ID	Customer Number	Pet Name	Type of Animal	Breed	Date of Birth	Gender	Colors
AC001-01	All Creatures	Bobo	RABBIT	Long Ear	Apr 92	M	Brown/Black/White
AC001-02	All Creatures	Presto Chango	LIZARD	Chameleon	May 92	F	Green
AC001-03	All Creatures	Stinky	SKUNK		Aug 91	M	Black/White
AC001-04	All Creatures	Fido	DOG	German Shepherd	Jun 90	M	Brown
AD001-01	Johnathan Adams	Patty	PIG	Potbelly	Feb 91	F	Brown
AD001-02	Johnathan Adams	Rising Sun	HORSE	Palomino	Apr 90	M	Black/White
AD002-01	William Adams	Dee Dee	DOG	Mixed	Feb 91	F	White/Grey/Brown
AK001-01	Animal Kingdom	Margo	SQUIRREL	Gray	Mar 86	F	Tan
AK001-02	Animal Kingdom	Tom	CAT	Tabby	Feb 85	M	Tan/White
AK001-03	Animal Kingdom	Jerry	RAT		Feb 88	M	Brown
AK001-04	Animal Kingdom	Marcus	CAT	Siamese	Nov 87	M	Brown/White
AK001-05	Animal Kingdom	Pookie	CAT	Siamese	Apr 85	F	Black
AK001-06	Animal Kingdom	Mario	DOG	Beagle	Jul 91	M	Black/Brown/White
AK001-07	Animal Kingdom	Luigi	DOG	Beagle	Aug 92	M	Black/Brown/White
BA001-01	Borderville Aquarium	Swimmy	DOLPHIN	Bottlenose	Jul 90	F	Grey
BA001-02	Borderville Aquarium	Charger	WHALE	Beluga	Oct 90	M	White
BA001-03	Borderville Aquarium	Daffy	DUCK	Mallard	Sep 83	M	Black
BA001-04	Borderville Aquarium	Toby	TURTLE	Box	Dec 90	M	Green
BA001-05	Borderville Aquarium	Jake	DOLPHIN	Bottlenose	Apr 91	M	Grey
BL001-01	Bird Land	Tiajuana	BIRD	Toucan	Sep 90	F	Blue/Green
BL001-02	Bird Land	Carlos	BIRD	Cockatoo	Jan 91	M	White
BL001-03	Bird Land	Ming	BIRD	Humming	Feb 88	F	Brown
BL001-04	Bird Land	Yellow Jacket	BIRD	Canary	Mar 83	F	Yellow
BL001-05	Bird Land	Red Breast	BIRD	Robin	Jun 90	M	Green
BL001-06	Bird Land	Mickey	BIRD	Parrot	May 91	M	Blue/Green/Yellow
BL001-07	Bird Land	Sally	BIRD	Parrot	Jul 85	F	Yellow/Green
BR001-01	Stephen Brown	Suzie	DOG	Mixed	Jan 92	M	Brown
BR002-01	James Brown	John Boy	DOG	Mixed	Apr 93	M	Brown/Grey
BW001-01	Bow Wow House	Spot	DOG	Basset Hound	Aug 85	M	Brown
BW001-02	Bow Wow House	Sweety	DOG	Terrier	Sep 82	F	Tan/White

Record: 1 of 130

Pet ID is entered as AA###-## (Customer Number-Sequence Number)

Figure 9-8: The datasheet with several fields.

Working with the datasheet

Access displays the dynaset in a datasheet. The techniques for navigating a query datasheet, as well as for changing its field order and working with its columns and rows, are exactly the same as for the other datasheets you worked with in Chapter 7.

Access 2000 allows you to sort and filter the results of a datasheet created by a query. All data in Access 2000 is editable all the time.

Changing data in the query datasheet

The query datasheet offers you an easy and convenient way to change data quickly. You can add and change data in the dynaset, and it will be saved to the underlying tables.

When you're adding or changing data in the datasheet, all the table properties defined at the table level are in effect. For example, you cannot enter a length value greater than 120 for any animal.

Returning to the query design

To return to the query design mode, select the Design button on the toolbar (the first one from the left).

Tip

You can also toggle between the design and datasheet mode by selecting View ⇨ Datasheet or View ⇨ Query Design from the Query menu.

On the CD-ROM

Clear the query grid by selecting Edit ⇨ Clear Grid. Next, add all the fields to the query grid by double-clicking the Pets data structure title bar and dragging all the selected fields to the query grid.

Working with Fields

There are times when you want to work with the fields you've already selected — rearranging their order, inserting a new field, or deleting an existing field. You may even want to add a field to the QBE design without showing it in the datasheet.

The *field selector row* is the narrow gray row above the Field: row. This row is approximately half the size of the others; it's important to identify this row because this is where you select columns, whether single or multiple. Recall that each column represents a field. To select the Pet Name field, move the mouse pointer until a small *selection arrow* (in this case, an outlined downward arrow) is visible in the selector row and then click the column. Figure 9-9 shows the selection arrow in the Pet Name column and the column after it is selected.

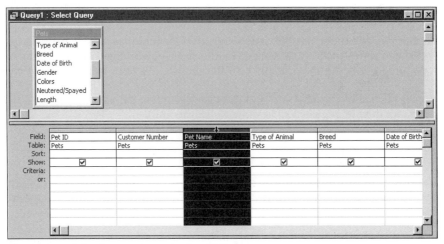

Figure 9-9: Selecting a column in the QBE pane.

If extend mode (F8) is on, the insertion point must be in the row whose column you want to select. If the insertion point is in an adjacent column and you select a column, you will select the adjacent column (containing the insertion point) as well. To deactivate extend mode (EXT), press the Esc key.

Changing field order

Two methods for changing the order of the fields in the QBE Design pane are to add them in the order you want them to appear in the datasheet, though this method is not always the easiest, or move fields after they are placed on the QBE design by selecting columns and moving them, just as you learned to move columns in a datasheet. Follow these steps to move a field:

1. Add several fields to the QBE pane.

2. Select the field you want to move (Breed) by clicking on the field selector above the field name. The column is highlighted.

3. Click and hold the field selector again; the QBE Field icon, a small graphical box, appears under the arrow.

4. While holding down the left mouse button, drag the column to its new position (to the left of Type of Animal).

5. Release the left mouse button to drop the field in its new position.

Figure 9-10 shows the Breed field highlighted (selected). As you move the selector field to the left, the column separator between the fields Pet Name and Type of Animal changes (gets wider) to show you where Breed will go.

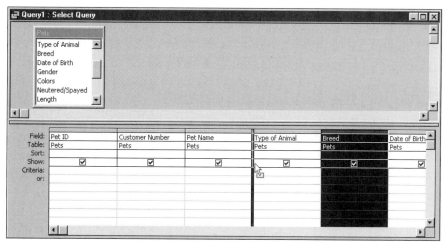

Figure 9-10: Moving the Breed field to between Pet Name and Type of Animal.

Removing a field

You can easily remove a field from the QBE Design pane. Select the field or fields to be deleted in the QBE Design pane, and then press Delete or select Edit ⇨ Delete. To remove the Customer Number field from the QBE Design pane, follow these steps:

1. Select the Customer Number field (or any other field) by clicking the field selector above the field name.

2. Press Delete.

Tip   If the field is not selected but the insertion point is in it, you can select Edit ⇨ Delete Column. You can delete all the fields in the QBE Design pane in a single operation: Select Edit ⇨ Clear Grid from the Query Design window's menu bar.

Inserting a field

You insert a field from the table/query entry pane in the QBE Design pane by first selecting the field(s) to be inserted from the table/query entry pane. Next, drag your field selection to the QBE Design pane. Follow these steps to insert the Customer Number field:

1. Select the Customer Number field from the field list in the table/query entry pane.

2. Drag the field from the field list to the column where you want the field to go.

3. Drop the field by releasing the left mouse button.

When you drag a field to the QBE Design pane, it is inserted wherever you drop the field. If you drop the field on top of another field, it is inserted before that field. If you double-click the field name in the table/query entry pane, the field is added to the end of the Field: list in the QBE Design pane.

Changing the field display name

To make the query datasheet easier to read, you may want to rename the fields in your query. The new names become the tag headings in the datasheet of the query. As an example, to rename the field Breed to Lineage, follow these steps:

1. Click to the left of the *B* in Breed in the Field: row of the QBE Design pane.

2. Type **Lineage** and then type a colon (:) between the new name and the old field name.

The heading now reads *Lineage:Breed*. When the datasheet is displayed, you'll see Lineage in place of *Breed*.

Note   Renaming the field by changing the datasheet caption changes *only* the name of the heading for that field in the datasheet. It does *not* change the field name in the underlying table.

Showing Table Names

When working with queries that have multiple tables, it can become difficult to determine where a field has come from. This is why Access has the capability to show the table where a field came from in the Table: row. Access automatically shows the Table: row, but you have the ability to turn it off so it is no longer visible.

When you select a field for display in the QBE pane, the name of the table that the field is from is shown in the row directly below the field name. If you want to turn this row off so that it is no longer visible, click View ➪ Table Names as shown in Figure 9-11 and the row with the table names disappears. To view the tables again, follow the same procedure to turn it on, and they will be displayed. It is a good idea to show the table names if you are working with a query that has multiple tables, so that you can easily tell what table the fields came from.

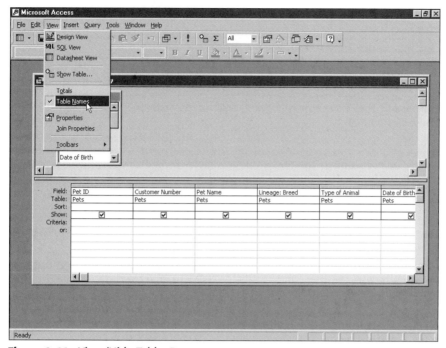

Figure 9-11: View/Hide Table: Row.

Showing a field

While performing queries, you may want to temporarily show only some of the fields. Suppose, for example, that you want to show only the fields Pet ID, Pet Name, and Breed. You can delete all other fields (and restore them when you're done with the temporary dynaset), or you can simply indicate which fields you want to see in the datasheet.

When you select fields, Access automatically makes every field a displayed field. Every Show: property is displayed with a check mark in the box.

To deselect a field's Show: property, simply click on the field's Show: box. The box clears, as you see in Figure 9-12. To reselect the field later, simply click on the Show: box again.

Field:	Pet ID	Customer Number	Pet Name	Type of Animal	Lineage: Breed	Dal
Table:	Pets	Pets	Pets	Pets	Pets	Pet
Sort:						
Show:	☑	☐	☑	☑	☑	
Criteria:						
or:						

Figure 9-12: The Show: row is checked only for the fields Pet ID, Pet Name, Breed, and Type of Animal.

Caution   If you save a query that has an unused field (its Show: box is unchecked), Access eliminates the field from the query pane.

Changing the Sort Order

When viewing a dynaset, you may want to display the data in a sorted order. You may want to sort the dynaset to make it easier to analyze the data (for example, to look at all the pets in order by Type of Animal).

Sorting places the records in alphabetical or numeric order. The sort order can be *ascending* (0 to 9 and A to Z) or *descending* (9 to 0 and Z to A).

Just as Access has a Show: property row for fields, there is a Sort: property row for fields in the QBE Design pane. In the following section, you learn to set this property.

Specifying a sort

To sort the records in the datasheet by Type of Animal in ascending order, perform these steps:

1. Click the Sort: cell for the Type of Animal field. An arrow appears in the cell.

2. Click the down arrow at the right of the cell.

3. Select Ascending from the list.

Figure 9-13 shows the QBE pane with the Type of Animal field selected for sorting by ascending order. Notice that the word *Ascending* is being selected in the field's Sort: cell.

Note   You *cannot* sort on a Memo or an OLE object field.

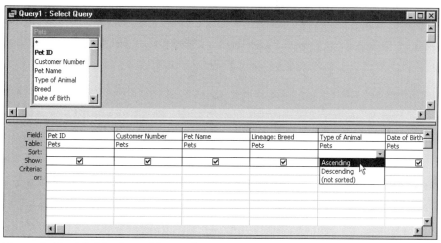

Figure 9-13: A field selected for sorting.

Sorting on more than one field

Access gives you the capability of sorting on multiple fields. You may, for example, want a primary sort order by Type of Animal and a secondary sort order by Breed. To create this query, start with the query illustrated in Figure 9-13. Then move the Breed field so that it is after the Type of Animal field. Finally, add a sort to the Breed field by selecting Ascending in the Sort: cell.

Access *always* sorts the leftmost sort field first. To make sure that Access understands how you want to sort your data, you must arrange the fields in order from left to right according to sort-order precedence. You can easily change the sort order by selecting a sort field and moving it relative to another sort field. Access corrects the sort order automatically.

That's all there is to it. Now the dynaset is arranged in order by two different fields. Figure 9-14 shows the multiple-field sort criteria. The sort order is controlled by the order of the fields in the QBE pane (from left to right); therefore, this dynaset is displayed in order first by Type of Animal and then by Breed, as shown in Figure 9-15. Also note that Breed has been renamed Lineage in the column header of the datasheet in Figure 9-15.

If you are following along with the examples, start a new query and select all the fields before continuing.

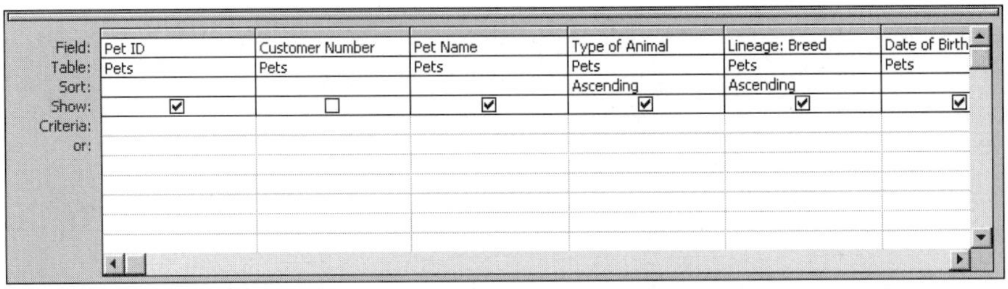

Field:	Pet ID	Customer Number	Pet Name	Type of Animal	Lineage: Breed	Date of Birth
Table:	Pets	Pets	Pets	Pets	Pets	Pets
Sort:				Ascending	Ascending	
Show:	☑	☐	☑	☑	☑	☑
Criteria:						
or:						

Figure 9-14: Multiple-field sort criteria.

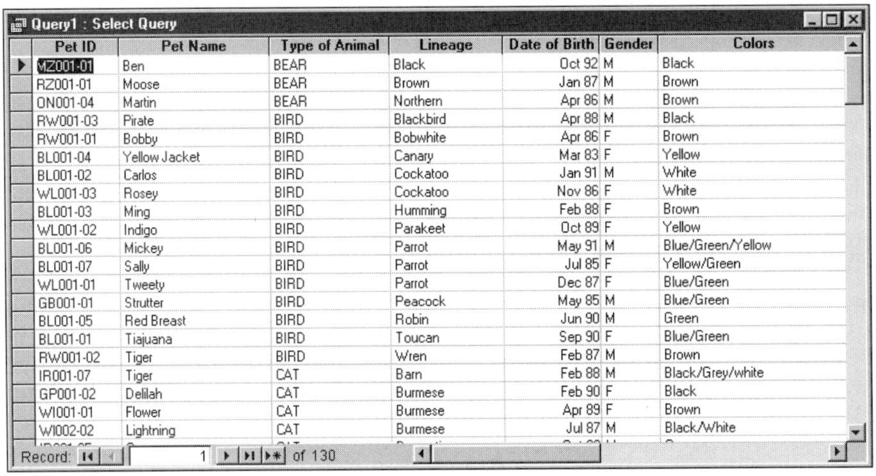

Query1 : Select Query

Pet ID	Pet Name	Type of Animal	Lineage	Date of Birth	Gender	Colors
MZ001-01	Ben	BEAR	Black	Oct 92	M	Black
RZ001-01	Moose	BEAR	Brown	Jan 87	M	Brown
ON001-04	Martin	BEAR	Northern	Apr 86	M	Brown
RW001-03	Pirate	BIRD	Blackbird	Apr 88	M	Black
RW001-01	Bobby	BIRD	Bobwhite	Apr 86	F	Brown
BL001-04	Yellow Jacket	BIRD	Canary	Mar 83	F	Yellow
BL001-02	Carlos	BIRD	Cockatoo	Jan 91	M	White
WL001-03	Rosey	BIRD	Cockatoo	Nov 86	F	White
BL001-03	Ming	BIRD	Humming	Feb 88	F	Brown
WL001-02	Indigo	BIRD	Parakeet	Oct 89	F	Yellow
BL001-06	Mickey	BIRD	Parrot	May 91	M	Blue/Green/Yellow
BL001-07	Sally	BIRD	Parrot	Jul 85	F	Yellow/Green
WL001-01	Tweety	BIRD	Parrot	Dec 87	F	Blue/Green
GB001-01	Strutter	BIRD	Peacock	May 85	M	Blue/Green
BL001-05	Red Breast	BIRD	Robin	Jun 90	M	Green
BL001-01	Tiajuana	BIRD	Toucan	Sep 90	F	Blue/Green
RW001-02	Tiger	BIRD	Wren	Feb 87	M	Brown
IR001-07	Tiger	CAT	Barn	Feb 88	M	Black/Grey/white
GP001-02	Delilah	CAT	Burmese	Feb 90	F	Black
WI001-01	Flower	CAT	Burmese	Apr 89	F	Brown
WI002-02	Lightning	CAT	Burmese	Jul 87	M	Black/White

Record: 1 of 130

Figure 9-15: A multiple-field sort order displayed.

Displaying Only Selected Records

So far, you've been working with all the records of the Pets table. There are times when you may want to work only with selected records in the Pets table. For example, you may want to look only at records where the value of Type of Animal is DOG. Access makes it easy for you to specify a record's criteria.

Understanding record criteria

Record criteria are simply some rule or rules that you supply for Access. These tell Access which records you want to look at in the dynaset. A typical criterion could be "all male animals," or "only those animals that are not currently vaccinated," or "all animals that were born before January 1990."

In other words, with record criteria, you create *limiting filters* to tell Access which records to find and which to leave out of the dynaset.

You specify criteria starting in the Criteria: property row of the QBE pane. Here you designate criteria with an expression. The expression can be simple example data or can take the form of complex expressions using predefined functions.

As an example of a simple data criterion, type **DOG** in the Criteria: cell of Type of Animal. The datasheet displays only records for dogs.

Entering simple character criteria

Character-type criteria are entered into fields that accommodate the Text data type. To use such criteria, you type in an example of the data contained within the field. To limit the record display to DOG, follow these steps:

1. Click the Criteria: cell in the Type of Animal column in the QBE Design pane.

2. Type **DOG** in the cell.

3. Click the Datasheet button.

Only the dogs are displayed. Observe that you did *not* enter an equal sign or place quotes around the sample text, yet Access added double quotes around the value. Access, unlike many other applications, automatically makes assumptions about what you want. This is an illustration of its flexibility. You could enter the expression in any of these other ways:

✦ Dog

✦ = Dog

✦ "Dog"

✦ = "Dog"

In Figure 9-16, the expression is entered under Type of Animal.

Figure 9-16 is an excellent example for demonstrating the options for various types of simple character criteria. You could just as well type **Not Dog** in the criteria column, to say the opposite. In this instance, you would be asking to see all records for animals that are not dogs, adding only Not before the example text Dog.

Generally, when dealing with character data, you enter equalities, inequalities, or a list of values that are acceptable.

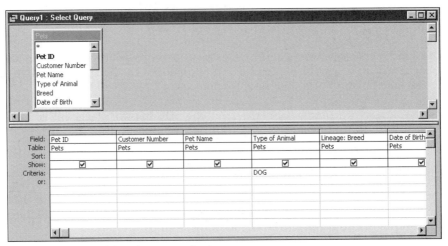

Figure 9-16: Specifying character criteria.

With either of these examples, Dog or Not Dog, you entered a simple expression in a Text-type field. Access took your example and interpreted it to show you all records that equal the example data you placed in the Criteria: cell.

This capability is a powerful tool. Consider that you have only to supply an example and Access not only interprets it but also uses it to create the query dynaset. This is exactly what *Query by Example* means: You enter an example and let the database build a query based on this data.

To erase the criteria in the cell, select the contents and press Delete, or select Edit ➪ Delete from the Query Design window's menu bar.

On the CD-ROM   If you are following the examples, delete the criterion in the Type of Animal field before continuing.

Entering other simple criteria

You can also specify criteria for Numeric, Date, and Yes/No fields. Suppose, for example, that you want to look only at records for animals born after January 1, 1993. To limit the display to records where the value of Date of Birth is greater than January 1, 1993, follow these steps:

1. Remove any existing fields in the QBE pane by selecting Edit ➪ Clear Grid from the menu.

2. Add the following fields: Pet Name, Type of Animal, Breed, and Date of Birth to the QBE grid.

3. Click the Criteria: cell in the Date of Birth column in the QBE Design pane.

4. Type > **01/01/93** in the cell.

5. Click the Datasheet button.

Access also compares Date fields to a value by using *comparison operators,* such as less than (<), greater than (>), equal to (=), or a combination thereof. Notice that Access automatically adds pound-sign (#) *delimiters* around the date value. Access recognizes these delimiters as differentiating a Date field from Text fields. Just as with entering text data examples, however, you don't have to enter the pound signs; Access understands what you want (based on the type of data entered in the field), and it converts the entry format for you.

Printing a Query Dynaset

After you create your query, you can quickly print all the records in the dynaset. Although you can't specify a type of report, you can print a simple matrix-type report (rows and columns) of the dynaset that your query created.

You do have some flexibility when printing a dynaset. If you know that the datasheet is set up just as you want, you can specify some options as you follow these steps:

1. Specify your record criteria in the query design mode.

2. Switch to the query datasheet mode by clicking the Datasheet button on the toolbar.

3. Select File ➪ Print from the Query Datasheet window's menu bar or click the Print button on the toolbar.

4. Specify the print options that you want in the Print dialog box.

5. Click the OK button in the Print dialog box.

Access now prints the dynaset for you. Assuming that you have set up a printer in Microsoft Windows, you can click OK to print your dataset. Your dataset prints out in the font selected for display or in the nearest equivalent your printer offers. The printout also reflects all layout options in effect when you print the dataset. Hidden columns do not print; gridlines print only if the Gridlines option is on. The printout does reflect the specified row height and column width.

Cross-Reference

Refer to Chapter 7 to review printing fundamentals. Chapter 7 covers printing the datasheet and using the Print Preview functions.

Saving a Query

To save a query while working in design mode, follow this procedure:

Select File ⇨ Save from the Query Design window or click the Save button on the toolbar. If this is the first time you're saving the query, enter a new query name in the Save As dialog box.

To save a query while working in datasheet mode, follow this procedure:

Select File ⇨ Save from the Datasheet File menu. If this is the first time you're saving the query, enter a new query name in the Save As dialog box.

Tip   The F12 key is the Save As key in Access. You can press F12 to save your work and continue working on your query.

Both of these methods save the query and return you to the mode you were working in. Occasionally, you want to save and exit the query in a single operation. To do this, select File ⇨ Close from the query or the datasheet and answer Yes to the question *Save changes to Query 'query name'?*. If this is your first time saving the query, Access prompts you to supply a query name and asks whether you want to save the query to the current database or to an external file or database.

You can leave the Query window at any time by any one of these ways:

✦ Select File ⇨ Close from the Query menu

✦ Select Close from the Query window control box

✦ Press Ctrl+F4 while inside the Query window

All three of these methods activate an Access dialog box that asks, *Save changes to Query 'Query1'?*.

Summary

In this chapter, you learned about the types of queries and the basics of using them. You had some practice creating simple queries and learned about some of the query options Access provides. The chapter covered these points:

✦ Queries ask questions about your data and return the answers in the form of information.

✦ Types of queries include select, total, crosstab, action, SQL, definition, and Top Values.

✦ Queries let you select tables, fields, sort order, and record criteria.

✦ Queries create a virtual view of the data, known as a dynaset. The data is displayed in a datasheet.

✦ A dynaset is the temporary answer set. Queries save only the instructions and not the data.

✦ The Query window has two panes. The top pane displays the Design view of your tables; the bottom pane is used for entering QBE instructions.

✦ When you add fields with the asterisk button, the query automatically changes if the underlying table changes.

✦ You can display field names differently in the datasheet by adding a new caption with a colon in front of the existing field name.

✦ You can limit records being displayed with record criteria, specifying character, numeric, date/time, and yes/no.

✦ You can use a query's dynaset datasheet just as you would any table—in forms, reports, and other queries.

In the next chapter, you learn to create and print simple reports.

✦   ✦   ✦

Creating and Printing Simple Reports

Reports provide the most flexible way for viewing and printing summarized information. Reports display information with the desired level of detail while letting you view or print your information in almost any format. You can add multilevel totals, statistical comparisons, and pictures and graphics to a report. In this chapter, you learn to use Report Wizards as a starting point. You also learn to create reports and what types of reports you can create with Access.

Understanding Reports

Reports are used for presenting a customized view of your data. Your report output can be viewed onscreen or printed to a hard-copy device. Reports provide the capability to control summarization of the information. Data can be grouped and sorted in any order and then presented in the order of the groupings. You can create totals that add numbers, calculate averages or other statistics, and display your data graphically. You can print pictures and other graphics as well as Memo fields in a report. If you can think of a report you want, Access can probably create it.

What types of reports can you create?

Four basic types of reports are used by businesses:

Tabular reports　　These print data in rows and columns with groupings and totals. Variations include summary and group/total reports.

Columnar reports	These print data as a form and can include totals and graphs.
Mail-merge reports	These create form letters.
Mailing labels	These create multicolumn labels or snaked-column reports.

Tabular reports

Figure 10-1 is a typical tabular-type report in the Print Preview window. *Tabular reports* (also known as *groups/totals reports*) are generally similar to a table that displays data in neat rows and columns. Tabular reports, unlike forms or datasheets, usually group their data by one or more field values; they calculate and display subtotals or statistical information for numeric fields in each group. Some groups/totals reports also have page totals and grand totals. You can even have *snaked columns* so that you can create directories (such as telephone books). These types of reports can use page numbers, report dates, or lines and boxes to separate information. They can have color and shading and can display pictures, business graphs, and Memo fields, just as forms can. A special type of tabular report, *summary reports* can have all the features of a tabular report but lack detail records.

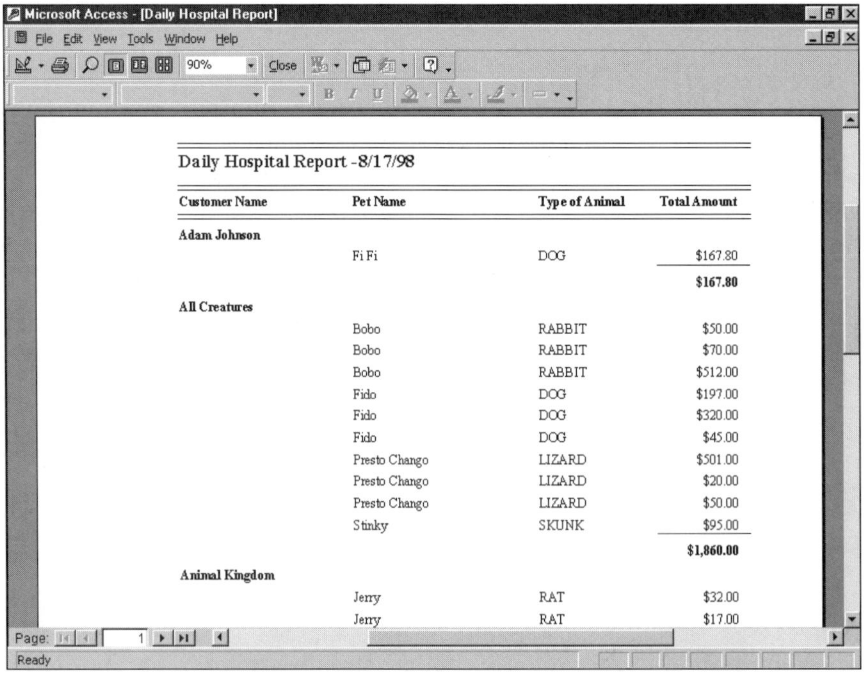

Figure 10-1: A tabular report in the Print Preview window of Access 2000.

Columnar reports

Columnar reports (also known as *form reports*) generally display one or more records per page, but do so vertically. Column reports display data very much as a data-entry form does, but the report is used strictly for viewing data and not for entering it. An invoice is a typical example. This type of report can have sections that display only one record and at the same time have sections that display multiple records from the *many* side of a one-to-many relationship — and even include totals. Figure 10-2 is part of a typical column report from the Mountain Animal Hospital database system in the Print Preview window.

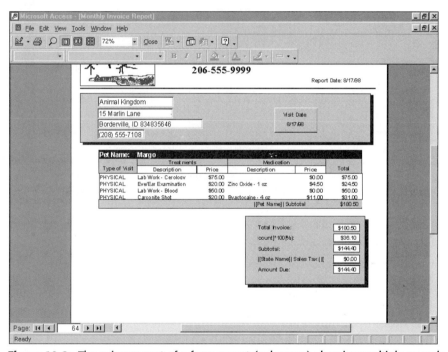

Figure 10-2: The primary part of a form report (columnar) showing multiple records.

Mailing labels

Mailing labels are also a type of report. You can easily create mailing labels, shown in Figure 10-3, using the Label Wizard to create a report in Access. The Label Wizard lets you select from a long list of Avery label paper styles, after which Access correctly creates a report design based on the data you specify to create your label. After the label is created, you can open the report in design mode and customize it as needed.

Cross-Reference   Mailing labels are covered in detail in Chapter 28.

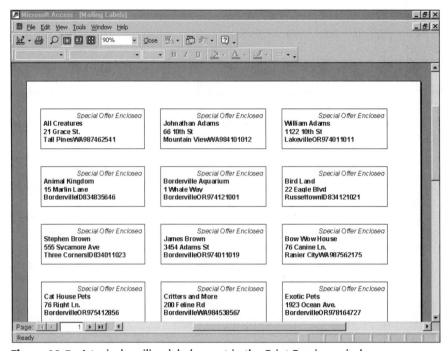

Figure 10-3: A typical mailing-label report in the Print Preview window.

The difference between reports and forms

The main difference between reports and forms is the purpose of the output. Whereas forms are primarily for data entry, reports are for viewing data (either onscreen or in hard-copy form). Calculated fields can be used with forms and can calculate an amount based on the fields in the record. With reports, you calculate on the basis of a common group of records, a page of records, or all the records processed during the report. Anything you can do with a form—except data input—can be duplicated by a report. In fact, you can save a form as a report and then customize the form controls in the Report Design window.

The process of creating a report

Planning a report begins long before you actually create the report design. The report process begins with your desire to view your data in a table, but in a way that differs from datasheet display. You begin with a design for this view; Access begins with raw data. The purpose of the report is to transform the raw data into a meaningful set of information. The process of creating a report involves several steps:

✦ Defining the report layout

✦ Assembling the data

✦ Creating the report design using the Access Report Design window

✦ Printing or viewing the report

Defining the report layout

You should begin by having a general idea of the layout of your report. You can define the layout in your mind, on paper, or interactively using the Access Report Design window. Figure 10-4 is a report layout created using the Access Report Designer. This report was first laid out on paper, showing the fields needed and the placement of the fields.

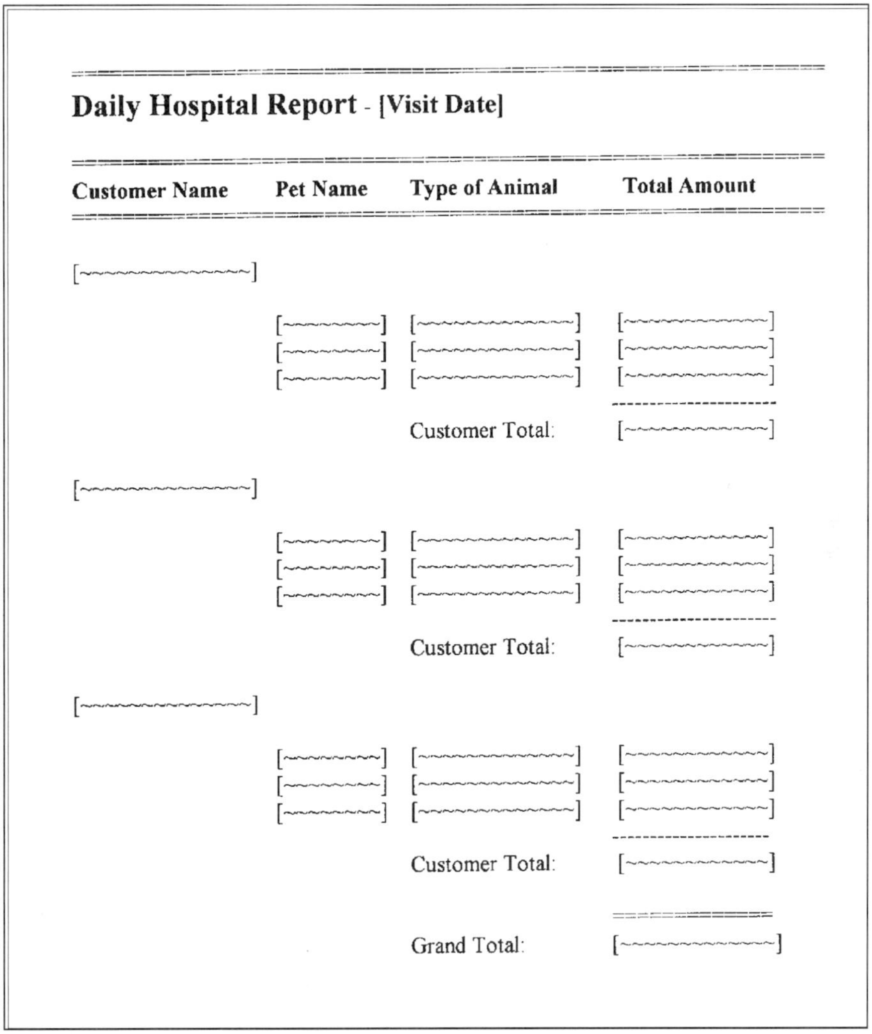

Daily Hospital Report - [Visit Date]

Customer Name	Pet Name	Type of Animal	Total Amount

[~~~~~~~~~~~~~]

	[~~~~~~~]	[~~~~~~~~~~]	[~~~~~~~~~]
	[~~~~~~~]	[~~~~~~~~~~]	[~~~~~~~~~]
	[~~~~~~~]	[~~~~~~~~~~]	[~~~~~~~~~]
		Customer Total:	[~~~~~~~~~]

[~~~~~~~~~~~~~]

	[~~~~~~~]	[~~~~~~~~~~]	[~~~~~~~~~]
	[~~~~~~~]	[~~~~~~~~~~]	[~~~~~~~~~]
	[~~~~~~~]	[~~~~~~~~~~]	[~~~~~~~~~]
		Customer Total:	[~~~~~~~~~]

[~~~~~~~~~~~~~]

	[~~~~~~~]	[~~~~~~~~~~]	[~~~~~~~~~]
	[~~~~~~~]	[~~~~~~~~~~]	[~~~~~~~~~]
	[~~~~~~~]	[~~~~~~~~~~]	[~~~~~~~~~]
		Customer Total:	[~~~~~~~~~]
		Grand Total:	[~~~~~~~~~]

Figure 10-4: A sample report layout.

Assembling the data

After you have a general idea of your report layout, you should assemble the data needed for the report. A report can use data from a single database table or from the results of a query dynaset. You can link many tables together with a query and then use the result of the query (its dynaset) as the record source for your report. A dynaset appears in Access as if it were a single table. As you learned, you can select the fields, records, and sort order of the records in a query. Access treats this dynaset data as a single table (for processing purposes) in datasheets, forms, and reports. The dynaset becomes the source of data for the report and Access processes each record to create the report. The data for the report and the report *design* are entirely separate. In the report design, the field names to be used in the report are specified. Then, when the report is run, Access matches data from the dynaset or table against the fields used in the report, and uses the data available at that moment to produce the report.

Consider the layout shown in Figure 10-4. You want to create a report that shows a daily total of all the pets the hospital treated during a specific day called the Daily Hospital Report. Looking at the layout, you see that you need to assemble these fields:

Visit Date from the Visits table	Used to select the visit date as a criterion in a query
Customer Name from the Customer table	Displays and groups customers on the report
Pet Name from the Customer table	Displays the pet name on the report table
Type of Animal from the Customer table	Displays the type of animal on the report
Total Amount from the Visits table	Displays and calculates totals for amounts charged

You begin the report by creating a query, as shown in Figure 10-5; notice the three tables linked together and the appropriate fields chosen for the report. The Visit Date field is limited to values of 8/4/98, indicating that this specific view of your data will be limited to customers who visited on August 4, 1998. The Customer Name field is being sorted in ascending sequence because the report is to be grouped by customer name.

After assembling the data, you create the report design. Figure 10-6 shows the results of this query. The datasheet shown in this figure is the dynaset created when you run the Daily Hospital Report query for 8/4/98.

On the CD-ROM

If you are following the examples, you may want to create a query and name it Hospital Report 8/4/98.

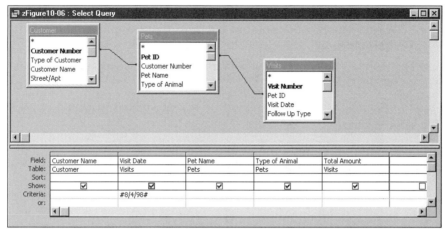

Figure 10-5: Creating a query for a report.

Customer Name	Visit Date	Pet Name	Type of Animal	Total Amount
Patricia Irwin	8/4/98	C.C.	CAT	$294.80
Patricia Irwin	8/4/98	Gizmo	CAT	$50.00
Patricia Irwin	8/4/98	Stripe	CAT	$45.00
Patricia Irwin	8/4/98	Romeo	CAT	$50.00
Patricia Irwin	8/4/98	Ceasar	CAT	$10.00
Patricia Irwin	8/4/98	Juliet	CAT	$20.00
Patricia Irwin	8/4/98	Tiger	CAT	$60.00
William Primen	8/4/98	Cleo	DOG	$80.00
Karen Rhodes	8/4/98	Golden Girl	ORSI	$50.00

Figure 10-6: The Daily Hospital Report dynaset datasheet.

Creating a Report with Report Wizards

With Access, you can create virtually any type of report. Some reports, however, are more easily created than others are when a Report Wizard is used as a starting point. Like Form Wizards, Report Wizards give you a basic layout for your report, which you can then customize.

Report Wizards simplify the layout process of your fields by visually stepping you through a series of questions about the type of report that you want to create and then automatically creating the report for you. In this chapter, Report Wizards create both tabular and columnar reports.

Creating a new report

You can choose from many ways to create a new report, including:

✦ Select Insert ➪ Report from the Database window menu

✦ Select the Reports object button and press the New toolbar button in the Database window

✦ Select the New Report object icon from the Database window, the datasheet, or the query toolbar

Regardless of how you create a new report, the New Report dialog box shown in Figure 10-7 appears.

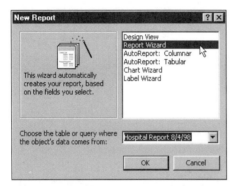

Figure 10-7: The New Report dialog box.

The New Report dialog box lets you choose from among six ways to create a report:

Design View	Displays a completely blank Report Design window for you to start with
Report Wizard	Helps you create a tabular report by asking you many questions
AutoReport: Columnar	Creates an instant columnar report
AutoReport: Tabular	Creates an instant tabular report
Chart Wizard	Helps you create a business graph
Label Wizard	Helps you create a set of mailing labels

To create a new report using a Report Wizard, follow these steps:

1. Create a new report by using any of the methods listed earlier.

2. Select Report Wizard.

3. Select the query Hospital Report 8/4/98 or the data source you created in the New Report dialog box.

 Chapter 20 discusses creating a new report without using a wizard.

Choosing the data source

If you begin creating the report with a highlighted table or from a datasheet or query, the table or query you are using is displayed in the Choose the table or query text box. Otherwise, you can enter the name of a valid table or query before continuing. You can also choose from a list of tables and queries by clicking on the combo box selection arrow. In this example, you use the Daily Hospital Report query you saw in Figure 10-5, which creates data for customer visits on the date 8/4/98.

 If you begin with a blank report, you don't need to specify a table or query before you start.

Choosing the fields

After you select the Report Wizard and click the OK button, a *field selection box* appears. This box is virtually identical to the field selection box used in Form Wizards (see Chapter 8 for detailed information). In this example, select all the fields except Visit Date, as shown in Figure 10-8.

1. Click the All Fields button (>) to place all the fields in the Selected Fields: area.

2. Select the Visit Date field and click the Remove Field button (<) to remove the field.

 You can double-click any field in the Available Fields list box to add it to the Selected Fields: list box. You can also double-click on any field in the Selected Fields: list box to remove it from the box. Access then redisplays the field in the Available Fields: box.

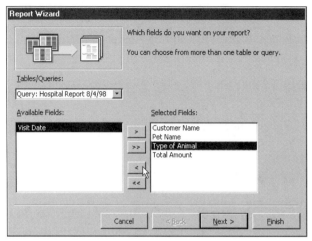

Figure 10-8: Selecting report fields.

In Access 2.0, once you selected the table or query to use with the Report Wizard, you were limited to those fields. In Access 2000, Access 97, and Access for Windows 95, however, you can continue to select other tables or queries by using the Tables/ Queries: combo box in this Wizard screen; you can also display fields from additional tables or queries. As long as you have specified valid relationships so that Access can link the data, these fields are added to your original selection and you can use them on the report. If you choose fields from tables that don't have a relationship, a dialog box will ask you to edit the relationship and join the tables. Or you can return to the Report Wizard and remove the fields.

Once you have selected your data, click the Next button to go to the next Wizard dialog box.

Selecting the view of your data

The next Wizard dialog box lets you set the view of your data, which can include a grouping. *View* means how you look at the overall data picture. In this example, there are three tables: Customer, Pets, and Visits. The purpose of this report is to look at visits for pets belonging to a specific customer. The visit, however, is the focus of the data because you are interested in why the Pet who happens to belong to a customer came to the veterinary hospital.

If you choose to view your report by Visits, all the data appears in the sample page on the right. If you choose to view it by Pets or by Customer, only the Total Amount field is shown on the page; the rest of the fields are shown grouped together. Later you group the data by Customer; for now, select to view the report by Visits, as shown in Figure 10-9.

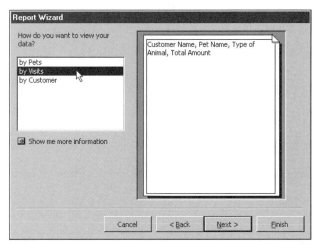

Figure 10-9: Selecting the view of your data.

Selecting the grouping levels

The next dialog box lets you choose which field(s) you want to use for a grouping. In this example, Figure 10-10 shows Customer Name as the only group field. This step designates the field(s) to be used to create group headers and footers. Using the Report Wizard, you can select up to four different group fields for your report; you can change their order by using the Priority buttons. The order you select for the group fields is the order of the grouping hierarchy.

Select the Customer Name field as the grouping field. Notice that the picture changes to graphically show Customer Name as a grouping field.

After you select the group field(s), click the Grouping Options button at the bottom of the dialog box to display another dialog box, which lets you further define how your report will use the group field.

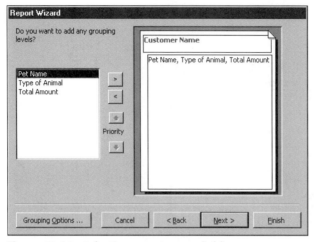

Figure 10-10: Selecting report group fields.

Defining the group data

The Grouping Options dialog box lets you further define the grouping. This selection can vary in importance, depending on the data type.

The list box displays different values for the various data types:

Text	Normal, 1st Letter, 2 Initial Letters, 3 Initial Letters, 4 Initial Letters, and so on
Numeric	Normal, 10s, 50s, 100s, 500s, 1000s, 5000s, 10000s, 50000s, 100000s, 500000s
Date	Normal, Year, Quarter, Month, Week, Day, Hour, Minute

Normal means that the grouping is on the entire field. In this example, use the entire Customer Name field. By selecting different values of the grouping, you can limit the group values. For example, suppose you are grouping on the Pet ID field. A typical Pet ID value is AP001-01. The first five characters represent the owner; the two after the hyphen represent the pet number for that owner. By choosing the Pet ID field for the grouping and then selecting 5 Initial Letters as the grouping data, you can group the pets by customer instead of by pet.

In this example, the default text-field grouping option of Normal is acceptable.

Click the OK button to return to the Grouping levels dialog box, and then click the Next button to move to the Sort order dialog box.

Selecting the sort order

Access sorts the Group record fields automatically in an order that helps the grouping make sense. The additional sorting fields specify fields to be sorted in the detail section. In this example, Access is already sorting the data by Customer Name in the group section. As Figure 10-11 shows, the data is also to be sorted by Pet Name so that the pets appear in alphabetical order in the detail section.

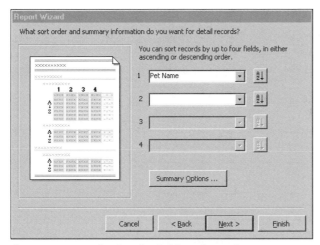

Figure 10-11: Selecting the field sorting order.

The sort fields are selected by the same method that is used for grouping fields in the report. You can select fields that you have not already chosen to group and use these as sorting fields. The fields chosen in this dialog box do not affect grouping; they affect only the sorting order in the detail section fields. You can determine whether the order is ascending or descending by clicking the toggle button to the right of each sort field.

Selecting summary options

At the bottom of the sorting dialog box is a button named Summary Options. Clicking this button displays the dialog box shown in Figure 10-12. This dialog box provides additional options for numeric fields. As you can see, the field Total Amount is to be summed. Additionally, you can display averages, minimums, and maximums.

You can also decide whether to show or hide the data in the detail section. If you select Detail and Summary, the report shows the detail data; selecting Summary Only hides the detail section showing only totals in the report.

Finally, checking the box labeled Calculate percent of total for sums adds the percentage of the entire report that the total represents below the total in the group footer. If, for example, you had three customers and their total was 15, 25, and 10, respectively, they would show 30%, 50%, and 20% below their total (that is, 50) — indicating the percentage of the total sum (100%) represented by their sum.

Clicking the OK button in this dialog box returns you to the sorting dialog box. There you can click the Next button to move on to the next Wizard dialog box.

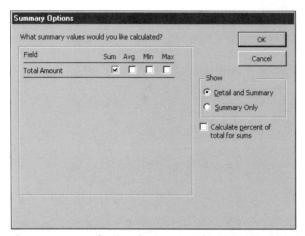

Figure 10-12: Selecting the summary options.

Selecting the layout

Two more dialog boxes affect the look of your report. The first (shown in Figure 10-13) lets you determine the layout of the data. The Layout area provides six layout choices; these tell Access whether to repeat the column headers, whether to indent each grouping, and whether to add lines or boxes between the detail lines. As you select each option, the picture on the left changes to show the effect.

The Orientation area lets you choose between a Portrait (up-and-down) and a Landscape (across-the-page) layout. This choice affects how it prints on the paper. Finally, put a check mark next to Adjust field width so that all fields fit on a page. You can cram a lot of data into a little area. (Magnifying glasses may be necessary!)

For this example, choose Stepped and Portrait, the default values, as shown in Figure 10-13. Then click on the Next button to move to the next dialog box.

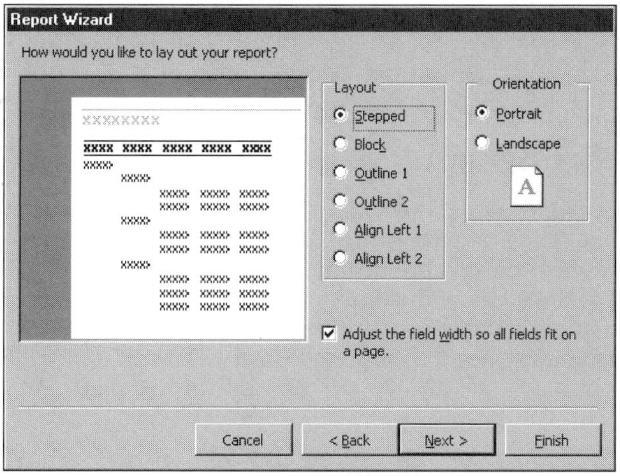

Figure 10-13: Selecting the page layout.

Choosing the style

After you choose the layout, you can choose the style of your report from the dialog box shown in Figure 10-14. Each style has different background shadings, font size, typeface, and other formatting. As each is selected, the picture on the left changes to show a preview. For this example, choose Compact (as shown in Figure 10-14). Finally, click the Next button to move to the last dialog box.

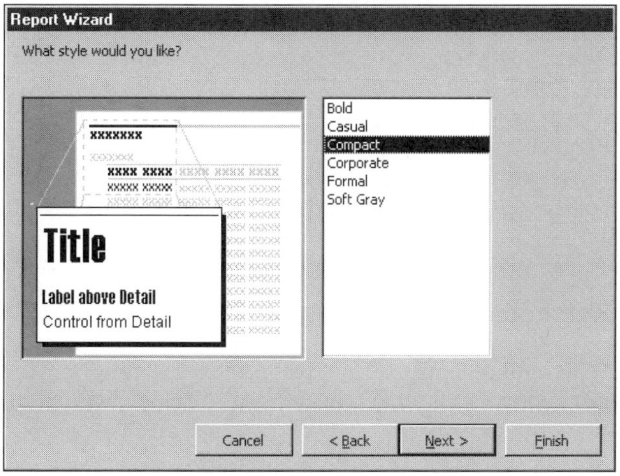

Figure 10-14: Choosing the style of your report.

Tip   You can customize any of the styles, or add your own, by using the AutoFormat menu option from the Format menu of the Report Design window and choosing Customize.

Opening the report design

Figure 10-15 is the final Report Wizard dialog box. The checkered flag lets you know that you're at the finish line. The first part of the dialog box lets you enter a title for the report. This title will appear once at the beginning of the report, not at the top of each page. The default is the name of the table you used initially. If you used a query, the name will be that of the table used for the view of the data (in this example, it was Visits). As you can see in Figure 10-15, *Daily Hospital Report* has been typed instead of *Visits*.

Figure 10-15: The final Report Wizard dialog box.

Next you can choose one of the option buttons at the bottom of the dialog box:

✦ Preview the report

✦ Modify the report's design

For this example, leave the default selection intact to preview the report. When you click the Finish button, your report is displayed in the Print Preview window.

Click Finish to complete the Report Wizard and view the report.

Using the Print Preview window

Figure 10-16 displays the Print Preview window in a zoomed view. This view lets you see your report with the actual fonts, shading, lines, boxes, and data that will be on the printed report. When the Print Preview mode is in a zoomed view, pressing the mouse button changes the view to a *page preview*, where you can see the entire page.

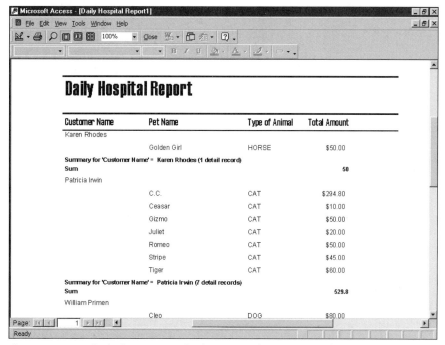

Figure 10-16: Displaying a report in the zoomed preview mode.

You can move around the page by using the horizontal and vertical scroll boxes. Use the Page controls (at the bottom-left corner of the window) to move from page to page.

Figure 10-17 shows an entire page of the report as seen in the page preview mode of Print Preview. By using the magnifying-glass mouse pointer, you can select a portion of the page and zoom in to that portion.

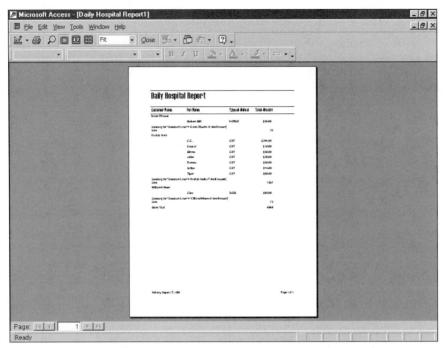

Figure 10-17: Displaying a report in Print Preview's page preview mode.

In Figure 10-17, you can see a representation of the printed page. Use the navigation buttons (in the lower-left section of the Print Preview window) to move between pages, just as you would to move between records in a datasheet. The Print Preview window has a toolbar with commonly used printing commands.

If, after examining the preview, you are satisfied with the report, select the Printer icon on the toolbar to print the report. If you are dissatisfied, select the Close button to return to the design window; Access takes you to the Report Design window to make further changes.

Viewing the Report Design window

When you select the first icon from the toolbar, Access takes you to the Report Design window, which is similar to the Form Design window. The major difference is in the sections that make up the report design. As shown in Figure 10-18, the report design reflects the choices you made using the Report Wizard.

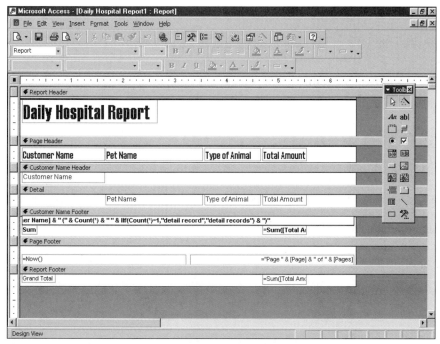

Figure 10-18: The Report Design window.

Cross-Reference

You may also see the Toolbox, Sorting and Grouping dialog box, property sheet, and Field List window, depending on whether you pressed the toolbar buttons to see these tools. You learn to change the design of a report in Chapters 20 and 21.

You can return to the Print Preview mode by selecting the Print Preview icon button on the Report Design toolbar or by selecting the Print Preview option on the File menu. You can also select Print or Page Setup from the File menu. This menu also provides options for saving your report.

Printing a Report

You can print one or more records in your report, exactly as they look onscreen, using one of these methods:

✦ File ➪ Print in the Report Design window

✦ Print button in the Preview window

✦ File ➪ Print in the Database window (with a report highlighted)

If you select File ➪ Print, a standard Microsoft Windows Print dialog box appears. You can select the print range, number of copies, and print properties. If you click the Print icon, the report goes immediately to the currently selected printer without displaying a Print dialog box.

Cross-Reference   For a complete discussion of printing, see Chapter 21.

Saving the Report

You can save the report design at any time by selecting File ➪ Save, or File ➪ Save As, or File ➪ Export from the Report Design window, or by selecting the Save button on the toolbar. The first time you save a report (or any time you select Save As or Export), a dialog box lets you select a name. The text box initially displays the default name from the Report Wizard, `Report1`.

Caution   Remember that Access saves only the report *design*, not the data or the actual report. You must save your query design separately if you created a query to produce your report. You can recreate the dynaset at any time by running the report that automatically reruns the query.

Creating a Report with AutoReport

From a table, datasheet, form, or nearly any design screen in Access, you can create a report instantly. Just click the AutoReport button from the New Object icon in the toolbar (it shows a form with a lightning bolt through it) and then select from the list of icons that drop down. Another method is to use the Insert ➪ Report command and then click one of the two AutoReport selections from the dialog box that appears. When you use the AutoReport button, the report appears instantly with no additional work from you. To create an AutoReport using the Pets table, follow these steps:

1. From the Mountain Animal Hospital or Mountain Animal Start Database Containers, click the Table button.

2. Select Pets.

3. Click the New Object button in the toolbar and select AutoReport.

The report instantly appears, as shown in Figure 10-19. Actually, the Picture property of the OLE control has been changed to Stretch to show the whole rabbit. (This was done in the Report Design screen, using the techniques you learned in Chapter 8.)

Using AutoReport is the quickest way to create a report. Generally, however, you want more control over the process. Other Report Wizards are available to help you create more customized reports.

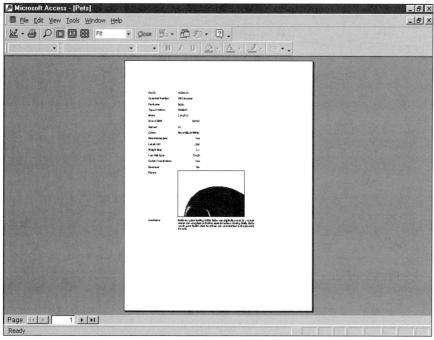

Figure 10-19: The AutoReport report.

Summary

In this chapter, you learned how easy it is to create reports in Access. You saw the basic types of reports and how the Report Wizards simplify the process. The chapter covered these points:

✦ The Access report writer lets you create tabular reports, columnar reports, business graphs, and mailing labels.

✦ The process of creating a report consists of defining the layout, assembling the data, creating the report design, and printing or viewing the report.

✦ Report Wizards let you create reports by filling in a series of dialog boxes.

✦ Reports can be printed or viewed onscreen in Print Preview mode.

In the next chapter, you learn to manipulate multiple tables with Access objects and how to relate tables to take full advantage of a relational database's capabilities.

✦　　✦　　✦

Setting Relationships Between Tables

So far, you have learned to create a simple table, to enter its data, and to display it in either a datasheet or a form. You have also learned to use simple queries and reports. All these techniques were demonstrated using only a single table. The Pets table has been an excellent sample of a single table; it contains many different data types that lend themselves to productive examples.

It's time now to move into the real world of relational database management.

Tables Used in the Mountain Animal Hospital Database

Figure 11-1 diagrams the database of the Mountain Animal Hospital system. There are eight tables in the figure, each of which requires its own table design, complete with field names, data types, descriptions, and properties.

On the CD-ROM

If you're following the examples, either use the Mountain Animal Start files on the CD-ROM that accompanies this book, or create these tables yourself. If you want to create each of these tables, you can use Appendix B as a reference for each table's description; then use the steps you learned in Chapter 6 to create each table.

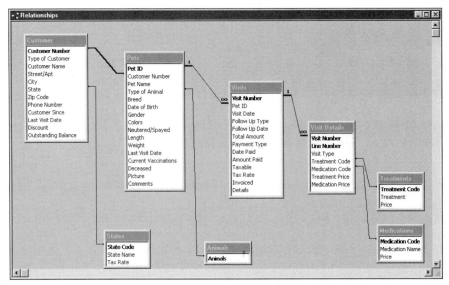

Figure 11-1: The database diagram for the Mountain Animal Hospital system.

Cross-Reference

In Figure 11-1, are lines joining the tables. These are the *relationship lines* between the tables. Each line indicates a separate relationship between two tables; these are established either at the table level (using the *Relationship Builder* feature of Access) or by using a query (Chapter 13 shows how to establish relationships in a query). In this chapter, you learn to use the Relationship Builder to establish a relationship at the table level.

Of the eight tables in the database diagram, four hold data about Mountain Animal Hospital and four are used for *lookups*. You can eliminate the lookup tables and still use the system if you want. The four main tables are:

Customer	Contains information about each customer
Pets	Contains information about each animal
Visits	Contains information about each visit
Visit Details	Contains multiple records about the details of each visit

The four lookup tables are:

States	Used by the Customer table to retrieve state name and tax rate
Animals	Used by the Pets table to retrieve a list of valid animal types

Treatments	Used by the Visit Details table to retrieve treatment name and price
Medications	Used by the Visit Details table to retrieve medication name and price

To set relations between tables, you must establish a link between fields that contain common information. The fields themselves do not need to have the same name. The field's data type and length must be the same, however, and (more importantly) the information contained within both fields for a specific record must be the same in both tables for the link to work. Generally, a relationship is established by linking these *key fields* between tables — the *primary* key in one table to a *foreign* key in another table.

Note In Figure 11-1, each table has one or more fields in bold. These are the fields that define each table's primary key.

Understanding Keys

Every table should have a *primary key* — one or more fields whose contents are unique to each record. For example, the Customer Number field is the primary key in the Customer table — each record in the table has a different Customer Number. (No two records have the same number.) This is called *entity integrity* in the world of database management. By having a different primary key in each record (such as the Customer Number in the Customer table), you can tell two records (in this case, customers) apart. This is important because you can easily have two individual customers named Fred Smith (or pet stores named Animal Kingdom) in your table.

Theoretically, you could use the customer name and the customer's address, but two people named Fred Smith could live in the same town and state, or a father and son (Fred David Smith and Fred Daniel Smith) could live at the same address. The goal of setting primary keys is to create individual records in a table that will guarantee uniqueness.

If you don't specify a primary key when creating Access tables, Access asks whether you want one. If you say yes, Access creates a primary key for you as an AutoNumber data type. It places a new sequential number in the primary key field for each record automatically. Table 11-1 lists tables and their primary keys.

Note In Access, you cannot use an AutoNumber data field to enforce referential integrity between tables. Therefore, it is important to specify another data type — such as Text or Numeric — for the primary key. (More about this topic later in this chapter.)

Table 11-1 **Tables and Primary Keys**	
Table	**Primary Key**
Customer	Customer Number
Pets	Pet ID
Visits	Visit Number
Visit Details	Visit Number; Line Number
States	State Code
Animals	Animals
Treatments	Treatment Code
Medications	Medication Code

Deciding on a primary key

Normally a table has a unique field (or combination of fields) — the primary key for that table — which makes each record unique; often it's an ID field that uses the Text data type. To determine the contents of this ID field, you specify a method for creating the value in the field. Your method can be as simple as using the first letter of the real value you are tracking along with a sequence number (such as A001, A002, B001, B002, and so on). The method may rely on a random set of letters and numbers for the field content (as long as each field has a unique value), or a complicated calculation based on information from several fields in the table.

Table 11-2 lists tables and explains how to define the primary key in each table.

As Table 11-2 shows, it doesn't take a great deal of work (or even much imagination) to create a key. Any rudimentary scheme and a good sequence number that are used together always work. Access automatically tells you when you try to enter a duplicate key value. To avoid duplication, you can simply add the value of 1 to the sequence number. You may think that all these sequence numbers make it hard to look up information in your tables. Just remember that *normally* you never look up information by an ID field. Generally, you look up information according to the *purpose* of the table. In the Customer table, for example, you would look up information by Customer Name. In some cases, the Customer Name is the same, so you can look at other fields in the table (ZIP code, phone number) to find the correct customer. Unless you just happen to know the Customer Number, you'll probably never use it in a search for information.

Table 11-2 **Deriving the Primary Key**	
Table	**Derivation of Primary Key**
Customer	Individuals: first two letters of last name, three-digit sequence number
	Pet Stores: first letter of first two major words, three-digit sequence number
	Zoos: first letter of first two major words, three-digit sequence number
Pets	Customer Number, a hyphen (–), and a sequential number
Visits	Four-digit year and the Julian day (sequential number)
Visit Details	Visit Number and another field that holds a three-digit sequence number (Line Number field)
Animals	Type of animal
Treatments	Four-digit unique number (arbitrarily selected)
Medications	Four-digit unique number (arbitrarily selected)

Benefits of a primary key

Have you ever placed an order with a company for the first time and then decided the next day to increase your order? You call the people at the order desk. Sometimes they ask you for your customer number. You tell them that you don't know your customer number. This happens all the time. So they ask you for some other information—generally, your ZIP code or telephone area code. Then, as they narrow down the list of customers, they ask your name. Then they tell you your customer number. Some businesses use phone numbers as a unique starting point.

Database systems usually have more than one table, and these tend to be related in some manner. For example, the Customer table and Pets table are related to each other via a Customer Number. The Customer table always has one record for each customer, and the Pets table has a record for each pet the customer owns. Because each customer is *one* physical person, you only need one record for the customer in the Customer table. Each customer can own several pets, however, which means you set up another table to hold information about each pet. Again, each pet is *one* physical animal (a dog, a cat, a bird, and so on). Each animal has one record in the Pets table. Of course, you relate the customers' pets in the Pets table to the right customer in the Customer table by using a common field between both tables. In this case, the field is the Customer Number (which is in both tables).

When linking tables, you link the primary key field from one table (the Customer Number in the Customer table) to a field in the second table that has the same structure and type of data in it (the Customer Number in the Pets table). If the link field in the second table is *not* the primary key field (and usually it isn't), it's known as a *foreign key* field (discussed later in the chapter).

Besides being a common link field between tables, a primary key field in Access has these advantages:

✦ A primary key field is an index that greatly speeds up queries, searches, and sort requests.

✦ When you add new records, you must enter a value in primary key field(s). Access will not allow you to enter Null values, which guarantees that you'll have only valid records in your table.

✦ When you add new records to a table that has a primary key, Access checks for duplicate data and doesn't let you enter duplicates for the primary key field.

✦ By default, Access displays your data in the order of the primary key.

If you define a primary key based on part of the data in the record, you can have Access automatically place your data in an understandable order. In the example, the Pet ID field is composed of the owner's Customer Number, followed by a hyphen and a two-digit sequence number. If the All Creatures Pet Store is the first customer on the list whose last name begins with AC, the store's customer number is AC001. If someone from this store brings in three pets, the Pet IDs are designated AC001-01, AC001-02, and AC001-03. This way, the Pet ID field provides you with data in the order of customers displayed alphabetically.

Tip   Primary key fields should be made as short as possible because they can affect the speed of operations in a database.

Creating a primary key

As discussed in Chapter 6, a primary key is created by selecting the field that you want to specify as a primary key and clicking the Primary Key button on the toolbar (the button with the key on it). If you are specifying more than one field, you specify the fields that you want for the primary key and again click the Primary Key button. Selecting each field while holding down the Ctrl key specifies the fields.

When you're specifying multifield primary keys, the selection order is important. Therefore, check your selection by clicking the Indexes button on the toolbar and looking at the field order. Figure 11-2 shows the two-field index for the Visit Details table. Notice that the Visit Number field is before the Line Number field in the index box.

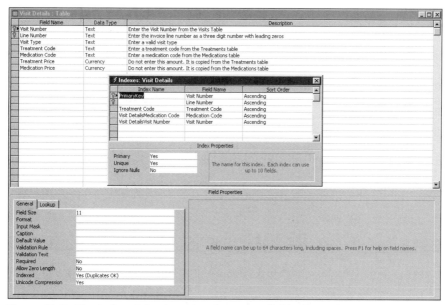

Figure 11-2: The index dialog box showing a two-field primary key.

Note
There are three additional index names in the index window. These are not keys but indexes used to speed sorts used in these tables. If you regularly sort data in tables by the same field or fields, you should create an index for that field. An *index* is an internal table of values that maintains the order of the records. This way, when you need to sort data or find a piece of data instantly, Access can search through the index keys in a known order rather than sequentially through the data.

Caution
Creating indexes slows data entry; each new record, deleted record, or change to the indexed field requires a change to the index. Use only the index fields you need, which will speed sorting your application and balance that need with data-entry speed.

Understanding foreign keys

Primary keys guarantee uniqueness in a table, and you use the primary key field in one table to link to another. The common link field in the other table may not be (and usually isn't) the primary key in the other table. The *common link field* is a field or fields that hold the same type of data as in the primary key of the link table.

The field (or fields) used to link to a primary key field in another table are known as foreign keys. Unlike a primary key, which must be created in a special way, a *foreign key* is any field(s) used in a relationship. By matching the values (from the primary key to the foreign key) in both tables, you can relate two records.

In Figure 11-1, you saw a relationship between the Customer and Pets tables. The primary key of Customer, Customer Number, is related to the Customer Number field in Pets. In Pets, Customer Number is the foreign key because it is the key of a related "foreign" table.

A relation also exists between the States and Customer tables. The primary key of States, State Code, is related to the State field in the Customer table. In the Customer table, State is the foreign key because it is the key of a related foreign table.

Understanding Relations Between Tables

At the beginning of this chapter, you saw eight tables in the Mountain Animal Hospital database and seven relationships. Before you learn to create these relationships, it is important to understand them.

A review of relationships

Relationships established at the table level take precedence over those established at the query level. If you can set a relationship at the table level, Access will recognize it automatically when you create a multiple-table query that uses fields from more than one table. Relationships between tables are grouped into four types:

- ✦ One-to-one
- ✦ One-to-many
- ✦ Many-to-one
- ✦ Many-to-many

Understanding the four types of table relationships

When you physically join two tables (by connecting fields with like information), you create a relationship that Access recognizes. Figure 11-3 shows the relationships between all the tables in the Mountain Animal Hospital system.

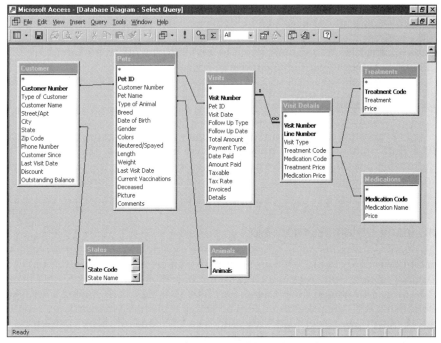

Figure 11-3: The Mountain Animal Hospital tables relationships.

The relationship that you specify between tables is important. It tells Access how to find and display information from fields in two or more tables. The program needs to know whether to look for only one record in a table or to look for several records on the basis of the relationship. The Customer table, for example, has a *one-to-many* relationship to the Pets table. There will *always* be one record in the Customer table for *at least* one record in the Pets table; there could be *many* related records in the Pets table. So Access knows to find only one record in the Customer table and to look for any in the Pets table (one or more) that have the same Customer Number.

The one-to-one relationship

The *one-to-one relationship*, though rarely used in database systems, can be a very useful way to link two tables together. A good example of a one-to-one relationship occurs in most billing systems; a billing file is created to allow additional information necessary to invoice customers at a location other than their listed addresses. This file usually contains the customer number and another set of address fields. Only a few customers would have a separate billing address, so you wouldn't add this information to the main customer table. A one-to-one relationship between a customer table and billing table may be established to retrieve the billing address for those customers who want to have a separate address. Although all the information on one table could be added to the other, the tables are maintained separately for efficient use of space.

The one-to-many relationship

The *one-to-many relationship* is used to relate one record in a table with many records in another. Examples are one customer to many pets or one pet to many visits. Both of these examples are one-to-many relationships. The Customer-Pets relationship links the customer number (the primary key of the Customer table) to the customer number in the Pets table (which becomes the foreign key of the Customer table).

The many-to-one relationship

The *many-to-one relationship* (often called the *lookup table relationship*) tells Access that many records in the table are related to a single record in another table. Normally, many-to-one relationships are not based on a primary key field in either table. Mountain Animal Hospital has four lookup tables, each having a many-to-one relationship with the primary table. The States table has a many-to-one relationship with the Customer table; each state record can be used for many customers. Although (in theory) this relationship is one-to-one, it is known as a many-to-one relationship because it does not use a primary key field for the link, and many records from the primary table link to a single record in the other table.

Some one-to-many relationships can be reversed and made into many-to-one relationships. If you set a relationship from Pets to Customers, for example, the relationship becomes many-to-one; many pets can have the same owner. So relationships depend on how the information in your tables is used and interpreted. Thus, one-to-many and many-to-one relationships can be considered the same — just viewed from opposite perspectives.

The many-to-many relationship

The *many-to-many relationship* is the hardest to understand. Think of it generally as a pair of *one-to-many relationships* between two tables, as happens in the tables Pets and Visits in the Mountain Animal Hospital database. A pet can be serviced at the hospital on many dates, so you see a one-to-many relationship between Pets and Visits. On the other hand, on each date, many pets can be brought into the hospital; this is also a one-to-many relationship. An individual pet may visit the hospital on many dates, and on a given date, many pets visit the hospital. Thus a pair of separate, two-way, one-to-many relationships creates a many-to-many relationship.

Understanding Referential Integrity

In addition to specifying relationships between tables in an Access database, you can also set up some rules that will help in maintaining a degree of accuracy between the tables. For example, you would not want to delete a customer record in your Customer table if there are related pet records in the Pets table. If you did delete a customer record without first deleting the customer's pets, you would have a system that has pets without an owner. This type of problem could be catastrophic.

Imagine being in charge of a bank that tracks loans in a database system. Now imagine that this system has *no* rules that say, "Before deleting a customer's record, make sure that there is no outstanding loan." It would be disastrous! So a database system needs to have rules that specify certain conditions between tables — rules to enforce the integrity of information between the tables. These rules are known as *referential integrity*; they keep the relationships between tables intact in a relational database management system. Referential integrity prohibits you from changing your data in ways that invalidate the links between tables.

Referential integrity operates strictly on the basis of the tables' key fields; it checks each time a key field, whether primary or foreign, is added, changed, or deleted. If a change to a key creates an invalid relationship, it is said to violate referential integrity. Tables can be set up so that referential integrity is enforced automatically.

When tables are linked together, one table is usually called the *parent* and the other (the table it is linked to) is usually called the *child*. This is known as a *parent-child relationship* between tables. Referential integrity guarantees that there will never be an *orphan*, a child record without a parent record.

 Cross-Reference If you connect to an SQL Server back end database or use the Microsoft Database Engine and create an Access Data Project, the relationship window is different. This is discussed in Chapter 33.

Creating Relationships

Unless you have a reason for not wanting your relationships always to be active, create your table relationships at the table level using the *Relationship Builder*. The table relationships can be broken later if necessary. For normal data entry and reporting purposes, however, having your relationships defined at the table level makes it much easier to use a system.

Access 2000 has a very powerful Relationship Builder tool. With it you can add tables, use drag-and-drop methods to link tables, easily specify the type of link, and set any referential integrity between tables.

Using the Relationship Builder tool

You create relationships in the Database window. From this window, you can select the menu item Tools ➪ Relationships or click the Relationships button on the toolbar. The main Relationships window appears, which lets you add tables and create links between them.

Figure 11-4 shows the main Relationships window. Notice the new toolbar associated with it. When first opened, the Relationships window is a blank surface. Tables are added to the window by using one of these methods:

✦ Add the tables before entering the Relationship Builder from the dialog box that's first displayed.

✦ Click the Show Tables button on the toolbar.

✦ Select Relationships ➪ Show Table from the menu bar.

✦ While in the Relationships window, click the right mouse button (which calls up the shortcut menu) and select Show Table from the menu.

To start the Relationship Builder and add tables to the Relationships window, follow these steps:

1. Click the Relationships button on the toolbar. Access opens a Show Table dialog box.

2. Select all the tables by double-clicking them — Customer, Pets, Visits, Visit Details, States, Animals, Medications, and Treatments.

3. Click the Close button on the Show Table dialog box. Your screen should look like the one in Figure 11-4. Notice that Access has placed each table in the Relationships window. Each table is in its own box; the title of the box is the name of the table. Inside the table box are the names of the fields for each table. Currently, there are no links between the tables. Now you are ready to set relationships between them.

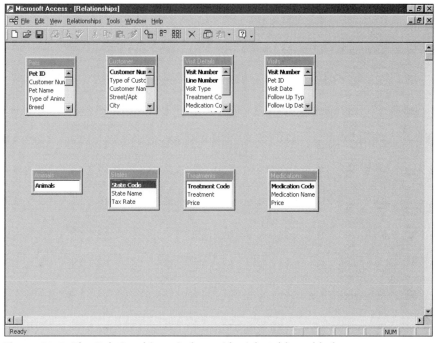

Figure 11-4: The Relationships window with eight tables added.

Note   If you select a table by mistake, it can be removed from the window by clicking in it and pressing the Delete key.

Tip   You can resize each table window to see all the fields, as shown in Figure 11-5.

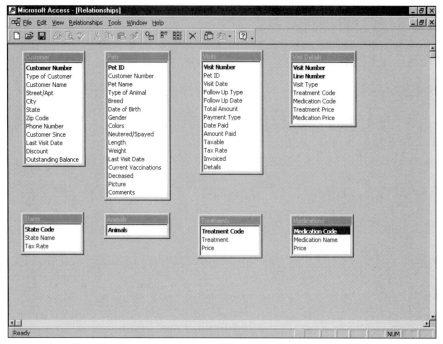

Figure 11-5: The Relationships window with tables sized.

Creating a link between tables

With the tables in the Relationships window, you are ready to create links between the tables. To create a link between two tables, select the common field in one table and drag it to the field in the table you want to link to and drop it on the common field.

Follow these steps to create a link between the tables:

1. Click the Customer Number field of the Customer table.

Note   If you select a field for linking in error, simply move the field icon to the window surface; it turns into the international No symbol. While it is displayed as this symbol, release the mouse button and field linking stops.

2. While holding down the mouse button, move the cursor to the Pets table. Notice that Access displays a field-select icon.

3. Drag the field-select icon to the Customer Number field of the Pets table. Access activates the Edit Relationships dialog box (see Figure 11-6).

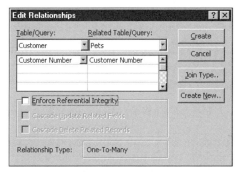

Figure 11-6: The Edit Relationships dialog box.

4. Click the Create button to create the relationship. Access closes the dialog box and places a join line between the Customer and Pets table.

Note
You can reactivate the Relationships dialog box for any *join* (link) by double-clicking the *join line* between the two tables. For example, double-clicking the join line between the Customer and Pets table reactivates the Edit Relationships dialog box for that link.

Specifying relationship options in the Relationships dialog box

The Edit Relationships dialog box has several options for the relationship between the Customer and Pets tables. Figure 11-6 shows the dialog box and all the options. The dialog box tells you which table is the primary table for the link and whether referential integrity is enforced. The dialog box also tells you the type of relationship (one-to-one or one-to-many) and lets you specify whether *cascading* updates and deletes (automatic key changes or deletions in related records) between linked tables when referential integrity is selected are allowed.

On the CD-ROM
For the following sections, activate the Edit Relationships dialog box for the link between the Customer and Pets tables. To do so, double-click the join line between the tables.

Specifying the primary table

The top of the dialog box has two table names — Customer on the left and Pets on the right. The Customer table is considered the primary table for this relationship. The dialog box shows the link fields for each table in a separate box immediately below the table names. Make sure that the correct table name is in both boxes (Customer and Pets) and that the correct link field is specified.

Caution   If you link two tables incorrectly, simply click the Cancel button in the dialog box. Access closes the dialog box and erases the join line, and you can begin again.

Tip   If you link two tables by the wrong field, simply select the correct field for each table by using the combo box under each table name.

Enforcing referential integrity

After specifying the link and verifying the table and link fields, referential integrity between the tables can be set by clicking the Enforce Referential Integrity checkbox below the table information. If you choose not to enforce referential integrity, you can add new records, change key fields, or delete related records without worrying about referential integrity. You can create tables that have orphans or parents without children. With normal operations (such as data entry or changing information), referential integrity rules should be in force. By setting this option, you can specify several additional options.

Clicking the checkbox in front of the option Enforce Referential Integrity activates the Cascading choices in the dialog box.

You might find, when you specify Enforce Referential Integrity and click the Create button (or the OK button if you've reopened the Edit Relationship window to create a relationship between tables), that Access will not allow you to create a relationship. The reason is that you are asking Access to create a relationship supporting referential integrity between two tables that have records that *violate* referential integrity (the child table has orphans in it). In such a case, Access warns you by displaying a dialog box similar to that shown in Figure 11-7. The warning happens in this example because there is a Pet record in the database with no Customer record. (There is also a Customer record with no Pet record. You will learn about these instances later.)

Figure 11-7: A dialog box warning that referential integrity cannot be set between two existing tables.

Access returns you to the Relationships window after you click the OK button; you need to recreate the relationship. If you are editing an existing join, Access also returns you to the Relationships window by removing the referential integrity option.

Tip

To solve any conflicts between existing tables, you can create a Find Unmatched query by using the Query Wizard to find the records in the *many*-side table that violate referential integrity. Then you can convert the Unmatched query to a Delete query to delete the offending records. You learn how to do this in Chapter 13.

With the offending records gone, you can set up referential integrity between the two tables.

Choosing the Cascade Update Related Fields option

If you specify Enforce Referential Integrity in the Edit Relationships dialog box, Access lets you select a checkbox option labeled Cascade Update Related Fields. This option tells Access that a user can change the contents of a link field (the primary key field in the primary table—Customer Number, for example).

When the user changes the contents of the primary key field in the primary table, Access verifies that the change is a new number (because there cannot be duplicate records in the primary table) and then goes through the related records in the other table and changes the link field value from the old value to the new value. Suppose you code your customers by the first two letters of their last names, and one of your customers gets married and changes the name that Access knows to look for. You could change the Customer Number, and all changes would ripple through other related records in the system.

If this option is not checked, you cannot change the primary key field in the primary table that is used in a link with another table.

Note

If the primary key field in the primary table is a link field between several tables, this option must be checked for all related tables or it will not work.

Choosing the Cascade Delete Related Records option

If you specify Enforce Referential Integrity in the Edit Relationships dialog box, Access lets you select the Cascade Delete Related Records checkbox. By selecting this option, you tel Access that if a user attempts to delete a record in a primary table that has child records, first it should delete all the related child records and then delete the primary record. This can be very useful for deleting a series of related records. For example, if you have chosen Cascade Delete Related Records and you try to delete a particular customer (who moved away from the area) by deleting the Customer record, Access goes out to the related tables—Pets, Visits, and Visit Details—and also deletes all related records for the customer. Access deletes all the records in the Visit Details for each visit for each pet owned by the customer, the visit records, the associated pet records, and the customer record, with one step.

If you do not specify this option, Access will not allow you to delete a record that has related records in another table. In cases like this, you must delete all related records in the Visit Details table first, then related records in the Visits table, then related records in the Pets table, and finally the customer record in the Customer table.

Note   To use this option, you must specify Cascade Delete Related Records for *all* of the table's relationships in the database. If you do not specify this option for all the tables in the chain of related tables, Access will not allow cascade deleting.

Caution   Use this option with caution! Access does not warn that it is going to do a cascade delete when you press the Delete key. The program just does it. Later you may wonder where all your records went. It is generally better to delete records programmatically, using macros or Visual Basic for Applications (formerly known as Access Basic).

Saving the relationships between tables

The easiest way to save the relationships you created between the tables is to click the Save button on the toolbar and then close the window. Another method is to close the window and answer Yes to the Save Relationships dialog box that appears.

Adding another relationship

After you specify all the tables, the fields, and their referential integrity status, you can add additional tables to the Relationships window by clicking the Relationships button on the toolbar and adding new tables.

Again, if data that violates referential integrity exists in the tables being linked, you must fix the offending table by removing the records before you can set referential integrity between the tables.

Deleting an existing relationship

To delete an existing relationship, go into the Relationships window, click the join line you want to delete, press the Delete key, and answer Yes to the question *Are you sure you want to delete the selected relationship?*.

Join lines in the Relationships window

When you create a relationship between two tables, Access automatically creates a thin join line from one table to another. Figure 11-8 shows the join line between States and Customer.

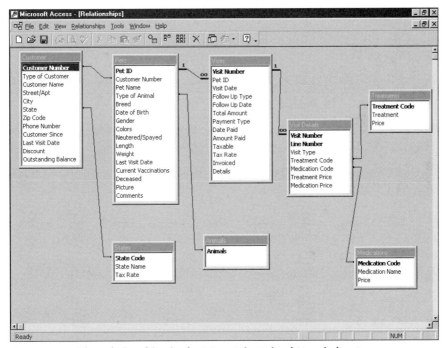

Figure 11-8: The relationships in the Mountain Animal Hospital system.

If you specify that you want to enforce referential integrity, however, Access changes the appearance of the join line. It becomes thicker at each end (alongside the table). It also has either a 1 or the infinity symbol (∞) over the thick bar of the line (on each side of the join line).

Tip
After referential integrity is specified, Access adds the thick lines to the join in any queries that use the tables. This gives you a visual way to know that referential integrity is active between the tables.

Creating the relationships for the Mountain Animal Hospital system

Table 11-3 shows the relationships between all the tables in the system. Referential integrity is set between three of the four primary tables. In addition to having referential integrity, each of the four main tables has the Cascade Delete Related Records option checked.

Table 11-3			
Relationships in the Mountain Animal Hospital System			
Primary Table/	*Related Table/*		
Field	**Field**	**Referential Integrity**	**Cascade Delete**
Customer	Pets		
Customer Number	Customer Number	No*	No*
Pets	Visits		
Pet ID	Pet ID	Yes	Yes
Visits	Visit Details		
Visit Number	Visit Number	Yes	Yes
State	Customer		
State Code	State	No	No
Animals	Pets		
Animals	Type of Animal	No	No
Medications	Visit Details		
Medication Code	Medication Code	No	No
Treatments	Visit Details		
Treatment Code	Treatment Code	No	No

*These will be changed in Chapter 13 after orphan records are deleted.

Using the Access Table Analyzer

Everything that you have read in this chapter assumes that your tables are designed and that the relationships are normalized in the entire database. With many new systems, however (and especially with new developers), this is not the case. Sometimes you might start by importing an Excel spreadsheet file into Access, or by importing a large mainframe file (commonly known as *flat files* because all the data is contained in a single file). When imported into Access, a flat file becomes one single table.

Access 2000 contains a tool called Table Analyzer that analyzes a single table and attempts to determine whether it is fully normalized. This tool then makes suggestions for splitting the data into related tables. It creates both primary and foreign keys, searches for misspellings of commonly used data, and suggests corrections. If, for example, you have a flat file that contains both sales items and customers, you might have the customer information (name, address, and so on) repeated over and over. Where the customer name Animals R Us is found many times, it might be listed as *Animals R Us Inc.* or *Animals R Us Company* or *Animals are Us* or even misspelled as *Aminals R Us*. The Table Analyzer splits your data into two or more tables and suggests corrections to the data.

To test this tool, create a single table consisting of fields from three different tables—Customer, Pets, and Visits. There is a special Make query that exists in both your Mountain Animals Hospital and Mountain Animal Start databases named MAKE: Customer-Pets-Visits. Run this query to create the Customer-Pet-Visit table. Use this table to learn how Table Analyzer tool works.

Starting Table Analyzer

You can start Table Analyzer by selecting Tools ⇨ analyze ⇨ Table from any design screen. This starts the Table Analyzer Wizard, as shown in Figure 11-9.

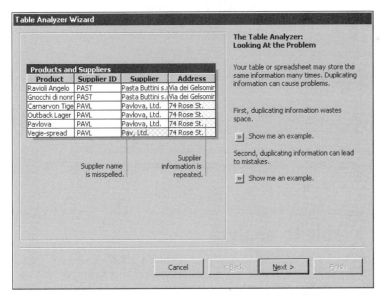

Figure 11-9: Looking At the Problem—Table Analyzer's first introductory screen.

Note   If you have already used the Analyzer, you may not see the introductory screens shown in Figures 11-9 and 11-10.

This first screen shown in Figure 11-9 is actually the first of two introductory screens. These introductory screens have no function other than to offer Help text. This first screen introduces the concepts performed by Table Analyzer. You can click the arrows in the right center of the screen to get a further explanation of why you should not duplicate information in a table.

Once you finish looking at that screen for the first time, click the Next button to move to the next screen. This screen tells you how Table Analyzer solves the potential problems you have in your table (Figure 11-10). The first screen's title is Looking At the Problem; the second screen's title is Solving the Problem. Figure 11-10 also has arrows to click for more detailed explanations about data normalization. Click the Next button to continue.

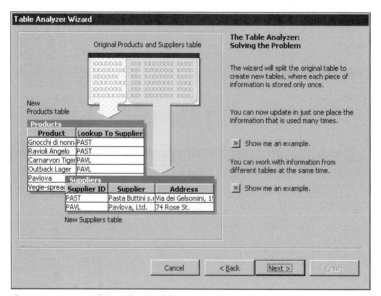

Figure 11-10: Solving the Problem — Table Analyzer's second introductory screen.

Selecting a table to analyze

After the introductory screens, Table Analyzer displays another screen. This screen is used to select the table to analyze. If you are following this example, select Customer-Pet-Visit from the list of tables, as shown in Figure 11-11.

Only tables can be analyzed, not queries.

Tip You don't have to look at the introductory screens each time you run Table Analyzer. As Figure 11-11 shows, there is a checkbox to turn the introductory screens on the next time you run Table Analyzer. The default is to turn it off once you have used the wizard once.

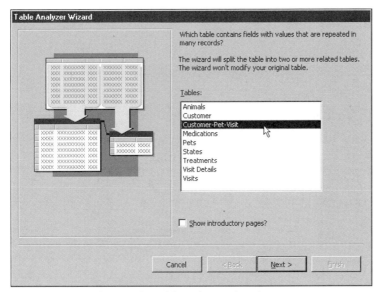

Figure 11-11: Selecting the table to be analyzed.

Analyzing the table

Once select the table is selected, click the Next button to move on. The next screen asks whether you want Access to analyze the tables and make decisions for you, or whether you want to make your own decisions. If you prefer to make your own choices, Access takes you to the Table Analyzer screen in a special version of the Relationships window. There you can drag and drop fields to create a new table, or drag fields from a related table into a parent table to undo a relationship. You learn about this screen later in this section.

At this point, accept the default value of Yes, and click the Next button. When you select *Yes, Let the Wizard Decide*, Table Analyzer performs a multistep analysis of your data, possibly displaying several progress meters onscreen. When the process is complete, the next Wizard screen appears automatically. It shows the proposed structure of the tables, their relationships, and the primary and foreign keys (Figure 11-12).

As Figure 11-12 shows, Table Analyzer has done a great job in splitting the flat file into several tables. The first table (named `Table1`) contains data about the Visit. The second table (named `Table2`) contains Pet information. The third table (Named `Table3`) contains Customer information, and the final table (named `Table4`) contains City/State information. Each table has a primary key assigned: the Pets and Customer tables have an existing field, the other two are assigned a Generated Unique Key. The relationships are already created between suggested tables.

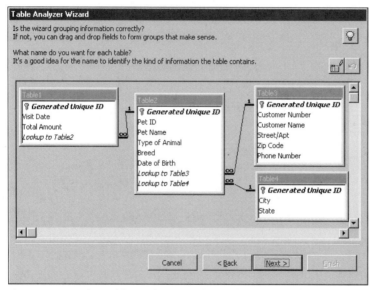

Figure 11-12: The Table Analyzer's Relationships window.

Analyzing a Flat-File Table

The following figure shows part of the data screen of the Customer-Pet-Visit table. As pointed out earlier, the data was created via a Make Table query that combined information from all three tables and eliminated the primary and foreign keys and many of the unimportant fields. The fields used from the Customer table are: Customer Number, Customer Name, Street/Apt, City, State, ZIP Code, and Phone Number. The Pet table fields are: Pet ID, Pet Name, Type of Animal, Breed, and Date of Birth. Finally, the fields from the Visit table: Visit Date and Total Amount.

If you study the information in the table, you will see repeating groups. For instance, the Customer information and individual Pet information are repeated across many records. The Table Analyzer should recognize this repetition and create a separate table for customers, pets, and visits because all the information is the same for multiple records. Table Analyzer can recognize information that is or is not part of a repeating group. When Table Analyzer looks at the Customer Name, Street/Apt, City, ZIP Code, and Phone Number fields, it finds many records with exactly the same data and moves this information into its own table.

Customer Num	Customer Nam	Street/Apt	City	State	Zip Code	Phone Numbe	
AC001	All Creatures	21 Grace St.	Tall Pines	WA	987462541	2065556622	AC
AC001	All Creatures	21 Grace St.	Tall Pines	WA	987462541	2065556622	AC
AC001	All Creatures	21 Grace St.	Tall Pines	WA	987462541	2065556622	AC
AC001	All Creatures	21 Grace St.	Tall Pines	WA	987462541	2065556622	AC
AC001	All Creatures	21 Grace St.	Tall Pines	WA	987462541	2065556622	AC
AC001	All Creatures	21 Grace St.	Tall Pines	WA	987462541	2065556622	AC
AC001	All Creatures	21 Grace St.	Tall Pines	WA	987462541	2065556622	AC
AC001	All Creatures	21 Grace St.	Tall Pines	WA	987462541	2065556622	AC
AC001	All Creatures	21 Grace St.	Tall Pines	WA	987462541	2065556622	AC
AC001	All Creatures	21 Grace St.	Tall Pines	WA	987462541	2065556622	AC
AD001	Johnathan Adar	66 10th St	Mountain View	WA	984101012	2065557623	AD
AD001	Johnathan Adar	66 10th St	Mountain View	WA	984101012	2065557623	AD
AD001	Johnathan Adar	66 10th St	Mountain View	WA	984101012	2065557623	AD
AD001	Johnathan Adar	66 10th St	Mountain View	WA	984101012	2065557623	AD
AD001	Johnathan Adar	66 10th St	Mountain View	WA	984101012	2065557623	AD
AD001	Johnathan Adar	66 10th St	Mountain View	WA	984101012	2065557623	AD
AD001	Johnathan Adar	66 10th St	Mountain View	WA	984101012	2065557623	AD
AD002	William Adams	1122 10th St	Lakeville	OR	974011011	5035556187	AD
AK001	Animal Kingdom	15 Marlin Lane	Borderville	ID	834835646	2085557108	AK
AK001	Animal Kingdom	15 Marlin Lane	Borderville	ID	834835646	2085557108	AK
AK001	Animal Kingdom	15 Marlin Lane	Borderville	ID	834835646	2085557108	AK
AK001	Animal Kingdom	15 Marlin Lane	Borderville	ID	834835646	2085557108	AK

Record: 1 of 86

Analyzing a flat-file table.

In addition to recognizing reoccurring information, Table Analyzer will also attempt to compare data for misspellings. If it finds misspellings, it reports them during the process of analyzing the table.

Before you use Table Analyzer, you may want to place your information in a sorted order. This will aid Table Analyzer in normalizing your data. For instance, the information stored in the table in the above figure is in order by Customer (Customer Number) first and then pet (Pet ID) second.

Changing the table and field definitions

In Figure 11-12, the fourth table has City and State information in it. Although Table Analyzer linked it to the Pets table, you know that it is really related to the Customer table. At this point, you can interactively work with Table Analyzer. You can rename the tables, move fields from table to table, and even delete or create tables from fields in the tables displayed.

All three of the main tables appear to have been split correctly (Visits [Table1], Pets [Table2], and Customer [Table3]) and to have been assigned the correct primary key fields (or to have created one). However, Table4 seems to have some problems. Following normalization rules, you could create a separate table that holds City, State, and ZIP Code information, and link it to a table that looks up cities according to the ZIP Code. To guarantee uniqueness of cities, you must use the US Postal Service 9-digit ZIP Code system. If you use 5-digit ZIP codes, it is possible to have multiple cities with the same ZIP Code. So for purposes of this session, you should move the two fields from the fourth table into Table3 (the customer information table).You can move a field from one table to another by dragging it from one table to another. Highlight the City and State fields in Table4 and click and drag them to Table3, between Street/Apt and ZIP Code. As you move them, the multifield icon appears and a horizontal cross bar appears between the Street/Apt and ZIP Code fields. Because all the fields except the Generated Unique ID field are moved out of the table, Table4 is removed from the screen.

Note Likewise, you can drag a field back from one table to another. You can also create a new table by dragging a field from one table to an empty area of the screen. This creates a new table, a primary key for the new table, and a new foreign key in the original table you dragged the field from. You can also change the order of the fields by selecting one and dragging it above or below other fields in the table.

With three tables now left in Table Analyzer, you should rename each of the tables. Logically you would rename them Customer, Pets, and Visits. However, these tables already exist, so instead give them the same name with the word "Analyze" before them — rename them from *Table1* to *Analyze Visit*, from *Table2* to *Analyze Pet*, and from *Table3* to *Analyze Customer*.

Note Although you can rename the table in Table Analyzer, you cannot rename any fields, such as the new primary and foreign key fields. You can rename the new key primary and foreign fields in the tables only by using the standard Table Design screen after the Wizard is complete.

Changing the key fields

Once you complete this Wizard screen, click the Next button to move to the next Wizard screen. This screen lets you change the key fields that Table Analyzer has created. Figure 11-13 shows this screen with the three tables created and renamed. Because the tables all have a correct primary key assigned, you are done with this screen.

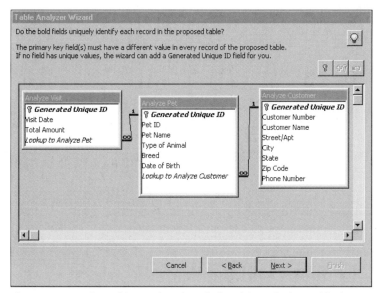

Figure 11-13: The Table Analyzer's Relationships window with the tables renamed.

If you need to create a new primary key, or to change a primary key to an existing field, this is where to do it. To assign a new unique key, click the Add Generated Unique Key button. This creates a new field and makes it the primary key. If you need to change the assigned primary key field, click the correct field that should be the primary field and then click the Set Unique Key button. This cancels the previously created primary key assignment. If the previous field was a generated field, it is removed from the table. Click the Next button to continue to the next step of Table Analyzer, which begins a search for aberrant data. Misspellings and inconsistencies in like data are the most common types of problem data Table Analyzer can find.

Figure 11-14 shows this type of analysis. If this type of analysis occurs, look for problems in your data. For example, if you had several SNAKES and one SHAKE, the system would detect that you probably made an error and let you correct it by selecting the correct animal type from the combo box list.

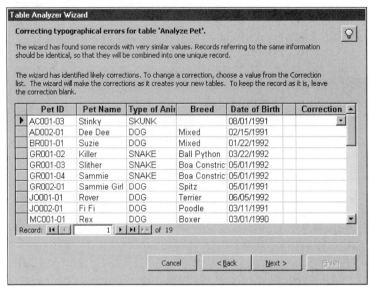

Figure 11-14: Warning message to go back and fix your tables.

Searching for typos and duplicate key data

If during the process of searching for aberrant data, Table Analyzer finds what it believes are inconsistencies or misspellings, it displays a series of screens that allow you to correct those apparent errors. You may see screens that make no sense, because Table Analyzer may make a wrong assumption about what to analyze. It might, for example, do some analysis on duplicate key data. The screens depend totally on the analysis of the data. In this example, Table Analyzer misses all the misspelled Cities and Companies but it keys in on the similar phone numbers.

Once the typos are corrected, and you click the Next button, you are taken to the final screen of Table Analyzer.

If Table Analyzer finds no apparent typos, you are immediately taken to the next, and final, screen.

Completing Table Analyzer

The final screen (Figure 11-15) lets you complete the analysis process. Notice that Table Analyzer offers to create a query using the original name of your table and rename the original table. If you accept this choice, any forms and reports that work with the old flat file table continue to work. This gives you the best of both worlds — you can start to work with the normalized tables while still being able to work with the old table. If you decide to accept this choice, you should NOT continue to add records to the old table!

Caution One problem Table Analyzer can cause is to render existing queries, forms, reports, and macros inoperable because all these objects are tied to specific table and field names. When you change the table name or field names within a table, Access reports an error when you try to run the form, report, or macro; they cannot automatically adjust. A solution is to create a new query (with the same name as the original table) that uses the new tables and creates a view identical to the original table.

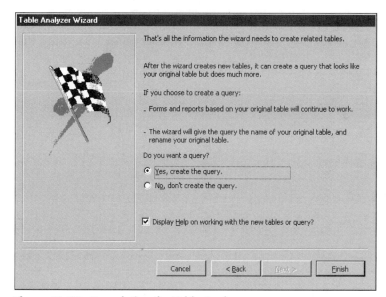

Figure 11-15: Completing the Table Analyzer process.

For the purpose of this exercise, select the choice *No, don't create the query* and click the Finish button.

Clicking the Finish button makes the Table Wizard disappear, and a tiled view of all the new tables appears. When you are finished looking at the new tables, close them.

If you want to change the names of any of the fields, you can open each table in Design view and rename any field names. Although the Table Wizard is not perfect, it is an outstanding way to normalize a data table with little effort.

Using the Lookup Wizard in the Table Designer

When you view one table that is related to another table, the table often contains a foreign key—generally the primary key of the other table. The foreign key field is often cryptic when looked at through the related table. Until you relate the two tables and look at the data from a Query view, you cannot tell the real value of the field.

For example, Figure 11-16 shows the Pets table sorted by Type of Animal and Breed. Notice the cryptic value in the Customer Number field. In Access versions 2.0 and earlier, the only way to see the Customer Name was to create a query and look at the resulting dynaset. In Access 2000, you can display the Customer Name in a table that contains only a foreign key lookup to the Customer table. This means that you can display, select, and immediately see a Customer Name, such as All Creatures, while in the Pets table, instead of using a foreign name such as AC001.

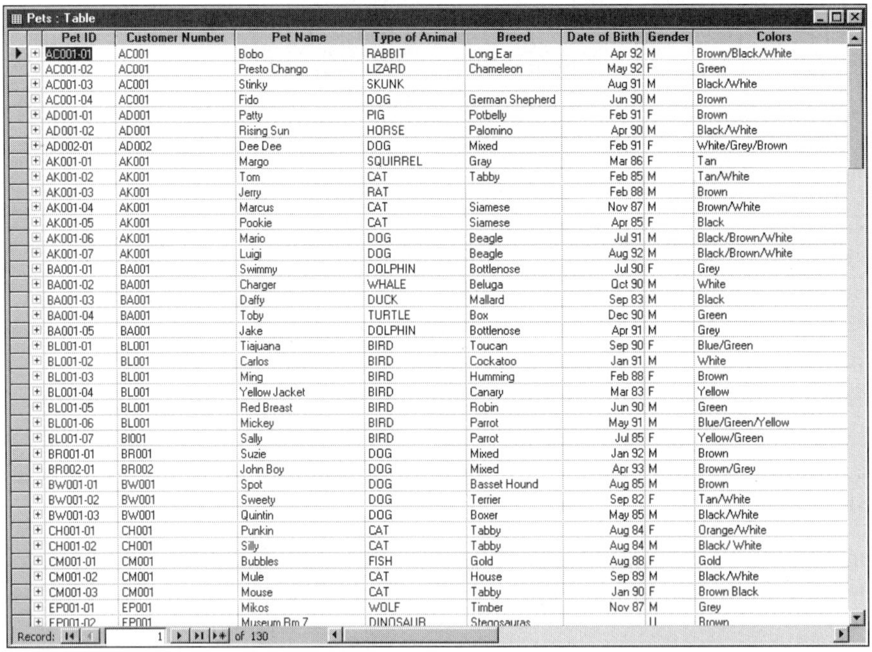

Pet ID	Customer Number	Pet Name	Type of Animal	Breed	Date of Birth	Gender	Colors
AC001-01	AC001	Bobo	RABBIT	Long Ear	Apr 92	M	Brown/Black/White
AC001-02	AC001	Presto Chango	LIZARD	Chameleon	May 92	F	Green
AC001-03	AC001	Stinky	SKUNK		Aug 91	M	Black/White
AC001-04	AC001	Fido	DOG	German Shepherd	Jun 90	M	Brown
AD001-01	AD001	Patty	PIG	Potbelly	Feb 91	F	Brown
AD001-02	AD001	Rising Sun	HORSE	Palomino	Apr 90	M	Black/White
AD002-01	AD002	Dee Dee	DOG	Mixed	Feb 91	F	White/Grey/Brown
AK001-01	AK001	Margo	SQUIRREL	Gray	Mar 86	F	Tan
AK001-02	AK001	Tom	CAT	Tabby	Feb 85	M	Tan/White
AK001-03	AK001	Jerry	RAT		Feb 88	M	Brown
AK001-04	AK001	Marcus	CAT	Siamese	Nov 87	M	Brown/White
AK001-05	AK001	Pookie	CAT	Siamese	Apr 85	F	Black
AK001-06	AK001	Mario	DOG	Beagle	Jul 91	M	Black/Brown/White
AK001-07	AK001	Luigi	DOG	Beagle	Aug 92	M	Black/Brown/White
BA001-01	BA001	Swimmy	DOLPHIN	Bottlenose	Jul 90	F	Grey
BA001-02	BA001	Charger	WHALE	Beluga	Oct 90	M	White
BA001-03	BA001	Daffy	DUCK	Mallard	Sep 83	M	Black
BA001-04	BA001	Toby	TURTLE	Box	Dec 90	M	Green
BA001-05	BA001	Jake	DOLPHIN	Bottlenose	Apr 91	M	Grey
BL001-01	BL001	Tiajuana	BIRD	Toucan	Sep 90	F	Blue/Green
BL001-02	BL001	Carlos	BIRD	Cockatoo	Jan 91	M	White
BL001-03	BL001	Ming	BIRD	Humming	Feb 88	F	Brown
BL001-04	BL001	Yellow Jacket	BIRD	Canary	Mar 83	F	Yellow
BL001-05	BL001	Red Breast	BIRD	Robin	Jun 90	M	Green
BL001-06	BL001	Mickey	BIRD	Parrot	May 91	M	Blue/Green/Yellow
BL001-07	BI001	Sally	BIRD	Parrot	Jul 85	F	Yellow/Green
BR001-01	BR001	Suzie	DOG	Mixed	Jan 92	M	Brown
BR002-01	BR002	John Boy	DOG	Mixed	Apr 93	M	Brown/Grey
BW001-01	BW001	Spot	DOG	Basset Hound	Aug 85	M	Brown
BW001-02	BW001	Sweety	DOG	Terrier	Sep 82	F	Tan/White
BW001-03	BW001	Quintin	DOG	Boxer	May 85	M	Black/White
CH001-01	CH001	Punkin	CAT	Tabby	Aug 84	F	Orange/White
CH001-02	CH001	Silly	CAT	Tabby	Aug 84	M	Black/White
CM001-01	CM001	Bubbles	FISH	Gold	Aug 88	F	Gold
CM001-02	CM001	Mule	CAT	House	Sep 89	M	Black/White
CM001-03	CM001	Mouse	CAT	Tabby	Jan 90	F	Brown Black
EP001-01	EP001	Mikos	WOLF	Timber	Nov 87	M	Grey
EP001-02	EP001	Museum Rm 7	DINOSAUR	Stegosaurus	U	Brown

Record: 1 of 130

Figure 11-16: A confusing foreign-key value.

To do this you need to change the display nature of the field from showing actual content to showing a lookup value from another table or list by redefining the properties of the field. For instance, to change the display of the Customer Number field in the Pets table so that it displays the actual Customer Name, you would change some properties at the database level of the Pets table.

To start this process, open the Pets table and switch to Design view. Select the data type of the Customer Number field, and click the down arrow to display the data type list. Notice the last item in the list is Lookup Wizard (as shown in Figure 11-17). This is actually not a data type, of course, but rather a way of changing the Lookup properties.

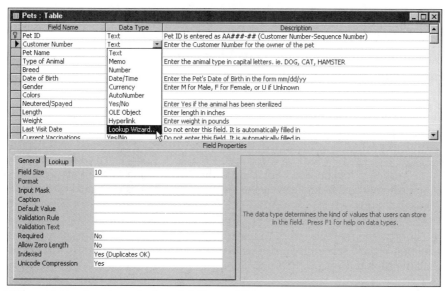

Figure 11-17: Creating a lookup field in a table.

In the Customer Number field, select the Lookup Wizard data type. This starts the Wizard, which takes you through a series of screens that help you create a lookup to another table instead of displaying the field value itself.

Figure 11-18 shows the first Lookup Wizard screen. There are two choices. The first choice lets you use data from another related table as the displayed value in the field.

The second option lets you type in a list of values. Use this option only when you enter a code such as the Type of Customer field in the Customer table. Later you learn how to change the Lookup properties of that field to display *Individual* if the code entered is 1, *Pet Store* if the code entered is 2, and *Zoo* if the code entered is 3.

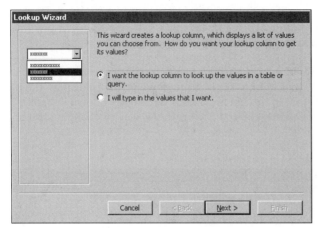

Figure 11-18: Selecting the type of lookup.

In this example, the Customer Name from the Customer table in the Customer Number field in the Pets table is displayed. Select the first choice and click the Next button.

Note   Creating a lookup does not change the stored value in the Pets table for the Customer Number field. Only the display of the value is changed.

The next screen asks *Which table or query contains the fields for the lookup?* and lets you choose the table or query to use for the lookup. This is the standard table-selection Wizard screen that is used in most Wizards. Select the Customer table and click the Next button.

The next Wizard screen displays a list of all of the fields in the Customer table and lets you select the fields to use in the lookup. This is also a standard field-selection screen. The accepted method is to select all the fields in the lookup table that will be used in the display when you select the combo box in the datasheet. You also need to add, but not display, the field that will hold the actual value. When you look at the datasheet, only the first nonkey field selected is displayed. When you press the combo box arrow, all of the nonkey fields that are selected are displayed; for example, you might want to display the customer name, address, and phone number. Though you can display more than one field in the table, generally you will display only one field. The key field is stored out of sight and used for the actual value that belongs to the table.

You need to select two fields from the Customer table. One field is the link field (used to link to the Pets table), and the other is the field that to be displayed in the

Pets table. Select the Customer Name and the Customer Number fields. Remember to click the > button after you select each field (which copies it from the Available Fields list to the Selected Fields list).

Tip   In Access 2000, the field selection order is NOT important. The Wizard automatically determines which field is the link field and which is the display field.

After you do this and click the Next button, the display and size screen shown in Figure 11-19 appears.

A list of the data is displayed from the Customer table. As Figure 11-19 shows, the only field visible is the Customer Name. The Customer Number field is hidden from view. If you want to see the hidden field, turn the *Hide key column* checkbox off. (Be sure to turn it back on before continuing.)

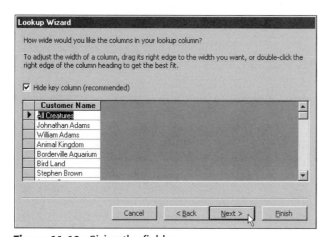

Figure 11-19: Sizing the fields.

Resize the Customer Name field to display all of its contents. When done, click the Next button.

The final screen asks what name to display when the table is viewed. The default name is the original name of the column. Accept the default name of Customer Number and click the Finish button to complete the Wizard. The Wizard displays a dialog box (Figure 11-20) telling you that the table must be saved before the relationship between the two tables (Customer and Pets) can be created. Accept the default action of Yes and the lookup table reference is created.

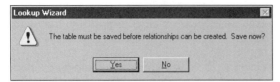

Figure 11-20: Dialog box to save relationship.

Figure 11-21 shows the new settings in the Pets table design window, in the fields set in the Field Properties Lookup tab sheet (bottom half of screen).

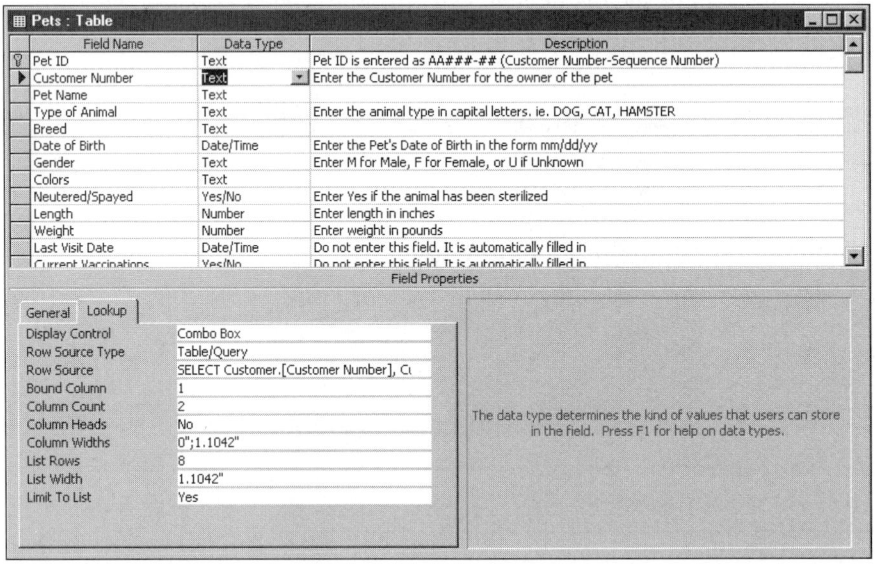

Figure 11-21: Understanding the Lookup properties.

The Lookup tab has changed significantly. The first property tells you that the field will now appear as a combo box whenever it is displayed in a table, or by default when it is placed on a form. The data type for the Customer Number field, however, is still Text. Even though you chose the Lookup Wizard from the Data Type list, it still creates a Text data type. The Lookup Wizard merely changes the Lookup properties.

The next two Lookup properties define the type of data for the record. In this case, the source of the data in the record is a table or query. Other choices are Value List (you type them into the Row Source property, separated by semicolons) and Field List (a list of fields in a table).

The Row Source displays a statement in SQL (Standard Query Language), an internal language that Access translates all queries into. You can see only a portion of the SQL statement in Figure 11-21. To see the entire SQL statement, open the Zoom window by pressing Shift-F2.

The entire statement is:

```
SELECT DISTINCTROW [Customer].[Customer Number],
[Customer].[Customer Name] FROM [Customer];
```

This command tells Access to use the Customer Name and Customer Number fields from the Customer table. The remaining values tell Access 2000 how many columns to use from the Customer table, which field to display (Customer Name, field 0), and which one is used for a link.

When you display the Pets table in a Datasheet view (as shown in Figure 11-22), Customer Name is shown in the Customer Number field instead of Customer Number. Using this method, you can display and limit the selection of any coded field in a table. You can even use fields found in only one table, such as the Gender field in the Pets table. Rather than display an M, F, or U, you can select from Male, Female, or Unknown, and still store the correct code in the field.

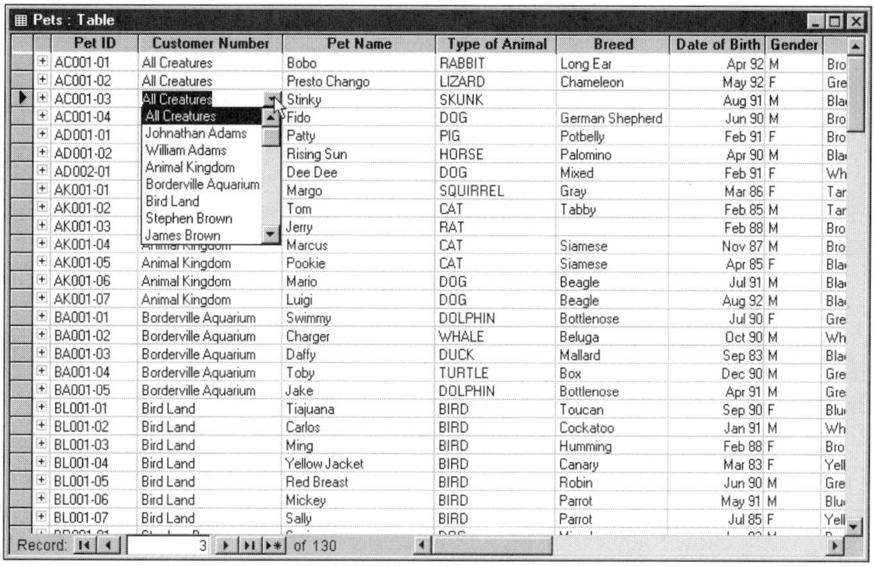

Figure 11-22: Displaying a lookup field in a datasheet.

Using Subdatasheets

Sometimes when viewing information in datasheets, you want to see records that are related to a record in one table that are in a separate table.

New Feature

Access 2000 has the capability to view hierarchical data in the datasheet view. You can setup the subdatasheets manually in the design of the table or you can have the database automatically determine them based on the relationships between tables. The subdatasheets can be viewed with a table, query, form and subform datasheets.

You will know that there has been a relationship with another table setup when you view records in a datasheet because there will be a new column added to the left-hand side of the datasheet with a + next to each row, as shown in Figure 11-23.

Pet ID	Customer Number	Pet Name	Type of Animal	Breed	Date of Birth	Gender	
AC001-01	All Creatures	Bobo	RABBIT	Long Ear	Apr 92	M	Bro
AC001-02	All Creatures	Presto Chango	LIZARD	Chameleon	May 92	F	Gre
AC001-03	All Creatures	Stinky	SKUNK		Aug 91	M	Bla
AC001-04	All Creatures	Fido	DOG	German Shepherd	Jun 90	M	Bro
AD001-01	Johnathan Adams	Patty	PIG	Potbelly	Feb 91	F	Bro
AD001-02	Johnathan Adams	Rising Sun	HORSE	Palomino	Apr 90	M	Bla
AD002-01	William Adams	Dee Dee	DOG	Mixed	Feb 91	F	Wh
AK001-01	Animal Kingdom	Margo	SQUIRREL	Gray	Mar 86	F	Tar
AK001-02	Animal Kingdom	Tom	CAT	Tabby	Feb 85	M	Tar
AK001-03	Animal Kingdom	Jerry	RAT		Feb 88	M	Bro
AK001-04	Animal Kingdom	Marcus	CAT	Siamese	Nov 87	M	Bro
AK001-05	Animal Kingdom	Pookie	CAT	Siamese	Apr 85	F	Bla
AK001-06	Animal Kingdom	Mario	DOG	Beagle	Jul 91	M	Bla
AK001-07	Animal Kingdom	Luigi	DOG	Beagle	Aug 92	M	Bla
BA001-01	Borderville Aquarium	Swimmy	DOLPHIN	Bottlenose	Jul 90	F	Gre
BA001-02	Borderville Aquarium	Charger	WHALE	Beluga	Oct 90	M	Wh
BA001-03	Borderville Aquarium	Daffy	DUCK	Mallard	Sep 83	M	Bla
BA001-04	Borderville Aquarium	Toby	TURTLE	Box	Dec 90	M	Gre
BA001-05	Borderville Aquarium	Jake	DOLPHIN	Bottlenose	Apr 91	M	Gre
BL001-01	Bird Land	Tiajuana	BIRD	Toucan	Sep 90	F	Blu
BL001-02	Bird Land	Carlos	BIRD	Cockatoo	Jan 91	M	Wh
BL001-03	Bird Land	Ming	BIRD	Humming	Feb 88	F	Bro
BL001-04	Bird Land	Yellow Jacket	BIRD	Canary	Mar 83	F	Yell
BL001-05	Bird Land	Red Breast	BIRD	Robin	Jun 90	M	Gre
BL001-06	Bird Land	Mickey	BIRD	Parrot	May 91	M	Blu
BL001-07	Bird Land	Sally	BIRD	Parrot	Jul 85	F	Yell

Record: 1 of 130

Figure 11-23: Displaying a datasheet that has related tables.

When you click the button for a row, the related records in the subdatasheet are shown. The tables that are setup to be subdatasheets may have subdatasheets for them, which allow the viewing of both related records for the main table that you are in and related records for the subdatasheet. Figure 11-24 is an example of this. It shows records from three different tables related to this one record in the Customers table.

	Customer	Typ	Customer Nam	Street/Apt	City	State	Zip Code	Phone Num	Custome
▶	⊟ AC001	2	All Creatures	21 Grace St.	Tall Pines	WA	987462541	(206) 555-66;	03/19/9!

		Pet ID	Pet Name	Type of Animal	Breed	Date of Birth	Gender	Colo
▶	⊟ AC001-01	Bobo		RABBIT	Long Ear	Apr 92	M	Brown/Black/Whi

	Visit Number	Visit Date	Follow Up Typ	Follow Up Dat	Total Amount	Payment Type
▶ ⊟	19990422-01	04/22/99	Exam	10/22/99	$512.00	

	Line Number	Visit Type	Treatment Coc	Medication Co	Treatment Pric	Medication
▶	001	INJURY	0404	0500	$230.00	$11.
	002	INJURY	0500	0402	$57.00	$14.
	003	INJURY	0408	0000	$120.00	$0.
	004	GROOMING	2003	0702	$25.00	$34.
	005	GROOMING	2002	0000	$20.00	$0.

Record: ◀ ◀ 1 ▶ ▶◀ ▶* of 4

	Customer	Typ	Customer Nam	Street/Apt	City	State	Zip Code	Phone Num	Custome
⊞	AD001	1	Johnathan Adar	66 10th St	Mountain View	WA	984101012	(206) 555-76;	01/01/99
⊞	AD002	1	William Adams	1122 10th St	Lakeville	OR	974011011	(503) 555-618	10/22/9;
⊞	AK001	2	Animal Kingdon	15 Marlin Lane	Borderville	ID	834835646	(208) 555-71(	05/22/9(
⊞	BA001	3	Borderville Aqua	1 Whale Way	Borderville	OR	974121001	(503) 555-26!	07/16/9;
⊞	BL001	2	Bird Land	22 Eagle Blvd	Russettown	ID	834121021	(208) 555-43!	08/09/9;
⊞	BR001	1	Stephen Brown	555 Sycamore /	Three Corners	ID	834011023	(208) 555-12;	09/01/9;
⊞	BR002	1	James Brown	3454 Adams St	Borderville	OR	974011019	(503) 555-12;	09/02/9;
⊞	BW001	2	Bow Wow Hous	76 Canine Ln.	Ranier City	WA	987562175	(206) 555-87;	09/08/9!
⊞	CH001	2	Cat House Pets	76 Right Ln.	Borderville	OR	975412856	(503) 555-43!	05/06/9;
⊞	CM001	2	Critters and Mol	200 Feline Rd	Borderville	WA	984538567	(206) 555-10!	01/01/99

Record: ◀ ◀ 1 ▶ ▶◀ ▶* of 49

Figure 11-24: Displaying subdatasheets in Datasheet view.

Setting up subdatasheets

You can setup subdatasheets in the design view of a table by clicking View ➪ Properties from the Access menu bar, or by clicking the Properties icon on your toolbar. This displays the Table properties as shown in Figure 11-25.

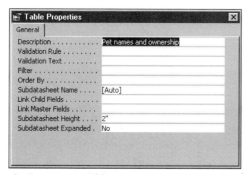

Figure 11-25: Table Properties.

Selecting a subdatasheet name

If you have used Access 97 previously, you will notice that five new properties have been added to the Table Properties dialog box. All of these properties are related to subdatasheets. Also notice the value entered for Subdatasheet Name, Auto. Auto automatically assigns the subdatasheet name based on relationships set up in the database. To display a list of Tables and Queries in the database, click anywhere in the Subdatasheet Name field and a combo box displays, as shown in Figure 11-26.

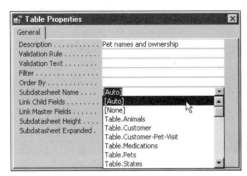

Figure 11-26: Displaying Table and Query names.

Entering the Link Child Fields and the Link Master Fields

The Link Child Fields and Link Master Fields property settings must have the same number of fields and must represent data of the same type. For example, if the Customer table and the Pets table both have Customer ID fields (one each) that contain the same type of data, enter **Customer ID** for both properties. The subform automatically displays all the pets found for the customer identified in the main table's Customer ID field.

Although the data must match, the names of the fields can differ. For example, the Customer ID field from the Customer table can be linked to the Customer Number field from the Pets table.

If you select the table or query that you would like to have related records displayed as, the Link Master Field and Link Child Field properties are automatically filled in if the linked fields have the same field name. If the linked field names are different, then these properties are left blank for you to fill in. If you are entering `Table.Pets` in as the subdatasheet, the field Customer Number is in both tables, so this is the field that will be used for both the Link Master Field and the Link Child Field.

If you change the name of the field Customer Number in the Customers table (which we don't recommend that you do) to Customer ID, and leave the Customer Number field in the Pets table, you will have to enter these field names into the correct property.

To create the link, follow these steps:

1. Enter Customer **Number** in the Link Child Fields property.
2. Enter **Customer ID** in the Link Master Fields property.

Without the link fields entered, no records will be displayed when you try to display your subdatasheet for the Pets table because Access doesn't know what fields to link.

Entering a subdatasheet height

The property for the subdatasheet height has a default value of 2 inches. This will show you the related records in a sheet that is 2 inches high. If the records don't fit in this space, scroll bars permit a view of all the records.

To change the height to a smaller or larger number, type in your preferred height in inches.

Expanding the subdatasheet

The Subdatasheet Expanded field is a Yes/No field. If you have Yes entered in this field, the subdatasheets are expanded, as shown in Figure 11-27.

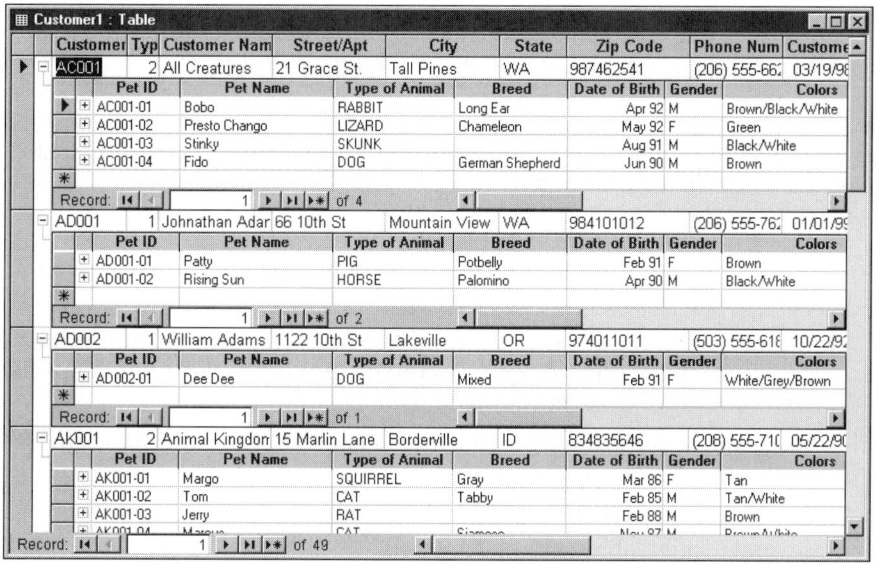

Figure 11-27: Subdatasheet Expanded option set to Yes.

Summary

Using multiple tables instead of a single table makes a system far more complex to work with. Throughout the rest of this book, you learn to use multiple tables to create more advanced types of forms, reports, and queries. A relational database management system can become quite complicated. By paying attention to details and applying the concepts you learned in this chapter, you can create a system of unlimited complexity with Access. This chapter covered these points:

✦ Eight tables make up the Mountain Animal Hospital example. The four main tables are Customer, Pets, Visits, and Visit Details; the four lookup tables are States, Animals, Treatments, and Medications.

✦ A primary key designates one or more fields that make a record unique. This uniqueness is called the entity integrity of a record.

✦ A primary key is an index that greatly speeds searches and query requests.

✦ You create primary keys in the Table Design window by clicking the Primary Key icon after selecting the primary key field.

✦ A multiple-field primary key is used when one field is not sufficient to guarantee uniqueness.

✦ A foreign key is a field that contains a value that matches another table's primary key.

✦ A primary key field and a foreign key field are linked to form a relation.

✦ The four types of relationships are one-to-one, one-to-many, many-to-one, and many-to-many.

✦ Referential integrity is a set of rules that prevents data entry if the result will be an invalid relationship.

✦ When data violates referential integrity, an error message displays.

✦ In a multiple-table system, records cannot be deleted without regard to referential integrity.

✦ Whenever you make changes to key-field data in a multiple-table system, the potential for violating referential integrity exists. You must follow special steps to change or delete key-field data.

✦ You create relationships by using the Relationships window from the Database window's Tools menu.

✦ The Access 2000 Table Analyzer lets you can normalize a flat-file table into several related tables automatically.

✦ Subdatasheets allow you to see related records in datasheets without having to create a form and subform.

✦ The Access 2000 Lookup Wizard lets you place lookup field properties in a table.

In the next chapter, you learn to use operators, functions, and expressions that are used throughout Access in forms, reports, and queries.

✦   ✦   ✦

Using Access in Your Work

Using Operators, Functions, and Expressions

Operators, functions, and expressions are the fundamental building blocks for Access operations. You use them in such operations as entering criteria in queries, creating calculated fields in forms, and creating summary controls in reports.

Operators

Operators let you add numbers, compare values, put text strings together, and create complex relational expressions. You use operators to inform Access that a specific operation is to be performed against one or more items. Access also uses several special operators to identify an object.

Types of operators

These are the types of operators discussed in this chapter:

- ✦ Mathematical (arithmetic) operators
- ✦ Relational operators
- ✦ String operators
- ✦ Boolean (logical) operators
- ✦ Miscellaneous operators

When are operators used?

Operators are used all the time. In fact, they are used every time an equation is created. In Access, operators specify data-validation rules for table properties, create calculated fields in forms, or specify criteria in queries.

Operators indicate that an operation needs to be performed on one or more items. Some common examples of operators are:

✦ =

✦ &

✦ And

✦ Like

✦ +

Mathematical operators

There are seven basic mathematical operators. These are also known as arithmetic operators because they are used for performing arithmetic calculations:

*	Multiply
+	Add
−	Subtract
/	Divide
\	Integer Divide
^	Exponentiation
Mod	Modulo

By definition, mathematical operators work with numbers. When you work with mathematical operators, numbers can be any numeric data type. The number can be the actual number or one that is represented by a memory variable or a field's contents. Furthermore, the numbers can be used individually or combined to create complex expressions. Some of the examples in this section are quite complex, but don't worry if you don't usually work with sophisticated mathematics. This chapter shows you how to work with mathematical formulas in Access.

The * (multiplication) operator

A simple example of when you use the *multiplication operator* is on an invoice entry form. A clerk enters the number of items and the per-item price; a calculated field calculates and displays the total price for that number of items. In this case, the text box contains the formula `[Price] * [Quantity]`. The field names are enclosed in brackets, which is standard notation for dealing with field names in an expression.

The + (addition) operator

If you want to create a calculated field in the same form, adding the values in fields such as Gross Amount and Tax, enter the expression `[Gross Amount] + [Tax]`. This simple formula uses the addition operator to add the contents of both fields and place the result in the object that contains the formula.

Besides adding two numbers, the *addition operator* can be used for concatenating two character strings. For example, you may want to combine the fields First Name and Last Name to display them as a single field. This expression is:

```
[First Name] + [Last Name]
```

Caution   Although you can *concatenate* (put two strings together) text strings by using the addition operator, you should use the ampersand (&). The reason for this appears in the section "String operators," later in this chapter.

The – (subtraction) operator

An example of using the *subtraction operator* on a form is the calculation of an invoice amount; you might offer a discount to certain customers. To determine the Net Amount, a formula that uses the subtraction operator would be used, such as

```
[Gross Amount] - ([Gross Amount]*[Discount]).
```

Note   Although parentheses are not mathematical operators, they play an integral part in working with operators, as discussed later, in the section "Operator precedence."

The / (division) operator

You can use the *division operator* to divide two numbers and (as with the previous operators) place the result wherever you need it. Suppose, for example, that a pool of 212 people wins the $1,000,000 lottery this week. The formula to determine each individual's payoff is `1,000,000 / 212`, resulting in $4,716.98 per person.

The \ (integer division) operator

Should you ever need to take two numbers, round them both to integers, divide the two rounded integers, and receive a nonrounded integer, the *integer division operator* does it in one step. Here is an example:

Normal Division	*Integer Conversion Division*
100 / 6 = 16.667	100 \ 6 = 16
100.9 / 6.6 = 15.288	100.9 \ 6.6 = 14

Tip   Access 2000 has the round function for rounding fractional numbers to whole numbers. You can also use this operator to round any number. Take the number you want to round and integer-divide (\) it by 1, as in 125.6 \ 1 = 126.

What Are Integer Values?

Integers are whole numbers (numbers that contain no decimal places), which in Access are between -32768 and +32767. They have no fractional part (after the dot — for example, 7.2 is not an integer because it has a fractional part — .2; 7 is the integer number!). Examples are 1, 722, 33, -5460, 0, and 22. They include all whole positive and negative numbers and 0. When you use the Int() function or the integer divide operator (\), to determine the integer part of any number, simply drop any decimal values. For example, the integer of 45.123 is 45; for 2.987, the integer is 2; and so forth.

This, the integer divide operator, can be a confusing operator until you understand just what it does. If you enter the following, it should become clear:

? 101 / 6 results in 16.833.

? 101.9 / 6.6 results in 15.439.

? 102 / 7 results in 14.571.

? INT(102 / 7) results in 14.

? 101.9 \ 6.6 results in 14.

The last entry uses the integer divide sign –(\) and is equivalent to rounding both numbers in the division operation (101.9 = 102 and 6.6 = 7), dividing 102 by 7, and converting the answer to an integer. In other words, it is equivalent to:

INT((101.9 \ 1) / (6.6 \ 1)) or INT(round(101.9)/ round(6.6))

Note   Access rounds numbers based on the greater-than-.5 rule: Any number with a decimal value of x.5 or less rounds down; greater than x.5 rounds up to the next whole number. This means that 6.5 becomes 6, but 6.51 and 6.6 become 7.

The ^ (exponentiation) operator

The *exponentiation operator* (^) raises a number to the power of an exponent. Raising a number simply means indicating the number of times that you want to multiply a number by itself. For example, multiplying the value 4 x 4 x 4 (that is, 4-cubed) is the same as entering the formula 4 ^ 3.

Relational operators

There are six basic relational operators (also known as comparison operators). They compare two values or expressions via an equation. The relational operators include:

=	Equal
<>	Not equal
<	Less than
<=	Less than or equal to
>	Greater than
>=	Greater than or equal to

The operators always return either a logical value or Null; the value they return says Yes (True), No (not True; that is, False), or it is a Null (unknown/no value).

Note   Access actually returns a numeric value for relational operator equations. It returns a −1 (negative 1) for True and a 0 (zero) for False.

If either side of an equation is a Null value, the resultant will always be a Null.

The = (equal) operator

The *equal operator* returns a logical True if the two expressions being compared are the same. Here are two examples of the equal operator:

`[Type of Animal] = "Cat"` is True if the animal is a cat; False is returned for any other animal.

`[Date of Birth] = Date()` is True if the date in the Date of Birth field is today.

The <> (not-equal) operator

The *not-equal operator* is exactly the opposite of the equal operator. Here the cat example is changed to not-equal:

`[Type of Animal] <> "Cat"` is True if Type of Animal is anything but a cat.

The < (less-than) operator

The *less-than operator* returns a logical True if the left side of the equation is less than the right side, as in this example:

`[Weight] < 10` is True if the Weight field contains a value of less than 10.

The <= (less-than-or-equal-to) operator

The *less-than-or-equal-to operator* returns a True if the left side of the equation is either less than or equal to the right side, as in this example:

[Weight] <= 10 is True if the value of Weight equals 10 or is less than 10.

Note   Access is not sensitive to the order of the operators. Access accepts either of these forms as the same: (<=) or (=<).

The > (greater-than) operator

The *greater-than operator* is the exact opposite of the less-than operator. This operator returns a True whenever the left side of the equation is greater than the right side; for example:

[Length (In)] > 22 returns True if the value of Length (In) is greater than 22.

The >= (greater-than-or-equal-to) operator

The *greater-than-or-equal-to operator* returns a True if the left side of the equation is either equal to or greater than the right side; for example:

[Weight (lbs)] >= 100 is return True if the field Weight (lbs) contains a value equal to or greater than 100.

Note   Access is not sensitive to the order of the operator. Access accepts either the form (>=) or (=>).

String operators

Access has two *string operators*. Unlike the other operators, these work specifically with the Text data type:

&	Concatenation
Like	Similar to...

The & (concatenation) operator

The *concatenation operator* connects or links (concatenates) two or more objects into a resultant string. This operator works similarly to the addition operator; unlike the addition operator, however, the & operator always forces a string concatenation. For instance, this example produces a single string:

[First Name] & [Last Name]

However, in the resultant string, no spaces are automatically added. If `[First Name]` equals "Fred" and `[Last Name]` equals "Smith," concatenating the field contents yields `FredSmith`. To add a space between the strings, you must concatenate a space string between the two fields. To concatenate a space string between first and last name fields, you enter a formula such as:

```
[First Name] & " " & [Last Name]
```

This operator can easily concatenate a string object with a number- or date-type object. Using the `&` eliminates the need for special functions to convert a number or date to a string.

Suppose, for example, that you have a Number field, which is House Number, and a Text field, which is Street Name, and that you want to build an expression for a report of both fields. For this, you can enter the following:

```
[House Number] & " " & [Street Name]
```

If `House Number` has a value of 1600 and `Street Name` is "Pennsylvania Avenue N.W.," the resultant concatenation of the number and string is:

```
"1600 Pennsylvania Avenue N.W."
```

Perhaps you have a calculated field in a report that prints the operator's name and the date and time the report was run. This is accomplished using syntax similar to the following:

```
"This report was printed " & Now() & " by " & [operator name]
```

If the date is March 21, 1999, and the time is 4:45 p.m., this concatenated line prints something like this:

```
This report was printed 3/21/99 4:45:40 PM by Michael R. Irwin
```

Notice the spaces at the end or the beginning of the strings. Knowing how this operator works makes maintenance of your database expressions easier. If you always use the concatenation operator for creating concatenated text strings, you won't have to be concerned with the data types of the concatenated objects. Any formula that uses the `&` operator converts all the objects being concatenated to a string type for you.

Note   Using the `&` with Nulls: If both objects are Null, the resultant is also a Null. If only one of the two objects is Null, Access converts the object that is Null to a string type with a length of 0 and builds the concatenation.

The Like (similar to) operator

The `Like` operator compares two string objects by using wildcards. This operator determines whether one object matches the pattern of another object. The resultant of the comparison is a True, False, or Null.

The `Like` operator uses the following basic syntax:

```
expression object Like pattern object
```

`Like` looks for the *expression object* in the *pattern object*; if it is present, the operation returns a True. (The `Like` operator is discussed in more detail in Chapter 14.)

Note   If either object in the `Like` formula is a Null, the resultant is a Null.

This operator provides a powerful and flexible tool for string comparisons. The pattern object can use wildcard characters to increase flexibility (see the sidebar "Using Wildcards").

Tip   If you want to match one of the wildcard characters in the `Like` operation, the wildcard character must be enclosed in brackets in the pattern object. In the example

```
"AB*Co" Like "AB[*]C*
```

the [*] in the third position of the pattern object will look for the asterisk as the third character of the string.

These are some examples that use the `Like` operator:

✦ `[Last Name] Like "M[Cc]*"` is True for any last name that begins with "Mc" or "MC." "McDonald," "McJamison," "MCWilliams" are all be True; "Irwin" and "Prague" are all False.

✦ `[Answer] Like "[!e-zE-Z]"` is True if the Answer is A, B, C, D, a, b, c, or d. Any other letter is False.

✦ `"AB1989" Like "AB####"` results in True. This string looks for the letters *AB* and any four numbers after the letters.

✦ `"#10 Circle Drive" Like "[#]*Drive"` results in True. The first character must be the pound sign (#), and the last part must be the word *Drive*.

Using Wildcards

Access lets you use these five wildcards with the Like operator:

Character	Matches
?	A single character (A to Z, 0 to 9)
F	Any number of characters (0 to *n*)
#	Any single digit (0 to 9)
[*list*]	Any single character in the list
[!*list*]	Any single character *not* in the list

Both [*list*] and [!*list*] can use the hyphen between two characters to signify a range.

Boolean (logical) operators

Access uses six *Boolean operators*. Also referred to as *logical operators*, these are used for setting conditions in expressions. Boolean operators are used to create complex multiple-condition expressions. Like relational operators, these always return either a logical value or a Null. Boolean operators include:

And	Logical and
Or	Logical inclusive or
Eqv	Logical equivalence
Imp	Logical implication
Xor	Logical exclusive or
Not	Logical not

The And operator

You use the *And operator* to perform a logical conjunction of two objects; the operator returns the value True if both conditions are true. The general syntax of an And operation is:

```
object expression 1 And object expression 2
```

Here is an example:

✦ `[State] = "MN" And [Zip Code] = "12345"` is True only if both conditions are True.

If the conditions on both sides of the `And` operator are True, the result is a True value. Table 12-1 demonstrates the results.

Table 12-1
And Operator Resultants

Expression 1	Expression 2	Return Resultant
True	True	True
True	False	False
True	Null	Null
False	True	False
False	False	False
False	Null	False
Null	True	Null
Null	False	False
Null	Null	Null

The Or operator

The *Or operator* is used to perform a logical disjunction of two objects; the operator returns the value True if either condition is true. The general syntax of an `Or` operation is:

```
object expression 1 Or object expression 2
```

The following two examples show how the `Or` operator works:

✦ `[Last Name] = "Williams" Or [Last Name] = "Johnson"` is True if Last Name is either Williams or Johnson.

✦ `[Animal Type] = "Frog" Or [Animal Color] = "Green"` is True if the animal is a frog or any animal that is green (a snake, bird, and so forth).

If the condition of either side of the `Or` operator is True, a True value is returned. Table 12-2 demonstrates the results.

	Table 12-2	
	Or Expression Resultants	
Expression 1	*Expression 2*	*Return Resultant*
True	True	True
True	False	True
True	Null	True
False	True	True
False	False	False
False	Null	Null
Null	True	True
Null	False	Null
Null	Null	Null

The Not operator

The *Not operator* is used for negating a numeric object; the operator returns the value True if the condition is not true. This operator reverses the logical result of the expression.

The general syntax of a `Not` operation is:

```
Not numeric object expression
```

The following example shows how to use the `Not` operator:

> `Not [Final Sales Amount] >= 1000` is true if Final Sales Amount is less than 1000.

If the numeric object is Null, the resulting condition is Null. Table 12-3 demonstrates the results.

	Table 12-3	
	Not Operator Resultants	
Expression	**Return Resultant**	
True	False	
False	True	
Null	Null	

Miscellaneous operators

Access has three very useful miscellaneous operators:

```
Between...And    Range
In               List comparison
Is               Reserved word
```

The Between...And operator

You can use the *Between...And operator* to determine whether an object is within a specific range of values. This is the general syntax:

```
object expression Between value 1 And value 2
```

If the value of the object expression is between value 1 and value 2, the result is True; otherwise, it is False.

The following is an example of the Between...And operator that uses the IIF function for a calculated control:

```
IIF([Amount Owed] Between 0 And 250, "Due 30 Days," "Due NOW")
```

This displays a 30-day-past due notice for values of $250 or less, and due-now notices for values over $250.

The In operator

The *In operator* is used to determine whether an object is equal to any value in a specific list. This is the general syntax:

```
object expression In (value1, value2, value3, ...)
```

If the object expression is found in the list, the result is True; otherwise, the result is False.

The following example also uses the `IIF` function. Here, the `In` operator is used for a control value in a form:

```
IIF([Animal Type] In ("Cat," "Dog"), "Common Pet," "Unusual
Pet")
```

This displays the message `Common Pet` if Animal Type is a cat or dog.

The Is (reserved word) operator

The *Is operator* is used only with the keyword Null to determine whether an object has nothing in it. This is the general syntax:

```
object expression Is Null, value 1
```

This example is a validation-check message in a data-entry form to force entry of a field:

```
IIF([Customer Name] Is Null, "Name Must be Entered,""")
```

Operator precedence

When you work with complex expressions that have many operators, Access must determine which operator to evaluate first, and then which is next, and so forth. To do this, Access has a built-in predetermined order, known as *operator precedence*. Access always follows this order unless you use parentheses to specify otherwise.

Parentheses are used to group parts of an expression and override the default order of precedence. Operations within parentheses are performed before any operations outside of them. Inside the parentheses, Access follows the predetermined operator precedence.

Precedence is determined first according to category of the operator. The operator rank by order of precedence is:

1. Mathematical
2. Comparison
3. Boolean

Each category contains its own order of precedence, which is explained next.

The mathematical precedence

Within the general category of mathematical operators, this order of precedence is in effect:

1. Exponentiation
2. Negation
3. Multiplication and/or division (left to right)
4. Integer division
5. Modulo
6. Addition and/or subtraction (left to right)
7. String concatenation

The comparison precedence

Comparison operators observe this order of precedence:

1. Equal
2. Not equal
3. Less than
4. Greater than
5. Less than or equal to
6. Greater than or equal to
7. Like

The Boolean precedence

The Boolean category follows this order of precedence:

1. Not
2. And
3. Or
4. Xor
5. Eqv
6. Imp

Precedence Order

Simple mathematics provides an example of order of precedence. Remember that Access performs operations within parentheses before operations that are not in parentheses. Also remember that multiplication and division operations are performed before addition or subtraction operations.

For example, what is the answer to this simple equation?

X=10+3*4

If your answer is 52, you need a better understanding of precedence in Access. If your answer is 22, you're right. If your answer is anything else, you need a calculator!

Multiplication is performed before addition by the rules of mathematical precedence. Therefore, the equation 10+3*4 is evaluated in this order:

3*4 is performed first, which yields an answer of 12. 12 is then added to 10, which yields 22.

Look at what happens when you add parentheses to the equation. What is the answer to this simple equation?

X=(10+3)*4

Now the answer is 52. Within parentheses, the values 10 and 3 are added first; then the result (13) is multiplied by 4, which yields 52.

What Are Functions?

Functions are small programs that always, by definition, return a value based on some calculation, comparison, or evaluation that the function performs. The value returned can be string, logic, or numeric, depending on the type of function. Access provides hundreds of common functions that are used in tables, queries, forms, and reports. You can also create your own user-defined functions (UDFs) using the Access Visual Basic language.

Using functions in Access

Functions perform specialized operations that enhance the utility of Access. Many times you find yourself using functions as an integral part of Access. The following are examples of the types of tasks functions can accomplish:

✦ Determine a default value in a table

✦ Place the current date and time on a report

✦ Convert data from one type to another

✦ Perform financial operations

✦ Display a field in a specific format

✦ Look up and return a value based on another

✦ Perform an action upon the triggering of an event

Access functions can perform financial, mathematical, comparative, and other operations. Therefore, functions are used just about everywhere—in queries, forms, reports, validation rules, and so forth.

Many Access functions evaluate or convert data from one type to another; others perform an action. Some Access functions require use of parameters; others operate without them.

Note   A parameter is a value that you supply to the function when you run it. The value can be an object name, a constant, or a quantity.

Access functions can be quickly identified because they always end with parentheses. If a function uses parameters, the parameters are placed inside the parentheses immediately after the function name.

Examples of Access functions are:

✦ Now( ) returns the current date and time.

✦ Rnd( ) returns a random number.

✦ Ucase( ) returns the uppercase of an object.

✦ Format( ) returns a user-specified formatted expression.

Types of functions

Access offers several types of functions. They can be placed in the following general categories:

✦ Conversion

✦ Date/Time

✦ Financial (SQL)

✦ Financial (monetary)

✦ Mathematical

✦ String manipulation

✦ Domain

What Is a Program?

A program is a series of defined steps that specify one or more actions the computer should perform. A program can be created by the user or can already exist in Access; all Access functions are already created programs. For example, a Ucase() function is a small program. If you employ Ucase () on a string, such as "Michael R. Irwin," Access creates a new string from the existing string, converting each letter to uppercase. The program starts at the leftmost letter, first converting *M* to *M* and then *i* to *I*, and so forth, until the entire string is converted. As it converts each letter, the program concatenates it to a new string.

Conversion

Conversion functions change the data type from one type to another. A few common functions are listed here:

Str() returns a numeric as a string:

> **Str(921.234)** returns "921.234".

> Val() returns a numeric value from a string:

> **Val("1234.56")** returns 1234.56.

> Val("10 Farmview Ct") returns 10.

Format() returns an expression according to the user-specified format:

> Format("Next,"">") returns NEXT.

> Format("123456789,""@@@-@@-@@@@") returns 123-45-6789.

> Format(#12/25/93#,"d-mmmm-yyyy") returns 25-December-1993.

Date/Time

Date/Time functions work with date and time expressions. The following are some common Date/Time functions:

Now() returns the current date and time: 3/4/99 12:22:34 PM.

Time() returns the current time in 12-hour format: 12:22:34 PM.

Date() returns the current date (vs. Now() which returns date and time): 3/4/99.

Financial (SQL)

Financial (SQL) functions perform aggregate financial operations on a set of values. The set of values is contained in a field. The field can be in a form, report, or query. Two common SQL functions are:

✦ Avg()   An example is Avg([Scores]).

✦ Sum()   An example is Sum([Gross Amount] + [Tax] + [Shipping]).

Financial (monetary)

Financial (monetary) functions perform financial operations. Two monetary functions are:

NPV() is the net present value, based on a series of payments and a discount rate. The syntax is:

> NPV(discount rate, cash flow array())

DDB() is the double-declining balance method of depreciation return. The syntax is:

> DDB(initial cost, salvage value, life of product, period of asset depreciation)

Mathematical

Mathematical functions perform specific calculations. The following are some mathematical functions, with examples of how to use them.

Int() determines the integer of a specific value:

> **Int(1234.55)** results in 1234.

> **Int(-55.1)** results in -56.

Fix() determines the correct integer for a negative number:

> **Fix(-1234.55)** results in -1234.

Sqr() determines the square root of a number:

> **Sqr(9)** returns 3.

> **Sqr(14)** returns 3.742.

String manipulation

String functions manipulate text-based expressions. Here are some common uses of these functions:

Right() returns the rightmost characters of a string:

> Right("abcdefg,"4) returns "defg."

Len() returns the length of a string:

> Len("abcdefgh") results in 8.

Lcase() returns the lowercase of the string:

> **Lcase("Michael R. Irwin")** returns michael r. irwin.

Domain

A *domain* is a set of records contained in a table, a query, or an SQL expression. A query dynaset is an example of a domain. Domain aggregate functions determine specific statistics about a specific domain.

Two examples of domain functions are:

DAvg() returns the arithmetic mean (average) of a set of values:

> DAvg("[Total Amount],""Visits") determines the average billing for patients.
>
> DCount() returns the number of records specified.

What Are Expressions?

In general, an *expression* is the means used to explain or model something to someone or something. In computer terminology, an expression is generally defined as a symbol, sign, figure, or set of symbols that presents or represents an algebraic fact as a quantity or operation. The expression is a representative object that Access can use to interpret something and, based on that interpretation, to obtain specific information. More simply put, an expression is a term or series of terms controlled by operators. Expressions are a fundamental part of Access operations.

You can use expressions in Access to accomplish a variety of tasks. You can use an expression as a property setting in SQL statements, in queries and filters, or in macros and actions. Expressions can set criteria for a query, filter, or control macros, or perform as arguments in user-defined functions.

Access evaluates an expression each time it is used. If an expression is in a form or report, Access calculates the value every time the form refreshes (as with changing records and so forth). This ensures accuracy of the results. If an expression is used as a criterion in a query, Access evaluates the expression every time the query is executed, thereby ensuring that the criterion reflects any changes, additions, or deletions to records since the last execution of the query. If an expression is used in the table design as a validation rule, Access executes the evaluation each time the field is trespassed to determine whether the value is allowed in the field; this expression may be based on another field's value!

To give you a better understanding of expressions, consider the examples that follow—all are examples of expressions:

```
=[Customer First Name] & " " & [Customer Last Name]
=[Total Amount] - ([Total Amount] * [Discount])
<25
[Deceased]=Yes
[Animal Type] = "Cat" And [Gender] = "M"
[Date of Birth] Between 1/91 And 12/93
```

Each is a valid expression. Access can use them in a variety of ways: as validation rules, query criteria, calculated controls, control sources, and control-source properties.

The parts of an expression

As the examples in the preceding section demonstrated, expressions can be simple or complex. They can include a combination of operators, object names, functions, literal values, and constants.

Remembering that expressions don't need to contain all these parts, you should have an understanding of each of the following uniquely identifiable portions of an expression:

Operators: `>, =, *, And, Or, Not, Like,` and so on.

Operators indicate what type of action (operation) will be performed on one or more elements of an expression.

Object names: `Forms![Add a Customer & Pets], [Customer Address], [Pet Name]`

Object names, also known as *identifiers*, are the actual objects: tables, forms, reports, controls, or fields.

Functions: `Date(), DLookUp(), DateDiff()`

Functions always return a value. The resultant value can be created by a calculation, a conversion of data, or an evaluation. You can use a built-in Access function or a user-defined function that you create.

Literal values: `100, Jan. 1, 1993, "Cat," "[A-D]*"`

These are actual values that you supply to the expression. Literal values can be numbers, strings, or dates. Access uses the values exactly as they are entered.

Constants: `Yes, No, Null, True, False`

Constants represent values that do not change.

The following illustration demonstrates the parts of an expression:

`[Follow Up Date] = Date() + 30`

`[Follow Up Date]` is an object name or identifier.

`=` is an operator.

`Date()` is a function.

`+` is an operator.

`30` is a literal.

Creating an expression

Expressions are commonly entered in property windows, action arguments, and criteria grids. As you create expressions, the area is scrolled so that you can continue to enter the expression. Although you can enter an expression in this manner, it is usually desirable to see the entire expression as you enter it. This is especially true when you are working with long, complex expressions. Access has a Zoom box that you can use to change how much of the expression you see as you enter it. Open this box by clicking where you want to enter your expression and pressing Shift+F2.

As you enter expressions, Access may insert certain characters for you when you change focus. Access checks your syntax and automatically inserts these characters:

✦ Brackets ([]) around control names that have no spaces or punctuation in the name

✦ Pound signs (#) around dates it recognizes

✦ Quotation marks (" ") around text that contains no spaces or punctuation in the body

Note   The term *changing focus* refers to the movement of the insertion point out of the location where you are entering the expression, which is accomplished by pressing Tab or by moving the mouse and clicking on another area of the screen.

Caution   Access reports an error when it changes focus under these conditions: Access doesn't understand the date form entered, the name of the control contains spaces, or a control is not placed in brackets.

Entering object names

Object names are identified by placing brackets ([]) around the element. Access requires the use of brackets when the object contains a space or punctuation in its name. If these conditions are not present, you can ignore the brackets — Access inserts them automatically. Therefore, the following expressions are syntactically identical:

```
Breed + [Type of Animal]
[Breed] + [Type of Animal]
```

Notice that in both cases the brackets are placed around Type of Animal because this object name contains spaces.

Although it isn't necessary to enter brackets around objects such as Breed in the second example, it is good programming practice to always surround object names with brackets for consistency in entry.

Entering text

Placing quotation marks around the text element of an expression identifies text. Access automatically places the quotation marks for you if you forget to add them.

As an example, you can type **Cat, Dog,** and **Frog** into separate criteria cells of a query, and Access automatically adds the quotation marks around each of these three entries. Access recognizes these as objects and helps you.

Entering date/time values

Placing pound signs (#) around the date/time element identifies date/time data. Access will evaluate any valid date/time format automatically and place the pound signs around the element for you.

Expression Builder

Access has added an *Expression Builder* tool to help you build complex expressions. You can use it anywhere you can build an expression (such as when specifying criteria for a query or creating a calculated field on a form or report). You can activate the builder tool in two ways:

✦ Press the Build button on the toolbar (the button with the ellipsis on it).

✦ Click the *right* mouse button and select Build from the shortcut menu.

Special identifier operators and expressions

Access has two special *identifier operators*: the dot (.) and the exclamation point (!). Access tables provide many ways to display and access objects. You can use fields and their contents, and any field object can be reused repeatedly. You can display the field object in numerous forms and reports by using the same reference, the field object name, in every form and report.

For example, the field Pet Name in the Pets table can be used in seven different forms. When you want to use the Pet Name field in an expression for a comparison, how do you tell Access which copy of the field Pet Name it should use for the expression? Because Access is a Windows database, it is possible to have several different forms in the same session on the same computer. In fact, it is possible to have multiple copies of Access running the same data and forms.

A Few Words About Controls and Properties

When you create a form or report, you place many different objects on the form — fields in text boxes, text labels, buttons, checkboxes, combo boxes, lines, rectangles, and so on.

As you select and place these objects on a form, each object is assigned a *control name*. Access supplies the control name according to predefined rules. For example, control names for fields default to a control-source name of the field name. The field name appears in the text box on the form. The label for the text box is assigned the control name Text, with a sequence number attached to it (for example, `Text11` or `Text12`). The sequence number is added to make each control name unique.

After all objects are placed on the form, you can identify any object on the form (line, button, text box, and so on) by its unique control name. This control name is what you use to reference a specific table field (or field on a form). You can change the name of the control that Access assigned to the object if you want. The only requirement for the new control name is that it must be unique to the form or report that contains it.

Every object on the form (and don't forget that the form itself is an object) has associated *properties*. These are the individual characteristics of each object; as such, they are accessible by a control name. Properties control the appearance of the object (color, size, sunken, alignment, and so forth). They also affect the structure, specifying format, default value, validation rules, and control name. In addition, properties designate the *behavior* of a control — for instance, whether the field can grow or shrink and whether you can edit it. Behaviors also affect actions specified for the event properties, such as On Enter and On Push.

With all this confusion, there must be a way to tell Access which Pet Name field object you want the expression to use. That is the purpose of the dot and exclamation point as operator identifiers. These symbols identify and maintain clarity in determining which field to use.

The ! (exclamation) identifier operator

The exclamation mark (!) is a key symbol that is used in conjunction with several reserved words. One such reserved word is Forms. When this word is followed by !, Access is being told that the next object name is the form object name that you want to reference.

As an example, say that you have a Date of Birth field that is in two forms — [Customer & Pets] and [Pet Specifics]. (These two form names are objects; you need to use brackets to reference them.) You want to refer to the Date of Birth field in the [Pet Specifics] form. The way to specify this form is by use of the ! and the *Forms* reserved word:

```
Forms![Pet Specifics]
```

Now that the form is specified, you need to further refine the scope to add the field Date of Birth.

Note   Although Chapter 15 covers controls and properties, by this point you should have a partial understanding of what properties and controls are (for a refresher, see the preceding sidebar).

Actually, what you are specifying is a control on the form. That control will use the field you need, which is Date of Birth. The control has the same name as the field. Therefore, you access this specific object by using the following expression:

```
Forms![Pet Specifics]![Date of Birth]
```

The second exclamation mark specifies a control on a form — one identified by the reserved word *Forms*.

By following the properties of each object, starting with the object Forms, you can trace the control source object back to a field in the original table.

In summary, the exclamation-point identifier is always followed by an object name. This object name is defined by using the name of a form, report, field, or other control name that was created in the database. If you don't use the existing name for the desired object, you can change the default value name of the source.

The . (dot) identifier operator

The . (dot) is also a key symbol that is used in conjunction with expression identification operators. Normally it is placed immediately after a user-defined object. Unlike the !, the . (dot) usually identifies a property of a specific object. Therefore, if you want to determine the value of the Visible property of the same control you worked with before, you specify it as follows:

```
Forms![Pet Specifics]![Date of Birth].Visible
```

This gives you the value for the Visible property of the specific field on the specific form.

Note   Normally the . (dot) identifier is used to obtain a value that corresponds to a property of an object. Sometimes, however, you can use it between a table name and a field name when you are accessing a value associated with a specific field in a specific table, as shown here:

```
[Pets].[Pet Name]
```

A thorough analysis of the two special identifier operators is beyond the scope of this book. Even so, you'll find that these identifiers enable you to find any object and the values associated with its properties.

Summary

In this chapter, you learned about the building blocks of Access operations: operators, functions, and expressions. The chapter covered these points:

✦ Operators let you add numbers, compare values, put strings together, and create complicated relational expressions.

✦ The many types of operators include mathematical, relational, string, Boolean operators, as well as a group of miscellaneous operators.

✦ The relational operators =, <>, >, >=, <, and <= make comparisons.

✦ To concatenate two strings, use the & operator.

✦ You can use five pattern-matching wildcards with the Like operator: *, ?, #, [list], and [!list].

✦ The Boolean operators are And, Or, Eqv, Imp, Xor, and Not.

✦ Operator precedence determines the order in which Access evaluates the various parts of an expression.

✦ Functions are small programs that return a value. Access has hundreds of built-in functions.

✦ Functions are classified as conversion, date/time, financial, mathematical, string, or domain.

✦ Expressions are used to create a calculation or to model a process.

✦ Expressions use operators, object names, functions, literal values, and constants.

✦ The Expression Builder tool can be used to create an expression.

✦ Object names are entered in brackets ([]) to identify them. Common objects include field names.

✦ The two special identifiers, the exclamation point and the dot, help identify Access objects, such as forms, reports, queries, and tables. These identifiers can also identify properties.

In the next chapter, you learn to create relationships and joins in queries.

✦   ✦   ✦

Creating Relations and Joins in Queries

In previous chapters, you worked with simple queries by using the single table Pets. Using a query to obtain information from a single table is common; often, however, information from several related tables is needed. For example, you may want to obtain a customer's name and the type of pets the customer owns. In this chapter, you learn how to use more than one table to obtain information.

Adding More Than One Table to the Query Window

In Chapter 11, you learned about the different tables in the Mountain Animal Hospital database system. This system is composed of four primary tables and four lookup tables. You learned about primary and foreign table keys and their importance for linking two tables together. You learned how to create relationships between two tables at the table level by using the Tools ⇨ Relationships menu choice in the Database window. Finally, you learned how referential integrity rules affect data in tables.

After you create the tables for your database and decide how the tables are related to one another, you are ready to begin creating multiple-table queries to obtain information from several tables at the same time.

By adding more than one table to a query and then selecting fields from the tables in the query, you can view information from your database just as though the information from the several tables was in one table. As an example, suppose you need to send a letter to all owners of snakes who brought their pets in for visits in the last two months. For this data, you need to get the information from three separate tables: Pets, Customer, and Visits. This can be done using the Pets and Visits tables and creating a query for all animals where the Type of Animal field equals snake and where Visit Date falls between today's date and today's date minus two months. The relationship between the Pets and Customer tables gives access to the customer information for each snake, permitting you to create a report form using the related information from the tables Pets, Visits, and Customer.

The first step in creating a multiple-table query is to open each table in the Query window. The following steps show how to open the Pets, Customer, and Visits tables in a single query:

1. Click the Query object in the Database window.
2. Click the New toolbar button to create a new query.
3. Select Design View and click the OK button in the New Query dialog box.
4. Select the Pets table (in the Show Table dialog box) by double-clicking the table name.
5. Select the Customer table by double-clicking the table name.
6. Select the Visits table by double-clicking the table name.
7. Click the Close button in the Show Table dialog box.

Note   You can also add each table by highlighting the table in the list separately and clicking Add.

Figure 13-1 shows the top pane of the Query Design window with the three tables you just added: Pets, Customer, and Visits.

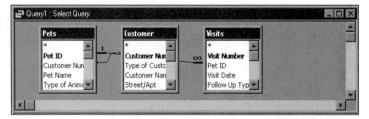

Figure 13-1: The Query Design window with three tables added.

Note   You can add more tables by selecting Query ➪ Show Table from the Query Design window or by clicking the Show Table icon.

Working with the Table/Query Pane

As Figure 13-1 shows, a single line from the primary key field to the foreign key field connects each table. Actually, on your screen it probably looks as if two lines connect Pets to Customer and a single line runs from Customer to Visits. Later you learn how to move the table design so that the lines appear correctly.

The join line

When Access displays each set of related tables, it places a line between the two tables. This line is known as a join line. A *join line* is a graphical line that represents the link between two tables. In this example, the join line goes from the Pets table to the Customer table to connect the two Customer Number fields. A join line also runs from Pets to Visits, connecting the Pet ID fields in these two tables.

This link is created automatically because a relationship was set in the Database window. If Access already knows what the relationship is, it automatically creates the link for you when the tables are added to a query. The relationship is displayed as a join line between two tables.

If Referential Integrity is checked in the relationship between two tables, Access displays a thick portion of the line right at the table window similar to the line in Figure 13-2. The line starts heavy and becomes thin between Pets and Visits (heavy on both ends). This line variation tells you that Referential Integrity has been set up between the two tables in the Relationship Builder. If a one-to-many relationship exists, the many relationship is denoted by an infinity sign ().

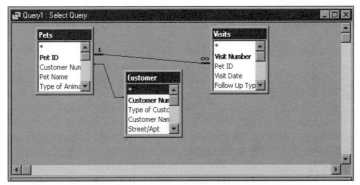

Figure 13-2: Resizing the Query Design panes. Note that the Table/Query pane is larger.

Note   If you have not specified a relationship between two tables and the following conditions are true, Access 2000 automatically joins the tables:

1. The tables have a field in both with the same name.

   The field with the same name in both tables is the same type (text, numeric, and so on).

2. The field is a *primary key* field in one of the tables.

Tip   Access 2000 automatically joins the table if a relationship exists. However, you can turn this property off by deselecting the default Enable AutoJoin option from the global options tabbed dialog box. To display this option, select Tools ⇨ Options, click the Tables/Queries tab in the options box, and deselect the Enable AutoJoin option (under the Query design section).

Manipulating the Table Design window

Each Table Design window begins at a fixed size, which shows approximately four fields and 12 characters for each field. Each Table Design window is a true window and behaves like one; it can be resized and moved. If you have more fields than will fit in the Table Design window, a scroll bar attaches to the table design. The scroll bar lets you scroll through the fields in the Table Design window.

Note   After a relationship is created between tables, the join line remains between the two fields. As you move through a table selecting fields, the graphical line will move relative to the linked fields. For example, if the scroll box moves down (toward the bottom of the window) in the Customer table, the join line moves up with the customer number, eventually stopping at the top of the table window.

When you're working with many tables, these join lines can become visually confusing as they cross or overlap. If you move through the table, the line eventually becomes visible, and the field it is linked to becomes obvious.

Resizing the Table/Query pane

When you place table designs on the Table/Query pane, they appear in a fixed size with little spacing between tables. When you add a table to the top pane, it initially shows five fields. If more fields are in the table, a scroll bar is added to the box (right side). The table box may show only part of a long field name, the rest being truncated by the box size. You can move the tables around the pane and resize them to show more field names or more of the field name. The first step, however, is to resize the pane itself. The Query Design window has two panes. The top pane displays your table designs, whereas the QBE (Query by Example) pane below lets you enter fields, sort orders, and criteria. Often the top pane is larger than the bottom pane; you may want more space for the design and less space for the QBE pane. The window tells you that you are creating a Select query (Query1: Select Query). If you change the query to another type of query (which you do in later chapters), it changes the name of the Query Design window to let you know what type of query you are creating.

You can resize the Table/Query pane by placing your cursor on the thick line below the elevator. This is the *window split bar*. The cursor changes to a double vertical arrow, as shown in Figure 13-2, which allows you to drag the split bar up or down. To resize the panes, follow these steps:

1. Place the cursor on the window split bar

2. Hold down the mouse button and drag the split bar down

3. Release the bar when it is two lines below the QBE row or:

The top pane is now much larger; the bottom pane is smaller but it still displays the entire QBE Design area. You now have space to move the table designs around and properly view the Table/Query pane.

Tip   You can build a database diagram so that you view only the table designs by moving the split bar to the bottom of the screen and then positioning the table designs as you want within the full-screen area.

Moving a table

You can move table designs in the Table/Query pane by placing the mouse pointer on the title bar of a table design (where the name of the table is) and dragging the table to a new location. You may want to move the table designs for a better working view or to clean up a confusing database diagram (like the one shown in Figure 13-2). To move table designs, follow these steps:

1. Place the mouse pointer on the title bar of the Customer table on the name *Customer*.

2. Drag the Customer table design straight down until the top of the table design appears where the bottom was when you started.

The screen should now look like Figure 13-3. You can see that each line is now an individual line that goes from one table's primary key to the foreign key in another table.

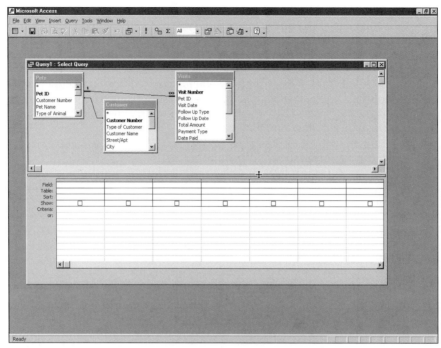

Figure 13-3: The repositioned Pets, Customer, and Visits tables.

You can move the table designs anywhere in the top pane. You can spread them out by moving the table designs farther apart. You can also rearrange the table designs. You may want to place the Customer table first, followed by the Pets table and then the Visits table. Remember that in this exercise you are trying to view the snakes that have been in for a visit in the last two months so that you can send a letter to the customer. So the sequence of Pets, Customer, and Visits makes sense. You generally want to view your diagram with a particular business purpose in mind. Pets is the main table in this business example and it needs to retrieve information from both the Visits and Customer tables.

Removing a table

There are times when you need to remove tables from a query. Any table can be removed from the Query window. Follow these steps to delete the Visits table, bearing in mind that you can restore it later:

1. Select the Visits table in the top pane of the Query window by clicking either the table or a field in the table.

2. Press the Delete key or select Edit ➪ Delete.

Note   Only one table can be removed at a time from the Query window. The menu choice Edit ➪ Clear Grid does *not* remove all tables; it removes all fields from the QBE pane. You can also remove a table by right-clicking a table and selecting Remove Table from the shortcut menu.

When you delete a table, any join lines to that table are deleted as well. When you delete a table, there is no warning or confirmation dialog box. The table is simply removed from the screen.

Adding more tables

You may decide to add more tables to a query or you may accidentally delete a table and need to add it back. You can accomplish this task by either selecting Query ➪ Show Table or clicking the *right* mouse button and selecting Show Table from the shortcut menu that appears. When you use one of these methods, the Show Table dialog box that appeared when you created the query is redisplayed. To restore the Visits table to the screen, follow these steps:

1. Move the mouse pointer to the top pane (outside of any existing tables) and press the right mouse button. Select Show Table from the menu.

2. Select the Visits table by double-clicking the table name.

3. Click the Close button in the Show Table dialog box.

Access returns you to the Table/Query pane of the Visits table and redisplays the join line.

Resizing a table design

You can also resize each of the table designs by placing the cursor on one of the table design borders. The table design is nothing but a window; thus, you can enlarge or reduce it vertically, horizontally, or diagonally by placing the cursor on the appropriate border. When you enlarge the table design vertically, you can see more fields than the default number (five). By making the table design larger horizontally, you can see the complete list of field names. Then, when you resize the Table/Query pane to take up the entire window, you can create a database diagram.

Creating a database diagram

Figure 13-4 is a database diagram for the three tables that displays all the fields. The more tables and relationships there are, the more important a database diagram is to viewing the data graphically with the proper relationships visible. In upcoming chapters, many different database diagrams are displayed as queries are used to assemble the data for various forms and reports.

In Figure 13-4, the Table/Query pane is expanded to almost its full size and the QBE pane is displayed (done at 800 x 600 resolution). It's OK if you can't see any of the QBE pane on your screen. You can get to the QBE pane by using the split bar to resize. When working with fields in the QBE pane, keep the screen split so that both panes are visible.

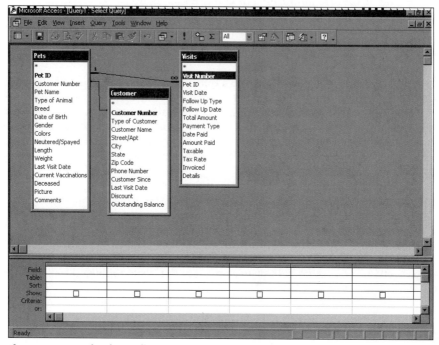

Figure 13-4: A database diagram.

 Caution   Although you can switch panes by pressing F6, you can't see where the insertion point is in the QBE pane while the Table/Query pane is displayed in full-screen size and the QBE pane is not visible.

 On the CD-ROM   If you are following the examples in this chapter, resize the panes so that you can see both the Table Design pane and the QBE pane.

Adding Fields from More Than One Table

You add fields from more than one table to the query in exactly the same way as when you're working with a single table. You can add fields one at a time, many fields grouped together, or all the fields from one or all tables.

Cross-Reference   Adding fields from a single table is covered in detail in Chapter 9; this chapter covers the topic in less detail, but focuses on the differences between single- and multiple-table field selection.

Adding a single field

You can select a single field from any table by using any of several methods:

✦ Double-click a field name in the Table/Query pane.

✦ Click a field name in the Table/Query pane and drag it to the QBE pane.

✦ Click an empty Field: cell in the QBE pane and type a field name.

✦ Click an empty Field: cell and select the field from the drop-down list.

Caution   If you type a field name in an empty Field: cell that is in both tables, Access enters the field name from the first table that it finds containing that field. Access searches the tables, starting from the left side in the top pane.

If you select the field from the drop-down list in the Field: cell, you see the name of the table first, followed by a period and the field name. For example, the field Pet ID in the Pets table is displayed as *Pets.Pet ID*. This helps you select the right field name. Using this method, you can select a common field name from a specific table.

The easiest way to select fields is still to double-click the query/table designs. To do so, you may have to resize the table designs to see the fields that you want to select. To select Customer Name, Pet Name, Type of Animal, and Visit Date, follow these steps:

1. Double-click Customer Name in the Customer table.

2. Double-click Pet Name in the Pets table.

3. Double-click Type of Animal in the Pets table.

4. Double-click Visit Date in the Visits table.

Viewing the table names

When you're working with two or more tables, the field names in the QBE pane can become confusing. You may find yourself asking, for example, just which table the field Customer Number is from.

Access automatically maintains the table name that is associated with each field displayed in the QBE pane. The default is to display the table name below the name of the field. If you do not want to show the table name of each field in the QBE pane, select View ➪ Table Names and the toggle will be turned off (unchecked).

This selection controls the display of table names immediately below the corresponding field name in the QBE pane. Figure 13-5 shows the QBE pane with the row Table: below the Field: row. It contains the name of the table for each field.

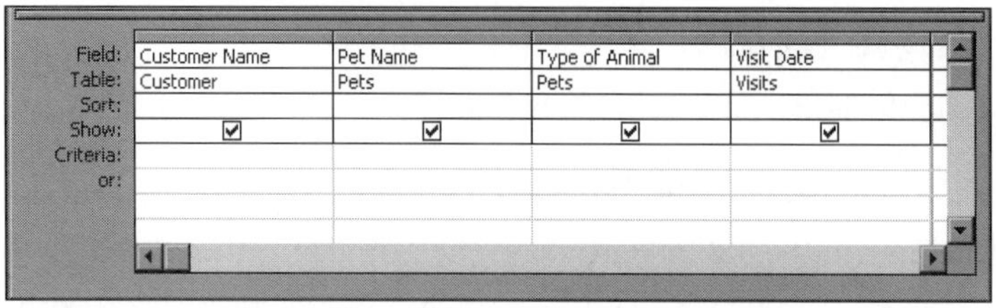

Field:	Customer Name	Pet Name	Type of Animal	Visit Date
Table:	Customer	Pets	Pets	Visits
Sort:				
Show:	☑	☑	☑	☑
Criteria:				
or:				

Figure 13-5: The QBE pane with table names displayed.

The display of the table name is only for your information. Access always maintains the table name associated with the field names.

After you add fields to a query, you can view your resultant data at any time. Although you eventually limit the display of data to snakes that have visited you during a specific two-month period, you can view all the data now by selecting the Datasheet icon. Figure 13-6 displays the data as currently selected. The fields are resized to show all the data values.

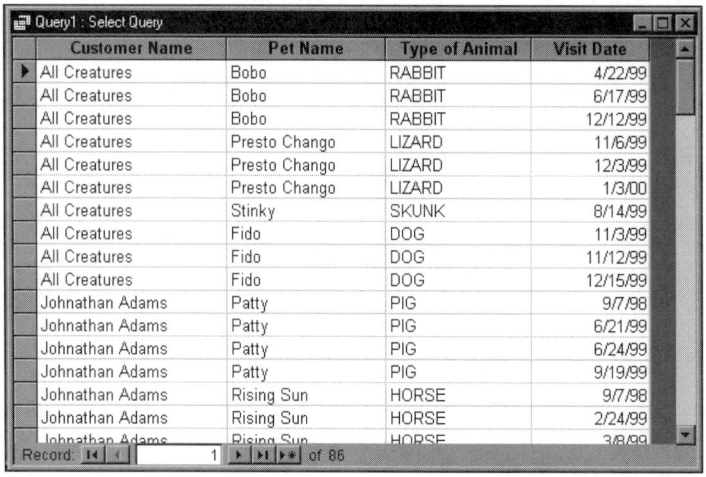

Query1 : Select Query

Customer Name	Pet Name	Type of Animal	Visit Date
All Creatures	Bobo	RABBIT	4/22/99
All Creatures	Bobo	RABBIT	6/17/99
All Creatures	Bobo	RABBIT	12/12/99
All Creatures	Presto Chango	LIZARD	11/6/99
All Creatures	Presto Chango	LIZARD	12/3/99
All Creatures	Presto Chango	LIZARD	1/3/00
All Creatures	Stinky	SKUNK	8/14/99
All Creatures	Fido	DOG	11/3/99
All Creatures	Fido	DOG	11/12/99
All Creatures	Fido	DOG	12/15/99
Johnathan Adams	Patty	PIG	9/7/98
Johnathan Adams	Patty	PIG	6/21/99
Johnathan Adams	Patty	PIG	6/24/99
Johnathan Adams	Patty	PIG	9/19/99
Johnathan Adams	Rising Sun	HORSE	9/7/98
Johnathan Adams	Rising Sun	HORSE	2/24/99
Johnathan Adams	Rising Sun	HORSE	3/8/99

Record: 1 of 86

Figure 13-6: Datasheet view of data from multiple tables.

Adding multiple fields at the same time

The process of adding multiple fields at the same time is identical to adding multiple fields in a single table query. When you're adding multiple fields from several tables, you must add them from one table at a time. The easiest way to do this is to select multiple fields and drag them together down to the QBE pane.

You can select multiple contiguous fields by clicking the first field of the list, then clicking the last field while holding down the Shift key (as you click the last field that you want to add). You can also select random fields in the list by holding down the Ctrl key while clicking individual fields with the mouse.

Adding all table fields

To add all table fields at the same time, select which table's fields you want to add and then select the fields to be added. You can select all the fields by either double-clicking the title bar of the table name or by selecting the Asterisk (*) field. These two methods, however, produce very different results.

Selecting all fields using the double-clicking method

One method of selecting all the fields is to double-click the title bar of the table whose fields you want to select.

This method automatically fills in each column of the QBE pane. The fields are added in the order of their position in the table, from left to right (based on their field order in the table). By default, Access displays only the first five fields. You can change the column width of each field to display more or fewer columns.

Selecting all fields using the Asterisk (*) method

The first object in each table is an asterisk (at the top of the field list), which is known as the *all-field reference tag*. When you select and drag the asterisk to the QBE pane, all fields in the table are added to the QBE pane, but there is a distinct difference between this method and the double-clicking method: When you add the all-field reference tag (*), the QBE pane shows only one cell with the name of the table and an asterisk. For example, if you select the * in the Pets table, you see *Pets.* * displayed in one field row cell.

Unlike selecting all the fields, the asterisk places a reference to all the fields in a single column. When you drag multiple columns, as in the preceding example, you drag actual table field names to the query. If you later change the design of the table, you also have to change the design of the query. The advantage of using the asterisk for selecting all fields is that the query doesn't need to be changed if you add, delete, or rename fields in the underlying table or query. Changing fields in the underlying table or query automatically adds fields to or removes fields from the query.

Caution   Selecting the * does have one drawback: You cannot perform criteria conditions on the asterisk column itself. You have to add an individual field from the table and enter the criterion. If you add a field for a criterion (when using the *), the query displays the field twice — once for the * field and a second time for the criterion field. Therefore, you may want to deselect the Show: cell of the criterion field.

Understanding the Limitations of Multiple-Table Queries

When you create a query with multiple files, there are limitations to what fields can be edited. Generally, you can change data in a query dynaset, and your changes are saved to the underlying tables. A primary key field normally cannot be edited if referential integrity is in effect and if the field is part of a relationship (unless Cascade Updates is set to Yes).

To update a table from a query, a value in a specific record in the query must represent a single record in the underlying table. This means that you cannot update fields in a Crosstab or Totals query because they both group records together to display grouped information. Instead of displaying the actual underlying table data, they display records of data that are calculated and stored in a virtual (nonreal) table called a *snapshot*.

Updating limitations

In Access, the records in your tables may not always be updatable. Table 13-1 shows when a field in a table is updatable. As Table 13-1 shows, queries based on one-to-many relationships are updatable in both tables (depending on how the query was designed). Any query that creates a *snapshot*, however, is not updatable.

Table 13-1
Rules for Updating Queries

Type of Query or Field	Updatable	Comments
One Table	Yes	
One-to-One relationship	Yes	
One-to-Many relationship	Mostly	Restrictions based on design methodology (see text)
Crosstab	No	Creates a snapshot of the data
Totals Query (Sum, Avg, etc.)	No	Works with Grouped data creating a snapshot
Unique Value property is Yes	No	Shows unique records only in a snapshot
SQL-specific queries	No	Union & Pass-through work with ODBC data
Calculated field	No	Will recalculate automatically
Read-only fields	No	If opened read-only or on read-only drive (CD-ROM)
Permissions denied	No	Insert, Replace, or Delete are not granted
ODBC Tables with no Primary Key	No	A primary key (unique index) must exist
Paradox Table with no Primary Key	No	A primary key file must exist
Locked by another user	No	Cannot be updated while a field is locked by another

Overcoming query limitations

Table 13-1 shows that there are times when queries and fields in tables are not updatable. As a general rule, any query that does aggregate calculations or is an ODBC (Open DataBase Connectivity)-based SQL (Structured Query Language) query is not updatable. All others can be updated. When your query has more than one table and some of the tables have a one-to-many relationship, there may be fields that are not updatable (depending on the design of the query).

Updating a unique index (primary key)

If a query uses two tables that have a one-to-many relationship, the one side of the join must have a unique (primary key) index on the field that is used for the join. If not, the fields from the one side of the query cannot be updated.

Replacing existing data in a query with a one-to-many relationship

Normally, all the fields in the many-side table are updatable in a one-to-many query; the one-side table can update all the fields *except* the primary key (join) field. Normally, this is sufficient for most database application purposes. Also, the primary key field is rarely changed in the one-side table because it is the link to the records in the joined tables.

At times, however, you may need to change the link-field contents in both tables (make a new primary key in the one table and have the database program change the link field in all the related records from the *many* table). Access 2000 lets you do this by defining a relationship between the two tables and using referential integrity. If you define a relationship and enforce referential integrity in the Relationship Builder, two checkboxes are activated. If you want to allow changes (updates) to the primary key field, check the Cascade Update Related Fields box, as shown in Figure 13-7. By checking this option, you can change the primary key field in a relationship; Access automatically updates the link field to the new value in all the other related tables.

To duplicate Figure 13-7, right-click anywhere in the top pane and select Relationships... from the shortcut menu (or Select Tools ⇨ Relationships...). The Relationships window appears. Click on the one-to-many link between the Pets and Visits tables to activate the Edit Relationships dialog box.

Design tips for updating fields in queries

✦ If you want to add records to both tables of a one-to-many relationship, include the join field from the *many*-side table and show the field in the datasheet. After doing this, records can be added starting with either table. The *one* side's join field is copied automatically to the *many* side's join field.

✦ If you do not want any fields to be updatable, set the Allow Edits property of the form to No.

✦ If you do not want to update some fields on a form, set the Tab Stop property for the control (field) to No for these fields.

✦ If you want to add records to multiple tables in a form (covered in later chapters), remember to include all (or most) of the fields from both tables. Otherwise, you will not have a complete record of data in your form.

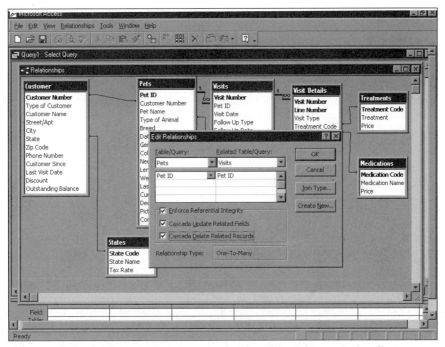

Figure 13-7: The Relationships dialog box with referential integrity in effect.

Temporary inability to update in a one-to-many relationship

When updating records on the one side of a one-to-many query, you will *not* be able to change the many-side *join* field until you save changes to the one side. You can quickly save changes to the one side by pressing Shift+Enter or selecting File ➪ Save Record. Once the one-side changes are saved, the join field in the *many*-side record can be changed.

Creating Query Joins

You can create joins between tables in these three ways:

✦ By creating relationships between the tables when you design the database (Select Tools ➪ Relationships from the Database window or click the Relationships button on the toolbar)

✦ By selecting two tables for the query that have a field that of the same type and name in both, and which field is a primary key field in one of the tables

✦ By creating joins in the Query window at the time you create a query

The first two methods are automatic. If you create relationships when designing the tables of your database, Access displays join lines based on those relationships automatically when you add the related tables to a query. It also creates an automatic join between two tables that have a common field, provided that field is a primary key in one of the tables.

There may be times when tables are added to a query that are not already related to a specific file, as in these examples:

✦ The two tables have a common field, but it is not the same name.

✦ A table is not related and cannot be related to the other table (for example, the Customer table cannot be directly joined to the Treatments table).

If you have two tables that are not automatically joined and you need to relate them, you join them in the Query Design window. Joining tables in the Query Design window does *not* create a permanent join between the tables. Rather, the join (relationship) will apply only to the table for the query you are working on.

Caution All tables in a query must be joined to at least one other table. If, for example, you place two tables in a query and *do not* join them, Access creates a query based on a *Cartesian product* (also known as the *cross product*) of the two tables. This subject is discussed later in this chapter. For now, note that a Cartesian product means that if you have 5 records in table 1 and 6 records in table 2, then the resulting query will have 30 records (5 × 6) that will probably be useless.

Joining tables

Figure 13-8 shows the joined Pets and Customer tables. Tables are not joined automatically in a query if they are not already joined at the table level, is they do not have a common named field for a primary key, or if the AutoJoin option is off. To join the Pets and Customer tables:

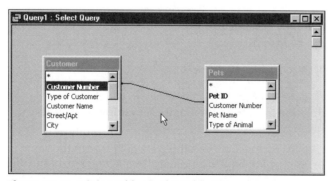

Figure 13-8: Joining tables in the Table/Query pane.

1. Select the Customer Number field in the Customer Table in the Table/Query pane.

2. Drag the highlighted field to the Pets table (as you drag the field, the Field icon appears).

3. Drop the Field icon on the Customer Number field in the Pets table.

Figure 13-8 shows the new join line after it is created. After selecting the field (Customer Number), the Field icon first appears in the Customer Number field of the Customer table; then it moves to the Pets table. As it moves between tables, the Field icon changes to the symbol that indicates the icon cannot be dropped in the area between the tables. When the icon is over the Customer Number field, it changes back to the Field icon, indicating that it can be dropped in that location. When you release the mouse button, the join line appears.

Of course, you can also create joins that make no sense, but when you view the data, you will get less-than-desirable results. If two joined fields have no values in common, you have a datasheet in which no records are selected or a Cartesian product in which each and every record is joined with each and every record in the second table. If one table has 100 records and the other has 200 records, the Cartesian join will create a table with 20,000 records and the results will make no sense.

Note   You can select either table first when you create a join.

You would never want to create a meaningless join. For example, you would not want to join the City field from the Customer table to the Date of Birth field in the Pets table. Although Access will let you create this join, the resulting dynaset will have no records in it.

Deleting joins

To delete a join line between two tables, you select the join line and press the Delete key. You can select the join line by placing the mouse pointer on any part of the line and clicking once. To practice, create a new query by adding the Customer and Pets tables, then follow these steps to delete the join line between the Pets and Customer tables:

1. Select the join line between the Customer Number field in the Pets table and the Customer table by clicking the line with the mouse button.

2. With the join line highlighted, press the Delete key.

After Step 2, the line should disappear. If you delete a join line between two tables that have a relationship set at the database level, the broken join is effective only for the query in which you broke the join. When you exit the query, the relationship between the two tables remains in effect for other operations, including subsequent queries.

You can also delete a join by selecting it and choosing Edit ➪ Delete.

Caution   If you delete a join between two tables and the tables remain in the Query window unjoined to any other tables, the solution will have unexpected results because of the Cartesian product that Access creates from the two tables. The Cartesian product is effective for only this query. The underlying relationship remains intact.

Note   Access enables you to create multiple-field joins between tables (more than one line can be drawn). The join must be between two fields that have the same data and data type; if not, the query will not find any records from the datasheet to display.

Understanding Types of Table Joins

In Chapter 11, you learned about table relationships. Access understands all types of table and query relations, including these:

- ✦ One-to-one
- ✦ One-to-many
- ✦ Many-to-one
- ✦ Many-to-many

When you specify a relationship between two tables, you establish rules for the type of relationship, not for viewing the data based on the relationship.

To view data in two tables, they must be joined through a link that is established via a common field (or group of fields) between the two tables. The method of linking the tables is known as *joining*. In a query, tables with established relationships are shown already joined. Within a query, you can create new joins or change an existing join line; just as there are different types of relationships, there are different types of joins. In the following sections, you learn about these types of joins:

- ✦ Equi-joins (inner joins)
- ✦ Outer joins
- ✦ Self-joins
- ✦ Cross-product joins (Cartesian joins)

Equi-joins (inner joins)

The default join in Access is known as an *equi-join* or *inner join*. It enables you to tell Access to select all records from both tables that have the same value in the fields that are joined together.

Note   The Access manuals refer to a default join as an equi-join (commonly referred to as an inner join in database relational theory). The terms equi-join and inner join are interchangeable and will be used interchangeably throughout this chapter.

Recall the Customer and Pets tables for an example of an equi-join. Remember that you are looking for all records from these two tables with matching fields. The Customer Number fields are common to both, so the equi-join does not show any records for customers that have no pets or any pets that do not relate to a valid customer number. The rules of referential integrity prevent pet records that are not tied to a customer number. Of course, it's possible to delete all pets from a customer or to create a new customer record with no pet records, but a pet should always be related to a valid customer. Referential integrity should keep a customer number from being deleted or changed if a pet is related to it.

Regardless of how it happens, it's possible to have a customer in the Customer table who has no pets. It's less likely, but still theoretically possible, to have a pet with no owner. If you create a query to show customers and their pets, any record of a customer without a pet or a pet record without a matching customer record will not be shown in the resulting dynaset.

It can be important to find these lost records. One of the features of a query is to perform several types of joins.

Tip   Access can help find lost records between tables. Use the Query Wizards to build a Find Unmatched Query (these are covered in Chapter 25).

Changing join properties

With the Customer and Pets tables joined, certain join behaviors (or *properties*) exist between the tables. The join property is a rule that says to display all records (for the fields you specify) that correspond to the characters found in the Customer Number field of the Customer table and in the corresponding Customer Number field of the Pets table.

To translate this rule into a practical example, this is what happens in the Customer and Pets tables:

✦ If a record in the Customer table has a number for a customer that is not found in the Pets table, then that Customer record is not shown.

✦ If a record in the Pets table has a number for a customer number that is not in the Customer table, then that Pets record is not shown.

This makes sense, at least most of the time. You don't want to see records for customers without pets — *or do you?*

A join property is a rule that is operated by Access. This rule tells Access how to interpret any exceptions (possible errors) between two tables. Should the noncorresponding records be shown?

Access has several types of joins, each with its own characteristics or behaviors. Access lets you change the type of join quickly by changing its properties. You can change join properties by selecting the join line between tables and double-clicking the line. When you do so, a Join Properties dialog box appears. If you double-click the join line between the Customer and Pets table, the dialog box in Figure 13-9 displays.

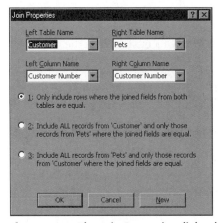

Figure 13-9: The Join Properties dialog box.

The Join Properties dialog box is has two parts: the four combo boxes and three option buttons. For now you focus on the three options buttons:

1. Only include rows where the joined fields from both tables are equal. (This is the default.)

2. Include ALL records from 'Customer' and only those records from 'Pets' where the joined fields are equal.

3. Include ALL records from 'Pets' and only those records from 'Customer' where the joined fields are equal.

The first choice is commonly known as an *inner join* and the other two are known as *outer joins*. These joins control the behavior of Access as it builds the dynaset from the query.

Inner and outer joins

Your Query Design window should display two tables in the top pane of the Query window — Customer and Pets. (If your query window does not have these two tables, create a new query and add them.) The following sections use these tables as examples to explain how inner and outer joins operate.

Displaying an inner join

To display an inner join, follow this procedure: In the QBE pane, select the fields Customer Number and Customer Name from the Customer table and the fields Pet Name and Type of Animal from the Pets table. Then display the dynaset by selecting the Datasheet button on the toolbar. The datasheet should now look like Figure 13-10, displaying each customer, all the customers' pets, and the type of animal for each pet. Scroll through the records until you reach the bottom of the datasheet.

Customer	Customer Name	Pet Name	Type of Animal
AC001	All Creatures	Bobo	RABBIT
AC001	All Creatures	Presto Chango	LIZARD
AC001	All Creatures	Stinky	SKUNK
AC001	All Creatures	Fido	DOG
AD001	Johnathan Adams	Patty	PIG
AD001	Johnathan Adams	Rising Sun	HORSE
AD002	William Adams	Dee Dee	DOG
AK001	Animal Kingdom	Margo	SQUIRREL
AK001	Animal Kingdom	Tom	CAT
AK001	Animal Kingdom	Jerry	RAT
AK001	Animal Kingdom	Marcus	CAT
AK001	Animal Kingdom	Pookie	CAT
AK001	Animal Kingdom	Mario	DOG
AK001	Animal Kingdom	Luigi	DOG
BA001	Borderville Aquarium	Swimmy	DOLPHIN
BA001	Borderville Aquarium	Charger	WHALE
BA001	Borderville Aquarium	Daffy	DUCK
BA001	Borderville Aquarium	Toby	TURTLE

Figure 13-10: The datasheet for an inner join.

Notice that each of the 129 records has entries in all four fields. This means that every record displayed from the Customer table has a corresponding record or records in the Pets table.

Return to query design mode by clicking the Design icon on the toolbar. When you double-click the join line between the Customer and Pets tables, you see that the join property for these two tables becomes the first selection shown in the Join Properties dialog box (see Figure 13-9). This is an inner join, or *equi-join*, the most common type. These joins show only the records that have a correspondence between tables.

Creating a right outer join

Unlike equi-joins (inner joins), *outer joins* are used for showing all records in one table while showing common records in the other. An outer join points graphically to one of the tables. When you look at the join line, it says, "Show all records from the main table (the one missing the arrow) while showing only matching records in the table being pointed to." For a further explanation, follow these instructions:

1. Return to the query design and again double-click the join line between Customer and Pets.

2. Select the second choice from the Join Properties dialog box, which includes all records from the Customer table and only those records from Pets where the joined fields are equal. (This may be the third choice if you have the Pets table to the left of the Customer table.) Then click the OK button. Notice that the join line now has an arrow at one end, pointing rightward to the Pets table. This is known in database terminology as a *right outer join*.

3. Click the Datasheet button to display this dynaset. Everything looks the same as before. Now move down the page until you can see record number 63. You should see a record for Customer Number JO003, Carla Jones, but no corresponding entry in the field Pet Name or Type of Animal (see Figure 13-11). This record results from selecting the join property that specifies "include all records from Customer 4."

Customer	Customer Name	Pet Name	Type of Animal
HP003	House Of Pets	Chili	DOG
IR001	Patricia Irwin	C.C.	CAT
IR001	Patricia Irwin	Gizmo	CAT
IR001	Patricia Irwin	Stripe	CAT
IR001	Patricia Irwin	Romeo	CAT
IR001	Patricia Irwin	Ceasar	CAT
IR001	Patricia Irwin	Juliet	CAT
IR001	Patricia Irwin	Tiger	CAT
JO001	Michael Johnson	Rover	DOG
JO002	Adam Johnson	Fi Fi	DOG
JO003	Carla Jones		
KP001	Kiddie Petting Zoo	Muncher	GOAT
KP001	Kiddie Petting Zoo	Whitey	LAMB
KP001	Kiddie Petting Zoo	Springer	DEER
MC001	Margaret McKinley	Rex	DOG
MC001	Margaret McKinley	Ceasar	DOG
MP002	Mount Pilot Zoo	Swinger	MONKEY
MP002	Mount Pilot Zoo	Prowler	WOLF

Record: 63 of 130

Figure 13-11: A datasheet with a right outer join.

There are now 130 records, with the extra record being displayed in a record in the Customer table. This person does not own any of the pets that have been entered into the tables.

Unlike equi-joins, outer joins show all corresponding records between two tables *and* records that do *not* have a corresponding record in the other table. In the preceding example, there was a record for Carla Jones but no corresponding record for any pet she owns.

If you've changed the display order of the tables since adding them to the Query window, Access does not follow the table order you set up; rather, it uses the original order in which you selected the tables. Because the information is normally the same in either table, it doesn't make a difference which field is selected first.

Select the Design button on the toolbar to return to the Query Design window. When you created the outer join for the Customer table with the Pets table, Access changed the appearance of the graphical join line to show an arrow at one end. As Figure 13-12 shows, the arrow is pointing toward the Pets table, which tells you that Access has created an outer join and will show *all* records in the Customer table but only those that match in the Pets table.

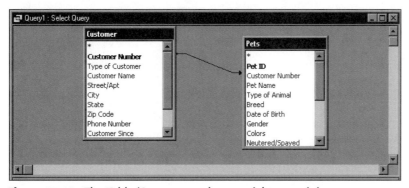

Figure 13-12: The Table/Query pane shows a right outer join.

Creating a left outer join

Return to the query design and again double-click the join line between the Customer and Pets tables.

Select the third choice from the Join Properties dialog box, which asks to "include all records from Pets." Then click the OK button. The join line now has an arrow pointing to the Customer table, as shown in Figure 13-13. This is known as a *left outer join*. (If the arrow points to the right in the top pane, the join is known as a right outer join; if the arrow points to the left, it's a left outer join.)

Select the Datasheet button to display this dynaset. Now move down the page until you can see record number 68, as shown in Figure 13-14. You should see a record with nothing in the fields Customer Number and Customer Name. All you see is Animal Name (which is Brownie) and the fact that it's a dog. This record results from selecting the join property to include all records from Pets. This is known as a left outer join in database terminology.

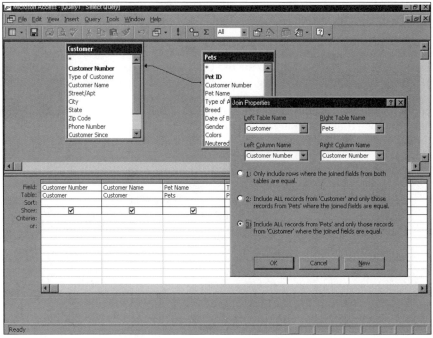

Figure 13-13: The Table/Query pane shows a left outer join.

Again, there are 130 records in this dynaset. However, unlike before, the extra record is not from the Customer table. Rather, this record (#68 in the dynaset) is in the Pets table. It is known as an orphan record. It is in the Pets table, but there is no Customer that owns it. Because referential integrity is not set up between the Customer and Pets tables this is possible. Referential integrity can't be set up in the Relationships window because of this record. If you remove the record, referential integrity can be set up between the two tables. This is covered more in Chapter 25.

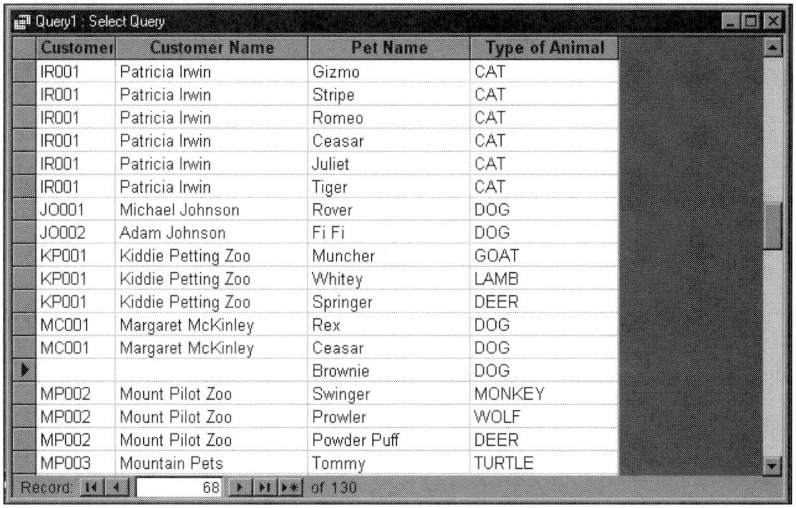

Customer	Customer Name	Pet Name	Type of Animal
IR001	Patricia Irwin	Gizmo	CAT
IR001	Patricia Irwin	Stripe	CAT
IR001	Patricia Irwin	Romeo	CAT
IR001	Patricia Irwin	Ceasar	CAT
IR001	Patricia Irwin	Juliet	CAT
IR001	Patricia Irwin	Tiger	CAT
JO001	Michael Johnson	Rover	DOG
JO002	Adam Johnson	Fi Fi	DOG
KP001	Kiddie Petting Zoo	Muncher	GOAT
KP001	Kiddie Petting Zoo	Whitey	LAMB
KP001	Kiddie Petting Zoo	Springer	DEER
MC001	Margaret McKinley	Rex	DOG
MC001	Margaret McKinley	Ceasar	DOG
		Brownie	DOG
MP002	Mount Pilot Zoo	Swinger	MONKEY
MP002	Mount Pilot Zoo	Prowler	WOLF
MP002	Mount Pilot Zoo	Powder Puff	DEER
MP003	Mountain Pets	Tommy	TURTLE

Figure 13-14: A datasheet with a left outer join.

Creating a Cartesian product

If you add both the Customer and Pets tables to a query but don't specify a join between the tables, Access takes the first Customer record and combines it with all the Pets records; then it takes the second record and combines it with all the Pets records; then it takes the third record and combines it with all the Pets records; and continues until all the Customer records have been combined with all of the Pets records. This combining of records between tables produces 6,321 records in the resultant dynaset. Combining each record in one table with each record in the other table results in a Cartesian product (cross-product) of both tables.

Summary

In this chapter, you learned about creating relationships between tables and how to use joins in queries. The chapter covered these points:

- ✦ Multiple tables can be added to a query, including multiple copies of the same table.
- ✦ Access creates join lines automatically for any tables that have their relationships set at table level.
- ✦ Fields from multiple-table queries can be added in any order. Multiple-table fields are moved and changed in the same way as fields from single tables.

✦ To view data from two or more tables, you must join them.

✦ Joins between two tables can be created by dragging and dropping a field from one table to another. Access draws a graphic join line between the fields.

✦ There are two types of joins — inner joins (equi-joins) and outer joins.

✦ An inner join (or equi-join) displays records that have a common field in both tables with corresponding data in those fields.

✦ An outer join displays all records having corresponding data in both fields and also displays records from one table that do not have corresponding records in the other table.

✦ The two types of outer joins are left and right. Access displays a pointer in the Table/Query pane to show the type of outer join you create.

In the next chapter, you learn to create select queries.

✦   ✦   ✦

Creating Select Queries

To this point, you have worked with queries based on criteria against a single field. You also added multiple tables to a query and joined tables together. This chapter focuses on extracting information from multiple tables in select queries.

Moving Beyond Simple Queries

Select queries are the most common type of query used; they select information (based on a specific criterion) from one or more related tables. With these queries, you can ask questions and receive answers about information stored in your database tables. So far, you have worked with queries that pose simple criteria for a single field in a table and with math operators, such as equal (=) and greater-than (>).

Knowing how to specify criteria is critical to designing effective queries. Although queries can be created against a single table for a single criterion, most queries extract information from several tables and more complex criteria. Because of this complexity, your queries retrieve only the data you need, in the order you need it. You may, for example, want to select and display data from the Mountain Animal Hospital database with these questions or limitations:

✦ All owners of horses or cows or pigs

✦ All animals that were given a specific medication during a specific week last year

✦ All owners whose dogs or cats had bloodwork performed over the past four months

✦ Only the first animal of each type that you have treated

✦ Any animal that has the word *color* in the Memo field comments

As your database system evolves, you will ask questions such as these about the information stored in the system. Although the system was not originally developed specifically for these questions, you can find the information needed to answer them stored in the tables. Because the information is there, you find yourself performing ad hoc queries against the database. The ad hoc queries you perform by using select queries can be very simple or quite complex.

Select queries are the easiest way to obtain information from several tables without resorting to writing programs.

Using query comparison operators

When working with select queries, you may need to specify one or more *criteria* to limit the scope of information shown. This is done by using *comparison operators* in equations and calculations. The categories of operators are mathematical, relational, logical, and string. In select queries, operators are used in either the Field: or Criteria: cell of the QBE (Query by Example) pane.

A good rule of thumb to observe is this:

✦ Use mathematical and string operators for creating calculated fields; use relational and logical operators for specifying scope criteria.

 Cross-Reference Calculated fields are discussed later in this chapter. An in-depth explanation of operators is found in Chapter 12.

Table 14-1 shows most of the common operators used with select queries.

Table 14-1 Common Operators Used in Select Queries				
Mathematical	**Relational**	**Logical**	**String**	**Miscellaneous**
* (multiply)	= (equal)	And	& (concatenate)	Between...And
/ (divide)	<> (not equal)	Or	Like	In
+ (add)	> (greater than)	Not		Is Null
– (subtract)	< (less than)			

Using these operators, you can ferret out such types of records as these:

✦ Pet records that have a picture associated with them

✦ A range of records, such as all patients seen between November and January

✦ Records that meet both And *and* Or criteria, such as all pets that are dogs *and* are not either neutered or have a current vaccination

✦ All records that do *not* match a value, such as any animal that is not a cat

When you supply a criterion to a query, you use the operator with an *example* that you supply. In Figure 14-1, the example is *PIG*. The operator is equal (=). Notice that the equal sign is *not* shown in the figure. The equal sign is the default operator for criteria selection.

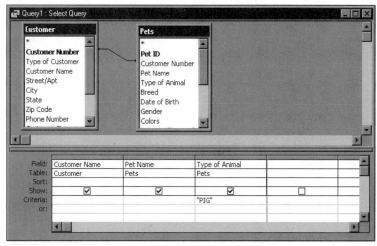

Figure 14-1: The QBE pane with a simple criterion.

When working with criteria for select queries, you supply an example of what type of information Access needs to find in the Criteria: cell of the Query by Example (QBE) pane.

Chapter 9 gives an in-depth explanation of working with queries.

Understanding complex criteria selection

As Table 14-1 shows, several operators can be used to build complex criteria. To most people, complex criteria consist of a series of Ands and Ors, as in these examples:

✦ State must be Idaho *or* Oregon

✦ City must be Borderville *and* state must be Washington

✦ State must be Idaho *or* Washington *and* city must be Borderville

These examples demonstrate use of both the logical operators `And`/`Or`. Many times, complex criteria can be created by entering example data in different cells of the QBE pane. Figure 14-2 demonstrates how to create complex `And`/`Or` criteria without having to enter the operator keywords `And`/`Or` at all. This example displays all customers and their pets who satisfy these criteria: *Live in the city of Borderville and live in either the state of Washington or the state of Idaho and whose pet is not a dog.*

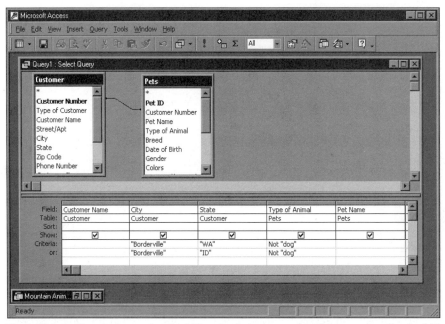

Figure 14-2: Creating complex And/Or criteria by example without using the And/Or operators.

Note   Sometimes you see a field name referred to by the table name first and then the field name, with a dot (.) between the two names. This nomenclature tells you which table a field belongs to. This is especially critical when you're describing two fields that have the same name but come from different tables. In a multiple-table query, this format is seen in the field list when you add a field to the QBE pane by clicking an empty column. This format is also seen when a multiple table form is created using the field list. The general format is *Table Name.Field Name*. If the field name or table name has spaces in it, you must surround the name with brackets [ ]. Examples are `Pets.[Type of Animal]` and `Customer.[Customer Name]`.

Tip   Although we use table and field names with spaces in them for better readability, it is really a good idea to not use spaces. This way, you don't have to use brackets around your field or object names.

If you build a mathematical formula for this query, it will look similar to this:

```
((Customer.City="Borderville") AND (Customer.State="WA") AND
(Not Pets.[Type of Animal]="DOG")) OR ((Customer.City=
"Borderville") AND (Customer.State="ID") AND (Not Pets. [Type
of Animal]="DOG"))
```

The city and pet example for each state line must be entered in the QBE pane of Figure 14-2. Later, you learn to use the And/Or operators in a Criteria: cell of the query, which eliminates the need for redundant entry of these fields.

Tip   To find records that *do not* match a value, use the Not operator with the value. For example, enter the expression Not Dog to find all animals except dogs.

The And/Or operators are the most commonly used operators when working with complex criteria. The operators consider two different formulas (one on each side of the And/Or operators) and then determine individually whether they are True or False. Then they compare the resultants of the two formulas against each other for a logical True/False answer. For example, take the first And statement in the formula just given:

```
(Customer.City="Borderville") AND (Customer.State="WA")
```

The first half of the formula, Customer.City = "Borderville", converts to a True if the city is Borderville (False if a different city; Null if no city was entered in the field).

Then the second half of the formula, Customer.State = "WA", is converted to a True if the state is Washington (False if a different state; Null if no state was entered). Then the And compares the logical True/False from each side against the other to give a resulting True/False answer.

Note   A field has a *Null value* when it has no value at all; it is the lack of entry of information in a field. Null is neither True nor False; nor is it equivalent to all spaces or zero—it has no value. If you never enter a city name in the City field, simply skipping it, Access leaves the field empty. This state of emptiness is known as Null.

When the resultant of an And/Or is True, the overall condition is True, and the query displays those records meeting the True condition. Table 14-2 reviews the True conditions for each operator.

Table 14-2			
Results of Logical Operators And/Or			
Left Side Is	*Operator Is*	*Right Side Is*	*Resultant Answer Is*
True	AND	True	True
True	OR	True	True
True	OR	False	True
True	OR	Null	True
False	OR	True	True
Null	OR	True	True

Notice that the And operator is True only when both sides of the formula are True, whereas the Or operator is True when either side of the formula is True. In fact, one side can be a Null value, and the Or operator will still be True if the other side is True. This is the difference between And/Or operators.

Cross-Reference   Refer to Chapter 12 for further details about logical operators.

Using functions in select queries

When you work with queries, you may want to use built-in Access functions to display information. For example, you may want to display such items as:

✦ The day of week (Sunday, Monday, and so forth) for visit dates

✦ All customer names in uppercase

✦ The difference between two date fields

You can display all this information by creating calculated fields for the query. Calculated fields are discussed in depth later in this chapter.

Referencing fields in select queries

When you work with a field name in queries, as you do with calculated fields or criteria values, you should enclose the field name in brackets([]). Access requires brackets around any field name that is in a criterion and around any field name that contains a space or punctuation. An example of a field name in brackets is the criterion [Visit Date] + 30. There are more examples later in this chapter.

Caution   If you omit the brackets ([]) around a field name in the criterion, Access automatically places quotes around the field name and treats it as text instead of a field name.

Entering Single-Value Field Criteria

There may be times when you want to limit query records on the basis of a single field criterion, as in these queries:

✦ Customer information for customers living in the state of Washington

✦ Animals you have treated from the local zoos in the area

✦ Customers and animals you treated during the month of January

Each of these queries requires a single-value criterion. Simply put, a single-value criterion is the entry of only one expression in a field. That expression can be example data or a function. "WA" or DatePart("m",[Visit Date])=1 are both examples of single-value criteria.

Criteria expressions can be specified for any type of data, whether Text, Numeric, Date/Time, and so forth. Even OLE Object and Counter field types can have criteria specified.

Cross-Reference   For a full explanation of expressions, operators, identifiers, literals, and functions, see Chapter 12.

On the CD-ROM   All the examples in this chapter rely on several tables: Customer, Pets, and Visits. The Mountain Start database contains only the tables used in this chapter. The majority of these examples use only the Customer and Pets tables. If you want to follow the examples, create a new query and add the Customer and Pets tables.

Each series of steps in this chapter tells you which tables and fields make up the query. For most examples, you should clear all previous criteria. Each example focuses on the criteria lines of the QBE pane. You can also view each figure to make sure you understand the correct placement of the criteria in each example. Only a few dynasets are shown; you can follow along and view the data.

Entering character (Text or Memo) criteria

Character criteria are used for Text or Memo data-type fields. These are either examples or data about the contents of the field. For example, to create a text criterion to display customers who own birds, follow these steps:

1. Select Customer Name from the Customer table and then Pet Name and Type of Animal from the Pets table.

2. Click the Criteria: cell of Type of Animal.

3. Type **BIRD** in the cell.

Your query should look similar to Figure 14-3. Notice that only two tables are open and only three fields are selected. You can click the Datasheet button to see the results of this query.

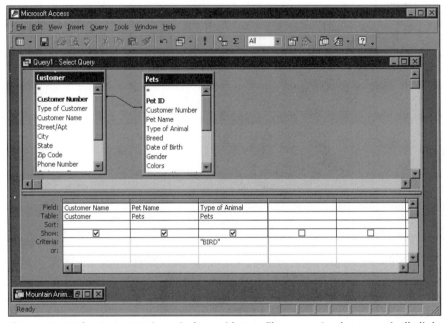

Figure 14-3: The Query Design window with two files open (and automatically linked).

Tip   When specifying example-type criteria, it is not necessary to match capitalization. Access defaults to case-insensitive when working with queries. Entering *BIRD, bird,* or *BiRd* provides the same results.

An equal sign was not needed before the literal word *bird* because Access uses the equal operator as the default. To see all animals except birds, use either the <> (not equal) or the Not operator before the word *bird*.

You also didn't have to place quotes around the word *bird*. Access understands that you are talking about the example literal *BIRD* and places the quotes for you automatically.

Tip   The double quotation mark should be used to surround literals. Access normally uses the single quotation mark as a remark character in its programming language. However, when you use the single quotation mark in the Criteria: cell, Access interprets it as a double quotation mark.

The Like operator and wildcards

To this point, you've been working with *literal* criteria. You specified the exact field contents for Access to find, which in the example was "Bird." Access used the literal to find the specific records. Sometimes, however, you know only a part of the field contents, or you may want to see a wider range of records on the basis of a pattern. For example, you may want to see all pet visits for pets that begin with the letter G; you want to check gerbils, goats, and so forth. Perhaps a more practical example is when you have a customer who owns a pig that was born Siamese. You remember making a note of it in the Comments field; you don't, however, remember which pig it was. This requires using a wildcard search against the Memo field to find any records that contain the word *Siamese*.

Access uses the string operator Like in the Criteria: cell of a field to perform wildcard searches against the field's contents. Access searches for a pattern in the field; you use the question mark (?) to represent a single character or the asterisk (*) for several characters. (This works just like with filenames at the DOS level.) In addition to the two characters (?) and (*), Access uses three other characters for wildcard searches. Table 14-3 lists the wildcards that the Like operator can use.

The question mark (?) stands for any single character located in the same position as the question mark in the example expression. An asterisk (*) stands for any number of characters in the same position in which the asterisk is placed. Unlike the asterisk at DOS level, Access can use the asterisk any number of times in an example expression. The pound sign (#) stands for any single digit found in the same position as the pound sign. The brackets ([ ]) and the list they enclose, stand for any single character that matches any one character of the list located within the brackets. Finally, the exclamation point (!) inside the brackets represents the Not word for the list — that is, any single character that does not match any character of the list within the brackets.

Table 14-3
Wildcards Used by the Like Operator

Wildcard	Purpose
?	A single character (0–9, Aa-Zz)
*	Any number of characters (0 to n)
#	Any single digit (0–9)
[list]	Any single character in the list
[!list]	Any single character not in the list

These wildcards can be used alone or in conjunction with each other. They can even be used several times within the same expression. The examples in Table 14-4 demonstrate how the wildcards can be used.

To create an example using the Like operator, let's suppose that you want to find the record of the Siamese pig. You know that the word *Siamese* is used in one of the records in the Comments field. To create the query, follow these steps:

1. Remove the criterion field for Type of Animal.

2. Double-click the Comments field in the Pets table.

3. Click the Criteria: cell of the Comments field.

4. Type ***Siamese*** in the cell (be sure to put asterisks before and after Siamese).

Table 14-4
Using Wildcards with the Like Operator

Expression	Field Used In	Results of Criteria
Like "Re?"	Pets.Pet Name	Finds all records of pets whose names are three letters long and begin with "Re"; examples: Red, Rex, Ren
Like "*Siamese*"	Pets.Comments	Finds all records with the word "Siamese" somewhere within the Comments field
Like "G*"	Pets.Type of Animal	Finds all records for animals of a type that begins with the letter G
Like "1/*/93"	Visits.Visit Date	Finds all records for the month of January 1993

Expression	Field Used In	Results of Criteria
Like "## Main St."	Customer.Street/Apt	Finds all records for houses with house numbers between 10 and 99 inclusively; examples: 10, 22, 33, 51
Like "[RST]*"	Customer.City	Finds all records for customers who live in any city with a name beginning with R, S, or T
Like "[!EFG]*"	Pets.Type of Animal	Finds all records for animals of types that do not begin with the letters E, F, or G; all other animals are displayed

When you click outside the Criteria: cell, Access automatically adds the operator Like and the quotation marks around the expression. Your query QBE pane should be similar to Figure 14-4.

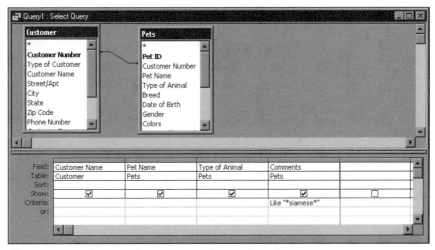

Figure 14-4: Using the Like operator with a selected query.

Access automatically adds the Like operator and quotation marks if you meet these conditions:

✦ There are no spaces in your expression.

✦ You use only the wildcards ?, *, and #.

✦ You use brackets ([ ]) inside quotation marks "   ".

If you use the brackets without quotation marks, you must supply the operator Like and the quotation marks.

Using the Like operator with wildcards is the best way to perform pattern searches through Memo fields.

Caution   The Like operator and its wildcards can be used only against three types of fields: Text, Memo, and Date. Using these with any other type can result in an error.

Specifying nonmatching values

To specify a nonmatching value, you simply use either the Not or the <> operator in front of the expression that you don't want to match. For example, you may want to see all customers and their pets for all states, but you want to exclude Washington. You see how to specify this nonmatching value in these steps:

1. Start with an empty query using the Customer and Pets tables.
2. Select the Customer Name and State fields from Customer and Pet Name from Pets.
3. Click on the Criteria: cell of State.
4. Type **Not "WA"** in the cell.

The query should look similar to Figure 14-5. The query will select all records *except* those for customers who live in the state of Washington.

Note   You can use the <> operator instead of Not in Step 4 of the instructions to exclude Washington. The resulting dynaset is the same with either operator. These two operators are interchangeable except with the use of the keyword Is. You cannot say Is <> Null. Rather, you must say Not Is Null.

Figure 14-5: Using the Not operator in criteria.

Entering numeric (Number, Currency, or Counter) criteria

Numeric criteria are used with Number, Currency, or Counter data-type fields. You simply enter the numbers and the decimal symbol, if required following the mathematical or comparison operator. For example, you may want to see all animals that weigh over 100 pounds. To create a query like this, follow these steps:

1. Start with a new query using the Customer and Pets tables.

2. Select the Customer Name in the Customer table, Pet Name, Type of Animal, and Weight in the Pets table.

3. Click in the Criteria: cell for Weight.

4. Type **>100** in the cell.

When you follow these steps, your query looks similar to Figure 14-6. When working with numeric data, Access does not enclose the expression with quotes, as it does with string or date criteria.

Field:	Customer Name	Pet Name	Type of Animal	Weight	
Table:	Customer	Pets	Pets	Pets	
Sort:					
Show:	☑	☐	☑	☑	
Criteria:				>100	
or:					

Figure 14-6: Criteria set for weight of animals.

Numeric fields are generally compared to a value string that uses comparison operators, such as less than (<), greater than (>), or equal to (=). If you want to specify a comparison other than equal, you must enter the operator as well. Remember that Access defaults to equal for all criteria. That is why you needed to specify greater than (>) 100 in the query for animals over 100 pounds.

Working with Currency and Counter data in a query is exactly the same as working with Numeric data; you specify an operator and a numeric value.

Entering Yes/No (logic) criteria

Yes/No criteria are used with Yes/No type fields. The example data you supply in the criteria can be for only Yes or No states. You can also use the Not and the <> operators to signify the opposite, but the Yes/No data also has a Null state you may want to check for. Access recognizes several forms of Yes and No. Table 14-5 lists all the positive and negative values you can use.

Thus, instead of typing Yes, you can type any of these in the Criteria: cell: **On**, **True**, **Not No**, **<> No**, **<No**, or **-1**.

Tip   In Access 2000, you can enter any number except 0 to represent TRUE or Yes.

Note   A Yes/No field can have only three criteria states: Yes, No, and Null. Null only occurs when no default value was set in a table and the value has not yet been entered. Checking for Is Null displays only records with no value, and checking for Is Not Null always displays all Yes or No records. After a Yes/No field checkbox is checked (or checked and then deselected) it can never be null. It will be Yes or No (-1 or 0).

Table 14-5 Positive and Negative Values Used in Yes/No Fields						
Yes	True	On	Not No	<> No	<No	-1
No	False	Off	Not Yes	<>Yes	>Yes	0

Entering a criterion for an OLE object

You can even specify a criterion for OLE objects: Is Not Null. As an example, suppose you don't have pictures for all the animals and you want to view only those records that have a picture of the animal—that is, those in which picture is not Null. You specify the Is Not Null criterion for the Picture field of the Pets table. Once you've done this, Access limits the records to those that have a picture in them.

Although Is Not Null is the correct syntax, you can also type Not Null and Access will supply the Is operator for you.

Entering Multiple Criteria in One Field

So far, you've worked with single-condition criteria on a single field at a time. As you learned, single-condition criteria can be specified for any field type. Now you'll work with multiple criteria based on a single field. You may be interested in seeing all records in which the type of animal is either a cat or a squirrel, for example, or perhaps you want to view the records of all the animals that you saw between July 1, 1999, and December 31, 1999.

The QBE pane has the flexibility to solve these types of problems. You can specify several criteria for one field or for several fields in a select query. Using multiple criteria, for example, you can determine which customers and pets are from Idaho or Washington (`"ID" or "WA"`) or which animals you saw for general examinations in the past 30 days (`Between Date() and Date()-30`).

The `And` and the `Or` operators are used to specify several criteria for one field.

Understanding an Or operation

You use an `Or` operation in queries when you want a field to meet either of two conditions. For example, you may want to see the customer and pet names of all rabbits and squirrels. In other words, you want to see all records where a customer owns a rabbit or a squirrel, or both. The general formula for this operation is:

```
[Type of Animal] = "Rabbit" Or [Type of Animal] = "Squirrel"
```

If either side of this formula is True, the resulting answer is also True. To clarify this point, consider these conditions:

✦ Customer One owns a rabbit but does not own a squirrel — the formula is True.

✦ Customer Two owns a squirrel but does not own a rabbit — the formula is True.

✦ Customer Three owns a squirrel and a rabbit — the formula is True.

✦ Customer Four does not own a rabbit and does not own a squirrel — the formula is False.

Specifying multiple values for a field using the Or operator

The `Or` operator is used to specify multiple values for a field. For example, you use the `Or` operator if you want to see all records of owners of fish or frogs or ducks. To do this, follow these steps:

1. Create a new query using the Customer and Pets tables.

2. Select the Customer Name field in the Customer table and then select Pet Name and Type of Animal in the Pets table.

3. Click on the Criteria: cell of Type of Animal.

4. Type **Fish Or Frog Or Duck** in the cell.

Your QBE pane should resemble Figure 14-7. Access automatically placed quotation marks around your example data — Fish, Frog, and Duck.

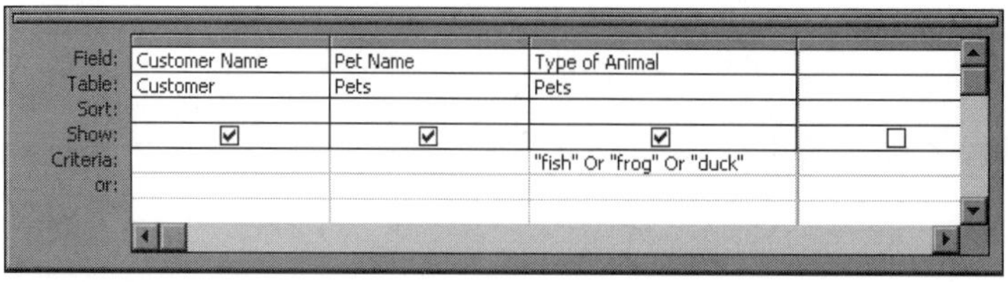

Figure 14-7: Using the Or operator.

Figure 14-8 shows this dynaset. Notice that the only records selected contain FISH, FROG, or DUCK in the Type of Animal column.

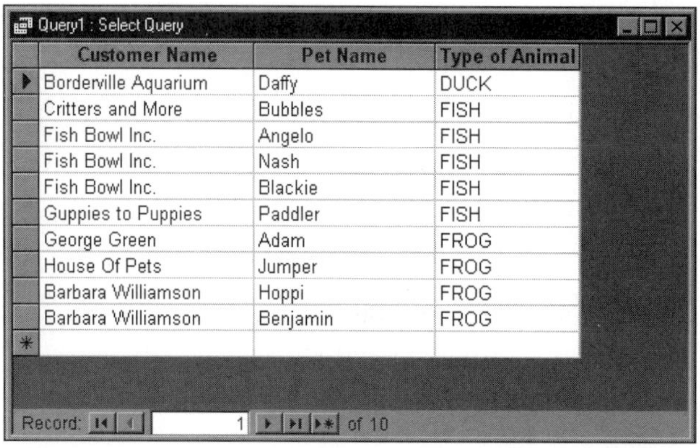

Figure 14-8: Selecting records with the Or operator.

Using the or: cell of the QBE pane

Besides using the literal Or operator, you can supply individual criteria for the field on separate lines of the QBE pane. To do this, enter the first criterion example in the Criteria: cell of the field, just as you have been. Then enter the criterion example in the or: cell of the field. Enter the next criterion in the cell directly beneath the first example; and continue entering examples vertically down the column. This is exactly equivalent to typing the Or operator between examples. Using the example in which you queried for fish, frogs, or ducks, change your QBE pane to look like the one in Figure 14-9. Notice that each type of animal is on a separate line in the query.

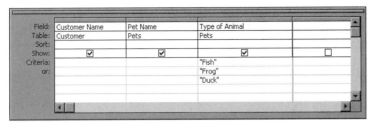

Figure 14-9: Using the or: cell of the QBE pane.

Tip

Access allows up to nine (depending upon the resolution you are using — 640 x 480, etc.) or: cells for each field. If you need to specify more `Or` conditions, use the `Or` operator between conditions (for example: `Cat Or Dog Or Pig`).

Using a list of values with the In operator

You can use another method for expressing the multiple values of a single field. This method uses the operator named `In`. The `In` operator finds a value that is one of a *list of values*. For example, type the expression **IN(FISH, FROG, DUCK)** under the Type of Animal field. This action creates a list of values, where any item in the list becomes an example criterion. Your query should resemble Figure 14-10.

In this example, quotation marks were automatically entered around Fish, Frog, and Duck.

Note

When you work with the `In` operator, each value (example data) must be separated from the others by a comma.

Field:	Customer Name	Pet Name	Type of Animal	
Table:	Customer	Pets	Pets	
Sort:				
Show:	☑	☑	☑	☐
Criteria:			In ("fish","frog","duck")	
or:				

Figure 14-10: Using the In operator.

Understanding an And query

You use `And` operations in queries when you want a field to meet both of two conditions that you specify. For example, you may want to see records of pets that had a visit date between July 1, 1999 and December 31, 1999. In other words, the animal had to be a patient during the last half of the year 1999. The general formula for this example is:

```
[Visit Date] >= 7/1/99 And [Visit Date] <= 12/31/99
```

Unlike the Or operator (which has several conditions under which it is True), the And operator is True only when both sides of the formula are True. When both sides are True, the resulting answer will also be True. To clarify use of the And operator, consider these conditions:

✦ Visit date (6/22/99) is not greater than 7/1/99, but it is less than 12/31/99 — the formula is False.

✦ Visit date (4/11/2000) is greater than 7/1/99, but it is not less than 12/31/99 — the formula is False.

✦ Visit date (11/1/99) is greater than 7/1/99 and it is less than 12/31/99 — the formula is True.

Both sides of the operation must be True for the And operation to be True.

An And operation can be performed in any of several ways against a single field in Access.

Specifying a range using the And operator

The And operator is frequently used in fields that have Numeric or Date/Time data types. It is seldom used in Text type, although it can be. For instance, you may be interested in viewing all animals whose names start with D, E, or F. The And operator can be used here, although the Like operator is better (Like" [DEF]*"). Using an And operator with a single field sets a range of acceptable values in the field. Therefore, the key purpose of an And operator in a single field is to define a range of records to be viewed. An example of using the And operator to create a range criterion is using it to display all animals that weigh between 100 and 300 pounds, inclusively. To create this query, follow these steps:

1. Create a new query using the Customer and Pets tables.

2. Select the Customer Name field in the Customer table, and Pet Name, Type of Animal, and Weight in the Pets table.

3. Click in the Criteria: cell of Weight.

4. Type **>=100 And <=300** in the cell.

The query should resemble Figure 14-11. You can change the formula to >99 And <301 with identical results.

Figure 14-11: Using the And operator with numeric fields.

Using the Between...And operator

There is another method for expressing a range of records from a single field. This method uses the operator `Between...And`. With the `Between...And` operator, you can find records meeting a range of values — for example, all pets `Between` Dog And Pig. Using the example of animals weighing between 100 and 300 pounds, create the query using the `Between...And` operator as shown in Figure 14-12.

Figure 14-12: Using the Between...And Operator.

Caution

When you use the `Between...And` operator, the values entered in the Criteria field (in this example 100 and 300) are (if they match) also included in the resulting dynaset.

Searching for Null data

A field may have no contents; perhaps the value wasn't known at the time of data entry, or the data-entry person simply forgot to enter the information, or the field's information has been removed. Access does nothing with this field; it simply remains an empty field. (A field is said to be *Null* when it's empty.)

Logically, a Null is neither True nor False. A Null is not equivalent to all spaces or to zero. A Null simply has no value.

Access lets you work with Null value fields by means of two special operators:

```
Is Null
Is Not Null
```

These operators are used to limit criteria based on Null values of a field. You worked with a Null value when you queried for animals having a picture on file. In the next example, you look for animal records that don't specify gender. To create this query, follow these steps:

1. Create a new query using the Customer and Pets tables.

2. Select the Customer Name field in the Customer table, and Pet Name, Type of Animal, and Gender field in the Pets table.

3. Click in the Criteria: cell of Gender.

4. Type **Is Null** in the cell.

Your query should look like Figure 14-13. Select the Datasheet button to see that there are no records without a gender.

Field:	Customer Name	Pet Name	Type of Animal	Gender	
Table:	Customer	Pets	Pets	Pets	
Sort:					
Show:	☑	☑	☑	☑	
Criteria:				Is Null	
or:					

Figure 14-13: Using the Is Null operator.

 Tip   When using the `Is Null` and `Is Not Null` operators, you can enter `Null` or `Not Null` and Access automatically adds the `Is` to the Criteria field.

Entering Criteria in Multiple Fields

To this point, you've worked with criteria specified in single fields. Now you'll work with criteria across several fields. When you want to limit the records based on several field conditions, you do so by setting criteria in each of the fields that will be used for the scope. Say, for example, that you want to search for all dogs or for all animals in Idaho. Or that you want to search for dogs in Idaho or Washington. Again, that you want to search for all dogs in Washington or all cats in Oregon. Each of these queries requires placing criteria in multiple fields and on multiple lines.

Using And and Or across fields in a query

To use And and Or across fields, place your example or pattern data in the Criteria: and the or: cells of one field relative to the placement in another field. When you want to use And between two fields, you place the example or pattern data across the same line. When you want to use Or between two fields, you place the example or pattern data on different lines in the QBE pane. Figure 14-14 shows the QBE pane and a conceptual representation of this placement.

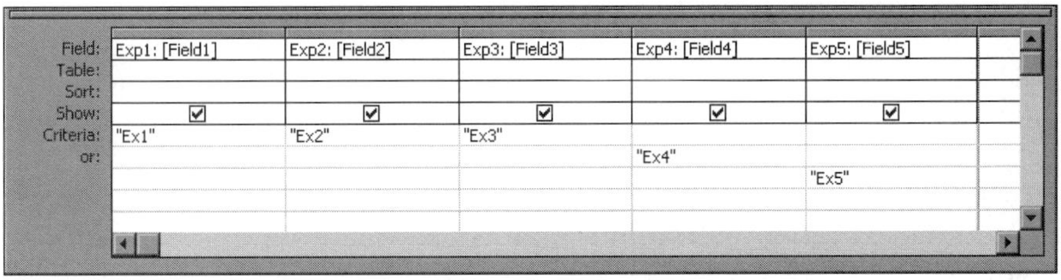

Figure 14-14: The QBE pane with And/Or criteria between fields.

Look at Figure 14-14. It shows that if the only criteria fields present were Ex1, Ex2, and Ex3 (with Ex4 and Ex5 removed), all three would be Anding between the fields. If only the criteria fields Ex4 and Ex5 were present (with Ex1, Ex2, and Ex3 removed), the two would be Oring between fields. As it is, the selection for this example is (EX1 AND EX2 AND EX3) OR EX4 OR EX5. Therefore, this query is True if a value matches any of these criteria:

EX1 AND EX2 AND EX3 (all must be true) or

EX4 (this can be true and either/both of the other two lines can be false) or

EX5 (this can be true and either/both of the other two lines can be false)

As long as one of these three criteria are True, the record will be selected.

Specifying And criteria across fields of a query

The most common type of condition operator between fields is the And operator. It is used to limit records on the basis of several field conditions. For example, you may want to view only the records of customers who live in the state of Washington and own rabbits. To create this query, follow these steps:

1. Create a new query using the Customer and Pets tables.

2. Select the Customer Name and State fields in the Customer table and then select Pet Name and Type of Animal fields in the Pets table.

3. Click the Criteria: cell of State.

4. Type **WA** in the cell.

5. Click the Criteria: cell for Type of Animal.

6. Type **RABBIT** in the cell.

Your query should look like Figure 14-15. Notice that both example data are in the same row.

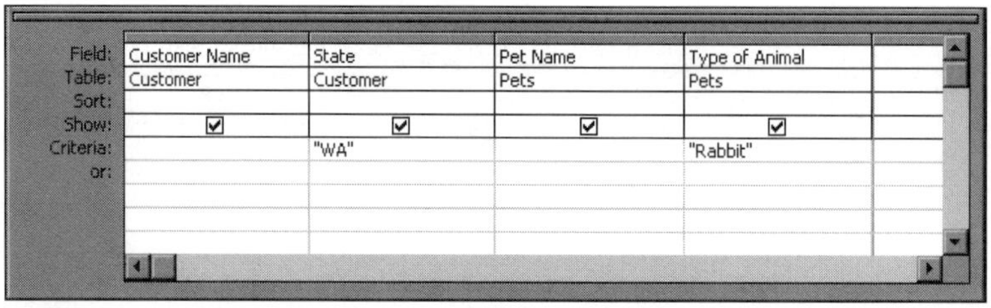

Figure 14-15: An And operator operation across two fields.

Because you placed data for both criteria on the same row, Access interprets this as an And operation.

Specifying Or criteria across fields of a query

Although the Or operator is not used across fields as commonly as the And operator, occasionally Or is very useful. For example, you may want to see records of any animals in Washington or you may want all rabbits regardless of the state they live in. To create this query, follow these steps:

1. Use the query from the previous example, emptying the two criteria cells first.

2. Click the Criteria: cell of State.

3. Type **WA** in the cell.

4. Click in the or: cell for Type of Animal.

5. Type **RABBIT** in the cell.

Your query should resemble Figure 14-16. Notice that the criteria entered this time are not in the same row for both fields.

When you place the criterion for one field on a different line from the criterion for another field, Access interprets this as an Or between the fields.

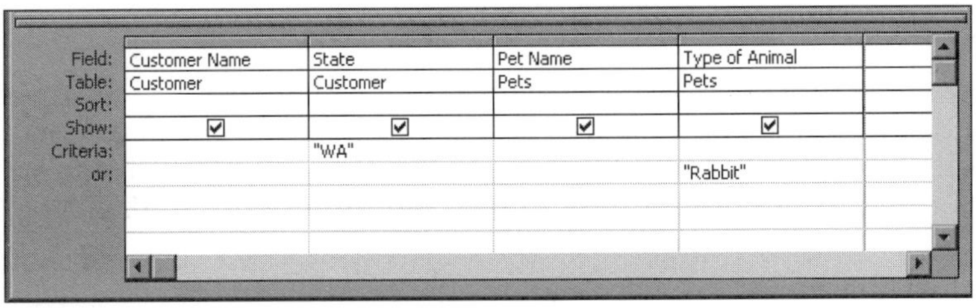

Figure 14-16: Using the Or operator between fields.

Using And and Or together in different fields

Now that you've worked with And and Or separately, you're ready to create a query using And and Or in different fields. In the next example, you want to display information for all skunks in Washington and all rabbits in Idaho. To create this query, follow these steps:

1. Use the query from the previous example, emptying the two criteria cells first.

2. Click the Criteria: cell of State.

3. Type **WA** in the cell.

4. Click the or: cell of State.

5. Type **ID** in the cell.

6. Click the Criteria: cell for Type of Animal.

7. Type **SKUNK** in the cell.

8. Click the or: cell for Type of Animal.

9. Type **RABBIT** in the cell.

Figure 14-17 shows how the query should look. Notice that WA and Skunk are in the same row; ID and Rabbit are in another row. This query represents two Ands across fields, with an Or in each field.

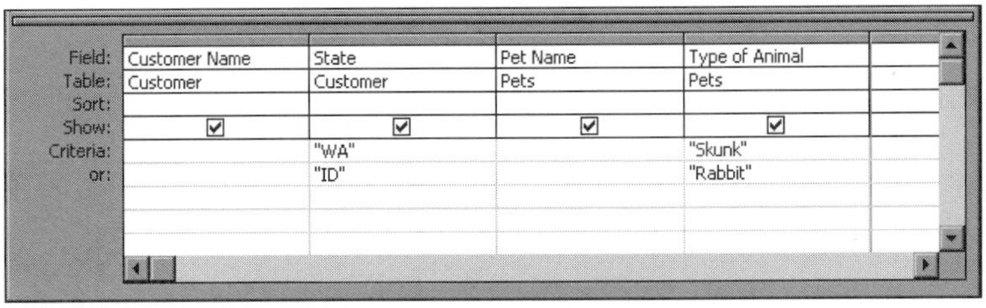

Figure 14-17: Using Ands and Ors across fields.

A complex query on different lines

Suppose you want to view all records of animals that are either squirrels or cats that were brought in by Animal Kingdom between July 1, 1999, and December 31, 1999. In this example, you use three fields for setting criteria: Customer.Customer Name, Pets.Type of Animal, and Visits.Visit Date. The formula for setting these criteria is:

```
(Customer.[Customer Name] = "Animal Kingdom" AND (Pets.[Type of
Animal] = "SQUIRREL" OR Pets.[Type of Animal]="CAT") AND
(Visits.[Visit Date] >= #7/1/99# AND <= #12/31/99#)
```

You can display this data by creating the query shown in Figure 14-18.

Field:	Customer Name	Pet Name	Type of Animal	Visit Date	
Table:	Customer	Pets	Pets	Visits	
Sort:					
Show:	☑	☑	☑	☑	
Criteria:	"Animal Kingdom"		"Squirrel"	Between #6/30/99# And #1/1/00#	
or:	"Animal Kingdom"		"Cat"	Between #6/30/99# And #1/1/00#	

Figure 14-18: Using multiple Ands and Ors across fields.

Note   You could have entered the date 1/1/2000 instead of 1/1/00 and Access 2000 would process the query exactly the same. Access 2000 is Year 2000 (Y2K) compliant. All Microsoft Office 2000 products process two-digit years from 00–30 as 2000 to 2030 while all two-digit dates between 31 and 99 are processed as 1931–1999.

A complex query on one line

Notice in Figure 14-18 that the Customer Name Animal Kingdom is repeated on two lines, as is the Visit Date of Between #6/30/99# And #1/1/00#. This is necessary because the two lines actually form the query:

```
Animal Kingdom AND SQUIRREL AND Between #6/30/99# And #1/1/00#
OR
Animal Kingdom AND CAT AND Between #6/30/99# And #1/1/00#
```

You don't have to repeat Animal Kingdom in a query such as this. Figure 14-19 shows another approach.

Notice that the criteria in Figure 14-18 have duplicate information in the or: cell of the Customer Name and Visit Date fields. Only the Type of Animal Field has different criteria—"SQUIRREL" or "CAT". By combining the Type of Animal information into a single criterion (using the Or), the Customer Name and Visit Date criteria will have to be entered only once, which creates a more efficient query.

Field:	Customer Name	Pet Name	Type of Animal	Visit Date	
Table:	Customer	Pets	Pets	Visits	
Sort:					
Show:	☑	☑	☑	☑	
Criteria:	"Animal Kingdom"		"Squirrel" Or "Cat"	Between #6/30/99# And #1/1/00#	
or:					

Figure 14-19: Using multiple Ands and Ors across fields on one line.

Creating a New Calculated Field in a Query

When you work with fields in a query, you are not limited to the fields from the tables that you use in the query. You can also create *calculated fields* to use in a query—for example, a calculated field named *Discount Amount* that displays an amount by multiplying the value of Discount times Outstanding Balance in the Customer table.

To create this calculated field, follow these steps:

1. Create a new query using the Customer table.

2. Select the Customer Name, Discount, and Outstanding Balance fields in the Customer table.

3. Click the empty Field: cell.

4. Type the following **Discount Amount: [Discount]*[Outstanding Balance]** and click in another cell.

If you did this correctly, the cell looks like Figure 14-20. The expression has changed to Discount Amount:[Discount]*[Outstanding Balance]. If you didn't type the field name, Expr1: would precede the calculation.

Note For two reasons, a calculated field has a name (supplied either by the user or by an Access default). First, a name is needed to supply a label for the datasheet column. Second, the name is necessary for referencing the field in a form, a report, or another query.

Notice that the general format for creating a calculated field is as follows:

✦ Calculated Field Name: Expression to build calculated field

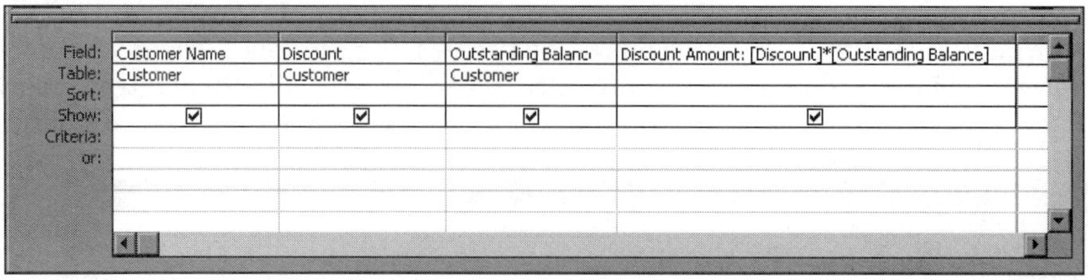

Figure 14-20: A calculated field.

Summary

In this chapter, you learned how to specify criteria to design select queries. You learned about the operators that help you query against fields for the exact information that you want. The chapter covered these points:

✦ Select queries let you select information from tables that you can use for datasheets, forms, reports, and other queries.

✦ You can specify record criteria for any type of field.

✦ You can build expressions in the Criteria: cell of a field based on literal data (examples) or with functions that build the example data.

✦ Access has five distinct wildcards it uses with the Like operator: ?, *, #, [], and !. You can use these operators independently or in conjunction with each other.

✦ The Not operator is similar to the <> operator and specifies nonmatching values as criteria.

✦ The And operator forms a True expression only when both sides of a formula are True. An Or operator is True when either side of the formula is True.

✦ The Or operator lets you specify a list of values for a field. The And operator lets you specify a range of values in a field.

✦ Often the In operator can be used instead of an Or operator; the Between...And operator can be used in place of the And operator.

✦ You can search fields for empty conditions by using the Is Null operator. A Null is the absence of any value in a field.

✦ Calculated fields are created from an expression. The expression can use one or more fields, functions, or other objects.

In the next chapter, you examine controls and properties.

✦   ✦   ✦

Understanding Controls and Properties

This is the first of eight chapters in Part III that examine forms and reports in detail. Forms are probably the most important type of object in any application. Forms allow you to display your raw data in a user-friendly format, validate data entry, and display it in a nicely formatted window. Microsoft Access forms can be used to create any Windows interface. While Autoforms are great as a starting point, the Microsoft Access's forms designer lets you create any imaginable design and then display it as a form.

Controls and properties form the basis of forms and reports. It is critical to understand the fundamental concepts of controls and properties before you begin to apply them to custom forms and reports.

On the CD-ROM

In this chapter, the Pets table in the Mountain Animal Hospital database is used. The chapter explains each control by examining one or more fields in the Pets table.

To create the first form you need for this chapter, follow these steps:

1. Open the Mountain Animal Hospital or Mountain Animal Start database.

2. Select Insert ➪ Form.

3. Select Design View from the New Form dialog box.

4. Select the Pets table from the combo box in the New Form dialog box.

5. Click the OK button to display the Form Design window.

6. Maximize the form by clicking the maximize button in the top-right corner of the window.

7. Expand the light gray area of the form to the full-window size by dragging the bottom-right corner of the light gray area to the bottom-right corner of the window.

What Is a Control?

A *control* has many definitions in Access. Generally, a control is any object on a form or report, such as a label or text box. These are the same controls that are used in any Windows application, such as Access, Excel, or Web-based HTML forms, or that are written in any language, such as Visual Basic or C++. While each language or product has different file formats and different items that are known as properties, a text box in Access is the same as a text box in another Windows product.

You enter values into controls and display them by using a control. A control can be bound to a table field, but it can also be an object, such as a line or rectangle. Calculated fields are also controls, as are pictures, graphs, option buttons, checkboxes, and objects. There are also controls that aren't part of Access but that are developed separately; these are *custom controls* (also known as *OCXs* or *ActiveX controls*). Custom controls extend the base feature set of Access 2000.

Cross-Reference　　ActiveXcontrols are covered in Chapter 19.

Whether you're working with forms or reports, essentially the same process is followed to create and use controls. In this chapter, controls are explained from the perspective of a form.

The different control types

There are many different control types on a form or report. You can create some of these controls by using the Toolbox shown in Figure 15-1. In this book, you learn to create and use the most-often-used controls (which are listed in Table 15-1). In this chapter, you learn when to use each control; you also learn how these controls work.

Table 15-1
Controls You Can Create in Access Forms and Reports

Basic Controls

Label	Literal text is displayed in a label control.
Text box	Data is typed into a text box.

Enhanced Data Entry and Data Validation Controls

Option group	This group holds multiple option buttons, checkboxes, or toggle buttons.
Toggle button	This is a two-state button, up or down, which usually uses pictures or icons instead of text to display different states.
Option button	Also called a radio button, this button is displayed as a circle with a dot when the option is on.
Checkbox	This is another two-state control, shown as a square that contains a check mark if it's on and an empty square if it's off.
Combo box	This box is a pop-up list of values that allows entries not on the list.
List box	This is a list of values that is always displayed on the form or report.
Command button	Also called a *push button*, this button is used to call a macro or run a Basic program to initiate an action.
Subform/Subreport	This control displays another form or report within the original form or report.
Tab control	This control can display multiple pages in a file folder type interface.

Graphic and Picture Controls

Image	Displays a bitmap picture with very little overhead.
Unbound object frame	This frame holds an OLE object or embedded picture that is not tied to a table field and includes graphs, pictures, sound files, and video.
Bound object frame	This frame holds an OLE object or embedded picture that is tied to a table field.
Line	This is a single line of variable thickness and color, which is used for separation.
Rectangle	A rectangle can be any color or size or can be filled in or blank; the rectangle is used for emphasis.
Page break	This is usually used for reports and denotes a physical page break.

Note   If the Toolbox is not displayed, display it by selecting View ➪ Toolbox or by clicking the Toolbox icon.

Tip   The Toolbox can be moved, resized, and anchored on the window. You can anchor it to any border, grab it, and resize it in the middle of the window. Figure 15-1 shows the resulting new form.

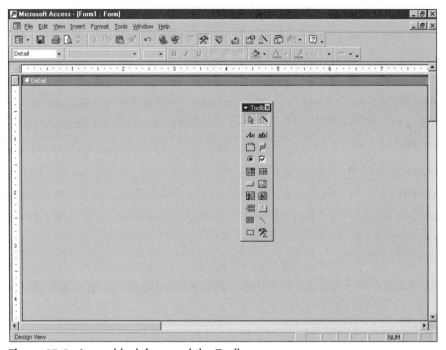

Figure 15-1: A new blank form and the Toolbox.

The Control Wizard icon in the Toolbox does not create a control; rather, it determines whether a Wizard is automatically activated when you create certain controls. The option group, combo box, list box, subform/subreport, object frame, and command button controls all have Wizards that Access starts when you create a new control. The More Controls icon is used to display a list of custom controls that you can add to Access 2000.

Understanding bound, unbound, and calculated controls

There are three basic types of controls:

✦ Bound controls

✦ Unbound controls

✦ Calculated controls

Bound controls are those that are bound to a table field. When you enter a value into a bound control, Access automatically updates the table field in the current record. Most of the controls that let you enter information can be bound; these include OLE (Object Linking and Embedding) fields. Bound controls can be most data types, including text, dates, numbers, Yes/No, pictures, and memo fields.

Unbound controls retain the value entered but do not update any table fields. You can use these controls for text display; for values to be passed to macros, lines, and rectangles; or for holding OLE objects (such as bitmap pictures) that are not stored in a table but on the form itself. Unbound controls are also known as *variables* or *memory variables*.

Calculated controls are based on expressions, such as functions or calculations. Calculated controls are also unbound as they do not update table fields. An example of a calculated control is =[Medication Price] + [Treatment Price]; this control calculates the total of two table fields for display on a form.

Figure 15-2 shows examples of these three control types. The picture of the mountain, which is the company's logo, and the text *Mountain Animal Hospital* are unbound controls. You can find bound controls that contain field names (including the picture) below the text and logo. The animal's age is a calculated control. You can see that the function DateDiff is used to calculate the number of years from the *Date of Birth* bound control to the function Now(), which returns the current date.

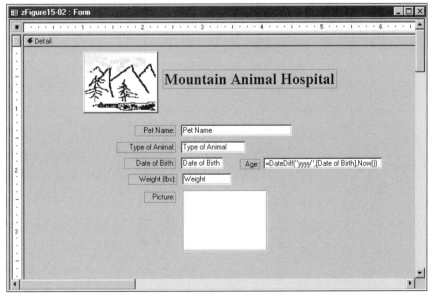

Figure 15-2: The three control types.

Standards for Using Controls

Most of you reading this book have used Microsoft Windows. You have probably used other applications in Windows as well, such as word processing applications (Word for Windows, WordPerfect for Windows, or WordPad) or spreadsheet applications (Excel, 1-2-3 for Windows, or Quattro Pro). There is a difference, however, between using a Windows application and designing one.

The controls in Access 2000 have specific purposes. Their uses are not decided by whim or intuition; a scientific method determines which control should be used for each specific situation. Experience will show you that correct screen and report designs lead to more usable applications.

Label controls

A *label control* displays descriptive text (such as a title, a caption, or instructions) on a form or report. Labels can be separate controls, as is common when they are used for titles or data-entry instructions. When labels are used for field captions, they are often attached to the control they describe.

You can display labels on a single line or on multiple lines. Labels are unbound controls that accept no input; you use them strictly for one-way communication (they are read and that's all). You can use them on many types of controls. Figure 15-3 shows many uses of labels, including titles, captions, button text, and captions for buttons and boxes. You can use different font styles and sizes for your labels, and you can boldface, italicize, and underline them.

You should capitalize the first letter of each word in a label, except for articles and conjunctions, such as *the*, *an*, *and*, *or,* and so on. There are several guidelines to follow for label controls when you use them in other controls. The following list explains some of these placement guidelines, which are shown Figure 15-3:

Command buttons	Inside the button
Checkboxes	To the right of the checkbox
Option buttons	To the right of the option button
Text box	Above or to the left of the text box
List or combo box	Above or to the left of the box
Group box	On top of and replacing part of the top frame line

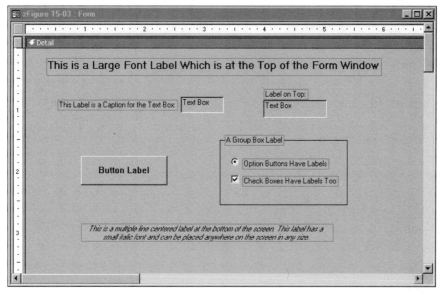

Figure 15-3: Sample label controls.

Text box controls

Text boxes are controls that display data or ask the user to type information at specific locations. In a text box, you can accept the current text, edit it, delete it, or replace it. Text boxes can accept any type of data, including Text, Number, Date/Time, Yes/No, and Memo, and they can be created as bound or unbound controls. Text box fields from tables or queries can be used, and the text box can contain calculated expressions. A text box is the most-used control because editing and displaying data are the main purposes of any database system.

Every text box needs an associated label to identify its purpose. Text boxes can contain multiple lines of data and often do (as when you use one to display Memo field data). Data that is too long for the width of the text field wraps automatically within the field boundaries. Figure 15-4 shows several different text boxes in Form view. Notice how the different data types vary in their alignment within the text boxes. The Comments text box displays multiple lines in the resized text box, which also has a scrollbar.

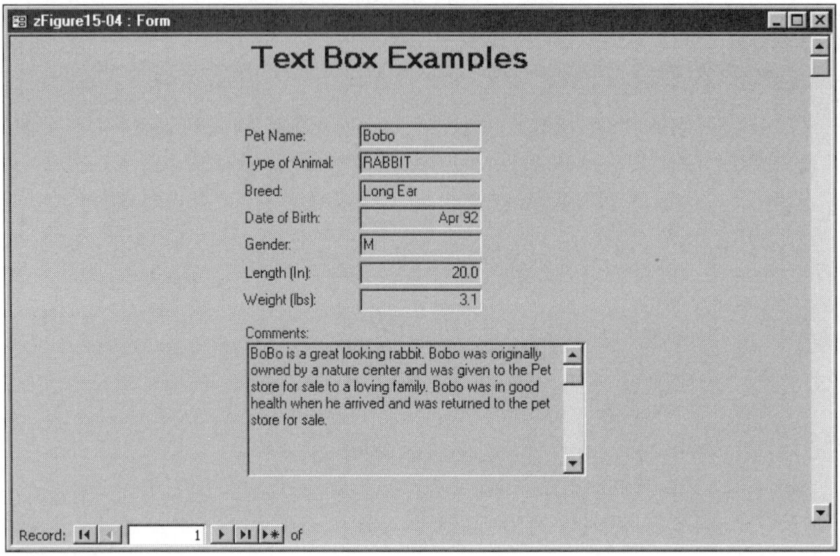

Figure 15-4: Sample text box controls.

Toggle buttons, option buttons, and checkboxes

There are three types of buttons that act in the same way, and yet their visual displays are very different:

✦ Toggle buttons

✦ Option buttons (also known as radio buttons)

✦ Checkboxes

These controls are used with Yes/No data types. Each can be used individually to represent one of two states: Yes or No, On or Off, or True or False. Table 15-2 describes the visual representations of these controls.

Toggle buttons, option buttons, and checkboxes return a value of –1 to the bound table field if the button value is Yes, On, or True; they return a value of 0 if the button is No, Off, or False. You can enter a default value to display a specific state. The control is initially displayed in a Null state if no default is entered and no state is selected. The Null state's visual appearance is the same as that of the No state.

Although Yes/No data types can be placed in a text box, it is better to use one of these controls. The values that are returned to a text box (–1 and 0) are very confusing, especially because Yes is represented by –1 and No is 0.

Table 15-2
Button Control Visual Displays

Button Type	State	Visual Description
Toggle button	True	Button is sunken
Toggle button	False	Button is raised
Option button	True	Circle with a large solid dot inside
Option button	False	Hollow circle
Checkbox	True	Square with a check in the middle
Checkbox	False	Empty square

Note As Figure 15-5 shows, using the special effects options from the Formatting toolbar can change the look of the option button or checkbox. See Chapter 17 for more details.

Tip You can format the display of the Yes/No values in Datasheet or Form view by setting the Format property of the text box control to Yes/No, On/Off, or True/False. If you don't use the Format property, the datasheet displays –1 or 0. Using a default value also speeds data entry, especially if the value selected most often is set as the default.

Option groups

An *option group* can contain multiple toggle buttons, option buttons, or checkboxes. When these controls are inside an option group box, they work together rather than individually. Instead of representing a two-state Yes/No data type, controls within an option group return a number based on the position in the group. Only one control within an option group can be selected at a time; the maximum number of buttons in such a group should be four. If you need to exceed that number, switch to a drop-down list box (unless you have plenty of room on your screen).

An option group is generally bound to a single field or expression. Each button inside it passes a different value back to the option group, which in turn passes the single choice to the bound field or expression. The buttons themselves are not bound to any field; instead, they are bound to the option group box.

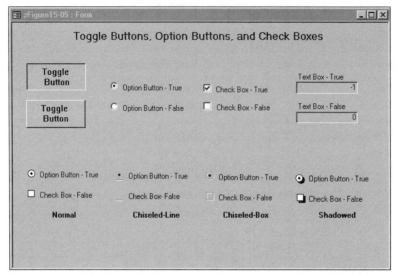

Figure 15-5: Sample toggle buttons, option buttons, and checkboxes.

Figure 15-6 shows three types of buttons; two of these types are shown in option group boxes. In the Toggle Buttons option group, the second choice is selected; the same is true of the Option Buttons option group. Notice, however, that the first and third choices are selected in the Check Boxes rectangle; the checkboxes are independent and are not part of an option group. When you make a new selection in an option group, the current selection is deselected. If (for example) you click on Option Button 3 in the option group box in the middle of Figure 15-6, the solid dot will appear to move to the third circle, and the second circle will become hollow.

Buttons in rectangles

The three types of buttons act very differently, depending on whether they are used individually or in an option group. You can create buttons that look like a group but that do not function as a single entity. Figure 15-7 shows a multiple-selection group. Notice that checkboxes 2 and 3 are simultaneously selected. This is not an option group; rather, this is a group of controls enclosed in a box. They act independently, so that they don't have to be in the same box; each control passes either a –1 (True) or a 0 (False) to the field, expression, or control to which it is bound. A common use for this type of grouping is to let a user select from a list of nonexclusive options, such as a list of reports or a list of days on which a process should occur.

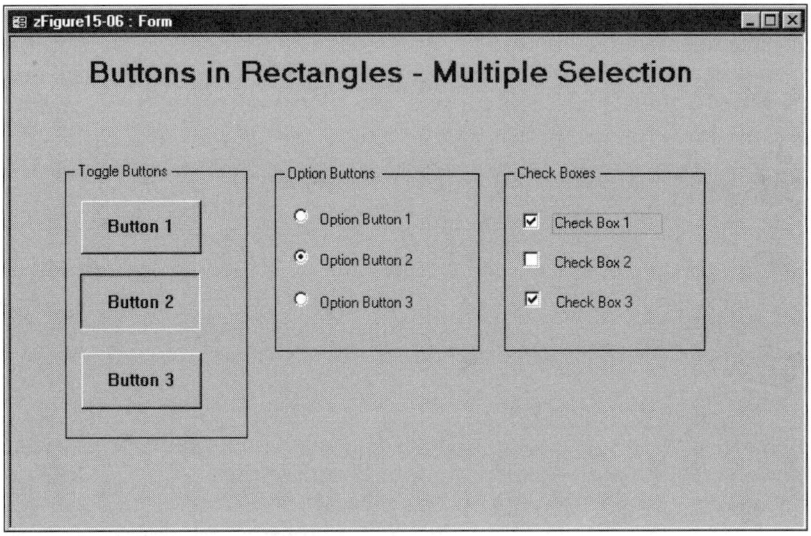

Figure 15-6: Three types of option groups.

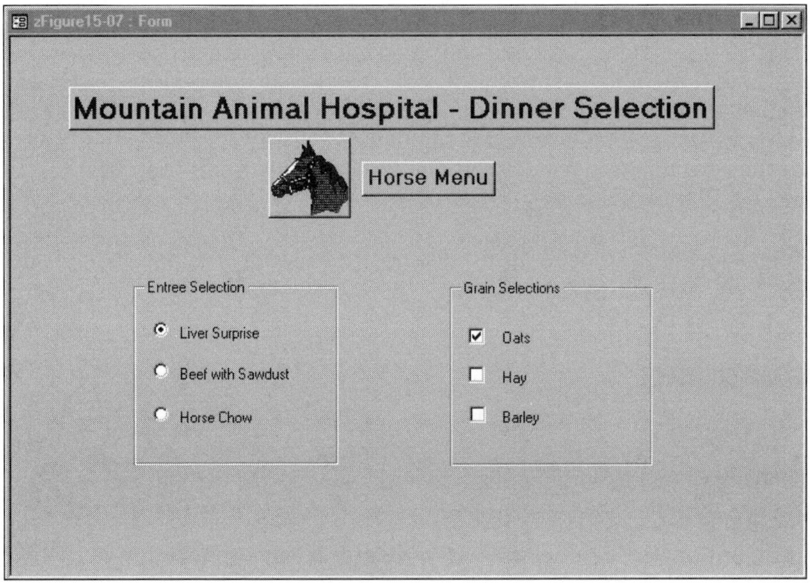

Figure 15-7: A multiple-selection group for selecting a meal.

Tip   You may want to create groups of buttons that look like option groups but have multiple selections. Rather than use an option button, simply enclose the group of buttons in a rectangle. Each button remains an individual entity instead of becoming part of a group.

List boxes

A *list box* control displays a list of data onscreen just as a pull-down menu does, but the list box is always open. An item in the list can be highlighted by moving the cursor to the desired choice and then pressing Enter (or clicking the mouse) to complete the selection. You can also type the first letter of the selection to highlight the desired entry. After you select an item, the item's value is passed back to the bound field.

List boxes can display any number of fields and any number of records. By sizing the list box, you can make it display more or fewer records.

Note   List boxes have a feature called *Multi-Select* property that allows you to select more than one item at a time. The results are stored in new properties and have to be used with Visual Basic for Applications.

List boxes are generally used when there is plenty of room onscreen and you want the operator to see the choices without having to click on a drop-down arrow. A vertical — and horizontal — scrollbar is used to display any records and fields not visible when the list box is in its default size. The highlighted entry is the one that is currently selected. If no entries are highlighted, either a selection has not been made or the selected item is not currently in view. Only items in the list can be selected.

You also have a choice of whether to display the column headings in list boxes. Figure 15-8 displays list boxes with three layout schemes.

Combo boxes

In Access, *combo boxes* differ from list boxes in two ways:

✦ The combo box is initially displayed as a single row with an arrow that opens the box to the normal size.

✦ As an option, the combo box lets you enter a value that is not on the list.

You see a list box and a combo box (shown both open and closed) in Figure 15-9.

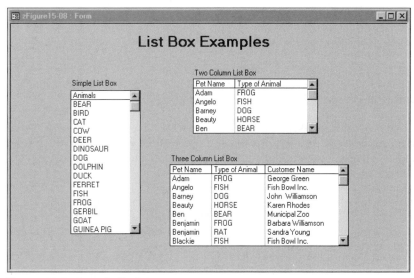

Figure 15-8: Sample list boxes.

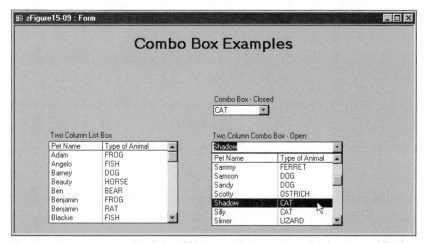

Figure 15-9: An example of the differences between combo boxes and list boxes.

Tab controls

The tab control is one of the most important controls because it allows you to create completely new interfaces using the tabbed dialog box look and feel.

Cross-Reference   Chapter 32 teaches you how to use the tabbed dialog box when creating a print dialog box example for Mountain Animal Hospital.

Today, most serious windows applications contain tabbed dialog boxes. Tabbed dialog boxes are very professional looking. They allow you to have many screens of data in a small area by grouping similar types of data and using tabs to navigate between the areas.

The tab control is called a tab control because it looks like the tabs on a file folder when you use it. Figure 15-10 shows the Access 2000 Tab Control icon and a tab control under construction on the design screen. As you can see, the tab control visually looks like the tabs seen in Form view.

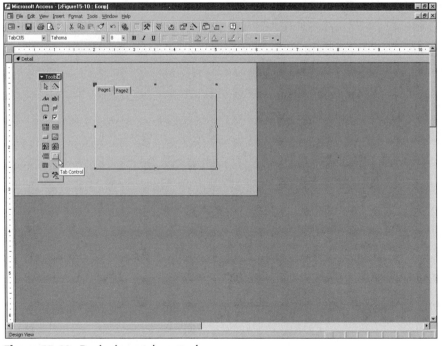

Figure 15-10: Designing a tab control.

A new tab control is created the same way you create any Access control. The tab control is selected, as shown in Figure 15-10, and then a rectangle is drawn to indicate the size of the control. When the tab control is initially shown, it is displayed with two tab pages. The tab control contains pages. Each tab you define creates a separate page. As you choose each tab in Design view, you see a different page. You can place other controls on each page of the tab control. The control can have many pages. In fact, you can have multiple rows of tabs, each having its own page. You can place new controls on a page or copy and paste them from other forms or other pages. You cannot drag and drop between pages of a tab control. To change the active page for the tab control, click the page you want and it becomes active (even in design mode).

New pages are inserted by right-clicking a tab and choosing the Insert command. The new page is inserted before the selected page. Pages are deleted by right-clicking a tab and choosing the Delete command. This deletes the active page and all the controls on it.

You can size the tab control but not individual pages. Individual pages don't have visual appearance properties — they get these from the tab control itself. Clicking the border of the tab control selects it. Clicking directly on a page selects that page. As with an Access detail section, you cannot size the tab control smaller than the control in the rightmost part of the page. You must move controls before resizing.

Creating New Controls

Now that you have learned about the controls that can be used on a form or report, you should learn how to add controls to a form and how to manipulate them in the Form Design window. Although the Form Wizard can quickly place your fields in the Design window, you still may need to add more fields to a form such as calculated fields.

The two ways to create a control

A control is created in either of two ways:

✦ Dragging a field from the Field List window to add a bound control

✦ Clicking a button in the Toolbox and then adding a new unbound control to the screen

Using the Field List window

The Field List window shown in Figure 15-11 displays all the fields in the open table/query that was used to create a form. This window is movable and resizable and displays a vertical scrollbar if there are more fields than will fit in the window.

Figure 15-11: The resized Field List window.

There are two methods for displaying the Field List window:

✦ Click the Field List button on the toolbar (this button looks like an Access table).

✦ Select View ➪ Field List... from the Form menu bar.

Note   After you resize or move the Field List window, it remains that size for all forms, even if toggled off or if the form is closed. Only if you exit Access is the window set to its default size.

Generally, dragging a field from the Field List window creates a bound text box in the Form Design window. If you drag a Yes/No field from the Field List window, you create a checkbox. If you drag a field which has a Lookup property, you create a list or combo box control. If you drag an OLE field from the Field List window, you create a bound object frame. Optionally, you can select the type of control by selecting a control from the Toolbox and dragging the field to the Form Design window.

Caution   When you drag fields from the Field List window, the first control is placed where you release the mouse button. Make sure that there is enough space to the left of the control for the labels. If there is insufficient space, the labels will slide under the controls.

There are several distinct advantages to dragging a field from the Field List window:

✦ The control is bound automatically to the field you dragged.

✦ Field properties inherit table-level formats, status-bar text, and data-validation rules and messages.

✦ The label text is created with the field name as the caption.

Using the Toolbox

By using the *Toolbox buttons* to create a control, you can decide what type of control is to be used for each field. If you don't create the control by dragging it from the Field List window, the field will be unbound and have a default label name such as Field3 or Option11. After you create the control, you can decide what field to bind the control to, enter text for the label, and set any properties.

The deciding factor of whether to use the field list or the Toolbox is this: does the field exist in the table/query or do you want to create an unbound or calculated expression. By using the Field List window and the Toolbox together, you can create bound controls of nearly any type. You will find, however, that some data types do not allow all the control types found in the Toolbox. For example, attempting to create a graph from a single field gets a text box.

In Access 2000, you can change the type of control after you create it; then you can set all the properties for the control. For example, suppose that you create a field as a text box control and you want to change it to list box. You can use Format ➪ Change To and change the control type. However, you can change only from some types of controls to others. Anything can be changed to a text box control; option buttons, toggle buttons, and checkboxes are interchangeable, as are list and combo boxes.

Dragging a field name from the Field List window

The easiest way to create a text box control is to drag a field from the Field List window. When the Field List window is open, you can click an individual field and drag it to the Form Design window. This window works in exactly the same way as a Table/Query window in QBE. You can also select multiple fields and then drag them to the screen together using these techniques:

✦ Select multiple contiguous fields by holding down the Shift key and clicking the first and last fields that you want.

✦ Select multiple noncontiguous fields by holding down the Ctrl key and clicking each field that you want.

✦ Double-click the table/query name in the window's top border to select all the fields.

After selecting one or more fields, drag the selection to the screen.

To drag the Pet Name, Type of Animal, Date of Birth, and Neutered/Spayed fields from the Field List window, follow the next set of steps. If you haven't created a new form, create one first and resize the form as instructed at the beginning of this chapter. When you complete those steps successfully, your screen should look like Figure 15-12.

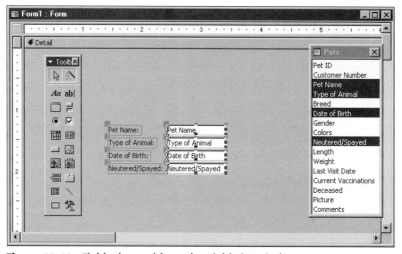

Figure 15-12: Fields dragged from the Field List window.

You can see four controls in the Form Design window, each made up of a label control and a text box control (Access attaches the label control to the text box automatically). You can work with these controls as a group or independently, and you can select, move, or delete them. To resize them, you must work with them separately. Notice that each is a text box control, each control has a label with a caption matching the field name, and the text box control displays the bound field name used in the text box.

You can close the Field List window by clicking the Field List button on the toolbar.

Creating unbound controls with the Toolbox

You can create one control at a time by using the Toolbox. You can create any of the controls listed in the Toolbox. Each control becomes an unbound control that has a default label and a name.

To create three different unbound controls, perform these steps:

1. Click the Text Box button in the Toolbox (the button appears depressed).

2. Place the cursor in the Form Design window (the cursor changes to the Text Box button).

3. Click and hold down the mouse button where you want the control to begin, and drag the mouse to size the control.

4. Click the Option Button icon on the toolbar (this button appears sunken).

5. Place the cursor in the Form Design window (the cursor changes to an Option button).

6. Click and hold down the mouse button where you want the control to begin, and drag the mouse to size the control.

7. Click the Check Box button on the toolbar (the button appears sunken).

8. Place the cursor in the Form Design window (the cursor changes to a checkbox).

9. Click and hold down the mouse button where you want the control to begin, and drag the mouse to size the control.

When you are done, your screen should resemble Figure 15-13.

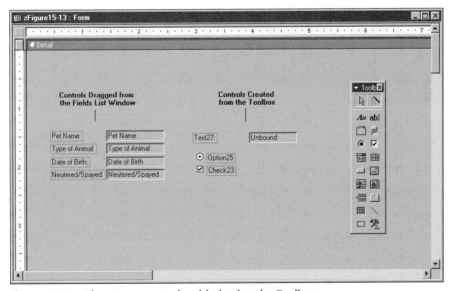

Figure 15-13: Three new controls added using the Toolbox.

Tip   If you just click the Form Design window, Access will create a default-sized control.

In Figure 15-13, notice the difference between the controls that were dragged from the Field List window and the controls that were created from the Toolbox. The Field List window controls are bound to a field in the Pets table and are appropriately labeled and named. The controls created from the Toolbox are unbound and have default names. Control names are assigned automatically according to the type of control and a number.

Later you learn how to change the control names, captions, and properties. Using properties speeds the process of naming controls and binding them to specific fields.

Selecting Controls

After a control is on the Form Design window, it can be worked with. The first step is to select one or more controls. Depending on its size, a selected control may show from four to eight *handles* (small squares that can be dragged) around the control box area at the corners and midway along the sides. The handle in the upper-left corner is larger than the other handles; use it to move the control. Use the other handles to size the control. Figure 15-14 displays these controls.

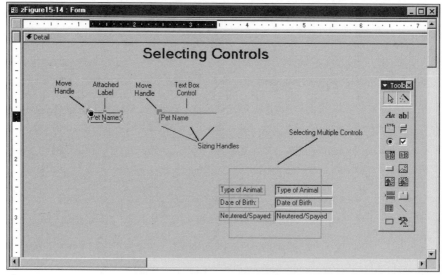

Figure 15-14: A conceptual view of selecting controls.

The Select Objects (also called the arrow or pointer) tool in the Toolbox must be on for you to select a control. The pointer always appears as an arrow pointing diagonally toward the upper-left corner. If the Toolbox is used to create a single control, Access automatically reselects the pointer as the default.

Deselecting selected controls

It is good practice to deselect any selected controls before you select another control. You can deselect a control by clicking an unselected area of the screen that does not contain a control. When you do so, the handles disappear from any selected control.

Selecting a single control

You can select any single control by clicking anywhere on the control. When you click a control, all the handles appear. If the control has an attached label, the handle for moving the label appears as well. If you select a single label control that is part of an attached control, all the handles in the label control are displayed, and only the *Move handle* (the largest handle) is displayed in the attached control.

Selecting multiple controls

Multiple controls can be selected in these ways:

✦ Click each desired control while holding down the Shift key.

✦ Drag the pointer through or around the controls that you want to select.

The screen in Figure 15-14 shows some of these concepts graphically. When you select multiple controls by dragging the mouse, a light gray rectangle appears as the mouse is dragged. When you select multiple controls by dragging the pointer through the controls, be careful to select only the controls that you want to select. Any control that is touched by the line or enclosed within it is selected. If you want to select labels only, you must make sure that the selection rectangle encloses only the labels.

Tip   When you click on a ruler, an arrow appears and a line is displayed across the screen. You can drag the mouse to widen the line. Each control that the line touches is selected.

Tip   If you find that controls are not selected when the rectangle passes through the control, you may have the Selection Behavior global property set to Fully Enclosed. This means that a control is selected only if the selection rectangle completely encloses the entire control. The normal default for this option is Partially Enclosed. You can change this option by first selecting Tools ⇨ Options... and then selecting Forms/Reports Category in the Options tabbed dialog box. The option Selection Behavior should be set to Partially Enclosed.

By holding down the Shift key, you can select several noncontiguous controls. This lets you select controls on totally different parts of the screen, cut them, and then paste them together somewhere else onscreen.

Manipulating Controls

Creating a form is a multistep process. The next step is to make sure that your controls are properly sized and moved to their correct positions.

Resizing a control

You can *resize* controls by using any of the smaller handles on the control. The handles in the control corners let you make the field larger or smaller — in both width and height — and at the same time. You use the handles in the middle of the control sides to size the control larger or smaller in one direction only. The top and bottom handles control the height of the control; the handles in the middle change the control's width.

When a corner handle is touched by the cursor in a selected control, the cursor becomes a diagonal double arrow. You can then drag the control size handles to the desired size. If the mouse pointer touches a side handle in a selected control, the pointer changes to a horizontal or vertical double-headed arrow. Figure 15-15 shows the Pet Name control after resizing. Notice the double-headed arrow in the corner of the Pet Name control.

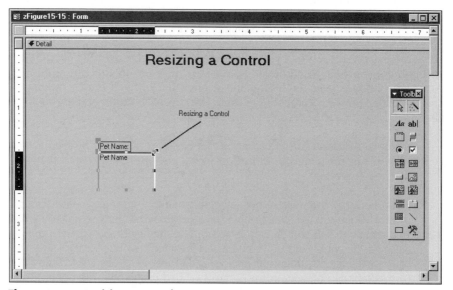

Figure 15-15: Resizing a control.

Tip   You can resize a control in very small increments by holding Shift and pressing the arrow keys. This also works with multiple controls selected. Using this technique, a control will change by only one pixel at a time.

Moving a control

After you select a control, you can easily move it, using either of these methods:

✦ Click the control and drag it to a new location.

✦ Select the control and place your mouse on the move handle in the upper-left corner of the control.

If the control has an attached label, you can move both label and control with either method. It doesn't matter whether you click the control or the label; they move together.

You can move a control separately from an attached label by grabbing the Move handle of the control and moving it. You can also move the label control separately from the other control by selecting the Move handle of the label control and moving it separately.

Figure 15-16 shows a label control that has been separately moved to the top of the text box control. The Hand button indicates that the controls are ready to be moved together. To see the hand, the control(s) must already be selected

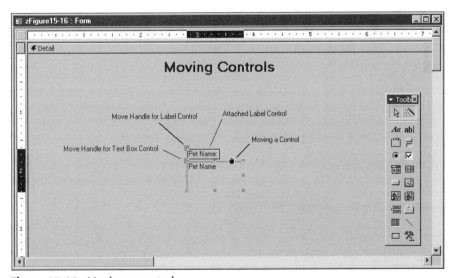

Figure 15-16: Moving a control.

Tip   You can move a control in small increments with the keyboard by holding Ctrl and pressing the arrow keys after you select a control or group of controls.

You can restrict the direction in which a control is moved so that it maintains alignment within a specific row or column by holding down the Shift key as you press the mouse button to select and move the control. The control will move only in the direction that you first move it, either horizontally or vertically.

You can cancel a move or a resizing operation by pressing Esc before you release the mouse button. After a move or resizing operation is complete, you can click the Undo button or select Edit ➪ Undo Move or Edit ➪ Undo Sizing to undo the changes.

Aligning controls

You may want to move several controls so that they are all *aligned* (lined up). The Format ➪ Align menu has several options, as shown in Figure 15-17 and described in the following list:

Left	Aligns the left edge of the selected controls with that of the leftmost selected control
Right	Aligns the right edge of the selected controls with that of the rightmost selected control
Top	Aligns the top edge of the selected controls with that of the topmost selected control
Bottom	Aligns the bottom edge of the selected controls with that of the bottommost selected control
To Grid	Aligns the top-left corners of the selected controls to the nearest grid point

Any number of controls can be aligned by selecting from this menu. When you choose one of the options, Access uses the control that is the closest to the desired selection as the model for the alignment. For example, suppose that you have three controls and you want to left-align them. They will be aligned on the basis of the control farthest to the left in the group of the three controls.

Figure 15-17 shows several sets of controls. The first set of controls is not aligned. The label controls in the second set of controls have been left-aligned. The text box controls in the second set have been right-aligned. Each label, along with its attached text box, has been bottom-aligned.

Each type of alignment must be done separately. In this example, you can left-align all the labels or right-align all the text boxes at once. However, you would have to align each label and its text control separately (three separate alignments).

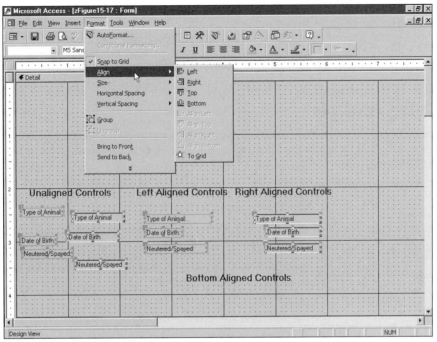

Figure 15-17: Aligning controls and the grid.

The series of dots in the background of Figure 15-17 is the *grid*. The grid assists in aligning controls. The grid is displayed by selecting View ⇨ Grid.

You can use the Format ⇨ Snap to Grid option to align new controls to the grid as you draw or place them on a form. It also aligns existing controls when you move or resize them.

When Snap to Grid is on and you draw a new control by clicking on and dragging the form, Access aligns the four corners of the control to points on the grid. When you place a new control by clicking the form or report, only the upper-left corner is aligned.

As you move or resize existing controls, Access 2000 lets you move only from grid point to grid point. When Snap to Grid is off, Access 2000 ignores the grid and lets you place a control anywhere on the form or report.

Tip

You can turn off Snap to Grid temporarily by pressing the Ctrl key before you create a control (or while creating or moving it).

The grid's *fineness* (number of dots) can be changed from form to form by using the GridX and GridY Form properties. The grid is invisible if its fineness is greater than 16 units per inch horizontally or vertically. (Higher numbers indicate greater fineness.)

Another pair of alignment options can make a big difference when you have to align the space between multiple controls. The options Horizontal Spacing and Vertical Spacing change the space between controls on the basis of the space between the first two selected controls. If the controls are across the screen, use horizontal spacing. If they are down the screen, use vertical spacing.

Sizing controls

The Size option on the Format menu has several options that assist in sizing controls based on the value of the data, the grid, or other controls. The options of the Size menu are:

To Fit	Adjusts the height and width of controls to fit the font of the text they contain
To Grid	Moves all sides of selected controls in or out to meet the nearest points on the grid
To Tallest	Sizes selected controls so that they have the same height as the tallest selected control
To Shortest	Sizes selected controls so that they have the same height as the shortest selected control
To Widest	Sizes selected controls so that they have the same width as the widest selected control
To Narrowest	Sizes selected controls so that they have the same width as the narrowest selected control

Tip   You can access most of the format menu by right-clicking after selecting multiple controls. When you right-click on multiple controls, a menu displays that is similar to the Format menu on the Access menu bar. This is a quick way to resize or align your controls.

Grouping controls

New Feature   A new feature to Access 2000 is the capability to *group* controls. When controls are grouped, you can select and format many controls at one time, instead of one at a time.

To group multiple controls, select the controls by holding down the Shift key and clicking them. Once the desired controls are selected, select Format ➪ Group from the Access menu bar, as shown in Figure 15-18.

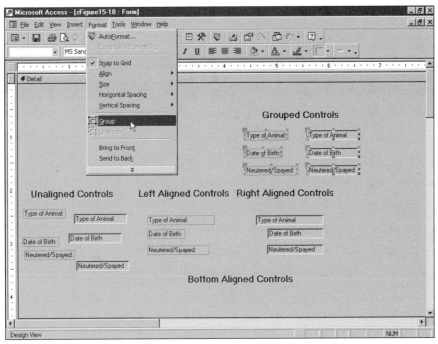

Figure 15-18: Grouping multiple controls together.

Once you have grouped the objects together, whenever you click any of the fields inside the group, the entire group is selected. If you click again, just the field is selected. If you want to resize the entire group, put your mouse on whichever side you want to resize and once the double arrow is displayed, click and drag until you reach the desired size, as shown in Figure 15-19.

To remove a group, select the group by clicking any of the fields inside the group and selecting Format ➪ UnGroup from your Access menu bar. This will ungroup the controls.

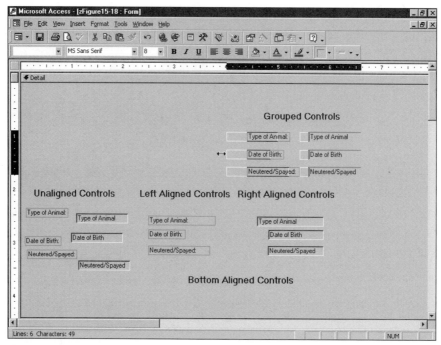

Figure 15-19: Resizing a group.

Deleting a control

If you find that you no longer want a specific control on the Form Design window, delete it by selecting the control and pressing Delete. You can also select Edit ⇨ Delete to delete a selected control or Edit ⇨ Cut to cut the control to the Clipboard.

You can delete more than one control at a time by selecting multiple controls and pressing one of the Delete key sequences. An entire group of controls can be deleted by selecting the group and pressing Delete on your keyboard or by selecting Edit ⇨ Delete. If you have a control with an attached label, you can delete only the label by clicking the label itself and then selecting a delete method. If you select the control, both the control and the label will be deleted. To delete only the label of the Pet Name control, follow the next set of steps (this example assumes that you have the Pet Name text box control in your Form Design window):

1. Select the Pet Name label control only.

2. Press Delete.

The label control is removed from the window.

Attaching a label to a control

If you accidentally delete a label from a control, you can reattach it. To create and then reattach a label to a control, follow these steps:

1. Click the Label button in the Toolbox.

2. Place the cursor in the Form Design window (the mouse pointer becomes the Text Box button).

3. Click and hold down the mouse button where you want the control to begin; drag the mouse to size the control.

4. Type **Pet Name:** and click outside the control.

5. Select the Pet Name label control.

6. Select Edit ➪ Cut to cut the label control to the Clipboard.

7. Select the Pet Name text box control.

8. Select Edit ➪ Paste to attach the label control to the text box control.

Copying a control

You can create copies of any control by duplicating it or by copying it to the Clipboard and then pasting the copies where you want them. If you have a control for which you entered many properties or specified a certain format, you can copy it and revise only the properties (such as the control name and bound field name) to make it a different control. This capability is useful with a multiple-page form in which you want to display the same values on different pages and in different locations.

What Are Properties?

Properties are named attributes of controls, fields, or database objects that are used to modify the characteristics of the control, field, or object. These attributes can be the size, color, appearance, or name. A property can also modify the behavior of a control, determining, for example, whether the control is editable or visible.

Properties are used extensively in forms and reports for changing the characteristics of controls. Each control has properties; the form itself also has properties, as does each of its sections. The same is true for reports; the report itself has properties, as does each report section and individual control. The label control also has its own properties, even if it is attached to another control.

Properties are displayed in a *property sheet* (also called a *Property window* because it is an actual window). The first column contains the property names; you enter properties in the second column. Figure 15-20 is the property sheet for the Date of Birth text box.

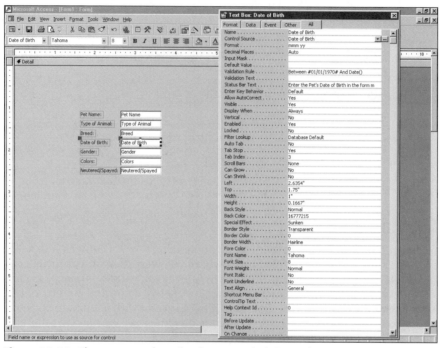

Figure 15-20: The property sheet for the Date of Birth text box.

Viewing a control's properties

There are several ways to view a control's properties:

✦ Click the control and select View ⇨ Properties from the menu bar.

✦ Click the control and then click the Properties button on the toolbar.

✦ Double-click any control.

✦ Right-click any control and select Properties from the menu.

To display the property sheet for the Date of Birth text box control, follow the steps below. First close the current form and don't save it. You will be creating a new blank form.

1. Create a new blank form using the Pets table.

2. Drag the fields Pet Name through Neutered/Spayed from the Field List window to the Form Design window.

3. Click the Date of Birth text box control to select it.

4. Click the Properties button on the toolbar.

As you can see in Figure 15-20, a partial property sheet is displayed. It has been resized larger. By widening the property sheet, you can see more of the its values; by increasing the vertical size, you can see more controls at one time. The vertical scrollbar lets you move between various properties. Only the text box control has more properties than can fit onscreen at one time. Because the property sheet is a true window, it can be moved anywhere onscreen and resized to any size. It does not, however, have Maximize or Minimize buttons.

As a tabbed dialog box, the property window lets you see all the properties for a control; you can also limit the view to specific properties. The specific groups of properties are:

Format	These determine how a label or value looks: font, size, color, special effects, borders, and scrollbars.
Data	These properties affect how a value is displayed and the control it is bound to: control source, formats, input masks, validation, default value, and other table-level properties.
Event	Event properties are named events, such as clicking a mouse button, adding a record, pressing a key for which you can define a response (in the form of a call to a macro or an Access Basic procedure), and so on.
Other	Other Properties shows additional characteristics of the control, such as the name of the control or the description that appears on the status bar.

Cross-Reference The number of properties available in Access has increased greatly since Access 2.0. The most important new properties are described in various chapters of this book. For a discussion of new event properties and event procedures, see Chapters 30–33.

The properties displayed in Figure 15-20 are the specific properties for Date of Birth. The first two properties, Name and Control Source, reflect the field name Date of Birth.

The Name is simply the name of the control itself. You can give the control any name you want. Unbound controls have names such as Field11 or Button13. When a control is bound to a field, Access names it automatically to match the bound field name.

The Control Source is the name of the table field to which the control is bound. In this example, the Date of Birth field is the name of the field in the Pets table. An unbound control has no control source, whereas the control source of a calculated control is the calculated expression, as in the example =[Weight] * .65.

The following properties are always inherited from the table definition of a field for a text box or other type of control. Figure 15-20 shows some of these properties inherited from the Pets table:

✦ Format

✦ Decimal Places

✦ Status Bar Text (from the field Description)

✦ Input Mask

✦ Caption

✦ Default Value

✦ Validation Rule

✦ Validation Text

Note   Changes made to a control's properties don't affect the field properties in the source table.

Each type of control has a different set of properties, as do objects such as forms, reports, and sections within forms or reports. In the next few chapters, you learn about many of these properties as you use each of the control types to create complex forms and reports.

Changing a control property

You can display properties in a property sheet, and you can use many different methods to change the properties, including:

✦ Entering the desired property in a property sheet

✦ Changing a property directly by changing the control itself

✦ Using inherited properties from the bound field

✦ Using inherited properties from the control's default selections

✦ Entering color selections for the control by using the palette

✦ Changing text style, size, color, and alignment by using the toolbar buttons

You can change a control's properties by clicking a property and typing the desired value.

Figure 15-20 displays an arrow and a button with three dots to the right of the Control Source property-entry area. Some properties display the arrow in the property-entry area when you click in the area. This tells you that Access has a pop-up list of values from which you can choose. If you click the down arrow in the Control Source property, you find that the choices are a list of all fields in the open table.

Three dots on a button constitute the Builder button, which opens one of the many Builders in Access. This includes the Macro Builder, the Expression Builder, and the Module Builder.

Some properties have a list of standard values such as Yes or No; others display varying lists of fields, forms, reports, or macros. The properties of each object are determined by the object itself and what the object is used for.

A feature in Access 2000 is the capability of cycling through property choices by repeatedly double-clicking on the choice. For example, double-clicking on the Display When property alternately selects Always, Print Only, and Screen Only.

Default properties

The properties shown in a specific control's property sheet are for that specific control. You can click a control to see its properties. You can also create a set of default properties for a specific type of control by clicking the toolbar button for that control type. For example, to view or change the default properties for a text box in the current form, follow these steps:

1. Make sure that the property sheet is displayed.
2. Click the Text Box button in the Toolbox.

Figure15-21 shows some of the default properties for a text box. You can set these properties; from then on, each new text box that you create will have these properties as a starting point. This set of default properties can determine the color and size for new controls, the font used, the distance between the attached label and the control, and most other characteristics.

Customized forms can be created much more quickly by changing the default property settings than by changing every control.

Access provides many tools for customizing your data-entry and display forms and your reports. In addition, you can apply the default properties to existing controls and save a set of default controls as a template. You can then use the template as the basis for a new form. Learning these techniques can save you even more time when you create new forms and reports.

Figure 15-21: Displaying default properties.

Cross-Reference   Chapter 17 covers saving control settings and using the AutoFormat tool to change settings globally.

Summary

In this chapter, you learned the basic usage of controls and properties for forms and reports. These points were examined:

✦ A new blank form is created by selecting Insert ➪ Form ➪ Design View.

✦ A control is an object on a form or report, such as a label or a text box.

✦ There are three types of controls: bound, unbound, and calculated.

✦ Text boxes, the most common type of control, let you enter and display data.

✦ The tab control helps you create tabbed user interfaces.

✦ Controls often have attached label controls to identify the purpose of the control.

✦ A new control is created by dragging a field from the Field List window or by using the Toolbox.

✦ The Field List window displays a list of all fields from the current table or query.

✦ A field can be dragged from the Field List window to create a bound control.

✦ A control is selected by clicking it. You can select multiple controls by clicking them while holding down the Shift key, by dragging a rectangle to enclose the controls, or by dragging the pointer through the controls.

✦ Controls are resized using the small resizing handles found in a selected control.

✦ Controls are moved by dragging. An attached control can be moved separately from its attached label by use of the larger Move handles in the upper-left corner of a selected control.

✦ Controls are aligned using the Align options of the Format menu. Controls can also be copied, duplicated, and deleted.

✦ The size of controls can be changed consistently using the Size options of the Format menu.

✦ Controls can be evenly spaced using the Horizontal and Vertical Spacing options in the Format menu.

✦ The Group feature, new to Access 2000, allows you to group controls together so that they can all be formatted at the same time.

✦ Properties are named attributes of controls, fields, or database objects. You can set properties that modify the characteristics of the control, such as size, color, or appearance.

✦ Properties are displayed in a property sheet. Each type of control has different properties.

✦ Although an individual control has its own properties, each form maintains a set of default properties for each type of control on the form.

In the next chapter, you learn to use controls to create a new form.

✦　　✦　　✦

Creating and Customizing Data-Entry Forms

In Chapter 15, you learned about all the tools necessary to create and display a form. In this chapter, you use all the skills that you acquired to create several types of data-entry and display forms.

This chapter uses the Customer and Pets tables in the Mountain Animal Start database to create several types of simple forms. Each control is explained by the use of one or more fields in these tables.

Creating a Standard Data-Entry Form

The first form created in this chapter is a simple data-entry form that uses two tables. In Chapter 8, a simple Pets data-entry form was created using a Form Wizard. In this section of the chapter, you create the more complex form shown in Figure 16-1. Generally, the more work that is done on a form, the easier it is for the ultimate user to use the form. This form demonstrates the use of label and text box controls from multiple tables as well as embedded pictures. You continue to modify this form in the next several chapters, adding more complex controls and emphasis, making the form increasingly more powerful and functional.

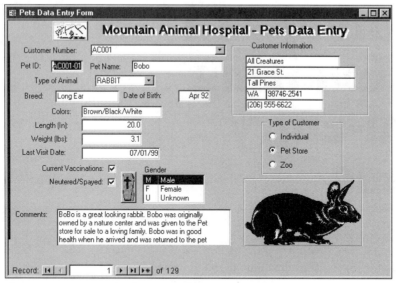

Figure 16-1: A complex data-entry form.

Assembling the data

With this design in mind, you need to assemble the data. To create this form, fields from the Customer and Pets tables are needed. Table 16-1 lists the necessary fields and their table locations.

To assemble this data, you first need to create a query called Pets and Owners, which includes all fields from both tables, even though you aren't going to use all the fields. These extra fields give you the flexibility to add a field later without redoing the query. You may need another field, for example, to derive a calculated control.

Table 16-1
Fields Needed for the Pets Data-Entry Form

Fields from Pets Table	*Fields from Customer Table*
Pet ID	Customer Name
Customer ID	Street/Apt
Pet Name	City
Type of Animal	State

Fields from Pets Table	Fields from Customer Table
Breed	ZIP Code
Date of Birth	Phone Number
Colors	Type of Customer
Length	
Weight	
Last Visit Date	
Current Vaccinations	
Deceased	
Neutered/Spayed	
Gender	
Comments	
Picture	

In this example, the data is sorted by the Pet ID. It's always a good idea to arrange your data into some known order. When you display a form, the data is listed in its physical order unless it is sorted.

To create the Pets and Owners query, follow these steps:

1. Click the Query object button in the Database window, and then click the New toolbar button to create a new query.

2. Select Design View in the New Query dialog box and click OK. The Show Table dialog box appears.

3. Add the Customer table.

4. Add the Pets table.

5. Close the Show Table dialog box.

6. Drag the asterisk (*) from the Customer field list to the first column in the QBE (Query by Example) design pane.

7. Drag the asterisk (*) from the Pets field list to the second column in the QBE design pane.

8. Drag the Pet ID field from the Pets field list to the third column in the QBE pane.

9. Click the Pet ID Show: box to turn it off.

10. Change the Sort to Ascending in the Pet ID field, as shown in Figure 16-2.

11. Select File ➪ Close, click Yes, and then name the query **Pets and Owners**.

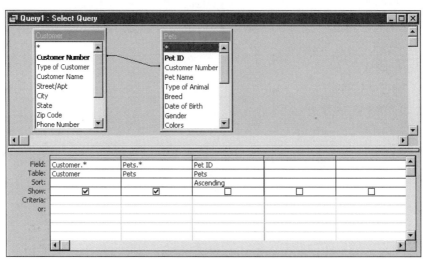

Figure 16-2: The Pets and Owners query.

 Note   The asterisk (*) is used to select all fields from each table.

Creating a new blank form and binding it to a query

Now that you've created the Pets and Owners query, you create a new blank form and bind it to the query. Later you add the controls. Follow these steps to complete this process:

1. Click the Database icon to display the Database window if it is not already displayed.

2. Click the Forms object button in the Database window and click the New toolbar button.

3. Select Design View in the Wizard list and then select the Pets and Owners query from the combo box at the bottom of the dialog box.

4. Click the OK button to create the new form.

5. Maximize the Form window.

Note   If the Toolbox and Property dialog boxes are not open, as they are in Figure 16-3, you can open them by selecting them from the View menu.

You now see a blank Form Design window, as shown in Figure 16-3. The form is bound to the query Pets and Owners as shown in the Property window on the screen. This means that the data from that query will be used when the form is viewed or printed. The fields from the query are available for use in the form design; they will appear in the Field List window.

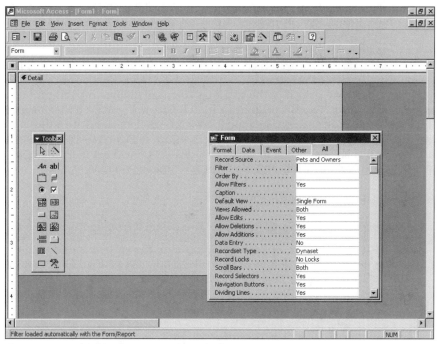

Figure 16-3: The blank Form Design window.

If you need to create a form that contains no field controls, you may want to create a blank form that is not bound to a query. This is done by not selecting a table/query when you select Design view in the New Form dialog box.

Defining the form display size

Now you must resize the workspace of the form. In Figure 16-3, the light gray area in the form is the workspace. If you place controls in the dark gray area outside it, however, the workspace expands automatically until it is larger than the area in which you placed the control. The workspace size you need depends on the size of your form. If you want the form to fill the screen, make it the size of your screen, and that depends on your screen resolution. More data can fit onscreen if you are using a SuperVGA screen size of 800 × 600 or 1024 × 768 than you can if you are using the standard VGA size of 640 × 480. Because you never know who may use a form you create; you should stay with the smallest size of any anticipated user.

A maximized standard VGA screen set to 640 × 480 in Microsoft Windows can display a full-screen size of approximately $6^1/4$ inches by $3^3/4$ inches. This includes the space for the title bar, menu bar, and toolbar at the top; the vertical scrollbar down the right side; and the navigation buttons/scrollbar and status line at the bottom. You can set form properties to control most of these elements. If you want to have the record pointer column down the left side, decrease the $6^1/4$-inch margin by approximately $1/8$-inch.

The easiest way to set the form size is to grab the borders of the light gray area with your mouse and drag it to the size that you want. If you grab either the top or bottom borders, your cursor becomes a double-arrow. If you grab the corner, the mouse pointer becomes a four-headed arrow and you can size both sides at the same time. (The four-headed arrow cursor is shown in Figure 16-4.) Next, set the form size to $6^1/4$ inches by $3^3/4$ inches by following the next set of steps, using Figure 16-4 as a guide. At this size, no form scrollbars should appear.

Follow these steps to change the form size:

1. Make sure that the ruler is on; otherwise, select it from the View menu.

2. Place the cursor in the bottom-right corner of the vertical and horizontal borders where the light gray area meets the dark gray area. The mouse pointer should appear as a four-headed arrow.

3. Grab the corner and (pressing the left mouse button) drag the borders until the size is exactly $6^1/4$ inches by $3^3/4$ inches.

4. Release the mouse button to accept the new size.

If controls are added beyond the right border, you have to scroll the form to see these controls. This is generally not acceptable in a form. If controls are added beyond the bottom border, you have to scroll the form to see these controls as well; this is acceptable because the form becomes a multiple-page form. Later in this chapter, you learn to control multiple-page forms.

Note   If you try the form and see a horizontal scroll bar along the bottom, either resize the right margin or turn the Record Selector property off for the form. This topic is covered later.

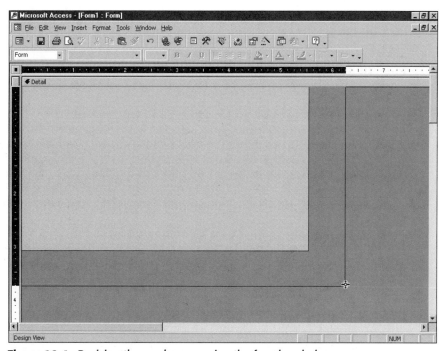

Figure 16-4: Resizing the workspace using the four-headed arrow cursor.

Working with form properties

You can set many form properties to change the way the entire form is displayed. Table 16-2 (in the "Eliminating the Record Selector Bar" section later in this chapter) discusses some of the most important properties. Changing default properties is relatively easy: you select the property in the Property dialog box (also known as the Property window) and set a new value. The following are some of the more important properties for the form.

Changing the title bar text with the Caption property

Normally the title bar displays the name of the form after it is saved. By changing the Caption property, you can display a different title on the title bar when the form is run. To change the title bar text, follow these steps:

1. Display the Property window if it is not already displayed and select the Format sheet by clicking the Format tab.

2. Click the Caption property in the Format sheet of the Property window.

3. Type **Pets Data Entry Form**.

4. Click any other property or press Enter.

You can display the blank form by selecting the Form button on the toolbar to check the result. The caption you enter here overrides the name of the saved form.

Specifying how to view the form

Two properties determine how your form displays records: *Default View* and *Views Allowed.*

The Views Allowed property has three settings: Form, Datasheet, and Both. The default setting is Both, which lets the user switch between Form and Datasheet view. If you set the Views Allowed property to Datasheet, the Form button and the View ⇨ Form menu selections cannot be selected; the data can be viewed only as a datasheet. If you set the Views Allowed property to Form, the Datasheet button and the View ⇨ Datasheet menu selections cannot be selected; the data can be viewed only as a form.

The Default View property is different; it determines how the data is displayed when the form is first run. Three settings are possible: Single Form, Continuous Forms, and Datasheet. Single Form displays one record per form page, regardless of the form's size. Continuous Forms is the default; it tells Access to display as many detail records as will fit onscreen. Normally you would use this setting to define the height of a very small form and to display many records at one time. Figure 16-5 shows such a form. The records have a small enough height that you can see a number of them at once. The final Default View setting, Datasheet, displays the form as a standard datasheet when run. Change this property setting to Single Form.

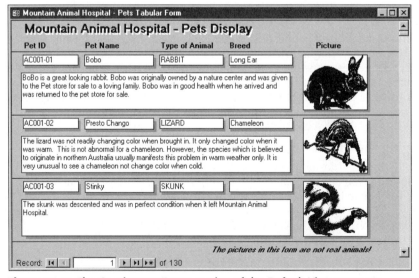

Figure 16-5: The Continuous Forms setting of the Default View property.

Eliminating the record selector bar

The Record Selector property determines whether you see the vertical bar on the left side of the form; this bar lets you select the entire record (you see the bar with the editing icon in datasheets). Primarily used in multiple-record forms or datasheets, a right-pointing triangle indicates the current record; a Pencil icon indicates that the record is being changed. Though the record selector bar is important for datasheets, you probably won't want it for a single record form. To eliminate it, simply change the form's Record Selector property to No.

Table 16-2 **Form Properties**		
Property	*Description and Options*	
Caption	Displayed on the title bar of the displayed form	
Default View	Determines the type of view when the form is run	
	Single Form	One record per page
	Continuous Forms	As many records per page as will fit (Default)
	Datasheet	Standard row and column datasheet view
Views Allowed	Determines whether user can switch between the two views	
	Form	Form view only allowed
	Datasheet	Datasheet view only allowed
	Both	Form or Datasheet view allowed
Allow Edits	Prevents or allows editing of data, making the form read-only for saved records	
	Yes/No	You can/cannot edit saved records
Allow Deletions	Used to prevent records from being deleted	
	Yes/No	You can/cannot delete saved records

Continued

Table 16-2 (continued)

Property	Description and Options	
Allow Additions	Used to determine whether new records can be added	
	Yes/No	You can/cannot add new records
Data Entry	Used to determine whether form displays saved records	
	Yes/No	Only new records are displayed/ All records are displayed
Recordset Type	Used to determine whether multitable forms can be updated; replaces Access 2.0's Allow Updating property	
	Dynaset	Only default table field controls can be edited
	Dynaset	All tables and fields are editable (Inconsistent Update)
	Snapshot	No fields are editable (Read Only in effect)
Record Locks	Used to determine multiuser record locking	
	No Locks	Record is locked only as it is saved
	All Records	Locks entire form records while using the form
	Edited Record	Locks only current record being edited
Scrollbars	Determines whether any scrollbars are displayed	
	Neither	No scrollbars are displayed
	Horizontal Only	Displays only horizontal scrollbar
	Vertical Only	Displays only vertical scrollbar
	Both	Displays both horizontal and vertical scrollbars
Record Selectors	Determines whether vertical record selector bar is displayed (Yes/No)	

Property	Description and Options	
Navigation Buttons	Determines whether navigation buttons are visible (Yes/No)	
Dividing Lines	Determines whether lines between form sections are visible (Yes/No)	
Auto Resize	Form is opened to display a complete record (Yes/No)	
Auto Center	Centers form on-screen when it's opened (Yes/No)	
Pop Up	Form is a pop-up that floats above all other objects (Yes/No)	
Modal	For use when you must close the form before doing anything else. Disables other windows; when Pop Up set to Yes, Modal disables menus and toolbar, creating a dialog box (Yes/No)	
Border Style	Determines form's border style	
	None	No border or border elements (scrollbars, navigation buttons)
	Thin	Thin border, not resizable
	Sizable	Normal form settings
	Dialog	Thick border, title bar only, cannot be sized; use for dialog boxes
Control Box	Determines whether control menu (Restore, Move Size) is available (Yes/No)	
Min Max Buttons		
	None	No buttons displayed in upper-right corner of form
	Min Enabled	Minimize button only is displayed
	Max Enabled	Maximize button only is displayed
	Both Enabled	Minimize and Maximize buttons are displayed

Continued

Table 16-2 *(continued)*

Property	Description and Options	
Close Button	Determines whether to display Close button in upper-right corner and a close menu item on the control menu (Yes/No)	
What's This Button	Determines whether Screen Tips appear when user presses Shift+F1 for Help	
Width	Displays the value of the width of the form; can be entered or Access fills it in as you adjust the width of the work area	
Picture	Enter the name of a bitmap file for the background of the entire form	
Picture Size Mode	Options:	
	Clip	Displays the picture at its actual size
	Stretch	Fits picture to form size (nonproportional)
	Zoom	Fits picture to form size (proportional); this may result in the picture not fitting in one dimension (height or width)
Picture Alignment	Options:	
	Top Left	The picture is displayed in the top-left corner of the form, report window, or image control
	Top Right	The picture is displayed in the top-right corner of the form, report window, or image control
	Center	(Default) The picture is centered in the form, report window, or image control
	Bottom Left	The picture is displayed in the bottom-left corner of the form, report window, or image control
	Bottom Right	The picture is displayed in the bottom-right corner of the form, report window, or image control

Property	Description and Options	
Picture Alignment (continued)	Form Center	The form's picture is centered horizontally in relation to the width of the form and vertically in relation to the topmost and bottommost controls on the form
Cycle	Options:	
	All Records	Tabbing from the last field of a record moves to the next record
	Current Record	Tabbing from the last field of a record moves to the first field of that record
	Current Page	Tabbing from the last field of a record moves to the first field of the current page
Menu Bar	Used to specify an alternate menu bar	
Shortcut Menu	Determines whether shortcut menus are active	
Shortcut Menu Bar	Used to specify an alternate shortcut menu bar	
Grid X	Determines number of points per inch when X grid is displayed	
Grid Y	Determines number of points per inch when Y grid is displayed	
Layout for Print	Determines whether form uses screen fonts or printer fonts	
	Yes	Printer Fonts
	No	Screen Fonts
Fast Laser Printing	Prints rules instead of lines and rectangles (Yes/No)	
Help File	Name of compiled Help file to assign custom help to the form	
Help Context ID	ID of context-sensitive entry point in the help file to display	

Continued

Table 16-2 *(continued)*

Property	Description and Options	
Record Source	Determines where the data to be displayed in the form is coming from, or where the data is going when you create a new record. Can be a table or a query.	
Filter	Used to specify a subset of records to be displayed when a filter is applied to a form. Can be set in the form properties, a macro, or in Visual Basic.	
Picture Type	Options:	
	Embedded	Picture is embedded in the form and becomes a part of the database file
	Linked	Picture is linked to the form. Access stores the location of the picture and retrieves it every time the form is opened.
Picture Tiling	Used when you want to overlay multiple copies of a small bitmap; for example, a single brick can become a wall (Yes/No)	
Toolbar	Use this property to specify the toolbar to use for the form. You can create a toolbar for your form by selecting the Customize option under the Toolbar command in the View menu.	
Tag	Use this property to store extra information about your form	
Has Module	Use this property to show if your form has a class module. Setting this property to No can improve the performance and decrease the size of your database	
Allow Design Changes	Options: Design View	Allows design edits in design view of the form only
	All Views	Allows design edits in all views.

Placing bound fields on the form

The next step is to place the necessary fields on the form. When you place a field on a form, it is called a *control* and it is bound to another field (its *control source*). Therefore, the terms *control* and *field* are used interchangeably in this chapter.

As you've learned, the process of placing controls on your form consists of three basic tasks:

- ✦ Display the Field List window by clicking the Field List button on the toolbar.
- ✦ Click the desired Toolbox control to determine the type of control that is created.
- ✦ Select each of the fields that you want on your form and drag them to the Form Design window.

Displaying the field list

To display the Field List window, click the Field List button on the toolbar (the icon that looks like a list sheet). The Field List window can be resized and moved around. The enlarged window (shown in Figure 16-6) displays all the fields in the Pets and Owners query dynaset.

Notice, in Figure 16-6, that the fields `Customer.Customer Number` and `Pets.Customer Number`, as well as `Customer.Last Visit Date` and `Pets.Last Visit Date` have the table name as a prefix. This prefix distinguishes fields of the same name that come from different tables within a query.

You can move the Field List window by clicking its title bar and dragging it to a new location.

Selecting the fields for your form

Selecting a field in the Field List window is the same as selecting that field from a query field list. The easiest way to select a field is to click it, which highlights it; then you can drag it to the Form window.

To highlight *contiguous* (adjacent) fields in the list, click the first field you want in the field list and move the mouse pointer to the last field you want; hold down the Shift key as you click the last field. The block of fields between the first and last fields is displayed in reverse video as you select it. Drag the block to the Form window.

Tip   You can highlight noncontiguous fields in the list by clicking each field while holding down the Ctrl key. Each field is then displayed in reverse video and can be dragged (as part of the group) to the Form Design window. One way this method differs from using the query Field List is that you *cannot* double-click a field to add it to the Form window.

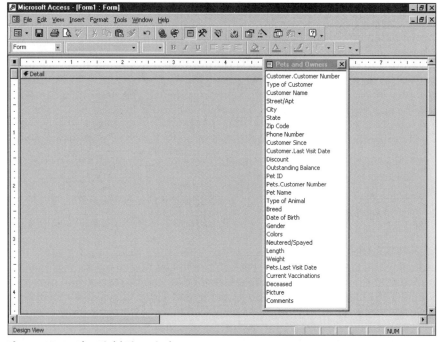

Figure 16-6: The Field List window.

You begin by selecting the Pets table fields for the detail section. To select the fields you need for the Pets Data Entry form, follow these steps:

1. Click on the Pet ID field.

2. Scroll down the field list until the Deceased field is visible.

3. Hold down the Shift key and click on the Deceased field.

The block of fields from Pet ID to Deceased should be highlighted in the Field List window.

Dragging fields onto your form

After you select the proper fields from the Pets table, drag the fields onto the form. Depending on whether you choose one or several fields, the mouse pointer changes to reflect your selection. If you select one field, you see a Field icon (a box containing text). If you select multiple fields, you see a Multiple Field icon instead. These are the same mouse pointer icons you saw on the Query Design screens.

To drag the Pets table fields onto the Form Design window, follow these steps:

1. Click within the highlighted block of fields in the Field List window.

2. Without releasing the mouse button, drag the mouse pointer onto the form, placing it under the 1¹/₂-inch mark on the horizontal ruler at the top of the screen and the ¹/₂-inch mark of the vertical ruler along the left edge.

3. Release the mouse button. The fields now appear in the form, as shown in Figure 16-7.

4. Close the Field List window by clicking the Field List button on the toolbar.

Notice that there are two controls for each field that you dragged onto the form. When you use the drag-and-drop method for placing fields, Access automatically creates a label control that displays the name of the field; it's attached to the text control that the field is bound to. If you followed along with Chapter 13, you changed the Customer Number field in the Pets table to a lookup field. Figure 16-7 shows this field displayed as a combo box (automatically because it is one of the properties that was changed in Chapter 11).

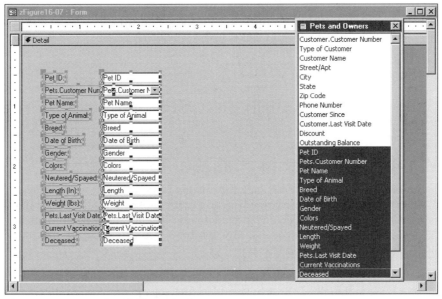

Figure 16-7: Dragging fields to the form.

Working with Label Controls and Text Box Controls

With the Text Box button selected in the Toolbox, dragging a field from the Field List window to a form creates a text box control with an attached label control automatically. Sometimes, however, you want to add text label controls by themselves to create headings or titles for the form.

Creating unattached labels

To create a new, unattached label control, you must use the Toolbox unless you copy an existing label. The next task in the example is to add the text header *Mountain Animal Hospital Pets Data Entry* to your form. This task is divided into segments to demonstrate adding and editing text. To create an unattached label control, follow these steps:

1. Display the Toolbox.
2. Click the Label button in the Toolbox.
3. Click just to the right of and above the label that says Pet ID and drag the cursor to make a small rectangle about 3 inches long and $1/4$-inch high.
4. Type **Pets Data**.
5. Press Enter.

To create a multiple-line label entry, press Ctrl+Enter at the cursor to force a line break in the control.

Modifying the text in a label or text control

To modify the text in a control, click the inside of the label and the mouse pointer changes to the standard Windows insertion point, an I-beam. Also notice that the Formatting toolbar icons become grayed out and cannot be selected. This is because within a label control — or any control — you cannot apply specific formatting to individual characters.

You can now edit the text. If you drag across the entire selection so that it is highlighted, anything new you type replaces the selected text. Another way to modify the text is to edit it from the control's Property window. The second item in the Property window is Caption. In the Caption property, you can edit the contents of a text or label control (for a text control, this property is called *Control Source*) by clicking the Edit box and typing new text. To edit the label so that it contains the proper text, follow these steps:

1. Click in front of the *P* in *Pets Data* in the label control.

2. Type **Mountain Animal Hospital -** before *Pets Data*.

3. Type **Entry** after *Pets Data*.

4. Press Enter.

If you want to edit or enter a caption that is longer than the space in the Property window, the contents will scroll as you type. Or you can press Shift+F2 to open a zoom box with more space to type.

The Formatting Toolbar

Access 2000 features a second toolbar known as the Formatting toolbar (which is described more fully in Chapter 17). Toolbars are really windows. You can move any toolbar by dragging it from its normal location to the middle of a form, and you can change its size and shape. Some toolbars can be docked to any edge of the screen (such as the left, right, or bottom). The Formatting toolbar, however, can be docked only at the top or bottom of the screen.

The Formatting toolbar integrates objects from the Access Form Design toolbar and the Palette. The first area of the Formatting toolbar (on the left side) selects a control or Form section, such as the Form or Page headers or footers, Detail, or the form itself. When you have multiple pages of controls and you want (for example) to select a control that's on page 3 or behind another control, this combo box makes it easy. The next few objects on the Formatting toolbar change text properties. Two more combo boxes let you change the font style and size. (Remember, you may have fonts others do not have. Do not use an exotic font if the user of your form does not have the font.) After the Font Style and Size combo boxes are icons for making a text control Bold, Italic, and Underlined. Beyond those are alignment icons for Left, Center, and Right text alignment. The last five pull-down icons change color properties, line types and styles, and special effects. See Chapter 17 for more complete descriptions.

Modifying the appearance of text in a control

To modify the appearance of text within a control, select the control by clicking its border (not in it). Then select a formatting style to apply to the label. Just click the appropriate button on the toolbar. To add visual emphasis to the title, follow these steps:

1. Click on the newly created form heading label.

2. Click on the **Bold** button on the Formatting toolbar.

3. Click on the drop-down arrow of the Font-Size list box.

4. Select **14** from the Font-Size drop-down list.

The label control needs to be resized to display all the text.

Sizing a text box control or label control

You can select a control by simply clicking it. Depending on the size of the control, from three to seven sizing handles appear. One appears on each corner except the upper left, and one appears on each side. When the cursor moves over one of the sizing handles, the mouse pointer changes into a double-headed arrow. When this happens, click and drag the control to the size you want. As you drag an outline the new size appears, indicating how large the label will be when the mouse button is released.

When you double-click on any of the sizing handles, Access usually resizes a control to a *best fit* for the text in the control. This is especially handy if you increase the font size and then notice that the text is cut off either at the bottom or to the right. For label controls, note that this *best-fit sizing* adjusts the size vertically and horizontally, though text controls are resized only vertically. This is because when Access is in form-design mode, it can't predict how much of a field to display — the field name and field contents can be radically different. Sometimes, however, label controls are not resized correctly and must be manually adjusted.

In the example, the text no longer fits within the label control but you can resize the text control to fit the enhanced font size. To do this, follow these steps:

1. Click the *Mountain Animal Hospital - Pets Data Entry* label control.

2. Move the mouse pointer over the control. Notice that the mouse pointer changes shape as it moves over the sizing handles.

3. Double-click one of the sizing handles.

The label control size may still need readjustment. If so, place the mouse pointer in the bottom-right corner of the control so that the diagonal arrow appears and drag the control until it is the correct size. You also need to move some of the controls down to make room to center the label over the form. You can select all the controls and move them down using the techniques you learned in the previous chapter.

You can also select Format ⇨ Size ⇨ To Fit to change the size of the label control text automatically.

As you create your form, you should test it constantly by selecting the Form button on the toolbar. Figure 16-8 shows the form in its current state of completion.

Now that you've dragged the Pets fields to the form design and added a form title, you can move the text box controls into the correct position. You then need to size each control to display the information properly within each field.

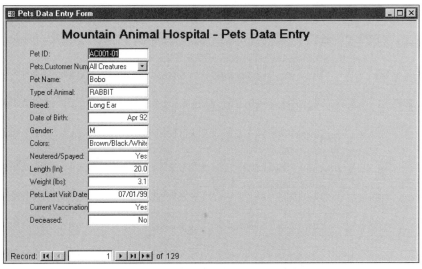

Figure 16-8: The form with bound and unbound controls.

Moving label and text controls

Before you move the label and text controls, it is important that you are reminded of a few differences between attached and unattached controls. When an attached label is created automatically with a text control, it is called a *compound control*— that is, whenever one control in the set is moved, the other control in the set is also moved.

To move both controls in a compound control, select one of the pair by clicking anywhere on it. Move the mouse pointer over either of the objects. When the pointer turns into a hand, you can click the controls and drag them to their new location.

Now place the controls in their proper position to complete the form design and layout, as shown in Figure 16-9. The Gender control's label has moved to a position above the text box control and some of the text labels are updated. Remember that you can do this by selecting the attached label control and then using the Move handle to move only the label. Also notice that some formatting was added, which you do in the next section.

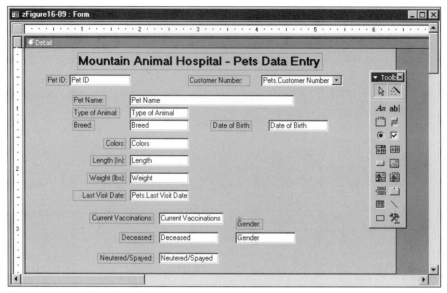

Figure 16-9: Selected and resized label controls in the Detail section.

Modifying the appearance of multiple controls

Changing the formatting of the labels may allow you to differentiate the label controls from the text controls. Although the standard is to leave the labels unformatted, you may change them to make your form unique. The following steps guide you through the process of changing the label controls to bold.

1. Select all the attached label controls in the form by clicking on them individually while holding down the Shift key. There are 14 label controls to select, as shown in Figure 16-9.

2. Click the Bold button on the toolbar.

3. Select Format ➪ Size ➪ to Fit to resize all the labels.

You cannot select the label controls in the steps given here if you use the drag-and-surround method and drag the rectangle through the text boxes because that method also selects all the text boxes; you only want to bold and resize the labels.

If you run the form now, the Length, Width, and Last Visit Date data items are all right-aligned within the text controls. You want to left-align these controls so that values appear left-aligned next to the label. To make this change, follow these steps:

1. Select the Length, Weight, and Pets. Last Visit Date text box controls only; drag to draw a box around the three text box controls.

2. Click the Left Align button on the toolbar.

Changing the control type

In Figure 16-9, the Customer Number field is a combo box (the default control type you defined in the table using the Lookup Wizard). Although there are times you may want to use a lookup field to display related data, this is not one of those times. In this example, you need to see the Customer Number for each Pet, not the Customer Name (you learn to display the Customer information later in this chapter). For now, use these steps to turn the combo box back into a text box control:

1. Select the Customer Number field.

2. Select Format ➪ Change To ➪ Text Box to change the control type.

Setting the tab order

Now that you've completed moving all your controls into position, you should test the form again. If you run the form and press Tab to move from field to field, the cursor does not move from field to field in the order you expect. It starts out in the first field, *Pet ID*, and then continues vertically from field to field until it reaches the *Date of Birth* field. Then the insertion point jumps down to *Gender*, back up to *Colors*, and then down again to *Neutered/Spayed*. This route may seem strange, but that is the original order in which the fields were added to the form.

This is called the *tab order* of the form. The form's *default tab order* is always the order in which the fields were added to the form. If you don't plan to move the fields around, this is all right. If you do move the fields around, however, you may want to change the order. After all, although you may make heavy use of the mouse when designing your forms, the average data-entry person still uses the keyboard to move from field to field.

When you need to change the tab order of a form, you can do so in either one of two ways. You may select the View ➪ Tab Order menu option or you may right-click any control and select Tab Order in the Design window to change the order to match your layout. To change the tab order of the form, follow the next set of steps (make sure that you are in the Design window before continuing):

1. Select View ➪ Tab Order or right-click any control and select Tab Order.

2. Click the Gender row in the Tab Order dialog box.

3. Click the gray area in front of the Gender row again; drag the row to the bottom of the dialog box to a point below the Deceased row, as shown in Figure 16-10.

4. Click the Neutered/Spayed row in the dialog box.

5. Click the Neutered/Spayed row again; drag the row to the bottom of the dialog box between the Deceased and Gender rows.

6. Click the OK button to complete the task.

Figure 16-10: The Tab Order dialog box.

The Tab Order dialog box lets you select either one row or multiple rows at a time. Multiple contiguous rows are selected by clicking the first row and dragging down to select multiple rows. After the rows are highlighted, the selected rows can be dragged to their new positions.

The Tab Order dialog box has several buttons at the bottom of the box. The Auto Order button places the fields in order from left to right and from top to bottom, according to their position in the form. This button is a good place to start when you have significantly rearranged the fields.

Each control has two properties that interact with this screen. The Tab Stop property determines whether pressing the Tab key lands you on the field. The default is Yes; changing the Tab Stop property to No removes the field from the tab order. When you set the tab order, you set the Tab Index property controls. In this example, the first field (*Pet ID*) is set to 1, *Customer Number* is set to 2, and so on. Moving the fields around in the Tab Order dialog box changes the Tab Index properties of those (and other) fields.

Adding multiple-line text box controls for Memo fields

Multiple-line text box controls are used for Memo data types such as the Comments field in the Pets table. When adding a Memo field to a form, make sure that there is plenty of room in the text box control to enter a large amount of text. There are several ways to make certain that you've allowed enough space.

The first method is to resize the text box control until it's large enough to accommodate any text you may enter into the Memo field, but this is rarely possible. Usually the reason you create a Memo field is to hold a large amount of text; that text can easily take up more space than the entire form.

One of the options in a text box control is a vertical scrollbar. By adding scrollbars to the Memo field's text box control, you can allow for any size of data entry. To create a Memo field text box control, follow these steps:

1. Display the Field List window.

2. Drag the Comments field to the bottom-left corner of the form below the Neutered/Spayed field.

3. Resize the Comments text box control so that the bottom of the control is about 1/2-inch high, and put the right side of the control just past the right side of the Gender text box control (as shown in Figure 16-11).

4. Close the Field List window.

The Comments text box by default displays a vertical scrollbar if the text in the box is larger than the display area. If you do not want to display a scrollbar, you can select the Scrollbar property in the Data sheet of the Property window and turn it off.

Figure 16-11 shows the added control.

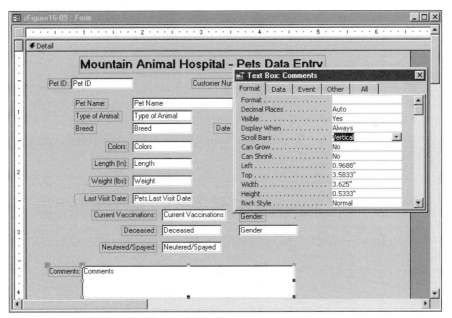

Figure 16-11: The form with a multiple-line text box control.

When you run the form, the scrollbar appears only once when you move into the Comments Memo field.

Adding a bound object frame to the form

When you drag a field that uses the OLE data type to a form, Access creates a bound object frame automatically. This control can be resized and moved the same as any control. To add the Picture OLE field to the form, follow these steps:

1. Display the Field List window.

2. Drag the Picture field to the center right area of the form.

3. Select the Picture attached label control by clicking the small solid box in the top-left corner of the text area.

4. Press Delete to delete the attached label control.

5. Move the left edge of the bound object frame just to the right of the Comments text box.

Note

One problem you may have when adding controls is that their default size exceeds the form's borders. When this happens, you must resize the control and also resize the border. If you don't resize the border, the form becomes scrollable outside the normal screen boundaries. This may work, but it doesn't create a well-displayed form.

To resize the bound object frame control and the form's border, follow these steps:

1. Select the Picture bound object frame.

2. Resize the control so that the right edge is just inside the original form border at $6^{1}/8$ inches on the top border. As you resize the control, you can follow the illustration in Figure 16-12.

3. Resize the form borders to make sure that they are at $6^{1}/4$ inches and $3^{3}/4$ inches.

When you're done, the design should look like Figure 16-12. Before you complete the OLE field, there is one more task to perform. The default value for the Size Mode property of a bound object frame is Clip. This means that a picture displayed within the frame is shown in its original size and truncated to fit within the frame. In this example, you need to display the picture so that it fits completely within the frame. Two property settings let you do this:

Zoom	Keeps picture in its original proportion but may result in extra white space
Stretch	Sizes picture to fit exactly between the frame borders

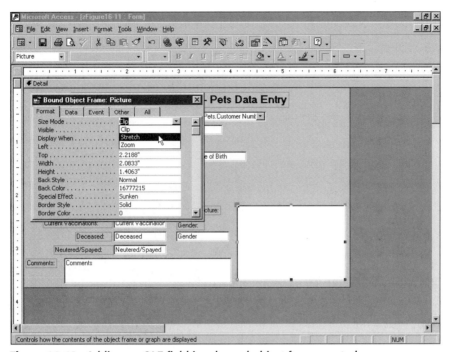

Figure 16-12: Adding an OLE field in a bound object frame control.

Although the Zoom setting displays the picture more correctly, the Stretch setting looks better, unless the picture's proportions are important to viewing the data. To set the Size Mode property of a bound object frame, follow these steps:

1. Select the Picture bound object frame.

2. Display the Property window.

3. Select the Size Mode property.

4. Select Stretch.

Figure 16-12 shows the form design as it currently is completed. Notice the Property window for the bound object frame control. The Size Mode property is set to Stretch.

When you complete this part of the design, you should save the form and then display it. You can now name this form **Pets Data Entry** if you want. Figure 16-13 shows the form.

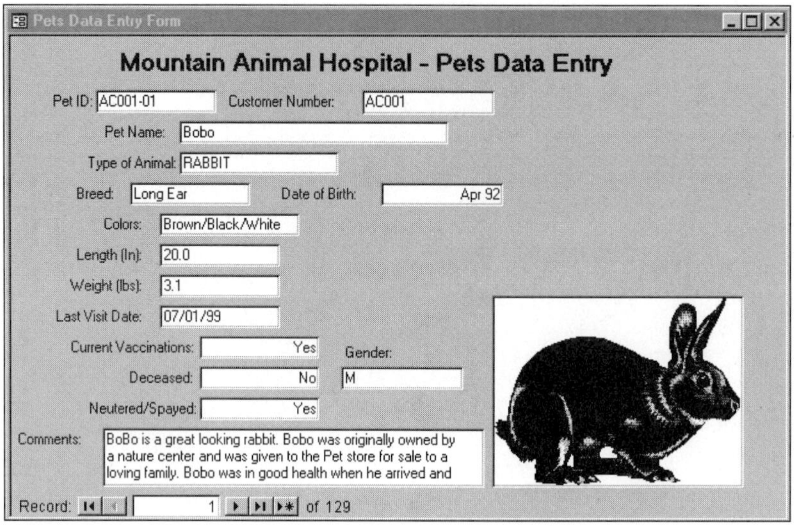

Figure 16-13: The form with a Memo and OLE field.

So far, you've created a blank form and added several types of controls to the form, but only fields from the Pets table are on the form. Originally, you created a query that linked the Pets and Customer tables. The Customer table can serve as a lookup table for each Pet record, which allows you to display customer information for each pet.

Using Fields from Multiple Tables in a Form

When you create a form from a single table, you use fields from the one table. When you create a form from multiple tables, fields from the second table are used as lookup fields to display additional information. In this section, you learn how to display the customer information.

Adding fields from a second table

You will now add the fields from the Customer table to the Pets form to display the customer name and address along with the Type of Customer field. These fields will be placed in the upper-right portion of the form. Follow these steps to add the customer fields to the form:

1. Display the Field List window.

2. Click the Type of Customer field.

3. Hold down the Shift key and click the Phone Number field.

4. Click within the highlighted block of fields in the Field List window.

5. Without releasing the mouse button, drag the fields to the form under the 5-inch mark on the ruler at the top of the screen and the ¹/₂-inch mark of the ruler along the left edge.

At this point, your form should look like Figure 16-14. Now all the fields needed for the Pets Data Entry form are in the form. You may have to adjust some of the other fields to make it look correct.

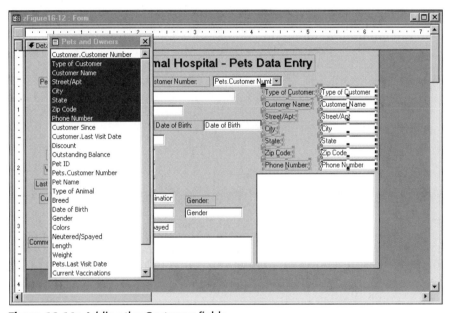

Figure 16-14: Adding the Customer fields.

As Figure 16-14 shows, the form begins with the Type of Customer field. Actually, you want that field separated from the others (you change it to a calculated field later). Use Figure 16-15 as a guide for the final placement of the field.

To move the Type of Customer control below the other customer controls, follow these steps:

1. Deselect all the selected controls by clicking any empty area of the form.

2. Select just the Type of Customer text box control and its attached label.

3. Move the control just below the Phone Number control so that it's just above the Picture bound object frame control.

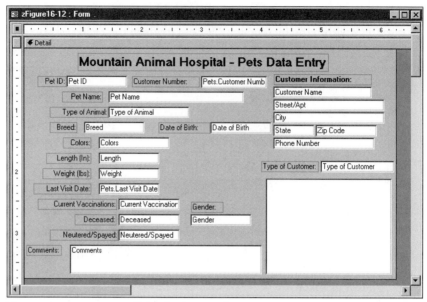

Figure 16-15: Customer fields in the Pets form.

Working with attached label and text controls

As Figure 16-15 shows, the remaining customer fields are displayed in a very small
area of the screen with no labels other than the label control Customer Information.
It is very easy to delete one or more attached label controls in a form. Simply select
the label control (or controls) to delete and press Delete. When deleting attached
controls, there are two choices:

✦ Delete only the label control.

✦ Delete both the label control and the field control.

If you select the label control and press Delete, only the label control is deleted. If
you select the field control and press Delete, both the label control and the field
control are deleted. To delete only the Customer label controls (that is, the
attached label controls), follow these steps:

1. Draw a box that surrounds only the six label controls from Customer Name
   through Phone Number.

2. Verify that only the label controls are selected (sizing handles are displayed in all
   the label controls; only the Move handle is displayed in the text box controls).

3. Press Delete.

To delete the field control yet keep the attached label control, first select the label control and Edit ➪ Copy. Then select the field control and press Delete to delete both the field control and the label control. Finally, choose Edit ➪ Paste to paste the copied label control to the form.

As you learned in Chapter 15, a label can be attached to an unlabeled control by cutting the unattached label control and then pasting it onto another control.

The final task is to move the customer controls to their final positions and add a label control, as shown in Figure 16-15. Follow these steps to complete this part of the form:

1. Rearrange the controls in the page header to resemble a typical mailing label's address format with State and Zip Code on the same line.

2. Move the Phone Number text box control under the State and Zip Code text box controls.

3. Move the block of name, address, and phone number controls into position so that it resembles Figure 16-15. Notice that all the control lines need to touch one another.

   • You can use the new Format ➪ Vertical Spacing ➪ Make Equal option to line up all the controls above each other. If there is still space between them, use the Decrease option.

4. Create a label control with the text **Customer Information**, as shown in Figure 16-15.

Creating a calculated field

The field Type of Customer is a numeric field that displays a 1 if the customer is an individual, 2 if the customer is a pet store, and 3 if the customer is a bird sanctuary, aquarium, or municipal zoo. Rather than have the number displayed, you can transform the value into a more recognizable text expression.

The easiest way to do this is to replace the original Type of Customer control with a calculated expression. In Chapter 12, you used the function called Immediate IF (IIf) that lets you transform one value to another. In this example, the expression uses two IIf functions together.

The expression must transform the value of 1 to "Individual," the value of 2 to "Pet Store," and the value of 3 to "Zoo." This is the complete expression:

```
=IIf([Type of Customer]=1,"Individual",IIf([Type of
Customer]=2,"Pet Store","Zoo"))
```

The first IIf function checks the value of the Type of Customer field; if the value is 1, the value of the calculated control is set to *Individual*. If the value is not 1, another IIf checks to see whether the value of Type of Customer is 2. If the value is 2, the value of the calculated control is set to *Pet Store*. If not 2, the value of the calculated control is set to the only other possibility, which is *Zoo*. To create this new calculated control, follow these steps:

1. Select the Type of Customer text box control.

2. Display the Property window and select the All sheet by clicking the All tab.

3. Change the Name property to Calculated Type of Customer.

4. Click the Control Source property and press Shift+F2 to display the zoom box.

5. In the Control Source property, type the following:

   =IIf([Type of Customer]=1,"Individual",IIf([Type of Customer]=2,"Pet Store","Zoo"))

6. Click OK.

7. Close the Property window.

Note   The Lookup Wizard for Access 2000 will help you create a control to display a different value from the value used in the control. You could use the Lookup Wizard in the Customer table and build a combo box to display *Individual*, *Pet Store*, or *Zoo* but store the values 1, 2, or 3. In Chapter 18, you create an option group, but this method is better for now.

Now that the form is complete, you can test it. Run the form and observe that the customer information is now displayed as you see the third record in Figure 16-16.

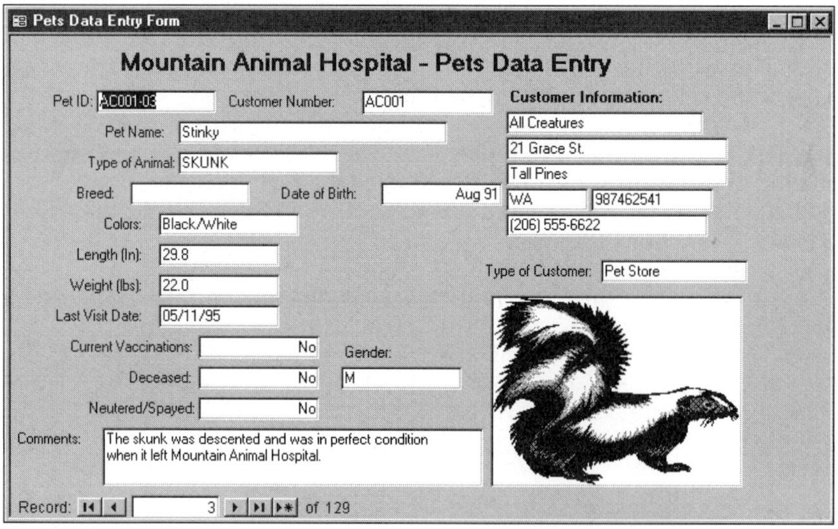

Figure 16-16: The Pets Data Entry form with customer information.

Changing the updatability of a multiple-table form

When you run the form you just created, you can edit the existing pet data or add new pet records. As you enter a new pet's valid customer number, the customer information is filled in automatically. You can, however, change the customer information. This information is being looked up in the customer table. Because it can affect all records for this customer, you don't want to allow changes to the information fields.

The Locked property prevents changes to the customer information fields. Select all the fields under Customer information. Change the Locked property, found on the Data sheet of the Property window, to Yes.

Updating a field such as Customer Name (which is on the one side of a one-to-many relationship) changes the one data field in the Customer table that changes a value for all records of pets owned by that customer.

Figure 16-17 shows the Locked property being changed to Yes for the Customer information in the Pets Data Entry form.

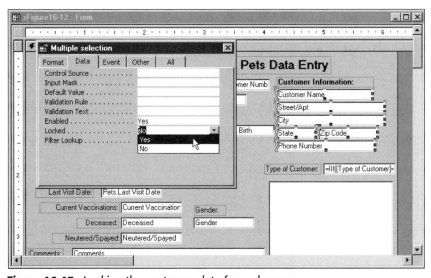

Figure 16-17: Locking the customer data from changes.

You should save this form with all the changes currently made. Name the form **Pets Data Entry Form - Without Formatting.** This form is used later in this chapter and again in the next few chapters, starting with the form in its current state.

Changing Defaults for Attached Label Positioning

Attached label controls are called compound controls because the two controls are attached. You can disable this feature by changing the default property named AutoLabel. When AutoLabel is set to Yes, a label control is automatically created that bears the name of the field the text control is bound to. With AutoLabel in effect, a label is created automatically every time you drag a field onto a form. Follow these steps to change the AutoLabel default:

1. Display the Toolbox if it is not already displayed.

2. Display the Property window if it is not already displayed.

3. Click the Text Box button on the toolbar. The title of the Property window should be Default Text Box.

4. Scroll down until you see the AutoLabel property.

5. Click the AutoLabel text box.

6. Change the contents in the text box to No.

The next property, AutoColon, automatically follows any text in a new label with a colon if the value of the property is set to Yes.

Two properties control where the label appears relative to the control itself. These are the Label X and Label Y properties. Label X controls the horizontal position of the label control relative to the text box control. The default is −1 (to the left of the text box control). As you make the value a smaller negative number, as with −0.5, you decrease the space from the attached label to the control. If you want the label after the control (as you may for an option button), you use a positive number, such as 1.5, to move the label to the right of the control.

Label Y controls the vertical position of the label control relative to the text box control. The default is 0, which places the label on the same line as the text box control. If you want to place the label above the control, change Label Y to −1 or a larger negative number.

The last option, Label Align, lets you control the alignment of the text within the label.

If you changed the AutoLabel default to No and you now drag fields from the Field List window to the form, no label controls attach. The AutoLabel property is in effect for only this form. Because you don't need to add further labeled fields to this form, you can leave the setting of AutoLabel as No.

Creating a Multiple-Page Form

Suppose that you want to add more information to the form. There is little room to add more fields or labels, but you may want to see a larger picture of the animal and to see all the comments at once in the multiple-line text box. Without getting a larger form, you can't do that. You can't just make the screen bigger unless you change to a higher screen resolution, which means getting the necessary hardware. One solution is to create a *multiple-page* form.

Why use multiple-page forms?

You use multiple-page forms when all your information won't fit on one page or when you want to segregate specific information on separate pages. Multiple-page forms allow you to display less information on a page so that a complicated form looks less cluttered. You can also place data items that are not always necessary on the second (or even the third) page, which makes data entry on the first page easier for the user.

You can have as many pages as you need on a form, but the general rule is that more than five pages make the form very tedious. There is also a 22-inch size limitation in the form. Another option is to use a macro to attach other forms to buttons on the form; then you can call up the other pages as you need them by selecting a button.

After you add pages to a form, you can move between them by using the PgUp and PgDn keys or you can use macros or Visual Basic for Applications to program navigation keys.

You can create a multiple-page form only when the Default View property of the form is set to Single Form.

Adding a page break

You can add *page breaks* to a form by adding a Page Break control (which is third from the bottom-left of the Toolbox). Use Figure 16-18 as a guide as you change the Pets Data Entry form to add a separate page for resized Picture and Comments controls.

Follow these steps to add a new page and a page break:

1. Increase the bottom margin of the form to $7^{1}/_{2}$ inches.

2. Move and resize the Comments text box control as shown in Figure 16-18.

3. Move and resize the Picture text box control.

4. Select the Pet Name text box control in the upper area of the control, and then select Edit ➪ Copy.

5. Select Edit ➪ Paste and move the copy to the second page of the form.

6. Display the Toolbox.

7. Click the Page Break button in the Toolbox.

8. Move the mouse pointer to the left corner of the intersection of the two pages (3^1/$_4$ inches).

9. Click the mouse to add the page break.

Figure 16-18 shows the completed design.

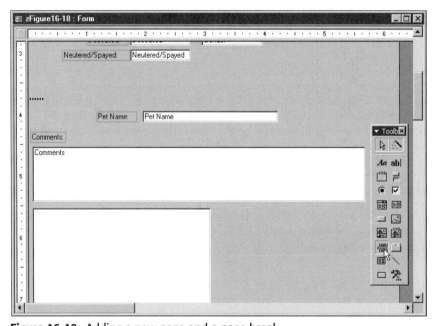

Figure 16-18: Adding a new page and a page break.

Notice that you copied *Pet Name* into the second page. This was for display-only purposes. Unless you change the properties of the second Pet Name control, you can also edit its value. When working with forms that require multiple pages, you may want to place controls that are used as headers in a form header section. If you are working with numeric data, you may also want to add a form footer section to display totals.

Figure 16-19 shows the second page of the form for the first record in the table.

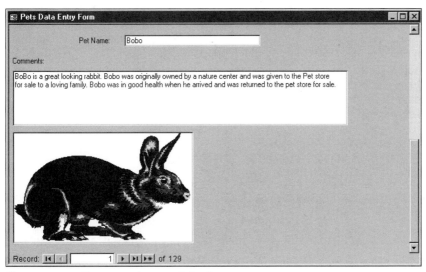

Figure 16-19: The second page of the form.

Do not save this last set of changes to create a multiple-page form. Reopen the form you saved as Pets Data Entry Form - Without Formatting.

Using Form and Page Headers and Footers

The most common use of a page or form header is to repeat identification information. In the Pets Data Entry form, for example, the text header is part of the form itself. When you have a second page, you don't see the text header. In Access forms, you can add both form and page sections. Sections include *headers* (which come before the detail controls) and *footers* (which come after the detail controls).

The different types of headers and footers

Several types of headers and footers can appear in a form:

Form header	Displayed at the top of each page when viewed and at the top when the form is printed
Page header	Displayed only when the form is printed; prints after the form header
Page footer	Appears only when the form is printed; prints before the form footer

Form footer   Displayed at the bottom of each page when viewed and at the bottom of the form when the form is printed

Form headers and footers are displayed in the form; you can use them optionally in a printed form. *Page headers and footers* are displayed only when a form is printed. Generally, unless you are printing the form as a report, you won't use the page headers or footers. Because you can create reports easily in Access (and even save a form as a report), you won't find much use for page headers and footers.

Creating a form header and footer

Form headers and footers are created by selecting View ➪ Form Header/Footer. When this menu option is selected, both the form header and form footer sections are added to the form.

To create a form header and move the text header label control into it, follow these steps:

1. Open the original Pets Data Entry Form - Without Formatting form in Design view.

2. Select View ➪ Form Header/Footer to display the form header and footer.

3. Select the label control Mountain Animal Hospital - Pets Data Entry.

4. Move the label control straight up from the detail section to the form header section.

5. Resize the form header to fit the label control properly, as shown in Figure 16-20.

6. Close the form footer area by dragging the form footer bottom border to meet the top border.

Sometimes when you display a form with an added header or footer, the equivalent amount of space is lost from the detail section. The size of your detail section must be adjusted to compensate for this lost space.

In this example, you might need to make the height of the detail section smaller because you moved the text label control to the form header section and moved the other controls up in the detail section. You are not using the form footer section, so close it.

The size of a section can be changed by placing the mouse pointer on the bottom border of the section, where it turns into a two-headed arrow, and dragging the section border up or down. You can only drag a section up to the bottom of the lowest control in the section.

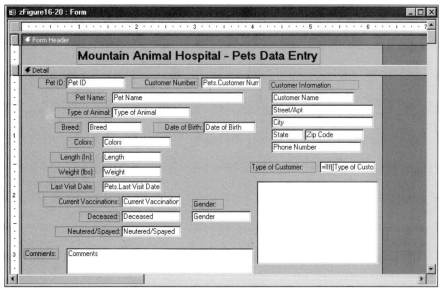

Figure 16-20: Adding a form header.

When you display a form with a header or footer section, the sections are separated from the detail section by a line. The form headers and footers are literally anchored in place. If you create a scrollable or a multiple-page form, the headers and footers remain where they are while the data in the detail section moves.

After completing the form, save it.

Printing a Form

You can print a form by selecting the File ⇨ Print option and entering the desired information in the Print dialog box. Printing a form is like printing anything; you are in a WYSIWYG ("What You See Is What You Get") environment, so what you see on the form is essentially what you get in the printed hard copy. If you added page headers or page footers, they are printed at the top or bottom of the printout.

You can also preview the printout by selecting the File ⇨ Print Preview menu option. This displays a preview of the printed page, as shown in Figure 16-21.

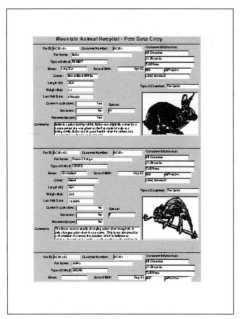

Figure 16-21: A preview of a form.

Converting a Form to a Report

By right-clicking a form name in the Database window and selecting Save As Report, you can save the form design as a report. The entire form is placed in the report form. If the form has form headers or footers, these are placed in the report header and report footer sections. If the form has page headers or page footers, these are placed in the page header and footer sections in the report. After the design is in the Report Design window, it can be enhanced using the report design features. This allows you to add group sections and additional totaling in a report without having to recreate a great layout!

Summary

In this chapter, you learned to create several types of forms without Form Wizards. In addition you learned that:

✦ When you create a form, you can adjust the form size by grabbing the borders and moving them.

✦ The Caption form property changes the text on the title bar.

✦ The Views Allowed form property lets you determine whether the user can switch to the Datasheet view.

✦ The Default View form property determines whether the form can display more than one record at a time.

✦ The Editing form properties determine whether the form is read-only and whether it allows only new records or records to be added, edited, or deleted.

✦ You can place fields on a form by using the Field List window and the Toolbox.

✦ The tab order determines the direction in which the insertion point moves within a data-entry form. You can change this order by selecting View ➪ Tab Order.

✦ Memo fields are generally displayed by use of a multiple-line text box control with a scrollbar.

✦ Generally, picture fields (which can be OLE objects or non-OLE bitmaps) are displayed in a bound object frame. The best way to display a picture is to set the Scaling control property to either Stretch or Zoom.

✦ The AutoLabel global properties let you determine where the labels, if any, appear when you create an attached label control.

✦ You can create a multiple-page form with the Page Break control.

✦ Page headers and footers appear only on the printed form.

✦ Form headers and footers appear at the top and bottom of each page in the form.

✦ You can print (or preview) a form by using the options on the File menu.

✦ You can save a form as a report design and later modify it by right-clicking a form name in the Database window and selecting Save As Report.

In the next chapter, you learn to add special effects to your forms. These special effects include colors, background shading, and other enhancements such as lines, rectangles, and a three-dimensional appearance.

✦   ✦   ✦

Creating Great-Looking Forms

In Chapter 16, you built a form that started with a blank Form Design screen. That form had no special formatting other than some label and text box controls. The most exciting object on the form was the picture of the rabbit. By using the various formatting windows and the Formatting toolbar, the line and rectangle controls, background pictures, and your own imagination, you can create great-looking forms with a small amount of work.

In this chapter, you learn to format the data-entry form you created in the preceding chapter to make it more readable and interesting to look at.

Making a Good Form Look Great

Just as a desktop publishing package can enhance a word-processing document to make it more readable, the form designer can enhance a database form to make it more usable. One way to make your database form more usable, is to draw attention to areas of the form that you want the reader to notice. Just as a headline in a newspaper calls your attention to the news, an enhanced section of a form makes the information it contains stand out.

The Access form designer has a number of tools to make the form controls and sections visually striking:

+ Lines and rectangles

+ Color and background shading

+ Three-dimensional effects (raised, sunken, etched, chiseled, shadowed)

+ Background pictures

+ Form headers and footers

In this chapter, you learn to add special text features to create shading, shadows, lines, rectangles, and three-dimensional effects. Figure 17-1 shows the form as it appears after some special effects are added.

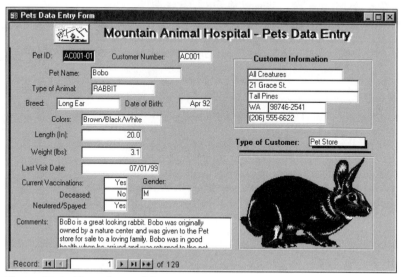

Figure 17-1: The enhanced form.

Understanding WYSIWYG

Access has a WYSIWYG (What You See Is What You Get) form designer. As your controls are created onscreen, you see instantly what they look like in your form. If you want to see what the data will look like during the form-design process, the onscreen preview mode lets you see the actual data in your form design without using a hard-copy device.

The Access form designer lets you add color and shading to form text and controls. You can also display them in reverse video, which shows white letters on a black background. You can even color or shade the background of form sections. As you specify these effects, you see each change instantly on the Design screen.

Using the formatting windows and toolbar

Important controls for enhancing a form are the formatting windows and the Formatting toolbar. There are five formatting windows, including:

✦ Fill/Background color for shading

✦ Font/Foreground color for text

✦ Line/Border Color for lines, rectangles, and control borders

✦ Line/Border Width for lines, rectangles, and control borders

✦ Special Effect, such as raised, sunken, etched, chiseled, or shadowed

Note The Formatting toolbar can be displayed or removed from the screen by selecting View ⇨ Toolbars and selecting Formatting or by right-clicking on the toolbar area and selecting Formatting. Figure 17-2 shows the five formatting windows pulled off the bar and opened. These windows can be used to format the different controls in a form.

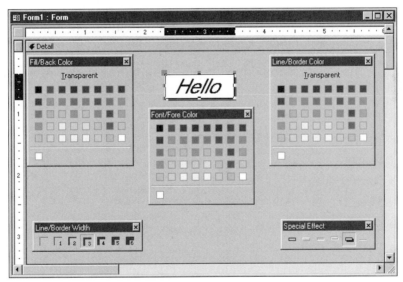

Figure 17-2: The five formatting windows.

Tip You can tell the selected color in the three color windows (Fill/Back Color, Font/Fore Color, and Line/Border Color) by looking at the small rectangle in each picture icon.

A *formatting window* is a window like the Toolbox or the Field List. You can move a formatting window around the screen, but you cannot anchor it the way a toolbar can be docked to a window border. To open the window and place it on the surface, click the formatting tool icon's down-arrow and then click the title bar and drag it to where you want it. A formatting window can remain onscreen all the time; you can use it to change the options for one or more controls. To close a formatting window, click the Close button or reselect its icon on the Formatting toolbar.

The appearance of a control is modified using a formatting window. To modify the appearance of a control, select it by clicking it, and then click the formatting window that that you need to change the control's options. (Refer to Figure 17-2 to see all five formatting windows.)

The Font/Fore Color (foreground text) and Fill/Back Color (background color) windows change the color of the text or background of a control. You can make a control's background transparent by selecting the Transparent button in the Fill/Back Color window. The Line/Border Color window changes the color of control borders, lines, and rectangles. Clicking the Transparent button in the Line/Border Color window makes the border on any selected control invisible.

The Line/Border Width window controls the thickness of control borders, lines, and rectangles. A line can be the border of a control or a stand-alone line control. The thickness of the line is defined with the thickness buttons. Available thicknesses (in points) are hairline, 1 point, 2 points, 3 points, 4 points, 5 points, and 6 points.

There is also a control property to designate the border style. The border styles include:

- ✦ Transparent
- ✦ Solid
- ✦ Dashes
- ✦ Short Dashes
- ✦ Dots
- ✦ Sparse Dots
- ✦ Dash Dot
- ✦ Dash Dot Dot

Note   A *point* (approximately $1/72$ inch) is a unit of measure for text and rule heights.

When you're finished with a formatting window, you can close it by clicking the X in its upper-right corner.

Creating special effects

Figure 17-3 shows some of the special effects that can easily be created for controls with the Special Effect formatting window. In the figure, you see that controls with gray as a background color display special effects much better than controls with white as a background color. In fact, a form background in gray or a dark color is almost mandatory to make certain special effects easy to see. The following sections describe each of these effects; you apply some of them later to modify the Pets Data Entry form.

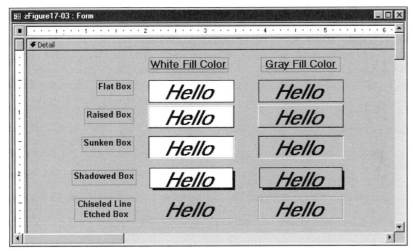

Figure 17-3: Special effects.

Special effects can be applied to rectangles, label controls, text box controls, checkboxes, option buttons, and option group boxes. Anything that has a box or circle around it can be raised, sunken, etched, chiseled, or shadowed. Figure 15-5 showed special effects applied to checkboxes and option buttons.

By simply selecting the control and adding the special effect, you can make your forms look much better and draw attention to their most important areas.

Flat

In Figure 17-3, the first pair of label boxes were created without any special effect. The flat box stands out better when set against the gray background.

Tip   You can also use the Border Width window to increase the width of the border lines, which makes the box more prominent. The Border Color window lets you change the color of the box. A thick white box also stands out.

Raised

The raised box is best used to set off a rectangle that surrounds other controls or for label controls. This box gives the best effect in a dark color against a dark background. As Figure 17-3 shows, the raised box is difficult to see with a white fill color. By increasing the width of the box, you can give the control the appearance of being higher than the surface of the onscreen background. The raised three-dimensional effect is achieved by contrasting the white left and top borders with the black right and bottom borders.

Sunken

The sunken special effect is the most dramatic and most often used. (It is the standard Windows 95 format in the Form Wizard and the default control format in the new version of Access.) As Figure 17-3 shows, either the white or the gray fill color looks very good on a gray form background. You can also increase the width of the border to give the effect of a deeper impression. The sunken three-dimensional effect is achieved by using black left and top borders and white right and bottom borders. The effect works well with checkboxes and option buttons.

Shadowed

The shadowed special effect places a solid, dark-colored rectangle behind the original control, which is slightly offset to give the shadowed effect. As Figure 17-3 shows, the black shadow works well behind a box filled with white or gray. You can change the border color to change the shadow color.

Etched

The etched effect is perhaps the most interesting of all the special looks. It is, in effect, a sunken rectangle with no sunken inside area.

Tip   Current Microsoft Windows 95, 98, and NT standards make heavy use of etched rectangles. Sunken rectangles are a Windows 3.1 standard and should only be used for text box controls. Groups such as option groups or rectangles around controls should use the etched look.

Chiseled

The chiseled effect adds a chiseled line underneath a selected control.

On the CD-ROM   In this chapter, you modify the form that you created in Chapter 16 so that it looks like Figure 17-1. If you are following the examples, you should have the *Pets Data Entry Form - Without Formatting* form open in the Form Design window.

Changing the forms background color

If your from will be primarily viewed onscreen instead of in print form, it may be beneficial to color the background. A light gray background (the Microsoft Windows default) seems to be the best neutral color in all types of lighting and visual conditions. To change the background for the form header and detail sections, select the desired section and then select the appropriate background color.

Tip   When changing the background color of form sections, also change the background of individual label controls for a more natural look. A label control generally doesn't look good if its background doesn't match the background of the form itself.

Enhancing Text-Based Controls

Generally, it's important to get the label text and data right before you start enhancing display items with shading or special effects. When your enhancements include label and text box control changes, begin with them.

Enhancing label and text box controls

You can enhance label and text box controls in several ways:

✦ Change the text font type style (Arial, Times New Roman, Wingdings)

✦ Change the text font size (4–200)

✦ Change the text font style (bold, italic, underline)

✦ Change the text color (using a formatting window)

✦ Add a shadow

Cross-Reference   In Chapter 16, you changed the title in the form header. You then changed the text font size and font style. Now you learn how to add a text shadow to the label control.

Creating a text shadow

Text shadows give text a three-dimensional look by making the text seem to float above the page while its shadow stays on the page. This effect uses the same basic principle as a shadowed box. Use this process to create text shadows:

1. Duplicate the text.

2. Offset the duplicate text from the original text.

3. Change the duplicate text to a different color (usually a lighter shade).

4. Place the duplicate text behind the original text.

5. Change the original text's background color to Clear.

To create a shadow for the title's text, follow these steps:

1. Select the label control that reads *Mountain Animal Hospital - Pets Data Entry*.

2. Select Edit ➪ Duplicate.

3. Select the white Fore color (second from the left) to change the duplicate text's color.

4. Drag the duplicate text up and to the right to create the offset from the text below it.

5. Select Format ➪ Send to Back.

After you complete the shadow, you may have to move the text and its shadow to accommodate the changes you made when you moved the controls. You also may have to move the section border. The text now appears to have a shadow, as shown in Figure 17-4.

Figure 17-4: The text with a shadow and reverse video.

Note   If you do not see the shadow, select the original text and then select the Transparent option on the Fill/Back Color Formatting toolbar.

Tip   The box around the label control is not visible when the form is printed because the Transparent button in the Border Color window is depressed.

When you duplicated the original text, the duplicate was automatically offset below the original text. When you place the duplicate text behind the original, it's hidden. You redisplay it by placing the original text in front. If the offset (the distance from the other copy) is too large, the effect will not look like a shadow. You can perfect the shadowed appearance by moving one of the label controls slightly.

Caution   Although the shadow appears correct onscreen and looks great, it won't print correctly on most monochrome printers. What you see normally is two lines of black text, which look horrible. If you plan to print your forms and don't have a printer that prints text in color (or prints many shades of gray by using graphics rather than text fonts), avoid using shadowed text on a form.

Changing text to a reverse video display

Text really stands out when you create white text on a black background. This setup is called *reverse video*; it's the opposite of the usual black letters on white. You can convert text in a label control or text box to reverse video by changing the Back Color to black and the Fore Color to white. To change the Pet Name text control to reverse video, follow these steps:

1. Select the Pet ID text box control (not the label control).

2. Select Black from the Back Color formatting window.

3. Select White from the Fore Color formatting window.

Tip

To make it more dramatic, you may want to set the font to Bold and resize the frame.

Caution

With some laser printers you may not see reverse video if you print your form because the printer's drivers cannot print it.

Displaying label or text box control properties

As you change values in a label control or text box control using a formatting window, you are actually changing the control's properties. Figure 17-5 displays the Property window for the text box control in the form header you just modified. As Figure 17-5 shows, a formatting window can affect many properties. Table 17-1 shows the various properties (and their possible values) for both label and text box controls.

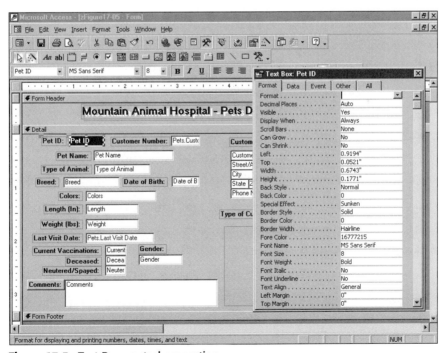

Figure 17-5: Text Box control properties.

Table 17-1
Label or Text Box Format Properties

Property	Options	Description
Format	Various Numeric and Date Formats	Determines how the data is displayed
Decimal Places	Auto, 1–15	How many decimal places, if any, you want to apply to this control
Visible	Yes/No	Yes: Control is displayed normally No: Control is invisible when displayed
Display When	Always, Print Only, Screen Only	Determines when the control is displayed
Scrollbars	None, Vertical, Horizontal, Both	Specifies when scrollbars are displayed
Can Grow	Yes/No	If multiple lines of text are in the control, does the text box get larger?
Can Shrink	Yes/No	If fewer lines of text are in the control than in its initial size, does the text box height get smaller?
Left	Position of the left corner of the control in the current measure (include an indicator, such as cm or in, if you use a different unit of measurement)	Specifies the position of an object on the horizontal axis
Top	Position of the top corner of the control in the current measure	Specifies the position of an object on the vertical axis
Width	The width of the control in the current unit of measure	Specifies the width of an object
Height	The height of the control in the current unit of measure	Specifies the height of an object
Back Style	Transparent, Normal	Determines whether a control's background is opaque or transparent
Back Color	Any available background color	Specifies the color for the interior of the control or section
Special Effect	Flat, Raised, Sunken, Shadowed, Etched, Chiseled	Determines whether a section or control appears flat, raised, sunken, shadowed, etched, or chiseled

Property	Options	Description
Border Style	Transparent or Solid, Dashes, Dots (Lines/Boxes Only)	Determines whether a control's border is opaque or transparent
Border Color	Any available border color	Specifies the color of a control's border
Border Width	Hairline, 1pt, 2pt, 3pt, 4pt, 5pt, 6pt	Specifies the width of a control's border
Fore Color	Any selection from a formatting window	Specifies the color for text in a control or the printing and drawing color
Font Name	Any system font name that appears on the toolbar; depends on fonts installed	Specifies the name of the font used for text or a control
Font Size	Any size available for a given font	Specifies the size of the font used for text or a control
Font Weight	Extra Light, Light, Normal, Medium, Semi-Bold, Bold, Extra Bold, Heavy	Specifies the width of the line Windows uses to display and print characters
Font Italic	Yes/No	Italicizes text in a control
Font Underline	Yes/No	Underlines text in a control
Text Align	General (default), Left, Center, Right	Sets the alignment for text in a control
Left Margin	Used to set margins on a control. Enter in inches for the left margin. Can only be used for text box and label controls	
Right Margin	Used to set margins on a control. Enter in inches for the right margin. Can only be used for text box and label controls	
Top Margin	Used to set margins on a control. Enter in inches for the top margin. Can only be used for text box and label controls	
Bottom Margin	Used to set margins on a control. Enter in inches for the bottom margin. Can only be used for text box and label controls	

Continued

Table 17-1 *(continued)*		
Property	*Options*	*Description*
Line Spacing	Used to specify line spacing for a control. Enter in inches for the amount of space between lines. Can only be used for text box and label controls	
Is Hyperlink		Used to specify if control is a hyperlink. If you select Yes, the text is blue and underlined. Can be used for a direct link to the Internet and for text box and label controls

Although you can set many of these controls from the property sheet, it's much easier to drag the control to set the Top, Left, Width, and Height properties or to use a formatting window to set the other properties of the control.

Tip   To move the selected control a very small amount, press Ctrl+arrow key; the control will move slightly in the direction of the arrow key used.

Displaying Images in Forms

You can display a picture on a form by using *image frames*. This method is different from the way a bound OLE (Object Linking and Embedding) control is used. Normally, an OLE object (sound, video, Word, or Excel document) is stored with a data record or with an unbound OLE object that is used specifically for storing OLE objects (those same sound, video, Word, or Excel documents) on a form.

Image controls in Access 2000 are used only for non-OLE objects such as Paintbrush (.BMP) pictures. Image controls offer a distinct advantage. Unlike OLE objects (which can be edited but use huge amounts of resources), the image control adds only the size of the bitmap picture to your computer's overhead. Using too many OLE objects in Access causes resource and performance problems. New and existing applications should use image controls only when displaying pictures that don't change or don't need to be edited within Access.

Tip   In Access 2.0, many people learned to select an unbound OLE object picture and then select Edit ⇨ Save As Picture. This technique broke the OLE connection but did not fix the resource problem.

On the
CD-ROM

You can add an image control to your form by either pasting a bitmap from the Clipboard or embedding a bitmap file that contains a picture. For example, you may want to add a logo for Mountain Animal Hospital. On the disk that accompanies this book is a bitmap file called MTN.BMP. In this section, you add this bitmap to the page header section of the form.

An image object can be displayed in one of three ways:

Clip	Displays picture in its original size
Stretch	Fits the picture into the control regardless of size; often displayed out of proportion
Zoom	Fits the picture into the control (either vertically or horizontally) and maintains proportions; often results in white space on top or right side

To add the logo to the form, follow these steps:

1. Display the Toolbox by selecting View ➪ Toolbox.

2. Click the Image button in the Standard Toolbox.

3. Click the left corner below the title; drag the box so that it is sized as shown in Figure 17-1. The Insert Picture dialog box appears, as shown in Figure 17-6.

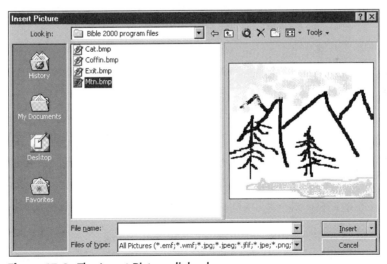

Figure 17-6: The Insert Picture dialog box.

- From this dialog box, you can select the type of picture object to insert into your form. The dialog box supports many picture formats, including .BMP, .TIF, .WMF, .PCX, .ICO, .WPG, .JPG, .PCT, as well as any other picture format that your copy of Microsoft Windows supports.

4. Select **Mtn.bmp** and click Insert. Then click Link to File, which is displayed if you click the arrow on the Insert button. Notice that when you click on a file, it is first displayed on the right part of the form for you to preview before the picture is inserted.

   If the file does not already exist and you want to create a new object (such as a Paintbrush picture), you must create an unbound OLE frame rather than an image.

   After you complete step 4, Access returns you to the Form Design window, where the picture is displayed. You must still change the Size Mode property to Stretch.

5. Display the property sheet.

6. Change the Size Mode property to Stretch.

   Now, you have to change the Border property so that the picture does not blend in with the background because there is so much white in it. This modification is made by changing the border color to black or by making the border three-dimensional, which is done by selecting the Raised toggle button in the Special Effect formatting window.

Display the Special Effect formatting window and click the Raised toggle button.

The image object frame is complete and should look like the one in Figure 17-1.

Working with Lines and Rectangles

You can use lines or rectangles (commonly called *boxes*), to make certain areas of the form stand out and attract attention. In Figure 17-1, several groups of lines and rectangles are being used for emphasis. In the present example, you need to add the lines and the rectangle. You can use Figure 17-7 as a guide for this procedure.

To create the rectangle for the customer information block, follow these steps:

1. Select the Rectangle button in the Toolbox.

2. Click to the left of the text *Customer Information* so that the rectangle encompasses the Customer fields and cuts through the middle of the text that reads *Customer Information*.

3. Drag the rectangle around the entire set of Customer text box controls and release the mouse button.

4. Select Format ➪ Send to Back to redisplay the text boxes.

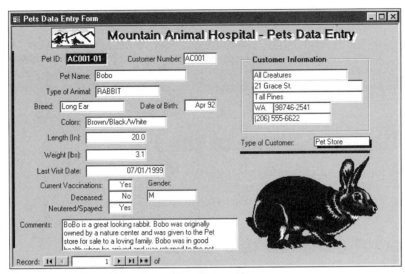

Figure 17-7: Completing the rectangles and lines.

Tip

Creating the rectangle blocks out the controls beneath it. Sending the rectangle to the background makes the controls reappear.

5. Select the etched effect in the Special Effect formatting window.

Tip

You can also redisplay the controls behind the rectangle by checking the Transparent button of the Background Color option in a formatting window. This method, however, does not allow you to add other shading effects. For a rectangle, you should always select Format ⇨ Send to Back.

You still need to create several lines for the form. You need to add a single horizontal line just below the Type of Customer control and a thick vertical line down the left side of the form (beginning with Pet ID and ending to the left of the Comments field). To add these lines, complete these steps (use Figure 17-7 as a guide):

1. Click the Line button in the Toolbox.

2. Create a new horizontal line just above the image picture control.

3. Select the 2 button in the Line Thickness window to make the line thicker.

4. Create a new vertical line, starting just to the left of the Pet ID field. To keep the line vertical, hold down the Shift key as you drag the line to just left of the Comments field (as shown in Figure 17-7).

5. Select the 3 button in the Border Width formatting window to make the line thicker.

 Tip   If you hold down the Shift key while creating the line, the line remains perfectly straight, either horizontally or vertically, depending on the initial movement you make when drawing the line.

Emphasizing Areas of the Form

If you really want to emphasize an area of the form, add a shadow to any control. The most common types of controls to which to add a shadow are rectangles and text boxes. Shadows are created with the Shadow special effect.

Adding a shadow to a control

If the background is light or white, a dark-colored rectangle is needed. If the background is dark or black, use a light-colored or white rectangle. To create a shadow for the Type of Customer text box, follow these steps:

1. Select the Type of Customer control.

2. Select the Shadow special-effects button.

If you want to give the form a Microsoft Windows look and feel, you need to change some other objects. The first object to change is the rectangle around the bound OLE object (displaying the rabbit in the first record). A Microsoft Windows look and feel has an etched gray rectangle rather than a sunken white one. Figure 17-7 shows this change.

Changing the header dividing line

Form headers and footers are automatically separated from the Detail section by a solid black line. In Access 2000, you can remove this line by changing the Dividing Lines form property to No. This action removes the line and makes the form appear seamless. This is especially important if you have a background bitmap on the entire form, you're using form headers or footers, and you want a single look.

Figure 17-7 shows the form after it has run. Notice both the etched rectangle around the Customer information and the two new lines. Also notice that the Mountain Animal Hospital logo appears in the form header.

Figure 17-8 shows the final form in the Form Design window.

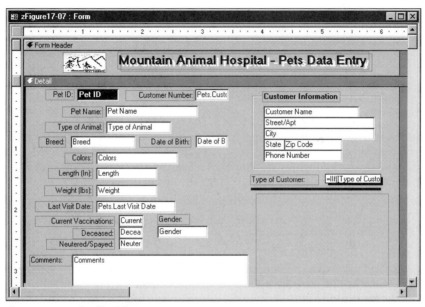

Figure 17-8: The final form.

You'll use this final form in the next chapter, so save it now. Select File⇨Save As/Export and name the form **Pets Data Entry - With Formatting**.

Adding a Background Bitmap

To emphasize a form even more (or add a really fun effect), you can add a background bitmap to any form, just as you added one control behind another. In Access 2000, this is done using the form's Picture properties. There are five properties that you can work with:

Picture	The name of the bitmap picture; it can be any image-type file.
Picture Type	Embedded or linked. The picture can be saved in the database or you can just save the location (pointer) of the picture.
Picture Size Mode	Clip, Stretch, or Zoom. Clip displays the picture only at its actual size starting at the Picture Alignment property. Stretch and Zoom fill the entire form from the upper-left corner of any header to the lower-right corner of any footer.

Picture Alignment	Top-Left, Top-Right, Center, Bottom-Left, Bottom-Right, and so on. Use this property only when you use the Clip option in Picture Size mode.
Picture Tiling	Yes/No. When a small bitmap is used with Clip mode, this repeats the bitmap across the entire form. For example, a brick becomes a brick wall.

For this example, you can add *Mtn.bmp* to the background of the form. Use these steps to add a background bitmap:

1. Select the form itself by clicking in the upper-left corner of the intersection of the two design rulers or by selecting Form from the combo box at the left margin of the Formatting toolbar.

2. Display the Properties window; click the Picture property that's on the Format sheet of the property window.

3. Enter **C:\ACCESS\MTN.BMP** (or the path to where you have placed your bitmap on the disk). When you move to another property, the Mountain Animal Hospital logo (or your bitmap) appears in the upper-left corner of the form background.

4. Click the Picture Size Mode property and change it from Clip to Stretch. The picture now occupies the entire form background.

If you are following the example, notice that the gray box for the Customer Information is still gray, the fields themselves still have white backgrounds, and the bitmap does not show through. If you want the bitmap to show through, check the Transparent background color of any control; the background will show through the form.

This is done by choosing Edit ➪ Select All to select all the controls and then selecting Transparent from the Fill Back Color formatting window. This action produces the effect shown in Figure 17-9. As Figure 17-9 shows, the white background of the picture (along with the thick, black lines) makes it difficult to see the fields.

Tip   Using background bitmaps adds some interesting capabilities to your form. For example, you can take this process a step further and incorporate the bitmap into your application. A bitmap can have buttons tied to macros (or Visual Basic for Applications code placed in the right locations). To help the office staff lookup a patient, for example, you can create a form that has a map with three states behind it. By adding invisible buttons over each state, you can give the staff the choice of clicking a state to select the patient records from that state.

You can also scan a paper form into your computer and use that image as the form background, by placing fields on top of the scanned form itself, without having to spend a great deal of time recreating the form (which gives the phrase *filling out a form* a whole new meaning).

Figure 17-9: A bitmap picture behind a form.

Using AutoFormat

You can change the format of an entire form by using the AutoFormat feature in Access 2000. This is the first menu option on the Format menu. AutoFormat lets you make global changes to all fonts, colors, borders, background bitmaps, and to virtually all other properties on a control-by-control-type basis. This feature works instantly and completely and is totally customizable.

When you select Format ➪ AutoFormat, a window appears, as shown in Figure 17-10. This window lets you select from the standard AutoFormats or any that you have created. The figure is shown after you click on the Options button. It lets you apply only fonts, colors, or border style properties separately.

In this example, you can choose the Blends AutoFormat type to change the style of the control fonts and colors and to change the background bitmap. As you move between the different AutoFormats, you can see an example of the look in the preview area to the right of the selections.

For this example, click the Options button and deselect the checkbox for color (turn it off). Then click OK.

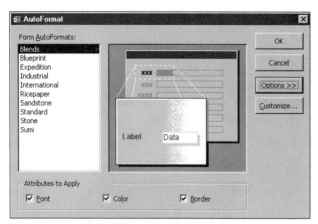

Figure 17-10: Selecting AutoFormat.

When you're done, the controls appear as shown in Figure 17-11. Notice that the title text size has changed and the shadow box around the Type of Customer has been removed. The reason is that the defaults for these controls are different from what you have selected.

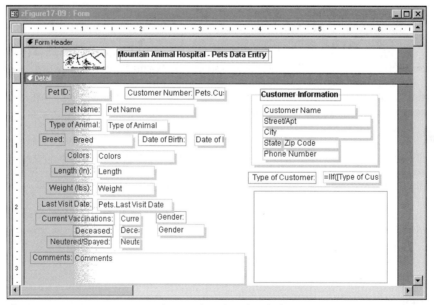

Figure 17-11: Pets Data Entry form using the Blends format.

Customizing and adding new AutoFormats

You can modify existing AutoFormats — or define new ones — by creating a form, setting various form properties, and starting AutoFormat. Although AutoFormat will change the look of your form totally, it does its job on one control type at a time. This means that it can format a label differently from a text box and differently from a line or rectangle. This capability also lets you define your own formats for every control type, including the background bitmap.

After you have created a form that you want to use as a basis for an AutoFormat, select AutoFormat and click the Customize button shown in Figure 17-10. Another window appears, as shown in Figure 17-12. This window allows you to create a new format, update the selected format, or delete the selected format.

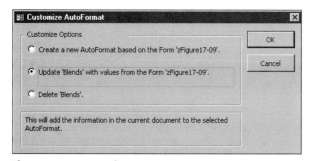

Figure 17-12: Creating your own AutoFormat.

Copying individual formats between controls

A subset of the AutoFormat technology is the Format Painter. This tool allows copying of formatting properties from one individual control to another. To use the Format Painter, first select the control whose properties you want to use. Then click the Format Painter icon on the toolbar (the picture of a paintbrush, next to the Paste icon). Your mouse pointer changes to a paintbrush. Click the control you want to update; Access copies the properties from the control you first selected to the newly selected control.

Summary

No matter which type of form you are creating with the tools in Access, you can get the job done readily and easily. In this chapter, these points were covered:

✦ The Access form designer is a WYSIWYG (What You See Is What You Get) form tool. What you see in the Design window is what you get when you run the form.

✦ A formatting window is a tool in the Form window that lets you set foreground and background colors, control line widths and line types, as well as add three-dimensional effects (such as a etched or sunken appearance) to controls.

✦ Label and text box control text can be enhanced by changing the font type style and size and by changing the font style to bold or italic. You can specify font color and even add a shadow by duplicating the text.

✦ Bound object frames (attached to a data field in the record), or image controls, or unbound object frames (which are embedded in the form) are used to display pictures in forms.

✦ Lines and rectangles let you separate areas of the form to add emphasis.

✦ Adding color, background shading, and three-dimensional effects can emphasize areas of the form. You can also use shadows and reverse video for emphasis.

✦ The Access 2000 AutoFormat tool lets you change the look of the entire form by applying a set of formatting properties to every control on the form, including the form itself and form selections.

✦ Formats cn be copied between controls with the Format Painter icon.

In the next chapter, you learn to add data-validation controls to your form, including list boxes, option buttons, checkboxes, and combo boxes.

✦   ✦   ✦

Adding Data-Validation Controls to Forms

In the preceding three chapters, you learned to create a basic form and to enhance it with visual effects to make data entry and display easier. In this chapter, you learn techniques for creating several *data-validation* controls; these controls help ensure that the data being entered (and edited) in your forms is as correct as possible.

On the CD-ROM

In this chapter, you modify your form from Chapter 17 to look like the one in Figure 18-1. If you are following the examples, open either the form you created in Chapter 17 (Pets Data Entry — With Formatting) or the form on the CD-ROM that comes with this book (Pets Data Entry Form — Without Validation).

Creating Data-Validation Expressions

Expressions can be entered into table design properties or a form control's property sheet to limit input to specific values or ranges of values. The limit is effective when a specific control or form is used. In addition, a status line message can be displayed that advises users how to enter the data properly when they move the insertion point into a particular field. Access can also show an error message dialog if a user makes an invalid entry. These expressions can be entered in a table design or in a form. Expressions entered in a table design are automatically inherited or used by any form that uses the table. If the expression is entered only in a form, only that form will have the validation.

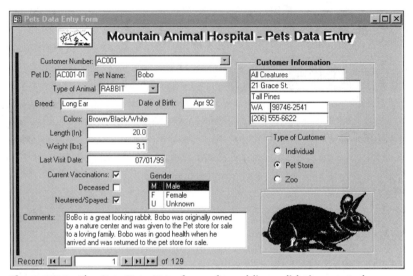

Figure 18-1: The Pets Data Entry form after adding validation controls.

Table-level validation

Several types of validation text can be entered into a table design, as shown in Table 18-1. When the user of a form or datasheet moves the cursor into the field, messages appear in the status line at the lower-left corner of the screen. In your table design, you enter these messages into the Description column, as shown in Figure 18-2. In this example, the status line message displays *Enter M for Male, F for Female, or U if Unknown* when the insertion point is in the Gender field.

<table>
<tr><td colspan="3" align="center">Table 18-1
Types of Validation Entered into a Table Design</td></tr>
<tr><td>*Type of Validation*</td><td>*Stored in*</td><td>*Displayed in Form*</td></tr>
<tr><td>Status line message</td><td>Description/Status Bar Text</td><td>Status bar</td></tr>
<tr><td>Validation expression</td><td>Validation rule</td><td>Not displayed</td></tr>
<tr><td>Error message</td><td>Validation text</td><td>Dialog box</td></tr>
<tr><td>Input mask</td><td>Input mask</td><td>Control text box</td></tr>
</table>

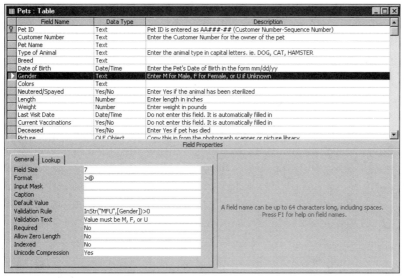

Figure 18-2: The validation properties for the Gender field in the table design.

Validation expressions are the rules the data must follow. Any type of expression can be entered into the Validation Rule property (found in the field properties area of the table design). In Figure 18-2, the expression `InStr("MFU",[Gender])>0` limits the valid entry to the three letters M, F, or U.

You can also display an error message in a dialog box when data entry does not pass the validation rule. This text is entered into the Validation Text property found in the field properties area of the table design. In this example, the dialog box will tell you *Value must be M, F, or U.* Figure 18-2 is a table design with the Gender field selected in the Pets table. The only properties that are displayed are for the highlighted field, although you can see all the descriptions in the upper part of the Table Design window.

Form-level validation

You can enter the same types of validation text into a form's property sheet. When you create a form, the table validation properties are copied into each bound field on the form. This way, if you enter them at the table level, you don't have to enter them for each form. If you want to override them for a particular form, you can do so here by simply entering a new value for any of the properties.

Note   Although you enter status bar instructions into a table design's Description column, they appear in the form design's Status Bar Text property.

Entering a validation expression

You can enter a validation expression in a number of different ways for each field in your table or control in your form. For a number field, you can use standard mathematical expressions such as *less than*, *greater than*, or *equal to*, using the appropriate symbols (<, >, =). For example, if you want to limit a numerical field to numbers greater than 100, you enter the following validation expression in the appropriate property box:

```
> 100
```

To limit a date field to dates before January 1999, you enter

```
< #1/1/99#
```

If you want to limit a numeric or date value to a range, you can enter

```
Between 0 And 1500
```

or

```
Between #1/1/70# And Date( )
```

Cross-Reference   You can use a series of the functions included within Access to validate your data. In Figure 18-2, Access interprets the validation expression used to limit the input in the Gender field as "allow only the letters M, F, or U." The Access function `InStr` means *in string*. Access will search the Gender input field and allow only those entries. Chapter 12 details the functions available for validation purposes.

Creating Choices with Option Buttons

Sometimes you don't want to allow a user to enter anything at all — only to pick a valid entry from a list. You can limit input on your form in this way by using an *option button* (also known as a *radio button*), a control that indicates whether a situation is True or False. The control consists of a string of text and a button that can be turned on or off by clicking the mouse. When you click the button, a black dot appears in its center, indicating that the situation is True; otherwise, the situation is False.

Generally, an option button is used when you want to limit data entry but more than two choices are available. You should limit the number of choices to four, however, when using option buttons. If you have more than four choices, use a list or combo box (described later in this chapter). If there is only one choice, true or false, use a checkbox.

Option buttons can increase flexibility in validating data input. For example, the current control for Type of Customer displays a number: 1 means individual, 2 means pet store, and 3 means zoo. It is much more meaningful to users if all these choices are displayed onscreen. Figure 18-1 shows the numerical field input changed to an option group box that shows the three choices available to users.

Only one of the option buttons can be made True for any given record. This approach also ensures that no other possible choices can be entered on the form. In an option group, the option group box itself is bound to a field or expression. Each button passes a different value back to the option group box, which in turn passes a single value to the field or expression. Each option button is bound to the option group box rather than to a field or expression.

Caution   Only fields with a Numeric data type can be used for an option group in a form. In a report, you can transform nonnumeric data into numeric data types for display-only option buttons (see Chapter 21). You can also display an alternative value by using the Lookup Wizard on the Table design window and displaying a combo box.

To create an option group with option buttons, you must do two things:

✦ Create the option group box and bind it to a field.

✦ Create each option button and bind each one to the option group box.

Creating option groups

In Access 2000, the easiest and most efficient way to create option groups is with the Option Group Wizard. You can use it to create *option groups* with multiple option buttons, toggle buttons, or checkboxes. When you're through, all your control's property settings are correctly filled out. This Wizard greatly simplifies the process and allows you to create an option group quickly, but you still need to understand the process.

Creating an option group box

When you create a new option group, the Option Group Wizard is triggered automatically. Clicking the Option Group icon on the toolbox and drawing the control box rectangle starts the process. Another method is to click the Option Group button and then drag the appropriate field from the field list window.

Caution   To start any of the Wizards that create controls, you must first click the Control Wizard button on the toolbox.

Before creating an option group for the Type of Customer field, highlight the current display of the field your mouse and click the Delete key to delete it. You may also want to delete the shadow (the thick line below the control) and narrow the height of the picture so that the option group box will fit. Use the completed option group in Figure 18-1 as a guide. If the toolbox and Field List are not open, open them now.

After you have deleted the existing Type of Customer text box control, you can create the Type of Customer option group box by following these steps:

1. Click the Option Group button from the toolbox. When you release the mouse button, the Option Group button will remain depressed.

2. Select and drag the Type of Customer field from the Field List window to the space under the Customer Information box.

   The first screen of the Option Group Wizard should be displayed (as shown completed in Figure 18-3). On this screen, you can enter the text label for each option button, checkbox, or toggle button that will be in your option group. Enter each entry as you would in a datasheet. You can press the down-arrow (↓) key to move to the next choice.

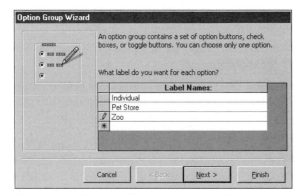

Figure 18-3: Entering the option group choices.

3. Enter **Individual**, **Pet Store**, and **Zoo**, pressing the down-arrow (↓) key between choices.

4. Click the Next button to move to the default option Wizard screen.

   The next screen lets you select the default control for when the option group is selected. Normally, the first option is the default. If you want to make a different button the default, select the *Yes, the default choice is* option button and then select the default value from the combo box that contains your choices. In this example, the first value will be the default automatically.

5. Click the Next button to move to the Wizard screen used for assigning values.

This screen (shown in Figure 18-4) displays the actual values you entered, along with a default set of numbers that will be used to store the selected value in the bound option group field (in this example, the Type of Customer field). The screen looks like a datasheet with two columns. Your first choice, *Individual*, is automatically assigned a 1, *Pet Store* a 2, and *Zoo* a 3. When Pet Store is selected, a 2 is stored in the Type of Customer field.

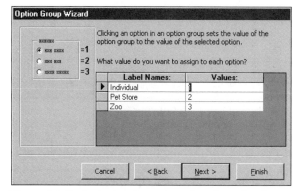

Figure 18-4: Assigning the value of each option button.

In this example, the default values are acceptable. Sometimes, however, you may want to assign values other than 1, 2, 3, etc. You may want to use 100, 200, and 500 for some reason. As long as you use unique numbers, you can assign any values you want.

6. Click the Next button to move to the next Wizard screen.

In this screen, you have to decide whether the option group itself is bound to a form field or unbound. The first choice in the Wizard — *Save the value for later use* — creates an unbound field. If you're going to put the option group in a dialog box that uses the selected value to make a decision, you don't want to store the value in a table field. Thus (in this example) the second value — *Store the value in this field* — is automatically selected because you started with the Type of Customer field. If you want to bind the option group value to a different table field, you can select from a list of all form fields. Again, in this example, the default is acceptable.

7. Click the Next button to move to the option group style Wizard screen.

For this example (as shown in Figure 18-5), select Option buttons and the Etched style. Notice that your actual values are used as a sample. The upper half of this Wizard screen lets you choose which type of buttons you want; the lower half lets you choose the style for the option group box and the type of group control. The style affects the option group rectangle. If you choose one of the special effects (such as Etched, Shadowed, Raised, or Sunken), that value is applied to the Special Effect property of the option group.

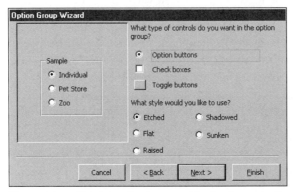

Figure 18-5: Selecting the type and look of your buttons.

Note　　As you change your selections, the Sample changes to show how it will look.

8. Click the Next button to move to the final Option Group Wizard screen.

This screen lets you give the option group control a label that will appear in the option group border. Then you can add the control to your design and (optionally) display help to additionally customize the control.

9. Enter **Type of Customer** as your caption for the Option Group.

10. Click the Finish button to complete the Wizard.

Your Wizard work is now complete. Eight new controls appear on the design screen: the option group, its label, three option buttons, and their labels. Even so, you may still have some work to do. You may want to move the option buttons closer together, or change the shape of the option group box as shown in Figure 18-6, or change the Special Effect property of some controls. As you learned, you can do this using the property sheet for the controls.

Figure 18-6 shows the option group controls and the property sheet for the first option button (as automatically created). Notice the Option Value property; it's found only in controls that are part of an option group.

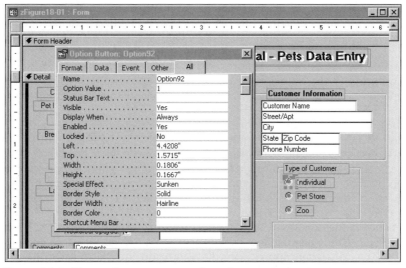

Figure 18-6: The option group controls and property sheet.

If you want to create an option group manually, the best advice is *don't*. If you must, however, the steps are the same as for creating any control. First create the option group box and then create each button inside it manually. You'll have to manually set all data properties, palette properties, and specific option group or button controls.

Caution   If you create the option buttons outside the option group box and then drag or copy them into the option group box, they will not work. The reason is that the automatic setting of the Option Value for buttons is left undone, and the option button control has not been bound to the option group box control.

After you finish this process, you can turn your attention to Yes/No controls.

Creating Yes/No Options

There are three ways to show data properly from Yes/No data types:

✦ Display the values *Yes* or *No* in a text box control, using the Yes/No Format property.

✦ Use a checkbox.

✦ Use a toggle button.

Although you can place values from Yes/No data types in a text box control and then format the control by using the Yes/No property, it's better to use one of the other controls. Yes/No data types require the values –1 or 0 to be entered into them. An unformatted text box control returns values (–1 and 0) that seem confusing, especially because –1 represents Yes and 0 represents No. Setting the Format property to Yes/No or True/False to display those values helps, but a user still needs to read the text *Yes/No* or *True/False*. A visual display is much better.

Toggle buttons and checkboxes work with these values *behind the scenes* — returning –1 to the field if the button value is on and 0 if the button is off — but they display these values as a box or button, which is faster to read. You can even display a specific state by entering a default value in the Default property of the form control. The control is displayed initially in a Null state if no default is entered and no state is selected. The Null state appears visually the same as the No state.

The checkbox is the commonly accepted control for two-state selection. Toggle buttons are nice (they can use pictures rather than a text caption to represent the two states) but not always appropriate. Although you could also use option buttons, they would never be proper as a single Yes/No control.

Creating checkboxes

A *checkbox* is a Yes/No control that acts the same as an option button but is displayed differently. A checkbox consists of a string of text (to describe the option) and a small square that indicates the answer. If the answer is True, a check mark is displayed in the box. If the answer is False, the box is empty. The user can toggle between the two allowable answers by clicking on the mouse with the pointer in the box.

The Pets Data Entry form contains three fields that have Yes/No data types. These are Current Vaccinations, Deceased, and Neutered/Spayed. The choices are easier to understand if they are shown as a checkbox (rather than as a simple text box control). To change these fields to a checkbox, first delete the original text box controls. The following steps detail how to create a checkbox for each of the Yes/No fields after you have deleted the original controls:

1. Click the Check Box icon in the toolbox.

2. While holding down the Ctrl key, select Current Vaccinations, Deceased, and Neutered/Spayed from the Field List window.

3. Using Figure 18-7 as a guide, drag these fields just below the Last Visit Date control. (This process creates each of the checkboxes and automatically fills in the Control Source property.)

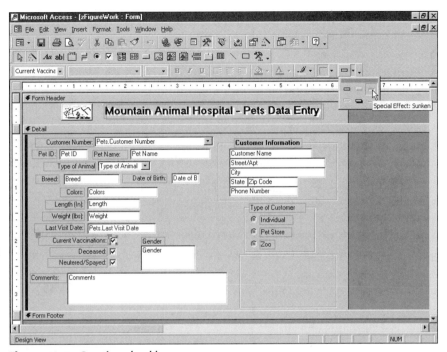

Figure 18-7: Creating checkboxes.

4. Rearrange the fields so that they look like Figure 18-7. (This example calls for the checkboxes to be on the right of the labels.)

5. Select each label control and modify it: change the labels to the appropriate text, add a colon to the end of the labels, and then size the controls to fit and align them as necessary.

Tip

While you can set the Display Control option of the Lookup tab in the Table Design to Check Box for any field with a Yes/No data type, you don't really need to. A checkbox is automatically created whenever you add a Yes/No field to a form. You can always change it to another type of control if you want.

Note

Before creating the checkbox controls, you could change the Default Check Box Label X property to a negative value; this would automatically place the checkboxes to the right of the labels when they are created. The value to enter depends on the length of the labels. To save several steps when creating a group of similar-looking controls, change the Add Colon property to Yes to add a colon automatically and change the Special Effect property to Sunken.

The completed checkboxes appear in Figure 18-7.

Creating visual selections with toggle buttons

A *toggle button* is another type of True/False control. Toggle buttons act like option buttons and checkboxes but are displayed differently. When a toggle button is set to True (in *pushed* mode), the button appears onscreen as depressed. When it is set to False, the button appears raised.

Toggle buttons provide a capability in addition to those other button controls offer. You can set the size and shape of a toggle button, and you can display text or pictures on the face of the button to illustrate the choice a user can make. This additional capability provides great flexibility in making your form user-friendly.

To learn to create a toggle button, follow these steps using the Deceased Yes/No field (this example is not part of the final form):

1. Select the Deceased checkbox label control and delete the label.

2. Select the Deceased checkbox and select Format ➪ Change To ➪ Toggle Button.

3. Resize the toggle button to the desired size.

4. Type the text **Deceased** for display on the face of the button and press Enter.

5. Using the keyboard arrows keys, change the size of the button to fit the text (or select Format ➪ Size ➪ To Fit) and move it below the other checkboxes.

Adding a bitmapped image to the toggle button

As mentioned earlier, you can display a picture on a toggle button rather than text. For example, you can modify the button you just created in the preceding steps, changing it to display a picture (included in the sample files). Use the following steps to modify the button for the Deceased field (this example assumes that you completed the steps to create this toggle button):

1. Select the toggle button.

2. Open the properties sheet and select the Picture property.

3. Click the Builder button (the button with three dots next to the property setting).

    The Picture Builder dialog box appears, which provides more than 100 predefined pictures. In this example, select the bitmap named COFFIN.BMP that came with your *Access 2000 Bible* disc; it should be in the same directory your Access book files were copied to (the example assumes that it's C:\ACCESS2000).

4. Click the Browse button in the Picture Builder dialog box.

5. Select COFFIN.BMP from the C:\ACCESS2000 directory; click the OK button. A sample of the picture appears in the Picture Builder dialog box, as shown in Figure 18-8.

6. Click the OK button to add the picture to the toggle button. The coffin appears on the toggle button on the design screen. You may need to move it on the screen to make it fit between other controls.

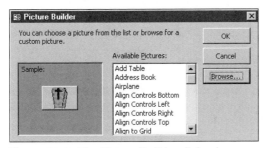

Figure 18-8: The Picture Builder dialog box.

Although option buttons, checkboxes, and toggle buttons are great for handling a few choices, they are not a good idea when many choices are possible. Access has other controls that make it easy to pick from a list of values.

Working with List Boxes and Combo Boxes

Access has two types of controls that let you show lists of data from which a user can select. These controls are *list boxes* and *combo boxes*.

The differences between list boxes and combo boxes

The basic difference between a list box and a combo box is that the list box is always open ready for selection, whereas the combo box has to be clicked to open the list for selection. Another difference is that the combo box allows you to enter a value that is not on the list.

Cross-Reference

Chapter 15 contains details on these controls. Review Figures 15-8 and 15-9 if you are not familiar with list boxes and combo boxes.

A closed combo box appears as a single text box field with a downward-pointing arrow on its far right side. A list box, which is always open, can have one or more columns, from one to as many rows as will fit onscreen, and more than one item to be selected. An open combo box displays a single-column text box above the first row, followed by one or more columns and as many rows as you specify on the property sheet. Optionally, a list box or combo box can display column headers in the first row.

Settling real-estate issues

Note

You have to consider the amount of space that is available on the form before deciding between a list box or combo box. If only a few choices are allowed for a given field, a list box is sufficient. However, if there is not enough room on the form for the choices, use a combo box (a list box is always open, but a combo box is initially closed). When you use a list box, a user cannot type any new values but instead must choose from the selection list.

When designing a list box, you must decide exactly which choices will be allowed for the given field and select an area of your form that has sufficient room for the open list box to display all selections.

Creating a single-column list box

List boxes and combo boxes can be even more difficult to create than option groups, especially when a combo box uses a query as its source and contains multiple columns. The List Box Wizard and Combo Box Wizard in Access make the process much easier. This first example uses the List Box Wizard to create a simple list box for the Gender field.

To create the single-column list box, follow these steps:

1. Delete the existing Gender text box field control and its label.

2. Click the List Box icon in the toolbox.

3. Display the field list and drag the Gender field to the right of the recently created checkboxes.

   The List Box Wizard starts automatically, as shown in Figure 18-9. The first screen lets you decide whether to have the values come from a table/query, type a list of values, or create a query-by-form list box to display all the unique values in the current table. Depending on your answer, you either select the number of columns (and type in the values) or select the fields to use from the selected table/query.

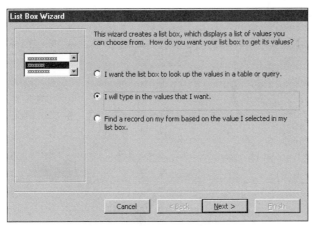

Figure 18-9: Selecting the data source for the list box.

4. Select the second option, *I will type in the values that I want*, and click on the Next button.

In the next screen, you can choose the number of columns and enter the values you want to use in the list box. You can also resize the column widths, just as in any datasheet. In this example, enter three values in a single column — **M**, **F**, and **U** — as shown in Figure 18-10.

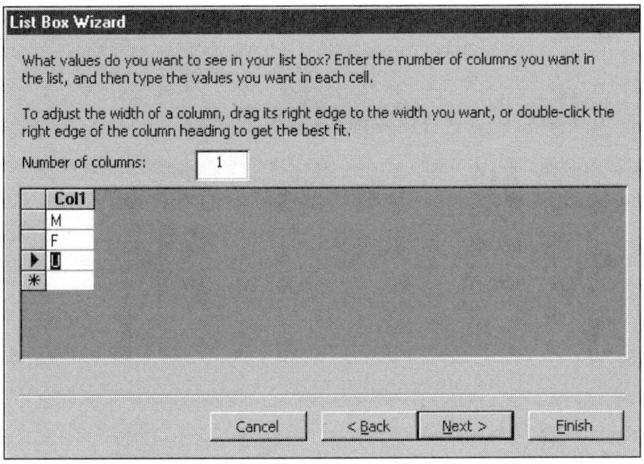

Figure 18-10: Entering the choices for the list box.

5. Enter **1** in the field that specifies Number of columns; then click in the first row under the Col1: header.

6. Enter **M**, press the down arrow (↓), enter **F**, press the down arrow (↓), and then enter **U**.

7. Resize the width of the column to match the single-character entry.

Tip   You can double-click on the right side of the column list to size the column automatically.

8. Click the Next button to move to the next screen.

   • Use this screen to specify the field that you will link to. It should currently say *Gender*. Accept this value.

9. Click the Next button to move to the final Wizard screen.

   Use this screen to give the list box control a label that will appear with your list box. When you click the Finish button, your control is added to your design; you can optionally display Help if you want to continue customizing the control.

10. Click the Finish button to complete the Wizard.

Your work with the Wizard is now complete and the control appears on the design screen. You need to move the label control and resize the list box rectangle because the Wizard does not do a good job of sizing the box to the number of entries.

Figure 18-11 shows the list box control and the property sheet for the list box.

Understanding list box properties

As Figure 18-11 shows, several properties define a list box. The Wizard takes care of these (except for the Column Heads property, which adds the name of the column at the top of the list box). Begin by setting the Row Source properties; the first of these is Row Source Type (shown later in this chapter), which specifies the source of the data type.

The Row Source properties are the first two properties that have to be set. Row Source Type determines the data type. Valid Row Source Type property options are listed in Table 18-2.

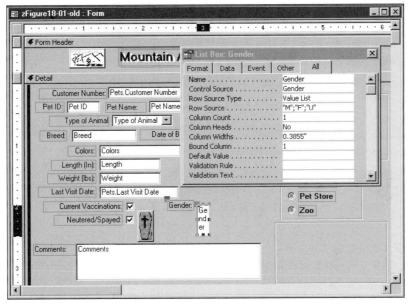

Figure 18-11: The list box control and property sheet.

Table 18-2
Row Source Type Settings

Row Source Type	Source of the Data Type
Table/Query	(Default setting) Data is from a table or is the result of a query or SQL statement
Value List	List of items specified by the Row Source setting
Field List	List of field names from the Table/Query named by the Row Source setting

The Row Source property settings depend on the source type specified by Row Source Type.

The method used to specify the Row Source property settings, as listed in Table 18-3, depends on the type of source (which you specified by setting the Row Source Type).

Table 18-3 Row Source Property Settings	
Row Source Type	**Method of Setting the Row Source Property**
Table/Query	Enter the name of a table, a query, or an SQL statement
Value List	Enter a list of items separated by semicolons
Field List	Enter the name of a table or query

In this example, you entered the values on the Wizard screen. Therefore, the Row Source Type is set to Value List, and the Row Source is set to `"M";"F";"U"`. As you can see, semicolons separate the entered values.

When the Table/Query or Field List is specified as the Row Source Type, you can pick from a list of tables and queries for the Row Source. The table or query must already exist. The list box displays fields from the table or query according to the order they follow in their source. Other settings in the property sheet determine the number of columns, their size, whether there are column headers, and which column is bound to the field's control source.

These settings include:

Column Count	The number of columns to be displayed.
Column Heads	Yes or No. Yes displays the first set of values or the field names.
Column Widths	The width of each column. Each value is separated by a semicolon.
Bound Column	The column that passes the value back to the control source field.

Suppose that you want to list Pet Name, Type of Animal, and Breed, returning Pet Name to the field control. You could enter **Table/Query** in the Row Source Type and **Pets** in the Row Source. You would then enter **3** for the Column Count, **1.5;1;1** in the Column Width, and 1 for the Bound Column.

These are valid entries for the Row Source property for a list box from the Value List:

For a one-column list with three rows (Column Count = 1):

    M;F;U

For a two-column list with three rows (Column Count = 2):

```
M;Male;F;Female;U;Unknown
```

For a two-column list with five rows of data and a column header (Column Count = 2, Column Heads = Yes):

```
Pet Name;Type of Animal;Bobo;Rabbit;Fido;Dog;Daffy;Duck;Patty;
Pig;Adam;Frog
```

Tip

If you want to use noncontiguous table/query fields in the list box, you should use a SQL statement rather than a list of field names. The Wizard can do this for you automatically. The following is an example of a SQL statement for a two-column list, drawn from the Pets table in the Mountain Animal Hospital database:

```
SELECT [Pet Name], [Type of Animal] FROM [Pets] ORDER BY
[Pet ID];
```

Creating a multiple-column list box

It's easy to create a list box with multiple columns of data. You could easily go back and run the Wizard again to create a two-column list box, but it's just as easy to modify the list box you already have on the design screen. Follow these steps to modify the list box control to change it to a two-column list:

1. Change the Row Source property to **M;Male;F;Female;U;Unknown**.

2. Set the Column Count property to **2**.

3. Enter the Column Widths property as **.25;.75**.

4. Set the Bound Column property to **1**.

5. Resize the list box control to fit the new column widths.

By changing the Number of Columns property to 2 and setting the Column Widths to the size of the data, you can display multiple columns. As Figure 18-12 shows, there are now multiple columns. The first column's value (specified by the Bound Column property) is passed back to the Gender field.

Note

You enter the column widths as decimal numbers; Access adds the abbreviation for inches (in) automatically. You can also change it to *cm* or any other unit of measurement.

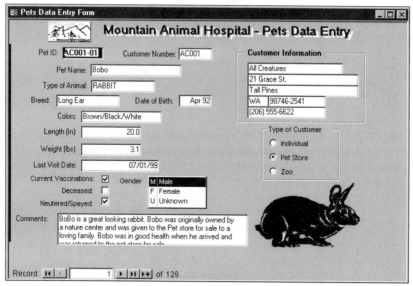

Figure 18-12: Creating a two-column list box.

Caution

If you don't size the list box wide enough to match the sum of the column widths, a horizontal scrollbar appears at the bottom of the control. If you don't size the list box deep enough to display all the items in the list (including the horizontal scrollbar), a vertical scrollbar appears.

When looking at this list box, you may wonder, "Why display the single-letter code at all?" You may think that you need it to pass the single-letter code back to the Gender field. That *is* the reason, in fact, for the first column, but there is no need to display it. Data in hidden *or* displayed columns can be used as a bound column.

Hiding a column in a list box

When you create a multiple-column list box, Access lets you *hide* any column you don't want displayed. This capability is especially useful when a list box is bound to a field that you don't want displayed. You can hide the first column in the list box you just created by following these steps:

1. Display the Properties sheet for the list box.

2. Change the Column Widths property to **0;.75**.

3. Resize the list box control to the new width.

When you display the list box, only the one column is visible; the hidden column is used as the bound column. You can bind a list box to a field that isn't even displayed onscreen.

Creating multiselection list boxes

An option in Access 2000 creates list boxes that allow more than one selection. You can build such a *multiselection* (or *multiselect*) list box by changing the Multi-Select property of a standard list box. To use the multiple selections, however, you must define a program by using Visual Basic for Applications to capture the selections.

The Multi-Select property has three settings:

None	(Default) Multiple selection isn't allowed.
Extended	Pressing Shift+click or Shift+arrow key extends the selection from the previously selected item to the current item. Pressing Ctrl+click selects or deselects an item.
Simple	Multiple items are selected or deselected by choosing them with the mouse or pressing the spacebar.

Creating and Using Combo Boxes

As mentioned earlier, a *combo box* is very similar to a list box; it's a combination of a normal entry field and a list box. The operator can enter a value directly into the text area of the combo box or else click on the directional arrow (in the right portion of the combo box) to display the list. In addition, the list remains hidden from view unless the arrow is activated, conserving valuable space on the form. A combo box is useful when there are many rows to display; a vertical scrollbar will give users access to the records that are out of sight.

In this next example, the Type of Animal control is changed from a text box to a combo box by using the Combo Box Wizard.

Creating a single-column combo box

To create a single-column combo box using the Wizard, follow these steps:

1. Delete the existing Type of Animal text box field control and its label.

2. Click the Combo Box icon in the toolbox.

3. Display the field list and drag the Type of Animal field to the area below Pet Name.

The Combo Box Wizard starts automatically; its first screen is exactly the same as the first list box screen. You decide whether the values will come from a table or query, or whether you want to type in a list of values. In this example, the values come from a table.

4. Select the first option, which displays the text *I want the combo box to look up the values in a table or query*; then click the Next button.

As shown in Figure 18-13, this Wizard screen lets you choose the table from which to select the values. By using the row of option buttons under the list of tables, you can view all the Tables, Queries, or Both tables and queries.

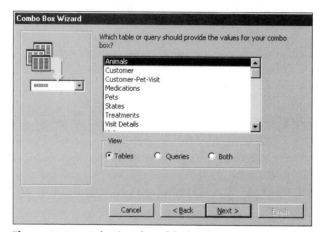

Figure 18-13: Selecting the table for the row source of the combo box.

5. Select the Animals table and click the Next button.

The next screen lets you pick the fields you want to use to populate the combo box. You can pick any field in the table or query and select the fields in any order; Access creates the necessary SQL statement for you. On this screen, only one field is shown. The Animals table has only one field (Animals), a list of valid animals.

6. Select the Animals field; click the Next button to add it to the Columns list.

7. Click the Next button to move to the next Wizard screen.

In this screen, a list of the actual values in your selected field appears (as shown in Figure 18-14). Here you can adjust the width of any columns for their actual display.

The rest of the Wizard screens are like the list box Wizard screens. First, you accept or change the name of the bound field; then the last screen lets you enter a label name, and the Wizard creates the combo box.

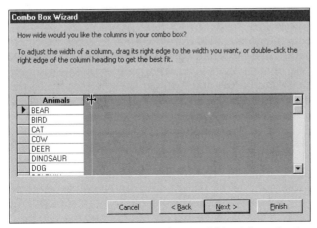

Figure 18-14: Adjusting the column width of the selection.

8. Click Finish to complete the entries with the default choices.

Figure 18-15 shows the combo box control in design view and the property sheet for the combo box.

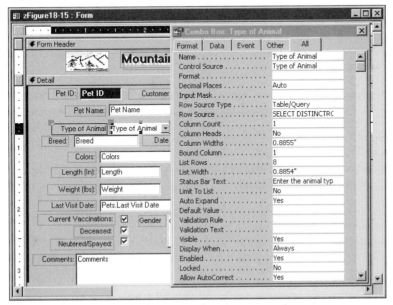

Figure 18-15: The combo box control and property sheet.

The Row Source Type property is set to Table/Query. The Row Source property is set to the SQL statement Select Distinctrow [Animals] From [Animals]. This statement selects the Animal field from the Animals table and limits it to unique values. There are two ways to display the animals in a sorted order: either enter the data into the Animals table in a sorted order or create a simple query to sort the data into the desired order and then use the query as the basis for the combo box. You can also add sorting directives to the SQL statement by adding Order By [Animals].

The List Rows property shows the number of rows when the combo box is opened set to 8, but the Wizard does not allow you to select this. The property, Limit To List, determines whether you can enter a value into the Pets table that is not in the list; this property is another one the Wizard does not let you set. You must set these directly from the property sheet. The default No value for Limit To List says that you can enter new values because you are not limiting the entry to the list.

Tip   Setting the AutoExpand property to Yes enables the user to select the combo box value by entering text into the combo box that matches a value in the list. As soon as Access finds a unique match, it displays the value without having to display the list. The default value is Yes for the AutoExpand property. To change it to No, you must do so in the property sheet.

Creating a multiple-column combo box from a query

Just as with list boxes, combo boxes may have multiple columns of information. These boxes are displayed when the operator activates the field list. Unless you are extracting fields from a single table — in the order in which they appear in the table — use a query.

Figure 18-16 shows the combo box you will create next. Notice that this combo box displays the Customer Number and Customer Name in the order of the Customer Name. A query accomplishes this task. Also notice (in Figure 18-16) that the Customer Number and Customer Name heads are displayed.

To understand the selection criteria of a multiple-column combo box, first create the query to select the proper fields.

Before continuing, minimize the form that you are working on and create a new query after selecting the Query object button in the Database container. The query you want to create is shown in Figure 18-17. After the query is created, save it as **Customer Number Lookup**. Note that the Customer table is related to the Pets table; the Customer Name field is selected to be used as the query's sorting field. When used for the combo box, this query selects the Customer Name from the Customer table, matches it with the Customer Number in the Customer table, and passes it to the Customer Number in the Pets table. When a Customer is selected, the Customer Number in the Pets table is updated and the correct name is displayed in the Customer area of the form. Thus, you can reassign the ownership of a pet or (more usefully) add a new pet to the system and correctly choose the pet's owner.

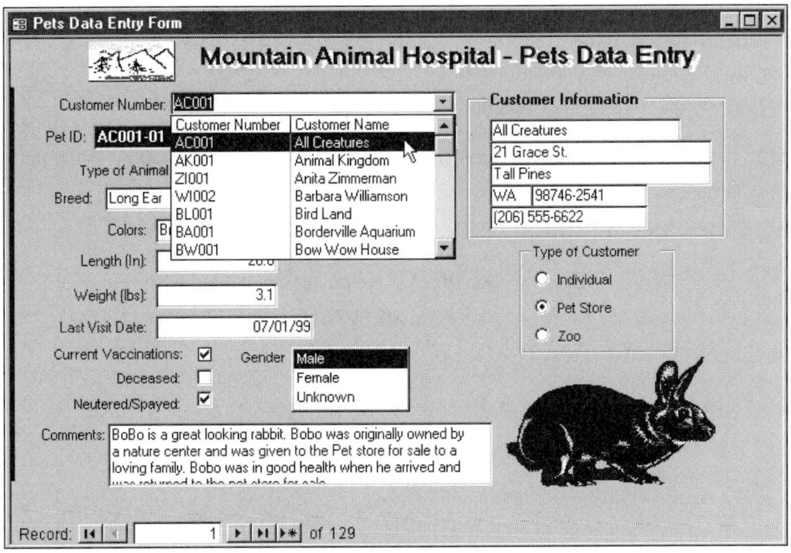

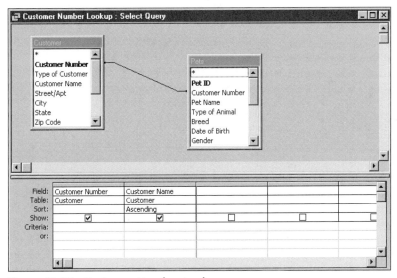

Figure 18-16: The multicolumn combo box.

Figure 18-17: Customer Number Lookup query.

The query shown in Figure 18-17 is the basis for a multiple-column combo box for the Pets.Customer Number field on the form. Before beginning, maximize the form to work on it. These steps describe how to create this new combo box without using the Wizard:

1. Select the Pets.Customer Number text box and then select Format ⇨ Change To ⇨ Combo Box from the menu.

2. Move the original Pet ID and Pet Name controls, as shown in Figure 18-18. Also resize the new Customer Number combo box control.

3. Select the Data sheet (Data tab) in the Property window. If the Property window is not open, open it.

4. Enter **Pets.Customer Number** in the Control Source property.

5. Select Table/Query in the Row Source Type property.

6. Set the Row Source property to the query Customer Number Lookup.

7. Set the Bound Column property to **1**.

8. Select the Format tab to activate the Format sheet.

9. Enter **2** in the Column Count property.

10. Set the Column Heads property to **Yes**.

11. Set the Column Widths property to **1;1.25**.

If you have followed the preceding steps properly, your Form design should resemble Figure 18-18, and the Form view should look like Figure 18-16.

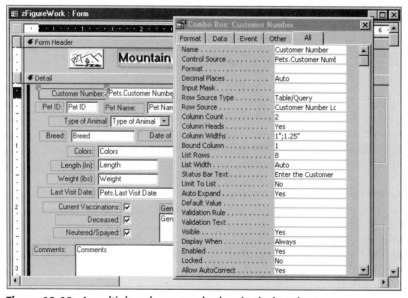

Figure 18-18: A multiple-column combo box in design view.

Summary

In this chapter, you learned many ways to create forms that accept only good data. Validation rules, option buttons, checkboxes, list boxes, and combo boxes make it easy. The Control Wizards in Access make creating these controls simple. This chapter covered these points:

✦ Data-validation expressions are entered in either tables or forms.

✦ The Description column in a table becomes the status-bar text on a form.

✦ The Validation Rule and Validation Text properties let you trap for errors and display error messages.

✦ Option buttons, checkboxes, and toggle buttons can be used individually to display a two-state choice or as part of an option group to display one of several possible choices.

✦ An option button is the preferred choice for showing three to four choices.

✦ Yes/No data is best shown with checkboxes.

✦ You can also use toggle buttons to display Yes/No data, and you can attach pictures to the face of the button.

✦ List boxes display choices in an open box.

✦ Combo boxes display choices in a closed box that a user must click to view the choices.

✦ List boxes and combo boxes can have one column or many.

In the next chapter, you learn to link and embed pictures and graphs in your forms and reports.

✦   ✦   ✦

Using OLE Objects, Graphs, and ActiveX Custom Controls

Access provides many powerful tools for enhancing your forms and reports. These tools let you add pictures, graphs, sound — even video — to your database application. Chart Wizards make it easy to build business graphs and add them to your forms and reports. OLE custom controls (OCXs or ActiveX controls) extend the power of Access 2000; new features borrowed from Microsoft Office 2000 make using Access forms more productive than ever. In this chapter, you learn about the different types of graphical and OLE objects you can add to your system. You also learn how to manipulate them to create professional, productive screen displays and reports. You will also learn how to use some of the new Office 2000 tools that work with Access 2000 forms.

Understanding Objects

Access 2000 gives you the capability of embedding pictures, video clips, sound files, business graphs, Excel spreadsheets, and Word documents; you can also link to any OLE (Object Linking and Embedding) object within forms and reports. Therefore, Access lets you not only use objects in your forms but also edit them directly from within your form.

Types of objects

As a general rule, Access can add any type of picture or graphic object to a form or report. Access can also interact with any application through DDE (Dynamic Data Exchange) or OLE. You can interact with OLE objects with great flexibility. For example, you can link to entire spreadsheets, ranges of cells, or even an individual cell.

Access can embed and store any binary file within an object frame control, including even sound and full-motion video. As long as you have the software driver for the embedded object, you can play or view the contents of the frame.

These objects can be bound to a field in each record (*bound*) or to the form or report itself (*unbound*). Depending on how you want to process the OLE object, you may either place (*embed*) the copy directly in the Access database or tell Access where to find the object (*link*) and place it in the bound or unbound object frame in your form or report. The following sections describe the different ways to process and store both bound and unbound objects by using embedding and linking.

Using bound and unbound objects

A *bound object* is an object displayed (and potentially stored) within a field of a record in a table. Access can display the object in a form or print it on a report.

A bound object is bound to an OLE object data type field in the table. If you use a bound object in a form, you can add and edit pictures or documents record by record, the same way you can with values. To display a bound OLE object, you use a *bound object frame*. In Figure 19-1, the picture of the pig is a bound object. Each record stores a photograph of the animal in the field named Picture in the Pets table. You can enter a different picture for each record.

An *unbound object* is not stored in a table; it is placed on the form or report. An unbound object control is the graphic equivalent of a label control. These are generally used for OLE objects in the form or report itself; they don't belong to any of the record's fields. Unbound objects don't change from record to record.

An *image control* that displays a picture is another example of an unbound object. Although an unbound OLE object frame allows you to edit an object by double-clicking on it and launching the source application (PC Paintbrush, Word, Excel, a sound or video editor or recorder, and so on), an image control only displays a bitmap picture (usually in .BMP, .PCX, or .WMF format) that cannot be edited.

Tip   Always use an image control for unbound pictures; it uses far fewer computer resources than an OLE control and significantly increases performance.

In Figure 19-1, the picture of the mountain is an image control. The pig is a bound OLE object; the graph is an unbound object. Though the graph is unbound, there is a data link from the graph template to the data on the form. This means the graph is updated each time data in the record changes.

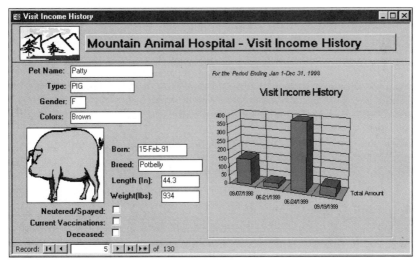

Figure 19-1: Bound and unbound objects.

Linking and embedding

The basic difference between linking and embedding objects within a form or report is that *embedding* the object stores a copy of it within your database. *Linking* an object from another application does not store the object in your database; instead, the external location of the object is stored.

Linking an object gives you two benefits:

✦ You can make changes using the external application, even without opening Access.

✦ The external file only uses space in the Access MDB database for the file path and file name of the external reference.

Caution If the external file is moved to another directory (or if the file is renamed), the link to Access is broken; opening the Access form may result in an error message.

One benefit of embedding is that you don't have to worry about someone changing the location or name of the linked file. Because it is embedded, the file is part of the Access MDB database file. Embedding does have its costs, however. The first is that it takes up space in your database — sometimes a great deal of it (some pictures can take several megabytes). In fact, if you embed an .AVI video clip of just 30 seconds in your database for one record, it can use ten or more megabytes of space. Imagine the space 100 records with video could use.

After the object is embedded or linked, you can use the source application (such as Excel or Paintbrush) to modify the object directly from the form. To make changes to these objects, you need only display the object in Access and double-click on it. This automatically launches the source application and lets you modify the object.

When you save the object, it is saved within Access.

Suppose that you've written a document management system in Access and have embedded a Word file in an Access form. When you double-click on the image of the Word document, Word is launched automatically and you can edit the document.

Note   When you use a linked object, the external application is started and when you modify the object, the changes are made to the external file, not within your database as they are with an embedded file.

Note   To edit an OLE object, you must have the associated OLE application installed in Windows. If you have embedded an Excel .XLS file but don't own Excel, you can view the spreadsheet (or use its values), but you won't be able to edit or change it.

On the CD-ROM   In the next section of this chapter, you use the form shown in Figure 19-2. You can find the form in the Mountain Animal Hospital database file, named *Pet Picture Creation - Empty.*

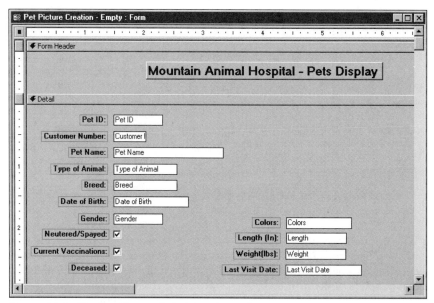

Figure 19-2: The Pet Picture Creation - Empty form.

Embedding Objects

You can embed objects in both unbound and bound object frames as well as in image frames. Embedding places the object in the Access database, where it is stored in the form, the report design, or a record of a table.

Embedding an unbound object

You can use two methods to embed an unbound object in a form or report:

✦ You can simply paste an object on the form or report; an image or unbound object frame is created that contains the object.

✦ You can create an unbound object frame or image frame and then insert the object or picture into the frame.

Pasting an unbound object

If the object you want to insert is not an OLE object, you *must* paste the object on the form. As an example, to cut or copy an object and then paste it into an image or unbound object frame, follow these steps:

1. Create or display the object by using the external application.

2. Select the object and choose Edit ➪ Cut or Edit ➪ Copy.

3. Display the Access form or report and select Edit ➪ Paste.

This process automatically creates an unbound object frame for an OLE object or an image frame for a picture and then embeds the pasted object in it.

If the object you paste into a form is an OLE object and you have the OLE application loaded, you can still double-click on the object to edit it. For example, you can highlight a range of cells in an Excel worksheet and paste the highlighted selection into an Access form or report. You can use the same highlight-and-paste approach with a paragraph of text in Word and paste it on the Access form or report. You can paste both OLE and non-OLE objects on a form or report with this method, but you'll see that there are other ways to add an OLE object.

Inserting an image-type object

You can also use another method to embed OLE objects or pictures into an unbound object frame or image frame. Suppose that you want to embed a file containing a Paintbrush picture. In Figure 19-1, the picture of the mountain appears on the form in the form header; this is an *image frame*. You can embed the picture by either pasting it into the image frame or by inserting the object into the image frame. Follow these steps to create an image frame:

1. Open the form Pet Picture Creation - Empty in Design view.

2. Select the Image Frame button on the toolbar.

3. Create the image frame, using the Image Frame button from the Toolbox to draw a rectangle, as shown in Figure 19-3.

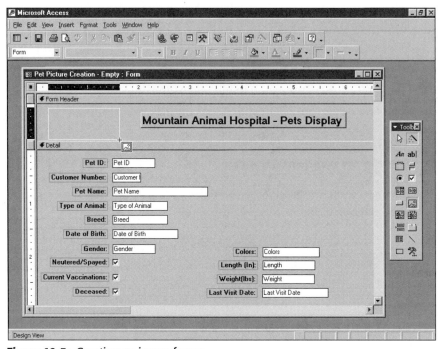

Figure 19-3: Creating an image frame.

When you create an image frame, the Insert Picture dialog box appears. This dialog box, shown in Figure 19-4, displays the image objects you have on your system. As you click on each file, a preview of the image apears to the right of the file selection list. If you don't see the preview, select Preview from the Tools menu in the Insert Picture toolbar.

To embed the existing Paintbrush file MTN.BMP in the image frame, follow these steps:

1. Using the standard file explorer dialog box, select MTN.BMP from the folder in which your other database files reside. (This file was installed when you installed files from the *Access 2000 Bible* CD-ROM.)

2. Click on Insert after the filename appears in the Insert Picture dialog box.

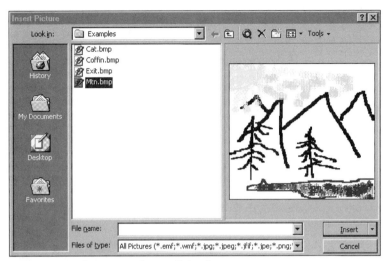

Figure 19-4: The Insert Picture dialog box.

Tip   If you had wished to not embed the picture but rather link it to the form, you could have used the combo box arrow on the right side of the Insert button and selected Link to File. While this would have saved some space in the Access database file, it would have made the application harder to move between computers because of the link to that file.

Access embeds and displays the picture in the unbound object frame, as you can see in Figure 19-5. Notice that in this figure the picture of the mountain does not seem to be displayed correctly. You can correct this by using the Size Mode property.

Notice some of the other properties of the Image control. The Picture property contains the path and filename of the image you selected. The Picture Type property below has two choices. The default is Embedded and saves a copy of the bitmap picture in the database container in a compressed form. When you save the form and have chosen Embedded, the Picture property will change to (bitmap) rather than the name of the path and file for the original location of the picture. The other Picture Type option is Linked. This would maintain a link to the original picture. However, if you move the bitmap, the picture will no longer be displayed and the link would be broken.

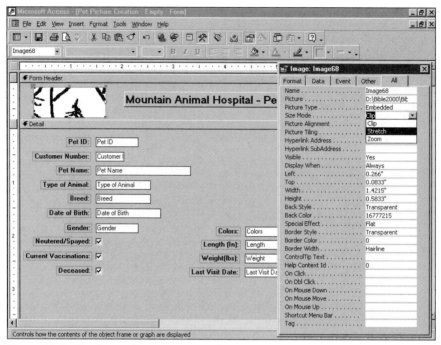

Figure 19-5: The image frame property sheet.

Changing the display of an image

After you add an image to a form or a report, you may want to change the size of the object or the object frame. If you embed a small picture, you may want to adjust the size of the object frame to fit the picture. Similarly, you might want to reduce the size of the picture to fit a specific area on your form or report.

To change the appearance and proportions of the object you embedded, you change the size of the image frame and set the Size Mode property. In Figure 19-6, you see three choices for the Size Mode property:

Clip	Shows the picture using the actual size, truncating both right and bottom
Stretch	Fits the picture within the frame, distorting the picture's proportions
Zoom	Fits the picture proportionally within the frame, possibly resulting in extra white space

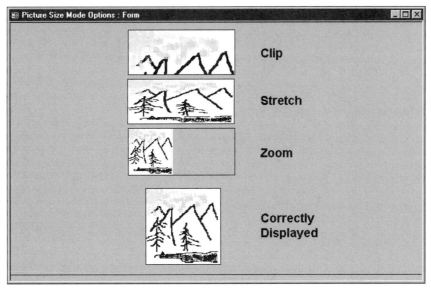

Figure 19-6: Results of using the various scaling options.

Use Clip only when the frame is the exact size of the picture or when you want to crop the picture. Stretch is useful when you have pictures where you can accept a slight amount of distortion. Although using Zoom fits the picture to the frame and maintains the original proportions, it may leave empty space in the frame. Figure 19-6 shows the MTN.BMP file using each of the property selections as well as the correct view of the picture.

To change the Size Mode options for the MTN.BMP file on the Pets form, follow these steps:

1. Select the image frame in Design view.

2. Display the property sheet.

3. Change the Size Mode setting to Stretch.

If you want to return the selected object to its original size, select it and choose Format ➪ Size ➪ To Fit.

When you have added a picture whose frame (border) is much larger than the picture itself and you have selected a Size Mode of Clip, the picture normally is centered within the frame. You can control this by using one of the Picture Alignment options, which include Center, Top Left, Top Right, Bottom Left, and Bottom Right. These options are also the same ones used when placing a picture in the background of a form using the form's Picture property. Using the Picture Tiling property, you can control how many copies of a picture will fit within a frame. For example, a brick wall is made up of many bricks. You can specify one brick (BRICKS.BMP) in your Windows system directory and then set the Picture Tiling option to Yes to build a wall within your frame. Access copies the bitmap as many times as it needs to fit within the frame.

Embedding bound objects

You can store pictures, spreadsheets, word-processing documents, or other objects as data in a table. You can store (for example) a Paintbrush picture, an Excel worksheet, or an object created in any other OLE application, such as a sound clip, an HTML document, or even a video clip from a movie.

You store objects in a table by creating a field that uses the OLE object data type. After you create a bound object frame, you can bind its Control Source to the OLE object field in the table.

You can then use the bound object frame to embed an object into each record of the table.

Note   You can also insert objects into a table from the Datasheet view of a form, table, or query, but the objects cannot be displayed in a view other than Form. When you switch to Datasheet view, you'll see text describing the OLE class of the embedded object. For example, if you insert a .BMP picture into an OLE object field in a table, the text *Picture* or *Paintbrush Picture* appears in Datasheet view.

Creating a bound OLE object

To create an embedded OLE object in a new bound object frame, follow these steps:

1. Select the Bound Object Frame button from the Toolbox.

2. Drag and size the frame, as shown in Figure 19-7.

3. Display the properties sheet.

4. Type **Picture** in the Control Source property. This is the name of the OLE field in the Pets table that contains pictures of the animals.

5. Set the Size Mode property to Zoom so that the picture will be zoomed proportionally within the area you define.

6. Select and delete only the bound object frame label (OLEBoundxx:).

7. Close and save the changes to this form.

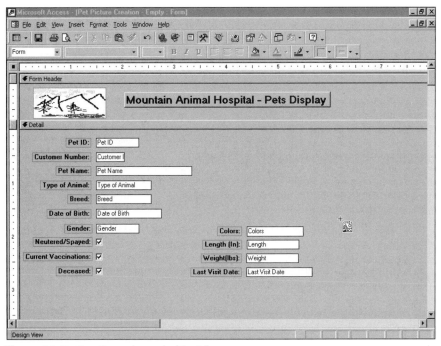

Figure 19-7: Creating a bound object frame.

Adding a picture to a bound object frame

After you define the bound object frame control and place it on a form, you can add pictures to it in several ways. You can paste a picture into a record or insert a file object into the frame. You insert the file object for a bound frame in nearly the same way you would insert an unbound object or image frame. The only difference is that where an image frame has a picture inserted in the design screen, a bound object frame has a picture inserted in Form view.

To insert a picture or other object into a bound object frame, display the form in Form view, move to the correct record (each record can have a different picture or object), select the bound object frame, and then choose Insert ⇨ Object from the Form menu. The dialog box is a little different. Because you can insert any OLE object (in this example, a picture), you first have to select Create from File and then choose the first option, Bitmap Image. You can then select the actual picture. When you're through, the picture or object appears in the space used for the bound object frame in the form.

Note

If you create the object (rather than embed an existing file), some applications display a dialog box asking whether you want to close the connection and update the open object. If you choose Yes, Access embeds the object in the bound object frame or embeds the object in the datasheet field along with text (such as *Paintbrush Picture*) that describes the object.

After you embed an object, you can start its source application and edit it from your form or report. Simply select the object in Form view and double-click on it.

Editing an embedded object

After you have an embedded object, you may want to modify the object itself. You can edit an OLE object in several ways. Normally, you can just double-click on it and launch the source application; then you can edit the embedded OLE object. As an example, follow these steps to edit the picture of the cat in Windows 95 Paintbrush:

1. Display the form Pets Picture Creation — Empty in Form view.

2. Move to record 12 and select the Picture bound object frame of the cat.

3. Double-click on the picture. The screen changes to an image-editing environment with Windows 95/98 Paint menus and functions available.

Note

As you can see in Figure 19-8, Windows 95 supports full in-place editing of OLE objects. Rather than launch a different program, it changes the look of the menus and screen to match Windows 95/98 Paint, temporarily adding that functionality to Access. Notice the different menus in Figure 19-8.

4. Make any changes you want to the picture.

5. Click on any other control in the form to close Paint.

If you make any changes, you will be prompted to update the embedded object before continuing.

Caution

In most cases you can modify an OLE object by double-clicking on it. When you attempt to modify either a sound or video object, however, double-clicking on the object causes it to use the player instead of letting you modify it. For these objects, you must use the Edit menu; select the last option, which changes (according to the OLE object type) to let you edit or play the object. You can also convert some embedded OLE objects to static images, which breaks all OLE links and simply displays a picture of the object.

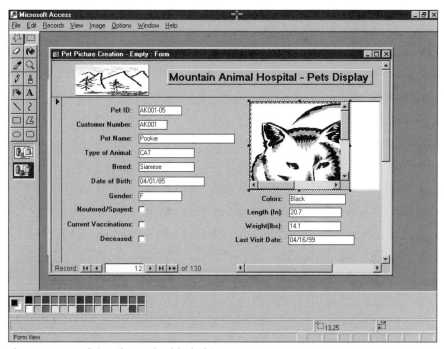

Figure 19-8: Editing the embedded object.

Linking Objects

Besides embedding objects, you can link them to external application files in much the same way as you would embed them. The difference is that the object itself is not stored in the form, the report, or the database table. Instead, Access stores information about the link in those places, saving valuable space in the MDB file. This feature also allows you to edit the object in its source application without having to go through Access.

Linking a bound object

When you create a link from a file in another application (for example, Microsoft Excel) to a field in a table, the information is still stored in its original file.

Suppose that you decide to use the OLE object field to store an Excel file containing additional information about the animal. If the Excel file contains history about the animal, you might want to link the information from the Pet record to this file.

Before linking information in a file to a field, however, you must first create and save the file in the source application.

On the CD-ROM

On your CD-ROM should be a file named PUNKIN.XLS, which is an Excel 2000 worksheet. You can use any spreadsheet or word-processing file in this example.

To link information to a bound object, use the following steps showing you how to use the Picture bound object frame to link a Pets table record to an Excel worksheet:

1. In the source application (Microsoft Excel), open the document that contains the information you want to link to.

2. Select the information you want to link, as shown in Figure 19-9.

3. Select Edit ⇨ Copy.

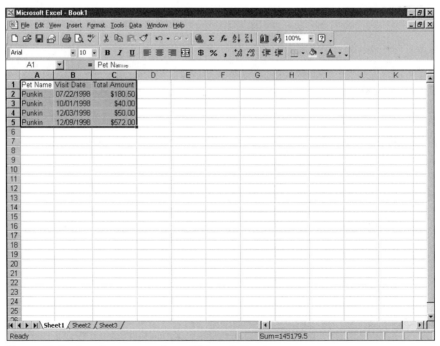

Figure 19-9: Copying a range from Microsoft Excel.

After you copy the range to the Clipboard, you can paste it into the bound object frame in the Access form by using the Paste Special option of the Edit menu.

4. Switch to Access and open the Pet Picture Creation - Empty form in Form view.

5. Go to record number 32 in the Access form.

6. Select the bound object frame containing the picture of the cat.

7. Select Edit ➪ PasteS.

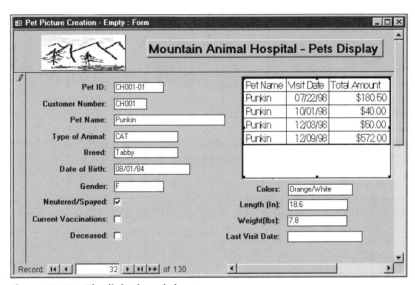

Figure 19-10: The linked worksheet.

The linked Excel worksheet appears in the bound object frame. Access creates the link and displays the object in the bound object frame or it links the object to the datasheet field, displaying text (such as Microsoft Excel) that describes the object. When you double-click on the picture of the worksheet, Excel is launched and you can edit the data.

Creating a Graph or Chart

You can use Microsoft Graph to chart data from any of your database tables or data stored within other applications (such as Microsoft Excel). You can create graphs in a wide variety of styles — bar graphs, pie charts, line charts, and others. Because Graph is an embedded OLE application, it does not work by itself; you have to run it from within Access.

Note   The terms Graph and Chart are used interchangeably in this chapter. Technically, you use Microsoft Graph to create a chart. There are many chart types that Microsoft Access cannot create. These have little to do with data, and include organization charts and flow charts. Since Microsoft Access creates data charts known as graphs, the term graph will be used throughout the chapter.

After you embed a graph, you can treat it as any other OLE object. You can modify it from the Design view of your form or report by double-clicking on the graph itself. You can edit it from the Form or Datasheet view of a form. The following sections describe how to build and process graphs that use data from within an Access table as well as from tables of other OLE applications.

The different ways to create a graph

Access provides two ways to create a graph and place it on a form or a report. Using the Graph form or Report Wizard, you can create a graph as a new form or report, add it to an existing form or report, or add it to an existing form and link it to a table data source. (To use this third method, click on the Unbound Object frame button in the Toolbox in the form design mode, and then choose Microsoft Graph 2000 Chart.) Unless you are already an experienced Graph user, familiar with it from previous versions of Access or Excel, you'll find it easier to create a new graph from the Toolbox. If you examine the Toolbox, however, you will not see a Chart Wizard icon. You must first customize the Toolbox so that you can add a graph to an existing form by using the Chart Wizard.

As a general rule (for both types of graph creation), before you enter a graph into a form or report that will be based on data from one or more of your tables, you must specify which table or query will supply the data for the graph. You should keep in mind several rules when setting up your query:

- ✦ Make sure that you've selected the fields containing the data to be graphed.
- ✦ Be sure to include the fields containing the labels that identify the data.
- ✦ Include any linking fields if you want the data to change from record to record.

Customizing the Toolbox

If you are an experienced Access 2.0 or Access 95 user, you may notice the Chart Wizard button is missing from the Access Toolbox. This is now an optional item, left for you to add. Fortunately, as with toolbars, the Toolbox can be customized.

The easiest way to customize the Toolbox is to right-click on it, display the shortcut menu, and choose Customize. The Customize Toolbars dialog box appears. Click on the Commands tab. You can then select Toolbox from the list of toolbars and then (as shown in Figure 19-11) click on the Chart... command and drag it to the Toolbox. This adds the missing icon permanently. You can rearrange Toolbox icons now by clicking on an icon and dragging it to the desired location in the Toolbox.

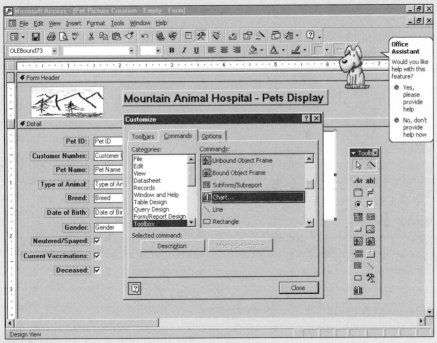

Figure 19-11: Customizing the Toolbox toolbar.

Embedding a Graph in a Form

As you learned earlier in this chapter, you can both link and embed objects in your Access tables, and you can create and display objects on your Access forms. Next you create and display a graph based on the Mountain Animal Hospital data and then display it on a form.

This graph will represent the visits of a pet, showing the visit dates and the dollars received for each visit. When you move through the Pets table, the form recalculates each pet's visits and displays the graph in a graph format. The graph is in the form that Figure 19-1 displayed, which was completed and displayed in Form view. You'll use a form that already exists but doesn't contain the graph: *Visit Income History - Without Graph*.

The form *Visit Income History - Without Graph* is in the Mountain Animal Hospital.MDB database, along with the final version (called Visit Income History) that contains the completed graph.

Assembling the data

As a first step in embedding a graph, make sure that the query associated with the form provides the information you need for the graph. In this example, you need both the Visit Date and the Total Amount fields from the Visits table as the basis of the graph. You also need the Pet ID field from the Visits table to use as a link to the data on the form. This link allows the data in the graph to change from record to record.

Sometimes you'll need to create a query when you need data items from more than one table. In this example, you can select all the data you need right from the Wizard; Access will build the query (actually an SQL statement) for you automatically.

Adding the graph to the form

The following steps detail how to create and place the new graph on the existing form (you should be in Design view of the form named *Visit Income History - Without Graph*):

1. Select the Chart button you added to the Toolbox, or select Chart from the Insert menu.

2. Position the new cursor at the upper left position for the new graph.

3. Click the mouse button and hold it down while dragging the box to the desired size on the righthand portion of the form.

After you size the blank area for the graph and release the mouse button, Access 2000 activates the Chart Wizard used to embed a graph in a form.

As shown in Figure 19-12, this Wizard screen lets you select the table or query from which you'll select the values. By using the row of option buttons under the list of tables, you can view all the Tables, all the Queries, or Both.

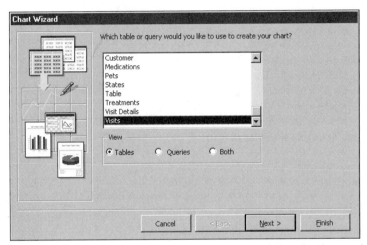

Figure 19-12: Selecting the table for the source of data for the graph.

The following steps take you through the Wizard to create the desired graph and link it to your form:

1. Choose the Visits table as the source for the graph.

2. Click on Next> to go to the next Wizard screen.

   The Chart Wizard lets you select fields to include in your graph.

3. Select the Visit Date and Total Amount fields by double-clicking on them to move them to the Fields for graph box.

4. Click on Next> to go to the next Wizard screen.

   This screen (Figure 19-13) lets you choose the type of graph you want to create and determine whether the data series are in rows or columns. In this example, select a column chart; you'll customize it later using the graph options. As you click on each of the graph types, an explanation appears in the box in the lower right corner of the screen.

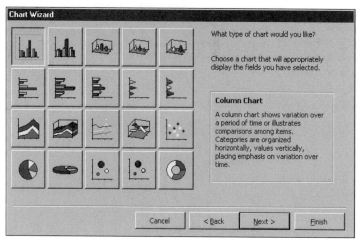

Figure 19-13: Selecting the type of chart.

5. Select the Column Chart (as shown in Figure 19-13), and then click on Next> to go to the next Wizard screen. (The Column Chart is easiest to work with.)

The next screen (Figure 19-14) makes choices for you automatically and lets you change the assumptions. Figure 19-14 shows that the Visit Date field has been used for the x-axis and that the Total Amount field is used in the y-axis to determine the height of the bars.

This screen gives you a graphical way to choose the fields you want for your graph; then you can drag them to the simulated graph window. Figure 19-14 shows the Wizard screen divided into two areas. The right side shows the fields you have selected to work with. The left side displays a simulated graph; you can drag fields from the list of fields on the right to the axis area on the left. If you want to change the Visit Date field chosen for you for the x-axis, drag it back from the left side to the right side. Likewise, to make a selection, drag a field name from the right side of the screen to its proper axis on the left side.

For this example, the assumptions made by Access are fine. You may notice (in Figure 19-14) that each of the fields on the left side of the screen is actually a button. When you double-click on one, you can further define how the data is used in the graph.

Generally, the x-axis variable is either a date or a text field. The y-axis field is almost always a number (though it can be a count of values). Only numeric and date fields (such as the y-axis variable Total Amount) can be further defined. If you double-click on the Total Amount field on the left side of the screen, the dialog box shown in Figure 19-15 appears; it lets you define options for summarizing the field. Remember that there may be many records for a given summary; in this example, many pets may have visits in a specific month.

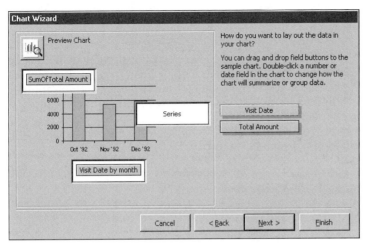

Figure 19-14: Laying out the chart's data elements.

Tip

If you had several numeric fields, you could drag them (or any multiple fields) to the left side for a multiple series; these would appear in a legend. You can also drag the same field to both the x-axis and the Series indicator, as long as you're grouping differently. For example, you could group the Visit Date by month and use it again in the Series grouped by year. Without using the Visit Date field a second time as the series variable, you would have one bar for each month in sequential order—for example, Jan95, Feb95, Mar95,... Dec95, Jan96, Feb96.... By adding the Visit Date as a series variable and grouping it by year, you could get pairs of bars. Multiple bars can be created for each month, each a different color and representing a different year and a legend for each year.

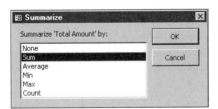

Figure 19-15: Selecting options to summarize the field.

As you can see in Figure 19-15, Sum has been chosen as the summarization type. You could change it to Average to graph the average amount of a visit instead of summing all the visit amounts.

Caution   You must supply a numeric variable for all the selections except Count, which can be any data type.

The dialog box shown in Figure 19-16 lets you choose the date hierarchy from larger to smaller roll-ups. The choices include Year, Quarter, Month, Week, Day, Hour, and Minute. If you have data for many dates within a month and want to roll it up by month, you would choose Month. In this example, you want to see all the detail data. Since the data is in Visits by date (mm/dd/yy), you would select Day to view all the detail records. For this example, change the default selection from Month to Day.

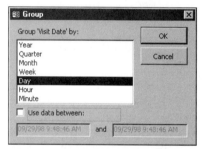

Figure 19-16: Choosing group options for a date field.

You can click on the Preview Chart button at any time to see the results of your choices.

6. Make sure that you changed the group options from Month to Day; click on Next> to go to the next Wizard screen.

Figure 19-17 shows the Field Linking box. If you run the Chart Wizard from inside an existing form, you have the option to link a field in the form to a field in the chart. Even if you don't specify the field when you select the chart fields, you can make the link as long as the field exists in the selected table.

In this example, Access has correctly selected the Pet ID field from both the Visit Income History form and the Visits table. This way, as you move from record to record (keyed by Pet ID) in the Visit Income History form, the graph changes to display only the data for that pet.

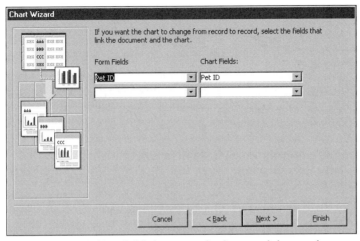

Figure 19-17: Linking fields between the form and the graph.

7. Select Next> to move to the last Wizard screen.

The last Chart Wizard screen, shown in Figure 19-18, lets you enter a title and determine whether a legend is needed. You won't need one for this example because you have only one data series.

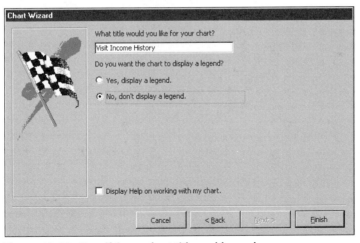

Figure 19-18: Specifying a chart title and legend.

8. Enter **Visit Income History** for the graph title.

9. Select the button next to the text *No, don't display a legend*.

10. Click on Finish to complete the Wizard.

After you complete all these entries, the sample chart appears in the graph object frame on the design screen (as shown in Figure 19-19). Until you display the form in Form view, the link to the individual pet is not established and the graph is not recalculated to show only the visits for the specific pet's record.

In fact, the graph shown is a sample preview; it doesn't use any of your data. If you were worried about where that strange-looking graph came from, don't be.

11. Click on the Form View button on the toolbar to display the Visit Income History form and recalculate the graph. Figure 19-20 shows the final graph in Form view.

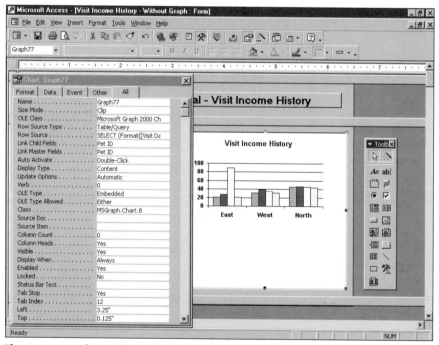

Figure 19-19: The graph in the Form Design window.

In Figure 19-19, you saw the graph and the property sheet. You display a graph by using a *graph frame*, which shows its data in either Form view or Design view. Take note of some properties in the property sheet. The Size Mode property is set initially to Clip. You can change this to Zoom or Stretch, although the graph should always be displayed proportionally. You can size and move the graph to fit on your form. When you work with the graph in the Graph window, the size of the graph you create is the same size it will be in the Design window.

The OLE Class property is Microsoft Graph 2000 Chart. This is linked automatically by the Chart Wizard. The Row Source comes from the table or query you used with the graph, but it appears as an SQL statement that is passed to the Graph. The SQL statement (more on this later) created for this graph is:

```
SELECT Format([Visit Date], "DDDDD"), SUM([Total Amount]) AS
[SumOfTotalAmount]
FROM [Visits] GROUP BY Int([Visit Date]), Format([Visit Date],
"DDDDD");
```

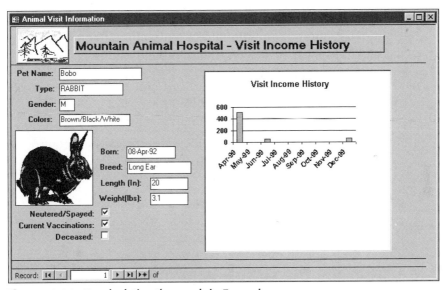

Figure 19-20: Recalculating the graph in Form view.

The next two properties, Link Child Fields and Link Master Fields, control linking of the data to the form data itself. Using the link properties, you can link the graph's data to each record in the form. In this example, the Pet ID from the current Pets record is linked to Visit Details records with the same Pet ID.

To change the appearance of the graph, you can double-click on the graph in Design view to open Microsoft Graph. After you make the changes you want, you can select File ➪ Exit, return to Microsoft Access, and go back to Design view.

Customizing a Graph

After you create a graph within Access, you can enhance it by using the tools within Microsoft Graph. As demonstrated in the preceding section, just a few mouse clicks will create a basic graph. The following section describes a number of ways to make your graph a powerful presentation and reporting tool.

In many cases, the basic chart you create presents the idea you want to get across. In other cases, however, it may be necessary to create a more illustrative presentation. You can accomplish this by adding any of these enhancements:

✦ Entering free-form text to the graph to highlight specific areas of the graph

✦ Changing attached text for a better display of the data being presented

✦ Annotating the graph with lines and arrows

✦ Changing certain graphic objects with colors and patterns

✦ Moving and modifying the legend

✦ Adding gridlines to reflect the data better

✦ Manipulating the 3-D view to show your presentation more accurately

✦ Adding a bitmap to the graph for a more professional presentation

✦ Changing the graph type to show the data in a different graphic format, such as Bar, Line, or Pie

✦ Adding or modifying the data in the graph

After the graph appears in the Graph application, you can begin to modify it.

Understanding the Graph window

The Graph or Chart window, shown in Figure 19-21, lets you work with and customize the graph. As you can see, the *graph* itself is highlighted and each object of the graph is active including titles, axis labels, and even the bars themselves. The data last displayed is shown in the graph. A *datasheet* containing the data for the last record used is also displayed. In Figure 19-21, there are three visit records for the graph.

Datasheet	A spreadsheet of the data used in the graph
Graph or Chart	The displayed chart of the selected data

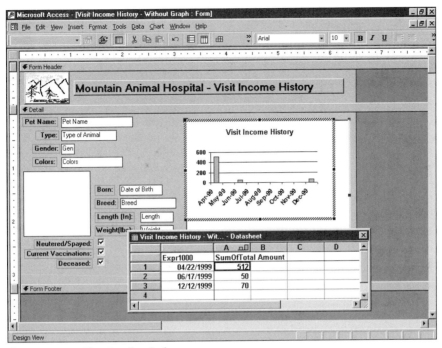

Figure 19-21: The Graph window.

In the datasheet, you can add, change, or delete data. Any data you modify this way is reflected immediately in the graph. After you change the datasheet in the Graph window, you can even tell Access whether to include each row or column when the graph is drawn.

Changing data in a linked record will change data in the graph for only as long as you are on that record. After you move off it, the changes are discarded.

More important, you can use the Chart portion of the Graph window to change the way the graph appears. By clicking on objects such as attached text (or on areas of the graph such as the columns), you can modify these objects. You can customize an object by double-clicking on an object to display a dialog box or by making selections from the menus at the top of the window.

Working with attached text

Text generated by the program is called attached text. These graph items are attached text:

✦ Graph title

✦ Value of y-axis

✦ Category of x-axis

✦ Data series and points

✦ Overlay value of y-axis

✦ Overlay value of x-axis

After the initial graph appears, you can change this text. Click on a text object to change the text itself, or double-click on any text item in the preceding list and then modify its properties.

You can choose from three categories of settings to modify an attached text object:

Patterns	Background and foreground colors, borders, and shading
Font	Text font, size, style, and color
Alignment	Alignment and orientation

Note   You can change attributes from the Format menu too.

The Font options let you change the font assignment for the text within the text object, as shown in Figure 19-22.

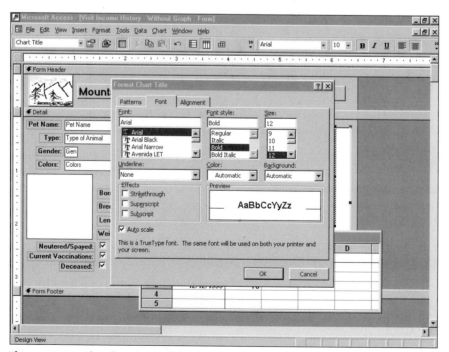

Figure 19-22: The chart fonts dialog box.

The chart fonts dialog box is a standard Windows font-selector box. Here you can select Font, Size, Font Style, Color, and Background effects. To change the text, follow these steps:

1. Double-click on the chart title *Visit Income History*.

2. Select the Font tab from the Format Chart Title dialog box.

3. Select Arial in the Font list box. (This is probably the default.)

4. Select Bold in the Font Style list box.

5. Select 12 in the Size list box.

6. Click on OK to complete the changes.

As you make the font changes, a sample of each change appears in the Preview box.

The Alignment tab in the dialog box lets you set the horizontal alignment (left, center, right, or justify), the vertical alignment (top, center, bottom, or justify), and the orientation (a control that lets you rotate your text on a compass).

Figure 19-23 shows the Alignment tab and the options available.

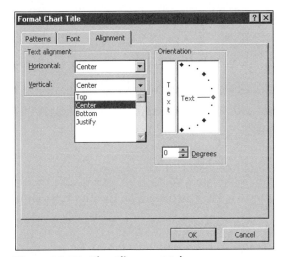

Figure 19-23: The Alignment tab.

The most important part of this dialog box is the Orientation setting. Although for some titles it is not important to change any of these settings, it becomes necessary to change them for titles that normally run vertically (such as axis titles).

Sometimes you may need to add text to your graph to present your data better. This text is called *free-form* (or *unattached*) text. You can place it anywhere on your graph and combine it with other objects to illustrate your data as you want. Figure 19-24 shows free-form text being entered on the graph, as well as the changes you previously made to the graph title.

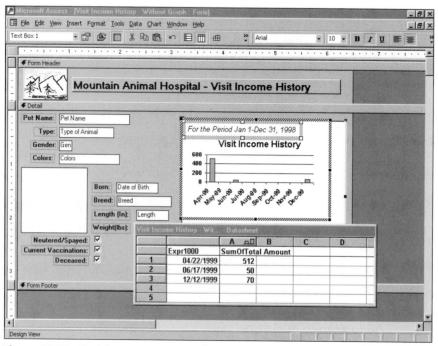

Figure 19-24: Free-form text on a graph.

In the next steps, you see how to add free-form text to the graph:

1. Type **For the Period Jan 1-Dec 31, 1998** anywhere on the graph, as shown in Figure 19-24.

   Microsoft Graph positions the text near the middle of the graph. The text is surrounded by handles so that you can size and position the text.

2. Drag the text to the upper left corner of the graph.

3. Right-click on the text, select Format ➪ Text Box, and change the font to Arial, 12 point, italic.

Changing the graph type

After you create your initial graph, you can experiment with changing the graph type to make sure that you selected the type that best reflects your data. Microsoft Graph provides a wide range of graphs to select from; a few mouse clicks can change the type of graph.

Table 19-1 shows the different types of graphs you can select:

Table 19-1 Types of Charts	
Two-Dimensional Charts	*Three-Dimensional Charts*
Column	3-D Column
Bar	3-D Bar
Line	3-D Line
Pie	3-D Pie
XY (Scatter)	3-D Area
Area	3-D Surface
Doughnut	3-D Cylinder
Radar	3-D Cone
Surface	3-D Pyramid
Bubble	
Stock	
Cylinder	
Cone	
Pyramid	

To select a different type of graph, select Chart ➪ Chart Type from the menu bar of the Chart window to display the various chart types. When you select any of the graph options, a window opens (as shown in Figure 19-25) to display all the different graphing options available within the selected graph type. Click on one of them to select your new graph type.

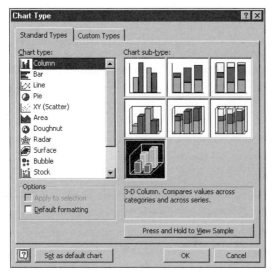

Figure 19-25: The chart types.

To display some different graph types, follow these steps:

1. Select Chart ➪ Chart Type, as shown in Figure 19-25.

2. Select Column from the Standard Types tab and select the 3-D Column type.

3. Click on OK to return to the Graph window.

Changing axis labels

You may want to change the text font of the x-axis so that you can see all the labels. Follow these steps to change axis labels:

1. Double-click on the x-axis (the bottom axis with the dates on it). You can see the Format Axis tabbed dialog box showing the Pattern tab in Figure 19-26.

2. Select the Font tab from the Format Axis dialog box.

3. Change the Size setting to 8 points by entering **8** in the Font Size box. (This probably will be the default.)

4. Click on OK to return to the chart.

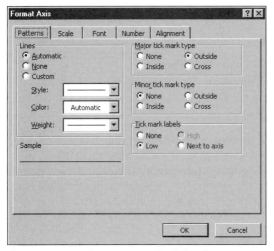

Figure 19-26: The Format Axis dialog box Pattern tab.

Changing a bar color, pattern, and shape

If you are going to print the graph in monochrome, you should always adjust the patterns so that they are not all solid colors. You can change the color or pattern of each bar by double-clicking on any bar in the category you want to select.

The Format Data Series dialog box is displayed. You can change the patterns and color of the bars from the first tab. If you press the Shape tab, as shown in Figure 19-27, you can select from cubes, pyramids, cylinders, or cones.

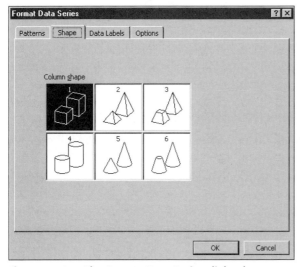

Figure 19-27: The Format Data Series dialog box showing the Shape tab.

Modifying gridlines

Gridlines are lines that extend from the axis across the plotting area of the graph to help you read the graph properly. You can add them for the x-axis and y-axis of your graph; if it's three-dimensional, an additional gridline is available for the z-axis. You can add gridlines for any axis on the graph. The *z-axis gridlines* appear along the back and side walls of the plotting area. The *x-* and *y-axis gridlines* appear across the base and up the walls of the graph.

Select Chart ➪ Chart Options... to begin working with gridlines. Select the Gridlines tab, as shown in Figure 19-28. Here, you can define which gridlines are shown. The y-axis gridlines are shown on the left wall; the z-axis gridlines are shown on the back wall; and the x-axis gridlines are shown on the floor. You can change the line type by double-clicking on the gridlines when you're in the normal Design view of the graph and working with the Format Gridlines dialog box to change the Patterns and Scale.

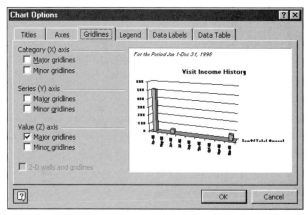

Figure 19-28: The Chart Options dialog box showing the Gridlines tab.

Manipulating three-dimensional graphs

In any of the three-dimensional chart options, you can modify the following graph-display characteristics:

- ✦ Elevation
- ✦ Perspective (if the Right angle axes option is turned off)
- ✦ Rotation
- ✦ Scaling
- ✦ Angle and height of the axes

You can change the 3-D view by selecting Chart ⇨ 3-D View. The dialog box shown in Figure 19-29 appears. Then you can enter the values for the various settings or use the six buttons to rotate the icon of the graph in real time. When you see the view you like, click on OK and your chart will change to that perspective.

Note The Elevation buttons control the height at which you view the data. The elevation is measured in degrees; it can range from –90 to 90 degrees.

An elevation of zero displays the graph as if you were level with the center of the graph. An elevation of 90 degrees shows the graph as you would view it from above center. A –90 degree elevation shows the graph as you would view it from below its center.

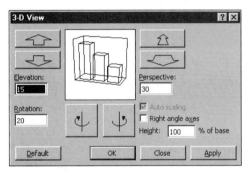

Figure 19-29: The 3-D View dialog box.

The Perspective buttons control the amount of perspective in your graph. Adding more perspective makes the data markers at the back of the graph smaller than those at the front of the graph. This option provides a sense of distance; the smaller data markers seem farther away. If your graph contains a large amount of data, you may want to use a larger perspective value (the ratio of the front of the graph to the back of the graph). This value can range from 0 to 100.

A perspective of 0 makes the back edge of the graph equal in width to the front edge. You can experiment with these settings until you get the effect you need.

The Rotation buttons control the rotation of the entire plotting area. The rotation is measured in degrees, from 0 to 360. A rotation of 0 displays your graph as you view it from directly in front. A rotation of 180 degrees displays the graph as if you were viewing it from the back. (This setting visually reverses the plotting order of your data series.) A rotation of 90 degrees displays your graph as if you were viewing it from the center of the side wall.

The Auto scaling check box lets you scale a three-dimensional graph so that its size is closer to that of the two-dimensional graph using the same data. To activate this option, click on the Auto scaling check box so that the X appears in the box. When this option is kept activated, Access will scale the graph automatically whenever you switch from a two-dimensional to a three-dimensional graph.

Two options within the 3-D View dialog box pertain specifically to display of the axes. The Right angle axes check box lets you control the orientation of the axes. If the check box is on, all axes are displayed at right angles to each other.

Caution   If the Right angle axes check box is selected, you cannot specify the perspective for the three-dimensional view.

The Height entry box contains the height of the z-axis and walls relative to the width of the graph's base. The height is measured as a percentage of the x-axis length. A height of 100 percent makes the height equal to the x-axis. A height of 50 percent makes the height half the x-axis length. You can set this height percentage at more than 100 percent; by doing so, you can make the height of the z-axis greater than the length of the x-axis.

Caution   If you change the Height setting, your change will not be displayed in the sample graph shown in the 3-D View dialog box.

After you have made the desired changes, you can select File ⇨ Exit and then select Return to (which will bring you back to the Form Design screen).

You might want to make one more change: A graph frame is really an unbound object frame, and you can change its border type and background (as you can for any unbound object frame). Figure 19-30 shows the final graph after the border has been changed to an etched special effect, and the background colored light gray to match the background of the form. This allows the graph to stand out more than it would if you used a sunken white background.

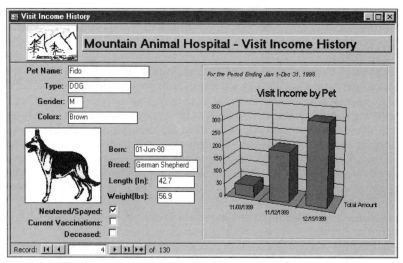

Figure 19-30: The final graph.

Integration with Microsoft Office

Access 2000 is not only integrated with Windows, it now shares many major components with Microsoft Office 2000. (If you are an Excel 2000 or Word 2000 user, you will be especially thrilled.) Access 2000 has an integrated Spell Checker that is used to make sure that the data stored in Access 2000 tables and database objects is spelled correctly. The dictionary is shared across all Office 2000 applications. There are also specific technical dictionaries for legal, medical, and foreign languages and also several custom dictionaries that you can maintain to store your own technical words. Access 2000 also shares the Office 2000 AutoCorrect features to fix errors while you type.

Checking the spelling of one or more fields and records

You can check the spelling of your data in either Form or Datasheet view. In Form view, you can spell-check only a single record — and field within the record — at a time. To check the spelling of data in Form view, you would select the field or text containing spelling you want to check, and then click on the Spell Check icon on the toolbar (the icon with the check mark and the small letters ABC above it).

When you click on the icon, Access checks the field (or selected text within the field) for spelling, as shown in Figure 19-31.

Figure 19-31: Spell-checking in Access.

In the Spelling dialog box that appears, you can click on Add if you want to add the word in the Not In Dictionary: box to the custom dictionary listed in the Add Words To: box.

You can select only one field at a time in Form view. You'll probably want to use only Form view to spell-check selected memo data. To select multiple fields or records, you must switch to Datasheet view. To check the spelling of data in

Datasheet view, you would select the records, columns, fields, or text within a field containing spelling you want to check and then click on the Spell Check icon.

You can also check the spelling in a table, query, or form in the Database window by clicking on the table, query, or form object containing spelling you want to check.

You only spell-check the data inside the objects. Access 2000 cannot spell-check control names.

Correcting your typing automatically when entering data

You can use the AutoCorrect feature to provide automatic corrections to text you frequently mistype and to replace abbreviations with the long names they stand for (also automatically). For example, you can create an entry "mah" for Mountain Animal Hospital. Whenever you type **mah** followed by a space or punctuation mark, Microsoft Access replaces *mah* with the text *Mountain Animal Hospital*.

You can activate AutoCorrect by selecting Tools ➪ AutoCorrect. The dialog box shown in Figure 19-32 appears. You can select the Replace text as you type check box. In the Replace box, type the text you want corrected. In the With box, type the corrected text. When you click on Add, the word replacement combination will be added to the AutoCorrect dictionary.

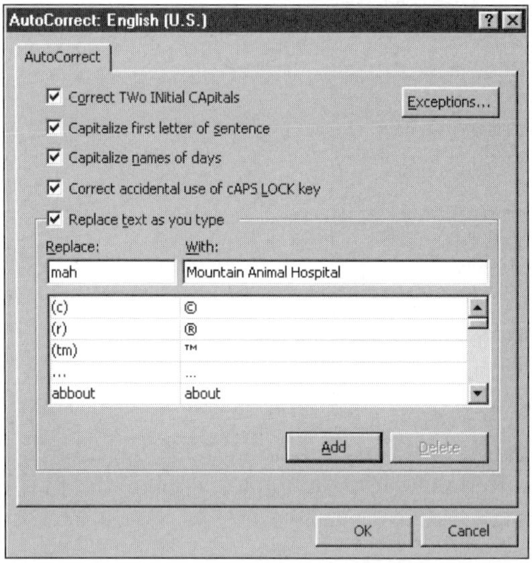

Figure 19-32: Using AutoCorrect in Access 2000.

AutoCorrect won't correct text that was typed before you selected the Replace text as you type check box.

Using OLE automation with Office 2000

Access 2000 takes advantage of drag and drop; you can do it from Datasheet view across Excel and Word. You can instantly create a table in a Word document (or add a table to an Excel spreadsheet) by simply copying and pasting (or dragging and dropping) data from an Access datasheet to a Word document or an Excel spreadsheet. (Obviously, you must have Word or Excel to take advantage of these features.)

Access 2000 contains a PivotTable Wizard to create Excel PivotTables based on Access tables or queries. A *PivotTable* is like a cross-tabulation of your data; you can define the data values for rows, columns, pages, and summarization. Figure 19-33 shows a conceptual figure of a PivotTable.

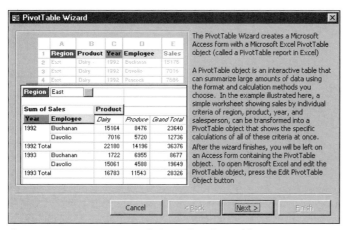

Figure 19-33: A conceptual view of a PivotTable.

A PivotTable can have multiple levels of rows, columns, and even pages. As you can see in the conceptual figure, the center of the table contains numeric data; the rows and columns form a hierarchy of unique data. In this figure, dates and employees are the row hierarchies, along with multiple levels of subtotals. The column headers are types of products, and each page of the PivotTable is a different region.

Cross-Reference   A PivotTable is like a crosstab query (see Chapter 24), but much more powerful.

You start creating a PivotTable from the New Form dialog box using the Pivot Table selection from the list of standard Wizards you can select. After you begin the PivotTable Wizard process, you will first see an introductory screen explaining how

a PivotTable works (Figure 19-33). After you view this screen, press the Next>
button. Figure 19-34 displays the table/queries dialog box.

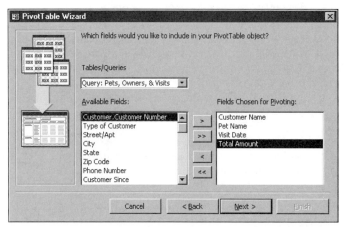

Figure 19-34: Selecting the Table/Query to supply data for the
Pivot Table.

This dialog box lets you select the tables or query to use in creating the PivotTable.
You can select from more than one table, but they must be joined at the database
level to create a valid PivotTable. In this example, the Pets, Owners, & Visits query
is being used. The PivotTable will use the Customer and Pet Name fields along with
the Visit Date and Total Amount spent.

**On the
CD-ROM**

In this example, you will select the query, *Pets, Owners, and Visits.*

After you press the Next> button, Microsoft Excel 2000 starts and the dialog box
shown in Figure 19-35 is displayed on the Excel screen.

The two important options in this dialog box are Layout… and Options…. Layout
lets you drag each of the fields you want into the desired position in the pivot table.
Options allows you to select various format and data options. These are described
in detail on the next few pages.

The Layout next dialog box displayed (shown in Figure 19-36) when you press the
Next> button lets you drag the fields to the PivotTable (using a technology similar
to the Chart Wizard you learned about earlier in this chapter). Unlike the Chart
Wizard, it makes no assumptions for you. You must drag each field from the list on
the right to the area on the left. As you can see, Customer Name will be used for the
page, Pet Name will be used for the column headers, Visit Date for the row names,
and Total Amount will be summed in the center of the PivotTable.

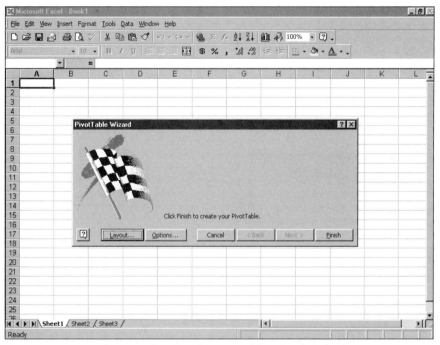

Figure 19-35: Excel screen showing the PivotTable Wizard dialog box.

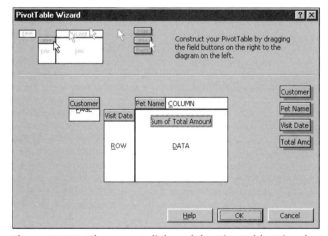

Figure 19-36: The Layout dialog of the PivotTable Wizard.

You can double-click on any of the field names in the field placement area to determine where a field is placed and how subtotals are created for each field (as shown in Figure 19-37). You can see in Figure 19-37 that you can also determine how subtotals are created for the field.

Finally, you can choose to hide any of the data items. Although this doesn't make sense for this example, if you were using date data, you could exclude a range of dates; or in the case of a few product lines, you could exclude selected products.

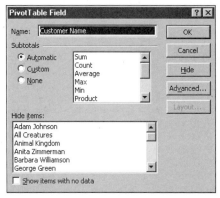

Figure 19-37: Hiding Pivot table fields and selecting Field orientation and totals.

After you complete this screen, you can display the Options dialog box. When you press the Options button, the Options screen appears, as shown in Figure 19-38.

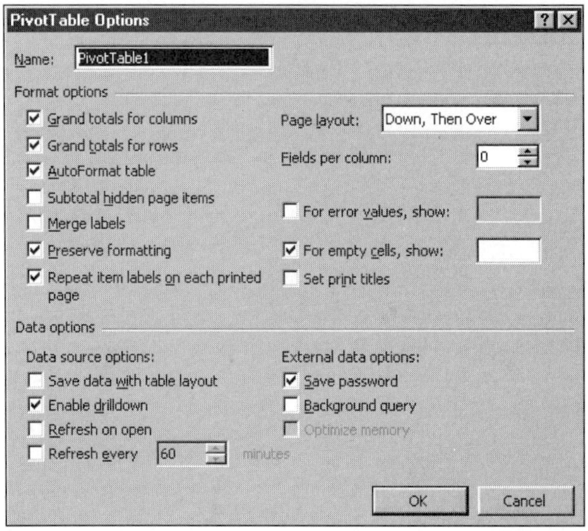

Figure 19-38: Using the PivotTable Wizard Options screen.

This screen lets you determine whether totals for columns and rows are displayed. You can also determine if the default AutoFormat is used when the PivotTable is created. After you return to the last screen and select the Finish button, a new form is created; you can see your results as shown in Figure 19-39.

The PivotTable in the figure shows the PivotTable in Excel 2000. The OLE link is then made to Access 2000 and the PivotTable is displayed in an Access form.

Note   You must have Excel to use this Wizard.

Using the new OLE capabilities, the Excel PivotTable Wizard appears to be integrated with Access; it's really an embedded Excel object. You can edit this table by pressing the large Edit PivotTable button, which switches to an Excel 2000 view (as shown in Figure 19-39) and displays the various options, including one that changes the PivotTable selections. The PivotTable toolbar appears in the lower portion of the screen. The page variable *Customer Name* appears as a combo box, initially set to All. This has been changed to show the customer name *All Creatures*. When this selection is made, the data below instantly changes to show only data for pets owned by All Creatures. Notice the row and column totals in the figure.

PivotTables are easy to create and provide a much better analysis than crosstabulation queries. When you save the form, the link to Excel remains.

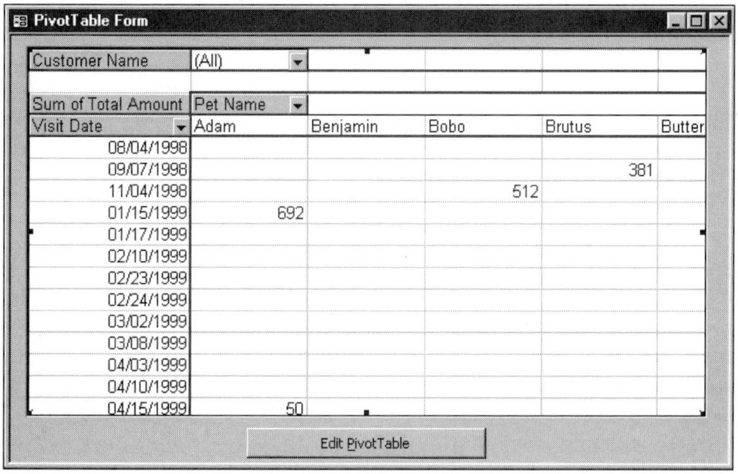

PivotTable Form					
Customer Name	(All)				
Sum of Total Amount	Pet Name				
Visit Date	Adam	Benjamin	Bobo	Brutus	Butter
08/04/1998					
09/07/1998				381	
11/04/1998			512		
01/15/1999	692				
01/17/1999					
02/10/1999					
02/23/1999					
02/24/1999					
03/02/1999					
03/08/1999					
04/03/1999					
04/10/1999					
04/15/1999	50				

Edit PivotTable

Figure 19-39: The completed PivotTable.

Another feature in Excel 2000 lets you create a new Access table directly from an Excel 2000 spreadsheet — automatically — and link them so that data changes are made with either product. This is not an Access feature, but an Excel feature you should know; it allows Excel users to update and manipulate Access data without knowing Access.

Using the Calendar ActiveX Control

ActiveX controls (also known as OCX and custom controls) are not new to Access. Custom controls extend the number of controls already found in Access. Some of the more popular controls are Calendars, Tab Dialog box controls, Progress Meters, Spin Box, Sliders, and many others. Though they existed in Access 2.0 (as 16-bit controls), they were seldom used; they required separate sets of properties and were not totally stable. Access for Windows 95 introduced support for the new 32-bit controls, and Access 2000 makes them even better. Access 2000 comes with several ActiveX controls. One of the most often used is the Calendar control. If you have Office 2000, you have many ActiveX controls from the new Microsoft Forms collection used to create Office forms without Access. There is expected to be a wealth of new ActiveX controls from third parties for Access 2000.

The Office Developers Edition is a separate product from Microsoft that allows you to create a run-time application without Access. It also includes the Help compiler, a printed-language reference manual, the Windows Setup Wizard, many other ActiveX controls, and many new tools for Access 2000 and Office 2000 developers, including many Internet tools.

You can select Insert ⇨ ActiveX Control... or select the More Tools icon from the Toolbox to see a list of all your ActiveX controls.

If you don't have the Office Developer's Edition or Office 2000, you probably will see only the Calendar control. You add a custom control as you would to any unbound OLE control. To add a Calendar custom control to a new blank form, follow these steps:

1. Open a new form in Design view and display the Toolbox. Don't select any table in the New Form dialog box.

2. Select Insert ⇨ Custom Control or choose the More Tools icon from the Toolbox.

3. Select Calendar Control 9.0 and click on OK.

The Calendar control appears on the new form. The calendar can be resized like any unbound control, and (of course) it has properties. Figure 19-40 shows the Calendar control and its basic properties.

Notice the Property window. This window appears showing the properties specific to a Calendar control. These are the properties displayed by the Other tab. With these properties, you can change some of the display characteristics of the calendar, including the following:

DayLength	Short (SMTWTFS), Medium (Sun, Mon, Tue, . . .), Long (Sunday, Monday, . . .)
FirstDay	First day of week displayed (default is Sunday)

GridCellEffect	Raised, Sunken, Flat
MonthLength	Long (January, February, . . .), Short (Jan, Feb, . . .)
ShowDateSelectors	Display a combo box for month and year in Form view

Many other properties control the various colors and fonts of calendar components. A number of value properties affect the display of the calendar and the selected date. Four properties change the display of the calendar data:

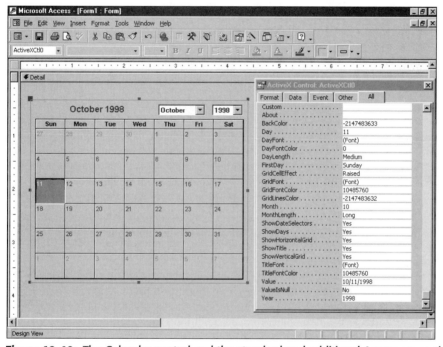

Figure 19-40: The Calendar control and the standard and additional Access properties.

Day	The day of the current month (11 in this example)
Month	The month of the current date (10 in this example)
Year	The year being displayed (1998 in this example)
Value	The date displayed (10/11/98 in this example)

Cross-Reference

The values can be changed in several ways. You can click on a date in the calendar in Form view, which changes the Value property. When the Value property changes, so do the Day, Month, and Year properties. You can also change these properties in the Property window or programmatically from a macro or Visual Basic for Applications. You'll learn how to do this in Chapters 31 and 34.

Another way to change properties in a custom control is to display the Calendar Properties dialog box, as shown in Figure 19-41. This provides combo-box access to certain control properties. You can display this dialog box by selecting Edit ➪ Calendar Control Object ➪ Properties or by right-clicking on the Calendar control and selecting Calendar Control Object ➪ Properties from the shortcut menu.

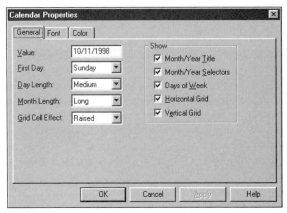

Figure 19-41: The Calendar Properties dialog box.

When you display the calendar in Form view, you can also display combo boxes (using the ShowDateSelectors property) to change the month or year because you can only click on a day in the calendar. These are the Month/Year Selectors in the Property dialog box.

The calendar's real power is that you can link it to a field. When the calendar is changed, the field value changes. Likewise, if the field value changes, the calendar display changes. You can easily do this by linking the calendar to a field by using its Control Source property.

Summary

In this chapter, you learned the differences between linking and embedding graphs and other OLE objects to your forms. You created a graph by using the Chart Wizard, and you used Microsoft Graph to customize the graph to fit your needs. Microsoft Access, because of its Windows compatibility, has the power to share data, pictures, and other objects with other OLE-compatible products. You also learned that you can embed or link a full range of graphs to your forms with just a few keystrokes. In this chapter, the following points were explained:

✦ Access adds any type of picture or graphic object to an Access table, including sound and video, a worksheet, or a document.

✦ A bound object is attached to a specific record, whereas an unbound object is attached only to a form or report.

✦ Embedded objects are stored in a table, form, or report, but linked objects merely link to an external file.

✦ You can embed an object by either pasting it into an object frame or inserting the object.

✦ If the embedded object supports OLE, you can double-click on the object to launch the source application and edit the object.

✦ The easiest way to create graphs is to use the Chart Wizard in a form.

✦ After you create a graph, you can customize the graph by using Microsoft Graph.

✦ To customize a graph, double-click on it; then you can change the graph type, text, axis labels, legend, gridlines, colors, patterns, and view of the graph.

✦ You can embed a graph in a form and link it to the data in the form by using the Chart button in the Toolbox of the Form or Report Design window; then you follow the steps in the Wizard.

✦ You can use various Office 2000 features, including spell-checking and AutoCorrect when you're working with Access data.

✦ You can create an Excel PivotTable to analyze your data by using the PivotTable Wizard.

✦ ActiveX controls extend the functionality of Access forms and reports. The Calendar control that comes with Access lets you add calendar functions to Access.

In the next chapter, you learn how to create reports.

✦   ✦   ✦

Creating and Customizing Reports

I n previous chapters, you learned to create a report from a single table by using a Wizard. You also learned to create multiple-table queries and work with controls. In this chapter, you combine and build on these concepts. While the wizards give you a good start, it is sometimes better to start with a blank report. This chapter teaches you to create — from scratch — a report that lets you view data from multiple tables, group the data, and sort it in meaningful ways. In subsequent chapters, you learn to create more powerful reports and different types of reports including reports that summarize and help analyze data, presentation reports with fancy formatting and graphics, and mail merge and labels created with reports.

Cross-Reference

In Chapter 10, you learned to create a report using an Access Report Wizard with a single table as the data source. Wizards are great for creating quick and simple reports, but they are fairly limited and give you little control over field type or placement. Although there are advantages to creating a report with a Wizard and then modifying the report, this chapter focuses on creating a report from a blank form without the help of the Wizards. If you haven't read Chapter 10, now is a good time to read or review it because the basic report concepts presented there are necessary to understand this chapter. You also need to be familiar with the basic controls and properties used in forms and reports presented in Chapter 15.

In This Chapter

Understanding the 11 tasks necessary to create a great report

Creating a report from a blank form

Sorting and grouping data

Adding label and text controls to your report

Modifying the appearance of text and label controls

Adding page breaks

Copying an existing report

Starting with a Blank Form

Previous chapters about forms introduced you to all the tools available in the Report Design window. When you create reports, you use some of these tools in a slightly different manner from the way they are used to create forms. Therefore, it is important to review some of the unique report menus and toolbar buttons.

Note   Because the Report Design window is set to a width of eight inches, most of the screen printouts in this chapter were taken with a Super VGA Windows screen driver (800 x 600 resolution) rather than with the standard VGA Windows driver (640 x 480). This higher resolution lets you see almost the entire screen in the screen figures.

You can view a report in three different views: Design, Layout Preview, and Print Preview. You can also print a report to the hard-copy device defined for Microsoft Windows. You have already seen the preview windows in previous chapters. This chapter focuses on the Report Design window.

The Report Design window is where you create and modify reports. The empty Report Design window, shown in Figure 20-1, contains various tools, including the Toolbox.

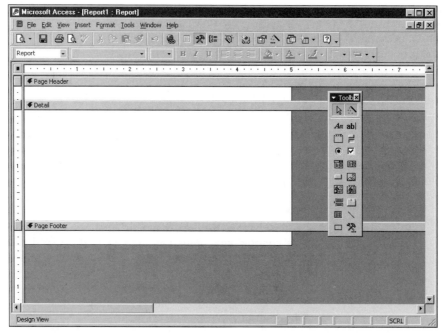

Figure 20-1: The Report Design window showing the Toolbox.

The Design Window Toolbar

The Report Design View toolbar is shown in Figure 20-2. You click the button you want for quick access to such design tasks as displaying different windows and activating Wizards and utilities. Table 20-1 summarizes what each item on the toolbar does. (The table defines each tool from left to right on the toolbar.)

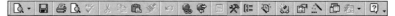

Figure 20-2: The Report Design toolbar.

The Report Design toolbar is distinct from the Format toolbar. To make such changes as font selection and justification, you must first make sure that the Format Form/Report Design toolbar is displayed.

Table 20-1 The Design View Toolbar	
Toolbar Item	**Description**
Report View button	Drop-down box displays the three types of previews available
Save button	Saves the current report design
Print button	Prints a form, table, query, or report
Print Preview button	Toggles to print preview mode
Spelling button	Spell-checks current selection or document
Cut button	Removes selection from the document and adds it to the Clipboard
Copy button	Copies the selection to the Clipboard
Paste button	Copies the Clipboard contents to the document
Format Painter button	Copies the style of one control to another
Undo button	Undoes the previous command
Insert Hyperlink button	Inserts hyperlink
Web Toolbar	Displays or hides Web toolbar
Field List button	Displays or hides the Field List window
Toolbox button	Displays or hides the Toolbox

Continued

Table 20-1 (continued)	
Toolbar Item	*Description*
Sorting and Grouping button	Displays or hides the Sorting and Grouping box
AutoFormat button	Applies a predefined format to a form or report
Code button	Displays or hides the module window
Properties button	Displays the properties sheet for the selected item
Build button	Displays the Builder or Wizard for selected control or item
Database window	Displays the Database window
New Object button	Creates a new object
Help button	Displays Access Help

Note   The tools on the Report Design screen are virtually identical to the Form Design tools.

Banded Report Writer Concepts

In a report, your data is processed one record at a time. Depending on how you create your report design, each data item is processed differently. Reports are divided into sections, known as *bands* in most report-writing software packages. (In Access, these are simply called *sections*.) Access processes each data record from a table or dynaset, processing each section in order and deciding (for each record) whether to process fields or text in each section. For example, the report footer section is processed only after the last record is processed in the dynaset.

A report is made up of groups of *details* — for example, all animals Johnathan Adams brought in on a certain day and how much he paid. Each group must have an identifying *group header*, which in this case is customer `Johnathan Adams`. Each group has a footer that calculates the total amount for each customer. For Johnathan Adams, this amount is `$375`. The *page header* contains column descriptions; the *report header* contains the report title. Finally, the *report footer* contains grand totals for the report, and the *page footer* prints the page number.

The Access sections are:

Report header   Prints only at the beginning of the report; used for title page

Page header   Prints at the top of each page

Group header	Prints before the first record of a group is processed
Detail	Prints each record in the table or dynaset
Group footer	Prints after the last record of a group is processed
Page footer	Prints at the bottom of each page
Report footer	Prints only at the end of a report after all records are processed

Figure 20-3 shows these sections superimposed on a report.

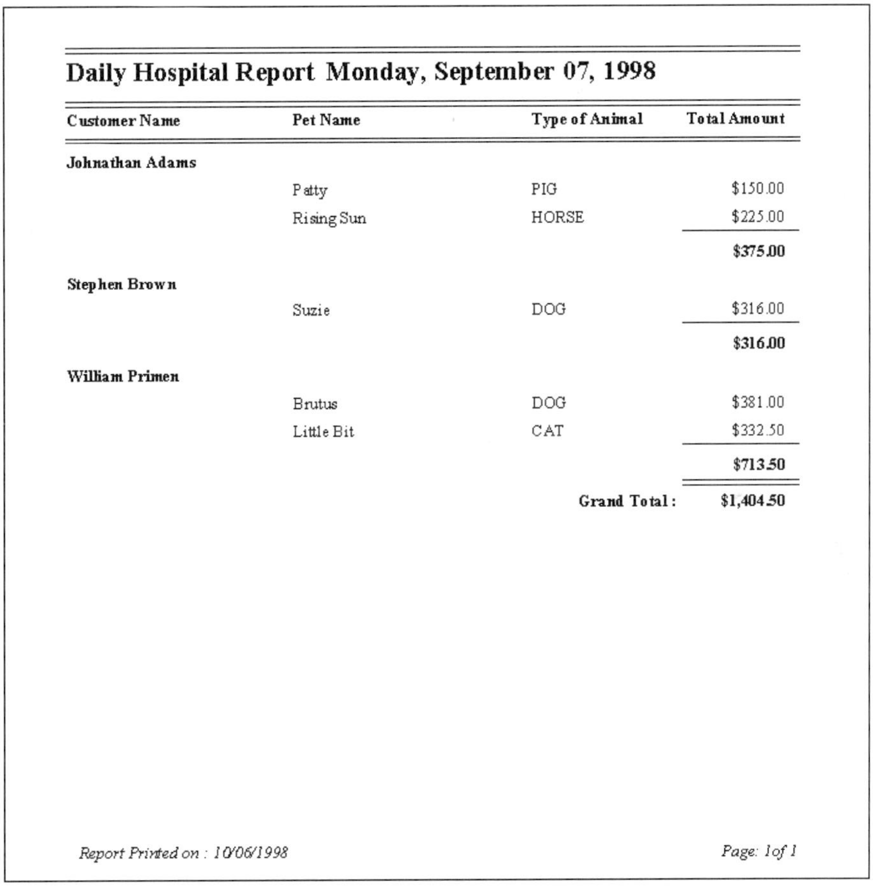

Daily Hospital Report Monday, September 07, 1998

Customer Name	Pet Name	Type of Animal	Total Amount
Johnathan Adams			
	Patty	PIG	$150.00
	Rising Sun	HORSE	$225.00
			$375.00
Stephen Brown			
	Suzie	DOG	$316.00
			$316.00
William Primen			
	Brutus	DOG	$381.00
	Little Bit	CAT	$332.50
			$713.50
		Grand Total :	$1,404.50

Report Printed on : 10/06/1998 *Page: 1of 1*

Figure 20-3: Typical Report Writer sections.

How sections process data

Most sections are triggered by the values of the data. Table 20-2 shows the five records that make up the dynaset for the Daily Hospital Report (*Yes* indicates that a section is triggered by the data).

Table 20-2							
Processing Report Sections							
Customer Name	**Pet Header**	**Report Header**	**Page Header**	**Group Detail**	**Group Footer**	**Page Footer**	**Report Footer**
Johnathan Adams	Patty	Yes	Yes	Yes	Yes	No	No
Johnathan Adams	Rising Sun	No	No	No	Yes	Yes	No
Stephen Brown	Suzie	No	No	Yes	Yes	Yes	No
William Primen	Brutus	No	No	Yes	Yes	No	No
William Primen	Little Bit	No	No	No	Yes	Yes	Yes

As you can see, Table 20-2 contains five records. Three groups of records are grouped by the customer name. Johnathan Adams has two records, Stephen Brown has one, and William Primen has two records. Each record in the table has corresponding columns for each section in the report. Yes means that the record triggers processing in that section; No means that the section is not processed for that record. This report has only one page, so it is very simple.

The report header section is triggered by only the first record in the dynaset. This section is always processed first, regardless of the data. The report footer section is triggered only after the last record is processed, regardless of the data.

For the first record only, Access processes the page header section after the report header section and then every time a new page of information is started. The page footer section is processed at the bottom of each page and after the report footer section.

Group headers are triggered only by the first record in a group. Group footers are triggered only by the last record in a group. Notice that the Stephen Brown record triggers both a group header and a group footer because it is the only record in a group. If three or more records are in a group, only the first or the last record can trigger a group header or footer; the middle records trigger only the detail section.

Access always processes each record in the detail section (which is always triggered, regardless of the value of the data). Most reports with a large amount of data have many detail records and significantly fewer group header or footer records. This small report has as many group header and footer records as it has detail records.

The Report Writer sections

Figure 20-4 shows what a report design looks like in Access. It is the Report Design window that produced the Daily Hospital Report. As you can see, the report is divided into sections. One group section displays data grouped by Customer Name, so that you see the sections Customer Name Header and Customer Name Footer. Each of the other sections is also named for the type of processing it performs.

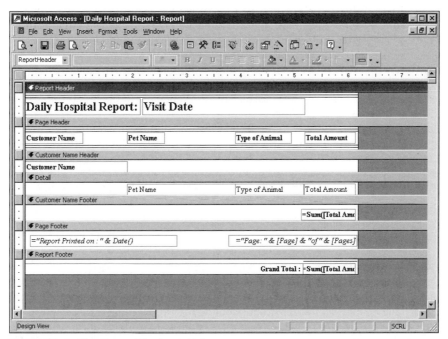

Figure 20-4: The Report Design window.

You can place any type of text or field controls in any section, but Access processes the data one record at a time. It also takes certain actions (based on the values of the group fields, the location of the page, or placement in the report) to make the bands or sections active. The example in Figure 20-4 is typical of a report with multiple sections. As you learned, each section in the report has a different purpose and different triggers.

Note   Page and report headers and footers must be added as pairs. To establish one without the other, simply resize the section you don't want to a height of zero; then set its Visible property to No.

Caution   If you remove a header or footer section, you also lose the controls in those sections.

Report header section

Anything in the *report header* is printed only once at the beginning of the report. In the report header section is a text control that places the words *Daily Hospital Report* in a large font size at the top of the report. Only the first page of the report has this text. You can also see the field control *Visit Date*; it places the value of the visit date from the first record in the report header. Figure 20-3 shows that this date is *Tuesday, September 8, 1998*. This was the value of the Visit Date field for the first record in the dynaset. It has been formatted using the long date format.

The report header section also has a double line placed before the text and field controls. You can place lines, boxes, shading, color, and special effects in any section. (You learn more about formatting and special effects in later chapters.)

You can also have anything in the report header section on a separate page, which allows you to create an entire page and include a graphic or picture in the section. A common use of a report header section is as a cover page or a cover letter. Because the header appears only once and doesn't have to contain any data, a separate page with the report header is a perfect place for a cover page or letter.

Note   Only data from the first record can be placed in a report header.

Page header section

Text or field controls in the *page header section* normally print at the top of every page. If a report header on the first page is not on a page of its own, the information in the page header section prints just below the report header information. Typically, page headers serve as column headers in group/total reports; they can also contain a title for the report. In this example, placing the Daily Hospital Report title in the report header section means that the title appears on only the first page; move it into the page header section if you want it to appear on every page.

The page header section seen in Figure 20-4 also has double lines above and below the text controls. Each of the text controls is separate; each can be moved or sized individually. You can also control special effects (such as color, shading, borders, line thickness, font type, and font size) for each text control.

Both the page header and page footer can be set for one of four settings (this setting can be found in the report's properties):

All Pages	Both the page header and page footer print on every page.
Not with Report Header	Neither the page header nor footer prints on a page with the report header.
Not with Report Footer	The page header does not print with the report footer. The report footer prints on a new page.
Not with Report Header/Footer	Neither the page header nor the footer prints on a page with the report header or footer.

Group header

Because *group headers* normally identify a specific value, you know that all the records displayed in a detail section belong to that group. In this example, the detail records are about animals and the cost of their treatments. The group header field control Customer Name tells you that these animals are owned by the customer who appears in the group header section. Group header sections immediately precede detail sections.

You may have multiple levels of group headers and footers. In this report, for example, the data is only for September 8, 1998. The detail data is grouped by the field Customer Name. If you want to see one report for the entire month of September 1998, you can change the query and add a second group section. In this second group section, you can group the data by date — and then, within each date, by customer. You can have many levels of groupings, but you should limit the number to between three and six; reports with too many levels become impossible to read. You don't want to defeat the purpose of the report, which is to show information clearly in a summarized format.

Note   To set group-level properties such as Group On, Group Interval, Keep Together, or something other than the default, you must first set the Group Header and Group Footer property (or both) to Yes for the selected field or expression.

Detail section

The *detail section* processes *every* record; this section is where each value is printed. The detail section frequently contains a calculated field such as a price extension that multiplies a quantity times a price. In this example, the detail section simply displays the Pet Name, Type of Animal, and Total Amount (which is the cost of the treatments). Each record in the detail section *belongs* to the value in the group header Customer Name.

> **Tip**   You can tell Access whether you want to display a section in the report by changing the section's Visible property in the Report Design window. Turning off the display of the detail section (or by excluding selected group sections) displays a summary report with no detail or with only certain groups displayed.

Group footer

Use the *group footer* to summarize the detail records for that group. In the Daily Hospital Report, the expression `=Sum([Total Amount])` adds the Total Amount fields for a specific customer. In the group for customer Johnathan Adams, this value sums the two Total Amount records ($225.00 and $150.00) and produces the value `$375.00`. This type of field is automatically reset to 0 every time the group changes. (You learn more about expressions and summary fields in later chapters.)

> **Tip**   You can change the way summaries are calculated by changing the Running Sum property of the field box in the Report Design window.

Page footer

The *page footer section* usually contains page numbers or control totals. In very large reports, you may want page totals as well as group totals (such as when you have multiple pages of detail records with no summaries). For the Daily Hospital Report, the page number is printed by combining the text and page number controls to show Page *x* of *y* where *x* is the current page number and *y* is the total number of pages in the report:

`="Page: " & [Page] & "of " & [Pages]`

(which keeps track of the page number in the report).

You can also print the date and the time printed. Figures 20-3 and 20-4 show the date printed in the Page Footer section as well as the page numbers.

Report footer

The *report footer section* is printed once at the end of the report after all the detail records and group footer sections are printed. Report footers typically display grand totals or other statistics (such as averages or percentages) for the entire report. The report footer for the Daily Hospital Report uses the expression =Sum([Total Amount]) to add the Total Amount fields for all treatments. This expression, when used in the report footer, is not reset to 0, as it is in the group footer. The expression is used only for a grand total.

When there is a report footer, the page footer section is printed after the report footer.

The Report Writer in Access is a *two-pass report writer*, capable of preprocessing all records to calculate the totals (such as percentages) needed for statistical reporting. This capability lets you create expressions that calculate percentages as Access processes those records that require foreknowledge of the grand total.

Cross-Reference   Chapter 22 covers calculating percentages.

Creating a New Report

Fundamental to all reports is the concept that a report is another way to view the records in one or more tables. It is important to understand that a report is bound to either a single table or a query that accesses one or more tables. When you create a report, you must select which fields from a query or table to place in your report. Unless you want to view all the records from a single table in it, bind your report to a query. If you are accessing data from a single table, using a query lets you create your report on the basis of a particular search criterion and sorting order. If you want to access data from multiple tables, you have almost no choice but to bind your report to a query. In the examples in this chapter, all the reports are bound to a query (even though it is possible to bind a report to a table).

Note   Access lets you create a report without first binding it to a table or object, but you will have no fields on the report. This capability can be used to work out *page templates*, which can serve as models for other reports. You can add fields later by changing the underlying control source of the report.

Throughout this chapter and the next chapter, you learn the tasks necessary to create the Mountain Animal Hospital Pets and Owners Directory (the first hard-copy page is shown in Figure 20-5). In this chapter, you design the basic report, assemble the data, and place the data in the proper positions. In Chapter 21, you enhance the report by adding lines, boxes, and shading so that certain areas stand out. You will also add enhanced controls (such as option buttons and checkboxes) to make the data more readable.

As with almost every task in Access, there are many ways to create a report without Wizards. It is important, however, to follow some type of methodology; creating a good report involves a fairly scientific approach. You can follow a set of tasks that will result in a good report every time and then arrange these tasks to create a checklist. As you complete each of task, check it off your list. When you are done, you will have a great-looking report. The following section outlines this approach.

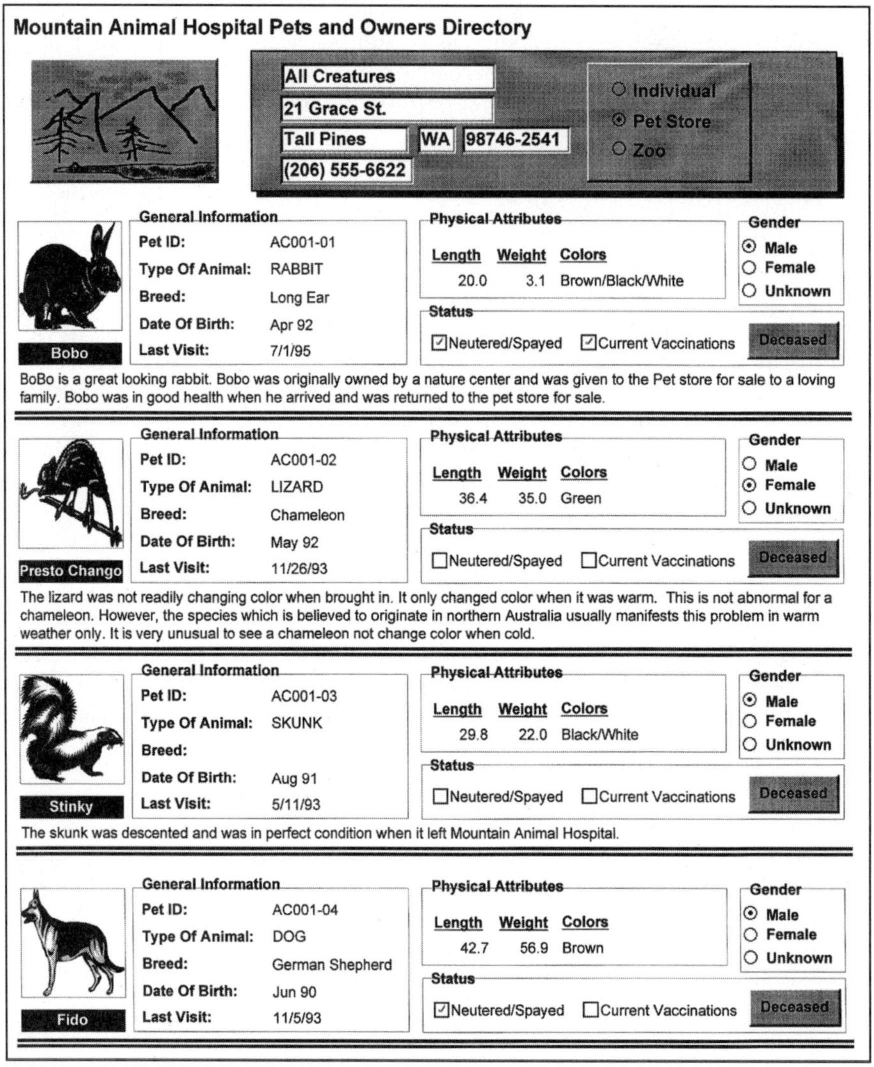

Mountain Animal Hospital Pets and Owners Directory

All Creatures
21 Grace St.
Tall Pines   WA   98746-2541
(206) 555-6622

○ Individual
◉ Pet Store
○ Zoo

General Information

Pet ID:	AC001-01
Type Of Animal:	RABBIT
Breed:	Long Ear
Date Of Birth:	Apr 92
Last Visit:	7/1/95

Bobo

Physical Attributes

Length Weight Colors
20.0   3.1   Brown/Black/White

Status
☑ Neutered/Spayed   ☑ Current Vaccinations   Deceased

Gender
◉ Male
○ Female
○ Unknown

BoBo is a great looking rabbit. Bobo was originally owned by a nature center and was given to the Pet store for sale to a loving family. Bobo was in good health when he arrived and was returned to the pet store for sale.

General Information

Pet ID:	AC001-02
Type Of Animal:	LIZARD
Breed:	Chameleon
Date Of Birth:	May 92
Last Visit:	11/26/93

Presto Chango

Physical Attributes

Length Weight Colors
36.4   35.0   Green

Status
☐ Neutered/Spayed   ☐ Current Vaccinations   Deceased

Gender
○ Male
◉ Female
○ Unknown

The lizard was not readily changing color when brought in. It only changed color when it was warm. This is not abnormal for a chameleon. However, the species which is believed to originate in northern Australia usually manifests this problem in warm weather only. It is very unusual to see a chameleon not change color when cold.

General Information

Pet ID:	AC001-03
Type Of Animal:	SKUNK
Breed:	
Date Of Birth:	Aug 91
Last Visit:	5/11/93

Stinky

Physical Attributes

Length Weight Colors
29.8   22.0   Black/White

Status
☐ Neutered/Spayed   ☐ Current Vaccinations   Deceased

Gender
◉ Male
○ Female
○ Unknown

The skunk was descented and was in perfect condition when it left Mountain Animal Hospital.

General Information

Pet ID:	AC001-04
Type Of Animal:	DOG
Breed:	German Shepherd
Date Of Birth:	Jun 90
Last Visit:	11/5/93

Fido

Physical Attributes

Length Weight Colors
42.7   56.9   Brown

Status
☑ Neutered/Spayed   ☐ Current Vaccinations   Deceased

Gender
◉ Male
○ Female
○ Unknown

Figure 20-5: The Mountain Animal Hospital Pets and Owners Directory — first page.

Eleven tasks to creating a great report

To create a good report, perform these 11 steps:

1. Design your report.

2. Assemble the data.

3. Create a new report and bind it to a query.

4. Define your page layout properties.

5. Place the fields on the report using text controls.

6. Add other label and text controls as necessary.

7. Modify the appearance, size, and location of text, text controls, and label controls.

8. Define your sorting and grouping options.

9. Save your report.

10. Enhance your report by using graphics and other control types.

11. Print your report.

Cross-Reference

This chapter covers tasks 1 through 9. Chapter 21 discusses task 10 and 11 — using other controls, such as group boxes, option buttons, and memo fields, as well as methods to enhance your report visually. It also covers printing and the use of images and graphical elements in your reports to give them a professional quality.

Designing the report

The first step in this process is to design the report. By the nature of the report name, Mountain Animal Hospital Pets and Owners Directory, you know that you want to create a report that contains detailed information about both the customer and the customer's pets. You want to create a report that lists important customer information at the top of a page followed by detailed information about each pet a customer owns, including a picture. You want no more than one customer on a page. If a customer has more than one pet, you want to see as many as possible on the same page. If a customer has more pets than will fit on one page, you want to duplicate the customer details at the top of each page. (The grouping section of this chapter discusses this task.)

Figure 20-6 is a design of this data. This is not the complete design for the report shown in Figure 20-5; rather, it is a plan for only the major data items, placed roughly where they will appear in this report. You can sketch this design by hand on a piece of paper or use any good word processor or drawing tool (such as Micrografx Draw or Word for Windows Draw) to lay out the basic design. Because Access has a WYSIWYG (What You See Is What You Get) report writer, you can also use that to lay out your report. (Personally, I like the pencil-and-paper approach to good design.)

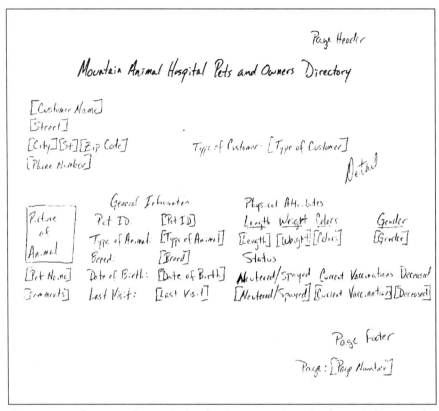

Figure 20-6: The report layout design for the Mountain Animal Hospital Pets and Owners Directory.

The report layout design is created only to lay out the basic data elements with no special formatting. Although this design may seem rudimentary, it is, nevertheless, a good starting point. This layout represents the report created in this chapter.

Assembling the data

With this design in mind, you now need to assemble the data. To create this report, you need fields from two tables: Customer and Pets. Table 20-3 lists the necessary fields and identifies the tables that contain them.

Table 20-3	
Tables and Fields Needed for the Pets and Owners Directory	
Fields from Pets Table	*Fields from Customer Table*
Pet ID	Customer Number
Picture	Customer Name
Pet Name	Type of Customer
Type of Animal	Street/Apt
Breed	City
Date of Birth	State
Last Visit Date	ZIP Code
Length	Phone Number
Weight	
Colors	
Gender	
Neutered/Spayed	
Current Vaccinations	
Deceased	
Comments	

To assemble this data, you need to create a query, which you can call Pets and Owners. This query includes *all* fields from both tables, but you won't use all of them. Some of the fields that don't appear on the report itself are used to derive other fields. Some fields are used merely to sort the data, although the fields themselves are not displayed on the report. In this example, you also create a sort by Pet ID. It is always a good idea to arrange your data in some known order. When reports are run, the data is used in its *physical* order unless you sort the data.

To create the Pets and Owners query, follow Figure 20-7.

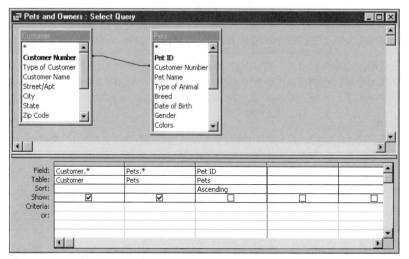

Figure 20-7: The Pets and Owners query.

Note   You use the asterisk (*) to select all fields from each table.

Creating a new report and binding it to a query

Now that you have created the Pets and Owners query, you need to create a new report and bind it to the query. Follow these steps to complete this process:

1. Press F11 to display the Database window if it is not already displayed.

2. Click the Reports object button.

3. Click the New toolbar button. The New Report dialog box appears.

4. Select Design View.

5. Click the combo box labeled Choose a table or query. A drop-down list of all tables and queries in the current database appears.

6. Select the Pets and Owners query.

7. Click OK.

8. Maximize the Report window.

A blank Report Design window appears (see Figure 20-8). Notice the three sections in the screen display: Page Header, Detail, and Page Footer. The report is bound to the query Pets and Owners. This means that the data from that query will be used when the report is viewed or printed. The fields from the query are available for use in the report design and appear in the Field List window.

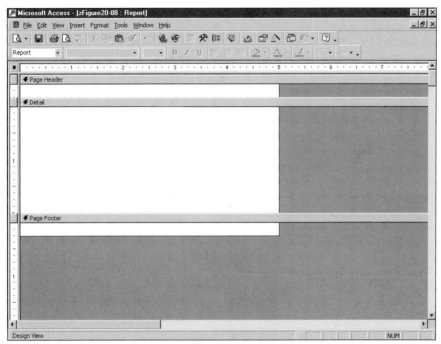

Figure 20-8: A blank Report Design window.

You can also create a new report by using any of these methods:

✦ Click the New Object toolbar button and then select New Report.

✦ Copy, paste, and rename an existing report.

✦ Start a New Report and then select one of the AutoReport options.

Note   There are two options for the AutoReport: Columnar and Tabular.

Defining the report page size and layout

As you plan your report, consider the page-layout characteristics as well as the kind of paper and printer you want to use for the output. If you use a dot-matrix printer with a wide-carriage feed, you design your report differently than for printing on a laser printer with $8\frac{1}{2}$ x 11-inch paper. After you make these decisions, you use several dialog boxes and properties to make adjustments; these items work together to create the desired output. You learn to use these tools in the next several chapters.

First, you need to select the correct printer and page-layout characteristics by selecting File ➪ Page Setup. The Page Setup dialog box, shown in Figure 20-9, lets you select your printer and set printer options.

Cross-Reference   Chapter 21 discusses Page Setup options in detail.

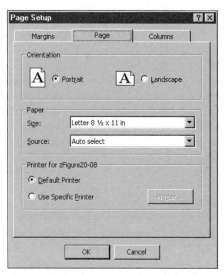

Figure 20-9: The Page Setup dialog box showing the Page tab.

This dialog box is a tab in the Page Setup dialog box. Layout tabs and page margins are also available under the Page Setup dialog box.

The Page dialog box is divided into three sections:

Orientation	Selects the page orientation you want
Paper	Selects the paper size and paper source you want
Printer	Selects the printer you want

Note   Select the Printer button; the Page Setup dialog box for the selected printer appears. Pressing Properties will then bring up a more extensive dialog box with all the applicable options.

For the Pets and Owners report, a *portrait* report, which is taller than it is wide. The paper is $8\frac{1}{2}$ x 11 inches; the left, right, top, and bottom margins are all set to 0.250.

Follow these steps to create the proper report setup for the Pets and Owners report:

1. Open the Page Setup dialog box and select the Page tab.

2. Click the Portrait option button.

   Next to the Orientation buttons are two sheet-of-paper icons with the letter A pictured on them. The picture of the sheet is an indication of its setting.

3. Click the Margins tab.

4. Click the Top margin setting and change the setting to 0.250.

5. Click the Bottom margin setting and change the setting to 0.250.

6. Click the Left margin setting and change the setting to 0.250.

7. Click the Right margin setting and change the setting to 0.250.

8. Click OK to close the Page Setup dialog box.

Tip　Access displays your reports in Print Preview view by using the driver of the active printer. If you don't have a good-quality laser available for printing, install the driver for a PostScript printer so that you can view any graphics that you create (and see the report in a high-resolution display). Later, you can print to your dot matrix or other available printer and get the actual hard copy in the best resolution your printer offers.

Caution　Figure 20-9 shows the option button (Printer…) in the bottom-right corner of the Page tab. If you are going to give your database or report to others, you should always select the first option, Default Printer. This way, if you have selected a printer the recipient doesn't have, the report will use their default printer. If you have selected the second option (Use Specific Printer), those who don't have that printer will get an error message and will not be able to use the report.

After you define your page layout in the Page Setup dialog box, you need to define the size of your report (which is not necessarily the same as the page definition).

To define the report size, place the mouse pointer on the rightmost edge of the report (where the white page meets the gray background). The pointer changes to a two-headed arrow. Drag the pointer to change the width of the report. As you drag the edge, a vertical line appears in the ruler to let you know the exact width if you release the mouse at that point. Be careful not to exceed the width of the page you defined in the Page Setup dialog box.

When you position the mouse pointer at the bottom of the report, it changes to a double-headed arrow similar to the one for changing width. This pointer determines the height not of the page length, but of the page footer section or other specified bottom section. (Predefining a page length directly in the report section doesn't really make sense because the detail section will vary in length, based on your groupings.) Remember that the Report Design view shows only a representation of the various report sections not the actual report.

To set the right border for the Pets and Owners report to 8 inches, follow these steps:

1. Click the rightmost edge of the report body (where the white page representation meets the gray background). The mouse pointer changes to a double-headed arrow.

2. Drag the edge to the 8-inch mark.

3. Release the mouse button.

Note   You can also select the Width property in the report's property sheet.

Because the Report Design screen is set to a width of 8 inches, most of the screen printouts in this chapter were taken with a Super VGA Windows screen driver (resolution: 800 × 600) rather than with the standard VGA Windows driver (640 × 480). This higher resolution lets you see almost the entire screen in the screen figures.

Placing fields on the report

Access takes full advantage of the Windows' drag-and-drop capabilities. The method for placing fields on a report is no exception. When you place a field on a report, it is no longer called a field; it is called a *control*. A control has a *control source* (a specific field) that it is bound to, so the terms *control* and *field* are used interchangeably in this chapter.

To place controls on your report:

✦ Display the Field List window by clicking the Field List toolbar button.

✦ Click the desired Toolbox control to determine the type of control that will be created.

✦ Select each of the fields that you want on your report and then drag them to the Report Design window.

Displaying the field list

To display the Field List window, click the Field List button on the toolbar. A small window with a list of all the fields from the underlying query appears. This window is called a *modeless* dialog box because it remains onscreen even while you continue with other work in Access. The Field List window can be resized and moved around the screen. This enlarged window is illustrated in Figure 20-10, showing all the fields in the Pets and Owners query dynaset.

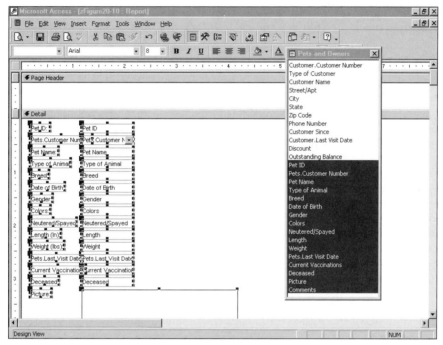

Figure 20-10: Dragging fields to the Design window.

Notice that in Figure 20-10 the fields `Customer.Customer Number` and `Pets.Customer Number` as well as `Customer.Last Visit Date` and `Pets.Last Visit Date` use the table name as a prefix. This nomenclature is necessary to distinguish fields of the same name that come from different tables used in the query.

Tip   You can move the Field List window by simply clicking on the title bar and dragging it to a new location.

Selecting the fields for your report

Selecting a field in the Report field list is the same as selecting a field in the Query field list. The easiest way to select a field is simply to click it. When you click a field, it becomes highlighted. After a field is highlighted, you can drag it to the Report window.

You can highlight *contiguous* (adjacent) fields in the list by following these steps:

1. Click the first field you want in the field list.
2. Move the mouse pointer to the last field you want from the list.
3. Hold down the Shift key and click the last field you want.

The block of fields between the first and last field you selected is displayed in reverse video indicating it is selected. You can then drag the block of fields to the Report window.

You can highlight noncontiguous fields in the list by clicking each field while holding down the Ctrl key. Each selected field will be displayed in reverse video; then you can drag the fields as a group to the Report Design window.

> **Note**   Unlike the Query field list, you *cannot* also double-click a field to add it to the Report window.

You can begin by selecting the Pets table fields for the detail section. To select the fields needed for the detail section of the Pets and Owners report, follow these steps:

1. Click the Pet ID field.
2. Scroll down the field list until the Comments field is visible.
3. Hold down the Shift key and click the Comments field.

The block of fields from Pet ID to Comments should be highlighted in the Field List window, as shown in Figure 20-10.

Dragging fields onto your report

After you select the proper fields from the Pets table, all you need to do is drag them to the detail section of your report. Depending on whether you choose one or several fields, the mouse pointer changes shape to represent your selection. If you select one field, you see a Field icon, which shows a single box with some unreadable text inside. If you select multiple fields, you see a set of three boxes. These are the same icons you saw when you were using the Query Design screens.

To drag the selected Pet table fields into the detail section of the Report Design window, follow these steps:

1. Click within the highlighted block of fields in the Field List window. You may need to move the horizontal scroll bar back to the left before starting this process.

2. Without releasing the mouse button, drag the mouse pointer into the detail section; place the icon under the $1\frac{1}{2}$-inch mark on the horizontal ruler at the top of the screen and next to the 0-inch mark of the vertical ruler along the left edge of the screen.

3. Release the mouse button.

The fields appear in the detail section of the report, as shown in Figure 20-10. Notice that for each field you dragged onto the report there are two controls. When you use the drag-and-drop method for placing fields, Access automatically creates a label control with the field name attached to the text control the field is bound to.

Note   Notice the OLE (Object Linking and Embedding) control for the field named `Picture`. Access always creates an OLE control for a picture or an OLE-type object. Also notice that the detail section automatically resizes itself to fit all the controls. Below the OLE control is the control for the memo field Comments.

You also need to place the desired field controls on the report for the customer information you need in the page header section. Before you do this, however, you need to resize the page header frame to leave room for a title you will add later.

Resizing a section

To make room on the report for both the title and the Customer table fields in the page header, you must resize it. You can resize a section by placing the mouse pointer at the bottom of the section you want to resize. The pointer turns into a vertical double-headed arrow; drag the section border up or down to make the section smaller or larger.

Resize the page header section to make it larger by following these steps:

1. Move the mouse pointer between the bottom of the page header section and the top of the detail section.

2. When the pointer is displayed as a double-sided arrow, hold down the left mouse button.

3. Drag the page header section border down until it intersects the detail section's ruler at the $1\frac{1}{2}$-inch mark.

4. Release the button to enlarge the page header section.

Now place the Customer table fields in the page header section by following these steps:

1. Click the `Customer.Customer Number` field.

2. Scroll down the field list until the Phone Number field is visible.

3. Hold down the Shift key and click on the Phone Number field.

4. Click within the highlighted block of fields in the Field List window.

5. Without releasing the mouse button, drag the pointer into the page header section; place the icon under the $1\frac{1}{2}$-inch mark on the horizontal ruler at the top of the screen and next to the $\frac{5}{8}$-inch mark of the vertical ruler along the left edge of the screen.

6. Release the mouse button; the fields now appear in the page header section of the report, as shown in Figure 20-11.

7. Close the Field List window by clicking the Field List toolbar button.

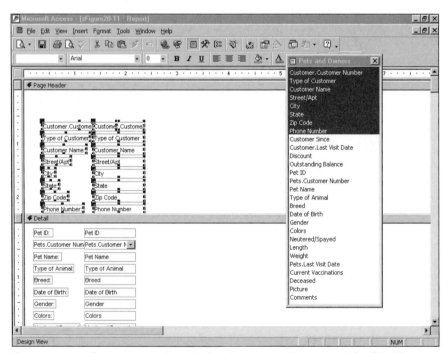

Figure 20-11: The Report Design window for Pets and Owners with all fields shown.

The page header section expanded to fit the fields that were dragged into the section. At this point, your report should look like Figure 20-11. All the fields needed for the Pets and Owners report are now placed.

Working with unattached label controls and text

When you drag a field from the Field List window to a report while the Text Box button is selected in the Toolbox, Access creates not only a text box control but also a label control that is attached to the text box control. At times, you will want to add text label controls by themselves to create headings or titles for the report.

Creating unattached labels

To create a new, unattached label control, you must use the Toolbox (unless you copy an existing label). The next task in the current example is to add the text header *Mountain Animal Hospital Pets and Owners Directory* to your report. This task is done in steps that demonstrate adding and editing text.

To begin creating an unattached label control, follow these steps:

1. Display the Toolbox.

2. Click the Label tool in the Toolbox.

3. Click near the top left edge of the page header at about the 1-inch mark on the ruler; then drag the mouse pointer downward and to the right to make a small rectangle about $2\frac{1}{2}$-inches wide and $\frac{1}{2}$-inch high.

4. Type **Mountain Animal Hospital Pets and Owners Directory**.

5. Press Enter.

Tip   To create a multiple-line label entry, press Ctrl+Enter to force a line break where you want it in the control.

Tip   If you want to edit or enter a caption that is longer than the space in the property sheet, the contents will scroll as you type. Otherwise, open a Zoom box that gives you more space to type by pressing Shift+F2.

Modifying the appearance of text in a control

To modify the appearance of the text in a control, select the control by clicking its border (not in the control itself). You can then select a formatting style to apply to the label by clicking the appropriate button on the Formatting toolbar.

To make the title stand out, follow these steps to modify the appearance of label text:

1. Click the newly created report heading label.

2. Click the Bold button on the Formatting toolbar.

3. Click the arrow beside the Font-Size drop-down box.

4. Select 18 from the Font-Size drop-down list box.

The label control appears. To display all the text, you need to resize it (which you do later in this chapter).

Working with text boxes and their attached label controls

So far you have added text box controls bound to fields in the tables and unbound label controls used to display titles in your report. There is another type of text box control that is typically added to a report: unbound text boxes that are used to hold expressions such as page numbers, dates, or a calculation.

After entering label controls to display text on the report, you want to place text box controls (fields) on the report. These text boxes can be bound to fields in tables, or they can be unbound, holding expressions such as the page number, date, or some calculation.

Creating and using text box controls

In reports, text box controls serve two purposes. First, they let you display stored data from a particular field in a query or table. Second, they display the result of an expression. Expressions can be calculations that use other controls as their operands, calculations that use Access functions (either built-in or user-defined), or a combination of the two. You have learned how to use a text box control to display data from a field and how to create that control. Next, you learn how to create new text box controls that use expressions.

Entering an expression in a text control

Cross-Reference

Expressions let you create a value that is not already in a table or query. They can range from simple functions (such as a page number) to complex mathematical computations. Chapters 12 and 22 cover expressions in greater detail; for the example in this chapter, you use an expression that is necessary for the report.

A *function* is a small program that when run returns a single value; it can be one of many built-in Access functions or it can be user-defined. For example, to facilitate page numbering in reports, Access has a function called Page that returns the value of the current report page. The following steps show you how to use an unbound text box to add a page number to your report:

1. Select the Text Box tool from the Toolbox.

2. Scroll down to the page footer section by using the vertical scroll bar.

3. Click in the middle of the page footer section, and then create a text box about three-quarters of the height of the section and about $\frac{1}{2}$-inch wide by resizing the default text box control.

4. Click the label control to select it. (It should say something similar to Text42.)

5. Click the beginning of the label control text, drag over the default text in the label control, and type **Page:** or double-click the text to highlight it and then replace it.

6. Click twice on the text box control (it says "unbound"); type **=Page** and press Enter. (Notice that the Control Source property changes on the data sheet of the Property window to =Page, as shown in Figure 20-12. If the Property window is not open, you may want to open it to see the change.)

7. Click the Page label control's Move handle (upper-left corner); move the label closer to the =Page text box control until the right edge of the label control touches the left edge of the text box control. (Later, you will move the entire control to the right side of the page.)

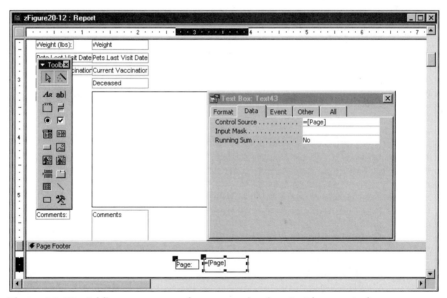

Figure 20-12: Adding a page-number expression in a text box control.

Tip   You can always check your result by clicking the Print Preview button on the tool-bar. Zoom in on the page footer section to check the page number.

Sizing a text box control or label control

You can select a control by simply clicking it. Depending on the size of the control, from three to seven sizing handles will appear — one on each corner except the upper-left corner and one on each side. When you move the mouse pointer over one of the sizing handles, the pointer changes into a double-headed arrow. When the pointer changes, click the control and drag it to the size you want. Notice that, as you drag, an outline appears; it indicates the new size the label control will be when you release the mouse button.

If you double-click any of the sizing handles, Access resizes a control to the best fit for the text in the control. This feature is especially handy if you increase the font size and then notice that the text is cut off, either on the bottom or to the right. Note that for label controls, this *best-fit sizing* resizes both vertically and horizontally, though text controls can resize only vertically. The reason for this difference is that in the report design mode, Access doesn't know how much of a field you want to display; the field name and field contents might be radically different. Sometimes label controls are not resized correctly, however, and have to be adjusted manually.

Changing the size of a label control

Earlier in this chapter (in the steps that modified the appearance of label text), you changed the characteristics of the Pets and Owners label; the text changed, but the label itself did not adjust. The text no longer fits within the label control. You can resize the label control, however, to fit the enhanced font size by following these steps:

1. Click the Mountain Animal Hospital Pets and Owners Directory label control.

2. Move your mouse pointer over the control. Notice how the pointer changes shape over the sizing handles.

3. To size the control automatically, double-click one of the sizing handles. The label control size may still need to be readjusted.

4. Place the pointer in the bottom-right corner of the label control so that the diagonal double-arrow appears.

5. Hold down the left mouse button and drag the handle to resize the label control's box until it correctly displays all of the text (if it doesn't already).

Tip   You can also select Format ⇨ Size ⇨ To Fit to change the size of the label control text automatically.

Before continuing, you should see how the report is progressing; do this frequently as you design a report. You can send a single page to the printer or view the report in a print preview. Figure 20-13 is a zoomed print preview of how the report currently looks. The customer information is at the top of the page; the pet information is below that and offset to the left. Notice the title at the top of the page. You can see the page number at the bottom if you click the magnifying-glass button to zoom out and see the entire page. Only one record per page appears on the report because of the vertical layout. In the next section, you move the fields around and create a more horizontal layout.

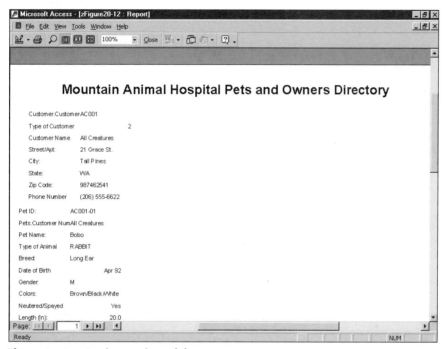

Figure 20-13: A print preview of the report.

Deleting attached label and text controls

As Figure 20-13 shows, the report begins with the Customer Number field. The original design in Figure 20-6 did not have the Customer Number field on the report. After talking to the report design's architect (who is usually yourself), you find that the Customer Number field is not wanted on the report, either in the page header section or the detail section. It's very easy to delete one or more attached controls in a report. Simply select the desired controls and press Delete. When deleting attached controls, there are two choices:

✦ Delete only the label control.

✦ Delete both the label control and the field control.

If you select the label control and press Delete, only the label control is deleted. If you select the field control and press Delete, both the label control and the field control are deleted. To delete an attached control (in this case, the Customer Number controls and their attached label), follow these steps:

1. Select the Close icon on the toolbar to exit print preview mode. Select the text box control `Customer.Customer (Customer Number)` in the page header.

2. Press Delete.

3. Select the text box control `Pets.Customer Num` in the detail section.

4. Press Delete.

If you accidentally selected the label control that precedes the text box control, the text box control is still visible. Simply click the control and press Delete.

Tip   If you want to delete only the field control and keep the attached label control, first select the label control and then select Edit ⇨ Copy. Next, to delete both the field control and the label control, select the field control and press Delete. Finally, select Edit ⇨ Paste to paste only the copied label control to the report.

Moving label and text controls

Before discussing how to move label and text controls, it is important to review a few differences between attached and unattached controls. When an attached label is created automatically with a text control, it is called a *compound control*. In a compound control, whenever one control in the set is moved, the other control moves as well. With a text control and a label control, whenever the text control is moved, the attached label is also moved. Likewise, whenever the label control is moved, the text control is also moved.

To move both controls in a compound control, select one of the pair by clicking the control. Move the mouse pointer over either of the objects. When the pointer turns into a hand, click the controls and drag them to their new location. As you drag an outline for the compound control moves with your pointer.

Cross-Reference   The concepts of moving controls are covered visually and in more detail in Chapter 15.

To move only one of the controls in a compound control, drag the desired control by its *Move handle* (the large square in the upper left corner of the control). When you click a compound control, it looks like both controls are selected, but if you look closely, you see that only one of the two controls is selected (as indicated by the presence of both moving and sizing handles). The deselected control displays only a moving handle. A pointing finger indicates that you have selected the Move handles and can now move only one control. To move either control individually, select the control's Move handle and drag it to its new location.

Cross-Reference

To move a label that is not attached, simply click any border (except where there is a handle) and drag it. You can also move groups of controls with the selection techniques you learned in Chapter 15.

To make a group selection, click with the mouse pointer anywhere outside a starting point and drag the pointer through (or around) the controls you want to select. A gray, outlined rectangle is displayed that shows the extent of the selection. When you release the mouse button, all the controls the rectangle surrounds are selected. You can then drag the group of controls to a new location.

Tip

The global option Tools ➪ Options – Form/Reports – Selection Behavior is a property that controls the enclosure of selections. You can enclose them fully (the rectangle must completely surround the selection) or partially (the rectangle must only touch the control), which is the default.

In the next steps, you begin to place the controls in their proper position to complete the report layout as designed (see Figure 20-5). You want this first pass at rearranging the controls to look like Figure 20-14. You will make a series of block moves by selecting several controls and then positioning them close to where you want them. Then, if needed, you fine-tune their position. This is the way most reports are done. Follow these steps to begin placing the controls where they should be.

To roughly position the page header controls:

1. Move the Type of Customer control to the right and down so that the top of the control intersects 1-inch on the vertical ruler and the left edge is under the *P* in *Pets* in the title.

2. Still in the page header, delete (only) the attached labels from all the text controls except Type of Customer.

3. Rearrange the controls in the page header to resemble a typical mailing-label address format; City, State, and ZIP Code should be on the same line.

4. Move the Phone Number text box control under the ZIP Code text box control.

5. Move the block of name, address, and phone number controls into position so that the top of the block intersects the $\frac{1}{2}$-inch mark on both the vertical and horizontal rulers.

6. Resize the page header section so that it intersects the $1\frac{1}{2}$-inch mark on the left vertical ruler.

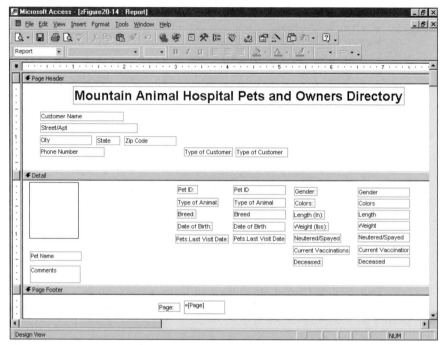

Figure 20-14: Rearranging the controls on the report.

Note   Some fields, such as Customer Name, Street/Apt, and Phone Number, may need to be adjusted. You can adjust them now or later.

To roughly position the detail controls:

1. Select the Pet ID, Type of Animal, Breed, Date of Birth, and Last Visit Date controls (and their attached labels) by clicking each text control while holding down the Shift key.

2. Drag the block of controls to the right so that the left edge intersects 3 inches on the top ruler.

3. Select (only) the Last Visit Date control and its attached label.

4. Drag the Last Visit Date control up so that it is just under the Date of Birth control.

5. Select the Gender control and its attached label.

6. Drag the control to the right so that the left edge intersects the 5"-inch mark on the top ruler and the "-inch mark on the left-side ruler.

7. Select the Colors, Length, and Weight controls and their attached labels by clicking on each text control while holding down the Shift key.

8. Drag the block of controls to the right so that the left edge intersects the 5"-inch mark on the top ruler and the "-inch mark on the left-side ruler.

9. Select the Neutered/Spayed, Current Vaccinations, and Deceased controls and their attached labels by clicking each text control while holding down the Shift key.

10. Drag the block of controls to the right so that they are just under the most recently moved block.

11. Select the Current Vaccinations and Deceased controls and their attached labels by clicking each text control while holding down the Shift key.

12. Drag the block of controls upward so that they are just under the Neutered/Spayed control.

13. Delete (only) the Pet Name label control.

14. Delete (only) the Picture label control.

15. Delete (only) the Comments label control.

16. Select the bottom-right handle to resize the Picture control to 1 inch × 1 inch.

17. Move the Picture control to $1/8$ inch × $1/8$ inch on the rulers (top-left corner) of the detail section.

18. Move the Pet Name text box control under the picture so that it intersects the left ruler at the 1"-inch mark.

19. Move the Comments text box control under the picture so that it intersects the left ruler at the 1"-inch mark.

20. Resize the detail section so that it intersects the 2"-inch mark on the left ruler.

At this point, you are about halfway done. The screen should look like Figure 20-14. (If it doesn't, adjust your controls until the screen matches the figure.) Remember that these screen pictures are taken with the Windows screen driver set at 800 × 600. If you are using normal VGA, you'll have to scroll the screen to see the entire report.

The next step is to refine the design to get as close as possible to the design created in Figure 20-6. The page header section is complete for now. Later in this chapter, you reformat the controls to change the font size and style. In the following steps, the detail section's layout is completed:

1. Group select all the fields starting with Pet ID through Last Visit date (in a column).

2. Select and drag that block to the right of the Picture OLE control, as shown in Figure 20-15.

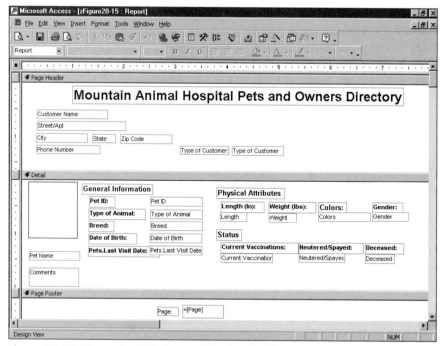

Figure 20-15: The resized label control in the detail section.

3. Drag the controls Neutered/Spayed, Current Vaccinations, and Deceased away from other controls to allow space to move the label controls above the text box controls, as shown in Figure 20-15.

4. Drag each of the label controls to locations above the text box controls by grabbing each Move handle individually and then moving the controls above the text box controls.

5. Select all three label controls and align them by selecting Format ⇨ Align ⇨ Bottom.

6. Repeat Steps 3 and 4 for the Length, Weight, Colors, and Gender controls, moving them into position as shown in Figure 20-15.

7. Move the Comments text box control so that it appears below all other controls.

Again, you may have to resize some of the controls to match the ones shown in Figure 20-15. There is still some text to add as label controls. If you compare the design shown in Figure 20-6 to your screen, you can see that you still need to add some label controls to define the groups. To add the label controls, follow these steps:

1. Double-click the Label Control button in the Toolbox so that you can add more than one label control.

2. Create a new label control above the Pet ID field and enter **General Information**. Make sure that you press Enter after entering the text of each label control so that the control is sized automatically to fit the text. You still may have to resize the label if it is bigger than the text.

3. Create a new label control above the Length field and enter **Physical Attributes**.

4. Create a new label control above the Neutered/Spayed field and enter **Status**.

5. Click the Pointer button in the Toolbox to unlock the Toolbox.

These steps complete the rough design for this report. There are still properties, fonts, and sizes to change. When you make these changes, you'll have to move fields around again. Use the design in Figure 20-6 only as a guideline. How it looks to *you*, as you refine the look of the report in the Report window, determines the real design.

Modifying the appearance of multiple controls

The next step is to change all the label controls in the detail section to bold and a 10-point font size. This will help to differentiate between label controls and text controls, which currently have the same text formatting. The following steps guide you through modifying the appearance of text in multiple label controls:

1. Select all label controls in the detail section by individually clicking them while holding down the Shift key. There are 15 label controls to select, as shown in Figure 20-15.

2. Click the Bold button on the toolbar.

3. Click the down-arrow in the Font Size drop-down box.

4. Select 10 from the Font Size drop-down list.

5. Select Format ⇨ Size ⇨ To Fit to resize all the labels.

Note

You cannot select all the label controls in the preceding steps by using the drag-and-surround method. This method would also select all the text boxes; you want only to bold and resize the labels.

You also need to make all the text box controls bold and increase their font size to 12 points in the page header section. To modify the appearance of text box controls, follow these steps:

1. Select all the controls except the title in the page header section by clicking the mouse pointer in the top-left corner of the section and then dragging the

pointer to surround all the controls. Include the Type of Customer label control.

2. Click the Bold button on the toolbar.

3. Click the Font Size box drop-down arrow.

4. Select 12 from the Font Size drop-down list.

5. Select Format ⇨ Size ⇨ To Fit to resize all the text box controls.

Notice that the text box controls do not display the entire field name. Remember that sizing to fit works only on the vertical height of a control. It is impossible to know how wide a field's value will be — you have to adjust these values manually. You can use the Print Preview window (shown in Figure 20-16) to check your progress.

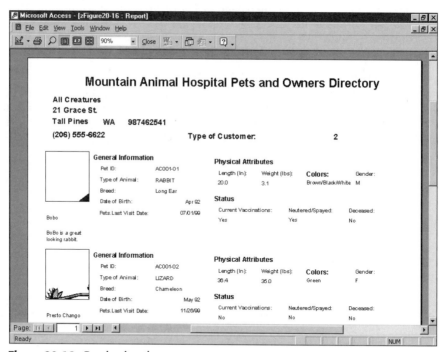

Figure 20-16: Previewing the report.

Looking at the print preview may show some minor problems. If you haven't already made any cosmetic changes, you should notice that these changes have to be made (some or all of these may need to be fixed on your form):

Page header section:

- ✦ The Customer Name text box is not wide enough.
- ✦ There is too much space after the State text box before the ZIP Code.
- ✦ The Phone Number text box is not wide enough.
- ✦ The Type of Customer label needs to be longer.
- ✦ The Type of Customer text box value needs to be left aligned.

Detail section:

- ✦ None of the text boxes in the detail section is 10-point; all are 8-point.
- ✦ The Pet Name needs to be bolded, centered, and moved closer to the picture.
- ✦ The data under General Information is not lined up properly.
- ✦ The Pets.Last Visit Date label needs to have the prefix Pets deleted.
- ✦ Pet ID, Type of Animal, and Breed are left aligned, whereas the other two values are right aligned.
- ✦ The Length and Weight values under Physical Attributes are right aligned and don't line up with the labels above them.
- ✦ The Gender control doesn't quite fit.
- ✦ The Picture OLE control is not correctly displayed.
- ✦ The Comments memo field displays only the first few words.

Page footer section:

- ✦ The Page Number control needs to be moved to the right edge of the page.
- ✦ The page number needs to be left aligned; both controls should be italicized.

Tip   Remember that you may have looked at the data for only one record. Make sure that you look at data for many records before completing the report design, and watch the maximum sizes of your data fields. Another suggestion is to create a dummy record to use only for testing; it should contain values that use each position of the field. For example, a great name to test a 24-character field is *Fred Rumpelstiltskin III*. (Of course, with proportional fonts, you really can't count characters because an *i* uses less space than an *m*.)

The problems just noted need to be fixed before this report is considered complete. You can fix many of them easily with the techniques you've already learned. Complete the changes as outlined in the list on the preceding pages. When you're through, your screen should look like Figure 20-17.

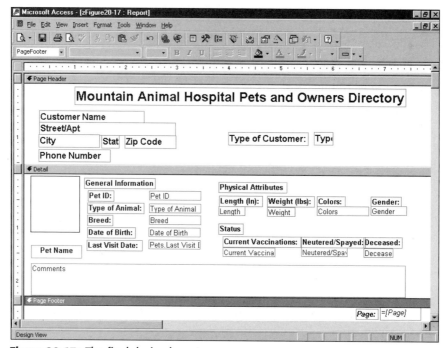

Figure 20-17: The final design layout.

After you make the final modifications, you are finished, except for fixing the picture. To do this, you need to change properties, which you do in the next section. This may seem to be an enormous number of steps because the procedures were designed to show you how laying out a report design can be a slow process. Remember, however, that when you click away with the mouse, you don't realize how many steps you are doing as you design the report layout visually. With a WYSIWYG layout like that of the Access report designer, you may need to perform many tasks, but it's still easier and faster than programming. Figure 20-17 shows the final version of the design layout as seen in this chapter. In the next chapter, you continue to improve this report layout.

Changing label and text box control properties

To change the properties of a text or label control, you need to display the control's property sheet. If it is not already displayed, perform one of these actions:

   ✦ Double-click the border of the control (anywhere except a sizing handle or Move handle).

✦ Click the Properties button on the toolbar.

✦ Select View ➪ Properties.

✦ Right-click the mouse and select Properties.

The *property sheet* lets you look at a control's property settings and provides an easy way to edit the settings. Using tools such as the formatting windows and text-formatting buttons on the Formatting toolbar changes the property settings of a control. Clicking the Bold button, for example, really sets the Font Weight property to Bold. It is usually much more intuitive to use the toolbar (or even the menus), but some properties are not accessible this way. Sometimes objects have more options available through the property sheet.

The Size Mode property of an OLE object (bound object frame), with its options of Clip, Stretch, and Zoom, is a good example of a property that is available only through the property sheet.

The Image control, which is a bound object frame, presently has its Size Mode property set to Clip, which is the default. With Clip, the picture is displayed in its original size. For this example, change the setting to Stretch so that the picture is sized automatically to fit the picture frame.

Cross-Reference   Chapter 19 covers the use of pictures, OLE objects, and graphs.

To change the property for the bound object frame control that contains the picture, follow these steps:

1. Click the frame control of the picture bound object.

2. Click the Size Mode property.

3. Click the arrow to display the drop-down list box.

4. Select Stretch.

These steps complete the changes so far to your report A print preview of a single record appears in Figure 20-18. Notice how the picture is now properly displayed; the Comments field now appears across the bottom of the detail section.

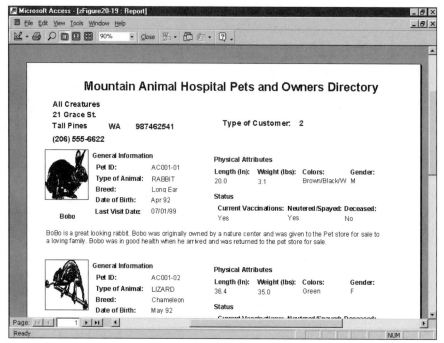

Figure 20-18: The final report print preview.

Formatting the display of text controls

Using the Formatting toolbar you can change the appearance of a control and its text. For example, you can make a control's value bold or change its font size. In addition, you can make changes by using the property sheet. Depending on the type of field a text box is bound to — or on whether it contains an expression — you can use various types of format masks. You can type the > character to capitalize all letters, or you can create an input mask to add parentheses and hyphens to a phone number. For numeric and date-formatting properties, you can select from a drop-down list box, which lets you add dollar signs to a number or format a date in a more readable way. If you want the data to always appear a certain way when used in all forms and reports, apply the format in the table design screen when you create the field.

New Feature

New to Access 2000 is the capability to add margins and line spacing to your text box and label controls in both forms and reports. This capability provides greater flexibility in how reports look. You can setup margins for these types of controls in the control's property sheet.

Growing and shrinking text box controls

When you print or print-preview fields that can have variable text lengths, Access provides options for enabling a control to grow or shrink vertically, depending on the exact contents of a record. The option Can Grow determines whether a text control adds lines to fit additional text if the record contains more lines of text than the control can display. The option Can Shrink determines whether a control deletes blank lines if the record's contents use fewer lines than the control can display. Although these properties are usable for any text field, they are especially helpful for memo field controls.

Table 20-4 explains the acceptable values for these two properties.

Table 20-4		
Text Control Values for Can Grow and Can Shrink		
Property	**Value**	**Description**
Can Grow	Yes	If the data in a record uses more lines than the control is defined to display, the control resizes to accommodate additional lines.
Can Grow	No	If the data in a record uses more lines than the control is defined to display, the control does not resize; it truncates the data display.
Can Shrink	Yes	If the data in a record uses fewer lines than the control is defined to display, the control resizes to eliminate blank lines.
Can Shrink	No	If the data in a record uses fewer lines than the control is defined to display, the control does not resize to eliminate blank lines.

To change the Can Grow settings for a text control, follow these steps:

1. Select the Comments text control.

2. Display the property sheet.

3. Click the Can Grow property, then click the arrow and select Yes.

Note   The Can Grow and Can Shrink properties are also available for report sections. Use a section's property sheet to modify these values.

As you near completion of testing your report design, you should also test the printing of your report. Figure 20-19 shows a hard-copy of the first page of the Customer and Pets report. You can see three pet records displayed for the Customer named All Creatures.

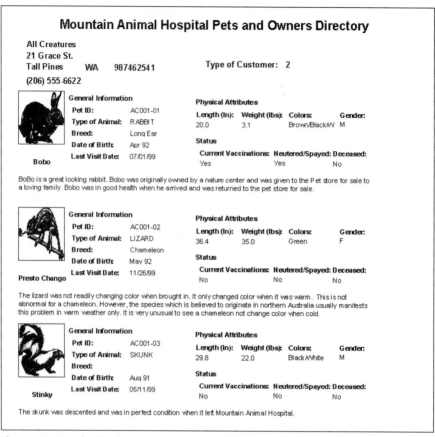

Figure 20-19: The final report's hard-copy printout.

You should, however, print several pages of the report. When you get to page 2, you may see a problem: The animals owned by Johnathan Adams are listed on the page for All Creatures, a pet store. What's wrong? The problem is that you haven't told Access how to group your data. Figure 20-19 displays three records on a page, but All Creatures brought in four pets. The next page begins again with All Creatures in the page header. Then the first record is Fido, the dog belonging to All Creatures. But the next record is Patty the Pig, which belongs to Johnathan Adams. This record needs to trigger a page break because the Customer record has changed (later in this chapter, you learn how to do this). You may also notice on page 2 that the Breed field is not fully displayed. You should expand the text box to display the entire text *German Shepherd*.

Caution If every even-numbered page is blank, you accidentally widened the report past the 8-inch mark. If you move a control to brush up against the right page-margin border or exceed it, the right page margin increases automatically. When it is past the 8-inch mark, it can't display the entire page on one physical piece of paper. The blank page you get is actually the right side of the preceding page. To correct this, make sure that all your controls are within the 8-inch right margin; then drag the right page margin back to 8 inches.

Sorting and grouping data

You have now completely designed the layout of your report. You may think that you're done, but some tasks still remain; one of these is sorting.

Sorting lets you determine the order in which the records are viewed in a datasheet, form, or report, based on the values in one or more fields. This order is important when you want to view the data in your tables in a sequence other than that of your input. For example, new customers are added to the Customer table as they become clients of the hospital; the physical order of the database reflects the date and time a customer is added. Yet, when you think of the customer list, you probably expect it to be in *alphabetical* order, and you want to sort it by Customer Number or Customer Name. By sorting in the report itself, you don't have to worry about the order of the data. Although you can sort the data in the query, it is more advantageous to do it in the report. This way, if you change the query, the report is still in the correct order.

You can take this report concept even further by *grouping;* that is, breaking related records into groups. Suppose that you want to list your customers first by Customer Name and then by Pet Name within each Customer Name group. To do this, you must use the Customer Number field to sort the data. Groupings that can create group headers and footers are sometimes called *control breaks* because changes in data trigger the report groups.

Before you can add a grouping, however, you must first define a *sort order* for at least one field in the report using the Sorting and Grouping box, which is shown completed in Figure 20-20. In this example, you use the `Customer.Customer Number` field to sort on first and then the `Pet ID` field as the secondary sort.

The Customer Name and Customer Number Fields

You may have noticed that the Customer Name field is not in last name/first name order and that the Customer Number is generally in a sorted order by the customer's last name. The Customer Number field begins with the first two characters of a customer's last name if the customer is an individual (Type of Customer = 1). If the customer is a pet store (Type of Customer = 2) or zoo (Type of Customer = 3), the Customer Number field begins with the first two logical characters of the pet store or zoo name.

For an illustration, examine the following list, which shows Type of Customer, Customer Name, and Customer Number for the first five records in the Customer table:

Type of Customer	Customer Name	Customer Number
2 - Pet Store	**All** Creatures	AC001
1 - Individual	Johnathan **Ad**ams	AD001
1 - Individual	William **Ad**ams	AD002
2 - Pet Store	**A**nimal **K**ingdom	AK001
3 - Zoo	**B**orderville **A**quarium	BA001

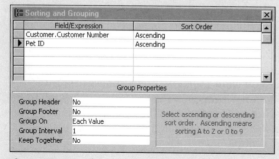

Figure 20-20: The Sorting and Grouping box.

To define a sort order based on Customer Number and Pet ID, follow these steps:

1. Click the Sorting and Grouping button on the toolbar to display the Sorting and Grouping box.

2. Click in the first row of the Field/Expression column of the Sorting and Grouping box. A downward-pointing arrow appears.

3. Click the arrow to display a list of fields in the Pets and Owners query.

4. Click the Customer.Customer Number field in the field list. Notice that Sort Order defaults to Ascending.

5. Click in the second row of the Field/Expression column.

6. Click the arrow to display a list of fields in the Pets and Owners query.

7. Scroll down to find the Pet ID field in the field list and select Pet ID. The Sort Order defaults to Ascending.

Tip

To see more of the Field/Expression column, drag the border between the Field/Expression and Sort Order columns to the right (as shown in Figure 20-20).

Note

You can drag a field from the Field List window into the Sorting and Grouping box Field/Expression column rather than enter a field or choose one from the field list in the Sorting and Grouping box Field/Expression column.

Although in this example you used a field, you can alternatively sort (and group) by using an expression. To enter an expression, click in the desired row of the Field/Expression column and enter any valid Access expression, making sure that it begins with an equal sign, as in =[Length]*[Weight].

To change the sort order for fields in the Field/Expression column, simply click the Sort Order column and click the down arrow to display the Sort Order list; then select Descending.

Creating a group header or footer

Now that you have added instructions to sort by the Customer Number and Pet ID, you will also need to create a group header for Customer Number to force a page break before each new customer page. This way, a customer page will display pet records for only that customer; customers who have more pets than will fit on one page will continue to generate new pages, with only the customer information and pets for that customer. You don't need a group footer in this example because there are no totals by customer number or other reasons to use a group footer.

To create a group header that lets you sort and group by Customer Number, follow these steps:

1. Click the Sorting and Grouping button on the toolbar if the Sorting and Grouping box is not displayed. The field Customer.Customer Number should be displayed in the first row of the Sorting and Grouping box; it should indicate that it is being used as a sort in Ascending order.

2. Click Customer.Customer Number in the Field/Expression column.

3. Click the Group Header property in the bottom pane; an arrow appears.

4. Click the arrow on the right side of the text box; a drop-down list appears.

5. Select Yes from the list.

6. Press Enter. (A header separator bar appears on the report.)

After you define a header or footer, the row pointer changes to the grouping symbol shown in Figure 20-21. This is the same symbol as in the Sorting and Grouping button on the toolbar. Figure 20-21 displays both the grouping row pointer and a newly created section. The Customer.Customer Number header section appears between the page header and detail sections. If you define a group footer, it appears below the detail section. If a report has multiple groupings, each subsequent group becomes the one closest to the detail section. The groups defined first are farthest from the detail section.

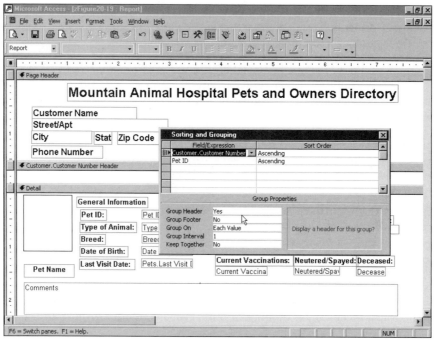

Figure 20-21: The group header definition.

The Group Properties pane (displayed at the bottom of the Sorting and Grouping box) contains these properties:

Group Header	Yes creates a group header. No removes the group header.
Group Footer	Yes creates a group footer. No removes the group footer.
Group On	Specifies how you want the values grouped. The options you see in the drop-down list box depend on the data type of the field on which you're grouping. If you group on an expression, you see all the options. Group On has more choices to make.

For Text data types, there are two choices:

Each Value	The same value in the field or expression
Prefix Characters	The same first *n* number of characters in the field

For Date/Time data types, there are additional options:

Each Value	The same value in the field or expression
Year	Dates in the same calendar year
Qtr	Dates in the same calendar quarter
Month	Dates in the same month
Week	Dates in the same week
Day	Dates on the same date
Hour	Times in the same hour
Minute	Times in the same minute

AutoNumber, Currency, or Number data types provide three options:

Each Value	The same value in the field or expression
Interval	Values falling within the interval you specify
Group Interval	Specifies any interval that is valid for the values in the field or expression you're grouping on
Keep Together	This option controls whats known as widows and orphans in the word processing world so you don't have a header at the bottom of a page with no detail until the next page
Whole Group	Prints header detail and group footer on one page
With First Detail	Prevents the contents of the group header from printing without any following data or records on a page
No	Do not keep together

On the CD-ROM

After you create the Customer Number group header, you are done with the Sorting and Grouping box for this report. You may need to make additional changes to groupings as you change the way a report looks; the following three sections detail how to make these changes. You should not make any of these changes, however, if you are following the examples. If you want to practice these skills, you can save the report before practicing and then retrieve the original copy of the report you saved. After the next three sections, you will have to size the group header section and change its properties.

Changing the group order

Access lets you easily change the Sorting and Grouping order without moving all the individual controls in the associated headers and footers. Here are the general steps to change the sorting and grouping order:

1. Click the selector of the field or expression you want to move in the Sorting and Grouping window.
2. Click the selector again and hold down the left mouse button.
3. Drag the row to a new location.
4. Release the mouse button.

Removing a group header or footer

To remove a page or report header/footer section, use the View ⇨ Page Header/Footer and View ⇨ Report Header/Footer toggles. To remove a group header or footer while leaving the sorting intact, follow these steps:

1. In the Sorting and Grouping window, click the selector of the field or expression that you want to remove from the grouping.
2. Click the Group Header text box.
3. Change the value to **No**.
4. Press Enter.

To remove a group footer, follow the same steps but click Group Footer in Step 2.

To permanently remove both the sorting and grouping for a particular field (and thereby remove the group header and footer sections), follow these steps:

1. Click the selector of the field or expression you want to delete.
2. Press Delete. A dialog box appears asking you to confirm the deletion.
3. Click OK.

Hiding a section

Access also lets you hide headers and footers so that you can break data into groups without having to view information about the group itself. You can also hide the detail section so that you see only a summary report. To hide a section, follow these steps:

1. Click the section you want to hide.
2. Display the section property sheet.
3. Click the Visible property's text box.

4. Click the drop-down list arrow on the right side of the text box.

5. Select **No** from the drop-down list box.

Note

Sections are not the only objects in a report that can be hidden; controls also have a Visible property. This property can be useful for expressions that trigger other expressions.

On the CD-ROM

If you are following the examples, complete the steps in the following section.

Sizing a section

Now that you have created the group header, you must decide what to do with it. Its only purpose in this example is to trigger a page break before a new customer record is displayed. (You learn how to do this later in this chapter.) For this example, you don't need to place any controls within the section. Unless you want to see the empty space on the report from the height of the group header section, close the section. You can do this by resizing the section height to 0.

To modify the height of a section, drag the border of the section below it. If, for example, you have a report with a page header, detail section, and page footer, change the height of the detail section by dragging the top of the page footer section's border. You can make a section larger or smaller by dragging the bottom border of the section. For this example, change the height of the group header section to zero with these steps:

1. Move your mouse pointer over the section borders. The pointer changes to a horizontal line split by two vertical arrows.

2. Select the top of the detail section border.

3. Drag the selected border until it meets the bottom of the header Customer.Customer Number. The gray line indicates where the top of the border will be when you release the mouse button.

4. Release the mouse button.

Adding page breaks

Access lets you add page breaks based on group breaks; you can also insert forced breaks within sections, except in page header and footer sections.

In some report designs, it's best to have each new group begin on a different page. A design criteria for the Pets and Owners report created in this chapter, is that no more than one customer will appear on a page (though a customer can appear on more than one page). You can achieve this effect easily by using the Force New Page property of a group section, which lets you force a page break every time the group value changes.

The four Force New Page settings are:

None	No forced page break (the default)
Before Section	Starts printing the current section at the top of a new page every time there is a new group
After Section	Starts printing the next section at the top of a new page every time there is a new group
Before & After	Combines the effects of Before Section and After Section

To create the report you want, you must force a page break before the Customer Number group by using the Force New Page property in the Customer Number header. To change the Force New Page property on the basis of groupings, follow these steps:

1. Click anywhere in the Customer.Customer Number header.

2. Display the Property window format sheet.

3. Select the Force New Page property.

4. Click on the drop-down list arrow on the right side of the edit box.

5. Select Before Section from the drop-down list box.

Figure 20-22 shows this property sheet.

If you run the report now, you'll see that page 2 has correctly printed only the last record from All Creatures. Page 3 now contains the two pets owned by Johnathan Adams.

Tip   Alternatively, you can create a Customer Number footer and set its Force New Page property to After Section.

Figure 20-22: Forcing a page break in a group header.

Sometimes you don't want to force a page break on the basis of a grouping but still want to force a page break. For example, you may want to split a report title across several pages. The solution is to use the Page Break tool from the Toolbox; just follow these steps:

1. Display the Toolbox.

2. Click the Page Break tool.

3. Click in the section where you want the page break to occur.

4. Test the results by using Print Preview.

Note   Be careful not to split the data in a control. Place page breaks above or below controls; do not overlap them.

Saving your report

After all the time you spent creating your report, you'll want to save it. It is good practice to save your reports frequently, starting as soon as you create them. This prevents the frustration that can occur when you lose your work because of a power failure or human error. Save the report as follows:

1. Select File ➪ Save. If this is the first time you have saved the report, the Save As dialog box appears.

2. Type a valid Access object name. For this example, type **Pets and Owners - Unformatted**.

3. Click OK.

If you already saved your report, Access saves your file with no message about what it is up to.

Summary

In this chapter, you learned the basic operations involved in creating a report. The concepts that were covered include:

✦ A report gives you a different way of viewing data in one or more tables.

✦ Because of the advanced capabilities of Access, you are limited only by your imagination and your printer in the types of reports you can create.

✦ Access provides powerful but easy-to-use tools in the Report Design window: the toolbars, the Properties window, the Sorting and Grouping box, and the Field List.

✦ The Report Design View toolbar provides quick access to such design tasks as displaying various windows and applying formatting styles.

✦ With the Toolbox, you can create, place, or select the controls on a report.

✦ The Field List window displays all fields available to a report from the query or table the report is bound to.

✦ Properties for a control can be viewed and edited from the control's property sheet.

✦ The Sorting and Grouping box lets you create group or summary sections on the report and define sort orders.

✦ Fields can be placed on a report by displaying the field list, selecting the fields, and then dragging the fields to the report.

✦ Control properties can be edited by direct manipulation (using the various tools in the Report Design window) or from the property sheet.

✦ Hiding the detail section can create a summary report.

✦ Sorting lets you organize your data in a different order from the order that was used during input.

✦ Grouping lets you organize your data in related groups that make the data easier to understand.

In the next chapter, you learn to publish your reports using the Access presentation quality printing features.

✦   ✦   ✦

Presentation Quality Reports and Printing

In Chapter 20, you built a report from a blank form. That report was fairly simple. You worked with only label and text box controls, and the report had no special formatting. There were no lines or boxes and no shading to emphasize any areas of the report. Although the report displays all the necessary data, you can make the data more readable by using checkboxes, option buttons, and toggle buttons to display certain fields.

In this chapter, you learn to complete the formatting of the report you created in the preceding chapter, enhancing it to make it more readable and presentable.

Note   Because the Report Design window is set to a width of 8 inches, most of the screen printouts in this chapter appear as though an 800 x 600-resolution Super VGA Windows screen driver is used rather than the standard 640 x 480 VGA Windows driver. This setup lets you see almost the entire screen in the figures.

Making Reports Presentation Quality

Once you have created a report that provides the correct data in a proper format, you can continue to format the report to make it presentation quality. The term *presentation quality* generally refers to the process of enhancing a report from a database by using special effects that desktop publishing packages provide. The Access Report Writer can accomplish with data, reports, and forms what any good desktop publishing package can do with words. Just as a desktop publishing application can enhance a word-processing document to make it more readable, a good report writer can enhance a database report to make it more usable.

You can, for example, draw attention to special areas of the report that you want the reader to notice. Just as a headline in a newspaper screams the news, an enhanced section of the report screams the information.

Cross-Reference

You accomplish database publishing in reports with a variety of controls and by enhancing the controls with color, shading, or other means of emphasis. In Chapters 17, 18, and 19, you learned to add to a form many of the controls that you work with in this chapter. However, you use a somewhat different process to add and enhance these controls in a report. One major difference is the ultimate viewing medium. Because the output of these controls is usually viewed on paper, you have design concerns that differ from those of creating a design to be viewed onscreen. Another difference is the use of each data control. In a form, you input or edit the data; in a report, you just view it.

Figure 21-1 shows the hard-copy of the final report that you create in this chapter. The report has been significantly enhanced with the addition of special effects and more control types than mere labels or text boxes. For example important information, such as the type of customer, gender, and current vaccinations, is easily understood because readers only need to glance at an option button or checkbox versus a numeric code or text.

The Access Report Writer offers a number of tools to make the report controls and sections stand out visually. These tools enable you to create such special effects as:

✦ Lines and rectangles

✦ Color and background shading

✦ Three-dimensional effects (raised, sunken, shadowed, flattened, etched, and chiseled)

In this chapter, you use all these features as you change many of the text box controls into option buttons, toggle buttons, and checkboxes. You also enhance the report with special text options: shading, shadows, lines, rectangles, and three-dimensional effects.

Caution

When you add shading to a report, you can increase printing time dramatically. Shading can also make data hard to read on all but the best black and white print-ers. Reverse video (white on black) loooks great but can also increase printing time. Also, avoid adding colors unless you plan to print on a color printer.

Mountain Animal Hospital Pets and Owners Directory

	All Creatures				Individual
	21 Grace St.				Pet Store
	Tall Pines	WA	98746-2541		Zoo
	(206) 555-6622				

General Information

Pet ID:	AC001-01
Type Of Animal:	RABBIT
Breed:	Long Ear
Date Of Birth:	Apr 92
Last Visit:	7/1/95

Bobo

Physical Attributes

| Length | Weight | Colors |
| 20.0 | 3.1 | Brown/Black/White |

Status
☑ Neutered/Spayed   ☑ Current Vaccinations   Deceased

Gender
⦿ Male
○ Female
○ Unknown

BoBo is a great looking rabbit. Bobo was originally owned by a nature center and was given to the Pet store for sale to a loving family. Bobo was in good health when he arrived and was returned to the pet store for sale.

General Information

Pet ID:	AC001-02
Type Of Animal:	LIZARD
Breed:	Chameleon
Date Of Birth:	May 92
Last Visit:	11/26/93

Presto Chango

Physical Attributes

| Length | Weight | Colors |
| 36.4 | 35.0 | Green |

Status
☐ Neutered/Spayed   ☐ Current Vaccinations   Deceased

Gender
○ Male
⦿ Female
○ Unknown

The lizard was not readily changing color when brought in. It only changed color when it was warm. This is not abnormal for a chameleon. However, the species which is believed to originate in northern Australia usually manifests this problem in warm weather only. It is very unusual to see a chameleon not change color when cold.

General Information

Pet ID:	AC001-03
Type Of Animal:	SKUNK
Breed:	
Date Of Birth:	Aug 91
Last Visit:	5/11/93

Stinky

Physical Attributes

| Length | Weight | Colors |
| 29.8 | 22.0 | Black/White |

Status
☐ Neutered/Spayed   ☐ Current Vaccinations   Deceased

Gender
⦿ Male
○ Female
○ Unknown

The skunk was descented and was in perfect condition when it left Mountain Animal Hospital.

General Information

Pet ID:	AC001-04
Type Of Animal:	DOG
Breed:	German Shepherd
Date Of Birth:	Jun 90
Last Visit:	11/5/93

Fido

Physical Attributes

| Length | Weight | Colors |
| 42.7 | 56.9 | Brown |

Status
☑ Neutered/Spayed   ☐ Current Vaccinations   Deceased

Gender
⦿ Male
○ Female
○ Unknown

Figure 21-1: An enhanced report.

Understanding WYSIWYG Printing

Access has a *WYSIWYG* (*What You See Is What You Get*) report writer. As you create controls onscreen, you see instantly how they will look in your report. If you want to see how the data will look, you can take advantage of several types of onscreen preview modes. These modes enable you to see the actual data without involving a hard-copy device.

The Access Report Writer lets you add color, shading, or reverse video (white letters on a black background) to your report text and controls. You can even color or shade the background of report sections and you see each effect immediately. Although what you see on the Report Design window *seems* to be exactly what you'll see when you print, there are some factors that affect just how close what you see is to what you really get.

The first problem is with fonts. If you use Microsoft Windows and TrueType fonts, generally about 95 percent of your fonts appear perfectly, both on the Report Design window onscreen and in the hard-copy report. A common problem is that not all letters fit on the report even though they appear to fit in the Report Design window. Another problem is that controls shift slightly from perfect alignment. For example, although the Report Design window shows that the word *Deceased* fits perfectly in the report, when you view the report in print preview mode or print it to a printer, only the letters *Decease* are printed. The final *d* simply vanishes.

Other problems occur when you place controls tightly within a rectangle or group box. Most of the time the print preview modes are perfect for determining what the hard-copy will look like, whereas the Report Design window view may differ slightly. The print preview (or hard-copy) should be your only method of determining when your report is complete. Make sure that you're using the correct Windows screen driver when you preview a report; you can get vastly different results depending on the driver. For example, a dot-matrix driver is probably only 100–150 dpi (dots per inch), whereas a laser Printer can be 600 dpi; higher values mean higher resolution (a clearer image).

In this chapter, you modify your report from Chapter 20 to look like the one shown in Figure 21-1. Before you begin, you should start with a design. Figure 21-2 is a sample design for enhancing the report. Lines and rectangles are drawn in the design. Changes to controls and their appearances are noted with instructions and arrows that point to the area to be changed.

On the CD-ROM

If you are following the examples, you should have the Pets and Owners report (created in Chapter 20) open in the Report Design window or the Pets and Owners - Unformatted report design that came in your Mountain Animal Hospital database open.

Enhancing Text-Based Controls

Before you begin using such display items as shading or three-dimensional effects, it's important to get the data right. If your enhancements include control changes, start with these changes.

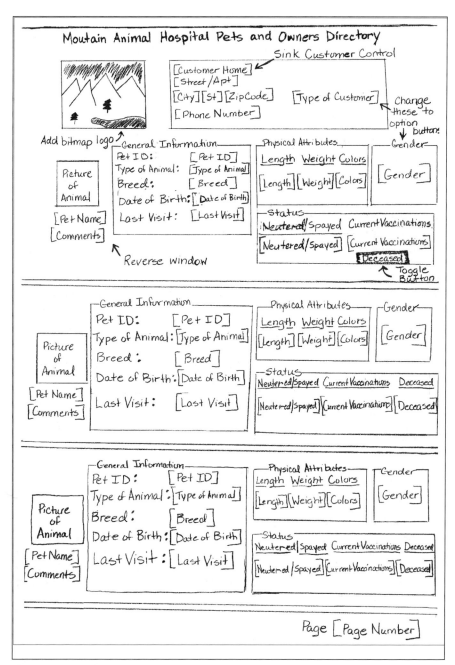

Figure 21-2: A design for report enhancements.

Enhancing label controls

You can enhance label controls in several ways, including:

✦ Change the type style of the text font (Arial, Times New Roman, Wingdings, etc.)

✦ Change the text font size (from 4 to 200 points)

✦ Change the text font style (bold, italic, underline)

✦ Change the text color (using the Fore Color button)

✦ Add a shadow

Changing text fonts and size

In Chapter 20, you learned to change the text font type, size, and style. Now you learn to make additional changes as you change the title to match the design shown in Figures 21-1 and 21-2.

These figures show that the text needs to be left-justified on the page and made one size smaller.

To change the font placement and size, follow these steps:

1. Select the label control with the text Mountain Animal Hospital Pets and Owners Directory.

2. Drag the label control to the left side of the Report window.

3. Change the control font size to 16 by changing the font size in the formatting toolbar.

Tip   You can select the font in the Properties window for the control but it is easier to use the formatting toolbar.

Tip   If you want to format controls the same way, then *group* them using the new Group function in Access 2000. This can be done the same way it is done in forms. Select the controls that you want to group by holding down the Shift key and clicking the controls that you want to group. Once grouped, these controls can be formatted at the same time by selecting the group, or one at a time by selecting a control inside the group.

Using the AutoFormat Button

As in the Form designer, Access has an AutoFormat feature in the Report Design window. The AutoFormat button can assign predefined styles to a report and its controls. To use the AutoFormat functions, click the AutoFormat button on the toolbar when you're in a report design. Access displays the AutoFormat dialog box for reports, as shown in Figure 21-3. Select the desired AutoFormat and click OK to complete the formatting. All your controls (and the overall look of the form) is changed, as shown in the AutoFormat preview.

Figure 21-3: The AutoFormat dialog box.

Creating a text shadow

Text shadows create a three-dimensional look. They make text seem to float above the page while text shadows stay on the page. You can create text shadows for a report using these techniques:

✦ Duplicate the text.

✦ Offset the duplicate text from the original text.

✦ Change the duplicate text to a different color (usually a lighter shade).

✦ Place the duplicate text behind the original text.

✦ Change the original text Back Color Transparent button.

Note   Access has a shadow effect on the Special Effects button under the Formatting toolbar. This effect creates a shadow only on boxes or on the text box, not on the text itself. Compare the Mountain Animal Hospital Pets and Owners Directory in Figure 21-4 with that in Figure 21-5.

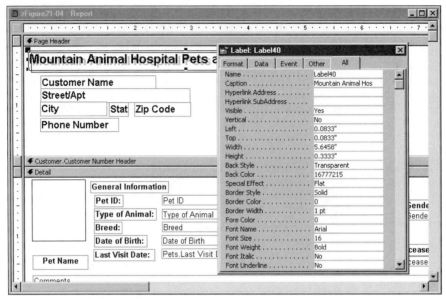

Figure 21-4: Label control properties.

To create a shadow for the title's text, follow these steps:

1. Select the label control with the text *Mountain Animal Hospital Pets and Owners Directory.*

2. Select Edit ➪ Duplicate.

3. Select light gray from the Foreground Color window to change the duplicate text color.

4. Drag the duplicate text slightly to the right and upward to lessen the offset from the original text below.

5. Select Format ➪ Send to Back.

6. Select the original copy of the text (the one now in front).

7. Click the Transparent button in the Back Color window.

The text now appears to have a shadow, as shown in Figure 21-4. The box around the label control is not visible when the report is printed or in print preview, as shown in Figure 21-5.

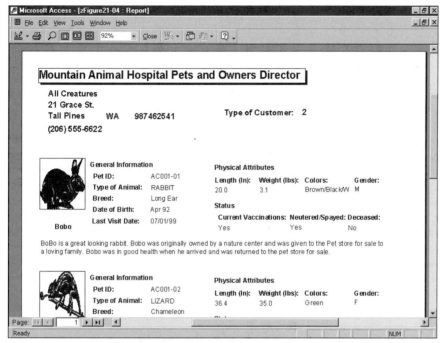

Figure 21-5: Displaying the Print Preview window.

Caution

Although the onscreen shadow looks great, it does not print correctly on most monochrome printers. Normally, you get just two lines of black text that look horrible. Unless you have a printer that prints text in shades of gray (using graphics rather than text fonts) or a color printer that prints in gray, avoid using shadowed text on a report. You may also notice in Figure 21-5, the entire word **Directory** is not displayed at the top of the report. Sometimes, you have to go back and make labels wider as they do not print (or print preview) correctly. Usually, it just needs to be a couple pixels wider.

On the
CD-ROM

For our purposes, select the shadow box you just created and remove it to continue with the tutorials.

Displaying label or text box control properties

As you use formatting to change values in a label or text box control, you change their properties. Figure 21-4 displays the property sheet for the label control you just created. As you can see in the figure, many properties (described in Chapter 17) can be affected by the formatting windows.

Although you can set many of these controls from the property sheet, it's much easier to drag the control to set the Top, Left, Width, and Height, and to use the Formatting toolbar to set the other properties of the control.

Tip   Access (like other Microsoft Office products) has a Format Painter on the standard toolbar. This excellent and convenient tool allows you to copy styles from one selection to the next. Simply click the item whose style you want to copy, then click the Format Painter icon, and then click the item that needs the style change.

Tip   A better idea than to shadow the text is to shadow the label box. You can do this easily by deleting the duplicate text label, selecting the original label, and using the Format bar to change the special effect to Shadowed. This technique displays a cleaner look, as shown in Figure 21-5.

Working with multiple-line text box controls

There are two reasons to use a multiple-line text box:

✦ To display a Text data type on multiple lines

✦ To display large amounts of text in a Memo data type

Displaying multiple lines of text using a text box

In the sample report, the Street/Apt text box control in the page header sometimes contains data that takes up more than one line. The way the text box control is sized, you can see only the first line of data. There are generally two ways to see multiple lines of text in a text box control:

✦ Resize the control vertically to allow more lines to be displayed

✦ Change the Can Grow or Can Shrink properties

When you resize a control by making it larger vertically, it uses as much space as you created for the field of the record. This leaves excess space for the field if the content's length changes from record to record. For example, most of the values of the Street/Apt text box control use one line; some use two. If you resize the Street/Apt text box control to display two lines, the control displays two lines for *every* customer. This leaves a blank line between the Street/Apt control and the City control whenever the Street/Apt value uses only one line.

One solution to this problem is to use the Can Grow or Can Shrink properties of the text box control instead of resizing the control. If you change the value of the Can Grow property to Yes, the control grows vertically if there are more lines than can be displayed in the default control. Another solution is to resize the control so that it's larger and then use the Can Shrink property to remove any blank lines if the value of the data does not use the full size of the control.

In addition to setting the Can Grow property in a text box control to Yes, the property can also be set for the detail, group header, group footer or report header or footer sections. This allows the entire section to grow or shrink along with the controls within it.

Displaying memo fields in multiple-line text box controls

The Memo data type fields generally use large amounts of text. You can display these fields on a report by simply placing the text box in the desired section (usually the detail section) and resizing it to the desired width and height.

In a form, you can add *scrollbars* to display any text that doesn't fit the space allotted. In a report, you don't have that option. So to display text properly, use the Can Grow and Can Shrink properties. In Chapter 20, you created a large text box control to accommodate several lines of memo text, and you set the Can Grow and Can Shrink properties to Yes. Check the Can Grow and Can Shrink properties to verify that they are set to Yes for the Comments text box control and resize the field. To do so, follow these steps:

1. Select the Properties button on the toolbar to display the property sheet.
2. Select the Comments text box control.
3. Change the height of the control to one line to fit the Comments caption.
4. Verify that the Can Grow property is Yes.
5. Verify that the Can Shrink property is Yes.
6. Shrink the detail section height by dragging the page footer border upward until it's just below the Comments control.

To see the effect of the Can Grow and Can Shrink properties, display the report in the Print Preview window. Notice the Comment line and the shadowed line in Figure 21-5, which shows the Print Preview window. Looking at the print preview in zoom mode shows that the spaces between the records are the same, regardless of the size of the Comments field. If no comment text is present, the next record begins immediately below the preceding record's information.

Tip
To enhance a control, use the new properties in Access 2000 that allow you to enter margins for all sides of a control (top, bottom, left, and right). You can also add line spacing to a control. To use these properties, display the property sheet for the control and select the format tab. Enter the margins and line spacing in inches.

Adding New Controls

You can change many data types to control types other than text boxes. These data types include Text, Number, and Yes/No. The other control types you can use are

✦ Option buttons

✦ Checkboxes

✦ Toggle buttons

Note   Access lets you change some control types from one type to another type. Generally, text box controls can become combo box or list box controls; checkboxes, option buttons, and toggle buttons are interchangeable.

Displaying values with option groups and option buttons

In your design, as shown in Figure 21-2, are two text box controls that should be changed to option buttons within an option group. These text box controls are the Type of Customer field in the page header section and the Gender field in the detail section.

An option group is generally bound to a single field or expression. Each button in the group passes a different value to the option group, which in turn passes the single choice to the bound field or expression. The buttons themselves are not bound to a field—only to the option group box.

Cross-Reference   If you haven't used an option button or option group yet, read Chapter 15 before continuing.

You can use only numeric data values to create an option button within an option group. The Type of Customer field is relatively easy to change to an option group; its values are already numeric, expressed as customer types 1, 2, or 3.

Creating the option group

To create the option group for the Type of Customer control, you must first delete the existing Type of Customer control. Then you can create a new option group and use the Option Group Wizard to create the option buttons.

Cross-Reference   Chapter 18 offers a more complete example of creating an option group and option buttons with the Option Group Wizard.

Follow these steps to create an option group using the Option Group Wizard:

1. Delete the existing Type of Customer control.

2. Select the Option Group button from the Toolbox.

3. Drag the Type of Customer field from the field list to the space in the page header section.

   The first screen of the Option Group Wizard should be visible (as shown completed in Figure 21-6). Enter the text label for each option button that will be in your option group, just as you would do in a datasheet. You can press the down-arrow (↓) key to move to the next choice.

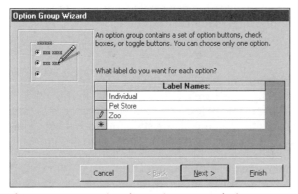

Figure 21-6: Entering the option group choices.

4. Enter **Individual**, **Pet Store**, and **Zoo**, pressing the down-arrow (↓) key between choices.

5. Click the Next button to move to the default option Wizard screen.

   The next screen lets you select the default control for when the option group is selected. Normally, the first option is the default. To make a different button the default, first select the Yes option button and then select the new default value from the combo box that shows your choices. In this example, the first value will be the default automatically.

6. Click the Next button to move to the Assigning Values screen of the Wizard.

   The next Wizard screen displays the actual values you entered, along with a default set of numbers that will be used to store the selected value in the bound option group field. The screen looks like a datasheet with two columns. In this example, this is the Type of Customer field. Your first choice, Individual, is automatically assigned a 1, Pet Store a 2, and Zoo a 3. When Pet Store is selected, a 2 is stored in the Type of Customer field.

In this example, the default values are acceptable. Sometimes you may want to assign values other than 1, 2, 3, and so on. For example, you might want to use 100, 200, and 500. As long as you use unique numbers, you can assign any values you want.

7. Click the Next button to move to the next Wizard screen.

In this Wizard screen, you have to decide whether to bind the option group itself to a form field or to leave it unbound. The first choice in the Wizard, *Save the value for later use*, creates an unbound field. When you are using the option group in a dialog box that uses the selected value to make a decision, you don't want to store the value in a table field. In this example, the second value, *Store the value in this field*, is selected automatically because you started with the Type of Customer field. If you want to bind the option group value to a different table field, you can select from a list of all form fields. Again, in this example, the default is acceptable.

8. Click the Next button to move to the Wizard screen that sets the option group style.

Again, as shown in Figure 21-7, the defaults are acceptable for this example. Notice that your actual values are used as a sample. In this Wizard screen, the upper half of the Wizard screen lets you choose which type of buttons you want. The lower half lets you choose the style for the option group box and the type of group control. The style affects the option group rectangle. If you choose Raised, Sunken, Etched, or Shadowed, that value is applied to the Special Effect property of the option group. Additionally, for Option buttons and Check boxes, if you choose any of the special effects, the property for each option button or checkbox is set to the special effect.

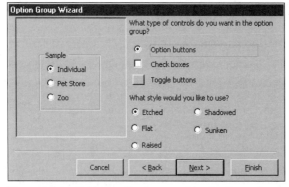

Figure 21-7: Selecting the type and look of your buttons.

Note   As you change your selections, the Sample changes as well.

9. Click the Next button to move to the final option group Wizard screen.

   The final screen lets you give the option group control a label that will appear in the option group border. You can then add the control to your design and optionally display help.

10. Accept Type of Customer as your label for the Option Group.

11. Click the Finish button to complete the Wizard.

   Your Wizard work is now complete, and the controls appear on the design screen. Eight controls have been created: the option group, its label, three option buttons, and their labels. In this example, you don't want the option group label.

12. Select the option group label Type of Customer, and click the Delete key to remove it.

Creating an option group with a calculated control

You also want to display the Gender field as a set of option buttons. There is one problem, however. The Gender field is a text field with the values of M, F, and U. You can create option buttons only with a numeric field. You can do this easily with the Type of Customer field, which is numeric. How can you solve this problem with the Gender field? The solution is to create a new calculated control that contains an expression. The expression must transform the values M to 1, F to 2, and U to 3. You create this calculation by using the Immediate IF function (IIf), with this expression:

```
=IIf([Gender]="M","1",IIf([Gender]="F","2","3"))
```

The first IIf function checks the value of Gender; if the value is "M," the value of the calculated control is set to 1. If the value is not "M," the second IIf checks for a Gender value of "F." If the value is "F," the calculated control value is set to 2. If the value is not "F," the value of the calculated control is set to 3. To create this new calculated control, follow these steps:

1. Create a new text box control alongside the Status text control, as shown in Figure 21-8.

2. Delete the attached label control.

3. Display the All sheet of the Properties window for the text box control.

4. Change the Control Name property to **Gender Number**.

5. Type =IIf([Gender]="M","1",IIf([Gender]="F","2","3")) in the Control Source property. (Remember that you can press Shift+F2 to zoom.)

6. Change the Visible property to No.

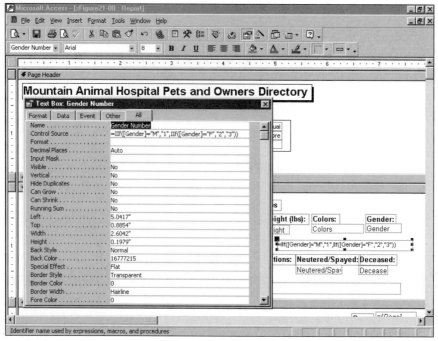

Figure 21-8: Creating a calculated control.

Because you change the Visible property of the calculated control to No, the control is not displayed when you produce the report. After you create the calculated control, you can use it as the control source for an option group. Figure 21-8 shows this new calculated control at the bottom-right of the screen. If you look at the report in print preview, you will see that the control is not visible.

To create the option group for Gender (based on this calculated control), follow these steps:

1. Delete the existing Gender text box and label control in the detail section.

2. Select the Option Group button from the Toolbox.

3. Drag the Option Group rectangle to the space in the detail section. The first screen of the Option Group Wizard should be displayed.

4. Enter **Male**, **Female**, and **Unknown**, pressing the down-arrow (↓) key between choices.

5. Click the Next button three times to move to the Control Source screen.

   In this Wizard screen, you have to decide whether the option group itself will be bound to a form field or unbound. In this example, you will use the first choice in the Wizard, Save the value for later use, which creates an unbound field. You cannot select a calculated field in the Wizard; after completing it, you will change the control source of the option group.

6. Click the Next button to move to the Option Group Style Wizard screen.

   Again, for this example, the defaults are acceptable. Notice that your actual values are used as a sample.

7. Click the Next button to move to the final Option Group Wizard screen.

8. Accept Gender.

9. Click the Finish button to complete the Wizard.

   Your Wizard work is now complete, and the controls appear on the design screen. Currently, as an unbound control, the Control Source property is blank. You must set this to the calculated control Gender Number.

10. Select the option group control and change the Control Source property to =[**Gender Number**], as shown in Figure 21-9.

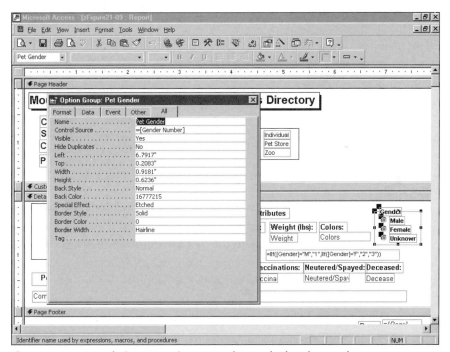

Figure 21-9: Completing an option group for a calculated control.

11. Name the control Pet Gender by changing the Name property to **Pet Gender**.

Caution   You must not name this control Gender. The pets table already has a field named Gender; if you duplicate the name as a control, you will receive an error.

You may need to change the size of the rectangle to fit within the 8-inch margin. If you have to make it smaller, remember to change the margin (which may be larger than 8 inches now).

12. Resize the option group rectangle and reset the right margin to 8 inches.

The last task is to enhance all the text on the control buttons to 12-point bold. To accomplish this, follow these steps:

1. Select the entire Gender option group box, all the buttons and their attached labels.

2. Click the Bold button on the toolbar.

3. Select Format ⇨ Size ⇨ To Fit to resize the label control boxes.

You may still need to align the labels before your task is complete. The final design for the option buttons is shown in Figure 21-9, including the option button properties.

Displaying Yes/No values with checkboxes

You can make Yes/No values more readable by using checkboxes. Although you could also use them in an option group, the primary purpose of a checkbox is to display one of two states for a single value; checkboxes are easier to create than option groups. You will now change the Neutered/Spayed and Current Vaccinations fields into checkboxes. As with option button controls, you must first delete the existing text box controls to create a checkbox that uses the fields. To create the checkboxes, use Figure 21-10 as a guide and follow these steps:

1. Select the Neutered/Spayed and Current Vaccinations text box controls (and their associated labels) in the detail section.

2. Press Delete to delete both the text box controls and the attached label controls.

3. Select the Check Box button from the Toolbox.

4. Using Figure 21-10 as a guide, drag the Neutered/Spayed and Current Vaccinations fields from the field list to create two new checkboxes.

5. Select both checkbox controls; change the font size to 10.

6. Size the controls to fit; move them as necessary.

The completed checkboxes are shown in Figure 21-10.

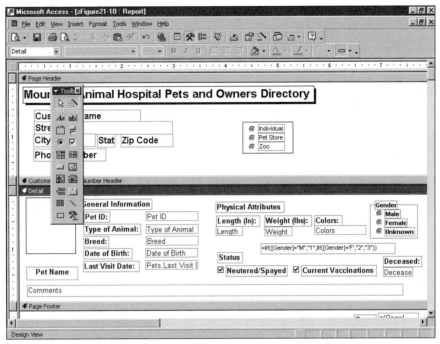

Figure 21-10: The completed checkboxes.

Displaying values as toggle buttons

You can use toggle buttons as another way to make Yes/No data types easier to read. A toggle button appears to sit above the screen if the value of the Yes/No data type is No. If the value is Yes, the button appears to be depressed. To create a toggle button for the Deceased field, follow these steps:

1. Select the Deceased text box control (and its associated label) in the detail section.

2. Press Delete to delete both the text box control and the attached label control.

3. Select the Toggle Button icon from the Toolbox and the field Deceased from the field list.

4. Using Figure 21-11 as a guide, create a new toggle button by dragging the Deceased field from the field list.

5. Double-click the toggle button and type **Deceased**.

6. Select Bold and the 10-point Font size from the Formatting toolbar.

7. Select Format ⇨ Size ⇨ To Fit to fit the button around the caption text.

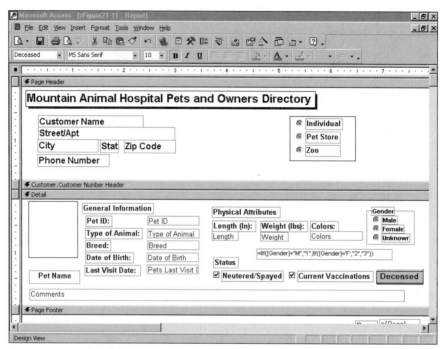

Figure 21-11: Creating a toggle button.

Though it looks like a command button, it is actually a toggle button that can be pressed and appear to be sunken and then pressed again and appear to be raised.

The toggle button is displayed with the caption centered within the control.

Note   A picture rather than text can be displayed on the face of the toggle button by entering the filename of a bitmap image in the Picture property of the toggle button. Use the builder button to display the Insert Picture dialog box, as shown in Figure 21-12.

Tip   Remember that Access allows you to change some controls from one type to another; first you select the control (right-click to display the shortcut menu) and then select the new control style from the Change To option.

Displaying bound OLE objects in reports

In the report you are creating in this chapter, a picture of each animal is shown in the detail section. Some animals are displayed as they look, but others appear stretched out of proportion. Presto Chango (who is not really a hunchbacked lizard) illustrates this distortion.

Pictures are stored in OLE controls. The two types of OLE controls are:

Bound object frames	Pictures are stored in a record
Image frames	Pictures are embedded or linked to a report section itself

In this report, there is already a bound object frame. The Picture field is an OLE data type that has bitmaps embedded in each record. The Picture bound object control gets its values from the Picture field in the Pets table.

Displaying an image in a report

On the CD-ROM

You can also add an image object to your report by pasting a bitmap from the Clipboard or by embedding or linking a bitmap file that contains a picture. Suppose that you have a logo for the Mountain Animal Hospital. On the disk that accompanies this book is a bitmap called MTN.BMP. In this section, you learn to add this bitmap to the page header section (if you copied it to your Access directory).

Using Figure 21-12 as a guide, you will move the customer information to the right side of the page header section and then add the bitmap to the left side after creating the image frame. To add an unbound object frame, follow these steps:

1. Select the customer information in the page header section and move it to the right, as shown in Figure 21-12.

2. Click the Image Frame button in the Toolbox.

3. Click the left corner below the title; drag the box so that it's sized as shown in Figure 21-12. The Insert Picture dialog box appears.

   From this dialog box, you can select the picture filename you want to insert into your report.

   Tip If you don't see the preview of the picture as shown in Figure 21-12, select Tools ⇨ Preview from the Insert Picture toolbar.

4. Select MTN.BMP from your Access directory (or wherever you copied the files for the book) and click OK.

5. Display the property sheet.

6. Change the Size Mode property to Stretch.

7. Finally, change the Border property so that the picture does not simply blend into the background (there is too much white in the picture); change the border color to black or make the border three-dimensional (as shown in the next step).

8. Click the Raised button in the Special Effect formatting window.

The image frame is now complete.

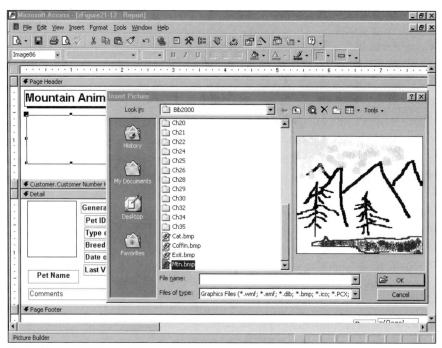

Figure 21-12: Adding a bitmap image to a report

Working with Lines and Rectangles

You can use lines and rectangles (commonly called boxes) to make certain areas of the report stand out or to bring attention to desired areas of the report. In Figure 21-1, are several groups of lines and rectangles that are used to emphasize data in the report. You need several rectangles and two different lines to complete the lines and boxes in this report. Figure 21-13 will be used as a guide for creating emphasis, boxes, and lines.

To create the rectangle for the page header, follow these steps, using Figure 21-13 as a guide:

1. Select the Rectangle button in the Toolbox.

2. Click the upper-left part of the page header section to the right of the picture and just below the title.

3. Drag the rectangle around the entire set of customer text boxes and option buttons.

4. Select Format ⇨ Send to Back to redisplay the text boxes and option buttons.

Tip You may notice that when you create the rectangle, it blocks out the controls beneath it. Sending the rectangle to the background makes the controls reappear.

You can also redisplay the controls by changing the Transparent button of the Back Color. This option, however, does not let you add other shading effects. For a rectangle, you should always select Send to Back.

The next three rectangles are in the detail section. You can create the rectangles by following the same steps you used to create the rectangle in the page header section. As you create them, you may find yourself rearranging some of the controls to fit better within the rectangles. Also change the label controls for Length, Weight, and Colors, as shown in Figure 21-13.

Several lines are needed for the report. A single line needs to be added to the top of the report above the title, and two lines need to be added below the Comments text box. To add these lines, complete the next set of steps, using Figure 21-13 as a guide (you can also take this opportunity to remove the shadow on the title if you added it earlier):

1. Click the title line (Mountain Animal Hospital Pets and Owners Directory).

2. Turn off the border shadow and make the background transparent using the Format bar.

3. Move the title line down, leaving sufficient room to place a thick line.

4. Click the Line button in the Toolbox.

5. Create a new line above the title in the page header, across the entire width of the report.

6. Select choice 3 from the Border Width window of the Formatting toolbar to make the line thicker.

7. Create a new line below the Comments text box in the detail section.

8. Again, make the line thickness 3 from the Border Width window to make the line thicker.

9. Duplicate the line below the comments and align it with the line above.

Tip If you hold down the Shift key while creating a line, the line remains perfectly straight, either horizontally or vertically, depending on the initial movement of drawing the line.

Note The toggle button does not display the text correctly in the button. At this size, no text font can display text correctly (in the previewed size) on a button. When the report is printed, however, the text will appear correctly.

Emphasizing Areas of the Report

The report is now almost complete, but several tasks remain. According to the original printout and design shown in Figures 21-1 and 21-2, you still need to shade the rectangle in the page header, add a shadow to the rectangle, sink the Customer text box controls, create an etched effect for the Type of Customer option group box, and change Pet Name to reverse video.

Adding background shading

A background shade can be added to any control. Adding background shading to a rectangle shades any controls contained within the rectangle. You can, however, add background shading to all controls that are selected at one time. To add background shading to the rectangle in the page header section, follow these steps:

1. Select the Rectangle control in the page header section.

2. Select the light gray Back Color.

Sinking controls

Generally, you cannot sink controls in a report; they don't look sunken on a white background. You can, however, use a gray background to enhance the depth of a control; both sunken and raised controls stand out on a gray background. Because you just added a gray background to the rectangle in the page header, you can sink or raise controls within the rectangle. To give the Customer text box controls a sunken appearance, follow these steps:

1. Select each of the Customer text box controls in the page header section.

2. Click the Sunken selection from the Special Effects button.

If you sink or raise a checkbox, Access uses a different, smaller checkbox that has the appearance of depth.

Etched controls

Next, give the rectangle inside the large rectangle an etched look. Like sunken controls, etched controls look much better on a gray or dark background. To give the Type of Customer option group control an etched look, follow these steps:

1. Select the Type of Customer option group control.

2. Click the Etched selection from the Special Effects button.

Creating a shadow on a rectangle

To emphasize an area of the report, add a shadow to any control. Most commonly, rectangles and text boxes are the types of controls given this effect. Shadows are created by adding a solid-color rectangle that is slightly offset and behind the original control. If the background is light or white, you need a dark-colored rectangle. If the background is dark or black, you need a light-colored or white rectangle. To create a shadow for the page header rectangle, follow these steps:

1. Select the rectangle in the page header.
2. Click the Special Effects button in the Formatting toolbar.
3. Select Shadow from the window.

Changing text to a reverse video display

Text really stands out when you create white text on a black background. This is called *reverse video*; it's the opposite of the usual black on white. You can convert text in a label control or text box to reverse video by changing the fill color to black and the text color to white. To change the Pet Name text control to reverse video, follow these steps:

1. Select the Pet Name text control (not the label control).
2. Click on the black Back Color button.
3. Click the white Fore Color button.

Figure 21-13 shows the final report in the Report Design window.

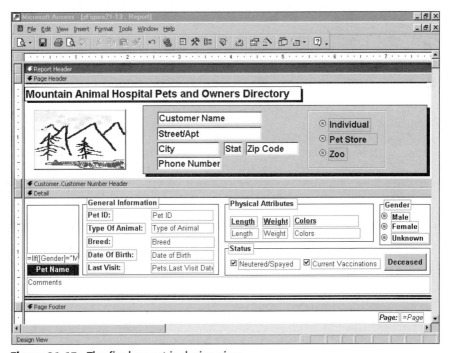

Figure 21-13: The final report is design view.

Seeing Your Output in Different Ways

You can see your output from a report in several ways:

✦ Print previewing

✦ Printing to hard copy

✦ Printing to a file

✦ Printing the report definition

Using the Print Preview window

Throughout this chapter, you used the Print Preview window to view your report. Figure 21-5 displayed your report in the Print Preview window in a zoomed view. This lets you see your report with the actual fonts, shading, lines, boxes, and data that will be on the printed report. When the print preview mode is in a zoomed view, you can press the mouse button to change the view to a page preview (where you can see the entire page).

You can use the horizontal and vertical scroll bars to move around the page or move from page to page by using the page controls in the bottom-left corner of the window.

The *page preview mode* of the Print Preview window displays an entire page of the report, as shown in Figure 21-14. The mouse pointer is shaped like a magnifying glass in Print Preview windows; using this pointer during page preview lets you select a portion of the page and then zoom in to that portion for a detailed view.

In Figure 21-14 is a representation of the printed page. You use the navigation buttons (located in the lower-left section of the Print Preview window) to move between pages, just as you would use them to move between records in a datasheet.

The first eight buttons displayed on the toolbar provide quick access to printing tasks:

Design	Switch between design view, print preview, or layout view
Print	Displays the Print dialog box
Zoom	Toggles in and out of Page Preview and Zoomed view
One Page	Displays a single page in the Print Preview window
Two Pages	Displays two pages in the Print Preview window

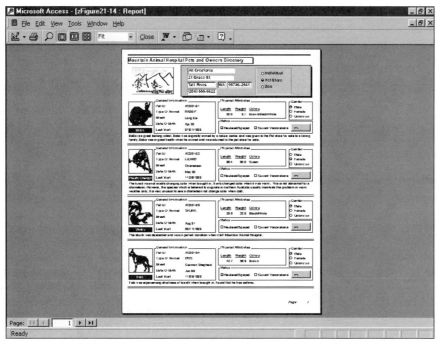

Figure 21-14: Displaying a report in page preview mode in the Print Preview window.

Multiple Pages	Displays from 1 x 1 to 2 x 3 pages in the Print Preview window
Zoom Control	Select Percent of Size to Zoom: 200%, 150%, 100%, 75%, 50%, 25%, 10%, Fit (you can also type a specific percentage in this control)
Close Window	Returns to Design view

You are not limited to a one- or two-page preview. As Figure 21-15 shows, the View ↪ Pages menu lets you select 1, 2, 4, 8, or 12 pages to preview. In Figure 21-15, eight pages have been selected and are visible. You can also right-click on the Print Preview page and select pages or the Zoom percentage. When you use the shortcut menus, you can select as many as 20 pages to preview at a time; you can also determine their arrangement in rows and columns (2 x 4, 5 x 4, 3 x 4, and so on).

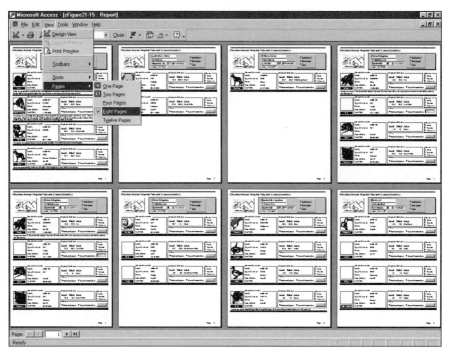

Figure 21-15: Multipage print preview mode.

If you are satisfied with the report after examining the preview, select the Print button on the toolbar and print it. If you are not satisfied with your report, select the Close button to return to the Report Design window and make additional changes.

Using layout previews

Layout preview is different from a print preview. A print preview uses a query's dynaset; layout preview displays sample data (ignoring criteria) or joins in an underlying query.

The purpose of a layout preview is strictly to show you field placement and formatting. Thus, you can create a report design without having to assemble your data properly; in a large query, this can save considerable time. You can see a sample preview by one of two methods: Select View ➪ Layout Preview, or click the Report View button and then select the Layout Preview icon (the bottom one) on the Report Design toolbar. You can switch back to the Report Design window by selecting the Close Window button if you entered the Print Preview from the Report Design window. If you entered from the Database window, you are returned there.

Note You can also zoom in to a layout page preview on the sample data or print the sample report from the Layout Preview window.

Printing a report

You can print one or more records in your form (exactly as they look onscreen) from several places:

✦ Select File ➪ Print in the Report Design window

✦ Select File ➪ Print in the Preview window

✦ Select File ➪ Print in the Database window with a report highlighted

Note If you are in the Print Preview window, the actual data prints. If you are in the Layout Preview window, only sample data prints.

Caution If you select the Print button in the Preview window, all your data starts printing immediately and you cannot control which data is to be printed.

The Print dialog box

After you decide to print your report, the Print dialog box is displayed, as shown in Figure 21-16. The Print dialog box lets you control several items by providing these choices:

Name	Lets you select the printer
Print Range	Prints the entire report or selected pages
Copies	Selects the number of copies
Collate	Selects whether to collate copies
Print to File	Prints to a file rather than to the printer

The Print dialog box that is displayed is specific to your printer and based on your setup in Microsoft Windows. Although each printer is different, the dialog box is essentially the same. Generally, dot matrix or impact printers have a few more options for controlling quality than do laser printers.

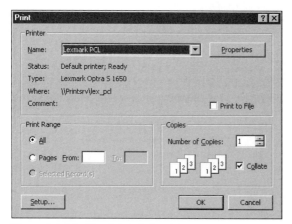

Figure 21-16: The Print dialog box.

Assuming that you set up a printer in Windows, you can click OK to print your form. Your form is printed using the font you selected for display (or the nearest printer equivalent). The printout contains any formatting in the form, including lines, boxes, and shading. Colors are converted to shades on a monochrome printer.

If you need to additionally set up your Windows printer options, choose the Properties button in the Print dialog box. This dialog box sets up your printer, not your report. To fine-tune the setup of your report, use the Setup button (which provides more options).

You can display print setup options in other ways as well, including:

✦ Select File ➪ Page Setup from the Report Design window

✦ Select File ➪ Page Setup from the Database window

The Page Setup dialog box

The Page Setup dialog box, shown in Figure 21-17, is divided into three tabbed dialog boxes: Margins, Page, and Layout. (You use the Layout tab in Chapter 29 when you work with labels and multicolumn reports.)

Margins	Sets the page margins; also has option for Print Data Only
Page	Selects page orientation, paper size and source, and printer device
Layout	Selects grid settings, item size, and layout items

Figure 21-17: The Page tab in the Page Setup dialog box.

The Page tab lets you control the orientation of the report. There are two choices: Portrait and Landscape. Clicking the Portrait button changes the report so that the page is taller than it is wide. Clicking the Landscape button changes the report orientation so that the page is wider than it is tall.

Tip   A good way to remember the difference between landscape and portrait is to think of paintings. Portraits of people are usually taller than they are wide; landscapes of the outdoors are usually wider than tall. When you click either button, the Page icon (the letter A) changes to show your choice graphically.

The Paper section indicates the size of the paper to use, as well as the paper source (for printers that have more than one source available). Clicking Source displays a drop-down list of paper sources available for the selected printer. Depending on the printer selected, you may have one or more paper trays or manual feed available. Click the source to use.

Clicking Size displays a drop-down list box showing all the paper sizes available for the selected printer (and paper source). Click the size to use.

If you click the Print Data Only checkbox on the Margins tab, Access prints only the data from your report and does not print any graphics. (This feature is handy if you use preprinted forms.) Also, printing complex graphics slows down all but the most capable printers; not printing them saves time.

The Margins section shown in Figure 21-18 displays (and allows you to edit) the left, right, top, and bottom margins. To edit one or more of these settings, click the appropriate text box and type a new number.

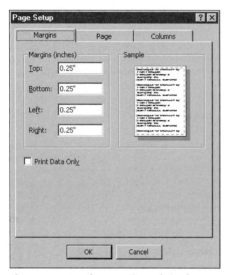

Figure 21-18: The Margins tab in the Page Setup dialog box.

Tip   Page Setup settings are stored with each report. It's therefore possible to use several different printers for various reports as long as you don't use the default Windows printer. This can be a problem, however, because if you exchange files with another user who doesn't have the same printer installed, the other user must modify the Page Setup settings.

Note   Someone may send you a report that you can't view or print because a Windows printer driver you don't have was used. If the report was created with a driver not installed on your system, Access displays a dialog box and lets you print with your default printer.

Summary

In this chapter, you learned to enhance your reports and to print them. The chapter covered these points:

✦ Presentation quality is a term that generally describes report formatting from a database application that offers lines, boxes, shading, and other types of desktop publishing enhancements.

✦ The Access Report Writer is a WYSIWYG (What You See Is What You Get) report writer. What you see in the Design window is generally what you get on the hard-copy report.

✦ The form- and report-formatting buttons in the Report window let you set text, fill colors, and control line widths, and add three-dimensional effects to controls, such as a raised, sunken, or etched appearance.

✦ You can enhance the text of label and text box controls by changing the font type style, font size, and such font style attributes as bold, italic, or font color. Use the new properties in Access 2000 to enter margins and line spacing for controls. You can even add a shadow by duplicating the text or selecting the special effects.

New Feature Use the new grouping feature in Access 2000 to group common controls together so that they can be formatted and moved together all at one time.

✦ Multiple-line text box controls can display large amounts of text. To avoid leaving blank lines, set the Can Grow and Can Shrink properties to control the precise amount of space needed.

✦ Controls such as option buttons, checkboxes, and toggle buttons make it easier to view your data. You must delete an existing control before you can create one of these controls using the same data field.

✦ When any of these controls is placed inside an option group, they act together rather than separately, and only one is active at a time.

✦ Option buttons are generally used to let a user select only one of a group, whereas checkboxes and toggle buttons represent a two-state selection from Yes/No data types.

✦ Pictures can be displayed in reports using object frames. The two types of object frames are bound (the objects are attached to a data field in each record) and unbound (the objects are embedded in the report itself).

✦ Lines and rectangles let you separate areas of the report to add emphasis.

✦ Areas of the report can be further emphasized by adding color, background shading, three-dimensional effects, shadows, and reverse video.

✦ View your report by previewing it or by printing it to a hard-copy device.

✦ View as many as 20 pages at a time on one screen in the Print Preview window.

✦ Two types of print previews are available: print preview and layout preview. With print preview, you see your actual data; a layout preview uses only portions of your table data, but it is very fast.

✦ Printing selections are set from the Page Setup dialog box.

In the next chapter, you learn to create reports with totals and summaries.

✦   ✦   ✦

Creating Calculations and Summaries in Reports

In the preceding two chapters, you learned to design and build reports from a blank form as well as to create striking and effective output using many of the advanced features in Access. In this chapter, you learn to use expressions to calculate results.

On the CD-ROM If you don't want to build the reports created in this chapter, they are included on your sample disk in the Reports object button. The reports are named Monthly Invoice Report – No Cover, Monthly Invoice Report, Monthly Invoice Report – Percentages, and Monthly Invoice Report – Running Sum.

Note Because the Report Design window is set to a width of eight inches, you see most of the screen printouts in this chapter taken with an 800 x 600 resolution Super VGA Windows screen driver (rather than the standard 640 x 480 VGA Windows driver), which lets you see almost the entire screen in the figures.

Designing a Multilevel Grouping Report with Totals

In this chapter, you create a report that displays information about visits to the hospital for each customer's pets on specific days. This report displays data in an invoice format that lists the type of visit, treatments given, medication dispensed, and the cost of each of these items. The data is totaled for each line item and summarized for each visit. The report can display multiple pets for the same customer on the same day. Finally, totals are shown for each visit by a customer, including the total amount spent, any discounts, and tax. Figure 22-1 is a sample printed page of the report. Later in this chapter, you learn to enhance this report to display individual line-item percentages and cumulative running totals.

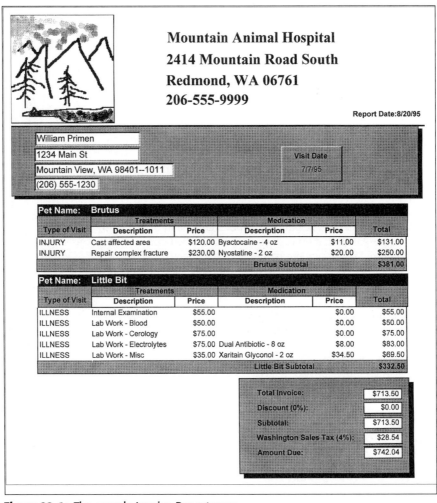

Figure 22-1: The sample Invoice Report page.

Designing the Invoice Report

The Invoice Report is an excellent example of the types of tasks necessary to create common types of reports. It uses many of Access's advanced report-writing features — sorting and grouping, group summaries, text expressions, and graphical objects. Invoice Report's design includes:

✦ The Mountain Animal Hospital name, address, phone number, and logo on the top of every page

✦ Owner detail information (customer name, street/apartment, city, state, ZIP code, and telephone)

✦ Visit date

✦ Pet name

✦ Visit detail information for each pet (including type of visit, treatment, treatment price, medication, medication price, and total cost)

✦ A subtotal that summarizes each pet's visit details (total cost subtotal for the pet)

✦ A subtotal that summarizes the total cost for each pet on a visit date for a particular owner and then calculates a total that lists and incorporates the owner's discount and proper state sales tax

The report design also must be shaped according to these considerations:

✦ The report must be sorted by the field's Visit Date, then Customer Number, and then Pet ID.

✦ No more than one visit date should appear per printed page.

✦ No more than one customer should appear per printed page.

✦ One or more pets belonging to the same owner can appear on each printed page.

✦ If there is more than one pet per invoice, the pets should be listed in Pet ID order.

The design for this report is shown in Figure 22-2. As you can see, each section is labeled, and each control displays either the field name control or the calculated control contents. With the exception of the Mountain Animal Hospital logo (an unbound object frame) and several lines and rectangles, the report consists primarily of text box controls.

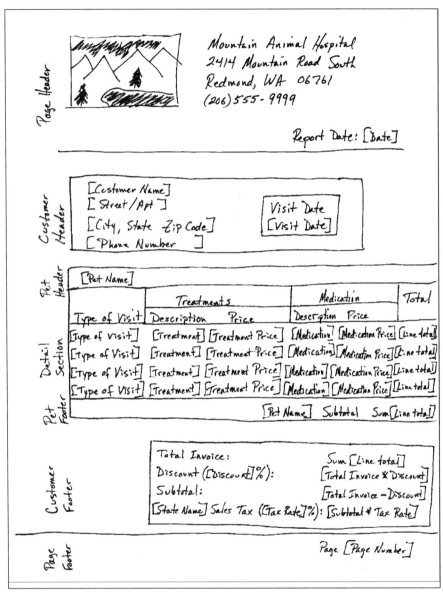

Figure 22-2: A design for the Invoice Report.

Designing and creating the query for the report

The Invoice Report uses fields from practically every table in the Mountain Animal Hospital database. Although the design in Figure 22-2 shows the approximate position and use of each control, it is equally important to perform a data design that lists each table field or calculated control. This data design should include the purpose of the field or control and the table in which the field originates. Using such a design plan, you can be sure to build a query that contains all the fields you may need. Table 22-1 lists these controls, the section in the report where they are used, and the originating table. Important: Do this type of data design *before* creating the query from which to build your report.

Table 22-1
The Data Design for the Invoice Report

Report Section	Control Purpose	Type of Control	Table Field/ Calculation	Table
Page header	Logo	Unbound object frame		
Page header	Name and address	Label controls (4)		
Page header	Report date	Calculated text box	Date Function	
Customer header	Customer name	Bound text box	Customer Name	Customer
Customer header	Street and apt.	Bound text box	Street/Apt	Customer
Customer header	City	Bound text box	City	Customer
Customer header	State	Bound text box	State	Customer
Customer header	ZIP code	Bound text box	ZIP Code	Customer
Customer header	Phone number	Bound text box	Phone Number	Customer
Customer header	Visit date	Bound text box	Visit Date	Visits
Pet header	Pet name	Bound text box	Pet Name	Pets
Pet header	Text labels	Label controls (8)		
Detail	Type of visit	Bound text box	Visit Type	Visit Details
Detail	Treatment	Bound text box	Treatment	Treatments
Detail	Treatment price	Bound text box	Treatment Price	Visit Details
Detail	Medication	Bound text box	Medication Name	Medications
Detail	Medication price	Bound text box	Medication Price	Visit Details
Detail	Line total	Calculated text box Price	Treatment Price + Medication	

Continued

Table 22-1 *(continued)*

Report Section	Control Purpose	Type of Control	Table Field/ Calculation	Table
Pet footer	Pet name	Calculated text box	Pet Name + Text	Pets
Pet footer	Line total sum	Calculated text box	Sum (Line Total)	
Customer footer	Text labels	Label controls (3)	Lines 1, 3, 5	
Customer footer	Discount label	Calculated text box	Text + Discount	Customer
Customer footer	State sales tax	Calculated text box	State Name + Tax Rate	States/Visits
Customer footer	Total invoice	Calculated text box	Sum (Line Total)	
Customer footer	Discount amount	Calculated text box	Total Invoice * Discount	
Customer footer	Subtotal	Calculated text box	Total Invoice − Discount	
Customer footer	Sales tax	Calculated text box	Subtotal * Tax Rate	Visits
Customer footer	Amount due	Calculated text box	Subtotal + Sales Tax	
Page footer	Page number	Calculated text box	Text + Page Number	

After you complete the data design for a report, you can skim the Table column to determine the tables necessary for the report. When you create the query, you may not want to select each field individually; if not, use the asterisk (*) field to select all the fields in each table. This way, if a field changes in the table, the query can still work with your report.

Caution   Remember that if a table field name changes in your query, you need to change your report design. If you see a dialog box asking for the value of a specific field when you run your report — or the text *#Error* appears in place of one of your values after you run it — chances are that a table field has changed.

After examining Table 22-1, you may notice that every table in the Mountain Animal Hospital database is needed for the report — with the exception of the Animals lookup table. You may wonder why you need *any* of the four lookup tables. The States, Animals, Treatments, and Medications tables are used primarily as lookup tables for data validation when adding data to forms, but they can also be used to look up data when printing reports.

In the Invoice Report, the State Name field from the States table is used for looking up the full state name for the sales tax label in the Customer footer. The Tax Rate field can also be found in the States table, but at the time of the visit, the current tax rate is copied to the Visits table for that record. Only the codes are stored in the Visit Details table, so Access looks up the Treatment and Medication Name fields from their respective tables.

These seven tables are all joined together using the Monthly Invoice Report query, as illustrated in Figure 22-3.

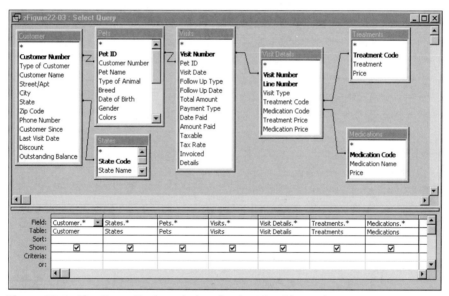

Figure 22-3: The Query Design window for the Monthly Invoice Report query.

After your query is completed, you can create your report.

Cross-Reference

Chapter 20 has a detailed explanation of how to create a new report from a blank form; it also shows you how to set page size and layout properly. If you are unfamiliar with these topics, read Chapter 20 before continuing. The present chapter focuses on multiple-level groupings, calculated and summarized fields, and expressions.

Designing test data

One of the biggest mistakes that can be made when designing and creating complex reports is not checking the results that the report displays. Before creating a complete report, you should have a good understanding of your data. One way is to create a query using the same sorting order the report will use and then create any detail line calculations. You can then check the query's datasheet results, using them to check the report's results. When you are sure that the report is using the correct data, you can be sure that it will always produce great results. Figure 22-4 is a simple query (the Monthly Invoice Report – Test Data) to use for checking the report that you create in this chapter.

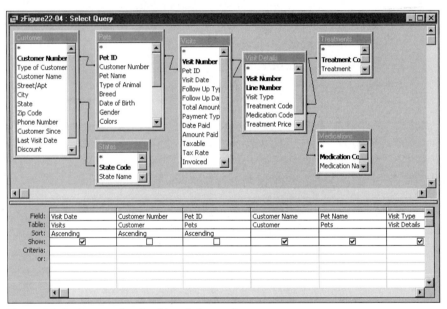

Figure 22-4: A query for checking data results.

The query in Figure 22-4 has three fields for sorting: Visit Date, Customer Number, and Pet ID. Only the first field is being viewed in the dynaset; the other two fields have the Show checkbox turned off. When you save this query and reopen it, the Customer Number and Pet ID fields will be moved to the end of the query skeleton.

Normally, you can make a copy of the report query, adding the sorting orders and using only the detail fields you need to check totals. You can then add the numbers manually or convert the query to a Total query to check group totals. Figure 22-5 shows the datasheet produced by this query; you can compare the results of each task in the report design to this datasheet.

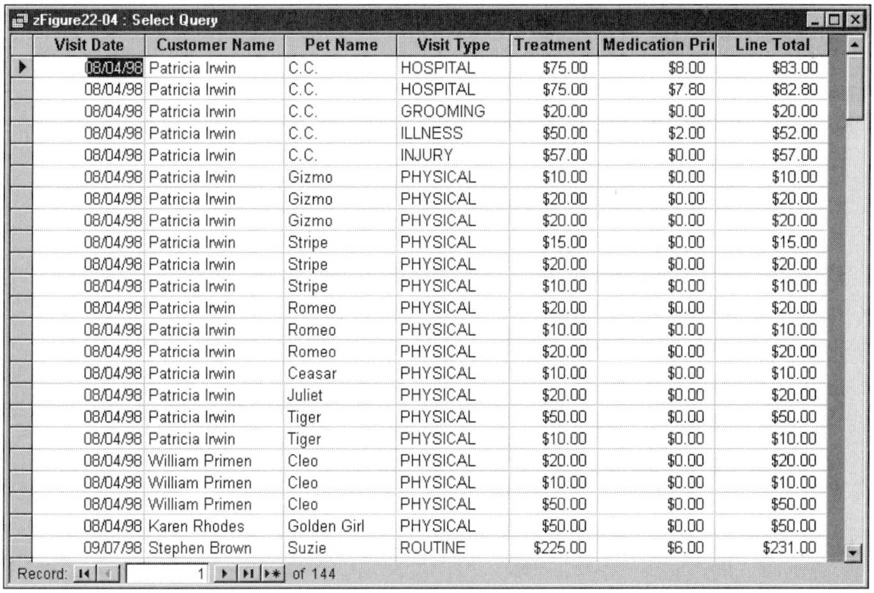

Visit Date	Customer Name	Pet Name	Visit Type	Treatment	Medication Pri	Line Total
08/04/98	Patricia Irwin	C.C.	HOSPITAL	$75.00	$8.00	$83.00
08/04/98	Patricia Irwin	C.C.	HOSPITAL	$75.00	$7.80	$82.80
08/04/98	Patricia Irwin	C.C.	GROOMING	$20.00	$0.00	$20.00
08/04/98	Patricia Irwin	C.C.	ILLNESS	$50.00	$2.00	$52.00
08/04/98	Patricia Irwin	C.C.	INJURY	$57.00	$0.00	$57.00
08/04/98	Patricia Irwin	Gizmo	PHYSICAL	$10.00	$0.00	$10.00
08/04/98	Patricia Irwin	Gizmo	PHYSICAL	$20.00	$0.00	$20.00
08/04/98	Patricia Irwin	Gizmo	PHYSICAL	$20.00	$0.00	$20.00
08/04/98	Patricia Irwin	Stripe	PHYSICAL	$15.00	$0.00	$15.00
08/04/98	Patricia Irwin	Stripe	PHYSICAL	$20.00	$0.00	$20.00
08/04/98	Patricia Irwin	Stripe	PHYSICAL	$10.00	$0.00	$10.00
08/04/98	Patricia Irwin	Romeo	PHYSICAL	$20.00	$0.00	$20.00
08/04/98	Patricia Irwin	Romeo	PHYSICAL	$10.00	$0.00	$10.00
08/04/98	Patricia Irwin	Romeo	PHYSICAL	$20.00	$0.00	$20.00
08/04/98	Patricia Irwin	Ceasar	PHYSICAL	$10.00	$0.00	$10.00
08/04/98	Patricia Irwin	Juliet	PHYSICAL	$20.00	$0.00	$20.00
08/04/98	Patricia Irwin	Tiger	PHYSICAL	$50.00	$0.00	$50.00
08/04/98	Patricia Irwin	Tiger	PHYSICAL	$10.00	$0.00	$10.00
08/04/98	William Primen	Cleo	PHYSICAL	$20.00	$0.00	$20.00
08/04/98	William Primen	Cleo	PHYSICAL	$10.00	$0.00	$10.00
08/04/98	William Primen	Cleo	PHYSICAL	$50.00	$0.00	$50.00
08/04/98	Karen Rhodes	Golden Girl	PHYSICAL	$50.00	$0.00	$50.00
09/07/98	Stephen Brown	Suzie	ROUTINE	$225.00	$6.00	$231.00

Record: ◀◀ ◀ 1 ▶ ▶▶ ▶* of 144

Figure 22-5: The datasheet showing test data.

Creating a Multilevel Grouping Report with Totals

With the report planning and data testing completed, it's time to create the new report. In Chapter 20, you learned how to create a report from a blank form. The steps to create a new report (and bind it to a query) are repeated here:

1. Press F11 to display the Database window if it is not already displayed.

2. Click the Report object button.

3. Click the New toolbar button. The New Report dialog box appears.

4. Select the Monthly Invoice Report query.

5. Select Design View.

6. Click OK.

7. Maximize the Report window.

A blank Report Design window showing three sections (Page Header, Detail, and Page Footer) appears. The report is bound to the query Monthly Invoice Report; data from that query is used when the report is viewed or printed. The fields from the query are available for use in the report design and appear in the Field List window.

You must also change the Printer Setup settings and resize the Report Design window area for the report (see Chapter 21 for details). The steps for specifying Page Setup settings are shown again here:

1. Select File ➪ Page Setup.

2. Select the Margins tab.

3. Click the Left Margin setting and change the setting to **0.250**.

4. Click the Right Margin setting and change the setting to **0.250**.

5. Click the Top Margin setting and change the setting to **0.250**.

6. Click the Bottom Margin setting and change the setting to **0.250**.

7. Click OK to close the Page Setup window.

Follow these steps to set the report width:

1. Click the rightmost edge of the report body (where the white area meets the gray).

2. Drag the edge to the 8-inch mark on the ruler.

3. Release the mouse button.

These steps complete the initial setup for the report. Next, you create the report's sorting order.

Creating the sorting orders

In a query, you can specify sorting fields as you did in the test query you created earlier. In a report, however, you must also specify the sorting order when you create groups; Access ignores the underlying query sorting. In the underlying query for this report, no sorting is specified because it must be entered here as well.

This report design has three sorting levels: Visit Date, Customer Number, and Pet ID. You need to use all these levels to define group headers, and you need the latter two for group footers. Look at the original design in Figure 22-2; Visit Date is not shown as a group. Later, you learn why a grouping to use the Visit Date header section is necessary.

Before you can add a grouping, you must first define the sort order for the report. You've already learned to do this task using the Sorting and Grouping box (shown completed in Figure 22-6).

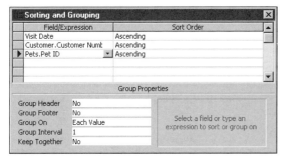

Figure 22-6: Creating the sorting orders.

To add the sorting orders as shown in Figure 22-6, follow these steps:

1. Click the Sorting and Grouping button on the toolbar to display the Sorting and Grouping box.

2. Click in the first row of the Field/Expression column of the Sorting and Grouping box. A downward-pointing arrow displays.

3. Click the arrow to display a list of fields in the Monthly Invoice Report query.

4. Select the Visit Date field in the field list. Notice that Sort Order defaults to Ascending.

5. Click in the second row of the Field/Expression column.

6. Click the arrow to display a list of fields in the Mountain Invoice Report query.

7. Select the Customer.Customer Number field in the field list. Notice that Sort Order defaults to Ascending.

8. Click in the third row of the Field/Expression column.

9. Click the arrow to display a list of fields in the Mountain Invoice Report query.

10. Select the Pets.Pet ID field in the field list. Notice that Sort Order defaults to Ascending.

Tip To see more of the Field/Expression column, drag the border between the Field/Expression and Sort Order columns to the right (as shown in Figure 22-6).

Cross-Reference You next learn to create the detail section for this report. Because this chapter focuses on expressions and summaries, be sure that you have read Chapters 20 and 21 and that you understand how to create and enhance the labels and text boxes in a report.

Creating the detail section

The detail section is shown in its entirety in Figure 22-7. The section has been completed and resized. Notice that there is no space above or below any of the controls, which allows multiple detail records to be displayed as one comprehensive section on a report. Because this section must fit snugly between the Pet header and Pet footer, as shown in Figures 23-1 and 23-2, it has been resized to the exact size of the controls.

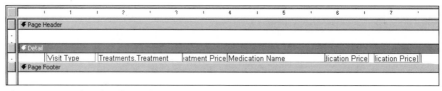

Figure 22-7: The detail section.

Creating the detail section controls

The detail section has five unlabeled bound text box controls, two line controls, and one calculated control:

- ✦ A Vertical line control
- ✦ Visit Details.Visit Type, bound text box control
- ✦ Treatments.Treatment, bound text box control
- ✦ Visit Details.Treatment Price, bound text box control
- ✦ Medications.Medication Name, bound text box control
- ✦ Visit Details.Medication Price, bound text box control
- ✦ Calculated unbound text control (formula is =[Treatment Price]+ [Medication Price])
- ✦ A Vertical line control

You need to drag each of these bound text box controls from the Report window field list onto the detail section and then properly size the controls. The default text box property Auto Label under the Format menu should be set to No.

The two line controls are vertical lines. One is on the left side of the detail section under the left edge of the Type of Visit text box control. The other is on the right side of the detail section under the right edge of the calculated control.

The last control is a calculated text box control. This control calculates the total of the Treatment Price and the Medication Price for each detail line. Enter this formula into a new unlabeled text box: =[Treatment Price]+[Medication Price]. A calculated control always starts with an equal sign (=), and each field name must be placed in brackets. Figure 22-7 also shows the property sheet for this calculated text box control, which is named Pet Line Visit Total. The Pet Line Visit Total control is formatted with the Currency format property so that the dollar signs appear. If any of the totals is over $1,000.00, the comma also appears. The Decimal Place property is set to Auto, which is automatically set to 2 for the Currency format.

Creating calculated controls

You can use any valid Access expression in any text control. Expressions can contain operators, constants, functions, field names, and literal values. Some examples of expressions are:

=Date()	Date function
=[Customer Subtotal]*[Tax Rate]	A control name multiplied by a field name
=Now()+30	A literal value added to the result of a function

The control (Control Source property), which is shown in Figure 22-7, calculates the total for each individual line in the detail section. To create this calculated control, follow these steps:

1. Create a new text control in the detail section, as shown in Figure 22-7.

2. Display the property sheet for the new text box control.

3. Enter =[Treatment Price]+[Medication Price] in the Control Source property cell.

4. Set the Format property to Currency.

Naming controls used in calculations

Every time you create a control, Access automatically inserts a name for it into the Control Name property of the control's property sheet. The name is really a description that defines which kind of control it is; for example, text controls show the name *Field* and label controls show the name *Text*. A sequential number follows each name. An example of a complete name is *Field13*. If the next control you create is a label, it is named *Text15*. These names can be replaced with user-defined names, such as Report Date, Sales Tax, or any other valid Access name, which lets you reference other controls easily (especially those containing expressions).

For example, if you have the fields Tax Rate and Subtotal and want to calculate Amount of Tax Due, you enter the expression =[Tax Rate]*[Subtotal] and call it Amount of Tax Due. You can then calculate Total Amount Due by entering the expression =[Subtotal]+[Amount of Tax Due]. This expression lets you change an expression in a calculated field without having to change all other references to that expression. To change the name of the control for Treatment Price + Medication Price Total, follow these steps:

1. Select the calculated control (=[Treatment Price]+[Medication Price]).

2. Display the property sheet.

3. Select the Name property.

4. Replace the default with **Pet Visit Line Total**.

Caution

Later, you learn that you cannot use a calculated control name in a *summary* calculation. Instead, you must summarize the original calculation. For example, rather than create an expression such as =Sum(Pet Visit Line Total), you must enter the summary expression =Sum([Treatment Price]+[Medication Price]).

Testing the detail section

As you complete each section, compare the results against the test datasheet you created, as shown in Figure 22-5. The easiest way to view your results is either to select the Print Preview button on the toolbar (to view the report onscreen) or to print the first few pages of the report. Figure 22-8 displays the Print Preview screen. If you compare the results to the test data in Figure 22-5, you'll see that all the records are correctly displayed. You may notice, however, that the records are not exactly in the right order. This is acceptable as long as groups of the same visit date for the same customer and pet are together. In Figure 22-5, the first five total amounts are $83.00, $82.80, $20.00, $52.00, and $57.00. In Figure 22-8, the first five totals are $83.00, $20.00, $52.00, $57.00, and, $82.80. Because the data is not yet sorted by the line number in the Visit Details table, the final sort is not precise.

Notice that the calculated control correctly calculates the sum of the two numeric price text box controls and displays them in the Currency format.

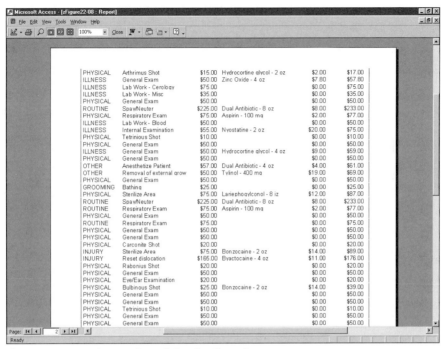

Figure 22-8: A print preview of the detail section.

Creating the Pet ID header and footer sections

When the detail section is complete, you can move *outward* to create the inner group headers and footers. The innermost group is the Pet ID group. You need to create both a header and a footer for this section.

To create group headers and footers for the Pet ID sort you already created, you only have to change the Group Header and Group Footer properties of the Pets.Pet ID Field/Expression to Yes (as shown in Figure 22-9). To make this change, follow these steps:

1. Display the Sorting and Grouping box if it is not displayed.

2. Click the Pets.Pet ID row in the window.

3. Click the Group Header property and change it to Yes.

4. Click the Group Footer property and change it to Yes.

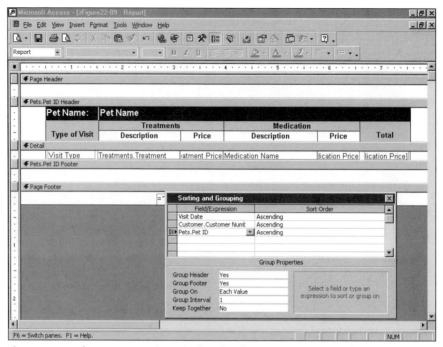

Figure 22-9: The Report Design window for the Pets.Pet ID group header.

Note After a group header or footer is defined, the first column of the Sorting and Grouping box for the field you created in the header or footer displays a grouping icon (the same icon you see when you select the Sorting and Grouping button on the toolbar).

The Pet ID header and footer sections should now be displayed.

Creating the Pet ID header controls

The Pets.Pet ID group header, shown in Figure 22-9 along with the Sorting and Grouping box, creates a group break on Pet ID, which causes each pet's individual visit details to be grouped together. This is the section where the pet's name is displayed, as well as labels that describe the controls that appear in the detail section.

No calculated controls are in this header. There are no lines or rectangles. With the exception of the pet name itself, in fact, all controls are label controls. Each label control is stretched so that the borders make perfect rectangles on the desired areas and the text is centered where appropriate. The Fore Color and Back Color buttons are then used for coloring the background and the text.

Notice the use of reverse video in the Pet Name label and text control. Also notice that the Type of Visit, Treatments, Medication, and Total label controls display black text on a light gray background. This setup, along with the borders, creates a visually appealing section. There is no room between the bottom of the controls and the bottom of the section. This (along with the lack of space in the detail section) creates the illusion that several sections are really one. You create the label controls Type of Visit and Total by pressing Ctrl+Enter before you enter the text, which makes it use two lines.

Creating the Pet ID footer controls

The Pets.Pet ID group footer, shown in Figure 22-10, is where you subtotal all the visit detail information for each pet. Thus, if a pet has more than one treatment or medication per visit, the report summarizes the visit detail line items in this section; even if there is only one detail record for a pet, a summary is displayed.

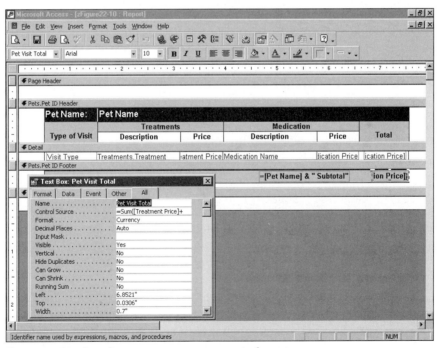

Figure 22-10: Creating a group summary control.

The Pets.Pet ID footer section contains three controls:

Rectangle	Displays the boundaries of the section and is shaded in light gray
Label control	Displays Pet Name and the text Subtotal
Summary text box control	Displays the total of all Pet Visit line totals for each pet

The rectangle completes the area displayed under the detail section; it serves as a *bottom cap* on the preceding two sections. Notice that there is no space between the top of the controls and the top of the section. Notice also how the edges line up, setting the entire section (Pet ID header, detail section, Pet ID footer) apart from other areas of the report.

The first control combines the Pet Name field with the text Subtotal. This is done using a process known as *concatenation*.

Using concatenation to join text and fields

Concatenation operators can combine two strings. (A string is either a field or an expression.) Several different operators can be used for concatenation, including these:

+	Joins two Text data type strings
&	Joins two strings; also converts non-Text data types to Text data

The + operator is standard in many languages, although it can easily be confused with the arithmetic operator used to add two numbers. The + operator requires that both strings being joined are Text data types.

The & operator also converts nonstring data types to string data types; therefore, it is used more than the + operator. If, for example, you enter the expression ="Today's Date Is:" & Date(), Access converts the result of the date function into a string and adds it to the text *Today's Date Is:*. If the date is August 26, 1998, the result returned is a string with the value *Today's Date Is:8/26/98*. The lack of space between the colon and the 8 is not an error; if you want to add a space between two joined strings, you must add one.

Access can join any data type to any data type using this method. If you want to create the control for the Pet Name and the text Subtotal using this method, you enter the expression =[Pet Name] & " Subtotal", which appends the contents of the Pet Name field to the text Subtotal. No conversion occurs because the contents of Pet Name and the literal value Subtotal are both already text. Notice that there is a space between the first double quotation mark and the text Subtotal.

Note   If you use the + operator for concatenation, you must convert any nonstring data types; an example is using the CStr( ) function to return a date with the Date( ) function to a string data type. If you want to display the system date with some text, you have to create a text control with the following contents:

```
="Today's Date Is:" +cstr(Date())
```

You can insert the contents of a field directly into a text expression by using the ampersand (&) character. The syntax is

```
="Text String "&[Field or Control Name]&" additional text
string"
```

or

```
[Field or Control Name]&" Text String"
```

Use this method to create the control for the Pet Name text box control by following these steps:

1. Create a new text control in the Pets.Pet ID footer section.

2. Enter the expression = [Pet Name]&" Subtotal" (as shown in Figure 22-10).

Calculating group summaries

Creating a sum of numeric data within a group is very simple. Following is the general procedure for summarizing group totals for bound text controls:

✦ Create a new text control in the group footer (or header).

✦ Enter the expression =Sum([Control Name]) where *Control Name* is a valid field name in the underlying query or the name of a control in the report.

If, however, the control name is for a calculated control, you have to repeat the control expression. Suppose that in the Pets.Pet ID footer you want to enter the following expression into the text box control to display the total of the detail line:

```
=Sum([Pets Line Visit Total])
```

If you try this, it won't work; that is simply a limitation of Access. To create a sum for the totals in the detail section, you have to enter:

```
=Sum([Treatment Price]+[Medication Price])
```

This is how the summary shown in Figure 22-10 was created.

Access 2000 knows to sum the detail lines for the Pet ID summary because you put the summary control in the Pets.Pet ID section. Each time the value of the Pet ID changes, Access resets the summary control automatically. Later, when you create this same summary control in the Customer ID footer section, Access resets the total only when the value of Customer ID changes.

You can use expressions in a report in two ways. The first is to enter the expression directly in a text control. For example, enter:

```
[Treatment Price]+[Medication Price]
```

The second way is to create the expression in the underlying query, as you saw in Figure 22-4, where you created a field named Line Total in the query itself. You can then use the calculated field of the query in a text control on the report. The advantage of the former method is that you have the flexibility to create your expressions *on the fly* as well as the ability to reference other report objects, such as text controls with expressions. The disadvantage is that you cannot use summary expressions on calculated controls.

If you add a calculated field to your underlying query, you can then refer to this field in the detail section or in any group section. The syntax you use is:

```
=Sum([Calculated Field Name])
```

If you want to create the detail section Line Total and Pet ID Subtotal by using the calculation from the query, first you create the query's calculated field as

```
Line Total: [Treatment Price]+[Medication Price]
```

Then you create the summary control in the report as

```
=Sum([Line Total])
```

Either method works and either method is acceptable.

Use the Print Preview window to check the progress of your report. Figure 22-11 displays the report created so far; notice how the three sections come together to form one area.

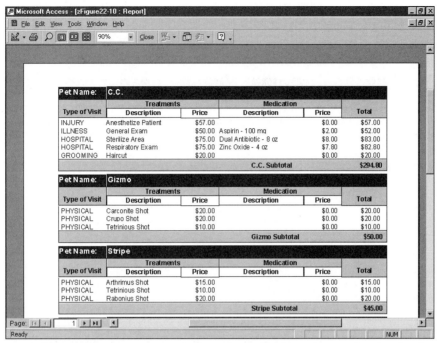

Figure 22-11: The Print Preview window of a report's Pet ID group header, the detail, and the group Pet ID footer sections.

Creating the Customer Number header and footer sections

When the Pet ID sections are complete, you can move outward again to create the next outer group header and footer. The next group as you move outward is Customer Number; you can create a header and footer for this section by following these steps:

1. Display the Sorting and Grouping box if it is not already displayed.

2. Click the Customer.Customer Number row in the window.

3. Click the Group Header property and change it to Yes.

4. Click the Group Footer property and change it to Yes.

One task remains: Each new customer for a specific date should be displayed on a separate page. As it currently exists, the report has no specific page breaks. You can create a page break every time the customer number changes by setting the

Force New Page property of the Customer.Customer Number header to Before Section. Doing so ensures that each customer's information is printed on a separate page.

Creating the Customer Number header controls

Figure 22-12 shows the Customer.Customer Number group header completed (at the top of the report design). This section is very similar to the Customer section created in Chapters 20 and 21. Seven fields are used in this section:

✦ Customer Name

✦ Street/Apt

✦ City

✦ State

✦ Zip Code

✦ Phone Number

✦ Visit Date

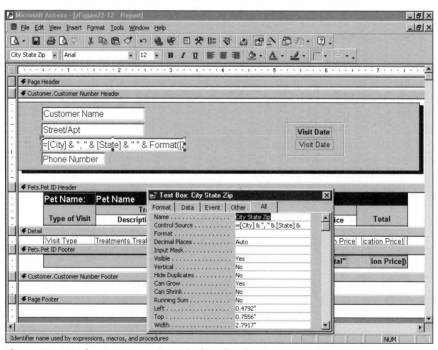

Figure 22-12: The Report Design window for the Customer.Customer Number group header.

The first six controls are from the Customer table; the Visit Date control is from the Visits table. The entire section is surrounded by a gray shaded rectangle and a shadow box.

Cross-Reference   Chapter 21 explains how to create this effect.

The Visit Date control has an attached label and is surrounded by a transparent rectangle (which you create by setting the Back Color window's Transparent button). The control uses the etched appearance option; the Customer controls are sunken (a three-dimensional effect created by selecting the Sunken button in the Special Effect window).

One change you can make is to rearrange the display of the City, State, and Zip Code fields. Rather than display these fields as three separate controls, you can concatenate them to appear together. You can save space by compressing any trailing spaces in the city name, adding a comma after city, and also by compressing the space between State and Zip Code. You can make these changes by creating a concatenated text box control. Follow these steps:

1. Delete the City, State, and Zip Code controls in the Customer Number header.

2. Create a new unlabeled text box control.

3. Enter `=[City]&", "&[State]&" "&[Zip Code]` in the Control Source property of the text box control.

The only problem with this expression is that the ZIP code is formatted in the Zip Code table field, using the @@@@@-@@@@ format to add a hyphen between the first five and last four characters. As currently entered, the control may display the following value when run: *Lakeville, OR 974011021.*

You still need to format the Zip Code field. Normally, the function Format( ) is used for formatting an expression. In this example, the function should be written as:

```
Format([Zip Code],"@@@@@-@@@@")
```

You can add this function to the concatenation expression, substituting the Format expression in place of the Zip Code field. To complete this example, change the control to:

```
=[City]&", "&[State]&" "&Format([Zip Code],"@@@@@-@@@@")
```

To check the Customer Number group heading, view the report in the Print Preview window, as shown in Figure 22-13.

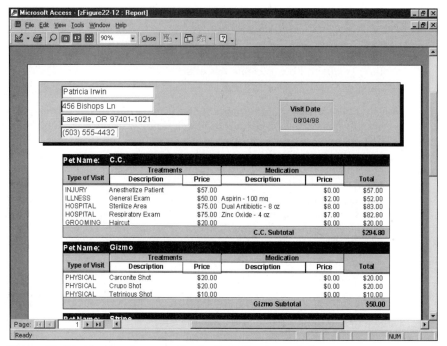

Figure 22-13: Viewing the report in the Print Preview window.

Creating the Customer Number footer controls

The Customer.Customer Number footer section contains 10 controls: 5 label controls and 5 text box controls. The text box control expressions (and their associated labels) are listed in Table 22-2.

Table 22-2
Expressions in the Customer Number Footer

Expression Name	Label Control	Text Box Control
Customer Total	Total Invoice:	=Sum([Treatment Price]+[Medication Price])
Discount Amount	="Discount	=[Customer Total] *[Discount] ("&[Discount]*100&"%):"
Customer Subtotal	Subtotal:	=[Customer Total]–[Discount Amount]
State Sales Tax	=[State Name]& "Sales Tax (" & [Visits.Tax Rate]* 100 & "%):"	=[Customer Subtotal] *[Visits.Tax Rate]
Amount Due	Amount Due:	=[Customer Subtotal]+[State Sales Tax]

Each of the concatenated label controls uses the same standard notation you learned in this chapter; each of the text box controls is a simple expression. Notice that Customer Total uses exactly the same expression as the Pet ID total, except that now it resets the total by Customer Number.

The Customer.Customer Number footer (shown in Figure 22-14) is where you create and summarize the line-item totals for each pet for a particular owner for a particular visit. You also want to display a customer's discount rate, the amount of the discount in dollars, the customer's state, the state sales tax as a percentage, the state sales tax in dollars, and (finally) a total for the amount due. All this information will appear in separate boxes with shadows; these boxes are created using the shadow special effect on the rectangle. The steps for each of the controls follow.

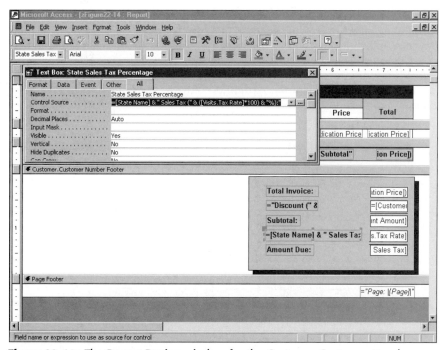

Figure 22-14: The Report Design window for the Customer.Customer Number group footer.

Because the first group has many pets and visit detail lines, you have to look at page 3 to see the first customer number footer. To create the label for Total Invoice (and for the text box controls), follow these steps:

1. Create a new label control.

2. Change the Caption property to **Total Invoice:**.

3. Create a new text box control.

4. Change the Name property to **Customer Total**.

5. Change the Control Source property to =Sum([Treatment Price]+
[Medication Price]).

Follow these steps to create the Discount Amount label and text box controls:

1. Create a new label control.

2. Change the Control Source property to ="Discount
("&[Discount]*100&"%):", which concatenates the word *Discount* with the
customer's discount rate and then multiplies by 100 to give a percentage.

3. Create a new text box control.

4. Change the Name to **Discount Amount**.

5. Change the Control Source to =[Customer Total]*[Discount], which
multiplies the customer's discount rate by the amount calculated in the
Customer Total control.

To check the Customer Number group footer, view the report in the Print Preview
window, as shown in Figure 22-15.

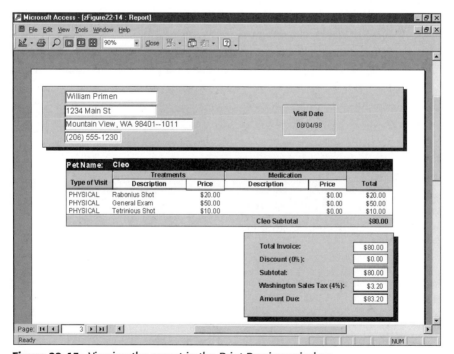

Figure 22-15: Viewing the report in the Print Preview window.

To create the Customer Subtotal label and text box controls, follow these steps:

1. Create a new label control.

2. Change the caption to **Subtotal:**.

3. Create a new text box control.

4. Change the Name to **Customer Subtotal**.

5. Change the Control Source to `=[Customer Total]-[Discount Amount]`, which subtracts the amount calculated in the Discount Amount control from the sum calculated in the Customer Total control.

Create the State Sales Tax label and text box controls with these steps:

1. Create a new label control.

2. Change the Control Source to `=[State Name] & " Sales Tax ("&[Visits.Tax Rate]*100&"%):"`, which concatenates the customer's state name (full spelling) and the words *Tax Rate* with the customer's tax rate, and then multiplies by 100 to give a percentage.

3. Create a new text box control.

4. Change the Name to **State Sales Tax**.

5. Change the Control Source to `=[Customer Subtotal]*[Tax Rate]`, which multiplies the customer's state tax rate by the amount calculated in the Customer Subtotal control.

Next, create the Amount Due label and text box controls:

1. Create a new label control.

2. Change the Caption to **Amount Due:**.

3. Create a new text box control.

4. Change the Name to **Amount Due**.

5. Change the Control Source to `=[Customer Subtotal]+[State Sales Tax]`, which adds the customer's calculated state sales tax to the amount calculated in the Customer Subtotal control.

Creating the Visit Date header

You have one more group header to create — Visit Date — but it won't display anything in the section. The section has a height of 0; essentially, it's *closed*. The purpose of the Visit Date header is to force a page break whenever the Visit Date changes. Without this section, if you were to have two customer records for the same customer on different dates that appear consecutively in the report's dynaset, the records would appear on the same page. The only forced page break you created so far is for Customer Number. By adding one for Visit Date, you complete the report groupings. To create the Visit Date grouping for the header and add the page break, follow these steps:

1. Display the Sorting and Grouping box if it is not already displayed.

2. Click the Visit Date row Field/Expression column.

3. Click the Group Header property.

4. Click the arrow and select Yes from the drop-down list.

5. Double-click the section to display its property sheet.

6. Change the Height property to **0**.

7. Change the Visible property to No.

8. Change the Force New Page property to Before Section.

Creating the page header controls

The page header appears at the top of every page in the Invoice Report. The page header and footer controls are not controlled by the Sorting and Grouping box; View ➪ Page Header/Footer have to be selected. In this report, the page header has been open all the time. This section contains a small version of the Mountain Animal Hospital logo in the upper-left corner, as well as the name, address, and phone number for the hospital. The section also contains the report date and a horizontal line at the bottom to separate it visually from the rest of the page. By default, the page header and footer are created and displayed automatically when a new report is created. All you have to do is change the height and add the proper controls.

In Chapter 21, you learned to add the unbound bitmap MTN.BMP to the report. The label controls that display the Mountain Animal Hospital page header are four separate controls. The only control that needs explanation is the Report Date control.

Access offers several built-in functions that let you display and manipulate date and time information. The easiest to start with is the Date( ) function, which returns the current system date when the report is printed or previewed. To add a text control to the report header that displays the date when the report is printed, follow these steps:

1. Create a new text control in the page header, as shown in Figure 22-16.

2. Display the control's property sheet.

3. In the Control Source property cell, type ="Report Date: "&Date( ).

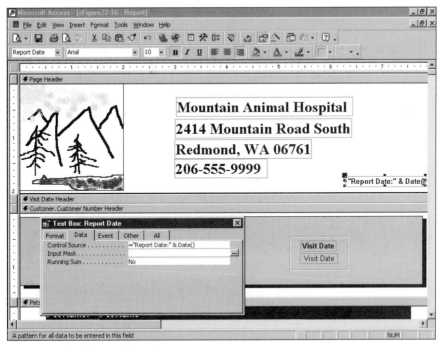

Figure 22-16: The page header.

This process concatenates the text Report Date with the current system date.

Another date function Access offers is DatePart( ), which returns a numeric value for the specified portion of a date. The syntax for the function is:

```
DatePart(interval,date,firstweekday,firstweek)
```

where *interval* is a string expression for the interval of time you want returned and *date* is the date to which you want to apply the function.

Table 22-3 lists some valid intervals and the time periods they represent.

The date can be a literal date (such as 1-Jan-1993) or a field name that references a field containing a valid date.

Table 22-3
DatePart( ) Intervals

Interval	Time Period
yyyy	Year
q	Quarter
m	Month
y	Day of year
d	Day
w	Weekday
ww	Week
h	Hour
n	Minute
s	Second

Expression	Result
=DatePart("yyyy",25-Dec-1999)	1999 (the year)
=DatePart("m",25-Dec-1999)	12 (the month)
=DatePart("d",25-Dec-1999)	25 (the day of the month)
=DatePart("w",25-Dec-1999)	6 (the weekday; Sunday=1, Monday=2 . . .)
=DatePart("q",25-Dec-1999)	4 (the quarter)

Creating the page footer controls

Normally, the page footer is used to place page numbers or to hold page totals. For this report, the footer's only purpose is to display a thick, horizontal line at the bottom of every page, followed by the page number in the bottom right corner.

To number the pages in your report, Access provides the Page function. You access it by using it in an expression in a text control that returns the current page of the report. As with all expressions, one that has the Page property in it must be preceded by an equal sign (=). To create a footer with a page number, follow these steps:

1. Create a new text control in the lower-right section of the page footer.

2. Display the control's property sheet.

3. In the Control Source property cell, type =`"Page: "&Page`.

4. Select the Italics button on the toolbar.

Although it makes the most sense to put the page number in the page header or page footer, you can place a control with the Page property in any section of your report. You can also use the Page property as part of an expression. For example, the expression =`Page*10` displays the result of multiplying the actual page number by 10.

You have now completed the Monthly Invoice Report. Compare your report design with the one shown originally in Figure 22-2 and then with the final output in Figure 22-17. Figure 22-17 shows page 14 of the report, a good example of displaying all the sections on one page. (Look back at Figure 22-1 to see a hard-copy of the report page.)

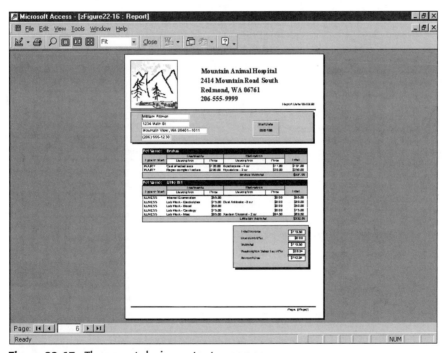

Figure 22-17: The report design output onscreen.

Before moving on, you need to create a few more controls. Because Access features a *two-pass report writer*, you can create controls based on knowledge of the final report. For example, you can create a control that displays the percentage of one total to a grand total or create a cumulative total to display cumulative totals.

Calculating percentages using totals

To determine what percent of the total cost for a pet's visit each line is, calculate a line percentage. By comparing the line item to the total, you can calculate the percentage of a particular item to a whole. To do so, you need to move all the controls for the Pet ID header and footer and the detail section to the far left side of the report. To create a new control that displays what percentage of the whole (Mountain Animal Hospital Charges) is for each pet, follow these steps:

1. Duplicate the Pet Visit Line Total control.

2. Position the duplicate to the right of the original.

3. Change the Control Source to =[Pet Visit Line Total]/[Pet Visit Total].

4. Change the Format property to Percent.

5. Create a new label control with the caption **Percent** above it, as shown in Figure 22-18.

The calculation takes the individual line total control [Pet Visit Line Total] in the detail section and divides it by the summary control [Pet Visit Total] in the page header section. The Percent format automatically handles the conversion and displays a percentage.

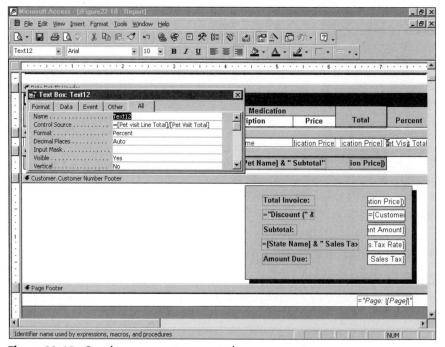

Figure 22-18: Creating a percentage control.

Calculating running sums

Access also lets you calculate *running sums* (also known as *cumulative totals*) easily; simply change the Running Sum property for a control. To create a running total of how much is spent as each pet's charges are totaled, follow these steps:

1. Duplicate the rectangle and its controls in the Pets.Pet ID footer section.

2. Display the new rectangle just below the existing one, as shown in Figure 22-19.

3. Select the label control and change the caption to =[Customer Name]&"'s Running Total".

4. Select the new control with this expression: =Sum([Treatment Price]+[Medication Price]).

5. Display the control's property sheet.

6. Change the Name to **Running Total**.

7. Click the Running Sum property.

8. Select Over Group from the drop-down list shown in Figure 22-19.

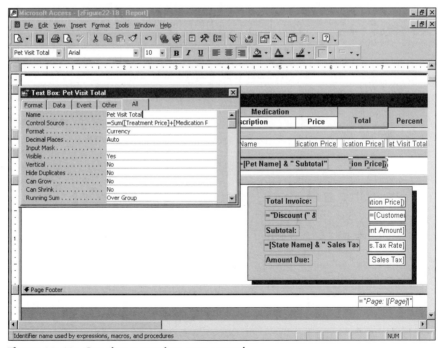

Figure 22-19: Creating a running sum control.

Access will now add the current subtotal to all previous subtotals for each owner. Alternatively, you can create a running sum across all values in a report. This is useful if you want to present an overall summary in the report's footer section.

You can display the percentages and the running total by performing a print preview, as shown in Figure 22-20.

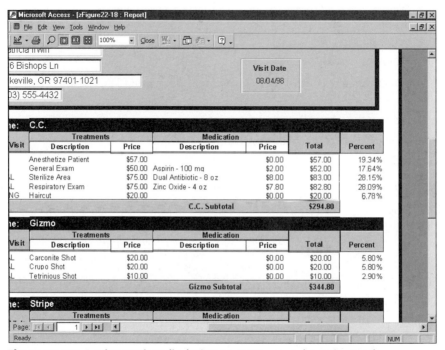

Figure 22-20: A print preview displaying percentages and running totals.

Creating a title page in a report header

The primary purpose of the report header (illustrated in Figure 22-21) is to provide a separate title page. From the report description given earlier, you know that the report header must contain Mountain Animal Hospital's logo, name, address, and phone, as well as a report title. In the sample Monthly Invoice Report file, all of these controls are created for you.

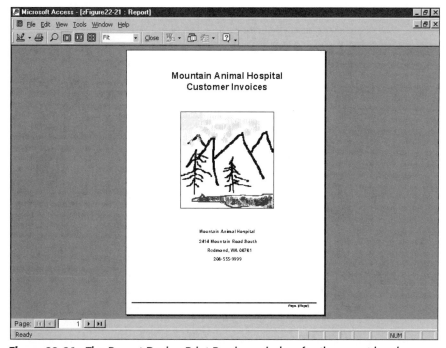

Figure 22-21: The Report Design Print Preview window for the report header.

If you created the report from scratch, you can follow these steps to create a report header:

1. Select View ➪ Report Header/Footer.

2. Click the report header section and then open its Properties sheet.

3. Resize the height of the report header section to about 9_ inches.

4. Set the Force New Page property of the report header section to After Section so that a page break occurs after the report header.

5. Create label controls for the report title, name, address, and phone.

6. Create an image picture control (using MTN.BMP) and change the Size Mode property to Stretch.

Using the report footer

The report footer is not actually used in this report; it's displayed because the report header cannot be displayed in Design view without it. The normal use of the report footer is for grand totals that occur once in the report. You can also use it in an accounting-type report or in a letter concerning the totals for an audit trail.

Summary

In this chapter, you learned to create multilevel reports. These points were covered:

✦ Access lets you easily create multilevel grouping reports.

✦ A calculated control contains mathematical expressions.

✦ Text box controls can contain field names or expressions.

✦ Text expressions use the concatenation operators + or & to combine text strings and/or text strings and other data types.

✦ The Date( ) function returns the current system date.

✦ The DatePart( ) function returns a numeric value for the specified portion of a date.

✦ Controls can, and should be, named. You can then reference them in other controls.

✦ When you use the =Sum( ) function in a group header or footer (or page or report header or footer), it summarizes all the values of a field within that group.

✦ Access can use summary totals to calculate line-item or group-total percentages.

✦ Access can perform running sums within a group as well as across groups.

In the next chapter, you learn to link to external data by attaching, importing, and exporting.

✦   ✦   ✦

Advanced Database Features

Working with External Data

So far, you have worked only with data in Access tables. In this chapter, you explore the use of data from other types of files. You learn to work with data from database, spreadsheet, and text-based files.

Access and External Data

Exchanging information between Access and another program is an essential capability in today's database world. Information is usually stored in a wide variety of application programs and data formats. Access (like many other products) has its own native file format, designed to support referential integrity and provide support for rich data types such as OLE objects. Most of the time, this format is sufficient; occasionally, however, you need to move data from one Access database file to another or even to or from a different software program's format.

Types of external data

Access has the capability to use and exchange data among a wide range of applications. For example, you may need to get data from other database files (such as FoxPro, dBASE, or Paradox files) or obtain information from an SQL Server, Oracle, or a text file. Access can move data among several categories of applications:

- ✦ Other Windows applications
- ✦ Macintosh applications (Foxbase, Foxpro, Excel5, and 98)
- ✦ Spreadsheets
- ✦ PC database management systems
- ✦ Server-based database systems (ODBC)
- ✦ Text or mainframe files

Methods of working with external data

Often you will need to move data from one application or file into your Access database. You may need to obtain information you already have in an external spreadsheet file. You can reenter all the information by hand — or have it *imported* into your database. Perhaps you need to put information from your Access tables into Paradox files. Again, you can reenter all the information into Paradox by hand or have the information *exported* to the Paradox table. Access has tools that allow you to move data from a database table to another table or file. It could be a table in Access, dBASE, or Paradox; it could be a Lotus 1-2-3 spreadsheet file. In fact, Access can exchange data with more than 14 different file types, including the following:

✦ Access database objects (all types, all versions)

✦ dBASE III+, IV, and 5

✦ FoxPro 2.*x* and 3.0

✦ Paradox 3.*x*, 4.*x*, and 5.0

✦ Text files (ANSI and ASCII; DOS or OS/2; delimited and fixed-length)

✦ Lotus 1-2-3 2.*x* and 3.*x*

✦ Excel 3.0 and greater

✦ ODBC (Microsoft SQL Server, Sybase Server, Oracle Server, and other ODBC 1.1-compliant databases)

✦ HTML tables and lists

✦ Outlook and Outlook Express

✦ IDC/HTX (Internet Information Services) resources

Access can work with these external data sources in several ways. Table 23-1 lists the methods available for working with external data along with a description of each method.

Table 23-1
Methods of Working with External Data

Method	Purpose
Link	Creates a link to a table in another Access database or uses the data from a different database format
Import	Copies data *from* a text file, another Access database, or another application's format into an Access table
Export	Copies data from an Access table *to* a text file, another Access database, or another application's format

Should you import or link data?

As Table 23-1 shows, you can work with data from other sources in two ways: linking or importing. Both methods allow you to work with the external data.

There is a distinct difference between the two methods:

✦ Importing makes a copy of the external data and brings the copy into the Access table.

✦ Linking uses the data in its current file format (such as a dBASE or Paradox file).

Each method has clear advantages and disadvantages.

Note   *Linking* in Access 2000 and 97 was called *attaching* in Access 2.0 and 1.*x*. When to import external dataAccess cannot link to certain file formats; these include 1-2-3 spreadsheet files. If you need to work with data from formats that cannot be linked to, you must import it. You can, however, link to Excel files in Access 2000.

Note   Access 2000 has the ability to link to HTML and text tables for read-only access. You can use and look at tables in HTML or text format; however, the tables cannot be updated nor records added to them using Access 2000.

Of course, importing data means that you have significantly increased the storage space required for that particular data because it now resides in two different files on the storage device.

Caution   Because importing makes another copy of the data, you may want to erase the old file after you import the copy into Access. Sometimes, however, you won't want to erase it. For example, the data may be sales figures from a spreadsheet still in use. In cases such as this, simply maintain the duplicate data and accept that storing it will require more space.

Working with Other Access Databases

Access can open only one database at a time; therefore, you can't work directly with a table in a different database. Even so, if you need to work with tables or other Access objects (such as forms and queries) from another Access database, you don't have to close the current one. Instead, simply import or link the object in the other database to your current database. You'll be able to view or edit data directly in more than one database table.

One of the principal reasons to import data is to customize it to meet your needs. You can specify a primary key, change field names (up to 64 characters), and set other field properties. With linked tables, on the other hand, you are restricted to setting very limited field properties. For example, you cannot specify a primary key, which means that you can't enforce integrity against the linked table.

Note   When you link to another Access database, you can do everything you can do with tables in the primary database, including defining primary keys and enforcing referential integrity.

When to link to external data

If you leave data in another database format, Access can actually make changes to the table while the original application is still using it. This capability is useful when you want to work with data in Access that other programs also need to work with. For example, you might need to obtain updated personnel data from a dBASE file (maintained in an existing networked dBASE application) so that you can print a monthly report in Access. Another example is when you use Access as a front end for your SQL database—you can link to an SQL table and update the data directly to the server, without having to "batch upload" it later.

The biggest disadvantage of working with linked tables is that you lose the internal capability of Access to enforce referential integrity between tables (*unless* you are linked to an Access database).

Linking External Data

Access can directly link to several database management system (DBMS) tables individually or simultaneously. After an external file is linked, Access builds and stores a link to the table.

Database connectivity

As the database market continues to grow, the need to obtain information from many different sources will escalate. If you have information captured in an SQL Server table or a Paradox table, you don't want to reenter the information from these tables into Access. Ideally, you want to open the table and use the information in its native format, without having to copy it or write a translation program to access it. For many companies today, this capability of accessing information from one database format while working in another is a primary goal.

Copying or translating data from one application format to another is both time-consuming and costly. The time it takes can mean the difference between success and failure. Therefore, you want a *heterogeneous* environment between your DBMSs and the data. Access provides this environment through linking tables.

Types of database management systems

Access lets you connect, or *link*, to several different DBMSs, directly accessing information stored in them. Following are the database systems Access supports:

✦ Other Access database tables

✦ dBASE (versions III, IV, and 5)

✦ FoxPro (versions 2.*x* and 3.0)

✦ Paradox (versions 3.0, 4.*x*, and 5.0)

✦ Microsoft SQL Server, Sybase Server, Oracle, or any ODBC-aware database

You can link to any of these table types, individually or mixed together. If you link to an external file, Access displays the filename in the Database Table window (just as it does for other Access tables), but the icon linked with the table will be different. It starts with an arrow pointing from left to right and points to an icon. A table icon tells you that it's an Access table, a dB icon tells you that it's a dBASE table, and so on. Figure 23-1 shows several linked tables at the top of the list, which are all external tables. These tables are linked to the current database. Notice that all the linked tables have an icon with an arrow. (The icon clues you in to the type of file that is linked).

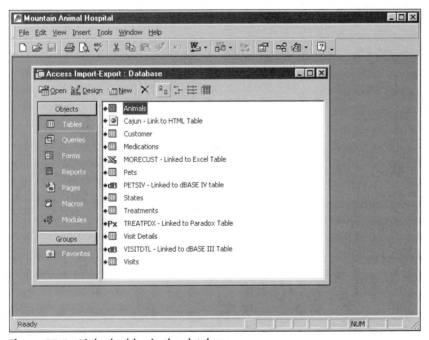

Figure 23-1: Linked tables in the database.

In Figure 23-1, the arrows that appear to the left of some of the table names indicate linked tables. In addition to the link arrow indicator, you can tell by their icon which type of file they are linked to. For instance, the web page displays the web icon, Excel has the X symbol, Paradox has the Px symbol, and dBASE tables have the dB symbol.

After you link a table to your Access database, you can use it as you would any other table. You can query against it, link another table to it, and so on. For example, Figure 23-2 shows a query design and dynaset using several linked tables Customer (from Excel), PETSIV (from dBASE), and Visits (from another Access database). Your application does not have to use Access tables at all; you can just as easily link to the Paradox and FoxPro tables.

Figure 23-2: A query design and dynaset of externally linked tables.

Caution

After you link an external table to an Access database, you *cannot* move the table to another drive or directory. Access does not actually bring the file into the MDB file; it maintains the link via the filename *and* the drive:path. If you move the external table, you have to update the link using the Linked Table Manager.

On the CD-ROM

The examples in this chapter use the database Access Import-Export.mdb. This database is included on your CD-ROM along with several different types of DBMS files: Paradox, dBASE IV, and dBASE III+with indexes.

Linking to other Access database tables

When you work with an Access database, normally you create every table you want to use in it. If the table exists in another Access database, however, you can link to the table in the other Access database (rather than re-creating it and duplicating its data). You may, for example, want to link to another Access table that is on a network.

After you link to another Access table, you use it just as you use another table in the open database. To link to the Visits table in the Mountain Animal Hospital Access database from the Access Import-Export.mdb database file, follow these steps:

1. Open the Access Import-Export.mdb database.

2. Select File ➪ Get External Data ➪ Link Tables... (as shown in Figure 23-3). Access opens the Link dialog box.

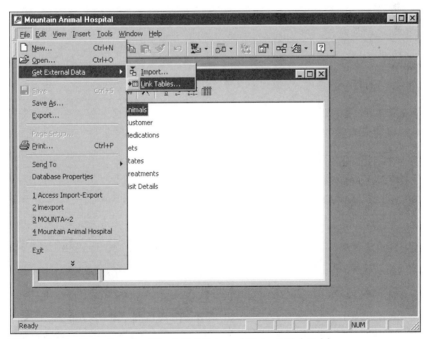

Figure 23-3: Selecting the File ➪ Get External Data ➪ Link Tables... menu commands.

You can select the .MDB file you want to link to. You can also change the type of files displayed in the Link dialog box; it can link to any type of external data. Though the default is to show only Access files (.MDB), you can link to any of the supported file types.

3. Find and select the Mountain Animal Hospital.MDB file in the dialog box. You may have to search for a different drive or directory.

4. Double-click on the Mountain Animal Hospital.MDB file (or select it and click on the Link button). Access will close the dialog box and display the Link Tables dialog box.

5. Select Visits and click on OK.

After you link the Visits table from the Mountain Animal Hospital database, Access returns to the Database window and shows you that the Visits table is now linked to your database. Figure 23-4 shows the Visits table linked to the current database. Notice the arrow on the Visits table's icon; it shows that the table has been linked from another source.

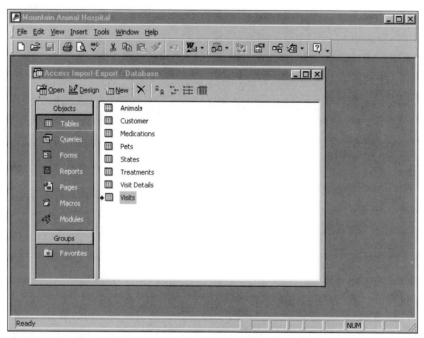

Figure 23-4: The Database window with the Visits table added.

Tip   You can link more than one table at a time by selecting each table before you click on the OK button. You can also use the Select All button to select all the tables.

Splitting an Access database into multiple linked databases

Generally, you split an Access application into two databases. One contains only your tables; the other contains all your queries, forms, reports, macros, and modules. This is extremely important when moving an application to a multiuser environment. The database with the queries, forms, reports, macros, and modules are installed on each client machine, and the database with the source tables is installed on the server. This arrangement has several major benefits:

✦ Everyone on the network shares one common set of data.

✦ Many people can update data at the same time.

✦ When you want to update the forms, reports, macros, or modules, you don't have to interrupt processing or worry about data corruption.

If you start with your database split when you create a new application, it's easier to complete your application later. Some things you just can't do with a linked table without doing a little extra work; these tasks include finding records and importing data. By using different techniques with linked tables, however, you can do anything you can do with a single database.

If you're starting from scratch, you first create a database with just the tables for your application. You then create another new database and link the tables from the first database to the second (as you learned in the preceding section).

After you have built a system with all your objects (including the tables) in one database file, however, it's a little more difficult to split your tables. One method is to create a duplicate copy of your database. In one version, you delete all objects leaving only the tables. In the other version, you delete only the tables. Then you use the database file without the tables as a starting point and then link to all the tables in the table database.

Access 2000 includes a Wizard, called the Database Splitter, that can do this for you automatically. Using the Mountain Animal Hospital database, for example, you can split all the tables into a separate database file. Later, you can import all the tables back into the original database if you want, or continue to use the split database files.

You start the Database Splitter Wizard by selecting Tools ⇨ -Database Utilities ⇨ Database Splitter. This displays a set of Wizard screens to help you split a single database into two files. The first Wizard screen simply confirms that you want to split the database, as shown in Figure 23-5.

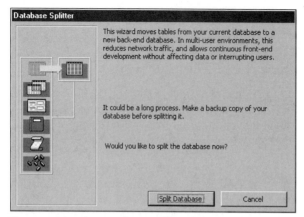

Figure 23-5: The Database Splitter Wizard.

When you click on the Split Database button, you see the standard Windows File Save dialog box (named the Create Back-end Database dialog). Here, you can enter the name of the new database you want Access to create with just the tables. When you're ready for Access to split the tables, click on the Split button.

Caution   The Database Splitter is not installed if you selected the standard installation option when you installed Office2000. You should have your Office2000 CD handy when you select this option.

Access creates the new database, copies all the tables from the original database to the new database, and then links to them. When the process is done, a message tells you that the database was successfully split. Figure 23-6 shows the original database file with linked tables.

Linking to dBASE and FoxPro databases (tables)

You can link to DBF files in either dBASE or FoxPro format. As with other Access database tables, after an *x*BASE (dBASE or FoxPro) file is linked, you can view and edit data in the DBF format.

dBASE and FoxPro save tables in individual files with the extension DBF. In *x*BASE, these DBF files are called databases. In Access, however, a *table* is equivalent to an *x*BASE *database*. (Access considers a *database* a complete collection of all tables and other related objects.) To maintain consistency in terminology, this book considers *x*BASE databases to mean the same thing as dBASE or FoxPro tables.

Figure 23-6: Linked tables in the Mountain Animal Hospital database.

Access and dBASE/FoxPro indexes

When you link a dBASE or FoxPro file, you can also tell Access to use one or more index files (NDX and MDX for dBASE, and IDX and CDX for FoxPro). The use of these indexes will improve performance of the link between *x*BASE and Access.

If you inform Access of the associated index files, Access will update the indexes every time it changes the DBF file. By linking a DBF file and its associated indexes, Access can link to DBFs in real time in a network environment. Access recognizes and enforces the automatic record-locking feature of dBASE and FoxPro as well as the file and record locks placed with *x*BASE commands and functions.

> **Tip** You should always tell Access about any indexes associated with the database. If you don't, it will not update them; dBASE or FoxPro will have unexpected problems if their associated index files are not updated.

When you tell Access to use one or more associated indexes (NDX, MDX, IDX, or CDX) of a dBASE or FoxPro file, Access maintains information about the fields used in the index tags in a special information file. This file has the same name as the dBASE or FoxPro file with an INF extension.

Caution If you link a dBASE or FoxPro file and associated indexes, Access must have access to the index files in order to link the table. If you delete or move the index files or the Access INF file, you will not be able to open the linked DBF file.

Linking to dBASE IV tables

Linking to FoxPro tables and dBASE tables works the same. For example, to link the dBASE IV table PETSIV.DBF and its associated memo file (DBT), follow these steps:

1. Open the Access Import-Export database and select File ➪ Get External Data ➪ Link Tables....

2. In the Link dialog box, select Files of type: dBASE IV. Access displays just the dBASE IV DBF files.

3. Double-click on PETSIV.DBF in the Select Index Files list box. (The memo file PETSIV.DBT is linked automatically and given the DBF extension.) Access activates the Select Index Files box and displays all NDX and MDX files.

4. Click on the Cancel button (there are no related indexes for this table). Access closes the Select Index Files box and displays a dialog box to indicate that the link was successful.

   Note: If there are any indexes to associate with this table, you select them here.

5. Click on the OK button. Access redisplays the Select File dialog box.

6. Click on the Close button to finish linking dBASE files. Access displays the Database window with the file PETSIV linked.

Note You can cancel linking at any time by clicking on the Cancel button in the Select File dialog box before you select a table.

Caution When you add index files, Access automatically creates and updates an Access information file. This file contains information about the index and associated dBASE or FoxPro file, has the same name, and ends in the extension INF.

Linking to Paradox tables

You can link DB files in either Paradox 3.x or Paradox 4.x formatAfter a Paradox file is linked, you can view and edit data the data just like an Access database table.

Access and Paradox index files

If a Paradox table has a primary key defined, it maintains the index information in a file that ends in the extension PX. When you link a Paradox table that has a primary key defined, Access links the associated PX file automatically.

Caution   If you link a Paradox table that has a primary key, Access needs the PX file in order to open the table. If you move or delete the PX file, you will not be able to open the linked table.

Tip   If you link a Paradox table to Access that does not have a primary key defined, you will not be able to use Access to update data in the table; you can only view it.

Access can link to DBs in real time in a network environment. Access recognizes and enforces the file- and record-locking features of Paradox.

Linking to nondatabase tables

You can also link to Excel, HTML tables, and text tables. When you select one of these types of data sources, Access will run a Link Wizard that will prompt you through the process.

If you link to an Excel table, you can update its records from within Access 2000 or any other application that can update Excel spreadsheets.

Linking to HTML and text tables will let you view and use tables in queries, forms, and reports. However, you cannot change the current record contents or add new records.

The Access 2000 Link Wizard

When you link to an Excel spreadsheet, HTML table, or text file, Access 2000 will automatically run a Link Wizard to help you. In each case, you will be asked whether the first line (record) contains the field names for the fields. If it does, click on the check box to turn it on. If the first record does not hold the field names, you will be given the option of specifying a name for each field or accepting the default names (field1, field2, field3, and so on).

Working with Linked Tables

After you link to an external table from another database, you can use it just as you would use another Access table.

After external tables are linked, you can use them with forms, reports, and queries. When working with external tables, you can modify many of their features; for example, you can rename the table, set view properties, and set links between tables in queries.

Setting view properties

Although an external table can be used like another Access table, you cannot change the structure (delete, add, or rearrange fields) of an external table. You can, however, set several table properties for the fields in a linked table:

✦ Format

✦ Decimal Places

✦ Caption

✦ Input Mask

Setting relationships

Access does not let you set permanent relations at the table level between non-Access external tables and Access tables. If you need to set a relationship between an external table and another Access table, you must do it in a query. Then you can use the query in a form, another query, or a report.

Setting links between external tables

To set a link between an external table and another Access table, simply create a query and use the drag-and-drop method of setting links. After a link is set, you can change the join properties from equi-join (inner join) to external join by double-clicking on the link.

Using external tables in queries

When using a query, you can join the external table with another table, internal or external. This gives you powerful flexibility when working with queries. Figure 23-7 shows a query using several different database sources:

✦ An Excel spreadsheet

✦ An HTML document (table)

✦ Access tables (both internal and linked)

✦ A Paradox table

✦ A dBASE IV table

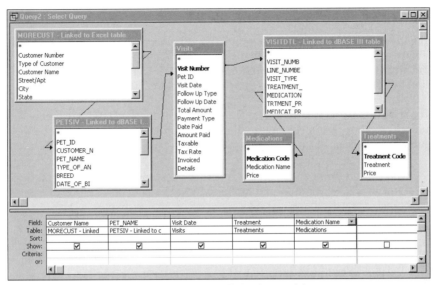

Figure 23-7: A query using several external database tables.

Notice that the query in Figure 23-7 has joins between all tables. This query will obtain information from all the tables and display a datasheet similar to the one in Figure 23-8.

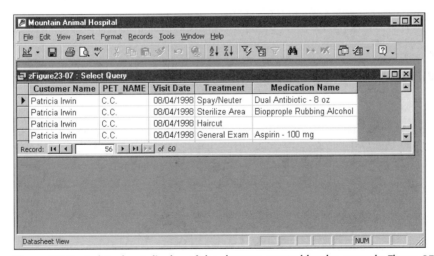

Figure 23-8: A datasheet display of the dynaset created by the query in Figure 23-7.

Renaming tables

You can rename a linked external table. Because Access lets you name a table with as many as 64 characters (including spaces), you may want to rename a linked table to be more descriptive. For example, you may want to rename the dBASE table called PETSIV to Pets Table from dBASE.

To rename a file, you can select Edit ⇨ Rename... from the Database menu. Another (quicker) method is to click on the filename, click on it again, and enter a new name.

Note   When you rename an external file, Access does not rename the actual DOS filename or SQL Server table name. It uses the new name only in the Table object list of the Access database.

Optimizing linked tables

When working with linked tables, Access has to retrieve records from another file. This process takes time, especially when the table resides on a network or in an SQL database. When working with external data, you can optimize performance by observing these points:

✦ *Avoid using functions in query criteria.* This is especially true for aggregate functions, such as DTotal or DCount, which retrieve all records from the linked table automatically and then perform the query.

✦ *Limit the number of external records to view.* Create a query specifying a criterion that limits the number of records from an external table. This query can then be used by other queries, forms, or reports.

✦ *Avoid excessive movement in datasheets.* View only the data you need to in a datasheet. Avoid paging up and down and jumping to the last or first record in very large tables. (The exception is when you're adding records to the external table.)

✦ *If you add records to external linked tables, create a form to add records and set the DataEntry property to True.* This makes the form an entry form that starts with a blank record every time it's executed.

✦ *When working with tables in a multiuser environment, minimize locking records.* This will free up records for other users.

Deleting a linked table reference

To delete a linked table from the Database window, follow these steps:

1. In the Database window, select the linked table you want to delete.

2. Either press the Delete key or select Edit ➪ Delete from the Database menu.

3. Click on OK in the Access dialog box to delete the file.

Note

Deleting an external table will delete only its name from the database object list. The actual file will not be deleted.

Viewing or changing information for linked tables

After a table is linked, neither it nor its associated indexes should be moved. If they are, Access will not be able to find them. You can use the Linked Table Manager to reestablish linked files.

If you move, rename, or modify tables or indexes associated with a linked table, you can use the Linked Table Manager to update the links. To use this tool, select Tools ➪ -Database Utilities ➪ Linked Table Manager. Access will display a dialog box similar to the one shown in Figure 23-9. Select the linked table that needs the information changed; Access will verify that the file cannot be found and will prompt you for the new information.

Figure 23-9: The Linked Table Manager.

Importing External Data

When you import a file (unlike when you link tables), you copy the contents from an external file into an Access table. You can import external file information from several different sources:

✦ Microsoft Access (other unopened database objects: forms, tables, and so on)

✦ Paradox 3.*x*, 4.*x*, and 5.0

✦ FoxPro 2.*x* and 3.0

✦ dBASE III, IV, and 5

✦ SQL databases (Microsoft SQL Server, Sybase Server, and Oracle Server)

✦ Delimited text files (fields separated by a delimiter)

✦ Fixed-width text files (specific widths for each field)

✦ Microsoft Excel (all versions)

✦ Lotus 1-2-3 and 1-2-3 for Windows (versions WKS, WK1, and WK3)

✦ An HTML document

✦ IDC/HTX (Microsoft Internet Information Server)

You can import information to either new tables or existing tables, depending on the type of data being imported. All data types can be imported to new tables, but only spreadsheet and text files can be imported to existing tables.

When Access imports data from an external file, it does not erase or destroy the external file. Therefore, you will have two copies of the data: the original file (in the original format) and the new Access table.

Note   If the filename of the importing file already exists in an Access table, Access adds a chronological number (1, 2, 3, and so on) to the filename until it has a unique table name. If an importing spreadsheet name is Customer.XLS (for example) and there is an Access table named Customer, the imported table name becomes Customer1. If Customer and Customer1 tables already exist, Access creates a table named Customer2.

Importing other Access objects

You can import other Access database tables or any other object in another database. You can therefore import an existing table, query, form, report, macro, or module from another Access database.

In addition to the standard Access objects, Access 2000 allows you to import custom toolbars and menus into the current database.

As an example, use these steps to import the States table from the Mountain Animal Hospital Access database:

1. Open the Access Import-Export database and select File ➪ Get External Data ➪ Import. (An Import dialog box appears.)

2. In the Import dialog box, select Files of type: Microsoft Access.

3. Double-click on Mountain Animal Hospital.MDB. Access closes the Import select database dialog box and opens the Import Objects dialog box, as shown in Figure 23-10. At the bottom of this selection box, you can click on the Options> button to specify import options.

4. In the box, select the States table by clicking on States and then clicking on the OK button.

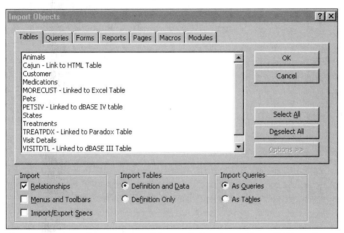

Figure 23-10: The Import Objects dialog box after clicking the Options button.

Access imports the States table into the Access Import-Export database and closes the Import Objects dialog box. You can select more than one item at a time, using the Select All and Deselect All buttons to select or deselect all the objects in a specific category or by control-clicking if you only desire a few. The Options> button lets you further define how to import Access data.

You can choose to import relationships, custom toolbars, and import/export specifications from an Access database. You can determine whether the tables you import come in with just the table design or with the data as well. Finally, the last set of options lets you decide whether queries you import come in as queries or run as make-table action queries to import a new table. (See Chapter 25 for details about make-table queries.)

The States table appears in the Database window display without a link symbol in the icon. Unlike linking the table, you have copied the States table and added it to the current database. Therefore, because it's not linked but instead an actual part of the database, it occupies space like the original Access table does.

Besides adding tables from other Access databases, you can also add other objects (including queries, forms, reports, macros, or modules) by clicking on each of the tabs in the Import Objects dialog box. You can select objects from each and then import them all at one time.

Importing PC-based database tables

When importing data from personal-computer-based databases, you can import two basic categories of database file types:

✦ *x*BASE (dBASE, FoxPro)

✦ Paradox

Each type of database can be imported directly into an Access table. The native data types are converted to Access data types during the conversion.

Importing a PC-based database

You can import any Paradox, dBASE III, dBASE IV, dBASE V, FoxPro, or Visual FoxPro database table into Access. To import one of these, simply select the correct database type in the Files of type: box during the import process.

After selecting the type of PC-based database, you select which file you want to import; Access imports the file for you automatically.

If you try to import a Paradox table that is encrypted, Access prompts you for the password after you select the table in the Select File dialog box. Enter the password and click on the OK button to import an encrypted Paradox table.

When Access imports *x*BASE fields, it converts them from their current data type into an Access data type. Table 23-2 lists how the data types are converted.

Table 23-2 Conversion of Data Types from *x*BASE to Access	
***x*BASE Data Type**	**Access Data Type**
Character	Text
Numeric	Number (property of Double)
Float	Number (property of Double)
Logical	Yes/No
Date	Date/Time
Memo	Memo

When importing any *x*BASE database file in a multiuser environment, you must have exclusive use of the file. If other people are using it, you will not be able to import it.

As with *x*BASE tables, when Access imports Paradox fields, the Paradox fields are converted from their current data type into an Access data type. Table 23-3 lists how the data types are converted.

Table 23-3 Conversion of Data Types from Paradox to Access	
Paradox Data Type	**Access Data Type**
Alphanumeric	Text
Number	Number (property of Double)
Short Number	Number (property of Integer)
Currency	Number (property of Double)
Date	Date/Time
Memo	Memo
Blob (Binary)	OLE

Importing spreadsheet data

You can import data from Excel or Lotus 1-2-3 spreadsheets to a new or existing table. The key to importing spreadsheet data is that it must be arranged in tabular (columnar) format. Each cell of data in a spreadsheet column must contain the same type of data. Table 23-4 demonstrates correct and incorrect columnar-format data.

Tip   You can import or link all the data from a spreadsheet, or just the data from a named range of cells. Naming a range of cells in your spreadsheet can make importing into Access easier. Often a spreadsheet is formatted into groups of cells. One group of cells may contain a listing of sales by customer, for example. The section below the sales listing may include total sales for all customers, totals by product type, or totals by month purchased. By naming the range for each group of cells, you can limit the import to just one section of the spreadsheet.

Table 23-4 represents cells in a spreadsheet, in the range A1 through F7. Notice that the data in columns A, B, and C and rows 2 through 7 is the same type. Row 1 contains field names. These columns can be imported into an Access table. Column D is empty and cannot be used. Columns E and F do *not* have the same type of data in each of their cells; they may cause problems when you try to import them into an Access table.

Table 23-4
Spreadsheet Cells with Contents

A	B	C	D	E	F
1	TYPE	WEIGHT	BDATE	JUNK	GARBAGE
2	DOG	122	12/02/92	123	YES
3	CAT	56	02/04/89	22	134.2
4	BIRD	55	05/30/90	01/01/91	DR SMITH
5	FROG	12	02/22/88	TEST	$345.35
6	FISH	21	01/04/93	══	══
7	RAT	3	02/28/93	$555.00	<══ TOTAL

Figure 23-11 shows an Excel spreadsheet named MORECUST.XLS (actually a spreadsheet with some of the same fields and data as other Mountain Animal Hospital tables).

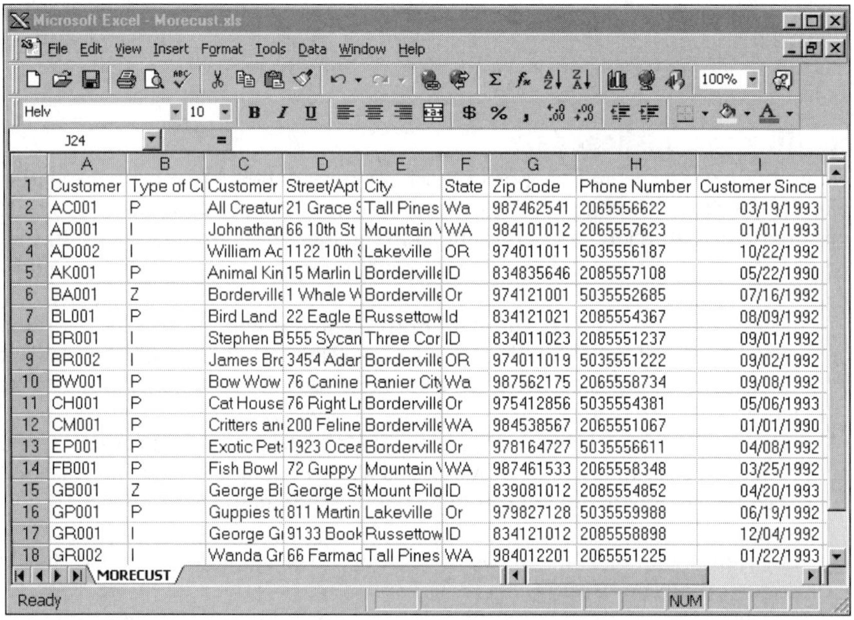

Figure 23-11: An Excel spreadsheet.

To import the Excel spreadsheet named MORECUST.XLS, follow these steps:

1. Open the Access Import-Export database and select File ⇨ Get External Data ⇨ Import.

2. In the Import dialog box, select Files of type: Microsoft Excel (*.xls). Then double-click on MORECUST.XLS in the select box. Access closes the Import box and displays the first Spreadsheet Import Wizard screen.

3. Access opens the first Import Spreadsheet Wizard screen for the table MORECUST.XLS; the screen resembles the one shown in Figure 23-12.

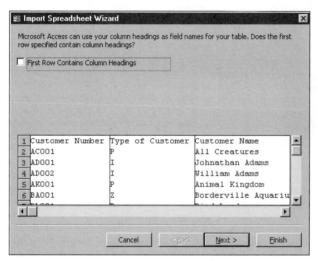

Figure 23-12: The first Import Spreadsheet Wizard screen.

This screen displays a sample of the first few rows and columns of the spreadsheet. You can scroll the display to see all the rows and columns if you want. Enter the starting row number to import the data. To use the first row of the spreadsheet to name fields in the table, use the check box.

4. Click on the First Row Contains Column Headings check box. The display changes to show the first row and column headings.

5. Click on Next> to display the second screen.

This screen lets you determine where the data will go. You can create a new table or add to an existing table.

6. Click on Next> to display the third screen.

   This screen (shown in Figure 23-13) lets you click on each column of the spreadsheet to accept the field name, change it, and decide whether it will be indexed; the Wizard determines the data type automatically. You can also choose to skip each column if you want.

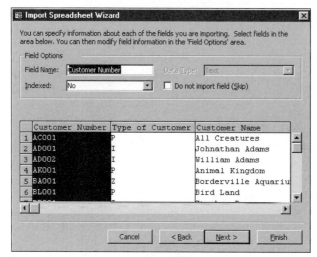

Figure 23-13: Determining the field names and data types.

7. Click on Next> to display the next Import Spreadsheet Wizard screen.

   This screen lets you choose a field for the primary key. You can let Access create a new AutoNumber field (by choosing Let Access add Primary Key), enter your own (by selecting Choose my own Primary Key and selecting one of the columns), or have no primary key. Figure 23-14 shows these options.

8. Select Choose my own Primary Key and select the Customer Number field.

9. Click on Next to display the last Import Spreadsheet Wizard screen.

   The last screen lets you enter the name for the imported table and (optionally) run the Table Analyzer Wizard.

10. Click on Finish to import the spreadsheet file. Access 2000 informs you that it imported the file successfully.

The filename now appears in the Access database window. A standard Access table has been created from the original spreadsheet file.

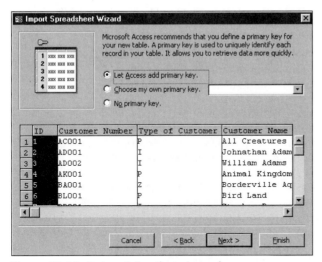

Figure 23-14: Determining the primary key.

Importing from word-processing files

Access does not offer a specific way to import data from word-processing files. If you need to import data from a word-processing file into Access, convert the word-processing file to a simple text file first and then import it as a text file. Most word processors have the capability to convert their formatted text to text files or ASCII files.

Importing text file data

Mainframe data is ordinarily output to a text file for use in desktop applications. You can import from two different types of text files: *delimited* and *fixed-width*. Access uses an *import/export specification* file as a guide in processing these types of files.

Access 2000 uses one Wizard for both types of text files. The Import Text Wizard assists you in identifying the fields for the import/export specification.

Delimited text files

Delimited text files are sometimes known as comma-delimited or tab-delimited files; each record is on a separate line in the text file. The fields on the line contain no trailing spaces, normally use commas as field separators, and require certain fields to be enclosed in a *delimiter* (such as single or double quotation marks). Usually the text fields are also enclosed in quotation marks or some other delimiter, as in these examples:

```
"Irwin","Michael","Michael Irwin Consulting",05/12/72
"Prague","Cary","Cary Prague Books and Software",02/22/86
"Zimmerman-Schneider","Audrie","IBM",01/01/59
```

Notice that the file has three records (rows of text) and four fields. Each field is separated by a comma, and the text fields are delimited with double quotation marks. The starting position of each field, after the first one, is different. Each record has a different length because the field lengths are different.

Tip   You can import records from a delimited text file that has fields with no values. To specify a field with no value, place delimiters where the field value would be, and put no value between them (for example, `"Irwin","Michael",,05/12/72`). Notice that there are two commas after the field content "Michael" and before the field content `05/12/72`. The field between these two has no value; it will be imported with no value into an Access file.

Fixed-width text files

Fixed-width text files also place each record on a separate line. However, the fields in each record are of a fixed length. If the field contents are not long enough, trailing spaces are added to the field, as shown in the following example:

```
Irwin      Michael        Michael Irwin Consulting  05/12/82
Prague    Cary   Cary Prague Books and Software   02/22/86
Zimmerman           Audrie IBM    01/01/59
```

Notice that the fields are not separated by delimiters. Rather, they start at exactly the same position in each record. Each record has exactly the same length. If a field is not long enough, trailing spaces are added to fill the field.

You can import either a delimited or a fixed-width text file to a new table or existing Access table. If you decide to append the imported file to an existing table, the file's structure must match that of the Access table you're importing to.

Note   If the Access table being imported has a key field, the text file cannot have any duplicate key values or the import will report an error.

Importing delimited text files

To import a delimited text file named MEDLIMIT.TXT, follow these steps:

1. Open the Access Import-Export database and select File ➪ Get External Data ➪ Import.

2. In the Import dialog box, select Files of type: Text files (*.txt).

3. Double-click on MEDLIMIT.TXT in the File Name list box. Access displays the first screen of the Import Text Wizard dialog box for the table MEDLIMIT.TXT. The dialog box resembles the one shown in Figure 23-15.

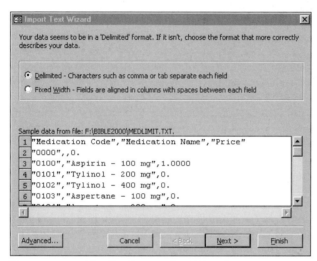

Figure 23-15: The first Import Text Wizard screen.

This screen displays the data in the text file and guesses whether the text file is delimited or fixed width. As you can see, the Wizard has determined correctly that the file is delimited.

Note Notice at the bottom of the screen the button marked Advanced. Click on it to further define the import specifications. You will learn more about this option in the upcoming section about fixed-width text files. Generally, it's not needed for delimited files.

4. Click on the Next> button to display the next Import Text Wizard screen.

As you can see in Figure 23-16, this screen lets you determine which type of separator to use in the delimited text file. Generally this separator is a comma, but you could use a tab, semicolon, space, or other character (such as an asterisk), which you enter in the box next to the Other option button. You can also decide whether to use text from the first row as field names for the imported table.

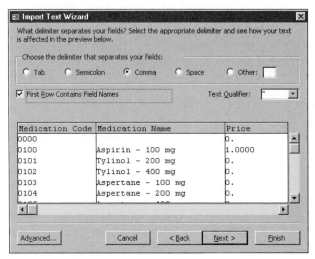

Figure 23-16: The second Import Text Wizard screen.

5. Click on the First Row Contains Field Names check box to use the first row for field names. Access will redisplay the text file with the first row as the column headers.

6. Click on the Next> button to display the next Import Text Wizard screen.

This screen lets you determine whether you're storing the imported data in a new table or an existing table. If you decide to use an existing table, you have to choose it from a list.

The next few screens are exactly the same as the Spreadsheet Import Wizard screens you saw earlier in this chapter.

7. Click on the Next> button to display the next Import Text Wizard screen, which lets you select each column of the Text Import grid, accept or change the field name, decide whether it will be indexed, and set the data type (which is also automatically determined by the Wizard). You can choose to skip a column if you want.

8. Click on Next> to display the next Import Text Wizard screen.

This screen lets you choose a field for the primary key. You can let Access create a new AutoNumber field (by choosing Let Access add Primary Key), enter your own (by selecting Choose my own Primary Key and selecting one of the columns), or have no primary key.

9. Click on the option button that says Choose my own Primary Key and select the field Medication Code.

10. Click on Next> to display the last Import Text Wizard screen.

The last screen lets you enter the name for the imported table and (optionally) run the Table Analyzer Wizard.

11. Click on Finish to import the delimited text file.

Access creates a new table, using the same name as the text file's name. The filename appears in the Access Database window, where Access has added the table MEDLIMIT.

Importing fixed-width text files

In *fixed-width* text files, each field in the file has a specific width and position. Files downloaded from mainframes are the most common fixed-width text files. As you import or export this type of file, you must specify an import/export setup specification. You create this setup file by using the Advanced options of the Import Table Wizard.

To import a fixed-width text file, follow these steps:

1. Open the Access Import-Export database and select File ⇨ Get External Data ⇨ Import.

2. In the Import dialog box, select Files of type: Text files (*.txt).

3. Double-click on PETFIXED.TXT in the File Name list box. Access opens the first screen of the Import Text Options Wizard dialog box for the table PETFIXED.TXT. (The dialog box resembles the one shown in Figure 23-15.)

This screen displays the data in the text file and guesses whether the type of text file is delimited or fixed width. As you can see, the Wizard has correctly determined that it's a fixed-width file.

4. Click on Next> to display the next Import Text Wizard screen.

This screen makes a guess about where columns begin and end in the file, basing the guess on the spaces in the file.

Figure 23-17 shows that Access has not done a good job in this file. It has recognized the first field correctly, but the second three fields have been lumped together. You'll need to add field break lines at positions 32, 33, and 34. You can do this on this screen by pointing between the columns of data and pressing the mouse button. The idea is to show the end of the Date field, the beginning and end of the Type of Animal field (1, 2, 3), the Gender field (M, F), and the beginning of the Weight field.

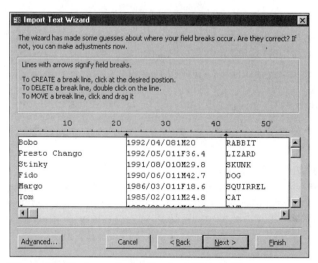

Figure 23-17: Importing a fixed-width text file.

As you can see in Figure 23-17, you can drag a field break line, add one, or delete one to tell Access where the fields really are.

As you you use these wizard tools to define the field widths, you're completing an internal data table known as Import/Export Specifications.

Figure 23-18 shows the Import Specification screen. If you click on the Advanced button in the Import Text Wizard, the Import Specification screen appears.

The section labeled Dates, Times, and Numbers describes how date, time, and numeric information is formatted in the import file. In this example, the date field is formatted with the year first, then the month followed by the day. Also the month and day include a leading zero for numbers less than 10. Choose YMD for Date Order and check the box labeled Leading Zeros in Dates.

The Field Information section lists the name, data type, and position of each field in the import table. Although you can manually type the specifications for each field in this file, in this example you can accept the field information that Access has created for you.

5. After you return to the Wizard, press the Next> button to move to the next screen.

This screen lets you determine whether the records should be added to a new table or an existing one.

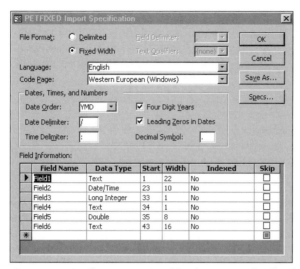

Figure 23-18: The Import Specification screen for fixed-width text files.

6. Click on the Next> button again to move to the next screen.

This screen lets you specify the field names and any indexes for the fields. You can type in fields for each one: Pet Name, Date of Birth, Neutered/Spayed, Gender, Length, and Pet Type. To move from field to field, click on the field heading or the field contents.

7. Click on the Next> button to move to the next screen.

This screen lets you specify a primary key. Click on No Primary Key.

8. Click on the Next> button.

This step takes you to the last screen. Again, you can name your file and then click on the Finish button to save the file to your database.

Using the Import Specification window

In earlier versions of Access, you had to specify the import/export specifications manually, specifying field lengths, delimited or fixed text, type of delimiter, how to export date fields, and so on. Although you can still specify this information by using the Import Specification window, it is easier to use the graphical tools in Access 2000.

Although the Import Text Wizard generally does a good job of importing your data correctly, at times you may need to specify field lengths and data types manually. If you use the Import Specification dialog box (shown in Figure 23-18), you can change or set all the options on one screen, which can be helpful.

One advantage of using this screen is the ability to specify the type of file to be imported from or exported to. The Language and Code Page fields determine the type of format. The default language is English. The Code Page combo box displays the code page types that are available for the language you select. Specifically, these choices are available for the English language:

✦ Unicode

✦ Unicode (Big-Endian)

✦ Unicode (UTF-7)

✦ Unicode (UTF-8)

✦ Western European (ISO)

✦ Western European (Windows)

The default value is the Western European (Windows). You may need to set this value if you are running a language that does not use the Roman character set used in English, French, German, etc. You can also specify the Field Delimiter option for delimited text files; the delimiter is used to separate the fields. You do this by using a special character such as a comma or semicolon. Four field-separator choices are available in this combo box:

;	Semicolon
{tab}	Tabulation mark
{space}	Single space
,	Comma

When working with delimited files, you can also specify your own field separator directly in this combo box.

Also, when working with delimited files, you can specify the Text Qualifier. It specifies the type of delimiter to be used when you're working with Text-type fields. Normally, the text fields in a delimited file are enclosed by specified delimiters (such as quotation marks). This is useful for specifying Number-type data (such as Social Security numbers) as Text type rather than Number type (it won't be used in a calculation). You have three list box choices:

{none}	No delimiter
"	Double quotation mark
'	Single quotation mark

The default value is a double quotation mark. This list box is actually a combo box; you can enter your own delimiter. If the one you want is not among these three choices, you can specify a different text delimiter by entering a new one directly in the combo box — for example, the caret symbol (^).

Tip If you use comma-delimited files, you should set the text qualifier to the double quotation mark (") and the field delimiter to a comma (,).

Caution If you specify your own delimiter, it must be the same on both sides of the text. For example, you can't use both of the curly braces ({ }) as user-specified delimiters; you can specify only one character. If you specify the left curly brace, Access looks for only the left curly brace as a delimiter — on both sides of the text:

{This is Text data enclosed in braces}

Notice that only the left brace is used.

When Access 2000 imports or exports data, it converts dates to a specific format (such as MMDDYY). In the example MMDDYY, Access converts all dates to two digits for each portion of the date (month, day, and year), separating each by a specified delimiter. Thus, January 19, 1999 would be converted to 1/19/99. You can specify how date fields are to be converted, using one of six choices in the Date Order combo box:

✦ DMY

✦ DYM

✦ MDY

✦ MYD

✦ YDM

✦ YMD

These choices specify the order for each portion of a date. The *D* is the day of the month (1-31), *M* is the calendar month (1-12), and *Y* is the year. The default date order is set to the American format of month, day, and year. When you work with European dates, the order must be changed to day, month, and year.

You use the Date Delimiter option to specify the date delimiter. This option tells Access which type of delimiter to use between the parts of date fields. The default is a forward slash (/), but this can be changed to any user-specified delimiter. In Europe, for example, date parts are separated by periods, as in 22.10.95.

Caution When you import text files with Date-type data, you must have a separator between the month, day, and year or else Access reports an error if the field is specified as a Date/Time type. When you're exporting date fields, the separator is not needed.

With the Time Delimiter option, you can specify a separator between the segments of time values in a text file. The default value is the colon (:). In the example 12:55, the colon separates the hours from the minutes. To change the separator, simply enter another in the Time Delimiter box.

You use the Four Digit Years check box when you want to specify that the year value in date fields will be formatted with four digits. By checking this box, you can export dates that include the century (such as in 1881 or 1999). The default is to include the century.

The Leading Zeros in Dates option is a check box where you specify that date values include leading zeros. You can specify, for example, that date formats include leading zeros (as in 02/04/93). To specify leading zeros, check this box. The default is without leading zeros (as in 2/4/93).

Importing HTML tables

Access 2000 lets you import HTML tables as easily as any other database, Excel spreadsheet, or text file. You simply select the HTML file you want to import and use the HTML Import Wizard.

Modifying imported table elements

After you import a file, you can refine the table in Design view. The following list itemizes and discusses some of the primary changes you may want to make to improve your table:

✦ *Add field names or descriptions.* You may want to change the names of the fields you specified when you imported the file. For example, *x*BASE databases allow no more than ten characters in names.

✦ *Change data types.* Access may have guessed the wrong data type when it imported several of the fields. You can change these fields to reflect a more descriptive data type (such as Currency rather than Number, or Text rather than Number).

✦ *Set field properties.* You can set field properties to enhance the way your tables work. For example, you may want to specify a format or default value for the table.

✦ *Set the field size to something more realistic than the 255 bytes Access allocates for each imported text field.*

✦ *Define a primary key.* Access works best with tables that have a primary key. You may want to set a primary key for the imported table.

Troubleshooting import errors

When you import an external file, Access may not be able to import one or more records, in which case it reports an error when it tries to import them. When Access encounters errors, it creates an Access table named Import Errors (with the user's name linked to the table name). The Import Errors table contains one record for each record that causes an error.

After errors have occurred and Access has created the Import Errors table, you can open the table to view the error descriptions.

Import errors for new tables

Access may not be able to import records into a new table for the following reasons:

- ✦ A row in a text file or spreadsheet may contain more fields than are present in the first row.

- ✦ Data in the field cannot be stored in the data type Access chose for the field.

- ✦ On the basis of the first row's contents, Access automatically chose the incorrect data type for a field. The first row is OK, but the remaining rows are blank.

- ✦ The date order may be incorrect. The dates are in YMD order but the specification calls for MDY order.

Import errors for existing tables

Access may not be able to append records into an existing table for the following reasons:

- ✦ The data is not consistent between the text file and the existing Access table.

- ✦ Numeric data being entered is too large for the field size of the Access table.

- ✦ A row in a text file or spreadsheet may contain more fields than the Access table.

- ✦ The records being imported have duplicate primary key values.

The Import Errors table

When errors occur, Access creates an Import Errors table you can use to determine which data caused the errors.

Open the Import Errors table and try to determine why Access couldn't import all the records. If the problem is with the external data, edit it. If you're appending records to an existing table, the problem may be with the existing table; it may need modifications (such as changing the data types and rearranging the field locations). After you solve the problem, erase the Import Errors file and import the data again.

Note   Access attempts to import all records that do not cause an error. If you reimport the data, you may need to clean up the external table or the Access table before reimporting. If you don't, you may have duplicate data in your table.

Tip   If importing a text file seems to take an unexpectedly long time, it may be because of too many errors. You can cancel importing by pressing Ctrl+Break.

Exporting to External Formats

You can copy data from an Access table or query into a new external file. This process of copying Access tables to an external file is called *exporting*. You can export tables to several different sources:

✦ Microsoft Access (other unopened databases)

✦ Delimited text files (fields separated by a delimiter)

✦ Fixed-width text files (specific widths for each field)

✦ Microsoft Excel (all versions)

✦ Lotus 1-2-3 and 1-2-3 for Windows (versions WKS, WK1, and WK3)

✦ Paradox 3.*x*, 4.*x*, and 5.0.

✦ FoxPro 2.*x* and Visual FoxPro 3.0

✦ dBASE III, dBASE IV, and dBASE 5

✦ Rich text formats (RTF)

✦ Word Mail Merge (.txt)

✦ ODBC Data Sources SQL databases (Microsoft SQL Server, Sybase Server, and Oracle Server)

✦ HTML document (as text HTML 1.1 or as tables HTML 2.0 or 3.0)

When Access exports data from an Access table to an external file, the Access table isn't erased or destroyed. This means that you will have two copies of the data: the original Access file and the external data file.

Exporting objects to other Access databases

You can export objects from the current database to another, unopened Access database. The objects you export can be tables, queries, forms, reports, macros, or modules. To export an object to another Access database, follow these steps:

1. Open the database that has the object you want to export and select File ⇨ AExport from the Database menu.

2. Access opens the standard Save As dialog box—the same one that appears whenever you save an object to another name. The difference is that you can specify a different format (Save as type). When you open the combo box, a list of formats appears. Select the one you want; Access will save the data to that format.

When this process is complete, Access copies to the other database the object you specified and immediately returns you to the Database window in Access.

Caution If you attempt to export an object to another Access database that has an object of the same type and name, Access warns you before copying. You then have the option to cancel or overwrite.

Exporting objects to other databases or to Excel, HTML, or text files

You can also export objects to databases (such as ODBC, dBASE, Paradox, and FoxPro) and text files (delimited and fixed width). To export any of these objects, simply follow these general steps:

1. Select File ⇨ Export... from the Database menu.

2. Select the type of file you want the object to be saved to and specify a name.

3. Click on the Save button.

Note If you save a table to an HTML table, Access 2000 will create the HTML document and then start your browser to show you the form it created.

Summary

This chapter explored the use of data from other types of files. You worked with data from database, spreadsheet, and text-based files. This chapter covered the following points:

✦ Access can work with various types of external data, including spreadsheets, PC-based databases, SQL Server tables, HTML and IDC/HTX documents, and text files.

✦ Access can link to other Access tables, *x*BASE (dBASE and FoxPro) databases, Paradox tables, and SQL Server tables. When you link to these tables through Access, you can view and edit the files in their native formats. You can also link to Excel spreadsheets, HTML documents, and text files. If you link to an HTML or text file, you can only view the records.

✦ You should always split your Access application into two databases: one with tables and one with all the other objects. You then link the tables from the second database to the first (the one that has only the tables). This approach makes multiuser systems more efficient.

✦ You can use linked tables for queries, forms, and reports. You can set relations between linked tables and Access tables. You can even rename a linked table for better clarity.

✦ When you're working with text files (delimited and fixed width), you have extensive flexibility for importing and exporting them by using the import/export specifications setup file.

✦ When you create an import/export setup file, you can set several options, such as a specific delimiter, the format of date fields, and so on.

✦ You can import data from other Access objects, dBASE databases, FoxPro databases, Paradox tables, SQL Server tables, Excel spreadsheets, Lotus 1-2-3 spreadsheets, HTML documents, and text files. All these file types can be imported to new tables.

✦ Spreadsheets and text files can also be appended to existing Access tables.

✦ You can export Access table data to several different external files: dBASE databases, FoxPro databases, Paradox tables, SQL Server tables, Excel spreadsheets, Lotus 1-2-3 spreadsheets, HTML documents, ActiveX Server, IDC/HTX resources, and text files.

In the next chapter, you examine advanced select queries.

✦   ✦   ✦

Advanced Select Queries

In this chapter, you work with advanced select queries. So far, you have worked with relatively simple select queries, in which you selected specific records from one or more tables based on some criteria. This chapter shows you queries that display totals, create cross-tabulations, and obtain criteria from the user at run-time.

Your queries have specified criteria for single or multiple fields (including calculated fields) using multiple tables. You also have worked with wildcard characters and fields not having a value (Is Null). You are already accustomed to using functions in queries to specify record criteria or to create calculated fields. Finally, you've realized that Access queries are a great tool for performing ad hoc "what-ifs."

This chapter focuses on three specialized types of advanced select queries:

- ✦ Total
- ✦ Crosstab
- ✦ Parameter

Using these queries, you can calculate totals for records, summarize data in row-and-column format, and run a query that obtains criteria by prompting the operator of the query.

Creating Queries That Calculate Totals

Many times, you want to find information in your tables based on total-type data. For example, you may want to find the total number of animals you've treated or the total amount of money each customer spent on animals last year. Access supplies the tools to accomplish these queries without the need for programming.

Access performs calculation totals by using nine aggregate functions that let you determine a specific value based on the contents of a field. For example, you can determine the average weight of all cats, the maximum and minimum length of all animals you have treated, or the total count of all records in which the type of animal is either a duck or a fish. Performing each of these examples as a query results in a dynaset of answer fields based on the mathematical calculations you requested.

To create a total query, you use a new row in the Query by Example (QBE) pane — the Total: row.

Displaying the Total: row in the QBE pane

To create a query that performs a total calculation, create a select query and then activate the Total: row of the QBE pane. You can activate the Total: row by using either of these two selection methods (but first, open a new query using the Pets table):

✦ Select View ⇨ Totals from the Design menu.

✦ Select the Totals button (the Greek sigma symbol button, Σ which is to the right of the midway mark) on the toolbar.

Figure 24-1 shows the Total: row after it is added in the QBE pane. The Totals button is selected on the toolbar and the Total: row is placed in the QBE pane between the Table: and Sort: rows.

Note   If the toolbar is not visible, select View ⇨ Toolbars... from the Query menu. Then select Query Design and close the dialog box.

If the Table: row is not present on your screen, the Total: row will be between the Field: and Sort: rows. You can activate the Table: row by selecting View ⇨ Table Names from the Design menu.

Removing the Total: row from the QBE pane

To deactivate the Total: row in the QBE pane, simply reselect either activation method (with the Totals button or the menu choice). The Totals button is a toggle that alternately turns the Total: row on and off.

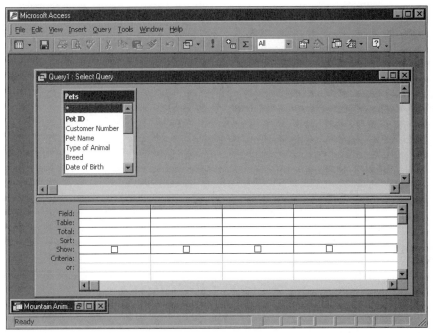

Figure 24-1: Activating the Total: row of the QBE pane.

The Total: row options

You can perform total calculations against all records or groups of records in one or more tables. To perform a calculation, you must select one of the options from the drop-down list in the Total: row for every field you include in the query, including any hidden fields (with the Show: option turned off). Figure 24-2 shows the drop-down list box active in the Total: row of the field Pet Name.

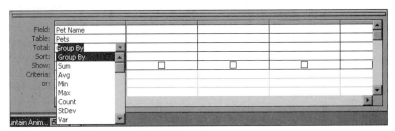

Figure 24-2: The drop-down list box of the Total: row.

What Is an Aggregate Function?

The word *aggregate* implies gathering together a mass (a group or series) of things and working on this mass as a whole—a total. Therefore, an *aggregate function* is a function that takes a group of records and performs some mathematical function against the entire group. The function can be a simple *count* or a complex *expression* you specify, based on a series of mathematical functions.

Although only 8 options are shown in Figure 24-2, you can choose from 12. You can view the remaining options by using the scroll bar on the right side of the box. The 12 options can be divided into four distinct categories:

✦ Group By

✦ Aggregate

✦ Expression

✦ Total Field Record Limit

Table 24-1 lists each category, its number of Total options, and its purpose.

Table 24-1
Four Categories of Total Options

Category	Number of Options	Purpose of Operator
Group By	1	Groups common records together against which Access performs aggregate calculations
Aggregate	9	Specifies a mathematical or selection operation to perform against a field
Expression	1	Groups several total operators together and performs the group totals
Total Field Record Limit	1	Limits records before record limit performing a total calculation against a field

The Aggregate category has nine options. Its options are used by the other three categories.

Group By category

This category has one option, the *Group By* option. You use this option to specify that a certain field in the QBE pane will be used as a grouping field. For example, if you select the field Type of Animal, the Group By option tells Access to group all cat records together, all dog records together, and so on. This option is the default for *all* Total: cells. In other words when you drag a field to the QBE pane, Access automatically selects this option. Figure 24-2 shows that this is also the first choice in the drop-down list box. These groups of records will be used for performing some aggregate calculation against another field in the query. This subject will be discussed in more detail later in this chapter.

Expression category

Like the Group By category, the *Expression* category has only one option: Expression. This is the second-from-last choice in the drop-down list. You use this option to tell Access that you will create a calculated field by using one or more aggregate calculations in the Field: cell of the QBE pane. For example, you may want to create a query that shows each customer and how much money the customer saved, based on the individual's discount rate. This query requires creating a calculated field that uses a sum aggregate against the Total Amount field in the Visits table, which is then multiplied by the Discount field in the Customer table. This type of calculation is discussed in detail later.

Total Field Record Limit category

The *Total Field Record Limit* category is the third category that has a single option: the *Where* option. This option is the last choice in the drop-down list. When you select this option, you tell Access that you want to specify limiting criteria against an aggregate type field, as opposed to a Group By or an Expression field. The limiting criteria is performed *before* the aggregate options are executed. For example, you may want to create a query that counts all pets by types of animals that weigh less than 100 pounds. Because the Weight field is not to be used for a grouping (as is Type of Animal) and won't be used to perform an aggregate calculation, you specify the Where option. By specifying the Where option, you are telling Access to use this field only as a limiting criteria field — before it performs the aggregate calculation (counting types of animals). This type of operation is also discussed in detail later in this chapter.

Aggregate category

The *Aggregate* category, unlike the others, has nine options: *Sum, Avg, Min, Max, Count, StDev, Var, First,* and *Last.* These options appear as the second through tenth options in the drop-down list. Each of these options performs some operation. Seven of the options perform mathematical operations, whereas two perform simple selection operations. When each option is executed, it finds (calculates or determines) some answer or value and supplies it to a cell in the resulting dynaset. For example, you may want to determine the maximum (Max) and minimum (Min) weight of each animal in the Type of Animal field in the Pets table. On the other hand, you may want the total number (Count) of animals in the Pets table. You use these aggregate options to solve these types of queries.

Options such as these are what most people think about when they hear the words *total query*. Each of the options performs a calculation against a field in the QBE pane of the query and returns a single answer in the dynaset. As an example, there can only be one maximum weight for all the animals. Several animals may have the same maximum weight, but only one weight is the heaviest.

The other three categories of options can be used against any type of Access field (Text, Memo, or Yes/No, for example). However, some of the aggregate options can be performed against only specific field types. For example, you cannot perform a Sum option against Text type data, and you cannot use a Max option against an OLE object.

Table 24-2 lists each option, what it does, and which field types you can use with the option.

Table 24-2
Aggregate Options of the Total: Row

Option	Finds	Field Type Support
Count	Number of non-Null values in a field	AutoNumber, Number, Currency, Date/Time, Yes/No, Text, Memo, OLE object
Sum	Total of values in a field	AutoNumber, Number, Currency, Date/Time, Yes/No
Avg	Average of values in a field	AutoNumber, Number, Currency, Date/Time, Yes/No
Max	Highest value in a field	AutoNumber, Number, Currency, Date/Time, Yes/No, Text
Min	Lowest value in a field	AutoNumber, Number, Currency, Date/Time, Yes/No, Text
StDev	Standard deviation of values in a field	AutoNumber, Number, Currency, Date/Time, Yes/No
Var	Population variance of values in a field	AutoNumber, Number, Currency, Date/Time, Yes/No
First	Field value from the *first* record in a number, table, or query	AutoNumber, Currency, Date/Time, Yes/No, Text, Memo, OLE object
Last	Field value from the *last* record in a number, table, or query	AutoNumber, Currency, Date/Time, Yes/No, Text, Memo, OLE object

Performing totals on all records

You can use total queries to perform calculations against all records in a table or query. For example, you can find the total number of animals in the Pets table, the average weight, and the maximum weight of the animals. To create this query, follow these steps:

1. Select the Pets table.

2. Click the Totals button on the toolbar to turn it on.

3. Double-click the Pet ID field in the Pets table.

4. Double-click the Weight field in the Pets table.

5. Double-click the Weight field in the Pets table again.

6. In the Total: cell of Pet ID, select Count.

7. In the Total: cell of Weight, select Avg.

8. In the second Total: cell of Weight, select Max.

Your query should look similar to Figure 24-3.

Field:	Pet ID	Weight	Weight		
Table:	Pets	Pets	Pets		
Total:	Count	Avg	Max		
Sort:					
Show:	☑	☑	☑	☐	
Criteria:					
or:					

Figure 24-3: A query against all records in the Pets table.

This query calculates the total number of pet records in the Pets table as well as the average weight of all animals and the heaviest weight of all the animals.

 Caution

The Count option of the Total: cell can be performed against any field in the table (or query). However, Count eliminates any records that have a Null value in the field you select. Therefore, you may want to select the primary key field on which to perform the Count total because this field cannot have any Null values, thus ensuring an accurate record count.

If you select the Datasheet button on the toolbar, you should see a query similar to Figure 24-4. Notice that the dynaset has only one record. When performing calculations against *all records* in a table or query, the resulting dynaset will have only one record.

Figure 24-4: This datasheet of a dynaset was created from a total query against all records in a table.

 Note   Access creates default column headings for all total fields in a totals datasheet, such as those shown in Figure 24-4. The heading name is a product of the name of the total option and the field name. Thus, in Figure 24-4 the heading names are CountOfPet ID, AvgOfWeight, and MaxOfWeight. You can change a column heading name to something more appropriate by renaming the field in the QBE pane of the Design window. As you do with any other field that you want to rename, place the insertion point at the beginning of the field cell to be renamed (to the left of the field name) and type the name you want to display followed by a colon.

Performing totals on groups of records

Most of the time, you need to perform totals on a group of records rather than on all records. For example, you may need to calculate the total number of animals you've treated for each type of animal. In other words, you want to create a group for each type of animal (bear, cat, dog, and so on) and then perform the total calculation against each of these groups. In database parlance, this is known as *control break* totaling.

Calculating totals for a single group

When you create your query, you specify which field or fields to use for grouping the totals and which fields to perform the totals against. Using the preceding example, to group the Type of Animal field, you select the Group By option of the Total: cell. Follow these steps to create the query:

1. Open a new query and select the Pets table.

2. Click the Totals button (the) on the toolbar to turn it on.

3. Double-click the Type of Animal field in the Pets table.

4. Double-click the Pet ID field in the Pets table.

5. In the Total: cell of Type of Animal, select Group By.

6. In the Total: cell of Pet ID, select Count.

The query in Figure 24-5 groups all like animals together and then performs the count total for each type of animal. Unlike performing totals against all records, this query produces a dynaset of many records — one record for each type of animal. Figure 254-6 demonstrates how the datasheet looks.

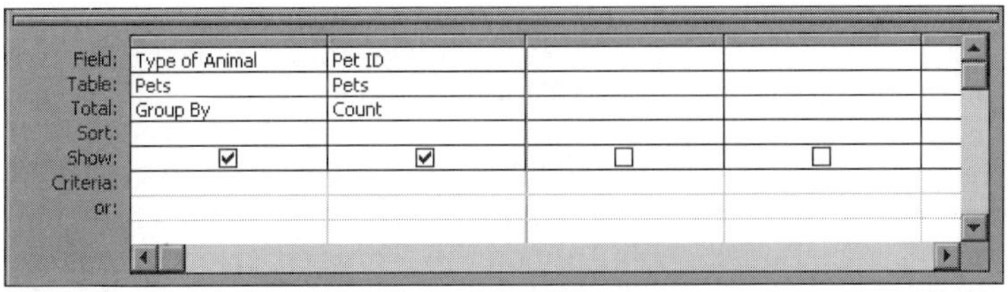

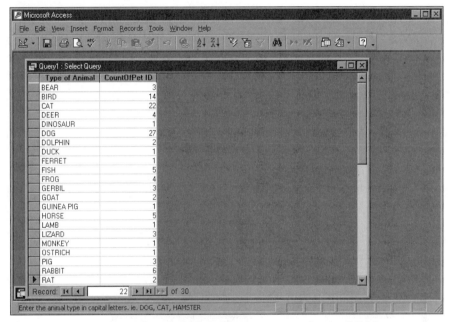

Figure 24-5: Totals against a group of records.

Figure 24-6: Datasheet of totals against the group Type of Animal field.

The dynaset in Figure 24-6 has a single record for each type of animal. The count was performed against each type of animal; there are 3 bears, 14 birds, and so on. The Group By field displays one record for each unique value in that field. The Type of Animal field is specified as the Group By field and displays a single record for each type of animal, showing Bear, Bird, Cat, Dog, and so on. Each of these records is shown as a row heading for the datasheet, indicating a unique record for each type of animal specified that begins with the Group By field content (bear, bird, and so on). In this case, each unique record is easy to identify by the single-field row heading under Type of Animal.

Calculating totals for several groups

You can perform group totals against multiple fields and multiple tables as easily as with a single field in a single table. For example, you may want to group by both customer and type of animal to determine the number of animals each customer owns by animal type. To create a total query for this example, you specify Group By in both Total: fields (Customer Name and Type of Animal).

This query, shown in Figure 24-7, uses two tables and also groups by two fields to perform the count total. First, the query groups by Customer Name and then by Type of Animal. When the Datasheet button on the toolbar is selected, a datasheet similar to the one shown in Figure 24-8 displays.

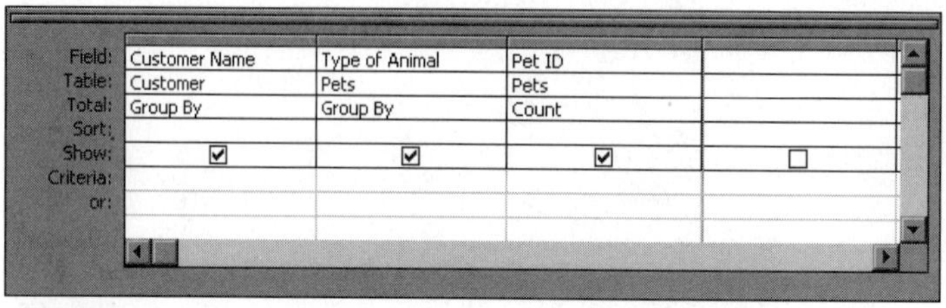

Figure 24-7: A multiple-table, multiple-field Group By total query.

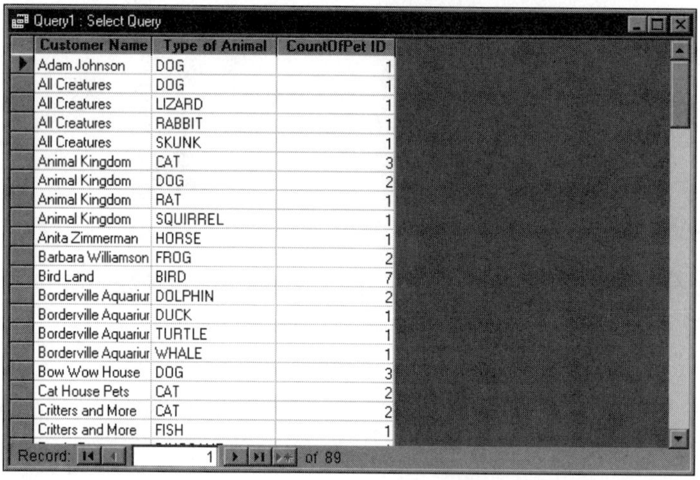

Figure 24-8: Datasheet of a multiple-field Group By query.

The datasheet in Figure 24-8 shows several records for the customer Animal Kingdom. This customer has three cats, two dogs, one rat, and one squirrel. This datasheet has a unique record based on two Group By fields: Customer Name and Type of Animal. Therefore, the unique row headings for this datasheet are created by combining both fields — first the Customer Name and then the Type of Animal.

Note   You can think of the Group By fields in a total query as fields that specify the row headings of the datasheet.

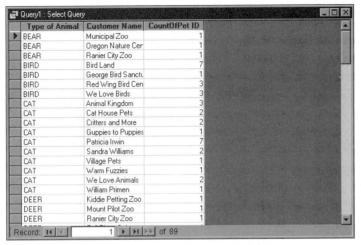

Figure 24-9: Changing the order of Group By fields.

Tip

Access groups records based on the order of the Group By fields in the QBE pane (from left to right). Therefore, you should pay attention to the order of the Group By fields. Although the order doesn't change the aggregate totals of the fields, the order of Group By fields does determine how the results are displayed in the datasheet. If you place the Type of Animal field before the Customer Name field, the resulting datasheet shows the records in order by animal first and then customer. Figure 24-9 demonstrates this setup, showing the bear records and their owners (with the total number) and then the bird records and their owners, and so on.

By changing the order of the Group By fields in a totals query, you can look at your data in new and creative ways.

Specifying criteria for a total query

In addition to grouping records for total queries, criteria to limit the records that will be processed or displayed in a total calculation can be specified. When you're specifying record criteria in total queries, several options are available. A criterion against any of these three fields can be created:

✦ Group By

✦ Aggregate Total

✦ Non-Aggregate Total

Using any one, two or all three of these criteria types, you can easily limit the scope of your total query to finite criteria.

Specifying criteria for a Group By field

To limit the scope of the records used in a grouping, specify criteria in the Group By fields. For example, to calculate the average length and weight of only three animals — bears, deer, and wolves — requires specifying criteria on the Group By field Type of Animal. This type of query looks like Figure 24-10.

Field:	Type of Animal	Pet ID	Length	Weight
Table:	Pets	Pets	Pets	Pets
Total:	Group By	Count	Avg	Avg
Sort:				
Show:	☑	☑	☑	☑
Criteria:	In ("bear","deer","wolf")			
or:				

Figure 24-10: Specifying criteria in a Group By field.

By specifying criteria in the Group By field, only those records that meet the Group By criteria will have the aggregate calculations performed. In this example, the count, average length, and average weight will be performed only for animals that are bears, deer, and wolves. This results in a three-record dynaset, with one record for each animal.

Specifying criteria for an Aggregate Total field

At times you will want a query to calculate aggregate totals first and then display only those totals from the aggregate calculations that meet a specified criterion. In other words, you want Access to determine all totals for each Group By field and then take the totals field and perform the criteria against the totals before creating the resulting dynaset.

For example, you may want a query to find the average length of all animals, grouped by type of animal, where the average length of any animal is greater than 20 inches. This query should look like Figure 24-11. Notice that the criterion >20 is placed in the Aggregate Total field, Length. This query calculates the average length of all animals grouped by type of animal. Then the query determines whether the calculated totals for each record are greater than 20. Records greater than 20 are added to the resulting dynaset, and records less than or equal to 20 are discarded. The criterion is applied *after* the aggregate calculations are performed.

Field:	Type of Animal	Pet ID	Length	
Table:	Pets	Pets	Pets	
Total:	Group By	Count	Avg	
Sort:				
Show:	☑	☑	☑	☐
Criteria:			>20	
or:				

Figure 24-11: A query with a criterion set against an Aggregate Total field.

Specifying criteria for a Non-Aggregate Total field

The preceding example limited the records *after* performing the calculations against total fields. You also can specify that you want Access to limit the records based on a total field *before* performing total calculations. In other words, limit the range of records against which the calculation is performed. Doing so creates a criterion similar to the first type of criteria; the field you want to set a criterion against is *not* a Group By field.

For example, you may want to display the total amount of money charged for each animal during the first half of 1999 after February 9. You want to use the Visit Date field to specify criteria, but you don't want to perform any calculations against this field or to use it to group by; you don't even want to show the field in the resulting datasheet.

Figure 24-12 shows how the query should look. Notice that Access automatically turned off the Show: cell in the Visit Date field.

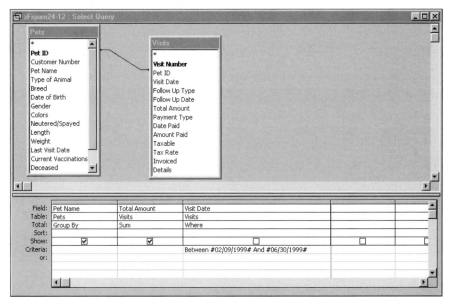

Figure 24-12: Specifying criteria for a Non-Aggregate field.

Note   Access automatically turns off the Show: cell whenever it encounters a Where option in the Total: cell of a field. Access understands that you are using the field only to specify criteria and that you don't want to see the actual field value displayed for the criteria field.

In the query you just completed, Access displays only those records for pets that have visited the hospital from February 9 to June 30, 1999. All other records are discarded.

Caution   When you specify a Where option in a Total: cell, you cannot show the field. The reason is that Access uses the field to evaluate the Where criteria before performing the calculation. Therefore, the contents are useful only for the limiting criteria. If you try to turn on the Show: cell, Access displays an error message.

Creating expressions for totals

In addition to choosing one of the Access totals from the drop-down list, you can create your own total expression based on several types of totals in an expression, such as using Avg and Sum or multiple Sums together. Or you can base your expression on a calculated field composed of several functions; or on a calculated field that is based on several fields from different tables.

Suppose that you want a query that shows the total amount of money each customer owed before discount. Then you want to see the amount of money these customers saved based on their discount. You want the information to be grouped by customer. Follow these steps to create this query:

1. Start a new query and select the Customer, Pets, and Visits tables.

2. Click the Totals button (the Σ) on the toolbar to turn it on.

3. Double-click the Customer Name field in the Customer table.

4. Double-click the Total Amount field in the Visits table.

5. In the Total: cell of Customer Name, select Group By.

6. In the Total: cell of Total Amount, select Sum.

7. Click on an empty Field: cell in the QBE pane.

8. Type `Total Saved:Sum([Visits].[Total Amount]*[Customer].[Discount])` in the cell.

9. In theTotal: cell of Total Saved expression, select Expression.

Note   Your query should be similar to Figure 24-13. Notice that the query uses two fields from different tables to create the Total Saved: calculated field. You had to specify both the table and the field name for each field the Sum function used.

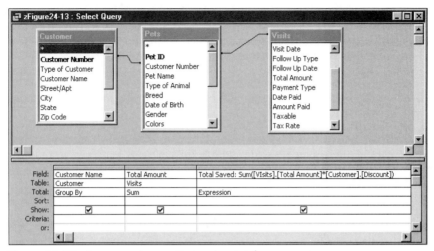

Figure 24-13: A query using an Expression total.

If you click the Datasheet button on the toolbar, your dynaset should be similar to Figure 24-14.

Query1 : Select Query

Customer Name	SumOfTotal Amc	Total Saved
Adam Johnson	$167.80	0
All Creatures	$1,860.00	372.00000554323
Animal Kingdom	$1,223.00	244.60000364482
Anita Zimmerman	$50.00	
Barbara Williamson	$100.00	0
George Green	$1,389.50	0
James Brown	$100.00	10.000000149012
Johnathan Adams	$936.00	46.800000697374
Karen Rhodes	$281.00	0
Margaret McKinley	$60.00	0
Michael Johnson	$70.00	0
Patricia Irwin	$1,340.80	0
Sandra Williams	$643.00	0
Sandra Young	$234.00	0
Stephen Brown	$316.00	0
Tyrone Potter	$106.00	0
Wanda Greenfield	$30.00	0
William Adams	$77.00	3.8500000573695
William Price	$385.00	0
William Primen	$843.50	0

Record: 1 of 20

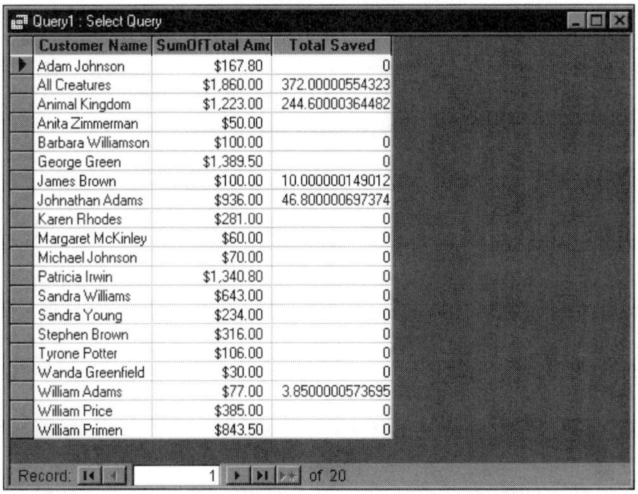

Figure 24-14: A datasheet created by an Expression total.

Tip   Notice in the datasheet in Figure 24-14 that the calculated field Total Saved shows as many as 12 decimal places. The number of decimal places can be limited by using the Format( ) function around the Sum( ) function. To do so, add the following line to the existing criteria formula in the calculated field cell:

```
Total Saved:Format(Sum([Visits].[Total
Amount]*[Customer].[Discount]), "Standard")Creating Crosstab
Queries
```

Access permits use of a specialized type of total query—the crosstab—to display summarized data in a compact and readable format. A *crosstab query* summarizes the data in the fields from your tables and presents the resulting dynaset in a row-and-column format.

Understanding the crosstab query

Simply put, a crosstab query is a spreadsheet-like summary of the things specified by the row header and column header that is created from your tables. This query presents summary data in a spreadsheet-like format created from fields that you specify. In this specialized type of total query, the Total: row in the QBE pane is always active. The Total: row cannot be toggled off in a crosstab query!

In addition, the Total: row of the QBE pane is used for specifying a Group By total option for both the row and the column headings. Like other total queries, the Group By option specifies the row headings for the query datasheet and comes from the actual contents of the field. However, unlike other total queries, the crosstab query also obtains its column headings from the value in a field (table or calculated) rather than from the field names themselves.

Caution   The fields used as rows and columns must always have Group By in the Total: row. Otherwise, Access reports an error when you attempt to display or run the query.

For example, you may want to create a query that displays the Type of Animal field as the row heading and the owner's state as the column heading, with each cell containing a total for each type of animal in each state. Table 24-3 demonstrates how you want the query to look.

In Table 24-3, the row headings are specified by Type of Animal: Bear, Bird, and so on. The column headings are specified by the state: ID, OR, and WA. The cell content in the intersection of any row and column is a summary of records that meets both conditions. For example, the Bear row that intersects the OR column shows that the clinic treats two bears in the state of Oregon. The Dog row that intersects with the WA column shows that the clinic treats 13 dogs in the state of Washington.

This table shows a simple crosstab query created from the fields Type of Animal and State, with the intersecting cell contents determined by a Count total on any field in the Pets table.

Table 24-3 A Typical Crosstab Query Format			
Type of Animal	*ID*	*OR*	*WA*
Bear	0	2	1
Bird	11	0	3
Cat	4	12	6
Dog	6	7	13
Pig	0	0	3

Creating the crosstab query

Now that you have a conceptual understanding of a crosstab query, it is time to create one. To create a crosstab query like the one described in Table 24-3, follow these steps:

1. Start a new query and select the Customer and Pets tables.

2. Double-click the Type of Animal field in the Pets table.

3. Double-click the State field in the Customer table.

4. Double-click the Pet ID field in the Pets table.

5. Select Query ⇨ Crosstab in the Query menu or press the Query Type button on the toolbar (this step displays a drop-down list showing the types of queries).

6. In the Crosstab: cell of Type of Animal, select Row Heading.

7. In the Crosstab: cell of State, select Column Heading.

8. In the Crosstab: cell of Pet ID, select Value.

9. In the Total: cell of Pet ID, select Count.

Your query should look similar to Figure 24-15. Notice that Access inserted a new row named Crosstab: between the Total: and Sort: rows in the QBE pane.

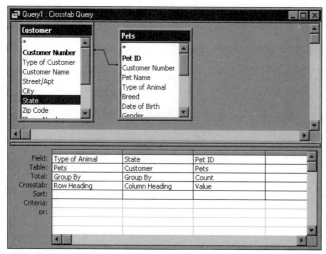

Figure 24-15: Creating a crosstab query.

As Figure 24-15 demonstrates, you *must* specify a minimum of three items for crosstab queries:

✦ The Row Heading field

✦ The Column Heading field

✦ The summary Value field

These three items are specified in the appropriate Crosstab: cells of the fields. After you specify the contents for the three Crosstab: cells, you specify Group By in the Total: cell of both the Row Heading and the Column Heading fields and an aggregate Total: cell operator (such as Count) for the Value field.

If you have done this procedure correctly, selecting the Datasheet button on the toolbar reveals a datasheet similar to Figure 24-16.

Notice that the dynaset is composed of distinct (nonrepeating) rows of animals, three columns (one for each state), and summary cell contents for each animal against each state; that is, the clinic treats no bears in the state of Idaho, but it does treat two in Oregon and one in Washington. When there are no values found, a null value is used rather than 0.

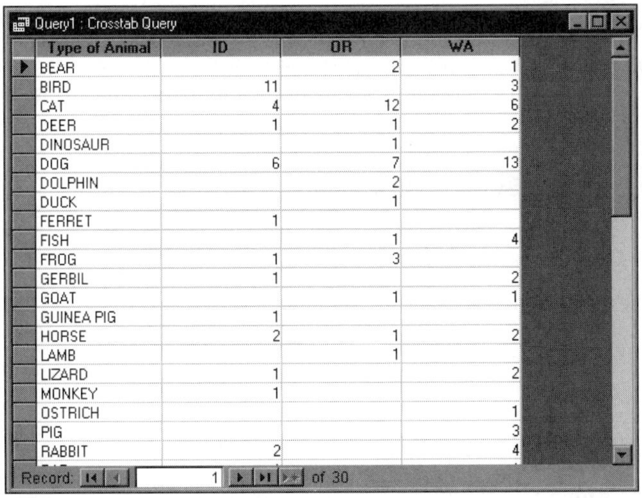

Type of Animal	ID	OR	WA
BEAR		2	1
BIRD	11		3
CAT	4	12	6
DEER	1	1	2
DINOSAUR		1	
DOG	6	7	13
DOLPHIN		2	
DUCK		1	
FERRET	1		
FISH		1	4
FROG	1	3	
GERBIL	1		2
GOAT		1	1
GUINEA PIG	1		
HORSE	2	1	2
LAMB		1	
LIZARD	1		2
MONKEY	1		
OSTRICH			1
PIG			3
RABBIT	2		4

Figure 24-16: Datasheet of a crosstab query.

Entering multiple-field row headings

When working with crosstab queries, only one summary Value field and one Column Heading field can be specified. You can add more than one Row Heading field, however. By adding multiple Row Heading fields, you can refine the type of data to be presented in the crosstab query.

Suppose that you're interested in seeing the types of animals from the last crosstab query further refined to the level of city. In other words, you want to see how many of each type of animal that you have from each city within each state. Such a query is shown in Figure 24-17. Notice that it has two Crosstab: cells that show Row Heading for the fields State and City. Access groups the Crosstab: rows first by the State and then by the City. Access specifies the group order from left to right. Effectively, you are changing the orientation of the row/column of the previous example.

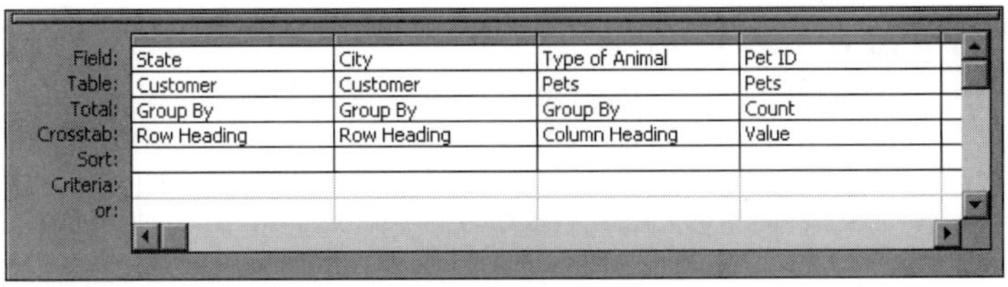

Field:	State	City	Type of Animal	Pet ID
Table:	Customer	Customer	Pets	Pets
Total:	Group By	Group By	Group By	Count
Crosstab:	Row Heading	Row Heading	Column Heading	Value
Sort:				
Criteria:				
or:				

Figure 24-17: Crosstab query using two fields for the row heading.

Access presents a datasheet similar to the one shown in Figure 24-18 when the Datasheet button on the toolbar is selected. The row heading depends on both the State and City fields. The dynaset is displayed in order: first by state (ID, OR, WA), and then by city within the state (Borderville, Mount Pilot, Russettown, and so forth).

State	City	BEAR	BIRD	CAT	DEER	DINOSAUR	DOG	DOLP
ID	Borderville			3			2	
ID	Mount Pilot		1		1		2	
ID	Russettown		7	1			1	
ID	Three Corners		3				1	
OR	Borderville			2		1	4	
OR	Lakeville	1		10	1		3	
OR	Small Tree	1						
WA	Borderville			2				
WA	Mountain View			3	1		5	
WA	Ranier City	1		1	1		4	
WA	Tall Pines		3				4	

Figure 24-18: Datasheet with multiple-field row headings of a crosstab query.

Tip   A crosstab query can have several row headings but only one column heading. To display a several-field column heading and a single-field row heading, simply reverse the heading types. Change the multiple-field column headings to multiple-field row headings and change the single-row heading to a single-column heading.

Specifying criteria for a crosstab query

When working with crosstab queries, you may want to specify record criteria for the crosstab. Criteria can be specified in a crosstab query against any of these fields:

✦ A new field

✦ A Row Heading field

✦ A Column Heading field

Specifying criteria in a new field

You can add criteria based on a new field that will not be displayed in the crosstab query itself. For example, you may want to create the crosstab query you see in Figure 24-17, in which the two fields, State and City, are used as the row heading. However, you want to see only records in which the type of customer is an individual (or the contents equal the number 1). To specify criteria, follow these additional steps:

1. Start with the crosstab query shown in Figure 24-17.

2. Double-click the Type of Customer field in the Customer table.

3. Select the Criteria: cell of Type of Customer.

4. Type **1** in the cell.

Note

The Crosstab: cell of the Type of Customer field should be blank. If it is not, select (not shown) to blank the cell.

Your query should resemble the one shown in Figure 24-19. Notice that you added a criterion in a field that will not be displayed in the crosstab query. The Type of Customer field is used as a grouping field and because nothing appears in the Crosstab row, the field value is not displayed.

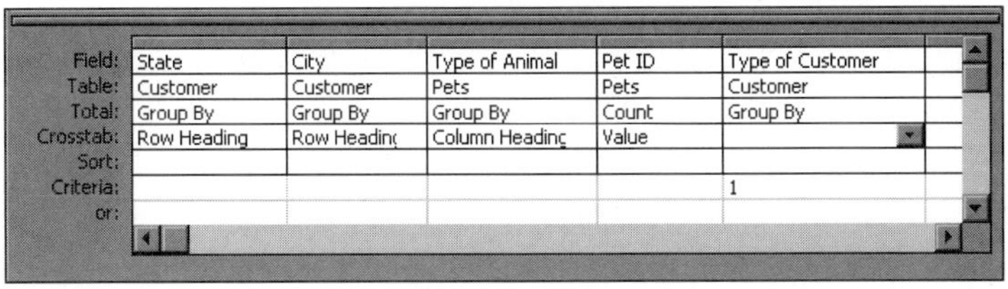

Field:	State	City	Type of Animal	Pet ID	Type of Customer	
Table:	Customer	Customer	Pets	Pets	Customer	
Total:	Group By	Group By	Group By	Count	Group By	
Crosstab:	Row Heading	Row Heading	Column Heading	Value		
Sort:						
Criteria:					1	
or:						

Figure 24-19: Specifying a criterion in a crosstab query on a new field.

Now that the new criterion is specified, you can click on the Datasheet button of the toolbar to see a datasheet similar to the one portrayed in Figure 24-20.

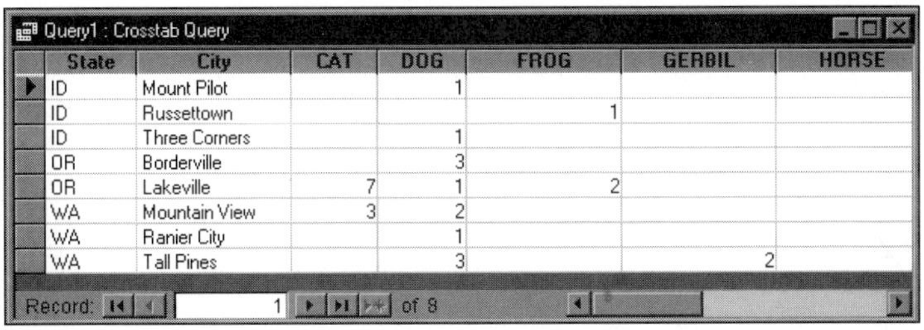

State	City	CAT	DOG	FROG	GERBIL	HORSE
ID	Mount Pilot		1			
ID	Russettown			1		
ID	Three Corners		1			
OR	Borderville		3			
OR	Lakeville	7	1	2		
WA	Mountain View	3	2			
WA	Ranier City		1			
WA	Tall Pines		3		2	

Record: ◄◄ ◄ 1 ► ►I ►* of 8

Figure 24-20: The datasheet after specifying a criterion on a new field.

The datasheet in Figure 24-20 shows only columns in which at least one of the intersecting row cells has a value. For example, only two gerbils appear in the Gerbil column. Several types of animal columns are gone. Bears, birds, deer, and others are missing because none of these types is owned by an individual.

Specifying criteria in a Row Heading field

You can specify criteria for not only a new field but also a field being used for a row heading. When you specify a criteria for a row heading, Access excludes any rows that do not meet the specified criteria.

For example, you may want to create a crosstab query for all animals where the state is Idaho (ID). To create this query, start with the crosstab query shown in Figure 24-17. If you created the last query, remove the Type of Customer column from the QBE pane. To create this query, make the QBE pane look like Figure 24-21. When this query is viewed, only records from Idaho are seen.

Field:	State	City	Type of Animal	Pet ID	
Table:	Customer	Customer	Pets	Pets	
Total:	Group By	Group By	Group By	Count	
Crosstab:	Row Heading	Row Heading	Column Heading	Value	
Sort:					
Criteria:	"ID"				
or:					

Figure 24-21: Criteria set against a Row Heading field.

You can specify criteria against any field used as a Row Heading field or for multiple Row Heading fields to create a finely focused crosstab query.

Specifying criteria in a Column Heading field

Criteria for the field used as the column heading can also be specified. When you specify the criteria for a column heading, Access excludes any columns that don't meet the specified criteria. For the next example, you want a crosstab query for any animal that is either a cat or a dog. To create this query, again start with the crosstab query shown in Figure 24-17. If you created the last query, remove the criteria for the State field from the QBE pane. The QBE pane should look similar to that in Figure 24-22.

Field:	State	City	Type of Animal	Pet ID	
Table:	Customer	Customer	Pets	Pets	
Total:	Group By	Group By	Group By	Count	
Crosstab:	Row Heading	Row Heading	Column Heading	Value	
Sort:					
Criteria:			"Cat" Or "Dog"		
or:					

Figure 24-22: A criterion specified against the Column Heading field.

The specified criterion is placed in the Criteria: cell of the Column Heading field Type of Animal. If you now select the Datasheet button on the toolbar, you should see a datasheet that has only two column headings: Cat and Dog. The other headings are eliminated.

Tip You cannot specify criteria in a field used as the summary Value field for the crosstab query. However, if you need to specify criteria based on this field, drag the field again to the QBE pane and set a criterion against this second copy of the field while keeping the Crosstab: cell empty.

Specifying criteria in multiple fields of a crosstab query

Now that you've worked with each type of criterion separately, you may want to specify criteria based on several fields. In the next example, you learn to create a crosstab query with complex criteria. You want a row heading based on the Type of Animal field, a column heading based on the Month value of the Visit Date field, and Value cells based on the Sum of Total Amount.

Finally, you want to limit the months to part of 1999. To create this complex crosstab query, make the QBE pane look like Figure 24-23. You need to use the Pets and Visits tables. Notice that you specified a column heading based on a calculated field.

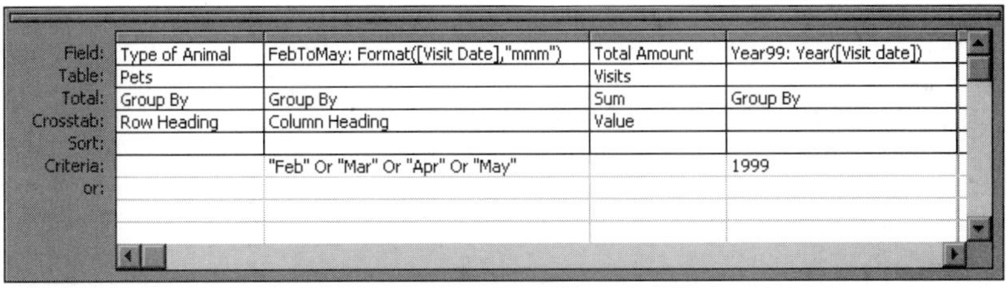

Field:	Type of Animal	FebToMay: Format([Visit Date],"mmm")	Total Amount	Year99: Year([Visit date])
Table:	Pets		Visits	
Total:	Group By	Group By	Sum	Group By
Crosstab:	Row Heading	Column Heading	Value	
Sort:				
Criteria:		"Feb" Or "Mar" Or "Apr" Or "May"		1999
or:				

Figure 24-23: A complex crosstab query.

This query should display a datasheet in which the columns are Feb, Mar, Apr, and May for the year 1999. When you select the Datasheet button on the toolbar, you should see a datasheet similar to Figure 24-24. The datasheet has four columns; the order of the columns is alphabetical, not the chronological, by-month order you entered in the Criteria: cell of the field. The next section shows you how to fix the column order so that the months display in chrononological order.

Type of Animal	Apr	Feb	Mar	May
▶ CAT		$100.00		$310.00
DOG	$30.00	$50.00		$167.80
FROG	$50.00			
HORSE		$20.00	$69.00	
PIG				$50.00
RABBIT	$512.00			
RAT			$32.00	$142.00
SNAKE	$150.00			$56.00

Record: I◀ ◀ 1 ▶ ▶I ▶* of 8

Figure 24-24: A datasheet of very complex crosstab criteria.

Note

As the preceding crosstab query shows, criteria can be set in the QBE pane for a number of fields, including calculated fields. Because of the ability to set either complex or focused criteria, very specific crosstab queries can be created.

Specifying fixed column headings

At times, you will want more control over the appearance of the column headings. By default, Access sorts column headings alphabetically or numerically. This sort order can be a problem, as in the preceding example and as illustrated in Figure 24-24. Your columns will be more readable if the columns are in chronological rather than alphabetical order. You can use the option Column Headings in the Query Properties box to solve this problem. This option lets you:

✦ Specify an exact order for the appearance of the column headings

✦ Specify fixed column headings for reports and forms that use crosstab queries

To specify fixed column headings, follow these steps:

1. Begin with the crosstab query shown in Figure 24-23. Move the pointer to the top half of the query screen and click it once.

2. Click the Properties button (a hand holding a piece of paper) on the toolbar or select View ➪ Properties... from the Query Design menu.

3. Select the Column Headings text box entry area.

4. Type **Feb, Mar, Apr, May** in the box.

Tip

If you double-click in step 1, the Properties window will automatically appear.

The Query Properties dialog box should look like the one shown in Figure 24-25. When you move to another entry area, Access converts your text into "Feb," "Mar," "Apr," "May" in the Query Properties dialog box.

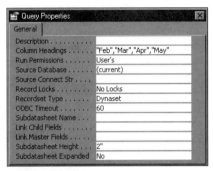

Figure 24-25: The Query Properties dialog box.

If you look at the datasheet, you see that it now looks like Figure 24-26. The order for the column headings is now chronological.

Type of Animal	Feb	Mar	Apr	May
CAT	$100.00			$310.00
DOG	$50.00		$30.00	$167.80
FROG			$50.00	
HORSE	$20.00	$69.00		
PIG				$50.00
RABBIT			$512.00	
RAT		$32.00		$142.00
SNAKE			$150.00	$56.00

Figure 24-26: The datasheet with the column order specified.

> **Note**
>
> The column names you enter *must* match the query headings exactly. If you enter February rather than Feb, Access accepts the heading without reporting an error. When you display the query, however, no records for that column appear.

You can enter column names without separating them by commas. To do so, enter each name on a new line (press Ctrl+Enter to move to a new line).

The Crosstab Query Wizard

Access 2000 employs several Query Wizards, which are helpful additions to the query design surface. One such Wizard, the Crosstab Query Wizard (see Figure 24-27), is an excellent tool to help you create a crosstab query quickly.

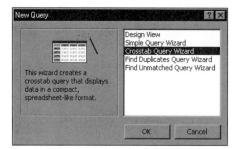

Figure 24-27: Selecting the Access Query Wizard from the New Query dialog box.

The Crosstab Query Wizard has some limitations, however:

✦ To use more than one table for the crosstab query, you need to create a separate query that has the tables you need for the crosstab query. For example, you may have a Group By row heading from the Pets table (Type of Animal) and a Group By column heading from the Customer table (State). The Crosstab Query Wizard allows you to select only one table or query for the row and column heading.

The workaround: Create a query of the Customer and Pets tables, selecting the All Fields reference for each, and save this intermediate query. Then use this intermediate query as the record source for the Wizard.

✦ The limiting criteria for the Wizard's query cannot be specified.

The workaround: Make the Wizard do the query and then go in and set the limiting criteria.

✦ Column headings or column orders cannot be specified.

The workaround: Again, have the Wizard create the query and then modify it.

To use the crosstab query wizard, click the New button in the database window toolbar after pressing the Queries Object button and then select the Crosstab Wizard (third from the top, Figure 24-27) in the dialog box. Click OK and then follow the prompts. Access asks for:

✦ The table or query name for the source

✦ The fields for the row headings

✦ The fields for the column headings

✦ The field for the body

✦ The title

After you specify these things, Access creates your crosstab query and then runs it for you.

Creating a Parameter Query

You can automate the process of changing criteria for queries that you run on a regular basis by creating *parameter queries*.

Understanding the parameter query

As the name *parameter* suggests, a parameter query is one you create that prompts the user for a quantity or a constant value every time the query is executed. Specifically, a parameter query prompts the user for criteria each time it is run, thereby eliminating the need to open the query in design mode to change the criteria manually.

Parameter queries are also very useful with forms or reports because Access can prompt the user for the criteria when the form or report is opened.

Creating a single-parameter query

You may have queries that require different values for the criteria of a field each time they are run. Suppose that you have a query that displays all pets for a specific customer. If you run the query often, you can design a parameter query to prompt the user for a customer number whenever the query runs. To create the query, follow these steps:

1. Starting with a select query, select the Customer and Pets tables.

2. Double-click the Customer Number field in the Customer table.

3. Double-click the Customer Name in the Customer table.

4. Double-click the Pet Name field in the Pets table.

5. Click the Criteria: cell for Customer Number.

6. Type **[Enter a Customer Number]** in the cell.

7. Deselect the Show: cell of Customer Number if you don't want this field to show in the datasheet. It has been left visible in the upcoming example figure.

That's all there is to creating a single-parameter query. Your query should resemble Figure 24-28.

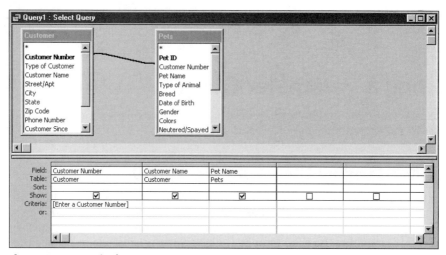

Figure 24-28: A single-parameter query.

In the preceding example, you created a parameter query that prompts the user for a customer number by displaying the message Enter a Customer Number each time the query is run. Access will convert the user's entry to an equals criteria for the field Customer Number. If a valid number is entered, Access will find the correct records.

Caution

When specifying a prompt message for the parameter, make the message meaningful but brief. When the parameter query is run, Access displays as many as 50 characters of any prompt message. If the message is longer than 50 characters, it is truncated to the first 50 characters.

Running a parameter query

To run a parameter query, select either the Run button or the Datasheet button on the toolbar. A parameter dialog box appears onscreen, such as the one shown in Figure 24-29, prompting the user for a value.

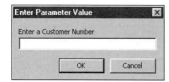

Figure 24-29: The Enter Parameter Value dialog box.

After the user enters a value or presses Enter, Access runs the query based on the criteria entered. If the criteria are valid, the datasheet shows records that match the criteria; otherwise, the datasheet displays no records.

If the user types **GR001** in the parameter dialog box, Access displays a datasheet similar to Figure 24-30.

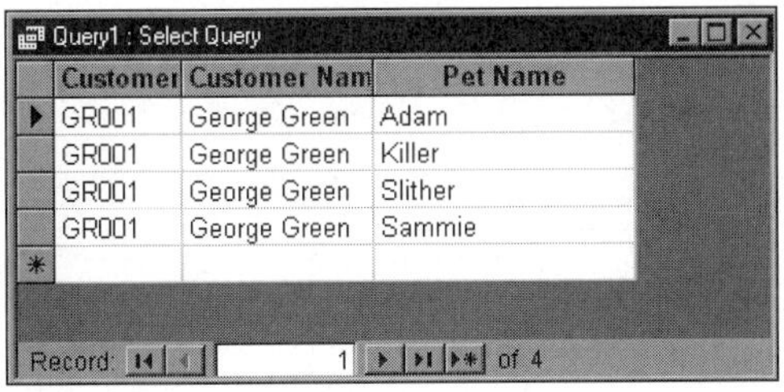

Figure 24-30: Datasheet of records specified by a parameter query.

The records displayed in Figure 24-30 are only those for George Green, whose customer number is GR001.

Creating a multiple-parameter query

You are not limited to creating a query with a single parameter. You can create a query that asks for multiple criteria. For example, you may want a query that displays all pet and visit information based on a type of animal and a range of visit dates. You can design this multiple-parameter query as simply as you designed the single-parameter query. To create this query, follow these steps:

1. Select the Pets and Visits tables.

2. Double-click the Pet Name field in the Pets table.

3. Double-click the Type of Animal field in the Pets table.

4. Double-click the Visit Date field in the Visits table.

5. Click in the Criteria: cell for Type of Animal.

6. Type **[Enter an Animal Type]** in the cell.

7. Click in the Criteria: cell for Visit Date.

8. Type **Between [Start Date] And [End Date]** in the cell.

Steps 6 and 8 contain the prompt messages for the prompt criteria. This query will display three parameter query prompts. Your query should resemble that shown in Figure 24-31.

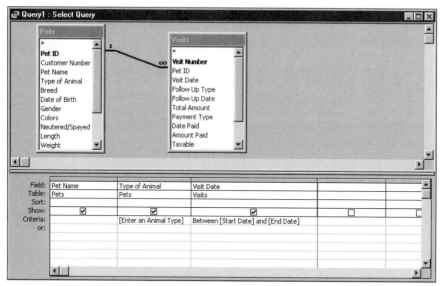

Figure 24-31: A parameter query with three criteria specified.

When this query runs, Access prompts the user for the three criteria in this order:

✦ Enter an Animal Type

✦ Start Date

✦ End Date

Like the single-parameter example, the user must enter valid criteria. If the user enters valid criteria in all three dialog boxes, Access displays all records meeting the specified criteria. Otherwise, it displays no records.

Tip   You can create parameter queries using any valid operator, including the `Like` operator with wildcards. For example, the query with the parameter `Like [Enter a State Abbr or Enter for all States] & *` lets the user run the query for a single state or for all states.

Viewing the parameter dialog box

Access defaults the prompt order to left to right, based on the position of the fields and their parameters. However, you can override the prompt order by selecting the Query ➪ Parameters... Query menu choice and specifying an order.

To specify a prompt order, enter the criteria on the QBE pane just as you have been doing. For example, to specify a prompt order of Start Date, End Date, and Animal Type, follow these steps:

1. Start with the query in Figure 24-31.

2. Select Query ➪ Parameters… from the Query menu.

3. Type **[Enter an Animal Type]** in the first cell under the Parameter column.

4. Press Tab to move to the Data Type column.

5. Enter **Text** or select the Text type from the drop-down list.

6. Press Tab to move to the Parameter column.

7. Type **[Start Date]** in the first cell under the Parameter column.

8. Press Tab to move to the Data Type column.

9. Type **Date/Time** or select the Date/Time type from the drop-down list box.

10. Press Tab to move to the Parameter column.

11. Type **[End Date]** in the first cell under the Parameter column.

12. Press Tab to move to the Data Type column.

13. Type **Date/Time** or select the Date/Time type from the drop-down list.

14. Press Enter or click OK to leave the dialog box.

Your Query Parameters dialog box should look like that shown in Figure 24-32.

Figure 24-32: The Query Parameters dialog box.

Notice that the message prompt in the Parameter column must match exactly the message prompt in each of the Criteria: cells of the QBE pane. If the prompt message does not match, the query will not work correctly.

Caution When specifying a parameter order, you must specify the correct data type for each parameter in the Query Parameters dialog box, otherwise Access reports a data type mismatch error.

Summary

In this chapter, you learned to work with complex select queries. You learned to use total, crosstab, and parameter queries. These points were discussed:

✦ The three specialized select query types are total, crosstab, and parameter.

✦ The Total: row of the QBE pane can be divided into four distinct total categories: Group By, Expression, Total Field Record Limit, and Aggregate.

✦ Access has nine Aggregate Total options. These operators perform mathematical or selection operations.

✦ Total queries can perform calculations against all records of a table or against groups of records in a table.

✦ Total queries can be used to specify criteria that limit the records that can be processed. These criteria can be against a Group By field, an Aggregate Total field after totaling is performed, or a Non-Aggregate Total field before totaling is performed.

✦ A total query based on an expression that uses one or more of the Aggregate Total options and/or a series of Access functions can be created.

✦ A crosstab query is a two-dimensional summary matrix that has field contents specified for both the row and column headings. Each intersecting cell between the row and column heading has a Value content (usually an Aggregate Total option).

✦ Crosstab queries can have multiple fields for specifying row headings but can have only one field for specifying column headings and one for specifying the total operation against the Value cell.

✦ The column heading order in a crosstab query is specified in the Query Properties dialog box by specifying the order in the Column Headings box.

✦ The new Crosstab Query Wizard simplifies the process of creating a crosstab query.

✦ A parameter query is used for obtaining user-specified criteria when the query is run. This eliminates the need to redesign the query every time a user runs it.

✦ A parameter query can prompt the user for more than one parameter. If the user wants the order of prompting to be different from the default, the order must be specified in the Query Parameter dialog box.

In the next chapter, you work with action queries and learn to make tables, perform global updates, and delete records by using queries.

✦   ✦   ✦

Creating Action Queries

Queries are tools that let you question or request information from your database. In this chapter, you learn about a special type of query, called the *action query*, which lets you *change* the field values in your records. For example, you can change a medications field to increase all prices by 10 percent or delete all information from the records of a deceased animal.

What Is an Action Query?

The term *action query* defines a query that does something more than simply select a specific group of records and then presents it to you in a dynaset. The word *action* suggests performing some operation — doing, influencing, or affecting something. The word is synonymous with operation, performance, and work. This is exactly what an action query does — some specific operation or work.

An action query can be considered a select query that is given a *duty* to perform against a specified group of records in the dynaset.

When you create any query, Access creates it as a select query automatically. You can specify a different type (such as action) from the Query Design menu. From this menu, you can choose from several types of action queries. (The menu's selections are *Make Table, Update, Append*, and *Delete*.)

Like select queries, action queries create a dynaset that you can view in a datasheet. To see the dynaset, click the Datasheet button on the toolbar. Unlike select queries, action queries perform an action — specified in the Query by

Example (QBE) pane of the query design — when you click the Run button (the button with the exclamation point) on the toolbar.

You can quickly identify action queries in the Database window by the special exclamation point icons that sit beside their names. There are four different types of action queries (see Figure 25-1); each has a different icon.

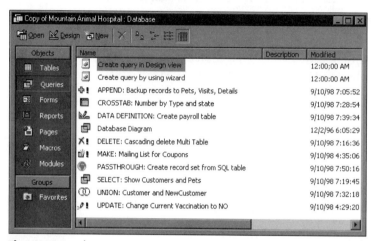

Figure 25-1: The query container of the Database window showing select and action queries.

Uses of Action Queries

Action queries can accomplish these tasks:

✦ Delete specified records from a table or group of tables

✦ Append records from one table to another

✦ Update information in a group of records

✦ Create a new table from specified records in a query

These examples describe some practical uses for action queries:

✦ You want to create history tables and then copy all inactive records to them. (You consider a record inactive if a customer hasn't brought a pet to the office in more than three years.) You decide to remove the inactive records from your active database tables.

- *What to do?* Use a make-table query to create the history tables and a delete query to remove the unwanted records.

✦ One of your old clients, whom you haven't seen in more than four years, comes in with a new puppy; you need to bring the old information back into the active file from the backup files.

- *What to do?* Use an append query to add records from your backup tables to your active tables.

Caution

Action queries change, add, or delete data. As a result, it's a good idea to observe the following rules.

To avoid changing the data:

✦ Always back up your table *before* performing the query.

✦ Always create and view the action query (use the Datasheet button on the toolbar) before *performing it.*

The Process of Action Queries

Because action queries are *irreversible*, follow this four-step process when you're working with them:

1. Create the action query specifying the fields and the criteria.

2. View the records selected in the action query by clicking on the Datasheet button on the toolbar.

3. Run the action query by clicking on the Run button on the toolbar.

4. Check the changes in the tables by clicking on the Datasheet button on the toolbar.

If you follow these steps, you can use action queries relatively safely.

Viewing the Results of an Action Query

Action queries perform a specific task—many times a destructive task. Be very careful when using them. It's important to view the changes that they will make before you run the action query and to verify afterward that they made the changes that you anticipated. Before you learn how to create and run an action query, it's also important to review the process for seeing what your changes will look like *before* you change a table permanently.

Viewing a query before using update and delete queries

Before actually performing an action query, you can click on the Datasheet View button to see which set of data the action query will work with. Meanwhile, when you're updating or deleting records with an action query, the actions take place on the underlying tables that the query is currently using. To view the results of an update or a delete query, click the Datasheet button to see whether the records will be updated or deleted before committing the action.

Note   If your update query made changes to the fields you used for selecting the records, you may have to look at the underlying table or change the selection query to see the changes. For example, if you deleted a set of records with an action button, the resulting select dynaset of the same record criteria will show that no records exist. By removing the delete criteria, you can view the table and verify that all the records specified have been deleted.

Switching to the result table of a make-table or append query

Unlike the update or delete queries, make-table and append queries copy resultant records to another table. After specifying the fields and the criteria in the QBE pane of the Query Design window, the make-table and the append queries copy the specified fields and records to *another* table. When you run the queries, the results take place in another table, not in the current table.

Pressing the Datasheet button shows you a dynaset of only the criteria and fields that were specified, not the actual table that contains the new or added records. To view the results of a make-table or append query, open the new table and view the contents to verify that the make-table or append query worked correctly. If you won't be using the action query again, do not save it. Delete it.

Reversing action queries

Action queries copy or change data in underlying tables. After an action query is executed, it cannot be reversed. Therefore, when you're working with action queries, create a select query first to make sure that the record criteria and selection are correct for the action query.

Caution   Action queries are destructive; before performing one, always make a backup of the underlying tables.

Scoping Criteria

Action queries can use any expression composed of fields, functions, and operators to specify any limiting condition that you need to place on the query. Scoping criteria are one form of record criteria. Normally, the record criteria serve as a filter to tell Access which records to find and/or leave out of the dynaset. Because action queries do not create a dynaset, you use *scoping criteria* to specify a set of records for Access to operate on.

Creating an Action Query

Creating an action query is very similar to creating a select query. You specify the fields for the query and any *scoping criteria*.

In addition to specifying the fields and criteria, you specify an action-specific property—Append to, Make new table, Update to, or Delete where.

Creating an Update Action Query to Change Values

In this section, you learn to handle an event that requires changing many records.

Suppose that the city of Mountain View has passed an ordinance that requires horses within its borders to receive a new type of vaccination starting this year. After all of the horses have been vaccinated, you want to update your records. To create this query, you work with the Customer and Pets tables. First, change the existing status of the Current Vaccinations field in the Pets table from No to Yes wherever the field shows a current vaccination status. Then enter **Horse** in the Criteria: row for Type of Animal and **Mountain View** in the Criteria: row for the City field.

It's possible to update each record in the table individually by using a form or a datasheet. Using a select query dynaset to make these changes, however, takes a very long time. The method is not only time-consuming but also inefficient—especially if you have many records to change. In addition, this method lends itself to typing errors as you enter new text into fields.

The best way to handle this type of event is to use an *update* action query to make many changes in just one operation. You save time and eliminate many of those typos that crop up in manually edited records.

To create an update query that performs these tasks, follow a two-phase process:

1. Create a select query. View the data you want to update by pressing the Datasheet button.

2. Convert the select query to an update query. Then run the update query after you're satisfied that it will affect only the records you want to affect.

Creating a select query before an update action

As outlined earlier, the first step in making an update query is to create a select query. In this particular case, the query is for all customers who live in Mountain View and own horses. Perform these steps to create this query:

1. Create a new query using the Customer and Pets tables.

2. Select the City field from the Customer table and Type of Animal and Current Vaccinations fields from the Pets table.

3. Specify a criterion of **Mountain View** in the City field and **Horse** in the Type of Animal field.

   The Select Query Design window should now resemble the one in Figure 25-2. Notice that the QBE pane shows all three fields but shows criteria in only the fields City and Type of Animal.

4. Examine the datasheet to make sure that it has only the records you want to change. Return to the design surface when you're finished.

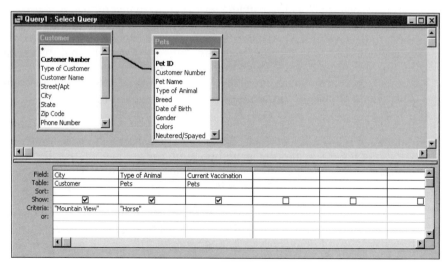

Figure 25-2: Entering a select query.

The select query datasheet should resemble the one shown in Figure 25-3. Notice that only the records for horses whose owners reside in Mountain View appear in the dynaset.

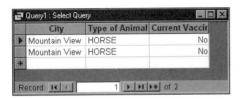

Figure 25-3: Dynaset showing only the records for horses whose owners live in Mountain View.

You are now ready to convert the select query to an update query.

Converting a select query to an update query

After you create a select query and verify the selection of records, it's time to create the update query. To convert the select query to an update query, follow these steps:

1. Select Update Query from the Query Type button on the toolbar or select Query ➪ Update from the menu.

   Access changes the title of the Query window from *Query1: Select Query* to *Query1: Update Query*. Access also adds the *Update To:* property row to the QBE pane.

2. In the Update To: cell of Current Vaccinations, enter **Yes** as shown in Figure 25-4.

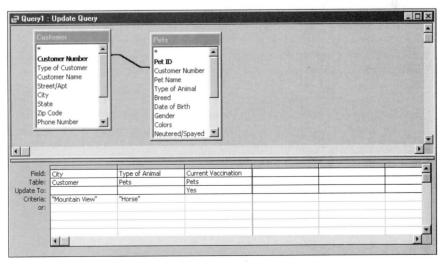

Figure 25-4: The design pane for the update query.

3. Click the Run button on the toolbar (or select Query ➪ Run from the menu).

Access displays the dialog box shown in Figure 25-5. This dialog box displays a message: *You are about to update x row[s]. Once you click Yes, you can't use the Undo command to reverse the changes. Are you sure you want to update these records?* Two command buttons are presented: Yes and No.

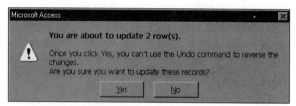

Figure 25-5: The dialog box for updating records.

4. Click the Yes button to complete the query and update the records. Selecting No stops the procedure (no records are updated).

Note If you're changing tables that are attached to another database, you *cannot* cancel the query.

Tip You can change more than one field at a time by filling in the Update To: cell of any field that you want to change. You can also change the field contents of fields that you used for limiting the records, that is, the criteria.

Checking your results

After completing the update query, check the results by changing the update query back to a select query (click on the Select Query button on the toolbar). After changing the query back to a select query, you can review the changes in the datasheet.

The update made *permanent* changes to the field Current Vaccinations for all horses whose owners live in Mountain View. If you did not back up the Pets table before running the update query, you cannot easily restore the contents to their original Yes or No settings. (You'll need a good memory if your query affects more than a few records!)

Note If you update a field that was used for a limiting criterion, you must change the criterion in the select query to the new value to verify the changes.

Creating a New Table Using a Make-Table Query

You can use an action query to create new tables based on scoping criteria. To make a new table, you create a *make-table* query. Consider the following situation as an example that might give rise to this particular task and for which you would create a make-table query.

A local pet-food company has approached you for a mailing list of customers who own dogs or cats. This company wants to send these customers a coupon for a free four-pound bag of food for each animal they own. The pet-food company plans to create the mailing labels and send the form letters if you supply a table of customer information, pet names, and type of animal. The company also stipulates that, because this is a trial mailing, only those customers you've seen in the past six months should receive letters.

You have decided to send the company the requested table of information, so now you need to create a new table from the Customer and Pets tables. A make-table query will perform these actions.

Creating the make-table query

You decide to create a make-table query for all customers who own dogs or cats and who have visited you in the past six months. (For this example, assume that six months ago was February 1, 1999.) Perform these steps to create this query:

1. Create a new query using the Customer and Pets tables.

2. Select Make Table from the Query Type button on the toolbar.

   Access displays the Make Table dialog box, as shown in Figure 25-6.

Figure 25-6: The Make Table dialog box with a table name entered.

3. Type **Mailing List for Coupons** in the Table Name: field; press Enter or click OK. Notice that the name of the window changes from *Query1: Select Query* to *Query1: Make Table Query*.

4. Select the mailing information fields (Customer Name through Zip Code) from the Customer table and the fields Pet Name, Type of Animal, and Last Visit Date from the Pets table.

5. Specify the criteria In("CAT","DOG") in the Type of Animal field and >#2/1/99# in the Last Visit Date field.

   The Query Design window should resemble the one shown in Figure 25-7. The fields are resized so that they all appear in the QBE pane. Two fields (Type of Animal and Last Visit Date) contain criteria.

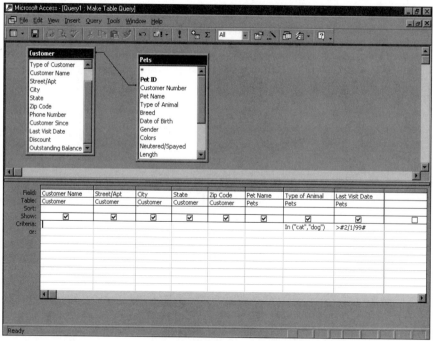

Figure 25-7: The Customer and Pets tables are in the top pane; the fields Customer Name, Street/Apt, City, State, Zip Code, Pet Name, Type of Animal, and Last Visit Date are in the bottom pane.

6. Click the Datasheet View button on the toolbar to view the dynaset (see Figure 25-8).

7. Make sure that the dynaset has only the records you specified.

8. Click the Design button to switch back to the Query Design view.

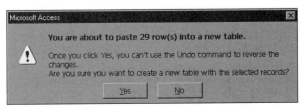

Customer Nam	Street/Apt	City	State	Zip Code	Pet Name	Type of Animal	Last Visit D
All Creatures	21 Grace St.	Tall Pines	WA	987462541	Fido	DOG	11/5
Animal Kingdon	15 Marlin Lane	Borderville	ID	834835646	Tom	CAT	10/11
Animal Kingdon	15 Marlin Lane	Borderville	ID	834835646	Marcus	CAT	2/26
Animal Kingdon	15 Marlin Lane	Borderville	ID	834835646	Pookie	CAT	4/16
Animal Kingdon	15 Marlin Lane	Borderville	ID	834835646	Mario	DOG	10/15
Animal Kingdon	15 Marlin Lane	Borderville	ID	834835646	Luigi	DOG	8/9
James Brown	3454 Adams St	Borderville	OR	974011019	John Boy	DOG	2/3
Bow Wow Hous	76 Canine Ln.	Ranier City	WA	987562175	Sweety	DOG	6/17
Bow Wow Hous	76 Canine Ln.	Ranier City	WA	987562175	Quintin	DOG	8/15
Cat House Pets	76 Right Ln.	Borderville	OR	975412856	Silly	CAT	4/14
Critters and Mor	200 Feline Rd	Borderville	WA	984538567	Mule	CAT	9/3
Wanda Greenfie	66 Farmaccess	Tall Pines	WA	984012201	Sammie Girl	DOG	2/23
Patricia Irwin	456 Bishops Ln	Lakeville	OR	974011021	C.C.	CAT	6/17
Patricia Irwin	456 Bishops Ln	Lakeville	OR	974011021	Gizmo	CAT	4/22
Patricia Irwin	456 Bishops Ln	Lakeville	OR	974011021	Stripe	CAT	5/4
Patricia Irwin	456 Bishops Ln	Lakeville	OR	974011021	Romeo	CAT	5/4
Patricia Irwin	456 Bishops Ln	Lakeville	OR	974011021	Ceasar	CAT	5/4
Patricia Irwin	456 Bishops Ln	Lakeville	OR	974011021	Juliet	CAT	5/5
Patricia Irwin	456 Bishops Ln	Lakeville	OR	974011021	Tiger	CAT	6/17
Michael Johnso	77 Farmaccess	Ranier City	WA	984012201	Rover	DOG	4/23
Adam Johnson	55 Childs Ave	Mount Pilot	ID	834121043	Fi Fi	DOG	3/7
Margaret McKin	5512 Green Acr	Borderville	OR	974121001	Rex	DOG	3/9
Margaret McKin	5512 Green Acr	Borderville	OR	974121001	Ceasar	DOG	3/9
Pet City	91 Main St.	Mount Pilot	ID	831875638	Sylvester	DOG	6/18
William Primen	1234 Main St	Mountain View	WA	98401-1011	Brutus	DOG	5/19
Village Pets	30 Murphy St.	Russettown	ID	830198573	Ren	DOG	6/28

Figure 25-8: The dynaset of cats and dogs you have seen since February 1, 1999.

9. Deselect the Show: property of the field *Last Visit Date*.

You do not want to copy this field to the new table Mailing List for Coupons. Only those fields selected with a checkmark in the checkbox of the Show: row are copied to the new table. By deselecting a field with a criteria set, you can base the scoping criteria on fields that will *not* be copied to the new table.

10. Click the Run button on the toolbar or select Query ➪ Run from the menu.

Access indicates how many records it will copy to the new table (see Figure 25-9).

11. Click the Yes button to complete the query and make the new table. Selecting No stops the procedure (no records are copied).

Figure 25-9: The dialog box for copying records.

When you're creating numerous make-table queries, you need to select Make Table Query from the Query Type button on the toolbar or select Query ➪ Make Table... from the menu; this command renames the make-table query each time. Access assumes that you want to overwrite the existing table if you don't reselect the make-table option. Access warns you about overwriting before performing the new make-table query; as an alternative, you could change the Destination table name on the Property sheet.

Checking your results

After you complete the make-table query, check your results by opening the new table Mailing List for Coupons, which was added to the database container (see Figure 25-10).

Customer Nam	Street/Apt	City	State	Zip Code	Pet Nam
All Creatures	21 Grace St.	Tall Pines	WA	987462541	Fido
Animal Kingdon	15 Marlin Lane	Borderville	ID	834835646	Tom
Animal Kingdon	15 Marlin Lane	Borderville	ID	834835646	Marcus
Animal Kingdon	15 Marlin Lane	Borderville	ID	834835646	Pookie
Animal Kingdon	15 Marlin Lane	Borderville	ID	834835646	Mario
Animal Kingdon	15 Marlin Lane	Borderville	ID	834835646	Luigi
James Brown	3454 Adams St	Borderville	OR	974011019	John Boy
Bow Wow Hous	76 Canine Ln.	Ranier City	WA	987562175	Sweety
Bow Wow Hous	76 Canine Ln.	Ranier City	WA	987562175	Quintin
Cat House Pets	76 Right Ln.	Borderville	OR	975412856	Silly
Critters and Mor	200 Feline Rd	Borderville	WA	984538567	Mule
Wanda Greenfie	66 Farmaccess	Tall Pines	WA	984012201	Sammie Gi
Patricia Irwin	456 Bishops Ln	Lakeville	OR	974011021	C.C.
Patricia Irwin	456 Bishops Ln	Lakeville	OR	974011021	Gizmo
Patricia Irwin	456 Bishops Ln	Lakeville	OR	974011021	Stripe
Patricia Irwin	456 Bishops Ln	Lakeville	OR	974011021	Romeo
Patricia Irwin	456 Bishops Ln	Lakeville	OR	974011021	Ceasar

Record: 1 of 29

Figure 25-10: The new table Mailing List for Coupons.

Note When you create a table from a make-table query, the fields in the new table inherit the data type and field size from the fields in the query's underlying tables; however, no other field or table properties are transferred. If you want to define a primary key or other properties, you need to edit the design of the new table.

Tip You can also use a make-table action query to create a backup of your tables before you create action queries that change the contents of the tables. Backing up a table using a make-table action query *does not copy* the table's properties or primary key to the new table.

To copy any database object (table, query, form, or other object) while you're in the Database window, follow these steps:

1. Highlight the object you need to copy.

2. Press Ctrl+C (or select Edit ⇨ Copy) to copy the object to the Clipboard.

3. Press Ctrl+V (or select Edit ⇨ Paste) to paste the object from the Clipboard.

4. Enter the new object name (table, form, and so forth) and click the OK button in the dialog box. If the object is a table, you also can specify Structure with or without the data and append it to an existing table.

Creating a Query to Append Records

As the word *append* suggests, an append query attaches or adds records to a specified table. An append query adds records from the table you're using to another table. The table you want to add records to must already exist. You can append records to a table in the same database or in another Access database.

Append queries are very useful for adding information to another table on the basis of some scoping criteria. Even so, append queries are not always the fastest way of adding records to another database. If you need, for example, to append all fields and all records from one table to a new table, the append query is *not* the best way to do it. Instead, use the Copy and Paste options on the Edit menu when you're working with the table in a datasheet or form.

Tip   You can add records to an open table. You don't have to close the table before adding records. However, Access does not automatically refresh the view of the table that has records added to it. To refresh the table, press Shift+F9. This action requeries the table so that you can see the appended records.

When you're working with append queries, be aware of these rules:

1. If the table you're appending records to has a primary key field, the records you add cannot have Null values or duplicate primary key values. If they do, Access will not append the records and you will get no warning.

2. If you add records to another database table, you must know the location and name of the database.

3. If you use the asterisk (*) field in a QBE row, you cannot also use individual fields from the same table. Access assumes that you're trying to add field contents twice to the same record and will not append the records.

4. If you append records with an AutoNumber field (an Access-specified primary key), do not include the AutoNumber field if the table you're appending to also has the field and record contents (this causes the problem specified in rule 1). Also, if you're adding to an empty table and you want the new table to have a new AutoNumber number (that is, order number) based on the criteria, do not use the AutoNumber field.

By following these simple rules, your append query will perform as expected and become a very useful tool.

Here's an example that will help illustrate the use of append queries: Every February you archive all records of animals that died during the preceding year. To archive the records, you perform two steps. First, you append them to existing backup files. Second, you delete the records from the active database.

In this case, you want to add records to the backup tables for deceased animals in your active tables. In other words, you will copy records to three tables: Pets, Visits, and Visit Details. You need three backup files to perform this exercise. To create the backup files, perform the following steps:

1. Press F11 or Alt+F1 to display the Database window.

2. Click the Tables object button to display the list of tables.

3. Click the Pets table to highlight it.

4. Press Ctrl+C (or select Edit ➪ Copy) to copy the object Pets table to the Clipboard.

5. Press Ctrl+V (or select Edit ➪ Paste) to display the Paste Table As dialog box.

6. Click Structure Only in the Paste Options section of the dialog box (or tab to the Paste Options section and click S).

7. Click the Table Name: box and type **Pets Backup**.

8. Click OK (or press Enter after typing the filename).

9. Open the Pets Backup table (it should be empty); then close the table.

Repeat this process for both the Visits and Visit Details tables, naming them **Visits Backup** and **Visit Details Backup**, respectively.

To create an append query that copies the deceased animals' records, follow a two-step process:

1. Create a select query to verify that only the records that you want to append are copied.

2. Convert the select query to an append query and run it.

Note When you're using the append query, only fields with names that match in the two tables are copied. For example, you may have a small table with six fields and another with nine. The table with nine fields has only five of the six field names that match fields in the smaller table. If you append records from the smaller table to the larger table, only the five matching fields are appended; the other four fields remain blank.

Creating the select query for an append query

To create a select query for all pets that died last year, along with their visit histories, follow these steps:

1. Create a new query using the Pets, Visits, and Visit Details tables.

2. Select the Deceased field from the Pets table.

3. Specify a criterion of **Yes** in the Deceased field.

   You may want to select some additional fields from each table, such as Pet Name, Visit Date, Visit Type, Treatment Code, and so forth. The Select Query Design window should resemble the one shown in Figure 25-11. Notice that all the fields are resized to appear in the QBE pane. The only field and criterion that must be in this select query is the first field: Deceased. If you add any other fields, make sure that you remove them before converting this query to an append query.

4. Go to the datasheet and make sure that all the Deceased field contents say Yes (see Figure 25-12).

5. Return to design mode. With the select query created correctly, you are ready to convert the select query to an append query.

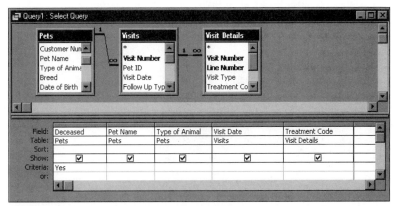

Figure 25-11: The tables Pets, Visits, and Visit Details are in the top pane, and selected fields are in the QBE pane.

Deceased	Pet Name	Type of Animal	Visit Date	Treatment Code
Yes	Tom	CAT	10/3/99	0300
Yes	Tom	CAT	10/3/99	0102
Yes	Tom	CAT	10/3/99	2002
Yes	Tom	CAT	10/4/99	0303
Yes	Tom	CAT	12/4/99	0300
Yes	Tom	CAT	12/4/99	2001
Yes	Tom	CAT	12/4/99	2004
Yes	John Boy	DOG	1/17/99	0300
Yes	John Boy	DOG	2/23/99	0300
Yes	Romeo	CAT	8/4/98	0100
Yes	Romeo	CAT	8/4/98	0101
Yes	Romeo	CAT	8/4/98	0102
Yes	Romeo	CAT	8/6/99	0100

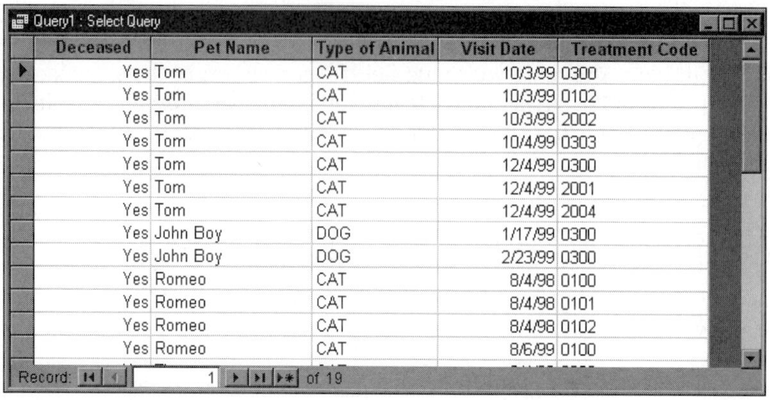

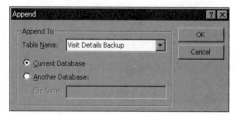

Figure 25-12: A dynaset of records for all deceased animals.

Converting to an append query

After you create the select query and verify that it is correct, you need to create the append query (actually, three different append queries — one each for the tables Visit Details, Visits, and Pets — because append queries work with only one table at a time). For this example, first copy all fields from the Visit Details table. Then copy all the fields from the Visits table. Finally, copy all the fields from the Pets table.

To convert the select query to an append query and run it, perform the following steps:

1. Deselect the Show: property of the Deceased field.
2. Select Append from the Query Type button on the toolbar, or select Query ➪ Append… from the Design menu.

   Access displays the Append dialog box, as shown in Figure 25-13.

Figure 25-13: The Append dialog box.

3. Type **Visit Details Backup** in the Table Name: field and either press Enter or click OK.

4. Drag the asterisk (*) field from the Visit Details table to the QBE pane to select all fields.

The QBE pane should look like Figure 25-14. Access automatically fills in the Append To: field under the All field-selector column.

5. Click the Run button on the toolbar (or select Query ➪ Run from the menu).

Access displays a dialog box that displays the message *You are about to append x row[s].* Then it presents two buttons (Yes and No). After you click Yes, the Undo command cannot be used to reverse the changes.

6. Click the Yes button to complete the query and copy (append) the records to the backup table. Selecting No stops the procedure (no records are copied).

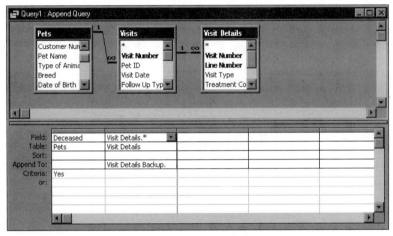

Figure 25-14: The QBE pane for an appended query.

Note After the Visit Details records for deceased animals are backed up, repeat Steps 2 through 5 for the Visits and Pets tables. Before you append fields from these other tables, however, you must remove the previous All selector field [Visit Details.*] from the QBE pane and the Visit Details table from the top pane. For example, to move the Visits records, delete the asterisk (*) field for the Visits Details table, remove the Visit Details table from the query, and select the asterisk (*) field for the Visits table. Reselect Query ➪ Append... and type **Visits Backup** for the name of the table to append to. Finally, click Run.

To create an Append query for the Pets table you will need to remove the Visits table from the query and the All selector field for the [Visits.*] QBE. Because you are using the Pets table field Deceased as your criteria, you need to select all the fields of the Pets table individually and add them to the query (except the Deceased field).

Caution If you create an append query by using the asterisk (*) field and you also use a field from the same table as the All asterisk field to specify a criterion, you must take the criteria field out of the Append To: row. If you don't, Access reports an error. Remember that the field for the criterion is already included in the asterisk field. If you leave the Show on, it tries to append the field twice, repeating an error, causing Access to halt the append query, with the result that no records are appended to the table.

Checking your results

After you complete the three append table queries, check your results. To do so, go to the Database window and select each of the three tables to be appended to (Pets Backup, Visits Backup, and Visit Details Backup); view the new records.

Creating a Query to Delete Records

Of all the action queries, the *delete query* is the most dangerous. Unlike the other types of queries you've worked with, delete queries wipe out records from tables permanently and *irreversibly*.

Like other action queries, delete queries act on a group of records on the basis of scoping criteria.

A delete action query can work with multiple tables to delete records. If you intend to delete related records from multiple tables, however, you must:

✦ Define relationships between the tables in the Relationships Builder.

✦ Check the Enforce Referential Integrity option for the join between tables.

✦ Check the Cascade Delete Related Records option for the join between tables.

Figure 25-15 shows the Relationships dialog box for the join line between tables. Notice that the options Enforce Referential Integrity and Cascade Delete Related Records are selected.

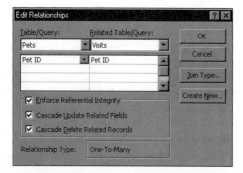

Figure 25-15: The Relationships dialog box.

When working with one-to-many relationships without defining relationships and putting Cascade Delete on, Access deletes records from only one table at a time. Specifically, Access deletes the *many* side of the relationship first. Then you must remove the many table from the query and delete the records from the *one* side of the query.

This method is time-consuming and awkward. Therefore, when you're deleting related records from one-to-many relationship tables, make sure that you define relationships between the tables and check the Cascade Delete box in the Relationships dialog box.

 Caution Because of the permanently destructive action of a delete query, always make backup copies of your tables before working with them.

The following example illustrates the use of Access action queries. In this case, you have a large number of records to delete.

You are going to delete all records of deceased animals. Recall that you already copied all deceased pet records to backup tables in the append query section. The tables you're dealing with have these relationships:

> ✦ One pet has many visits.
>
> ✦ One visit has many visit details.

Both of these are one-to-many relationships. As a result, if you don't define permanent relationships between the tables and turn on Cascade Delete, you'll need to create three separate delete queries. (You would need to delete from the Visit Details, Visits, and Pets tables — in that order.)

With relations set and Cascade Delete on, however, you have to delete only the records from the Pets table; Access automatically deletes all related records. Assume for this example that you have already appended the records to another table — or that you have made a new table of the records that you're about to delete, set up permanent relationships among the three tables, and turned on Cascade Delete for both relationships (that is, between Pets and Visits and between Visits and Visit Details).

Creating a cascading delete query

To create a *cascading delete* query for all pets that died last year, along with their visit histories, perform these steps:

1. Create a new query using the Pets, Visits, and Visit Details tables.

2. Select Query ⇨ Delete from the Design menu.

   The name of the window changes from *Select Query:Query1* to *Delete Query:Query1*.

3. Select the Deceased field from the Pets table.

4. Specify the criterion **Yes** in the Deceased field.

The Delete Query Design window is shown in Figure 25-16. The only field and criteria that must appear in this delete query is the first field, Deceased.

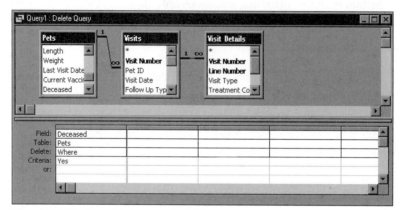

Figure 25-16: The delete query's QBE pane.

5. Go to the datasheet and verify that only records which say *Yes* are there.

6. Return to the Design window.

7. Click the Run button on the toolbar (or select Query ⇨ Run from the menu).

Access displays a dialog box with the message: *You are about to delete x row[s] from the specified table (Pets). After you click Yes, you can't use the Undo command to reverse the changes. Are you sure that you want to delete the selected records?* Access does not specify how many rows will be deleted from the other tables that may be linked to the table you selected.

8. Click the Yes button to complete the query. The records are removed from all three tables. When you click Yes, Access deletes the records in the Pets table and then automatically deletes the related records in the Visits and Visit Details tables. Selecting No stops the procedure (no records are deleted).

Remember that a delete query permanently and irreversibly removes the records from the table(s). Therefore, it is important that the records to be deleted are backed up *before* they are deleted.

Checking your results

After completing the delete query, you can check your results by pressing the Datasheet button on the toolbar. If the delete query worked correctly, you will see no records in the datasheet.

You have now deleted all records of deceased animals from the database tables Pets, Visits, and Visit Details.

Note Delete queries remove entire records, not just the data in specific fields. If you need to delete only values in specific fields, use an update query to change the values to empty values.

Creating Other Queries Using the Query Wizards

In the preceding chapter, you learned to use a Query Wizard to create a crosstab query. Access has two other Wizards that can help maintain your databases:

✦ Find Duplicate Query Wizard, which shows duplicate records in a single table on the basis of a field in the table.

✦ Find Unmatched Query Wizard, which shows all records that do not have a corresponding record in another table (for example, a customer with no pets or a pet with no owner).

The Find Duplicate Query Wizard works on a single table. The Find Unmatched Query Wizard compares records from one table with another.

These Wizards (along with all the others, such as the Crosstab Wizard) are listed when you first start a new query.

Find Duplicate Query Wizard

This Wizard helps you create a query that reports which records in a table are duplicated using some field or fields in the table as a basis. Access asks which fields you want to use for checking duplication and then prompts you to enter some other fields that you may want to see in the query. Finally, Access asks for a title and then it creates and displays the query.

This type of Wizard query can help you find duplicate key violations, a valuable trick when you want to take an existing table and make a unique key field with existing data. If you try to create a unique key field and Access reports an error, you know that you have either Nulls in the field or duplicate records. The query helps find the duplicates.

Find Unmatched Query Wizard

This Wizard helps you create a query that reports any orphan or widow records between two tables.

An *orphan* is a record in a *many*-side table that has no corresponding record in the one-side table. For example, you may have a pet in the Pets table that does not have an owner in the Customer table (the pet is an orphan).

A *widow* is a record in the *one* side of a one-to-many or one-to-one table that does not have a corresponding record in the other table. For example, you may have a customer who has no animals in the Pets table.

Access asks for the names of the two tables to compare; it also asks for the link field name between the tables. Access prompts you for the fields that you want to see in the first table and for a title. Then it creates the query.

This type of query can help find records that have no corresponding records in other tables. If you create a relationship between tables and try to set referential integrity but Access reports that it cannot activate the feature, some records are violating integrity. This query helps find them quickly.

Saving an Action Query

Saving an action query is just like saving any other query. From design mode, you can save the query and continue working by clicking the Save button on the toolbar (or by selecting File ➪ Save from the Query menu). If this is the first time you're saving the query, Access prompts you for a name in the Save As dialog box.

You can also save the query and exit by either selecting File ➪ Close from the menu or double-clicking on the Control menu button (in the top-left corner of the Query window) and answering Yes to this dialog box question: *Save changes to the design of '<query name>'?* You also can save the query by pressing F12.

Running an Action Query

After you save an action query, you can run it by double-clicking its name. Access will warn you that an action query is about to be executed and ask for confirmation before it continues with the query.

Troubleshooting Action Queries

When you're working with action queries, you need to be aware of several potential problems. While you're running the query, any of several messages may appear, including messages that several records were lost because of *key violations* or that records were *locked* during the execution of the query. This section discusses some of these problems and how to avoid them.

Data-type errors in appending and updating

If you attempt to enter a value that is not appropriate for the specified field, Access doesn't enter the value; it simply ignores the incorrect values and converts the fields to Null values. When you're working with append queries, Access will append the records, but the fields may be blank!

Key violations in action queries

When you attempt to append records to another database that has a primary key, Access will not append records that contain the same primary key value.

Access does not let you update a record and change a primary key value to an existing value. You can change a primary key value to another value under these conditions:

✦ The new primary key value does not already exist.

✦ The field value you're attempting to change is not related to fields in other tables.

Access does not let you delete a field on the *one* side of a one-to-many relationship without first deleting the records from the *many* side.

Access does not let you append or update a field value that will duplicate a value in a *unique index field*—one that has the Index property set to Yes (No Duplicates).

Record-locked fields in multiuser environments

Access will not perform an action query on records locked by another user. When you're performing an update or append query, you can choose to continue and change all other values. But remember this: If you allow Access to continue with an action query, you won't be able to determine which records were left unchanged!

Text fields

When appending or updating to a Text field that is smaller than the current field, Access truncates any text data that doesn't fit in the new field. Access does not warn you that it truncated the information.

Summary

In this chapter, you learned to create and use a special type of query called the action query. This type of query goes beyond performing searches; it can make changes to the data. This chapter covered these points:

✦ Action queries perform some operation on the tables you're using. The operation can be deleting records, changing the contents of records, adding records to another table, or making new tables.

✦ The various types of action queries include make-table, append, update, and delete.

✦ Action queries do not create a dynaset. To view the results of an action query, you must convert it to a select query (if it's a delete or update query) or view the affected table.

✦ Always back up your tables before you work with action queries.

✦ When you create an action query, it's best to create a select query first to make sure that the action will affect the correct records.

✦ Append action queries can work with only one table at a time.

✦ Append action queries must already have an existing table to append to. The query does not create a table if one doesn't already exist.

✦ The append query is not the best method for appending all records from one table to another. It's better to copy the table to the Clipboard and paste it to the other table.

✦ Make-table action queries can take fields from one or many tables and combine them into a single table.

✦ Delete action queries can delete records from multiple tables that have one-to-one relationships.

✦ Delete action queries for tables with one-to-many relationships require deleting the *many*-side records first; then the *one*-side record can be deleted.

✦ Unless an action query will be executed over and over, do not save it.

✦ Access enforces all referential rules when performing action queries. If an action query attempts to perform an operation that violates referential integrity, Access halts the operation.

In the next chapter, you examine advanced query topics.

✦   ✦   ✦

Advanced Query Topics

In this chapter, you work with queries in greater detail and complexity than in earlier chapters. So far, you have worked with all types of queries: select, action, crosstab, and parameter. You have not, however, worked with all the options that can be used with these types of queries.

This chapter focuses on a wide range of advanced query topics. You will read several topics that were explained in other chapters; this chapter addresses them in greater detail. A firm understanding of advanced queries can prevent unexpected problems.

Using Lookup Tables and Joins

A lookup table is used to validate the entry of data or find additional information based on a key value. Such a table uses, by definition, a many-to-one relationship; many records in the primary table can reference information from one record in the lookup table. A lookup table can be permanent or transient:

Permanent	Created solely for lookup purposes
Transient	Used as either a lookup table or a primary table

The Mountain Animal Hospital database has four permanent lookup tables: States, Pets, Treatments, and Medications.

The Customer table is an example of a *transient lookup table*. When you're working with a form to add pet personal information (name, type, and so on), the Customer table becomes a lookup table based on the customer number. Although the Customer table is a primary table of the database, in this case it becomes a lookup table for the Pets table.

Working with lookup tables in queries does require an understanding of joins and how they work. For example, you may be interested in displaying visit details along with the specific treatment and medication given for each visit. Treatment and medication information comes from the lookup tables — in this case, Treatments and Medications. To create this query, follow these steps:

1. Select the Visit Details, Treatments, and Medications tables and join them if they are not already joined using standard inner joins (the value must be found in both tables from Visit Details to Treatments and Visit Details to Medications).

2. Double-click the Visit Number field in the Visit Details table.

3. Double-click the Visit Type field in the Visit Details table.

4. Double-click the Treatment field of the Treatments table.

5. Double-click the Medication Name field of the Medications table.

Your query should look like Figure 26-1. Notice that Visit Details uses both Treatments and Medications as lookup tables.

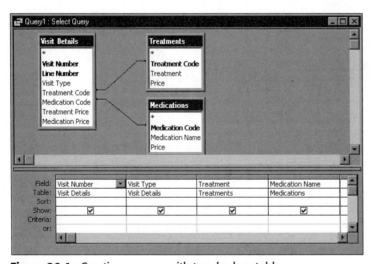

Figure 26-1: Creating a query with two lookup tables.

After you create the query, select the Datasheet option from the Query View button on the toolbar to display a dynaset similar to the one in Figure 26-2. (Clicking once toggles back and forth between the Design view and the Datasheet. Clicking the drop-down arrow displays all three options: Query View, Datasheet, and SQL.)

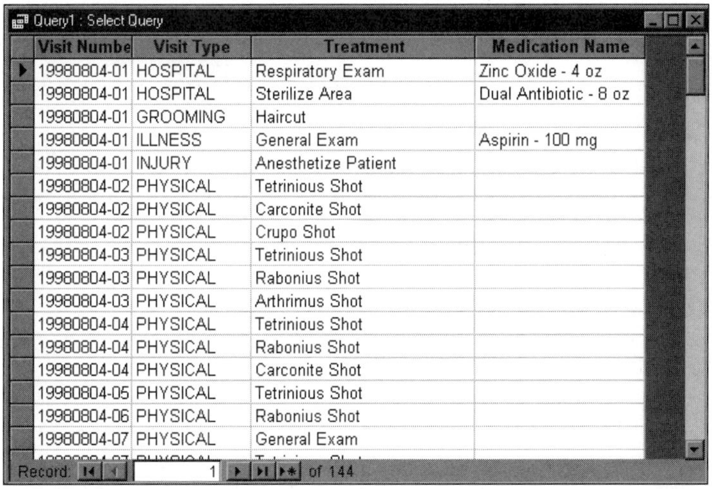

Figure 26-2: Datasheet of a query with two lookup tables.

Using the DLookUp( ) Function for Lookup Tables

Another way to find specific lookup information based on a field is to create a calculated field using the DLookUp( ) function. DLookUp( ) finds information in a table that is not currently open. While it can be easy to program and works well with small amounts of records, if your tables contain more than 5,000 records you should do this with DAO code (see Chapters 34 and 35). The general syntax for the DLookUp( ) function is:

```
DLookUp("[Field to display]", "[Lookup Table]", "<Criteria for
Search>")
```

"[Field to display]" in quotation marks is the field in the lookup table you want to find.

"[Lookup Table]" in quotation marks is the table containing the field you want to display.

"<Criteria for Search>" in quotation marks signifies criteria used by the lookup function.

Access suggests that *Criteria for Search* is not necessary, but if you want to use a different criterion for each record, it is essential. When you use DLookUp( ), the format of your criteria is critical. The syntax of *Criteria for Search* is as follows:

```
"[Field in Lookup Table] = '<Example Data>' "
```

You can replace the equal operator with any valid Access operator.

'<Example Data>' in single quotation marks is usually a literal, such as 'DOG' or 'AC001'. If the data is a field in the current table, you must use the following syntax:

```
" & [Field in This Table] & "
```

Continued

(continued)

Notice that the field is surrounded with double quotation marks (") and ampersands (&).

Although using the DLookUp( ) function to build a calculated field seems complex, it can be a simple way to create a query for use by a form or report. To create a query that finds the medication name and treatment in the Treatments and Medications tables, follow these steps:

1. Select the Visit Details table.

2. Double-click on the Visit Type field in the Visit Details table.

3. In an empty field in the QBE pane, type: `TreatmentType:DLookUp ("[Treatment]", "[Treatments]","[Treatment Code]='"&[Visit Details]. [Treatment Code]&"'").`

4. In another empty field in the QBE pane, type `MedicationType: DLookUp ("[MedicationName]", "[Medications]","[Medication Code] = '"&[Visit Details]. [Medication Code]&"'").`

When you enter the field name of the current table in the criteria for the DLookUp( ) function, you must not use spaces. After the equal sign, type the entry in this format:

```
single quote - double quote - ampersand - [field name] -
ampersand - double quote - single quote - double quote
```

No spaces can be entered between the quotation marks (single or double).

Figure 26-3 shows how the query looks after the calculated fields Treatment Type and Medication Type are entered. Notice that you don't see the entire formula you entered.

If you're having problems typing in Steps 3 or 4, press Shift+F2 to activate the Zoom window. After activating the window, the entire contents will be highlighted; press F2 again to deselect the contents and move to the end of them.

If you now select the Datasheet option using the Query View button on the toolbar, you see a datasheet similar to Figure 26-4. Notice that several records have no medication name, because these treatments required no medication. The results should be identical with the method shown in Figure 26-2.

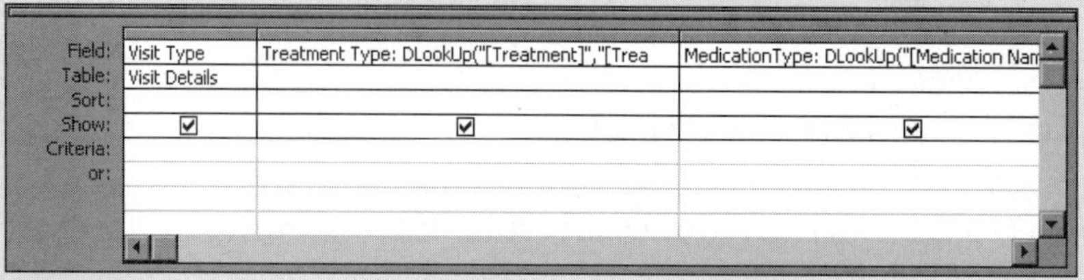

Field:	Visit Type	Treatment Type: DLookUp("[Treatment]", "[Trea	MedicationType: DLookUp("[Medication Nam
Table:	Visit Details		
Sort:			
Show:	☑	☑	☑
Criteria:			
or:			

Figure 26-3: The QBE pane showing two calculated fields using the DLookUp( ) function.

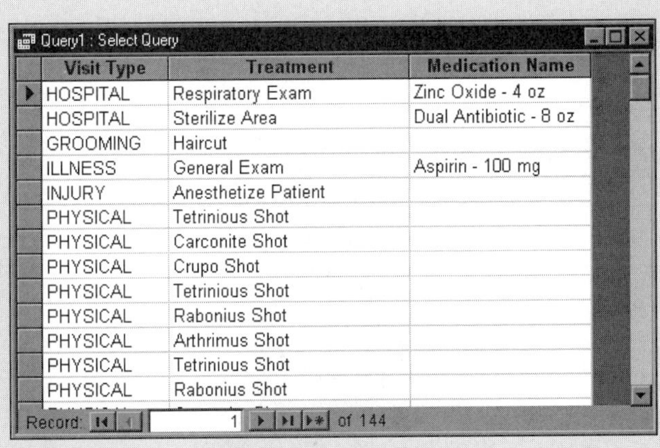

Query1 : Select Query

Visit Type	Treatment	Medication Name
HOSPITAL	Respiratory Exam	Zinc Oxide - 4 oz
HOSPITAL	Sterilize Area	Dual Antibiotic - 8 oz
GROOMING	Haircut	
ILLNESS	General Exam	Aspirin - 100 mg
INJURY	Anesthetize Patient	
PHYSICAL	Tetrinious Shot	
PHYSICAL	Carconite Shot	
PHYSICAL	Crupo Shot	
PHYSICAL	Tetrinious Shot	
PHYSICAL	Rabonius Shot	
PHYSICAL	Arthrimus Shot	
PHYSICAL	Tetrinious Shot	
PHYSICAL	Rabonius Shot	

Record: 1 of 144

Figure 26-4: A datasheet using the DlookUp method.

Using Calculated Fields

Queries are not limited to actual fields from tables; you can also use *calculated fields* (created by performing some calculation). A calculated field can be created in many different ways, for example:

✦ Concatenating two Text type fields using the ampersand (&)

✦ Performing a mathematical calculation on two Number type fields

✦ Using an Access function to create a field based on the function

In the next example, you create a simple calculated field, Total Due, from the Outstanding Balance and Discount fields in the Customer table by following these steps:

1. Create a new query by using the Customer table.
2. Select the Outstanding Balance and Discount fields from the Customer table.
3. Click an empty Field: cell of the QBE pane.
4. Press Shift+F2 to activate the Zoom box (or right mouse click and select Zoom…).
5. Type `Total Due: Format([Outstanding Balance]-[Outstanding Balance]* [Discount],"currency")`.
6. Click the OK button in the Zoom box (or press Enter).

Figure 26-5 shows the expression from Step 5 being built in the Zoom window. Total Due is the calculated field name for the expression. The field name and expression are separated by a colon.

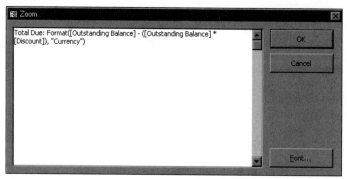

Figure 26-5: Creating a simple calculated field.

Access 2000 has an *Expression Builder* that helps you create any expression, such as a complex calculated field for a query. In the following example, you create a calculated field named Next Visit Date that displays a date six months in the future. You can use this date for a letter you plan to send to all customers; the date is based on the Last Visit Date field of the Pets table. To create this calculated field, follow these steps:

1. Create a new query using the Pets table.

2. Select the Type of Animal and Last Visit Date fields from the Pets table.

3. Click an empty Field: cell in the QBE pane.

4. Activate the Expression Builder by clicking the Build button on the toolbar (the wand). Another method is to *right*-click to display the shortcut menu and select Build.

   Access displays the Expression Builder dialog box, as shown in Figure 26-6.

   Now build the expression DateAdd("m",6,[Pets]![Last Visit Date]) for the calculated field. The DateAdd function adds a specified number of days, weeks, months, quarters, or years to another date. In this example, it is adding 6 months to the Last Visit Date value.

5. Go to the bottom-left window of the Expression Builder dialog box and expand the Functions tree by double-clicking it.

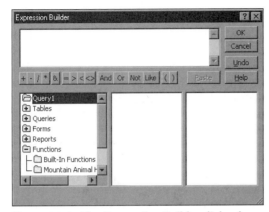

Figure 26-6: The Expression Builder dialog box.

6. Select the Built-in Functions choice (double-click it).

   Access places information in the two panes to the right of the one you're in (see Figure 26-7).

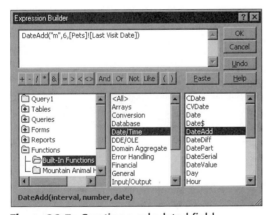

Figure 26-7: Creating a calculated field.

7. Go to the third window (which lists all the functions).

8. Select the DateAdd function (double-click it).

   Access places the function in the top-left window, with information about the necessary parameters.

9. Go to the top-left window and click the parameter `<interval>`.

10. Type "**m**".

11. Click ⟨number⟩ and replace it with **6**.

12. Click ⟨date⟩ and highlight it.

    The function should look like the one in Figure 26-7.

13. Go back to the bottom-left window; double-click Tables.

14. Select the Pets table (click it).

15. Select [Last Visit Date] from the middle window on the bottom (double-click it).

    Access places the table and field name in the last part of the DateAdd function.

16. Click OK in the Expression Builder.

    Access returns you to the QBE pane and places the expression in the cell for you.

17. Access assigns a name for the expression automatically, labeling it *Expr1*. Should your field now show this name, change it from *Expr1* to **Next Visit Date** by overwriting it.

If you perform these steps correctly, the cell looks like Figure 26-8. The DateAdd( ) function lets you add six months to Pets.Last Visit Date. The *m* signifies that you are working with months rather than days or years.

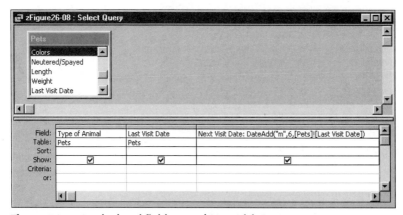

Figure 26-8: A calculated field named Next Visit Date.

Of course, you could type in the calculated field, but the Expression Builder is a valuable tool when you're creating complex, hard-to-remember expressions.

Finding the Number of Records in a Table or Query

To determine quickly the total number of records in an existing table or query, use the Count(*) function. This is a special parameter of the Count( ) function. For example, to determine the total number of records in the Pets table, follow these steps:

1. Start a new query using the Pets table.
2. Click the first empty Field: cell in the QBE pane.
3. Type **Count(*)** in the cell.

Access adds the calculated field name *Expr1* to the cell in front of the Count( ) function. Your query should now look like Figure 26-9.

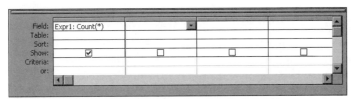

Figure 26-9: Using the Count(*) function.

The datasheet now has a single cell that shows the number of records for the Pets table. The datasheet should look like the one in Figure 26-10.

Figure 26-10: The datasheet of a Count(*) function.

If you use this function with the asterisk wildcard (*), this is the only field that can be shown in the datasheet. That is why you entered the expression Count(*) in an empty QBE pane.

The Count(*) function can also be used to determine the total number of records that match a specific criterion. For example, you may want to know how many cats you have in the Pets table. Follow these steps to ascertain the number of cats in the table:

1. Start a new query and select the Pets table.

2. Click the first empty Field: cell in the QBE pane.

3. Type **Count(*)** in the cell.

4. Double-click the Type of Animal field of the Pets table.

5. Deselect the Show: cell for Type of Animal.

6. Type **CAT** in the Criteria: cell for Type of Animal.

Figure 26-11 shows how the query should look. If you select the Datasheet option from the Query View button on the toolbar, Access again displays only one cell in the datasheet; it contains the number of cats in the Pets table. You could have given the Count(*) expression a name such as "Total Cats" instead of using the default Exp1, by overwriting Exp1 after step 6. For example: Total Cats: Count(*).

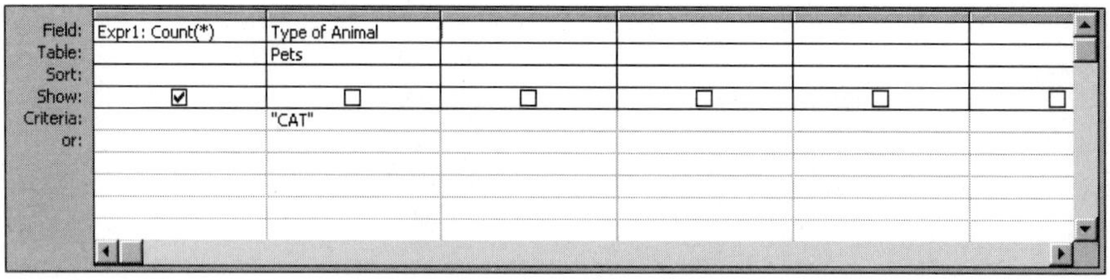

Field:	Expr1: Count(*)	Type of Animal				
Table:		Pets				
Sort:						
Show:	☑	☐	☐	☐	☐	☐
Criteria:		"CAT"				
or:						

Figure 26-11: The query to show the number of cats.

Remember that only the field that contains the Count(*) function can be shown in the datasheet. If you try to display any additional fields, Access reports an error.

Finding the Top (*n*) Records in a Query

Access 2000 not only enables you to find the number of records in an existing table or query, but also provides the capability of finding the query's first (*n*) records (that is, a set number or percentage of its records).

Suppose that you want to identify the top 10 animals that you have treated — in other words, for which animal has which owner paid the most to your business? To determine the top 10 animals and their owners, follow these steps:

1. Create a new query using the Customer, Pets, and Visits tables.

2. Select Customer Name from the Customer Table, Type of Animal and Pet Name from the Pets table, and Total Amount from the Visits table.

3. Click the Totals button () on the toolbar.

4. Change Group By (under the Total Amount field) to Sum.

5. Sort the Total Amount field in Descending order.

The resulting query should look like the one in Figure 26-12.

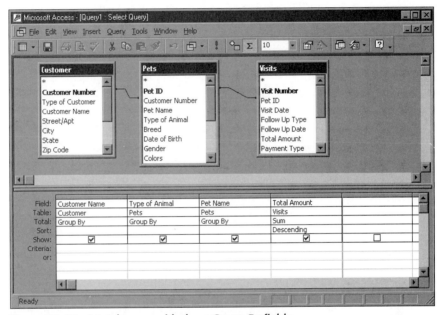

Figure 26-12: A total query with three Group By fields.

6. Click the Top Values combo box next to the button on the toolbar.

7. Enter **10** in the Top Values property cell.

You are ready to run your query. When you click on the Query View button on the toolbar, you should see the top 10 money-producing records in the dynaset, which should look like Figure 26-13. The three Group By columns sum any data with the Customer Name, Type of Animal, and Pet Name. While the Pet Name is theoretically unique, this technique allows you to display each of the values so that you can see the Customer Name and Type of Animal.

Customer Name	Type of Animal	Pet Name	SumOfTotal A
George Green	FROG	Adam	$1,239.50
Animal Kingdom	SQUIRREL	Margo	$842.50
All Creatures	RABBIT	Bobo	$632.00
Johnathan Adams	PIG	Patty	$622.00
All Creatures	LIZARD	Presto Chango	$571.00
All Creatures	DOG	Fido	$562.00
Patricia Irwin	CAT	C.C.	$495.80
William Primen	DOG	Brutus	$431.00
Patricia Irwin	CAT	Tiger	$410.00
Sandra Williams	CAT	Flower	$360.00

Figure 26-13: Dynaset of the top ten records in a query.

SQL-Specific Queries

Access 2000 has three query types that cannot be created by using the QBE pane; instead, you type the appropriate SQL (Structured Query Language) statement directly in the SQL view window. These *SQL-specific* queries are:

✦ *Union query:* Combines fields from more than one table or query into one recordset.

✦ *Pass-through query:* Allows you to send SQL commands directly to ODBC (Open Database Connectivity) databases using the ODBC database's SQL syntax.

✦ *Data definition query:* Lets you create or alter database tables or create indexes in a database, such as Access databases directly.

To create any of these queries, select from the Query ➪ SQL Specific menu the type you want to create. (No applicable button is available on the toolbar.)

In addition to these three special SQL-specific queries, you can use SQL in a subquery (inside a standard Acess 2000 query) to define a field or define criteria for a field.

Cross-Reference The "Understanding SQL" section at the end of this chapter provides a primer on SQL. You may want to read it before diving into the following SQL Queries.

Creating union queries

Union queries let you quickly combine fields from several tables or queries into one field. The resultant *snapshot* (like a dynaset) is not updatable.

For example, a competing veterinarian retires and gives you all the client records from her practice. You decide to create a union query to combine the data from both practices. Figure 26-14 shows a union query that returns the customer name and city in order (by city).

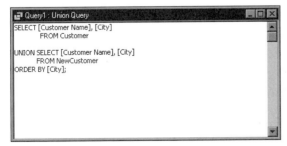

```
Query1 : Union Query
SELECT [Customer Name], [City]
        FROM Customer

UNION SELECT [Customer Name], [City]
        FROM NewCustomer
ORDER BY [City];
```

Figure 26-14: An SQL union query.

Notice that a union query has two or more SQL SELECT statements. Each SELECT statement requires the same number of fields, in the same order.

Tip When you use Union command in the SQL SELECT statement, it only copies records that are NOT duplicates when it joins the tables. If you want to copy *all* records simply use the keyword ALL after the UNION command: i.e., `UNION ALL SELECT`.

Creating pass-through queries

A *pass-through query* sends SQL commands directly to an SQL database server (such as Microsoft SQL Server, Oracle, and so on). You send the command by using the syntax required by the particular server. Be sure to consult the documentation for the appropriate SQL database server.

You can use pass-through queries to retrieve records or change data, or to run a server-side stored procedure or trigger. It can even be used to create new tables at the SQL server database level (vs. local tables).

When you create a pass-through query you can specify a connection string in the ODBCConnectStr property of the query property sheet. If you do not specify a connection string you are prompted for the connection infomration at the time you run the query.

Figure 26-15 shows a pass-through query for a Microsoft SQL Server that creates a new table named Payroll and defines the fields in the table.

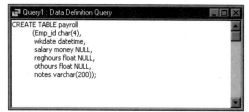

Figure 26-15: A pass-through query for SQL Server.

Caution   Never attempt to convert a pass-through query to another type of query. If you do, Access erases the entire SQL statement you had typed in.

When working with pass-through queries, you should not perform operations that change the state of the connection. Halting a transaction in the middle, for example, may cause unexpected results.

Creating data definition queries

Of the three SQL-specific queries, the *data definition query* is the least useful. Everything that can be done with it also can be done using the design tools in Access. The data definition query is, however, an efficient way to create or change database objects. With a data definition query, any of these SQL statements can be used:

✦ CREATE TABLE

✦ ALTER TABLE

✦ DROP TABLE

✦ CREATE INDEX

✦ DROP INDEX

For example, the following code creates a local Access table named TelephoneList:

```
CREATE TABLE TelephoneList
( [TeleID] integer, [FullName] text, [Address1] text,
[Address2] text, [Address3] text, [Country] text, [Phone 1]
text, [Phone 2] text, [FaxPhn 1] text, [Notes] memo,
CONSTRAINT [Index1] PRIMARY KEY ([TeleID]) );
```

Note   You can only have one SQL statement in each Data-Definition Query. If you want to create a new index for the TelephoneList table that you just created, you will need to create another Data-Definition Query to create the index such as:

```
CREATE INDEX CountryName ON TelephoneList ([Country],
[FullName]);
```

Creating subqueries in an Access query

Access 2000 lets you create an SQL SELECT statement inside another select query or action query. You can use these SQL statements in the Field row to define a new field, or in the Criteria row to define criteria for a field. Using subqueries, you can:

✦ Find values in the primary query that are equal to, greater than, or less than values returned by the subquery using the ANY, IN, or ALL reserved words.

✦ Test for the existence of a result from a subquery using the EXISTS or NOT EXISTS reserved words.

✦ Create nested subqueries (subqueries within subqueries).

How Queries Save Field Selections

When you open a query design, you may notice that the design has changed since you last saved the query. When you save a query, Access rearranges (even eliminates) fields on the basis of several rules:

✦ If a field does not have the Show: box checked but has criteria specified, Access moves it to the rightmost columns in the QBE pane.

✦ If a field does not have the Show: box checked, Access eliminates it from the QBE pane column unless it has sorting directives or criteria.

✦ If you create a totaling expression with the Sum operator in a total query, Access changes it to an expression using the Sum function.

Because of these rules, your query may look very different after you save and reopen it. In this section, you learn how this happens (and some ways to prevent it).

Hiding (not showing) fields

Sometimes you won't want certain fields in the QBE pane to show in the actual dynaset of the datasheet. For example, you may want to use a field such as Customer Number to specify a criterion or a sort without showing the actual field.

To *hide*, or exclude, a field from the dynaset, you simply click off the Show: box under the field you want to hide. Figure 26-16 demonstrates this procedure. Notice that the field Type of Customer is used to specify a criterion of displaying only individuals ("1"). Because you don't want the Type of Customer field in the actual datasheet, you deselect the Show: cell for the Type of Customer field.

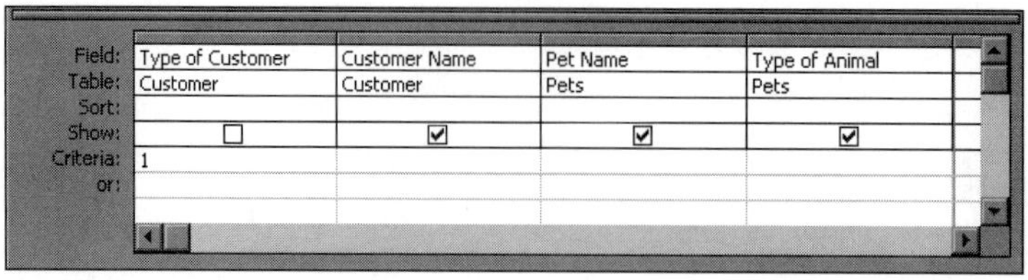

Figure 26-16: Hiding a field.

Any fields that have the Show: cell turned off (and for which you entered criteria) are placed at the end of the QBE pane when you save the query. Figure 26-17 shows the same query as Figure 26-16 after it is saved and redisplayed on the design screen. Notice that the Type of Customer field has been moved to the end (extreme right) of the QBE pane. The location of a hidden field will not change the dynaset. Because the field is not displayed, its location in the QBE pane is unimportant. You always get the same results, even if you've placed a hidden field in the QBE pane.

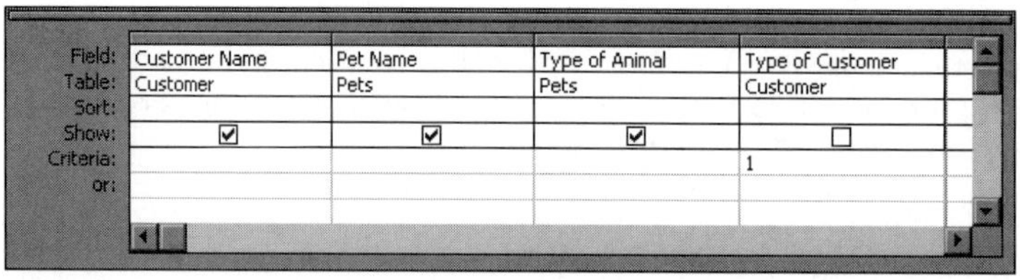

Figure 26-17: A query that has been saved with a hidden field.

Note If you hide any fields in the QBE pane that are not used for sorts or criteria, Access eliminates them from the query automatically when you save it. If you want to use these fields and need to show them later, you'll have to add them back to the QBE pane.

Caution If you're creating a query to be used by a form or report, you *must show any fields it will use*, including any field to which you want to bind a control.

Renaming fields in queries

When working with queries, you can rename a field to describe the field's contents more clearly or accurately. For example, you may want to rename the Customer Name field to Owner Name. This is useful for working with calculated fields or calculating totals; Access automatically assigns nondescript names such as *Expr1* or *AvgOfWeight*, but it's easy to rename fields in Access queries. To change the display name of the Customer Name field, for example, follow these steps:

1. Select the Customer table.

2. Double-click the Customer Name field.

3. Place the cursor in front of the first letter of Customer Name in the Field: cell.

4. Type **Owner Name:** (be sure to include the colon).

Figure 26-18 shows the query field renamed. The field has both the display name, which is *Owner Name*, and the actual field name, which is *Customer Name*.

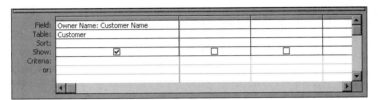

Figure 26-18: Renaming a query field.

Note When naming a query field, delete any names assigned by Access (to the left of the colon). For example, remove the name *Expr1* when you name the calculated field.

If you rename a field, Access uses only the new name for the heading of the query datasheet; it does the same with the control source in any form or report that uses the query. Any new forms or reports you create on the basis of the query will use the new field name. (Access does not change the actual field name in the underlying table.)

When working with renamed fields, you can use an *expression name* (the new name you specified) in another expression within the same query. For example, you may have a calculated field called First Name that uses several Access functions to separate an individual's first name from the last name. For this calculated field, use the field called Owner Name that you created earlier.

Caution When you work with referenced expression names, you cannot have any criteria specified against the field you're referencing. For example, you cannot have a criterion specified for Owner Name if you reference Owner Name in the First Name calculation. If you do, Access will not display the contents for the expression field Owner Name in the datasheet.

Hiding and unhiding columns in the QBE pane

Sometimes you may want to hide specific fields in the QBE pane. This is not the same as hiding a field by clicking on the Show: box. Hiding a column in the QBE pane is similar to hiding a datasheet column, which is easy: you simply resize a column (from right to left) until it has no visible width. Figure 26-19 shows several fields in the QBE pane; in the next example, you hide one of its columns.

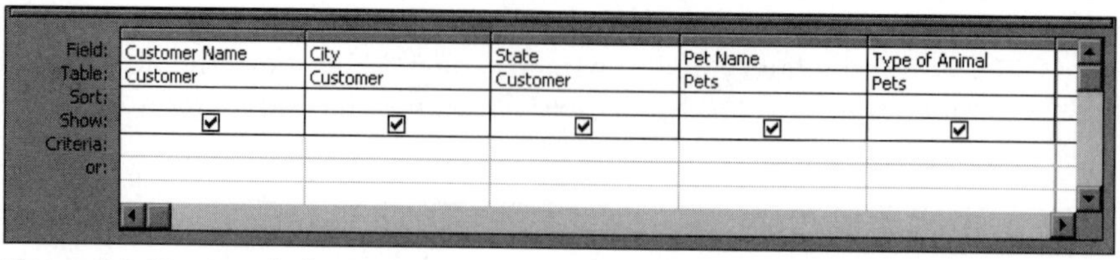

Field:	Customer Name	City	State	Pet Name	Type of Animal	
Table:	Customer	Customer	Customer	Pets	Pets	
Sort:						
Show:	☑	☑	☑	☑	☑	
Criteria:						
or:						

Figure 26-19: A typical QBE pane.

Follow these steps to hide the City column:

1. Move the mouse pointer to the right side of the City field on the *field selector*. The double-arrow sizing pointer displays.

2. Click the right side of the City field and drag it toward the Customer Name field until it totally disappears.

Figure 26-20 shows the QBE pane with the City field hidden. In the picture, the field wasn't 100% hidden so that you can see where the column has been moved to (next to Customer Name).

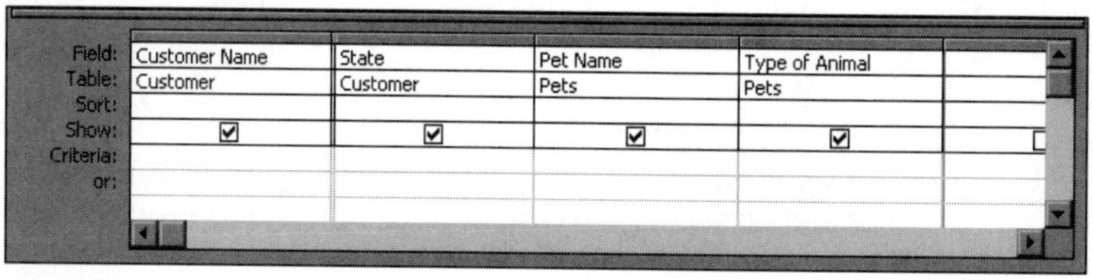

Field:	Customer Name	State	Pet Name	Type of Animal	
Table:	Customer	Customer	Pets	Pets	
Sort:					
Show:	☑	☑	☑	☑	
Criteria:					
or:					

Figure 26-20: The QBE pane with a column hidden.

After you hide a field, you can *unhide* it by reversing the process. If you want to unhide the City column, follow these steps:

1. Move the mouse pointer to the left side of the field State on the selector bar (the bar with arrows appears). Make sure that you are to the right of the divider between Customer Name and State.

2. Click the left side of State and drag it toward the Pet Name field until you size the column to the correct length.

3. Release the button; the field name *City* will appear in the column you unhide.

Query Design Options

There are three specifiable default options when working with a query design. These options can be viewed and set by selecting Tools ⇨ Options from the main Query menu and then selecting the Tables/Queries tab. Figure 26-21 shows this Options dialog box.

These four items can be set for queries:

✦ Show Table Names

✦ Output All Fields

✦ Enable AutoJoin

✦ Run Permissions

Generally, the default for Show Table Names is Yes, and the default for Output All fields is No. Run Permissions offers a choice of either the Owner's permission or the User's (the default). Finally, Enable AutoJoin controls whether Access will use common field names to perform an automatic join between tables that have no relationships set. Table 26-1 describes each option and its purpose.

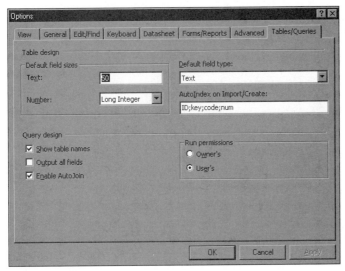

Figure 26-21: The Options dialog box.

Note   When you set query design options, they specify actions for new queries only; they do not affect the current query. To show table names in the current query, select View ➪ Table Names from the main Query menu. To specify the other two options for the current query, select View ➪ Properties....

	Table 26-1
	Query Design Options

Option	Purpose
Output All Fields	Shows all fields in the underlying tables or only the fields displayed in the QBE pane
Run Permissions	Restricts use in a multiuser environment; a user restricted from viewing the underlying tables can still view the data from the query
Enable AutoJoin	Uses common field names to perform an automatic join between tables that have no relationships set
Show Table Names	Shows the Table: row in the QBE pane when set to Yes; hides the Table: row if set to No.

Setting Query Properties

To set query properties, either click the Properties button on the toolbar, or *right-click* on Properties and choose it from the shortcut menu, or select View ➪ Properties from the main Query menu. Access displays a Query Properties dialog box. Your options depend on the query type and on the table or field with which you're working. Table 26-2 shows the query-level properties you can set.

You can use the *query-level properties* just as you would the properties in forms, reports, and tables. Query-level properties depend on the type of query being created.

Table 26-2
Query-Level Properties

Property	Description	Query	Select	Crosstab	Update	Delete	Make-Table	Append
Description	Text describing table or query	X	X	X	X	X	X	
Output All Fields	Show all fields from the underlying tables in the query	X				X	X	
Top Values	Number of highest or lowest values to be returned	X					X	
Unique Values	Return only unique field values in the dynaset	X				X	X	
Unique Records	Return only unique records for the dynaset	X		X	X		X	
Run Permissions	Establish permissions for specified user	X	X	X	X	X	X	
Source Database	External database name for all tables/queries in the query	X	X	X	X	X	X	
Source Connect Str	Name of application used to connect to external database	X	X	X	X	X	X	
Record Locks	Records locked while query runs (usually action queries)	X	X	X	X	X	X	
ODBC Time-out	Number of seconds before reporting error for opening DB	X	X	X	X	X	X	
Filter	Filter name loaded automatically with query	X						
Order By	Sort loaded automatically with query	X						

Continued

Table 26-2 (continued)

Property	Description	Query	Select	Crosstab	Update	Delete	Make-Table	Append
MaxRecords	Max number of records returned by ODBC database	X						
SubDatasheet Name	Identify subquery	X	X	X		X	X	
Link Child Fields	Field name(s) in subquery	X	X	X		X	X	
Link Master Fields	Field name(s) in main table	X	X	X		X	X	
Subdatasheet Height	Maximum height of subdatasheet	X	X	X		X	X	
Subdatasheet Expanded	Records initially in their expanded state?	X	X	X		X	X	
Column Headings	Fixed column headings	X						
RecordSet Type	Which tables can be edited	X						
Use Transaction	Run action query in transaction?		X	X	X	X	X	
Fail on Error	Fail operation if errors occur			X	X			
Destination Table	Table name of destination					X	X	
Destination DB	Name of database					X	X	
Dest Connect Str	Database connection string					X	X	

Understanding SQL

When you use graphical Query by Example, Access 2000 converts what you create into a *Structured Query Language (SQL)* statement. This SQL statement is what Access actually executes when the query runs.

Many relational databases use SQL as a standardized language to query and update tables. SQL is relatively simple to learn and use. Even so, Access does not require you know it or use it — though Access uses it, you won't ever have to know that it's there.

Viewing SQL statements in queries

If you're familiar with SQL, you can view and/or edit an SQL statement. If you make changes to an SQL statement, Access reflects them automatically in the QBE pane.

To view an SQL statement that Access creates, select View ➪ SQL View from the Query menu. Figure 26-22 shows a typical SQL statement that will display the fields Customer Name and State for dogs in Idaho or Oregon.

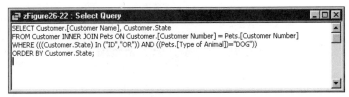

Figure 26-22: An SQL statement in Access.

Note   If you want to modify an existing SQL statement or create your own, enter changes directly into the SQL dialog box. To add new lines in the dialog box, press Ctrl+Enter.

SQL statements can be used directly in expressions, macros, forms, and reports, as in the RowSource or RecordSource properties of a form or report. You don't have to "know the language" to use SQL statements directly. You can create the needed statement (for such purposes as selecting specific records) in the Query window. Then activate the SQL dialog box and copy (Ctrl+C) the entire SQL statement you created. Switch to where you want to use the statement and paste it (Ctrl+V) where you need it (for example, the RowSource property of the property sheet).

Tip   You can create SQL statements in the SQL dialog box. Whether you write your own statement or edit one, Access updates the Query window when you leave the dialog box. Tables are added to the top portion; fields and criteria are added to the QBE pane.

An SQL primer

Until now, you have created queries using the query designer of Access. You have even been told that you can examine the SQL statement Access builds by selecting View ⇨ SQL View from the menu.

As you already know, one way to learn SQL statements is to build a query graphically and then view the corresponding SQL statement. Earlier, for example, Figure 26-22 showed this SQL statement:

```
SELECT DISTINCTROW Customer.[Customer Name], Customer.State
FROM Customer
INNER JOIN Pets ON Customer.[Customer Number] = Pets.[Customer
Number]
WHERE (((Customer.State) In ("ID","OR"))
AND ((Pets.[Type of Animal])="DOG"))
ORDER BY Customer.State;
```

Four common SQL commands

This statement uses the four most common SQL commands. Table 26-3 shows each command and explains its purpose.

Table 26-3 Four Common SQL Keywords/Commands	
Command	*Purpose in SQL Statement*
SELECT	This command/keyword starts an SQL statement. It is followed by the names of the fields that will be selected from the table or tables (if more than one is specified in the FROM clause/command). This is a required keyword.
FROM	This clause/keyword specifies the name(s) of the table(s) containing the fields specified in the SELECT command. This is a required keyword.
WHERE	This command specifies any condition used to filter (limit) the records that will be viewed. This keyword is used only when you want to limit the records to a specific group on the basis of the condition.
ORDER BY	This command specifies the order in which you want the resulting dataset (the selected records that were found and returned) to appear.

Using these four basic commands, you can build very powerful SQL statements to use in your Access forms and reports.

The DISTINCTROW keyword

The DISTINCTROW keyword in the preceding SQL statement is an *optional* predicate keyword. Access uses it as a *restricter keyword* to specify which records should be returned. This predicate keyword is not used by other SQL database languages. In Access, it limits the display of duplicate records, basing its restrictions on the values of the entire duplicate record. It works like the DISTINCT predicate of other SQL languages, except that DISTINCT works against duplicate fields within the SELECT statement. DISTINCTROW works against their records (even fields that are not in the SELECT statement). This is covered in more detail later.

The SELECT command

The SELECT command (*or clause*) is the first word found in two query types; in a select query or make-table query, the SELECT clause specifies the field(s) you want displayed in the Results table.

After specifying the keyword SELECT, you need to specify the fields you want to display (for more than one, use a comma between the fields). The general syntax is

```
SELECT Field_one, Field_two, Field_three ...
```

where *Field_one, Field_two*, and so on are replaced with the names of the table fields.

Notice that commas separate each field in the list from the others. For instance, if you want to specify customer name and city using fields from the Customer table, you would specify:

```
SELECT [Customer Name], City
```

If you need to view fields from more than one table, then specify the name of the tables in which to find the fields. The SELECT clause would, for example, look like this to select fields from both the Customer and Pets table:

```
SELECT Customer.[Customer Name], Customer.City, Pets.[Type of
Animal], Pets.[Pet Name]
```

When you build a query in Access, it places the table name before the field name automatically. In reality, you need only specify the table name if more than one table in the SQL statement have fields with the same name. For instance, a field named Customer Number appears in both the Customer table and the Pets table. If you want to SELECT a *[Customer Number]* field in your SQL statement, you *must* specify which of these to use — the one in Customer or the one in Pets.

The following SQL SELECT clause illustrates the syntax:

```
SELECT Customer.[Customer Number], [Customer Name], City, [Type
of Animal], [Pet Name]
```

Note   Although table names are *not* required for nonduplicate fields in an SQL state-ment, it's a good idea to use them for clarity.

Tip   You can use the asterisk wildcard (*) to specify that all fields should be selected. If you're going to select all fields from more than one table, specify the table, a period (.), and then the name of the field — in this case, the asterisk.

Using the Brackets Around Field Names

The SELECT clause just described uses brackets around the field name Customer Name. Any field name that has spaces within it requires the use of brackets.

Specifying SELECT Predicates

When you create an SQL SELECT statement, several predicates can be associated with the SELECT clause:

✦ ALL

✦ DISTINCT

✦ DISTINCTROW

✦ TOP

The predicates are used to restrict the number of records returned. They can work in conjunction with the WHERE clause of an SQL statement.

The ALL predicate is the default. It selects all records that meet the WHERE condition specified in the SQL statement. Selecting it is optional (it's the default value).

Use the DISTINCT predicate when you want to omit records that contain duplicate data in the fields specified in the SELECT clause. For instance, if you create a query and want to look at both the Customer Name and the Type of Animal the customer owns, *without* considering the number of animals of a given type, the SELECT statement would be:

```
SELECT DISTINCT [Customer name], [Type of Animal]
```

If a customer owns two dogs — that is, has two Dog records (one named Bubba and one named Killer) in the Pets table — only one record will appear in the resulting datasheet. The DISTINCT predicate tells Access to show only one record if the values in the selected fields are duplicates (that is, same customer number and same type of animal). Even though two different records are in the Pets table, only one is shown. DISTINCT eliminates duplicates on the basis of the fields selected to view.

The DISTINCTROW predicate is unique to Access. It works much like DISTINCT, with one big difference: It looks for duplicates on the basis of *all* fields in the table(s), not just the selected fields. For instance, if a customer has two different Dog records in the Pets table and uses the predicate DISTINCTROW (replacing DISTINCT) in the SQL statement just described, *both* records are displayed. DISTINCTROW looks for duplicates in all the fields of the Customer and Pets tables. If any field is different (in this case, the name of the pet), then both records are displayed in the datasheet.

The TOP predicate is also unique to Access. It lets you restrict the number of displayed records, basing the restriction on the WHERE condition to the TOP <number> of values. For instance, TOP 10 will display only the first 10 records that match the WHERE condition. You can use TOP to display the top five customers who have spent money on your services. For instance, the following SELECT clause will display the top five records:

```
SELECT TOP 5 [Customer Name]
```

The TOP predicate has an optional keyword, PERCENT, that displays the top number of records on the basis of a percentage rather than a number. To see the top two percent of your customers, you would use a SELECT clause like this one:

```
SELECT TOP 2 PERCENT [Customer Name]
```

The FROM clause of an SQL statement

As the name suggests, the FROM clause (command) specifies the tables (or queries) that hold the fields named in the SELECT clause. This clause is required; it tells SQL where to find the records.

When you're working with one table (as in the original example), the FROM clause simply specifies the table name:

```
SELECT [Customer Name], City,
FROM Customer
```

When you are working with more than one table, you can supply a TableExpression to the FROM clause to specify which data will be retrieved. The FROM clause is where you set the relationship between two or more tables for the SELECT statement. This link will be used to display the data in the resulting data sheet.

The TableExpression can be one of three types:

✦ INNER JOIN ... ON

✦ RIGHT JOIN ... ON

✦ LEFT JOIN ... ON

Use INNER JOIN ... ON to specify the traditional equi-join of Access. For instance, to join Customers to Pets via the Customer Number field in the FROM clause, the command would be:

```
SELECT Customer.[Type of Customer], Pets.[Type of Animal]
FROM Customer INNER JOIN pets ON Customer.[Customer Number] =
Pets.[Customer Number]
```

Notice that the FROM clause specifies the main table to use (Customer). Then the INNER JOIN portion of the FROM clause specifies the second table to use (Pets). Finally, the ON portion of the FROM clause specifies which fields will be used to join the table together.

The LEFT JOIN and RIGHT JOIN work exactly the same, except that they specify an outer join instead of an inner join (equi-join).

The WHERE clause of an SQL statement

Use the WHERE clause (command) of the SQL statement only when you want to specify a condition. (This clause is optional, unlike SELECT/DELETE ... and FROM.)

The original SQL statement you started with (for example) specified the following WHERE clause:

```
WHERE ((((Customer.State) In ("ID","OR"))
AND ((Pets.[Type of Animal])="DOG"))
```

The WHERE condition can be any valid expression. It can be a simple, one-condition expression (such as the one just given) or a complex expression based on several criteria.

Note   If you use the WHERE clause, it *must* follow the FROM clause of the SQL statement.

The ORDER BY clause

Use the ORDER BY clause to specify a sort order. It will sort the displayed data by the field(s) you specify after the clause, in ascending or descending order. In the original example, you specified a sort order by Customer Number:

```
ORDER BY Customer.[Customer Name];
```

Specifying the end of an SQL statement

Because an SQL statement can be as long as 64,000 characters, a way is needed to tell the database language that you've finished creating the statement. End an SQL statement with a semicolon (;).

Tip Access is very forgiving about the ending semicolon. If you forget to place one at the end of an SQL statement, Access will assume that it should be there and run the SQL statement as if it were there.

Caution If you place a semicolon *inside* an SQL statement accidentally, Access will report an error and attempt to tell you where it occurred.

Using SELECT, FROM, WHERE, and SORT BY, you can create some very powerful SQL statements to display and view data from your tables.

For instance, you can build an SQL statement that will:

1. Select the Customer Name and City, Pet Name, and Type of Animal fields.

2. Join FROM the Customer and Pets tables, where the Customer and Pets tables are linked ON the Customer Number.

3. Display only records where the Type of Customer is a pet store (type = 2).

4. Sort the data in order by the Customer Number.

The SQL statement could be:

```
SELECT [Customer Name], City, [Pet Name], [Type of Animal]
FROM Customer INNER JOIN Pets ON Customer.[Customer Number] =
Pets.[Customer Number]
WHERE [Type of Customer] = 2
ORDER BY Customer.[Customer number];
```

This is a quick overview of SQL statements and how to create them in Access 2000. Various other clauses (commands) can be used with SQL statements. SQL is relatively easy to understand and work with.

Summary

In this chapter, you worked with queries in greater detail than in earlier chapters. The chapter covered these points:

✦ When working with lookup tables, always set an outer join that points to the lookup table. An alternative is to use the DLookUp( ) function.

✦ When using tables in queries, open (use) only the tables whose fields you will use. Because Access creates equi-joins automatically, you may not see all the records unless you set outer joins.

✦ Calculated fields can be created for display, and you can set criteria against them and sort on them in a query.

✦ When a field is hidden and the query saved, Access moves the hidden field to the end of the display. If you don't use a hidden field for a criterion or sort and you save the query, Access deletes the hidden field from the QBE pane.

✦ Columns in the QBE pane can be hidden and unhidden by clicking the side of the field on the selector bar and dragging it until the field disappears.

✦ Query properties are optional for all queries except the make-table and append queries.

✦ SQL statements can be viewed and modified. If you modify an SQL statement, Access updates the QBE pane automatically to reflect the changes.

✦ SQL statements can be used in expressions, macros, forms, and reports by copying and pasting them where you need them.

In the next chapter, you learn to create multiple-table forms.

✦   ✦   ✦

Creating and Using Subforms

Subforms give you great flexibility in displaying and entering data with multiple tables. You can still edit all the fields without worrying about integrity problems. With a subform, you can even enter data into a one-to-many form relationship.

What Is a Subform?

A *subform* is simply a form within a form. It lets you use data from more than one table in a form; you can display data from one table in one format while using a different format for data from the other table. You can, for example, display one customer record on a form while displaying several pet records on a datasheet subform.

Although you can edit multiple tables in a typical form, using a subform gives you the flexibility to display data from several tables or queries at one time.

As you may recall, you can display data on a form in several ways:

Form	Display one record on a form
Continuous	Display multiple records on a form
Datasheet	Display multiple records using one line per record

Including a subform on your form enables you to display your data in multiple formats, as shown in Figure 27-1. This figure shows a form for entering visit details. It shows data from a query that lists information from the Customer, Pets, and Visits tables at the top, in a Form view. At the bottom is a subform that displays information from the Visit Details table. Notice that both the form and the subform have record selectors; each acts independently.

The subform contains data from three tables. In addition to its data from Visit Details, the subform shows descriptions of each treatment from the Treatments table, and medication listings from the Medications table. As you'll learn when you create this form later in this chapter, a drop-down list box appears when you select either of these latter fields in the datasheet. Each one is a combo box that lets you select a description from the Treatments or Medications table; then it will store the appropriate code in the Visit Details table for you.

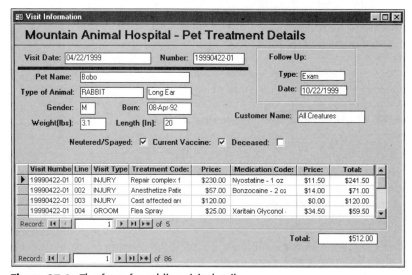

Figure 27-1: The form for adding visit details.

When you create a subform, you link the main form to it by a common field of expression. The subform will then display only records that are related to the main form. The greatest advantage of subforms is their ability to show the one-to-many relationship. The main form represents the *one* part of the relationship; the subform represents the *many* side.

You can create a subform in several ways:

✦ Use the Form Wizard when you create a new form.

✦ Use the Subform Wizard in an existing form.

✦ Use the Subform button in the toolbox and modify control properties.

✦ Drag a form from the Database window to another form.

Creating Subforms with the Form Wizard

The Access Form Wizard can create a form with an embedded subform if you choose more than one table (or use a query with more than one table). If you don't use the Wizard, you have to create both the form and subform separately; then you embed the subform and link it to the main form.

Creating the form and selecting the Form Wizard

Both the form and the subform are created automatically by the Form Wizard when you specify more than one table in a one-to-many relationship. In this example, you create a form that displays information from the Customer table on the main form; the subform shows information from the Pets table. To create the form, follow these steps:

1. Create a new form by selecting the Forms object button in the Database window and clicking on the New toolbar button.

2. Select Form Wizard in the New Form dialog box and select the Customer table from the tables/queries combo box, as shown in Figure 27-2.

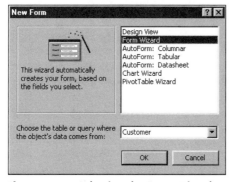

Figure 27-2: Selecting the Form Wizard.

Note   Access 2.0 users should note that there is no longer a Main/Subform Wizard in Access 2000. The standard Form Wizard automatically handles the process of creating a new form with a subform.

After you select the Form Wizard and the table or query to use for the new form, you need to select the fields for the main part of the form.

Choosing the fields for the main form

You then select each of the fields you want on the main form. The Customer table will be used for these fields. Figure 27-3 shows the completed field selection. To select the fields for this example, follow these steps:

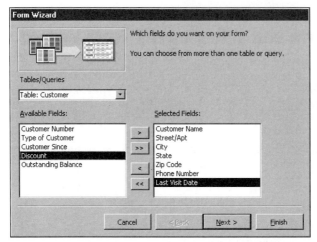

Figure 27-3: Selecting the fields for the main form.

1. Select Customer Name and select the > button.

2. Select Street/Apt and select the > button.

3. Select City and select the > button.

4. Select State and select the > button.

5. Select Zip Code and select the > button.

6. Select Phone Number and select the > button.

7. Select Last Visit Date and select the > button.

Selecting the table or query that will be the subform

Because a subform uses a data source separate from the form, you have to select the table or query to be used on the subform. To select another table/query, select the Pets table from the combo box, as shown in Figure 27-4. This table will be the subform of the primary form.

You will notice after a few seconds that the field list below in the Available Fields list box changes to display fields in the Pets table. The fields already selected from the Customer table in the Selected Fields list box remain.

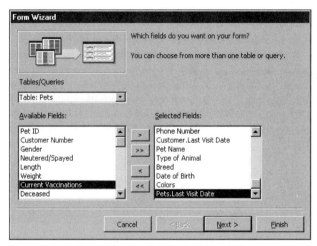

Figure 27-4: Selecting the fields for the subform.

Choosing the fields for the subform

Fields for the subform are selected in exactly the same way as fields for the main form. Those you select from the Pets table will be added to the list of fields already selected from the Customer table.

To select the fields for the subform, follow these steps:

1. Select Pet Name and select the > button.

2. Select Type of Animal and select the > button.

3. Select Breed and select the > button.

4. Select Date of Birth and select the > button.

5. Select Colors and select the > button.

6. Select Last Visit Date and select the > button.

7. Select the Next > button to move to the next dialog box.

Note   Notice the Pets.Last Visit Date field in the Selected Fields list box. Because both tables have a field named Last Visit Date, a prefix is added from the table that uniquely identifies the field.

After you select the fields for the Pets table, you can move to the next Wizard screen to decide how the linkage between forms will be built and how the data on the form will look.

Selecting the form data layout

The next dialog box is shown as part of a conceptual diagram in Figure 27-5. A multi-table relationship gives you many ways to lay out the data. The top part of the figure shows an automatic decision Access makes on the basis of the one-to-many relationship between Customer and Pets. The data is viewed by Customer, with a subform with the Pets data.

On the left side of the dialog box, you can choose how you want to view your form. Below the field view diagram, you can select whether you want to see your data as a Form with subform(s) or as Linked forms.

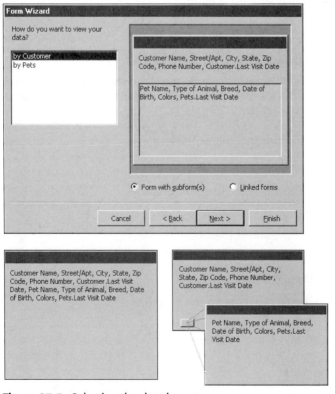

Figure 27-5: Selecting the data layout.

In the top part of the figure that shows the entire Form Wizard dialog box, you can see the form with a subform: Customer fields are on the main form, and Pets fields are on the subform. The bottom left part of the diagram shows conceptually what the data would look like if you viewed the data by Pets instead. The data from both tables would be placed on a single form. The bottom right part of the figure shows how it would look if you chose to view the data by Customer but chose Linked forms instead. Rather than creating a Customer form with an embedded Pets subform, Access would create a Customer form with a button to display the Pets form.

After you select the type of form you want (the data is viewed by *Customer*, with *a Form with subform(s)* with the Pets data), you can click on the Next> button to move to the subform layout screen.

Selecting the subform layout

When you create a form with an embedded subform, you must decide which type of layout to use for the subform. The two possibilities are *tabular* and *datasheet*. The datasheet is the default, but it may not be the choice you want to accept. Datasheets are rigid by nature; you cannot change certain characteristics (such as adding multiline column headers or precisely controlling the location of the fields below). You can choose a tabular layout for added flexibility. Whereas a datasheet combines the headers and data into a single control type (the datasheet itself), a tabular form places the column headers in a form header section, placing the field controls in the form's detail section.

Select the Datasheet layout, as shown in Figure 27-6.

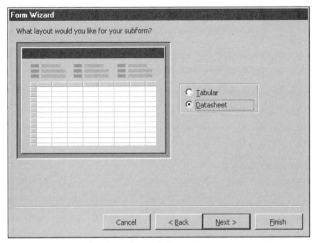

Figure 27-6: Selecting the subform layout.

Selecting the form style

As with other Form Wizards, you can determine how the form will look by selecting one of the AutoFormat choices. The style applies to the main form. The subform, displayed as either a separate tabular form or a datasheet, has the same look.

Cross-Reference Chapter 8 explains in more detail the process of determining a form's look, and Form Wizards in general.

You can accept the default Standard style and click on the Next > button to move to the final dialog box. This box lets you select the title for the form and the subform.

Selecting the form title

You can accept the default titles (the table names Access gives the main form and subform), or you can enter a custom title. The text you enter appears in the form header section of the main form. (See Figure 27-7.)

Note In this example, you will see the names *Customer1* and *Pets Subform1* if you are using the Mountain Animal Hospital example database because there are already forms with the names *Customer* and *Pets Subform*. The 1's indicate that there are already forms with this name. If you were using a database where there were no Customer or Pets Subforms, the names would not have a 1 appended to them and would look like Figure 27-7.

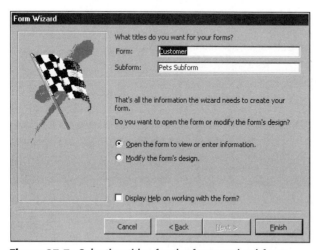

Figure 27-7: Selecting titles for the form and subform.

Note   When you accept the names (or enter a name of your choice), the subform is saved as a form; it will appear in the Database window when you select Forms. You should try to name your forms and subforms something similar so that you can tell that they go together. After you complete this step, you can view your form or its design.

Displaying the form

After the subform is named, the screen displays either the form or its design, depending on the option button you choose. In this example, you see the form, as shown in Figure 27-8.

The datasheet form layout was chosen for the subform. Whether you create your subform through a Wizard, by dragging one to the form, or by using the toolbox, Access creates either a datasheet or a tabular (continuous) form. You can change it by changing the Default View property to either Single Form, Continuous Form (Tabular), or Datasheet.

You can change the look of the subform by moving to Design view and double-clicking on the subform control. This action displays the subform's main form; there, you can change the subform all you like. You can move fields around, adjust column widths, change the formatting, modify the distance between rows, and rearrange columns. When you make these changes, you'll see them in effect the next time you view the subform. If you scroll down to the bottom of the subform, you'll notice that the asterisk (*) appears in the record selector column. As with any continuous form or datasheet, you can add new records by using this row.

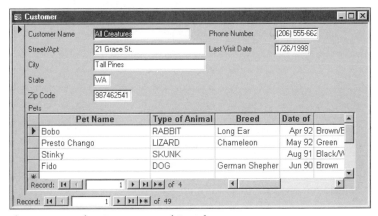

Figure 27-8: The Customer and Pets form.

Both the main form and the subform have record selectors because they are separate forms. As you use the outer record selector on the main form, you move from one customer record to another, and the link automatically changes which pets are displayed. This way, when you look at the record for All Creatures, you see pets for All Creatures. When you switch to Animal Kingdom, its pets are displayed.

When you use the inner record selector of the subform, you can scroll the records within the tabular form or datasheet. This capability is especially important if more records are on the subform than can be displayed in the subform area. You can use the scrollbar, too.

Displaying the main form design

To understand how the forms are linked from main form to subform, view the main form in Design view, as shown in Figure 27-9.

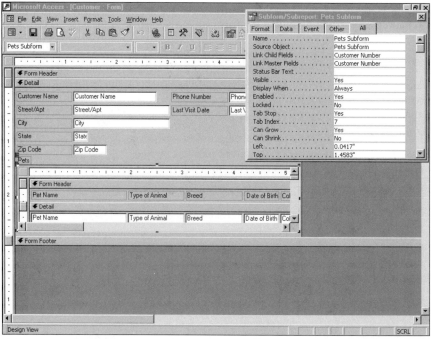

Figure 27-9: The Customer and Pets main form design.

The design for the main form shows the fields from the Customer table at the top and the subform control at the bottom. The subform control is similar to other controls (such as the unbound object control). It stores the name of the subform, and displays the fields in the subform.

New Feature If you are used to using any older version of Microsoft Access, you previously saw only a gray box indicating the subform. You had to double click on the subform control to see the subform form itself.

Caution If you do not use the wizard to create your forms and subforms, you must always first create the form you intend to use as a subform; the main form will not be usable until the subform form is created.

The Subform control property sheet is also shown. Notice the two properties Link Child Fields and Link Master Fields; these properties determine the link between the main form and the subform. The field name from the main table/query is entered in the Link Master Fields property. The field name from the subform table/query is entered in the Link Child Fields property. When the form is run, the link determines which records from the child form are displayed on the subform.

Tip In previous versions of Microsoft Access, you could double-click on the subform and instantly open the subform form. Access 2000 improves this by letting you work with the subform live in the main form. However, the subform control limits the space in which you have to work. You may find it easier to close the main form containing the subform control and open the subform form itself.

Note The subform control is used for both subforms and subreports.

Displaying the subform design

To understand how the subform is built, view the subform form in Design view (as shown in Figure 27-10). You should close the Customer form and open the Pets Subform form.

A subform is simply another form; it can be run by itself without a main form. You should always test your subform by itself, in fact, before running it as part of another form.

In Figure 27-10, you can see that all the fields are from the Pets table. You can also create a subform design with fields from multiple tables by using a query as the data source.

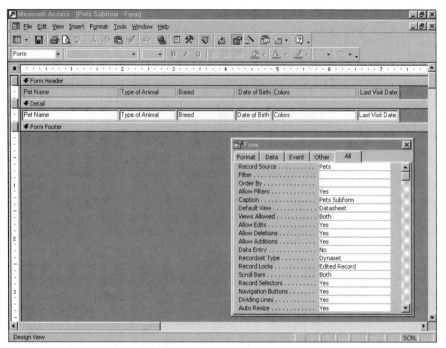

Figure 27-10: The Pets subform design.

Notice that in the Form property sheet for the Pets subform, the Default View property is set to Datasheet. This will print the data in a datasheet view which gives you little control over how the data looks and virtually no control over validation. For this example, you will change it to Continuous Forms. This means that the subform is displayed as a continuous form displaying multiple records, whether it is run by itself or used in a form. You can change it to a datasheet if you want or create a multiple-line form (which would then display its multiple lines on a subform).

Tip   A subform that will be viewed as a datasheet needs only to have its fields added in the order you want them to appear in the datasheet. Remember that you can rearrange the fields in the datasheet.

Tip   You can use the form footer of a subform to calculate totals or averages and then use the results on the main form. You learn how to do this later in this chapter.

The Form Wizard is a great place to start when creating a form with a subform. In the next section, however, you learn to create a subform without using a Form Wizard. Then you customize the subform to add combo box selections for some of the fields as well as calculate both row and column totals.

Creating a Simple Subform Without Wizards

As mentioned, there are several ways to create a subform without Wizards. You can drag a form from the Database window to a form, or you can use the Subform tool in the toolbox. The most desirable way is to drag the form from the Database window, because Access will try to create the links for you.

On the CD-ROM

In this section, you create the form shown in Figure 27-11. The entire form is on the CD-ROM that accompanies this book, in the Mountain Animal Hospital database, and is called Adding Visit Details. The completed subform is called Data for Subform Example.

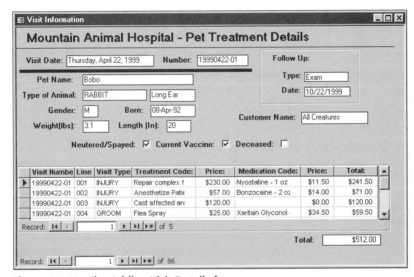

Figure 27-11: The Adding Visit Details form.

In this chapter, you'll work with only the Adding Visit Details form as a main form; you create and embed the Data for Subform Example form as a subform. (You may want to copy the Adding Visit Details form from the example disk and then delete the subform and subform totals box. You can use that copy to create the main form for this section of the chapter and save yourself a great deal of work.)

The Adding Visit Details form is divided into several sections. The top half uses the query Pets, Owners, and Visits to display data from the Pets, Customer, and Visits tables. The Adding Visit Details form's only purpose is to let you add or review details about an existing visit. The middle of the form contains the subform that displays information about the visit details in a datasheet. Data in this subform comes from the query Data for Subform Example. Finally, there is a total for the data in the subform displayed in a text box control in the main form.

Creating a form for a subform

The first step in creating an embedded subform is to create the form to be used as the subform. Of course, this process begins with a plan and a query. The plan is what you see in Figure 27-11. This datasheet, however, is not just a few fields displayed as a datasheet. The field Visit Type is a combo box that uses a value list; you create that layer in this section. The fields Treatment Code and Medication Code do not display codes at all; instead, they display the treatment description and the medication description. The Price fields come from the Treatments table and Medications table by way of links. Finally, Total is a calculated field.

To create this datasheet, you start by writing the query. Figure 27-12 shows the query used for the subform.

Note   This figure is a composite of two screen shots to show all the fields selected in the query.

At the top of the query, you can see the three necessary tables. Notice that the Visit Details table is joined to both the Treatments and Medications tables using a right outer join. You learned about this subject in Chapter 13. This is necessary so that if a Visit Detail record has either no treatment or no medication, it will not appear because of referential integrity.

Cross-Reference   Chapter 11 discusses the implications of referential integrity on a system using lookup tables.

The bottom pane of the query shows the fields that can be used for the datasheet. These fields include the Visit Number, Line Number, Visit Type, Treatment Code, and Medication Code fields from the Visit Details table. The fields Treatment and Price (from the Treatments table) and the fields Medication Name and Price (from the Medications table) can be used to display the actual data they name rather than the codes. This datasheet can be further enhanced by using combo boxes, as you'll soon see.

The final field in the query, `Total: [Treatments].[Price]+[Medications].` `[Price]`, names the field Total and sets the calculation to the total of both Price fields — the one in the Treatments table and the one in the Medications table. This field displays the line totals for each record in the datasheet.

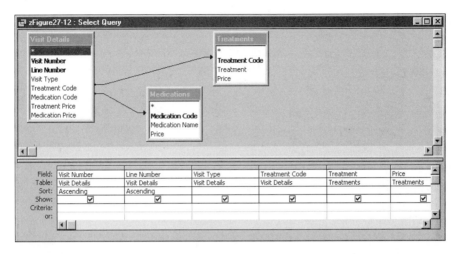

Figure 27-12: A composite figure showing the subform query.

Creating a *subform datasheet* is an iterative process; you have to see how many fields can fit across the screen at one time. If your goal is not to use a horizontal scrollbar, you'll have to use only as many fields as you can fit across the screen.

You can create the basic subform either by using a Form Wizard or by creating a new form and placing all the needed fields in it.

To create the initial subform, follow these steps:

1. Create a new blank form, using the query Data for Subform Example as the Record Source.

2. Open the Field List window and drag all the fields to the form.

3. Change the Default View property to Datasheet, if it is not already, as shown in Figure 27-13.

4. Display the form as a datasheet to check the results.

When you display the datasheet, you see that the fields don't even come close to fitting. There simply isn't enough room to display all of them. There are two solutions: Use a scrollbar or get creative. By now, you have learned enough to get creative!

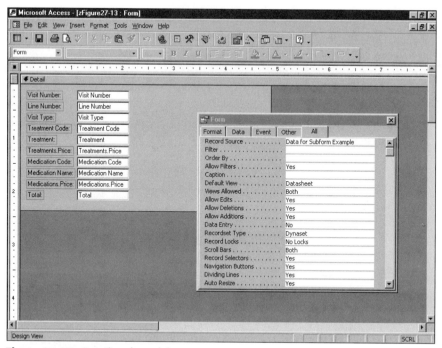

Figure 27-13: Creating the subform.

First, which fields are absolutely necessary to the entry of data, and which are strictly lookup fields? The first necessary field is Visit Number — it's used to link to the main form and must be included. Next is Line Number, the second field that makes up the multiple-field key in Visit Details. You must enter a Visit Type for each record, so that field needs to stay. Next come the details themselves. To enter a treatment, you must enter a treatment code and a medication code (if any). The codes themselves are used to look up the description and price. Therefore, you need only Treatment Code and Medication Code. Even so, you also want to display the prices and the line total. So the only fields you can eliminate are Treatment and Medication Name — and even then the datasheet doesn't fit across the page. To make it all fit, follow these steps:

1. Switch to Form Design view.

2. Delete the fields Treatment and Medication Name.

3. Change the labels for Treatments.Price and Medications.Price to simply **Price**.

4. Switch back to Datasheet view.

5. The fields still don't fit. By changing the column widths, however, you can fix that. Adjust the column widths, as shown in Figure 27-14.

6. Save the form as **Data for Subform Example**.

This is usually a good starting point. Notice that in Figure 27-14 some extra space shows on the right side. Because this datasheet will be placed in the center of another form, you must take into consideration the space the record selector column and scrollbar of the main form will use. After you view the datasheet in the main form, you can make final adjustments. You may also wonder why so much space was left for the Treatment Code and Medication Code columns. Later, when you change these columns into combo boxes, you'll need this amount of space. (Normally, you might not have realized this yet.)

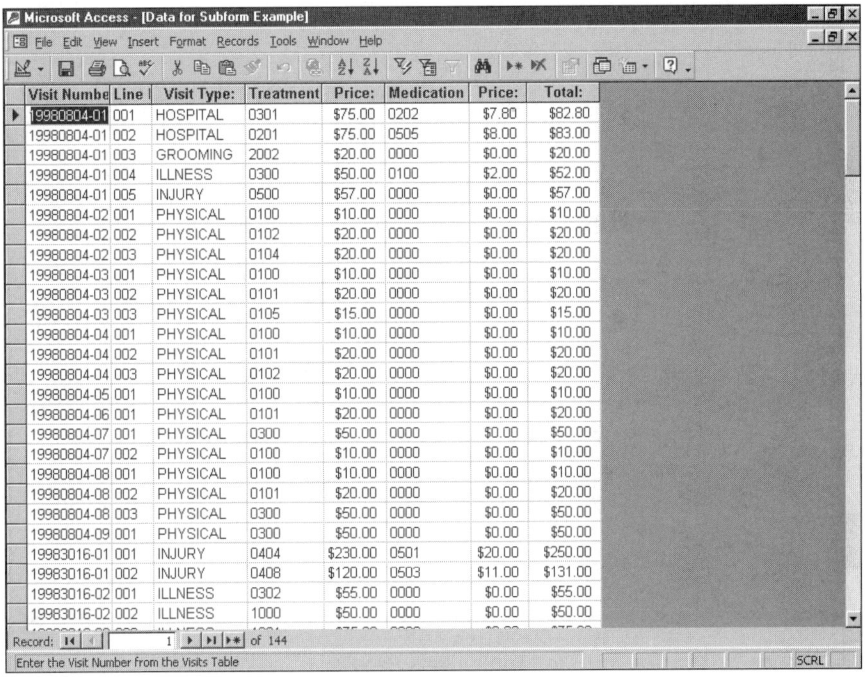

Visit Numbe	Line	Visit Type:	Treatment	Price:	Medication	Price:	Total:
19980804-01	001	HOSPITAL	0301	$75.00	0202	$7.80	$82.80
19980804-01	002	HOSPITAL	0201	$75.00	0505	$8.00	$83.00
19980804-01	003	GROOMING	2002	$20.00	0000	$0.00	$20.00
19980804-01	004	ILLNESS	0300	$50.00	0100	$2.00	$52.00
19980804-01	005	INJURY	0500	$57.00	0000	$0.00	$57.00
19980804-02	001	PHYSICAL	0100	$10.00	0000	$0.00	$10.00
19980804-02	002	PHYSICAL	0102	$20.00	0000	$0.00	$20.00
19980804-02	003	PHYSICAL	0104	$20.00	0000	$0.00	$20.00
19980804-03	001	PHYSICAL	0100	$10.00	0000	$0.00	$10.00
19980804-03	002	PHYSICAL	0101	$20.00	0000	$0.00	$20.00
19980804-03	003	PHYSICAL	0105	$15.00	0000	$0.00	$15.00
19980804-04	001	PHYSICAL	0100	$10.00	0000	$0.00	$10.00
19980804-04	002	PHYSICAL	0101	$20.00	0000	$0.00	$20.00
19980804-04	003	PHYSICAL	0102	$20.00	0000	$0.00	$20.00
19980804-05	001	PHYSICAL	0100	$10.00	0000	$0.00	$10.00
19980804-06	001	PHYSICAL	0101	$20.00	0000	$0.00	$20.00
19980804-07	001	PHYSICAL	0300	$50.00	0000	$0.00	$50.00
19980804-07	002	PHYSICAL	0100	$10.00	0000	$0.00	$10.00
19980804-08	001	PHYSICAL	0100	$10.00	0000	$0.00	$10.00
19980804-08	002	PHYSICAL	0101	$20.00	0000	$0.00	$20.00
19980804-08	003	PHYSICAL	0300	$50.00	0000	$0.00	$50.00
19980804-09	001	PHYSICAL	0300	$50.00	0000	$0.00	$50.00
19983016-01	001	INJURY	0404	$230.00	0501	$20.00	$250.00
19983016-01	002	INJURY	0408	$120.00	0503	$11.00	$131.00
19983016-02	001	ILLNESS	0302	$55.00	0000	$0.00	$55.00
19983016-02	002	ILLNESS	1000	$50.00	0000	$0.00	$50.00

Figure 27-14: Adjusting the subform datasheet.

Adding the subform to the main form

After the subform is complete, you can add it to the main form. The easiest way is to display the main form in a window and then drag the subform to the main form. This action automatically creates the subform object control and potentially links the two forms.

To add the Data for Subform Example to the Adding Visit Details form you're using as the main form, follow these steps:

1. Display the Adding Visit Details form in a window in Design view so that you can also see the Database window.

2. Display the form objects in the Database window.

3. Click on the form name Data for Subform Example and drag it to the Adding Visit Details form, as shown in Figure 27-15.

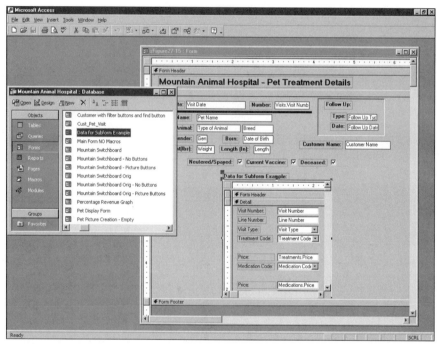

Figure 27-15: The form for Adding Visit Details.

4. Maximize the Form window.

The subform is displayed showing the form view. However, you will want to see it in a datasheet. Because the Default View of the Data for Subform form is Datasheet, you will see this when the form is displayed in Form view.

Tip   Sometimes, to resize a control properly, you must display it in form view, note the height or width to change, switch to design view, make your changes, and then start the process over again. You should not feel that this is design by trial and error but a perfectly normal development process.

5. Resize the subform so that it fits on-screen below the three check boxes. It should begin around the 2-inch mark and go down to the 3-inch mark. The width should be approximately $6^1/4$ inches.

6. Delete the subform label control.

7. Display the property sheet for the subform control to see if there was an automatic link. If not, you will manually link the fields.

The form should look like Figure 27-16. Notice that the Link Child Fields and Link Master Fields sections are not filled in. This means that the main form (Master) and the subform (Child) are not linked because the primary key for the Visit Details table is a multiple-field key. Access cannot automatically link this type of primary key.

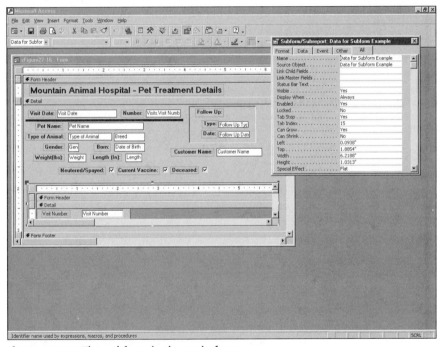

Figure 27-16: The subform in the main form.

Linking the form and subform

When you drag a form from the Database window onto another form to create a subform, Access tries automatically to establish a link between the forms. This is also true when you drag a form or report onto a report.

Access establishes a link under these conditions:

✦ Both the main form and subform are based on tables, and a relationship has been defined with the Relationships command.

✦ The main form and the subform contain fields with the same name and data type, and the field on the main form is the primary key of the underlying table.

If Access finds a relationship or a match, these properties show the field names that define the link. You should verify the validity of an automatic link. If the main form is based on a query, or if neither of the conditions just listed is true, Access cannot match the fields automatically to create a link.

The Link Child Fields and Link Master Fields property settings must have the same number of fields and must represent data of the same type. For example, if the Customer table and the Pets table both have Customer ID fields (one each) that contain the same type of data, you enter Customer ID for both properties. The subform automatically displays all the pets found for the customer identified in the main form's Customer ID field.

Although the data must match, the names of the fields can differ. For example, the Customer ID field from the Customer table can be linked to the Customer Number field from the Pets table.

To create the link, follow these steps:

1. Enter **Visit Number** in the Link Child Fields property.
2. Enter **Visit Number** in the Link Master Fields property.

Without the link, if you display the form, you see all the records in the Visit Details table in the subform. By linking the forms, you see only the visit details for the specific visit being displayed on the main form.

Display the form, as shown in Figure 27-17. Notice that the only visit numbers displayed in the datasheet are the same as the visit numbers in the main form. In Figure 27-17, you may notice that the user will have to enter the Treatment Code and Medication Code. In the type of systems that Access lets you create, you should never have to enter a code that can be looked up automatically. You can change some of the fields in the datasheet to use lookup tables by creating combo boxes in the subform.

Adding lookup tables to the subform fields

You can change the way the data is displayed on a subform of a main form by changing the design of the subform itself. You now make three changes:

✦ Display the Visit Type field as a value list combo box.

✦ Display the Treatment Code as a combo box showing the Treatment Name, letting Access enter the Treatment Code automatically.

✦ Display the Medication Code as a combo box showing the Medication Name, letting Access enter the Medication Code automatically.

Cross-Reference

Combo boxes are discussed in detail in Chapter 18.

By changing a field in a subform to a combo box, when you click on the field in the datasheet of the subform, the list will drop down and you can select from the list.

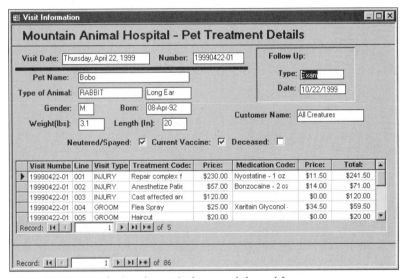

Figure 27-17: Displaying the main form and the subform.

The first control to change is the Visit Type field. To create a value list combo box without using the Wizard, follow these steps:

1. Display the subform in the Design view.

2. Select the existing Visit Type text box control.

3. From the menu bar, select Format ⇨ Change To ⇨ Combo Box.

4. With the Visit Type combo box selected, display the property sheet.

5. Select Value List for the Row Source Type property.

6. Enter **INJURY;PHYSICAL;GROOMING;HOSPITAL** in the Row Source property.

7. Set the Column Count property to **1** and the Column Widths to **1"**.

8. Set the Bound Column property to **1** and the List Rows property to **8**.

9. Set the Limit To List property to **No** to allow an alternative treatment type to be added.

This combo box and property sheet are shown in Figure 27-18.

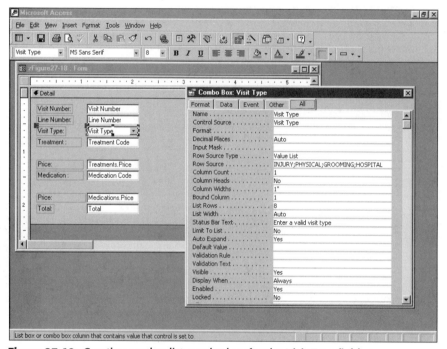

Figure 27-18: Creating a value list combo box for the Visit Type field.

Note   You can also display fields in a datasheet as check boxes or as individual option buttons. You cannot display an option button group, a list box, or a toggle button in a datasheet.

When a user clicks on the Visit Type field in the datasheet, the combo box appears. When a user selects the arrow, the list box is displayed with the values *INJURY; PHYSICAL; GROOMING;* or *HOSPITAL.* Because the Limit To List property is set to No, a user can also add new values to the Visit Details table.

The next two combo boxes are very similar. You want to create two combo boxes. The first one allows you to see the treatment descriptions rather than the treatment codes. When you select a treatment description, the code is entered automatically. The second combo box is the same, except that it uses the Medications table rather than the Treatments table.

To create these combo boxes, you need to create several queries. Figure 27-19 shows the query for the Treatment Code combo box. You have to create this query and name it Treatment Lookup.

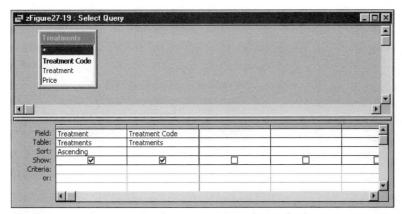

Figure 27-19: The query for the Treatment Code combo box.

As you can see, both fields come from the Treatments table. The fields appear in the combo box in order of the value of Treatment. This is the treatment name. This is an alphabetical listing because the field is a Text field data type. Notice that two fields are used in the query. The treatment code will be hidden so that only the treatment name is displayed.

After you create the query, you can create the combo box. To create the combo box for the treatment code, follow these steps:

1. Display the subform in the Design view.

2. Select the existing Treatment Code text box control.

3. From the menu bar, select Format ➪ Change To ➪ Combo Box.

4. With the Treatment Code combo box selected, display the property sheet.

5. Select Table/Query for the Row Source Type property.

6. Enter **Treatment Lookup** in the Row Source property.

7. Set the Column Count property to **2** and the Column Heads property to **Yes**.

8. Set the Column Widths property to **2";0"**.

9. Set the Bound Column property to **2** and the List Rows property to **4**.

10. Set the List Width property to **2"**.

11. Set the Limit To List property to **Yes** so that the user must select from the list.

Figure 27-20 shows this combo box completed. When the form is run and the user selects the Treatment Code field, the list of valid treatment codes is shown. Because the Bound Column is 2 (the hidden Treatment Code column), Access places the value of the Treatment Code in the Treatment Code field in the Visit Details table.

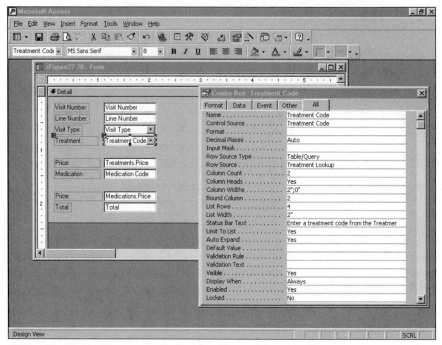

Figure 27-20: Creating a combo box for the Treatment Code.

The Medication Code lookup table is virtually identical to the Treatment Code lookup table; only the field name is different. To create this combo box, you also need to create a query. Figure 27-21 shows the query for the Medication Code combo box.

As you can see, all these fields come from the Medications table. They appear in the combo box in order of the value of the Medication Name (an alphabetical listing because the field uses the Text data type). Notice that two fields are used in the query. The Medication Code is hidden; only the Medication name is displayed.

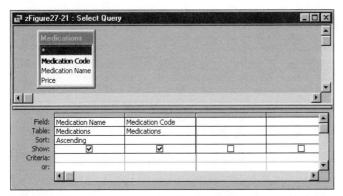

Figure 27-21: The query for the Medication Code combo box.

After you create the query, you can create the combo box. To create the combo box for the Medication Code, follow these steps:

1. Display the subform in Design view.

2. Select the existing Medication Code text box control.

3. From the menu bar, select Format ⇨ Change To ⇨ Combo Box.

4. With the Medication Code combo box selected, display the property sheet.

5. Select Table/Query for the Row Source Type property.

6. Enter **Medications Lookup** in the Row Source property.

7. Set the Column Count property to **2** and the Column Heads property to **Yes**.

8. Set the Column Widths property to **2";0"**.

9. Set the Bound Column property to 2 and the List Rows property to **4**.

10. Set the List Width property to **2"**.

11. Set the Limit To List property to **Yes** so that the user must select from the list.

Figure 27-22 shows this combo box completed. When the form is run and the user selects the Medication Code field, the list of valid medication codes is shown. Because the Bound Column is 2 (the hidden Medication Code column), Access places the value of the Medication Code in the Medication Code field in the Visit Details table.

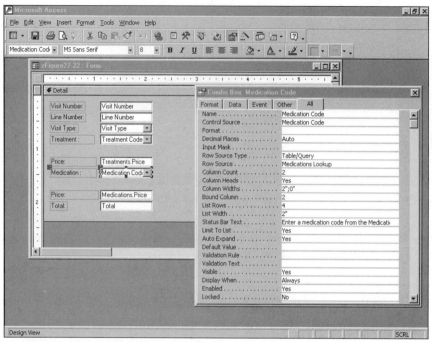

Figure 27-22: Creating a combo box for the Medication Code.

After you make these changes, you can test your changes. You may want first to display the form as a datasheet in the Form view of the subform. You can also close the form and display the subform in the main form. Close the subform and run the main form named Adding Visit Details.

First, you can test the combo boxes. Click on the Visit Type field. An arrow should appear. When you click on the arrow, the list of valid visit types is displayed. You can then select the desired visit type or enter a new one in the combo box. When the combo box is closed, Access enters this data into the Visit Type field of the Visit Details table.

When you select the Treatment Code field and select the arrow, a combo box is also displayed, as shown in Figure 27-23. The combo box displays only three columns because the List Rows property is set to 4 and the Column Heads property is set to Yes.

The treatment description is shown in its entirety, even though the Treatment Code field entry area is smaller. This is controlled by setting the List Width property to 2. If you leave this property set to the default (Auto), your data may be truncated (displayed with too much white space after the values) because the list width will be the size of the actual combo box control on the subform. When you select the desired treatment, Access automatically enters the hidden value of the treatment code in the Treatments table into the Treatment Code field in Visit Details.

The Medication Code field works in exactly the same way. Notice that as you select various treatments, the price is updated automatically in each line to reflect the selection. As either Treatment Price or Medication Price changes, the Total field is also updated.

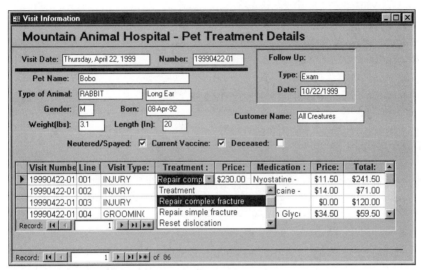

Figure 27-23: Displaying the subform.

The last change to make to the form is to create a field to display totals of all the line items in the datasheet.

Creating totals in subforms

To create a total of the line items in the subform, you have to create an additional calculated field on the form you're using as a subform. Figure 27-24 shows a new field being created in the form footer on this form.

Just as you can create summaries in reports, you can create them in forms. Use the form footer; that way, the calculation occurs after all the detail records are processed. When the form is displayed in Single-form view, this total is always equal to the detail record. In Continuous-form or Datasheet view, however, this calculation is the sum of the processed record.

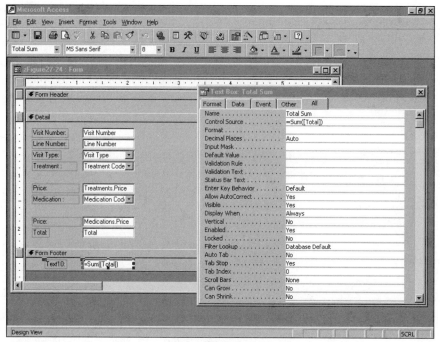

Figure 27-24: Creating a summary calculation.

As shown in Figure 27-24, the text box Control Source property is the expression =Sum([Total]). This is the sum of all the values in the Total field. To display the data as a dollar amount, the field's Format property should be set to Currency and the number of decimal places set to 2.

Although the text box control was created in the subform, it's displayed by a text box control (which references the subform control) placed in the main form. This control is shown in Figure 27-25.

Because the field is in another form, it must be referenced with the fully qualified terminology (Object type![Form name]![Subform name].Form![Subform field name]).

As you can see in the property sheet, the Control Source property is as follows:

```
=[Forms]![Adding Visit Details]![Data for Subform
Example].[Form]! [Total Sum]
```

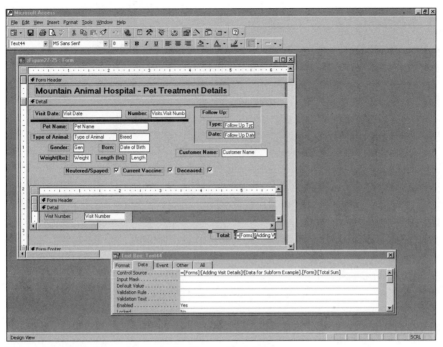

Figure 27-25: Referencing a control in another form.

The first part of the reference specifies the name of the form; `Form` tells Access that it's the name of a form. By using the ! character, you tell Access that the next part is a lower hierarchy. The control name `[Total Sum]` contains the value to be displayed.

Caution If you are an experienced Access 2.0 user, you may find that many of the field reference calculations you enter no longer work; they just display the `#Name?` `Symbol` message in your calculated or referenced text boxes. A major change was introduced in Access for Windows 95 that makes it mandatory to fully qualify all references. In Access 2.0, you could leave off the first part of the reference (`Forms![formname]`). In the example just given, you could have used just the subform name first, leaving out the `Forms![Adding Visit Details]` part.

The final form, including the total for the subform, is shown in Figure 27-26.

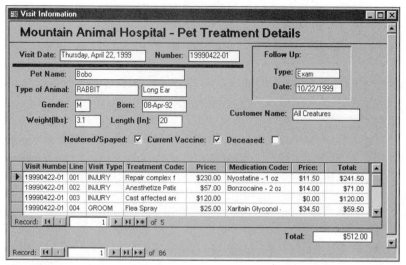

Figure 27-26: Displaying the totals.

Summary

In this chapter, you learned how to use subforms to make displaying data from multiple tables easier. You learned how to create a subform with a Wizard as well as how to create subforms by dragging the form from the Database window to another form. You also learned how to change the display of the subform. This chapter covered the following points:

✦ A subform is simply a form within a form.

✦ There are several ways to create a subform:

  • Use the Form Wizard.

  • Drag a form from the Database window to another form.

  • Use the toolbox and the Form Wizard.

✦ A subform can be displayed as a single form, a continuous form, or a datasheet.

✦ Before adding a subform to an existing form, you must create the subform.

✦ By using the Form Wizard, you can create a form with an embedded subform datasheet.

✦ When you create a subform by dragging a form from the Database window, you may have to link the form to the subform manually.

✦ You link a form and subform by entering the field names for the link in the Link Master Fields and Link Child Fields properties.

✦ You can add lookup tables and even combo boxes to the datasheet used in a subform.

In the next chapter, you learn how to create mailing labels, snaked column reports, and mail-merge reports.

✦　　✦　　✦

Creating Mailing Labels and Mail Merge Reports

For correspondence, you often need to create mailing
labels and form letters, commonly known as *mail merges*.
The Access Report Writer helps you create these types of
reports as well as reports with the multiple columns known as
snaked column reports.

Creating Mailing Labels

You create mailing labels in Access by using a report. You can
create the basic label by starting from a blank form, or you
can use the Label Wizard. This Wizard is much easier to use
and saves you a great deal of time and effort.

Access 2000 has no special report for creating mailing labels.
Like any other report, the report for a mailing label is made up
of controls; the secret to the mailing label is using the margin
settings and the Page Setup screen. In previous chapters, you
learned how to use the Page Setup dialog box to change your
margins. One of the tabs in the dialog box is Columns. When
you select this tab, the Columns dialog box expands to reveal
additional choices you use to control the number of labels
across the report as well as how the data is placed on the
report. You learn how to use this dialog box later in this
chapter.

The best way to create mailing labels is to use the Label
Wizard.

Creating the new report with the Label Wizard

You create a new report to be used for a mailing label just as you create any other report (see Figure 28-1). To create a new report for a mailing label, follow these steps:

1. From the Database window, click on the Reports object button.

2. Click on the New toolbar button to create a new report.

3. Select Label Wizard.

4. Select Customer from the table/query combo box.

5. Click on OK.

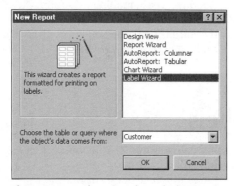

Figure 28-1: Choosing the Label Wizard.

The Label Size dialog box will now display.

Selecting the label size

The first Wizard dialog box you see will ask you to select a label size. You can select the type of label stock you want to print to. Nearly a hundred Avery label stock forms are listed. (Avery is the world's largest producer of label paper.)

New Feature

Other types of labels that you can select from are:

EXPE

Herma

Tab1

Tab2

Zweckform

To select a different type of label other than Avery, then click on the Filter by Manufacturer combo box to display the manufacturers listed above.

You can find in these lists nearly every type of paper these manufacturers make. You can select from lists of English or metric labels. You can also select sheet feed for laser printers or continuous feed for tractor-fed printers. Select between the two using the option buttons below the label sizes.

Note   If you do not see the Avery labels in the Label Wizard, click in the customized sizes check box to turn it off.

The list box shown in Figure 28-2 contains three columns:

Avery number	The model number on the Manufacturer label box
Dimensions	The height and width of the label in either inches or millimeters
Number across	The number of labels that are physically across the page

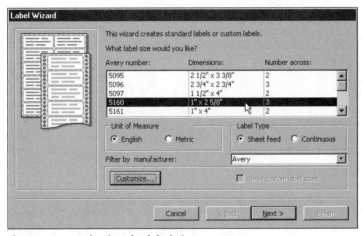

Figure 28-2: Selecting the label size.

When you select a label size, you're actually setting the Page Setup parameters, as you learn later in this chapter.

Select Avery number 5160, as shown in Figure 28-2. Notice that there are three labels across and that the size is shown as 1" x 2 $5/8$". You'll see these values again when you examine the Page Setup dialog box. After you select the label size, you can again click on the Next> button to go to the next dialog box.

Note   You can also select the Customize button to create your own label specifications if the labels you're using are not standard labels.

Selecting the font and color

The next dialog box (shown in Figure 28-3) displays a set of combo boxes to let you select various attributes about the font and color of the text to use for the mailing label. For this example, click on the Italic check box to turn on the italic effect. Notice that the sample text changes to reflect the difference. Accept the remaining default choices of Arial, 8, Light, and black text. Click on the Next> button to move to the next dialog box.

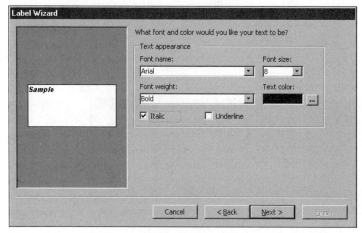

Figure 28-3: Selecting the font type, size, and color.

Creating the mailing-label text and fields

The next dialog box lets you choose the fields from the table or query to appear in the label. You can also add spaces, unbound text, blank lines, and even punctuation.

The dialog box is divided into two areas. The left area, titled Available fields:, lists all the fields in the query or table. Figure 28-4, shown completed, displays the fields from the Customer table. The right area, titled Prototype label:, shows the fields used for the label and displays a rough idea of how the mailing label will look when it's completed.

Note   The fields or text you use in this dialog box serve only as a starting point for the label. You can make additional changes later in the Report Design window.

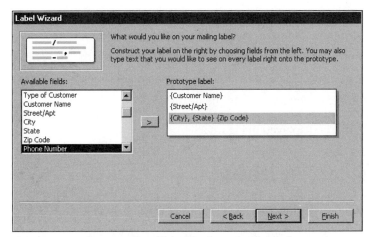

Figure 28-4: The completed label in the Label Wizard.

You can select a field either by double-clicking on the field name in the Available fields: area or by selecting the field name and then clicking on the > command button between the two areas. You can remove a field by highlighting it and then pressing Delete on your keyboard. You move to the next line by pressing the Tab key.

Note   You may enter text at any point by simply placing your cursor where you want to insert the text and then typing the text, including spaces and punctuation marks.

Caution   If you add a new line to the label and leave it blank, it will appear only as a blank line on the label (provided you have also manually changed the Can Shrink property to No for the unbound text box control you created to display that blank line). The default property for this control is Yes; the blank line is not displayed, and the lines above and below the blank line appear together.

To create the label as shown completed in Figure 28-4, follow these steps:

1. Double-click on the Customer Name field in the Available fields: list.

2. Press the Tab key to go to the next line.

3. Double-click on the Street/Apt field in the Available fields: list.

4. Press the Tab key to go to the next line.

5. Double-click on the City field in the Available fields: list.

6. With your cursor on the space after the City field type a comma (,) to add a comma to the label.

7. Press the spacebar to add a blank space to the label after the comma.

8. Double-click on the State field in the Available fields: list.

9. Press the spacebar to add a blank space to the label after the State field.

10. Double-click on the Zip Code field in the Available fields: list.

11. Click on the Next> button to go to the next dialog box.

The completed label is displayed in Figure 28-4.

Sorting the mailing labels

The next dialog box will prompt you to select a field on which to sort, as shown in Figure 28-5. Depending on how you have your database set up (and on how you want to organize your information), you may sort it by one or more fields. The dialog box consists of two sections; one lists the available fields, the other, the selected sort fields. To select a field, double-click on it (it will appear in the right-side column labeled Sort by:) or use the arrow buttons (> and >). The single > means that only the highlighted field will be selected; the double > means that every field showing in the column will be selected. In this example, you will select Customer Name as the field to sort by. When you're done, click on Next> to bring up the final dialog box.

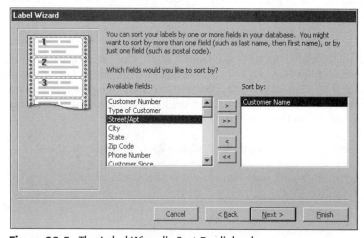

Figure 28-5: The Label Wizard's Sort By dialog box.

Note The order in which the fields are listed in the Sort by: column represents the order in which they will be sorted, from the top down. If you have a database set up in which you have first and last name, you can select the last name and then the first name as the sort order.

The last dialog box in the Label Wizard sequence lets you decide whether to view the labels in the Print Preview window or to modify the report design in the Report Design window. The default name is the word Label followed by the table name. In this example, that's Labels Customer. Change it to a more meaningful name, such as Customer Mailing Labels. This final dialog box is shown in Figure 28-6.

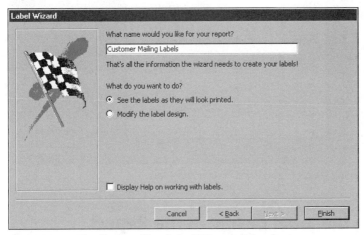

Figure 28-6: The final mailing Label Wizard dialog box.

Displaying the labels in the Print Preview window

When you click on the Finish button, you are taken directly to the Print Preview window (as shown in Figure 28-7). This is the normal Print Preview window for a report. By using the magnifying-glass mouse pointer, you can switch to a page view to see an entire page of labels at one time, or you can zoom in to any quadrant of the report. By using the navigation buttons in the bottom left corner of the window, you can display other pages of your mailing label report.

Note Remember that a mailing label is simply a report; it behaves as a report normally behaves.

You can print the labels directly from the Print Preview window, or you can click on the first icon on the toolbar to display the Report Design window.

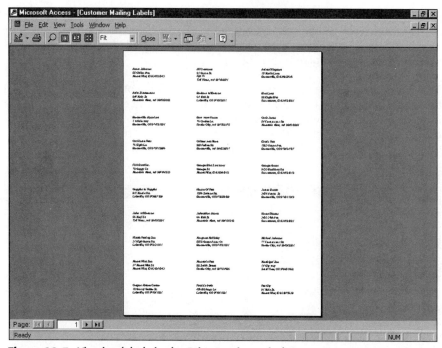

Figure 28-7: Viewing labels in the Print Preview window.

Modifying the label design in the Report Design window

When you click on the Close Window icon, the label design is displayed in the Report Design window, as shown in Figure 28-8. Notice that the height of the detail band is set at 1 inch and that the right margin of the report is set at 2 $3/8$ inches. This gives you the measurement you defined when you chose the label size of 1" × 2 $5/8$". The difference between 2 $3/8$ and 2 $5/8$ is the settings in the page setup box (discussed later in this chapter).

If you look at the report print preview, you notice that the first record's ZIP code value is 834121043. The Zip Code field is normally formatted using the @@@@@-@@@@ format. This format displays the stored sequence of nine numbers with a hyphen placed where it properly goes.

The Label Wizard uses the ampersand (&) type of concatenation when working with text strings; any formatting is missing. In the property sheet for the third line text box, you must change the control by adding the format function inside the Trim( ) function. Change the source to this:

```
=Trim([City] & ", " & [State] & " " & Format([Zip Code],"@@@@@-
@@@@")).
```

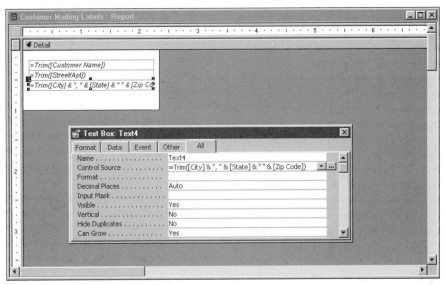

Figure 28-8: The Report Design window.

This control source correctly displays the ZIP code as 83412-1043 when it's printed or displayed. You can make this change by simply selecting the control and adding the Format( ) function.

Another change you could make is to the font size. In this example, Arial (the Helvetica TrueType font) with a point size of 8 is used. Suppose that you want to increase the text size to 10 points. You select all the controls and then click on the Font Size drop-down list box and change the font size to 10 points. The text inside the controls becomes larger, but the control itself does not change size. As long as the text is not truncated or cut off on the bottom, you can make the font size larger.

You can also change the font style of any text. For example, if you want only the Customer Name text to appear in italics, you will need to select the other two text box controls and deselect the Italics button on the toolbar. Earlier, you specified in the Wizard that all three fields should be italics.

Now that you've changed your text as you want, it's time to print the labels. Before you do, however, you should examine the Page Setup window.

To display the Page Setup window, select File ➪ Page Setup. The Page Setup window appears. Here, you can select the printer, change the orientation to Portrait or Landscape (have you *ever* seen landscape label paper?), change the Paper Size or Source settings, and set the margins. The margin setting controls the margins for the entire page. These affect the overall report itself, not just the individual labels.

To view the settings of each label and determine the size and number of labels across the page, you need to select the Columns tab. The window then displays additional options, as shown in Figure 28-9.

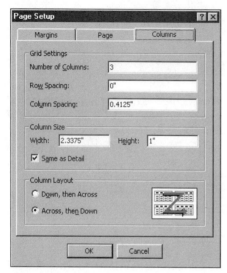

Figure 28-9: The Columns tabbed dialog page from the Page Setup window.

Note   Figure 28-9 shows the Columns tab active. You first need to click on the Margins tab and make sure the top and bottom margins are set to to 0.5″ and the left and right margins to 0.3″.

Several items appear in the Columns dialog box. The first three items (under the Grid Settings) determine the spacing of the labels on the page:

Number of Columns	Number of columns in the output
Row Spacing	Space between the rows of output
Column Spacing	Amount of space between each column (this property is not available unless you enter a value greater than 1 for the Items Across property)

The Column Size settings determine the size of the label:

Width	Sets the width of each label
Height	Sets the height of each label

Same as Detail	Sets the Width and Height properties to the same width and height as the detail section of your report

The Column Layout section determines in which direction the records are printed:

Down, then Across	Prints consecutive labels in the first column and then starts in the second column when the first column is full
Across, then Down	Prints consecutive labels across the page and then moves down a row when there is no more room

After the settings are completed, you can print the labels.

Printing labels

After you create the labels, change any controls as you want, and view the Page Setup settings, you can print the labels. It's always a good idea to preview the labels one last time. Figure 28-10 shows the final labels in the Print Preview window. The ZIP code is correctly displayed.

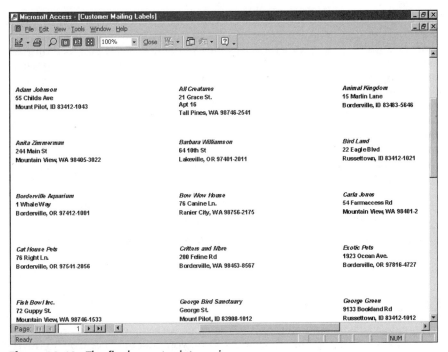

Figure 28-10: The final report print preview.

You can print the labels by simply selecting the Print button on the toolbar and then clicking on OK in the Print dialog box. You can also print the labels directly from the Report Design window by selecting File ⇨ Print.

Of course, you must insert your label paper first. If you don't have any #5160 label paper, you can use regular paper. If you want the labels to be printed in consecutive format, like a telephone directory, select Down, then Across in the Columns tab shown in Figure 28-9. In fact, that's another feature of Access reports — the capability to create what is known as a snaked column report.

Creating Snaked Column Reports

All the reports discussed in this book so far are either form-based (that is, free-form) or single-column lists. (*Single column* means that each column for each field appears only once on each page.) Often this is not the best way to present your data. Access gives you another option: *snaking columns*. This option lets you define the sections of a report so that they fit in an area that is less than half the width of the printed page. When the data reaches the bottom of the page, another column starts at the top of the page; when there is no more room on the page for another column, a new page starts.

This technique is commonly used for text in telephone directories or newspapers and other periodicals. An example of a database use is a report that prints several addresses, side by side, for a page of adhesive mailing labels you feed through your laser printer. You just learned how to create labels for mailing. Now you will learn how to apply these same techniques in a report. Snaked column reports have a major difference from mailing labels: They often have group sections, page headers, and footers; mailing labels have only data in the detail section.

The general process for creating a snaked column report is as follows:

✦ Decide how you want your data to be displayed: How many columns do you want? How wide should each column be?

✦ Create a report that has detail and group section controls no wider than the width of one column.

✦ Set the appropriate options in the Page Setup dialog box.

✦ Verify your results by using print preview.

Creating the report

You create a snaked column report in the same way you create any report. You start out with a blank Report Design window. Then you drag field controls to the report design and add label controls, lines, and rectangles. Next, you add any shading or special effects you want. Then you're ready to print your report. The major difference is the placement of controls and the use of the Page Setup window.

Figure 28-11 shows a completed design for the Customers by State (three snaking columns) report. The report displays a label control and the date in the page header, along with some solid black lines to set the title apart from the directory details. The detail section contains information that lists the customer number, customer name, address, and phone number. Then, within this section, you see three information fields about the customer's history with Mountain Animal Hospital. The page footer section contains another solid black line and a page number control.

What's important here is to make sure that the controls in the detail section use no more space for their height or width than you want for each occurrence of the information. Because you're going to be printing or displaying multiple detail records per page in a snaked-column fashion, you must note the size. In this example, you can see that the detail section data is about 13/4 inches high and about 2 inches wide. This is the size of the item you will define in the Columns dialog box.

Before continuing, you have to specify a sort order for the report. The report should be placed in order by State and then by Customer Number. You can do this by clicking on the Sorting and Grouping button on the toolbar and typing the names of the fields in the dialog box.

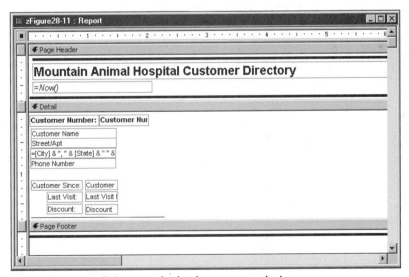

Figure 28-11: Defining a snaked column report design.

Defining the page setup

Earlier in this chapter, in the "Creating Mailing Labels" section, you learned how to use Page Setup settings. Since you created the labels by using the Label Wizard, the values for the Page Setup were automatically adjusted for you. Next, you learn how to enter these values manually. Figure 28-12 shows the Page Setup dialog box and the settings used to produce the Customer Directory report. Again, it doesn't show you the settings for the margins. Before continuing, click on the Margins tab and set the left and right margins to 0.5" (the top and bottom should be 1"). Then click on the Columns tab to continue.

The first group of settings (Grid Settings) to change are the Number of Columns, Row Spacing, and Column Spacing. Notice that the Number of Columns setting is set to 3. This means that you want three customer listings across the page. This and the other two settings actually work together. As you learned in the section about mailing labels, these controls set the spacing between groups of data and how the data is to be shown (the number of columns). The Row Spacing should be set to 0.2" and the Column Spacing set to 0.4". This is one way to set up the multiple columns and allow enough space between both the rows and the columns.

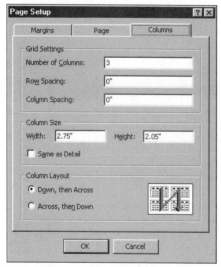

Figure 28-12: Defining the layout setup for a snaked column report.

The next grouping is the Column Size settings. In this example, the data is $^{13}/_4$ inches high and about 2 inches wide in the detail section. You can define Width as **2.75 in** and Height as **2.05 in**. By adjusting the Grid Settings and Column Sizes, you control how your columned report will look.

Notice that the final grouping, Column Layout section, offers two settings: Down, then Across or Across, then down. The icon under Column Layout shows the columns going up and down. You saw in Figure 28-9 that when the setting is Across, then Down, the icon shows rows of labels going across. In this customer directory, you want to fill an entire column of names first before moving to the right to fill another column. Therefore, you select the Down, then Across setting.

Printing the snaked column report

After the expanded Page Setup dialog box settings are completed, you can print your report. Figure 28-13 shows the top half of the first page of the final snaked column report in the Print Preview window. The data is sorted by state and customer number. Notice that the data snakes down the page. The first record is for Customer Number AK001, in Idaho. Below that is customer BL001. There are five customers in the first column. After the fifth customer, the next customer (Customer Number JO002) is found at the top of the middle column.

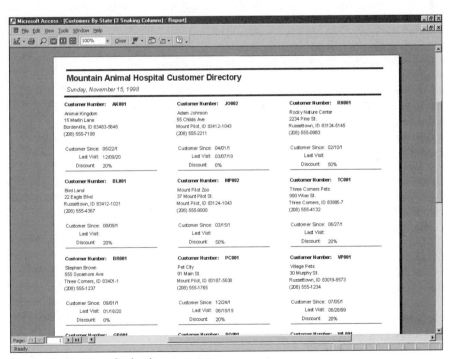

Figure 28-13: A snaked column report.

Creating Mail Merge Reports

Now that you have learned how to create snaked column reports and mailing labels (actually, they are the same thing), there is one more type of report to create—the *mail merge report* (also known as a *form letter*). A mail merge report is simply a report containing large amounts of text that have embedded database fields. For example, a letter may contain within the body of the text the amount a customer owes and the name of a pet.

The problem is how to control the *word wrap*. This means that the text may occupy more than one line, depending on the length of the text and the embedded field values. Different records may have different length values in their embedded fields. One record may use two lines in the report, another may use three, and another may require only one.

Access 2000 contains a Report Wizard that exports your data to Microsoft Word and launches the Word Print Merge feature. Why would you want to use a word processor, however, when you're working in a database? What happens if you don't use Word? Most word processors can perform mail merges using database data. Access itself does not have a specific capability to perform mail merging. Even so, as you see in this section, Access can indeed perform mail merge tasks with nearly the same precision as any Windows word processor!

In the first section of this chapter, you created mailing labels that indicated a special offer. You can use these labels to address the envelopes for the mail merge letter you now create. Suppose that you need to send a letter to all your customers who have an outstanding balance. You want to let them know that you expect payment now.

Figure 28-14 shows a letter created with Access. Many of the data fields embedded in this letter come from an Access query. The letter was created entirely with the Access Report Writer, as were its embedded fields.

Mountain Animal Hospital
2414 Mountain Road South
Redmond, WA 06761
(206) 555-9999

Aug 26, 1998

All Creatures
21 Grace St.
Tall Pines, WA 98746-2541

Dear All Creatures:

It has come to our attention that you have an outstanding balance of $2,000.00. We must have payment within 10 days or we will have to turn this account over to our lawyers. We give great service to your pets. In fact, according to our records, we have helped care for your animals since March 1998.

The entire staff is very fond of your animals. They especially like Bobo, and they would be very upset if your pet was no longer cared for by us. Since your last visit date on November 26, 1998, we have tried to contact you several times without success. Therefore, we are giving you 10 days to pay at least half of the outstanding balance, which comes to $1,000.00.

In advance, thank you, and we look forward to hearing from you and receiving your payment by September 05, 1998.

Sincerely,

Fred G. Rizzley

President
Mountain Animal Hospital

Figure 28-14: A letter created with the Access Report Writer.

Assembling data for a mail merge report

You can use data from either a table or a query for a report. A mail merge report is no different from any other report. As long as you specify a table or query as the control source for the report, the report can be created. Figure 28-15 shows a typical query used for the letter.

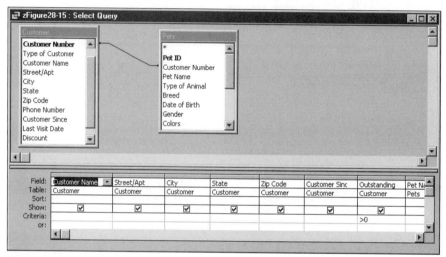

Figure 28-15: A typical query for a mail merge report.

Table 28-1 shows the fields or functions embedded in the text blocks used to create the letter. Compare the values in each line of the letter (shown in Figure 28-14) to the fields shown in the table. Later in this chapter, you'll see how each field or function is embedded in the text.

	Table 28-1	
	Fields Used in the Mail Merge Report	
Field Name	*Table*	*Usage in Report*
Date( )	Function	Page header; displays current date; formatted as mmmm dd, yyyy
Customer Name	Customer	Page header; displays customer name
Street/Apt	Customer	Page header; displays street in the address block
City	Customer	Page header; part of city, state, ZIP code block

Field Name	Table	Usage in Report
State	Customer	Page header; part of city, state, ZIP code block
Zip Code	Customer	Page header; part of city, state, ZIP code block; formatted as @@@@@-@@@@
Customer Name	Customer	Detail; part of salutation
Outstanding Balance	Customer	Detail; first line of first paragraph; formatted as $#,##0.00
Customer Since	Customer	Detail; fourth line in first paragraph; formatted as mmmm yyyy
Pet Name	Pets	Detail; first line in second paragraph
Last Visit Date	Customer	Detail; second and third lines in second paragraph; formatted as mmm dd, yyyy
Outstanding	Customer	Detail; fifth line in second paragraph; formatted as $#,##0.00 Balance *.5 Calculation
Date Add( );	Function	Detail; second line in third paragraph; Date Add adds ten days Now( ) Function to system date Now( ); formatted as mmmm dd, yyyy

Creating a mail merge report

After you assemble the data, you can create your report. Creating a mail merge report is much like creating other reports. Frequently a mail merge has only a page header and a detail section. You can use sorting and grouping sections, however, to enhance the mail merge report (although form letters normally are fairly consistent in their content).

Usually the best way to begin is with a blank report. Report Wizards don't really help you create a mail merge report. After you create a blank report, you can begin to add your controls to it.

Creating the page header area

A form letter generally has a top part that includes your company's name, address, and possibly a logo. You can print on preprinted forms that contain this information, or you can scan in the header and embed it in an unbound object frame. Usually, the top part of a form letter also contains the current date along with the name and address of the person or company to whom you're sending the letter.

Figure 28-16 shows the page header section of the mail merge report. In this example, an unbound bitmap picture is inserted that contains the Mountain Animal Hospital logo. The text for the company information is created with individual label controls. As you can see in the top half of the page header section, the current date is also displayed along with a line to separate the top of the header from the body of the letter. You can see the calculated text box control's properties at the bottom of Figure 28-16. The Format( ) and Date( ) functions are used to display the date with the full text for month, followed by the day, a comma, a space, and the four-digit year.

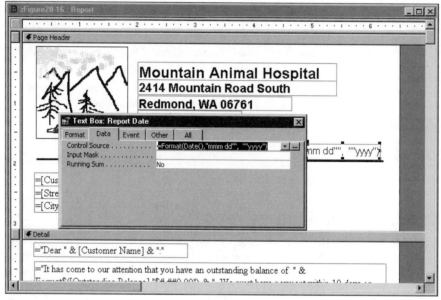

Figure 28-16: The page header section of a mail merge report.

The date expression is entered as

```
=Format(Date( ),"mmmm dd, yyyy")
```

and then automatically changed to

```
=Format(Date(),"mmmm dd""," ""yyyy")
```

This expression takes the system date of 8/26/98 and formats the date as Aug 26, 1998.

The customer name and address fields are also displayed in the page header. The standard concatenated expression is used to display the city, state, and ZIP code fields:

```
=[City] & ", " & [State] & " " & Format([Zip Code],"@@@@@-
@@@@")
```

Working with embedded fields in text

The body of the letter is shown in Figure 28-17. Each paragraph is one large block of text. A standard text box control is used to display each paragraph. The text box control's Can Grow and Can Shrink properties are set to Yes, which allows the text to take up only as much space as needed.

Embedded in each text block are fields from the query or expressions that use the fields from the query. In the page header section, the & method is used to concatenate the city, state, and ZIP code. Although this method works for single concatenated lines, it does not allow word wrapping, which is critical to creating a mail merge report. If you use this method in large blocks of text, you get only a single, truncated line of text.

Cross-Reference

As you learned in Chapter 22, the & method of concatenation handles word wrap within the defined width of the text box. When the text reaches the right margin of a text box, it shifts down to the next line. Because the Can Grow property is turned on, the text box can have any number of lines. It's best to convert nontext data to text when you concatenate with the & method. Although this conversion isn't mandatory, the embedded fields are displayed more correctly when they are correctly converted and formatted.

The first text block is a single-line text box control that concatenates the text "Dear" with the field Customer Name. Notice the special symbols within the first text box control. Remember that each text box is made up of smaller groups of text and expressions. By using the & character, you can concatenate them.

The expression =**"Dear" & [Customer Name] & ":"** begins with an equal sign and a double quote. Because the first item is text, it's surrounded by " characters. [Customer Name] needs to be enclosed in brackets because it's a field name; it should also be surrounded by & characters for concatenation. The colon at the end of the expression appears in the letter; it too is text and must be surrounded by double quotes.

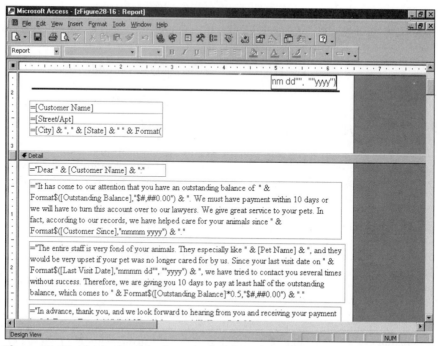

Figure 28-17: The body of the letter in the Report Design window.

The next control produces the first paragraph of the letter. Notice that there are five lines in the text box control but only four lines in the first paragraph of the letter (as shown in Figure 28-14). If you compare the two figures carefully, however, you'll see that the text box for the date is on the fifth line of the paragraph in the text control, whereas it's in the fourth line of the paragraph in the printed letter. This is a good example of word wrap. The lines shrank to fit the data.

The first line of the text control simply displays a text string. Notice that the text string is both enclosed in double quotes *and* concatenated to the next expression by the & character. The second line begins with an expression:

```
Format$([Outstanding Balance],"$#,##0.00") & "."
```

The expression converts the numeric expression to text and formats the field Outstanding Balance so that it shows a dollar sign, a comma (if the value is 1,000 or more), and two displayed decimal places. Without the format, the field would have simply displayed 381 rather than $381.00 for the first record.

The rest of the second line of the paragraph through the end of the fourth is one long text string. It's simply enclosed in double quotes and concatenated by the & character. The last line of the first paragraph contains an expression that formats and converts a date field. The expression Format$([Customer Since],"mmmm yyyy") formats the date value to display only the full month name and the year. (The date format in the page header demonstrated how to display the full month name, day, and year.)

Caution The maximum length of a single concatenated expression in Access is 254 characters between a single set of quotes. To get around this limitation, just end one expression, add an & character, and start another. The limit on the length of an expression in a single text box is 2,048 characters (almost 40 lines)!

The last line of the second paragraph formats a numeric expression, but it also calculates a value within the format function. This is a good example of an expression within a function. The calculation [Outstanding Balance] * .5 is then formatted to display dollar signs, and a comma if the number is 1,000 or more.

The last paragraph contains one text string and one expression. The expression advances the current date Now() by 10 days by using the expression DateAdd("d",10,Now()).

The bottom of the letter is produced using the label controls, as shown in Figure 28-17. These label controls display the closing, the signature, and the owner's title. The signature of Fred G. Rizzley is created here by using the Script font. Normally, you would scan in the signature and then use an unbound frame object control to display the bitmap picture that contains the signature.

One thing you must do is set the Force New Page property of the detail section to After Section so that a page break is always inserted after each letter.

Printing the mail merge report

You print a mail merge report in exactly the same way you would print any report. From the Print Preview window, you can simply click on the Print button. From the Report Design window, you can select File ➪ Print. The report is printed out like any other report.

Using the Access Mail Merge Wizard for Word for Windows 6.0, 7.0/95, or 8.0/97, or 9.0/2000

Another feature in Access 2000 is a Wizard to open Word automatically and start the Print Merge feature. The table or query you specify when you create the new report is used as the data source for the Word for Windows 6.0, Word for Windows 7.0/95, Word 8.0/97, or Word 9.0/2000 print merge.

To use the Mail Merge Wizard in Access 2000, you must have either Word 6.0 for Windows 3.1, Word for Windows 95 Version 7.0, 8.0, 9.0, or the Word in Office 95 Office 97, or Office 2000.

1. From the Database container window, click on either the Tables or Queries object button.

2. Select the table or query you want to merge with Word.

3. Click on the OfficeLinks drop-down button on the toolbar.

4. Click on Merge It to start the MS Word Mail Merge Wizard, as shown in Figure 28-18.

   After you select the MS Word Mail Merge Wizard, Access displays the Microsoft Word Mail Merge Wizard screen, as shown in Figure 28-19.

   This screen lets you decide whether to link your data to an existing Word document or to create a new document. If you select the option that says to Link your data to an existing Microsoft Word document, Access displays a standard Windows file-selection box that lets you select an existing document. The document is retrieved, Word is displayed, and the Print Merge feature is active. You can then modify your existing document.

   In this example, you start with a new document.

5. Select the option Create a new document and then link the data to it.

6. Click on OK to launch Word and display the Print Merge toolbar.

You may also see a dialog box asking for the field and record delimiter, usually a quote (") and a comma (,), with some type of merged data. You can now create your document, adding merge fields where you want them. As you can see in Figure 28-20, you simply click on the Insert Merge Field button whenever you want to display a field list from your Access table or query. The fields appear with a pair of carets around them.

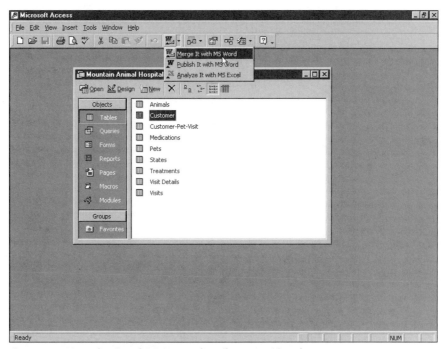

Figure 28-18: Selecting the MS Word Mail Merge Wizard.

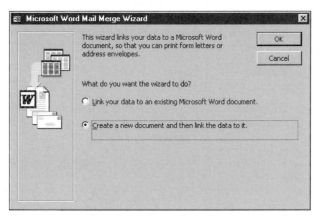

Figure 28-19: The Microsoft Word Mail Merge Wizard screen.

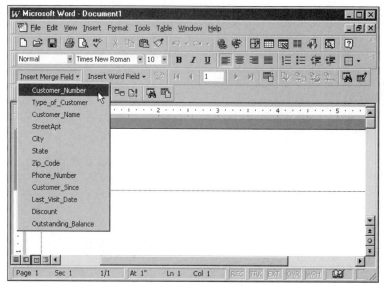

Figure 28-20: The Word Print Merge screen.

When you're through, you can use the Mail Merge command button to merge the data and print your mail merge letters. There are some advantages to using the Microsoft Word print merge facility to create your letters. You have the availability of a spell checker, you can properly justify your paragraphs, and you can individually change the font type, size, or weight of individual words or characters. The negatives are that you have to use a word processor, you can't format numeric or date data, and you can't embed other Access objects, such as datasheets or graphs.

An example of a document created using the Mail Merge feature is shown in Figure 28-21. The merged fields have been highlighted in bold to make them stand out. An example of the hard-copy printout of the form letter is shown in Figure 28-22.

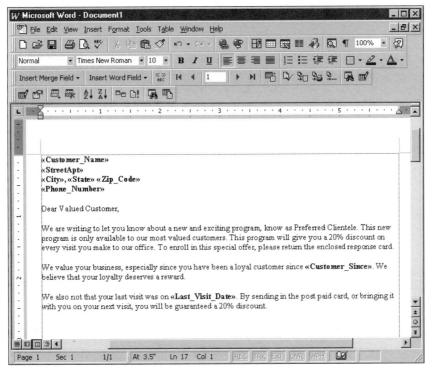

Figure 28-21: An example of a document created with the Mail Merge feature.

To see the merged fields in your document while in Word, you can click on the Merged Data button on the Word format bar.

When you're through editing and printing your letter, you can return to Access by selecting File ⇨ Close or File ⇨ Exit.

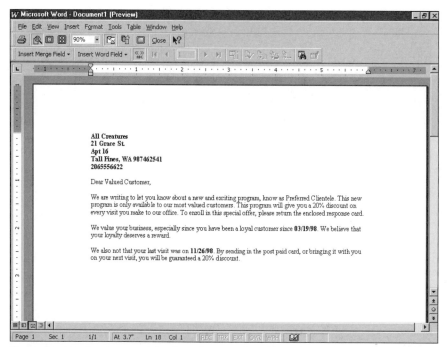

Figure 28-22: A printout of the form letter using the Mail Merge function.

Summary

In this chapter, you learned how to create mailing labels, snaked column reports, and mail merge reports. The following concepts were discussed:

✦ Mailing labels are most easily created using the Access Label Wizard.

✦ The Label Wizard lets you select the fields for the mailing label and also select from six different label manufacturers including Avery.

✦ Using the Report Design window, you can further customize the mailing label.

✦ The secret to mailing labels is changing the settings in the expanded Page Setup dialog box.

✦ Snaked column reports can be snaked vertically or horizontally.

✦ Snaked column reports are essentially large labels on paper; they are used for such things as customer directories.

✦ You can create mail merge reports with the Access Report Writer.

✦ By using concatenated text boxes, you can create paragraphs of text with embedded fields that word-wrap to create form letters.

✦ You can use the Format( ) function to reformat numeric and date fields in a mail merge report.

✦ The Word for Windows 6.0, 7.0/95,8.0/95, or 9.0/2000 Mail Merge Wizard makes exported Access data easy to use with the Print Merge feature in Word (all versions after 6.0).

This chapter completes Part IV, which deals with advanced Access query, form, and report topics. Part V covers the use of Access macros you can use to automate tasks without programming.

✦   ✦   ✦

Applications in Access

An Introduction to Macros and Events

◆ ◆ ◆ ◆

In This Chapter

Understanding how macros work

Examining the components of the Macro window

Creating and running a macro

Editing, deleting, and renaming macros

Creating macro groups

Creating a macro that starts automatically

Supplying conditions to macros

Troubleshooting macros

Understanding how events work

Learning how events are triggered

◆ ◆ ◆ ◆

When working with a database system, the same tasks may be performed repeatedly. Rather than doing the same steps each time, you can automate the process with macros.

Database management systems continually grow as you add records in a form, perform ad hoc queries, and print new reports. As the system grows, many of the objects are saved for later use — for a weekly report or monthly update query, for example. You tend to create and perform many tasks repetitively. Every time you add customer records, for example, you open the same form. Likewise, you print the same form letter for customers whose pets are overdue for their annual shots.

You can create Access *macros* to perform these tasks. After you have created these small programs, you may want certain macros to take effect whenever a user performs some action (such as pressing a button or opening a form). Access uses *events* to trigger macros automatically.

Understanding Macros

Access *macros* automate many repetitive tasks without your having to write complex programs or subroutines. In the example of the form letter for customers whose pets are overdue for annual shots, a macro can perform a query and print the results for all such customers.

What is a macro?

A macro is an object like other Access objects (tables, queries, forms, and reports), except that you create it to automate a particular task or series of tasks. Think of each task as the result of one or more steps; each step is an action not found on the Access menu but in the Visual Basic for Applications (VBA) language. You can also use Access macros to simulate menu choices or mouse movements.

Unlike macros in spreadsheets, Access macros normally are not used to duplicate individual keystrokes or mouse movements. They perform specific, user-specified tasks, such as opening a form or running a report.

Every task you want Access to perform is called an *action*. Access 2000 provides 53 actions that can be selected and performed in your macros. For example, you may have a macro that performs the actions shown in Figure 29-1:

- ✦ Place the hourglass on the screen

- ✦ Automatically open a form

- ✦ Display a message box that says that the macro is complete

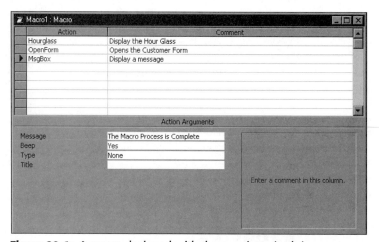

Figure 29-1: A macro designed with three actions (tasks).

Macro actions are created in a Macro Design window. The macros are run by entering the macro name in the Event properties of a form or report.

When to use a macro

Macros can be used for any repetitive task that you do in Access, saving time and energy. In addition, because the macro performs the actions the same way each time, macros add accuracy and efficiency to the database. Macros can perform such tasks as:

✦ Running queries and reports together

✦ Opening multiple forms and/or reports together

✦ Checking for data accuracy on validation forms

✦ Moving data between tables

✦ Performing actions when you click on a command button

As an example, a macro can find and filter records for a report, which allows you to add a command button to a form that when clicked tells the macro to perform a user-specified search. Macros such as this example can be used throughout the Access database system.

The Macro Window

As with other Access objects, a macro is created in a graphical design window. To open a new Macro window, follow these steps:

1. In an open database, press F11 (or Alt+F1) to select the Database window.

2. Click the Macros object button.

3. Click the New toolbar button in the Database window.

After you complete these steps, Access displays an empty Design window, similar to that in Figure 29-2. Notice the different parts of the window in this figure.

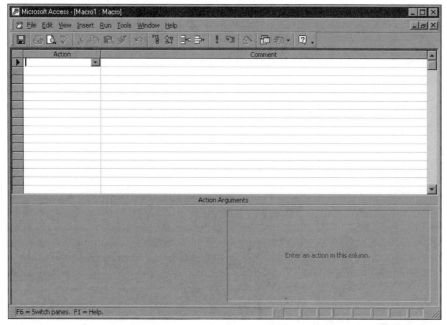

Figure 29-2: An empty Macro Design window.

As Figure 29-2 shows, the Macro Design window has four parts: a menu and a toolbar above the Design window, and two windowpanes:

✦ Action pane (top portion of the window)

✦ Argument pane (bottom portion of the window)

The Action pane

By default, when you open a new Macro Design window, as in Figure 29-2, Access displays two columns in the *Action pane* (top pane): Action and Comment. Two more columns, Macro Name and Condition, can be displayed in the Action pane by selecting View ⇨ Macro Names and View ⇨ Conditions, or by clicking on the equivalent icons on the toolbar.

Note   If you want to change the default so that all four columns are open, select Tools ⇨ Options, click the View tab, and place a check mark next to both items in the Show in macro design.

A macro object can contain many different names each containing their own actions. The Names column shows the name of each macro within the macro object. Checking the Conditions column lets you run or skip a macro based on a condition you enter such as SALEAMT > 200.

Each macro can have one or many actions (individual tasks for Access to perform). You add individual actions in the Action column, and you can add a description of each action in the Comment column. Access ignores the comments when the macro is run.

The Argument pane

The *Argument pane* (lower portion of the window) is where you supply the specific *arguments* (properties) needed for the selected action. Most actions need additional information to carry out the action, such as which object should be used. For example, Figure 29-3 shows the action arguments for a typical action named OpenForm, which opens a specific form and has six different arguments that can be specified:

Form Name	Specifies the form for Access to open
View	Specifies the view mode to activate: Form, Design, Print Preview, Datasheet
Filter Name	Applies the specified filter or query
Where Condition	Limits the number of records displayed
Data Mode	Specifies a data-entry mode: Add, Edit, or Read Only
Window Mode	Specifies a window mode: Normal, Hidden, Icon, or Dialog

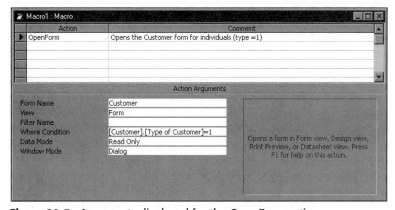

Figure 29-3: Arguments displayed for the OpenForm action.

Note   Some actions, such as Beep and Maximize, have no arguments, but most actions require at least one argument.

Creating a Macro

To create a macro, you use both the Action and Argument panes of the Macro window. After you supply actions and associated arguments, you save the macro for later use.

Entering actions and arguments

Actions are added to a macro in any of several ways:

✦ Enter the action name in the Action column of the Macro window.

✦ Select actions from the drop-down list of actions (in the Action column).

✦ Drag and drop an object from the Database window into an action cell.

The last method, drag and drop, is useful for common actions associated with the database. For example, you can drag a specific form to an action cell in the macro Action column; Access automatically adds the action OpenForm and its known arguments (such as the form name).

Selecting actions from the combo box list

The easiest way to add an action is by using the combo box, which you can access in any action cell. For example, to open a form, specify the action OpenForm. To create the OpenForm action, follow these steps:

1. Open a new Macro Design window.

2. Click the first empty cell in the Action column.

3. Click the arrow that appears in the action cell.

4. Select the OpenForm action from the combo box.

Note   You don't have to add comments to the macro, but it's a good idea to document the reason for each macro action (as well as providing a description of the entire macro).

Specifying arguments for actions

After entering the OpenForm action, you can enter the arguments into the bottom pane. Figure 29-3, which displays the completed arguments, shows that the bottom pane has six action arguments associated with this specific action. The arguments View, Data Mode, and Window Mode have default values. Because Access does not know which form you want to open, you must enter at least a form name. To open the form named Customer as a dialog box in read-only mode, enter the three arguments Form Name, Data Mode, and Window Mode, as shown in Figure 29-3.

To add the arguments, follow these steps:

1. Click the Form Name cell (or press F6 to switch to the Argument pane).
2. Select the Customer form from the drop-down list (or type the name).
3. Click the Data Mode cell.
4. Select the Read Only choice from the drop-down list (or type the choice).
5. Click the Window Mode cell.
6. Select the Dialog choice from the drop-down list (or type the choice).

Your macro should now resemble the one in Figure 29-3. Notice that the Form Name is specified and the default values of the Data Mode and Window Mode cells are changed.

Selecting actions by dragging and dropping objects

You can also specify actions by dragging and dropping objects from the Database window. When you add actions in this manner, Access adds the appropriate arguments automatically. To add the same form (Customer) to an empty Macro window, follow these steps:

1. Start with an empty Macro Design window.
2. Select Window ⇨ Tile Vertically from the Design menu. Access places the Macro and Database windows side by side.
3. Click on the Forms object button in the Database window. Access displays all the forms, as shown in Figure 29-4.
4. Click and drag the Customer form from the Database window. Access displays a Form icon as it moves into the Macro window.
5. Continue to drag and drop the Form icon in any empty action cell of the Macro window.

Access displays the correct action and arguments automatically.

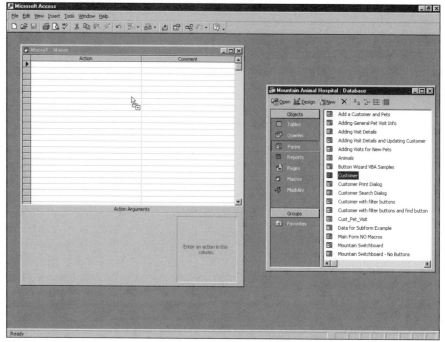

Figure 29-4: The Macro and Database windows are tiled side-by-side.

Note

After using the drag-and-drop method to select actions, you may need to modify the action arguments to further refine them from their default values. Recall that in the last example that Data Mode and Window Mode were changed for the form.

Adding multiple actions to a macro

A macro can have multiple actions assigned to it, not just a single action. For example, you may want to display an hourglass and then, while it's displayed, open two forms. Then you can have the computer beep for the user after completing the macro. To accomplish these multiple actions, follow these steps:

1. Open a new Macro Design window.

2. Click the first empty cell in the Action column.

3. Select the Hourglass action from the drop-down list or type it.

4. Click in the Comment cell alongside the Hourglass action.

5. Type **Display the hourglass while the macro is running**.

6. Click the next empty cell in the Action column.

7. Select the OpenForm action from the drop-down list or type the name of the action.

8. Click the argument cell Form Name.

9. Select the Add a Customer and Pets form.

10. Click the Comment cell alongside the OpenForm action.

11. Type **Open the Add a Customer and Pets form**.

12. Click the next empty cell in the Action column.

13. Select the OpenForm action from the drop-down list or type the action.

14. Click the argument cell Form Name.

15. Select the Adding Visit Details form.

16. Click the Comment cell alongside the OpenForm action.

17. Type **Open the Adding Visit Details form**.

18. Click the next empty cell in the Action column.

19. Select the Beep action from the drop-down list or type the action.

Your macro design should now look similar to Figure 29-5. This macro opens both forms as it displays the hourglass. After both forms are open, the macro beeps to signal that it is finished.

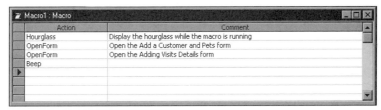

Figure 29-5: Adding multiple actions to a single macro.

 Tip   When you're adding more than one action, you can specify each action, one after the other, with several rows of spaces between them. These blank rows can contain additional lines of comments for each macro action.

Rearranging macro actions

When you work with multiple actions in a macro, you may change your mind about the order of the actions. For example, you may decide that the macro created in

Figure 29-5 should have the Beep action come first in the macro. To move the action, follow these steps:

1. Select the action by clicking the row selector to the left of the action name.

2. Click the highlighted row again and drag it to the top row.

Deleting macro actions

If you no longer need an action in a macro, you can delete the action. In the example of the macro shown in Figure 29-5, to delete the action to open the form Adding Visit Details, follow these steps:

1. Select the action by clicking the row selector to the left of the action's name.

2. Press Delete or select Edit ➪ Delete Row from the menu.

Tip   You can also delete a row by using the right-click shortcut menu: Select the row to delete, press the *right* mouse button, and select Delete Row.

Saving macros

Before you can run a macro, it must be saved. After you save a macro, it becomes another database object that can be opened and run from the Database window. To save a macro, follow these steps:

1. Select File ➪ Save from the Macro Design menu or click the Save button on the toolbar.

2. If the macro has not been saved, you must enter a name in the Save As dialog box. Press Enter or click OK when you're through.

Tip   The fastest way to save a macro is to press F12 or Alt+F2 and give the macro a name. Another way is to double-click the Macro window's Control menu (top-left corner) and answer the appropriate dialog box questions.

Editing existing macros

After a macro is created, it can be edited by following these steps:

1. In the Database window, select the Macros object button.

2. Highlight the macro you want to edit.

3. Click the Design button in the Database window.

Copying entire macros

To copy a macro, follow these steps:

1. Click the Macros object button in the Database window.
2. Select the macro to copy.
3. Press Ctrl+C or select Edit ⇨ Copy to copy the macro to the Clipboard.
4. Press Ctrl+V or select Edit ⇨ Paste to paste the macro from the Clipboard.
5. In the Paste As dialog box, type its new name.

Renaming macros

Sometimes you need to rename a macro because you changed the event property in the form or report property. To rename a macro, follow these steps:

1. Select the Database window by pressing F11 or Alt+F1.
2. Click the Macros object button to display all the macro names.
3. Highlight the macro name to change.
4. Choose Edit ⇨ Rename from the Database menu or right-click and choose Rename from the shortcut menu.
5. Enter the new name.

Running Macros

After a macro is created, it can be run from any of these locations within Access:

✦ A Macro window

✦ A Database window

✦ Other object windows

✦ Events such as a form opening or closing

✦ Another macro

Cross-Reference

The many events in Access 2000 are covered later in this chapter and in Chapter 30.

Running a macro from the Macro window

A macro can run directly from the Macro Design window by clicking the toolbar's Run button (the exclamation mark) or by choosing Run from the Design menu.

Running a macro from the Database window

A macro can be run from the Database window by following these steps:

1. Click the Macros object button in the Database window.

2. Select the macro to run.

3. Either double-click the macro or choose the Run button.

Running a macro from any window in the database

To run a macro from any window in the database, follow these steps:

1. Select Tools ⇨ Macro from the menu.

2. In the Macro dialog box, enter the name or select it from the drop-down list.

3. Click OK or press Enter.

Running a macro from another macro

To run a macro from another macro, follow these steps:

1. Add the action RunMacro to your macro.

2. Enter the name of the macro you want to run in the Macro Name argument.

Running a macro automatically when you open a database

Access can automatically run a macro each time a database is opened; there are two ways to do this. One way is by using a special macro name, *AutoExec,* that Access recognizes. If Access finds it in a database, it executes this macro automatically each time the database is opened. For example, you may want to open some forms and queries automatically and immediately after opening the database.

To run a macro automatically when a database is opened, follow these steps:

1. Create a macro with the actions you want to run when the database is opened.

2. Save the macro and name it **AutoExec**.

If you close that database and reopen it, Access runs the AutoExec macro automatically.

Tip   If you have a macro named AutoExec but you *don't* want to run it when you open a database, hold down the Shift key as you select the database in the Open Database dialog box.

The second method makes use of Access 2000's option for setting Startup properties. As shown in Figure 29-6, you can enter the name of a form that you want to start when Access is opened. This form can contain the name of a macro to run when the form is loaded (more about form events later). The Startup properties window is displayed by selecting Tools ➪ Startup from any window. The options that you set in the Startup properties window are in effect for as long as the Access database is open. You can set many options from the Startup properties window; for instance, you can change the title bar of all windows, specify the name of an icon file to use when Access is minimized, and affect many Access custom menus and toolbars.

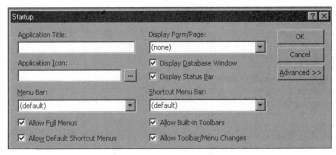

Figure 29-6: Using the Startup properties.

Macro Groups

As you create macros, you may want to group a series of related macros into one large macro. To do this, you need some way of uniquely identifying the individual macros within the group. Access lets you create a *macro group* (a macro file that contains two or more macros).

Creating macro groups

Like individual macros, macro groups are database objects. When you look in the macro object list in the Database window, you see only the macro group's name. Inside the group, each macro has a unique name that you assign (along with the actions for each macro).

You may, for example, want to create a macro that is a group of all macros that open forms. To create this type of macro, follow these steps:

1. In the Database window, select the Macros object button.

2. Click the New toolbar button in the Database window. Access opens the Macro Design window.

3. Select View ⇨ Macro Names or select the Macro Names button on the toolbar. Access adds the Macro Name column to the Action pane.

4. In the Macro Name column, enter a name for the macro.

5. In the Action column, next to the macro name that you just entered, enter an action for the macro.

6. Select the Action column under the action that you just entered so that you can enter the next action.

7. Enter the next action (if the macro has more than one) in the Action column. Continue to enter actions until all are specified for a certain macro. To add another macro to the group, repeat Steps 4 through 7.

8. Save the macro group, naming it **Open and Close Forms**.

Figure 29-7 shows how a macro group will look. Notice that five separate macros are in it: Customer, Visits, Details, Close All Forms, and Exit. The Arguments pane shows only the arguments for the highlighted macro name.

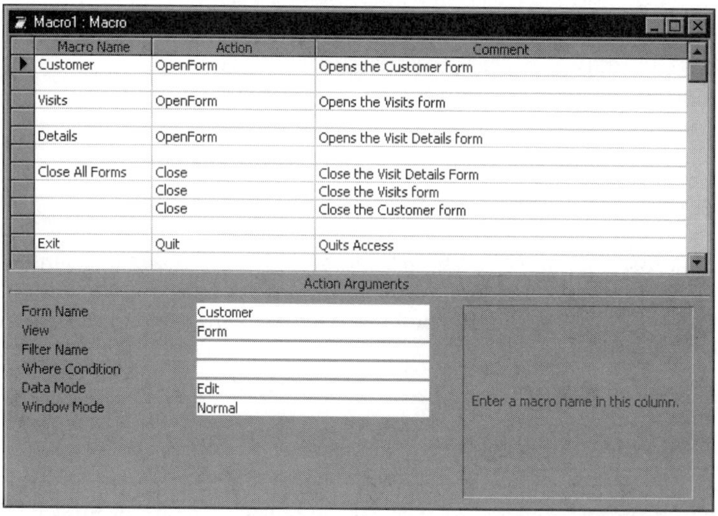

Macro Name	Action	Comment
Customer	OpenForm	Opens the Customer form
Visits	OpenForm	Opens the Visits form
Details	OpenForm	Opens the Visit Details form
Close All Forms	Close	Close the Visit Details Form
	Close	Close the Visits form
	Close	Close the Customer form
Exit	Quit	Quits Access

Action Arguments

Form Name	Customer
View	Form
Filter Name	
Where Condition	
Data Mode	Edit
Window Mode	Normal

Enter a macro name in this column.

Figure 29-7: A macro group.

Tip   Although not necessary, it's a good idea to leave a blank line between macros to improve readability and clarity.

Running a macro in a macro group

After you create a macro group, you'll want to run each macro inside the group. To run one, you must specify both the group name and the macro name.

Cross-Reference   Later in this chapter, you learn to use the events that run macros.

To specify both group and macro names, enter the group name, a period, and then the macro name. If you type **Open and Close Forms.Visits**, for example, you are specifying the macro Visits in the group macro named Open and Close Forms.

Caution   If you run a group macro from the Macro Design window or from the Database window, you cannot specify a macro name inside the macro group. Access will run only the first macro or set of actions specified in the group macro. Access stops executing actions when it reaches a new macro name in the Macro Name column.

To run a macro inside a group macro, using the other windows in the database or another macro, you enter both the macro group name and macro name, placing a period between the two names.

Tip   You also can run a macro by selecting Macro from the Tools menu and typing the group and macro name.

Supplying Conditions for ActionsIn some cases, you may want to run some action or actions in a macro only when a certain condition is true. For example, you may want to display a message if no records are available for a report and then stop execution of the macro. In such a case, you can use a condition to control the flow of the macro.

What is a condition?

Simply put, a *condition* is a logical expression that is either True or False. The macro follows one of two paths, depending on the condition of the expression. If the expression is True, the macro follows the True path; otherwise, it follows the False path. Table 29-1 shows several conditions and the True/False results.

Table 29-1
Conditions and Their Results

Condition	True Result	False Result
Forms!Customer!State="WA"	If the state is Washington	Any state except Washington
IsNull(Gender)	If no gender is specified	Gender is male or female (not Null)
Length <= 10	If length is less than or equal to 10 inches	If length is greater than 10
Reports![Pet Directory]![Type animal] = "CAT" OR Reports! [Pet Directory]! [Type of Animal] = "DOG"	If type of animal is cat or dog	Any animal other than cat or dog

Activating the Condition column in a macro

As Table 29-1 demonstrates, a condition is an expression that results in a logical answer of Yes or No. The answer must be either True or False. You can specify a condition in a macro by following these steps:

1. Enter the Macro Design window by creating a new macro or editing an existing one.

2. Select View ➪ Conditions or click on the Conditions button on the toolbar. The Condition column is inserted to the left of the Action column. If the Macro Name column is visible, the Condition column is between the Macro Name and the Action columns (see Figure 29-8).

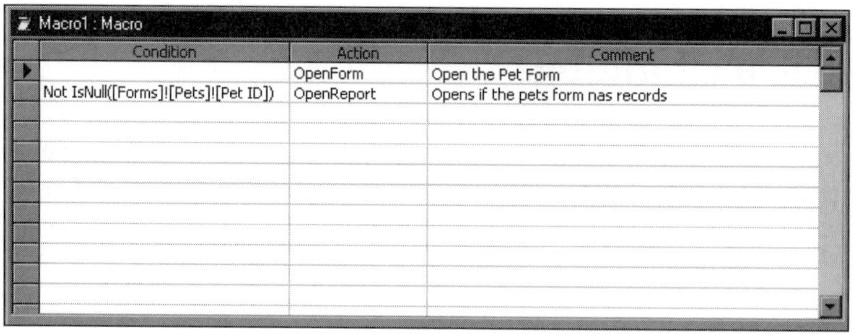

Condition	Action	Comment
	OpenForm	Open the Pet Form
Not IsNull([Forms]![Pets]![Pet ID])	OpenReport	Opens if the pets form nas records

Figure 29-8: The Condition column added to the Macro Design window.

With the Condition column visible, you can specify conditions for one or many actions within a macro.

 Tip   In Figure 29-8, you can see that the Condition and Comment columns are wider than the Action column. You can widen or shrink columns by positioning the mouse pointer on the column border and dragging the column line. You can also resize the height between the rows but that resizes all of the rows.

Referring to Control Names in Expressions

When working with macros, you may need to refer to the value of a control in a form or report. To refer to a control in a form or report, use this syntax:

```
Forms!formname!controlname
Reports!reportname!controlname
```

If a space occurs within the name of a form, report, or control, you must enclose the name in brackets. For example, Forms![Add a Customer and Pets]!State refers to the State control (field on a form) on the currently open form called Add a Customer and Pets.

If you run a macro from the same form or report that contains the control, you can shorten this syntax to the control name.

Note: To reference a control name on a form or report, first make sure that the form or report is open.

Specifying a condition for a single action

You may want to specify a condition for a single action. An example is activating the report Pet Directory only when there are records in the form Pets, based on a query named Only Cats and Dogs. If no records are present, you want the macro to skip activation of the report. To have the macro specify this condition, as shown in Figure 29-8, follow these steps:

1. In the Macro window, click the Conditions button on the toolbar.
2. In the first action cell of the Action pane, select OpenForm.
3. In the Form Name cell of the Argument pane, select Pets.
4. In the next Action cell of the Action pane, select OpenReport.
5. In the Report Name cell of the Argument pane, select Pet Directory.
6. Click the Condition cell next to the action OpenReport.
7. Type Not IsNull(Forms![Pets]![Pet ID]).

At the completion of these steps, your macro should resemble the one shown in Figure 29-8.

In this example, the condition specified is True if there are no records (the first Pet ID is Null) in the open form Pets. If the condition is True, when the macro is run, the action OpenReport is not performed; otherwise, the report is opened in print preview mode.

Caution   When you specify conditions in a macro and reference a control name (field name), the source (form or report) of the control name must already be open.

Specifying a condition for multiple actionsBesides specifying a condition for a single action, you can specify a condition that is effective for multiple actions. That is, a single condition that causes several actions to occur. In this way, you can also create an If-Then-Else condition.

If you want Access to perform more than one action, add the other actions below the first one. In the Condition column, place an ellipsis (...) beside each action. Figure 29-9 is a macro in which two actions are performed based on a single condition. Notice that the condition has been changed from `Not IsNull` to `IsNull`.

Condition	Action	Comment
	OpenForm	Open the Pets Form
IsNull(Forms![Pets]![Pet ID])	MsgBox	(Then) If there are NO records display a message box
...	StopMacro	and stop the macro.
	OpenReport	(Else) If the Pets form has records, run the report in the Print Preview mode

Figure 29-9: This macro performs two actions based on a single condition.

In Figure 29-9, the condition `IsNull(Forms![Pets]![Pet ID])` performs the two actions MsgBox and StopMacro if the condition is True. Notice the ellipsis (...) in the cell immediately under the specified condition, which is the Condition cell for the action StopMacro.

When you run the macro, Access evaluates the expression in the Condition cell. If the expression is True, Access performs the action beside the expression and then all the following actions that have an ellipsis in the Condition column. Access continues the True actions until it comes to another condition (using the new condition from that point on).

If the expression is False, Access ignores the action (or actions) and moves to the next action row that does not have an ellipsis.

Caution If Access reaches a blank cell in the Condition column, it performs the action in that row regardless of the conditional expression. The only way to avoid this is to control the flow of actions by use of a *redirection action* such as RunMacro or StopMacro. For example, if the second conditional action (StopMacro) is not after the MsgBox action, the OpenReport action is executed regardless of whether the conditional expression is True or False. On the other hand, the MsgBox action takes effect only if the field Pet ID is Null (True).

Controlling the flow of actions

By using conditional expressions, the flow of action in the macro is controlled. The macro in Figure 29-9 uses the action StopMacro to stop execution of the macro if the field is Null, thereby avoiding opening the report Pet Directory if the table is empty.

Several macro actions can be used to change or control the flow of actions based on a condition. The two most common are the actions StopMacro and RunMacro; they also control the flow of actions within a macro.

Troubleshooting Macros

Access has two tools to help troubleshoot macros:

✦ Single-step mode

✦ The Action Failed dialog box

Single-step mode

If unexpected results occur while running a macro, you can use *single-step mode* to move through the macro one action at a time, pausing between actions. Single-step mode lets you observe the result of each action and isolate the action or actions that caused the incorrect results.

To use single-step mode, click the Single-Step button on the toolbar. To use this feature on the macro in Figure 29-9, follow these steps:

1. Edit the macro by opening the macro in the macro design window.

2. Click the Single-Step button on the toolbar or select Run ⇨ Single Step.

3. Run the macro as you normally do or by clicking the Run button on the toolbar.

Access displays the Macro Single Step dialog box, showing the macro name, the action name, and the arguments for the action (see Table 29-2). Figure 29-10 is a typical Macro Single Step dialog box.

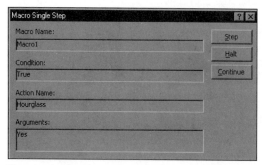

Figure 29-10: The Macro Single Step dialog box.

Table 29-2		
Macro Single-Step Button Options		
Button	**Purpose**	
Step	Runs the action in the dialog box. If no error is reported, the next action appears in the dialog box.	
Halt	Stops the execution of the macro and closes the dialog box.	
Continue	Turns off single-step mode and runs the remainder of the macro.	

The Action Failed dialog box

If a macro action causes an error (either during single-step mode or when running normally), Access opens a dialog box that looks exactly like the Macro Single Step dialog box, except that the only available button is the Halt button.

To correct the problem, choose Halt and return to the Macro Design window.

Understanding Events

With the actions stored in macros, you can run the macro either via a menu choice or by naming the macro AutoExec. The AutoExec macro runs automatically each time the database is opened. Access also offers another method to activate a macro: Base it on a user action.

For example, a user can activate a macro by clicking on a command button or by the action of opening a form. To accomplish this, Access takes advantage of something known as an *event*.

What is an event?

An Access event is the result or consequence of some user action. An Access event can occur when a user moves from one record to another in a form, closes a report, or clicks on a command button on a form.

Your Access applications are *event driven*. Objects in Access respond to many types of events. Access responds to events with behaviors that are built in for each object. Access events can be recognized by specific object properties. For example, if a user clicks the mouse button with the pointer in a checkbox, the property OnMouseDown recognizes that the mouse button was clicked. You can have this property run a macro when the user clicks the mouse button.

Events in Access 2000 can be categorized into seven groups:

✦ *Windows (Form, Report) events:* Opening, closing, and resizing

✦ *Data events:* Making current, deleting, or updating

✦ *Focus events:* Activating, entering, and exiting

✦ *Keyboard events:* Pressing or releasing a key

✦ *Mouse events:* Clicking or pressing a mouse button down

✦ *Print events:* Formatting and printing

✦ *Error and timing events:* Happening after an error has occurred or some time has passed

In all, 53 events can be checked in forms and reports to specify some action after they take place.

How do events trigger actions?

You can have Access run a macro when a user performs any one of the 53 events that Access recognizes. Access can recognize an event through the use of special properties for forms, controls (fields), and reports.

For example, Figure 29-11 shows the property sheet for a form. This form has many properties, which may be used to respond to corresponding events. Forms aren't the only objects to have events; form sections (page header, form header, detail, page footer, form footer) and every control on the form (labels, text boxes, check boxes, and option buttons, for example) have events, too.

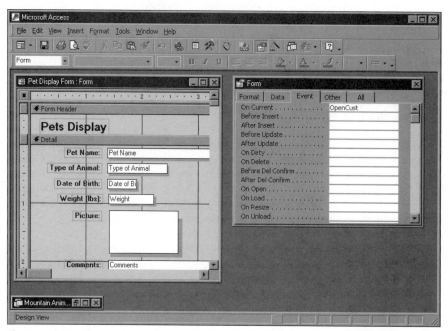

Figure 29-11: The property sheet for a form, showing the OnOpen property entered. This figure shows the form Pets Display Form in Design mode with the property sheet open.

Where to trigger macros

In Access, you can run event-driven macros by using properties in forms and reports. There are no event properties for tables or queries.

Even so, when you work with forms, you can run macros based on Access switchboards (full-screen button-type menus), command buttons, and pull-down menus. These features make event-driven macros powerful and easy to use. In the next several chapters, you learn about many events and the macro actions that events can use.

Summary

In this chapter, you learned the basics of macros and events:

✦ An Access macro is a database object that lets you automate tasks without writing complex programs. Macros are used to automate repetitive tasks. In Access, the tasks that are performed are known as *actions*.

✦ Two panes comprise the Macro Design window: Action and Argument. Access actions are specified in the Action pane. You can add them from a pull-down list box or by dragging and dropping common objects.

✦ Access requires arguments (variables) to perform actions.

✦ Macros can be saved, renamed, edited, and copied just like any other Access object.

✦ Access has a special macro called AutoExec that runs automatically when the database is opened. Holding down the Shift key can deactivate the AutoExec macro when opening the database.

✦ The Startup window can control many options in an Access database when it's first opened.

✦ When you create macros, you can consolidate them into a group macro. Group macros use a column in the Action pane called the Macro Name column.

✦ When you work with macros, you can specify a condition for one or more actions. If the condition is True, the action is performed; if False, the action is skipped.

✦ Access offers two methods for troubleshooting macros: single-stepping and the Action Failed dialog box. With these tools, you can trace any errors in your macros or halt a faulty macro.

✦ An event (a result or consequence of some action performed by the user) can run a macro. In Access, events are recognized by use of special properties. The only objects in which Access recognizes events are forms and reports.

The next chapter introduces the many uses of macros and how they are generally run from triggered events. In Chapter 31, you learn to create menu-based systems by using events and macros.

✦ ✦ ✦

Using Macros in Forms and Reports

At this point you should know how to create and run macros, and you should know how to start a macro automatically when you open a database. In addition, you should be able to create and specify conditions for macros.

Now you're going to learn how to use macros in real examples by using tables, forms, queries, and reports that you created in previous chapters.

Types of Macros

Cross-Reference

In Chapter 29, you learned how to create macros, and you learned how to associate a macro with a form or report property. *Macros* are Access objects consisting of one or more actions such as opening a dialog box, running a report, or even finding a record.

Usually, you create macros to perform repetitive tasks or a series of required actions following an initial action. For example, macros can synchronize two forms while a user moves from record to record. They can also validate new data after it is entered by a user.

Before activating a macro, you need to decide where and how you will use it. For example, you may have a macro that opens the Customer form, and you want Access to run the macro every time a user opens the Pets form. In this case, you place the name of the macro in the On Open property of the Pets form. Then, every time a user opens the Pets form, the On Open property will trigger the macro that opens the Customer form.

Or you may want to trigger another macro every time a user presses an accelerator key (also known as a hot key). For example, if you want an Import dialog box to be activated when a user presses Ctrl+I, you should attach the macro to the key combination Ctrl+I in a hot-key macro file.

Although the second macro performs some tasks or actions, it is different from the first macro. The second macro is activated by a user action (pressing a hot key); the first one is activated when a user performs some specific action recognized by a form property.

Macros can be grouped together based on their usage. The four basic groups are:

- ✦ Form
- ✦ Report
- ✦ Import/Export
- ✦ Accelerator keys

The most common macros are those used in forms and reports. Using macros in these objects lets you build intelligence into each form and report. Macros are also used for importing or exporting data to and from other data sources. Finally, macros can be activated by the use of hot keys.

A Review of Events and Properties

Simply put, an *event* is some user action. The event can be an action such as opening a form or report, changing data in a record, selecting a button, or closing a form or report. Access recognizes nearly 50 events in forms (37 for the form, itself, and more for the controls on the form) and reports (10 for the report and report sections; more for the controls on the report).

To recognize one of these events, Access uses form or report *properties*. Each event has an associated form or report property. For example, the On Open property is associated with the event of opening a form or report.

You trigger a macro by specifying the macro name. The name is specified as a parameter for the event property you want to have the macro run against. For example, if you want to run a macro named OpenPets every time a user opens the Customer form, you place the macro name in the parameter field alongside the property On Open in the form named Customer.

Macros for forms

You can create macros that respond to *form events*. These events are triggered by some user action, which may be opening a form or clicking a command button on a form. Access knows when a user triggers an event through its recognition of event-specific form properties. Forms let you set properties for field controls. These properties can be quite useful during the design phase of a form, such as when you use a property to set a format or validation rule.

However, macros give you added power by letting you specify actions to be performed automatically based on a user-initiated event. The event is recognized by Access by use of event properties such as Before Update, On Delete, or On Enter. Unlike a simple format or field-level validation rule, a macro can perform multiple-step actions based on the user event. For example, after a user presses the Delete key to delete a record but before the deleted record is removed from the table, you can have a macro that automatically runs and asks the user to verify that the record should be deleted. In this case, you use the On Delete property to trigger execution of the macro.

Macros for forms can respond both to *form events* and *control events*. Form events take effect at the form level; control events take effect at the individual control level. Form events include deleting a record, opening a form, or updating a record. These events work at the form and record levels. Control events, on the other hand, work at the level of the individual control. These controls are the ones you specify when you create your form and include such items as a field (text box), a toggle button, or an option button — even a command button. Each control has its own event properties that can trigger a macro. These events include selecting a command button, double-clicking a control, and selecting a control.

By specifying a macro at the control level, you can activate a customer form when the user double-clicks a field object or its label object. For example, you may have a form that identifies the customer by name but gives no additional customer information. When the user double-clicks the customer's name, your macro can activate a customer form that shows all the customer information. To accomplish this, you use the field object property On Dbl Click to specify a macro that opens the customer form. Then the macro will run and open the Customer form each time the user double-clicks the Customer field.

Figure 30-1 shows the Cust_Pet_Visit form with a label named Customer Name; note the field containing the name Animal Kingdom. When the user double-clicks either the label (Customer Name) or the name (Animal Kingdom), the Customer form opens.

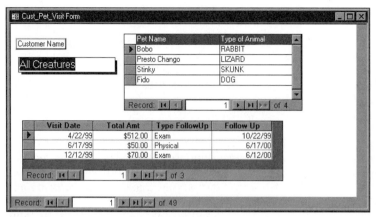

Figure 30-1: A typical form with labels and controls (fields).

The form in Figure 30-1 does not display any outward sign that a user can initiate a macro by double-clicking the label or field. However, the On Dbl Click property is set for the field to automatically execute the macro that opens the Customer form. Figure 30-2 shows that the macro is specified in the On Dbl Click property. The macro group name is Update Form, and the specific macro name in the group is ShowCustomer.

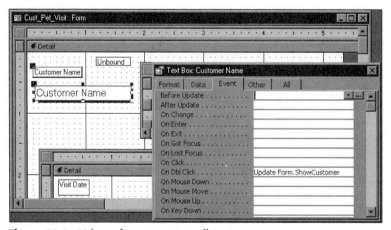

Figure 30-2: Using a form event to call a macro.

Tip

By using the properties of text boxes, the event is triggered when it occurs on the text box (field) or its associated label.

Macros for reports

Just as with forms, macros can also enhance the use of the reports. You may, for example, want to prompt a user for a range of records to be printed before printing the report. You may want to display a message on the report whenever a certain condition is met. You may even want to underline or highlight a field on the basis of its value, such as when the value is too small or too large. Macros give you this type of refined control in reports.

Macros for reports can respond both to *report events* and *report section events.* Report events take effect at the report level; report section events take effect at the section level of the report.

Macros for accelerator keys

A macro can also be associated with a specific key or combination of keys. When a macro is assigned to a key combination, a user pressing that key or key combination activates it. For example, you may assign the key combination Ctrl+P to print the current record displayed onscreen. Another example is assigning the key combination Ctrl+N to skip to the next record in the report or form. Creating hot keys gives you additional capabilities in your forms and reports without requiring you to write complicated programs.

You use most hot-key macros when you work with forms and reports, although hot-key macros can be used in queries or other Access objects.

Form-Level Event Macros

When you work with forms, you can specify macros based on events at the form level, the section level, or the control level. If you attach a macro to a form-level event, whenever the event occurs, the action takes effect against the form as a whole (such as when you change the record pointer or leave the form).

Attaching macros to forms

To have your form respond to an event, you write a macro and attach it to the event property in the form that recognizes the event. Many properties can be used to trigger macros at the form level. Table 30-1 shows each property, the event it recognizes, and how the property works.

Many form-level events can trigger a macro. These events work only at the level of forms or records. They take effect when the pointer is changed from one record to another or when a form is being opened or closed. Control at a level of finer detail (such as the field level) can be obtained by using the control-level events covered later in this chapter.

Table 30-1
The Form-Level Events and Associated Properties

Event Property	When the Macro Is Triggered
On Current	When you move to a different record and make it the current record
Before Insert	After data is first entered into a new record but before the record is actually created
After Insert	After the new record is added to the table
Before Update	Before changed data is updated in a record
After Update	After changed data is updated in a record
On Dirty	When a record is modifiedOn Delete When a record is deleted but *before* the deletion takes place
Before Del Confirm	Just before Access displays the Confirm Delete dialog box
After Del Confirm	After the Delete Confirm dialog box closes and confirmation has happened
On Open	When a form is opened, but the first record is not displayed yet
On Load	When a form is loaded into memory but not yet opened
On Resize	When the size of a form changes
On Unload	When a form is closed and the records unload and before the form is removed from the screen
On Close	When a form is closed and removed from the screen
On Activate	When an open form receives the focus, becoming the active window
On Deactivate	When a different window becomes the active window but before it loses focus
On Got Focus	When a form with no active or enabled controls receives the focus
On Lost Focus	When a form loses the focus
On Click	When you press and release (click) the left mouse button on a control in a form
On Dbl Click	When you press and release (click) the left mouse button twice on a control/label in a form
On Mouse Down	When you press the mouse button while the pointer is on a form
On Mouse Move	When you move the mouse pointer over an area of a form
On Mouse Up	When you release a pressed mouse button while the pointer is on a form

Event Property	When the Macro Is Triggered
On Key Down	When you press any key on the keyboard when a form has focus; when you use a SendKeys macro
On Key Up	When you release a pressed key or immediately after the SendKeys macro
On Key Press	When you press and release a key on a form that has the focus; when you use the SendKeys macro
Keyview	(YES or NO) Evoke keyboard macros for forms before keyboard events for macros
On Error	When a run-time error is produced
On Filter	When a filter has been specified but before it is applied
On Apply Filter	After a filter is applied to a form
On Timer	When a specified time interval passes
TimerInterval	Specify the Interval in milliseconds

Opening a form with a macro

Sometimes you may want to open a form with a macro. For example, each time you open the Pets Display form, you may also want to open the Customer form, enabling a user to click either form to see information from both at one time.

To accomplish this, create a macro named OpenCust and attach it to the On Open property of the Pets Display form.

To create the macro, follow these steps:

1. Click the Macros object button in the Database window to select the Macro Object list.

2. Click the New toolbar button to display the Macro Design window.

3. Click the first empty Action cell.

4. Select the OpenForm action from the drop-down menu of the Action cell.

5. Click in the Form Name cell of the Action Arguments (bottom part of window).

6. Select or type **Customer**.

7. Save the macro by clicking the Save button on the toolbar and naming the macro **OpenCust**.

Notice that in Figure 30-3 the OpenCust macro has only one action — OpenForm, with the action argument Form Name of Customer.

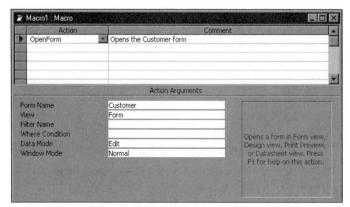

Figure 30-3: A macro to open a form.

The macro in Figure 30-3 has only a single action associated with it, which is the OpenForm action. This action has six possible arguments, although you entered only the form name Customer in the example. You accepted the default values of the other arguments. This action opens the specified form (Customer) for you automatically.

With the OpenCust macro created, you need to enter design mode for the Pets Display form to attach the macro OpenCust to the form property On Open.

Attaching a macro to a form

With the OpenForm macro saved, you are now ready to *associate*, or *attach*, it with the On Open property of the form Add a Customer and Pets. To attach the OpenCust macro to the form, follow these steps:

1. Click the Forms object button in the Database window to select the Form list.

2. Select the form named Pet Display Form and bring it into design mode.

3. Display the property sheet by clicking on the Properties button on the toolbar.

   The title of the Property window dialog box should be Form. If it isn't, select the form by clicking the gray box in the top-left corner of the form (where the rulers intersect).

4. Select the Event tab from the tabs at the top of the Property window.

5. Move to the On Open property in the Form property window. Select or type the macro name **OpenCust** in the On Open property cell.

   The property sheet should look similar to the one in Figure 30-4. Notice that the macro name OpenCust is placed in the property area of the On Open property.

6. Save the form and return to the Database window.

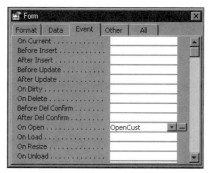

Figure 30-4: Entering a macro in the On Open property of a form.

With the OpenCust macro attached to the form Pets Display, you are ready to try running it. Open the Pets Display form. Notice that Access automatically opens the Customer form for you, placing it alongside the Pets Display form. Now you can use either form by clicking it to look at the individual records. Figure 30-5 shows both forms open.

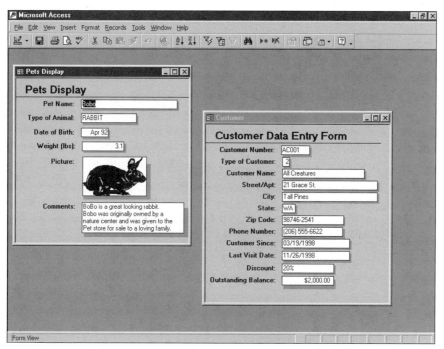

Figure 30-5: Two forms open; one form is opened automatically by a macro attached to the On Open property of the other form.

The only problem with these two forms is that they are not related. Each time you change the pet, it would be nice if the Customer form showed you the correct owner of the pet.

Of all the form-level events, the most common are On Open and On Current. Although the other events are available for use, these two are used for 80 percent of all form-level macros.

Synchronizing two forms with On Current

The forms in Figure 30-5 are independent of each other. Therefore, when you skip through the Pets Display form, the Customer form is not automatically updated to display the related owner information for the pet. To make these two forms work together, you synchronize them by relating the data between the forms with the On Current property.

You can use the same macro you used before (OpenCust), but now you must specify a Where condition for the OpenForm action. The condition on which to synchronize these two forms occurs when the Customer Number is the same in both forms. To specify the synchronizing condition between these two forms, follow these steps:

1. Open the macro OpenCust in design mode.

2. Click on the Where Condition box of the Action Arguments.

3. Type **[Customer Number] = Forms![Pet Display Form]![Customer Number]**.

4. Resave the OpenCust macro.

Note   Notice in Step 3 that you typed **[Customer Number]**, which is the control name for the Customer Number field in the Customer form. You typed this name on the left side of the expression without reference to the form name. The left side of the Where expression in an OpenForm action uses the form specified in the Form Name action argument (three lines above). The right side of the expression requires the keyword *Forms*, the form name, and the control name.

Caution   If you specify an unopened form in the Where Condition box, you will get an error message at run time, but not as you create the macro.

Now that you have modified the macro, you need to set the On Current property of the Pets Display form.

To add the OpenCust macro to the form, follow these steps:

1. Open the Pets Display form in design view.

2. Remove the macro from the On Open property of the form.

3. Move to the On Current property of the Property window.

4. Type **OpenCust** in the On Current parameter box.

5. Save the changes to the form.

Now, when you open the Pets Display form and a pet record is displayed, the Customer form also opens and displays the correct owner for that pet. As you change pets, the Customer form automatically displays the new owner information. These two forms are now synchronized.

Note   Even though the two forms are synchronized on the basis of the On Current property, you must still close both forms separately. Closing one form does not automatically close the other. If you want to close both forms at the same time automatically, you need to specify another macro for the On Close property.

To see how these two forms work together, open the Pets Display form and then click on the Datasheet button on the toolbar. The Customer form becomes active. If you click a different pet record in the Pets datasheet, the Customer form is updated automatically to reflect the new owner. Figure 30-6 demonstrates how this process works.

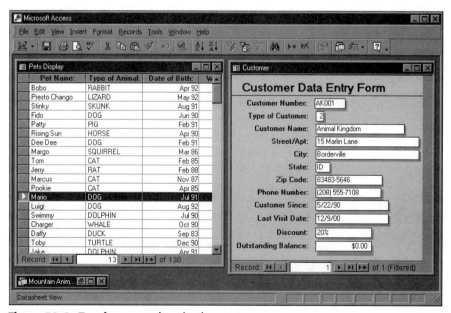

Figure 30-6: Two forms synchronized.

As Figure 30-6 demonstrates, you are not limited to a single-record view when synchronizing forms. The Pets Display form has been set to Datasheet; as you click on different records in the datasheet, the Customer form is updated automatically to reflect the new owner.

The On Current property of the Pets form triggers the OpenCust macro every time the record changes. If you click on the next navigation button, you see that the Customer form shows only one record — the owner record related to the current individual pet record in the Pets form. Notice that in the bottom of the Customer form in Figure 30-6, the record number shows *Record 1 of 1 (Filtered).* The Where condition in the macro acts as a filter to the Customer form.

If you know this, you can easily understand the use of the On Current property: It activates a macro that performs actions based on the specific record indicated by the form that is using the On Current property. In this case, the current pet record triggers the macro that finds the correct owner in the Customer form. Every time the pet record changes, the On Current property is activated and the next owner is found.

Running a macro when closing a form

At times, you'll want to perform some action when you close or leave a form. For example, you may want Access to keep an automatic log of the names of everyone using the form. Or, using the two forms from the preceding examples, you may want to close the Customer form automatically every time a user closes the Pets Display form.

To close the Customer form automatically every time the Pets Display form is closed, you need to create a new macro to perform the actions. Then you need to attach the macro to the On Close property of the Pets Display form.

To create a macro that closes a form, follow these steps:

1. Select the OpenCust macro and enter design mode.

2. Activate the Macro Name column by clicking on the Macro Name button on the toolbar. This step lets you create a macro group.

3. Select a blank Macro Name cell below the OpenForm action.

4. In the empty Macro Name cell, type **Close Customer**.

5. Select the empty Action cell alongside the Close Customer macro name.

6. Select the Close action from the pull-down menu.

7. Select the action argument Object Type.

8. Type (or select) **Form**.

9. Select the action argument Object Name.

10. Type (or select) the form name **Customer**. The macro should now look similar to Figure 30-7.

11. Resave the macro with the new changes.

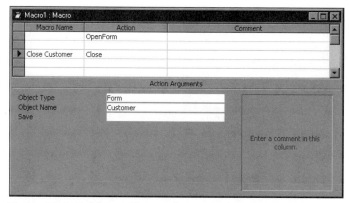

Figure 30-7: Adding a Close action macro to a macro group.

Figure 30-7 shows the new macro Close Customer added to the macro OpenCust. Until now, the OpenCust macro has been a single-purpose macro. Adding another macro has made it into a group macro of two macros. The first macro is the default macro, which opens a form, and the second is a macro named Close Customer.

Cross-Reference
Macro groups are covered in Chapter 29.

The Close Customer macro has only one action: Close. This action has two arguments, both of which must be entered. The first argument is the Object Type, which specifies the type of object to close (form or report, for example). The second argument is the Object Name, which specifies by name the object to close (in this case, the form named Customer).

Now that the Close Customer macro is created, attach it to the form named Pets Display by following these steps:

1. Select the Pets Display form and click on Design.

2. Activate the property sheet for the form.

3. Select the On Close property in the property sheet.

4. Type **OpenCust.Close Customer** in the On Close property parameter box. The property sheet should look like Figure 30-8.

5. Save the form with the new changes.

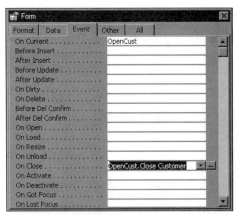

Figure 30-8: The property sheet with the
On Close property set.

Note
As Figure 30-8 shows, when typing the macro name in the On Close parameter
box, you specify the macro group name. Then you type a period (.) followed by the
name of the macro.

Opening the Pets Display form continues to maintain the current owner information
in the Customer form because you left the macro with its On Current property set.
Now, however, the On Close property is also set. Because you specified On Close
with the Pets Display form, the Customer form closes automatically when you close
the Pets Display form.

The macro attached to the On Close property simply closes the Customer form. If a
user accidentally closes the Customer form and then the Pets Display form, Access
does not report an error. Therefore, you don't have to specify an On Close for the
Customer form to allow closing only via the Pets Display form. Using this principle,
you can have one form that specifies the closing of many forms. If the forms are
open, Access closes them; otherwise, Access issues the Close command with no
harm done.

Confirming a delete with On Delete

The On Delete property can be used to execute a macro that displays a message
and confirms that a user wants to delete a record. For example, to create a macro
named ConfirmDelete, follow these steps:

1. Enter the macro design mode, create a new macro, and click the Condition
   column.

2. Select the first Condition cell.

3. Type **MsgBox("Do you Want to Delete this Record?", 273, "Delete")<>1**.

4. Select the Action cell next to the Condition box.

5. Select or type the **CancelEvent** action.

6. Select the next Condition cell.

7. Type an ellipsis, which is three periods (…).

8. Select the Action cell next to the Condition box.

9. Select or type the **StopMacro** action.

10. Select the next Action cell.

11. Select or type the **SendKeys** action.

12. Select the Keystrokes action argument.

13. Type **{Enter}**.

14. Save the macro, naming it **ConfirmDelete**.

The macro should look like the one in Figure 30-9. Notice that this macro also uses the CancelEvent action. The condition for this macro uses the MsgBox( ) function (for a detailed explanation, see the sidebar "Using the MsgBox( ) function," later in this chapter).

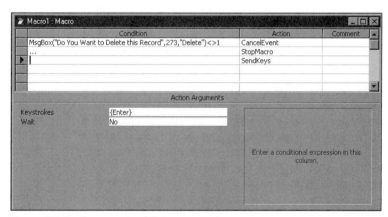

Figure 30-9: A macro to delete a record.

The macro in Figure 30-9 shows the use of another new action: SendKeys. This action lets you send prearranged keystrokes to Access or another active application. The passed keystrokes are processed just as though you pressed them while working in an application. In this case, Access displays a message box like the one in Figure 30-10. Notice that the message box has two buttons: OK and Cancel. Access displays the box and waits for a keystroke. When a user selects the Cancel button, the macro cancels the delete event and stops the macro.

Figure 30-10: A message box for the delete macro.

If a user clicks the OK button in the message box, the macro performs the SendKeys action. In this case, the macro sends the Enter keystroke. If the user does not take this action, Access displays its Delete message dialog box, forcing the user to verify again that the record should be deleted. Using SendKeys sends the Enter keystroke to the Access Delete message box, telling it to accept the deletion.

Caution   This macro does not bypass referential integrity between tables. If you have referential integrity set between the Customer table and the Pets table and have not
authorized Cascade Delete through the entire application, the macro fails. To override this, either set up cascade deletes through all the tables or expand the macro
to perform a cascade delete by creating an SQL statement and running the SQL
statement (use the RunSQL action).

Next, with the delete macro ConfirmDelete completed, attach it to the Pets Display form by placing the macro name in the entry box of the On Delete property of the form. Figure 30-11 shows the property sheet for the Pets Display form with the On Delete property set.

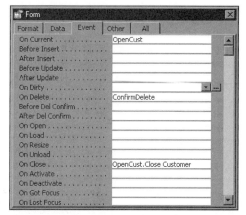

Figure 30-11: Setting an On Delete property.

To see how this macro and the On Delete property work, follow these steps:

1. Display the first record in the Pets Display form.

2. Select Edit ➪ Delete Record from the main menu.

   Access responds with the message box you saw in Figure 31-10. In this message box, the Cancel button is the default.

3. Click the Cancel button to not delete this record.

Control Event Macros

So far, you have worked with event macros at the form level. You can also trigger macros at the control level, using an event as a basis. When you attach a macro at the control level, the macro takes effect against the control. For example, you can immediately verify complex data validation at the field level (rather than when the record is exited) by using the field's Before Update property rather than the property at the form level.

Using the MsgBox( ) Function

The MsgBox( ) function is a very powerful function that can be used to display a message in a dialog box, wait for a user response, and then return a value based on the user's choice. The function has three arguments:

```
MsgBox("message" [, type of msg [, box title ] ] )
```

✦ The *message* here is the string displayed in the dialog box as a message.

✦ The *type of msg* is the numeric expression controlling the buttons and icons in the dialog box.

✦ The *box title* is the string displayed on the title bar of the dialog box.

Only the message is required. If you don't specify *type of msg* or *box title*, Access displays one button: OK. There is no icon and no title.

Access offers a wide range of type of message numbers. The type of message number specifies three message parts:

✦ Number and type of buttons

✦ Icon style

✦ Default button

The following table describes each:

Number and Button Type

Value	Display Button
0	OK
1	OK, Cancel
2	Abort, Retry, Ignore
3	Yes, No, Cancel
4	Yes, No
5	Retry, Cancel

Icon Style

Value	Display	Icon
0	None	
16	x Critical	X in a circle

Value	Display	Icon
32	? Warning	Question mark in a balloon
48	! Warning	Exclamation sign in a triangle
64	i	Information in a balloon

Default Button

Value	Button
0	First
256	Second
512	Third

Using the preceding table, specify the second parameter of the MsgBox( ) function by summing the three option values. For example, you can have a message box show three buttons (Yes, No, and Cancel [3]), use the Question mark (?) [32], and make the Cancel button the default [512]. Just add the three values (512+32+3) to get the second parameter number, which is 547.

If you omit *type of msg* in the function, MsgBox displays a single OK button and makes it the default button with no icon displayed.

Besides displaying the message box with all the options, the MsgBox() function also returns a value that indicates which button the user selects. The number it returns depends on the type of button selected. The following table shows each button and the value that MsgBox() returns:

Button Selected	Value Returned
OK	1
Cancel	2
Abort	3
Retry	4
Ignore	5
Yes	6
No	7

If the dialog box displays a Cancel button, pressing the Esc key is the same as selecting the Cancel button.

Attaching macros to controls

To have a control respond to an event, you write a macro and attach the macro to the property in the control that recognizes the event. Several properties can be polled to trigger macros at the control level. Table 30-2 shows each property, the event it recognizes, and how it works.

As Table 30-2 demonstrates, you can use any of the control-level events to trigger a macro. One of these, On Click, works only with command buttons.

Table 30-2	
The Control-Level Events and Associated Properties	
Event Property	*When the Macro Is Triggered*
Before Update	Before changed data in the control is updated to the table
After Update	After changed data is updated in the control to the data
On Change	When the contents of a text box or combo box's text changes
On Updated	When an OLE object's data has been modified
On Not In List	When a value that isn't in the list is entered into a combo box
On Enter	Before a control receives the focus from another control
On Exit	Just before the control loses focus to another control
On Got Focus	When a nonactive or enabled control receives the focus
On Lost Focus	When a control loses the focus
On Click	When the left mouse button is pressed and released (clicked) on a control
On Dbl Click	When the left mouse button is pressed and released (clicked) twice on a control/label
On Mouse Down	When a mouse button is pressed while the pointer is on a control
On Mouse Move	When the mouse pointer is moved over a control
On Mouse Up	When a pressed mouse button is released while the pointer is on a control
On Key Down	When any key on the keyboard is pressed when a control has the focus or when the SendKeys macro is used
On Key Press	When a key is pressed and released on a control that has the focus or when the SendKeys macro is used
On Key Up	When a pressed key is released or immediately after the SendKeys macro is used

Forms have several different types of objects on them: labels, text boxes, OLE (Object Linking and Embedding) objects, subforms, command buttons, checkboxes, and so on. Each of these has several event properties associated with it. You can attach a macro, an expression, or Visual Basic code to any of them. To see any object's event properties, simply activate the Properties dialog box and select event properties while working with the object.

Working with Macros on Forms

You can group macros for forms into six categories according to their functions:

✦ Validating data

✦ Setting values

✦ Navigating between forms and records

✦ Filtering records

✦ Finding records

✦ Printing records

Each category uses specific macro actions to perform its job.

Validating data

You already worked with macros to validate data at both the form level and control level. When validating data, you worked with several macro actions: MsgBox, CancelEvent, StopMacro, and GoToControl.

The most common event properties that trigger validation macros are the On Delete and Before Update properties, although any property can be used.

Displaying a message

To display a message, you use the MsgBox action. This action has four arguments:

Message	Specifies the user message in a dialog box
Beep	Sounds a computer beep when the dialog box is opened
Type	Specifies the type of icon displayed in the dialog box, such as the stop sign, a question mark, and so on
Title	Specifies a user-entered title for the box

Canceling events

To cancel an event, use the CancelEvent action. This action has no arguments — it simply cancels the event that triggers the macro to run. For example, if the macro is attached to the Before Update property of a form, the update is canceled.

Stopping a macro

To stop execution of a macro, use the StopMacro action. This action stops execution of the macro immediately and returns the user to the calling form. This action is useful for stopping a macro based on a condition specified in the macro.

Going to a specific control

If you need to return to a specific control (field) in a form, use the GoToControl action. This action has one argument: the control name. If you supply a control name, this action takes you to that control. You normally use this action just before you use the StopMacro action.

Setting values

By setting control, field, and property values with macros, data entry is easier and more accurate. Besides these advantages, several forms, databases, and reports can be linked to make them work together more intelligently.

Setting values with a macro can accomplish these tasks:

✦ Hide or display a control on the basis of a value in the form (Visible property).

✦ Disable or lock a control on the basis of a value in the form (Enable and Locked properties).

✦ Update a field in the form on the basis of the value of another control.

✦ Set the value of a control in a form on the basis of the control of another form.

The SetValue action is used to set values with a macro. This action has two arguments:

Item	The name of the control or property
Expression	The expression used to set the value

Tip   If you use the SetValue action to change the value of a control (field) being validated, do not attach it to the Before Update property. Access cannot change the value of a control while it is being validated; it can change the value only after it has been saved. Use the After Update property instead.

Caution   You cannot use the SetValue macro action on bound or calculated controls on reports; the same is true for calculated controls on forms.

Converting a field to uppercase

If you allow entry of a field in either uppercase or lowercase, you may want to store it in uppercase. To accomplish this, create a macro that uses the SetValue action to set the value of the field for you. In the Item argument box, enter the name of the field to convert to uppercase. In the Expression argument box, enter the function UCase( ) with the name of the field to be converted. The function UCase( ) must already exist. Figure 30-12 shows the arguments for converting the field Customer Name to uppercase.

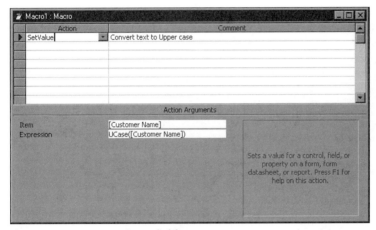

Figure 30-12: Converting a field to uppercase.

After creating the macro, place the macro name in the After Update property sheet.

If the user enters a customer name in lowercase or mixed case, Access automatically runs the macro and converts the field to uppercase when the user completes the update.

Assigning values to new records

When you add new records to a form, it is often convenient to have values automatically filled in for fields using values from another open form. SetValue is also used to do this.

For example, after adding a new customer in the Customer form, you may immediately want to add a pet record in another form and have the Customer Number automatically filled in.

For example, the After Update event on the Customer form can be programmed to add a pet record after the customer record's Pet Name value is changed. A macro opens the Pets Display form in the Add Mode using the OpenForm action. The next macro action, SetValue, automatically sets the value of Customer Number in the Pets Display form to the Customer Number in the Customer form. Figure 30-13 shows the arguments for this macro.

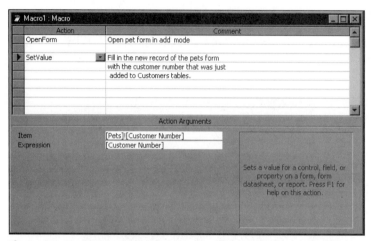

Figure 30-13: Macro arguments to set a field value in another form on the basis of a value in the current form.

Tip

The Item argument can also use its full syntax instead of the abbreviation shown in Figure 30-13. The syntax is:

```
Forms![Pets]![Customer Number]
```

The Expression argument references the Customer Number in the open form, which is the Customer form. When working with the SetValue action in this way, you must specify the entire syntax for the name of the field being replaced in the Item box.

Navigating in forms and records

Whenever you need to move to a specific control (field), record, or page in a form, you use the GoTo*XXXX* actions, where *XXXX* represents the control, record, or page.

Moving to a specific control

To move to a specific control, use the GoToControl action. This action has one argument, which is Control Name. To move to a specific field, supply the control name in the argument.

Moving to a specific record

To move to a specific record in a table, query, or form, use the GoToRecord action. This action has four arguments:

Object Type	Type of object (form, table, or query)
Object Name	Name of the object specified in Object Type
Record	Specifies which record to go to (preceding, next, new, first, last, and so on)
Offset	The number of records to offset from (if 10, go back 10 records)

Using this action, you can move to any record in a form, query, or table.

Moving to a specific page

To move to a specific page and place the focus in the first control of the page, use the GoToPage action. This action has three arguments:

Page Number	Specifies the page number you want to move to
Right	The upper-left corner of the page (horizontal position)
Down	The upper-left corner of the page (vertical position)

This action is useful for working with multiple-page forms.

Filtering records

You can create a macro or series of macros to filter records in a form. For example, you may want to have a Customer form with four buttons to limit the form's records to a single state or to allow all states. (Even though you haven't learned about buttons yet, you can learn how they would interact with a group of macros.) The form will look similar to Figure 30-14. Notice that four buttons are in the box named Filter Records.

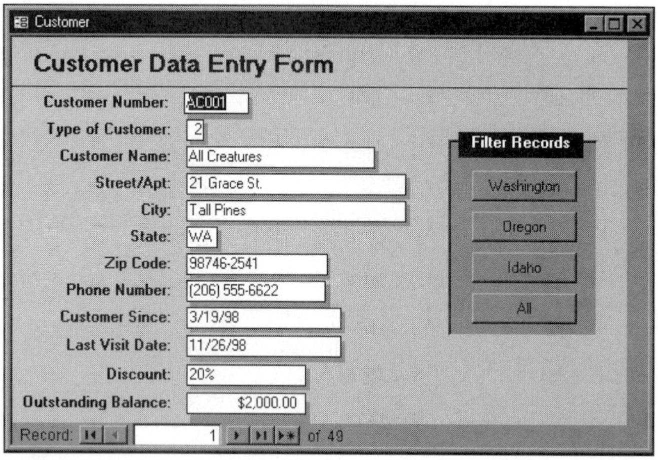

Figure 30-14: A form with buttons used to activate filter macros.

Each button in Figure 30-14 is attached to a different macro. Three of the macros use the ApplyFilter action, and one uses the ShowAllRecords action.

Using the ApplyFilter action

To set a filter condition in a macro, use the ApplyFilter action. This action has two arguments: Filter Name and the Where Condition. You can use either one, but you should use only one unless you predefine a filter and want to filter the filter. For this example, you use the Where Condition argument. To create a macro named StateFilter.WA, follow these steps:

1. Enter the Macro Design window.

2. Enter the macro name **WA** into the group macro StateFilter.

3. Select or type **ApplyFilter** for the action.

4. Type **[State]** = **"WA"** in the Where Condition argument box.

After you create this macro, create two more macros: one named StateFilter.ID the other named StateFilter.OR. These macros set a condition equal to the individual state.

Using the ShowAllRecords action

When you create filter conditions with macros, you should always create another macro that uses the ShowAllRecords action. This action removes an existing filter set by another macro. This action has no arguments. For the next example, create a macro named StateFilter.All with the ShowAllRecords action. When you complete this process, all four macros should look like the ones in Figure 30-15.

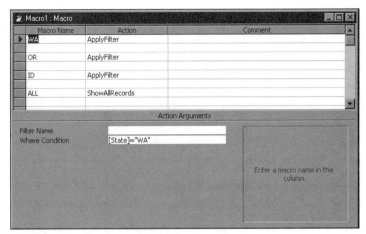

Figure 30-15: A macro group with four filter macros.

Running filter macros

To run a filter macro, attach the macro name to the On Click property of the appropriate command button. Then the macro will execute and implement the filter condition every time the button is selected.

Finding records

One of the most powerful ways of using macros is to locate user-specified records. This type of macro uses two macro actions: GoToControl and FindRecord. For example, you can add a search routine to the Customer form, as shown in Figure 30-16. You can create an unbound combo box; as you can see in Figure 30-17, it is named CustomerSelect. Once created, attach a macro to the AfterUpdate event of the control to move the record pointer in the table.

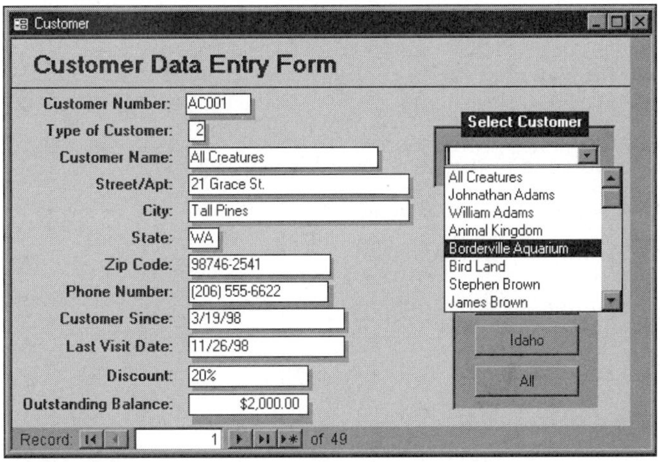

Figure 30-16:
The Customer form with a combo box used to find records.

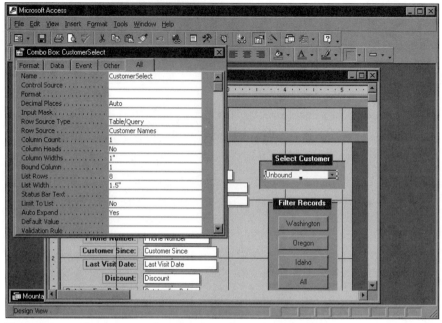

Figure 30-17: The property sheet for the unbound combo box.

Your property sheet for the combo box should look similar to Figure 30-17.

After creating the unbound combo box, you can beautify the label and combo box area (as a look back at Figure 30-16 shows). These enhancements aren't required.

Once the combo box is created, you are ready to create the FindRecord macro to find the customer record by the Customer Name field. Before you can attach the macro, you must first create the macro. Create a new macro by first selecting New from the macro section of the database container. Once in the macro design screen, you can create the macro by following these steps:

1. Select or type **GoToControl** in the first empty Action cell.

2. Type **[Customer Name]** in the Control Name argument cell.

3. Select or type **FindRecord** in the next empty Action cell.

4. Type =**[CustomerSelect]** in the Find What argument box.

5. Save the macro, naming it **FindRecord**.

That's it! Your macro should now resemble the one in Figure 30-18.

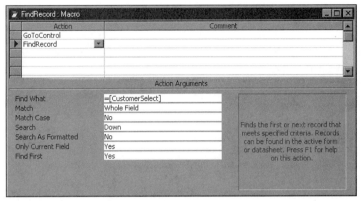

Figure 30-18: A macro to find a record based on the customer's name.

In the GoToControl argument, you placed the form control name [Customer Name], which is the same as the field name, to limit the scope of the search to the current field (Customer Name). Then, in the FindRecord argument Find What, you placed the control name for the unbound combo box. By placing the unbound combo box in the Find What box, you specify that the macro will find the name via the combo box but update the record on the basis of Customer Name.

Caution

Note that you entered an equal sign before the control name CustomerSelect in the Find What argument box. If you don't enter the equal sign, the macro will not work.

Now that you have created the macro, you're ready to attach it to the After Update property for the unbound combo box. To attach the macro, follow these steps:

1. Move to the After Update property of the CustomerSelect control (unbound combo box).

2. Type **FindRecord** in the Action Arguments cell (the name of the macro).

The form now uses the combo box to find any customer!

Report Event Macros

Just as with forms, reports can also use macros that perform actions based on events you specify. You can work with macros at the report level or the section level. If you attach a macro at the report level, it takes effect when the event occurs against the report as a whole, such as when you open or close the report. If you attach the macro at the section level, it takes effect when the event occurs within a section (such as when you format or print the section).

Several event properties can be used for report-level macros. Table 30-3 shows each property, the event it recognizes, and how it works.

As Table 30-3 illustrates, you can use any of the report-level events to trigger a macro. These events can be used just as you use their counterparts in forms.

Table 30-3	
The Report-Level Events and Associated Properties	
Event Property	*When the Macro Is Triggered*
On Open	When a report is opened but before it prints
On Close	When a report is closed and removed from the screen
On Activate	When a report receives the focus and becomes the active window
On Deactivate	When a different window becomes the active window
On No Data	When the report has no data passed to it from the active table or query
On Page	When the report changes pages
On Error	When a run-time error is produced in Access

Opening a report with a macro

You may want to use the On Open property of a report to run a macro that prompts the user to identify the records to print. The macro can use a filter or use the ApplyFilter action.

For example, you may want to activate a form or dialog box that prompts the user to identify a state or to print the report Customer Mailing Labels. To accomplish this task, create a filter macro similar to the one in the section on forms and attach it to the On Open property of the report.

Report Section Macros

Besides the report-level properties, Access offers three event properties that you can use at the section level for a report macro. Table 30-4 shows each property, the event it recognizes, and how it works.

<table>
<tr><td colspan="3" align="center">Table 30-4
The Report Section-Level Events and Associated Properties</td></tr>
<tr><td>*Event Property*</td><td>*Event*</td><td>*When the Macro Is Triggered*</td></tr>
<tr><td>On Format</td><td>Format</td><td>When Access knows what data goes in a section (but before laying out the data for printing)</td></tr>
<tr><td>On Print</td><td>Print</td><td>After Access lays out the data in a section for printing (but before printing the section)</td></tr>
<tr><td>On Retreat</td><td>Retreat</td><td>After the Format event but before the Print event; occurs when Access has to "back up" past other sections on a page to perform multiple formatting passes</td></tr>
</table>

Using On Format

You use the On Format property when a user's response can affect page layout or when the macro contains calculations that use data from sections you don't intend to print. The macro will run before Access lays out the section (following your other property settings for the report, such as Keep Together, Visible, or Can Grow).

You can set the On Format and On Print properties for any section of the report. However, the On Retreat is not available for the page header or page footer sections.

For example, you may want to highlight some data on the form, based on a certain condition the macro determines. If the condition is met, the macro uses the SetValue action to change a control's Visible property to Yes.

Using On Print

You use the On Print property when no user's response affects page layout or when the macro depends on what page it finds the records to be printed. For example, you may want to have a total calculation placed in either the header or footer of each page.

Report Properties

When you work with macros that use the On Print and On Format properties of report sections, you may need to use two special conditional printer properties:

✦ Format Count

✦ Print Count

These two conditional printer properties are used in the Condition Expression column of a macro. Both are read-only properties; Access sets their values. Therefore, you can check these properties, but you cannot change their values. These properties determine when an event occurs twice.

Using Format Count

The Format Count property is used as a macro condition to determine the number of times the On Format property setting is evaluated for the current line on the report.

It is possible for a line to be formatted more than once. For example, when the labels are printed, the last label may not fit on a page; there may be room for only one line of a two-line label. If the label won't fit on the page, Access prints it on the next page. The Format Count for any lines moved from the bottom of the page to the top of the next page is set to 2 because the lines are formatted twice.

If you are accumulating a count of the number of labels being printed, you use the Format Count property in the Condition box of the macro to disregard counting the label a second time.

Using Print Count

Like the Format Count property, the Print Count property is used as a macro condition. This property determines the number of times the On Print setting is evaluated for the current line of the report.

It is possible for part of a record to be printed on one page and the remainder to be printed on the next page. When that occurs, the On Print event occurs twice, so the Print property is incremented to 2. When this occurs, you don't want to have the macro perform its action twice; therefore, you check to see whether the Format Count has changed, and then you stop the macro action.

To understand how this works, suppose that you have a macro that counts the number of records being printed on a page. The record number is placed in the page footer section of each page of the report. If a record is printed across two pages, you want the records counted on only one of the pages.

Working with macros in reports

Like form macros, report macros can be triggered at two levels — report and section. A macro triggered at the report level can prompt a user for a range of records to print before doing anything with the report.

On the other hand, a section-level macro can be used for printing messages on a report when a condition is met. For example, if a customer has not paid on his or her bill in 30 days, the report may print a reminder line that a partial payment is overdue.

Report-level macros can be executed before or after a report is printed or previewed. Section-level macros can be executed before or after a section of the report is printed or previewed. Thus, section-level macros tend to be used for actions that are more refined, such as including conditional lines of text in the report.

Underlining data in a report with a macro

You can use a macro to underline or highlight data dynamically in a report. This is accomplished by hiding or displaying controls and sections.

Suppose that you print the Monthly Invoice Report and you want to underline the Amount Due control if the total amount is more than $500.00. You do this by adding a control to the group footer named Customer.Customer Number Footer and creating a macro that toggles the Visible property for the control.

Figure 30-19 shows a line added below the Amount Due control. This control is named AmtDueLine.

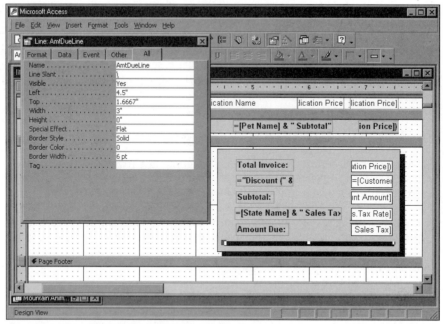

Figure 30-19: A report form with a line added.

In Figure 30-19, the Visible property is set to Yes in the property sheet for the control AmtDueLine.

With the control (line) placed on the report, create a macro that sets the Visible property for this control. This macro requires two conditions — one for [Amount Due]>500 and the other for not being greater than this amount. To create the macro, follow these steps:

1. Create a macro named PrtLine.

2. Select an empty cell in the Condition column.

3. Type **[Amount Due]>500** in the Condition cell.

4. Select the associated Action cell.

5. Select or type **SetValue**.

6. Select the Item argument.

7. Type **[AmtDueLine].Visible**.

8. Select the Expression argument.

9. Type **Yes**.

10. Select another empty Condition cell.

11. Typc **Not [Amount Due]>500**.

12. Select the associated Action cell.

13. Select or type **SetValue**.

14. Select the Item argument.

15. Type **[AmtDueLine].Visible**.

16. Select the Expression argument.

17. Type **No**.

18. Save the macro, naming it **PrtLine**.

The macro should look similar to the one in Figure 30-20. Notice that the macro in this figure has a separate condition to turn the Visible property on (set to Yes) and off.

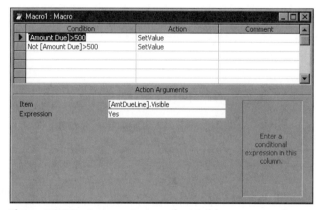

Figure 30-20: A macro to turn the Visible property of a control on or off.

Now that the macro is created, it needs to be attached to the group section named Customer.Customer Number Footer in the Monthly Invoice Report. The macro is attached to the On Format property of the section. Figure 30-21 shows the property sheet with the macro added to the On Format property.

Figure 30-21: A property sheet with a macro name in the On Format property.

Hiding data in a report with a macro

Data in a report can be hidden with the same method you just used to display or hide a line — setting the Visible property to Yes or No in a macro. After you set the property to Yes or No in a macro, attach the macro to the On Format property of the section where the data resides.

Filtering records for a report with a macro

Creating a macro and attaching it to the On Open property of the report can filter records for a report. This provides a consistent way of asking for criteria. The On Open property runs the macro no matter how the user opens the report. For example, a user can double-click the report name, choose a command from a custom menu, or select a command button on a form. If the On Open property is used to trigger the macro, you have to run the dialog box against only this single property.

Chapter 31 shows a menu and dialog box that perform this type of filtering.

Importing and Exporting Macros

You can easily use data from other formats in Access. You can import, export, and attach tables via commands from the File menu in the Database window. However, if you consistently transfer the same data, you may want to automate the process in a macro.

Using command buttons to import or export

If you create a macro to transfer data, you can activate the macro by using a command button and the On Click property of the button.

When you create the macro, Access provides three actions to help you transfer the data. Essentially, these actions save your data in a database, spreadsheet, or text type format:

✦ TransferDatabase

✦ TransferSpreadsheet

✦ TransferText

By using these actions and their arguments, you can create very powerful (but simple) transfer-data macros.

Creating Accelerator Keys (Hot Keys)

A macro can be assigned to a specific key or combination of keys, such as Ctrl+P. After a macro is assigned to a key, the key is known as a hot key. By assigning *hot keys*, you can create one macro to perform an action no matter which form, view, or table you're in. For example, the Ctrl+P key combination can be used to print the current record.

You can assign macros to any number of hot keys. All hot-key macros are stored in a single group macro that Access uses. That group macro is known as a key assignment macro. When you open a database, Access looks for a macro named AutoKeys. If the macro exists, it runs automatically, assigning macros to hot keys. Figure 30-22 shows several hot-key assignments in an AutoKeys macro.

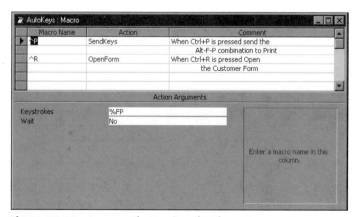

Figure 30-22: A macro that assigns hot keys.

Creating a hot-key combination

To create a hot-key combination and assign actions to it requires creating a special macro named AutoKeys and using macro names based on the key combination you want to use to specify an action. The macro names can be based on a specific Access syntax called SendKeys syntax; otherwise, they can use the typical macro actions.

Using SendKeys syntax for key assignments

When you enter a key combination in the Macro Name column, you specify the key combination by using a specific syntax known as SendKeys syntax. Table 30-5 shows several key combinations and their corresponding SendKeys syntax. When you assign actions to a key combination, you enter the SendKeys syntax in the Macro Name column.

Using Table 30-5 as a reference, you see that to assign some macro actions to the Tab key, you name a macro {TAB} in the group macro AutoKeys.

Table 30-5 SendKeys Syntax			
Key Combo	*SendKeys Syntax*	*Key Combo*	*SendKeys Syntax*
Backspace	{BKSP} or {BS}	F2	{F2}
Caps Lock	{CAPSLOCK}	Ctrl+A	^A
Enter	{ENTER} or ~	Ctrl+F10	^{F10}
Insert	{INSERT}	Ctrl+2	^2
Left Arrow	{LEFT}	Shift+F5	+{F5}
Home	{HOME}	Shift+Delete	+{DEL}
PgDn	{PGDN}	Shift+End	+{END}
Escape	{ESC}	Alt+F10	%{F10}
PrintScreen	{PRTSC}	Alt+Up arrow	%{UP}
Scroll Lock	{SCROLLLOCK}	Left arrow 10 times	{LEFT 10}
Tab	{TAB}	Shift+BA together	+(BA)

Creating a hot key

To create a hot key, follow these steps:

1. Create a macro named AutoKeys.

2. Type the key combination in the Macro Name column.

3. Type the set of actions you want to associate with the key combination.

4. Repeat Steps 2 and 3 for each hot key to which you want to assign actions.

5. Save the macro.

Access makes the key assignment immediate. When you press the key combination, Access runs the macro actions. In the preceding steps, you can also make several key assignments, creating a macro for each key combination. Just remember to name the macro group AutoKeys.

Summary

This chapter provided an in-depth explanation of macro usage. You learned to use macros in forms and reports and to create hot keys. These topics were covered:

✦ An event is some user action. The action may be opening a form, changing data in a record, or clicking a command button.

✦ Access recognizes user events by using a corresponding property of a form or report. For example, the On Open property is associated with the event of opening a form.

✦ You can attach form macros to the form or to individual controls. Forms can use form-level events and control-level events.

✦ Form-level macros can display messages, open a form, synchronize two forms, and validate data entry.

✦ The two most common form properties for validating data at the form level are On Delete and Before Update.

✦ With the MsgBox( ) function, you can specify conditions in macros. This powerful function displays messages and command buttons to obtain user input.

✦ Control-event macros can be triggered when a user enters or exits a control, clicks a button, or double-clicks a control.

✦ The SetValue action is used in macros to hide a control, update a field on the basis of another field value, or disable a control.

✦ Report macros can be triggered at the report level or at the report-section level. Only two event properties are used at the report level; two are used at the report-section level.

✦ By using macros in reports, you can apply a filter to a report, hide or print a line, or hide some other object on a report, basing the macro on a condition.

✦ Macro actions can be assigned to combinations of keys by using a key assignment macro and macro names based on the SendKeys syntax of Access.

In the next chapter, you work with macros in menus, switchboards, and dialog boxes to further automate your database system.

✦   ✦   ✦

Creating Switchboards, Command Bars, Menus, Toolbars, and Dialog Boxes

In prior chapters, you created individual Access objects: tables, queries, forms, reports, and macros. You worked with each object interactively in Access, selecting the Database window and using the assorted objects.

In this chapter, you tie these objects together into a single database application — without having to write or know how to use a complex database program. Rather, you automate the application through the use of switchboards, dialog boxes, and menus. These objects make your system easier to use, and they hide the Access interface from the final user.

What Is a Switchboard?

A switchboard is fundamentally a form. The switchboard form is a customized application menu that contains user-defined command buttons. With these command buttons, you can run macros that automatically select such actions as opening forms or printing reports.

Using a switchboard button, you replace many interactive user steps with a single button selection (or *click*). For example, if you want to open the form Add a Customer and Pets interactively, you must perform three actions: Switch to the Database window, select the Forms tab, and open the form. If you use a switchboard button to perform the same task, you simply click the button. Figure 31-1 shows the switchboard window with several buttons. Each command button triggers a macro that performs a series of steps, such as opening the Customer form or running the Hospital Report.

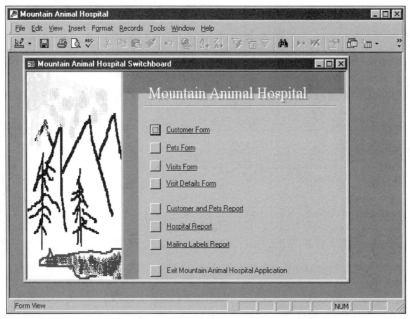

Figure 31-1: A switchboard with several command buttons for forms and reports.

By using a switchboard and other objects covered in this chapter, you can tie your database objects together in a single database application. Rather than the Access interactive interface, the application will have a user interface that you create. A primary component of that user-defined interface is the switchboard you create.

Using a switchboard

A switchboard's primary use is as an application interface menu. The switchboard in Figure 31-1 is the application interface menu for the Mountain Animal Hospital database. As the figure shows, the switchboard contains several command buttons. When the user clicks on any switchboard button, a macro is triggered that performs some action or a series of actions.

Creating the basic form for a switchboard

You create a switchboard by adding command buttons to an existing Access form. The form in Figure 31-1 is a standard Access 2000 display form. Forms can have many uses, including data entry, data display, and switchboards.

Because switchboard forms are used as application menus, they tend to use a limited number of form controls. Typically, you find command buttons, labels, object frames (OLE objects, such as pictures), lines, and rectangles. Normally, switchboards lack the other types of form controls, such as text boxes (bound to fields), list and combo boxes, graphs, subforms, and page breaks.

To create a basic switchboard form, you place labels like titles and group headings on the form. In addition to the labels, you may also want to place lines, rectangles, and pictures on the form to make it aesthetically appealing. You create the basic switchboard form by using the techniques you already learned in chapters covering form objects.

Consider, for example, the switchboard in Figure 31-1. Minus the command buttons, this is a typical Access application form. Its major components are a title, some other text controls, various colored rectangles, a line, and a picture (image control).

Working with command buttons

Command buttons are the type of form control that is used to run macros or VBA routines. Command buttons are the simplest type of form controls, having the single purpose of executing a macro or VBA procedure that can exist *behind* a form or in a module procedure.

In this example, you will create command buttons that will run macros. As you have learned, macros perform a multitude of tasks in Access, including:

✦ Opening and displaying other forms

✦ Opening a pop-up form or dialog box to collect additional information

✦ Opening and printing reports

✦ Activating a search or displaying a filter

✦ Exiting Access

On your CD-ROM in the Mountain Animal Hospital database is a form named Mountain Switchboard-No Buttons. You can use that as a starting point to create your switchboard.

Figure 31-2 shows a command button named Command01 and its property sheet. In this property sheet are the event properties available for a command button.

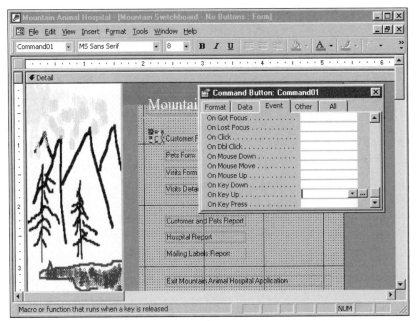

Figure 31-2: A single-button switchboard form with its open property sheet.

Each event property can trigger a macro. For example, to trigger a macro named OpenCust when the user clicks on the button, place the macro name OpenCust in the parameter box for the On Click property. The keyword *On* identifies an event property. The property identifies the user event that must occur to trigger an action.

On Click and On Dbl Click are mutually compatible. If you activate both the On Click property (giving it a macro name) and the On Dbl Click property, Access follows this order of precedence for the mouse clicking and trapping:

1. On Click (single click)

2. On Dbl Click (double-click)

3. On Click (single click)

In other words, Access processes an On Click first and then an On Dbl Click and, finally, an On Click *again*. Access *always* processes the On Click if it is defined. To prevent the second On Click macro from running, place a CancelEvent action in the On Dbl Click macro.

In addition, if the macro you call from an On Click opens a dialog box (message box, pop-up form, and so forth), the second click is lost and the On Dbl Click is never reached! If you use On Click and On Dbl Click, the On Click should not open a dialog box if you need to capture the On Dbl Click.

What Is focus?

To understand the terminology associated with command buttons, you need to know the term *focus*. The two command button properties On Enter and On Exit gain or lose focus. In other words, the focus represents the next item of input from the user. For example, if you Tab from one button to another, you lose the focus on the first button as you leave it, and you gain the focus on the second as you enter it. In a form with several command buttons, you can tell which button has focus by the dotted box around the label of the button. Focus does not denote the state of input, as when you press a button; rather, focus is the object that is currently active and awaiting some user action.

The focus for mouse input always coincides with the button down, or pointer, location. Because focus occurs at the moment of clicking on a command button, the property On Enter is not triggered. The reason is that On Enter occurs just before the focus is gained; that state is not realized when you select a command button by using a mouse. The On Enter state never occurs. Rather, the focus and On Click occur simultaneously, bypassing the On Enter state.

Creating command buttons

A command button's primary purpose is to activate, or run, a macro. Access gives you two ways to create a command button:

✦ Click the Command Button icon in the Form Toolbox.

✦ Drag a macro name from the database container to the form.

In this chapter, both these methods are used at least once as you learn to create the eight command buttons shown in Figure 31-1 (four buttons to display a form, three to display a report, and one to exit the application). In this first example, you learn to create the first form button using the Command Button Wizard.

When using the Command Button Wizard, in addition to creating a command button, you can also automatically display text or embed a picture on the button. More importantly, you can create VBA modules to perform tasks, including Record Navigation (Next, Previous, First, Last, Find), Record Operations (Save, Delete, Print, New, Duplicate), Form Operations (Open, Close, Print, Filter), Report Operations (Print, Preview, Mail), Applications (Run Application, Quit, Notepad, Word, Excel), and Miscellaneous (Print Table, Run Query, Run Macro, AutoDialer), even if you don't know a single command in VBA.

 Cross-Reference In Chapter 33, you learn to create and edit Visual Basic code with the Command Button Wizard.

To create the Customer button using the Command Button Wizard, follow these steps:

1. Open the form Mountain Switchboard - No Buttons in design mode.

2. Make sure that the Control Wizard icon is toggled on.

3. Click on the Command Button icon in the Toolbox.

4. Place the mouse pointer on the form in the upper-left corner of the Form Display rectangle and draw a small rectangle.

Note   Command buttons have no control source. If you try to create a button by dragging a field from the Field List, a text box control (not a command button) is created. You must draw the rectangle or drag a macro to create a command button.

The Command Button Wizard displays the dialog box shown in Figure 31-3. You can select from several categories of tasks. As you choose each category, the list of actions under the header *When button is pressed* changes. In addition, the sample picture changes as you move from action to action. In Figure 31-3, the specified category is Form Operations and the desired action is Open Form.

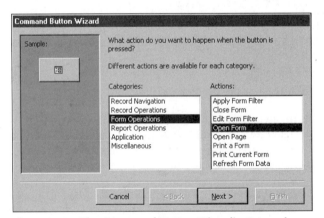

Figure 31-3: The Command Button Wizard's Categories and Actions dialog box.

5. Choose the Form Operations category and the Open Form action.

6. Click Next> to move to the next screen.

The Wizard displays a list of the Mountain Animal Hospital database's forms.

7. Select the Customer form and Click Next> to move to the next Wizard screen.

The next screen is a specific dialog box for this button. Because you have chosen the Open Form action, Access uses built-in logic to ask what you want to do now with this form. As Figure 31-4 shows, Access can automatically write a VBA program behind the button to open the form and show all records; if necessary, it can let you specify fields to search for specific values after the form is opened.

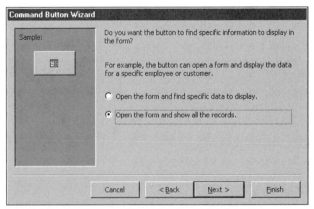

Figure 31-4: The Command Button Wizard open form with a specific data question.

8. Select Open the form and show all the records. Then Click Next> to move on.

The next screen lets you decide what you want to appear on the button. You can display text or a picture on the button. The button can be resized to accommodate any size text. The default is to place a picture on the button. You can choose from the default button for the selected action, or you can click in the Show All Pictures checkbox to select from over 100 pictures. You also can click on the Browse button to select an icon (.ICO) or bitmap (.BMP) file from your disk. For this example, simply display the text Customer on the button.

9. Click on the Text option button and erase the text Open Form in the text box.

The sample button displays nothing instead of the picture (see Figure 31-5).

10. Click Next> to move to the final Wizard screen, which lets you enter a name for the button and then display the button on the form.

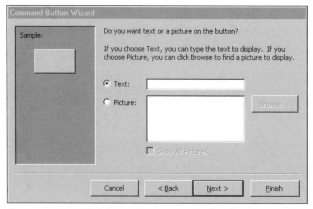

Figure 31-5: Selecting a picture or text for the button.

11. Enter **Customer** as the name of the button and Click Finish.

The button appears on the Form Design screen, as shown in Figure 31-6.

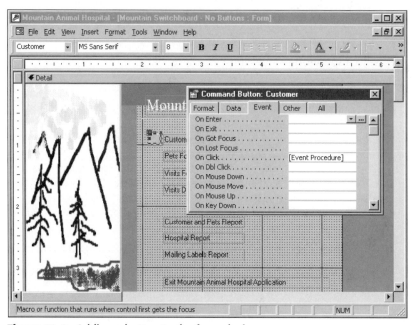

Figure 31-6: Adding a button to the form design.

Notice the property sheet displayed in Figure 31-6. The On Click property displays *Event Procedure*, which means that a module is stored *behind* the form. You can see this VBA module library by pressing the Builder button (three dots) next to the

[Event Procedure] text. When the Customer button is clicked, the VBA program is run and the Customer form is opened.

Cross-Reference

A module window appears with the specific VBA program code that's necessary to open the Customer form (see Figure 31-7). There is no need to look at this code unless you plan to change the program. This topic is discussed in Chapter 32.

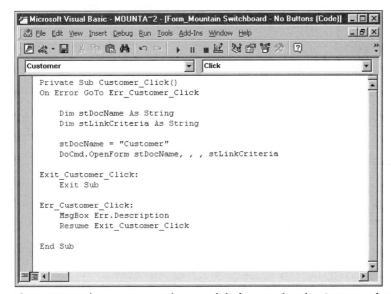

Figure 31-7: The event procedure module for opening the Customer form.

You can create a command button and attach a macro very easily — or attach pictures — without using the Wizard. If you want to dabble in Visual Basic, the Command Button Wizard is a great place to start.

You may want to create buttons for all the forms and reports. You can use the Command Button Wizard, as shown on the previous page (except for the reports for which you would use the Report Operations options). If you are planning on using a macro or want to create an event procedure yourself, click on the first button and choose Edit ⇨ Duplicate from the menu bar to duplicate the button.

Note   This only duplicates the button itself, not the code behind the button.

After you duplicate the Customer button for all the other text entries except the last one, your screen should look like Figure 31-8.

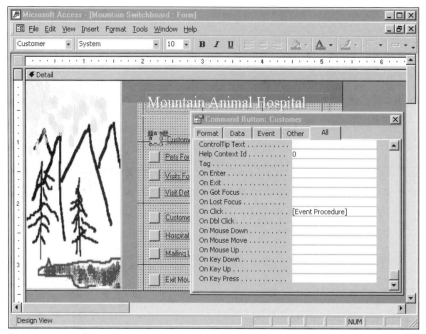

Figure 31-8: All buttons on screen.

Linking a command button to a macro

As soon as you create a command button in the Design window, it is already active. You can click on it, although it doesn't perform any action unless you created it with the Wizard. Switching to the Form window by clicking on the Form button on the toolbar displays the switchboard. You can use any of the seven buttons that you created in design mode.

Each time you click on a button, it graphically pushes down, showing that it is selected. Except for the Customer button, however, nothing else occurs; only the button movement happens. By switching back to design mode and clicking on the Design button on the toolbar, you can link a macro to the button.

To link a command button to a macro, enter the macro name into the property cell of one of the command button's event properties. To see the property sheet for a command button, follow these steps:

1. In design mode, click on the Pets command button.

2. Click on the Properties button on the toolbar or select View ➪ Properties.

A property sheet similar to the one in Figure 31-8 should be visible on your screen. Notice that the event properties that begin with the word *On* in the property sheet.

The property most commonly used to link a command button to a macro is On Click. This property runs a macro whenever a user clicks on the button. When the button is selected, the On Click property becomes True and the specified macro is run. To associate the macro named Pets in the macro group Mountain Switchboard, follow these steps:

1. Click on the Pets command button.

2. Click on the On Click property cell in the property sheet for the command buttons.

3. Select **Mountain Switchboard. Pets** from the list of macros in the cell and press Enter.

Make sure that both the macro group name and then the macro name separated by a period display in the On Click property.

Tip

When you enter a macro name, the macro does not have to exist. You can enter the name of a macro that you create later. In this way, you can create the switchboard first and the macros later. If the macro name you enter in the On Click cell does not exist when you open the form and click on the button, Access displays an error message.

Using these methods, you can now complete the properties for seven of the form's buttons, assigning a macro for each button on the basis of the On Click property. Table 31-1 shows each button name and the macro it calls.

Table 31-1		
The Seven Buttons and Their Macro Names		
In Rectangle	*Button Name*	*Macro for On Click*
Form	Customer	Event Property (created by Button Wizard)
Form	Pets	Mountain Switchboard.Pets
Form	Visits	Mountain Switchboard.Visits
Form	Visit Details	Mountain Switchboard.Visit Details
Report	Customer and Pets	Mountain Switchboard.Customer and Pets
Report	Hospital Report	Mountain Switchboard.Hospital Report
Report	Customer Labels	Mountain Switchboard.Customer Labels

The macros for the Mountain Switchboard

In this example, each command button opens either a form or a report by using the OpenForm or OpenReport macro actions. The Exit button closes the form with the Quit macro action.

You can create each macro and its actions by following these general steps:

1. Enter a macro name in the Macro Name column.

2. Enter a macro action in the Action column (such as OpenForm, OpenReport, or Close) or select the macro action from the drop-down list box.

3. Enter a macro argument (name of form or report) for each action.

4. Optionally, enter a remark (as a reminder) in the Comment Column.

Another way to add a macro action and argument is to drag the form or report from the Database window to the macro's Action column. Access automatically adds the correct action in the Action column, which is OpenForm or OpenReport. Access also adds the correct argument in the Name cell of the arguments.

If you want to create the group macro for this chapter, follow Table 31-2. This table shows each macro name, the action for each macro, and the form or report name. (These are shown in Figure 31-9.) The macro Mountain Switchboard should already exist in the Macro Object list of the Database window.

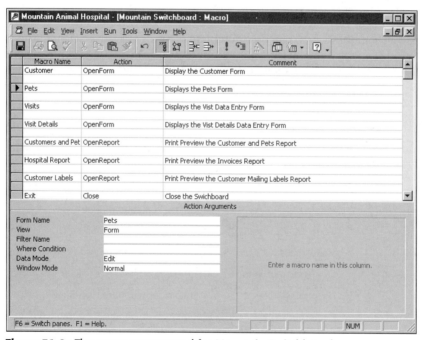

Figure 31-9: The seven macros used for Mountain Switchboard.

Table 31-2
Macros Used in the Group Macro

Macro Name	Action	Argument Name (Form, Report, Object)
Pets	OpenForm	Pets
Visits	OpenForm	Adding General Pet Visit Info
Visit Details	OpenForm	Adding Visit Details
Customer and Pets	OpenReport	Pets & Owners
Hospital Report	OpenReport	Invoices
Customer Label	OpenReport	Customer By State (three snaking columns)
Exit	Close	Mountain Switchboard

Table 31-2 shows that the action Close will close the form named Mountain Switchboard. These macros work with the actual form named Mountain Switchboard. The Exit command button will be created next.

Dragging a macro to the form to create a button

The form Mountain Switchboard does not have an Exit command button. You already learned one way to add a command button in the Form Design window. Another way to create a command button is by dragging and dropping a macro name from the macro Database window to a position on the switchboard.

For example, to create an Exit command button for the form Mountain Switchboard by using the drag-and-drop method, follow these steps:

1. Enter the design mode for the form Mountain Switchboard - No Buttons.

2. Activate the Database window by pressing F11 or Alt+F1.

3. In the Database window, click on the Macro object button to display all macros.

4. Highlight Mountain Switchboard on the Macro Object list.

5. Click on the macro Mountain Switchboard; drag and drop it onto the form below the rectangles.

6. Click on the button name and change it to **Exit**.

7. Click in the cell of the On Click property of the Exit button.

8. Move to the end of the macro group name and type **.Exit**.

Your screen should now look similar to Figure 31-10. Notice that when you added the macro to the form by the drag-and-drop method, Access automatically created a command button, named it the same as the macro, and placed the macro name (in this case, a group name) in the On Click property of the button.

When you added the macro name to the On Click property, you did not have to add the macro group name. Rather, you moved to the end and placed a period after the group name and then the macro name. Access automatically brought the group name into the On Click property for you.

Tip   If you drag and drop a macro that is not a group macro, Access correctly places the macro name in the On Click property and names the button the same as the macro.

Caution   If you drag a macro group, as you did in this example, and do not add a macro name to the On Click property, Access runs the first macro in the macro group.

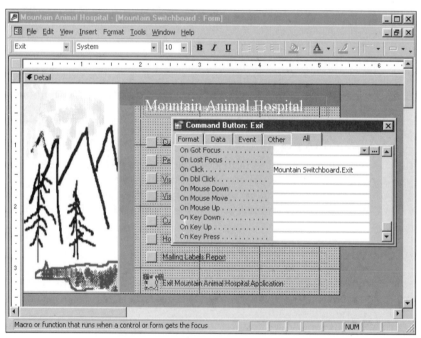

Figure 31-10: The new button created by dragging and dropping a macro onto the form.

Adding a picture to a command button

On the CD-ROM   The first seven command buttons you created contained nothing in the Caption property of the button. This last button currently contains the text Mountain in the Caption property of the command button. However, you can have any button display a picture instead. For example, the CD-ROM in the back of the book contains a file named EXIT.BMP (as well as a sampler of pictures for command buttons), which is a bitmap of an exit sign. You can have the Exit command button show the picture EXIT.BMP rather than the word Exit.

To change a command button to a picture button, use one of these methods:

✦ Type the name of the bitmap (.BMP) containing the picture into the Picture property of the button.

✦ Use the Picture Builder to select from an icon list that comes with Access.

✦ Specify the name of an icon or bitmap file.

To change the Exit command button to the picture button EXIT.BMP, follow these steps:

1. In the Mountain Switchboard form, click on the Exit command button.

2. Display the Property window.

3. Select the *Picture* property for the Exit button.

4. Click on the Builder button (three dots on a little button).

   The Picture Builder dialog box appears. No picture appears because the button you are modifying has none. Because you are adding a picture for an Exit button, you may want to see if there is an Exit button in Access. You can scroll down the list of Available Pictures, as shown in Figure 31-11. Access has an Exit picture, but it may not be what you want. You can select any bitmap or icon file on your disk.

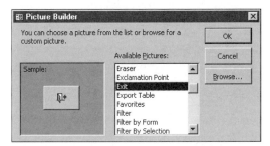

Figure 31-11: The Picture Builder.

5. Click on the Browse button.

   The Select Bitmap dialog box shows a standard Windows directory list. Select the directory that contains your file.

6. Select the directory that contains the file EXIT.BMP, select the file, and click on Open (see Figure 31-12). The bitmap appears in the sample area. Although it doesn't fit in the sample, it should fit on the button when it is displayed.

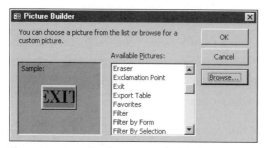

Figure 31-12: Viewing a sample bitmap in Picture Builder.

7. Click OK to accept the bitmap.

Access places the path of the bitmap in the Picture property. Once you save the application, however, the bitmap no longer is required to exist in the path.

8. Resize the button so that the picture shows only the word *Exit*.

Your form should look like Figure 31-13. Notice that Access added the path and filename of the bitmap to the Picture cell for the button Exit.

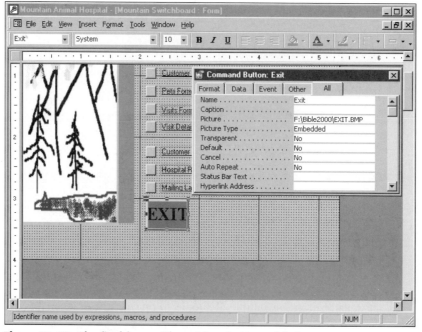

Figure 31-13: The final form with a picture button added.

You also can type the filename directly into the Picture property. If Access cannot find the picture file, it displays a dialog box stating that it couldn't find your file. If you know the drive and directory where the file is located, enter them in the Picture cell with the filename (for example, C:\BIBLE2000\EXIT.BMP).

You may want to make all of the buttons into pictures. Click on each button and select the Picture property. Some of the pictures in the Access Picture Builder are 32×32 pixels (1½-inch × ½-inch), and others are 16x16 pixels (0.18 inch × 0.18 inch).

Tip　Database Creations, Inc. offers two libraries of over 1,500 button-size pictures, each like the 100 that come with the Access 2000 Picture Builder. If you would like to purchase the Picture Builder Add-On Picture Pack, call Database Creations at 860-644-5891 or FAX them at 860-648-0710. For complete information, visit Database Creation's Website at www.databasecreations.com. This product normally costs $99.95. Mention the *Access 2000 Bible* and you can buy it for only $59.95!

This action completes the Mountain Switchboard. Save your switchboard. The next task is to customize the menu bar to correspond to the buttons on the switchboard so that the choices can be made from the menu or the buttons.

Creating Customized Menu Bars

Besides creating switchboards with Access, you can create a custom drop-down menu bar that adds functionality to your system. You can add commands to this menu that are appropriate for your application. These commands may be the actions specified in your switchboard command buttons. When you create a custom drop-down menu bar, the new bar replaces the Access menu bar.

Tip　Only a form references the menu bar; you can create a single menu bar and use it for several forms.

Figure 31-14 shows the Mountain Switchboard with a custom drop-down menu bar attached. Each of the three choices on the bar menu (File, Forms, and Reports) has a drop-down menu attached.

There are two ways to create custom menus in Access 2000:

✦ Use the Access 2000 CommandBar Object.

✦ Use macros (this was the only way to create menus in Access 2.0 and Access 95).

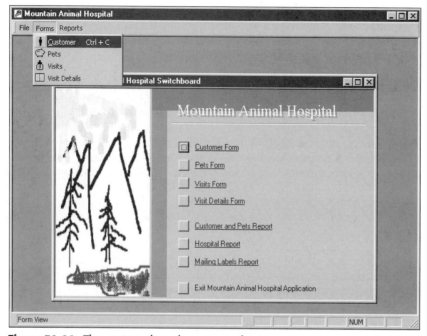

Figure 31-14: The custom drop-down menu bar.

Tip If you previously created menus in Access 2.0 or Access 95, you can convert them to the new menu bar object by selecting the macro to be converted and then by choosing Tools ⇨ Macro ⇨ Create Menu from Macro. You also can use the other two options, Create Toolbar from Macro and Create Shortcut Menu from Macro, to create those objects.

If you have menus previously created in Access 97, however, you do not need to convert them. Access 97 menus can be used as is in Access 2000.

Understanding command bars

The Access 2000 Command Bar object lets you create three types of menus:

Menu Bars	Menus that go along the top of your forms and that can have drop-down menus too
ToolBars	Groups of icons generally found under the menu bars
Shortcut Menus	Pop-up menus that display when you right-click on an object

This enables you to duplicate the Access 2000 user interface, including adding pictures to your menus.

Creating custom menu bars with command bars

You create the custom menu bar shown in Figure 31-14 by first creating the top-level menu consisting of three elements — File, Forms, and Reports. The top-level menu is created by selecting View ➪ Toolbars ➪ Customize. . . , as shown in Figure 31-15.

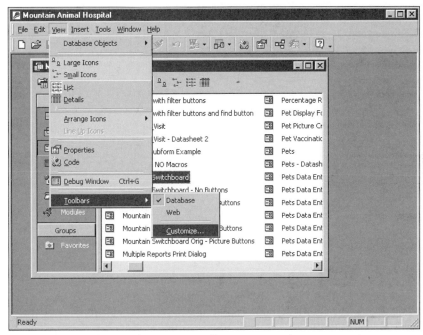

Figure 31-15: Selecting the View ➪ Toolbars ➪ Customize menu option.

If you've never really looked at an Access 2000 menu bar, this is a good example because many of the menu bars have pictures in front of the text. Notice the separator lines on the View menu. You will learn how to add these lines. Also notice the checkbox on the Toolbars cascading menu. This option indicates whether the menu bar is displayed. In this example, only the database menu bar is displayed. The Web menu bar is hidden.

You learn about Access 2000 and the World Wide Web in Chapter 32.

Select Customize. . . and the dialog box shown in Figure 31-16 appears. Notice that your Office Assistant, if it is enabled, also is displayed to help you because this is a new feature. Microsoft has decided that you will need help.

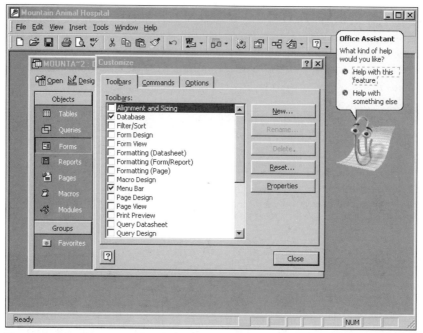

Figure 31-16: The Customize dialog box for toolbars.

Changing existing menus

From this dialog box, you can also select any of the preexisting menus and customize them by adding, removing, or moving menu items. You can also change
pictures and the purpose of the menu.

To change the menu items, display the toolbar or menu that you want to change and
then directly change it by clicking on the menu items that you want to manipulate. If
you click and hold the mouse on a menu item, a submenu item, or a toolbar icon, a
little gray button appears over the top of the item. You can then move the icon to a
different location by dragging it to the new location. To remove the menu item or
icon, simply drag it to a place away from the toolbar. To add a new item, select the
Commands tab in the Customize dialog box, find the category that contains the item
you want, and then drag the item to the toolbar or menu.

You can create a whole new item by selecting All Macros or New Menu and dragging
it to the menu or toolbar you want it to be on. See the next section to learn to add a
new menu.

Creating a new menu bar

To create a new menu bar, select New... from the Customize dialog box, as shown
in Figure 31-16. A dialog box appears asking you to name the custom toolbar. The

default is Custom 1. Name this new menu bar **Mountain Custom Command Bar** and click OK.

A small, gray rectangle appears in the center of the screen, on top of the Customize menu. The new command bar name also appears in the list at the bottom of the Customize menu list, as shown in Figure 31-17.

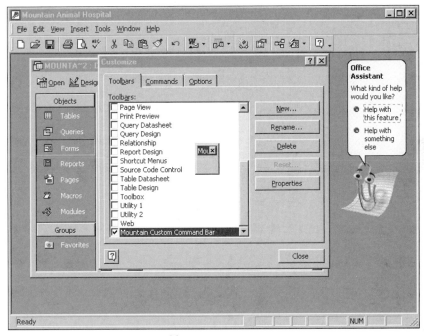

Figure 31-17: A new command bar.

Tip

You can move this menu to the top of the screen by dragging it so that it looks like a normal menu bar with no items as shown in Figure 31-18. The Mountain bar is at the top, above the standard menu bar.

Before you begin to drag commands or text to the command bar, you must decide what type of command bar it is. Select the menu bar (Mountain Custom Command Bar) on the Toolbars tab in the Customize dialog box and then click on the Properties button.

Figure 31-18 shows the Toolbar Properties dialog box. Here you can select each of the command bars in your system. The important portion of this dialog box is the middle portion. The first option is Type.

There are three Type choices:

Menu Bar   Used for drop-down menus of commands containing text and, optionally, pictures

Toolbar   Used for button bars of pictures only

Popup   Used either for drop-down menu lists or shortcut menus; can
                 contain pictures and text

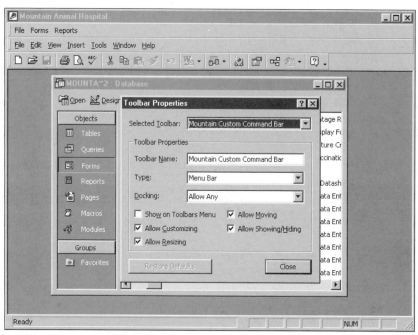

Figure 31-18: The Toolbar Properties dialog box.

For this example, you want to create a menu, so choose the Menu Bar option.

The next option, Docking, has four options:

Allow Any	Allows docking horizontally or vertically
Can't Change	Cannot change where the command bar is docked
No Vertical	Can dock only horizontally (across the screen)
No Horizontal	Can dock only vertically (up and down the screen)

The rest of the options are five checkboxes:

Show on Toolbars Menu	Displays the selected toolbar on the View ⇨ Toolbars menu list
Allow Customizing	Allows the user to change this through the Customize menu

Allow Resizing	Allows you to resize a floating toolbar or menu bar
Allow Moving	Lets you move the menu or toolbar between floating or docking
Allow Showing/Hiding	Lets you show/hide the menu through the View ➪ Toolbars menu

For this example, you can select all the choices to give the menu maximum flexibility.

Adding a submenu to a custom menu bar

Most menu commands are placed on submenus. It is rare for a top-level menu item to do anything but display a submenu. The submenu contains the actual menu item that, when clicked on, runs the desired action, such as opening a form or printing a report.

To create a submenu, you essentially repeat the steps that you used to create the Mountain Custom Command Bar. To create the submenu menu bar, select New. . . from the Customize dialog box, as originally shown in Figure 31-16, drag it to the Mountain Custom Command Bar, and drop it. The text New Menu appears on the menu bar. Click on it again, and a gray rectangle appears, as shown in Figure 31-19. This is the submenu.

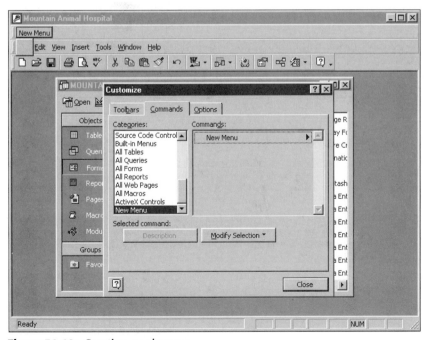

Figure 31-19: Creating a submenu.

Edit the name of the submenu by right-clicking on it. Name it File by clicking in the Name area and changing the name from New Menu to File. Repeat these steps for two additional new submenus, and name them Forms and Reports.

After you have defined your three menus you can add commands to the submenus. Again, you can drag the menu commands directly to the submenu area.

Note Dragging the New Menu item to another menu automatically links the main menu and the submenu and makes the original menu choices nonselectable. The main menu (Mountain Custom Command Bar) is now permanently a menu bar. You can still change the defaults for the submenu items as you create them to display text, pictures, or both.

Caution After you add submenus to a menu bar, you cannot change it to a toolbar or pop-up menu.

Adding commands to a submenu

You can add commands to a custom menu bar by dragging any of the preexisting commands to the menu bar, or you can add any of your tables, queries, forms, reports, or macros to the menu bar.

Using a preexisting command fills in all the options for you. However, unless you are planning to use an action found on one of the Access 2000 menus, you should create your own menus by first creating a new command bar and making it a menu bar, as discussed in the previous section.

After you have defined the blank submenus on the menu bar, you can drag controls to them. For this example, you might want to add the Forms menu items first. Follow these steps to add an item to display the Customers form when the first item is selected on the Forms menu:

1. Select Commands from the View ⇨ Toolbars ⇨ Customize dialog box.

2. Select All Forms from the Categories list.

3. Select Customer from the Commands list and drag it to the Forms menu bar. When you drop it, the text Customer appears on the menu bar.

4. Repeat the process for the Pets command, as shown in progress in Figure 31-20.

5. Repeat the process for the Adding General Pet Visit Info form and name it **Visits**.

6. Repeat the process for the Adding Visit Details form and name it **Visit Details**.

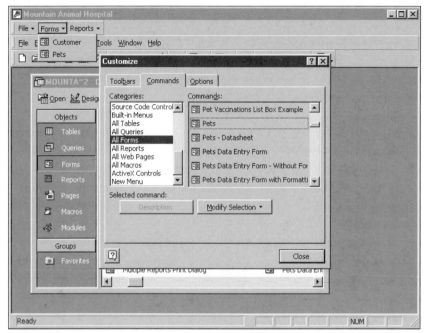

Figure 31-20: Creating a submenu item.

Changing the look of the submenu items

When you click on the Forms menu, each of the items has a form icon. If you right-click on any of the submenu items with the View ➪ Toolbars ➪ Customize menu active, you can change the picture, or even change whether a picture is displayed at all. Figure 31-21 shows the Change Button Image selection of the View ➪ Toolbars ➪ Customize menu. Notice that all four of the button images have been changed by simply right-clicking on each menu item, selecting Change Button Image, and then selecting the desired picture.

The shortcut menu contains five options for changing pictures on menus or toolbar icons:

Copy Button Image	Copies the current button face image to the Clipboard
Paste Button Image	Copies the current picture in the Clipboard to the button face
Reset Button Image	Changes the button face image to the default image
Edit Button Image	Uses the internal image editor to change an image
Choose Button Image	Changes the button face image from a list of images stored in Access

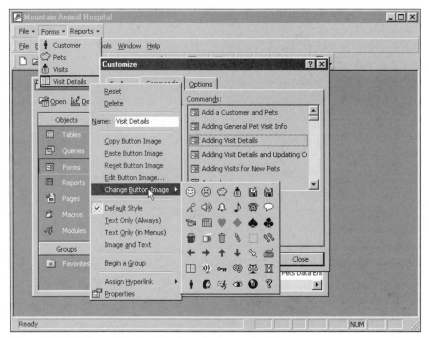

Figure 31-21: Changing the display of a menu bar item.

There are several ways to change the button image. The easiest is to select from a set of button images that Access stores internally, as shown in Figure 31-21. When you choose a picture and click OK, the button image changes.

As Figure 31-21 shows, there are not too many pictures to choose from. You can, however, create your own image and copy it to the Clipboard. After you have an image on the Clipboard, you can use the Paste Button Image option of the short-cut menu to add the image to the button. The image must be sized to fit the button. You can also use the Edit Button Image to change the image after it is on the button face. You can edit the button face by moving the image around and changing individual pixels of color.

As Figure 31-21 also shows, you can change the caption of the text and the way it is displayed. There are four additional options for displaying the menu or toolbar option:

Default Style	Displays image and text for menu bars, pictures for toolbars, and both for pop-ups
Text Only (Always)	Displays text only for menu bars and pop-ups

| Text Only (in Menus) | Displays text on menu bars and graphics on toolbars and both on pop-ups |
| Image and Text | Displays pictures and text on menu bars and pop-ups |

Tip

To remove the images and display just text, select the Text Only choice for each submenu item.

Tip

If you check the Begin a Group checkbox, Access places a horizontal separator line before the menu item.

You can further customize each item for the specific purpose you need. You can display the Properties for any menu by clicking on the Properties button, shown at the bottom of Figure 31-21. Figure 31-22 shows the properties for the Customer Item that has been enhanced. Here you set the rest of the actions for the menu item.

Each menu item has a list of properties, as shown in Figure 31-22. After the Control Properties window is displayed, you can change the Selected Control to any of the menu items without returning to the previous menu. Changing the caption changes the text on the menu.

Tip

To define a hot key for the menu item, you can add an & in front of the hot-key letter.

The caption has been changed with the addition of an & in front of the *C*. This allows you to press the letter *C* after displaying the Forms menu in this example. If you set up an AutoKeys macro list, you can specify the shortcut text, as shown in Figure 31-22. Notice the Ctrl + C next to the Customer menu item as well as in the shortcut text area.

You also can define the tool tip text for the control by entering text in the ToolTip area.

The most important option is normally the On Action item. This allows you to specify a VBA function or macro that should run when the menu item is selected. Because you dragged each form from the forms list to the menu, the action is already known in the Properties sheet for the item. In fact, the name of the form to open is stored in the Parameter option of the window.

The other options let you choose the Help File name and entry point if you click on Help while selecting the menu. The Parameter entry is used to specify optional parameters when calling a VBA function.

Note

You can complete the Reports menu items by dragging the desired reports to the Reports menu item from the All Reports commands. You can add the Exit function to the File menu by dragging the Exit command from the File category.

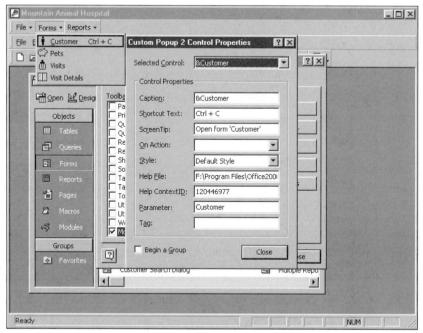

Figure 31-22: Changing the display of a menu bar item.

Attaching the menu bar to a form

After you have completed the menu bar named Mountain Custom Command Bar and its submenus, you are ready to attach the menu bar to a form.

To attach a menu bar to a form, open the form in design mode and set the Menu Bar property of the form to the menu bar name. To attach the menu bar named Mountain Custom Command Bar to the switchboard form Mountain Switchboard – No Buttons, follow these steps:

1. Open the form Mountain Switchboard – No Buttons in design mode.

2. Display the property sheet by clicking on the Properties button on the toolbar.

3. Click on the small blank box to the left of the ruler (immediately below the toolbar).

   Access displays the title *Form* for the property sheet.

4. Click on the Menu Bar property of the Property window.

5. Select the Mountain Custom Command Bar from the pull-down menu (or type the menu bar name).

By following these steps, you attached the menu bar named Mountain Custom Command Bar with its drop-down menus to the form. You should have a design screen similar to the one in Figure 31-23.

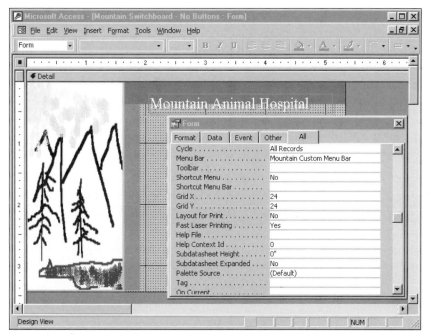

Figure 31-23: Attaching a menu bar to the form using the Menu Bar property.

Creating shortcut menus

Access 2000 allows you to create *custom shortcut menus* that open when the right mouse button is clicked. These menus can replace the standard shortcut menus in Access 2000. Shortcut menus can be defined for the form itself or for any control on the form. Each control can have a different shortcut menu.

A shortcut menu is simply another type of command bar. You can begin a shortcut menu by selecting View ➪ Toolbars ➪ Customize and then choosing the New... button from the Toolbars tab of the Customize dialog box. In this example, you can name the new menu **Pets Shortcut**.

After you create the new command bar, you can select it and click on the Properties button. The Toolbar Properties dialog box is displayed. Change the Type to Popup, as shown in Figure 31-24.

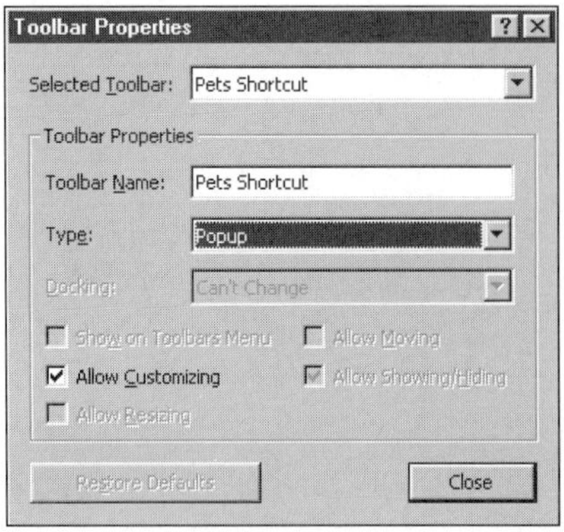

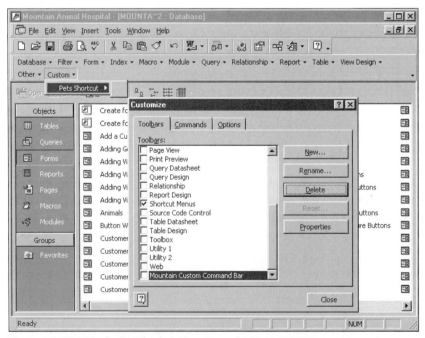

Figure 31-24: Changing a new toolbar to a pop-up shortcut menu.

Change the type of the toolbar from the default Menu Bar to Popup raises a message warning you that you have to edit the menu items in the Shortcut Menus Custom section. Shortcut Menus is a standard Access 2000 toolbar, as shown in Figure 31-25. When you click on Shortcut Menus, a list of all menu bars appears on a command bar. By selecting any of these menu items, such as Database, Filter, or Form, which are shown on the left side of the menu bar in Figure 31-25, a submenu of all the shortcut menus available on the standard Access design screens is displayed.

Figure 31-25: Displaying the list of custom shortcut menus.

The last item on the command bar is Custom. When you click on this item, a list of all the shortcut (pop-up) menus that you have defined is displayed. The only shortcut menu defined so far is the Pets Shortcut. Notice the blank menu bar in Figure 31-25, to the right of the Pets Shortcut menu. This is where you will drag your selections.

You add menu items to a shortcut menu in exactly the same way that you add any menu item. While the empty Pets Shortcut menu rectangle is displayed as shown in Figure 31-25, click on the Commands tab in the Customize dialog box and then select All Forms in the Categories list. You can then drag any command to the shortcut menu. For this example, add four forms (Pets, Customers, Visits, and Visit Details) by dragging the four forms (Pets, Customers, Adding General Pet Visit Info, and Adding Visit Details) to the menu. Then add three items for the reports—Customer and Pets, Hospital Reports, and Customer Labels—by first selecting All Reports in the Categories list.

As you add each of the forms and reports, it appears on the shortcut menu. Notice that the forms and reports display a different icon next to the menu text. You can display the menu to change the details of each of these menu items by clicking on the item and then right-clicking. The shortcut menu in Figure 31-26 has been defined and each of the original form and report names has been changed to the more standard names for the example. Also notice the separator line between the forms and reports. This line was created by selecting the Begin a Group option while on the first report, as shown in Figure 31-26. If you wanted to, you could change the pictures for each of the icons next to the menu item by using the button image options.

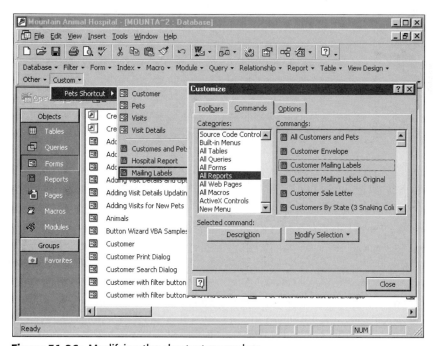

Figure 31-26: Modifying the shortcut menu bar.

Tip   By clicking on Properties for any of the menu items, you can set the shortcut keys, ToolTips, actions, and Help file.

After you create the menu definition and save the shortcut menu, you can attach the shortcut menu to either the form or any control on the form. If you attach the shortcut menu to a form, it will override the standard shortcut menu for the form. If you attach a shortcut menu to a control, it is displayed only when you right-click while on that control. Figure 31-27 shows the Pets shortcut menu being attached to the Shortcut Menu Bar property of the Mountain Switchboard – No Buttons.

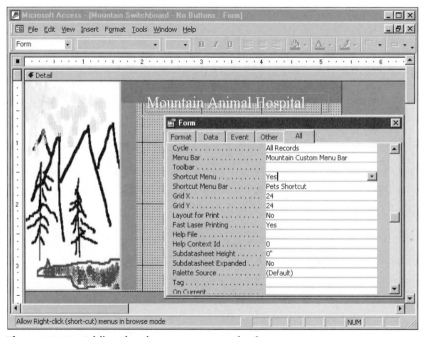

Figure 31-27: Adding the shortcut menu to the form.

You may also notice that the Shortcut Menu property is set to Yes. This is for either the default shortcut menus or the shortcut menus that you create. If it is set to No, you will not see any shortcut menus when you right-click.

Figure 31-28 shows the shortcut menu on the Mountain Switchboard – No Buttons form. The menu will be displayed to the right of wherever the mouse was clicked, even if it extends beyond the window. Now when you select the desired menu item the actions listed in the menu macro will be run.

Tip   If you want to delete a shortcut menu, you must first select the shortcut menu by displaying the list of toolbars in the View ⇨ Toolbars ⇨ Customize dialog box and then click on the Properties button. The Shortcut menus are visible only by then opening the Selected Toolbar combo box. You must change the type from Popup to Menu Bar. After you do this, you can return to the Toolbars tab, where you will now be able to see the shortcut menu and press the Delete button. Remember that when you change a command bar to a pop-up menu, it is visible only on the shortcut menu's Custom tab or in the Selected Toolbar list in the Toolbar Properties dialog box.

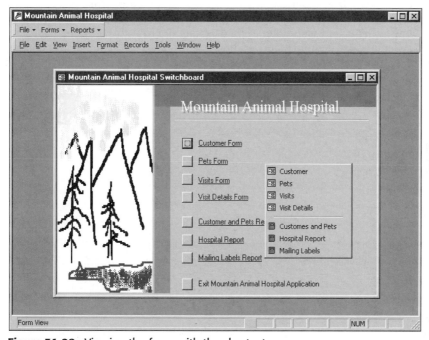

Figure 31-28: Viewing the form with the shortcut menu.

Creating and using custom toolbars

Access has always let you define new toolbars for your application and customize existing toolbars. However, Access 2000 also adds features such as customizing the pictures on the buttons (known as button faces). For example, suppose that when you display the Mountain Switchboard, you want a toolbar that lets you open the various forms with one button push. You can create a new toolbar or even add some icons to the standard form toolbar. For this example, you will create a new toolbar.

A toolbar is just another type of command bar.

To create a custom toolbar, follow these steps:

1. Select View ➪ Toolbars ➪ Customize.
2. Click on the New button from the Toolbars window.

3. Enter **Mountain Toolbar** in the New Toolbar dialog box and click OK.

4. Select Properties.

You can see that the new command bar is created as a toolbar. You can close the properties window and drag the four forms to the toolbar. You use the same technique to do this as you saw when creating menu bars and shortcut menus. While the empty Mountain Toolbar rectangle is displayed, click on the Commands tab in the Customize dialog box and then select All Forms in the Categories list. You can then drag any command to the shortcut menu. For this example, add four forms (Pets, Customers, Visits, and Visit Details) by dragging the four forms (Pets, Customers, Adding General Pet Visit Info, and Adding Visit Details) to the menu and change the button face for each button. When you are done, you can see the toolbar completed, as shown in Figure 31-29. This figure also shows how to change a button image on the last item by first selecting the item and then right-clicking on the item.

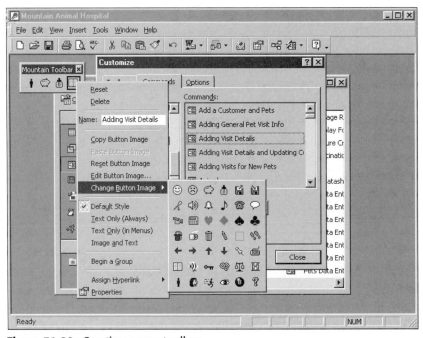

Figure 31-29: Creating a new toolbar.

Tip

You can add a space and a separator line between icons by selecting Begin a Group on the icon you want the line to the left of.

Attaching the toolbar to a form

After the toolbar named Mountain Toolbar is completed, you are ready to attach the toolbar to a form.

To attach a toolbar to a form, open the form in design mode and set the Toolbar property of the form to the toolbar name. To attach the toolbar named Mountain Toolbar to the switchboard form Mountain Switchboard – No Buttons, follow these steps:

1. Open the form Mountain Switchboard – No Buttons in design mode.
2. Display the property sheet by clicking on the Properties button on the toolbar.
3. Click on the small blank box to the left of the ruler (immediately below the toolbar).

    Access displays the title *Form* for the property sheet.

4. Click on the Toolbar property in the Property window.
5. Select the **Mountain Toolbar** from the pull-down menu (or type the toolbar name).

By following these steps, you attached the Mountain Toolbar with its picture buttons to the form. You should have a design screen similar to the one in Figure 31-30.

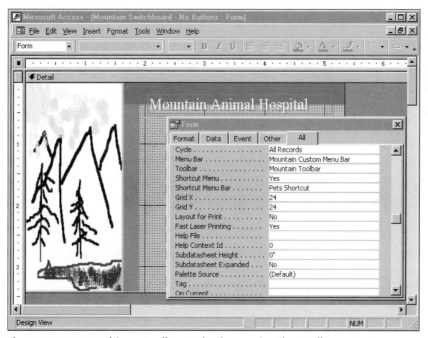

Figure 31-30: Attaching a toolbar to the form using the Toolbar property.

When you set a form's menu bar or toolbar to a custom menu bar or toolbar, the menu bar and toolbar display automatically when the form opens. When focus changes to another form, the custom menu bar and toolbar for the previous form are removed. The menu bar and toolbar are replaced with the newly displayed form's menu bar and toolbar if the form's properties specify them.

After you have made these changes, you can display the Mountain Switchboard – No Buttons, as shown in Figure 31-31. Mountain Toolbar is displayed on the screen. When you hold the mouse pointer over one of the toolbar buttons the tool tip displays.

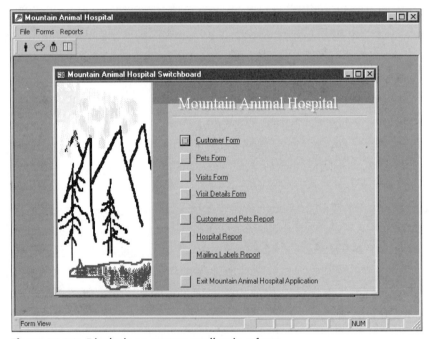

Figure 31-31: Displaying a custom toolbar in a form.

Adding control tips to any form control

Although tool tips must be added using the toolbar customization windows, you can add a tool tip known as a *control tip* to any control. When you place your mouse pointer on a control, textual help resembling a tool tip is displayed with a yellow background. You can create a control tip by entering text into the ControlTip Text property of any control. Whatever you enter into this property is displayed when you place the mouse pointer on a control and leave it there for about a second.

Running a macro automatically when you start Access

After you create the switchboard, a menu bar, and the associated submenus and toolbars, you may want Access to open the form automatically each time you open the database. One method to automatically load a form at startup is to write an AutoExec macro. When Access opens a database, it looks for a macro named AutoExec. If the macro exists, Access automatically runs it. To create an AutoExec macro to open the switchboard automatically, follow these steps:

1. Create a new macro (you'll name it AutoExec later).
2. Type **Minimize** (or select the action) in the next empty Action cell.
3. Type **OpenForm** (or select the action) in the next empty Action cell.
4. Type **Mountain Switchboard** (or select the switchboard form name) in the Form Name cell in the Action Arguments pane.

Save the macro with the name AutoExec. After you do so, Access will run the macro automatically each time you open the database.

The AutoExec macro shows two actions. The Minimize action minimizes the Database window and the OpenForm action opens the switchboard.

Tip To bypass an AutoExec macro, simply hold down the Shift key while selecting the database name from the Access File menu.

In early versions of Access, the Autoexec method was the only way to launch a form at startup. Access 95 and later versions provide an easier way to automatically launch a form at startup.

Controlling options when starting Access

Rather than run a macro to open a form when Access starts, you can use the Access 2000 startup form to control many options when you start Access including:

✦ Changing the text on the title bar

✦ Specifying an icon to use when Access is minimized

✦ Global custom menu bar

✦ Global custom shortcut menu bar

✦ Display a form on startup (for example, the application's switchboard)

✦ Control the display of default menus, toolbars, the Database window, and the status bar

Figure 31-32 shows the Access 2000 Startup dialog box. You can display this by selecting Tools ⇨ Startup or by right-clicking on the border of the Database window and selecting Startup.

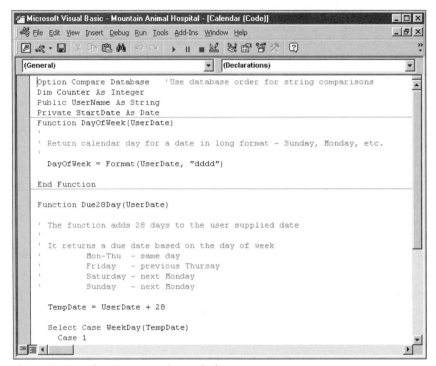

```
Microsoft Visual Basic - Mountain Animal Hospital - [Calendar (Code)]
File  Edit  View  Insert  Debug  Run  Tools  Add-Ins  Window  Help

(General)                              (Declarations)

Option Compare Database    'Use database order for string comparisons
Dim Counter As Integer
Public UserName As String
Private StartDate As Date
Function DayOfWeek(UserDate)
'
' Return calendar day for a date in long format - Sunday, Monday, etc.
'
  DayOfWeek = Format(UserDate, "dddd")


End Function


Function Due28Day(UserDate)

' The function adds 28 days to the user supplied date
'
' It returns a due date based on the day of week
'         Mon-Thu  - same day
'         Friday   - previous Thursay
'         Saturday - next Monday
'         Sunday   - next Monday

  TempDate = UserDate + 28

  Select Case WeekDay(TempDate)
    Case 1
```

Figure 31-32: The Startup options window.

When you click Advanced>, you can specify whether to enable special Access keys to view Database or Code windows.

Tip   This tool replaces both the AutoExec macro and items formerly specified in the Access 2.0 INI file.

Creating a Print Report Dialog Box Form and Macros

A dialog box is also a form, but it is unlike a switchboard; the dialog box usually displays information, captures a user entry, or lets the user interact with the system. In this section, you create a complex dialog box that prints reports and labels.

By using a form and some macros, you can create a dialog box that controls print-ing of your reports. This dialog box can display a list of pets and their owners (see Figure 31-33), so that you can print only a single page of the Pets Directory without having to change the query.

Figure 31-33: A Print Reports dialog box.

Although this dialog box is more complex than a switchboard, it uses the same types of Access objects, which include the following:

✦ Forms

✦ Form controls and properties

✦ Macros

Creating a form for a macro

The form you use in this example displays the various controls. There are three basic sections to the form.

The upper-left corner of the form contains three option buttons, which are placed within an option group. The option buttons let you select one of the three listed reports. Each of the reports is already created and can be seen in the Database window. If you select All Customers and Pets or the Daily Hospital Report, you can print or preview that report. If you select Pet Directory, as shown in Figure 31-33, you see a list box of pets and their owners. You can then choose a pet name for a printout from the Pet Directory report for only that one pet. If you don't choose a pet name, records for all pets are printed from the Pet Directory report.

The upper-right corner of the form contains three buttons. Each button runs a different macro in the Print Report macro library. The first option button, Print Preview, runs a macro that opens the selected report in a Print Preview window. The second option button, Print, runs a macro that prints the selected report to the default printer. The last button, Close, simply closes the form without printing any reports.

To create a form for your macro, first create a blank form and size it properly by following these steps:

1. Create a new blank form unbound to any table or query.

2. Resize the form to $3^1/_2$ inches x 3 inches.

3. Change the Back color to dark gray.

Three rectangles will be placed on the form to give it a distinctive look. You can create the three rectangles (as shown in Figure 31-33) by following these steps:

1. Click on the Rectangle button in the Toolbox.

2. Using Figure 31-33 as a guide, create three separate rectangles.

   Each rectangle in this example is shown with the Raised special effect. To create this effect, follow these steps:

3. Select a rectangle.

4. Change the Back color to light gray.

5. Click on the Raised special-effect button in the Special Effect window.

6. Click on the Transparent button in the Border Color window.

7. Repeat Steps 3 through 6 for the second and third rectangles.

8. Finally, to enhance the Raised special effect, drag each rectangle away from the adjacent rectangles so that the darker background of the form shows between the rectangle borders. You may need to resize one of the rectangles to line up the edges.

Creating the option group

After you create the form and the special effects, you can create the necessary controls.

The first set of controls is the option group. In Chapter 18, you learned to use the Option Group Wizard to create option buttons. To create the option group and option buttons, follow the steps given here and use Figure 31-34 as a guide. In this example, the option group buttons are not bound to a field; they are used to select the report to print, not to enter data:

1. Click on the Option Group button in the Toolbox, making sure that the Control Wizard icon is on.

2. Draw an option-group rectangle within the upper-left rectangle, as shown in Figure 31-34.

3. Enter **All Customers and Pets, Daily Hospital Report**, and **Pet Directory** as three separate labels in the first Option Group Wizard.

4. Click on the Finish button to go to the last Wizard screen.

Your option buttons and the option group appear in the first rectangle. You may need to move or resize the option group's box to fit properly.

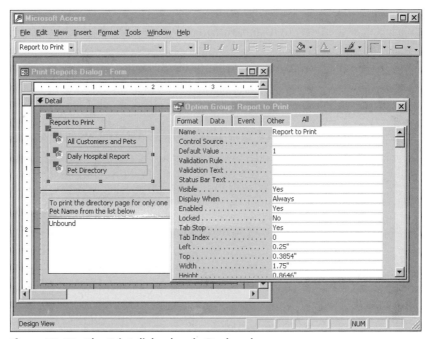

Figure 31-34: The Print dialog box in Design view.

Creating command buttons

After you complete the option group and the option buttons, you can create the command buttons. These pushbuttons trigger the actions for your dialog box. As you can see in Figure 31-33, there are three buttons:

Print Preview	Displays the selected report in the Print Preview window
Print	Prints the selected report to the default print device
Close	Closes the dialog box

To create each command button, follow the next set of steps. Because each button will be the same size, duplicate the second and third buttons from the first:

1. Turn the Wizard off, then Click on the command button in the Toolbox.

2. Create the first command button, as shown in Figure 31-34.

3. Select Edit ➪ Duplicate to duplicate the first command button.

4. Move the button, as shown in Figure 31-34.

5. Select Edit ➪ Duplicate to duplicate the second command button.

6. You may need to move the button into position as shown in Figure 31-3.

   You now need to change the command button captions. The remaining steps show how to make these changes.

7. Select the first command button and change the Caption property to **Print Preview**.

8. Select the second command button and change the Caption property to **Print**.

9. Select the third command button and change the Caption property to **Close**.

Creating a list box on the print report form

The last control that is needed in the dialog box is the list box that displays the pet name and customer name when the Pet Directory option button is clicked on. To create the list box, follow these steps, using Figure 31-35 as a guide. In this example, you create the list box without using the Wizard:

1. Click on the list box button in the Toolbox. Make sure that the Control Wizard icon is off.

2. Using Figure 31-35 as a guide, create the list box rectangle.

3. Move the label control to a position above the list box.

4. Resize the label control so that the bottom-right corner is just above the list box, as shown in Figure 31-35.

5. Using the formatting windows, change the Back color of the label to light gray to match the background of the bottom rectangle.

6. Change the Caption property for the list box by clicking on the label of the field (the caption in the label itself) and typing **To print the directory page for only one pet, select the Pet Name from the list below**. The text in the label will wrap automatically as you type.

After the list box and label are created, you must define the columns of the list box. To define the columns and data source for the list box, follow these steps, using Figure 31-35 as a guide:

1. Change the Name property to **Select Pet**.

2. Make sure that the Row Source Type indicates **Table/Query**.

3. Change the Row Source to **Pets Report**.

4. Change the Column Count to **2**.

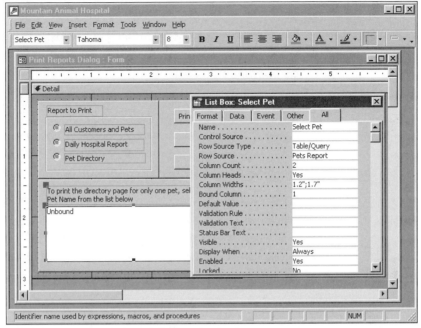

Figure 31-35: The list box definition on the form.

Note   The Pets Report must be created before you try to run this form. The Pets Report is a simple query that requires an interesting technique to create (see the sidebar, "The Pets Report query for the Print Reports form list box," for more information).

5. Change Column Heads to **Yes**.

6. Change the Column Widths to **1.2**, **1.7**.

7. Make sure that the Bound Column property indicates **1**.

Before continuing, you should save the form. Save the file but leave the form onscreen by selecting the menu option File ➪ Save. Name the form **Print Reports Dialog Box**.

When the form is completed, you are halfway done. The next task is to create each of the macros you need and create the macro library. When you complete that task, you can add the macros to the correct event properties in the form.

Creating the print macros

As you've learned, macros are attached to the events of controls or objects. These events include entering, exiting, updating, or selecting a control. In this example, macros are attached to several controls and objects. Table 31-3 shows the macros you create for this example and how they run.

Table 31-3
Macros for the Print Reports Form

Macro Name	Attached to Control/Object	Attached to Property	Description
Show List	Form	On Open	Displays list box if the third option button is on
Show List	Option group	After Update	Displays list box if the third button is selected
Print Preview	Print Preview	On Click	Displays selected report in print-preview mode when Print Preview button is selected
Print	Print button	On Click	Prints selected report if Print button is selected
Close	Close button	On Click	Closes form if Close button is selected

The Pets Report Query for the Print Reports Form List Box

The Pets Report is a simple query that has the Customer and Pets tables related by the Customer Number field. The query has two fields displayed: Pet Name from the Pets table and Customer Name from the Customer table. The data is sorted first by Customer Number and second by Pet Name. Figure 31-36 shows the partial datasheet for this list box.

In Figure 31-36, the Pet Name field is in the first column and the Customer Name field is in the second column. The data is sorted first by the customer number and second by the pet name. As you learned previously, to sort data by two fields, you must place the fields in the Query Design window in the order in which you want the two fields sorted. To sort by the customer number first and then by the pet name, you must place the Customer Number field first in the query but not select it to show. You then place the Customer Name field third in the query and select it. The query would place Customer Name first in the datasheet. The query design after it is saved and reopened is shown in Figure 31-37. Remember, Access will rearrange fields when a field is not selected to be viewed because the Show checkbox is unchecked.

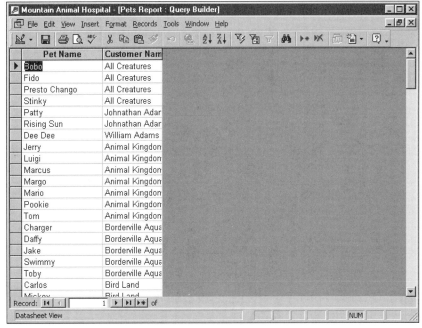

Figure 31-36: The partial datasheet for the Pets Report query.

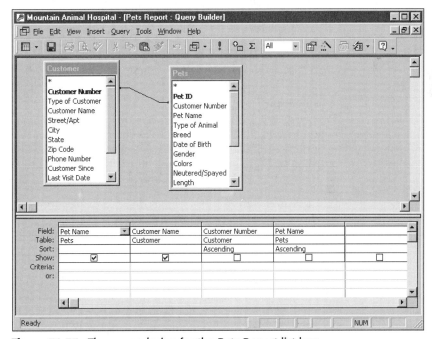

Figure 31-37: The query design for the Pets Report list box.

Creating the Print macro library

In the preceding two chapters, you learned that creating a macro library is the same as creating any macro. You create a macro library by following these steps:

1. From the Form window toolbar, click on the New Object icon and select New Macro to create a new macro.

2. Select View ➪ Macro Names or click on the Macro Names button on the toolbar to display the Macro Names column.

3. Select View ➪ Conditions or click on the Conditions button on the toolbar to display the Condition column.

As you may recall, the Macro Names and Conditions menu options add two columns to the basic Macro window. You use these columns to enter more parameters into the macro. The Macro Name column is used for creating the individual macro entry points in a macro library. The Condition column determines whether the action in the Action column should be run (on the basis of the conditions). To create the macro, follow these steps:

1. In the third row of the Macro Name column, type **Show List**.

2. In the sixth row of the Macro Name column, type **Print Preview**.

3. In the ninth row of the Macro Name column, type **Print**.

4. In the twelfth row of the Macro Name column, type **Close**.

5. Select File ➪ Save As/Export and name the macro **Print Reports**.

You can see these macro names along with their conditions and actions in Figure 31-38.

Creating the Show List macro

The Show List macro either displays or hides the list box that lists the pet names and customer names. This macro uses the SetValue macro command to run from either the form object or the option group control. The SetValue macro command lets you set a property of a control in the form. In this example, the list box is named Select Pet. The Visible action argument is set to Yes to display the list box or No to hide the list box.

Two conditions are needed for the Show List macro. The first condition holds if the third option button has been clicked on; the second condition holds if the button has not been clicked on. The Macro Name column has already been set to Show List.

In the first line of the Show List macro, set the Condition column to [Report to Print]=3 to reflect the third option button being clicked on in the option group. This line will display the list box, so the action of the macro is set to SetValue, the Item action argument is set to [Select Pet].Visible, and the Expression action argument is set to Yes. Figure 31-38 displays these settings.

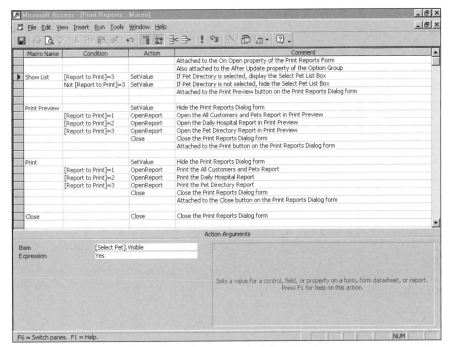

Figure 31-38: Creating the Show List macro and the Print Reports macro group.

You can also see the second line of the Show List macro and comments in Figure 31-38. Notice in the second line that the Condition column indicates that the third option button in the option group has not been clicked on and is therefore set to Not [Report to Print]=3. This line will hide the list box, so the action of the macro is SetValue, the Item property is set to [Select Pet].Visible, and the Expression property is set to No. To create the macro, follow these steps:

1. Type the first two lines in the Comment column, as shown at the top of Figure 31-38.

2. Move the cursor to the first line of the Show List macro row.

3. Place the cursor in the Condition column and type **[Report to Print]=3**.

4. Place the cursor in the Action column and either select or type **SetValue**.

5. Press F6 to move to the Item property in the Action Arguments pane and type **[Select Pet].Visible**.

6. Move to the Expression property and type **Yes**.

7. Press F6 to return to the Action column and then move to the Comments column.

8. Enter the comments in the Comment column, as shown in Figure 31-38.

9. Move your cursor to the second line of the Show List macro row.

10. In the Condition column, type **Not [Report to Print]=3**.

11. In the Action column, type (or select) **SetValue**.

12. Press F6 to move to the Item box in the Action Arguments pane and type **[Select Pet].Visible**.

13. Move to the Expression property and type **No**.

14. Press F6 to return to the Action column and then move to the Comment column.

15. Enter the comments in the Comment column, as shown in Figure 31-38.

When you complete the Show List macro, you can enter the calls to the macro in the form events properties. After this task is completed, test the macro. Before continuing, select File ⇨ Save to save the Print Reports macro library and leave it open on screen.

Entering the Show List macro calls

You are now ready to enter the macro calls for the Show List macro. This macro is called from two places:

✦ The On Open property of the form object

✦ The After Update property of the option group control

As you've learned, these properties are found in the property sheet of the form. To enter the two macro calls, follow these steps:

1. From the Print Reports Macro window, select Window ⇨ 2 Print Reports Dialog: Form.

2. Make sure that the Property window is displayed. If not, click on the Properties button on the toolbar.

3. Display the form's Property window by clicking on the gray square next to the intersection of both form rulers.

4. Enter **Print Reports.Show List** in the On Open property of the Form property sheet.

5. Click on the Option Group control.

6. Enter **Print Reports.Show List** in the After Update property of the Option Group property sheet, as shown in Figure 31-39.

Test this macro by clicking on the Form View button on the toolbar. As you click on the first and second option buttons, the list box should become invisible. When you select the third option button, the list box should appear. Return to the Design window before continuing.

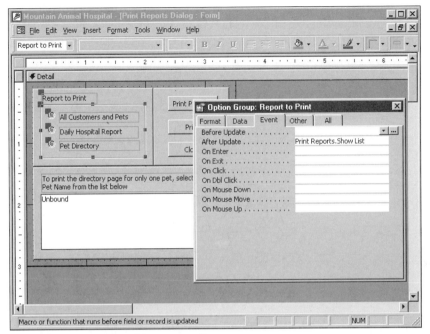

Figure 31-39: Entering the macro call.

Creating the Print Preview macro

The Print Preview macro is the next macro you need to create. Switch to the Macro window by selecting Window ➪ 3 Print Reports: Macro. This macro is fairly complicated, although it uses only three different macro commands. As you enter the macro commands, you may need to add more lines to the Macro window. Select Insert ➪ Row whenever you need to add a new row to the Macro window.

Note   You must first select a row to add a new row.

Figure 31-40 shows the completed Print Preview, Print, and Close macros in the Macro window. You can enter all the comments and create the first macro row by following these steps:

1. Type all the lines in the Comment column, as shown in Figure 31-40.

2. Move the cursor to the first line of the Print Preview macro row.

3. In the Action column, type (or select) **SetValue**.

4. Press F6 to move to the Item property of the Action Arguments pane and type **Visible**.

5. Move to the Expression box in the Action Arguments pane and type **No**.

Because no control is specified, it defaults to the form itself. This hides the entire Form window when the Print Reports macro is started.

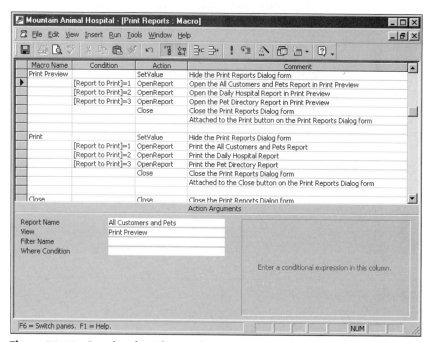

Figure 31-40: Creating the Print Preview macro.

The next three lines of the macro determine the actions to be taken when the Print Preview button is selected for each of the possible option button choices. The first two choices simply display the selected report in a print preview mode. The third choice displays a report by selecting the pet name chosen from the list box. To create the next row, follow these steps:

1. Move your cursor to the second row of the Print Preview macro.

2. In the Condition column, type **[Report to Print]=1**.

3. In the Action column, type (or select) **OpenReport**.

   The OpenReport macro command opens the report specified in the Action Arguments pane of the Macro window.

4. Press F6 to move to the Report Name box in the Action Arguments pane of the Print Preview macro and type **All Customers and Pets**.

5. Move to the View box in the Action Arguments pane and type **Print Preview**.

6. Press F6 to return to the Action column.

These action arguments specify to open the report named All Customers and Pets in a Print Preview window. The second Print row of the Print Preview macro is very similar to the first, except that you must reference the second option button being selected. To create the next row, follow these steps:

1. Move the cursor to the third row of the Print Preview macro.

2. In the Condition column, type **[Report to Print]=2**.

3. In the Action column, type (or select) **OpenReport**.

4. Press F6 to move to the Report Name box in the Action Arguments pane and type **Daily Hospital Report**.

5. Move to the View box in the Action Arguments pane and type **Print Preview**.

6. Press F6 to return to the Action column.

The third OpenReport row contains an extra action argument that the first two rows do not use. The Pet Directory report must use the results of the list box selection to determine whether to print the entire Pets Directory report or to print only the report for the specific pet selected. To create the next row, follow these steps:

1. Move the cursor to the fourth row of the Print Preview macro and insert a row.

2. In the Condition column, type **[Report to Print]=3**.

3. In the Action column, type (or select) **OpenReport**.

4. Press F6 to move to the Report Name box in the Action Arguments pane and type **Pet Directory**.

5. Move to the View box in the Action Arguments pane and type **Print Preview**.

6. Move to the Where Condition box and type the following:

=IIF(Forms![Print Reports Dialog]![Select Pet]Is Null,"","[Pet Name] = Forms![Print Reports Dialog]![Select Pet]")

The Where Condition specifies the condition when the pet name is selected. The condition has two parts. The first part of the IIf (Immediate IF) function handles the condition when no pet name is selected, and it forms the object hierarchy. The hierarchy is:

Object	Forms
Form name	Print Reports Dialog box
Control name	Select Pet (the list box)
Selection	Is Null

Note   Each of the hierarchy objects is separated by an exclamation mark (!).

If there is no selection, all the pet records are used. The second half of the IIf function is used when a pet name is selected. The second half of the function sets the value of Pet Name to the value chosen in the list box control.

Creating the Print macro

You can create all the macro code for the Print macro by copying each line from the Print Preview macro. Then substitute **Print** for Print Preview in the View box of the Action Arguments pane for each OpenReport action.

Creating the Close macro

The Close macro simply uses Close for the action. Enter **Form** for the Object Type and **Print Reports Dialog** for the Action Arguments object name.

Entering the Print Preview, Print, and Close macro calls

You use the command buttons to trigger an action. Each uses the On Click property. To enter the three macro calls, follow these steps:

1. From the Print Reports Macro window, select Window ⇨ 2 Form: Print Reports Dialog.

2. Make sure that the property sheet is displayed. If not, click on the Properties button on the toolbar.

3. Display the Print Preview command button property by clicking on the Print Preview button.

4. Enter **Print Reports.Print Preview** in the On Click property of the button's property sheet, as shown in Figure 31-41.

5. Display the Print command button property sheet by clicking on the Print button.

6. Enter **Print Reports.Print** in the On Click property of the button's property sheet.

7. Display the Close command button property sheet by clicking on the Close button.

8. Enter **Print Reports.Close** into the On Click property of the button's property sheet.

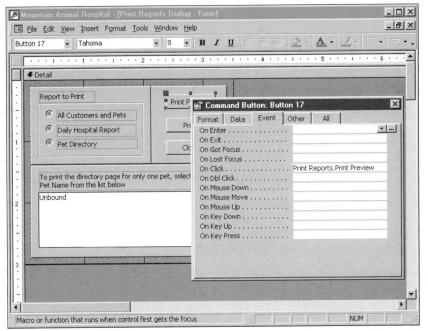

Figure 31-41: Entering the Print Preview macro call into the command button's property sheet.

Sizing the dialog box and changing form properties

The last step in creating a dialog box is to change the Form window properties and size and place the window. You need to set several form properties. The properties and their explanations are listed in Table 31-4.

Table 31-4
Properties for a Form Dialog Box

Property	Value	Description
Default View	Single Form	Displays the form as a single form; necessary for forms that take up less than half a page
Views Allowed	Form	User cannot switch into datasheet mode
Scroll Bars	Neither	(Scroll bars should be omitted in a dialog box)
Navigation Buttons	No	Record navigation buttons are not displayed
Record Selectors	No	Does not display standard record selectors at the bottom left of the form

Continued

Table 31-4 *(continued)*		
Property	**Value**	**Description**
Auto Resize	Yes	Automatically resizes the form when opened
Auto Center	Yes	Automatically centers the form when opened
Border Style	Dialog	Makes border nonsizable
Pop Up	Yes	Allows the form to be displayed on top of other windows as a pop-up dialog box
Modal	Yes	User must make a choice before leaving the dialog box

Set the Pop Up property to No if the dialog box will call any other windows. If this property is set to Yes, the dialog box is always displayed on top; you can't get to other windows without first closing the dialog box.

Using the Access 2000 Tab Control

Today, most serious Windows applications contain tabbed dialog boxes. Tabbed dialog boxes are very professional looking. They allow you to have many screens of data in a small area by grouping similar types of data and using tabs to navigate between the areas.

Access 2000 provides a built-in tab control similar to the one that has been in Visual Basic for many years.

Note   Access 2.0 and 95 do not contain a tab control, but Microsoft provided a free .OCX tab control, which was available on CompuServe for the past several years. There were several other methods for creating tabbed dialog boxes such as by using lines, rectangles, and either command buttons or label controls.

Creating a new form with the Access 2000 Tab control

The Access 2000 Tab control is available on the Form Design toolbar. This control is called a tab control because it looks like the tabs on a file folder when you use it. Figure 31-42 shows the Access 2000 Form Design window with the toolbar showing the tab control icon and a tab control already under construction on the design screen.

In this example, you create a Print Reports Dialog form that contains a tabbed dialog box that shows a larger view of the Pet Directory so that you can see more data.

You create a new tab control the way you create any Access control. You select the tab control as shown in Figure 31-42 and then draw a rectangle to indicate the size of the control.

The tab control contains pages. When you first place a new tab control, it initially contains two tab pages. Each tab you define creates a separate page. As you choose each tab in Design view, you see a different page. You can place other controls on each page of the tab control. The control can have many pages. You can have multiple rows of tabs, each with its own page. You can place new controls onto a page or copy and paste them from other forms or other pages. You cannot drag and drop between pages of a tab control, however. To change the active page for the tab control, click on the page you want; it will become active (even in design mode).

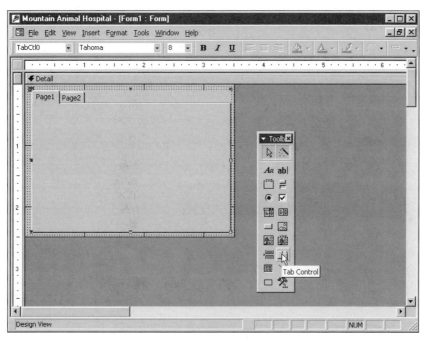

Figure 31-42: Creating an Access 2000 Tab control.

You insert new pages by selecting the Insert ➪ Tab Control Page option or by right-clicking on a tab and choosing the Insert command. The new page is inserted before the selected page. You delete pages by selecting a tab and pressing the Delete key or by choosing the Edit ➪ Delete menu option or by right-clicking on a tab and selecting the Delete command.

Caution   This deletes the active page and all the controls on it.

You can size the tab control but not individual pages. Individual pages don't have visual appearance properties — they get these from the tab control itself. You can click on the border of the tab control to select it. You can click directly on a page to select that page. As with an Access detail section, you cannot size the tab control smaller than the control in the rightmost part of the page.

Tip   You must move controls before resizing.

Tip   For this example, you can copy all the controls from the original Print Report Dialog except the List Box and its caption and paste them on Page1 of the tab control. Copy and paste the List Box control and its caption to Page2 of the tab control. Remember that you move between tab pages by clicking on the tab — even in Form Design view. When you are done, your tabbed dialog box should look like Figure 31-43.

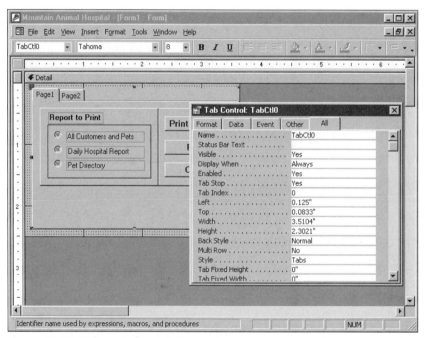

Figure 31-43: Tab control properties.

Access 2000 Tab control properties

Like any control, the tab control has a variety of properties. The tab control has a separate set of properties for the tab control itself as well as for each page of the tab control. Figure 31-43 shows the property window for the tab control itself. Notice that there is no Control Source property. The tab control is only a container for other controls. The form itself can be bound to a table or query, and each control placed on a tab page can be bound to a table field, but the tab control and its pages cannot be bound by themselves to a data source.

The tab control itself has many properties found in most controls, such as a Name, Status Bar Text, Visible, Enabled, Tab Stop, and the position and size properties. The tab control also has several unique properties. Notice the last four properties in the Property window. These properties are found only in tab control.

Working with multiple rows

The first unique property is Multi Row. This is either Yes or No. The default is No. When you change the value to Yes and you have more tabs than will fit in the width of the tab control, the tabs will jump to a new row (see Figure 31-44). If you make the tab control wider, the tab may return to a single row. You can create as many rows as you have vertical space. The tab control itself can be as wide as the form width allows. Figure 31-44 shows one-, two-, and three-row tab controls. The middle tab control has an uneven number of tabs on each row. This is perfectly acceptable; the tabs will grow to fill the available space. The tab control at the bottom was sized too small to fit the number of tabs and the Multi Row property was set to No. Navigation buttons appear to fill the space.

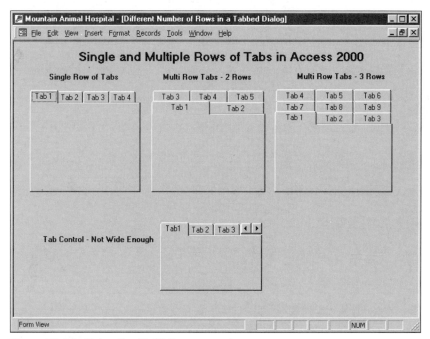

Figure 31-44: Using the Multi Row property.

Setting the height and width of the tabs

Two properties affect the size of the tabs in the tab control. These are the Tab Fixed Height and Tab Fixed Width properties. The default for both of these properties is 0. When the properties are set to 0, each tab is just wide enough and tall enough to accommodate its contents. If the properties are greater than 0, the tab will be the exact size specified.

The style of a Tab control

The next unique property is the Style property, which has three settings — Tabs, Buttons, and None — as shown in Figure 31-45. The Tabs setting is the default and creates the standard square tabs. Using the Buttons setting makes the tabs look like raised and sunken command buttons. The effect shown in Figure 31-45 looks more like a toolbar than a set of tabbed folders. You cannot see the rectangle, as with the Tabs setting. The third setting, None, removes the tabs from the tab control and leaves an empty gray area. When using this setting, the tab control can act like a multipage form. Using this method provides more control than a standard multipage form because you don't have to worry about navigation from one page to the next.

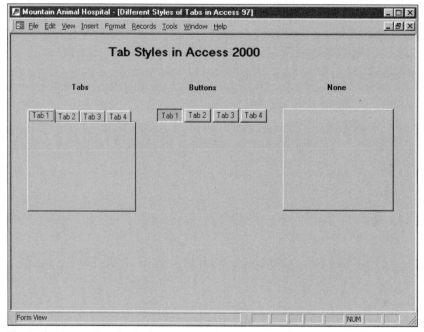

Figure 31-45: Using the Style property.

Changing the page order

Another feature of the tab control is the ability to change the order of the pages (tabs) in the same way that the tab order of the controls on the form can be changed. Figure 31-46 shows the Page Order dialog box. It lists the text on each tab and lets you use the Move Up and Move Down buttons to rearrange the pages on the tab control.

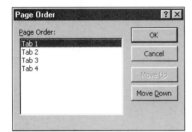

Figure 31-46: Changing the page order.

Changing the tab order for controls on a tab page

When you select a form and choose View ⇨ Tab Order, the Tab Order dialog box shows only the name of the tab control. The controls inside the tab control do not show in this dialog box.

To set the tab order for controls within a particular page of a tab control, choose the Tab Order command from the tab control's right-click menu, or select a control on the tab page then select View ⇨ Tab Order. You must set the tab order for each page individually.

Tabbing out of the last control inside a tab control page brings you to the next control in the tab order for the form itself. You cannot jump between pages.

Adding pictures to the tab control

A picture can be added to each tab using the page properties for the tab control. You can display the page properties for a particular tab by selecting the tab on the tab control and choosing View ⇨ Properties. To add a picture to the tab, use the Picture property just as you would for a command button, toggle button, image control, or unbound OLE object. When you specify a caption and a picture for a tab, the picture displays to the left of the tab caption.

You can type the full path and name of the bitmap or icon file or use the Access 2000 Picture Builder to select a picture. Figure 31-47 illustrates adding a picture to a tab in the Print Reports Tabbed Dialog form. In the figure, the picture of a printer displays on Page 1.

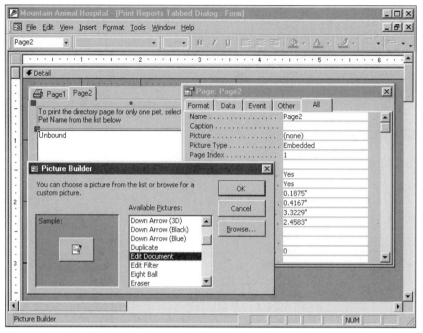

Figure 31-47: Adding a picture to a tab.

Summary

In this chapter, you learned to use Access forms to create switchboards and dialog boxes. You also learned to create your own custom menu. These points were discussed:

✦ Switchboards are forms that usually contain command buttons.

✦ Switchboards are used as menus to help you navigate within your system.

✦ You can create command buttons by using the Toolbox, by dragging a macro onto a form, or by using the Command Button Wizard.

✦ Command buttons trigger macros through several properties.

✦ The best way to create multiple command buttons that are all the same size is by duplicating the first button that you created.

✦ You link a command button to a macro by entering the macro name in the On Click property.

✦ You can create macro actions by entering them into the Macro window, selecting them from the Action pull-down menu, or dragging a form or report into a macro's Action cell.

✦ You can have a command button display a picture instead of a text caption by entering the bitmap name into the command button's Picture property or by using the Picture Builder.

✦ The Access View ⇨ Toolbars ⇨ Customize dialog box helps you create a menu bar, toolbar, or shortcut menu.

✦ Each menu item can contain a submenu. You can specify bar separators and hot keys in a submenu.

✦ You can activate a custom bar menu by entering a menu bar name in the Menu Bar property of a form or report.

✦ You can create a macro that runs automatically when you open a database by naming the macro AutoExec or by using the Startup Properties window.

✦ You can bypass a macro that runs automatically by holding down the Shift key when you open the Database window.

✦ You can create control tips that work like tool tips but can be used with any control.

✦ A dialog box is nothing more than a form that is used as a pop-up window; usually it contains various controls, such as option buttons, list boxes, and command buttons.

✦ Access 2000 provides a tab control that can be used for multipage forms.

✦ You can set the Access 2000 Tab control's style, size, and number of rows.

✦ You can add pictures to a tab control tab.

✦ A dialog box's pop-up property should be set to No if you are going to open any other windows from the dialog box.

As the last chapter demonstrated, menus, toolbars, and dialog boxes provide powerful uses to navigate your application. In the next chapter, you learn about Access 2000 and the Internet.

✦   ✦   ✦

Using Data Access Pages, Intranets, and the Internet

The Internet, and particularly the World Wide Web, has become an important part of all businesses today. Whether you simply use the Internet to search for information or are part of a vast corporate intranet, there is a need to be able to use Microsoft Acccess to store and disseminate the data that is moved across the network wire.

Note

An *intranet* is simply the use of Internet technologies within an organization (or company). Intranets help in cutting costs and offer fast and easy accessibility to day-to-day information. It offers some features that are often lacking in Internet technology — speed, security, and control. It is a network (or networks), that works on a local or wide area network that that uses TCP/IP, HTTP, and other Internet protocols, and looks like a private version of the Internet. You can use an intranet much as you use the World Wide Web to store information on home pages and Websites. One of the leading methods of creating World Wide Web pages is through use of the HyperText Markup Language (HTML) language. This is the de facto language of the Web. Web browsers (like Amaya, Internet Explorer, Netscape, Opera, and others) read and interpret this HTML code to display the text and graphics on the screen.

Access 2000 contains many new features that allow you to store data found on the Internet in your database container in standard Access tables. You can also create a table, form, or report in Access 2000 and save it as an HTML-based table that can be used in any Website. In addition, Access 2000 has a new feature known as Data Access Pages. These are a special type of Web page. They allow you to view and work with data using Microsoft's Internet Explorer browser, which gives you access to live and stagnant information across an intranet or the Internet itself. This data can be stored in a Microsoft Access database or a Microsoft SQL Server database.

What Is HTML?

If you're unfamiliar with HTML, you should make this topic your next learning experience. Web pages are formatted using a special language called HyperText Markup Language (HTML). With HTML you can create a Web page containing text, pictures, or links to other Web pages. Each Web page is identified by its address, which is called a Uniform Resource Locator (URL), for example, `http://www.databasecreations.com` or `http://www` `.geocities.com/Tokyo/Towers/4385/`. Using Access 2000's Internet tools, you can translate Access 2000 objects and data into HTML-compatible format.

Using the Web Toolbar with Access 2000

Figure 32-1 shows the Access 2000 database container with the Web toolbar, which can be turned on by right-clicking on the toolbar and selecting Web or by selecting View ⇨ Toolbars ⇨ Web from any menu. After the Web toolbar is displayed, you can use it to access Websites on the Internet or on your local intranet. When you use the Web toolbar, you launch the default Web browser on your system.

Figure 32-1: The Web toolbar on the Access database container screen.

Tip

You can also activate/deactivate the Web toolbar at anytime by right-clicking on any active toolbar and selecting the Web toolbar from the popup menu. To take advantage of the Internet features of the Web toolbar in Access 2000, you need the Microsoft Internet Explorer 5.0 Web browser, a modem, and an Internet connection or other network connection to access the Internet. Once active, the Web toolbar is available at all times. It is normally the last toolbar displayed in the toolbar area of Access 2000. Like other tool bars it can also be undocked as in Figure 32-2. Once undocked you can place it anywhere along the bottom, right, or left side of the Access 2000 window, or simply let it float on the Windows surface, as in Figure 32-2.

Figure 32-2: The Web toolbar undocked from the toolbar area of Access 2000.

Once the Web toolbar is active it is available from any View mode of Access. This includes Datasheet, View, and Design. You can use it to quickly activate your Web browser (IE 5.0) and perform local (intranet) and remote (Internet) Web operations. Figure 32-3 shows Internet Explorer 5.0 active in Access 2000 with a Home Page displayed.

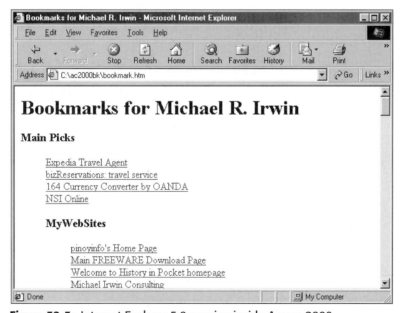

Figure 32-3: Internet Explorer 5.0 running inside Access 2000.

It appears that you are running IE 5.0 independently, but you are actually running the Web browser inside Access 2000. If you click the Back button or press Alt + Right Arrow (→), you will be returned to the Access database that you were working with (in the Access 2000 window).

Tip   You can use the Back and Forward buttons to move back and forth through the browser pages of IE 5.0 and the Access database that you are working with.

The Web toolbar

The Web toolbar contains several buttons specific to working with the Web, as shown in Figure 32-4.

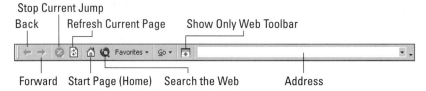

Figure 32-4: The Web toolbar.

The Favorites and Go buttons are actually pull-down menus of additional actions that are Web oriented. The Favorites choice displays a series of choices specific to your environment. The Go menu has several choices that you may use:

Open …	Open an Internet address
Back	Go back to the page that called the current page
Forward	Go forward to previously viewed page
Start Page	Go to the start page (you specify it below)
Search the Web	Go to the search page (you specify it below)
Set Start Page …	Specify a new default start page
Set Search Page …	Specify a new default search page
(Current open database)	Go back to the current open database

Several of these choices are also available via the buttons on the Web toolbar. The two that you may want to use from the Go menu because they are not accessible via the toolbar buttons are Set Start Page and Set Search Page.

You can set the default home page by using the Set Start Page... option from the Go menu on the Web toolbar. In Figure 32-1, the initial URL is `http://www.databasecreations.com`, theDatabase Creations home page.

Tip   When specifying a home page, you are not limited to specifying a Web-based address (such as `http://www.databasecreations.com`). You can also specify a local file, such as your bookmark or favorites file that the browser uses.

Because this book is about Access 2000 and not specifically about the Internet, it is assumed that you own a browser and have some experience visiting Websites on the World Wide Web. This chapter uses Microsoft's Internet Explorer 5.0 for its discussion.

Data Access Pages

In the simplest sense, Data Access Pages are a combination of forms and reports for the Web.

New Feature   Data Access Pages are new to Access 2000. They are HTML documents that are attached directly to data in the database. They can be attached to a single table or several tables via a query. They can be used like Access forms except that Data Access Pages are designed to run in the Internet Explorer 5.x Web browser.

In the simplest sense, Data Access Pages are a combination of forms and reports for the Web. In Access 97, you could create a form or report and publish it to an HTML document viewable on the Web. Access 2000 still lets you create stagnant data pages from your tables, queries, forms, and reports (discussed later in this chapter), but Data Access Pages remove this interim step because they are HTML documents from the start.

Unlike Access 2000 forms, Data Access Pages are stored in the Windows file system, rather than in the Access database or project.

Once created you can use these Data Access Pages directly in an Access program or within the Web browser. These files are specifically designed for Internet Explorer 5.0 and make use of dynamic HTML and XML technology.

Note   At the time of this writing, Data Access Pages only work with Microsoft's Internet Explorer 5.0 or greater.

Tip   Access 2000 can open any existing HTML file in the Data Access Page designer. Once a page is opened in Access, you can add data-bound fields to the page easily and quickly. To build a Data Access Page, users work with the new Data Access Page designer.

Data Access Pages are more than simple forms for the Internet. They offer a totally new way for the user to interact with live data. Using the browser, you can display summarized data, such as Sales By Product or Sales By Month. With a mouse click you can also display the detail information for each summarized item, for example, individual sales by invoice. The tools to summarize, expand, sort, and filter the data are available in the browser itself. These pages let you work with dynamic information; that is, your browser can access live data from within your databases in an interactive fashion.

Working with dynamic and static views of Web-based data

When working with data in Web-based files, you can access the data statically (data that never changes) or dynamically (data that can change). If the data does not change, the HTML file can display the information statically. However, if the data that is to be displayed in the HTML page changes often, you will want to display the data dynamically.

How Web applications use static HTML pages

Web applications, specifically browsers, use static HTML pages to display data that was originally in a database table or series of tables. It is static; that is, nonchanging. Once the HTML page is created, the data in the page will not change. The data, itself, is a physical part of the page. It is actually embedded in the page.

Access 2000 lets you create a static Web page from any table or query by exporting the datasheet results to an HTML page.

To create a static Web page from any table or query, simply select the table or query object that you want to export from within the correct database container (table or query object type). Once the table or query object is highlighted, select File ➪ Export... from the menu. An alternate method is to right mouse click on the object (table or query name) and select Export... from the popup menu. This activates an Export As dialog box that allows you to specify a name for the new file and how you want to save it.

For example, Figure 32-5 shows the exporting of the Customer table to an HTML page. It shows the active Export [table or query name] As dialog box.

As Figure 32-5 shows, you can specify a specific format for the HTML page that will be created. To specify a specific format, simply click the Save formatted checkbox and when you click the Save button, you will be given another dialog box, the HTML Output options, as in Figure 32-6. You can specify a specific HTML template format file by typing in a name or by clicking the browse button and selecting from existing HTML templates.

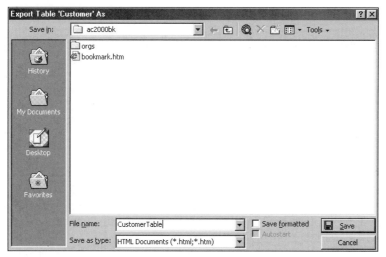

Figure 32-5: Exporting a table to an HTML page.

Figure 32-6: Specifying an HTML template format file for saving a table in HTML format.

What are HTML template files?

An HTML template file is a file that you create in HTML and that is used by Access to enhance the appearance and navigation of your HTML-generated files. It can be used to include a company logo in the header section, a background image in the body section, and your own navigation buttons in the footer section of an HTML report.

It is a text file that includes HTML tags and tokens that are unique to Access 2000. The tokens are used to tell Access where to insert output and other information in the generated HTML files.

If you specify an HTML template file in the dialog box, Access 2000 merges the HTML template file with the .html, .asp, and .htx output files, replacing the tokens with the appropriate items.

How Web applications use dynamic HTML pages

In contrast to static pages, dynamic HTML pages support viewing and working with live, up-to-date data. There are several ways that a Web application can display and work with live data from databases. Traditionally, this was accomplished using server-side technology. Methods such as CGI (Common Gateway Interface) and Microsoft's ASP (Active Server Pages) do the job. These are programming methodologies that allow you write code and store it at the server level where the database application resides. Then, when the user wants to look at live data, the user sends a CGI script or ASP query to the database sitting on the Web server. The server takes this request and processes it, returning the requested data to the end user.

Previously, the data being sent back was up-to-date, but not live, and it was stored in an HTML file that your browser displayed. This has changed with Access 2000, which uses ASP technology tied together with Microsoft's implementation of the new Extensible Markup Language (XML).

Working with dynamic HTML

Dynamic HTML is used when you need to access data that changes frequently and you or your users need to enter and retrieve live data from an Access database using a Web form.

Access 2000 lets you create dynamic HTML pages from within Access and display them in Access 2000 or Microsoft's Internet Explorer 5.0.

These pages can be created to display and work with your data in either datasheet or form mode.

Once created, you can add new records, modify existing information stored in the tables, or simply view records in the Access tables from the Web. You can even move between records in the table, from within the browser, using ActiveX controls that are on the dynamic HTML Web form.

Working with the Data Access Page

Data Access Pages can be used like any another Access object — select them from the Pages Object container and use them. Unlike other Access objects, however, they can also be used independent of Access with Microsoft's Internet Explorer 5.0 Web browser.

It is easy to create a new Data Access Page. You can build one from scratch, using the Page Designer, or use a Wizard to create new page.

New Feature   Access 2000 has added the new object type Pages to the Object Bar of the database container. Figure 32-7 shows the Pages Object type in the database container.

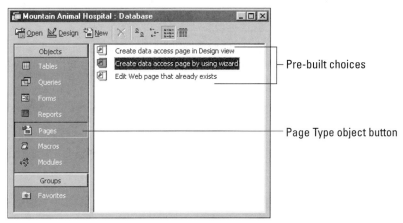

Figure 32-7: The Pages object of a database container.

Figure 32-7 shows the three choices available in the Page container — two let you create a new Data Access Page (Create data access page … in design view / by using Wizard), one lets you edit an existing page (Edit Web page that already exists).

Remember that a Data Access Page is simply an Access form or report that starts as an HTML document that is immediately usable in a Web browser. Access 2000 utilizes Microsoft Internet Explorer 5.0 technology (in edit mode) as the actual design environment to create the form within Access.

Creating a Data Access Page is very similar to creating a form or report in Access. You use the Data Access Page design mode to place ActiveX controls on the page. When you have finished designing the page, the page becomes a fully functional HTML document.

Creating a Data Access Page using the Page Wizard

The easiest way to create a Data Access Page is to let the Data Access Page Wizard help you. For instance, to create a new Data Access Page for the Customers table, follow these steps:

1. Select the Pages object type from the Object Bar of the database.

2. Double-click on Create data access page by using a Wizard.

3. Select the Customer table from the Tables/Queries drop-down combo box. Figure 32-8 shows the new Page Wizard.

4. Select Type of Customer, Customer Name, City, State, and Phone Number from the Available fields list box. You can select them by highlighting each field and pressing the right arrow button (>) or by double clicking the field name.

5. Click Next> to move to the next page.

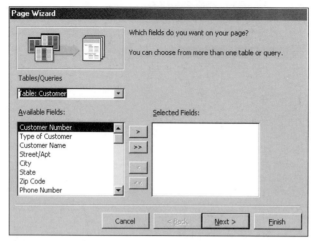

Figure 32-8: The first page of the Page Wizard.

6. Select Type of Customer for a grouping level, by double clicking the field name. Figure 32-9 shows the grouping level set.

7. Click Next> to move to the next page.

8. Specify Customer name for the sort order on this page.

9. Click Next> to move to the next page.

10. Specify "Customer Info" as the title for the new page.

11. While still on this page, choose the Open the page radio button.

12. Click Finish and be patient. The Wizard performs many steps to create the new Data Access Page.

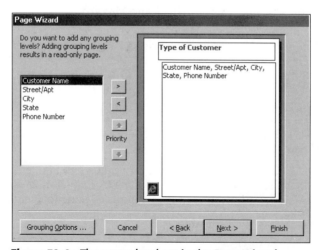

Figure 32-9: The group level set in the Page Wizard.

Access 2000 will create a new Web document, giving it a title name of Customer Info (on the title bar when the HTML document is open). It has not saved the file to disk yet.

Figure 32-10 shows the newly created Customer Data Access Page running in Access. As Figure 32-10 shows, only the Customer Type is initially displayed on the form. When the page is initially created (using the Wizard), the expand button (plus (+) sign) displays next to Group of Customer-Type of Customer. When you click the plus (+) sign, it is replaced by the collapse button (minus (–) sign) and the detail information for each customer displays below the Type of Customer heading.

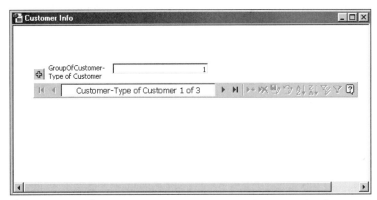

Figure 32-10: The new Customer Data Access Page running in Access 2000.

The form in Figure 32-10 also has a record management control (ActiveX) along the bottom of the page. If you click the expand button alongside of the Customer type, you will see two displayed — one for the type of customer level and the other for all the records that match that customer type. These are used to perform several functions, including:

✦ Moving between records in the page

✦ Adding new records to the underlying table(s)

✦ Deleting records

✦ Sorting records by a specific field

✦ Setting filter conditions for viewing records

In addition to these record management controls, the page also has an expand control (ActiveX) next to the Type of Customer text (top-left corner). It is the small box that displays either a plus (+) sign or a negative (–) sign. It is used to expand and close a level of information in the page. In this case, it is used to display individual customer information (level 2) when the negative sign is showing, or only the Customer type information when the positive sign is showing (as in Figure 32-10). When you run the form, clicking the expand control toggles between expanded (+) and closed (–) modes.

You can change the default action of this expand control before saving your new Data Access Page by making a change to the page in the design view window. Follow these steps to change the default behavior of the expand control:

1. Click the View button (first button on the toolbar) or select View ⇨ Design View from the menu.

2. Click the Sorting and Grouping button (the seventh button from the right side of toolbar) or select View ⇨ Sorting and Grouping on the menu. Figure 32-11 shows the Sorting and Grouping dialog box.

3. With the Customer-Type of Customer Group Record Source selected (the first choice in the top pane should have a small right-pointing triangle in the row selector column as in Figure 32-11), change the Expanded By Default Group property in the lower pane to Yes. Figure 32-12 shows setting this property.

4. Close the Sorting and Grouping dialog box. At this point you can make any other cosmetic changes that you would like to the Data Access Page. Perhaps you may want to change the text title for the Type of Customer, or move some fields around.

5. Click the View button to see the changes. Figure 32-13 shows the new Data Access Page with the expand button's default action changed to open (Yes).

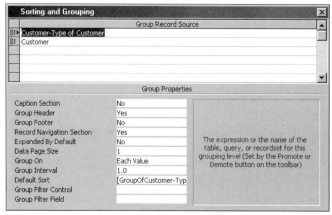

Figure 32-11: The Sorting and Grouping dialog box.

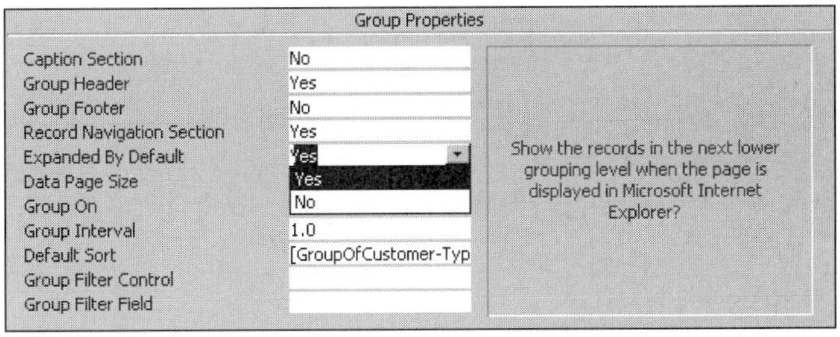

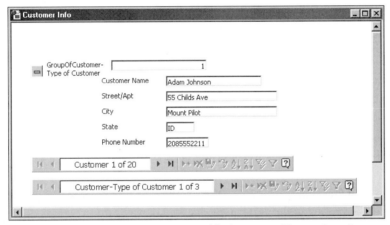

Figure 32-12: The Expanded By Default property changed to Yes.

Figure 32-13: The Data Access Page with the expand button's action set to open (Yes).

With the changes made to your Data Access Page the last thing to do is save it to an HTML document. To save your work, select File ➪ Save (or press Ctrl-S, or close the window and answer yes to the save changes dialog box). You can save it to a file named Customer Info — Microsoft Access will add the extension .htm to the file. Access will store a pointer to the HTML file in the Pages container of the database — not the file itself.

The HTML file is not stored in the database container. Rather, it is stored in the Windows file system in a subdirectory. Microsoft's Internet Explorer 5.x can be used to display and work with these files. Figure 32-14 shows the HTML file for the Customer Data Access Page in IE 5.0.

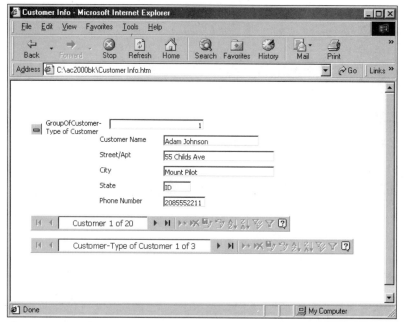

Figure 32-14: The Customer Info.html page running in IE 5.0.

As Figure 32-14 shows, you can use the ActiveX controls to move through the records of the Customer table. You can even add a new record or delete an existing record.

Creating a Data Access Page using Page Design View

Although the easiest way to create a Data Access Page is to use the Page Wizard, it is also good to know how to build a page using the Design View tools. For example, follow these steps to create a new Data Access Page for the Customers and Pets table:

1. Select the Page object type from the Object Bar of the database.

2. Double-click on Create data access page in Design View.

3. Click in the area labeled Click here and type title text then type **Customer and Pets Information**.

4. Click in the area labeled Unbound section to select it. Notice that the area has been selected.

5. With the Unbound section selected in the Design View, select View ⇨ Field List... from the menu (or click the Field List button).

6. Double-click the Tables folder to show all the table names in the list.

7. Double-click the Customer table to show all the fields from this table. Figure 32-15 shows what your screen should now look like.

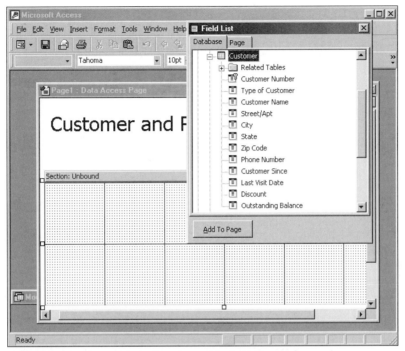

Figure 32-15: The Page Design view with Field List open.

8. Select Type of Customer field and drag it to the section on the page labeled Section: Unbound. A simple bound Input Box is created and the section is renamed Header: Customer. It also added a Navigation section below the Header section for the Customer table and placed the Record management toolbar object within it.

9. Select Customer Name, City, and State fields, dropping them on the same area — Header: Customer. (You can move them around and resize them if you want to make the document aesthetically pleasing.)

10. Click the related tables Folder in the Field List to expand the folder.

11. Grab the Pets table (the whole thing — don't worry about drilling in to see the details) and drag it onto the Customer Section. A dialog box will pop up with two choices (Individual Controls and Pivot Table List).

12. Select Pivot Table List from the Layout Wizard dialog box and press OK. Your page should now look like Figure 32-16. (Figure 32-16 shows the final layout with many of the fields resized before continuing.)

13. Save your work and name it **Customer and Pets.html**.

Once your data is saved, you can use it in Access or IE 5.0. Figure 32-17 shows the page you just created running in IE 5.0.

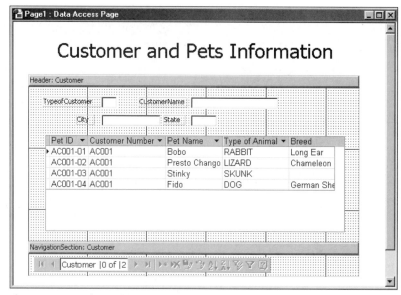

Figure 32-16: The Page Design view with both tables placed on the form.

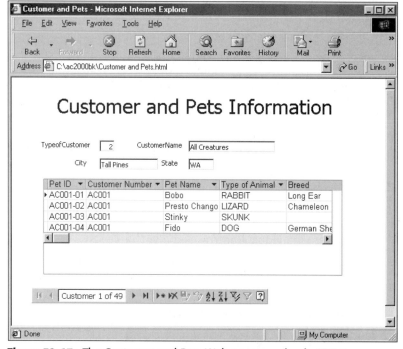

Figure 32-17: The Customer and Pets Web page running in IE 5.0.

Editing a Web page that already exists

You can bring any preexisting HTML document into Access by selecting the third choice in the Pages object container — Edit Web page that already exists.

When you select this option, a Locate Web Page dialog box is displayed so that you can select and open the Web page (*.htm, *.html) file that you want to link to in Access 2000. Once the HTML document is selected, Access displays it. When you close the file, you will receive a dialog box offering to save the changes made to the design of the Data Access Page. If you answer yes, the file is saved and a pointer to the file is stored in the Pages object container for use later.

Note   If the HTML document that you are editing does not contain any Extended Markup Language (*.xml) code, then the Data Access Page will display stagnant data only. If it contains Microsoft's Internet Explorer 5.x-understandable XML code, then it will create a table that will display dynamic Web pages.

Exporting Tables, Queries, Forms, and Reports to HTML Format

The Data Access Page Wizard creates Web pages in Access and the dynamic HTML files that are necessary to create interactive Web pages using live Access data. Because Data Access Pages use live data, they can only use tables and queries as a data source. Sometimes, however, you may want to output information from an Access form or report. Using the File Export option, you can export individual tables, forms, reports, and datasheets to static HTML format. Access 2000 creates one Web page for each report page, datasheet, and form that you export. Exporting objects to HTML format is useful for creating a simple Web application, verifying the format and appearance of an object's output, or adding files to existing Web applications.

When you export an object, you can also specify an HTML template file along with your output files. An HTML template contains HTML tags and special tokens unique to Access 2000 that enhance the appearance, consistency, and navigation of your Web pages.

Exporting a datasheet to static HTML format

If you want to export a datasheet to static HTML format, follow these steps:

1. In the Database window, click the name of the table, query, or form that you want to export, and then on the File menu, click Export.

2. In the Export dialog box, in the Save as type box, click on HTML Documents (*.html;*.htm), as shown in Figure 32-18.

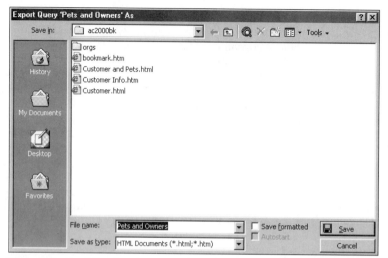

Figure 32-18: Selecting the HTML format in the Export dialog box.

3. If you want to save the file to a different folder or drive, click the arrow to the right of the Save in combo box and select the drive or folder to export to.

4. In the File name box, enter the filename.

5. Select Save Formatted if you want to save the datasheet using a specific HTML template file to enhance the appearance of the Web page. If you select Save Formatted, Access automatically displays the HTML output options dialog box, which lets you specify an HTML template to use for saving the document. Select AutoStart if you want to display the results in your default Web browser.

6. Click Save.

If you selected Save Formatted in Step 5, the HTML Output Options dialog box is displayed. You can specify an HTML template to use. The HTML file is based on the recordset behind the datasheet, including any current Order By or Filter property settings. If the datasheet contains a parameter query, Access 2000 first prompts you for the parameter values and then exports the results. Values from most fields (except OLE objects and hyperlink fields) are output as strings and are formatted similarly to how they appear in the datasheet, including defined Format or Input Mask properties. Fields with a Hyperlink data type (see the section "Hyperlinks Connect Your Application to the Internet," later in this chapter) are output as HTML links using <A HREF> tags. All unformatted data types, except Text and Memo, are saved with right alignment as the default. Text and Memo fields are saved with left alignment by default.

The layout of the HTML page simulates the page orientation and margins that are set for the datasheet. To change these settings, display the datasheet and use the Page Setup command on the File menu before you export it. A large datasheet may take a long time to output and to display through a Web browser. Consider reducing the size of the datasheet, dividing the datasheet into smaller datasheets by using criteria such as a date field, or using a report or form to view the data.

Figure 32-19 shows the first portion of the HTML that's generated when exporting the data from the Pets and Owners query. Notice that the figure shows the data for part of the first record in the file.

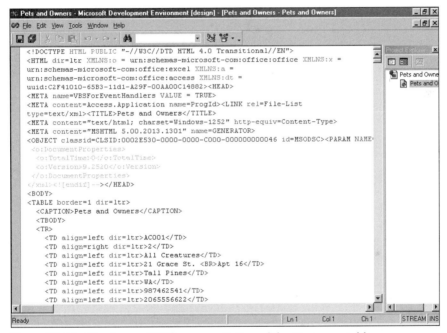

Figure 32-19: Viewing an HTML representation of the Customer table.

Tip

You can view the HTML source code of any HTML document being viewed in Access 2000 by selecting View ➪ HTML source from the file menu while the HTML document is active.

Exporting a datasheet to dynamic HTML format

The process of exporting a dynamic HTML format is essentially the same as exporting a static format except that you choose the Microsoft IIS 1-2 (*.htx; *.idc) or Microsoft ActiveX Server (*.asp) server choice instead of the HTML Documents choice.

Note   Exporting to an ActiveX Server or IIS 1-2 document is not the same as an Active Data page. These options create both an HTML document and an appropriate related file for access by the corresponding server (an IIS or an ASP server).

To export a datasheet to dynamic HTML format, follow these steps:

1. In the Database window, click on the name of the table, query, or form that you want to export, and then click Export on the File menu.

2. In the Export dialog box, in the Save as type box, click Microsoft IIS 1-2 (*.htx;*.idc) or Microsoft ActiveX Server (*.asp), depending on which dynamic HTML format you want to use.

3. If you want to save to a different drive or directory, click the down arrow at the right of the Save in combo box and select the drive or folder to export to.

4. In the File name box, enter the filename.

5. Click Save.

6. In the HTML Output Options dialog box, specify an HTML template to use.

You must specify the machine or file data source name that you will use on the World Wide Web server, and, if required, a username and password to open the database. If you are exporting to ASP file format, you must enter the full destination URL for the ASP file's directory (folder). For example, if you are storing the ASP files in the \SalesApp folder on the \\Pubweb server, type **http://pubweb//salesapp/**. Figure 32-20 shows the Microsoft Active Server Pages Output Options dialog box that is displayed if you attempt to save an object as an ASP type.

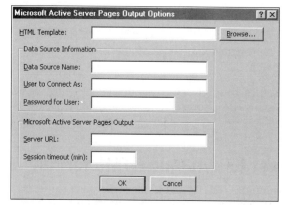

Figure 32-20: The ASP Output Options dialog box for creating a dynamic ASP file (export to ASP type).

If a form is in Datasheet view or its Default View property is set to Datasheet when you export to ASP file format, Access 2000 outputs the form as a datasheet. If the form is in Form or Design view, or its Default View property is set to Single Form or Continuous Forms, Access 2000 outputs the form as a form. The layout of the HTML page simulates the page orientation and margins that are set for the datasheet. To change these settings, display the datasheet and then use the Page Setup command on the File menu before you export it.

Exporting a report to static HTML format

Reports are always output in a static file format type. To export a report, follow these steps:

1. In the Database window, click on the name of the report that you want to export, and then click Export on the File menu (or right mouse click and select Export…).

2. In the Export dialog box, in the Save as type box, click on HTML Documents (*.html; *.htm).

3. Change the drive or folder to export to, if desired, by clicking on the Save in: combo box.

4. In the File name box, enter the filename.

5. Select AutoStart to display the results in your default Web browser.

6. Click Save.

   In the HTML Output Options dialog box, you can specify an HTML template to use. If you do not specify an HTML template file containing navigation tokens, Microsoft Access 2000 provides a default navigation scheme. If the HTML output is from a report, the default scheme includes adding page number and several text navigation links (first, previous, next, and last) at the bottom of each page. If it the HTML output is from any other type of Access object, a simple table is created. If you selected AutoStart in Step 5, only the first page is displayed and the remaining pages are accessible by using the attached navigation links at the bottom of the page. Figure 32-21 shows the bottom of page one (of four pages) of the "Customers By State (3 Snaking Columns)" report.

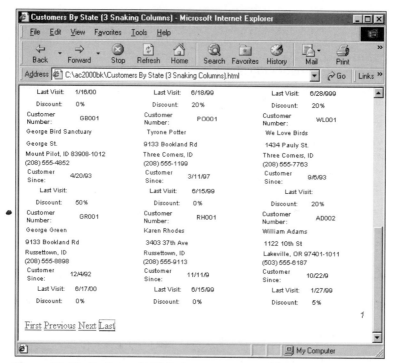

Figure 32-21: Bottom of HTML document created from a report using the Export... choice. It displays the text navigation bars that were added to each page.

The HTML file is based on the recordset behind the report, including any current Order By or Filter property settings. If the datasheet contains a parameter query, Access 2000 first prompts you for the parameter values and then exports the results. Most controls and features of a report, including subreports, are supported except for these: lines, rectangles, OLE objects, and subforms. However, you can use an HTML template file to include report header and footer images in your output files.

The output files simulate as closely as possible the appearance of the report by creating the appropriate HTML tags to retain attributes such as color, font, and alignment. Fields with a Hyperlink data type are output as HTML links using <A HREF> tags. Access outputs a report, unlike a datasheet, as multiple HTML files, one file per printed page, using the object name and an appendix to create each filename; for example, Products.htm, ProductsPage1.htm, ProductsPage2.htm, and so on. The layout of the HTML pages simulates the page orientation and margins set for the report. To change these settings, display the report in Print or Layout Preview, and then use the File menu's Page Setup command before you export it.

You cannot output a report to dynamic HTML format.

Exporting a form to dynamic HTML format

You can design an Access 2000 form for use in a World Wide Web application and then save it to dynamic HTML format. Several types of forms can be outputted: view forms (to display records), switchboard forms (to act as the home page or to navigate to related pages, such as all reports), and data-entry forms (to add, update, and delete records).

To export a form in dynamic HTML format, follow these steps:

1. In the Database window, click on the name of the form that you want to export, and then click Export on the File menu.

2. In the Export dialog box, in the Save as type box, click Microsoft IIS 1-2 (*.htx; *.idc) or Microsoft ActiveX Server (*.asp), depending on which dynamic HTML format you want to use.

3. Change the drive or folder to export to, if desired, by clicking the Save in: combo box.

4. In the File name box, enter the filename.

5. Click Save.

You must specify the machine or file data source name that you will use on the Web server, and, if required, a username and password to open the database. If you are exporting to ASP file format, you must enter the full destination URL for the ASP file's directory (folder). For example, if you are storing the ASP files in the \SalesApp folder on the \\Pubweb server, type **http://pubweb//salesapp/**.

Access 2000 outputs a continuous form as a single form. Access outputs most controls as ActiveX controls but ignores any Visual Basic code behind them. The output files simulate as closely as possible the appearance of the form by creating the appropriate HTML tags to retain attributes such as color, font, and alignment. However, all data types are output unformatted, and all Format and InputMask properties are ignored.

If a form is in Datasheet view or its Default View property is set to Datasheet when you export to ASP file format, then Access outputs the form as a datasheet. If the form is in Form or Design view, or its Default View property is set to Single Form or Continuous Forms, then Access outputs the form as a form.

HTML template files

You can create an HTML template file that contains some specific code (called *tokens*) that is specific to Microsoft Access. These tokens can be used to input specific information into the final HTML document that is created when you export a table, query, form, or report.

There are eight specific template tokens that Access recognizes:

✦ <!—AccessTemplate_Title—>, which is used to place the name of the object in the Browser title bar.

✦ <!—AccessTemplate_Body—>, which is used to designate where the output of the object is to be placed in the <body> of the HTML document.

✦ <!—AccessTemplate_FirstPage—>, which is used to create an HTML anchor tag (<a href= ...>) in the document to point to the first page of a multipage document.

✦ <!—AccessTemplate_NextPage—>, which is used to create an HTML anchor tag (<a href= ...>) in the document to point to the next page, after the current page, of a multipage document.

✦ <!—AccessTemplate_PreviousPage—>, which is used to create an HTML anchor tag (<a href= ...>) in the document to point to the previous page, after the current page, of a multipage document.

✦ <!—AccessTemplate_LastPage—>, which is used to create an HTML anchor tag (<a href= ...>) in the document to point to the last page of a multipage document.

✦ <!—AccessTemplate_PageNumber—>, which is used to display the current page number of the document.

Each of these tokens can be placed in an HTML document that can be used as a template to tell Access 2000 how to format or display the object being exported to HTML code. It lets you enhance the appearance and navigation of your static HTML documents. For instance, you can add images, backgrounds, specify foreground and background colors, and so on to the document.

Figure 32-22 shows a simple HTML template file named MyTemp01.htm.

As Figure 32-22 shows, there are several HTML Access tokens placed in the HTML code of the template. It uses the token <!—AccessTemplate_Title—> to display the title of the table in the Browser when the HTML document is created. It also uses two of the navigational tokens – <!—AccessTemplate_FirstPage—> and <!—AccessTemplate_LastPage—> to place links for multipage documents.

Once the template file is created, you can use it by specifying it in the HTML Output options dialog box that appears when you specify Save Formatted in the Export dialog box. Figure 32-23 shows the top part of an HTML document that is running in Internet Explorer 5.x and that was Exported from a query created on the customer table. It used the HTML template file MyTemp01.htm to create the HTML document.

Notice that the exported HTML code shows a graphic and two navigational links (TopPage and LastPage). It also shows the name of the query object (Customer List) that was used for the HTML export.

```
<html>
 <head>
   <title><!--AccessTemplate_Title--></title>
 </head>
 <body bgcolor=cyan>
   <img src = "sunnwatr.jpg" height =50 width =80>
   <br>
      
   <a href = "<!--AccessTemplate_FirstPage-->">TopPage</a>
   <a href = "<!--AccessTemplate_LastPage-->">LastPage</a>
   <p>
   <!--AccessTemplate_Body-->
 </body>
 <p>
 <img src = "sunnwatr.jpg" height =50 width =80>
 <br>
    
 <a href = "<!--AccessTemplate_FirstPage-->">TopPage</a>
 <a href = "<!--AccessTemplate_LastPage-->">LastPage</a>
</html>
```

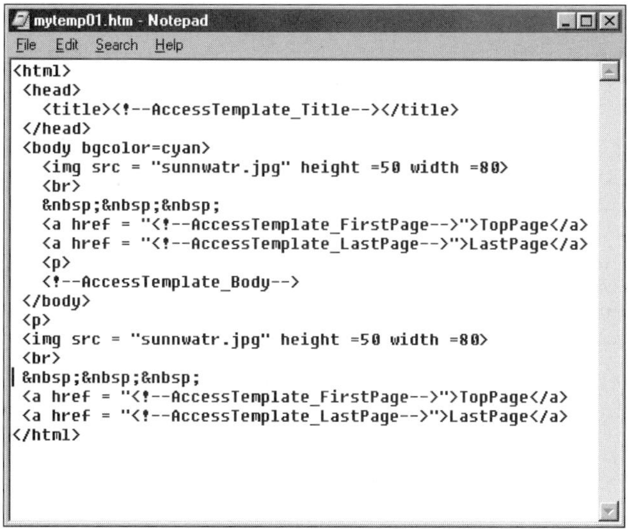

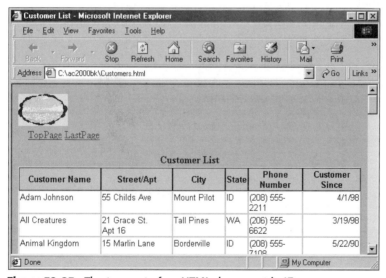

Figure 32-22: An HTML template file.

Customer Name	Street/Apt	City	State	Phone Number	Customer Since
Adam Johnson	55 Childs Ave	Mount Pilot	ID	(208) 555-2211	4/1/98
All Creatures	21 Grace St. Apt 16	Tall Pines	WA	(206) 555-6622	3/19/98
Animal Kingdom	15 Marlin Lane	Borderville	ID	(208) 555-	5/22/90

Figure 32-23: The top part of an HTML document in IE.

Import or Link (Read-Only) HTML Tables and Lists

In addition to exporting an HTML table, you can import or link to an HTML table. This process uses the standard Import or Linked Table Wizard shown in Chapter 22. Figure 32-24 shows the Import dialog box. To do this, follow these steps:

1. Open a database or switch to the Database window for the open database.

2. Do one of the following:

   - To import HTML tables or lists, from the File menu point to Get External Data and click on Import. To link (formerly known as attaching) HTML tables or lists, from the File menu point to Get External Data and click on Link Tables.

   - In the Import or Link dialog box, in the Files of Type box, click on HTML Documents (*.html; *.htm).

   - Click the arrow at the right of the Look In box, select the drive and folder where the HTML file that you want to import or link is located, and then double-click on the filename.

   - Follow the instructions for the Import HTML Wizard or the Link HTML Wizard. Click the Advanced button if you want to edit an import/export specification, or if you want to specify different file and field formats.

If your HTML file contains more than one table or list, repeat the steps for each table or list that you want to import or link.

Figure 32-24: The Import dialog box.

A table that is embedded within a table cell in an HTML file is treated as a separate table when you import or link. A list embedded in a table cell is treated as the contents of a cell, and each item in the list is delimited with the carriage return/line feed characters.

If the data being imported contains a URL link or file hyperlink, Access converts HTML links to a Hyperlink data-type column, but only if all values in a table column or list contain hyperlink addresses defined by an <A HREF> tag. You can change the data type when using the Import HTML Wizard or the Link HTML Wizard. Access ignores GIF and JPEG images embedded in the HTML tables or lists. For data that spans rows or columns, Access 2000 duplicates the data in each cell. On the other hand, Microsoft Excel 2000 stores the data in the first or upper-left cell and then leaves other cells blank.

Hyperlinks Connect Your Application to the Internet

Microsoft Access 2000 includes hyperlinks that help you connect your application to the Internet or to an intranet. A hyperlink can jump to a location on the Internet or on an intranet, to an object in your database or in another database, or to a document on your computer or on another computer connected by a network. Normally, you embed a hyperlink in a form. However, by storing hyperlinks in a table, you can programmatically move to Internet URLs or Office objects such as a Word document using a bookmark, an Excel spreadsheet using a sheet or range, a PowerPoint presentation using a slide, or an Access object such as a table, form, or report.

Using the Hyperlink data type

Microsoft Access provides a Hyperlink data type that can contain a hyperlink address. You can define a table field with this data type in order to store hyperlinks as data in a table. Imagine, for a moment, the future where all patients have e-mail addresses or even their own Websites. You would want to include a patient's e-mail address or Website in a linkable file much as automatic phone dialer code is commonly added to a customer's phone number today.

Figure 32-25 shows the Hyperlink data type being defined.

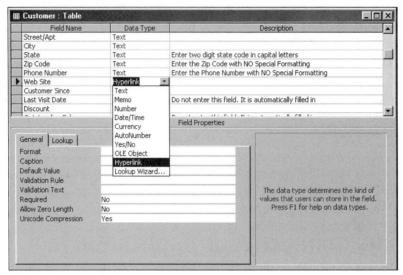

Figure 32-25: Creating a hyperlink in a table design.

Using the Hyperlink data type lets you input text or combinations of text and numbers stored as text and used as a hyperlink address. A hyperlink address can have as many as three parts:

Displaytext	The text that appears in a field or control
Address	The path to a file (UNC path) or Web page (URL)
Subaddress	A location within the file or page

The easiest way to insert a hyperlink address in a field or control is to click on Hyperlink on the Insert menu. The Insert Hyperlink dialog box appears as shown in Figure 32-26.

There are many options available in the dialog box. You can specify an existing file or Web page, an Object in the database, Create a new page, or an e-mail address.

The dialog box in Figure 32-26 shows adding an existing Web page (on the World Wide Web) as a URL for All Creatures.

The Hyperlink data type can contain as many as 2,048 characters.

When you click on a hyperlink field, Access jumps to an object, document, Web page, or other destination.

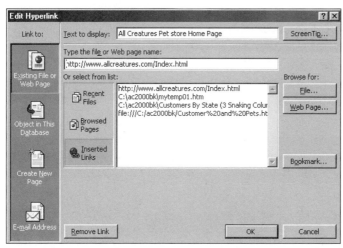

Figure 32-26: Inserting a hyperlink in a table.

Add a hyperlink to a form, report, or datasheet

You can use hyperlinks in forms and datasheets to jump to objects in the same or another Access database; to documents created with Microsoft Word, Microsoft Excel, and Microsoft PowerPoint; and to documents on the global Internet or on a local intranet. You can also add hyperlinks to reports. Although hyperlinks in a report won't work when viewed in Access, the hyperlinks will work when you output the report to Word or Excel, or to HTML.

You can store hyperlinks in fields in tables, just as you store phone numbers and fax numbers. For example, the Suppliers table in the Northwind sample database stores hyperlinks to home pages for some of the suppliers.

You can also create a label or picture on a form or report or a command button on a form that you can click to follow a hyperlink path. For example, the labels in the Mountain Animal Hospital switchboard can be modified to use the hyperlink address and subaddress properties.

Figure 32-27 shows how to modify the Customer Form label into a hyperlink. When connecting an object in the current database, leave the Hyperlink Address field blank and fill in the Hyperlink SubAddress with the object type and the object name.

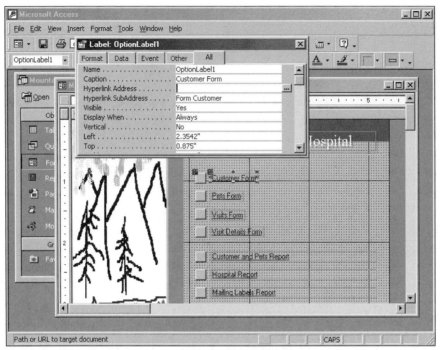

Figure 32-27: Specifying a hyperlink address and subaddress in a form.

Creating a label using the Insert Hyperlink button

If you want to automatically create a label using the Insert Hyperlink button on a form, follow these steps:

1. Open a form or a report in Design view.

2. Click on Insert Hyperlink on the toolbar.

3. In the Insert Hyperlink dialog box, specify a UNC path or a URL in the Link to File or Web Page dialog box. If you are unsure of the file name, click the File button to navigate to a file on your hard drive, on a local area network, or on an FTP server that you've registered. For a Web Page name, click the Web Page button to navigate to the Web page that you want to use.

   To jump to a location in a file, enter a location. For example, type a bookmark name for a Microsoft Word document or a slide number for a PowerPoint presentation.

   To jump to an Access object, enter the object type and object name (for example, Form Customer), or click on the Browse button. The Browse button displays a list of the objects in the current database. Select the object that you want to open.

4. Click OK in the Insert Hyperlink dialog box.

Access adds a label to the form or report. To test the link, click the label with the right mouse button, point to Hyperlink on the shortcut menu, and click Open.

When you create a label this way, Access sets the Hyperlink Address property of the label to the value you specified in the Link to File or URL box, and the Hyperlink SubAddress property to the value (if any) that you specified in the Named Location in File box. Access 2000 uses the Caption property for the display text that you see in the label itself. You can change any of these properties to modify the hyperlink.

You can also add hyperlinks to a picture (Image Control) or command button control in the same way.

In Figure 32-28, the hand icon indicates that the label is pointing to a link on a Web site. In this example, it will link to the Customer form in the Mountain Animal Hospital database.

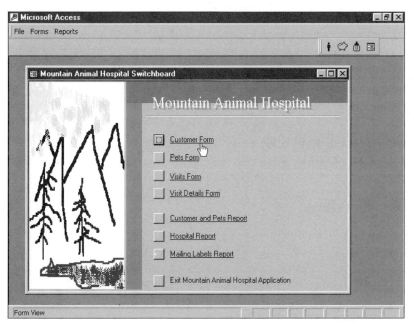

Figure 32-28: Moving to a hyperlink address and subaddress in a form.

Browsing Web Pages with the Web Browser Control

The Microsoft Web Browser control lets you browse the World Wide Web; view Web pages; access other documents on your computer, the network, or the Internet; and download data from the Internet, all through a single form in your application.

The Microsoft Web Browser control is an ActiveX control that enables you to view Web pages and other documents on the Internet or an intranet from an Access 2000 form. The Web Browser control is provided by Microsoft Internet Explorer 5.0, which is included with Microsoft Office 2000. You can also download Microsoft Internet Explorer from the Microsoft corporate Website (http://www.microsoft.com/) free of charge. You can obtain further documentation about the Web Browser control at the URL http://www.microsoft.com/intdev/sdk/docs/iexplore/.

If you purchased Microsoft Office 2000 on CD-ROM, there is a Help file that contains this information. You can view the information by copying it from the Office 2000 ValuPack. For information about obtaining the Web Browser control Help file from the ValuPack, see About the Office 2000 ValuPack.

The Web Browser control is automatically registered with the operating system when you install Internet Explorer, so you can use it from Access 2000 without first registering it. To add the Web Browser control to a form, click on ActiveX Control on the Insert menu, and then click on Microsoft Web Browser Control in the list of ActiveX controls, as shown in Figure 32-29.

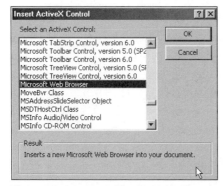

Figure 32-29: Inserting the Web Browser control in Access 2000.

After you've added the Web Browser control to a form, you can use the control's Navigate method to open a Web page within the Web Browser window. For example, if you've added a Web Browser control named ActiveXCt27 (which was named automatically by Access) to a form, you could create this Load event procedure for the form:

```
Private Sub Form_Load
   Me!ActiveXCt27.Navigate "http://www.databasecreations.com/"
End Sub
```

This procedure would display the Database Creations home page within the control. In Figure 32-30, the Microsoft Explorer logo represents the area of the Web browser window. When the form opens, the Web page information appears in place of the Explorer logo. The area can be resized as you desire.

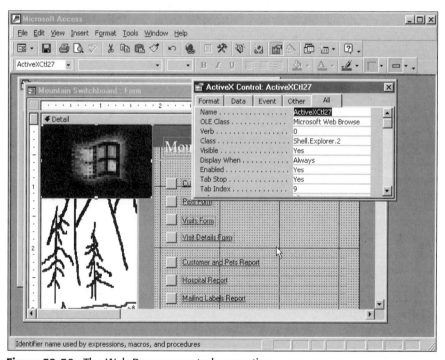

Figure 32-30: The Web Browser control properties.

The Internet is a continuously evolving technology. The ability to access it and program your Microsoft Access 2000 environment to take advantage of Internet technology has become very important today.

Summary

In this chapter, you learned to use Internet technology to publish your Access data and to link to both World Wide Web sites as well as internal intranets. These points were discussed:

✦ The Internet, and particularly the World Wide Web, has become an important part of all businesses today.

✦ The Web toolbar can be turned on by selecting View ➪ Toolbars ➪ Web from any menu. After the Web toolbar is displayed, you can use it to access Websites on the Internet or your local intranet. When you use the Web toolbar, you launch the default Web browser on your system.

✦ To take advantage of Internet technology, you must have a Web browser installed (Microsoft Internet Explorer or Netscape Navigator).

✦ Access 2000 has added a new object — the Data Access Page object. This object can be used by Access or Internet Explorer 5.0 to view and work with live Access data.

✦ You can create static HTML pages from table, query, and form datasheets, and from reports. The resulting HTML files are a snapshot of the data at the time you published your files. If your data changes, you must republish your files to view the new data in your Web application.

✦ If your data changes frequently and your Web application needs to store and retrieve live data from your Access 2000 database using a form, then you must use the dynamic HTML format. You must have a Web server such as the Microsoft Internet Information Server (IIS) (IDX/HDC) or the ActiveX Server (ASP) to create Web forms.

✦ You can export individual objects to HTML using the Export menu item from the File menu.

✦ You can import HTML data by using the Get External Data option from the File menu to import or attach to data tables on the Web.

✦ You can create a new data type, known as a hyperlink, which can store a Web URL or Microsoft Office object address.

✦ The Hyperlink Address and Subaddress properties in a form label, command button, or image control let you automatically link to a URL or database object and automatically jump to those objects.

✦ The Web Browser control is an ActiveX control that lets you view a Web page within your Access 2000 application.

As you saw in this chapter, the Internet is an important part of applications. See the chapters on using Visual Basic to learn the basics of programming and to move beyond macros with Access 2000.

✦   ✦   ✦

Using Access with the Microsoft Database Engine and SQL Server

New in Access 2000 is the Microsoft Database Engine (MSDE). MSDE offers a client/server environment that is compatible with Microsoft SQL Server 7.0. If you anticipate your small workgroup application to eventually accommodate hundreds or thousands of users, you will want to use MSDE.

Understanding the Microsoft Database Engine

MSDE is an alternative database engine to the Microsoft Jet database engine, which is the default database engine included with Access 2000. If you have developed applications in previous versions of Microsoft Access, you should be familiar with Microsoft Jet.

MSDE is a client/server database engine that is designed to be compatible with the SQL Server database engine. Think of MSDE as a scaled-down version of SQL Server. With some exceptions, it provides all of the power of SQL Server, yet it has been optimized to run on desktop computers running Windows 95, Windows 98, or Windows NT 4.0 or later.

Applications developed using MSDE can be run under SQL Server without modification. This capability is a great advantage to both application developers and their customers.

In the rapidly changing business environments of today, many software development projects start out targeting a handful of users. Within a relatively short span of time, the application needs to be available across the enterprise consisting of possibly hundreds or thousands of users. In a typical scenario such as this, the customer faces expensive development costs and lost time when having the application modified to accommodate the larger environment. Or, in the worse case scenario, the customer may be forced to abandon the smaller application and reengineer it using a client/server toolset. MSDE provides the scalability required by growing business environments.

Developers who do not have access to a network running SQL Server can build client/server applications using MSDE on a personal computer. Some simple changes to the connection information are all that is required when the time comes to connect the application to SQL Server.

Comparing MSDE and Jet

MSDE is a client/server database engine. That is, the interface objects (forms, reports, and shortcuts to data access pages) are stored locally on the workstations in a Microsoft Access project. The data, however, is stored on a local or network server. Additionally, much of the processing of data (running queries and stored procedures) occurs on the server. This architecture minimizes the work of both the client and the server and cuts down on the amount of information traveling over the network.

Jet is the data manager behind the Microsoft Access database. A Microsoft Access database can store all of an application's database objects, including the interface objects and the data. Jet moves the data back and forth between tables and forms and reports. Jet is described as a file server database engine because it's job is merely to store and retrieve data. There is no distribution of processing between server and workstation as occurs in the client/server architecture.

While MSDE provides the optimum in power and flexibility, there are many situations where Jet is the appropriate environment.

Choosing the right database engine

Designing a database application requires careful consideration of the business environment's current situation as well as strategic planning for expansion either in the number of users, or in the volume of data to be stored and retrieved. Delivering an application that is unable to handle the growing needs of the business or, worse, that cannot handle even the initial needs of the business environment, can be a real career-buster. Although it is tempting to design every application with a "sky's the limit" approach so that it can accommodate the full spectrum of business environments, there is a need to find the right balance between maximum flexibility and simplicity.

When selecting the database engine that is most appropriate for your application, consider these four criteria:

✦ Simplicity

✦ Data Integrity

✦ Number of Users

✦ Volume of Data

In the simplicity category, Jet gets the score. As the default database in Access 2000, creating a Jet database is much easier than creating one for MSDE. It is also the most compatible with previous versions of Access. Although Access provides built-in security administration, Jet databases do not require security (user ids and passwords). MSDE does require security and uses the Windows NT security model. The memory and disk space requirements for Jet databases are low as compared to MSDE.

Tip　　You can always upsize a Jet database to SQL Server later on using the Upsizing Wizard. Some modifications to the application may be necessary, however.

When considering data integrity, MSDE is the most reliable choice. MSDE includes the same data integrity technology that is provided in SQL Server 7. All changes made to the database are logged to a transaction file. In the event of a database disaster — a hardware failure or power interruption — the database can repair itself using the log file. With Jet, however, this kind of disastrous event can permanently corrupt the database. As anyone who has ever tried to repair an Access database knows, a reliable backup strategy is a must. For some mission-critical applications, though, restoring from yesterday's backup would result in a major business interruption. For those types of applications, MSDE is the best option.

Note　　When addressing the limitations of MSDE, remember that it is 100 percent compatible with SQL Server 7.

Both Jet and MSDE are designed for the single workstation or small workgroup. As a client/server database engine, MSDE has the performance advantage over Jet even in a small workgroup situation. MSDE processes queries on the server and moves only the resulting data to the client workstation. Jet, on the other hand, must move the data to the client so that the client workstation can process the query.

Both Jet and MSDE have a maximum database size of 2GB. For applications that accumulate a large volume of data over a long period of time, consider including an archive/purge utility in the application. For many business situations, only a relatively small volume of data needs to be active at any point in time.

Table 33-1 compares the capabilities of SQL Server/MSDE and Jet. The table comes from the "Microsoft Access 2000 Data Engine Options" whitepaper and is reprinted with permission from Microsoft.

Table 33-1 Comparison of SQL Server/MSDE and Jet		
Requirement	**SQL Server**	**Microsoft Access (Jet) (Use MSDE if These Are Future Requirements)**
Scalability	SMP support	No SMP support
	Virtually unlimited number of concurrent users	Maximum of 255 users
	Terabyte levels of data	2 GB of data
	Transaction logging	No transaction logging
Business Critical	7X24 support and QFE	No 7X24 support or QFE
	Point-in-time recovery	Recoverable to last backup
	Guaranteed transaction integrity	No transaction logging
	Built-in fault tolerance	No integrated security with Windows NT
	Security integrated with Windows NT	
Rapid Application Prototyping	Access is UI for both engines and offers WYSIWIG database tools and built-in forms generation	

Once you have determined that MSDE is the right database engine to utilize in your database application, you are ready to begin working with this new and powerful feature of Access 2000.

Installing MSDE

MSDE is not installed automatically when you install Office 2000. It is provided as a separate installation process included on the Office 2000 CD-ROM.

Hardware requirements

Chances are, if you are successfully running Office 2000 on your personal computer, your hardware meets the minimum requirements for MSDE.

MSDE requires approximately 45MB of hard disk space for a typical installation — 25MB for program files and 20MB for its data files. Optionally, you can store the program files and data files on separate drives. Remember that additional space is needed for your database files.

Software requirements

MSDE requires that Microsoft Windows 95 or later, or Windows NT 4.0 or later, be installed on your computer. MSDE does not run on OS/2 or Windows 3.1.

Installing MSDE

To install MSDE, insert the Office 2000 CD-ROM into your CD-ROM drive and select Run from the Start menu. In the Run box, type **D:\SQL\X86\SETUP\Setupsql.exe** (or use whatever letter corresponds to the drive containing your installation CD-ROM). Click OK to begin the installation.

Note　These installation instructions correspond to the installation procedure provided by Microsoft's beta-testing staff at the time this chapter was written. Actual installation instructions may be revised by the time the product is released.

Because some Windows programs interfere with the Setup program, the installation program may warn you to shut down any applications currently running. You can simply click on the Continue button to continue the setup, or you can click on the Exit Setup button to cancel the installation and run the installation later. The installation program displays the Welcome screen, as shown in Figure 33-1.

Figure 33-1: The MSDE Setup Welcome screen.

The Setup program now requires some information from you. If you are installing for the first time, you are asked to customize your copy of the program by entering your name and (optionally) a company name, as shown in Figure 33-2.

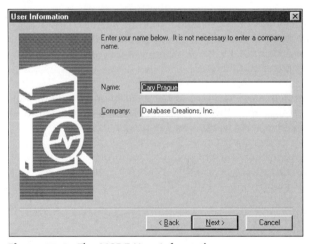

Figure 33-2: The MSDE User Information screen.

Setup then checks for available disk space or existing copies of MSDE. When this verification step is complete, Setup wants to know where you want to install MSDE (as shown in Figure 33-3). The default location for the Program and Data files is

C:\MSSQL7. If this location is satisfactory, click Next> to continue with the installation. If you want to change the location for either the Program or Data files, type the new drive letter and folder name. Or select the Browse button and then a drive and folder from the list. If you type the name of a folder that does not exist, it will be created.

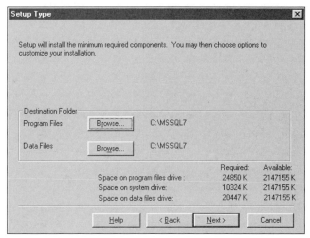

Figure 33-3: The MSDE Setup Type screen.

Next, the Character Set/Sort Order/Unicode Collation screen displays, as shown in Figure 33-4. This screen lets you customize MSDE to accommodate the multilingual features available in MSDE. The defaults are already selected for U.S. locations.

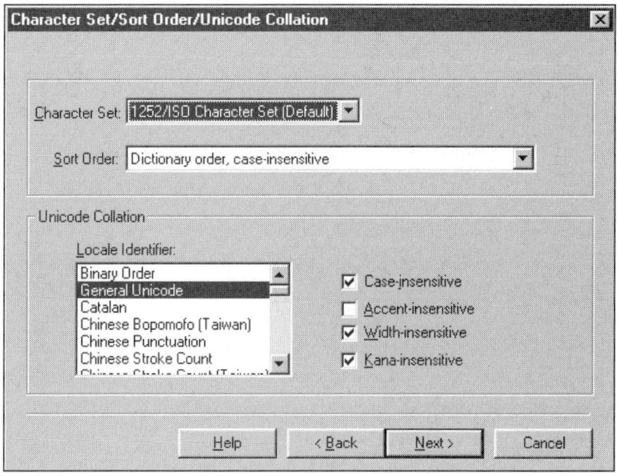

Figure 33-4: The Character Set/Sort Order/Unicode Collation screen.

The Network Libraries screen, as shown in Figure 33-5, tells MSDE how to connect to your network environment.

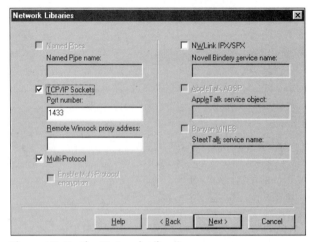

Figure 33-5: The Network Libraries screen.

Setup now has enough information to install the necessary files. If you want to review your setup information, select the Back button, as shown in Figure 33-6. Otherwise, click Next> to continue with the installation.

Figure 33-6: The Start Copying Files screen.

When all of the MSDE files have been installed, the Setup complete screen displays, as shown in Figure 33-7. Click Finish to complete the installation.

Figure 33-7: The Setup Complete screen.

Starting MSDE

When setup has completed, the SQL Server Service Manager opens, as shown in Figure 33-8, and starts the MSDE database engine. To work with an MSDE database, you must first start the SQL Server Service Manager.

Figure 33-8: Using SQL Server Service Manager.

When you install MSDE, SQL Server Service Manager starts automatically. You can run the SQL Server Service Manager any time by choosing it from your Start menu under the MSDE folder.

To start MSDE, select MSSQLServer for Services. Then click Start/Continue.

 Tip   Selecting the option **Auto-Start service when OS starts** in the SQL Server Service Manager automatically starts the service when you boot up Windows 95 or later.

When MSDE has started, an arrow displays next to the server in SQL Server Service Manager, as shown in Figure 33-9.

Figure 33-9: Starting MSDE.

Now that you have successfully installed MSDE and started the server, it's time to get started building a database.

Creating an MSDE database

To create an MSDE database, you start by creating a Microsoft Access project. A Microsoft Access project (.adp) is a new type of file in Access 2000. Using a project, you can create and access Microsoft SQL Server 6.5, Microsoft SQL Server 7.0, or Microsoft Data Engine (MSDE) databases. This section shows how creating a client/server application is very similar to creating a Microsoft Access database.

Creating a project

To begin creating a project, start Microsoft Access. Then select File ➪ New from the main Access menu, or click on the first icon in the toolbar.

 Tip   You can also create a new project by clicking on the New Database icon. This is the first icon in the toolbar. It looks like a sheet of paper with the right-top corner bent down.

Caution　To create a new project that accesses an SQL database, Microsoft SQL Server Service Manager must be running. Refer to the topic on Starting MSDE to learn how to start the service manager.

The New dialog box appears, as shown in Figure 33-10. You will see two tabs labeled General and Databases. The General tab contains four icons: Database, Data Access Page, Project (Existing Database), and Project (New Database). Select the Project (New Database) icon and click OK.

Tip　When you first start Access, a Database selection window appears automatically. You can choose the option Access database wizards, pages, and projects on this screen.

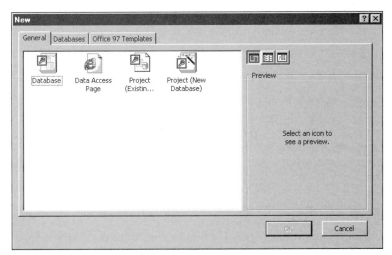

Figure 33-10: The New dialog box.

The File New Database dialog box displays where you must create a name and location for the database. Figure 33-11 shows the standard Windows file dialog box, which has several information areas to complete. A default name adp1.adp displays next to the File name combo box. Adding the .adp file extension is optional; Access adds it automatically during the creation process. Because the database is a standard Windows file, its file name can be any valid Windows long file name. You may also see existing .adp files in the file list area if any projects were previously created. Although the Save in combo box may be set to My Documents, you can change this to any folder name. In this example, the folder name is Microsoft Office 2000.

Figure 33-11: Entering a file name for the new database.

Type **My Mountain StartCS** in place of adp1.adp as the name for your new database.

Caution   If you enter a file extension other than ADP, Access saves the database file, but does not display it in the list of files when you want to open the database later. By default, Access searches for and displays only those files with an ADP file extension.

If you are following along with the examples in this book, note that we have chosen the name My Mountain StartCS for the name of the database you create in this chapter. The database in the examples for this section is for our hypothetical business, the Mountain Animal Hospital. The CD-ROM that comes with your book contains the project database file named Mountain StartCS.

After you enter the file name, select the Create button. Access begins the process of creating the new database. To create a new project database, Access needs some additional information about the connection information required for your new client/server database.

Access displays the Microsoft SQL Server Database Wizard to collect the required connection information. The Wizard screen is shown in Figure 33-12.

In the Microsoft SQL Server Database Wizard, Access needs the name of the server that you would like to use, the logon ID and password of an account with Create Database privileges on the server, and the name of the new SQL Server database.

In this example, we are creating an MSDE database on a personal computer. Type **(local)** as the server name. Type **sa** for the logon ID. Type **My Mountain Start SQL Database** for the database name. Then click Next> to create the new database. The completed Wizard screen is shown in Figure 33-13.

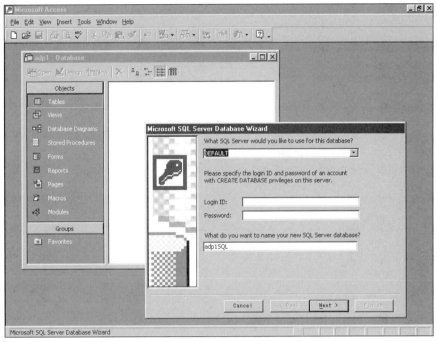

Figure 33-12: The Microsoft SQL Server Database Wizard.

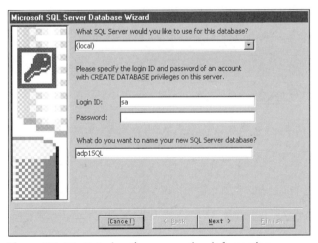

Figure 33-13: Entering the connection information.

The Microsoft SQL Server Database Wizard verifies the entered connection information. When verification is complete, the final Wizard screen displays as shown in Figure 33-14. Click Finish to create the new database.

Figure 33-14: The final Microsoft SQL Server Database Wizard screen.

The Microsoft SQL Server Database Wizard creates the new database. This process may take a few minutes to complete. When the process is complete, Access displays the Database window for the new empty project database.

The empty Database window is shown in Figure 33-15. This window appears similar to the Access database window. If you have ever created an Access database, you are familiar with most of the object buttons in this window.

Figure 33-15: The Database window and the empty project.

Understanding projects

An Access project file contains only the user-interface objects for an application. It contains only the objects that interact directly with the user: the forms, reports, data access pages, macros, and modules. Creating forms, reports, data access pages, macros, and modules is virtually the same as creating them in an Access database.

The objects that contain data or describe the definitions of the data — the tables, views, stored procedures, and database diagram — are stored in the SQL Server or MSDE database file.

In our example, the Access project file name is Mountain StartCS.adp. The MSDE database file name is Mountain Start SQL Database.mdf. The MSDE file is created automatically when you create a new project file.

Even though the data objects are not stored in the Access project file, you can create and work with data objects through an Access project. Although the design tools are different than the tools in Access databases, you will find them just as easy to use.

Table 33-2 compares the objects in a Microsoft Access database to the objects in a Microsoft Access project.

Table 33-2 Comparison of Objects in an Access Database and an Access Project	
Access Database	**Access Project**
Table	Table
Select Query	View
Action Query	Stored Procedure
Parameterized Query	Stored Procedure
Relationship	Database Diagram
Form	Form
Report	Report
Data Access Page	Data Access Page
Macro	Macro
Module	Module

Project objects

The Database window contains a list of the object types available for an Access project. You can select among any of these nine available object types:

✦ Tables

✦ Views

✦ Database Diagrams

✦ Stored Procedures

✦ Forms

✦ Reports

✦ Pages

✦ Macros

✦ Modules

Click on any one of the objects listed to display a list of existing items for that object type or to create a new item.

Creating a New Table

Creating a table in an Access project is very similar to creating a table in an Access database. Because creating tables, queries, forms, and reports is covered in detail in other chapters, this section focuses on the design tool methods that differ from Access database design tool methods.

To create a new table, first make sure that the Tables object is selected. Then select the item labeled *Create table in Design view*. The Choose Name window displays. Enter **Pets** for the name of the new table, then click OK. The Table Design window displays.

The Table Design window

The Table Design window is shown in Figure 33-16. The table design tool is quite different from the Access database table design tool. The Table Design window consists of two areas:

✦ The field properties area

✦ The field entry area

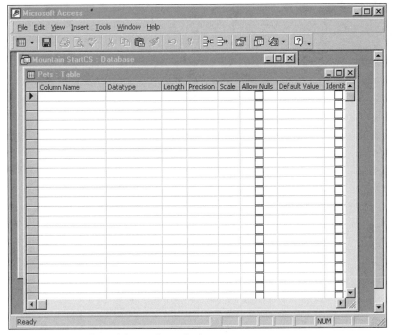

Figure 33-16: The Table Design window.

The *properties area* is a set of column headings that are used to label each of the items of information that describes each field, which are called *properties*. The *field entry area* is for entering each field's name and the values for each of the field's properties.

Working with fields

Fields are created by entering a *field name* and a *field data type* in each row of the field entry area of the Table Design window. You must enter a data type and length for each field name that you enter. You can further describe each field by completing any of the additional properties available for the data type you selected.

Table 33-3 describes the data types available for SQL databases and how they compare to Access data types.

Table 33-3
Comparison of Access and SQL Server Data Types

Microsoft Access Data Type	SQL Server Data Type
Yes/No	Bit
Number	Tinyint, smallint, int, real, float, decimal, numeric
Currency	Money, Smallmoney
Date/Time	Datetime, Smalldatetime
AutoNumber	int (with **Identity** property defined)
Text	Varchar(n), Nvarchar(n)
Memo	Text
OLE Object	Image
Hyperlink	Ntext (but Hyperlink is not active)
(no equivalent)	Nchar
(no equivalent)	varbinary
(no equivalent)	User-defined
(no equivalent)	timestamp
(no equivalent)	Char, nchar

Table 33-4 describes some of the remaining properties that you can set for each field.

Table 33-4
Additional Properties

Field Property	Description
Length	Default value provided based on data type. Modifiable for binary, char, varbinary, or varchar.
Precision	Maximum number of digits. Default value provided based on data type.
Scale	Maximum number of digits to the right of the decimal point. Default is 0.
Identity	Autonumbers the records in a table.
Identity Seed	The first number to assign to an identify record. Default is 1.
Identity Increment	The amount to increment each identity record.

The Table Properties window

Figure 33-17 shows the Table Properties window. The Table Properties window includes three tabs. The Tables tab allows you to categorize your tables and text files into group files. You can also set up constraints for the table's values. Constraints are similar to validation rules in an Access database. The Relationships tab (Figure 33-18) shows the relationships defined for this table. The Indexes/Keys tab (Figure 33-19) shows the primary key columns and other indexes created for the table.

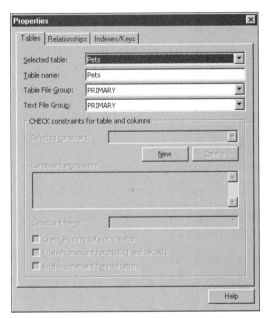

Figure 33-17: Setting the Tables properties.

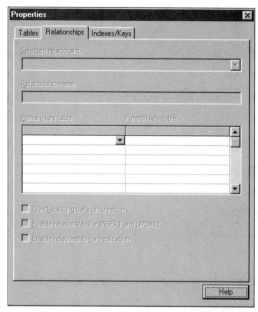

Figure 33-18: Setting the Relationships properties.

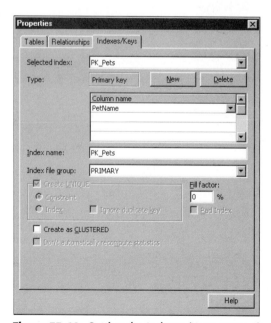

Figure 33-19: Setting the Indexes/Keys properties.

Working with Database Diagrams

The Database Diagrams object is similar to Relationships in an Access database. Figure 33-20 shows a database diagram for the Mountain StartCS project. Although the process of adding tables to the diagram and setting relationships between the tables is similar to how relationships are set in an Access database, database diagrams provide several other powerful features.

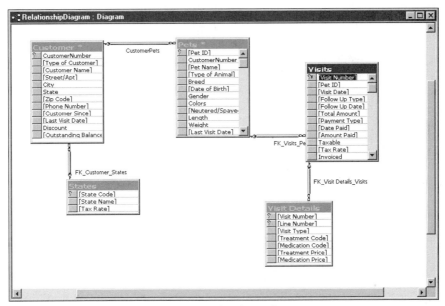

Figure 33-20: Setting relationships in a database diagram.

The relationship lines between the tables and their icons make it easy to see how the tables relate to each other. In addition, labels for each relationship can be displayed. To display relationship labels, right-click on the database diagram, then select Show Relationship Labels.

When you display relationships, default names are assigned. You can change the default names by assigning a new name in the Properties window for each relationship. To display the Properties window, right-click on a relationship line. Then select Properties. The relationship name can be changed using the Relationships tab of the Properties window as shown in Figure 33-21.

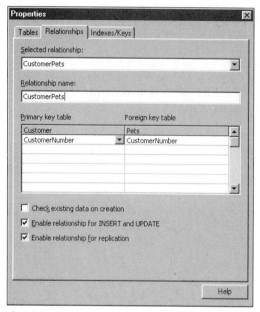

Figure 33-21: Assigning a name to a relationship.

For applications that have dozens of tables, it can be difficult to manage all of the relationships in one diagram. In Access projects, you can create multiple diagrams. All of your application's relationships can be organized into manageable sections that store each section in a separate diagram. In a sales order application, for example, you can have one diagram named Sales Relationships that includes the Customers, Sales Orders, and Sales Order Line Items tables and another diagram named Inventory Relationships that includes the Inventory, Inventory Receipts, and Inventory Suppliers tables.

Another powerful feature of Database Diagrams is the capability to create, edit, or delete tables and table-column definitions. Database Diagram can be used as a graphical table designer to modify the columns in a single table, or you can work with the design of multiple tables all at the same time. To modify a table's design, select the table's title bar in the Database Diagram window, then select the Table Modes toolbar button. Then select Column Properties from the Table Modes list as shown in Figure 33-22.

When you display the column properties for a table, the view of the selected table transforms into a table design view. You can then change any of the properties for a field, or even add or delete fields the same way you work with fields in the Table Design window.

Note   When you make changes to a table in a database diagram, the changes are not actually applied to the database until you save the database diagram. An asterisk (*) displays next to any table name with pending changes to remind you that the changes have not yet been applied.

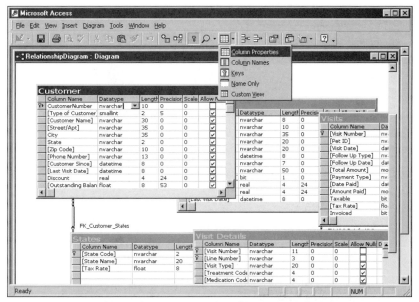

Figure 33-22: Modifying the structure of a table in a Database Diagram.

When you save a database diagram, a confirmation message box displays listing the tables that will be updated with the changes. An example message box is shown in Figure 33-23. When you modify a table in a database diagram, your modifications are also saved in every other diagram that the table appears in.

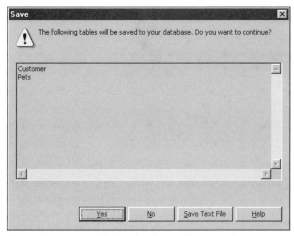

Figure 33-23: Applying database diagram changes to the database.

Understanding Views

A view is just like an Access query. You can create, open, and modify a view the same way you work with Access queries.

To create a view, select the Views object, then select *Create view in designer*. The Query Designer opens. To add a table to the Query Designer window, right-click in the Query Designer window and select Show Table from the short-cut menu. The Show Table window displays as shown in Figure 33-24.

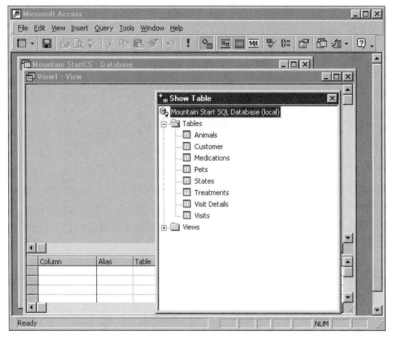

Figure 33-24: The Show Table window in the Query Designer window.

You can select columns and enter criteria the same way you design queries in an Access database. Figure 33-25 shows the All Pets query in the Query Designer window.

With views, you can retrieve information stored in tables or related tables, or even from other views. You can retrieve all the rows and columns from a table, or select individual columns and specify criteria to filter the rows to retrieve. When you select columns and specify criteria, symbols display next to the table's column name to indicate the type of operation to be performed on the field. Figure 33-26 shows that criteria have been specified for the Type of Animal column.

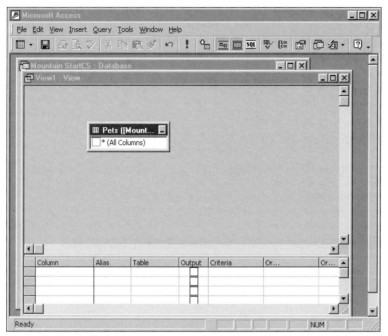

Figure 33-25: The Query Designer window with the Pets table displayed.

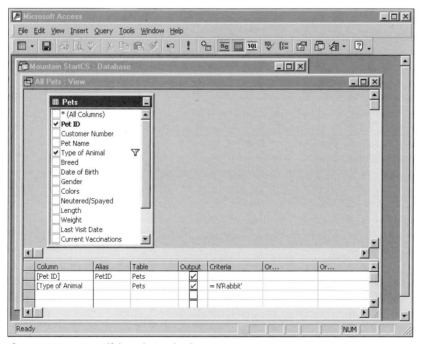

Figure 33-26: Specifying view criteria.

Views support only SELECT queries. If you need to use commands such as UPDATE, INSERT, or APPEND, you must create a stored procedure.

Creating Stored Procedures

A stored procedure is a special type of query that allows you to use commands that update data in the database. Creating a stored procedure is very different than the process of creating a view or an Access database query.

To create a new stored procedure, first make sure that the Store Procedures object is selected. Then select the item labeled *Create procedure in designer*. The stored procedure design window displays, as shown in Figure 33-27.

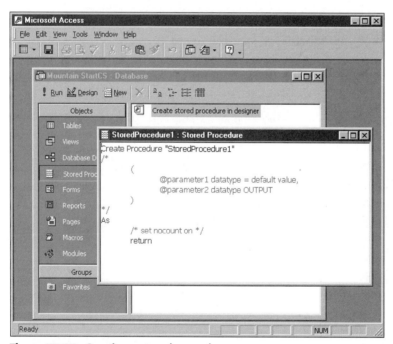

Figure 33-27: Creating a stored procedure.

Creating stored procedures is a lot like writing a Visual Basic procedure. Instead of writing Visual Basic code, however, you use SQL statements. You can also use control-of-flow statements like IF-THEN-ELSE. They can accept input parameters, return single or multiple rows of data, and even return a value. The Monthly Visits Report stored procedure, shown in Figure 33-28, accepts two date parameters to return a list of the visits that occurred for the time period.

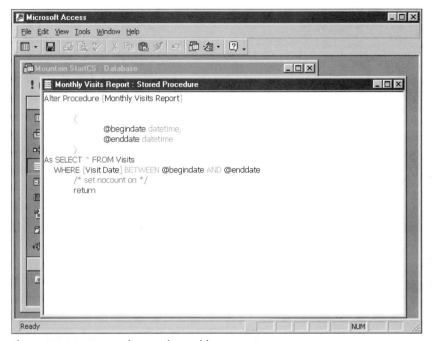

Figure 33-28: A stored procedure with parameters.

The Monthly Visits Report stored procedure could be used as a record source for a report called Monthly Visits. When the Monthly Visits report runs, it passes the two dates for the time period to the stored procedure.

Tip   You can use a form or report's InputParameters property to pass the values to a stored procedure's parameters. The Monthly Visits report InputParameters property might be something like `begindate datetime=[Form]![BeginDate]`, `enddate datetime=[Form]![EndDate]`.

Stored procedures provide a handy container for storing all of the SQL statements that you use throughout your application. Instead of writing SQL statements in your code, you can store them here and call them from your code in much the same way that you call a function stored in a module. Some of the many benefits of stored procedures are:

   ✦ Can contain multiple SQL statements

   ✦ Can call another stored procedure name

   ✦ Can receive parameters and return a value

   ✦ Are stored in a compiled state on the server so they execute faster than if they were embedded in your code

   ✦ Are stored in a common container in your application so that others can maintain them more easily

Creating Triggers

A trigger is a special kind of stored procedure that runs when you modify data in a table. You have already seen how to enforce referential integrity using database diagrams. Triggers are another powerful tool to help enforce referential integrity throughout the database.

Triggers are attached to individual tables. To create a new trigger, first make sure that the Tables object is selected. Then right-click the table name and choose Triggers… from the shortcut menu. The Trigger Name window displays. Enter a name for the new trigger and select the New button. The trigger design window displays as shown in Figure 33-29.

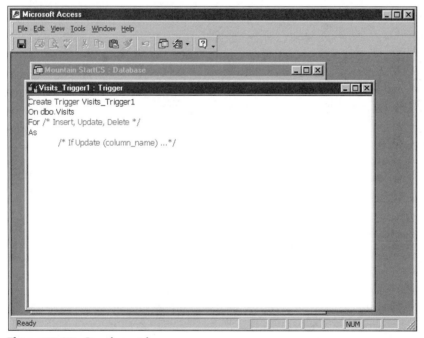

Figure 33-29: Creating a trigger.

One of the most commonly used triggers in a database is the update trigger. You can use an update trigger to validate the data being updated in a table. Figure 33-30 shows the update trigger *Pets_Utrig* for the Pets table.

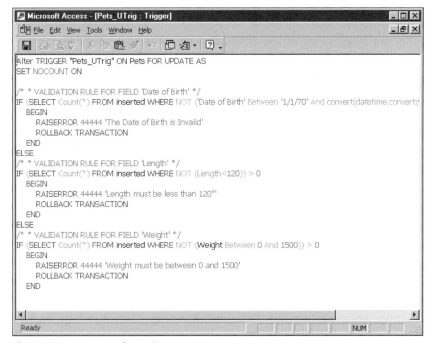

Figure 33-30: An update trigger.

Before a new record is added to the Pets table, the Pets_Utrig trigger checks the new data to make sure it passes the tests for birth date, length, and weight. If any test fails, the insert process is canceled and an error number and error message are returned to the object performing the update. The object could be a form in your application or a procedure.

Using the Upsizing Wizard

You can convert an existing Microsoft Access database (.mdb) to a client/server application automatically using the Microsoft Access Upsizing Wizard. The Upsizing Wizard takes a Jet database and creates an equivalent database on SQL Server with the same table structure, data, and many other attributes of the original database. It will recreate table structures, indexes, validation rules, defaults, autonumbers, and relationships, and takes advantage of the latest SQL Server functionality wherever possible. At the same time, the Upsizing Wizard can also convert your forms, reports, macros, and modules to a Microsoft Access project.

Before upsizing an application

You should perform these steps prior to converting an application using the Upsizing Wizard:

✦ **Backup your database** Although the Upsizing Wizard doesn't remove any data or database objects from your Access database, it's a good idea to create a backup copy of your Access database before you upsize it.

✦ **Ensure that you have adequate disk space** At a minimum, you must have enough disk space to store the new SQL Server database. Plan to allow at least twice the size of your Access database to allow room for future growth. If you expect to add a lot of data to the database, make the multiple larger.

✦ **Set a default printer** You must have a default printer assigned because the Upsizing Wizard creates a report snapshot as it completes the conversion.

✦ **Assign yourself appropriate permissions on the Access database** You need read/design permission on all database objects to upsize them.

Starting the Upsizing Wizard

Now that you have completed the steps to prepare for the conversion, you are ready to upsize your application. First, open the Microsoft Access database that you want to convert. This example upsizes the Mountain Animal Hospital database. Second, select Tools Database Utilities Upsizing Wizard from the Access menu. The first screen of the Upsizing Wizard displays as shown in Figure 33-31.

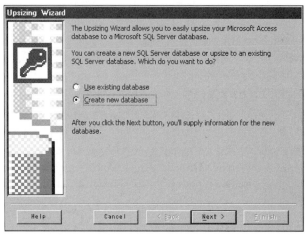

Figure 33-31: The Upsizing Wizard.

In the first Upsizing Wizard screen, you can choose to either copy your existing data to an SQL Server database that already exists, or to create a new SQL Server database. For this example, choose *Create new database*. Then click Next>. The second Upsizing Wizard screen displays as shown in Figure 33-32.

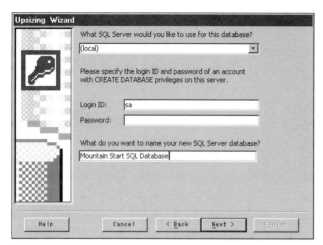

Figure 33-32: Setting up the new SQL Server database.

In this Wizard screen, you define the connection information for the new SQL Server database. For this example, type **(local)** as the name of the SQL Server. Type **sa** as the login ID. Type **Mountain Start SQL Database** as the name of the new SQL Server database. Then click Next> to continue.

The next Wizard screen, shown in Figure 33-33, allows you to select the tables to upsize to the new SQL Server database. Click the > button to export all of the tables. Then click Next> to continue.

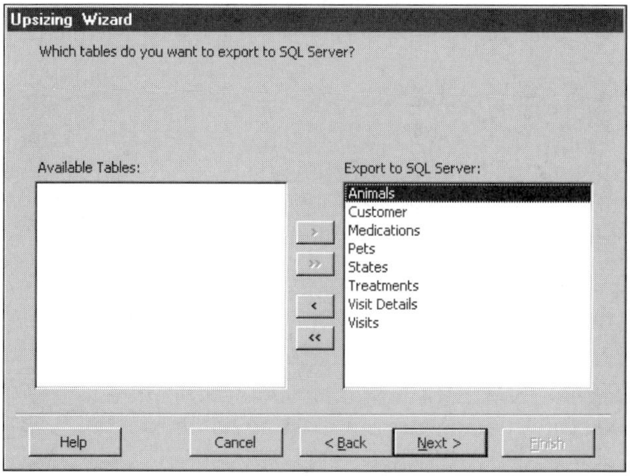

Figure 33-33: Selecting the files to export.

In this next screen, which is shown in Figure 33-34, you can take advantage of many of the new database features available in SQL Server including:

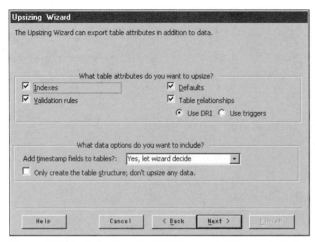

Figure 33-34: Selecting the SQL Server database attributes.

✦ **Indexes** — The Upsizing Wizard converts Microsoft Access primary keys to Microsoft SQL Server nonclustered, unique indexes and marks them as SQL Server primary keys. Other indexes are converted unchanged.

✦ **Validation rules** — The Upsizing Wizard upsizes all table, record, and field validation rules, and field required properties as update and insert triggers.

✦ **Defaults** — The Upsizing Wizard upsizes all default values as ANSI defaults.

✦ **Table relationships** — Choose this option to preserve the relationships that you have defined for your tables. If your Access application uses cascading updates or deletes, also select the Use Triggers option. Use Declared Referential Integrity (DRI) if your application does not make use of cascading updates and deletes.

✦ **Timestamp fields** — Microsoft SQL Server uses a timestamp field to indicate that a record was changed (not when it was changed) by creating a unique value field, and then updating this field whenever a record is updated. In general, a timestamp field provides the best performance and reliability. Without a timestamp field, SQL Server must check all the fields in the record to determine whether the record has changed, which slows performance. If you choose **Yes, let wizard decide**, timestamp fields are created only for tables that contain floating-point (Single or Double), memo, or OLE object fields.

✦ **Don't upsize any data** — Choose this option if you only want to create the SQL Server database structures using your existing database.

When you have made all of your selections, click Next> to continue.

Figure 33-35 shows the next Wizard screen. Here you can automatically create a Microsoft Access project file to store the application objects for your new client/server application. Choose the option Create a new Access client/server application. The Wizard automatically assigns a default name for your new project by adding the suffix "CS" to your Access database file name. Leave the option *Save password and user ID* unchecked to force the user to enter a logon ID and password whenever the project is opened. When you have completed the information for this screen, click Next>.

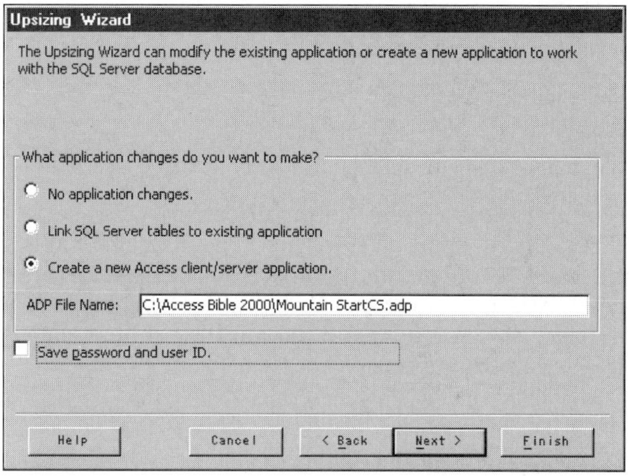

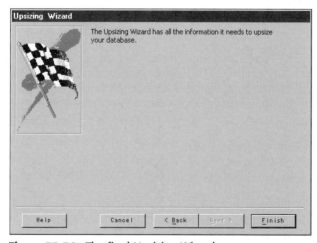

Figure 33-35: Automatically creating an Access project.

You have now reached the final Wizard screen, which is shown in Figure 33-36. The Upsizing Wizard now has all of the information that it needs to create both the SQL Server database and the Access project. Click Finish to begin the conversion.

Figure 33-36: The final Upsizing Wizard screen.

The conversion process takes several minutes to complete. A message box displays the progress of the conversion as shown in Figure 33-37.

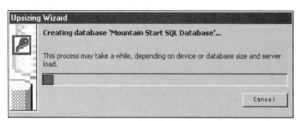

Figure 33-37: Waiting for the Upsizing Wizard to complete the conversion process.

If the Upsizing Wizard encounters any referential integrity errors while converting your data to the new SQL Server database, an error message displays that is similar to the one shown in Figure 33-38. If you encounter an error message like this one, you can click Yes to proceed with the conversion. Any problem data will not be converted to the new database. If you do not want to omit the problem data, you must click No to cancel the conversion process.

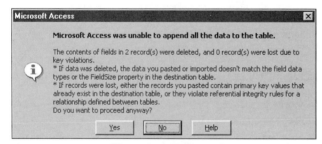

Figure 33-38: Handling referential integrity errors.

When the conversion process completes, the Upsizing Wizard automatically displays a report snapshot. An example of the report snapshot is shown in Figure 33-39. The report snapshot includes information about each step of the conversion process for your application. The Upsizing Wizard report contains information about the following:

✦ Database details, including database size.

✦ Upsizing parameters, including what table attributes you chose to upsize and how you upsized.

✦ Table information, including a comparison of Access and SQL Server values for names, data types, indexes, validation rules, defaults, triggers, and whether or not timestamps were added.

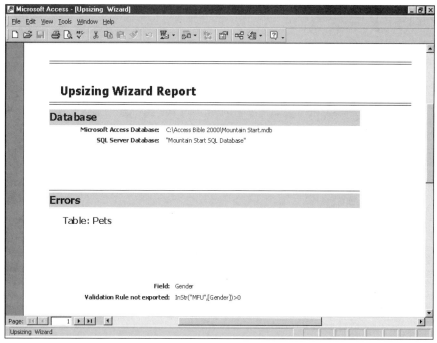

Figure 33-39: The Upsizing Wizard report.

✦ Any errors encountered, including database or transaction log full, inadequate permissions, device or database not created, table, default, or validation rule skipped, relationship not enforced, query skipped (because it cannot be translated to SQL Server syntax), and control and record source conversion errors in forms and reports.

When you are finished reviewing the report, close it. When you close the report, the Upsizing Wizard automatically loads the new Access project.

Tip The report snapshot is stored in the same folder as your application so that you can refer to it later.

Note After you upsize, you need to manually convert code from Data Access Objects (DAO) to ActiveX Data Objects (ADO) in your modules, and convert queries that did not upsize (such as those that were nested too deeply). See Chapter 35 for more information on working with ADO.

Summary

In this chapter, you learned to maximize the potential of your applications by creating client/server databases. This chapter discussed these points:

✦ Access 2000 offers two database engines: Jet and MSDE.

✦ Jet is used when a file/server environment is sufficient. MSDE provides a client/server environment.

✦ The SQL Server Service Manager manages the connection between your application and the SQL Server database.

✦ Projects allow you to take full advantage of the client/server development environment.

✦ Views allow you to SELECT information from one or more tables.

✦ Triggers are used to maintain referential integrity and validate data.

✦ You can pass parameters from forms and reports to stored procedures.

✦ Table structures can be modified in the Database Diagram window.

✦ The Upsizing Wizard automatically converts an Access database to a client/server application.

✦   ✦   ✦

Introduction to Applications with VBA

You've learned how to create macros to automate operations. You can, however, program Access in other ways. Writing VBA modules is the best way to create applications. Adding error routines, setting up repetitive looping, and adding procedures that macros simply can't perform give you more control of application development. In this chapter, you learn what a module is and how to begin to use VBA.

Instant Applications Using the Access 2000 Database Wizard

It's 3 p.m. on a Friday. A potential new client has just called and said he hears that you do great work. The client wants a custom system to do whatever — and wants to see a prototype of what you can do by Monday morning at 10 a.m. Do you cancel the weekend picnic with the family? Do you reschedule your golf or tennis match and order plenty of Jolt Cola? No. There's a great way to get started: the Access 2000 Database Wizard!

Table Wizards in Access 2000 allow you to choose business and personal table definitions — expenses, contact management, order entry, time and billing, and so on — from a list. Some definitions contain multiple tables, such as Orders and Items. After you select your table(s), Access displays a set of fields and allows you to choose which ones to include. The program then builds the table for you. Optionally, you can also have a simple AutoForm created. Although this feature is a real time-saver, it pales in comparison with this new generation of Access.

The Access 2000 Database Wizard takes the concept of Table Wizards to a new dimension by combining the best features of Access Wizards with the amazing power of an application generator. *Application generators* have been popular for many years in some products. These products enable you to create a custom table design, create a form or report, and then automatically generate code to tie everything together.

The Access 2000 Database Wizard doesn't require you to define a table design first; it doesn't make you create a form or report; it simply builds a complete, customizable application, including tables, forms, modules, reports, and a user-modifiable switchboard. The Wizard doesn't build just one table or form. The Database Wizard builds groups of tables; adds the table relationships; builds forms for each table, including one-to-many forms, where appropriate; and even adds critical reports for the type of application you are building. This process means that the Wizard creates an entire ready-to-run application. As you go through the Wizard process, you determine which fields from each table definition are used; some fields are mandatory, and some are optional. You can always make changes after the application is built.

The order-entry application you build in this chapter creates 10 tables, 14 forms, and 8 reports, including customer reports, sales reports, and even an aged-receivables statement — everything you need to start a basic order-entry system.

You start the Database Wizard by choosing File ➪ New Database. Access 2000 displays the General tab in the New dialog box that contains the Blank Database icon for creating a new database. Select the Databases tab, as shown in Figure 34-1. Each icon represents a different application the Database Wizard can create. When you create an application, that application is created in its own database container.

The Database Wizard allows you to choose among a wide variety of applications, as follows:

✦ Asset Tracking

✦ Order Entry

✦ Contact Management

✦ Resource Scheduling

✦ Event Management

✦ Service Call Management

✦ Expenses

✦ Time and Billing

✦ Inventory Control

✦ Ledger

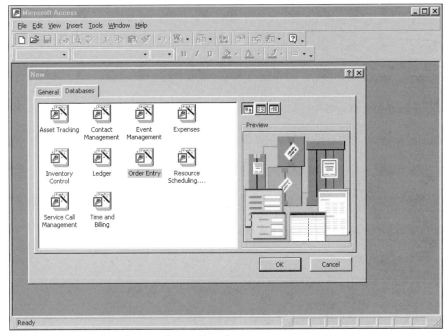

Figure 34-1: Starting the Database Wizard.

When you decide which application is closest to the one you want to create, double-click on it to start defining your own application. For the example in this chapter, choose the Order Entry application.

Getting started

When you choose the Order Entry application, a dialog box appears. Enter a name for the database. This dialog box is a standard File navigation-type dialog box that allows you to select the drive, directory, and database name. The default name is the name of the application. In this example, the name is Order Entry1.mdb. You can make the name anything you want, and you can change it later by renaming the database with the Windows Explorer. Press the Create button to create the new database.

When the Wizard starts, the dialog box shown in Figure 34-2 appears, showing a pictorial representation of the system. In this example, the dialog box tells you that six basic functions will be created: Customer information, Order information, Order Details, Payment information, Product information, and My company information. These functions generally are tables or forms. After you view this introductory dialog box, you can click on the standard Next> button to go to the next dialog box.

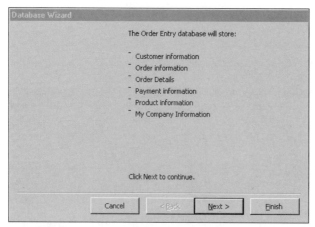

Figure 34-2: Learning what the database will create for you.

Working with tables and fields

The next Wizard screen (see Figure 34-3) enables you to work with the tables and fields of the database. Most of the fields and tables are mandatory, but you also can select optional fields for each table. The tables are listed on the left side of the dialog box, and the fields that make up the table are on the right side of the dialog box.

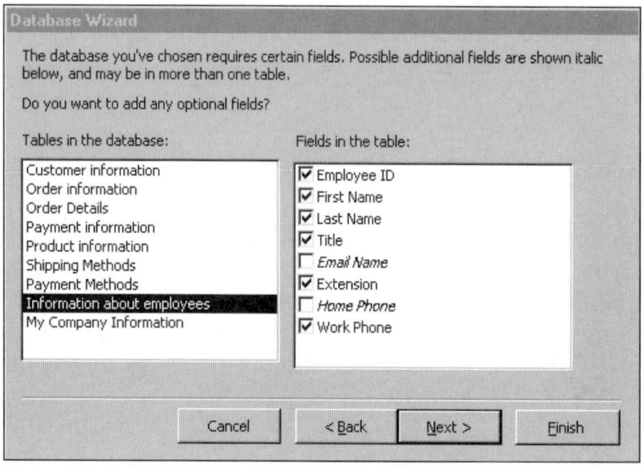

Figure 34-3: Working with tables and fields.

As you select each table, the list of fields changes. Fields that are optional appear italicized. When you check the fields, the Wizard includes them in the table design.

Selecting AutoFormat styles

After you make your selections, you can move to the next Wizard screen, which allows you to select the style for your forms. You can choose any of the AutoFormat options. If you created your own AutoFormats, they are listed here, too.

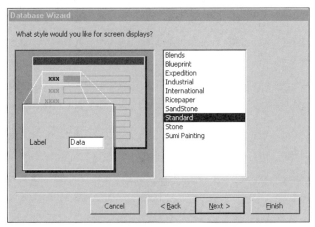

Figure 34-4: Selecting an AutoFormat for the screens.

After you select the style of your forms, you can do the same for reports. The next Wizard screen (see Figure 34-5) allows you to select an AutoFormat style for the printed report. You can add your own formats for each of the reports the Wizard creates.

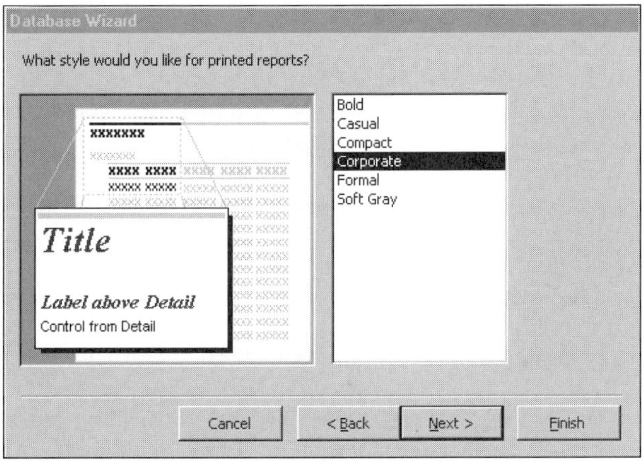

Figure 34-5: Selecting an AutoFormat for a report.

Customizing by selection

After you select the style of forms and reports, you see a Wizard screen that enables you to give your application a title and even a bitmap picture. In Figure 34-6, the standard title of Order Entry has been changed to Mountain Scenes Order Entry System, and the client's logo (a small sun rising over a mountain, the same one as Mountain Animal Hospital) has been included. This is found on your CD-ROM and is called MTN.BMP. You can scan a logo or select any standard Windows 95 image file for inclusion in the application. When you click on the Picture button, the Database Wizard displays a dialog box you can search to find the desired picture. The picture appears on all your reports.

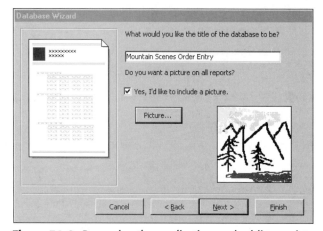

Figure 34-6: Renaming the application and adding a picture.

When you complete this Wizard screen and click the Next> button, the last Database Wizard screen appears. This Wizard screen, which displays a checkered flag, asks whether you want to learn how to use a database (developers never ask for help, do they?) and whether you want to start the application after it is built. Clicking on the Finish button clears the screen and builds the application.

As the creation process progresses, you see a dialog box displaying the Wizard's magic wand and two progress meters. The top progress meter displays the overall progress. The bottom progress meter displays the progress Access is making with creating each object — first the tables and then the relationships, queries, forms, switchboards, reports, and even database properties. Below this dialog box, you can see the Database window magically filling with names as each new object is created.

Note　　If this is the first time you are using the Database Wizard, you will be asked for your company name, address, and related information. To avoid errors in creating the new database, be sure to complete all of the requested information. After you complete this screen, the switchboard is displayed.

Using the switchboard system

If you elected on the last Wizard screen to start the application, the main switchboard appears (as shown in Figure 34-7), and the Database window is minimized. Otherwise, the Database window is displayed.

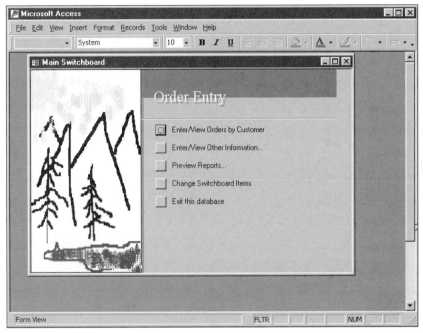

Figure 34-7: The main switchboard.

The main switchboard is your gateway to the system functions. As you see in Figure 34-7, the switchboard displays five main items. The first item — Enter/View Orders by Customer — displays the one-to-many orders form (see Figure 34-8), where you can review or edit all the orders sorted by your customer's name. The next item — Enter/View Other Information — displays another switchboard screen that allows you to display all the peripheral forms for editing all the support tables. In this example, those tables include Employees, Company Information, Products, Payment methods, and Shipping methods. At the bottom of each switchboard screen (other than the main switchboard) is the option *Return to Main Switchboard.*

In Figure 34-8, you see a form that actually is a summary of a specific customer's orders. At the bottom of the form are several buttons for displaying an order, displaying a payment, or printing an invoice for the customer. If you look at the order form itself, you see that it has several supporting tables, such as products, employees, payment methods, and shipping methods. The form has embedded subforms that allow you to select data from these lookup tables. From the data-entry switchboard screen, you can even set various global company options, such as company name and address, payment terms, and other information used for invoices and other reports.

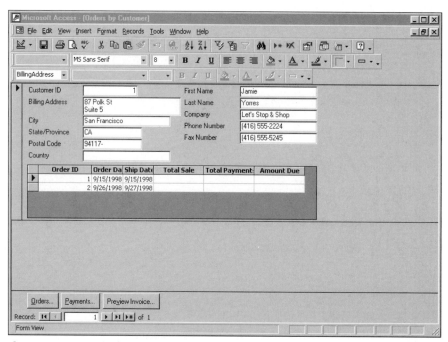

Figure 34-8: A typical one-to-many form.

Besides the data-entry switchboard, a switchboard is available for viewing and printing your reports. For the Order Processing example, the reports include Customer Listing; Invoice; Receivables Aging Report; and Sales by Customer, Employee, or Product. The company name and logo (if specified) appear at the top of each report.

Although the forms and reports are simplistic, they serve as a great starting point for creating more robust applications. Obviously, the Wizard decides the choices of forms and reports, but you can create your own forms and reports and then add them to the Order Entry switchboard. One of the options in the main switchboard allows you to customize the switchboards themselves.

Customizing the switchboards

The Database Wizard contains a series of hierarchical screens (similar to the Menu Builder) that allow you to create and maintain switchboard items. Unfortunately, this technology works only in the Database Wizard. If you are creative, you can copy the switchboards and the supporting tables to other applications, but you must have access to the Access 2000 Wizard libraries because some of the code resides in the common areas.

Figure 34-9 shows one of the screens used to customize the switchboards. This screen shows the switchboard definition for Figure 34-7. To customize a switchboard, you start with the Switchboard Page definitions, which list the switchboard's name. In Figure 34-9, this switchboard is named Main Switchboard. Each page contains the items shown in Figure 34-9, and you can edit each item. When you edit an item, you enter the item name (text) and the command, which is similar to the macro commands but more explanatory. There are only eight commands: GoTo Switchboard, Open Form in Add Mode, Open Form in Edit Mode, Open Report, Design Application, Exit Application, Run Macro, and Run Code. With these eight commands, you can do almost anything. Based on which of the eight commands you select, the last entry area changes to display the name of the switchboard, form, report, macro, or VBA function.

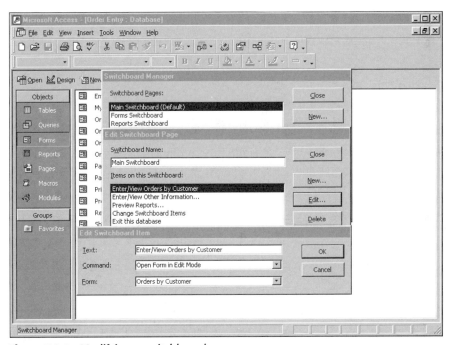

Figure 34-9: Modifying a switchboard.

Although the Database Wizard allows you to create instant applications, these applications are very simple — good only for the most basic business or personal applications. As a starting point, though, they are excellent for new users and even for developers who need to prototype a system fast. Because you can customize everything (especially the switchboards), you can develop a custom solution quickly to get started or impress your customers.

Building Applications from Scratch

Access has an excellent variety of tools that allow you to work with databases and their tables, queries, forms, and reports without ever having to write a single line of code. At some point, you may begin building more sophisticated applications. You may want to make your applications more "bulletproof" by providing more intensive data-entry validation or implementing better error handling.

Some operations cannot be accomplished through the user interface, even with macros. You may find yourself saying, "I wish I had a function that would. . . ." or "There just has to be a function that will let me. . . ." At other times, you find that you are continually putting the same formula or expression in a query or filter. You may find yourself saying, "I'm tired of typing this formula into. . . ." or "Doggone it, I typed the wrong formula in this. . . ."

For situations such as these, you need the horsepower of a structured programming language. Access provides a programming language called Visual Basic, Applications Edition, which most often is referred to as *VBA*. VBA extends the capabilities of Access, offering power beyond the scope of macros.

Getting started with programming in Access requires an understanding of its event-driven environment.

Understanding events and event procedures

In Access, unlike traditional *procedural* programming environments, the user controls the actions and flow of the application. The user determines what to do and when to do it, such as changing information in a field or clicking a command button.

Using macros and event procedures, you implement the responses to these actions. Access provides event properties for each of the controls you place on the form. When you attach a macro or event procedure to a control's event property, you do not have to worry about the order of actions a user may take on a particular form.

In an event-driven environment such as Access, the objects — forms, reports, and controls — respond to events. Basically, an event procedure is program code that executes when an event occurs. The code is directly attached to the form or report that contains the event being processed. An Exit command button, for example, exits the form when the user clicks that button. Clicking on the command button triggers its On Click event. The event procedure is the program code (or macro) that you create and attach to the On Click event. Every time the user clicks on the command button, the event procedure runs automatically.

Up to this point, you have used macros to respond to an object's events. In addition to macros, Access provides a built-in programming language for creating procedures.

Creating programs in Visual Basic for Applications

VBA has become the common language for all Microsoft applications. VBA is in all Microsoft Office 2000 applications, including Access, Word, Excel, PowerPoint, and Outlook. It is also in Visual Basic and Project. VBA is a modern, structured programming language that offers many of the programming structures programmers are accustomed to: If. . .Then. . .Else, Select Case, and so on. VBA allows a programmer to work with functions and subroutines in an Englishlike language. The language also is extensible (capable of calling Windows or Windows NT API routines) and can interact through ADO (Active Data Objects) or DAO (Data Access Objects) with any Access or Visual Basic data type.

Using the Module window, you can create and edit VBA code or procedures. Each procedure is a series of code statements that performs an operation or calculation.

Note   A *procedure* is simply some code, written in a programming language, that follows a series of logical steps in performing some action. You could, for example, create a Beep procedure that makes the computer beep as a warning or notification that something has happened in your program.

There are two types of procedures:

✦ Subs

✦ Functions

Sub procedures

A *sub* procedure is program code that does not return a value. Because it does not return a value, a sub procedure cannot be used in an expression or be called by assigning it to a variable. A sub procedure typically runs as a separate program called by an event in a form or report.

You can use a sub to perform actions when you don't want to return a value. In fact, because you cannot assign a value to a control's event properties, you can only create sub procedures for an event.

You can call subs and pass a data value known as a *parameter*. Subs can call other subs. Subs also can call function procedures.

The code statements inside the sub procedure are lines of Visual Basic statements. (Remember that this statement refers to the Visual Basic language, not to the product.) These statements make up the code you want to run every time the procedure is executed. The following example shows the Exit command button's sub procedure:

```
Sub Button_Click ()
  DoCmd.Close
End Sub
```

The `Button_Click ()` sub procedure is attached to the Exit command button's On Click event. When the user clicks the Exit command button, the command `DoCmd Close` executes to close the form.

Function procedures

A *function* procedure returns a value. The value can be Null, but the procedure always returns a value. You can use functions in expressions or assign a function to a variable.

Like subs, functions can be called by other functions or by subs. You also can pass parameters to a function.

You assign the return value of a function to the procedure name itself. You then can use the value that is returned as part of a larger expression. The following function procedure calculates the square footage of a room:

```
Function nSquareFeet (dblHeight As Double, dblWidth As Double)
As Double
  nSquareFeet = dblHeight * dblWidth
End Function
```

This function receives two parameters for the height and width of the room. The function returns the results to the procedure that called it by assigning the result of the calculation to the *procedure name* (nSquareFeet).

To call this function, you could use code like this:

```
dblAnswer = nSquareFeet(xHeight, xWidth)
```

Sub and function procedures are grouped and stored in modules. The Modules object button in the Database window stores the common procedures that any of your forms can access. You can store all your procedures in a single module. Realistically, though, you'll probably want to group your procedures into separate modules, categorizing them by the nature of the operations they perform. An Update module, for example, might include procedures for adding and deleting records from a table.

Creating a new module

To create a new module, follow these steps:

1. Click on the Module object button in the Database window.

2. Click on the New toolbar button.

Access opens Microsoft Visual Basic and creates a new module, named Module1, in a Module window. This new module should look like the one shown in Figure 34-10. In this figure, notice that Access places two lines of text in the first line in the window, beginning with `Option Compare Database` and then `Option Explicit`.

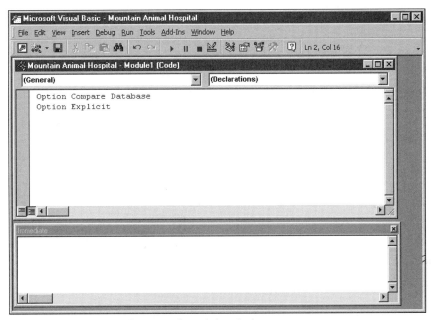

Figure 34-10: The newly opened module window.

Notice that the Module window in Figure 34-10 displays the tools for the Visual Basic editor. Also notice the two combo boxes just below the toolbar. The right combo box displays *Declarations* because you currently are in the declarations part of the module.

Each module includes two or more sections:

✦ A single declarations section

✦ A section for each procedure

Note
Is there a difference between a module and a procedure? *Modules* are the containers used to organize your code. You can think of a module as being a library of procedures. You can create many modules for an Access database.

Note
Each form has its own module. Every form or report you create in your database contains a built-in form module or report module. This module is known as *code-behind-form*, or CBF (the same for reports). This form or report module is an integral part of each form or report; it is used as a container for the event procedures you create for the form or report. The module is a convenient way to place a form's event procedures in a single collection. Generally, if the module will be used by only a single form or report object, it should go behind the form or report. If the module will be needed more globally or will be used by common menus or toolbar definitions, it should be placed in a *global module.*

The declaration section

You can use the declaration section to *declare* (define) variables you want to use in procedures. You can declare variables that will be used only by the procedures in a module or by all procedures across all modules within a database.

You are not required to declare variables in this section because variables can also be declared in the individual procedures. In fact, if you remove the Option Explicit line from a procedure or function, you don't have to declare a variable at all. Access allows *implicit* variable declarations — that is, declarations created on the fly. If you enter a variable name in an expression and the variable hasn't been declared, Access accepts and declares it for you, giving it the data typeconsistent with its first use.

Caution   If you have the line of code Option Explicit in your module, which is the default in Access 2000 VBA, you must explicitly declare your variables or you will get an error when you try to use them. This speeds up execution of VBA modules. If you have a small application, you might want to remove the Option Explicit line of code, which will allow you to use variables without first defining their name and data type.

Tip   Entering the declaration statement Option Explicit forces you to declare any variables you will use when creating procedures for the module. Although this procedure involves a little more work, it speeds execution of module code by Access. For others who may need to work with your code later on, declaring variables provides assistance in documenting your code.

Creating a new procedure

After you complete any declarations for the module, you are ready to create a procedure. Follow these steps to create a procedure called BeepWarning:

1. Go to any empty line in the Module window.

2. Type **Sub BeepWarning** to name the module. The module window should look similar to Figure 34-11.

3. Press Enter.

If you enter the name of a function you previously created in this module (or in another module within the database), Access informs you that the function already exists. Access does not allow you to create another procedure with the same name.

Notice that when you pressed Enter, Access did two things automatically:

✦ Placed the procedure named BeepWarning in the Procedure combo box in the toolbar

✦ Placed parentheses at the end of the procedure name

✦ Added the End Sub statement to the procedure

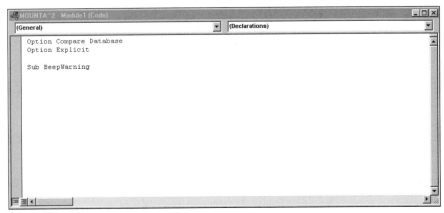

Figure 34-11: Entering a new procedure in the Module window.

You are no longer in the declarations section of the module; you are now in an actual procedure.

Now you can enter the lines of code needed for your procedure. Enter the following lines of code into the module:

```
Dim xBeeps, nBeeps As Integer
nBeeps = 5
For xBeeps = 1 To nBeeps
  Beep
Next xBeeps
```

In this example, you are running the program five times. Don't worry about what the procedure does—you'll learn more about how to program specific tasks in the next chapter.

Your completed function should look like the one shown in Figure 34-12.

When BeepWarning runs, it beeps for the number of times specified.

Using the Access 2000 Module Help

Suppose that you know you want to use a specific command but can't remember the syntax (*syntax* is computer grammar). Access 2000 features two types of help called Auto List Members and Auto Quick Info to help you create each line of code.

Auto List Members is automatically displayed when you type the beginning of a command that has objects, properties, and methods following the main object. For example, if you enter DoCmd, a list of the possible commands is displayed, as shown in Figure 34-13. You can scroll through the list box and select the option you want.

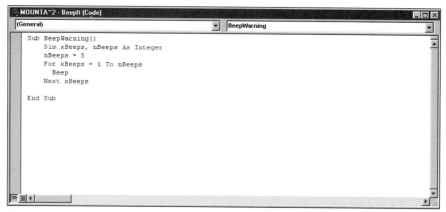

Figure 34-12: The BeepWarning procedure completed.

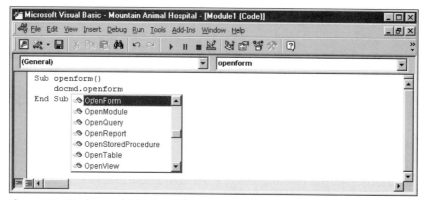

Figure 34-13: Access 2000 Auto List Members help in a module.

In this example, the OpenForm command is being chosen. After you choose an option, either more Auto List Members help is displayed or, if the rest of the command options are parameters for the other type of module help, Auto Quick Info is displayed, as shown in Figure 34-14.

Auto Quick Info help guides you through all the options for the specific command. The bold word is the next parameter to be entered. Figure 34-14 shows that there are many parameters in the OpenForm command. When you enter the form name, the next section will become bolded. As you enter each parameter or a comma to skip a parameter, the next section in the help becomes bolded. You can remove the help by pressing Esc.

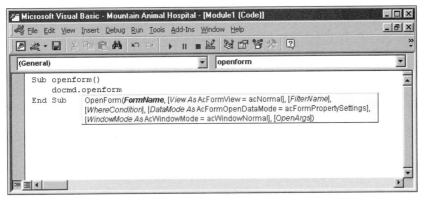

Figure 34-14: Access 2000 Auto Quick Info help in a module.

Compiling procedures

After you create all the procedures, you should compile them by choosing Debug ⇨ Compile from the module menu. This action checks your code for errors (a procedure known as *syntax checking; syntax* is computer grammar) and also converts the programs to a form your computer can understand. If the compile operation is not successful, an error window appears.

Note   Access compiles all uncompiled procedures, not just the current procedure.

Saving a module

When you finish creating your procedures, you should save them by saving the module. As you do any other Access object, you can save the module by choosing File ⇨ Save or else they will be saved automatically when you close the window. You should consider saving the module every time you complete a procedure.

Creating procedures in the Form or Report Design window

All forms, reports, and their controls can have event procedures associated with their events. While you are in the design window for the form or report, you can add an event procedure quickly in one of three ways:

✦ Choose Build Event from the shortcut menu (see Figure 34-15).

✦ Choose Code Builder in the Choose Builder dialog box when you click on the ellipsis button to the right of an event in the Property dialog box.

✦ Enter the text **Event Procedure** or select it from the top of the event combo box (see Figure 34-16).

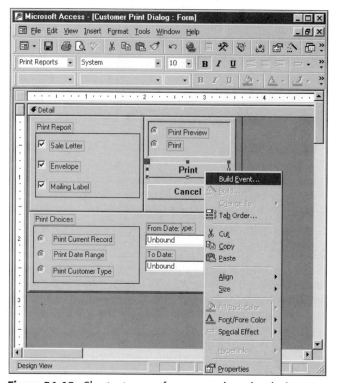

Figure 34-15: Shortcut menu for a control on the design surface of a form.

Whether you choose the Build Event from the shortcut menu choice or click the ellipsis button in the Property dialog box, the Choose Builder dialog box appears. Choosing the Code Builder item opens the Module window in Visual Basic, as shown in Figure 34-17. In Visual Basic, if you click on the View Microsoft Access button, you can toggle back and forth between the Access form designer and the Visual Basic Module window.

Note   If an event procedure is already attached to the control, the text [Event Procedure] is displayed in the event area. Clicking on the Builder button instantly displays the procedure for the event in a Visual Basic Module window — hence the name Event Procedure.

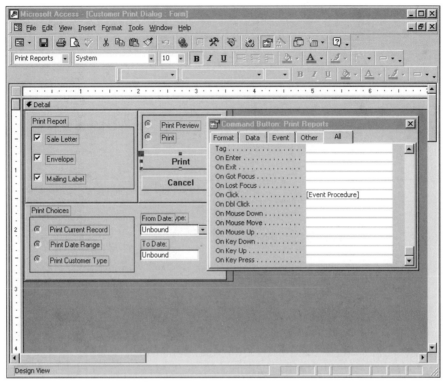

Figure 34-16: Properties dialog box for the Form Designer.

Editing an existing procedure

To edit an existing procedure, follow these steps:

1. Click on the Module object button in the Database window.

2. Double-click on the module name that contains the procedure. The declaration portion of the module appears.

3. Find the procedure you want and select it from the pull-down menu on the right of the module window.

Tip After you are in a module, you can select any procedure in another module quickly by pressing F2 or choosing View ➪ Object Browser. Access displays the Object Browser dialog box, shown in Figure 34-18. Highlight a different module name in the Modules section of the View Procedures dialog box to see the names of all procedures in the new module. When you select a module, you then can select a method and display the function call, as shown in Figure 34-18.

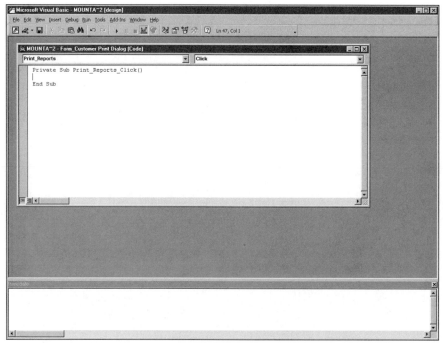

Figure 34-17: A form module open in the Form Designer.

Figure 34-18: Selecting a procedure to edit.

Working in the Module window

Whenever you create Visual Basic procedures for your Access applications, you write that code in a Module window. Although the Module window is confusing at first, it is easy to understand and use.

Parts of the Module window

When you enter Design mode of a module — whether it is via a form or report module or the module object (Database window) — the Visual Basic module window and its associated menu and toolbar open to allow you to create or edit your procedures.

When you open a module from the Modules object button of the Database window, the Module window has the same features as the Module window for a form or report design window. The only difference between the two is that for a form (or report) module, the Object and Procedure combo boxes on the toolbar list the form's objects and events. You can select these objects and events to create or edit event procedures for the form. The object combo box for a module you open from the Database window displays only one choice: General. The Procedure combo box contains only the names of existing procedures.

The Module window has four basic areas:

    ✦ Menu bar (command bar)

    ✦ Toolbar

    ✦ Code window

    ✦ Debug window

The Menu bar

The menu bar of the Module window has ten menus: File, Edit, View, Insert, Debug, Run, Tools, Add-Ins, Window, and Help.

The Toolbar

The Module window's toolbar (refer to Figure 34-17) helps you create new modules and their procedures quickly. The toolbar contains buttons for the most common actions you use to create, modify, and debug modules.

The Code window

The code window — the most important area of the Module window — is where you create and modify the VBA code for your procedures.

The code window has the standard Windows features that enable you to resize, minimize, maximize, and move the window. You also can split the window into two areas. At times, you want to edit two procedures at the same time; perhaps you need to copy part of one procedure to another. To work on two procedures simultaneously, simply choose Window ⇨ Split. You can resize the window by moving the split bar up and down. Now you can work with both procedures at the same time. To switch between windows, press the F6 key or click the other window.

The Debug window

When you write code for a procedure, you may want to try the procedure while you are in the module, or you may need to check the results of an expression. The Debug window allows you to try your procedures without leaving the module. You can run the module and check variables. You could, for example, type **?** and the name of the variable.

To view the Debug window, choose View ⇨ Debug Window. Figure 34-19 shows the Debug window.

Note   Before Access 2000, the Debug included the Locals and Watch windows. The Locals and Watch windows are now independent of the Debug window.

After you create a sub procedure, you can run it to see whether it works as expected. You can test it with supplied arguments.

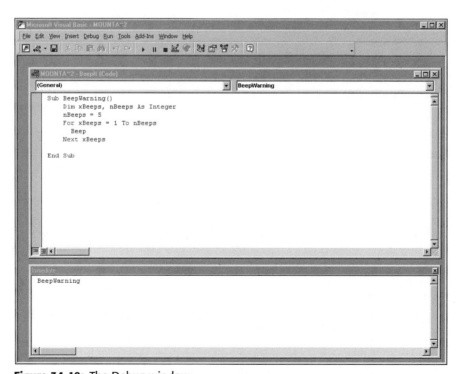

Figure 34-19: The Debug window.

To run the BeepWarning Sub procedure, follow these steps:

1. Activate the Debug pane by selecting it from the View menu.

2. Type BeepWarning and press Enter. The BeepWarning sub runs.

You may have heard five beeps or (if you have a really fast machine) only a few beeps because the interval between beeps is short.

Figure 34-19, earlier in this section, shows this command.

Migrating from Macros to VBA

Because you can accomplish many tasks by using macros or the user interface, without the need for programming, should you now concentrate on using Visual Basic for your applications? The answer depends on what you are trying to accomplish. The fact that Access 2000 includes VBA does not mean that Access macros are no longer useful. Access developers will want to learn VBA and add it to their arsenal of tools for creating Access applications.

VBA is not always the answer. Although VBA enables you to create programs that can eliminate the need for most macros, macros are appropriate in some cases. Some tasks, such as assigning global key assignments, can be accomplished only via macros. You can perform some actions more easily and effectively by using a macro.

Depending on the task you need to accomplish, a Visual Basic procedure may offer better performance. The opposite also is true: A VBA procedure may run at the same speed as a macro counterpart or even slower. Simply deciding to use VBA for performance proves to be ineffective in most cases. In fact, most people may find that the time needed to create an application actually increases when they rely on using VBA to code everything in their application.

Knowing when to use macros and procedures

In Access, you will want to continue to use macros at times because they offer an ideal way to take care of many details, such as running reports and forms. Because the arguments for the macro actions are displayed with the macro (in the bottom portion of the Macro window), you can develop applications and assign actions faster. You won't have to remember complex or difficult syntax.

Several actions you can accomplish via VBA are better suited for macros. The following actions tend to be more efficient when they are run from macros:

◆ Using macros against an entire set of records — for example, to manipulate multiple records in a table or across tables (such as updating field values or deleting records)

◆ Opening and closing forms

◆ Running reports

Note
Visual Basic supplies a DoCmd Object you can use to accomplish most macro actions. This object actually runs the macro task. You could, for example, specify DoCmd.Close to run the close macro and close the current active form. Even this method has flaws. DoCmd cannot perform at least eight macro actions: AddMenu, MsgBox, RunApp, RunCode, SendKeys, SetValue, StopAllMacros, and StopMacro. Some of these actions have VBA equivalents.

Although macros sometimes prove to be the solution of choice, VBA is the tool of choice at other times. You probably will want to use Visual Basic rather than macros when you want to perform any of the following tasks:

◆ *Create and use your own functions.* In addition to using the built-in functions in Access, you can create and work with your own functions by using VBA.

◆ *Create your own error routines and messages.* You can create error routines that detect an error and decide what action to take. These routines bypass the cryptic Access error messages.

◆ *Use OLE and DDE to communicate with other Windows applications or to run system-level actions.* You can write code to see whether a file exists before you take some action, or you can communicate with another Windows application (such as a spreadsheet), passing data back and forth.

◆ *Use existing functions in external Windows DLLs.* Macros don't allow you to call functions in other Windows Dynamic Link Libraries.

◆ *Work with records one at a time.* If you need to step through records or to move values from a record to variables for manipulation, code is the answer.

◆ *Maintain the application.* Unlike macros, code can be built into a form or report, making maintaining the code more efficient. Additionally, if you move a form or report from one database to another, the event procedures built into the form or report move with it.

✦ *Create or manipulate objects.* In most cases, you'll find that it's easiest to create and modify an object in that object's Design view. In some situations, however, you may want to manipulate the definition of an object in code. Using Visual Basic, you can manipulate all the objects in a database, including the database itself.

✦ *Pass arguments to your Visual Basic procedures.* You can set arguments for macro actions in the bottom part of the Macro window when you create the macro, but you can't change arguments when the macro is running. With Visual Basic, however, you can pass arguments to your code at the time it's run or use variables for arguments — something you can't do with macros. This capability gives you a great deal of flexibility in the way your Visual Basic procedures run.

✦ *Display a progress meter on the status bar.* If you need to display a progress meter to communicate progress to the user, VBA code is the answer.

Tip

If you create a form or report that will be copied to other databases, it is a good idea to create your event procedures for that form or report in Visual Basic rather than use macros. Because macros are stored as separate objects in the database, you have to remember which ones are associated with the form or report you are copying. On the other hand, because Visual Basic code can be attached to the form or report, copying the form automatically copies the VBA event procedures associated with it.

Converting existing macros to Visual Basic

After you become comfortable with writing VBA code, you may want to rewrite some of your application macros as Visual Basic procedures. As you set off on this process, you quickly realize how mentally challenging the effort can be as you review every macro in your various macro libraries. You cannot merely cut the macro from the Macro window and paste it into a Module window. For each condition, action, and action argument for a macro, you must analyze the task it accomplishes and then write the equivalent statements of VBA code in your procedure.

Fortunately, Access provides a feature that converts macros to VBA code automatically. One of the options in the Save As dialog box is Save As Visual Basic Module; you can use this option when a macro file is highlighted in the Macros object window of the Database window. This option allows you to convert an entire macro library to a module in seconds. To start this process, choose File ➪ Save As, as shown in Figure 34-20.

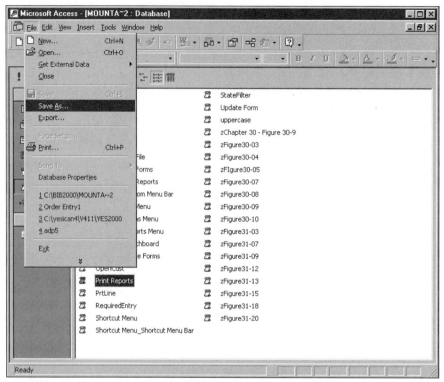

Figure 34-20: Choosing File ➪ Save As.

To try the conversion process, you can convert the Print Reports macros in the Mountain Animal Hospital database. Figure 34-21 displays the macros for the Print Reports macro library.

Follow these steps to run the conversion process:

1. Click on the Macros object button of the Database window.

2. Select the Print Reports macro library.

3. Choose File ➪ Save As. The Save As dialog box appears, as shown in Figure 34-22.

4. Choose Save as Module and click on OK. The Convert Macro dialog box appears, as shown in Figure 34-23.

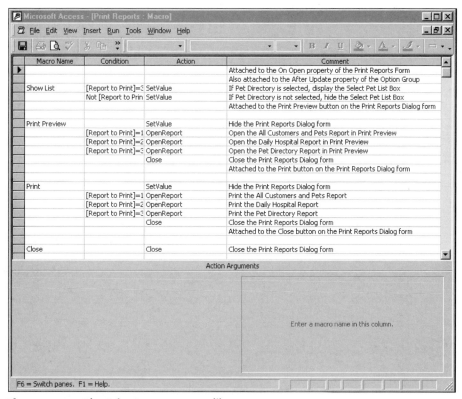

Macro Name	Condition	Action	Comment
			Attached to the On Open property of the Print Reports Form
			Also attached to the After Update property of the Option Group
Show List	[Report to Print]=3	SetValue	If Pet Directory is selected, display the Select Pet List Box
	Not [Report to Prin	SetValue	If Pet Directory is not selected, hide the Select Pet List Box
			Attached to the Print Preview button on the Print Reports Dialog form
Print Preview		SetValue	Hide the Print Reports Dialog form
	[Report to Print]=1	OpenReport	Open the All Customers and Pets Report in Print Preview
	[Report to Print]=2	OpenReport	Open the Daily Hospital Report in Print Preview
	[Report to Print]=3	OpenReport	Open the Pet Directory Report in Print Preview
		Close	Close the Print Reports Dialog form
			Attached to the Print button on the Print Reports Dialog form
Print		SetValue	Hide the Print Reports Dialog form
	[Report to Print]=1	OpenReport	Print the All Customers and Pets Report
	[Report to Print]=2	OpenReport	Print the Daily Hospital Report
	[Report to Print]=3	OpenReport	Print the Pet Directory Report
		Close	Close the Print Reports Dialog form
			Attached to the Close button on the Print Reports Dialog form
Close		Close	Close the Print Reports Dialog form

Action Arguments

Enter a macro name in this column.

F6 = Switch panes. F1 = Help.

Figure 34-21: The Print Reports macro library.

Save As

Save Macro 'Print Reports' To:

Print Reports

A_s

Module

OK   Cancel

Figure 34-22: The Save As Visual Basic
Module dialog box.

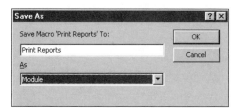

Convert macro: Print Reports

☑ Add _e_rror handling to generated functions
☑ _I_nclude macro comments

Convert   Cancel

Figure 34-23: The Convert Macro dialog box.

5. Select the options that include error handling and comments and click on Convert.

Access briefly displays each new procedure as it is converted. When the conversion process completes, the Conversion Finished message box appears.

6. Click on OK to remove the message box.

7. Access displays the Modules object window of the Database window, as shown in Figure 34-24. Access names the new module Converted Macro - Print Reports.

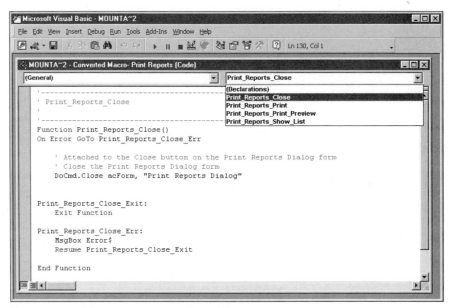

Figure 34-24: The newly converted module.

When you open the Module window for the new module, you can view the procedures created from the macros. As you can see in Figure 34-24, Access created four functions from the Print Reports macro: Print_Reports_Close, Print_Reports_Print, Print_Reports_Print_Preview, and Print_Reports_Show_List. Figures 34-25 and 34-26 show samples of the new procedures.

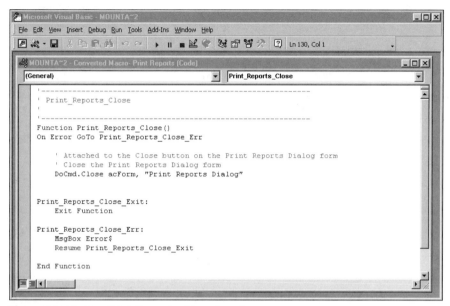

Figure 34-25: The Print_Reports_Close function.

At the top of each function, Access inserts four comment lines for the name of the function. The Function statement follows the comment lines. Access names the functions, using the macro library's name as a prefix (Print_Reports); the macro name (if one is supplied) for the suffix; and Close for the Close function.

Cross-Reference

When you specify that you want Access to include error processing for the conversion, Access automatically inserts the OnError statement as the first command in the procedure. The OnError statement tells Access to branch to other statements that display an appropriate message and then exit the function. Error processing is covered in more detail in Chapter 35.

The statement beginning with DoCmd is the actual code that Access created from the macro. The DoCmd methods run Access actions from Visual Basic. An action performs important tasks, such as closing windows, opening forms, and setting the value of controls. In the Close macro, for example, Close Print Reports Dialog closes the Print Reports dialog box. Access converts the Close macro action arguments to the properly formatted parameters for the DoCmd methods.

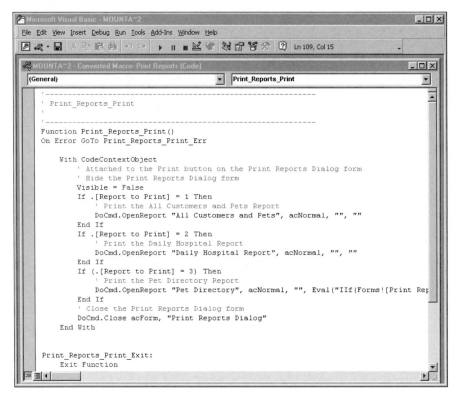

Figure 34-26: The Print_Reports_Print function.

In the `Print_Reports_Print` function, the group of statements beginning with the With command retrieves the settings of some of the controls in the Print Reports dialog box. The `DoCmd` action prints various reports based on the value of the settings in the dialog box. Chapter 35 covers conditional structures, such as the `If...End If` statements you see in these functions.

Tip You also can convert macros that are used in a form by choosing Tools ➪ Macro ➪ Convert Form's Macros to Visual Basic in Forms Design view.

Using the Command Button Wizard to create VBA code

A good way to learn how to write event procedures is to use the Command Button Wizard, which was covered in Chapter 32. When Access creates a command button with a Wizard, it creates an event procedure and attaches it to the button. You can open the event procedure to see how it works and then modify it to fit your needs.

The Wizard speeds the process of creating a command button because it does all the basic work for you. When you use the Wizard, Access prompts you for information and creates a command button based on your answers.

You can create more than 30 types of command buttons by using the Command Button Wizard. You can create a command button that finds a record, prints a record, or applies a form filter, for example. You can run this Wizard by creating a new command button on a form. Figure 34-27 shows a command button being created in the Record Operations category, with the Delete Record action.

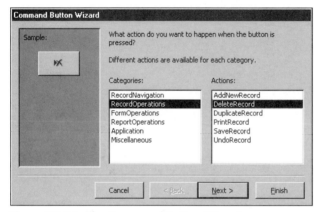

Figure 34-27: The Command Button Wizard.

Note   In the Mountain Animal Hospital database is a form named *Button Wizard VBA Samples*. This form, shown in Figure 34-28 in Design mode, contains the result of running the Button Wizard with several selections. The Button Wizard VBA Samples form contains a dozen command buttons created with the Command Button Wizard. You can review the procedures for each command button on the form to see how powerful Visual Basic code can be.

To view the sample code, follow these steps:

1. Display the Button Wizard VBA Samples form in Design view.

2. Display the Property window for the desired button.

    Click on the Builder button (. . .) for the On Click event property to display the command button's Module window, with the procedure.

Figure 34-29 shows the code for the Delete Record command button.

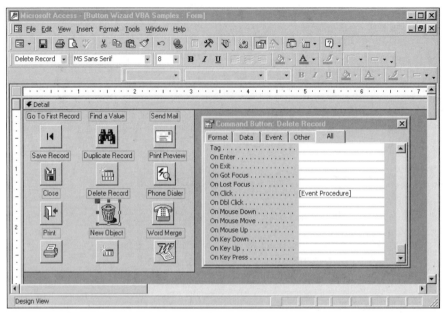

Figure 34-28: Examples of Command Button Wizard buttons.

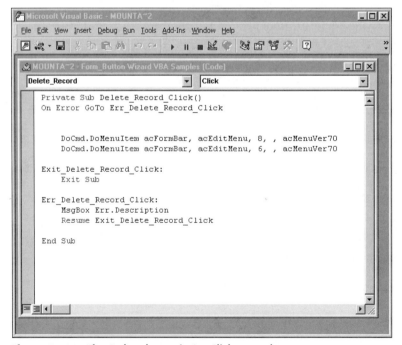

Figure 34-29: The Delete button's On Click procedure.

Figure 34-30 shows the code for a Dialer command button. The Dialer_Click procedure retrieves the text in the current field and then passes the text to a utility that dials the telephone.

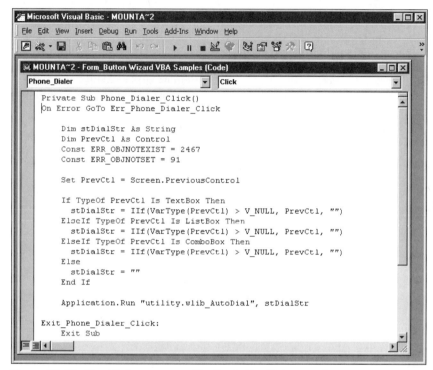

Figure 34-30: The Dialer command button's On Click procedure.

Summary

In this chapter, you learned how to create instant applications, use the Module window, and convert macros to VBA code. The following topics were covered:

✦ You can use the Database Wizard to create an application by clicking on an icon and answering a few questions.

✦ The Database Wizard features a customizable switchboard for adding new forms and reports to the application the Wizard creates for you.

✦ Module code can be created in a global module container or stored behind a form or report.

✦ Modules provide their own type of help to assist you as you enter a command.

✦ Sub procedures are called from events. Functions also are called from events or expressions and are used to return a value.

✦ You can use the Debug window to test your program.

✦ The Command Button Wizard enables you to create more than 30 types of buttons by selecting options from a list.

✦ You can convert a macro group to a VBA module library by selecting the macro and then choosing File ➪ Save As.

In the next chapter, you learn how to create modules, add variables, use logical constructs (If Then, While, Case), add error checking, and use recordset manipulation.

✦   ✦   ✦

The Access 2000 Programming Environment

✦ ✦ ✦ ✦

In This Chapter

Understanding modules

Using variables and data types

Working with Visual Basic logical constructs

Handling errors

Filtering data programmatically

Programming list and combo boxes

Updating tables

Using ADO and DAO

✦ ✦ ✦ ✦

T he Visual Basic language offers a full array of powerful commands for manipulating records in a table, controls on a form, or just about anything else. This chapter continues Chapter 34's discussion of working with procedures in forms, reports, and standard modules.

Understanding Modules

In the preceding chapter, you created a few procedures and became somewhat familiar with the Visual Basic programming environment. You probably are a little uncomfortable with modules and procedures, however, as well as unsure when and how to create them.

Modules and their procedures are the principal objects of the Visual Basic programming environment. The programming code that you write is placed in procedures that are contained in a module. The *procedures* can be independent procedures, unrelated to a specific form or report, or they can be integral parts of specific forms and reports.

Two basic categories of modules can be stored in a database:

Standard Modules	(Stored in the Module Object)
Form/Report	(CBF - Code Behind Form/CBR - Code Behind Report)

As you create Visual Basic procedures for your Access applications, you use both types of modules.

Form and report modules

All forms, reports, and their controls can associate event procedures with their events. These event procedures can be macros or Visual Basic code. Every form or report you create in your database contains a form module or report module. This *form or report module* is an integral part of the form or report, and is used as a container for the event procedures you create for the form or report. This method is a convenient way to place all of a form's event procedures in a single collection.

Creating Visual Basic event procedures in a form module can be very powerful and efficient. When an event procedure is attached to a form, it becomes part of the form. When you need to copy the form, the event procedures go with it. If you need to modify one of the form's events, you simply click on the ellipsis button for the event, and the form module window for the procedure appears. Figure 35-1 illustrates accessing the event procedure of the First Record button's On Click event shown in the form named Button Wizard Visual Basic Samples. Notice that in the On Click property is the text [Event Procedure]. When you click on the Builder button next to [Event Procedure], you will see the module window for that form (and specifically the On Click event for that button control).

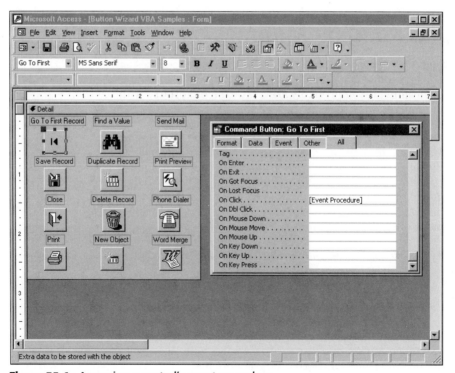

Figure 35-1: Accessing a control's event procedure.

Cross-Reference You learned about the Button Wizard Visual Basic Samples form in Chapter 34.

Standard modules

Standard modules are independent from form and report objects. These modules can be used to store code, in the form of procedures, that can be used from anywhere within your application. In early versions of Access (1.0 through 2.0), standard modules were known as *global modules*.

You can use standard procedures throughout your application for expressions, macros, event procedures, and even other procedures. To use a standard procedure, you simply call it from a control as a function or an event based on an event procedure, depending on the type of procedure that it is. Remember that two basic types of procedures are stored in modules:

✦ *Subs*, which perform actions without returning a value

✦ *Functions*, which always return a value

Tip Procedures run — modules contain. A procedure is executed; it performs some action. You create the procedures that your application will use. Modules, on the other hand, simply act like containers, grouping procedures and declarations together. A module cannot be run; rather, you run the procedures that are contained in the module. These procedures can respond to events or can be called from expressions, macros, and even other procedures.

You use the Modules container of the database to store your standard procedures. The module container is the section of the database that has a object button labeled Modules.

Although you can place any type of procedure in any module, you should group your procedures into categories. Most modules contain procedures that are related in some way. Figure 35-2 shows a standard module called Calendar. The Calendar module contains some procedures for working with dates, called DayOfWeek and Due28Day.

Event procedures that work with a single form or report belong in the module of the form or report. A specific form's module should contain only the declarations and event procedures needed for that form and its controls (command buttons, check boxes, text labels, text boxes, combo boxes, and so on). Placing another form's or report's event procedures in this form's module doesn't make sense.

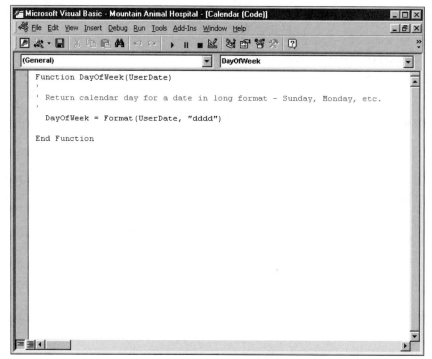

Figure 35-2: A standard module containing date-manipulation procedures.

To begin creating more sophisticated procedures with Visual Basic, you need to understand some of Visual Basic's fundamental programming elements. These basic elements include the following:

✦ Variables and how they interact with data

✦ Data types

✦ Programming syntax for logical constructs

Although this book is not a how-to programming book, it attempts to explain the concepts of the Visual Basic environment in Access and how you can use it to manipulate Access objects.

Using Variables

One of the most powerful concepts in programming is the variable. A *variable* is a temporary storage location for some value and is given a name. You can use a variable to store the result of a calculation, or you can create a variable to make the value of a control available to another procedure.

To refer to the result of an expression, you create a *name* to store the result. The named result is the variable. To assign an expression's result to a variable, you use the = operator. Following are some examples of calculations that create variables:

```
counter = 1
counter = counter + 1
today = Date()
```

Naming variables

Every programming language has its own rules for naming variables. In Visual Basic, a variable name must meet the following conditions:

✦ Must begin with an alphabetical character

✦ Can't contain an embedded period or type-declaration character

✦ Must have a unique name; the name cannot be used elsewhere in the procedure or in modules that use the variables

✦ Must be no longer than 255 characters

Although you can make up almost any name for a variable, most programmers adopt a standard convention for naming variables. Some common practices include:

✦ Using uppercase and lowercase characters, as in TotalCost.

✦ Using all lowercase characters, as in counter.

✦ Preceding the name with the data type of the value. A variable that stores a number might be called nCounter.

Tip When creating variables, you can use uppercase, lowercase, or mixed-case characters to specify the variable or call it later. Visual Basic variables are not case-sensitive. This fact means that you can use the Todayis variable later without having to worry about the case that you used for the name when you created it; TODAYIS, todayis, and tOdAyis all reference the same variable. Visual Basic automatically changes any explicitly declared variables to the case that was used in the declaration statement (Dim statement).

When you need to see or use the contents of a variable, you simply use its name. When you specify the variable's name, the computer program goes into memory, finds the variable, and gets its contents for you. This procedure means, of course, that you need to be able to remember the name of the variable.

Visual Basic, like many other programming languages, allows you to create variables on the fly. In the Counter = 1 example, the Counter variable was not *declared* before the value 1 was assigned to it.

Declaring variables

Declaring a variable before assigning anything to it sets up a location in the computer's memory for storing a value for the variable ahead of time. The amount of storage allocated for the variable depends on the type of data that you plan to store in the variable. More space is allocated for a variable that will hold a currency amount (such as $1,000,000) than for a variable that will never hold a value greater than, say, 255.

Caution   Even though Visual Basic does not require you to declare your variables before using them, it does provide various declaration commands. Getting into the habit of declaring your variables is good practice. Declaring a variable assures that you can assign only a certain type of value to it — always a number or always characters, for example. In addition, you can attain real performance gains by predeclaring variables. For purposes of maintenance, most programmers like to declare their variables at the top of the procedure.

Although Visual Basic does not require initial declaration of variables, you should avoid using undeclared variables. If you do not declare a variable, the code may expect one type of value in the variable when another is actually there. If, in your procedure, you set the variable TodayIs to *Monday* and later change the value for TodayIs to a number (such as TodayIs = 2), the program generates an error when it runs.

The Dim statement

To declare a variable, you use the Dim statement. When you use the Dim statement, you must supply the variable name that you assign to the variable. The format for the Dim statement is:

```
Dim variable name [As type]
```

Figure 35-3 shows the Dim statement for the variable xBeeps. Notice that the variable name follows the Dim statement. In addition to naming the variable, you can use the optional As clause to specify data type for the variable. The data type is the kind of information that will be stored in the variable: String, Integer, Currency, and so on. The default data type is known as *variant*. A variant data type can hold any type of data.

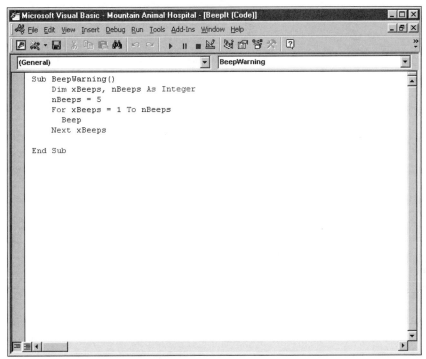

Figure 35-3: Using the Dim statement to declare a variable.

When you use the Dim statement to declare a variable in a procedure, you can refer to that variable only within that procedure. Other procedures, even if they are stored in the same module, do not know anything about the variable. This is known as a *private* variable because it was declared in a procedure and is only known in the procedure where it was declared and used.

Variables can also be declared in the *declarations* section of a module. Then, all the procedures in the module can access the variable. Procedures outside the module in which you declared the variable however, cannot read or use the variable.

The Public statement

To make a variable available to all modules in the application, use the Public keyword when you declare the variable. Figure 35-4 illustrates using the Public keyword to declare a variable. Notice that the statement is in the declarations section of the module. Public variables must be declared in the declarations section of the module.

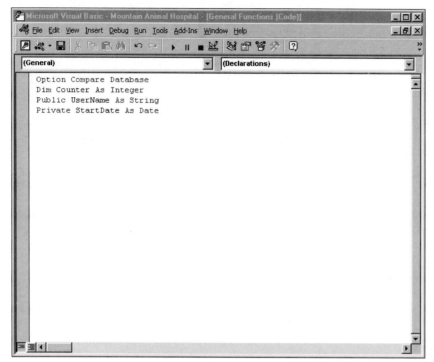

Figure 35-4: Declaring a public variable.

Although you can declare a public variable in any module, it seems logical to declare public variables only within the module that will use them the most. The exceptions to this rule are true global variables that you want to make available to all procedures across modules and that are not specifically related to a single module. You should declare global variables in a single standard module so you can find them easily.

Caution   You cannot declare a variable public within a procedure. It must be declared in the declarations section of a module. If you attempt to declare a variable public within a procedure, you receive an error message.

Tip   In a standard, report, or form module, you can refer to a public variable from a different form or report module. To access the value of a public variable from another module, you must qualify the variable reference, using the name of the form or report object. Employee_MainForm.MyVariable, for example, accesses a form named Employee_MainForm and obtains the value of the variable MyVariable.

The Private statement

The declarations section in Figure 35-4, earlier in this chapter, shows the use of the Dim and Private statements to declare variables. Technically, there is no difference between Private and Dim, but using Private at the module level to declare variables that are available to only that module's procedures is a good idea. Declaring private variables does the following things:

✦ Contrasts with Dim, which must be used at the procedure level, distinguishing where the variable is declared and its scope (Module versus Procedure)

✦ Contrasts with Public, the other method of declaring variables in modules, making understanding your code easier

Tip
You can go to the declarations section of a module while you are creating an event procedure in a form by selecting declarations from the Procedure combo box. Another way to move to the declarations section is to select (general) in the Object combo box. Figure 35-5 shows the Module window combo boxes.

When you declare a variable, you use the AS clause to assign a data type to the variable. Data types for variables are similar to data types in a database table definition.

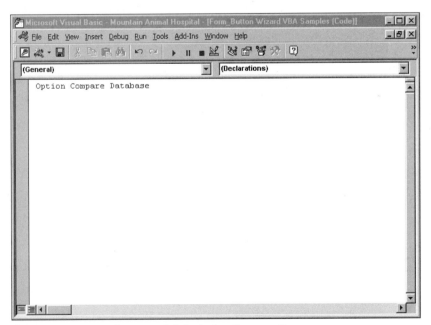

Figure 35-5: Accessing a module's declarations section.

Working with Data Types

When you declare a variable, you also can specify the data type for the variable. All variables have a data type. The type of variable determines what kind of information can be stored in the variable.

A *string variable* — a variable with a data type of string — can hold any values ranging from A–Z, a–z, and 0–1, as well as formatting characters (#, -, !, and so on). Once created, a string variable can be used in many ways: comparing its contents with another string, pulling parts of information out of the string, and so on. If you have a variable defined as a string, however, you cannot use it to do mathematical calculations. Conversely, you cannot assign a number to a variable declared as a string.

Table 35-1 describes the 11 data types that Visual Basic supports.

Table 35-1		
Data Types Used in Visual Basic		
Type	**Range**	**Description**
Boolean	True or false	2 bytes
Byte	0 to 255	1-byte binary data
Currency	−922,337,203,685,477,5808 to 922,337,203,685,477,5807	8-byte number with fixed decimal point
Decimal	+/-79,228,162,514,264,337,593,543,950,335 with no decimal point	
	+/-7.9228162514264337593543950335 with 28 places to the right of the decimal; smallest non-zero number is +/0.0000000000000000000000000001	14 bytes
Date	01 Jan 100 to 31 Dec 9999	8-byte date/time value
Double	−1.79769313486231E308 to −4.94065645841247E−324	8-byte floating-point number
Integer	−32,768 to 32,767	2-byte integer
Long	−2,147,483,648 to 2,147,483,647	4-byte integer
Object	Any object reference	4 bytes

Type	Range	Description
Single	negative values: −3.402823E38 to −1.401298E − 45 positive values: 1.401298E −45 to 3.402823E38	4-byte floating-point number
String (variable-length)	0 to approximately 2,000,000,000	10 bytes plus length of string
String (fixed-length)	1 to approximately 65,400	Length of string
Variant (with numbers)	Any numeric value up to the range of Double	16 bytes
Variant (with characters)	0 to approximately 2,000,000,000	22 bytes plus length of string
User-defined (using Type)	Same as Range of its data type	Number required by elements

Most of the time you use the string, date, integer, and currency or double data types. If a variable always contains whole numbers between −32,768 and 32,768, you can save bytes of memory and gain speed in arithmetic operations if you declare the variable an integer type.

When you want to assign the value of an Access field to a variable, you need to make sure that the type of the variable can hold the data type of the field. Table 35-2 shows the corresponding Visual Basic data types for Access field types.

Table 35-2
Comparative Data Types of Access and Visual BasicVisual Basic

Access Field Data Type	Visual Basic Data Type
AutoNumber (Long Integer)	Long
AutoNumber (Replication ID)	—
Currency	Currency
Computed	—
Date/Time	Date
Memo	String

Continued

Table 35-2 *(continued)*	
Access Field Data Type	*Visual Basic Data Type*
Number (Byte)	Byte
Number (Integer)	Integer
Number (Long Integer)	Long
Number (Single)	Single
Number (Double)	Double
Number (Replication ID)	—
OLE object	Array of bytes
Text	String
Yes/No	Boolean

Note   If a variable may have to hold a value of Null, it must be declared as variant. Variant is the only data type that can accept Null values.

Now that you understand variables and their data types, you're ready to learn how to use them in writing procedures.

Understanding Visual Basic Logical Constructs

One of the real powers of a programming language is the capability to have a program make a decision based on some condition. Often, a program in Visual Basic performs different tasks based on some value. If the condition is True, the code performs one action. If the condition is False, the code performs a different action. This procedure is similar to walking down a path and coming to a fork in the path; you can go to the left or to the right. If a sign at the fork points left for home and right for work, you can decide which way to go. If you need to go to work, you go to the right; if you need to go home, you go to the left. Conditional processing of code works the same way. A program looks at the value of some variable and decides which set of code should be processed.

When writing code, you need to be able to control which actions execute. You may want to write some statements that execute only if a certain condition is True.

Conditional processing

An application's capability to look at a value and, based on that value, decide which code to run is known as *conditional processing*.

Visual Basic offers two sets of conditional processing statements:

✦ If. . .Then. . .Else. . .End If

✦ Select Case

The If. . .Then. . .Else. . .End If statement

The If. . .Then and If. . .Then. . .Else statements allow you to check a condition and, based on the evaluation, perform a single action. The condition must evaluate to True or False. If the condition is True, the program moves to the next statement in the procedure. If the condition is False, the program skips to the statement following the Else statement, if present, or the End If statement if there is no Else clause.

In Figure 35-6, the Print Reports dialog box displays an option group, called Report to Print, that displays three reports. When you choose the Pet Directory report, a list of pets appears at the bottom of the dialog box. When you choose either of the other two reports, the list of pets disappears. Figure 35-7 shows the dialog box with the All Customers and Pets report option selected and nothing displayed in the now-invisible list box.

Figure 35-6: Choosing the Pet Directory report in the Print Reports dialog box.

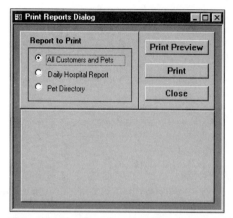

Figure 35-7: Choosing the All Customers and
Pets report in the Print Reports dialog box.

In Chapter 34, you learned how to make the Select Pet list box visible and invisible
in the Print Reports dialog box. Figure 35-8 illustrates the Show List macro for the
Print Reports dialog box. The two condition statements determine which SetValue
action to use to set the Select Pet list box's Visible property to Yes when the Pet
Directory option is selected and to No when another report option is selected.

You can write a procedure to perform the same actions as the Show List macro.
Figure 35-9 shows the Print_Reports_Show_List procedure. Notice that the
If. . .Then. . .End If construct replaces the Condition statement used in the macro.

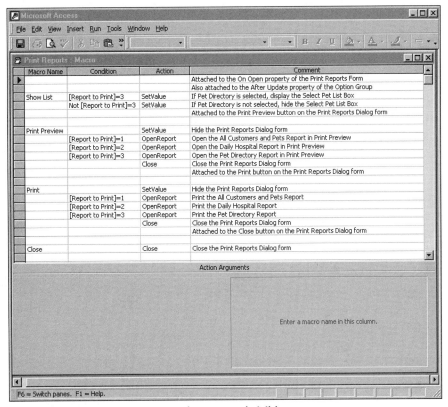

Figure 35-8: Using a macro to make a control visible.

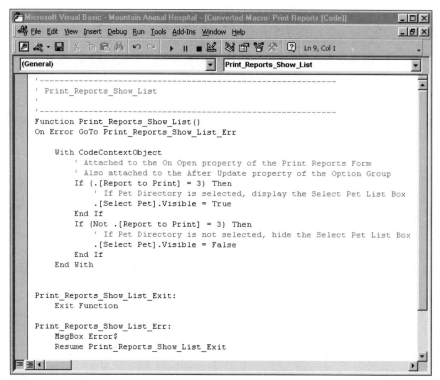

Figure 35-9: Using the If. . .Then. . .End If statement.

The Else statement is optional. You can use Else to test for a second condition when the If statement evaluates to False or just to perform an alternate set of actions when the If statement is false. When the If statement is True, the program executes the statements between the If statement and the Else statement. When the If statement evaluates to False, the program skips to the Else statement, if it is present. Then, if the Else statement is True, the program executes the following statement. If the Else statement is False, the program skips to the statement following the End If statement.

Figure 35-10 illustrates the Print_Reports_Show_List procedure with an Else statement.

When you have many conditions to test, the If. . .Then. . .Else statements can get rather complicated. A better approach is to use the Select Case construct.

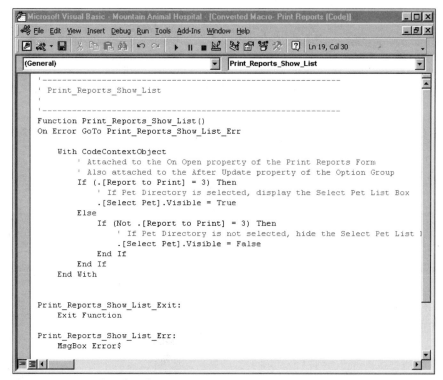

Figure 35-10: Using the Else statement.

The Select Case. . .End Select statement

In addition to the If. . .Then statements, Visual Basic offers a command for checking more than one condition. You can use the Select Case statement to check for multiple conditions. Following is the general syntax of the statement:

```
Select Case test_expression
    Case expression value1
        code statements here (test expression = value1)
    Case expression value2
        code statements here (test expression = value2) ...
    Case Else
        code statements (test expression = none of the values)
End Select
```

Notice that the syntax is similar to that of the If. . .Then statement. Instead of a condition in the Select Case statement, however, Visual Basic uses a test expression. Then each Case statement inside the Select Case statement tests its value against the test expression's value. When a Case statement matches the test value, the program executes the next line or lines of code until it reaches another Case statement or the End Select statement. Visual Basic executes the code for only one matching Case statement.

Note   If more than one Case statement matches the value of the test expression, only the code for the first match executes. If other matching Case statements appear after the first match, Visual Basic ignores them.

The Print Reports dialog box prints a different report for each of the three Report to Print options. Figure 35-11 shows the Print command button's Print macro. The three condition statements determine which OpenReport action is used to print the appropriate report.

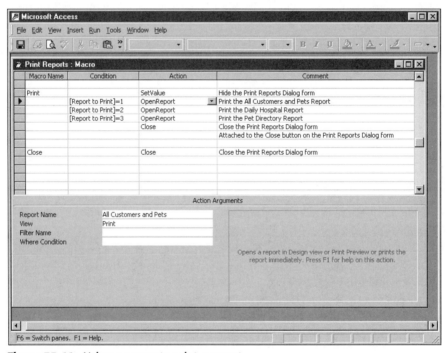

Figure 35-11: Using a macro to print a report.

The Print_Reports_Print procedure, illustrated in Figure 35-12, performs the same actions as the Print macro. Notice that the procedure replaces each of the macro's Condition statements with a Case statement.

The Select Case statement looks at the value of the control Report to Print and then checks each Case condition. If the value of Report to Print is 1 (All Customers and Pets), the Case 1 statement evaluates to True, and the All Customers and Pets report prints. If Report to Print is not 1, Visual Basic goes to the next Case statement to see whether Report to Print matches that value. Each Case statement is evaluated until a match occurs or the program reaches the End Select statement.

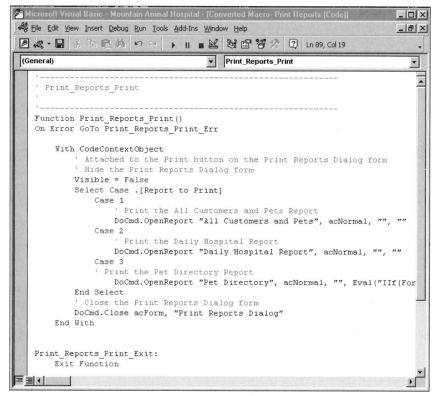

Figure 35-12: Using the Select Case statement.

The Case Else statement is optional. The Case Else clause always is the last Case statement of Select Case. You use this statement to perform some action when none of the Case values matches the test value of the Select Case statement.

In some procedures, you may want to execute a group of statements more than one time. Visual Basic provides some constructs for repeating a group of statements.

Repetitive looping

The capability to determine conditions and then process a statement or group of statements based on the answer can be very powerful.

Another very powerful process that Visual Basic offers is *repetitive looping*—the capability to process some series of code over and over. The statement or group of statements is processed continually until some condition is met.

Visual Basic offers two types of repetitive-looping constructs:

✦ Do. . .Loop

✦ For. . .Next

The Do. . .Loop statement

The Do. . .Loop statement is used to repeat a group of statements while a condition is true or until a condition is true. This statement is one of the most common commands that can perform repetitive processes.

Following is the format of the Do. . .Loop statement:

```
DO [While | Until condition]
      code statements [for condition = TRUE]
      [Exit DO]
      code statements [for condition = TRUE]
LOOP [While | Until condition]
```

Notice that the Do. . .Loop statement has several optional clauses. The two While clauses tell the program to execute the code inside Do. . .Loop as long as the test condition is True. When the condition evaluates to False, the program skips to the next statement following the Loop statement. The two Until clauses work in just the opposite way; they execute the code within Do. . .Loop as long as the condition is False. Where you place the While or Until clause determines whether the code inside Do. . .Loop executes at least once.

The Exit Do clause is used to terminate Do. . .Loop immediately. The program then skips to the next statement following the Loop statement.

The Print_Reports_Print2 procedure, illustrated in Figure 35-13, prints multiple copies of the report, based on the value of the Number of Copies control on the form. Notice that the procedure declares a Counter variable. The program increments the Counter variable each time the report prints. When Counter is greater than Number of Copies, Do. . .Loop stops printing copies of the report.

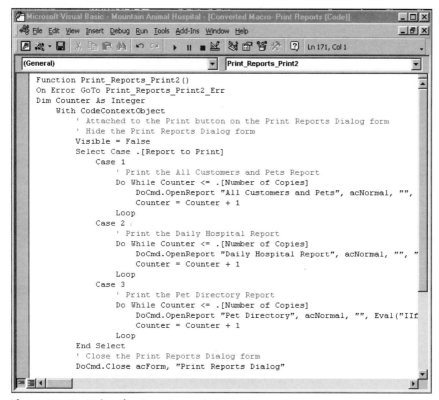

Figure 35-13: Using the Do. . .Loop statement.

The While clause causes the Do...Loop to exit when Counter reaches the limit. Using the While or Until clause is equivalent to using the Exit Do statement within the loop. The following is the same Do...Loop example using the Exit Do statement:

```
Do
        Docmd.OpenReport …
        Counter = Counter + 1
        If Counter > .[Number of Copies] Then
                Exit Do
        End If
Loop
```

The While and Until clauses provide powerful flexibility for processing Do. . .Loop in your code. Table 35-3 describes the various alternatives for using the While and Until clauses and how they affect the processing of code:

	Table 35-3
	Repetitive Looping Using Do. . .Loop with the While and Until Clauses

Pseudo Code	Purpose of Do. . .Loop

Do	Code starts here
	`If condition Then`
	`Exit Do`
	`End If`

Loop	The code always runs. The code has some conditional statement (If. . .Then) that, if True, runs the Exit Do statement. The Exit Do statement allows the user to get out of Do. . .Loop. If that statement were missing, the code inside the loop would run forever.
Do	While condition code starts here for the condition on the Do While line being TRUE
Loop	The code inside the Do While loop runs only if the condition is True. The code runs down to the Loop statement and then goes back to the top to see whether the condition is still True. If the condition is initially False, Do. . .Loop is skipped; if the condition becomes False, the loop is exited when the code loops back to the Do While line. Exit Do is not needed for this purpose.
Do	Until condition code starts here for the condition on the Do Until line being FALSE
Loop	This code works the opposite way from Do While. If the condition is False (not True), the code begins and loops until the condition is True; then it leaves the loop. Again, the loop and its code are skipped if the Until condition is True.
Do	Code starts here
Loop While	This code always runs at least one time. First, the code is executed condition and reaches the Loop While line. If the condition is True, the code loops back up to process the code again; if not, the code loop ends.
Do	Code starts here
Loop Until	This code works similarly to the preceding one. The code always condition runs at least one time. When the code reaches the Loop Until line, it checks to see whether the condition is True. If the condition is True, the code drops out of the loop. If the condition is False, the code loops back up to redo the code.

The second repetitive-looping construct is the For. . .Next statement.

The For. . .Next statement

For. . .Next is a shortcut method for the Do. . .Loop construct. You can use For. . .Next when you want to repeat a statement for a set number of times. The Step clause followed by an increment lets you process the loop in a nonsingle step amount. For example, if start number was 1 and end number was 100 and you wanted to increment the counter by 10 each time you would use Step 10. Though the loop would only be executed 10 times (or is it 11?) the value of the counter would be 1, 11, 21, and so on, instead of 1, 2, 3, and so on.

Following is the general syntax of the For. . .Next statement:

```
For counter variable name  = start number  To end number
[Step increment]
code statements begin here and continue to Next If condition
code
[Exit For]
End If code can continue here after the Exit for
Next [counter]
```

You can code the Print_Reports_Print2 procedure by using the For. . .Next construct. In Figure 35-14, notice that the For. . .Next statements replace the Do While. . .Loop statements of the Print_Reports_Print3 procedure. Notice also that the statement Counter = Counter + 1 is omitted.

At the start of the For. . .Next loop, the program initializes Counter to 1; then it moves on and executes the DoCmd statement. Whenever the program encounters the Next statement, it automatically increments Counter and returns to the For statement. The program compares the value of Counter with the value in the Number of Copies control. If Counter is less than or equal to Number of Copies, the DoCmd executes again; otherwise, the program exits the loop.

Whenever you write your own procedures, it is a good idea to plan for any error conditions that may occur when your procedure runs.

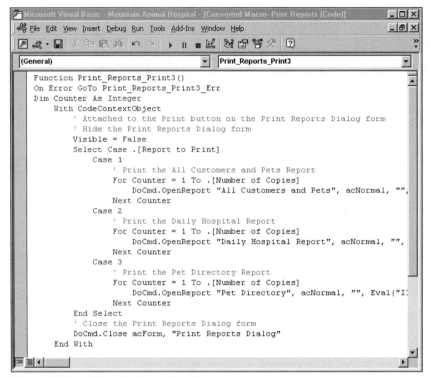

Figure 35-14: Using the For. . .Next loop.

Planning for Runtime Errors

If an error occurs when you run a procedure, Access displays an error message and stops executing the program. When the procedure terminates, your application can end up in a state of flux, depending on the nature of the error.

Chapter 34 covered compiling procedures to make sure that the syntax of your code is correct. Running the procedure yourself to make sure that it does what you expect it to is good practice. Even though the syntax of your procedure may be exactly right, you may have omitted a necessary statement or misnamed a reference to some control on your form.

Even though you may have tested and retested the procedures in your application, things still can go wrong. Reports and forms can be deleted, and tables can become corrupted. When you write your procedures, you cannot alleviate situations like these. You can, however, provide a means of recovering from errors gracefully.

The Print_Reports_Close procedure, illustrated in Figure 35-15, closes the Print Reports dialog box. If the Print Reports dialog box is missing when the procedure runs, an error occurs. The On Error statement at the top of the procedure provides a way to recover from errors.

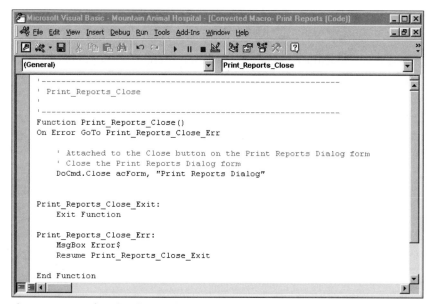

Figure 35-15: Planning for runtime errors.

Adding an On Error subroutine to a procedure

If any error occurs when you run your procedure, and you did not include an On Error statement, Access displays a message and stops running the procedure. Adding an On Error statement to a procedure allows the procedure to keep running even if an error occurs.

Following is the syntax for the On Error statements:

```
On Error GoTo labelname
On Error Resume Next
```

Using the On Error GoTo statement signals Access that you want it to perform some special instructions if an error occurs anywhere in the procedure. The GoTo labelname clause tells Access where to look for the special instructions. You replace the keyword labelname with a label name.

On Error Resume Next tells Access that you want to ignore the error and go on to the next statemment. This can be dangerous if the statement that gets ignored because of an error contained an important instruction like to multiply two numbers. With the calculation not performed, all sorts of things can begin to go wrong. You should only use On Error Resume Next in procedures where this can't happen.

A label name is used to identify a special section of code somewhere in your procedure. A label name can be any combination of characters that start with a letter and end with a colon. In Figure 35-15, earlier in this chapter, the On Error statement for the Print_Reports_Close function points to the line label Print_Reports_Close_Err. At the bottom of the function, you see Print_Reports_Close_Err:. If an error occurs when Print_Reports_Close runs, Access looks for the section of code that starts with Print_Reports_Close_Err: and executes the statements that follow.

The lines of code that follow a label name are called a *subroutine*. A subroutine is like a procedure within a procedure. The commands in a subroutine can be executed multiple times by the sub or function that contains the commands; or they may not execute at all, depending on the purpose of the error-handling routine. An error-handling subroutine, such as Print_Reports_Close_Err, runs only if an error occurs in the Print_Reports_Close function.

You can add subroutines anywhere in your procedure. Usually, you add subroutines to the bottom of your procedure, somewhere after the Exit Sub (or Exit Function) statement and before the End Sub (or End Function). Be careful of where you add subroutines to your procedure, however, because Access runs all the lines of code in your procedure until it reaches an Exit or End statement. Even though you have labeled a section of code, Access skips line labels and runs the subroutine's lines of code as though they are part of the main procedure. In the example in Figure 35-15, the Print_Reports_Close_Err subroutine was added below the Exit Function statement because the subroutine is to run only if an error occurs.

A subroutine can branch to another subroutine within a procedure. Notice that the Print_Reports_Close_Err subroutine calls the Print_Reports_Close_Exit subroutine, using the Resume command. The Print_Reports_Close_Exit subroutine simply exits the function.

The Resume command tells Access to exit the error subroutine and continue running the code in the main procedure. You must tell Access when to end an error-handling subroutine by using a Resume statement or an Exit Sub (or Exit Function) statement. If you do not end your subroutine appropriately, Access assumes that any statements in the rest of the procedure are part of the subroutine and continues running the lines of code in the procedure until it reaches the End statement. If Access encounters an End Sub (or End Function) statement during an error-handling subroutine, an error occurs.

In the Print_Reports_Close function, the Print_ Reports_Close_Exit subroutine contains the Exit Function statement. If no error occurs when the procedure runs, Access automatically runs the Print_Reports_Close_Exit subroutine and exits the function. If an error occurs, Access runs the Print_Reports_Close_Err subroutine and then branches to Print_Reports_Close_Exit.

Including only one Exit statement in your procedure is good programming practice. Instead of branching to another subroutine, you could just as easily have added the statement Exit Function to Print_Reports_Close_Err. By using a subroutine to exit the function, you can exit from anywhere in the procedure without inserting multiple Exit statements.

In addition to providing a means of recovering from runtime errors, you may want to notify the user that an error occurred.

Displaying meaningful runtime error messages

Even though recovery from most errors that occur in your application is possible, it is important to notify the user any time an error occurs. That way, if what the user sees next on-screen seems to be abnormal, he or she has some idea why. If an error occurs in retrieving data from a table, for example, and the next screen displays empty controls, the error message alerts the user that something has gone wrong with the application.

When you notify the user that an error has occurred, you also should supply an appropriate message that gives the user some idea what the problem is. You can determine the cause of any error condition by using the built-in error-trapping mechanism in Access. Access has a code and message assigned for any possible error situation that could occur. You can retrieve this information to display a meaningful message in a message box.

To retrieve the message for an error, use the Err.Description command. As shown in Figure 35-16, the error subroutine for the Find_Record_Click sub uses the Msgbox command to display a message box whenever an error occurs in the procedure. The Err.Description command tells the message box to retrieve and display the text of the error.

Note   In previous versions of Access, the Error$ statement returned the description for an error code. Visual Basic includes Error$ so that Access 2000 can be compatible with code from earlier versions of Access. Even though Error$ is a valid command, you should use Err.Description in any new procedures that you write.

Sometimes, for certain error conditions, you may want to display your own message text instead of using the messages built into Access.

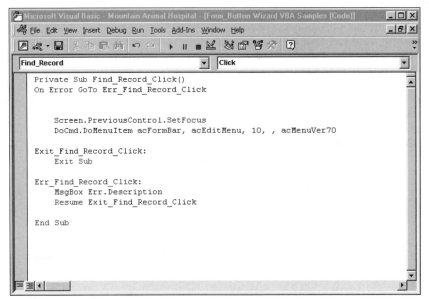

Figure 35-16: Displaying a runtime error message.

Trapping for specific error codes

Even though Access supplies a complete set of generic message codes and descriptions, you sometimes want to be even more specific about the error condition. You can test for a specific error code and then display your own message whenever that error occurs. For other errors, you may want to use the generic message descriptions.

In Figure 35-17, the RoundIt_Err subroutine first checks the value of the error code. For Error Code 13, a more meaningful message than the generic message Type mismatch appears. For any error code other than 13, the Err.Description command displays the generic message text.

One of the most common features you will want to provide in your applications is the capability to locate data quickly. Having multiple ways to search for a specific record quickly is important and productive.

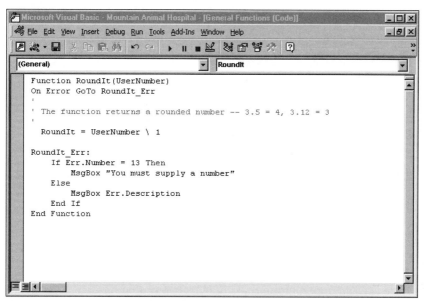

Figure 35-17: Trapping a specific error.

Filtering Records in Procedures

You can create intelligent search dialog boxes to locate and display or print records, using different search types. In this section, you learn how you can use Visual Basic code to locate and display or print a specific record or a set of records, using search criteria.

Displaying a dialog box for selecting a record

You can add a Find button to the Customers form to display the Search for Customer dialog box, shown in Figure 35-18. This dialog box provides two ways of searching for a customer. Each method displays a list of customers. The contents of the list box change, depending on the type of search that you select. When you select a customer in the list box (by clicking an entry in the list box and then clicking the OK button, or by double-clicking an entry in the list box), the Search for Customer dialog box closes, and the Customers form displays the selected customer record.

Figure 35-18: Searching for a customer.

Refreshing the items for a list box

This form uses an option group that contains two option buttons, a list box, and two command buttons. The secret to changing the contents of the list box is manipulating its Row Source property each time you click on an option button. When you click on one of the option buttons, a simple procedure updates the contents of the list box at the bottom of the form.

The bottom rectangle of the form is a list box. When you click on an option button in the Type of Search option group, the list box displays the customer list, using a different set of fields and in different order.

Figure 35-19 illustrates Design view for the dialog box, showing the properties for the By Search Type list box. The Row Source property is a select query instead of a table. You can build a select query by using the standard query screen. When you select the Row Source property and click on the ellipsis button (. . .), the SQL statement translates back to its query equivalent, and the query design screen appears.

Tip
Notice in Figure 35-19 that the Bound Column property is set to 3 and that the list box displays only two columns. The third column is the Customer Number field. The Customer Number is used in the search procedure. Even though the Customer Number is not visible in the dialog box, you can access its value along with the other visible fields in the selected list box row.

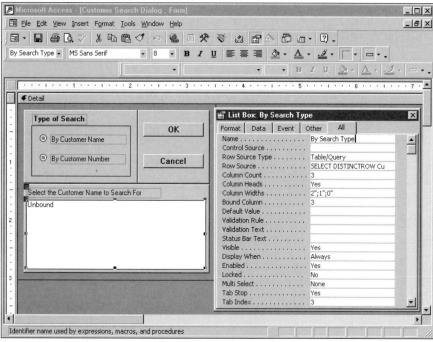

Figure 35-19: Designing a list box for search criteria.

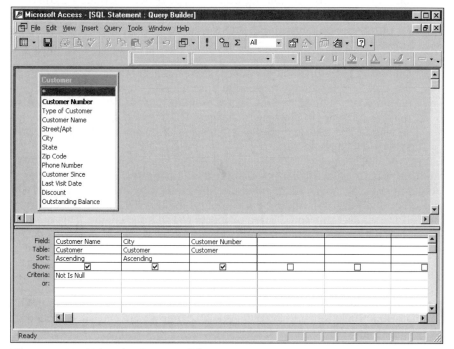

Figure 35-20: Using the Query Builder to generate an SQL statement.

If you want to view the SQL statement that Access creates for you, choose View ➪ SQL View in the Query Builder window. The SQL statement window, shown in Figure 35-21, appears when you choose View ➪ SQL View.

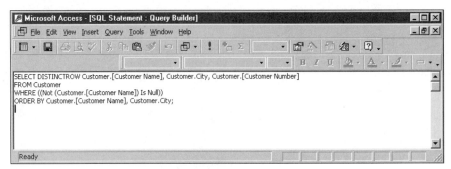

Figure 35-21: Viewing the SQL statement for a query.

The Type of Search option group has an associated After Update event procedure that changes the Row Source query each time the option button changes. Figure 35-22 shows the Type_of_Search_AfterUpdate procedure.

The Type_of_Search_AfterUpdate procedure displays the Customer Name and City fields when the By Customer Name option button (Type of Search.Value = 1) is selected. The By Customer Number option (Type of Search.Value = 2) displays the Customer fields Customer Number and Customer Name in the list box, in Customer Number order. The procedure sets the Row Source property to the appropriate select query for each Type of Search option.

Tip   One secret to this method of updating the contents of the list box is to initially set the Row Source property to Null. Because Access reruns the query as you specify each property setting, the Row Source property must be set to Null; otherwise, the query is run as each property is changed. This method speeds the query by preventing Access from unnecessarily retrieving the query results for each property setting in the procedure.

Another way to make the list box display itself faster is to store the queries as actual queries. You can create and name the queries by using the Queries object button of the Database window. Instead of typing the SQL statement in the procedure, you set the Row Source property to the query name. This method runs the query 10 percent to 40 percent faster.

Finding the selected record

The OK command button in the Customer Search dialog box runs a simple Visual Basic program that locates the record that you selected in the list box and displays the record in the associated form. Figure 35-23 shows the OK_Click procedure for the OK button.

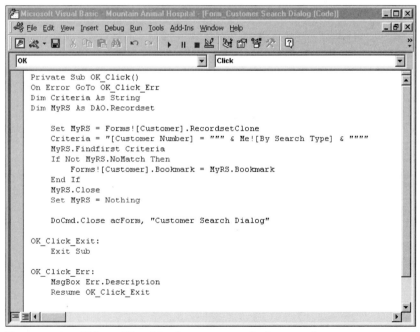

Figure 35-22: Updating the properties of a list box.

```
Private Sub Type_of_Search_AfterUpdate()
    With CodeContextObject
    If .[Type of Search] = 1 Then
        .[By Search Type].RowSource = ""
        .[Search Text].Caption = "Select the Customer Name to Search For
        .[By Search Type].ColumnCount = 3
        .[By Search Type].ColumnWidths = "2 in;1 in;0 in"
        .[By Search Type].BoundColumn = 3
        .[By Search Type].RowSource = "SELECT Customer.[Customer Name],Cus
    ElseIf .[Type of Search] = 2 Then
        .[By Search Type].RowSource = ""
        .[Search Text].Caption = "Select the Customer Number to Search For
        .[By Search Type].ColumnCount = 2
        .[By Search Type].ColumnWidths = "1 in;2 in"
        .[By Search Type].BoundColumn = 1
        .[By Search Type].RowSource = "SELECT [Customer Number],[Customer
    End If
    End With
End Sub
```

```
Private Sub OK_Click()
On Error GoTo OK_Click_Err
Dim Criteria As String
Dim MyRS As DAO.Recordset

    Set MyRS = Forms![Customer].RecordsetClone
    Criteria = "[Customer Number] = """ & Me![By Search Type] & """"
    MyRS.Findfirst Criteria
    If Not MyRS.NoMatch Then
        Forms![Customer].Bookmark = MyRS.Bookmark
    End If
    MyRS.Close
    Set MyRS = Nothing

    DoCmd.Close acForm, "Customer Search Dialog"

OK_Click_Exit:
    Exit Sub

OK_Click_Err:
    MsgBox Err.Description
    Resume OK_Click_Exit
```

Figure 35-23: Using a Visual Basic program to find a record.

The OK_Click procedure uses the FindFirst method to locate a record. The FindFirst method works just like the Find command (Edit menu). The criteria is the same as the fields in the Find dialog box.

The RecordsetClone method makes a copy of the recordset used in the Customer form. The FindFirst method searches the cloned recordset for the first record that meets the specified criteria. If a match is found, then the form's recordpointer jumps to the bookmark that matches the cloned recordset's bookmark value. An object's bookmark property contains a value that uniquely identifies each record for the object.

Using *intelligent search* dialog boxes, you can easily provide your user a multitude of ways to search for a record. You can have as many intelligent search dialog boxes in an application as you need, each dialog box working with a different form and a different set of tables and fields.

Another useful feature in professional applications is the capability to print reports quickly and easily, without having to sit in front of a computer and select one report after another. You can create an intelligent Print dialog box to print reports, envelopes, and mailing labels for one record or for a set of records.

Selecting a set of records to print

You can add a Print button to a form to display the Print dialog box, shown in Figure 35-24. This Print dialog box can print up to three reports at the same time and also provides three methods of selecting the records to be printed. Different options for filtering records appear, depending on the type of criteria you select. When you click on the OK button, the Print dialog box closes, and the report or reports print for the selected customers.

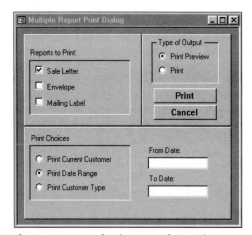

Figure 35-24: Selecting records to print.

This form uses a group of check boxes, two option groups, and two command buttons. You use the check boxes—named Sale Letter, Envelope, and Mailing Label—to select the report or reports to be printed. You can select one or more reports to print at the same time. The three reports are called Customer Sale Letter, Customer Envelope, and Customer Mailing Label. You can view the reports from the Database container.

Using Visual Basic to display and hide controls

The Print Choices option group, named Print Criteria, runs a Visual Basic procedure that displays and removes form controls, based on the selected option button. When the dialog box opens, the From Date, To Date, and Customer Type controls are hidden. Figure 35-25 shows the dialog box in Design view. The Customer Type combo box displays beneath the From Date text box.

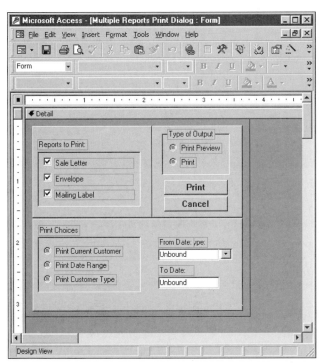

Figure 35-25: Displaying and hiding controls on a form.

The Visual Basic procedure for the Print Choices option group is shown in Figure 35-26. When you select the Print Current Record option, the procedure hides the From Date, To Date, and Customer Type controls. The report or reports print only for the current record. When you select the Print Date Range option (Print Criteria = 2), the From Date and To Date text boxes appear. You then specify a beginning date and ending date to print all customers whose Last Visit Date falls between the two dates. When you select the Print Customer Type option (Print Criteria = 3), the Customer Type combo box appears, allowing you to print the selected reports for all customers whose Customer Type matches the type you selected. Notice that the procedure sets the Visible property for the controls to either True or False, which displays or hides them.

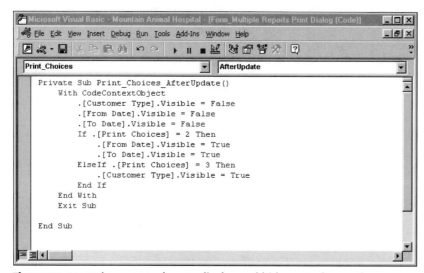

Figure 35-26: Using a procedure to display and hide controls on a form.

Printing records by using selection criteria

The Print command button in the dialog box runs the Print_Customers_Click procedure. Figure 35-27 shows the procedure, which is triggered by the command button's On Click event property.

Notice that the Print_Customers_Click procedure uses the Select Case structure to test the value of the Print Criteria option group. Each Case statement includes three sets of If. . .End If statements for testing which of the reports is selected. Separate If. . .End If statements were used instead of a single If. . .Else. . .End If structure, because you can select multiple reports to print.

```
Private Sub Print_Customers_Click()
Dim ReportDest As String
    'Hide the Customer Multiple Report Print Dialog
    Me.Visible = False
    ' Destination is Print Preview
    If Me![Type of Output] = 1 Then
        ReportDest = acPreview
    Else        ' Destination is printer
        ReportDest = acNormal
    End If
    ' Determine Print Criteria selected
    Select Case [Print Criteria]
        Case 1     ' Current Customer
            ' Print Sale Letter
            If Me![Sale Letter] = -1 Then
                DoCmd.OpenReport "Customer Sale Letter",
ReportDest, , "[Customer]![Customer
Number]=Forms![Customer]![Customer Number]"
            End If
            ' Print Envelope
            If Me![Envelope] = -1 Then
                DoCmd.OpenReport "Customer Envelope",
ReportDest, , "[Customer]![Customer
Number]=Forms![Customer]![Customer Number]"
            End If
            ' Print Mailing Label
            If Me![Mailing Label] = -1 Then
                DoCmd.OpenReport "Customer Mailing Labels",
ReportDest, , "[Customer]![Customer
Number]=Forms![Customer]![Customer Number]"
            End If
        Case 2       ' Date Range
            If Me![Sale Letter] = -1 Then
                DoCmd.OpenReport "Customer Sale Letter",
ReportDest, , "[Customer]![Last Visit Date] Between me![From
Date] and me![To Date]"
            End If
            ' Print Envelope
            If Me![Envelope] = -1 Then
                DoCmd.OpenReport "Customer Envelope",
ReportDest, , "[Customer]![Last Visit Date] Between me![From
Date] and me![To Date]"
            End If
            ' Print Mailing Label
            If Me![Mailing Label] = -1 Then
                DoCmd.OpenReport "Customer Mailing Labels",
ReportDest, , "[Customer]![Last Visit Date] Between me![From
Date] and me![To Date]"
            End If
```

Continued

Figure 35-27: Opening a report by using a procedure.

```
            Case 3       ' Customer Type
                ' Print Sale Letter
                If Me![Sale Letter] = -1 Then
                    DoCmd.OpenReport "Customer Sale Letter",
ReportDest, , "[Customer]![Type of Customer]=me![Customer
Type]"
                End If
                ' Print Envelope
                If Me![Envelope] = -1 Then
                    DoCmd.OpenReport "Customer Envelope",
ReportDest, , "[Customer]![Type of Customer]=me![Customer
Type]"
                End If
                ' Print Mailing Label
                If Me![Mailing Label] = -1 Then
                    DoCmd.OpenReport "Customer Mailing Labels",
ReportDest, , "[Customer]![Type of Customer]=me![Customer
Type]"
                End If
        End Select
```

Figure 35-27: *(continued)*

Working with Combo-Box and List-Box Controls

You have seen in previous examples how combo boxes and list boxes provide an effective method of validating data entry in a form. These boxes can display a list of values that the user can choose so that the user does not have to memorize customer numbers, for example, or remember the spelling of a customer's name.

Figure 35-28 shows the Select a Pet combo box for the Add a New Visit Entry form. In the Mountain Animal Hospital database, the name of the form is Adding Visits for New Pets.

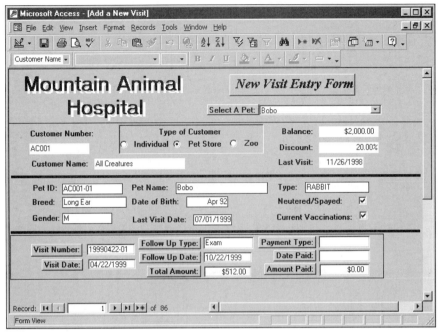

Figure 35-28: Using a combo box to validate data entry.

Handling a combo-box entry that is not in the list

As an option, you can set up a combo box to accept a value that is not in the list. Suppose that a customer brings in a new pet for a visit. The Select a Pet combo box in the New Visit Entry form displays only pets that have visited Mountain Animal Hospital before. Instead of making the user exit the New Visit Entry form and enter the new-patient pet in the Pets form, you can allow the user to type the name of the pet in the combo box. When the user types in the combo box a value that is not in the list of values, the Pets Data Entry form automatically appears. When the user completes the information for the pet and closes the Pets Data Entry form, the New Visit Entry form appears, and the combo box displays the pet in the list.

Entering in the combo box an item that is not in the list of valid values triggers the NotInList event. Figures 35-29 and 35-30 show the properties for the Select a Pet combo box. By connecting an event procedure to the NotInList event, you can override the normal Not in list error that is built into Access and allow the user to add the new value to the list. Notice that you also must set the LimitToList property to Yes.

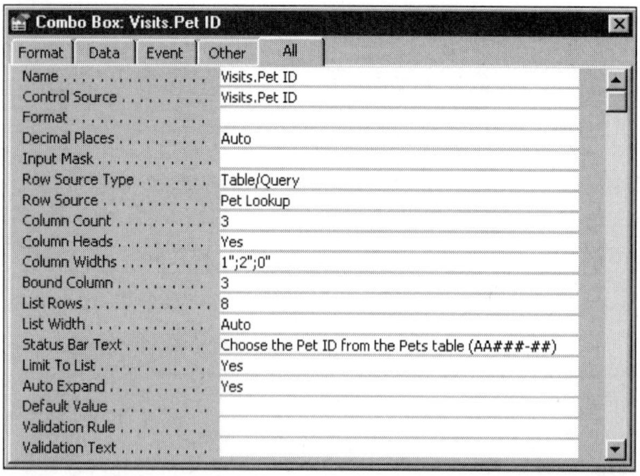

Figure 35-29: Limiting combo-box values to items in the list.

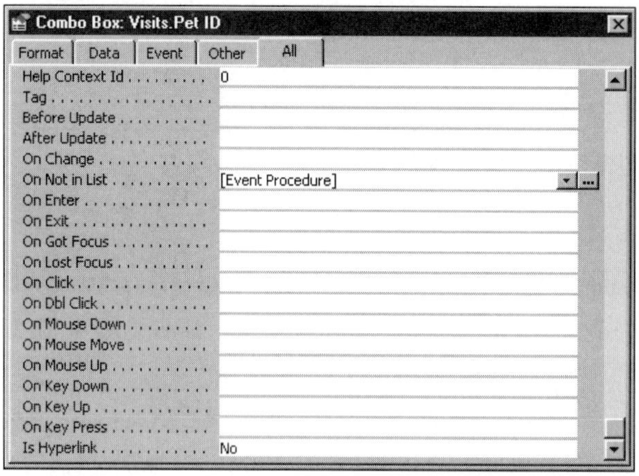

Figure 35-30: Handling combo-box values that are not in the list.

The LimitToList property determines how Access responds to entries that do not match any of the list items. When you set LimitToList to No, Access accepts anything that the user enters, as long as the entry conforms to the ValidationRule property, if one exists. When you set LimitToList to Yes and the user enters an invalid value, Access checks to see whether an event procedure exists for the NotInList event property. If no procedure is attached, Access displays the standard Item Not In List error message; otherwise, Access does not display the error message and runs the procedure instead. Figure 35-31 shows the NotInList procedure, called Visits_Pet_ID_NotInList, for the Select a Pet combo box.

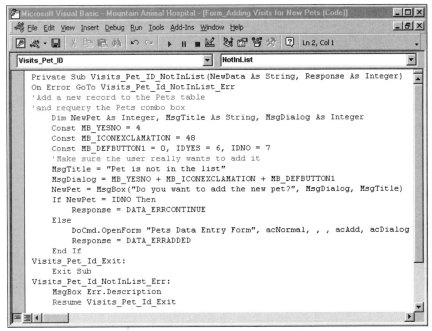

Figure 35-31: A procedure for combo-box values that are not in the list.

Caution

Make sure that you change the Limit To List property in the combo box to No before using the On Not in List event.

The Const declarations at the top of the Visits_Pet_ID_NotInList procedure are called symbolic constants. *Constants* are variables whose values do not change during execution of the procedure, and *symbolic constants* are names for certain constants.

Symbolic constants are names for certain values that are available anywhere in your Visual Basic procedures. The actual values may be 0, 1, or 2, but providing a meaningful name makes it easier to understand what your code is doing Using all-uppercase characters to name symbolic constants helps to differentiate them from variables. Constants that are built into Access are upper and lower case and begin with the letters ac.

The constants used in this procedure are used as the arguments for the MsgBox function. Instead of using numbers such as 52 and 0 as the arguments, you can create a meaningful name that makes it easier to understand what your code is doing.

This procedure first displays a confirmation message to make sure that the user really wants to add the new item. If the user chooses No (they do not want to add the item), the procedure ends. The user then must choose a valid item from the list. Before exiting a NotInList procedure, you must set the Response variable to one of three values. The Response variable tells Access what to do with the invalid item.

The three values for the Response variable are represented by symbolic constants. These symbolic constants are built into Access and are available to any of your Visual Basic programs. The following table describes the three Response values:

Value	Description
acDataErrDisplay	Displays the standard error message and does not add the item to the list
acDataErrContinue	Does not display the standard error message and does not add the item to the list
acDataErrAdded	Does not display the standard error message and reruns the query for the RecordSource

Tip   If you use acDataErrContinue or acDataErrAdded as Response values, you need to make sure that you display a message to the user at some point in your procedure. Otherwise, the user will not be able to leave the field and will not know why.

If the user does want to add the new item to the combo box, the Visits_Pet_ID_NotInList procedure displays a blank Pets Data Entry form. When the user closes the Pets Data Entry form, Visits_Pet_ID_NotInList sets the value for the Response variable before exiting. Setting Response to acDataErrAdded tells Access to query the list of items for the combo box again. When Access requeries the Select a Pet combo box list, it retrieves the newly added pet from the Pets table.

Handling MultiSelect list boxes

Sometimes, it makes sense for a field to have more than one value at a time. With MultiSelect list boxes, you can provide a list of values for a field and allow the user to select one or more items.

In the Pet Vaccinations List Box Example form, shown in Figure 35-32, you can select one or more vaccination types in the list box on the left. When you click the Add button, the selected items appear in the Current Vaccinations list box on the right. When you select one or more items in this list box and click on the Remove button, the selected items disappear from the Current Vaccinations list box.

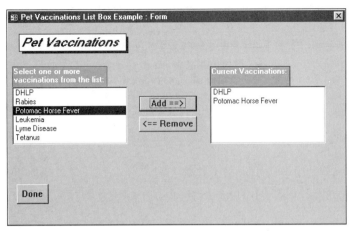

Figure 35-32: Making multiple selections in a list box.

You use the MultiSelect property of a list box to specify whether, and how, a user can make multiple selections in a list box. Figure 35-33 shows the properties of the Vaccinations list box for the Pet Vaccinations form. Notice that the MultiSelect property is set to Extended.

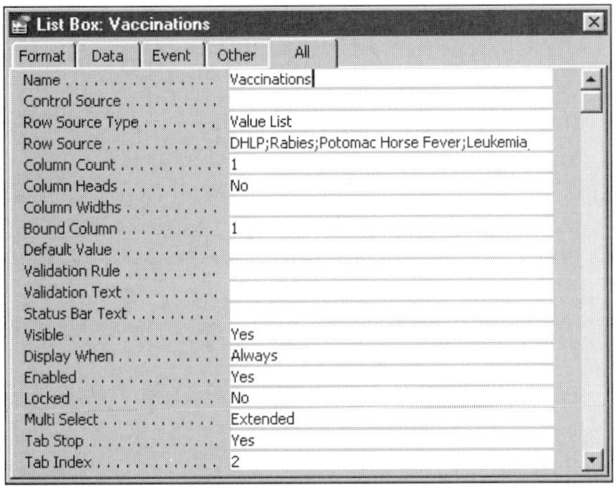

Figure 35-33: Setting the properties for a MultiSelect list box.

Setting MultiSelect to Simple or Extended allows the user to select multiple items. If you want to use the normal single-selection list box, set MultiSelect to None. The following table lists the MultiSelect property settings:

Setting	Visual Basic	Description
None	0	(Default) Multiple selection isn't allowed.
Extended	1	Shift+click or Shift+arrow key extends the election from the previously selected item to the current item. Ctrl+click selects or deselects an item.
Simple	2	Multiple items are selected or deselected by clicking them with the mouse or pressing the spacebar.

The Add command button in the Pet Vaccinations form runs the Add_Button_Click procedure, shown in Figure 35-34. The procedure is triggered by the command button's On Click event.

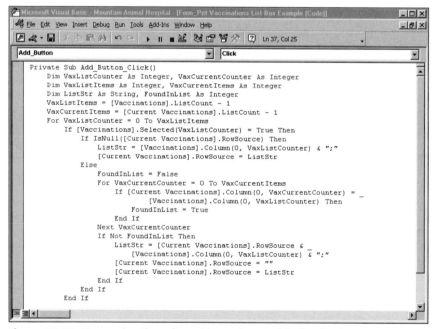

Figure 35-34: Processing the selected items in a MultiSelect list box.

The Add_Button_Click procedure checks each item in the Vaccinations list box to see whether the item is selected. The list box's ListCount property tells you how many items are in the list. To refer to an individual item in the list, you refer to its numbered position in the list. The position numbers start at 0, so the first item is 0, the second is 1, and so on. An item is selected when its Selected property is True and unselected when the Selected property is False. To find out whether the first item in the Vaccinations list is selected, for example, you use the following statement:

```
If [Vaccinations].Selected(0) = True Then
```

The parentheses following the Selected property indicate which items in the list you are interrogating.

If a Vaccinations item is selected, the procedure copies it to the Current Vaccinations list box. If the item is already in the Current Vaccinations list box, however, it cannot be copied again. The OK_Button_Click procedure checks each item in the Current Vaccinations list to see whether it matches the selected item in the Vaccinations list. To refer to the items listed in a list box, you use the Column property. When you use the Column property, you supply a column number and a row number. Column numbers and row numbers also start at 0. The Current Vaccinations list box uses only one column (0). To refer to the second item in the Current Vaccinations list, you use the following syntax:

```
[Current Vaccinations].Column(0, 1)
```

If the selected Vaccinations item is in the Current Vaccinations list, the procedure does not add it to the Current Vaccinations list. The procedure loops back to the top and checks the next Vaccinations item.

If the selected Vaccinations item is not in the Current Vaccinations list, the procedure adds the item to the Current Vaccinations list box. To add an item to a list box, you concatenate it to the RowSource property. Because the RowSource property and the list box item are strings, you add them together, using the & operator. To delimit one list-box item from another, you also must add a semicolon (;) to the end of the string.

The Remove button on the Pet Vaccinations form runs the Remove_Button_Click procedure. The procedure is shown in Figure 35-35.

The Remove_Button_Click procedure removes items from the Current Vaccinations list box. Basically, the procedure adds all the unselected items to a string variable, ignoring any selected items; then it assigns the string variable to the RowSource property of the Current Vaccinations list box.

In previous chapters, you saw how to update data in a table by using a form. Using Visual Basic and some special data-access tools built into Access, you can update data in a table that is not part of a form.

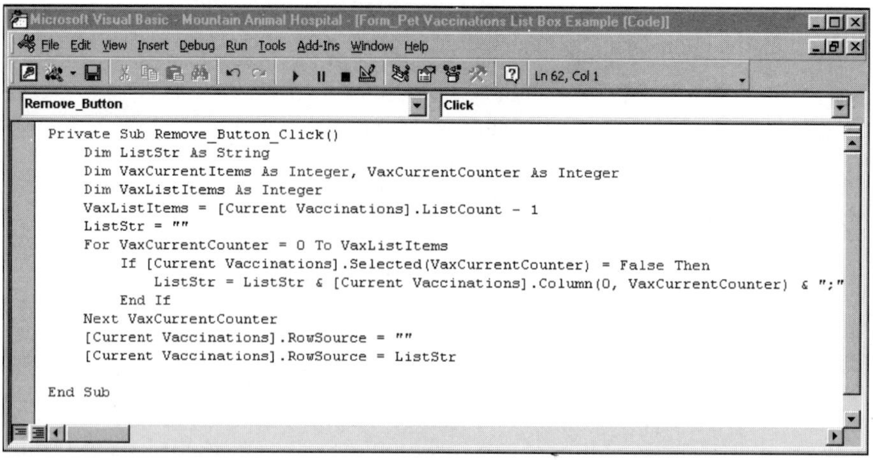


```
Private Sub Remove_Button_Click()
    Dim ListStr As String
    Dim VaxCurrentItems As Integer, VaxCurrentCounter As Integer
    Dim VaxListItems As Integer
    VaxListItems = [Current Vaccinations].ListCount - 1
    ListStr = ""
    For VaxCurrentCounter = 0 To VaxListItems
        If [Current Vaccinations].Selected(VaxCurrentCounter) = False Then
            ListStr = ListStr & [Current Vaccinations].Column(0, VaxCurrentCounter) & ";"
        End If
    Next VaxCurrentCounter
    [Current Vaccinations].RowSource = ""
    [Current Vaccinations].RowSource = ListStr

End Sub
```

Figure 35-35: Removing items from a list box.

Creating Programs to Update a Table

Updating data in a table by using a form is easy; you simply place controls on the form for the fields of the table that you want to update. Figure 35-36 shows the Visit Information form. The name of the form for this example is Adding Visit Details and Updating Customer. The fields that you see on the form update the Pets, Customer, and Visits tables.

Sometimes, however, you want to update a field in a table that you do not want to display on the form. When information is entered in the Visit Information form, for example, the Last Visit Date field in the Customer table should be updated to reflect the most recent date on which the Customer visited the animal hospital. When you enter a new visit, the value for the Last Visit Date field is the value of the Visit Date field on the Visit Information form.

Because the Last Visit Date field can be derived from the Visit Date field, you do not want the user to have to enter it. Theoretically, you could place the Last Visit Date field as a calculated field that is updated after the user enters the Visit Date field. Displaying this field, however, could be confusing and really has nothing to do with the current visit.

The best way to handle updating the Last Visit Date field is to use a Visual Basic procedure.

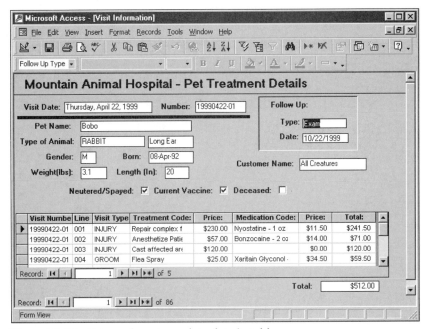

Figure 35-36: Using a form to update data in tables.

Updating a record

You can create a Visual Basic procedure to update a field in a table. The AfterUpdate event for the Visit Information form runs a procedure to update the Customer table. The procedure is shown in Figure 35-37.

The Form_AfterUpdate procedure for the Visit Information form updates the Last Visit Date in the Customer table. This procedure uses special programming language to operate directly on a table in the Mountain Animal Hospital database.

The programming language used to access and manipulate the data in a database is called *ActiveX Data Objects*, or ADO. When you update data by using a form, Access itself uses an entire system of programs, written in ADO, to access and update the database.

The Mountain Animal Hospital examples you have seen so far show you how you can use Access to update data in a local Access database. That is, all of the tables, queries, forms, and reports are stored in one Access database located either in a folder on your desktop or on a server.

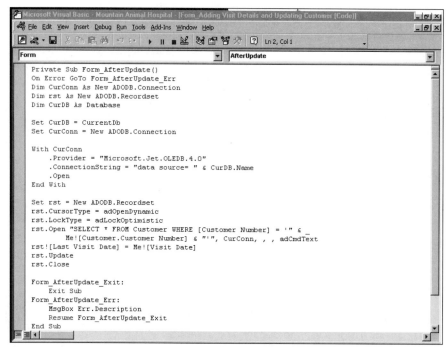

Figure 35-37: Using ADO to update a table.

As a client-server development tool, Access can interact with all kinds of databases. You can develop forms and reports in one Access database that get their data from an entirely separate Access database that may be on your local desktop or on a remote server. You can even link to non-Access databases like Oracle and SQL Server just as easily as linking to an Access database.

ADO is a data access interface that allows you to write programs to manipulate data in local or remote databases. Using ADO, you can perform database functions including querying, updating, data-type conversion, indexing, locking, validation, and transaction management.

Earlier versions of Access included the Data Access Objects, or DAO, data access interface. Improvements in data access technology have taken Access to new levels as a client-server development tool. ADO, a refinement of DAO, represents these improvements and provides a simpler, more powerful array of data access tools. Figure 35-38 shows the same Form AfterUpdate procedure using DAO code.

Caution   Visual Basic currently supports DAO. However, Microsoft does not plan to provide any future DAO enhancements. All new features will be incorporated only into ADO. You should use ADO for any new development projects.

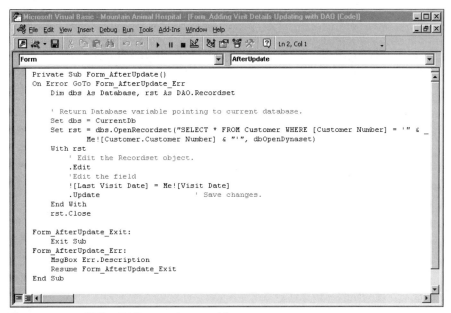

Figure 35-38: Using DAO to update a table.

As you can see in the Form_AfterUpdate procedures, you can combine Visual Basic code with methods and functions from ADO and DAO.

Writing An ADO Procedure

To use ADO functions and methods, you first declare ADO variables, using the Dim and Set statements. The Dim statements in this example declare ADO variables for the name of the connection (CurConn) and the recordset that the procedure wants to access (rst). A *connection* is a communication line into the database. A *recordset* is simply a set of records from a database table or the set of records that result from running a query. The Set statement assigns a value to an ADO variable. The variable CurDB is assigned to the current database — Mountain Animal Hospital, in this example. You use CurrentDb to refer to the currently active database. You use the Open method to establish a link to a database or recordset.

When you use data access objects, you interact with data almost entirely by using Recordset objects. Recordset objects are composed of rows and columns, just like database tables.

Before you can open a connection, you need to define its properties. The Provider and ConnectionString properties describe what kind of database to connect to and the name of the database.

Tip   With DAO, the Provider property was unnecessary. DAO was designed for Access, or Jet, databases. Since ADO is a generic interface, you must specify the Provder name. For Access 2000, or Jet 4.0, databases, the Provider name is Microsoft.Jet.OLEDB.4.0.

Once you have set the connection properties, you can open the connection. The Open method establishes the connection. When the Open method executes, it inherits the properties that have already been set for the connection. You can make a recordset updatable by setting its properties prior to executing the Open method. The CursorType and LockType properties determine how ADO can access and modify the recordset.

Table 35-4 describes the recordset properties you can set.

Table 35-4 Recordset Properties			
ADO Cursor Type	**ADO Lock Type**	**DAO Type**	**Description**
adOpenForwardOnly	adLockReadOnly	DbOpenSnapshot with dbForwardOnly option	You can only scroll forward through records. This improves performance in situations where you do not need to update, as in finding records and printing reports.
adOpenKeyset	adLockOptimistic	dbOpenDynaset	You can't see records that other users add, although records that other users delete are inaccessible from your recordset. Data changes by other users are automatically applied to the recordset.
adOpenStatic	adLockReadOnly	dbOpenSnapshot	A static copy of a set of records that you can use to find data or generate reports. Additions, changes, or deletions by other users are not visible.

Writing a DAO Procedure

The Dim statements in the DAO example declare DAO variables for the name of the database (dbs) and the recordset that the procedure wants to access (rst). The Set statement assigns a value to a DAO variable. The variable dbs is assigned to the current database — Mountain Animal Hospital, in this example. You use the OpenRecordset function to retrieve data from a table or query.

Tip　DAO and ADO share some data types. Since both ADO and DAO have a Recordset type, you must precede the variable name with the appropriate class. When you are referring to a DAO recordset, you use the DAO.Recordset data type. ADO recordsets are referred to as type ADODB.Recordset.

The first argument for the OpenRecordset function is the table name, query name, or an SQL statement. In Chapter 27, you learned about writing SQL statements to retrieve data from a table. The example in this section uses an SQL statement to retrieve the Customer record for the customer referred to in the Visit Information form.

You can choose the type of Recordset object that you want to create by using the second argument of the OpenRecordset method. If you don't specify a type, the Microsoft Jet database engine attempts to create a table-type Recordset. The table recordset type usually is the fastest of the three types, because you are opening the table directly and don't require the overhead of filtering records. When the source for the Recordset is a query or SQL statement, as in the example, you cannot use the Table type. The Dynaset type makes the most efficient use of memory, because it loads only the unique key values from the table.

When the Recordset has been opened, you can begin working with the values in its rows and columns. The statements between the With and End With commands apply to the Rst object — the Recordset of data from the Customer table.

Before you can modify any of the data in a Recordset, you need to tell Jet ahead of time, using the DAO command Edit. The Edit command copies the current record to a buffer so you can change any of the fields in the record.

Note　With ADO, the recordset opens in Edit mode automatically. In DAO, you must explicitly issue the Edit method for each record to edit.

Before you enter the Edit command, however, you need to make sure you are in the record you want to edit. When a Recordset opens, the current record is the first record. Because the SQL statement in the example in this section is based on the table's unique key, you know that the first record in the Recordset is the only record.

To update a field in the current record of the Recordset, you simply assign a new value to the name of the field. In this example, you assign the value of the Visit Date field on the Visit Information form to the Last Visit Date field in the Recordset.

After you make the desired changes in the record, use DAO's Update method to save your changes. The Update method copies the data from the buffer to the Recordset, overwriting the original record.

Caution　This is one of the biggest differences between DAO and ADO. In ADO, changes are automatically saved when you move to another record or close the recordset. In DAO, If you edit a record and then perform any operation that moves to another record without first using Update, you lose your changes without warning. In addition, if you close a recordset or end the procedure that declares the recordset or the parent Database object, your edited record is discarded without warning.

Tip   To cancel pending changes to a recordset in either ADO or DAO, use the CancelUpdate method. In ADO, you must issue the CancelUpdate method before moving to another record.

The Close statement at the end of the Form_AfterUpdate procedure closes the Recordset. Closing recordsets when you finish using them is good practice.

You can use ADO and DAO to add a record to a table just as easily as you can update a record.

Adding a new record

To use ADO and DAO to add a new record to a table, you use the AddNew method. Figure 35-39 shows the ADO procedure for adding a new customer to the Customer table.

```
Private Sub New_Customer_Click()
On Error GoTo New_Customer_Click_Err
Dim CurConn As New ADODB.Connection
Dim rst As New ADODB.Recordset
Dim CurDB As Database

Set CurDB = CurrentDb
Set CurConn = New ADODB.Connection

With CurConn
    .Provider = "Microsoft.Jet.OLEDB.4.0"
    .ConnectionString = "data source= " & CurDB.Name
    .Open
End With

Set rst = New ADODB.Recordset
rst.CursorType = adOpenDynamic
rst.LockType = adLockOptimistic
rst.Open "Customer", CurConn, , , adCmdTable
    With rst
        ' Add new record to end of Recordset object.
        .AddNew

                                               Continued
```

Figure 35-39: Adding a new record to a table using ADO.

```
                ![Customer Number] = "JN-001"
                ![Customer Name] = "Jacob Nottingham"    ' Add data.
                .Update                        ' Save changes.
        End With
        rst.Close
        New_Customer_Click_Exit:
            Exit Sub
        New_Customer_Click_Err:
            MsgBox Err.Description
            Resume New_Customer_Click_Exit
        End Sub
```

Figure 35-39: *(continued)*

Figure 35-40 shows the DAO procedure for adding a new customer to the Customer table.

```
        Private Sub New_Customer_Click()
        On Error GoTo New_Customer_Click_Err
            Dim dbs As Database, rst As Recordset
            ' Return Database variable pointing to current database.
            Set dbs = CurrentDb
            Set rst = dbs.OpenRecordset("Customer", dbOpenDynaset)
            With rst
                ' Add new record to end of Recordset object.
                .AddNew
                ![Customer Number] = "JN-001"
                ![Customer Name] = "Jacob Nottingham"   ' Add data.
                .Update                       ' Save changes.
            End With
            rst.Close
        New_Customer_Click_Exit:
            Exit Sub
        New_Customer_Click_Err:
            MsgBox Err.Description
            Resume New_Customer_Click_Exit
        End Sub
```

Figure 35-40: Adding a new record to a table using DAO.

As you see in this example, using the AddNew method is very similar to using the Edit method. The AddNew method creates a buffer for a new record. After entering the AddNew command, you simply assign values to the fields. When you enter the Update command, the new record buffer is added to the end of the Recordset.

As you might imagine, you also can use ADO and DAO methods to delete a record.

Deleting a record

To remove a record from a table, you use the ADO or DAO method Delete. Figure 35-41 shows the ADO procedure for deleting a record from the Customer table.

Figure 35-42 shows the DAO procedure for deleting a record from the Customer table.

Notice that for both ADO and DAO you need to code only one statement to delete a record. You do not precede the Delete method with Edit or follow it with Update. As soon as the Delete method executes, the record is removed from the Recordset permanently.

```
Private Sub Delete_Customer_Click()
On Error GoTo Delete_Customer_Click_Err
Dim CurConn As New ADODB.Connection
Dim rst As New ADODB.Recordset
Dim CurDB As Database

Set CurDB = CurrentDb
Set CurConn = New ADODB.Connection

With CurConn
    .Provider = "Microsoft.Jet.OLEDB.4.0"
    .ConnectionString = "data source= " & CurDB.Name
    .Open
End With

Set rst = New ADODB.Recordset
rst.CursorType = adOpenDynamic
rst.LockType = adLockOptimistic
rst.Open "SELECT * FROM Customer WHERE [Customer Number] = '"
& _
        Me![Customer.Customer Number] & "'", CurConn, , ,
adCmdText    With rst
        ' Delete the record.
        .Delete
    End With
    rst.Close
Delete_Customer_Click_Exit:
    Exit Sub
Delete_Customer_Click_Err:
    MsgBox Err.Description
    Resume Delete_Customer_Click_Exit
End Sub
```

Figure 35-41: Deleting a record from a table using ADO.

```
Private Sub Delete_Customer_Click()
On Error GoTo Delete_Customer_Click_Err
    Dim dbs As Database, rst As Recordset
    ' Return Database variable pointing to current database.
    Set dbs = CurrentDb
    Set rst = dbs.OpenRecordset("SELECT * FROM Customer WHERE
[Customer Number] ='" Me![Customer.Customer Number] & "'",
dbOpenDynaset)
    With rst
        ' Delete the record.
        .Delete
    End With
    rst.Close
Delete_Customer_Click_Exit:
    Exit Sub
Delete_Customer_Click_Err:
    MsgBox Err.Description
    Resume Delete_Customer_Click_Exit
End Sub
```

Figure 35-42: Deleting a record from a table using DAO.

Using ADO to manipulate data in your database can be very powerful. Figure 35-43 shows a more complex example of the capabilities of ADO. The Clone_Customer_ Click procedure creates a new record from an existing record.

This procedure uses a record from the Customer table as a template to create a new Customer record. The procedure first opens a recordset containing the template customer's information. The template recordset is copied to another new recordset by using the clone method.

The clone method creates an exact copy of the original recordset. Any changes made to one recordset are automatically applied to the other. In other words, if you change the information for the State field in the cloned recordset for Customer Number "AN-001", the State information is automatically changed for Customer Number "AN-001" in the original recordset.

Next, the procedure adds a new record to the cloned recordset. The Customer Number, Customer Name, and Phone Number fields are set to the information for the new customer. The City, State, and Zip Code fields are set to the information for the original template customer.

The Update method saves the information for the new customer. Saving the new customer record in the cloned recordset automatically adds the new record to the original recordset.

```
Private Sub Clone_Customer_Click()
On Error GoTo Clone_Customer_Click_Err
Dim CurConn As New ADODB.Connection
Dim rst As New ADODB.Recordset, rstCln As New ADODB.Recordset
Dim CurDB As Database

Set CurDB = CurrentDb
Set CurConn = New ADODB.Connection

With CurConn
    .Provider = "Microsoft.Jet.OLEDB.4.0"
    .ConnectionString = "data source= " & CurDB.Name
    .Open
End With

Set rst = New ADODB.Recordset
rst.CursorType = adOpenKeyset
rst.LockType = adLockOptimistic
rst.Open "SELECT * FROM Customer WHERE [Customer Number] = '"
& _
        Me![Customer.Customer Number] & "'", CurConn, , ,
adCmdText

Set rstCln = rst.Clone

    With rstCln
        .AddNew
        ![Customer Number] = "JN-001"
        ![Customer Name] = "Jacob Nottingham"    ' Add data.
        ![Phone Number] = "(413)555-3322"
        ![City] = rst![City]
        ![State] = rst![State]
        ![Zip Code] = rst![Zip Code]
        .Update                      ' Save changes.

    End With
    rstCln.Close
    rst.Close
Clone_Customer_Click_Exit:
    Exit Sub
Clone_Customer_Click_Err:
    MsgBox Err.Description
    Resume Clone_Customer_Click_ExitEnd Sub
```

Figure 35-43: Cloning a record.

Summary

This chapter provided an in-depth explanation of programming in Access. You learned how to create procedures to select and update data by using Visual Basic with ADO and DAO. The chapter covered the following topics:

✦ Modules are the principal objects of the Visual BasicVisual Basic programming environment. Form-level modules contain the procedures that apply only to a specific form. Standard modules are available throughout the application.

✦ You use the Dim statement to declare a variable. Declaring variables makes your programs more bugproof.

✦ When you declare a variable, you also specify its data type. Visual Basicdata types are similar to Access field types.

✦ Conditional processing and repetitive looping allow your programs to execute code on the basis of certain conditions.

✦ By using the On Error statement, you can plan for runtime errors.

✦ You set the RowSource property in a procedure to change the contents of a list box on a form. The list box displays faster if you set the RowSource property to null before updating any of the other list-box properties.

✦ You set a control's Visible property in a procedure to display or hide the control.

✦ The LimitToList and NotInList properties of a combo box allow you to use a procedure to add an item to the combo-box list.

✦ You use the ListCount property in a procedure to count the number of items in a list box and the Selected property to see whether an item is selected.

✦ Using Visual Basic with ADO and DAO, you can update data that is not displayed on an active form.

✦   ✦   ✦

Advanced Access Topics

Optimizing Performance

Thisfinal part of the book contains advanced level
material intended to allow you to master some diverse
and important topics. The examples in each of the chapters
are self contained and use the Mountain Animal Hospital
database. As you become a more experienced developer, you
will find these topics more and more useful. Because each of
the remaining chapters deal with separate topics, you can
study them in any order you want.

When Microsoft introduced 32 bit Access, a number of new
performance concerns came part and parcel with the new
features and functions. Microsoft has made a conscious effort
to improve the performance of Access 2000 with improvements in compilation techniques and features such as light
forms. The end result is that Microsoft has helped ease your
burden, but in no way has it completely taken it from you.

> **Tip** The published minimum RAM requirement for a computer
> to run Access for Windows 2000 on Windows 95/98 is
> 16MB — with an emphasis on *minimum.* On a Windows NT
> machine, the published minimum is 32MB of RAM. If
> you are going to do serious development with Access
> for Windows 2000, you should have at least 64MB of RAM
> or, preferably, 128MB or more. With today's computers
> and memory prices this amount of memory is a valuable
> investment.

Lightweight Forms and Reports — Less Filling, Runs Great!

Access 2000 gives you the ability to create forms and reports
with class modules as a part of them (physically stored in
them). When a form doesn't have a code module (default
action), it is called a *lightweight form object.* Lightweight forms

load and display faster than forms with class modules because no code needs to be loaded or compiled when the form is loaded. When you create a new form, it is created as a lightweight form by default. You can always create a class module for a form by setting the form's Has Module property (in the Other container of the Properties dialog box) to Yes (see Figure 36-1).

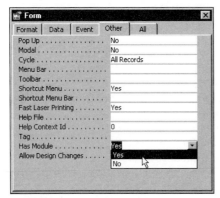

Figure 36-1: A form with the Has Module property set to Yes (True).

If your form does not use event procedures (code that you create and attach to an event property), you should make sure that this property is set to No (False).

Caution   If you create a form that has event procedures and later delete the procedures, Access will keep the property Has Module set to Yes (True). Deleting all of the event procedures in a code module does not turn the form into a lightweight form. In fact, Access automatically sets the Has Module property to Yes (True) as soon as you attempt to view an object's module (form or report), even if no code is actually created for the module. Once a form has a module behind it, the only way to remove the reference to the code module and make the form a lightweight form is to change the form's Has Module property to No (False).

Just because a lightweight form or report does not have code behind it doesn't mean that it is useless; you can attach macros or specify functions that are stored in standard modules from the events of the form or report and its controls. For example, if you have a switchboard form, you will need to have the form's events run functions (open other forms, run a report, etc.) when the buttons on the form are clicked. Instead of attaching code directly to the form in the class module, thus setting the form's Has Module property to Yes, you can call a function in a standard module by creating an expression in the button's click event. Figure 36-2 shows how to call the function `ShowInventory()` when a button is clicked.

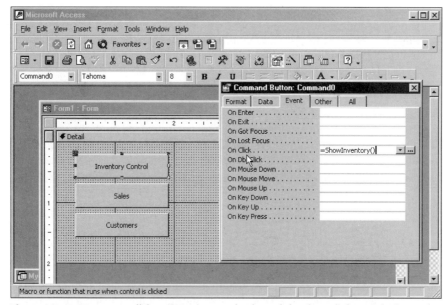

Figure 36-2: You can call functions in standard modules from lightweight forms by specifying the name of the function (assigning it using an equal sign) in the expression space next to the event name.

When a function is assigned to an event in this manner, the module containing the function will only be loaded and compiled when the event procedure (function you specified) is triggered. Thus, in the example above, the module containing the procedure ShowInventory() is not loaded until the button is clicked.

Note   This technique only works for functions; you cannot call a procedure declared with Sub because it does not return a value and therefore cannot be used as part of an expression.

Understanding Module Load on Demand

One of the great features of Visual Basic for Applications (the core language that replaced Access Basic in Access 2.0) is the *load on demand* functionality of VBA. Using load on demand, Access loads code modules only as they are needed or referenced. In Access 95, load on demand of modules wasn't fully realized because loading a module loaded the entire module's potential call tree. With Access 2000, the load on demand feature truly does help reduce the amount of RAM needed and helps your program run faster.

Tip   Because Access does not unload code after it has been loaded into memory, you should periodically close your application while you develop. When developing, there is a tendency to open and work with many different procedures in many different modules. These modules stay in memory until you close Access.

Organizing your modules

First, be aware that when any procedure or variable is referenced in your application, the entire module that contains the procedure or variable is loaded into memory. To minimize the number of modules loaded into memory, you need to organize your procedures and variables into logical modules. For example, it is a good idea to place all Global variables in the same module. If only one Global variable is declared in a module, the entire module is loaded into memory. By the same token, you should put only procedures that are always used by your application (such as start-up procedures) into the module containing the Global variables.

Access 2000 prunes the call tree

The way in which Access 95 performed load on demand imposed serious performance concerns. In Access 95, not only was an entire module loaded when a procedure within it was called, but the potential call tree for that procedure was also called.

Remember, when a procedure or function is called, the entire module in which that function is stored is placed in memory.

Therefore, a potential call tree consists of all the procedures that *could* be called by the current procedure you are calling. In addition, all the procedures that could be called from *those* procedures and so forth are part of the potential call tree as well. For example:

1. If you call Procedure A, the entire module containing Procedure A is loaded.

2. Modules containing variable declarations used by Procedure A are loaded.

3. Procedure A has lines of code that call Procedures B and C — the modules containing Procedure B and Procedure C are loaded. (Even if the call statements are in conditional loops and are never executed, they are still loaded because *potentially* they could be called.)

4. Any procedures that could be called by Procedure B and Procedure C are loaded, as well as the entire modules containing those potential procedures.

5. And so on and so on and . . .

What is a call tree

The call tree for a procedure is any additional functions or procedures that the current procedure (or function) has referenced within it as well as those referenced by the newly loaded functions and procedures and so forth. Since a procedure may reference numerous additional functions/procedures (stored in different modules) based on the action taken by the procedure, this loading of all potentially called functions/procedures takes a lot of time and memory.

Fortunately for all Access developers, this complete loading of a potential call tree has been addressed in Access 2000. Access 2000 automatically compiles modules upon demand, rather than the entire potential call tree. However, you can turn this feature off, thus making Access 2000 compile all modules at one time. Do this in the Visual Basic for Applications program (rather than in Access itself). Access 2000 links directly to VBA's development environment for working with Visual Basic code. To check the status of the Compile on Demand option, follow these steps:

1. Select the Modules object type from the Object Bar of the database.

2. Click the NEW object button to activate the Visual Basic Development Environment.

3. Select Tools ➪ Options... The Options dialog box will appear.

4. Select the General tab.

5. Verify that the check box Compile on Demand is checked. It is located on the bottom right side of the dialog box. If not, select it. Figure 36-3 shows the dialog box with the option selected.

6. Click the OK button.

7. Select File ➪ Close and Return to Microsoft Access (Alt + Q) or click the Access button (first button on toolbar) if you want to return to Access and leave the VBA window open.

Tip　Unless you have a specific reason to do so, never deselect the Compile on Demand option. When you deselect that option, you could conceivably cause *all* of the modules in a database to load and compile by simply calling just one procedure.

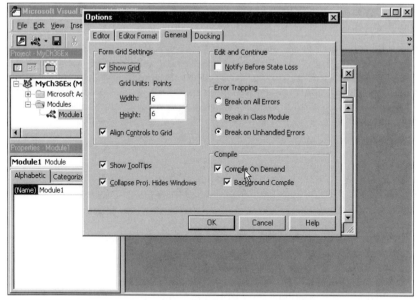

Figure 36-3: For maximum performance, leave the Compile on Demand box selected.

With the Compile on Demand option selected, Access 2000 will not load the entire call tree of a module but will load a portion of the call tree of the executed procedure. For example, if you call procedure A in module A, any modules that contain procedures referenced in procedure A are loaded and compiled. However, Access 2000 doesn't take into consideration procedures that may be called from other procedures in module A, and it doesn't look at the potential call tree of the modules loaded because one of their procedures is referenced in procedure A. Because Access 2000 only loads modules one-deep from the executed procedure's immediate call tree — not the module's call tree — your applications should load and execute many times faster than they did in Access 95.

Even though there has been a significant improvement in the way modules are loaded and compiled in Access 2000, there are still a number of things you can do to reduce the number of modules loaded and compiled. For instance, you should never place infrequently called procedures in a module with procedures that are called often. At times, this may make your modules less logical and harder to conceptualize. For example, you may have a dozen functions that perform various manipulations to contact information in your application. Ordinarily, you might make one module called `mdlContacts` and place all the contact-related procedures and variables into this one module. Because Access loads the entire module when one procedure or variable in it is called, you may want to separate the contact-related procedures into separate modules (one for procedures that are commonly used and one that contains procedures that are rarely used).

Tip

You need to be aware at all times that all modules having procedures referenced in a procedure of a different module are loaded when that procedure is called. In your application, if any of your common procedures reference a procedure that is not commonly used, you will want to place the uncommon procedure in the same module with the common procedures to prevent a different module (containing the uncommon procedures) from being loaded and compiled. You may even decide to use more than two modules if you have very large amounts of code in multiple procedures that are rarely called. Although breaking related procedures into separate modules may make your code a little harder to understand, it can greatly improve the performance of your application.

To fully take advantage of Compile on Demand, you have to carefully plan your procedure placement. Third-party tools, such as Total Access Analyzer from FMS, print a complete module reference report. This can be invaluable for visualizing where all the potential calls for various procedures are located.

Distributing MDE Files

One way to ensure that your application's code is always compiled is to distribute your database as an .MDE file. When you save your database as an .MDE file, Access compiles all code modules (including form modules), removes all editable source code, and compacts the database. The new .MDE file contains no source code, but continues to work because it does contain a compiled copy of all of your code. Not only is this a great way to secure your source code, it allows you to distribute databases that are smaller (because they contain no source code) and always keep their modules in a compiled state. Because the code is always in a compiled state, less memory is used by the application, and there is no performance penalty for code being compiled at run time.

In addition to not being able to view existing code because it is all compiled, the following restrictions apply:

✦ You cannot view, modify, or create forms, reports, or modules in Design view.

✦ You cannot add, delete, or change references to object libraries or databases.

✦ You cannot change your database's VBA project name using the Options dialog box.

✦ You cannot import or export forms, reports, or modules. Note, however, that tables, queries, and macros can be imported from or exported to non-MDE databases.

Because of these restrictions, it may not be possible to distribute your application as an .MDE file. For example, if your application creates forms at run time, you would not be able to distribute the database as an .MDE file.

Caution

There is no way to convert an .MDE file into a normal database file. Always save and keep a copy of the original database! When you need to make changes to the application, you must open the normal database and then create a new .MDE before distribution. If you delete your original database, you will be unable to access any of your objects in design view!

Note

There are some prerequisites to be met before a database can be saved as an .MDE file. First, if security is in use, the user creating the .MDE file must have all applicable rights to the database. In addition, if the database is replicated, you must remove all replication system tables and properties before saving the .MDE file. Finally, you must save all databases or add-ins in the chain of references as .MDE files or your database will be unable to use them.

To create an .MDE file:

1. Close the database if it is currently open. If you do not close the current database, Access will attempt to close it for you, prompting you to save changes where applicable. When working with a shared database, all users must close the database; Access needs exclusive rights to work with the database.

2. Select Tools ⇨ Database Utilities and then click Make MDE File (see Figure 36-4).

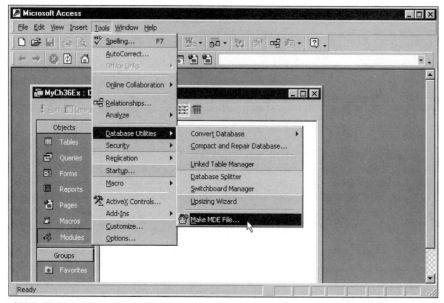

Figure 36-4: Access doesn't convert the existing database into an .MDE file, it creates a new .MDE file for the database.

3. In the Database To Save As MDE dialog box, specify the database you want to save as an .MDE file, and click Make MDE (see Figure 36-5).

If you had a database opened when you selected Make MDE File, this step is skipped and Access assumes you want to use the previously opened database. If you wish to use a different database, you need to cancel creating the .MDE file, close the database, and select Make MDE File again. At that time, you will be asked for the database to save as an .MDE file.

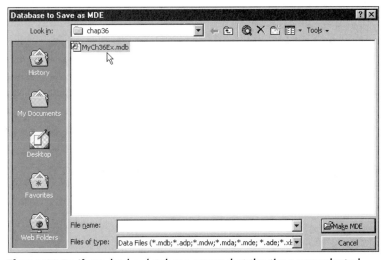

Figure 36-5: If you had a database opened at the time you selected Make MDE File, you will not see this form.

4. In the Database to Save as MDE dialog box, specify a name, drive, and folder for the database. Do not attempt to save the .MDE file with the same filename as the original database.

Caution　Do not delete or overwrite your original database! As stated previously, there is no way to convert an .MDE file to a normal database, and you cannot edit any objects in an .MDE file. If you delete or otherwise lose your original database, you will never again be able to access any of the objects in the design environment!

Understanding the Compiled State

Understanding how Access performs Compile on Demand is critical to achieving maximum performance from your Access application. However, it is also paramount that you understand what compilation is and what it means for an application to be in a compiled state. There are actually two types of code in Access, code that you write and code that Access can understand and execute. Before a procedure of VBA code that you have written can be executed, the code must be run through a compiler to generate code in a form that Access can understand — compiled code. Access lacks a true compiler and instead uses partially compiled code and an interpreter. A true compiler converts source code to machine-level instructions which are executed by your computer's CPU. Access converts your source code to an intermediate state which it can rapidly interpret and execute. The code in the converted form is known as compiled code, or as being in a compiled state.

If a procedure is called that is not in a compiled state, the procedure must first be compiled and then the compiled code is passed to the interpreter for execution. In reality, as previously stated, this does not happen at the procedure level, but at the module level; when you call a procedure, the module containing the procedure and all modules that have procedures referenced in the called procedure are loaded and compiled. You can manually compile your code, or you can let Access compile it for you on the fly. It takes time to compile the code, however, so the performance of your application will suffer if you let Access compile it on the fly.

In addition to the time it takes for Access to compile your code at run time, decompiled programs use considerably more memory than compiled code. When your application is completely compiled, only the compiled code is loaded into memory when a procedure is called. If you run an application that is in a decompiled state, Access loads the decompiled code and generates the compiled code as needed (explained previously). Access does not unload the decompiled code as it compiles, so you are left with two versions of the same code in memory.

There is one drawback to compiled applications: They use more disk space than their decompiled versions. This is because both the compiled and decompiled versions of the code are stored on disk.

Disk space should not often become a problem, but if you have an application with an enormous amount of code, you can save disk space by keeping it in a decompiled state. Remember, there is a trade-off between disk space used and the performance of your database. Most often, when given the choice, a user would rather give up a few megabytes of disk space in exchange for faster applications.

Tip   You may use this space-saving technique to your advantage if you need to distribute a large application and your recipients have a full development version of Access. By distributing the uncompiled versions, you will need much less disk space to distribute the application, and the end users can compile it again at their location. If you are going to do this, you should put the entire application into a decompiled state. Fully decompiling an application is discussed later in this chapter.

Putting your applications code into a compiled state

There is only one way to put your entire application into a compiled state: use the Compile [mdb name] menu item from the Debug menu on the Modules toolbar in the Visual Basic for Applications development window (see Figure 36-6). To access the Debug menu, you must have a module open. Generally, you should always use the Compile [mdb name] command to ensure that all of the code is saved in a compiled state. It can take a long time to compile complex applications, and, in general, you should only perform a Compile [mdb name] before you distribute your application or before performing benchmark tests.

Access 2000 has an added a new option for compiling code to the Visual Basic for Applications program — Background Compile. (Figure 36-3 shows this option under Compile on Demand. The default value for this option is True (selected). This option tells Access to compile code in background rather than compile it all at one time.

Tip   It is especially important to close your application after performing a Compile [mdb name]. To compile all your modules, Access needs to load every single one of them into memory. All this code stays in memory until you close down Access.

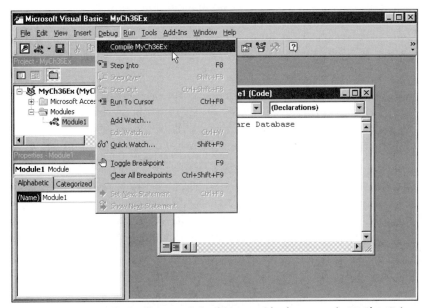

Figure 36-6: Compile [mdb name] (in this example the name is MyCh36Ex) is the only way to fully compile your application.

Losing the compiled state

One of the greatest roadblocks to increasing the performance of Access 95 applications was the too-easy way in which an application could be decompiled. When the Access 95 application was in a decompiled state, Access had to constantly compile code as it was called. Losing the compiled state was so easy to do in Access 95, it would often happen without developers even realizing they had done it.

In Access 2000, only portions of code affected by certain changes are put into a decompiled state — not the entire application. This is in itself a tremendous improvement over Access 95.

The following will cause portions of your code to be decompiled:

✦ Modifying a form, report, control, or module. (If you don't save the modified object, your application is preserved in its previous state.)

✦ Adding a new form, report, control, or module (includes adding new code behind a form).

✦ Deleting or renaming a form, report, control, or module.

✦ Adding or removing a reference to an object library or database by using the References command on the Tools menu.

Okay, so you think you have a handle on code that loses its compiled state? Well, here are a couple of "gotchas" that you need to consider:

✦ If you modify objects such as reports or forms at run time through VBA code, portions of your application are put into an uncompiled state when the objects are modified. (Wizards often do this.)

✦ If your application creates objects such as reports or forms on the fly, portions of your application are put into an uncompiled state when the objects are created. (Wizards often do this, as well.)

Another serious flaw of Access 95 was that an application's entire compiled state was tied to the filename of the database itself. This feature meant that your entire application would lose its compiled state and all code would have to be compiled at the time it was called if you renamed your database, compacted your database into a database of a different name, or copied your database to a database with a different name.

Fortunately, Access 97 fixed this serious problem and it does not exist in Access 2000. The compiled state of an application is still tied to its name, but now it is tied to its project name rather than its filename. By default, the project name of a database is the same as the filename of the database. You can change the project name of a database by selecting Tools ⇨ [mdb name/database] Properties ... in the Visual Basic development Window and clicking the General tab, as shown in Figure 36-7.

Caution When you change a project name (but not when you change the filename), the entire application loses its compiled state. Because of this, you should change the project name only if absolutely necessary, and you should perform a Compile [mdb name] immediately after changing the project name.

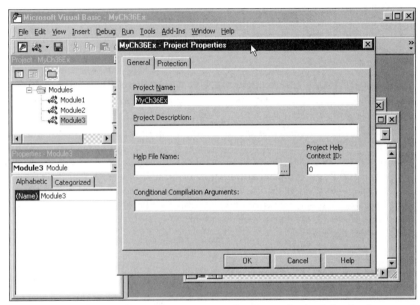

Figure 36-7: Change the project name on the General tab of the [mdb name/ database] Project properties dialog – but only if absolutely necessary.

Distributing applications in a compiled or decompiled state

There are a couple of issues concerning compilation that you should take into consideration when distributing your Access application.

Distributing source code for your application

First and foremost, if you distribute source code and allow your users access to modify or add objects, you must make them completely aware of the compilation issues. If your users do not fully comprehend what is happening with your application's compiled state, you can be sure you will receive phone calls about how your program seems to be getting slower the more the users make changes to objects.

Putting an application in a decompiled state

If your application is the type that will be constantly changing its compiled state (due to creating forms and reports dynamically), or end users will be making modifications to the application's objects often, or distributed file size is an issue, you may want to consider distributing the database in a fully decompiled state.

To put your entire application into a decompiled state

1. Create a new database.

2. Import all of your application objects into the new database.

3. Compact the new database.

Organizing commonly used code that is never modified into a library

After your application is finished and ready for distribution, you may want to consider placing all commonly used code that will never be modified by an end user into a library database. A library database is an external database that your application database can reference and access. A little overhead is incurred by having to call code from the library rather than accessing it directly in the parent application, but the benefit is that the library code will never be put into a decompiled state — even if your application creates or modifies objects on the fly or your users add new or modify existing objects. This technique can greatly increase an application's performance and keep the performance relatively consistent over time.

The first step for referencing procedures in an external database is to create the external database with all its modules just as you would an ordinary Access database.

Caution   Any procedures that you declare as Private are not made available to the calling application, so plan carefully what you want and don't want to expose to other databases.

After you have created the database and its modules, you must create a reference to that database in your application database (the database your users will run). To create a reference, first open any module in your application database in Design view. When you have a module in Design view, a new command is available from the Tools menu — References (see Figure 36-8). Select Tools ➪ References to access the References dialog box (see Figure 36-9).

In the References dialog box, you specify all the references your application needs for using OLE automation or for using other Access databases as library databases. When making a reference to another Access database as opposed to an OLE server created with another development tool such as Visual Basic, you will probably need to Browse for the database. Use the Browse dialog box as though you were going to open the external database. After you have selected the external Access database, it shows up in the References dialog box with a check mark to indicate that it is referenced.

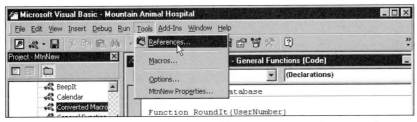

Figure 36-8: The References option only appears on the Tools menu when you have a module open and selected in Design view.

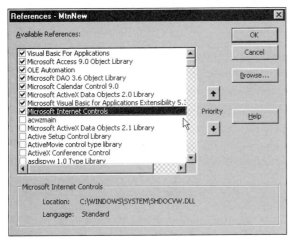

Figure 36-9: The References dialog box is where you resolve references to OLE automation servers and Access library databases.

To remove a reference, access the References dialog box again and deselect the referenced item by clicking its check box. After you have made all the references you need to make, click the OK button.

After a database is referenced, you can call the procedures in the referenced database as though they existed in your application database. No matter what happens in your application database to cause code to decompile, the referenced database always stays in a compiled state unless it is opened and modified directly using Access.

To reference an external Access database to call its procedures, follow these steps:

1. Create the library database and its modules.

2. Open the database in which you want to use the external procedures.

3. Open any module in Design view.

4. Select Tools ➪ References.

5. Select the OLE server you wish to register. If it is an Access database, you will probably have to use Browse to locate the database.

Tip

If your application uses add-in databases (a special type of library database), open the add-in database for read-only access. Opening add-ins for read-only access increases performance because Jet does not have to maintain locking information for the add-in database in an .LDB file.

Creating a library reference for distributed applications

If you are distributing your application, references stay intact only if the calling database and the library database are in the same or relative path. For example, if on your machine the main database is in C:\MYAPP and the library database is in C:\MYAPP\LIBRARY, the reference remains intact if the library database is located in the same relative path, such as in C:\NEWDIR for the main database and C:\NEWDIR\LIBRARY for the library database. If the relative path will not remain consistent upon distribution, your application's users will have to add the reference manually or you will have to create the reference using VBA code.

In Access 95, it was impossible to create a reference using code. If you distributed your Access 95 application, the end user *had* to create the reference manually. If you distributed your Access 95 application using the Access Developer's Toolkit, it was impossible for the end user to create the reference! Access 2000 has a References collection that you can use to programmatically create references at run time. The following procedure creates a reference to the file whose name is passed to it. For this function to work, the full filename with path must be passed:

```
bResult = CreateReference("c:\My Documents\MyLib.mdb").
```

The function is:

```
Public Function CreateReference(szFileName As String) As
Boolean
    On Error GoTo CreateReferenceError
    Dim ref As Reference

    Set ref = References.AddFromFile(szFileName)
    CreateReference = True

Exit Function

CreateReferenceError:
    MsgBox Err & ": " & Err.Description
    CreateReference = False
    Exit Function

End Function
```

Tip   You can verify that a reference is set by using the `ReferenceFromFile` function. To verify a reference, pass the function the full path and filename like this:

```
bResult = ReferenceFromFile("C:\Windows\System\mscal.ocx").
```

The function returns True if the reference is valid, False if it is not.

With the References collection, the primary concern of using and distributing libraries — losing references upon distribution — is now gone. There is, however, still one major drawback to library databases: Access does not support circular references. This means that code in your library databases cannot reference variables or call procedures that exist in your parent database.

Whether you distribute your application as one database or as a primary database that uses library databases, if your applications are static (they don't allow modification of objects by end users or wizards and don't perform object modifications on themselves), you should always distribute the databases in a fully compiled state so that your users experience the highest level of performance possible.

Improving Absolute Speed

When discussing an application's performance, the word performance is usually synonymous with speed. In software development, there are actually two different types of speed: absolute and perceived. Absolute speed refers to the actual speed at which your application performs a function, such as how long it takes to run a certain query. Perceived speed is the phenomenon of an end user actually perceiving one application to be faster than another application, even though it may indeed be slower. This phenomenon of perceived speed is often a direct result of visual feedback provided to the user while the application is performing a task. Absolute speed items can be measured in units of time; perceived speed cannot.

Of course, some of the most important items for increasing actual speed are

- ✦ Keeping your application in a compiled state
- ✦ Organizing your procedures into "smart" modules
- ✦ Opening databases exclusively
- ✦ Compacting your databases regularly

You should always open a database exclusively in a single-user environment. If your application is a standalone application (nothing is shared over a network), opening the database in exclusive mode can really boost performance. If your application is run on a network and shared by multiple users, you will not be able to open the database exclusively. (Actually, the first user can open it exclusively, but if they do, no other user can access the database until the first user closes it.) The preferred method for running an application in a network environment is to run Access and the main code .MDB file locally, and link to a shared database containing the data on the server. If your application is used in this manner, you can open and run the code database exclusively, but you cannot use exclusive links to the shared data.

To open a database exclusively in Access 2000, select the pull-down Open button and select Open Exclusive in the Open Database dialog box (see Figure 36-10).

Figure 36-10: Selecting the Open Exclusive button on the pull-down Open button to open a database in a single-user environment to increase the performance of the database.

Tip   You can set the default open mode for a database on the Advanced tab of the Options dialog box to Exclusive. The default open mode is Shared.

Another often-overlooked way of maximizing your database's performance is to compact your database regularly. When records are deleted from a database, the disk space that held the deleted data is not recovered until a compact is performed. In addition, a database becomes fragmented as data is modified in the database. Compacting a database defragments the database and recovers used disk space.

All of the preceding methods are excellent (and necessary) ways to help keep your applications running at their optimum performance level, but these are not the only things you can do to increase the absolute speed of your application. Almost every area of development, from forms to modules, can be optimized to give your application maximum absolute speed.

Tuning your system

One important aspect of performance has nothing to do with the actual application design; that is, the computer on which the application is running. Although it is impossible to account for all the various configurations your clients may have, there are some things you can do for your computer and recommend that end users do for theirs:

✦ Equip the computer with as much RAM as possible. This step often becomes an issue of dollars. However, RAM prices continue to decrease, and adding to a computer's RAM is one of the most effective things you can do to increase the speed of Access.

✦ Make the WinCacheSize parameter for SmartDrive as small as possible, and disable SmartDrive completely on computers with little memory. You need to determine the size to set this at yourself based on your system and its memory configuration. Please consult your Windows manuals for more information on SmartDrive.

✦ Don't use wallpaper. Removing a standard Windows wallpaper background can free up anywhere from 25K to 250K of RAM, and removing complicated bitmaps or high-color bitmaps can free up even more space.

✦ Eliminate unnecessary TSRs (Terminate and Stay Resident programs). TSRs can be real memory hogs and should not be used unless absolutely needed.

✦ Close all applications that aren't being used. Windows makes it very handy to keep as many applications as you wish loaded for just the odd chance you may need to use one of them. Although Windows 95 and Windows 98 are pretty good at handling memory for multiple open applications, each running application still uses RAM. On machines with little RAM, unnecessary open applications can significantly degrade performance.

✦ Ensure that your Windows swap file is on a fast drive with plenty of free space. If possible, you should also set the minimum disk space available for virtual memory to at least 25MB of RAM and make it a permanent swap file.

✦ Defragment your hard drive often. Defragmenting a hard drive allows data to be retrieved from the drive in larger sections, causing fewer direct reads and less repositioning of the read heads.

Adjusting the Jet registry settings

Access 2000 includes a number of registry settings that allow you to tailor Jet functions for maximum performance. The `MaxBufferSize` and the `ReadAheadPages` settings are still there, as well as a group of new settings that affects various elements of the Jet engine.

Tip

Most of the preceding registry entries are found in the \HKEY_LOCAL_MACHINE\ SOFTWARE\Microsoft\Jet\4.0\Engines\Jet 4.0 key of the Windows Registry. You may also find some of them in the other two Jet sites. They follow the same path as the Jet 4.0 key except that the end keys are ...\Jet\4.0\Engines\Jet 2.0 and ...\Jet\4.0\Engines\Jet 3.x.

Where appropriate they will be referenced as \Engines\Jet 2.0, \Engines\Jet 3.x, and \Engines\Jet 4.x.

Caution

Unless you are comfortable with editing the Windows 95/98 or NT registry you should not perform the following changes. If you decide to edit the registry, make sure that you make a back up copy *before* making changes using REGEDIT.exe or another registry editing program.

Making changes improperly can possibly cause your computer to *stop* working and, without a backup copy of the registry, could require re-installing all software on your computer.

MaxBufferSize

Key is found in \Engines\Jet 4.0. The MaxBufferSize setting in the Windows registry controls how Jet uses memory in some operations. The MaxBufferSize setting controls the maximum size of the Jet database engine's internal cache (the cache used to store records in memory). The Jet engine reads data in 2K pages and places the data in the cache. After the data has been placed in the cache, it can be used wherever it is needed (in tables, queries, forms, or reports). The default setting for MaxBufferSize is 0, which means that Jet calculates the settings based on the formula ((Total RAM in K - 12,288)/4 + 512K). On a computer with 16MB of RAM, this equates to a MaxBufferSize of 1,536. For computers with minimal memory (8MB), you should set the value to something less than 512K to free up more memory for Access operations. However, for computers with more memory, increase the MaxBufferSize.

There is no hard-and-fast rule for the MaxBufferSize setting, but some general guidelines are 2,048K for computers with 16MB, 4,096 for computers with 32MB, and 8,092 for computers with 64KB. Increasing the MaxBufferSize enables Jet to read more records into the memory cache, which in turn minimizes disk reads/writes. Note: A higher setting does not always imply a more efficient setting. Setting the value higher than 8MB has not been found to increase performance.

ReadAheadPages

Key is found in \Engines\Jet 2.0. The ReadAheadPages setting controls the number of 2K data pages Jet reads ahead when doing sequential page reads. A sequential page read occurs when Jet detects that the data in a current read request is on a data page located on the hard disk adjacent to the data page of the previous request. The default setting for ReadAheadPages is 8; you can set the value anywhere between 0 and 31. If you change the setting to 0, Jet does not read ahead pages during sequential scans of data. A low setting frees more memory for other

Access operations; a higher setting uses more memory but enables Jet to access more records quickly in operations performed on sequential records. This setting is most efficient immediately after a database is compacted, because compacting defragments the data (makes the data contiguous).

UserCommitSync

Key is found in \Engines\Jet 4.0. The UserCommitSync registry setting is used to choose whether Jet processes transactions *synchronously* or *asynchronously*. Setting the UserCommitSync setting to Yes (default) forces Jet to process transactions synchronously; setting it to No forces Jet to process transactions in asynchronous mode. In synchronous mode, Jet processes the entire transaction before returning control to the application. In asynchronous mode, Jet caches the changes to its memory buffer and immediately returns control to the application while writing the transaction results to disk using background processing. The FlushTransaction-Timeout, the SharedAsyncDelay, and the ExclusiveAsyncDelay settings all affect how Jet commits transactions in asynchronous mode.

> **Note**   By default, the UserCommitSync registry setting is set to Yes; that is, synchronous mode. You should not change this setting to No, asynchronous mode, because in such a case, control will return to your application before all transactions are committed to disk. Your application won't know whether the transaction was completed properly or not.

ImplicitCommitSync

Key is found in \Engines\Jet 4.0. Jet processes add, delete, and update operations as transactions, even if they are not explicitly wrapped in a transaction. These transactions are known as implicit transactions. The ImplicitCommitSync setting affects implicit transactions in much the same way that the UserCommitSync setting affects explicit transactions. However, the ImplicitCommitSync is set to No, asynchronous mode, by default. If you change this setting to Yes to process implicit transactions synchronously, you will get behavior similar to Access 2.0, in that all add, delete, and update operations are performed immediately and not as a transaction (unless explicitly wrapped in a transaction with BeginTrans and CommitTrans). Changing this setting to Yes yields much slower performance, so you should leave the setting at its default.

FlushTransactionTimeout

Key is found in \Engines\Jet 4.0. The FlushTransactionTimeout setting is the number of milliseconds after which Jet starts committing (writing) a cached transaction to disk. The setting is 500 milliseconds by default. Increasing the setting in a shared database environment can increase performance because more information is cached before writing to disk, causing fewer disk writes. Jet will commit the cached transactions to disk after the FlushTransactionTimeout interval is achieved or if the cache exceeds the MaxBufferSize setting.

ExclusiveAsyncDelay

Key is found in \Engines\Jet 4.0. The `ExclusiveAsyncDelay` setting is the maximum amount of time in milliseconds that is allowed to pass before asynchronous mode changes start to be committed to disk for a database that is opened exclusively. The default setting is 2,000 (2 seconds), and increasing the value will probably not boost performance unless there is over 32MB of RAM on the computer.

SharedAsyncDelay

Key is found in \Engines\Jet 4.0. The `SharedAsyncDelay` setting is the maximum amount of time in milliseconds that is allowed to pass before asynchronous mode changes start to be committed to disk for a database that is opened in shared mode. The default setting is 50 milliseconds, and increasing this value can yield faster performance. The higher the value, however, the longer it takes to commit changes so other users can see them and free the locks on the cached records.

PageTimeout

Key is found in \Engines\Jet 4.0. The `PageTimeout` setting is how long Jet waits before checking to see if other users have made changes to the database. After the `PageTimeout` interval has passed, Jet refreshes any changed data into its memory buffer and restarts the interval. The default `PageTimeout` setting is 5,000 milliseconds (5 seconds). Increasing this value can yield faster performance but creates more lag time from when a user changes a record to when you see the change. The Refresh Interval (sec) setting on the Advanced tab of the Options dialog box overrides the `PageTimeout` setting.

Tip You can cause Jet to immediately update its cache by using the `dbRefreshCache` argument of the `Idle` method in DAO code in a line such as this: `DBEngine. Idle dbRefreshCache`.

LockDelay

Key is found in \Engines\Jet 4.0. The `LockDelay` setting determines how long Jet waits to reattempt a record lock after a record lock attempt has been denied, such as when another user has locked the record. If the time it takes to return a lock denial message is longer than the `LockDelay`, the `LockDelay` setting is ignored and an immediate retry is attempted. The default `LockDelay` setting is 100 milliseconds, and increasing this value on computers accessing a database with frequent locks over a busy network may help reduce network traffic.

MaxLocksPerFile

Key is found in \Engines\Jet 4.0. The `MaxLocksPerFile` setting determines the maximum number of locks that Jet places on a single file. Jet will immediately commit to disk all pending transactions along with associated locks and free their locks if a queued transaction requires more locks than are currently available. By default, the MaxLocksPerFile setting is set for 9,500 locks. On a network, if Jet attempts to create more locks than the server can handle, the server returns an error message or may appear to lock up. If this occurs on your network, decrease the MaxLocksPerFile setting.

RecycleLVs

Key is found in \Engines\Jet 4.0. Jet uses Long Value pages (LVs) to store data in fields of Memo, OLE Object, and Hyperlink data types. LVs are also used to store data that defines forms, reports, and modules. Databases increase in size when opened in shared mode because Access LVs are constantly being replaced with new LVs as certain database objects are manipulated. The ReclyceLVs setting determines when discarded LVs become available for reuse. The default RecycleLVs setting is 0, meaning that discarded LVs are recycled only when the last user closes the database. If set to 1, Jet recycles LVs when it determines that there is only one user left using the database — this slows down performance.

Tip   The only way to free the disk space used by discarded LVs is to compact the database — another reason you should compact your databases frequently.

Getting the most from your tables

In addition to all of the technical issues discussed in the preceding sections, it is advantageous to get back to the basics when designing your applications. Tools such as Access enable novices to create relational databases quickly and easily, but they do not teach good database design techniques in the process. An exception to this statement is the Table Analyzer Wizard. Even though the Table Analyzer Wizard offers suggestions that are often helpful in learning good design technique, its recommendations should *never* be taken as gospel. The Table Analyzer has proven to be wrong on many occasions.

Entire volumes of text have been devoted to the subject of database theory. Teaching database theory is certainly beyond the scope of this chapter (or even this book). There are, however, many basics of good database design with which you should be familiar.

Creating efficient indexes

Indexes help Access find and sort records more efficiently (in other words, faster). Think of these indexes as you would think of an index in a book. To find data, Access looks up the location of the data in the index and then retrieves the data from its location. You can create indexes based on a single field or based on multiple fields. Multiple-field indexes enable you to distinguish between records in which the first field may have the same value. If they are defined properly, multiple-field indexes can be used by Microsoft's Rushmore query optimization to greatly speed queries. Rushmore is the technology Jet uses to optimize the speed at which queries execute based on the search and sort fields of the queries and indexes of the tables included in the queries.

Deciding which fields to index

Two typical mistakes made by people new to database development are, first, not using indexes and, second, using too many indexes (usually putting them on every field in a table). Both of these mistakes are serious — sometimes a table with indexes on every field may give *slower* performance than a table with no indexes. Why? When a record is saved, Access also must save an index entry for each defined index. This can take time and use a considerable amount of disk space. The time used is usually unnoticed when there are just a few indexes, but many indexes can require a huge amount of time for record saves and updates. In addition, indexes can slow some action queries (such as append queries) when the indexes for many fields need to be updated while performing the query's operations. Figure 36-11 shows the index property sheet for a sample Customer table.

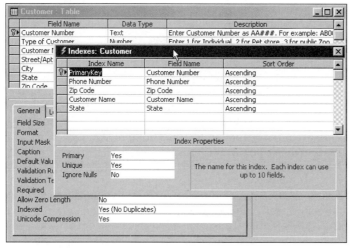

Figure 36-11: Note that common search fields such as Zip Code and State are indexed.

When you create a primary key for a table, the field (or fields) used to define the key is automatically indexed, and you can index any field unless the field's data type is Memo or OLE Object. You should consider indexing a field if all the following apply:

✦ The field's data type is Text, Number, Currency, or Date/Time.

✦ You anticipate searching for values stored in the field.

✦ You anticipate sorting records based on the values in the field.

✦ You will join the field to fields in other tables in queries.

✦ You anticipate storing many different values in the field. (If many of the values in the field are the same, the index may not significantly speed up searches or sorting.)

When defining an index, you have the option of creating an ascending (the default) or a descending index.

Tip Jet can use a descending index when optimizing queries only when the equal sign (=) operator is used. If you use an operator other than the equal sign, such as <, >, <=, or >=, Jet cannot use the descending index. If you plan on using operators other than an equal sign on an index, you should define the index as an ascending index.

Using multiple-field indexes

If you often search or sort by two or more fields at the same time, you can create an index for that combination of fields. For example, if you often set criteria for LastName and FirstName fields in the same query, it makes sense to create a multiple-field index on both fields.

When you sort a table by a multiple-field index, Access first sorts by the first field defined for the index. If there are records with duplicate values in the first field, Access then sorts by the second field defined for the index, and so on. This creates a drill-down effect. For a multiple-field index to work, there *has* to be search criteria defined for the first field in the index, but not for additional fields in the index. In the preceding example, if you were to search for someone with the first name *Robert* but don't specify a last name to use in the search, the second field in the index would not be used. If you need to perform searches on the second field in a multiple-field index, but are not always specifying criteria for the first field in the index, you should create an index for the second field in addition to the multiple-field index.

Continuing with the LastName, FirstName index, if you wanted to search for the first name *John*, the multiple-field index would not be used because you would be attempting to search only on the second field in the index.

Getting the most from your queries

The performance problems of many Access applications lie in the design of their queries. Database applications are all about looking at and working with data, and queries are the heart of determining what data to look at or work with. Queries are used to bind forms and reports, fill list boxes and combo boxes, make new tables, and for many other functions within an Access application. Because they are so widely used, it is extremely important to optimize your queries. A query that is properly designed can provide results minutes to hours faster than a poorly designed query that returns the same result set. The following are things to consider:

✦ When designing queries and tables, you should create indexes for all fields used in sorts, joins, and criteria fields. Indexes enable Jet to quickly sort and search through your database.

> **Tip**
>
> Sorting and searching is much faster if the indexes are unique rather than nonunique. Also, if you are using conditions in your queries, you will find it faster if the index is based on Ascending order (versus reverse, z to a, descending order).

✦ When possible, use a primary key in place of a regular index when creating joins. Primary keys don't allow nulls and give the Rushmore query optimizer more ways to use the joins.

✦ Limit the columns of data returned in a select query to only those you need; if you don't need the information from a field, don't return it in the query. Queries run much faster when they must return less information.

> **Tip**
>
> If you need to use a field for a query condition *and* it is not necessary to display the field in the results table, deselect the view check box to suppress displaying the field and its contents.

✦ When you need to return a count of the records returned by an SQL statement, use Count(*) instead of Count([FieldName]); Count(*) is considerably faster. Count(*) counts records that contain null fields; Count([FieldName]) checks for nulls and disqualifies them from being counted. If you specify a field name instead of using the asterisk, Count does not count records that have a null in the specified field.

> **Tip**
>
> You may also replace `FieldName` with an expression, but this slows down the function even further.

✦ Avoid using calculated fields in nested queries. A calculated field in a subordinate query considerably slows down the top-level query. You should use only calculated fields in top-level queries, and then only when necessary.

✦ When you need to group records by the values of a field used in a join, specify the Group By for the field that is in the same table as you are totaling. You can drag the joined field from either table, but using Group By on the field from the table you are totaling yields faster results.

✦ Domain Aggregate functions, such as DLookup or DCount, used as expressions in queries, slow down the queries considerably. Instead, you should add the table to the query or use a subquery to return the information you need.

✦ As with VBA code modules, queries are compiled. To compile a query, Jet's Rushmore query optimizer evaluates the query to determine the fastest way to execute the query. If a query is saved in a compiled state, it runs at its fastest the first time you execute it. If it is not compiled, it takes longer the first time it executes because it must be compiled, but it then runs faster in succeeding executions. To compile a query, run the query by opening it in Datasheet view and then close the query without saving it. If you make changes to the query definition, run the query again after saving your changes and then close it without saving it.

✦ If you really want to squeeze the most out of your queries, you should experiment by creating your queries in different ways (such as specifying different types of joins). You will be surprised at the varying results.

Getting the most from your forms and reports

Forms and reports can slow an application by taking a long time to load or process information. You can do a number of things to increase the performance of forms and reports.

Minimizing form and report complexity and size

One of the key elements to achieving better performance from your forms and reports is reducing their complexity and size. To reduce a form's or report's complexity and size:

✦ Minimize the number of objects on a form or report. The fewer objects used, the less resources needed to display and process the form or report.

✦ Reduce the use of subforms. When a subform is loaded, two forms are in memory — the parent form and the subform. Use a list box or a combo box in place of a subform whenever possible.

✦ Use labels instead of text boxes for hidden fields; text boxes use more resources than labels. Hidden fields are often used as an alternative to creating variables to store information.

Tip　You cannot write a value directly to a label like you can to a text box, but you can write to the label's caption property like this: `Label1.Caption = "MyValue"`.

✦ Move some code from a form's module into a standard module. This enables the form to load faster because the code doesn't need to be loaded into memory. If the procedures you move to a normal module are referenced by any procedures executed upon loading a form (such as in the form load event), moving the procedures will not help because they are loaded anyway as part of the potential call tree of the executed procedure.

✦ Don't overlap controls on a form or report.

✦ Place related groups of controls on form pages. If only one page is shown at a time, Access does not need to generate all the controls at the same time.

✦ Use lightweight forms and reports whenever possible. Lightweight forms have no code module attached to them, so they load and display considerably faster than forms with code modules.

Cross-Reference

See the Lightweight Forms and Reports section earlier in this chapter for a more detailed explanation.

✦ Use a query that returns a limited result set for a form's or report's RecordSource rather than using a table or underlying query that uses tables. The less data returned for the RecordSource, the faster the form or report loads. In addition, return only those fields actually used by the form or report. Do not use a query that gathers fields that will not be displayed on the form or report (except for a conditional check).

Using bitmaps on forms and reports

Bitmaps on forms and reports make an application look attractive and can also help convey the purpose of the form or report (as in a wizard). However, graphics are always resource intensive, so you should use the fewest number of graphic objects on your forms and reports as possible. This helps minimize form and report load time, increase print speed, and reduce the resources used by your application.

Often you will display pictures that a user never changes and that are not bound to a database. Examples of such pictures would be your company logo on a switchboard or static images in a wizard. When you want to display an image such as this, you have two choices:

✦ Use an Unbound Object Frame.

✦ Use an Image control.

If the image will never change and you don't need to activate it in Form Design view, use an Image control. Image controls use fewer resources and display faster. If you need the image to be a linked or embedded OLE object that you can edit, use an Unbound Object Frame. You can convert OLE images in Unbound Object Frames.

Tip

If you have an image in an Unbound Object Frame that you no longer need to edit, you can convert the Unbound Object Frame to an Image control by selecting Change To Image from the Format menu.

Tip

When you have forms that contain unbound OLE objects, you should close the forms when they are not in use to free resources. Also avoid using bitmaps with many colors—they take considerably more resources and are slower to paint than a bitmap of the same size with fewer colors.

If you want to display an Unbound OLE object but don't want the user to be able to activate it, set its `Enabled` property to False.

Speeding up list boxes and combo boxes

It is important to pay attention to the optimization of list boxes and combo boxes when optimizing your application. There are a number of steps you can take to make your combo boxes and list boxes run faster.

✦ When using multipage forms that have list boxes or combo boxes on more than one page, consider not setting the RowSource of the list boxes or combo boxes until the actual page containing the control is displayed.

✦ Index the first field displayed in a list box or combo box. This enables Access to find entries that match text entered by the user much faster.

✦ Although not always practical to do so, try to refrain from hiding a combo box's bound column. Hiding the bound column causes the control's searching features to slow down considerably.

✦ If you don't need the search capabilities of AutoExpand, set the AutoExpand property of a combo box to No. Access is then relieved of constantly searching the list for entries matching text entered in the text portion of the combo box.

✦ When possible, make the first nonhidden column in a combo or list box a text data type, not a numeric one. To find a match in the list of a combo box or list box, Access must convert a numeric value to text in order to do the character-by-character match. If the data type is text, Access can skip the conversion step.

✦ Often overlooked is the performance gain achieved by using saved queries for RecordSource and RowSource properties of list boxes and combo boxes. A saved query gives much better performance than an SQL SELECT statement because an SQL query is optimized by Rushmore on the fly.

Tip   There is one problem with combo boxes present in Access 2000 that poses a performance concern. Because Access 2000 supports hyperlinks, Access has to perform a little additional work when first painting a combo box; it needs to determine the data type of the combo box.

The result is that the combo box takes a little longer to paint—up to a couple of seconds on some computers. If your combo box is a bound combo box, this is not a problem because Access gets the data type from the `ControlSource`'s data type. In addition, if you save a `RowSource` for the combo box when you save the form, Access determines the data type from the `RowSource` and doesn't need to determine the data type at run time. The only time this paint delay is an issue is when you have an unbound combo box that has its `RowSource` set programmatically. When this is the case, the combo box will take slightly longer to paint the first time it is displayed.

Getting the most from your modules

Perhaps the area where you'll be able to use smart optimization techniques most frequently is in your modules. For example, in code behind forms, you should use the Me keyword when referencing controls. This approach takes advantage of Access 2000 capabilities; using Me is faster than creating a form variable and referencing the form in the variable. Other optimization techniques are simply smart coding practices that have been around for many years. You should try to use the optimum coding technique at all times. When in doubt, try different methods to accomplish a task and see which one is fastest.

Tip

Consider reducing the number of modules and procedures in your application by consolidating them whenever possible. There is a small memory overhead incurred for each module and procedure you use, so consolidating them may free up some memory.

Using appropriate data types

You should always explicitly declare variables using the Dim function rather than arbitrarily assign values to variables that have not been Dimmed. To ensure that all variables in your application are explicitly declared before they are used in a procedure, while in Visual Basic for Application's design surface, select Tools ➪ Options, the Editor tab, and then set the Require Variable Declarations option on the tab (second from the top in the Code settings section).

Use integers and long integers rather than singles and doubles when possible. Integers and long integers use less memory, and they take less time to process than singles and doubles. Table 36-1 shows the relative speed of the different data types available in Access.

Table 36-1	
Data Types and Their Mathematical Processing Speed	
Data Type	*Relative Processing Speed*
Integer/Long	Fastest
Single/Double	Next to Fastest
Currency	Next to Slowest
Variant	Slowest

In addition to using integers and long integers whenever possible, you should also use integer math rather than precision math when applicable. For example, to divide one long integer by another long integer, you could use the following statement:

```
x = Long1 / Long2
```

This statement is a standard math function that uses floating-point math. The same function could be performed using integer math (notice that the mathematical sign is the regular slash versus the backward slash) with the following statement:

```
x = Long1 \ Long2
```

Of course, integer math isn't always applicable. It is, however, commonly applied when returning a percentage. For example, you could return a percentage with the following precision math formula:

```
x = Total / Value
```

However, you could perform the same function using integer math by first multiplying the Total by 100 and then using integer math like this:

```
x = (Total * 100) \ Value
```

You should also use string functions ($) where applicable. When you are manipulating variables that are of type String, use the string functions (for example, Str$()) as opposed to their variant counterparts (Str()). If you are working with variants, use the non-$ functions. Using string functions when working with strings is faster because Access doesn't need to perform type conversions on the variables.

When you need to return a substring by using Mid$(), you can omit the third parameter to have the entire length of the string returned. For example, to return a substring that starts at the second character of a string and returns all remaining characters, use a statement like this:

```
szReturn = Mid$(szMyString, 2)
```

When using arrays, use dynamic arrays with the Erase and ReDim statements to reclaim memory. By dynamically adjusting the size of the arrays, you can ensure that only the amount of memory needed for the array is allocated.

Tip   In addition to using optimized variables, consider using constants when applicable. Constants can make your code much easier to read and will not slow your application if you compile your code before executing it.

Writing faster routines

There are a number of ways you can make your procedures faster by optimizing the routines they contain. If you keep performance issues in mind as you develop, you will be able to find and take advantage of situations like those discussed here.

Some Access functions perform similar processes but vary greatly in the time they take to execute. You probably use one or more of these regularly, and knowing the most efficient way to perform these routines can greatly affect your application's speed:

✦ For/Next statements are normally faster than Select Case statements. They tend to process less logic.

✦ The IIF() function is much slower than a standard set of If/Then/Else statements.

✦ The With and For Each functions accelerate manipulating multiple objects and/or their properties.

✦ Change a variable with Not instead of using an If . . . Then statement. (For example, use x = Not(y) instead of If y = true then x= false.)

✦ Instead of comparing a variable to the value True, use the value of the variable. (For example, instead of saying If X = True then . . ., say If X then . . .)

✦ Use the Requery method instead of the Requery action. The method is significantly faster than the action.

✦ When using OLE automation, resolve references when your application is compiled rather than resolve them at run time using the GetObject or CreateObject functions.

Using control variables

When referencing a control on a form many times in a loop, it is much faster to first dimension a control variable to reference the control like this:

```
Dim ctrl as Control
set ctrl = Me![CustomerNumber]
```

You can then reference the variable rather than reference the actual control. Of course, if you don't need to set values in the control but rather use values from a control, you should simply create a variable to contain the value rather than the reference to the control.

Tip　If you need to set the value of a property of a control but the property may already contain the value, check the value first and write to the property only if its current value is not correct.

Using field variables

The preceding technique also applies to manipulating field data when working with a `Recordset` in VBA code. For example, you may ordinarily have a loop that does something like this:

```
...
Do Until tbl.EOF
MyTotal = MyTotal + tbl![OrderTotal]
Loop
```

If this routine loops through many records, you should use the following code snippet instead:

```
Dim MyField as Field
...
Set MyField = tbl![OrderTotal]
Do Until tbl.EOF
MyTotal = MyTotal +MyField
Loop
```

The preceding code executes much faster than code that explicitly references the field in every iteration of the loop.

Increasing the speed of finding data in code

Use the `FindRecord` and `FindNext` methods on indexed fields. These methods are much more efficient when used on a field that is indexed. Also, take advantage of bookmarks when you can. Returning to a bookmark is much faster than performing a `Find` method to locate the data.

The procedure shown in Listing 36-1 is an example of using a bookmark. Bookmark variables must always be Dimmed as variants, and you can create multiple bookmarks by Dimming multiple variant variables. The following code opens the `tblCustomers` table, moves to the first record in the database, sets the bookmark for the current (first) record, moves to the last record, and finally repositions back to the bookmarked record. For each step, the `debug.print` command is used to show the relative position in the database as evidence that the current record changes from record to record.

Listing 36-1: **Using a Bookmark to Mark a Record**

```
Public Sub BookmarkExample()
Dim rs As Recordset, bk As Variant
Set rs =
Workspaces(0).Databases(0).OpenRecordset("tblCustomers", _
dbOpenTable)
```

Continued

Listing 36-1: *(continued)*

```
' Move to the first record in the database
    rs.MoveFirst
    ' Print the position in the database
    Debug.Print rs.PercentPosition

' Set the bookmark to the current record
    bk = rs.Bookmark

' Move to the last record in the database
    rs.MoveLast
    ' Print the position in the database
    Debug.Print rs.PercentPosition

' Move to the bookmarked record
    rs.Bookmark = bk
    ' Print the position in the database
    Debug.Print rs.PercentPosition

rs.Close
Set rs = Nothing

End Sub
```

Using transactions

Transaction processing is the act of queuing multiple database transactions, such as record updates, and then committing them as a whole. If any one of the queued transactions fails, all successful transactions are undone and any remaining transactions are canceled.

Transactions are typically used in applications dealing with financial data to maintain data integrity. For example, if you transfer money from one account to another, you would subtract an amount from one table and add the amount to another table. If either update fails, the accounts no longer balance. By wrapping these record updates in a transaction, you assure that the data remains intact, because if either update fails, neither update is performed. In Access 2.0, you could greatly increase the speed of your application by wrapping Recordset operations in transactions. In Access 2000, Access uses transactions internally, and wrapping your code in transactions tends to decrease the transaction's performance.

Eliminating dead code and unused variables

Before distributing your application, remove any *dead code* — code that is not used at all — from your application. Oftentimes you will find entire procedures, or even modules, that once served a purpose but are no longer called. In addition, it is not uncommon to leave variable declarations in code after all code that actually uses the variables has been removed. By eliminating dead code and unused variables, you reduce the amount of memory your application uses and the amount of time it takes to compile code at run time.

Tip   Although not easy and often impractical, removing large numbers of comments from your code can decrease the amount of memory used by your application.

Other things you can do to increase the speed of your modules include opening any add-ins your application uses for read-only access and replacing procedure calls within loops with in-line code. Also, don't forget one of the most important items: Deliver your applications with the modules compiled.

Increasing Network Performance

The single most important action you can take to make sure your networkable applications run at their peak performance is to run Access and the application database on the workstation and link to the shared network database. Running Access over the network is much slower than running it locally.

Using the Performance Analyzer

Access includes a wonderful tool to help you better optimize your applications: the Performance Analyzer Wizard. The Performance Analyzer looks at the objects in your application and makes suggestions about things you can do to optimize your objects. Often the Performance Analyzer alerts you to a potential problem discussed in this chapter. For example, the Performance Analyzer tells you which modules in your database don't have Option Explicit set. It then recommends that you set Option Explicit and tells you why.

To run the Performance Analyzer Wizard, select Tools ➪ Analyze ➪ Performance, as shown in Figure 36-12.

On the CD-ROM   You can use any database you have. Mountain Animal Hospital contains many objects and is a good example.

When you first run the Performance Analyzer, you need to select the type of objects to analyze by using the tabs at the top of the dialog box. To view all of the objects in the database, click the All tab. After selecting the type of object (such as Form, Report, Table, or All), you must select the specific objects to analyze. You can use the Select All and Deselect All buttons to save time. Figure 36-13 shows a large Access database with all its forms selected for analysis.

Note   Notice in Figure 36-13 the tab labeled "All Object Types." Clicking on this tab will display all the objects in the current database.

Figure 36-12: Select the Performance Analyzer Wizard using the Tools menu.

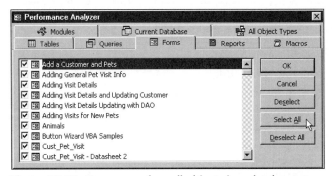

Figure 36-13: You can analyze all objects in a database or just a few specific objects.

Figure 36-14 shows the results of analyzing all the forms in a database. Notice that the suggestions in the figure are all covered in depth in this chapter. The Performance Analyzer can make suggestions and recommendations, offer hints, and fix things automatically. If you have a question about its recommendation for a certain item, click that item. The Performance Analyzer gives you more information about what it thinks needs to be done with the object.

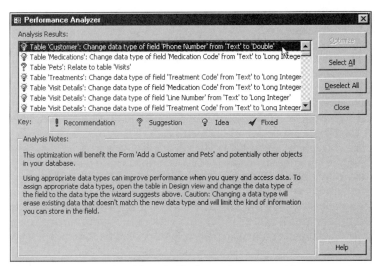

Figure 36-14: You should periodically analyze your objects to make sure you take advantage of all possible optimization strategies.

As the analysis shows in Figure 36-14, the Performance Analyzer will offer three comments that are signified by a graphic next to the suggestion — exclamation point (!): Recommendation, question mark (?): Suggestion, and light bulb: Idea. Selecting any exclamation point and question mark will activate the Optimize button. If you click the Optimize button, the Analyzer will perform the recommended/suggested action, placing a checkmark alongside the suggestion.

The more you are exposed to the issues expressed by the Performance Analyzer Wizard, the more it becomes second nature to use the optimization strategies as you work.

Improving Perceived Speed

Perceived speed is how fast your application appears to run to the end user. Many techniques can increase the perceived speed of your applications. Perceived speed usually involves supplying visual feedback to the user while the computer is busy performing some operation, such as constantly updating a percent meter when Access is busy processing data.

Using a splash screen

Most professional Windows programs employ a splash screen as shown in Figure 36-15. Most people think the splash screen is simply to show the product's name and copyright information as well as the registered user's information; this is not entirely correct. The splash screen greatly contributes to the perceived speed of an application. It shows the user that something is *happening*, and it gives users something to look at (and hence occupy their time) for a few seconds while the rest of the application loads.

Note   In large applications, you may even display a series of splash screens with different information such as helpful hints, instructions on how to use the product, or even advertisements. These are known as billboards.

To create a splash screen, create a basic form with appropriate data, such as your application information, logo, and registration information. Then set this form as the Display Form in the Start Up dialog box. Setting the form as the Display Form ensures that the splash screen is the first form that is loaded. You then want to call any initialization procedures from the On Open event of the splash form. You may find that a light form that calls code or a macro displays faster than putting the startup code in the form's module.

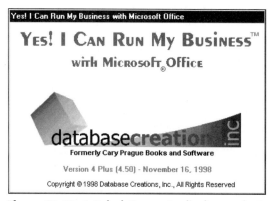

Figure 36-15: A Splash Screen to display product and version information.

After all the initialization code has been run, close down the splash form. There are a few issues to remember when using splash forms:

✦ Never use custom controls in a startup form. Custom controls take time to load and consume resources.

✦ Minimize code in startup forms. Use only code that is absolutely necessary to display your startup form; use a light form if possible.

✦ The startup form should call only initialization procedures. Be careful about call trees; you don't want your startup form triggering the loading of many modules in your application.

Loading and keeping forms hidden

If there are forms that are displayed often, consider hiding them rather than closing them. To hide a form, set its Visible property to False. When you need to display the form again, set its Visible property back to True. Forms that remain loaded consume memory, but they display more quickly than forms that must be loaded each time they are viewed. In addition, if you are *morphing* a form or report (changing the way the form or report looks by changing form and control properties), keep the form hidden until all changes are made so that the user doesn't have to watch the changes take place.

Using the hourglass

When your application needs to perform a task that may take a while, use the hourglass. The hourglass mouse pointer shows the user that the computer is not locked up but is merely busy. To turn on the hourglass cursor, use the Hourglass method like this:

```
DoCmd.Hourglass True
```

To turn the hourglass back to the default cursor, use the method like this:

```
DoCmd.Hourglass False
```

Using the progress meter

In addition to using the hourglass, you should consider using the progress meter when performing looping routines in a procedure. The progress meter gives constant visual feedback that your application is busy, and it shows the user in no uncertain terms where it is in the current process. The following code demonstrates using the percent meter in a loop to show the meter starting at 0 percent and expanding to 100 percent, 1 percent at a time:

```
Dim iCount As Integer, iCount2 As Long
Dim Result As Integer

Result = SysCmd(acSysCmdInitMeter, "Running through loop", 100)
For iCount = 1 To 100
    Result = SysCmd(acSysCmdUpdateMeter, iCount)
    For iCount2 = 1 To 50000: Next iCount2' This creates a  _
pause so the meter is readable
Next iCount

Result = SysCmd(acSysCmdRemoveMeter)
```

The first step for using the percent meter is initializing the meter. You initialize the meter by calling the `SysCmd` function like this:

```
Result = SysCmd(acSysCmdInitMeter, "Running through loop", 100)
```

The `acSysCmdInitMeter` in this line is an Access constant that tells the function that you are initializing the meter. The second parameter is the text you want to appear to the left of the meter. Finally, the last value is the maximum value of the meter (in this case, 100 percent). You can set this value to anything you want. For example, if you were iterating through a loop of 504 records, you could set this value to 504. Then you could pass the record count at any given time to the `SysCmd` function; Access decides what percentage the meter shows as filled.

After the meter has been initialized, you can pass a value to it to update the meter. To update the meter, you call the `SysCmd` function again and pass it the `acSysCmdUpdateMeter` constant and the new update meter value. Remember, the value that you pass the function is not necessarily the percent displayed by the meter.

There are two types of progress meters included in Chap36.MDB. The first is a pop-up form which uses a colored rectangle to show the progress of an activity. The other is created using the standard Microsoft Access progress meter which is displayed in the status bar.

Creating a Progress Meter With a Pop-up Form

To run the sample Progress Meter: Open the form `Progress Meter Form` and press the Search button. You will see the progress meter form appear and the bar grow from 0 to 100%. This should take about 10 seconds on a high-end Pentium machine, a little longer on a slower machine.

The Progress Meter form in progress is shown in Figure 36-16.

This progress meter has some advantages over the standard Microsoft Access progress meter. The progress meter supplied with Access uses the status bar to display the meter and is not always as visible as you may want it. The progress meter above pops up in the middle of the screen and is immediately visible to the user. The meter supplied with Access, however, usually displays faster because it requires less overhead to run, although with longer tasks the difference may not be noticeable. The speed of the pop-up meter can be controlled by updating the meter every *x* percent. Therefore, if the form meter is set for fast execution, it will display with comparable speed to that of the built-in meter.

The progress meter form itself (named **Progress Meter** in Chap36.MDB file) is created from a few simple controls, as shown in Figure 36-17. There is one rectangle and several label controls. The labels controls on top are shown for 0, 50, and 100. If you want, you could create a more detailed scale. The label control at the bottom can be updated as the meter progresses.

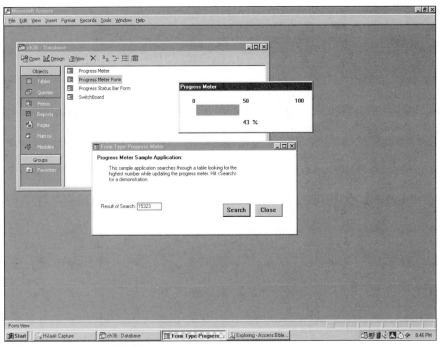

Figure 36-16: A graphical progress meter.

In Figure 36-17, you can see that the rectangle is shown completed. In reality, the width of the rectangle is manipulated by the program that is used to display the meter's progress. The width is reset to 0 when the progress meter starts and it is slowly built back to its original width.

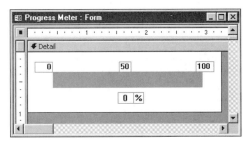

Figure 36-17: The Progress Meter form.

Here is a procedure to display and control the progress of the meter: Simply pass the procedure used to display the meter a percentage from 0 to 100. Any invalid percentage will be corrected by the procedure. You must pass a 0 to initialize the meter. The meter will close when the percentage reaches 100. This procedure, shown in Figure 36-18, is named Progmeter and is located in the Progress module in Chap36.MDB. Using the form in Figure 36-17 to create the meter, you can make the meter look any way you want as long as the meter is a rectangle. For example, you can make a vertical meter instead a horizontal one.

Note   Notice the line *X = Percent * 35.* This code makes the bar proportional to the form and should be changed for custom meters. This distance is measured in twips. There are 1440 twips to an inch; therefore, because the meter is 2.5 inches long, it is about 3500 twips. The rest of the subroutine changes the width of the filled rectangle, and then updates the percent text on the meter. The form is then repainted in order to update the meter on the screen.

This routine is called whenever you want to update the progress meter. It is up to you as to when to do this. A normal method is to call the progress meter only when it is likely to be updated. If you know there are 1000 records, you may call the meter every 10 records; if there are 10,000 records you may call the meter every 100 records.

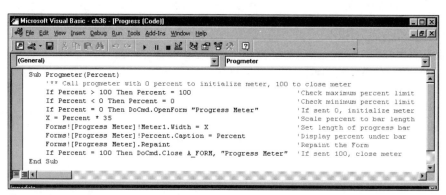

Figure 36-18: The Progmeter procedure.

The code in Figure 36-19 is that of the sample application named *Progress Meter Form.* Many of the statements can be ignored. What you want to concentrate on are the statements that call the progress meter code.

The first few statements open the recordset. In this example, it is a table named Sample Application Data. You would substitute your table or query here. The next statement counts the total number of records in the recordset. This step is necessary in order to know what percent of the file you have processed. The next few lines are specific to your application. If you are deleting or processing the data, those lines would go next. This example is searching for the highest value.

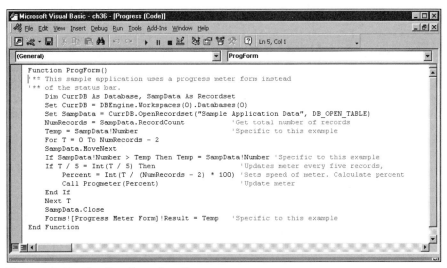

Figure 36-19: The ProgForm function.

In Figure 36-19, the progress meter update routine is being called every five records. You can speed up the meter execution by changing the line *If T/5 = Int(T / 5),* which displays every pass divisible by 5 evenly. This change means the meter is not refreshed as often as it could be, resulting in faster execution. There are many ways of controlling meter execution, all application-dependent.

The next line determines the percent to be passed to the Progmeter procedure. This must be calculated by using information in your application; the Progmeter procedure does not calculate percentages. The only two things required when copying this meter into your application are the meter form and the Progmeter procedure. The percentage could be calculating in the Progmeter form if you want it to. This would require you to pass the number of records to the subprocedure when initializing it.

Follow these steps to integrate the Progress Meter into your application:

1. Import the Form **Progress Meter** into your application.

2. Import the Module **Progress** into your application.

3. Change the Progress Module Procedure **Progform** to interact with your application.

Using the Standard Progress Meter

To run the standard Access progress meter: Run the form **Progress Status Bar Form** and press Search.

You will see the progress meter change from 0 to 100 percent in the status bar. This should take about 3 seconds on a high-end Pentium machine, a little longer on a slower machine.

Caution   The internal Access progress meter is much faster than creating your own.

The code shown in Figure 36-20 is the same sample application, but using the progress meter provided by Access. There is no progress meter form or a subprocedure to handle the drawing of the meter. Everything is controlled by the three SYSCMD statements you previously learned about.

The first: SysCmd(SYSCMD_INITMETER, Msg, CountRecs) initializes the meter with a message and the number of total records. The two statements directly preceding the call sets the message for the status bar and gets the total number of records. The second: SysCmd(SYSCMD_UPDATEMETER, T) updates the meter with the current record. The value T is the number of the record being processed while the meter calculates the percentage. The third line closes the meter: SysCmd(SYSCMD_REMOVEMETER).

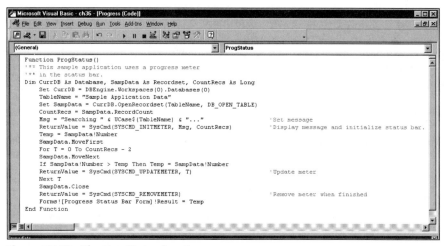

Figure 36-20: The ProgStatus function.

This type of meter is easier to call than the form meter. It only requires information to initialize and process and a call to close the meter. Also mentioned before, this type of meter may not be as noticeable as the pop-up form meter. This type of meter does offer some advantages over the one previously discussed. Since the total number of records is passed to the function when it is initialized, the percentage is calculated when you update the meter with the record you are currently on. A message telling the user what is happening can also be displayed. With a little more coding, the form meter can also provide these functions but may slow the meter down a bit.

Use the following steps to integrate the Access Status Bar Progress Meter into your application:

1. Import the Module **Progress** into your application.

2. Change the Progress Module Procedure **Progstatus** to interact with your application.

Working with Large Program Databases in Access 2000

When someone mentions large databases in Microsoft Access, they are generally thinking about a database with tables that contain hundred of thousands of data records. Though that could be considered a large database, another definition is a database that contains hundreds of objects — tables, queries, forms, reports, and thousands of lines of VBA program code. While you can sometimes solve data performance problems by changing the back end from Jet to SQL Server, there are much more complex problems that you will probably have if you create applications with many queries, forms, reports, and lots of VBA module code.

If your database has hundreds of objects, especially forms and reports, you may have run into problems that cause your database to exhibit strange behavior. These include:

✦ Not staying compiled or not compiling at all

✦ Growing and growing and growing in size, even after compiling and compacting

✦ Running slower and slower

✦ Displaying the wrong record in linked subforms

✦ Displaying compile errors when you know the code is correct

✦ Corrupting constantly

Compacting your database doesn't always work as advertised. Compiling and Saving All Modules becomes a long wait with a seemingly perpetual hourglass. After you compact and open the database, it is uncompiled again. If you work with large databases, chances are these are well-known experiences. If you have one of these out of control databases, this section will teach you how to solve these problems and get you up and running fast again.

How databases grow in size

There are many things that can cause a database to grow. Each time you add an object to an Access 2000 database (.MDB) file, it gets larger. And why shouldn't it? You are certainly using more space to define the properties and methods of the object. Reports and forms take the most space because the number of properties associated with each form or report and each control on a form or report uses space. Table attachments (links) and queries take up very little space, while VBA code grows proportionally to the number of lines in both modules and code behind forms and reports. If you store data in your program database this also takes up space proportionally to the number of records in the table. There are many other reasons why a database grows.

When you first create an Access 2000 database file, it will use about 60KB depending on your hard disk type and size. As you add objects, the database will start to grow. Adding a very simple form takes about 6K while a simple report uses about 25K of hard disk space. Each time you add another new form or report, more space is used. Each time you add a new control and define some properties, even more space is used. When you define any event in a form or report that contains even a single line of VBA code, more overhead is used, as the form or report is no longer a lightweight object but one that is VBA aware. This requires more space and resources than a lightweight form or report containing no VBA code. If you embed images into your forms and reports these also use space. Embedding bound OLE aware data, such as pictures, sound, video, or Word or Excel documents, use more space than unbound objects or images.

Each time you make a change to any object, even a simple one, a duplicate copy of the object is created until you compact the database. Within even a few hours of work, Access 2000 databases can begin to grow larger and larger. If the database contains thousands of lines of VBA code, the database can grow to two or three times its original size very quickly, especially when compiled and before it is compacted.

Simply compiling and compacting may not be enough

As you add, delete, and modify objects, Access doesn't always clean up after itself. You have probably learned that after you make changes to your objects, especially VBA code, you should open any module and select Debug ➪ Compile and Save All Modules. After you do this, you should close the module and select the database container and select Tools ➪ Database Utilities ➪ Compact Database. This will compact the database to the same name and reopen the database running any Startup commands or Autoexec macro you may have. For the less aggressive, you may want to close the database first and compact the database to a different name, effectively creating a compacted backup. You can then use the new database or delete the old and rename the new database to the original name.

Compiling and Compacting may not be enough to solve some of the problems mentioned at the beginning of the section. In a large database we've worked with and had originally converted from Access 2.0, we noticed it started at 15MB. After hundreds of minor changes, it was growing at of rate of 50K each time we compiled and compacted it, even if we added no new objects, properties, methods, or VBA code. Out of necessity, this author has experimented with a variety of techniques to understand this phenomenon and solve our problems. More importantly, strange things started happening.

While we noticed that the database was growing larger, it took several compiles and compacts to get it to compile, and frequently after we compacted the database it was no longer compiled. It also ran slower the first time we opened it. When the database displayed compile errors on perfectly written code, it was time to try new techniques.

Rebooting gives you a clean memory map

We have always noticed that strange behavior in any program gets better when you reboot your system. Access is particularly bad at *memory leaks*, especially if you are going in and out of form, report, and module design. If you don't want to reboot, at least close your database and exit Access before beginning the examination of your problem.

Repair does nothing if the database is not corrupt

We started by trying to repair the database. Though it was not corrupt, we thought maybe that would help. While the repair utility ran fine and automatically compacted the database, it did nothing else, and the database was still growing.

Create a new database and import all of the objects

It is important to have your database as clean as possible. While we are not sure if gremlins crawl into some obscure portion of the database file, we are sure that you can't import or export them. A technique that usually proves successful is to simply create a new database and then import all of the objects from the original database. Access 2000 makes it easy to import all of your objects by using the Select All button found in the Import Objects dialog box. You can get to this dialog box by first going to the database container of the new empty database file you create and then selecting File ➪ Get External Data ➪ Import, selecting the original program database and then pressing the Import button. You can then import all of your objects.

If you have any custom menus and toolbars or have defined any Import/Export specifications you should remember to use the Options button and check off those options as shown in Figure 36-21. The default for these options is false. If you have created any Startup properties in the database, you will have to create them again as they are not importable.

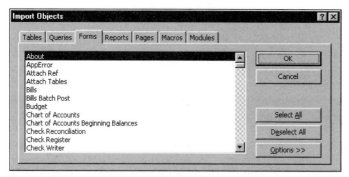

Figure 36-21: Importing Database Objects.

Caution   If you use externally referenced libraries or add-ins you must manually reference these libraries in the new database. You can display a module and use the Tools ⇨ References menu to do this

After some time working in our large database, even creating a new database and importing all of the objects failed to help the database stay compiled or get smaller.

The undocumented decompile option in Access 2000

There is an undocumented startup command-line option called /decompile. You may have seen many of the command-line options such as /nostartup, /cmd, and /compact. This option starts Access 2000 in a special way, and, when a database is opened, saves all VBA modules as text. This works with module objects and all the code behind forms and reports.

To do this, go to the Windows Start menu Run command and type **msaccess /decompile** as shown in Figure 36-22.

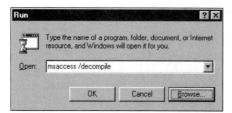

Figure 36-22: Starting Access 2000 with the **decompile** command-line option.

Access appears to start as usual. It takes about 3 minutes to open a database and decompile all of the objects in a 20MB database. The real question now is whether the database will get sufficiently smaller, run faster, and stay compiled after it is compiled and compacted.

Caution Make sure you immediately exit Access 2000 after it finishes decompiling and then start Access normally before running Compile and Save All Modules and Compact Database.

After you exit Access, you can restart Access normally. You can then open your database, open any module, and select Debug ⇨ Compile and Save All Modules. After the database compiles, you should close the module, return to the database container, and select Tools ⇨ Database Utilities ⇨ Compact Database. You will find that Access will run these procedures much faster than usual.

Using our test database, we then went to Windows Explorer and checked the size of the database. It had shrunk from 22Mb to 15Mb, a reduction of over 30 percent, and it has stayed compiled every time we compact it. The first time we ran the application, it seemed to run faster than ever. We are not sure why it works faster or differently than manually opening and saving each VBA module as text, but it simply does. Even more strangely, the database no longer seems to be growing each time we make a minor change, recompile, and compact it. While the decompile option may be a small miracle, it is always a good idea to follow the six steps to success before releasing any application to the ultimate users.

Summary — six steps to large database success

If you are ready to release your application for a real test by the users, you should follow the steps below to insure a clean-running system:

1. Reboot your computer to clean up memory.

2. Create a new access database and import all the objects.

3. Restart Access using the /decompile option.

4. Restart Access normally.

5. Recompile the database.

6. Compact the database.

By releasing a clean, fully compiled and compacted system you will have fewer problems, your application will run faster, and you will have less technical or maintenance problems.

An interface for detecting an uncompiled database and automatically recompiling

It is very important to make sure that a database is always in a compiled state. If you release your application as a modifiable .MDB file, your customers may make simple or even complex changes to your application, and then complain because their system is running slowly. While some of your customers may be serious developers, our experience is that many customers who make changes to Access databases do not know about compilation or compacting.

To solve this problem, you can create an interface that automatically detects if the database is not in a compiled state and then gives the user the option of compiling the application. This is run each time the database is opened. The user still has to compact the database, but the hard part is compiling. Figure 36-23 shows the message that is automatically displayed if the database is uncompiled. The code is shown below.

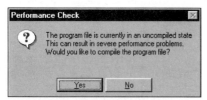

Figure 36-23: A dialog box to help the user compile your application.

The code uses the Access 2000 built-in function IsCompiled to determine the compiled state of the application. If the application is not compiled, the MsgBox is displayed as shown in Figure 36-23. Users have two choices. If they are still testing, they may not want to compile yet. If they want to compile, they simply have to press the Yes button.

Following is the VBA Module to detect and automatically compile an application:

```
Dim MsgTxt As String
     If Not IsCompiled() Then
       MsgTxt = "The program file is currently in an uncompiled
state" & Chr$(13) & Chr$(10)
       MsgTxt = MsgTxt & "This can result in severe performance
problems." & Chr$(13) & Chr$(10)
       MsgTxt = MsgTxt & "Would you like to compile the program
file?"
       Response = MsgBox(MsgTxt, vbYesNo+vbQuestion,
"Performance Check")
       If Response = vbYes Then
         'You could display a message box that tells the user
to be patient while the database is compiled
         DoCmd.Echo False    'Stop screen display to
eliminate seeing the module open and close
         DoCmd.OpenModule "anymodulename"    'Open any module
you have in the database
         DoCmd.SelectObject acModule, "anymodulename"    'You
must select the module after you open it
         RunCommand (acCmdCompileAndSaveAllModules)    'This
command does the compile and save
```

```
            DoCmd.Close acModule, "anymodulename"      'Close the
module after the compile and save is done
            DoCmd.Echo True      'Start screen display again
            MsgTxt = "          The program file has been
compiled" & Chr$(13) & Chr$(10)
            MsgTxt = MsgTxt & "You should now select Tools |
Database Utilities | Compact Database" & Chr$(13) & Chr$(10)
            MsgTxt = MsgTxt & "from the menu above the database
container. "
            Response = MsgBox(MsgTxt, vbInformation, "Compile
Completed Successfully")
        End If
    End If
```

Although there is no easy way that we know of to automatically compact the open program file, the user can be instructed to simply select Tools ⇨ Database Utilities ⇨ Compact Database. When the program database is open, this also reruns the startup or Autoexec macro file after compacting the database.

Making small changes to large databases — one word — export

One final tip for working with large databases: always work with a copy of the program file and export the changed objects. When you are making lots of changes to a few objects to try a new technique or to get a stubborn algorithm to work, you are constantly opening and closing objects. This tends to negatively affect large databases. Work with a copy of the database, and then when you have the changes just the way you want, you can export the changed objects from the test database to the production database. Any object you export with the same name as the production database will be exported with a 1 at the end of the name. You can then open the production database, delete the original objects and rename the changed objects that have a 1 on the end of their name. New objects are obviously exported with their name intact.

Anything you can do to make fewer changes to a large database, the better off you are. By following the tips and techniques in this section you will have fewer problems and will be more productive.

Through judicious use of the techniques discussed in this chapter, you will be able to increase the performance of your Access application to the highest level possible.

Summary

Access 2000 provides improved compilation techniques and new features, such as lightweight forms and load on demand functionality of VBA. Improvements such as these make it possible for you to dramatically increase an Access application's performance. This chapter explained how to:

✦ Increase performance by keeping your code in a compiled state

✦ Use lightweight forms

✦ Use MDE databases for better performance

✦ Adjust Jet registry settings

✦ Get the most from your tables

✦ Tune your queries for maximum speed

✦ Get the most out of your forms and reports

✦ Increase performance by optimizing your VBA code

✦ Use techniques to increase the perceived speed of your application

✦ Work with large databases and use the Decompile command

In the next chapter, you will learn how to use and program Access security.

✦   ✦   ✦

Securing an Access Application

Although security options can be maintained in Access, Access is manipulating security at the Jet engine level. The Jet security model has changed little since Access 95. Jet's security is still a workgroup-based security model; all users in a workgroup are bound to the same security rules. The rules enforced for individual users may vary from user to user, based on the permissions assigned each user.

Understanding Jet Security

Jet security is defined at the object level for individuals or groups of users. This security model of Jet/Access is rather complex, but it isn't too difficult to understand when broken down into its core components, which are as follows:

- ✦ Workgroups
- ✦ Groups
- ✦ Users
- ✦ Object owners
- ✦ Object permissions

Understanding workgroups

Jet stores security information for databases in workgroup files, usually named SYSTEM.MDW. The *workgroup file* is a special Access database that contains a collection of user names and passwords, user group definitions, object owner assignments, and object permissions. You can use the same workgroup file for multiple databases; after you enable security for a database, however, users must use the workgroup containing the security information. If users use a workgroup other than the one used to define security, they are limited to logging in to the database as the Admin user — with whatever permissions the database administrator left for the Admin user.

> **Tip**
>
> When securing a database, one of the first things you need to do is remove all permissions for the Admin user. Removing these permissions prevents other users from opening the database as the Admin user by using another Access workgroup file and obtaining the rights of the Admin user. Users can still open the database as the Admin user using a different workgroup, but they will not have any object permissions. This measure is discussed later in this chapter in the section "Working with workgroups."

Understanding permissions

The permissions in Jet security are defined at the object level; each object, such as a form or report, has a specific set of permissions. The system administrator defines what permissions each user or group of users has for each object. Users may belong to multiple groups, and they always inherit the highest permission setting of any of the groups to which they belong.

For example, every table object has a set of permissions associated with it: Read Design, Modify Design, Read Data, Update Data, Insert Data, Delete Data, and Administrator. (See Table 37-1, which appears later in this chapter, for a complete list of permissions and their meanings.) The database administrator has the ability to assign or remove any or all of these permissions for each user or group of users in the workgroup. Because the permissions are set at the object level, the administrator may give a user the ability to read data from Table A and read data from and write data to Table B, and prevent the user from even looking at Table C. In addition, this complexity allows for unique security situations, such as having numerous users sharing data on a network, each with a different set of rights for the database objects. All security maintenance functions are performed from the Tools ➪ Security menu item (see Figure 37-1).

Understanding security limitations

You need to be aware that you cannot depend on the Jet security model to be foolproof. For example, security holes have been previously discovered in Access 2.0 and exposed, in effect, *un*protecting every database distributed under the assumption that the code and objects were protected. Often, the amount of resources involved in developing an application is huge, and protecting that investment is essential. The most you can do for protection is to fully and properly implement the Jet 4.0 security model and use legally binding licensing agreements for all your distributed applications. Unfortunately, the future security of your databases is at the mercy of software hackers. As of the printing of this book, no *published* holes exist in the Jet 4.0 security model; however, as proven in the past, you are not guaranteed that this condition will not change.

Figure 37-1: All Jet security functions are performed from the Tools ➪ Security menu.

Tip It is recommended that you use Microsoft Access security to lock up your tables and prevent access to the design of your forms, reports, queries, and modules. However, if you want to control data at the form level — for example, you want to hide controls or control access to specific form-level controls or data — you have to write your own security commands. You can also use the operating system (Windows) to prevent access to directories themselves.

Choosing a Security Level to Implement

As an Access developer, you must decide the level of security required for your application; not every database even needs security. If your application is used solely in-house, you may not need the powerful permission protection of Jet's security. When you do have an application database that you want to secure, you need to make the following decisions:

✦ What users are allowed to use the database?

✦ What groups do you need to create in the workgroup and what users will belong to each group?

✦ What object permissions need to be limited for each group or user?

After you have made these determinations, you are ready to begin implementing security in your application. Access includes a tool to help you implement security — the User-Level Security Wizard (available from the Tools ➪ Security menu choice). This chapter teaches you how you can implement security by using Access's interface, discussing each security element in detail. Understanding the workings of the security model will greatly help you in your quest for total security. (The wizard is discussed later in this chapter.)

Creating a Database Password

You can use Jet security at its most basic level simply by controlling who can open the database. You control database access by creating a password for the databases you want to protect. When you set a database password for a database, users are prompted to enter the password each time they attempt to access the database. If they do not know the database password, they are not allowed access to the database. When using this form of security, you are not controlling specific permissions for specific users, you are merely controlling who can and cannot access the secured database.

To create a database password, follow these steps:

1. In Access, open the database that you want to secure exclusively. You *must* open the database exclusively in order to set the database password. To open a database exclusively, select the Open Exclusive button from the Open pull-down menu in the lower-right corner of the Open dialog box.

2. Select Tools ➪ Security ➪ Set Database Password (refer to Figure 37-1).

3. In the Password field, type the password that you want to use to secure the database (see Figure 37-2). Access does *not* display the password, rather it shows an asterisk (*) for each letter.

4. In the Verify field, type the password again. This security measure ensures that you do not mistype the password (because you cannot see the characters you type) and mistakenly prevent everyone, including yourself, from accessing the database.

5. Click OK to save the password.

Tip   For maximum security, when entering a password you should follow standard password naming conventions. That is, you should make it some combination of letters and numbers that will not represent any easily known or deduced combination. Often people use a birthday and name, or address number and name of themselves, a child, or someone they know. On the other hand, you should not make the password so difficult to remember that you and others accessing the database will have to write it down to use it. A written password is a useless password.

Figure 37-2: Creating a database password is the simplest way to secure your database.

Caution   You cannot synchronize replicated databases that have database passwords. If you plan on using Jet's replication features and you need database security, you must use user-level security.

After you save the database password, Access prompts every user of the database to enter the password prior to being allowed access to the database. Although this method controls *who* can access the database, it does not control *what* users are allowed to do with the objects and data after they have opened the database. To control objects, you need to fully implement Jet's user-level security, which is discussed in the following section.

Tip　Once you have assigned a password to the database, you may want to protect your database further by encrypting it. Encrypting a database makes it unreadable by other programs such as word processors. Encrypting is discussed in detail later in the chapter.

Note　Once a database has been protected using a database-level password, you must supply the password before you link to a table in the database. This password will be stored in the information used to define the link to the table.

To remove a database password, follow these steps:

1. In Access, open the database you want to unsecure. You must open the database exclusively to be able to unset the database password.

2. Select Tools ⇨ Security ⇨ Unset Database Password. This menu item was previously labeled Set Database Password but was changed when the database password was set.

3. In the password field, type the password of the database (see Figure 37-3).

4. Click OK to unset the password.

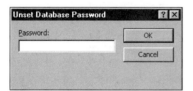

Figure 37-3: You can remove a database password by retyping the password in the Unset Database Password dialog box.

If you remove a database password from an Access database, users are no longer required to enter a password to access the database unless you have enabled user-level security.

Note　Any user who knows the database password has the ability to change or remove the database password. You can prevent this situation by removing the Administer permissions from the database for all users except the database administrator. This is discussed in more detail later in the chapter.

Using the /runtime Option

If you're not concerned with protecting your application but simply want to prevent users from mistakenly breaking your application by modifying or deleting objects, you can force your application to be run in Access's *runtime mode*. When a database is opened in Access in runtime mode, all the interface elements that allow changes to objects are hidden from the user. For example, it is impossible for a user to access the Database window in runtime mode. You must ensure your application has a startup form that gives the users access to whatever objects you want them to be able to access. Normally this would be the main menu of your application, or main switchboard.

Note   You must purchase and install the Microsoft Office 2000 Developer (MOD) tools to use the /runtime switch. This version of Office includes a runtime version of the program allowing you to distribute a royalty-free licensed copy of your Access 2000 applications to users, whether they have Access on their machines or not.

To assign a form as a startup form, choose Tool ⇨ Startup and select the form you want to be the startup form from the Display Form drop-down list (see Figure 37-4).

To create a shortcut to start your application in Access's runtime mode, follow these steps:

1. Create a shortcut to start Microsoft Access (MSACCESS.exe).

2. Right-click the shortcut, select Properties, and then click the Shortcut tab.

Figure 37-4: When running a database in Access's runtime mode, you must designate a startup form, usually a switchboard form from which your users can navigate your application.

3. In the Target field, append to the path of MSACCESS.exe (program) a space, the path and filename of the database to open in runtime mode, another space, and then /runtime.

For example, the following command line starts Access and opens the Northwind database in runtime mode:

C:\Program Files\Microsoft Office\Access\MSAccess.exe "c:\Program Files\Microsoft Office\Access\Samples\Northwind.mdb" /runtime

Note The path and filename for MSAccess.exe, as well as the /runtime switch, are not enclosed in quotes. However, you must enclose the path and filename for the database to open in quotes if you are using Windows 95. Windows 98 omits this requirement. If you enclose the /runtime switch in quotes, an error occurs when you attempt to execute the shortcut.

4. Distribute or re-create the shortcut for each user installation.

You also can set database passwords by using VBA code. The following code changes the database password of the currently opened database:

```
Public Sub ChangeDatabasePassword()
On Error GoTo ChangeDatabasePasswordErr
Dim szOldPassword As String, szNewPassword As String
Dim db As Database

Set db = CurrentDb
szOldPassword = ""
szNewPassword = "shazam"

db.NewPassword szOldPassword, szNewPassword

Exit Sub

ChangeDatabasePasswordErr:
    MsgBox Err & ":  " & Err.Description
    Exit Sub

End Sub
```

If no database password is set, you pass a zero-length string ("") as the old password parameter. If there is a database password assigned and you want to remove the password, pass the database password as the old password parameter and pass a zero-length string ("") as the new password.

Using a Database's Startup Options

A slightly more secure alternative to using the /runtime option is to set a database's Startup options. Although this provides greater security than the /runtime option, it is not a complete solution for situations where tight security is paramount. Figure 37-5 shows the Startup options dialog box with the Advanced options displayed. To access the Startup options dialog box, select Tools ➪ Startup.

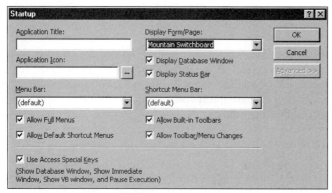

Figure 37-5: Using the Startup options dialog box gives you more security control than using the /runtime option.

By making the appropriate specifications in the Startup options dialog box, you can do the following:

✦ Prevent the Database window from being displayed.

✦ Prevent the status bar from being displayed.

✦ Designate a menu bar to be used on startup of your application.

✦ Designate a shortcut menu to be used on startup of your application.

✦ Prevent Access's built-in menus (full menus) from being displayed.

✦ Prevent Access's built-in shortcut menus from being displayed.

✦ Prevent Access's built-in toolbars from being displayed.

✦ Prevent users from modifying toolbars (toolbar/menu changes).

✦ Prevent users from using Access's special keys to display the Database window, display the debug window, or pause execution.

Distributing a Database as an .MDE File

One way to ensure the security of your application's code, forms, and reports is to distribute your database as an .MDE file, as discussed in the prior chapter. When you save your database as an .MDE file, Access compiles all code modules (including form modules), removes all editable source code, and compacts the database. The new .MDE file contains no source code but continues to work because it does contain a compiled copy of all of your code. Not only is this a great way to secure your source code, it enables you to distribute databases that are smaller (because they contain no source code) and always keep their modules in a compiled state.

In addition to not being able to view your source code, end users cannot do the following to an .MDE file database:

✦ View, modify, or create forms, reports, or modules in Design view.

✦ Add, delete, or change references to object libraries or databases.

✦ Change your database's VBA project name using the Options dialog box.

✦ Import or export forms, reports, or modules. Note, however, that tables, queries, and macros can be imported from or exported to database types other than .MDE databases.

Because of these benefits/restrictions, it may not be possible to distribute your application as an .MDE file. For example, if your application creates forms at runtime, you would not be able to distribute the database as an .MDE file.

Caution   There is no way to convert an .MDE file into a normal database file. Always save and keep a copy of the original database! When you need to make changes to the application, you must open the normal database and then create a new .MDE file before distribution. If you delete your original database, you will be unable to access any of your objects in Design view!

Note   Your database has to meet some requirements before it can be saved as an .MDE file. First, if security is in use, the user creating the .MDE file must have all applicable rights to the database. In addition, if the database is replicated, you must remove all replication system tables and properties before saving the .MDE file; you cannot create an .MDE file from a replicated database, but you can replicate an .MDE database. Last, you must save all databases or add-ins in the chain of references as .MDE files, or your database will be unable to use them.

Note   If you have a database open when you select Make MDE File, this step is skipped and Access assumes you want to use the database that's open. If you want to use a different database, you need to cancel creating the .MDE file, close the database, and select Make MDE File again. Then you will be asked for the database to save as an .MDE file.

To create an .MDE file, follow these steps:

1. Close the database if it is currently opened. If you do not close the current database, Access attempts to close it for you, prompting you to save changes where applicable. When working with a shared database, all users must close the database; Access needs exclusive rights to work with the database.

2. Select Tools ⇨ Database Utilities and then click Make MDE File (see Figure 37-6).

3. In the Database to Save as MDE dialog box, specify the database you want to save as an .MDE file, and click Make MDE (see Figure 37-7).

4. In the Database to Save as MDE dialog box, specify a name, drive, and folder for the database. Do not attempt to save the .MDE file with the same filename as the original database.

Figure 37-6: Access doesn't convert the existing database into an .MDE file, it creates a new .MDE file for the database.

Figure 37-7: If you have a database open at the time you select Make MDE File, you do not see this dialog box.

Caution   Do not delete or overwrite your original database! As stated previously, there is no way to convert an .MDE file to a normal database, and you cannot edit any objects in an .MDE file. If you delete or otherwise lose your original database, you will never again be able to access any of the objects in the design environment!

Using the Jet User-Level Security Model

Most often when security is required, setting a database password is simply not enough; you need to fully implement the user-level/object permissions security of Jet 4.0. To do this, you need to complete the following functions:

1. Select or create a workgroup database.
2. Define the workgroup database's security groups.
3. Create the users of the workgroup database.
4. Define permissions for each user and security group.
5. Enable security by setting an Admin user password.

Enabling security

Jet security is always on. When a new workgroup database is created, a user by the name of Admin is automatically created within the workgroup. This Admin user has no password assigned to it. When the Admin password is blank, Access assumes any user attempting to open the database is the Admin user, and that user is automatically logged in to the database as the Admin user. To force Access/Jet to ask for a valid user name and password to log in to the database (see Figure 37-8), you simply need to create a password for the Admin user. To "turn security off," simply clear the Admin user's password. The security permissions you have designed are still in effect, but Access does not ask for a user name and password—it logs on all users as the Admin user with whatever permissions were assigned to the Admin user. Be careful about clearing the Admin user's password when you have modified the permissions of your users.

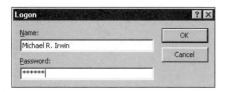

Figure 37-8: When you activate security, Jet forces all users to enter a valid user name and password to use the secured database.

Tip   If you have cleared the Admin password, only to find out that some or all of the Admin user's permissions have been revoked, and you need access to the restricted objects, or if you need to log on as a different user, open the database and create a password for the Admin user, then exit and restart Access 2000 (not the database). When you restart Access, you are prompted to enter a user name and password. Changes you make to security will not take effect until you restart Access.

Working with workgroups

A *workgroup* is a collection of users, user groups, and object permissions. You can use a single workgroup file for all your databases, or you may use different workgroups for different databases. The method you use depends on the level of security you need. If you give Administrative rights to users of some databases but not to users of other databases, you need to distribute separate workgroup files with each database. Access always uses a workgroup file when you open it. By default, this workgroup file is the SYSTEM.MDW workgroup file. This file comes with Access 2000.

Creating a new workgroup

You can create new workgroups or join existing ones by using the Workgroup Administrator program that comes with Access 2000 (see Figure 37-9). This is a separate program (WRKGADM.EXE) that is located in the same directory as MSACCESS; normally it can be found in the c:\program files\microsoft office\office\1033\WRKGADM.EXE directory (if you installed Access using the default directory). However, Office places a shortcut to this file in the office directory (same as the preceding directory minus the \1033\).

Figure 37-9: Use the Workgroup Administrator program to create new workgroups and to join existing workgroups.

Note   You should completely close down Access when creating new or joining existing workgroups. When you use the Workgroup Administrator to join a workgroup, that workgroup is not actually used until the next time you start Access.

To create a new workgroup file, follow these steps:

1. Start MS Access Workgroup Administrator from the Taskbar or from Microsoft Explorer. If you use Explorer, the executable name to run is "MS Access Workgroup Administrator," located in the directory in which you installed Access.

2. Click the Create button in the Workgroup Administrator dialog box to display the Workgroup Owner Information dialog box.

3. The workgroup you create is identified by three components: Name, Organization, and Workgroup ID (see Figure 37-10).

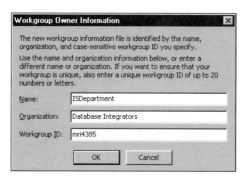

Figure 37-10: Workgroups are identified by these three key pieces of information. A workgroup cannot be re-created without all three of these items.

Caution In order to re-create the workgroup file in the event that it becomes corrupt or deleted, you need all three pieces of information. For this reason, to ensure that no other user can create your workgroup and access your secured database, you should supply a unique, random string for the Workgroup ID. Someone may possibly guess the name and organization used in your workgroup file if he or she knows who you are, but to guess all three items, especially if you create a random, unique ID, is almost impossible.

4. When you are satisfied with your entries, click OK to display the Workgroup Information File dialog box.

5. Enter the name to save the new workgroup file as and click OK to save the workgroup (see Figure 37-11). If you choose the existing file, SYSTEM.MDW, you will receive a confirmation box requesting that you confirm replacing the existing file.

Figure 37-11: After defining your workgroup file, you need to give it a name in order to save it.

6. The Workgroup Administrator shows you a confirmation dialog box (see Figure 37-12) that contains the information you entered for the new workgroup and explains the importance of writing down and storing the information. If you are satisfied with your entries, click OK to save your workgroup. If you wish to change anything, click the Change button and you will be returned to Step 3.

7. Finally, you will receive an information box that informs you that you have created the workgroup information file correctly. If you have Access open, you receive a different dialog box informing you it could not create the file — clicking this returns you to Step 6. If this happens, close Access and continue from Step 6.

Tip In order to ensure that you can recover from the loss of your workgroup file, you should immediately make a copy of the workgroup file. In addition, you should write down the three pieces of information used to create the workgroup file exactly as they were entered in the event that you have to re-create the workgroup file from scratch. Store both the backup file copy and the written information in a secure place.

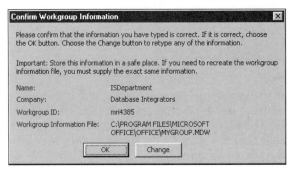

Figure 37-12: Do as this dialog box says and write down this information! You may need it if you ever have to re-create the workgroup file.

Joining an existing workgroup

When you create a new workgroup, Access automatically joins the new workgroup. If you do not want to use the new workgroup right away, or if at any time you need to use a workgroup other than the current workgroup, you need to join the desired workgroup by using the Workgroup Administrator.

To join an existing workgroup, follow these steps:

1. Run the Workgroup Administrator program.

2. The Workgroup Administrator dialog box shows you the currently joined workgroup (refer back to Figure 37-9). Click the Join button to select a workgroup file. If you are not sure of the filename, click the Browse button to display a File dialog box in which to locate the workgroup file.

3. A prompt appears, enabling you to confirm or cancel joining the selected workgroup. Click OK and then click Exit to close the Workgroup Administrator program.

Working with users

Every time a user opens an Access (Jet) database, Jet must know the user opening the database. When security is "off" (in reality, security is never off — see the following section on enabling security), Jet always assumes that the Admin user is opening the database. When a new workgroup is created, Access automatically creates a default user with the name Admin; the Admin user is given full permissions to all objects in the database. Obviously, when you secure a database, you do not want everyone to be able to open the database with full permissions on all objects, so you must create additional users in the workgroup.

Adding and deleting user accounts

You add, delete, and edit user information with the User and Group Accounts dialog box (see Figure 37-13), accessed through the Tools ➪ Security ➪ User and Group Accounts menu item. The Users page (Users tab active) of the User and Group Accounts dialog box consists of two sections. You use the first section to maintain user names and passwords; use the second section to assign users to security groups. Assigning users to groups is discussed in detail later in this chapter.

To fully secure your database with users and groups, follow these steps:

1. Create a new user.

2. Add the new user to the Admins group.

3. Remove the Admin user from the Admins group.

4. Assign all object ownerships to the new user.

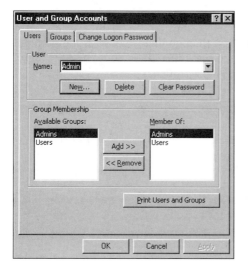

Figure 37-13: Users are maintained in the User and Group Accounts tabbed dialog box.

When you create a user, you supply the user name and a personal identifier. Jet then combines these two items and processes them in a special algorithm, producing a unique security ID (SID). It is this SID that Jet uses to recognize users. In order to re-create a user in the workgroup, you need to know the user name and the personal ID (PID) used to create the user. Consequently, you should always write down and store all names and PIDs of users you create in a safe place.

To create a new user in a workgroup, follow these steps:

1. Open the database to secure in Access.

2. Select Tools ➪ Security ➪ User and Group Accounts to display the User and Group Accounts dialog box.

3. Click the New button in the User section to display the New User/Group dialog box (see Figure 37-14).

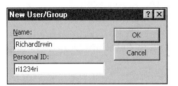

Figure 37-14: Jet employs the user name and personal identifier to create a unique SID for the user.

4. Enter the name of the user and a unique personal ID. Write this information down and store it in a safe place; you will need it to re-create the user in the workgroup.

5. Click OK to save the new user.

Caution

In order to fully secure your database, you must remove all permissions for the Admin user. All Admin users share the same SID in all workgroups, on all machines. If you do not remove the permissions for the Admin user, an unauthorized user using a different workgroup can open the database as the Admin user, with all permissions of the Admin user. The Admin user cannot be deleted, so the Admin user account needs to be adjusted accordingly.

Creating and changing user passwords

Any member of the Admins group can remove a password from any user account; however, no user can change or create a password for anyone other than himself; each user has the ability to change or create only his or her own password, regardless of security permissions.

Caution

If a password has been assigned to any user, then Access will start by first presenting the Logon Dialog box (refer back to Figure 37-8).

However, if no passwords are assigned to any of the users, Access 2000 will automatically start with the user Admin.

This means that any other user you create in Security will *not* be able to assign themselves a password without first logging in via the Logon Dialog box (it will not appear). To correct this, you will need to create a password for the Admin user, and then quit Access and restart, logging in as the user whose password you want to change.

To create or change a user password, follow these steps:

1. Log on to the database as the user whose password you want to change.

2. Select Tools ⇨ Security ⇨ User and Group Accounts.

3. Click the Change Logon Password tab (see Figure 37-15).

Figure 37-15: The Change Logon Password page of the User and Group Accounts dialog box. Notice that the name is Admin and cannot be changed.

4. If a password exists for the user you logged on as (the first time you will be Admin), enter it in the Old Password field. If no password is assigned to the user, leave the Old Password field blank.

5. Enter the new password in the New Password field.

6. You must enter the new password a second time in the Verify field in order to prevent typing errors, because you cannot see the characters you type for the password.

7. Click the Apply button to save the new password for the user.

8. Click the OK button to close the User and Group Accounts dialog box.

Tip Once you have created a password for the user, as in Figure 37-15, you will have to quit Access 2000 and restart for the changes to take effect.

Initially, the user Admin must have a password assigned to make sure Access displays the Logon screen when it starts up.

Users cannot create or change passwords for users other than themselves, regardless of their permission settings.

Any user who has Admin rights can clear the password of another user so that second user can log in if he or she has forgotten his or her password.

Working with groups

In addition to users, workgroups contain groups. *Groups* are collections of users; any user may belong to one or more groups. Groups enable you to easily set up object permissions for sets of users — enabling you to define the permissions once, versus having to assign them separately for each user. When you want a user to have the security permissions of a particular group, you simply add the user to the desired group.

For example, you may have a number of users in a credit department and in a sales department. If you want to allow all of these users to look at a customer's credit history but restrict the sales staff to viewing basic customer information, you have the following options:

✦ Allow all users in the credit department to log on as one user, and allow all users in the sales department to log on as a different user. You could then restrict the object permissions for each of these two users.

✦ Create an individual user account for all users in each department and assign object permissions for each user.

✦ Create an individual user account for all users in each department, and create a group account for each department. You could then make the permissions assignments for each of the two groups and place each user into his or her respective group to inherit the group's permissions.

The first method is straightforward and simple but presents many problems. If a user transfers from one department to another, he has user names and passwords for both departments and may be able to retrieve data he is no longer authorized to view. In addition, if an employee leaves, the user name and password need to be changed, and each user of the workgroup has to be made aware of the change. In a multiuser environment, creating a unique user account for each user and then grouping them accordingly is a much better solution.

Although the second method — creating a unique user account and assigning specific permissions to each user — would work, it is an administrator's nightmare. If policy dictates that one of the departments needs to have permissions added or revoked, the change has to be made to each user's account for that department. With the third option, the change can be made to the department group once, and all users inherit the new permission settings.

Adding and deleting groups

Just as Access creates a user called Admin in all new workgroups, it also creates two groups: Users and Admins. Every user account in the system belongs to the Users group; you cannot remove a user from the Users group. The Admins group is the all-powerful, "Big Daddy" group. Users of the Admins group have the ability to add and delete user and group accounts, as well as to assign and remove permissions for any object, for any user or group in the workgroup. In addition, a member of the Admins group has the ability to remove other user accounts from the Admin group. For this reason, you need to carefully consider which users you allow as members of the Admins group. The Admins group and the Users group are permanent groups; they can never be deleted.

Tip Access does not enable you to remove all users from the Admins group; one user must belong to the Admins group at all times. If you were allowed to remove all users from the Admins group, you could set up security so tight that you would never be able to bypass it yourself! In general, when securing a database, you should only place one or two users in the Admins group.

Note Unlike the Admin user's SID, which is identical in every Access workgroup, the Admins group's SIDs are not identical from workgroup to workgroup, so unauthorized users using a workgroup other than the one you used to define security cannot access your database as a member of the Admins group. The Users group's SIDs are the same throughout all workgroups, however, so you need to remove all permissions for the Users group. If you do not remove permissions from the Users group, any user with any workgroup can open your database with the Users group's permissions.

To create a new group, follow these steps:

1. Select Tools ➪ Security ➪ User and Group Accounts to display the User and Group Accounts dialog box.

2. Click the Groups tab.

3. Click New to display the New User/Group dialog box (see Figure 37-16).

4. Just as you do to create users, enter a group name and personal ID. Also, just as before, write down this information and put it in a safe place; you will need it to re-create the group at a later time.

5. Click OK to save the new group.

6. Once this is complete, you can click the OK button of the Accounts dialog box to save your work.

To delete a group, follow these steps:

1. Select Tools ➪ Security ➪ User and Group Accounts to display the User and Group Accounts dialog box.

2. Click the Groups tab (refer to Figure 37-16).

3. From the drop-down list, select the group to delete.

4. Click the Delete button to delete the selected group.

Assigning and removing group members

Assigning users to and removing users from groups is a simple process. All assignments and removals are performed under the Users tab of the User and Group Accounts dialog box. You may place any user in any group, and users may belong to more than one group. As stated earlier, you cannot remove a user from the Users group, nor can you remove all users from the Admins group; you must always have at least one user in the Admins group.

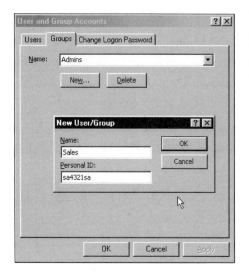

Figure 37-16: Jet uses the group name and personal identifier to create a unique SID for the security group, just as it does for user accounts.

To add or remove a user from a group, follow these steps:

1. Select Tools ⇨ Security ⇨ User and Group Accounts to display the User and Group Accounts dialog box.

2. From the drop-down list, select the user whose group assignments you want to modify.

3. If you want to assign users to a group or groups to which they do not currently belong, select the group(s) in the Available Groups list and click the Add button (see Figure 37-17). The selected group (or groups) is then removed from the Available Groups list and moved to the Member Of list.

4. If you want to remove a user from a group or groups, select the group (or groups) in the Member Of list and click the Remove button. The selected group is then removed from the Member Of list and moved to the Available Groups list.

5. Click OK to save the new group assignments.

Figure 37-17: Assigning users to groups makes controlling object permissions much easier for the system administrator.

Because Jet uses the same SIDs for all Admin user accounts throughout all workgroups, you always need to remove the Admin user from the Admins group when securing a database. Figure 37-17 shows the user RichardIrwin removed from the Admins group. After removing the user from the Admins group, all that is left to do is to verify that the Users group does not contain any permissions that you do not want unauthorized users to have and that no explicit permissions are assigned to the Admin user account (see the next section, "Securing objects by using permissions").

Securing objects by using permissions

After you have defined your users and groups, you must decide on the specific object permissions a user or group is to have. Permissions control who can view data, update data, add data, and work with objects in Design view. Permissions are the heart of the Jet security system and can only be set by a member of the Admins group, by the owner of the object (see the next section), or by any user who has Administrator permission on the object in question.

Setting an objects owner

Every object in the database can have an owner. The *owner* is a user account in the workgroup that is designated to always have administrator rights to the object, regardless of the group to which they belong or the permissions explicitly applied to them for the object. You can designate one user to be the owner of all the objects in a database, or you may assign different owners to different objects.

OwnerAccess queries require special consideration when assigning owners to objects. When creating a query, you can set the `Run Permissions` property of the query to either `User's` or `Owner's` (see Figure 37-18). By default, this permission is set to `User's`, which limits the users of the query to seeing only the data that their security permissions permit. If you want to enable users to view or modify data for which they do not have permissions, you can set the `Run Permissions` property to `Owner's`. When the query is run with the Owner's permissions (`WITH OWNERACCESS OPTION` in an SQL statement), users inherit the permissions of the owner of the query when they run the query. These permissions are applicable only to the query and not to the entire database.

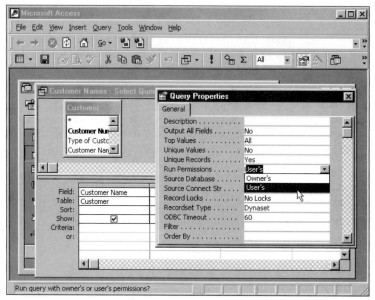

Figure 37-18: Judicious use of OwnerAccess queries enables you to temporarily grant object permissions to users who don't currently have those permissions.

Tip

When a query's `Run Permissions` property is set to `Owner's`, only the owner can make changes to the query. If this restriction poses a problem, you may want to set the owner of the query to a group, rather than to a user account. Note that only the owner of an OwnerAccess query can change the query's owner.

To change the owner of an object, follow these steps:

1. Select Tools ➪ Security ➪ User and Group Permissions (the second choice in the Security menu) to display the User and Group Permissions dialog box.

2. Click the Change Owner tab (see Figure 37-19).

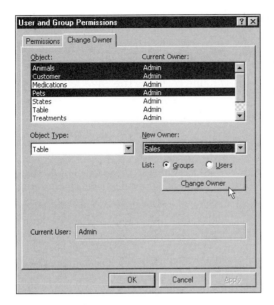

Figure 37-19: Controlling an object's owner is an important step in securing a database. This figure demonstrates changing the selected table object's ownership from the Admin user to the new Group Sales.

3. Select the object (or objects) whose ownership you want to transfer. You can select the type of objects to display by changing the Object Type field.

4. Select the user or group that you want to make the owner of the selected object.

5. Click the Change Owner button to change the object's owner to the selected user or group.

Note

In addition to the objects within a database each having an owner, the database itself has an owner. You can view the owner of the database by selecting Database from the Object Type drop-down list. You cannot change an object's owner by using Access's interface; the only way to change a database's owner is to log on as the user that you want to make the owner of the database, create a new database, and import the original database into the new database using the Import Database add-in. When you import a database, the current user is assigned as the new owner of the database and all of the database objects; this is essentially what the Security Wizard (discussed later in this chapter) does for you.

Setting object permissions

Object permissions are the heart of Jet security. One or more object permissions at a time can be set for users and groups. When assigning permissions, you must keep in mind that some permissions automatically imply other permissions. For example, if you assign a user Read Data permission for a table, the Read Design permission is also granted, because a table's design must be available to access the data.

An object's permission assignments are persistent until one of the following conditions occurs:

✦ A member of the Admins group changes the object's permissions.

✦ The object is saved with a new name by using the Save As command from the File menu.

✦ The object is cut and pasted in the Database window.

✦ The object is imported or exported.

If any of the preceding actions occur, all permissions for the manipulated object are lost, and you have to reassign them. This loss of permissions occurs because you are actually creating a new object when you perform any of the actions (versus editing and saving the same object), and new objects are assigned the default permissions defined for the object's type.

Understanding the two types of permissions is important:

✦ **Explicit permissions** are permissions granted directly to a user. When you explicitly assign a permission to a user, no other user's permissions are affected.

✦ **Implicit permissions** are permissions granted to a group. All users belonging to a group implicitly have the permissions of that group.

Note   Because permissions can be assigned implicitly, and some permissions grant other permissions (as mentioned in the previous discussion of the Read Data and Read Design permission relationship), users may be able to grant themselves permissions that they don't currently have. Because of this possibility, you must plan carefully when assigning permissions to groups of users and to individual users themselves.

To assign or revoke a user's permissions for an object, follow these steps:

1. Select Tools ➪ Security ➪ User and Group Permissions to display the User and Group Permissions dialog box. Make sure the Permissions tab is active (the first tab).

2. Select the type of object whose permissions you want to change from the Object Type drop-down list (located on the right side and center of the dialog box).

3. Select the user or group account for which you want to modify the permissions (from the User/Group Name list box).

4. Select the object (or objects) for which you want to modify the permissions (from the Object Name list box).

5. Select or deselect the permissions of the object (under the Permissions group of the dialog box).

6. Click Apply to commit the permission assignments.

Remember that Admin user SIDs are identical throughout all workgroups, so you need to remove all permissions for the Admin user in order to secure your database. Figure 37-20 shows the Admin user's permissions for all tables in the database. Note how all check boxes have been cleared, preventing an Admin user from doing anything with the table object.

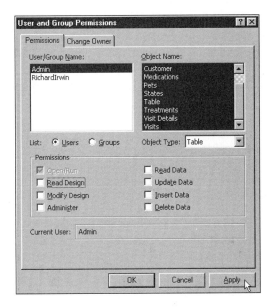

Figure 37-20: Removing all permissions for the Admin user is critical to securing your database.

Setting default object permissions

You can create default permission assignments for each type of object in a database. These default permissions are assigned when a new object is created, imported, or cut and pasted within the database container. You set the default permissions just as you would set any other object's permissions. You must select the user or group to which to assign default permissions, but you do not select a specific object. When you select the Object Type from the drop-down list, the first item in the Object Name list is <New OBJECT>, where OBJECT is replaced with the actual object type selected, such as <New Forms>. When you assign permissions for users and groups to these <New> items, the permissions are used as defaults for all new objects of that type.

Tip

When removing default permissions for table objects, if you have created make table queries, you must ensure that any users running the make table query have the ability to create new tables. If you remove a user's permission to create new tables, that user will not able to execute a make table query.

Setting database permissions

Each database has permissions, just as the objects in the database do. Selecting Database from the Object Type drop-down list will display the database permissions that can be modified (see Figure 37-21). The database permissions enable you to control who has administrative rights to the entire database, who can open the database exclusively (locking out other users), and who can open or run the database.

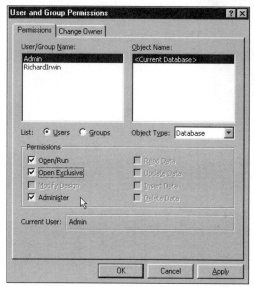

Figure 37-21: You can assign permissions for the entire database, not just for individual objects.

Securing your database for distribution: A basic approach

If you are securing a database for distribution, setting up detailed security for multiple users for all objects in your database may not be important to you. Often, the only concern with shipping a secured database is protecting your development investment by securing the design of your objects and code. If you need this protection, you can distribute your application as an .MDE file (see the section "Distributing a Database as an .MDE File"), or you can follow these steps:

1. Create a workgroup to distribute with your database.

2. Remove the Admin user from the Admins group.

3. Remove all permissions for the Users group.

4. Remove any and all design permissions for the Admin user for all objects in the database.

5. Do not supply a password for the Admin user.

By not supplying a password for the Admin user, you tell Access to log on all users as the Admin user. Because the Admin user has no rights to the design of any objects, users cannot access your objects or code in Design view.

If you use this method to secure the design of your objects, and you need to modify objects using DAO that the Admin user does not have rights for (such as Query-Defs, TableDefs, or reading data from a secured table), you need to create a temporary workspace as a user with administrative rights for the object.

For example, if you have a table called tblRegistration in which you keep registration and licensing information that you do not want the Admin user to be able to update, you can remove the Update Data permissions for the table. However, if you attempt to update the table using DAO, you receive an error because the logged-in user — the Admin user — does not have sufficient rights to manipulate the table. You can avoid this error by using a temporary workspace. Creating a temporary workspace is essentially logging in to the database as a user in Visual Basic; the login is valid for the scope of the workspace object that you dimension. The following is sample code that creates a temporary workspace and edits the data in tblRegistration. This example assumes that a valid user by the name of "David Hawkings" exists in the current workgroup and has the password "TheHawk":

```
Dim TempWorkspace As Workspace, MyDB As Database, tbl As Table
Set TempWorkspace = DBEngine.CreateWorkspace("TempWs", _
"David Hawkings", "TheHawk")

    DBEngine.Workspaces.Append TempWorkspace

    Set MyDB = TempWorkspace.OpenDatabase(CurrentDB().Name)
    Set tbl = MyDB.OpenTable("tblUsers")

    tbl.Edit
    tbl![Reg Name] = "John Davis"
    tbl.Update
```

The `CreateWorkspace` method of the `DBEngine` object accepts three parameters:

1. **A name to call the temporary workspace.** In the preceding code sample, the name assigned to the workspace is TempWs, but you can choose any name.

2. **The user name to use for logging in.** The preceding example creates a temporary workspace for the user David Hawkings.

3. **The user's password.** In the preceding example, David Hawkings's password is TheHawk.

Tip Because you must supply the user's password when creating a temporary workspace, and the user has additional rights (or you wouldn't be following this procedure), it is absolutely critical that you secure the View Design permissions for all modules or forms that use the preceding code. If you do not secure objects that contain the code to create the temporary workspace, users can get the user name and password from your code and log in to the database as that user.

Table 37-1 summarizes permissions that you can assign.

Table 37-1 Summary of Assignable Permissions		
Permission	**Permits a User To**	**Applies To**
Open/Run	Open a database, form, or report, or run a macro.	Databases, forms, reports, and macros
Open Exclusive	Open a database with exclusive access.	Databases
Read Design reports	View objects in Design view.	Tables, queries, forms, macros, and modules
Modify Design reports	View and change the design of objects, or delete them.	Tables, queries, forms, macros, and modules
Administer	For databases, set database password, replicate a database, and change start-up properties. For database objects, have full access to objects and data, including the ability to assign permissions.	Databases, tables, queries, forms, reports, macros, and modules
Read Data	View data.	Tables and queries
Update Data	View and modify but not insert or delete data.	Tables and queries
Insert Data	View and insert but not modify or delete data.	Tables and queries
Delete Data	View and delete but not modify or insert data.	Tables and queries

Using the Access Security Wizard

Access includes a tool to help you secure your databases: the Security Wizard. The Security Wizard enables you to select the objects to secure, and then it creates a new database containing secured versions of the selected objects. The Security Wizard assigns the currently logged-in user as the owner of the objects in the new database and removes all permissions from the Users group for those objects. Finally, the Security Wizard encrypts the new database. The original database is not modified in any way. Only members of the Admins group and the user who ran the Security Wizard have access to the secured objects in the new database.

Tip   When you use the Security Wizard, make sure you are logged in as the user whom you want to become the new database's owner.

To run the Security Wizard, select Tools ⇨ Security ⇨ User-Level Security Wizard (refer back to Figure 37-1 to see the menu choice). The wizard first informs you that you will need to use either the existing workgroup information file or create a new one for the current open database (see Figure 37-22).

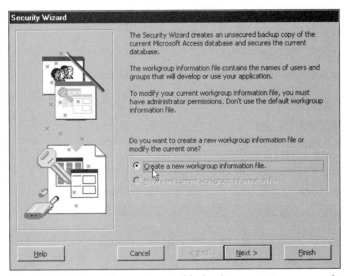

Figure 37-22: The Security Wizard helps jump-start your security implementation.

Tip   If you select Create a new workgroup information file, you will be taken to a page that asks you for the filename of the file, a Workgroup ID number (WID — this must be remembered to re-create it later), and, optionally, your name and company. Figure 37-23 shows the Security Wizard screen that enables you to create a new workgroup information file.

As Figure 37-23 shows, you can choose to make this the new default file for all databases, or have Access 2000 create a shortcut to use this file only for this database (default). Selecting the default and assigning a shortcut will associate this file with only one database.

By default, the wizard secures all existing database objects. If you deselect an object type (such as Tables or Forms), none of the objects of that type are exported to the secured database. Figure 37-24 shows this page of the wizard. If you do not want to restrict security permissions for a set of objects but still want those objects included in the new, secured database, you need to select the objects in the wizard and then modify the user and group permissions for those objects in the new, secured database. When you are satisfied with your object selections, click OK to continue.

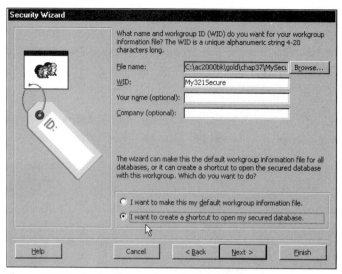

Figure 37-23: Assigning a unique WID and name to new workgroup information file.

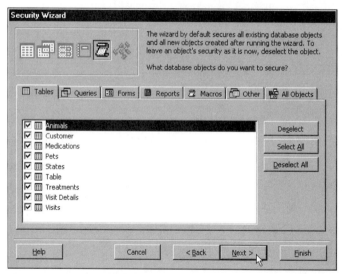

Figure 37-24: The Security Wizard helps jump-start your security implementation by asking which objects you want to protect.

Now the wizard asks you for a password you want to assign for all your Visual Basic for Applications (VBA) modules that are contained in your database. Figure 37-25 shows this screen with a password entered.

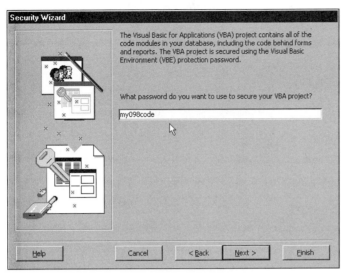

Figure 37-25: The Security Wizard asks for a password to use for all your VBA code in the database.

The next screen of the wizard asks you to input an optional security group account for a series of group actions. These include:

- ✦ Backup Operators — Can open the database exclusively for backing up and compacting.
- ✦ Full Data Users — Can edit data, but not alter design.
- ✦ Full Permissions — Has full permissions for all database objects, but cannot assign permissions.
- ✦ New Data Users — Can read and insert data only (no edits or deletions).
- ✦ Project Designers — Can edit data and objects, and alter tables or relationships.
- ✦ Read-Only Users — Can read data only.
- ✦ Update Data Users — Can read and update, but cannot insert or delete data or alter design of objects.

Figure 37-26 shows this page with all groups checked (default is off). Notice that the next page of the wizard lets you choose to grant permissions to the Users group (the default is no permissions). By selecting yes, you are able to assign rights to all object types in the database. Figure 37-27 shows this page active with Yes selected. The default choice is No, the Users group should not have any permissions.

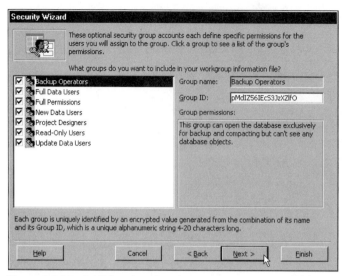

Figure 37-26: Additional optional security groups created for the database.

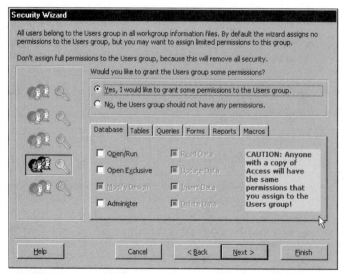

Figure 37-27: The ability to assign permissions to the Users group.

Caution   If you decide to grant some permissions to the Users group, you should be aware that anyone with a copy of Access will have the same permissions that you assign to this group. Thus you are opening the database to a security breach if you assign rights to this group.

Figure 37-28 shows the next page of the wizard. This page lets you add users to the workgroup information file. To add a user, you have to put their name and password in the correct fields and click the Add this user to the list button.

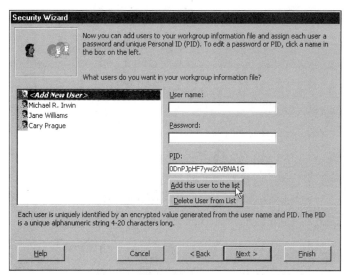

Figure 37-28: Adding users and passwords to the database information file.

As Figure 37-28 shows, you can also remove users from the list by simply selecting their name from the list box on the left side and pressing the Delete User from the list button.

The wizard then takes you to a page that enables you to assign users to groups in your workgroup information file. If you added optional groups from the earlier page (shown in Figure 37-26), you can now assign each user in your group to these groups by turning the check box on. To select a user to assign rights to, simply select the user from the combo box and then assign that user to groups using the check boxes. The default value for all users, except the person creating the wizard, is that they belong to all groups. Figure 37-29 shows this page.

After going through these pages, the Security Wizard finally asks you to provide a name for the old, now unsecure, database (see Figure 37-30). Technically, the Security Wizard does not make any modifications to the current database; rather, it makes a backup copy using the name you specify and creates an *entirely new* database with secured objects. However, the new database is given the name of the original database. When you distribute your secured application, make sure to distribute the database that the Security Wizard created for you.

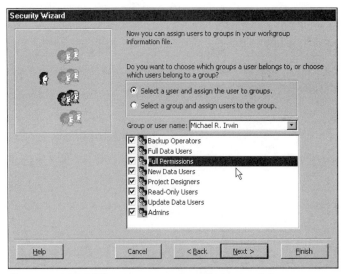

Figure 37-29: Adding users to groups for group rights.

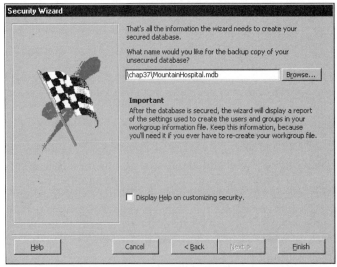

Figure 37-30: In the Final dialog box, the Security Wizard asks you to assign a name to the old database.

Tip

After the database is secured, a report is generated that has all the settings used to create the users and groups in the workgroup information file. You should keep this information. Should you ever need to re-create the workgroup file, you will have to have this information.

Generally, making a copy of the original database but working with the secured database is a good idea. If you make changes to the original database, you will need to run the Security Wizard again to create a secured version of the database. In addition, making a copy of the original database and then removing it from development helps prevent accidentally distributing the unsecured database. After entering the new database name, click Save to save the secured database.

After supplying a name for the backup unsecured database (the original), the Security Wizard creates the database with the secured objects and gives you a summary of everything it did

Encrypting a Database

When security is of utmost importance, one final step you need to take is to *encrypt* the database. Although it would take a great deal of skill (far more than the average computer user — or developer — possesses), using tools to view the actual database structure on the hard disk of the computer is possible. A skilled hacker could use this information to reconstruct SIDs and gain full access to your secured database.

Encrypting a database makes using such tools to gain any useful information about the database virtually impossible. Only the database owner or a member of the Admins group (or a really good computer hacker) can encrypt or decrypt a database.

To encrypt a database, follow these steps:

1. With no database open, select Tools ➪ Security ➪ Encrypt/Decrypt Database (see Figure 37-31).
2. Select the database to encrypt from the Encrypt/Decrypt dialog box.
3. Provide a name for the new encrypted database.

Access does not modify the original database when it encrypts it; rather, it creates a clone of the database and encrypts the clone. As when using the Security Wizard, you should make a backup copy of the original database and store it somewhere safe to prevent accidentally distributing the unencrypted database. Remember that in a world of rapidly changing data, your backup will rapidly become out of date.

In addition to encrypting a database using Access's interface, it is possible to encrypt a database using VBA code. The following code example can be used to encrypt a database:

```
Public Sub EncryptDatabase()
On Error GoTo EncryptDatabaseErr
Dim szDBName As String, szEncryptedDBname As String
```

```
szDBName = _
"c:\Program Files\Microsoft
Office\Access\Samples\northwind.mdb"
szEncryptedDBname = _
"c:\Program Files\Microsoft
Office\Access\Samples\encrypted.mdb"

DBEngine.CompactDatabase szDBName, szEncryptedDBname,
dbLangGeneral, _ dbEncrypt

Exit Sub

EncryptDatabaseErr:
    MsgBox Err & ":  " & Err.Description
    Exit Sub

End Sub
```

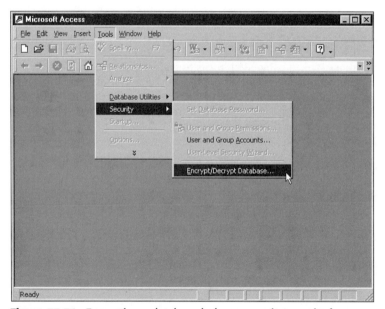

Figure 37-31: Encrypting a database helps ensure its security from highly skilled hackers.

As stated previously, few people have the ability or drive to hack a database in the way that encryption prevents, but encryption is a necessary step for securing highly sensitive databases. If you choose to encrypt a database, you have to accept the following drawbacks:

✦ Encrypted databases do not compress from their original size when used with compression programs such as PKZIP or the ODE Setup Wizard; encryption modifies the way the data is stored on the hard disk and renders the compression algorithms useless.

✦ Encrypted databases suffer some performance degradation (up to 15 percent). Depending on the size of your database and the speed of your computer, this loss may not be noticeable.

Note Encrypting a database should be performed as an *additional* step to securing a database using users, groups, and permissions. Simply encrypting a database does nothing to secure the database from users using Access. Encryption is an addition, not a complete solution, to securing a database.

Decrypting a Database

Access 2000 lets you decrypt a previously encrypted database. To decrypt a database, follow these steps (similar to the encrypting process):

1. With no database open, select Tools ➪ Security ➪ Encrypt/Decrypt Database.

2. Select the database to decrypt from the Encrypt/Decrypt dialog box.

3. Provide a name for the new decrypted database.

That is all there is to reversing an encryption.

Manipulating Security Objects Using DAO

An example presented earlier in this chapter demonstrates how to create temporary workspaces to gain the permissions of users other than the user you are logged in as. In addition, it is possible to create users and groups, remove or change passwords, change ownership of objects, and assign permissions for objects — all using DAO in Visual Basic for Applications code.

Creating a user account using DAO

DAO includes a number of security objects that you can manipulate. First and foremost are the User and Group objects. Using these objects, you can create or delete users as well as change or remove user passwords. Users and Groups are created by defining the user or group and then appending it to the User or Group collection. The following code creates a new user account using DAO:

```
Public Sub CreateUser()
Dim usrNew As User, szUserName As String, szPID As String
Dim szPassword As String

szUserName = "Tabatha Thrush"
```

```
szPID = "MYPID105"
szPassword = "Shadow"

' Create a new user account.
Set usrNew = DBEngine.Workspaces(0).CreateUser(szUserName, _
szPID, szPassword)

' Save the new user account by appending it to Users
collection.
DBEngine.Workspaces(0).Users.Append usrNew

End Sub
```

Changing a users password using DAO

The password parameter of the `CreateUser` method is an optional parameter. Using the password property of the user object, the password can also be set as follows:

```
usrNew.PassWord = "Shadow"
```

This property must be set after the `CreateUser` method and prior to the `Append` method. To change the password of an existing user account, you need to use the `NewPassword` method of the `Users` object, as shown in the following procedure:

```
Public Sub ChangePassword()
On Error GoTo ChangePasswordErr
Dim szUserName As String, szOldPassword As String,
szNewPassword As _ String

szUserName = "Tabatha Thrush"
szOldPassword = "Shadow"
szNewPassword = "Katie"

Workspaces(0).Users(szUserName).NewPassword szOldPassword, _
szNewPassword

Exit Sub

ChangePasswordErr:
    MsgBox Err & ":  " & Err.Description
    Exit Sub

End Sub
```

The `NewPassword` method accepts three arguments:

✦ The name of the user whose password is to be changed

✦ The existing password for the user

✦ The new password to assign to the user

If you create procedures that add or change passwords in code, you must protect or delete the code prior to distributing the application to prevent a user from obtaining other users' passwords.

Creating a group account using DAO

Creating a group account is much like creating a user account. The difference is that the Group object and collection are used in place of the User object and collection. The following code creates a new group account:

```
Public Sub CreateGroup()
On Error GoTo CreateGroupErr
Dim grpSales As Group, szGroupName As String, szPID As String

szGroupName = "Sales"
szPID = "GroupPID0456"

' Create the new Group object.
 Set grpSales = DBEngine.Workspaces(0).CreateGroup(szGroupName,
_
 szPID)
' Create the new group by appending it to Groups collection.
 Workspaces(0).Groups.Append grpSales

Exit Sub

CreateGroupErr:
    MsgBox Err & ":  " & Err.Description
    Exit Sub

End Sub
```

Changing an object's owner using DAO

Ownership entitles users to certain irrevocable rights to objects in the database. You should take great care in protecting the ownership of the objects in your database. If you need to change an ownership through VBA code, you use the Owner property of a Document object, as follows:

```
Public Sub ChangeOwner()
On Error GoTo ChangeOwnerErr
Dim db As Database, ctrTemp As Container, docModule As Document
Dim szNewOwner As String

szNewOwner = "Tabatha Thrush"

' Return Database variable that points to current database.
 Set db = CurrentDb
' Return Container variable that points to Modules container.
 Set ctrTemp = db.Containers!Forms
```

```
' Return Document object that points to mdlUtilities module.
 Set docModule = ctrTemp.Documents!frmSwitchBoard
' Change the owner by setting the Owner property of the
Document _ object
docModule.Owner = szNewOwner

Exit Sub

ChangeOwnerErr:
    MsgBox Err & ":  " & Err.Description
    Exit Sub

End Sub
```

Assigning object permissions using DAO

Permissions are manipulated by using the `UserName` and `Permissions` properties of a document or container object. For example, the function in the following code assigns full permissions on all modules for the user Laura Thrush:

```
Sub SetPermissions()
' This procedure is to demonstrate changing user permissions
' programmatically.
On Error GoTo SetPermissionsErr
Dim db As Database, ctr As Container, szUserName As String

szUserName = "Tabatha Thrush"

Set db = CurrentDb()
' Set the container to the table objects
 Set ctr = db.Containers!Modules

' Set UserName property to valid existing user account.
 ctr.UserName = szUserName

' Set permissions for all table objects
 ctr.Permissions = dbSecFullAccess

Exit Sub

SetPermissionsErr:
    MsgBox Err & ":  " & Err.Description
    Exit Sub

End Sub
```

Tables 37-2, 37-3, and 37-4 show all available permission constants. If you want to set multiple permissions, add the properties together as follows:

```
ctr.Permissions = dbSecDelete + dbSecReadSec
```

Table 37-2
General DAO Permissions Constants

Constant	Description
dbSecNoAccess	No access to the object
dbSecFullAccess	Full access to the object
dbSecDelete	Can delete the object
dbSecReadSec	Can read the object's security-related information
dbSecWriteSec	Can alter access permissions
dbSecWriteOwner	Can change the Owner property setting

The possible settings or return values for the Tables Container object or any Document object in a Documents collection are shown in Table 37-3.

Table 37-3
Constants Applicable Only to Tables, Containers, and Their Documents

Constant	Description
dbSecCreate	Can create new documents (valid only with a Container object)
dbSecReadDef	Can read the table definition, including column and index information
dbSecWriteDef	Can modify or delete the table definition, including column and index information
dbSecRetrieveData	Can retrieve data from the Document object
dbSecInsertData	Can add records
dbSecReplaceData	Can modify records
dbSecDeleteData	Can delete records

The possible settings or return values for the Databases Container object or any Document object in a Documents collection are shown in Table 37-4.

	Table 37-4 **Constants Applicable Only to Databases, Containers, and Their Documents**
Constant	*Description*
dbSecDBAdmin	Gives the user permission to make a database replicable and to change the database password
dbSecDBCreate	Can create new databases (valid only on the Databases Container object in the system database [SYSTEM.MDW])
dbSecDBExclusive	Exclusive access
dbSecDBOpen	Can open the database

With a full understanding of the Jet security model and how to manage it, you can create databases that protect your development investment and your users' data.

Summary

Access 2000 offers Jet security, a workgroup-based security model that binds all the users in a workgroup to the same security rules of the workgroup itself. This is accomplished by defining Jet security at the object level for individuals or groups of users. This chapter explained the following:

✦ How permissions are assigned to objects

✦ How you can distribute the application as a protected .MDE file

✦ The Security Wizard, a tool that helps you secure an Access database

✦ How to encrypt a database

In the next chapter, you will learn how to create HTML-based help, which can now be used in Access 2000.

✦   ✦   ✦

Creating Help Systems in Access 2000

One item of an application that is often overlooked entirely is the inclusion of a comprehensive Help system. Creating a complete and useful Help system is a skill unto itself, and often programmers don't take the time necessary to learn how to do it right. Understanding what makes a good Help system and how to create one can be a powerful tool in your development arsenal.

Understanding the Windows Help Structure

Great Help systems are more than just online documentation. A Help system needs to explain the how-to of your application in bits and pieces, and the user needs to be able to access a specific bit or piece of information related to the task at hand with minimum effort. In addition, these bits and pieces — called topics — need to be linked in a comprehensive web enabling a user to easily travel from one related topic to another. Each topic can be linked to a form or control's `HelpContextId` property (see Figure 38-1) to provide instant access to the topic when the user presses F1 while the control or form has the focus.

Help systems may consist of simple linked text topics, or they may contain graphics and multimedia to help educate the user. A good application of graphics in a Help system is the use of hotspot graphics to help explain an application's toolbars. Hotspot graphics, or hypergraphics, are graphic pictures that have links assigned to various regions of the graphic. Often, these regions are invisible; the user knows when the cursor is over a hotspot because the pointer turns into a pointing hand. When the user clicks the hotspot, the topic linked to the hotspot is displayed. When creating a hypergraphic of a toolbar, you can link a related topic to each tool button in the toolbar graphic. Then users can simply click the button they want help on to display the appropriate Help topic, just as they would click the button on the toolbar.

Figure 38-1: You can link Help topics to the form or control they relate to by using the HelpContextId property.

The Help interface consists of numerous components, and understanding these components is key to mastering the designing of great Help files as well as to getting the most out of using a Help file.

The Help Viewer

The Help Viewer is the application that displays the Help system. The Help Viewer contains three panes (see Figure 38-2):

✦ The Topic pane displays on the right side of the Help Viewer. This is where the topic information displays.

✦ The Navigation pane on the left side of the Help Viewer. You can customize this pane to display a table of contents, an index, a list of favorite help topics, or a full-text search tab.

✦ The toolbar, at the top of the viewer, allows users to display or hide the Navigation pane, or move forward to the next topic or back to the previous topic. Stop, Refresh, Locate, and Home buttons are also available.

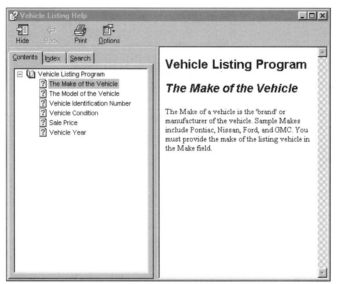

Figure 38-2: The Help Contents is where users of your Help file find the topics they're interested in.

You can customize the appearance of the Help Viewer to include or exclude the Index or Search tabs in the Navigation pane. However every Help system must have a Contents tab. A Contents tab lists the topics that are available when a user clicks Help Topics in your application's Help menu, clicks the Contents tab of any Help topic, or double-clicks your Help file in Windows Explorer. The Contents feature of a Help system is similar to the table of contents in a book.

The Contents tab

The Contents tab displays the Contents items in a collapsible outline format. Contents items that can be expanded are shown with a closed book icon. To expand a Contents item, select an item, and then select the Open button—or simply double-click the Contents item. When you expand a Contents item, the closed book icon changes to an open book icon, and the individual topics that can be viewed display. Each topic is preceded by a document icon. When users locate the items they want help on, they can double-click the Help topic or select it and click the Display button to view the Help topic. To view a specific Help Topic, select the Help Topic item, and then select the Display button—or double-click the item. The Help Topic displays in the Help Topics dialog box.

The Topic pane

Help topics are the core element of a Help system. Each topic covered in your Help System should be contained in its own Help topic. Help topics are displayed in the Help Topics dialog boxes (see Figure 38-3). A Help Topics dialog box contains information specific to the topic, such as pertinent text, graphics, animation, or sound, and it may contain links to other topics.

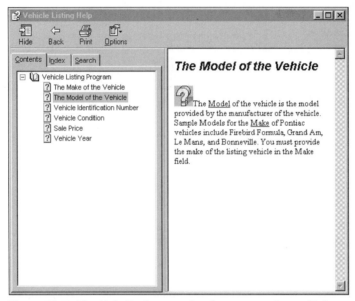

Figure 38-3: The Help Topics pane is where users of your Help system get the topical information they need.

Office 2000 Developer includes Microsoft HTML Help Workshop. Microsoft HTML Help 1.2 is the next-generation online help authoring system based on Microsoft WinHelp 4.0. If you've used WinHelp or Help Workshop before, you will be familiar with many of the features of HTML Help and HTML Help Workshop.

Like WinHelp, HTML Help uses a project file to combine topic, contents, index, image, and other source files into one compiled help file. HTML Help also provides you with HTML Help Workshop, an authoring tool that makes it easy to view, manage, and edit your files in an enhanced user interface. Unlike WinHelp, HTML Help has no practical help system limits. Help file size, topic size, contents entry limits, and keyword limits have all been (essentially) eliminated.

If you want even more control over how HTML Help is displayed and integrated into your solution, you can work directly with Html Help application programming interface (API) calls from your Visual Basic for Applications (VBA) code.

> **Tip** Implementing a Help button in Access requires you to use an API call to the HTML Help or WinHelp engine to display the Help topic.

Other help tools included in Microsoft Developer 2000:

✦ The Answer Wizard Software Development Kit (SDK)—lets you add your own help topics to the ones provided by the Microsoft Office Assistant.

✦ The HTML Help ActiveX control—for creating help pages on the Web.

These new tools greatly enhance the usability of the Help interface for the end user of your application.

Creating a Windows Help System

Creating Help systems for Windows involves the following:

✦ Author Help topic files in HTML. You can use Microsoft Word, or any authoring tool, to create HTML files as long as you create standard Version 3.2 HTML source code.

✦ Create a Help project file (.hhp) to manage the interface objects that make up your help system—topics, graphics, contents (.hhc), index (.hhk), and other source files—and to define the overall style of these objects.

✦ Create window definitions to define the style of window for displaying the help information.

✦ Create a table of contents file for easy navigation to Help topics.

✦ Create an index file for indexing Help topics.

✦ Compile your Help file. (Optional if you are using the HTML Help ActiveX control.)

✦ Test the Help system.

> **Tip** You do not need to include all your Help topics in one Help file. The Help engine has the capability to use one index and one table of contents for multiple Help files—very useful when you have an application that consists of modular components. If the Help engine does not locate a referenced Help file on the end user's computer, that Help file's topics will not show up in the table of contents.

Creating Help topics

The most fundamental element in a Help file is the Help topic. The documents you author are created using a special formatting language known as Hypertext Markup Language (HTML). HTML topic files have an .htm or .html file name extension.

Although each help topic or Web page you author appears to be a document with text, graphics, or animated images on it, .htm files are actually text documents that have special HTML formatting codes. These codes, called tags, tell a browser how to display each page. Only the text that appears in a topic or Web page is actually in the .htm file. Any graphics, sounds, animated images, or other elements that appear are separate files that your HTML file points to. The browser copies or downloads the graphics, sounds, or other elements when it sees the tags telling it to do so.

Before you begin typing the descriptive text for your topics, you should define a list of all the topics you want to include in your Help system. When you have created such a list, organize it as best as possible (see Figure 38-4). This organization, in effect, creates a level 1 outline for your topics. After the topics are organized, simply type the descriptive text below each topic. Creating your topics this way simplifies the effort in designing your topic structure.

The easiest way to author your help system is to create a new HTML file for each help topic. HTML Help is designed to work with multiple files, each containing a single topic. For larger help systems, however, you may find it easier to develop one HTML file that contains all of the topics. Using the HTML Help Workshop, you can split the large file into individual HTML files later.

To create an HTML topic file, follow these steps:

1. Create a new document in Microsoft Word (or another product supporting HTML files).

2. Enter the text to be displayed for each topic.

3. Identify separate topic sections with a hard page break. You can create a hard page break in Microsoft Word by selecting Insert ➪ Break and then selecting Page Break.

4. Save the file as a Web page.

Tip   You can create a document template to use when creating your HTML files. A template is a file that contains all the font, style, heading, and design elements you use most frequently. You can distribute the template to all of the authors who will be creating the help content files.

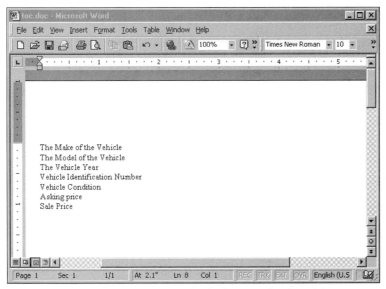

Figure 38-4: Organizing your topic list before you begin writing simplifies the design process.

Creating a Help project file

Once you have authored all of the help contents files that you will use in your Help system, you can create an HTML Help Workshop project file. A Help project (.hhp) file contains information about the location of your HTML topic files, contents (.hhc) files, index (.hhk) files, image (.png, .jpg, .gif) files, and other files. Project files also contain help window definitions and other options that customize the way a Help system functions.

To create a Help project file, follow these steps:

1. Open the HTML Help Workshop.

2. Select File ➪ New Project. The New Project Wizard opens.

3. Follow the instructions on the wizard pages that follow to begin creating the new project.

4. On the Existing Files page of the wizard, as shown in Figure 38-5, select the HTML files option to import your existing help files into the project. The HTML Files Page displays.

5. On the HTML Files page, shown in Figure 38-6, use the Add button to select the files to import. When you have selected all of the HTML files to include, select the Next button.

Figure 38-5: Using the New Project Wizard to import HTML files into a new project.

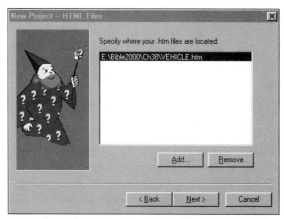

Figure 38-6: Selecting the HTML files to import into a new project.

6. When the Finish page displays, select the Finish button to create the new project. The new project displays as shown in Figure 38-7.

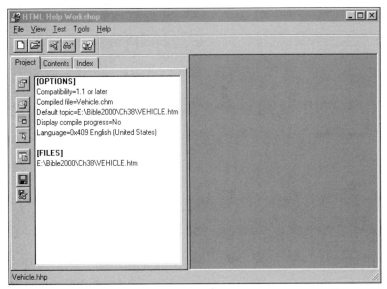

Figure 38-7: A new HTML Help Workshop project.

When you create a new project, contents, or index file, the minimum necessary settings are added automatically. The project file is divided into sections; for example, [FILES] and [OPTIONS] are included in every help project file. You can edit these sections by double-clicking the section title.

Adding graphics to a topic

Although most of your Help topics will consist primarily of text, it is often beneficial to include graphics in your Help topics. For example, if you use lots of buttons with images on them (such as toolbar images), you can display the picture with its Topic text to help the user associate the image with its function.

You can include the following types of graphics in your Help Topics: .gif, .jpg, and .png. To insert a graphic in an HTML file using Microsoft Word, do this:

1. Place the cursor where you want the graphic to appear in the topic.

2. Select Insert ⇨ Picture ⇨ From file from the menu.

3. Select the image file to insert.

Setting the Help project options

The first thing you should do when you create a new Help project is define the Options for the project. Click the Change Project Options button on the HTML Help Workshop main screen to access the project Options dialog box (see Figure 38-8).

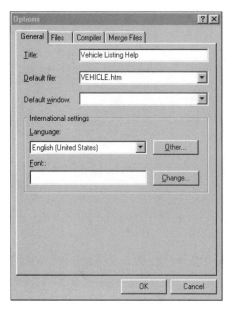

Figure 38-8: The Options dialog box is where you define parameters for your Help project, such as the title for the Help system.

Setting the General tab options

The two main tabs to be concerned with at first are the General and the Files tabs. The General tab is the tab displayed when you first click the Options button. On the General tab, you can modify these settings:

✦ Title. This is the text string that appears in the title bar of your Help system. The words "Windows Help" are used if you leave this field blank and the contents (.htm) file does not have a title specified. You should always provide a title specific to your Help program.

✦ Default File. This is the first HTML file that will open in the Help system.

Setting the Files tab options

Clicking the Files tab on the HTML Help Workshop Options dialog box displays the page used to enter information about files associated with the current project (see Figure 38-9). The information you supply on this tab is discussed next, item by item. You need to be aware, however, that you must specify the Contents file to use on this tab, or your Help system will not have a Contents! Although you may not have created the Contents file yet, you may still specify the name of the Contents file you plan to create (with full path), or you may create the Contents file first and then reopen the project and supply the name.

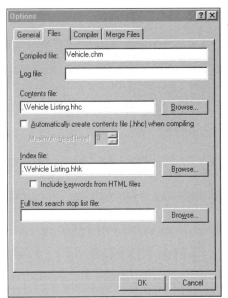

Figure 38-9: To include a Contents in your Help file, you must specify the Contents file name here.

The information you supply on the Files tab consists of the following:

✦ Compiled file. This is where you specify the name for your project when it compiles. You can name the file anything you want, as long as it has the extension .CHP. Prefixing the filename with a .\ causes the Help file to be created in the same directory as the HTML Help Workshop.

✦ Log file. You can have a text log file created when your Help project is compiled by specifying a valid filename here. This log file contains the information printed to the screen during compilation. For small projects, you may not need a log file, so you can leave this box blank. For larger projects, you may want to create a log file so you can review errors encountered when compiling the project.

✦ Contents file. You should always include a Contents for your Help project. Creating a Help Contents is discussed later in this chapter, but this is where you specify the full name and the path of the Contents file.

✦ Index file. You should also include an Index for your Help project. Creating a Help Index is discussed later in this chapter, but this is where you specify the full name and the path of the Index file. The specified Help Index must exist when you compile the Help file.

Setting up window definitions

The Help Viewer is the three-paned window in which topics will automatically appear. You never have to create a Help Viewer, but you can customize it. You can make changes to just one of the panes or all of them. Window definitions change the size of the Help Viewer window, its position, background color, and other attributes.

To specify the Help Viewer definition, follow these steps:

1. Select the Add/Modify Window Definitions button on the Project page. The Window Types dialog box displays as shown in Figure 38-10.

2. In the General tab, type a name for the window in the Window Type field, in this case type **Main**.

3. In the Title bar text field, enter an appropriate title for the Main window.

4. In the Navigation Pane tab, select the check box labeled *Window with navigation pane, topic pane, and button.*

5. Make sure that the *Search Tab* and *Auto sync* options are selected as shown in Figure 38-11.

6. Click the OK button to save the window definition.

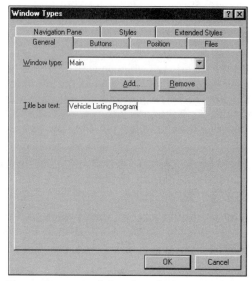

Figure 38-10: Defining the window type for the Help Viewer.

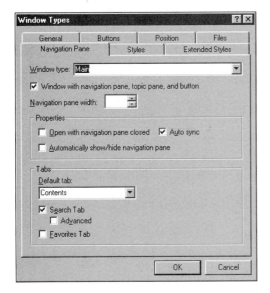

Figure 38-11: Selecting the display options for the window definition.

Adding topic files to a Project file

When you create a new project, you can automatically load existing files. If you create additional HTML files later, you can always add these to your project. You must supply at least one topic file in order to compile a Help project into a help file. To add topic files to, or remove topic files from, a Help project, use the Add/Remove Topic Files button on the HTML Help Workshop main screen (see Figure 38-12).

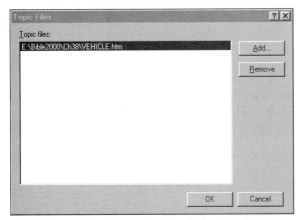

Figure 38-12: Use the Topic Files dialog box to add topics to or remove topic files from your Help project.

To add topic files to your Help project, first select the Add/Remove Topic Files button to display the Topic Files dialog box. Then follows these instructions:

1. Click the Add button.

2. Select the topic file you want to add to the Help project.

3. Click the Open button to add the topic file to the project file. Files that you add to the project appear in the Help project definition script (see Figure 38-13).

To remove a topic file from your Help project, select the Add/Remove Topic Files button to display the Topic Files dialog box, and then do the following:

1. Select the file name you want to remove from the Help project.

2. Click the Remove button.

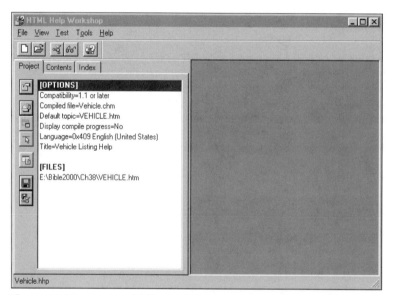

Figure 38-13: As you add files and change options, the text script that defines your Help project changes.

Saving and compiling the Project

In order to ensure that you are shipping a Help system without errors or broken links, you need to test your help. In HTML Help Workshop, the help project file compiles all of the necessary files into a compiled help (.chm) file. When you compile a Help project, all the included topic files, bitmap files, and Contents file are placed into one Help file with the extension .CHM.

The compiled help file can then be placed on your hard disk, a 3.5-inch disk, a compact disc, a server location, an Internet location, or an intranet location.

During compilation, HTML Help Workshop uses the Help project (.hhp) file to determine how HTML topic files, contents (.hhc) files, index (.hhk) files, image (.jpg, .gif, .png) files, and any other elements you have added to the project file will look in the single, compressed help file. If any errors are found during the compilation, compiler messages are generated that point a help author to the problems.

HTML Help Workshop performs these tasks during the compilation process:

> ✦ Reports missing topics or other errors in contents and index files.

> ✦ Reports broken links in topic, index, and contents files.

> ✦ Removes unnecessary white space or comments.

To save and compile the project, select the *Save all files and compile* button on the Project page. As the project compiles, a progress report displays in the right pane of the HTML Help Workshop (see Figure 38-14).

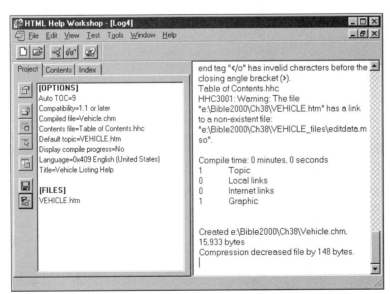

Figure 38-14: The right pane of the HTML Help Workshop displays the results of compilation.

Creating a Table of Contents

When you have finished adding all the topic files your help project will use, you need to create a Contents for your Help system. It is critical that you create a clear, concise, and comprehensive Contents to make it easy for users to locate the topics they need to get their job done.

Creating a new Help Contents file

Contents files are ASCII files saved with the extension .hhc. Contents files consist of specifications of three items:

- ✦ Headings
- ✦ Topics
- ✦ Commands

To create a new contents file using the HTML Help Workshop, follow these steps:

1. Select the Change Project Options button.

2. Select the Files tab.

3. Specify a file name for the new Contents file.

4. Select the *Automatically create contents file (.hhc) when compiling* check box, as shown in Figure 38-15. In the *Maximum head level* box, click the maximum heading level for which you want entries generated in your contents file. For example, if you click 3 for the maximum head level, entries will be generated with <H1>, <H2>, and <H3> heading tags.

5. Save and compile the project. The new Contents items display on the Contents page as shown in Figure 38-16.

Caution   If you make changes to a Contents file that has been automatically generated, you will lose them if you compile the project again. To prevent this, make sure the *Automatically create contents file when compiling* check box is cleared before you recompile.

Help Contents are just like tables of contents in books: They are essentially outlines. Headings appear with book pictures in the Help Contents. If the user clicks the book or the heading text, the Contents expands to show all items under the heading. When the HTML Help Workshop automatically creates the Contents file, it looks for text formatted as headings within the HTML files you have included in the project. The hierarchy of the HTML file's styles becomes the hierarchy of the Contents items. For example, you have formatted your HTML file title as Heading 1, and have formatted each topic under the title as Heading 2. When the HTML Help Workshop creates the Contents, it uses the Heading 1 items as Contents Headings, and the Heading 2 items as Page items under each respective heading.

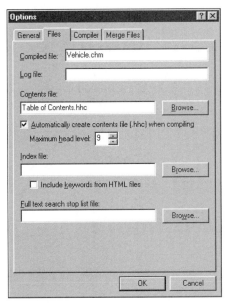

Figure 38-15: Automatically creating a Contents file.

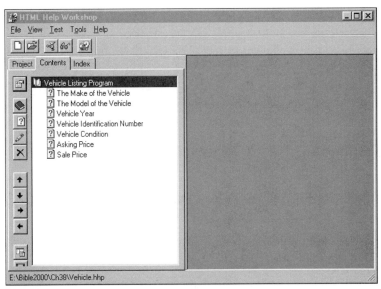

Figure 38-16: The help system's Table of Contents.

Modifying the Contents items

You can add new Contents headings and pages to the ones that were automatically generated. To add another heading entry to the Contents, follow these instructions:

1. Position the cursor in the Contents page on the item below where you want to add the new heading.

2. Select the Insert A Heading button to add the heading above the selected item in the Contents page. The Table of Contents Entry dialog box displays (see Figure 38-17).

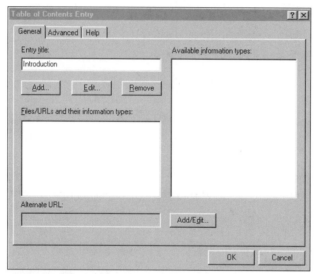

Figure 38-17: Defining a new Table of Contents heading.

3. Enter a title for the new heading.

4. Select the Add button. The Path or URL dialog box displays, as shown in Figure 38-18.

5. Select the HTML file to use for the new heading, then select the OK button. The file name displays in the Table of Contents Entry dialog box.

6. Select the OK button to create the heading.

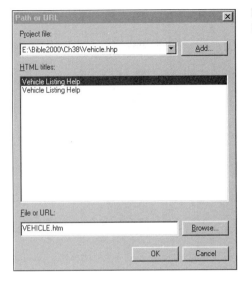

Figure 38-18: Selecting the HTML file for a new heading.

Creating a Help Index

Put yourself in the user's seat for a little while and ask yourself this question: If I needed to find this information, what keywords would I expect to find it under? In general, you should specify any and all keywords a user might use to search for each topic.

Adding keywords to an index

Topic keywords are words that are listed in the index of a Help system. These keywords are used to quickly locate Topics; finding by keywords is faster than performing a full-text search. In addition, you can create keywords that do not even appear in the text of a topic, thereby allowing for many different ways to locate a topic of interest.

Consider using the following types of keywords:

✦ Nontechnical terms that are likely to occur to a beginning user.

✦ Technical terms that are likely to occur to an advanced user.

✦ Common synonyms for technical terms.

✦ Words that describe the topic in a general manner.

✦ Words that describe specific subjects within the topic.

✦ Inverted forms of keyword phrases, such as "combining Help files" and "Help files, combining."

To add a keyword to the Index, follow these steps:

1. Select the Insert a Keyword button on the Index page. The Index Entry dialog box displays as shown in Figure 38-19.

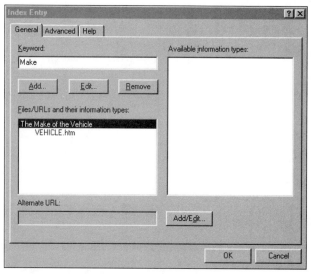

Figure 38-19: Adding a keyword to the Index.

2. Enter the keyword to include in the Keyword field, and then select the Add button. The Path or URL dialog box displays as shown in Figure 38-20.

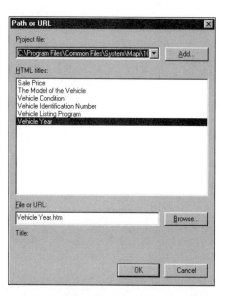

Figure 38-20: Selecting the HTML file source for the keyword.

3. Select the HTML file, or files, that contain the information for the keyword. Then select the OK button. The Index Entry dialog box displays the selected file name.

4. Select the OK button to save the new keyword.

5. Compile and save the project. Then select View Compiled File. The keyword displays in the Index page of the Help system as shown in Figure 38-21.

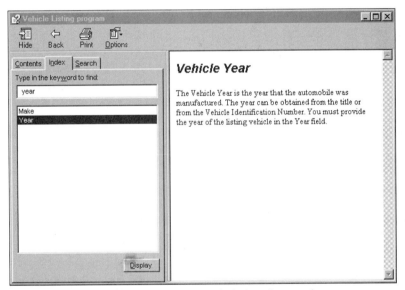

Figure 38-21: Using the Index to locate help by a keyword.

Implementing a full-text search

Index keywords allow you to connect help files to predefined search words. Often, users want to locate information on a topic that does not appear in the predefined keyword list. A powerful feature of any Help system is the capability to perform full-text searches. The Search tab of the Help system allows the user to search using any word or combination of words or letters.

Ordinarily, when a user runs your Help system and clicks the Search tab for the first time, the Find Setup Wizard appears. The wizard helps users set up a full-text search index on their computers. A full-text search index lists all the unique words in the Help file.

You can create the full-text index for your users and ship it with your Help files. The disadvantage to this technique is that it can greatly add to the disk space needed to distribute your Help file. You define your full-text search file by using the *Compile full-text search information* check box in the Help project Options dialog box Compiler tab (see Figure 38-22).

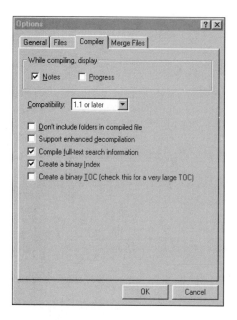

Figure 38-22: Use the Help project Options dialog box to define full-text search files.

When you compile your project with *Compile full-text search information* turned on, a full-text search (.fts) file is created for your Help system. You need to distribute this file with your Help file.

When using HTML Help Workshop, the number of topic files you can view and add is limited to 5,000. Projects with more than 5,000 files will compile correctly, and links from entries in the index and contents files will work, but you will need to use a text editor to view, add, or edit them.

Running your compiled Help file

To run your compiled Help file, click the View compiled file button on the toolbar (the button with the eyeglasses on it). When you click this button, HTML Help Workshop displays the View compiled file dialog box (see Figure 38-23). In this dialog box, you tell HTML Help Workshop what Help file to run.

Remember to save and compile your Help system whenever you make any changes.

Figure 38-23: It is very important to thoroughly test your Help file before distributing it to users.

When you have selected the compiled help file name, select the View button to run the Help file. The Help system displays (see Figure 38-24).

You can now test the contents and topic jumps in the Help file. If you click the Index tab of the Help file's main window, you see a searchable list of all the keyword index entries you created for the topics (see Figure 38-25).

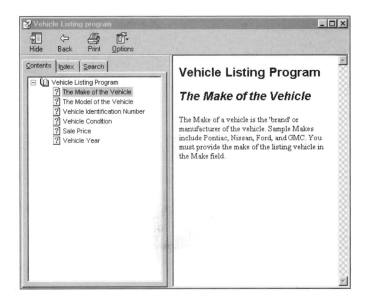

Figure 38-24:
A finished Help file showing the Contents tab.

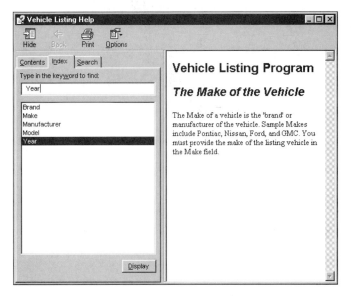

Figure 38-25:
The keywords you created for topics appear in the index for the Help file.

Integrating a Help File with Your Application

After you have created and compiled a working Help file, it's time to integrate it with your Access application. You can tie controls, forms, command buttons, and menu items to specific Help topics by using the techniques described here.

Displaying Form-Level Help

The most common way to link an application to a Help file is to link forms or specific controls to topics in the Help file. You accomplish this task in two stages: first by specifying the Help file to use and then by setting the Help Context ID property on the forms and controls. See Figure 38-26 for an example of setting the properties for the form.

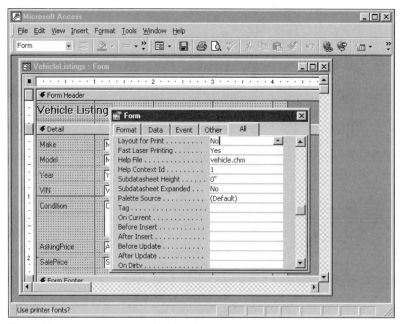

Figure 38-26: Setting up Help for a form.

You must specify the Help file name on each form in your application to prevent Access Help from displaying. If you are distributing your application with the Office 2000 Developer tools and you do not supply a Help filename, an error occurs when the user attempts to access help. If the Help file is located in a different folder than the running Access application, the Help File property on the form must include the full path to the Help file.

After you have set the Help File property on each form, you need to set the Help Context ID for the form. This should be the ID of a topic that talks about the form in general.

Displaying Control-Level Help

After you have set the form's Help Context ID, you can set the Help Context IDs of all controls. Specify a unique number for each control that will display a different topic than the topic to which the form is linked. If you do not want a control to display a unique topic, leave its Help Context ID as 0. When the control's Help Context ID is 0, the form's topic displays when the user presses F1 while the control has the focus; otherwise, the topic whose ID matches the Help Context ID of the control with the focus is displayed when the user presses F1. See Figure 38-27 for an example of setting up Help for a control.

Make sure that you set Help Context IDs for the labels as well as the controls. Some users click the text box to get help, while others click the label for the control. This way, the Help topic will display regardless of where the user attempts to locate help.

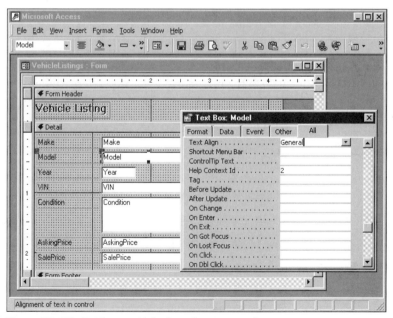

Figure 38-27: Setting up Help for a form control.

Tip   If the user presses F1 in a control that has its Help Context ID set to 0, and the form's Help Context ID is also set to 0, Access help is displayed. If your application is distributed with the Office Developer Tools, Access's Help will not be displayed and an error will occur. For this reason, you should always link each form's Help Context ID to a valid topic.

Mapping a Help Context ID to a Help Topic

Now that you have established Help Context IDs for your forms and controls, you need to map each Help Context ID to its corresponding topic in the Help file. The HTML Help Workshop provides a tool for assigning a unique number to each of your Help file's topics.

The HTMLHelp API, included in HTML Help Workshop, provides information to applications about the Help file. This information enables an application to display a help window.

Before you can use the HTMLHelp API to map your Help Context IDs, you must first create a header file. The header file establishes a link between the Help Context ID you set in the application to a symbolic ID that can be used by the HTMLHelp API.

To create the header file, follow these steps:

1. Open Notepad (or your favorite text editor).

2. Create an entry for each symbolic ID, followed by its corresponding numeric ID, using the following format:

   ```
   #define IDH_symbolicID 1000
   ```

3. You can name the symbolic ID anything you want. You should name it something that indicates the name of the topic that it refers to — VehMake, for example. The number 1000 in the previous line of code refers to the Help Context ID in your application. See Figure 38-28 for an example header file.

4. Save the file with a .h extension.

Tip   If you use an IDH prefix with the symbolic ID, as shown in the example above, HTML Help Workshop will automatically check that the topics mapped in your project file actually exist in your compiled help (.chm) file, and that your context-sensitive help topics are all mapped in your project file.

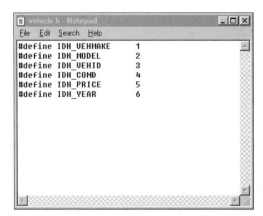

Figure 38-28: Creating a header file.

Now that you have created the header file, you can set up the HTMLHelp API to use the header file. To set up the HTML Help API, follow these steps:

1. Click the HtmlHelp API information button in the HTML Help Workshop. The HTMLHelp API dialog box displays as shown in Figure 38-29.

Figure 38-29: Setting up the HtmlHelp API information.

2. Click the Header file button in the Map page of the HTMLHelp API dialog box. The Include File dialog box displays.

3. Enter the name of the header file you created. Then select the OK button. The header file name displays in the Map page.

4. Select the Alias page of the HtmlHelp API dialog box (see Figure 38-30).

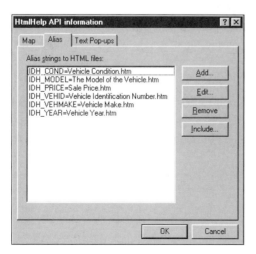

Figure 38-30: Mapping the symbolic IDs to Topics.

5. Select the Add button on the Alias page. The Alias dialog displays as shown in Figure 38-31.

6. Enter the first symbolic ID you created in the header file.

7. Select the HTML file that contains the Topic that the symbolic ID refers to. Then select the OK button.

8. Repeat the Alias definitions for each of the symbolic IDs you created in the header file.

9. When you have created all of the Alias definitions, select the OK button to save the HTMLHelp API information.

10. Save and compile the project.

Figure 38-31: Adding an HtmlHelp API map definition.

The Map page of the HTMLHelp API allows you to include the header file information in your project. The Alias definitions establish the link between the symbolic IDs and the individual Help topics in the Help system.

Testing the HTMLHelp API

Once you have defined the HtmlHelp API information, you can use the HTML Help Workshop to test the API connections. To test each API connection, follow these steps:

1. Select the Test-HtmlHelp API button in the HTML Help Workshop. The Test HtmlHelp API dialog box displays as shown in Figure 38-32.

2. In the Compiled file box, make sure the correct file displays. If not, select the current project to test. In the command field, select HH_HELP_CONTEXT. In the Map Number field, enter the Help Context ID you want to test.

3. Select the Test button. The Help Viewer displays the Topic you entered in the test dialog box.

Figure 38-32: Testing the HtmlHelp API definitions.

If you encounter problems when testing the HtmlHelp API information, use the following checklist to locate and solve the problem:

✦ Have you included the numeric ID in the header file?

✦ Have you included the proper header file in the HtmlHelp API dialog box?

✦ Does each symbolic ID you included in the header file match the alias?

✦ Is the alias mapped to the proper HTML file?

✦ Have you saved and recompiled the project?

Testing Help in Access

Now that you have created the connections between your Access application and your Help system, you should now be able to request help directly from a form in your Access application. To try out your new Access Help system, run the Access form. Then press F1 on any field for which you have set a Help Context ID. The field's Help Topic will display in the Help Viewer, as shown in Figure 38-33.

What's This? Help

Clicking the What's This button on the title bar of a form causes the question-mark mouse pointer to appear. With the question-mark pointer, you can click any control to access its custom Help topic specified by the control's Help Context ID property. If the control doesn't have a custom Help topic, the form's custom Help topic is displayed. If neither the form nor the control has a custom Help topic, Microsoft Access Help is displayed.

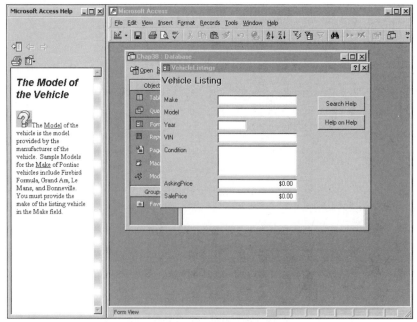

Figure 38-33: Displaying Help in an Access form.

Third-Party Help Tools

A number of tools on the market are designed specifically for creating Help files. Two of the most popular are Doc-2-Help and RoboHelp. These tools will save you days or weeks of work when creating large Help files. The only reason not to invest in one of these tools is cost; they can be rather expensive. If you need to create large, in-depth Help files, however, you should invest in a Help authoring tool.

By supplying complete, accurate Help that is fully linked with your application, you will be providing a professional program that lowers the amount of support required for the application and greatly increases the application's usability.

Summary

This chapter covered the Help system in Access 2000. You learned:

✦ The Windows Help structure.

✦ The steps involved in creating a Help system.

✦ How to integrate the Help system with your Access 2000 application.

In the next chapter, you learn to use the Microsoft Office Developer.

✦   ✦   ✦

Using the Microsoft Office Developer

CHAPTER

39

✦ ✦ ✦ ✦

In This Chapter

Defining the startup parameters of the application

Testing and Polishing the application

Creating comprehensive and intuitive menus and toolbars

Bulletproofing the application

Separating code objects from tables in the application

Documenting the application

Creating a help system for the application

Implementing a security structure for the application

Using productivity tools

Packaging and deploying the application

✦ ✦ ✦ ✦

You are indeed lucky if you have the luxury of developing only single-user, in-house applications and never have to worry about distributing an application within a company or across the country. Most developers have to worry about application distribution sooner or later. You don't have to develop commercial software to be concerned with distribution — when you develop an application to be run on a dozen workstations in one organization, you need to distribute your application.

This chapter covers all the preceding points to some degree. However, because some of the listed items, such as splitting tables and creating Help systems, are covered in detail in other chapters, this chapter focuses primarily on using the Package and Deployment Wizard in Microsoft Office 2000 Developer.

Preparing Your Application for Distribution

There are many issues to be concerned with when preparing an Access application for distribution. Distributing your application properly not only makes installing and using the application easier for the end user but also makes updating and maintaining the application easier for you. In addition, you can decrease the support required for your application by including comprehensive online help.

Defining the startup parameters of the application

An Access database has a number of startup parameters that can greatly simplify the process of preparing your database for distribution (see Figure 39-1). You can access the startup parameters for a database by selecting Tools ➪ Startup or by right-clicking the database window and selecting Startup. You can still use an Autoexec macro to execute initialization code, but the Startup parameters dialog box enables you to set up certain aspects of your application, reducing the amount of startup code you have to write. It is extremely important to set up the startup parameters correctly before distributing your Access application.

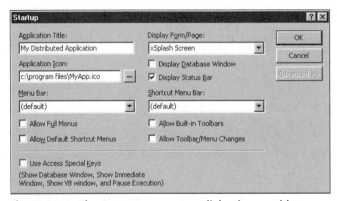

Figure 39-1: The Startup parameters dialog box enables you to take control of your application from the moment a user starts it.

Application Title

The text you provide in the Application Title box displays on the main Access title bar. You should always specify an application title for your distributed applications. If you do not, Microsoft Access appears on the title bar of your application.

Application Icon

The icon you specify in the Startup dialog box is displayed on the title bar of your application and in the task switcher (Alt+Tab) of Windows. If you do not specify your own icon, Access displays the default Access icon, so you should always provide an application-specific icon for your application. You can create small bitmaps in Windows Paint and use available conversion tools to convert a .BMP file to an .ICO file format. You can also create icons or choose from tools such as IconMaker or the Command Bar Image Editor, available in many Internet sites or from www.databasecreations.com.

Menu Bar

The Menu Bar box is used to specify a custom menu bar as the default menu bar. If you do not supply a custom menu bar, Access uses its own default menu bar, which may be inappropriate for your application.

Allow Full Menus

This setting determines whether Access displays its menus with all options available to the user or if it disables items used to create or modify objects. If you supply custom menus for all your forms and reports and set the Menu Bar property to a custom menu bar, this setting has no effect.

Tip   If you supply your own menu bars or use Access's menu bars but do not allow full menus, you must deselect Allow Built-in Toolbars or supply your own custom toolbars for each form. If you do not, the built-in toolbars may make available features to which you do not want users to have access.

Allow Default Shortcut Menus

The Allow Default Shortcut Menus setting determines whether or not Access displays its own default shortcut menus when a user left-clicks an object.

Display Form

The form you select in this field displays automatically when your application is run. When the form loads, the Form Load event fires if there is any code in it, eliminating the need to use an Autoexec macro. You should consider using a splash screen (discussed later in this chapter) as your startup Display Form.

Display Database Window

With most distributed applications, you may never want your users to have direct access to any of your forms or other database objects. Deselecting this option hides the Database Window from the user at startup. Unless you also deselect the option Use Access Special Keys (discussed later), users can press F11 or select Window ➪ Unhide to unhide the database window.

Display Status Bar

You can deselect the Display Status Bar option to completely remove the status bar from the screen. However, the status bar is an incredibly informative and easy-to-use tool; it displays the various key-states automatically, as well as displaying status bar text for the active control. Instead of hiding the status bar, you should make full use of it and only disable it if you have a very good reason to do so.

Shortcut Menu Bar

This setting is similar to the Menu Bar option discussed previously, except it enables you to specify a menu bar to use as the default shortcut menu bar when a user right-clicks an object. Using custom shortcut menus that have functionality specific to your application is always preferable.

Allow Built-in Toolbars

Deselecting this option prevents Access from displaying any of its built-in toolbars. In general, you should always deselect this option and provide your own custom toolbars that you can display using the Toolbar property for the form.

Allow Toolbar/Menu Changes

Deselecting this option prevents users from modifying either Access's built-in toolbars or your own toolbars, whichever you choose to use. Once again, you almost always want to deselect this item to prevent your users from gaining access to features that you do not want them to have.

Use Access Special Keys

If you select this option, users of your application can use keys specific to the Access environment to circumvent some security measures, such as unhiding the database window. If you deselect this option, the following keys are disabled:

- ✦ **F11 and Alt+F1** — These keys show the database window if it is hidden and bring it to the front.
- ✦ **Ctrl+G** — This key displays the Immediate window.
- ✦ **Ctrl+Break** — In Access projects, this key causes Access to stop retrieving records from the server database.
- ✦ **Ctrl+F11** — This key is used to toggle between using a custom menu bar for a form and using a built-in menu bar.

You should always deselect this option when distributing the application.

Using the Startup options saves you many lines of code that you would ordinarily need to perform the same functions and enables you to control your application's interface from the moment the user starts it. Always verify the Startup options before distributing your application.

Testing the application before distribution

After you finish adding features and have everything in place within your application, you need to take some time to thoroughly test the application. Testing may sound obvious, but this step apparently is overlooked by many developers and is evident by the amount of buggy software appearing on the shelves of your local software stores. If you don't believe this to be true, check out the software support forums on the Internet; almost every major commercial software application has some patch available or known bugs that need to be addressed.

Distributing an application that is 100 percent bug free is almost impossible. The nature of the beast in software development is that if you write a program, someone can and will find a way to break it. Specific individuals even seem to have a black cloud above their heads and can usually break an application (hit a critical bug) within minutes of using it. If you know of such people, hire them! They can be a great asset when testing your application.

While working through the debugging process of an application, categorize your bugs into one of three categories:

✦ **Category 1: Major ship-sinking bug.** These bugs are absolutely unacceptable, such as numbers in an accounting application that don't add up the way they should or a routine that consistently causes the application to terminate unexpectedly. If you ship an application with known Category 1 bugs, prepare yourself for a lynch party from your customers!

✦ **Category 2: Major bug that has a workaround.** Category 2 bugs are fairly major bugs, but they do not stop users from performing their tasks. For instance, a toolbar button that does not call a procedure correctly is a bug. If the toolbar button is the only way to run the procedure, this bug is a Category 1 bug. If, however, a corresponding menu item calls the procedure correctly, the bug is a Category 2 bug. Shipping an application with a Category 2 bug is sometimes necessary. Although shipping a bug is officially a no-no, deadlines sometimes dictate that exceptions need to be made. Category 2 bugs will annoy your users but should not send them into fits.

If you ship an application with known Category 2 bugs, document them! Some developers have a don't-say-anything-and-act-surprised attitude when users find a Category 2 bug. This attitude can frustrate users and waste considerable amounts of their time by forcing them to discover not only the problem but also the solution. For example, if you were to ship an application with the Category 2 bug just described, you could include a statement in your application's README file that reads something like this:

The foobar button on the XYZ form does not correctly call procedure suchandsuch. Please use the corresponding menu item suchandsuch found on the Tools menu. A patch will be made available as soon as possible.

✦ **Category 3: Small bugs and minor nits.** Category 3 bugs are small issues that in no way affect the workings of your application. They may be misspellings of captions or incorrect colors of text boxes. Category 3 bugs should be fixed whenever possible but should never take precedence over Category 1 bugs, and they should take precedence over Category 2 bugs only when they are so extreme that the application looks completely unacceptable.

By categorizing your bugs and approaching them systematically, you can create a program that looks and behaves as its users think it should. Sometimes you may feel like you will never finish your Category 1 list, but you will. You will surely be smiling the day you check your bug sheet and realize that you're down to a few Category 2s and a dozen or so Category 3s! Although you may be tempted to skip this beta testing phase of development, don't. You will only pay for it in the long run.

Tip   Not all Access features are available when an application is run within the Access runtime environment (discussed with the Setup Wizard later in this chapter). You can operate in the runtime environment and use the full version of Access to test for problems with your code and with the runtime environment by using the /Runtime command line option when starting your Access application. Click Run on the Windows Start menu or create a shortcut. The following example command line starts Access and opens the Invoices database in the runtime environment:

```
C:\OFFICE2000\ACCESS\MSACCESS.EXE /RUNTIME
C:\MYAPPS\INVOICES.MDB
```

You should always test and debug your application in the runtime environment if you plan to distribute the application with the Office 2000 Developer Package and Deployment Wizard.

Polishing your application

When your application has been thoroughly tested and appears ready for distribution, spend some time polishing your application. Polishing your application consists of

✦ Giving your application a consistent look and feel

✦ Adding common, professional components

✦ Adding clear and concise pictures to buttons

✦ Using common, understandable field labels and button captions

Giving your application a consistent look and feel

First and foremost, you should decide on some design standards and apply them to your application. This is incredibly important if you want your application to look professionally produced. Figure 39-2 shows a form with samples of different styles of controls.

You must make design decisions such as the following:

✦ Will text boxes be sunken, flat with a border, flat without a border, chiseled, or raised?

✦ What backcolor will the text boxes be?

✦ What color will the forms be?

✦ Will you use chiseled borders to separate related items or opt for a sunken or raised border?

✦ What size will buttons on forms be?

✦ For forms that have similar buttons, such as Close and Help, in what order will the buttons appear?

✦ Which accelerator keys will you use on commonly used buttons such as Close and Help?

Making your application look and work in a consistent manner is the single most important thing you can do to make it appear professional. For ideas on design standards to implement in your applications, spend some time working with some of your favorite programs and see what standards they use. In the area of look and feel, copying from another developer is generally not considered plagiarism but rather often looked upon as a compliment. Copying does not extend, however, to making use of another application's icons or directly copying the look and feel of a competitor's product; this is very bad practice. An example of a good look-and feel-environment is provided by the Microsoft Office Compatible program.

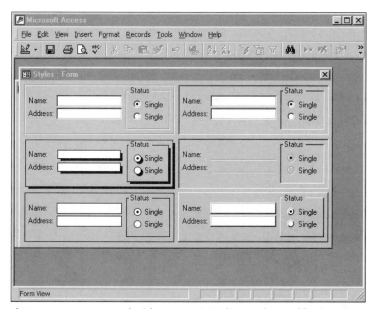

Figure 39-2: You can decide on any interface style you like for your application. However, once you decide on a style, use it consistently.

An application may be certified Office Compatible by meeting certain user-interface requirements laid out by Microsoft Corporation. An Office-compatible application uses the same menu structures as all the Office applications such as Word, Access, Excel, and so on. In addition, toolbars are also similar and, where applicable, the same button image as Microsoft uses. Making an application look like an Office application results in the benefits of saving the developer time, by giving clear and concise guidelines for interface features, and helping end users, by lowering the learning curve of the application.

Although you may not want to have your application independently tested and certified Office Compatible, you may want to check out the specifications and use some of the ideas presented to help you get started designing your own consistent application interfaces.

Adding common professional components

Most commercial/professional applications have some similar components. The most common components are the splash screen, about box, and switchboard. Be aware that the splash screen, an example of which is shown in Figure 39-3, not only aids in increasing perceived speed of an application but also gives the application a polished, professional appearance from the moment a user runs the program. Figure 39-4 shows the implementation of Database Creation's splash screen.

Figure 39-3: A splash screen not only increases perceived speed of your application but also gives your application a professional appearance.

Figure 39-4 shows the design window for a splash screen template that you can use when building your own applications. This form is included in the database Ch39Gold.mdb on the CD-ROM that comes with this book. Import this form into your application and use it as a template for creating your own splash screen.

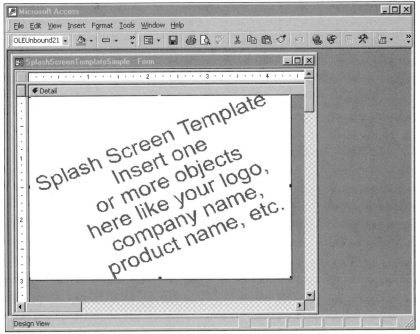

Figure 39-4: Use this form as a template to create your own splash screens for your applications.

Your splash screen should contain the following items:

✦ The application's title

✦ The application's version number

✦ Your company information

✦ A copyright notice

In addition, you may want to include the licensee information and/or a picture on the splash screen. If you use a picture on your splash screen, make it relevant to your application's function. For example, some coins and an image of a check could be used for a check writing application. If you like, you can use clip art for your splash screen; just be sure that the picture is clear and concise and doesn't interfere with the text information presented on your splash screen.

To implement the splash screen, have your application load the splash form before it does anything else (consider making your splash screen the Startup Display Form). When your application finishes all its initialization procedures, close the form. Make the splash form a light form and be sure to convert any bitmaps you place on your splash screen to pictures to decrease the splash form's load time.

The second component that you should implement is an application switchboard. The switchboard is the steering wheel for users to find their way throughout the functions and forms available in the application. You can use the switchboard itself as a data entry form, as in the switchboard example shown in Figure 39-5. You can also use a command button to display another form.

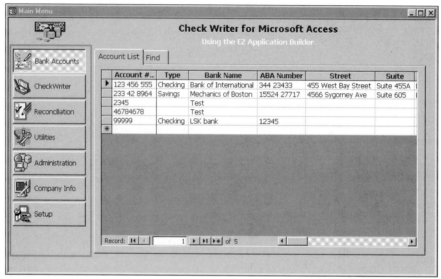

Figure 39-5: The switchboard provides a handy way to navigate throughout the application.

Make sure that whenever the user closes a form, the switchboard redisplays. The switchboard provides a familiar place where the user can be assured he or she won't become lost in the application.

The second component that you should implement is an about box (see Figure 39-6). The about box should contain your company and copyright information, as well as the application name and current version. Including your application's licensee information (if you keep such information) in the about box is a good idea as well. The about box serves as legal notice of your ownership and makes your application easier to support by giving your users easy access to the version information. Some advanced about boxes call other forms that display system information (Figure 39-6 has an additional button — System Info). You can make the about boxes as fancy as you want, but usually a simple one works just fine.

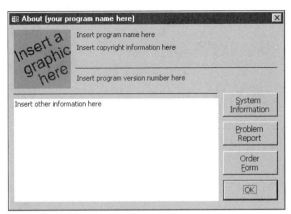

Figure 39-6: The implementation of an about box is a polishing technique that also provides useful information to the user and protects your legal interests.

Most users love pictures, and most developers love to use pictures on buttons. Studies have shown that clear and concise pictures are more intuitive to understand and are more easily recognizable than textual captions. Most developers, however, are not graphic artists and usually slap together buttons made from any clipart images that are handy. These ugly buttons make an application look clumsy and unprofessional. In addition, pictures that do not clearly show the function of the button make the application harder to use.

Select or create pictures that end users easily recognize. Avoid abstract pictures or pictures that require specific knowledge to understand them, such as wiring symbology. If your budget permits, consider hiring a professional design firm to create your button pictures. A number of professional image galleries and a number of tools to create and edit buttons are available.

Tip A great third-party library of pictures specifically designed for Microsoft Access is the Picture Builder Add-On Picture Pack (3000 .BMP pictures specifically sized for buttons) and the Command Bar Image Editor to edit and resize pictures. These are available from Database Creations (www.databasecreations.com).

Well-thought-out picture buttons can really make your application look outstanding, as well as easier to use.

On the
CD-ROM
The form shown in Figure 39-7 is a template about box that can be found in the database Ch39Gold.mdb on the CD-ROM that accompanies this book. Import this form into your application and customize it to fit your needs. The about box should be a modal form (it should keep the focus until the form is closed) and should not have minimize or maximize buttons available to the user.

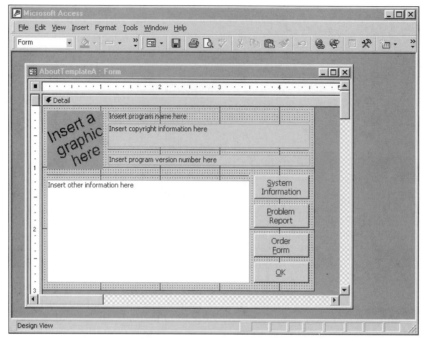

Figure 39-7: You can import and customize this about box template form to meet your needs.

The about box should be accessible from a Help menu on all menu bars. The submenu title should be About MyApplication. Of course, substitute *Your program name here* with your application's actual name.

The splash screen, about box, and switchboard may seem trivial, but they can greatly enhance your application's appeal. They take little time to implement and should be included in all your distributed applications.

Creating comprehensive and intuitive menus and toolbars

Before you even consider distributing an application, you need to make the application as intuitive as possible. Menus and toolbars are absolutely vital for usability with any Windows application.

Bulletproofing an application

Bulletproofing your application is an additional stage that should be completed parallel with debugging and performed again after the application is working and debugged. Bulletproofing an application is the process of making the application idiot-proof. It involves trapping errors that can be caused by users, such as invalid data entry, attempting to run a function when the application is not ready to run the function, and allowing users to click a Calculate button before all needed data has been entered.

Using error trapping on all VBA procedures

An error handling routine provides a chance for you to display a friendlier message to the user other than some unintuitive default message box like the one shown in Figure 39-8.

Figure 39-8: A error message resulting from a procedure with no error handling routine.

One of the most important elements of bulletproofing an application is making sure that the application never crashes — that is, never ceases operation completely and unexpectedly. Although Access provides built-in error processing for most data entry errors, characters entered into a currency field for example, there is no automatic processing for VBA code errors. You should include error handling routines in every VBA procedure, even if you use just `On Error Resume Next`.

When running an application distributed with the Office Developer Package and Deployment Wizard, any untrapped error encountered in your code causes the program to terminate completely. Your users cannot recover from such a crash, and serious data loss may occur. Your users have to restart the application after such an application error.

Separating the code objects from the tables in the application

You should separate your code objects (forms, reports, queries, modules, and macros) from your table objects. Many benefits are gained from distributing these objects in separate .MDB files:

✦ Network users benefit from speed increases by running the code .MDB (the database containing the queries, forms, macros, reports, and modules) locally and accessing only the shared data on the network.

✦ Updates can easily be distributed to users.

✦ Data can be backed up more efficiently because only one file is needed to back up, and disk space and time are not used to continuously back up the code objects.

All professionally distributed applications, especially those intended for network use, should have separate code and data database (.MDB) files.

Documenting the application

Most developers dislike writing documentation; it's simply no fun and can be quite frustrating and time-consuming. However, taking the time and effort now to prepare thorough documentation can save hours of technical support time down the road. Even if you do not plan to distribute a full user's manual, take time to document how to perform the most common functions in your application. If you have created shortcuts, make sure to share them with the users.

Creating a help system

Although documentation is extremely important for getting users started with your application, well-written and thorough context-sensitive help is just as important. Help puts pertinent and informative information at users' disposal with just a click of the mouse or a push of a button.

Implementing a security structure

The final item to consider before distributing your application is the level at which you wish to secure your application. You can secure specific individual objects or secure your entire application. If it is important to you to secure design permissions for all your objects to protect your source code, you need to be aware that you cannot rely solely on Microsoft's word that the security in Access works. The security model of Access 2.0 was touted by Microsoft as being the most secure available. It was discovered that an average Access developer can unsecure an Access 2.0 database in about five minutes, with only minimum coding! Although no method for unsecuring a secured Access 97 or Access 2000 application has yet been discovered, a method may be uncovered in the future. You must understand and accept this risk when you distribute a secured Access application.

Using VBA Productivity Tools to Streamline the Development Environment

Office 2000 Developer provides several new tools that can help you create efficient and bomb-proof VBA programs. These tools can be integrated into the VBA development environment, enabling you to develop better code in less time.

What is Office 2000 Developer?

Office 2000 Developer replaces the Office Developer Edition Tools, or ODE Tools, available with earlier versions of Office. Office Developer is the edition of Office geared for Office 2000 developers building professional applications. When you purchase Office 2000 Developer, you get Microsoft Office Premium edition along with a rich set of productivity tools.

The new Office Developer features include the following:

✦ **COM Add-in Designer** allows developers to create and debug stand-alone VBA COM add-ins (DLL's) without having to leave the VBA development environment.

✦ **Microsoft Visual SourceSafe** delivers version control and code management tools that professional developers need to manage source code in team and individual development environments.

✦ **VBA Error Handler** automates creating standardized error handler code with input dialog boxes that capture basic information and insert standardized error handling code using a customizable template.

✦ **VBA Code Commenter** creates well-commented code by automatically adding comments and headers to procedures using customizable templates.

✦ **Code Librarian** provides a centralized repository for prewritten code that can be reused across development teams.

✦ **VBA Multi-Code Import/Export** enables you to easily copy Office objects from one project to another.

✦ **VBA String Editor** makes it easier to create strings to embed long scripts or complicated SQL statements into VBA code.

✦ **VBA WinAPI Viewer** enables you to browse through Declares, Constants, and Types that are included in a Text API file or a Jet database.

✦ **VBA Source Code Control** provides check in/check out, versioning, history, and other important source code management functions for use in the Visual Basic for Applications environment.

✦ **VBA Package and Deployment Wizard** helps you create installation packages for your Office 2000 and VBA applications and install them on your users' computers.

Installing the VBA productivity tools

The Office Developer VBA productivity tools are offered as wizards and add-ins. Wizards and add-ins are extensions that you can add to your VBA development environment to simplify the many tasks involved in developing an application. Because these wizards and add-ins are available only through the Office Developer, they are not installed through the normal Access and VBA installation process. You must install them using the Add-In Manager.

To install an add-in, follow these steps:

1. Select Add-Ins ➪ Add-In Manager from the menu. The Add-In Manager dialog box displays as shown in Figure 39-9.

Figure 39-9: Using the VBA Add-In Manager to install an add-in.

2. Highlight an add-in from the list and click the desired behaviors in Load Behavior. To unload an add-in or prevent it from loading, clear all Load Behavior boxes.

3. When you are finished making your selections, click OK. The Add-Ins menu displays the tools you selected to load as shown in Figure 39-10.

Depending on your Load Behavior selections, Visual Basic connects the selected add-ins and disconnects the cleared add-ins. Visual Basic saves your add-in selections between editing sessions.

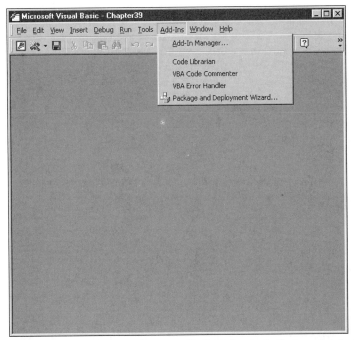

Figure 39-10: The Add-ins menu displays the tools that are loaded.

Creating distribution disks using the Office Developer Package and Deployment Wizard

When you finish your application, you need to find a way to distribute it to your customers. Distribution includes delivering all files necessary to run your application on some form of media, such as floppy disk or CD-ROM, or via electronic distribution channels such as the Internet. The media should include some sort of setup program that automates copying the files to the user's computer, sets up any shortcut items, registers necessary controls, and sets values in the system registry. The Office Developer Package and Deployment Wizard guides you through the process of building the distribution program.

You may be thinking, What if my users do not own Access? When you distribute your application with the Package and Deployment Wizard, end users can run your application using the Access runtime environment without needing to purchase a full version of Access. The Package and Deployment Wizard makes it easy to package and distribute all of the necessary runtime files. This is all (mostly) transparent to users; they do not realize that Access is running in the background. Certain design interfaces are hidden from users so that they cannot create Access applications with the runtime executable. Purchasing Office Developer gives you the licensing rights to distribute your application with the runtime environment to an unlimited number of users, with no royalty fees! So, even if you plan to create your setup program with a third-party tool, you need to purchase one copy of Office Developer for the legal rights to distribute your application with the runtime files.

Tip Note that the runtime version of Access can't be used to open .adp or .ade files; however, you can use the Packaging and Deployment Wizard to create a setup program to distribute .adp or .ade files to users who already have the full version of Access installed.

When you distribute your application using the Package and Deployment Wizard, you can configure your custom Setup program to do the following:

✦ Copy your application's files to specified locations on a user's hard disk.

✦ Create Windows shortcuts that start your application or program files.

✦ Add Windows Registry keys and entries for your application.

✦ Group files, shortcuts, and registry keys and entries into components that users can select to install or uninstall.

✦ Install other Access files, such as drivers for accessing various data sources and any .OCX custom controls used by your application.

✦ Run an application or open a file after the Setup program is finished installing your application.

Restrictions of the Package and Deployment Wizard

The Access runtime environment is an excellent (and currently the only) way to distribute your applications to users who do not own a licensed copy of Microsoft Access. As stated earlier, the Access runtime is almost transparent to the user. Unfortunately, some limitations do exist with the release version of the Office Developer. Some of these issues affect the behavior of your application; some are problems inherent in the Package and Deployment Wizard itself. You need to be aware of the limitations, and you probably want to make your end users aware of some of them as well.

Some key points and pitfalls to be aware of when designing your setup routine include the following:

✦ Runtime applications that do not include custom help files generate errors when referring to the Access help file. As stated earlier, you should always attempt to distribute applications with help systems. Even a rudimentary help system is better than no online help at all.

Tip If you elect not to ship a help file with your application, you can avoid Access generating an error by not providing a Help menu item on any of your custom menus and by creating an Autokeys Macro that traps the F1 key. The F1 key does not have to do anything in the macro. Simply including it in the Autokeys macro causes the macro to trap the F1 key when it is pressed. This prevents it from being passed to the Access runtime, calling up the help file.

✦ Attempting to close a runtime application with the `CloseCurrentDatabase` method generates an error. The runtime version of Access does not run without an application loaded and therefore generates the error if you attempt to close the current database. To terminate your application, use the `Quit` method of the `DoCmd` object.

✦ Uninstalling Microsoft Access 2000 breaks applications installed with a custom Setup program. Unfortunately, Access's uninstall program does not know when a runtime Access application is installed on the computer, and it changes registry settings that are crucial to running your runtime Access application.

Tip You should include the file MSARNREG.EXE in your list of files to distribute. This file is located in C:\PROGRAM FILES\COMMON FILES\MICROSOFT SHARED\MICRO-SOFT ACCESS RUNTIME folder under Windows and in the C:\WINDOWS\MSAPPS\ MICROSOFT ACCESS RUNTIME folder on Windows NT /2000 machines. The file installs when you install the ODE Tools on your computer. This program fixes the registration database so that your Access runtime application works again. You will want to document the program for your users, and you may want to consider creating a shortcut or adding a menu item to your start menu to run the program.

✦ The Package and Deployment Wizard does not support Administrative (setup /a) and Run From Network Server installations. Performing a network installation places all the Setup files onto a server drive so that all workstations on the network can run the Setup program from the server rather than from floppy disk. If you distribute your application to run in a network environment, instruct your users to copy all files from each disk in the distribution set to the same directory on the network and then run the Setup program in this directory from each workstation.

✦ Reinstalling your application with the custom Setup program fails if the user has performed a Maintenance Removal of Workgroup Administrator. A user can do this by rerunning the Setup program and deselecting the Workgroup Administrator component (discussed later). If a user removes the Workgroup Administrator component and attempts to reinstall your Access runtime application, the installation fails. Attempting to run the Setup program again after the failure results in a successful installation.

Tip   You can prevent end users from removing the Workgroup Administrator component by setting the component to Hidden on the Components page of the Setup Wizard. This setting is discussed later in this chapter.

✦ Very large components (+100MB) show negative numbers in your custom setup program. This bug does not affect the installation or workings of your setup routine, but it may confuse end users. Most developers almost never have components this large. However, if you experience this problem, consider breaking the offending component into smaller components.

✦ Removing the component in single-component setup does not remove the entire application. There is no workaround for this. If users want to remove the application completely, they must use the Remove All button.

The Package and Deployment Wizard is unable to use exclusively locked files. If you try to add a file in the wizard that is exclusively locked by another user or another application, the wizard responds with an application-defined or object-defined error. When users trigger this error, Access cancels the creation of your custom Setup program disk images. When creating disk images with the Package and Deployment Wizard, you should close all possible applications in order to avoid potential lock conflicts.

Using the Package and Deployment Wizard to create distribution disks

The Visual Basic Package and Deployment Wizard makes it easy for you to create the necessary .cab files and setup programs for your application. Like other wizards, the Package and Deployment Wizard prompts you for information so that it can create the exact configuration you want.

Tip   Any time you create a package, you should be sure that the version number for your project has been set on the Make tab of the Project Properties dialog box. This is especially important if you are distributing a new version of an existing application: Without the appropriate change in version numbers, the end user's computer may determine that critical files do not need to be updated.

Setting up the Package and Deployment Wizard

1. Open the project you want to package or deploy using the wizard.

Note If you are working in a project group or have multiple projects loaded, make sure that the project you want to package or deploy is the current project before starting the wizard.

2. Use the Add-In Manager to load the Package and Deployment Wizard, if necessary: Select Add-In Manager from the Add-Ins menu, select Package and Deployment Wizard from the list, and then click OK.

Creating a package

Once you have loaded the Package and Deployment Wizard add-in into your project workspace, you are ready to begin the process of creating a setup routine for your application.

1. Select Package and Deployment Wizard from the Add-Ins menu to launch the wizard. The first screen of the Package and Deployment wizard displays as shown in Figure 39-11.

Figure 39-11: The first page of the Package and Deployment Wizard enables you to select between packaging, deploying, or managing a script for the project.

The Package option helps you package a project's files into a .cab file that can then be deployed, and in some cases creates a setup program that installs the .cab files. The wizard determines the files you need to package and leads you through all the choices that must be made in order to create one or more .cab files for your project.

The Deploy option helps you deliver your packaged applications to the appropriate distribution media, such as floppies, a shared network installation, or a Web site.

The Manage Scripts option lets you view and manipulate the scripts you have saved from previous packaging and deployment sessions in the wizard. Each time you use the wizard, you save a script that contains all the choices you made. You can reuse these scripts in later sessions if you want to use similar settings and make the same choices as you did previously.

2. Select Package to create a package for the selected project. The Package Type page of the wizard displays as shown in Figure 39-12.

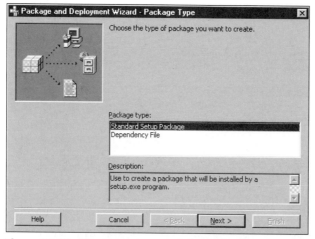

Figure 39-12: The second page of the Package and Deployment Wizard enables you to select the type of package to create.

A standard package is a package that is designed to be installed by a setup.exe program. You create standard packages for Windows-based applications that will be distributed through disks, CD, or over a network.

A dependency (.dep) file contains information about the runtime requirements of an application or component — for example, which files are needed, how they are to be registered, and where on the user's machine they should be installed.

3. Select Standard Setup Package, then select the Next button. The Package Folder page of the wizard displays as shown in Figure 39-13.

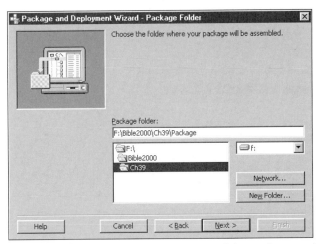

Figure 39-13: The Package Folder page of the Package and Deployment Wizard enables you to specify the location for the package files.

The Package Folder page lets you choose the location, on a local or network drive, where the wizard should place the files for your packaged solution. This is a temporary staging area for your package, prior to deployment. After packaging is complete, you will use the deployment portion of the wizard to move your package from the package folder to its final location.

4. Select the drive and directory for the package files, then select the Next button. The Included Files page displays as shown in Figure 39-14.

The Included Files page displays a list of the files that will be included in the package and enables you to add additional files to the package or to remove unwanted files. The Include Access Runtime option allows you to distribute the runtime files in your setup routine. The Files list shows the filenames that will be packaged. You can deselect any file that you do not wish to include. Notice that a ToolTip displays over each filename describing the purpose of each file.

5. Select the Next button. The Cab Options page displays as shown in Figure 39-15.

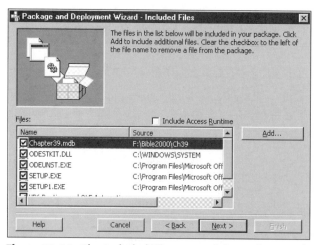

Figure 39-14: The Included Files page of the Package and Deployment Wizard enables you to verify the files to be included in the setup routine.

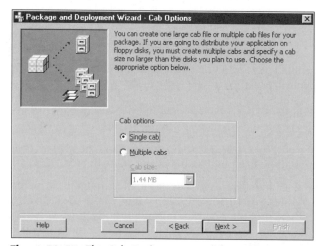

Figure 39-15: The Cab Options page of the Package and Deployment Wizard enables you to create one large file or many smaller files.

The Cab Options page of the wizard enables you to choose whether the wizard creates one large .cab file for your package or a series of smaller .cab files that break your package into a series of manageable units. If you are planning to deploy using floppy disks, you must choose the Multiple cabs option. If you are planning to deploy using any other method, such as the network, a CD, or the Internet, you can choose either the Single cab or Multiple cabs option, depending on your preferences.

A .cab, or cabinet file, is a file that acts as a container for other files. It serves as a compressed archive for a group of files. Typically, .cab files are used as a way of compressing files for installation on a user's machine. You compress all your control, component, or application's files into one or more .cab files and distribute those to your users. The user's computer decompresses the .cab file and installs your component.

6. Select the Single cab option, and then select the Next button. The Installation Options page displays as shown in Figure 39-16.

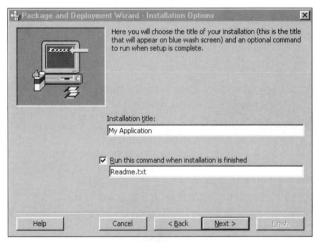

Figure 39-16: Use the Installation Options page to customize the installation screen.

In the Installation Options page, you can specify a title for your installation welcome screen. Optionally, you can also specify a command to run when the installation completes.

7. Enter a title for the application, and then select the Next button. The Start Menu Items page displays as shown in Figure 39-17.

In the Start Menu Items page, you specify the Start menu groups and group items that should be created on the user's computer during installation of your solution. You can create groups and items for your solution in one of two locations: on the main level of the Start menu, or within the Programs subdirectory of the Start menu.

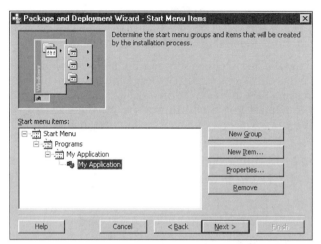

Figure 39-17: Specifying where to place the Start menu icon.

In addition to creating new Start menu groups and items, you can edit the properties for an existing item, or you can remove groups and items.

8. Make your Start Menu selections, and then select the Next button. The Install Locations page displays as shown in Figure 39-18.

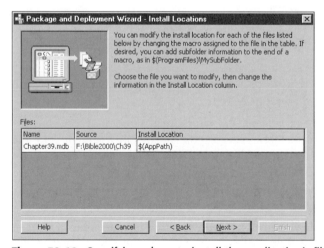

Figure 39-18: Specifying where to install the application's files.

Use the Install Locations page to change the location where your project files will be installed on the user's computer. You can choose from a series of predefined folder variables that indicate installation locations on the user's machine:

- **$(AppPath)** — This folder is designated by the user running your custom Setup program. Think of AppPath as being a variable used to specify the user-selected folder. Your main application database should always be placed in the AppPath folder. In addition, you should always place your help files with the application files, so the help files should also have AppPath specified as their destination folder.

- **$(WinPath)** — This is the Windows folder on the user's machine. Once again, think of WinPath as a variable. At runtime, the Wizard determines in what folder Windows resides and places all files that have WinPath as their destination folder in that Windows folder. You should generally avoid placing a file in the Windows folder unless that file is an update to a file that already resides in the Windows folder.

- **$(WinSysPath)** — This folder is the System folder found below the Windows folder. WinSysPath is similar to WinPath in that at runtime the Setup Wizard resolves where the Windows System folder resides and places the appropriate files there. You should place .DLL and .OCX files in the system folder because these files are common components. Avoid placing application-specific files in the System folder.

- **$(ProgramFiles)** — This folder is the folder where application files are usually installed (that is, C:\Program Files).

- **$(CommonFiles)** — Where shared files are usually installed (for example, C:\Program Files\Common Files).

- **$(MSDAOPath)** — Location that is stored in the registry for Data Access Objects (DAO) components. You should not use this for your files.

Although not immediately apparent, you are not limited to placing your files in only these folders. You may also specify a subfolder below your AppPath folder. To do this, use the following syntax:

```
$(AppPath)\subfolder
```

Replace the word `subfolder` with the actual folder name. For example, if you want to create a folder called DATA under your main application folder, specify the following folder as the destination folder: When the Setup program is complete, it informs

```
$(AppPath)\DATA
```

The Setup Wizard determines the AppPath folder name at runtime by letting the user specify the folder. It then creates the folder if it does not currently exist and creates any subfolders specified in the `Destination Folder` property of included files.

Tip   If you include a large number of files and offer many components for installation, consider grouping the files or components into subfolders. Grouping makes future updates much easier and makes your application component architecture easier to understand when troubleshooting — if you need to replace a file for component A, you know in which subfolder to look. Keeping only the main application files in the application folder is best whenever possible.

9. Choose the Install Locations for your application, then select the Next button. The Shared Files page displays as shown in Figure 39-19.

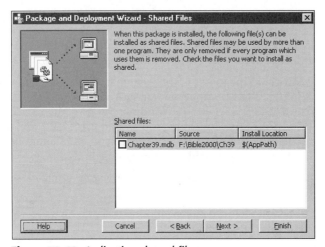

Figure 39-19: Indicating shared files.

The selections you indicate on the Shared Files page determine which files to install as shared. A *shared file* is one that can be used by other applications on the user's machine. Such a file will not be removed when the user uninstalls your application if any other applications that use the file still exist on the computer.

The system determines the files that can be shared by looking at the installation location you have indicated. Any files can be shared except those that are installed as system files. All files that are not marked to be installed into the $(WinSysPath) directory have the potential to be shared.

10. Select any files that should be installed as shared files, then select the Next button. The Finished page displays as shown in Figure 39-20.

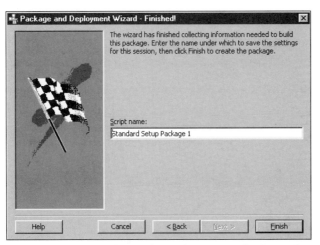

Figure 39-20: Completing the Package Wizard information.

The Package and Deployment Wizard has collected the information necessary to begin building your package. When you click Finish, the Package and Deployment Wizard saves the settings you chose as a script. Scripts serve three purposes:

- A script enables you to package the project again later, using the same settings.

- A script provides a way of identifying a package for deployment purposes. When you begin the deployment portion of the wizard, the first step will ask you to select a package to deploy. Packages are referred to by the script name they were given in the packaging process.

- A script allows you to package your project in silent mode. When you run the wizard in silent mode, you must give the wizard the name of a script that it should use.

Tip You should assign your script a descriptive name that will make it easy to recognize later in the process.

11. Select the Finish button to complete the package. The Package Wizard will create the .CAB files. When the Package Wizard has finished creating the files, the Packaging Report window displays as shown in Figure 39-21.

The Packaging Report window confirms that the .CAB package file was created and indicates the directory where it is located. The Packaging Report also lists any other files that were created along with a description of each file.

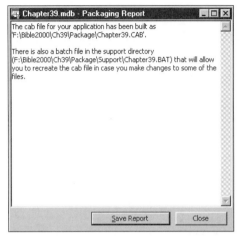

Figure 39-21: Displaying the results of the Package Wizard.

12. When you are finished reviewing the summary information, select the Close button. When you close the Packaging Report window, the initial screen of the Package and Deployment wizard redisplays.

Deploying an application

The Package Wizard allows you to identify the files to install and how you want them to be loaded into the user's environment. Then the Package Wizard combines all the files and information into one or more .cab files. These .cab files, however, are not executable. The Deployment Wizard uses the package files to create an executable file that users can run to install the application. The executable file is created in a folder that you specify.

1. Select Deploy from the initial page of the Package and Deployment Wizard. If the Package and Deployment Wizard is not open, follow Step 1 in the section "Creating a package." The Package to Deploy page displays as shown in Figure 39-22.

The Package to Deploy page of the Package and Deployment Wizard enables you to choose the package you want to deploy. Each package displayed in the list is identified by the name of the corresponding packaging script. Only packages for the current project are shown.

2. Select the package to deploy, and then select the Next button. The Deployment Method page displays as shown in Figure 39-23.

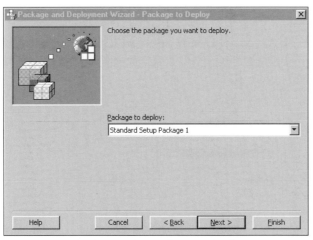

Figure 39-22: Selecting the package to deploy.

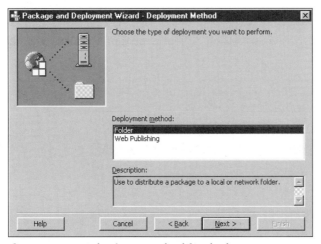

Figure 39-23: Selecting a method for deployment.

The Deployment Method page lists the types of deployments supported for the package you selected to deploy. The Folder method deploys the package to a folder on a local or network drive. The Web Publishing method deploys the package to a Web server.

3. Select the Folder method, and then select the Next button. The Folder page displays as shown in Figure 39-24.

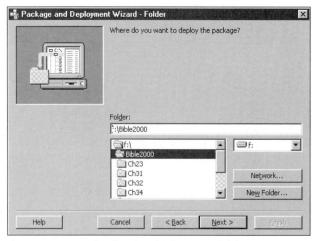

Figure 39-24: Selecting the deployment folder.

Use the Folder page to choose the folder on a local or network drive to which you want to deploy your package. This screen is available only when you have selected Folder as your method of deployment on the Deployment Method page.

4. Select a folder on your local drive, or select the Network button to select a network folder. Then select the Next button. The Finished page displays as shown in Figure 39-25.

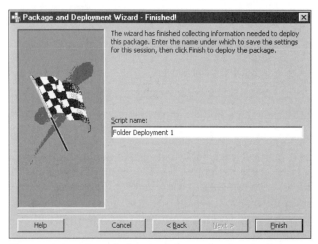

Figure 39-25: Completing the information for deployment.

The Package and Deployment Wizard has collected the information necessary to begin deploying your package. When you click Finish, the Package and Deployment Wizard saves the settings you chose as a script.

5. Select the Finish button to complete the deployment. The Deployment wizard will create the setup files in the folder you selected. When the Deployment wizard has finished creating the files, the Deployment Report window displays as shown in Figure 39-26.

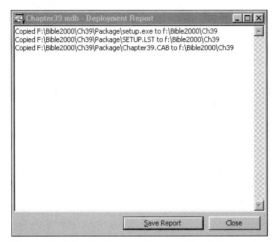

Figure 39-26: Reviewing the results of the deployment.

The Deployment Report window confirms that the installation files were created and shows the directory where they are stored.

6. When you are finished reviewing the summary information, select the Close button. When you close the Deployment Report window, the initial screen of the Package and Deployment Wizard redisplays.

Testing the setup program

Whenever you create a new setup program, or make changes to an old one, you should take the time to run the setup program before releasing it to the users. By running the Package and Deployment Wizard using your saved scripts, it is quick and easy to make any last minute adjustments.

To run the setup program, locate the Setup.exe file in the directory you indicated to use in the Deployment Wizard. When you run Setup.exe, a professional welcome screen displays as shown in Figure 39-27.

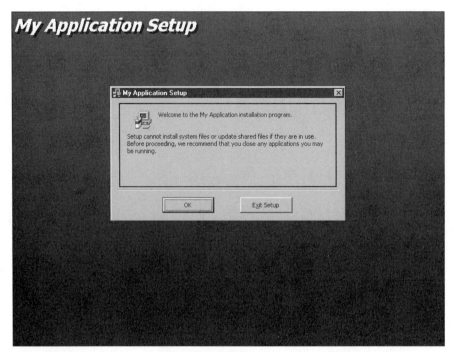

Figure 39-27: The Setup program starts with a welcome and a warning about shared files.

When the user clicks OK to continue with the installation, the Application Setup page displays as shown in Figure 39-28.

On this page, the user can accept the recommended installation folder that you designated in the Package and Deployment Wizard, or they can select Change Directory to choose another folder.

When the user selects the large button at the top of the Application Setup page, the Setup program copies the installation files to the selected folder.

When all the files have been copied, the user can select a Program Group for the application's icon, as shown in Figure 39-29.

The Setup program confirms that the installation has been successfully completed, as shown in Figure 39-30.

The Package and Deployment Wizard makes it easy to create a setup routine for any Access application. It virtually eliminates the guesswork involved in identifying all the files that an application needs to run correctly. Additionally, it automatically builds a professional installation interface that adds that final finishing touch to a well-built application.

Figure 39-28: The Setup suggests the installation folder you specified in the Wizard.

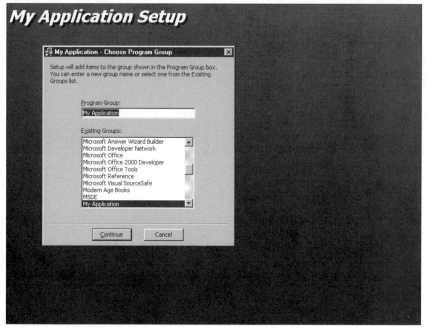

Figure 39-29: Choosing a Program Group for the new application.

Although deciding what to distribute to your users and how to distribute it takes some time and considerable thought, taking the time to learn the Package and Deployment Wizard enables you to create perfect installations every time!

Many different steps are discussed here that are required to produce a top-notch distributed Access application. For each step, you can take dozens and dozens of shortcuts, but don't. It is not uncommon for a company to devote an entire week or longer just to prepare an application for distribution (not writing core code). It really shows when you take your time and do these things right, and your users will have a smooth-running, intuitive, dependable application that makes their tasks just a little bit easier.

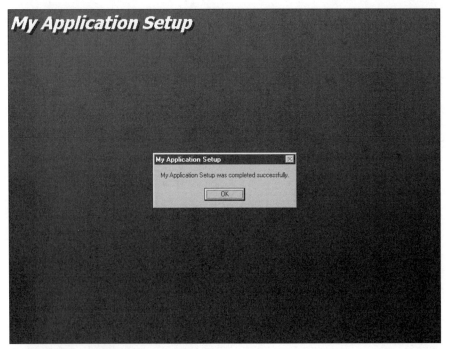

Figure 39-30: When the Setup program is complete, it informs the user that it completed successfully.

Summary

Many different steps are required to produce a professionally developed and packaged application. For each step, you can take many shortcuts, but resist the temptation. It is not uncommon for a company to devote a week or more to preparing an application for distribution. Using the Office Developer tools, you can ready your application for distribution without Microsoft Access. In this chapter you learned how to do the following:

✦ Prepare an application for distribution.

✦ Polish an application.

✦ Add menus and toolbars to an application.

✦ Create a Setup.EXE file using the Office Developer Tools.

✦ Use the Access Runtime System.

✦ Use VBA Productivity tools to streamline development.

In the next chapter, you learn how to integrate Access with other Microsoft Office applications.

✦   ✦   ✦

Integrating with Microsoft Office 2000

As companies standardize their computer practices and software selections, it is becoming more and more important to develop *total* solutions: solutions that integrate the many procedures of an organization. Usually, various procedures are accomplished by using different software packages, such as Word for letter writing, Exchange and Outlook for mailing and faxing, and Excel for financial functions. If the organization for which you are developing has standardized on the Microsoft Office suite, you can leverage your knowledge of Visual Basic for Applications to program for all these products.

Note　Automation, formerly called OLE Automation, is a means by which an application can expose objects, each with it's own methods and properties, that other applications can create instances of and control through code. Not all commercial applications support Automation, but more and more applications are adopting Automation to replace the outdated DDE interface. Consult with a specific application's vendor to find out if it supports or plans to support OLE Automation in the program.

Using Automation to Integrate with Office

The Microsoft Office 2000 applications mentioned all support Automation (sometimes referred to as OLE Automation). Using Automation, you can create objects in your code that represent other applications. By manipulating these objects (setting properties, calling methods), you can control the referenced applications as though you were programming directly in them; you can create seamless integrated applications using Automation.

Creating Automation references

Applications that support Automation provide information about their objects in an *Object Library*. The Object Library contains information about an application's classes (its internal objects), and their properties and methods. To reference an application's objects, Visual Basic must determine the type of object to which an object's variable in your code belongs. The process of determining the type of an object variable is called *binding*. You have two methods available to bind an object, *early binding* and *late binding*.

Early binding an object

Using the References dialog box in the Visual Basic for Applications window of Access, you can explicitly reference an object library. When you explicitly reference an object library, you are performing early binding. Automation code executes more quickly when you use early binding.

Note   To access the References dialog box of VBA you need to activate the window by either creating a new module or displaying the design of an existing module.

To create a reference, first open any module in your application database in the Visual Basic for Applications Design screen. When you have a module in Design view, a new command is available from the Tools menu — References (see Figure 40-1). Select Tools ➪ References to access the References dialog box (see Figure 40-2).

In the References dialog box, you specify all the references your application needs for using Automation or for using other Access databases as library databases. To select or deselect a reference, click its check box.

After you reference an application for Automation, you can explicitly dimension an object variable. The new coding help feature displays the available objects as you type, as shown in Figure 40-3. In addition, after you have selected the primary object and have entered a period (.), the help feature of Access 2000 enables you to select from the available class objects (see Figure 40-4).

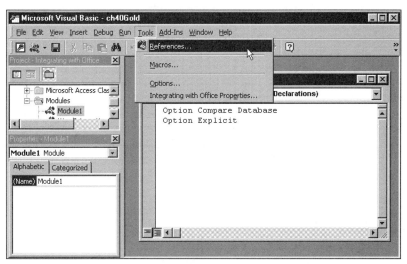

Figure 40-1: The Tools ⇨ References menu item is only available when in the module Design or New view of Access. This activates the VBA window.

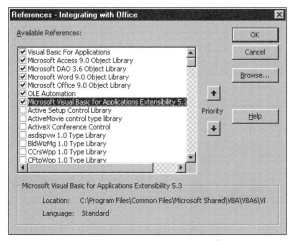

Figure 40-2: Early binding by setting references is the most efficient way to perform Automation.

Late binding an object

If you do not explicitly reference an object library using the References dialog box, you set an object's reference in code by first declaring a variable as an object and then using the Set command to create the object reference. This process is known as *late binding*.

To create an object to reference Microsoft Word 2000, for example, you use code such as the following:

```
Dim WordObj As Object
Set WordObj = New Word.Application
```

The Set command is discussed in the next section.

Note   If you create an object for an application that is not referenced, no drop-down help box, such as the ones shown in Figures 40-3 and 40-4, is displayed.

Figure 40-3: When an Automation Server is referenced, its objects are immediately known by Visual Basic.

Figure 40-4: The new drop-down syntax help of Visual Basic makes using referenced Automation Servers easy.

Figure 40-3 shows the automatic drop-down box that will appear immediately after you type the word "new" in the Dim statement. At this point you can select one of the application object name types displayed (such as word) or enter a new application object name type you define. Figure 40-4 shows the new drop-down box that will appear when you type a period (.) after the object type "word." This box will help you by displaying all known object types that can be associated with the particular primary object name. In this case, clicking the Application object type will add this to the "word." portion of the object, thus word.application.

Creating an instance of an Automation object

To perform an Automation operation, the operating system needs to start the application — if it isn't already started — and obtain a reference, or handle, to it. This reference will be used to access the application. Most applications that support Automation, called *Automation Servers,* expose an Application object. The Application object exists at the top of the object application's hierarchy and often contains many objects itself.

Using the New keyword to create a new instance

The simplest (and most efficient) method to create an Automation object is to bind the Automation Server: set a reference to it in Tools ➪ References and then create a new instance of the object by using the New keyword in Visual Basic. In the preceding example, shown in Figure 40-3 and Figure 40-4, the variable WordObj is set to a new instance of Word's Application object.

Caution If you do not create a reference to the Automation Server by using the References dialog box, Visual Basic does not recognize the object type and generates an error on compile.

Every time you create an instance of an Automation Server by using the New keyword, a new instance of the application is started. If you do not want to start a new instance of the application, use the GetObject function discussed in the section "Getting an Existing Object Instance."

Not all Automation Servers support the New keyword. Consult the specific Automation Server's documentation to determine whether it supports the New keyword. If the New keyword is not supported, you need to use the CreateObject function discussed in the next section to create an instance of the Automation Server.

Using the CreateObject function to create a new instance

In addition to creating an instance of an object library by using the New keyword, you can create an instance of an object library using the CreateObject function. You use the CreateObject function to create instances of object libraries that do not support the New keyword. To use the CreateObject function, first declare a variable of the type equal to the type of object you want to create. Then use the Set statement in conjunction with the CreateObject function to set the variable to a new instance of the object library.

For example, Microsoft Binder does not support the New keyword, but it does provide an object library, so you can reference it by using the References dialog box. To early bind the object library of Binder, use the CreateObject function as shown in the following code:

```
Dim BinderObj As OfficeBinder.Binder
Set BinderObj = CreateObject("Office.Binder")
```

Note   In the preceding example, the object library name for Binder is OfficeBinder. Binder, and the class instance is "Office.Binder." You can view the names of object libraries and their available classes by using the Object Browser.

You can create an object instance with the CreateObject function that is late bound by not declaring the object variable as a specific type. For example, the following code creates an instance of the Binder object using late binding:

```
Dim BinderObj As Object
Set BinderObj = CreateObject("Office.Binder")
```

Note   If you have different versions of the same Automation Server on your computer, you can specify the version to use by adding it to the end of the class information. For example, the following code uses Office 2000 as the Automation Server:

```
Dim BinderObj As Object
Set BinderObj = CreateObject("Word.Application.9")
```

Tip   Although you could perform Automation in Word 95, Word 95 was not a true Automation Server. Word 97 was the first true Automation Server, and, like it, Word 2000 does not require you to specify a version when creating instances of Word 2000 object libraries; Word 2000 is always used regardless of the other versions of Word on the computer. As a matter of fact, you get an error if you try to specify a version number.

Getting an existing object instance

As stated earlier, using the New keyword or the CreateObject function creates a new instance of the Automation Server. If you do not want a new instance of the server created each time you create an object, use the GetObject function. The format of the GetObject function is as follows:

```
Set objectvariable = GetObject([pathname][, class])
```

The pathname parameter is optional. To use this parameter, you specify a full path and file name to an existing file for use with the Automation Server.

Note   The specified document is then opened in the server application. Even if you omit the parameter, you must still include the comma (,).

The *class* parameter is the same as that used with the `CreateObject` function. See Table 40-1 for a list of some class arguments used in Microsoft Office.

Table 40-1
Class Arguments for Common Office Components

Component	Class Argument	Object Returned
Access	`Access.Application`	Microsoft Access Application object
Excel	`Excel.Application`	Microsoft Excel Application object
	`Excel.Sheet`	Microsoft Excel Workbook object
	`Excel.Chart`	Microsoft Excel Chart object
Word	`Word.Application`	Microsoft Word Application object
	`Word.Document`	Microsoft Word Document object

For example, to work with an existing instance of Microsoft Word but not a specific Word document, you use code such as the following:

```
Dim WordObj as Word.Application
Set WordObj = GetObject(, "Word.Application")
```

To get an instance of an existing Word document called `MyDoc.Doc`, you can use code such as the following:

```
Dim WordObj as Word.Application
Set WordObj = GetObject("c:\MyDoc.Doc", "Word.Application")
```

Of course this code is always placed in a new function or sub that you declare in your module.

Working with Automation objects

After you have a valid instance of an Automation Server, you manipulate the object as though you were writing code within the application itself, using the exposed objects and their properties and methods.

For example, when developing directly in Word, you can use the following code to change the directory Word uses when opening an existing file:

```
ChangeFileOpenDirectory "D:\My Documents\"
```

Note Consult the development help for the Automation Server for specific information on the objects, properties, and methods available.

Just as in Access, Word is implicitly using its `Application` object; the command `ChangeFileOpenDirectory` is really a method of the `Application` object. Using the following code, you create an instance of Word's `Application` object and call the method of the object:

```
Dim WordObj As New Word.Application
WordObj.ChangeFileOpenDirectory "D:\My Documents\"
```

Tip When using Automation, you should avoid setting properties or calling methods that cause the Automation Server to ask for input from the user via a dialog box. When a dialog box is displayed, the Automation code stops executing until the dialog is closed. If the server application is minimized or behind other windows, the user may not even be aware that he or she needs to provide input and might assume that the application is locked up.

Closing an instance of an Automation object

Automation objects are closed when the Automation object variable goes out of scope. Such a closing, however, does not necessarily free up all resources used by the object, so you should explicitly close the instance of the Automation object. You can close an Automation object by doing either of the following:

✦ Using the `Close` or `Quit` method of the object (consult the specific Automation Server's documentation for information on which method it supports).

✦ Setting the object variable to nothing, as follows:

```
Set WordObj = Nothing.
```

The best way to close an instance of an Automation object is to combine the two techniques, like this:

```
WordObj.Quit
Set WordObj = Nothing
```

An Automation example using Word 2000

Perhaps the most common Office application used for Automation from a database application, like Access, is Word. Using Automation with Word, you can create letters that are tailored with information from databases. The following is an example of merging information from an Access database to a letter in Word by using Automation. This example is included in the thanks.dot template file on the CD-ROM that accompanies this book.

Note When you attempt to run this example, you must make sure that the path for the template in the Visual Basic code is the actual path in which the thanks.dot template file resides. This path may vary from computer to computer.

Items discussed in this Word Automation example include the following:

✦ Creating an instance of a Word object

✦ Making the instance of Word visible

✦ Creating a new document based on an existing template

✦ Using bookmarks to insert data

✦ Activating the instance of Word

✦ Moving the cursor in Word

✦ Closing the instance of the Word object without closing Word

This example prints a thank-you letter for an order. Figure 40-5 shows the data for customers; Figure 40-6 shows the data entry form for orders; Figure 40-7 shows the thanks.dot template; and Figure 40-8 shows a completed merge letter.

Figure 40-5: Customer data used in the following Automation example is entered on the Customers form.

 Caution

If you click "Print Thank-You Letter" in Access while Word is open with an existing document, the fields will simply be added to the text inside Word 2000 at the point where the cursor is currently sitting.

Figure 40-6: Each customer can have an unlimited number of orders. Thank-you letters are printed from the Orders form.

Figure 40-7: The thanks.dot template contains bookmarks where the merged data is to be inserted.

Figure 40-8: After a successful merge, all the bookmarks have been replaced with their respective data.

When the user clicks the Print Thank You Letter button on the Orders form, Word 2000 generates a thank-you letter with all the pertinent information. Listing 40-1 shows the MergetoWord function in its entirety:

Listing 40-1: The MergetoWord Function

```
Public Function MergetoWord()
' This method creates a new document in MS Word 2000 using
Automation.
On Error Resume Next
Dim rsCust As Recordset, iTemp As Integer
Dim WordObj As Word.Application
Set rsCust =
DBEngine(0).Databases(0).OpenRecordset("Customers", _
dbOpenTable)
rsCust.Index = "PrimaryKey"
rsCust.Seek "=", Forms!Orders![CustomerNumber]
    If rsCust.NoMatch Then
        MsgBox "Invalid customer", vbOKOnly
        Exit Function
    End If
DoCmd.Hourglass True
Set WordObj = GetObject(, "Word.Application")
If Err.Number <> 0 Then
    Set WordObj = CreateObject("Word.Application")
End If
WordObj.Visible = True
WordObj.Documents.Add
Template:="D:\office2000\Templates\thanks.dot",
NewTemplate:=False
WordObj.Selection.Goto what:=wdGoToBookmark, Name:="FullName"
    WordObj.Selection.TypeText rsCust![ContactName]
WordObj.Selection.Goto what:=wdGoToBookmark,
Name:="CompanyName"
    WordObj.Selection.TypeText rsCust![CompanyName]
WordObj.Selection.Goto what:=wdGoToBookmark, Name:="Address1"
    WordObj.Selection.TypeText rsCust![Address1]
WordObj.Selection.Goto what:=wdGoToBookmark, Name:="Address2"
    If IsNull(rsCust![Address2]) Then
        WordObj.Selection.TypeText ""
    Else
        WordObj.Selection.TypeText rsCust![Address2]
    End If
WordObj.Selection.Goto what:=wdGoToBookmark, Name:="City"
    WordObj.Selection.TypeText rsCust![City]
WordObj.Selection.Goto what:=wdGoToBookmark, Name:="State"
    WordObj.Selection.TypeText rsCust![State]
WordObj.Selection.Goto what:=wdGoToBookmark, Name:="Zipcode"
    WordObj.Selection.TypeText rsCust![Zipcode]
```

Continued

Listing 40-1 *(continued)*

```
WordObj.Selection.Goto what:=wdGoToBookmark,
Name:="PhoneNumber"
    WordObj.Selection.TypeText rsCust![PhoneNumber]
WordObj.Selection.Goto what:=wdGoToBookmark, Name:="NumOrdered"
    WordObj.Selection.TypeText Forms!Orders![Quantity]
WordObj.Selection.Goto what:=wdGoToBookmark,
Name:="ProductOrdered"
    If Forms!Orders![Quantity] > 1 Then
        WordObj.Selection.TypeText Forms!Orders![Item] & "s"
    Else
        WordObj.Selection.TypeText Forms!Orders![Item]
    End If
WordObj.Selection.Goto what:=wdGoToBookmark, Name:="FName"
    iTemp = InStr(rsCust![ContactName], " ")
    If iTemp > 0 Then
        WordObj.Selection.TypeText Left$(rsCust![ContactName],
iTemp _ - 1)
    End If
WordObj.Selection.Goto what:=wdGoToBookmark, Name:="LetterName"
    WordObj.Selection.TypeText rsCust![ContactName]
DoEvents
WordObj.Activate
WordObj.Selection.MoveUp wdLine, 6
' Set the Word Object to nothing to free resources
Set WordObj = Nothing
DoCmd.Hourglass False
Exit Function
TemplateError:
    Set WordObj = Nothing
    Exit Function
End Function
```

Creating an instance of a Word object

The first step in using Automation is to create an instance of an object. The sample creates an object instance with the following code:

```
On Error Resume Next
...
Set WordObj = GetObject(, "Word.Application")
If Err.Number <> 0 Then
    Set WordObj = CreateObject("Word.Application")
End If
```

Obviously, you wouldn't want a new instance of Word created every time a thank-you letter is generated, so some special coding is required. This code snippet first attempts to create an instance by using an active instance (running copy) of Word 2000. If Word 2000 is not a running application, an error is generated. Because this function has `On Error Resume Next` for error trapping, the code does not fail but rather proceeds to the next statement. If an error is detected (the `Err.Number` is not equal to 0), an instance is created by using `CreateObject`.

Making the instance of Word visible

When you first create a new instance of Word 2000, it runs invisibly. This approach enables your application to exploit features of Word without the user even realizing Word is running. In this case, however, it is desirable to let the user edit the merged letter, so Word needs to be made visible by setting the object's `Visible` property to True by using this line of code:

```
WordObj.Visible = True
```

Note

If you do not set the object instance's `Visible` property to True, you may create hidden copies of Word that use system resources and never shut down. A hidden copy of Word does not show up in the Task tray or in the Task Switcher.

Creating a new document based on an existing template

Now that Word is running, a blank document needs to be created. The following code creates a new document using the supplied template thanks.dot:

```
WordObj.Documents.Add _
Template:="D:\office2000\Templates\thanks.dot", _
NewTemplate:=False
```

The thanks.dot template contains bookmarks that tell this function where to insert data, as well as a generic thank-you paragraph. You create bookmarks in Word by highlighting the text you want to make a bookmark, selecting Edit ➪ Bookmark, entering the bookmark name, and clicking Add.

Using Bookmarks to insert data

Using Automation, you can locate bookmarks in a Word document and replace them with the text of your choosing. To locate a bookmark, you use the `Goto` method of the `Selection` object. When a bookmark is located, the text making up the bookmark is selected. By inserting text (using Automation or simply by typing directly into the document), you replace the bookmark text. To insert text, use the `TypeText` method of the `Selection` object, as shown here:

```
WordObj.Selection.Goto what:=wdGoToBookmark, Name:="FullName"
WordObj.Selection.TypeText rsCust![ContactName]
```

Note   You cannot pass a null to the TypeText method. If there is a possibility that a value may be Null, check ahead and make allowances. The preceding sample code checks the Address2 field for a Null value and acts accordingly. If you do not pass text to replace the bookmark, even just a zero length string (" "), the Bookmark text remains in the document.

Activating the instance of Word

To enable the user to enter data in the new document, you must make Word the active application. If you do not make Word the active application, the user has to switch to Word from Access. You make Word the active application by using the Activate method of the Word object, as follows:

```
WordObj.Activate
```

Tip   Depending on the processing that is occurring at the time, Access may take the focus back from Word. You can help to eliminate this annoyance by preceding the Activate method with a DoEvents statement. Note, however, that this does not always work.

Moving the cursor in Word

You can control the cursor in Word. To move the cursor, use the MoveUp method of the Selection object. The following example moves the cursor up six lines in the document. The cursor is at the location of the last bookmark when this code is executed:

```
WordObj.Selection.MoveUp wdLine, 6
```

Closing the instance of the Word object

To free up resources taken by an instance of an Automation object, you should always close the instance. In this example, the following code is used to close the object instance:

```
Set WordObj = Nothing
```

This code closes the object instance but not the instance of Word as a running application. In this example, the user needs access to the new document, so closing Word would defeat the purpose of this function. You could, however, automatically print the document and then close Word. If you were to do this, you might choose to not even make Word visible during this process. To close Word, use the Quit method of the Application object, as follows:

```
WordObj.Quit
```

Inserting pictures by using Bookmarks

It is possible to perform other unique operations by using Bookmarks. Basically, anything you can do within Word, you can do using Automation. The following code locates a bookmark marking where a picture goes, and inserts a .PCX file from disk. You can use code such as the following to insert scanned signatures into letters:

```
WordObj.Selection.Goto what:=wdGoToBookmark, Name:="Picture"
WordObj.ChangeFileOpenDirectory "D:\GRAPHICS\"
WordObj. ActiveDocument.Shapes.AddPicture
Anchor:=Selection.Range, _ FileName:= _
        "D:\GRAPHICS\PICTURE.BMP", LinkToFile:=False,
SaveWithDocument _
        :=True
```

Using Office's Macro Recorder

Using Automation is not a difficult process when you understand the fundamentals. Often, the toughest part of using Automation is knowing the proper objects, properties, and methods to use. Although the development help system of the Automation Server is a requirement for fully understanding the language, there is an even easier way to quickly create Automation for Office applications: the Macro Recorder.

Office 2000 applications have a Macro Recorder located on the Tools menu (see Figure 40-9). When activated, the Macro Recorder records all events, such as menu selections and button clicks, and creates Visual Basic code from them.

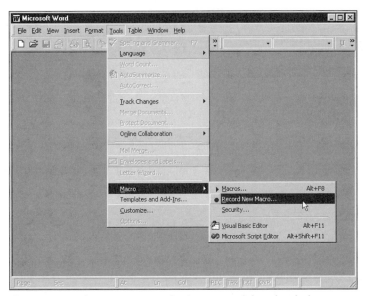

Figure 40-9: The Macro Recorder is a powerful tool to help you create Automation code.

After selecting Tools ➪ Macro ➪ Record New Macro, you must give your new macro a name (see Figure 40-10). In addition to a name, you can assign the macro to a toolbar or keyboard combination and select the template in which to store the macro. If you are creating the macro simply to create the Visual Basic code, the only thing you need to be concerned with is the macro name.

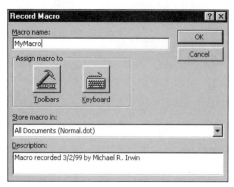

Figure 40-10: Enter a macro name and click OK to begin recording the macro. In this example the macro is named "MyMacro."

After entering a macro name and clicking OK, the Macro Recorder begins recording events and displays a Stop Recording window, as shown in Figure 40-11. You can stop recording events by clicking the Stop button (the button with a square on it). To pause recording events, click the other button, which is the Pause button.

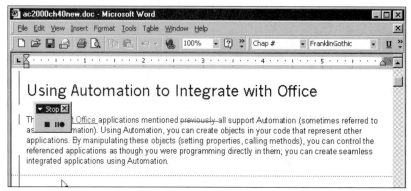

Figure 40-11: The Macro Recorder records all events until you click the Stop button.

After you have finished recording a macro, you can view the Visual Basic code created from your events. To view the code of a macro, select Tools ➪ Macro ➪

Macros to display a list of all saved macros. Then select the macro you recorded and click the Edit button to display the Visual Basic editor with the macro's code. Figure 40-12 shows the Visual Basic editor with a macro that recorded creating a new document using the Normal template, and inserting a picture using the Insert ➪ Picture ➪ From File menu item.

In the application for which a macro is created, the Application object is used explicitly. When you use the code for Automation, you must create an Application object accordingly. For example, the preceding macro uses the following code to create a new document:

```
Documents.Add Template:="C:\Windows\Application
Data\Microsoft\Templates\Normal.dot", _ NewTemplate:= False,
DocumentType:=0
```

This code implicitly uses the Application object. To use this code for Automation, copy the code from the Visual Basic editor, paste it into your procedure, and create an object that you use explicitly, as follows:

```
Dim WordObj as New Word.Application
WordObj.Documents.Add Template:="C:\Windows\application
data\microsoft\Templates\Normal.dot", _ NewTemplate:= False,
DocumentType:=0
```

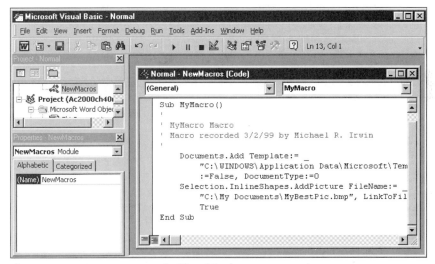

Figure 40-12: Macros are really Visual Basic event procedures.

The Macro Recorder enables you to effortlessly create long and complete Automation code without ever needing to read the Automation Server's documentation.

Programming the Office Assistant

Perhaps the most fun Automation Server yet is the Office Assistant. That's right, the Office Assistant is a fully programmable Automation Server! Using the techniques described in this chapter, you can completely control the Office Assistant. Included in the database for this chapter on the companion CD-ROM is an Office Assistant Automation Example form with all the code necessary to control the Office Assistant (see Figure 40-13).

To program the Office Assistant using Automation, you must first ensure that the Office Assistant is installed, and then you must create a reference to the Microsoft Office 9.0 Object Library (see Figure 40-14). To reference the library you must be in the VBA window. The fastest way to activate Visual Basic for Applications is to design or create a new module from Access.

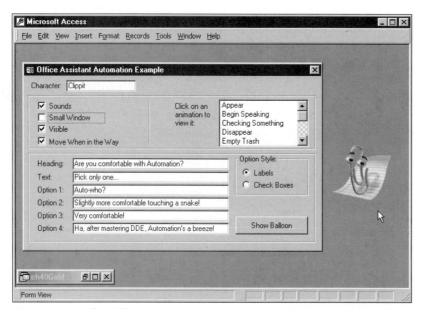

Figure 40-13: The Office Assistant Automation Example form contains all the code you need to control the Office Assistant.

Note   The program, Office Assistant, shown in Figure 40-13 shows a check box for Small Window. Note that this will only work in Access 97. Office 2000's Office Assistant is not displayed in a window as in previous versions of Office. Therefore, activating this check box will have no effect in Office 2000.

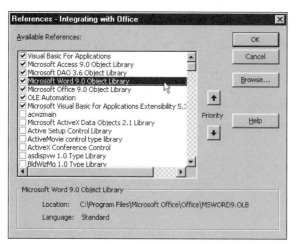

Figure 40-14: Programming the Office Assistant requires that the Office Assistant be installed and referenced in the database.

Tip If you have installed the Office Assistant and the form, Office Assistant, still cannot access the Office Assistant, you will need to activate it. To activate the Office Assistant select Help ➪ Show Office Assistant. From this point on it will work correctly.

Hiding and showing the Office Assistant

You can completely hide the Office Assistant at any time by setting its Visible property to False, as follows:

```
Assistant.Visible = False
```

To show the Office Assistant, simply set the Visible property to True.

Keeping the Assistant out of the way

You can give the Office Assistant some smarts by instructing it to stay out of the way of other windows. To do this, use the following to set the Assistant's MoveWhenInTheWay property:

```
Assistant.MoveWhenInTheWay = True
```

When you set the `MoveWhenInTheWay` property to True, the Assistant recognizes when it is in the way of other windows — as they appear — and it attempts to move itself to a less obtrusive location. If you set the `MoveWhenInTheWay` property to False, the Office Assistant never moves itself.

Enabling and disabling the Assistant's sounds

You can programmatically enable and disable the Assistant's sounds by setting the Assistant's `Sounds` property. For example, to enable Assistant sounds, set the property to True, as follows:

```
Assistant.Sounds = True
```

To disable all Assistant sounds, set the property to False.

Displaying an Assistant animation

Of course, the coolest thing about the Office Assistant is its animation. To display an animation, you simply set the `Animation` property to the appropriate animation number. For example, to display the Empty Trash animation shown in Figure 40-15, you set the `Animation` property to 116, as follows:

```
Assistant.Animation = 116
```

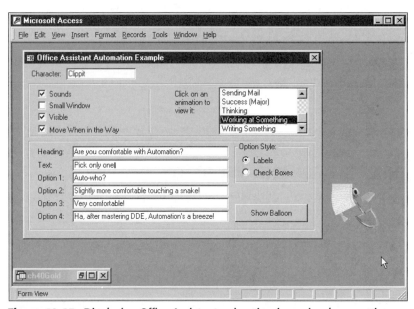

Figure 40-15: Displaying Office Assistant animation is as simple as setting a property.

Note   The sample database on the companion CD-ROM contains a table of all of the animations and their respective reference numbers.

There are a number of different Assistants, ranging from a bouncing paper clip to a talking computer. Not every Office Assistant has an animation associated with each entry in the Animations table.

Displaying information and getting user input using balloons

The Office Assistant isn't just a passive object taking up space on the desktop. You also can use the Assistant to display dialog boxes and to get user input (see Figure 40-16). These Assistant dialog boxes are called *balloons,* and you create them by using the `NewBalloon` method of the `Assistant` object.

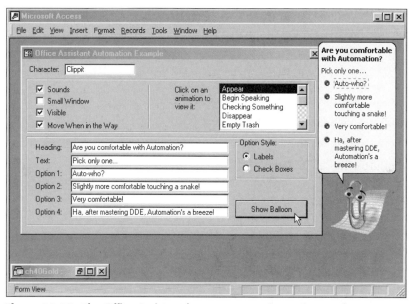

Figure 40-16: The Office Assistant becomes an active assistant when you use balloons.

Creating a new balloon

To create a balloon, first dimension a variable as a `Balloon` object. Then set the variable to a new balloon object by using the `NewBalloon` method of the `Assistant` object, as follows:

```
Dim objBalloon As Balloon
Set objBalloon = Assistant.NewBalloon
```

Specifying a balloons heading and text

You then specify the heading and body text by using the `Heading` and `Text` properties of the new balloon object, as in the following example:

```
objBalloon.Heading = "This is heading text!"
objBalloon.Text = "This is body text."
```

Specifying a balloon's buttons

Specifying the buttons to be displayed is similar to specifying buttons for dialog boxes — you use a constant. Buttons are defined by setting the `Buttons` property, as follows:

```
objBalloon.Button = buttonconstant
```

The following are valid constants to use in place of `buttonconstant`:

- ✦ msoButtonSetAbortRetryIgnore
- ✦ msoButtonSetBackClose
- ✦ msoButtonSetBackNextClose
- ✦ msoButtonSetBackNextSnooze
- ✦ msoButtonSetCancelmsoButtonSetNextClose
- ✦ msoButtonSetNonemsoButtonSetOK
- ✦ msoButtonSetOkCancel
- ✦ msoButtonSetRetryCancel
- ✦ msoButtonSetSearchClose
- ✦ msoButtonSetTipsOptionsClose
- ✦ msoButtonSetYesAllNoCancel
- ✦ msoButtonSetYesNoCancel
- ✦ msoButtonSetYesNo

Creating balloon labels and check boxes

You give the user selections from which to choose by defining a labels or check boxes item. In Figure 40-16, labels are used. Labels are similar to option buttons in that the user can select only one of a given set of labels. Instead of labels, you can allow a user to select a number of items by making them check boxes (see Figure 40-17).

For each labels or check boxes item on a balloon, you set a labels or check boxes array item in code, as in the following:

```
objBalloon.Labels(1).Text = "Text for label 1"
objBalloon.Labels(2).Text = "Text for label 2"
...
or
objBalloon.checkboxes(1).Text = "Text for checkbox 1"
objBalloon.checkboxes(2).Text = "Text for checkbox 2"
...
```

Note　There can be up to five labels and five check boxes on a balloon.

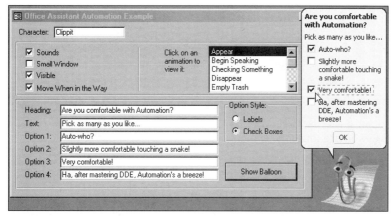

Figure 40-17: You can let a user select a number of items by using the check boxes item.

Displaying a balloon

After the balloon is completely defined, you display the balloon by using the Show method of the Balloon object, as follows:

```
intRetval = objBalloon.Show
```

Note that the Show method returns a value. If the balloon contains labels, the return value is the index of the selected label. To find out which check boxes are selected, you must look through the check boxes items for the balloon, as follows:

```
Dim iCount as integer
For iCount = 1 To objBalloon.Checkboxes.Count
If objBalloon.Checkboxes(iCount).Checked = True Then
MsgBox "Checkbox #" & iCount & " is selected!", vbOKOnly
End If
Next iCount
```

Figure 40-18 shows the result of determining the selected item and creating a new balloon object to tell the user what it was.

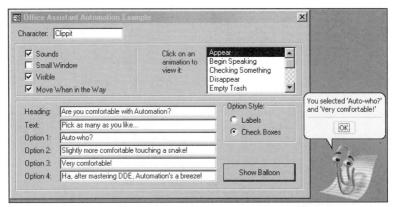

Figure 40-18: To display a new balloon, create a new balloon object.

Using the techniques discussed in this chapter, you can leverage your Visual Basic knowledge and create intelligent and powerful integrated applications.

Summary

In this chapter you learned how to integrate Microsoft Access with other Office products. You learned:

How to use automation to create references to other Office products

How to integrate Access data in a Word document

How to program the Microsoft Office assistant

In the next chapter, you learn about Database Replication.

✦   ✦   ✦

Exploring Replication

The *replication* feature of Microsoft Jet 4.x provides a method for distributing your database, including all its objects, to other users. The users of a replicated database may have read-only or read-write access, depending on the permissions you assign to the replica.

If a replicated database has been created as read-write, the changes made to it can be synchronized with the changes made to other replicas. This enables a database to be distributed to other machines and kept up-to-date with other distributed databases. Database changes can be synchronized directly among two replicas or, if direct connection is not possible, the changes can be stored for later update by the target Synchronizer. This feature goes well beyond a simple copy of the database, because changes to a copy are not easily synchronized back into the master database.

You can use replication to distribute your application code, tables, queries, forms, and reports. You can distribute your application's tables separately from the rest of your database objects, even if your master database contains all objects in a single database. Beginning with Access 97, you have the capability to create and synchronize partial replicas, which provide a means of distributing only the data required by a receiving site.

Replication may be used to provide a database or a part of a database to a portable computer, to other machines on the network, or to stand-alone machines. Even though other network-attached machines can be set up to access the same database, instances occur where you may want to have some of these machines access a replica of the database to improve performance.

You should precede the use of replication with solid planning. Replication does not come free. Several points within the scheme of replication require serious consideration before adopting this feature. This chapter addresses those considerations and looks at the components of replication and their management.

The Components of Replication

When you create a replica of your database, the database changes in several ways to support the synchronization of changes between the replica you create and the master database. Understanding these changes is your first task in deciding whether or not to use replication.

At the time you create a replica, Access needs to add several fields and objects to your database in order to track and synchronize updates. These additions increase the size of the database as described in the "Design Master" section of this chapter.

The original database that you are replicating becomes the *Design Master*. If you make any changes to the design of the database, meaning changes to the design of any object in the database, those changes should be made to the Design Master and then propagated to the replicas.

A replica of the Design Master can receive data changes, including additions, modifications, and deletions, but does not support changing the design of any of its replicated objects. Changes to the design of local objects, those created at the replica, are supported, however.

Multiple replicas can be created from either the Design Master or any replica created from the Design Master. All replicas related to the same Design Master are part of a group called the *Replica Set*.

Nonreplicable database

Your database requires the addition of several system tables, fields, and properties before it can be replicated. Without this additional information in your database, Access cannot keep track of changes and therefore cannot replicate those changes.

If your database has a password attached to it, you need to remove that password before making the database replicable. A password on the database prevents the synchronization of replicas among the replica set.

Making a database replicable

When you make a database replicable, you are creating a *Design Master* database. For example, to make the database named CstPtLit.mdb a Design Master, follow these steps:

1. Open the CstPtLit database.

2. Select Tools ➪ Replication ➪ Create Replica from the file menu. Access 2000 displays a dialog box stating: "This database must be closed before you can create a replica" and another message informing you that it will convert the database to a Design Master.

3. Click the Yes button of the dialog box. Access will respond with another dialog box suggesting that it should make a backup of your database for you and will give the backup an extension of .BAK. You may also see a conversion dialog box.

4. Click the Yes button of this dialog box. Access responds with the save file dialog box, titled "Location of New Replica."

5. You should accept the default name of file "Replica of cstptlit.mdb" by pressing the OK button. If you want to select a different name for the new file, you can do it here. However, Access will still convert the original table as well as the new name you enter (thus it will automatically create a replica of the table at the same time).

6. If you selected an existing filename, Access will inform you that the file already exists and ask if you want to replace it. Answer Yes if you did not accept the default name.

7. Access will convert the table and display another dialog box saying it completed the job. Click the OK button.

Caution   If you enter the original name of "CstPtLit.mdb" in the File Name field, Access will respond with a verification dialog box and then refuse to allow you to convert the file, because the original and destination are the same file. This means that you will need to create a file under a different name resulting in Access 2000 creating two tables that are converted (the original and the backup).

Once completed, Access will have converted the table and created a second copy (or replica table) of the Design Master (original).

Tip   You can convert the original table *without* creating a second copy (replica) of a Design Master by simply clicking the Cancel button in Step 5. Access will immediately convert the table and skip to Step 7.

Once converted, all the objects of your database will have a small yellow circle with two arrows attached to the icons as displayed in Figure 41-1.

Notice that the icon for all the tables in Figure 41-1 has been changed, to include a small circle to the right side of the icon.

Figure 41-1: The database converted to a Design Master.

Design Master

After your database has been made replicable, it is known in the newly created replica set as the Design Master database.

The Design Master and all replicas created from it contain internal IDs that are unique within the replica set. This set ID enables the replica set members to update each other but prevents updating members of other replica sets, even if those sets were created from the same nonreplicable database.

Any changes in design of replicated objects must be made at the Design Master. These changes are replicated to all the replicas in the set at the time of the next synchronization.

When the Design Master is created, new object tables are added to your tables container to support the replication of changes.

Note These objects are *not* initially visible to you in the table design surface or from the Property dialog box of any of the objects. However, you can view these system objects by selecting Tools ➪ Options and clicking the System objects box.

The table object named MSysAccessObjects has several fields added to track changes to tables — s_Generation, s_GUID, and s_Lineage.

The field named s_Generation is added to track the number of changes occurring in a row. This field is incremented each time its containing row is updated, and is used during synchronization to satisfy conflicts among other members of the replica set having updates to the same row.

An s_GUID field is added to give each row in a table a unique identifier. This field is an AutoNumber data type with a Replication ID field size, a 16-byte randomly generated field.

The s_GUID field is a Globally Unique ID generated by the operating system using time and machine information. A row existing at the time of replication is given an s_GUID that appears in all members of the replica set. New rows added to a table in a replica set member are given an ID that is randomly generated. Although unlikely, rows added to the same table in different replicas may possibly end up having the same s_GUID value. If this occurs, the synchronization process treats the rows as being one row instead of two different rows and selects one of the rows to keep in the replicas, whereas the other row is written to a *conflict table* for your review.

The s_Lineage field is added to hold information regarding the history of changes made to the row. This field plays a role in determining which changes to apply when multiple updates to the same record have been detected during synchronization.

Memo and OLE objects are each given an additional field named Gen_fieldname. This field tracks changes to these objects separately from the rest of the row. If a row's changes do not include its memo or OLE object fields, those objects are not updated, which reduces the amount of traffic between the source and target of a synchronization process.

The conversion and synchronization processes add new system tables to your database, as described in Table 41-1.

When errors are detected during synchronization, they are recorded in the MSysErrors system table. When conflicts are detected, the conflicting records are added to the table indicated in the MSysSideTables. Conflict tables have names such as *tablename Conflict*, where *tablename* is the name of the table where the conflict was detected.

New properties arc added to your database to give each replica set member a unique ID and to indicate whether the member is replicable or not. DesignMasterID is the GUID of the Design Master database, and ReplicaID is the ID of a replica database. A `True` value in the Replicable property indicates that the database is replicable.

Tip If you have objects that you do not want to replicate, you can create a `KeepLocal` property and set it to `True` prior to creating the replica set.

Table 41-1
System Tables Added by the Creation and Synchronization of a Replica Set

Table Name	Description
MSysErrors	Holds the errors that occurred during the synchronization process. The table is not displayed unless there are errors.
MSysExchangeLog	Holds information about exchanges between replicas in the set.
MSysGenHistory	Holds information about the generations of the containing replica.
MSysOthersHistory	Holds information about the generations of other replicas the containing database has synchronized with.
MSysRepInfo	Holds information about the replica set.
MSysReplicas	Holds information about each replica in the replica set.
MSysSchChange	Holds Design Master schema (design) changes to be replicated.
MSysSchedule	Holds synchronization schedule and details.
MSysTableGuids	Holds information about tables and their GUIDs used in synchronization.
MSysTombstone	Holds information about deletions to be replicated.
MSysTranspAddress	Holds information about replica set Transporters.
MSysSideTables	Holds the GUIDs of tables involved in conflicts and the names of their associated conflict tables holding the conflict records. Created at time of first conflict.
MSysSchemaProb	Holds information about schema (design) errors detected during synchronization.

Any object with a KeepLocal property set to True does not appear in the replicas. If you later want to replicate these objects, add a Replicable property to the object and set it to True. When you next synchronize the database with other members, the object is replicated into the target replica. This also applies to objects created after a database becomes replicable, but only objects from the Design Master. Objects created within replicas cannot be replicated to other members.

Caution   If any of your tables have AutoNumber fields whose new values are assigned incrementally, these fields are changed to be assigned randomly during the conversion to the Design Master. If the AutoNumber field is a key field, keys are assigned randomly instead of sequentially to prevent the same key from being added in multiple replicas. Even though random values are assigned, the same value may possibly be generated in different replicas and may cause a data error when the replicas are synchronized. To eliminate this risk, use the s_GUID field as the key or a value that you can guarantee to be unique among all replicas in the set.

The addition of new fields and tables to your database increases the size of the database and raises some issues that you need to be aware of (see Table 41-2).

The addition of three fields, plus an additional field for each OLE Object and Memo field in the table, reduces the number of fields that your application can use due to the limit of 255 fields per table. Likewise, the additional data added to support replication could put the record size over the limit of 2,048 bytes and, depending on update activity, could put the database over the total size limit of one gigabyte. Additionally, disk management needs to be addressed to ensure that sufficient space is available not only to add records but also to accommodate the replication support data.

Table 41-2
New Field Overhead

Field Name	Description
s_Generation	Long integer used to track changes to a record since the last synchronization
s_GUID	16-byte globally unique identifier
s_Lineage	OLE object used to track the versions and replicas updating a record
Gen_xxx	Long integer for each Memo or OLE field used to track changes to these fields in a record

After you convert a nonreplicable database to a Design Master, you may then create as many replicas as needed.

Caution You should not allow users to access the Design Master database. Keep this database protected so that no one can change it and cause those changes to be replicated to other replicas. Likewise, you should not allow the original nonreplicated database to be accessed so that new Design Masters and replica sets can be created. Too many replicas and multiple replica sets of the same database may cause confusion and possibly an environment that is out of synchronization.

Replicas can be created from the Design Master or from another replica in the set. Before creating a new replica, compress the database and synchronize all members of the set. Doing this ensures that the replica is created quickly and is up to date.

The replicas of a set can be synchronized only with the other members of the same set, including the Design Master. An error occurs if you attempt to synchronize a replica of one set with a replica of a different set.

If objects are created within a replica, they are marked as local and cannot be made replicable. If these objects are required to be replicated to other members, either create them in the Design Master or import them from their source database and set their `Replicable` property to `True`.

Creating a Replica

You have four options for creating a replica set for your database, as follows:

✦ **Access replication** — Access provides a Replication command on the Tools menu. From this menu, you can create the Design Master and the first replica, create additional replicas, and synchronize and resolve conflicts.

✦ **Briefcase replication** — Dragging an Access .MDB file and dropping it on the Windows Briefcase creates a Design Master and a replica, given that Access is installed on the machine. The Briefcase can also be used to synchronize the replica with the Design Master.

✦ **Replication using DAO** — DAO provides replication methods that enable you to create and maintain either full or partial replicas from code. The Replication Lab in CH41Gold.MDB on the CD-ROM accompanying this book illustrates the use of these methods.

✦ **Replication Manager 4.0 Utility** — Microsoft Office 2000 Developer contains a utility called Replication Manager. This utility provides access to all the replication functions, with the exception of creating a partial replica, which must be done in code, and offers a facility for scheduling the synchronization of replicas.

Access replication

To convert your database to a Design Master and create the first replica from within Access, select Tools ⇨ Replication ⇨ Create Replica. This is the same process described earlier in this chapter.

Steps to create a replica of a Design Master table:

1. Open the Design Master table CstPtLit.

2. Select Tools ⇨ Replication ⇨ Create Replica from the menu. Access will open the Location of New Replica dialog box.

3. Select a name for the replica — (Default is "replica# of [table name]"). For this example, type **My Replica of Customer Pets Lite** as shown in Figure 41-2.

4. Click the OK button.

5. Access displays a new dialog box informing you that the new replica will not appear in the potential synchronization partners until the database is closed and reopened, and which asks whether Access should close and reopen the database now. Click Yes in this dialog box.

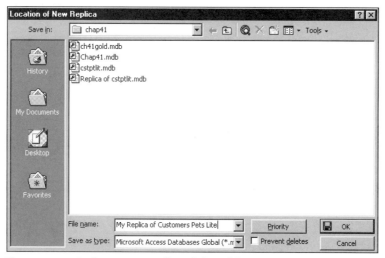

Figure 41-2: Saving a new replica of the table CstPtLit.

Note that once a Design Master table is opened, the Access title bar identifies your opened database as the Design Master. Click the Tables object button in the database window and select Show System Objects from the Tools ➪ Options menu to see the new tables added to your database during conversion. Figure 41-3 shows the system tables after converting the database named CstPtLit.

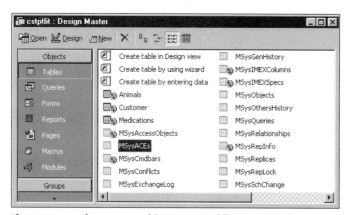

Figure 41-3: The system objects created for a Design Master database named CstPtLit.

Notice that the system objects used by the Design Master are now visible in Figure 41-3. They all begin with MSys.

If you now open the database My Replica of Customer Pets Lite, you will see that the title bar identifies your open database as a *Replica* (see Figure 41-4).

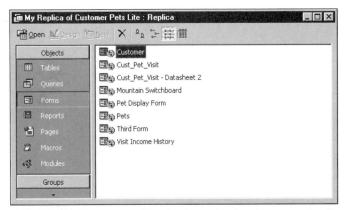

Figure 41-4: An open replica database (notice the name Replica at the end of the table).

Briefcase replication

If you installed the Briefcase Replication component when installing Access, you can use the Windows 95/98 Briefcase to convert your database to a replicable form and to synchronize that database with the briefcase replica.

When you install the Briefcase Replication component, it registers a reconciler ClassID with the briefcase, to be launched whenever an .MDB file is dropped onto the briefcase. The reconciler handles the database conversions and the synchronization of the briefcase replica with its associated replica whenever the user requests an update from the briefcase menu.

You can establish a briefcase icon on your Windows desktop by right-clicking the mouse and selecting New Briefcase from the shortcut menu.

Convert your database by dragging it from the Explorer window and dropping it on the Briefcase icon. The reconciler converts your database to the Design Master, leaving it in the source directory and creating a replica in the Briefcase. During this process, you are prompted to make two decisions: Do you want to create a backup of the nonreplicable database before conversion, and which of the two databases should be the Design Master — the original in the source directory or the one in the Briefcase?

You can send the Briefcase to the floppy disk drive, for example, load it onto another computer, and update the replica. When you return the Briefcase to the desktop, you'll want to synchronize the replica updates in the Briefcase with the other replica in the source directory. See the section "Synchronizing from the Briefcase," later in this chapter, for details on Briefcase synchronization.

Replication using DAO

DAO provides methods that you can use to support either full or partial replication from code. Using these methods, you can convert a database to a Design Master, create additional replicas, synchronize replica members, and resolve conflicts.

Note   CHAP41Gold.MDB on the CD-ROM contains a replication lab form that illustrates the use of the replication methods, as shown in Figure 41-5.

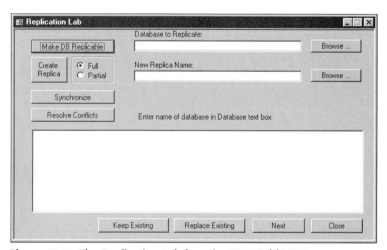

Figure 41-5: The Replication Lab form in CH41Gold.MDB.

To convert a database to a replicable form, type a database name into the Database text box or click the Browse button to select one.

Click the Make DB Replicable button to create and set the Replicable property on the selected database. This is done in the MakeDesignMaster procedure shown in Listing 41-1.

Listing 41-1: **Function to Create and Set the Replicable Property**

```
Public Function MakeDesignMaster(sDatabase As String)
On Error GoTo MDSErrHandler

Dim dbDatabase As Database
Dim dbProperty As Property

Set dbDatabase =
DBEngine.Workspaces(0).OpenDatabase(sDatabase, _      True)
Set dbProperty = dbDatabase.CreateProperty("Replicable",
dbText)
dbProperty.Value = "T"
dbDatabase.Properties.Append dbProperty
dbDatabase.Close
MakeDesignMaster = True
Exit Function
MDSErrHandler:
MsgBox Err.Description, vbCritical + vbOKOnly, "Conversion _
Error"
MakeDesignMaster = False
Exit Function
End Function
```

The `MakeDesignMaster` procedure creates the Replicable property and assigns the string value "T" to it. When the database is closed at the end of this procedure, the conversion to the Design Master occurs. Note that the database was opened exclusively.

Note   Prior to converting a database, you should ensure that it has been reviewed to remove unwanted data. The existence of unnecessary data only lengthens the conversion process and makes replicas carry the burden of additional records that will never be used. Getting rid of these records prior to conversion is best, because then the system does not need to replicate the removal of these records across all replica set members some time after conversion.

To create a replica, enter the name of the database that will be the source of the replica in the Database to Replicate text box, and enter the path and name of the resulting replica in the New Replica Name text box. The database entered in the Database text box is expected to be either the name of the Design Master or of another existing replica.

Click either the Full or Partial option button and click the Create Replica button to create the replica database. Selecting the Full option executes the `CreateReplica` procedure shown in Listing 41-2. The Partial option procedure is shown in Listing 41-3.

Listing 41-2: **Function to Create a Full Replica of a Database**

```
Public Function CreateReplica(sDatabase As String, sReplicaName
As _ String)
 On Error GoTo CRErrHandler
 Dim dbDatabase As Database
 Dim sDescription As String

 Set dbDatabase =
DBEngine.Workspaces(0).OpenDatabase(sDatabase)
 sDescription = "Replica of " & sDatabase
 dbDatabase.MakeReplica sReplicaName, sDescription
 dbDatabase.Close
 CreateReplica = True
 Exit Function
CRErrHandler:
 MsgBox Err.Description, vbCritical + vbOKOnly, "Create Error"
 CreateReplica = False
 Exit Function
 End Function
```

The CreateReplica procedure assigns a description to the replica, and then uses the MakeReplica method of the database object assigned by the OpenDatabase method on the database you entered in the Database text box.

If you want the replica to be read-only, you can uncomment the dbRepMake ReadOnly constant, which can be passed as the third parameter to the MakeReplica method. You may want to add this as an option on the form.

When you designate a table as replicable and create a full replica of the database containing that table, all records in the table are replicated to the replica member. You may not need all records for a particular replica user. If this is the case, you can create a partial replica using the code in Listing 41-3.

CreatePartial first creates a replica database to hold the partial replica. You do this by using the MakeReplica method of the source database.

The next step is to set the filter in the replica database. You accomplish this task by first collecting from the user the table to set a filter on and the filter specification. The lab example only allows one table and filter to be specified. The specifications collected from the CollectPartialFilter form are used to set the ReplicaFilter property of a table in the replica database.

After the ReplicaFilter is set, you can set relationships to pull records related to the filtered records. You do this by setting the PartialReplica property on all relations to participate in the partial population. The lab does not show the code to carry out this task.

Listing 41-3: **Function to Create a Partial Replica of a Database**

```
Public Function CreatePartial(sDatabase As String, sReplicaName
As _ String)
    Dim db As Database, dbReplica As Database
    Dim td As TableDef
    Dim frmFilter As Form

    Set db = OpenDatabase(sDatabase)

    ' Create a replica to hold the partial data
    db.MakeReplica sReplicaName, _
        "Partial Replica of " & sReplicaName, dbRepMakePartial
    db.Close

    ' Set the ReplicaFilter property

    Set dbReplica = OpenDatabase(sReplicaName, True)

    ' Show modal dialog to collect table filter
    DoCmd.OpenForm ("CollectPartialFilter")
    Set frmFilter = Forms("CollectPartialFilter")
    Set td = dbReplica.TableDefs(frmFilter.sFilterTable)
    td.ReplicaFilter = frmFilter.sFilter
    dbReplica.Close

    ' Set the PartialReplica property on relationships here

    ' Create the partial replica
    Set dbReplica = OpenDatabase(sReplicaName, True)
    dbReplica.PopulatePartial sDatabase
    dbReplica.Close
    Exit Function
End Function
```

The last step in creating a partial replica is to populate the replica with data according to the filter specification. The PopulatePartial method is used on the replica database to cause the ReplicaFilter on each table object to be applied to the database specified in the PopulateReplica method. This action pulls records from tables containing a ReplicaFilter property and related records in relations with a PartialReplica property. No other data is pulled into the partial replica. To remove a ReplicaFilter from a table, set the property to False.

Replication Manager utility

The Replication Manager utility found in Microsoft Office Developer enables you to manage replica sets from the point of creating the set or additional replica members to synchronizing the set through a scheduled or manual synchronization. There is no facility for resolving conflicts, but you can determine which replicas experienced conflicts or errors and launch Access from within the Manager to resolve them.

Figure 41-6 shows the Replication Manager Synchronizer window displaying one Synchronizer. The CstPtLit replica set is opened and is managed by the local Synchronizer named Michael Irwin's Synchronizer. This Synchronizer has two members that it is managing (you cannot currently see the names of the databases being managed). One of those replicas is the Design Master, as indicated by the Design Master icon. Tthe replica set member is also managed by the Synchronizer.

In Figure 41-6, note at the bottom of the Manager window a status message indicating that the Synchronizer is idle. Later in this chapter, you see how the Synchronizer is scheduled.

A Synchronizer, MSTRAN40.EXE, is responsible for monitoring and synchronizing the replicas within one or more replica sets. You can assign as many replicas as necessary to a Synchronizer. As shown in Figure 41-6, when a replica set is opened, the number of replica members in that set managed by a Synchronizer is shown in parentheses below the Synchronizer icon.

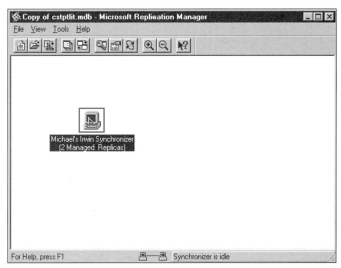

Figure 41-6: The Replication Manager utility window displaying one of its managed replica members.

When you first start the Replication Manager, it asks you to configure the Manager. This configuration designates various options the utility will use in managing replicas, such as the name of a shared network folder that will be used to cache transactions if a remote replica set member cannot be accessed during a synchronization and the path to the log file the Transporter will use to log its activity.

After the configuration is complete, the Synchronizer for the machine can be started and the Replication Manager can do its work. If the Synchronizer cannot be started, you cannot synchronize replicas with the utility; however, you can still synchronize by using one of the other methods discussed in this chapter.

Replicas may be located in any folder on the local machine and assigned to the local machine's Synchronizer, or they may be located in folders of other machines on the network and assigned to other Synchronizers, as is the case in Figure 41-6. The key to keeping these replicas in sync with each other is the knowledge of the Synchronizers regarding the member locations.

Note   When using the Replication Manager to manage your replica sets, do not move replicas or create replicas outside of the Manager. Instead, use the Manager to create replicas and to move them to other folders on the network to ensure integrity of the set.

To start managing or to stop managing replicas, use the Managed Replicas tab of the Replication Manager (shown in Figure 41-7). The replicas selected in this dialog box will be managed by the machine's Synchronizer.

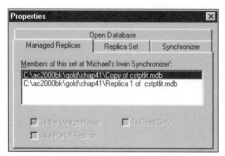

Figure 41-7: The Managed Replicas tab in the Replication Manager.

Figure 41-8 shows the dialog box in the Configuration Wizard for specifying the location of the *Dropbox*, or shared network folder, where the Synchronizer leaves messages for a replica that cannot be accessed during a synchronization process.

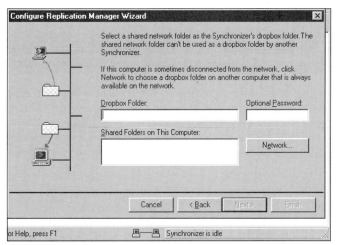

Figure 41-8: The Dropbox folder selection dialog box of the Replication Manager Configuration Wizard.

The Synchronizer attempts to synchronize all managed members of a set by directly accessing the members itself and applying the necessary changes. If a replica in the set cannot be accessed for any reason, the Synchronizer cannot synchronize the replica with the other members of the set. In this case, the Synchronizer will leave messages for the remote Synchronizer of the disconnected member. The messages are placed in a Dropbox to be picked up at a later time. Choose a Dropbox folder to be available when the Synchronizer runs (see Figure 41-8). If the folder is not accessible when the Synchronizer launches, it does not start.

If the Synchronizer does run into problems during synchronization, it logs the problems, along with other messages regarding the status of the synchronization, in a Synchronizer Log file. This file and the path to it are specified in the Configure Replication Manager Wizard. You should choose a file location on the Synchronizer machine so that the log can be written, even if network connections are down.

You can enter a name for the Synchronizer in the last dialog box of the wizard, which appears under the icon of the Synchronizer in the Replication Manager Synchronizer window. The machine name is a good choice for the Synchronizer name, although for this example we used the name Michael Irwin's Synchronization.

After the configuration is completed, you are ready to start using the Manager to convert your databases and create and synchronize your replicas.

Note   The Replication Manager does *not* require you to use its facilities for converting your database or creating new replicas. You may use any method presented in this chapter to create the replicas. After they are created, assign the replicas to a Synchronizer in the utility.

Using the Replication Manager to convert a database

If you do choose to convert your database with the utility, select Convert Database To Design Master from the Replication Manager Tools menu. After selecting the database to convert, the Convert Database to Design Master Wizard appears.

In the first dialog box of the wizard, you are prompted to choose between making a backup of the selected database or not. If you haven't yet done so, have the wizard create a backup. The next dialog box asks you to enter a description for the entire replica set, as shown in Figure 41-9. This description appears in the title bar of the Replication Manager window whenever you select a member of the replica set.

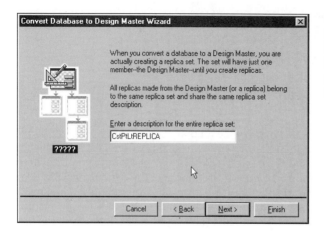

Figure 41-9: The second dialog box of the Convert Database Wizard is used to specify a description for the replica set.

The next dialog box of the wizard, shown in Figure 41-10, enables you to select the database objects you want replicated. You can choose to replicate all objects in the database or select specific objects. Consider the target users of the replicas and the objects they will need. Also consider the time required to synchronize replicas in making your choice of objects.

If the data in your database supports partitioning, you could create separate partitions (tables) of the main database and then replicate those partitions to their target users. For example, if your database supports an organization that is broken down into regions, you may have data that is accessed only by users in a particular region and no one else. By creating a database that maintains only that subset of data, you could reduce the size of the replica and the time required to synchronize it. These partitions would need to be synchronized only with the main database tables to support global reporting and queries, because none of the replica data would overlap. Opportunities for other types of partitioning may exist as well, so give some thought to your target group and the data you need to support their requirements before you begin replicating databases. As an alternative to this approach, you can create partial replicas in DAO code.

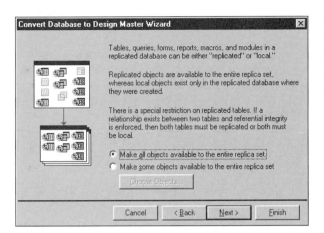

Figure 41-10: The third dialog box of the Convert Database Wizard enables you to select database objects to replicate.

Note In the next step of the Conversion Database Wizard, you are asked to choose between read-only and read-write replicas, as shown in Figure 41-11. Select the appropriate option for your intended usage of the replicas.

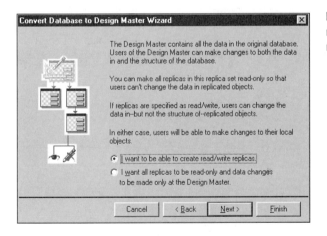

Figure 41-11: Replicas may be designated as read-only or read-write.

As shown in Figure 41-12, you have a choice of managing the Design Master with the local Synchronizer or deferring assignment to a Synchronizer until later.

Clicking the Finish button starts the conversion process and then opens the Design Master. Unlike the Access method and the Briefcase method, the Replication Manager does not automatically create a first replica member when it converts your database. The outcome of this process is the Design Master only.

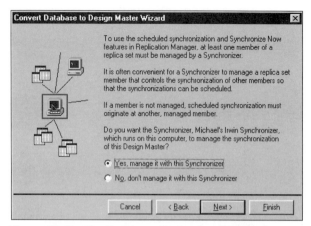

Figure 41-12: The Database Conversion Wizard gives you the opportunity to synchronize the Design Master with the local Synchronizer or to defer the assignment to later.

Creating replicas of the converted database

To create replicas of your converted database, select New Replica from the File menu. The New Replica Wizard will ask you to select the Design Master as the source of the new replica or another member replica. The wizard will then prompt you to choose between read-only and read-write attributes for the new replica, as shown in Figure 41-13.

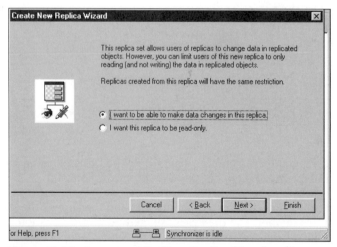

Figure 41-13: A screen of the New Replica Wizard used to designate the new replica as read-only or read-write.

Next the Wizard asks you to choose the local Synchronizer or defer Synchronizer assignment for the new replica member, as shown in Figure 41-14. At least one member of the replica set needs to be assigned to a Synchronizer. If you have already assigned the Design Master to a Synchronizer, then you can defer assignment for this replica.

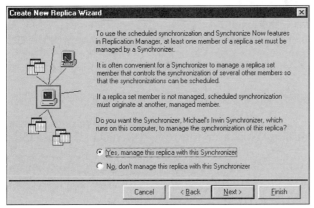

Figure 41-14: Assign the local Synchronizer to manage the new replica or defer assignment.

When you have finished using the Wizard to create the new replica, an additional count will be added to the Synchronization window if you requested it to manage replicas. If you did not request it to manage replicas, they will be placed in the Replication Manager window as unmanaged replica icons. Figure 41-15 shows an unmanaged replica added to the system.

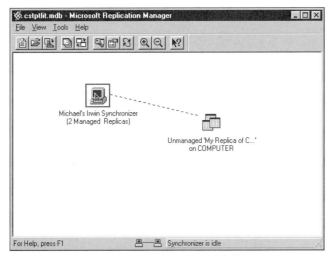

Figure 41-15: An unmanaged replica added to system.

To view the objects contained in a replica, select the replica member in the Synchronization window and double-click or right-click the mouse to view properties. On the Open Database tab, click the View Object Status button. The Object Status dialog box displays the objects contained in the replica set and their status.

Synchronizing Replicas

All the replication facilities previously discussed—Access, Briefcase, DAO, and Replication Manager—offer the capability to synchronize members of the replica set. This next topic presents synchronization in each of these four facilities.

Synchronizing with Access

You can synchronize your open replica member with another selected member of the set by choosing Synchronize Now from the Tools ➪ Replication menu in Access.

From the Synchronize Database dialog box, select another replica member to synchronize with from the drop-down list box, or click the Browse button to specify a member not yet in the list, as shown in Figure 41-16.

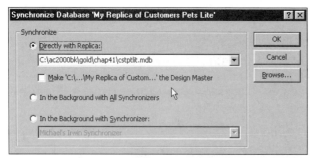

Figure 41-16: The Synchronize Database dialog box asks you to choose a target replica member to synchronize with the current database.

Tip   Replica set member names reside in the MSysReplicas table within each member database. A replica member becomes known to another member if one is created from the other or synchronized with the other. If a replica named Replica xxx1 creates a member replica named Replica xxx2, Replica xxx2 is immediately known to Replica xxx1 but is not known to Replica xxx or any other member until Replica xxx2 and Replica xxx are synchronized with each other. At that time, the existence of Replica xxx2 is entered into the MSysReplicas table of Replica xxx and vice versa.

Tip You can remove a replica from a set by deleting the physical .MDB file. This action, however, does not remove the replica entry from the MSysReplicas table in remaining replica member databases, and the Synchronize Database dialog box continues to list the removed replica member in its drop-down list as a candidate for synchronization. To remove a replica from a set and from the candidate list in the Synchronize dialog box, attempt to synchronize the current open replica with the deleted replica. Access will detect the missing database and remove the member from the replica set by removing the entry from the MSysReplicas table.

After deleting the file and removing it from the replica set, open Replication Manager and the managed replica set member or choose Refresh Synchronization Window from the Tools menu. You will no longer see the deleted replica member in the window. Attempting to remove a deleted replica from a managed set with the Replication Manager utility will only report a problem in its synchronization history details. It does not have the same effect as the synchronization from within Access.

Synchronizing from the Briefcase

Select the Details view from the Briefcase View menu to display the replica status information. To start the synchronization process, choose Update All or Update Selection from the Briefcase menu. For the .MDB replica in the Briefcase, a dialog box is presented that depicts the Briefcase replica and its target as well as the source from which the Briefcase replica was created. Click the Update button to start synchronization.

When the synchronization process ends, the status of the replica in the Briefcase changes to Up-to-date. Open the target database to verify that the briefcase database changes have been updated or to deal with the conflicts that may have been recorded. Be sure to check the Briefcase database as well if a bidirectional synchronization, changes passed between Briefcase and target and vice versa, has been performed.

If you subsequently make a design change to the Design Master, you again can select Update from the Briefcase menu to synchronize the design change with the replica

Synchronizing with DAO

Note On the Replication Lab form (frmReplicationLab) in CH41.MDB, included on the CD-ROM with this book, enter the names of the replicas in the Database and Replica Name text boxes and click the Synchronize button.

The `SyncDBs` procedure (shown in Listing 41-4) called from the Synchronize button's click event uses the `Synchronize` method of the database object. The `sSyncWithDB` string passed into the procedure is the name from the Replica Name text box, and it designates the other member with which the database object is to synchronize.

You may specify the direction of synchronization between the database object (`dbDatabase`) and the replica (`sSyncWithDB`) with the second parameter of the `Synchronize` method.

Use the `dbRepImpExpChanges` constant to replicate the changes in the `dbDatabase` database into the `sSyncWithDB` database.

Use `dbRepImportChanges` to replicate the changes in the `sSyncWithDB` database into the `dbDatabase` database.

The `dbRepImpExpChanges` constant used in the `SyncDBs` procedure yields a bidirectional exchange of changes between the two databases.

Listing 41-4: Function to Synchronize Two Replicas Using the Synchronize Method

```
 Public Function SyncDBs(sDatabase As String, sSyncWithDB As
String, _
   RepType As Integer)
   On Error GoTo SDBErrHandler
   Dim dbDatabase As Database
   If RepType = 0 Then

      ' Full replica
      Set dbDatabase = _
   DBEngine.Workspaces(0).OpenDatabase(sDatabase)
      dbDatabase.Synchronize sSyncWithDB, dbRepImpExpChanges
   Else

      ' Partial replica
      Set dbDatabase = _
   DBEngine.Workspaces(0).OpenDatabase(sSyncWithDB)
      dbDatabase.PopulatePartial sDatabase
   End If
   dbDatabase.Close
   SyncDBs = True
   Exit Function
 SDBErrHandler:
  MsgBox Err.Description, vbCritical + vbOKOnly,
"Synchronization _
      Error"
  SyncDBs = False
   Exit Function
 End Function
```

Note in Listing 41-4 the use of the `PopulatePartial` method to synchronize the changes contained in a partial replica indicated in the Replica Name text box with the database indicated in the Database Name text box. You use this method if you select the Partial option.

`PopulatePartial` synchronizes the changes in the partial replica member with the full database, clears the partial replica, and then repopulates it using the currently specified ReplicaFilter contained in the replica database. This portion of the `PopulatePartial` method is the same behavior used to create the partial replica, as discussed in the section "Replication using DAO," previously in this chapter.

Using `PopulatePartial` instead of `Synchronize` ensures that the partial is up to date with the full replica and that no orphaned records are left in the partial replica. Orphaned records can be created whenever a change in the partial replica data causes a record to no longer have the characteristics specified in the ReplicaFilter. Say, for example, your ReplicaFilter asks for all customers in Arizona at the time the partial replica was created. If the replica is updated to change a customer's state to New York, that customer no longer meets the Filter specifications. At synchronize time, `PopulatePartial` will pass the change to the full database and then receive new customers according to the current ReplicaFilter. If the ReplicaFilter still specifies Arizona customers, the customer changed to New York will not be pulled into the replica. Had the synchronization process merely exchanged changes, the New York customer would never be updated and therefore would be orphaned from the Arizona customers.

Synchronizing with Replication Manager

Using the Replication Manager, you have two options for synchronizing replicas. You can synchronize on demand or through a synchronization schedule, which you can customize to run on any 15-minute interval within a 24-hour clock.

To synchronize on demand, choose Synchronize Now from the Tools menu. This displays the Synchronize Now dialog box shown in Figure 41-17.

In the Synchronize Now dialog box, you specify the members to synchronize with the selected replica icon. You can synchronize with all other members managed by a Synchronizer, with all members of the set at the local Synchronizer, or with a specific member.

If you select the option *All members of the set managed by a Synchronizer*, you can select the exchange options in the Options frame. Only a bidirectional exchange is possible with the *All members of the set at this Synchronizer* option.

To set up a schedule for synchronizing members of replica sets managed by the local Synchronizer, right-click a replica icon and select Edit Locally Managed Replica Schedule from the pop-up menu (see Figure 41-18).

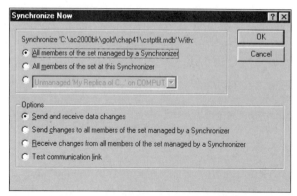

Figure 41-17: The Synchronize Now dialog box in Replication Manager enables you to specify the members to synchronize.

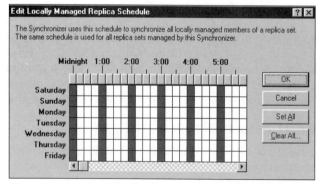

Figure 41-18: The Edit Locally Managed Replica Schedule can be set to automatically synchronize replica members at the local Synchronizer.

Click the cells representing the time of day you want to schedule a synchronization. Click the button at the top of the schedule grid to select all cells for the indicated time and have synchronization run at that time on every day of the week.

It is not necessary to have Replication Manager running for the synchronization schedule to take effect, but you do need to have the Synchronizer running.

Resolving Conflicts

When you synchronize replicas, you may detect conflicting changes that prevent one of the change records from being applied, or you may detect errors such as referential integrity errors or key errors.

Conflicts arise when the same record, identified by the GUID, is updated at two replica members in the set. The synchronization process selects one of the records to be applied to the two members being synchronized and writes the other record as a conflict record into a side table created in the database that owns the conflict.

In the case of a conflict, Jet selects the record to apply to the table based on the version number in the record's s_Lineage field. This version number is updated each time the record is changed in each replica, and Jet selects the record having the highest version number, which is the record changed the most. If the version numbers are identical, then Jet must select one of the records to apply and write the other to the conflict side table.

Errors can result whenever an update or design change from the Design Master violates a Jet- or Access-enforced rule, such as a unique key error or referential integrity error. The error is written into the MSysErrors table of the replica member where the error occurred. Before the members can be considered safely in sync, you must research and resolve all errors among the replicas and resynchronize the set to the point of no errors or conflicts.

Although you can use Replication Manager to determine the outcome of a synchronization, you cannot resolve the conflicts or errors within the utility. You can use Access or code your own DAO procedures to handle the resolution of problems.

To view the synchronization results of a replica, right-click a replica icon and select View Local Synchronization History from the pop-up menu.

Resolving conflicts in Access

Opening a database after synchronization displays a message box informing you of any synchronization problems that occurred. You have the option to resolve the problems in this message box, or you can resolve the problems at a later time by choosing Resolve Conflicts from the Tools menu. Access displays a dialog box showing you the tables having problems and the types of problems experienced. Figure 41-19 shows a message that appears when there is a conflict.

Figure 41-19: A conflict between two databases.

Resolving conflicts displays a dialog box showing the existing record and the conflict record, as shown in Figure 41-20. You are shown a list of tables with conflicts and the number of conflicts in each table. Figure 41-20 shows one conflict (as designated by the number 1 in parentheses) in the table Customers.

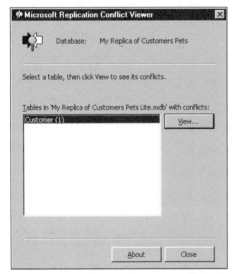

Figure 41-20: The Replication Conflict Viewer dialog box shows one conflict in the table Customers.

If you click the View button, you will see a dialog box similar to the one in Figure 41-21.

You are asked to choose between keeping the existing data, keeping revised data, overwriting data with the conflict record, or overwriting data with the revised data. Once you choose what to do, you can process the choice by pressing the Resolve button. Either choice deletes the entry from the conflict side table and either moves to the next conflict record or informs you that all conflicts have been processed.

The Data Errors dialog box shows you the error details, such as duplicate values in a key field resulting from the same key being added to a table in the replicas. This error can arise if the key fields are not AutoNumber fields. The action you take depends on the type of error reported and may involve some extensive research with the replica users to determine how to resolve the error.

After resolving the reported problems, you should resynchronize the set to ensure that all problems have been resolved before releasing the databases into the production environment.

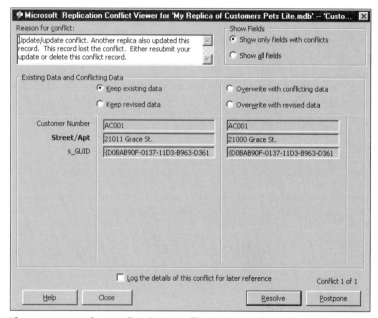

Figure 41-21: The Replication Conflicts Viewer dialog box asks you either to choose to keep the existing record or to overwrite the existing record with the conflict record.

Resolving conflicts with DAO

If conflicts or errors result from the synchronization process, you can resolve them with your own procedures.

The Replication Lab form presents a method to resolve conflicts that is similar to the one used when you chose Resolve Conflicts from the Access Replication menu, but the method only illustrates the handling of conflicts. You can add procedures to handle errors by processing the MSysErrors table.

Processing the MSysErrors table enables you to find the tables that experienced conflicts and step through each conflict. The Replication Lab method asks you to choose either to keep the existing record (the one that was chosen by the synchronization process) or to overwrite it with the conflict record (the one that lost in the battle to become a row in the table).

On the Replication Lab form, enter the name of the database for which you want to resolve conflicts in the Database text box and click the Resolve Conflicts button. The click event procedure for the Resolve Conflicts button calls the ProcessConflicts function to manage the display of conflicts.

The ProcessConflicts function shown in Listing 41-5 sets up the Recordsets needed to inspect the conflicts in all tables having conflicts. You can determine these tables by inspecting a table property called ConflictTable, which returns the name of the side table holding the conflict records. Because this method would require visiting each TableDef in the database, the Replication Lab uses a more direct route to the conflicts by reading MSysSideTables. This system table records the names of the side tables holding the conflict records along with the GUID of the base table in which those conflicts occurred. To determine the name of the base table, another system table is used, MSysTableGuids, which holds the GUIDs and names of all tables in the database.

Listing 41-5: **ProcessConflicts Manages the Collection and Display of Database Conflicts**

```
Public Function ProcessConflicts(sDatabase As String)

On Error GoTo PCErrHandler

Set dbDatabase =
DBEngine.Workspaces(0).OpenDatabase(sDatabase, _
True)
' Process Conflicts
On Error Resume Next
sSQLStmt = "SELECT [SideTable],[TableName] FROM _
MSysSideTables,MSysTableGuids WHERE MSysSideTables![TableGuid]
= _
MSysTableGuids![s_GUID]"
Set rsSideTables = dbDatabase.OpenRecordset(sSQLStmt, _
dbOpenSnapshot)
    If Err = 0 Then
      If NextSideTable() = False Then
          rsSideTables.Close
            MsgBox "All conflicts have been processed"
      Else
          rc = NextConflict()
      End If
    End If
' Put Your Process Errors Code Here
```

```
ProcessConflicts = True
Exit Function

PCErrHandler:
ProcessConflicts = False
Exit Function
End Function
```

Replication Lab steps through each conflict record in the current side table, presents each conflict record along with the existing record in the base table, and asks you to choose between those records. The base table record is selected using the conflict record's GUID field. This process is found in the NextConflict procedure shown in Listing 41-6.

Listing 41-6: **Routine to Display the Existing Records and Associated Conflict Records**

```
Public Function NextConflict()
If Not rsConflicts.EOF Then
    Me!OLEControl10.ListItems.Clear
    rsBaseTable.Index = "s_GUID"
    rsBaseTable.Seek "=", rsConflicts![s_GUID]
    If rsBaseTable.NoMatch Then
'Record updated in Source not present in Target
    Else
'Record found is in conflict with the conflict table record
'Add existing record to view
        Set liItem = OLEControl10.ListItems.Add(, "K" & _
CStr(rsBaseTable.Name), CStr(rsBaseTable.Name))
        For i = 1 To rsBaseTable.Fields.Count
          liItem.SubItems(i) = rsBaseTable.Fields(i -1)   .Value
        Next i
      ' Add conflict record to view
        Set liItem = OLEControl10.ListItems.Add(, "K" & _
CStr(rsConflicts.Name), _
CStr(rsConflicts.Name))
        For i = 1 To rsConflicts.Fields.Count
          liItem.SubItems(i) = rsConflicts.Fields(i - 1).Value
        Next i
    End If
    rsConflicts.MoveNext
    NextConflict = True
Else
    NextConflict = False
End If
Exit Function
End Function
```

After all conflicts for a table are resolved, the next side table is selected. The resolution process repeats until all side tables have been inspected. The NextSideTable procedure in Listing 41-7 implements this process.

Listing 41-7: Function to Open a Conflict Table and Its Corresponding Base Table

```
Public Function NextSideTable()
 If Not rsSideTables.EOF Then
 ' Open the Conflict Table
    Set rsConflicts = _
 dbDatabase.OpenRecordset(rsSideTables![SideTable],
 dbOpenDynaset)
  ' Open the Base Table where conflict occurred
    Set rsBaseTable = _
 dbDatabase.OpenRecordset(rsSideTables![TableName],
 dbOpenTable)
    Me!OLEControl10.ColumnHeaders.Clear
    Set colHeader = Me!OLEControl10.ColumnHeaders.Add(,
 "Table", _
 "Table", 2000)
    For i = 0 To rsBaseTable.Fields.Count - 1
       Set colHeader = Me!OLEControl10.ColumnHeaders.Add(, _
 (rsBaseTable.Fields(i).Name), _
 (rsBaseTable.Fields(i).Name), 2000)
    Next i
 ' Get the next sidetable holding conflicts
    rsSideTables.MoveNext
    NextSideTable = True
 Else
    NextSideTable = False
 End If
 Exit Function
 End Function
```

If you click the Replace Existing button, the existing record in the base table is replaced with the conflict record in the side table. This process is found in the ReplaceExistingRec procedure listed in Listing 41-8.

After the conflict is resolved, the conflict record is removed from the side table. When the side table is empty, the table is deleted from the database. This process is implemented in the RemoveConflict procedure shown in Listing 41-9. This same function is also called when you elect to keep the existing record.

Listing 41-8: **Function Used to Replace a Base Table Record with a Conflict Record**

```
Public Function ReplaceExistingRec()
 'Replace existing base table record with conflict record
 On Error Resume Next
 rsConflicts.MovePrevious
 rsBaseTable.Edit
 For i = 0 To rsConflicts.Fields.Count - 1
    rsBaseTable.Fields(i).Value = rsConflicts.Fields(i).Value
 Next i
 rsBaseTable.Update
 rsConflicts.MoveNext
 Exit Function
 End Function
```

Listing 41-9: **Function to Remove a Conflict Record from a Side Table**

```
Public Function RemoveConflict()
 ' This procedure deletes the current conflict record. When the
_
conflict
 ' table is empty, the table itself is deleted.
 On Error Resume Next
 rsConflicts.MovePrevious
 rsConflicts.Delete
 rsConflicts.MoveNext
 If rsConflicts.EOF Then
    rsConflicts.Close
    rsSideTables.MovePrevious
    dbDatabase.TableDefs.Delete rsSideTables![SideTable]
    rsSideTables.MoveNext
 End If
 Exit Function
 End Function
```

Building a New Design Master

If the Design Master becomes corrupted or lost, you can designate one of the other replicas as the new Design Master.

With one of the replica databases open in Access, choose Recover Design Master from the Tools ➪ Replication menu. A message box appears, as in Figure 41-22, informing you of the current Design Master name and asking you to verify that it has been lost or corrupted. Click Yes to continue.

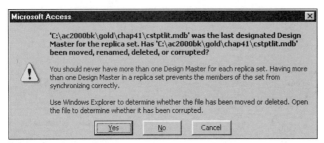

Figure 41-22: Creating a new Design Master.

Access next tells you to synchronize the current database with all other replica members before designating it as the new Design Master. If you have already done this, click Yes.

Access designates the current replica as the Design Master, which enables you to make design changes to the database and replicate those changes to other members in the set.

To designate the current database as the Design Master, Access changed the DesignMasterID property of the database to the ID of the replica. This can be accomplished in your own DAO procedures by assigning the current database ReplicaID value to the DesignMasterID property.

After changing a replica to the Design Master, you need to synchronize the replica with all other members of the set to update their DesignMasterIDs to point to the new Design Master.

Summary

Replication is useful for distributing your Access application code, tables, queries, forms, and reports to others. You can use replication to supply an Access database or part of a database to a portable computer, to computers on a network, or to a stand-alone machine. Depending on the permissions you assign to the replica, users of a replicated database may have read-only or read-write access. This chapter explained the following:

✦ The components of replication

✦ How to synchronize replicas

✦ How to use briefcase replication

✦ Resolving replica conflicts

In the next and last chapter, you learn about add-ins and libraries.

✦   ✦   ✦

Exploring Add-Ins and Libraries

Access 2000 add-ins are databases containing procedures and associated objects that you can add to Access using the Add-In Manager. By doing so, you can enhance the functionality of Access or a custom application developed for the Access environment. There are three types of Access add-ins: menu add-ins, builder add-ins, and wizard add-ins. This chapter provides an overview of the various add-ins prepackaged with Access and presents a hands-on look at building a custom add-in wizard that creates a table, form, and report.

Understanding Types of Add-Ins

Some add-ins are context-specific and are launched when the user attempts to perform some action in a particular context. Examples of context-specific add-ins include the Access Form Wizards, invoked when a user builds a new Autoform, and Control Wizards, invoked when a user inserts a new control on a form with the Control Wizards enabled. Context-specific add-ins are usually represented as wizard add-ins or builder add-ins.

Add-ins that are not context-specific are generally classified as menu add-ins. They appear on the submenu when you choose Tools ➪ Add-Ins. In Access 2000, many of the add-ins are found in submenus under the Tools menu. For instance, the User-Level Security Wizard can be found under the Security menu of the Tools menu.

You can see the built-in menu add-ins and wizards installed by Access 2000 by inspecting the system registry. Using the Registry Editor, expand the tree HKEY_LOCAL_MACHINE\Software\Microsoft\Office\9.0\Access. In this subtree, you see two subkeys, labeled Menu Add-Ins and Wizards. Expand these subkeys to see the various built-in add-ins in Access 2000.

Later in this chapter, you'll explore a custom menu add-in and discover how to register this add-in in the registry. For now, expand the Wizards subkey, the Control Wizards subkey, and the CommandButton subkey. Click once on the subkey labeled MSCommandButtonWizard to see the values registered for this add-in. Note the Library value. This is the database location of the database housing this add-in, the Command Button Wizard. Also note the Function value, which specifies the function in the add-in that Access will call when a user invokes the add-in. You'll become more familiar with these entries when you explore the custom add-in. Figure 42-1 shows this value.

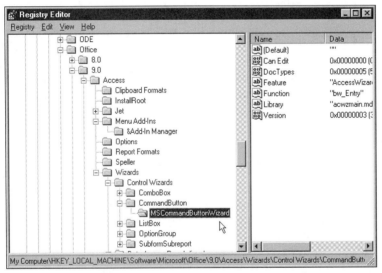

Figure 42-1: Viewing the values registered for a wizard of Access 2000 using the RegEdit program.

A *wizard* is an add-in that helps you create objects such as tables, queries, reports, and forms. Some wizards create entire applications or sets of routines that you can integrate into your database. Access 2000 has several built-in wizards, as you saw in the Registry, that you should find helpful. You'll find many more wizards available from third-party vendors. Wizards either are sold directly for an end-user's use, perhaps to produce a query or report, or are sold to enhance the productivity of

Access application developers. As mentioned earlier, you also can build your own wizards.

Another type of add-in is a *builder*. Builders are tools that help simplify a task, such as building a formula for a control on a form or report or setting a control property. Builders are usually simpler than wizards in terms of the user interface and the resulting output of the add-in. Access 2000 installs Property builders and an Expression builder, which you will use quite often as you build your applications.

The third type of add-in is the *menu* add-in. This type of add-in is not associated with any particular context in using Access. You install it, and it becomes a choice found on the Tools ⇨ Add-Ins menu (although you can place the add-in on other menus). An example of a menu add-in is one that you would create and add to Access.

Although not actually another type of add-in, there are several tools that can be found under the appropriate section of the Tools menu. For example, the Switchboard Manager can be found under the Database Utilities menu of the Tools menu. This is an add-in; however, it is no longer found under the Add-In section of the Tools menu. In Access 97 and earlier versions, it was found under the Add-In menu.

Understanding Libraries

Add-ins live in a standard Access database and usually have either an .MDA or an .MDE extension. These databases are built with the sole purpose of housing one or more add-in procedures and associated database objects, such as forms, queries, and tables. These types of databases are known as *add-in databases* but sometimes are referred to as *libraries*.

Although add-ins can be considered library databases, the term *library* is generally reserved for databases that hold Visual Basic routines that provide utility across several Access applications. Using libraries will enable you to provide procedures that are customized for your business to all Access applications developed for the business, as well as to maintain the procedures in one common source, the library database.

Referencing library databases

To be used by Access 2000 databases, library databases must be in Access 2000 format and require that a reference be made to them from the calling database. Circular references are not allowed, meaning that you cannot establish a reference from YourAccountingLib.MDA to YourMathLib.MDA and have YourMathLib.MDA reference YourAccountingLib.MDA. These libraries can reference each other but not at the same time.

To establish a reference by using Access menus from YourApp.MDB to YourLib.MDA for example, follow these steps:

1. Open a module window in YourApp.MDB.

2. Choose References from the Tools menu and then click the Browse button in the References dialog box.

3. In the Files of Type box, select Databases (*.mdb, *.mda, *.mde).

4. Locate your library database (YourLib.MDA in this example).

5. Click OK.

Tip You should see your library database name in the list of available references in the References dialog box. If your library contains a procedure with a name that is also found in another referenced library, a call to this procedure will invoke the first library in the references list to contain the procedure name. If your code is not being called, you can move your library higher on the list of referenced libraries or rename the procedure so that conflicts do not occur. You should take care in naming library procedures to reduce the risk of collisions with other libraries. Use a naming convention that has a good chance of being unique.

If you want to establish a reference at runtime in Visual Basic code, use one of the `Create reference` methods of the `References` collection.

Tip Your application database can now call routines in the referenced database. The procedures called in your library must be Public procedures and must be resident in standard modules within the library database. Although your library procedures can use Private procedures in the library, the referencing database cannot use those Private procedures. Additionally, you cannot call functions contained in class modules within the library database. To use your library class methods, call public functions contained in standard modules that use the library class modules. Your library routines can be set up to return a calculated result and open Access objects stored in the library database. You can even use a library database to store custom toolbars.

The section "Exploring .MDE files," later in this chapter, introduces the .MDE file type, which enables you to save your database as a compressed file with your source code removed. If you choose to save your library database as an .MDE file and your database references other databases, those referenced databases must also be in .MDE format before your save operation can be successful.

Calling functions in Dynamic Link Libraries

As you gain experience developing Access applications and libraries, sooner or later you'll find yourself needing a function that resides in a Windows Dynamic Link Library (DLL) or some third-party DLL. It is quite common today to find Access applications containing calls to the Windows Application Programming Interface (API) to take advantage of the power provided by the API.

To use functions contained in DLLs, you need to declare the functions to VBA. You use the `Declare` statement for this purpose. `Declare` informs VBA of the name of the DLL containing the function being declared as well as the arguments and argument types the function expects. This information enables VBA to check your function call at compile time for proper argument types. The following `Declare` statement is specified in the CH42.MDA General Declarations section of the `General Functions` module to declare the common dialog `GetOpenFileName` function for opening a file (this code is included on the CD-ROM with this book):

```
Declare Function GetOpenFileName Lib "comdlg32.dll" Alias _
"GetOpenFileNameA" _
(pOpenfilename As OPENFILENAME) As Long
```

In the preceding `Declare` statement, `GetOpenFileName` is the name of the function being declared and is specified as residing in the DLL named by the `Lib` argument, comdlg32.dll.

The `Alias` argument specifies that `GetOpenFileNameA` is the actual name of the function in the comdlg32.dll. The program will use `GetOpenFileName`, but the actual function called will be `GetOpenFileNameA`.

The parentheses contain the arguments expected by the `GetOpenFileNameA` function. In this case, the function expects an OPENFILENAME structure to be passed into it. You need to declare this structure before the reference to it in the `Declare` statement.

The final `As Long` indicates to Visual Basic that `GetOpenFileNameA` returns a value of type `Long`. Alternatively, you can specify this return type as follows:

```
Declare Function GetOpenFileName& Lib "comdlg32.dll" Alias _
"GetOpenFileNameA" (pOpenfilename As OPENFILENAME)
```

Note the use of the & symbol at the end of the function name to designate the return type.

You can specify the arguments as `Optional`, `ByVal`, `ByRef`, or `ParamArray` to indicate the means of passing the arguments to the function, and each variable specified can also designate a type. Note that the variables specified in the `Declare` statement need not match those used in the actual call to the function, but the variables used in the call must match the type specified by position.

If you use `Optional` to specify an argument that may be passed to the function or omitted, you must designate the type of the argument as `Variant` and specify all remaining arguments as `Optional` also.

`ByVal` causes the variable's value to be passed to the function instead of to the variable's address. If an argument is designated as `ByVal`, the function cannot modify the argument variable (with the exception of `String` arguments, which are covered shortly).

ByRef causes the variable's address to be passed to the function. Argument variables passed in this manner can be modified by the called function. This is the manner in which you pass a variable to receive a return value other than that passed by the function's As Type specifier. In other words, some functions pass back a value indicating the success of the function execution in the function's As Type return value but also return other values into variables passed ByRef. If you don't specify an argument-passing method, the ByRef method is assumed.

The ParamArray specification can only be used as the last argument specifier and implies an Optional array of Variant elements. You may pass any number of arguments in place of this argument specification.

If a function does not require any arguments, you need only specify the parentheses with nothing inside of them.

Indicate the type of the argument after the argument name by using As Type, where Type can be any of the valid Visual Basic types, a user-defined structure as used in the GetOpenFileName function, an object type, or the generic type Object. If you use ByVal in front of a String type, Visual Basic passes a C-Type string, that is, a reference to a null-terminated string. This type of argument can be modified by the calling function.

Take a look at the OpenFileDlg function in the Ch42.MDA General Functions module. The function first sets up a string variable with the filters that will appear in the File of Type drop-down list in the OpenFile dialog box. These are the file types that will be listed in the directories chosen by the user of the File Open dialog box.

Next, various string variables are initialized, which will be assigned to members of the OPENFILENAME structure passed to the GetOpenFileName function. The DlgTitle string variable, for example, will be assigned to the lpstrTitle member of OPENFILENAME to display a custom title in the FileOpen dialog box when it appears.

After the initializations, the members of the variable pOpenfilename declared as an OPENFILENAME structure are given values before the actual call to the GetOpenFileName function. Note that some of the structure variables are assigned a value that is returned from another function, the lstrcpy function.

The lstrcpy function is another Windows API function found in kernel32.dll, as declared in the Declare Function statement in the General Declarations. This function copies the second argument string to the first argument string and returns the address (pointer) of the first argument string as a Long. This address is assigned to various member variables of the OPENFILENAME structure, which require an address value. Note that all these member variables begin with the letters *lp,* which stand for *long pointer.* This naming scheme is generally followed throughout the Win32 API.

Tip   Not all structure members with names beginning with the letters *lp* are assigned the return value of `lstrcpy`. Some are assigned a value of zero. A zero value in variables storing long pointers is interpreted as a null pointer. If you are working with API calls that require input address values or pointers and they will accept null-valued pointers, you can assign zero and the function should be able to accept it.

When the OPENFILENAME structure has been set up for the call, the actual call to `GetOpenFileName` is made to open the `FileOpen` dialog box. The address of the filename chosen by the end user is returned in the `lpstrFile` member of OPENFILENAME. Again, `lstrcpy` assigns the filename to a string variable within the function. Because the `lpstrFile` points to a null-terminated string, one ending in `Chr$(0)`, the function strips the null character at the end of the filename using the `InStr` and `Left$` functions of VBA. The resulting string is passed back to the caller of `OpenFileDlg`. This filename contains the full path of the file.

Win32 API calls, and calls to other DLLs, can be valuable in your Access applications. Of course, you have to know the API functions and their syntax before using them successfully in your application, and some are easier to use than others. If you do decide to use a Win32 API call, you can pick up its declaration statement, structure declarations, and constant declarations from the Win32 API Viewer application that ships with the Office Developers Edition. This application is located in the Office\ODE Tools\Win32 API Viewer directory. It's a handy tool for reducing function declaration errors as a result of typing the declaration statements manually.

An Overview of a Few Access 2000 Add-Ins

This section presents an overview of some of Access's built-in add-ins. Three add-ins are explored here to give you a feel for the power of these tools: the Switchboard Manager add-in, the Form Wizard, and the Command Button Control Wizard.

Using the Switchboard Manager

Switchboards are forms in an application that present a road map of the application components or subsystems. Using a switchboard, the end user can easily choose the part of the application he or she wants to use, usually by clicking a button on the form. The switchboard is a main form presented to the user when the application starts up, or it can be a form buried in the application to help the end user through a series of tasks and can act as a checklist.

You can use the Switchboard Manager to build one or more switchboards for your application or to edit an existing switchboard built previously with the Manager. Use the following steps to create a new switchboard:

1. Click Tools ➪ Database Utilities and then select the Switchboard Manager.

2. If the Switchboard Manager doesn't find its Switchboard Items table resident in your database, it displays a dialog box that asks if you would like to build a new switchboard. Click Yes.

3. In the Switchboard Manager dialog box, the default switchboard, referred to as a page, is highlighted (see Figure 42-2). Click the Edit button to add items to this switchboard.

Figure 42-2: The Switchboard Manager dialog box.

4. In the Edit Switchboard Page dialog box, you can type a name for the switchboard in the Switchboard Name box to change the default name, or you can use the default name Main Switchboard (see Figure 42-3). Click the New button to add a new item to this switchboard. The Edit Switchboard Item dialog box appears.

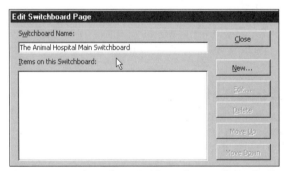

Figure 42-3: The Edit Switchboard Page dialog box.

5. The Edit Switchboard Item dialog box presents three choices for the switchboard item (see Figure 42-4). In the Text box, enter a name for the item. This name will appear on a switchboard button. In the Command combo box, select the command you want to activate when the user clicks this button.

Figure 42-4: The Edit Switchboard Item dialog box.

What you enter in the third entry, the Form box, varies with the selection in the Command combo box. If you select the command Go To Switchboard, for example, the third entry needs to specify the name of the switchboard to activate. If you specify a command of Run Code, the third entry needs to be the name of the function to run. Some command selections, such as Design Application, do not need a third entry.

6. After entering your choices for this switchboard item, click OK. Repeat adding new items until you have completed your switchboard entries for this switchboard.

7. In the Edit Switchboard Page dialog box, you can edit an item by clicking the Edit button, delete an item by clicking the Delete button, or reposition an item by clicking the Move Up or Move Down buttons.

8. When you have completed your switchboard, click the Close button.

After you have completed these steps, you will notice that the Switchboard Manager has created a Switchboard Items table in your database and a form with the name you selected in the Edit Switchboard Page dialog box. Open the form to see the result of your work. Try out the choices to ensure they do what you intended; if they don't, you can reopen the Switchboard Manager to edit your choices. Figure 42-5 shows a single action switchboard.

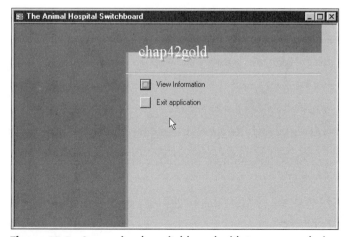

Figure 42-5: A very simple switchboard with two menu choices.

Note If you use the Switchboard Manager to create a switchboard form, you should also use the Manager to edit the form. This practice keeps the Manager's table of switchboard items in sync with the form and makes it easier to manage your switchboards.

Using the Form Wizard

The Form Wizard is one of seven wizards you can choose from when you elect to build a new form. This wizard is an example of an add-in that creates a form object and controls based on selected fields from the table or query you name in the New Form dialog box before launching the wizard.

The first page of the Form Wizard asks you to select the fields you want on the form (see Figure 42-6). You can choose to add all fields from the Available Fields list by clicking the > button, or you can choose specific fields and click the > button for each field to move it to the Selected Fields list box.

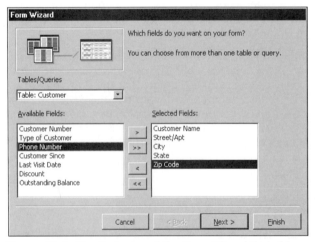

Figure 42-6: The first page of the Form Wizard that ships with Access.

If you have relationships established in your database, you can choose fields from multiple tables, simply by selecting the appropriate query using multiple tables from the Tables/Queries drop-down combo box. You can also select fields from numerous tables. If you select tables not in the relationships, the wizard asks if you want to edit the relationships.

Note If you do elect to edit relationships at that point, you will need to restart the Form Wizard to build your form.

The next page displayed by the wizard depends on the selections you made on the first page. If you selected fields from only one table or query, the second page displayed asks you what layout you want for the form (see Figure 42-7). You can choose from the options shown in Table 42-1.

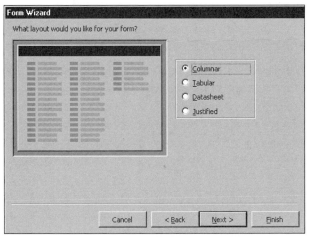

Figure 42-7: The Layout page of the Form Wizard.

Table 42-1 Form Wizard Layout Types	
Layout Type	**Description**
Columnar	The selected fields are laid out in a column down the form; one record is displayed at a time.
Tabular	The selected fields are laid out across the form; multiple records are displayed.
Datasheet	The selected fields are laid out in datasheet format across the form width; multiple records are displayed.
Justified	The selected fields are laid out in tabular fashion across the form, but the fields are joined or justified on multiple lines and only one record is displayed at a time.

If you selected fields from multiple tables/queries on page one of the wizard, the second page asks you for the type of view you want for each field source (see

Figure 42-8). If a table selected in the list box is a one-side table in the defined relationships (a parent table), you can select the *Form with subform(s)* option or the *Linked forms* option for a view. Selecting a many-side table (a child table) in the list box enables you to choose *Single form* as a view.

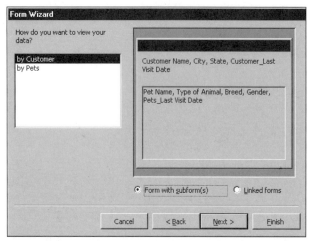

Figure 42-8: The View Selection page of the Form Wizard prompts you for a view type when you have selected fields from multiple related tables/queries.

For a parent table, choosing *Form with subform(s)* creates a parent form containing the fields you selected from the one side of the related tables and a subform for the fields you selected from the many side of the related tables. Selecting *Linked forms* as a view type creates a parent form for the one-side fields and a separate child form for the many-side fields linked by a command button on the parent form.

Choosing *Form with subform(s)* causes the next page of the wizard to prompt you for a layout of the subform. You can choose between the options Tabular or Datasheet.

After selecting the fields, the optional view, and the layout, the wizard asks you to select a style for the form and controls (see Figure 42-9). You have ten choices for styles. Selecting the styles from the list displays a preview in the left pane of the page.

The last page of the wizard asks you for a title for your form (see Figure 42-10). If you have linked forms, you can enter a title for each form. The last choice you have before creating the form is to open the form and view the data the form is based on or open the form in Design view to make changes. Click the Finish button after making these choices to start the build process.

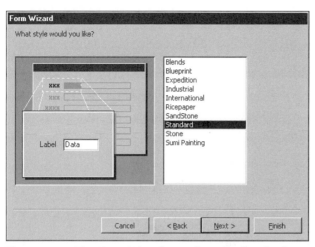

Figure 42-9: The Form Wizard page for selecting the form style applied to the form and controls.

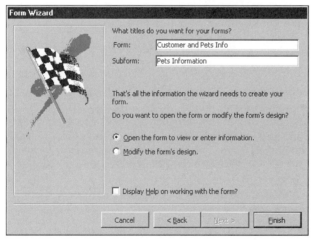

Figure 42-10: The last page of the Form Wizard prompts for a title and for the way you want the new form to open.

The Form Wizard does a good job with the information it collects, but like many of the wizards, you most likely will use the wizard as a starting point and make your own design changes to get the result you want.

Using the Command Button Wizard

If you enable Control Wizards by clicking the Control Wizards button on the Toolbox in form design mode, the Command Button Wizard will be launched when you insert a command button onto a form (see Figure 42-11).

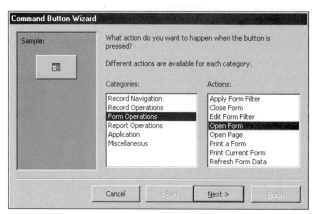

Figure 42-11: The first page of the Command Button Wizard asks you for an action to be associated with the click event of the command button.

The first page of the Command Button Wizard asks you to choose an action to run when a user clicks the command button. There are six categories to choose from in the Categories list box. Selecting one of the categories causes the Actions list to be filled with actions in the selected category. Select an action and click the Next button at the bottom of the wizard form. The available action categories are listed here:

✦ **Record Navigation:** Includes the actions Find Next, Find Record, Go to First Record, and others

✦ **Record Operations:** Includes the actions Add New Record, Delete Record, and others

✦ **Form Operations:** Includes the actions Edit Form Filter, Open Form, Print a Form, and others

✦ **Report Operations:** Includes the actions Preview Report, Print Report, Send Report to File, and others

✦ **Application:** Includes the actions Quit Application, Run Application, Run MS Excel, and others

✦ **Miscellaneous:** Includes the actions Print Table, Run Macro, Run Query, and others

Subsequent pages of the wizard depend on the selected action. For example, if you choose the Open Form action from the Form Operations category, the next page prompts you for a form name to be associated with the Open command. If you choose Run Query from the Miscellaneous category, the wizard prompts you for the query name to run.

Eventually, you get to choose between having text or a picture on the button (see Figure 42-12). If you choose Text, you can enter the text to be displayed on the button face. If you choose Picture, you can select a picture from the list or click the Browse button to find a picture file to be loaded and displayed on the button face.

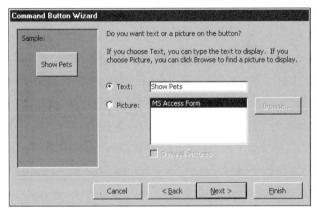

Figure 42-12: The Command Button Wizard dialog page for specifying your choice of having text or a picture displayed on the button face.

The final page of the wizard asks for the name you want to give to the command button. After entering the name, click the Finish button to set the chosen properties. Canceling from this page only cancels the wizard; it does not cancel the insertion of the command button onto the form. To use the wizard again for this button, delete the button and reinsert a new one onto the form.

The Command Button Wizard is a good example of a property wizard that can help you set up your applications quickly. It also gives you an indication of what you can do with add-in technology.

Creating Your Own Add-Ins

This section presents an overview of the steps for creating and installing an add-in. The CD-ROM at the back of this book contains the file CH42Gold.MDA as a sample add-in, which creates a table, form, and report object based on the selections you make in the wizard.

Following are the basic steps you take in developing an add-in:

1. Consider the purpose of the add-in and what type of add-in would best fit this purpose.

2. Design the add-in user-interface and the flow of control for the add-in.

3. Code the add-in by using code-behind-forms and modules.

4. Test your add-in.

5. Implement your add-in. This step includes the preparation of the add-in for use with the Add-In Manager.

The following sections discuss each step in order.

Considering the add-in purpose and type

The first task in developing your add-in is to decide what the add-in will do. What is the purpose of the add-in? Will it help the end user create some object, such as a report or form? Will it guide the end user through a series of steps toward the completion of some task? Will it aid in setting some property value or in selecting a value for a control?

Thinking about the purpose of the add-in and how it will be used helps you determine how to design the add-in and how it should be invoked.

If your add-in will create an Access object, such as a form or report, you may want to consider a form or report wizard invoked from the New button on the Form or Report tab of the database window. For this type of add-in, you need to query the end user for information about controls, such as their names and types, about data sources for the form, and about the look and feel of the form layout — just as the built-in Form Wizard does.

If you need to provide an aid to creating a property value or help deciding on a value for a field based on the answers to a set of questions and values in the database, you might consider using a builder as an add-in launched in the context of a control on a form or in design mode for a form or report.

When your analysis determines that the add-in is not associated with any particular object or control context and should be generally available to the end user of Access or your application, you can choose to implement a menu add-in that end users can choose whenever they need the tool.

Designing the add-in user interface and flow of control

In designing the add-in user interface and the flow of control within the add-in, you need to consider how the user will interact with the add-in to enter information in a logical manner as well as the dependencies among the information collected.

In this phase of the design process, you decide where to place prompts for information, which prompts to group together on a form, and in which order to present the prompts. As in the Form Wizard discussed earlier in this chapter, the second page to appear in the wizard is dependent on the user's selection(s) on the first page. When the user selects fields from only one data source, the wizard displays the page prompting for the layout to apply to the form. When the user selects fields from multiple data sources, the wizard displays a prompt for the type of view to use. This dependent action by a wizard may also be necessary in your add-in.

Diagramming flow of control

You may find it helpful to design your add-in flow of control on paper first. Start by drawing boxes to represent pages of dialog to present to the user. Connect those boxes by a line denoting direct passage of control from one page to the next, or by a diamond shape denoting one or more decisions. A diamond may be connected to any number of other boxes, one being chosen by the decision outcome.

The decisions you specify can range from very simple to very complex and may include decisions based on the outcome of edits on the entered data. If you need to perform edits on the entered data on a page-by-page basis, a decision point in the flow of control may direct the flow back to the same page if the edits fail (see Figure 42-13).

As you draw the boxes, label them with their names and purposes. When you are satisfied with the flow and the decisions controlling that flow, you can go back to the diagram and start designing the user interface for each page.

Note
You may find that some add-ins need to present a means for the user to jump from one part of the add-in to another, possibly to skip a section that is not necessary for the task the end user wants to perform. In this case, you may provide a set of buttons on the add-in form to enable the end user to jump to the page of interest, or, if there are many choices, a drop-down list of pages from which the end user can choose. On your design diagram, you can designate the direct jump entry points by an arrow or other symbol at the page where the end user may jump to or enter.

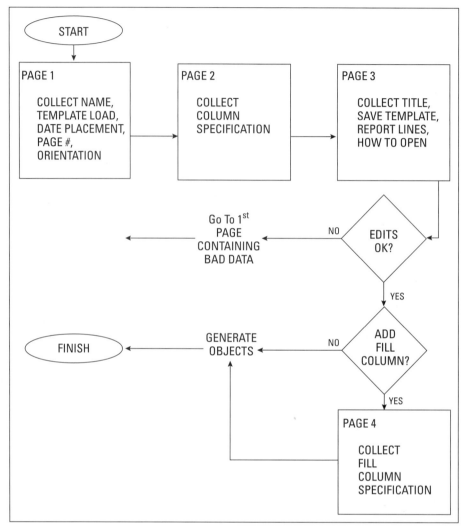

Figure 42-13: An example of a flow of control design for an add-in showing dialog pages and decision points.

Designing the interface

You may again want to do the preliminary design for each page by drawing a layout of controls on paper, labeled by the page name to correspond to the flow diagram, or you may want to design a prototype directly in Access form design mode to help you get the look you are after.

In designing your interface, try to keep it simple and consistent with the interface found in other Access add-ins. Don't try to cram too much into one dialog page. Keep the interface logical and collect information in a manner consistent with the way the typical end user would assume in entering the data. Be forgiving. If the end user makes a mistake, don't blow out of the add-in, making them reenter all the work they did up to that point. Instead, provide a message indicating the problem and give them a chance to fix it.

Tip We find it helpful in the design of our add-ins to put navigation buttons in a form footer and develop the pages of the interface as multiple pages of the same form. We usually provide a means for the end user to save and reload information entered into the wizard. This is especially useful when the add-in collects information that could be used in subsequent uses of the add-in. In a Form Wizard, for example, the end user may enter information to create a particular form and then want to go back later and create basically the same form but with some different choices. End users are very appreciative if they can simply load the add-in choices they made for the previous form and then make the changes they want for the new form.

Coding your add-in

When coding your add-in, you need to be aware of which objects you are referring to, those in the database that called the add-in or those in the database containing the add-in.

Note An example of the two reference requirements is found in the sample add-in from CH42Gold.MDA on the CD-ROM. This add-in needs to refer to local tables in the add-in database for saving user entries that will be used in building the form and report. It doesn't make sense to create this table in the end user's database, because it is needed by the add-in only for creating the output objects. The output objects, table, form, and report, however, must be stored in the end-user database. You need a way to point your add-in to either the add-in database or the end-user database.

The CodeDb function returns a Database object that refers to the database in which the code is running. Because your add-in code is running to make the reference to the CodeDb function, the database returned is your add-in database. The Name property of this Database object is the full path and name of the add-in database. This is useful if you need to know where your add-in database resides on the user's hard disk.

The Generate_Table function in the CH42Gold.MDA sample wizard needs a database object for the user database calling the wizard and a database object for the wizard database. The function starts out by setting two database objects using the familiar DBEngine.Workspaces(0).Databases(0) to refer to the user database and the CodeDb function to refer to the wizard database. The syntax is as follows:

```
Dim dbDatabase As Database, userdb As Database
. . .
```

```
Set dbDatabase = CodeDb()
Set userdb = DBEngine.Workspaces(0).Databases(0)
```

Access 97 provides several functions that you will find useful in coding your add-in. Table 42-2 shows these functions and their purpose.

Table 42-2
Add-In Functions for Creating Forms, Reports, and Controls

Function Name	Purpose
CreateForm	Creates a form in the user database and returns a Form object.
CreateReport	Creates a report in the user database and returns a Report object.
CreateControl	Creates a control on a form and returns a Control object. The form on which the control is placed must be open in design mode.
CreateReportControl	Creates a control on a report and returns a Control object. The report on which the control is placed must be open in design mode.
CreateGroupLevel	Creates a group on a report. The report must be open in design mode.

You may specify a template in both the CreateForm and CreateReport functions. The template is typically used to provide a new form or report with a standard set of properties and controls. This reduces the amount of work the add-in must do to create the final result. If the Create functions do not specify a template, the one designated in the Forms/Reports tab of the Options dialog box is used as a template.

The sample wizard uses these functions to create the data entry form and the report, both of which are based on the table created in the user database. Refer to the functions Generate_Form, Generate_Controls, and Generate_Report to see these functions in action.

In addition to using DAO methods and the preceding functions for creating and manipulating database objects, you may find that you need to generate code to provide some special processing in the resulting objects. In the sample wizard, the Generate_Code function creates a series of statements that make up the Print event of the Detail section of the newly created report. This code draws lines around the report columns if the user specified this option in the wizard dialog box. Refer to the next section, "Coding on the run," to learn about the powerful module-editing capabilities you have available to your add-in.

You can run a preliminary test of your add-in by running the entry point function that's called by Access when your add-in is invoked by the user. Any objects generated by the add-in will end up in the add-in database because the user database and add-in (CodeDb) database are one and the same. Using this testing technique, you can at least test out the flow of control and generation of objects — but you must wait until after installation into a user environment to complete the tests.

Coding on the run

Your wizard or add-in may need to build or edit modules at run time. You may need to add code to a form module or, as the sample wizard does, add code to a report module. Or maybe you want to build some functions in a stand-alone module based on information entered by the user. Access has added many new module-editing methods to help you build your modules at runtime. This section explains these new methods associated with Module objects.

An Access application contains a Modules collection of all open standard and class modules. Each Module object in the Modules collection can be accessed in any of the standard syntax for referencing collection members. Forms and Reports have Module properties that return a Module object that refers to their respective code modules. This property is used in the following discussion of the InsertText method. Within a Modules collection, an open form can also be referenced by using the following syntax:

```
Modules!Form_formname
```

Using InsertText

One method you can use to add code to a module at runtime is the InsertText method. The syntax is as follows:

```
Module object.InsertText string
```

The object to which the InsertText method applies is either a form, report, standard module, or class module in your application database. This method inserts the text at the end of the designated module. You have no control over where to insert the code lines with this method.

The following example adds a command button and inserts a Click Event Sub procedure called New_Customer_Click into the Account form:

```
Dim sProcText As String
Dim cmdButton As Control

sProcText = "Private Sub New_Customer_Click()" & vbCrLf
sProcText = sProcText & "MsgBox ""A New Customer Added""" &
vbCrLf
sProcText = sProcText & "End Sub" & vbCrLf
```

```
DoCmd.OpenForm "Account", acDesign

Set cmdButton = CreateControl("Account", acCommandButton,
acDetail, _ "", "", (3.25 * 1440), (0.9583 * 1440), (1.0417 *
1440), (0.25 * 1440))
cmdButton.Name = "New_Customer"
cmdButton.OnClick = "[Event Procedure]"
cmdButton.Caption = "New Customer"
Forms![Account].Module.InsertText sProcText

DoCmd.Close acForm, "Account", acSaveYes
DoCmd.OpenForm "Account"
```

sProcText holds the text to be inserted into the module. vbCrLf is a constant defined by Visual Basic representing a carriage-return line-feed pair that forces line ends within the string.

Note   This example only inserts a subprocedure that does nothing but present a message box when called, but you can code any valid statements to build a complete, meaningful procedure for your application. InsertText fails unless you insert at least one statement — even if it's no more than a comment — within the procedure being inserted.

The form that receives the text is opened in design mode by using the DoCmd object's OpenForm method. Use of the InsertText statement requires that the form be open in design mode.

After opening the form in design mode, the CreateControl function adds a command button that is used to add a new customer. CreateControl returns a Control object, which is assigned to an Object variable called cmdButton.

The cmdButton control sets the name of the command button and its caption and designates that the OnClick event references an event procedure.

The InsertText method is then executed to insert the click event procedure into the form's module. The click event procedure receives the same name as the command button.

Now that the command button is on the form and tied to an event procedure, you can close the form by using the Close method of the DoCmd object. You specify an acSaveYes argument to save the form changes without prompting the user.

The Accounts form is then reopened to display the form with the new button. Clicking the New Customer button displays the message inserted into the event procedure.

Using AddFromFile

Another method available to you for adding code to a module is the `AddFromFile` method, which adds lines from a text file into a module object. The syntax is as follows:

```
Module object.AddFromFile filename
```

Unlike the `InsertText` method — which inserts lines at the end of the module — the lines of the text file are inserted immediately after the declarations section and before the first procedure in the module designated by the module object. As in all module-editing methods, the module object must be open in design mode to enable editing.

The `AddFromString` method works exactly like the `AddFromFile` method but specifies a string as the source of the text lines instead of a filename.

Using CreateEventProc

The sample add-in discussed in this chapter needs to add an `OnPrint` event procedure to the report module being generated by the wizard. This procedure creates borders around the printed text whenever the `OnPrint` event is fired by Access. As you see in the add-in, the entire procedure is built using the `InsertText` method. Another way to add event procedures to form or report modules starts off by using the `CreateEventProc` method. Its syntax is as follows:

```
Form/Report Module object.CreateEventProc(name of event, name
of _ object)
```

`CreateEventProc` adds an event subprocedure shell for the event specified by the first argument to the object specified by the second argument. This method doesn't specify any code lines, so you need to use other methods of the `Module` object to insert the code you want to execute when the event is fired. To help in this endeavor, `CreateEventProc` returns the line number of the first line of the procedure. This line number is relative to other procedures in the module.

Using InsertLines, ReplaceLine, and DeleteLines

To insert a line of code into the event procedure created with `CreateEventProc`, you can use the `InsertLines` method with the line number returned from the `CreateEventProc`. The syntax is as follows:

```
Module object.InsertLines starting line, string to insert
```

If you use a starting line number where code already resides, that code is pushed down below the inserted text. To replace a line, use the `ReplaceLine` method, which replaces the specified line number with the string argument. Its syntax is as follows:

```
Module object.ReplaceLine starting line, string to add
```

You may decide to house a module in your add-in database that contains a set of procedures you can use as templates in creating the code your add-in will insert into the target database. It's likely that these template procedures will contain more code than is necessary for a given target module, and you'll need some way to delete certain lines from the templates as you build the target code. The module's DeleteLines method will come in handy for this purpose. Following is the syntax:

```
Module object.DeleteLines starting line, line count
```

DeleteLines deletes the number of lines specified by the line count argument, starting at the line specified by the starting line argument. Note that there is no designation of the procedure name in this method. The method works entirely by line numbers. If you know the name of the routine you want to delete, or maybe an offset from the first line of the routine, how do you get the line number so you can start deleting? The Find method is one method that can come to the rescue. Use the following syntax:

```
Module object.Find(text to find, starting line, starting
column, _ ending line, ending column, _
optional wholeword, optional matchcase, optional pattern)
```

Tip

The text to find argument specifies the text to search for. When you have a module being used to hold template procedures in an add-in, as discussed previously, you can add comment lines or labels to the procedures or parts of procedures that designate sections you want to work with. To get the starting position of these procedures or sections, specify the label or keyword in the comment as the text to find in the Find method and nothing in the starting line argument. The Find method will return the line number of the text you are searching for, and you can add one to get the line after it.

If you know the text to find is beyond a given line in the module, you can set the starting line argument to that line number and Find will start its search at that line number. Whether the starting line argument is preset or not, the Find method returns the line number at which the search text was found in this argument. The starting column can be preset to the column of the starting line in which you want to start the search. Find will set the column number of the search text in this argument when it returns with a found condition.

Ending line and ending column work in a manner similar to starting line and starting column. You can specify the line you want the search to stop on in ending line and the column to stop search on in ending column. On return, Find will set the ending line argument to the line number the search text ends on and ending column to the column of that line at which the search text ends. The last three arguments are optional. Wholeword tells Find to search for whole words only. If you specify port as a text to find argument and set the wholeword argument to True, Find searches for port as a whole word. Setting wholeword to False or not specifying it at all causes Find to stop searching on any word containing port, such sup*port* or re*port*.

Setting the `matchcase` argument to `True` causes `Find` to match the case of the text to find, and a setting of `False` disregards case.

You can use wildcard characters such as * and ? in the text to find argument to do a pattern-matching search. To initiate pattern matching, set the `pattern` argument to `True`.

Tip   You can use `Find` to search through all occurrences of a text string by issuing the `Find` method with an empty `starting line` argument or an argument of `0`. If the `Find` method returns `True`, the text was found and the `starting line` argument is set to the line number where the text was found. Issuing the `Find` method again with this line number preserved in the `starting line` argument and `starting column` set to a value at least one greater than the value returned by `Find` causes the method to find the next occurrence of the text string. Continue with this technique until `Find` returns `False`.

Using ProcBodyLine and ProcStartLine

The `ProcBodyLine` property also returns the starting line number of a given procedure name. The syntax is as follows:

```
Module object.ProcBodyLine(name of proc, kind of proc)
```

Use one of the following predefined constants in the `kind of proc` argument:

Constant	Procedure Type
vbext_pk_Get	Property Get
vbext_pk_Let	Property Let
vbext_pk_Set	Property Set
vbext_pk_Proc	Sub or Function

`ProcBodyLine` returns the line number of the `Proc` statement. If you want the line number of the start of the procedure, which may include comments and compiler constants placed before the procedure statement, use the `ProcStartLine` property with the same arguments used in the `ProcBodyLine`.

If you need to retrieve one or more lines from a module, use the `Lines` property with the first argument set to the starting line number you want to retrieve and the second argument set to the number of lines to retrieve. Use this syntax:

```
Module object.Lines(starting line, number of lines)
```

Use any of the methods previously discussed to get the starting line number and then the `Lines` property to retrieve the number of lines you need into a string variable. You can then edit the string with standard VBA string editing functions and place the lines back into the module or into another module.

Finding the number of lines in a module

Two properties are available to find the number of lines within a module. The `ProcCountLines` property returns the number of lines in a given procedure, including any comments and compiler constants immediately above the procedure statement. Following is the syntax:

```
Module object.ProcCountLines(name of proc, kind of proc)
```

The `kind of proc` argument is specified in the same way as for `ProcBodyLine`, discussed previously.

The `CountOfDeclarationLines` property is the second property that returns a line count. This property returns the number of lines in the declaration section of the referenced module. The syntax is as follows:

```
Module object.CountOfDeclarationLines
```

The number of lines returned is effectively the line number of the end of the module's `Declaration` section.

Compiling modules

After completing your module editing, you can force a compile of the modules by using the `RunCommand` method of the `DoCmd` or `Application` object. For example, to compile and save all modules, execute the following `RunCommand` before closing the edited modules:

```
DoCmd.RunCommand acCmdCompileAndSaveAllModules
```

When your add-in has finished its work, you should refresh the user's database window to display any new objects your add-in has added to their database. To do this, execute the `RefreshDatabaseWindow` method. This is a method of the application object, and there are no arguments to provide.

Preparing your add-in for installation

Now that you have your add-in designed, coded, and tested, you can turn your attention to distribution. This section deals with two topics: 1) Preparing your add-in database so that the Add-In Manager can install it, and 2) Saving your add-in as an .MDE file to protect your work and make a smaller file for distribution.

The first task to consider is setting up the necessary information in your database so that the Add-In Manager can determine what kind of add-in you want to install and provide the end user doing the installation with helpful information about your add-in.

Using the USysRegInfo table

The Add-In Manager uses a table called USysRegInfo and several database properties when installing your add-in. You can build the USysRegInfo from scratch or import it from any of the add-ins that ship with Access 97. The layout of the USysRegInfo table is shown in Table 42-3.

Table 42-3 Definition of the USysRegInfo Table		
Field Name	*Field Type*	*Field Size*
SubKey	Text	255
Type	Number	Long Integer
ValName	Text	255
Value	Text	255

The records you insert into the USysRegInfo table depend on the type of add-in you have built. The first record in this table creates a key in the registry to register your add-in.

The SubKey field of the first record is the key name and must be the same value on all records in the USysRegInfo table describing a given add-in. The SubKey starts with the root of the registry tree under which you want to install your add-in. This value can be HKEY_LOCAL_MACHINE, or, if you are using a profile, use the value HKEY_CURRENT_ACCESS_PROFILE. The next part of the SubKey entry depends on the type of add-in you are installing. If you are installing a builder, Control Wizard, or ActiveX Control Wizard, the next part of the SubKey must specify Wizards as the subkey under the root you previously chose, followed by the type of wizard, the subtype of wizard, and the name of the wizard, as shown here:

```
HKEY_LOCAL_MACHINE\Wizards\type wizard\subtype wizard\wizard
name
```

For a Control Wizard, the type of wizard part of the string will be Control Wizards and the subtype of wizard will be the name of the control the wizard is associated with. Here is a list of valid control names:

✦ BoundObjectFrame

✦ CheckBox

✦ ComboBox

- ✦ CommandButton
- ✦ Image
- ✦ Label
- ✦ Line
- ✦ ListBox
- ✦ OptionButton
- ✦ OptionGroup
- ✦ PageBreak
- ✦ Rectangle
- ✦ SubformSubreport
- ✦ TextBox
- ✦ ToggleButton
- ✦ UnboundObjectFrame

If you are installing a builder, the type of wizard will be Property Wizards and the subtype of wizard will be the name of the property to associate the builder with. You can refer to the properties dialog box for an object in design mode to find the property name. Enter that name without spaces as the subtype of wizard.

For ActiveX Control Wizards, the type of wizard is ActiveX Control Wizards and the subtype of wizard is the value of the ActiveX control's Class property. To find the class name, select the ActiveX control in design mode and view its properties dialog box.

The SubKey format is a little different for wizards that create Access objects such as tables, forms, and reports. With these wizards, the SubKey specifies a type of wizard and wizard name but no subtype of wizard. The format of the SubKey is as follows:

```
HKEY_LOCAL_MACHINE\Wizards\type of wizard\name of wizard
```

The type of wizard may be one of the following values:

- ✦ Form Wizards
- ✦ Query Wizards
- ✦ Report Wizards
- ✦ Table Wizards

Menu add-ins have a SubKey format that registers your add-in under a Menu Add-Ins subkey rather than a Wizards subkey in the registry. The format of the SubKey is the following:

```
HKEY_LOCAL_MACHINE\Menu Add-Ins\name of add-in
```

The name of the wizard for Access Object Wizards will appear in the New Object dialog box, and for a menu add-in, the name of the add-in will appear in the Add-Ins submenu. For many of these menu add-ins, you will see an underlined letter in the add-in name. This is an access key for the add-in that enables the end user to access the menu add-in via the keyboard: Pressing Alt and then the underlined key launches the add-in. For example, to launch the Switchboard Manager add-in via the keyboard, you hold down the Alt key and press T for Tools, I for Add-Ins, and W for Switchboard Manager. To set an access key for your menu add-in, type & before the letter you want for an access key.

The Type field of the first record must be zero to denote that the subkey is to be added to the Registry, and the ValName and Value fields must be blank.

After the first record has been defined, subsequent records define values that are entered into the add-in entry in the registry. All records must have the same SubKey value as the first record to identify them as belonging to that add-in.

The Type field on records following the first record denote the type of value to be entered into the registry. These types can be the following:

Type Field Value	Type of Registry Value
1	REG_SZ (String)
4	DWORD (REG_DWORD in the Windows NT registry)

ValName specifies the name of the value to be entered, and Value contains the value itself. The number of values to add to the USysRegInfo table depends on the type of add-in being added. Table 42-4 lists the values you need to add for the various add-in types. (Remember that all SubKeys are the same as the first record in USysRegInfo for the add-in being defined.)

Table 42-4
Values to Add to the USysRegInfo Table for Add-Ins

Type Field	ValName Field	Value Field
Add-in Type: Control, ActiveX, or Builder Wizards		
4	Can Edit	1 = Wizard can modify control or property. 0 = Wizard cannot modify.
1	Description	Text displayed in the Choose Builder dialog box when more than one add-in has been defined for the same control or property.
1	Function	Indicates the name of the function that starts the add-in.
1	Library	Specifies the path and name of the add-in database.
Add-in Type: Access Object Wizards		
1	Bitmap	Specifies the path and name of the bitmap that is displayed for the wizard in the New Object dialog box.
4	Datasource Required	1 = User must specify a table or query name as the source of data for the object to be created by the wizard. 0 = datasource not required; this value is only necessary for Form and Report Wizards.
1	Description	Text displayed in the New Object dialog box.
1	Function	Indicates name of the function that starts the add-in.
4	Index	Specifies the order of the Description text displayed in the New Object dialog box; 0 = The first entry in the dialog box.
1	Library	Specifies the path and name of the add-in database.
Add-in Type: Menu Add-In		
1	Expression	Specifies the name of the function that starts the add-in preceded by an equal sign.
1	Library	Specifies the path and name of the add-in database.

On the CD-ROM

The CH42Gold.MDA sample add-in on the CD-ROM is an Object Wizard that creates a table, form, and report. The USysRegInfo records for this add-in are shown in Table 42-5.

Table 42-5
USysRegInfo Records Defining the CH42.MDA Sample Add-In

Subkey	Type	ValName	Value
HKEY_CURRENT_ACCESS_ PROFILE \Menu Add-Ins\ Bible Sample Wizard	0		
HKEY_CURRENT_ACCESS_ PROFILE \Menu Add-Ins\ Bible Sample Wizard	1	Expression	=StartWiz()
HKEY_CURRENT_ACCESS_ PROFILE \Menu Add-Ins\ Bible Sample Wizard	1	Library	ch42.mda

Setting database properties

Your second task in preparing your add-in for installation is to set some database properties. The information you provide in these properties will appear in the Add-In Manager dialog box to identify your add-in and your company. To set these properties, follow these steps:

1. Open the Database Properties dialog box by selecting Database Properties from the File menu or by right-clicking the database container window and selecting Properties.

2. Click the Summary tab in the Database Properties dialog box.

3. Enter a title for your add-in, your company name, and comments. The title will appear in the Available Add-Ins list in the Add-In Manager dialog box and in the Add-Ins menu after the end user adds your add-in. The company name will appear below the Available Add-Ins list box, and the comments will appear directly below your company name.

4. Click OK to close the Database Properties dialog box.

Now that you have prepared your add-in for installation by the Add-In Manager, you can create an installation disk set. Before you build your installation disk set, however, you may want to save your add-in in a smaller file size and at the same time protect your secrets by removing source code. The next section discusses how to save your database in a new format in Access 97: an .MDE file.

Exploring .MDE files

Saving your database as an .MDE file causes Access to compile your database, save it, remove source code, and compact the database. These actions result in a smaller, more efficient database due to source code removal and optimizations.

In the .MDE file format, your database code and objects cannot be viewed or modified by others, nor can they import the database forms, reports, and modules to another database. They can import tables, queries, and macros from your database, however. With these exceptions, your design is essentially locked up.

Tip   A drawback of the .MDE format is that because your source code is removed from the file, there is nothing to edit should your procedures use the module-editing features of VBA, as discussed in the "Coding on the run" section in this chapter. If your add-in needs to use module editing to add or change add-in code on the fly, you can't use the MDE format. If your add-in uses these VBA features to modify objects generated into the user database, however, an .MDE format is okay to use. This is generally what you will be doing in an add-in anyway.

If your database references other databases, such as a library database or another add-in database, those databases must also be in .MDE format. You cannot access .MDA formatted files from an .MDE file. Access will complain when you attempt to make an .MDE file that contains references to .MDB or .MDA files.

Building an .MDE file

To build the .MDE file, follow these steps:

1. Ensure that the database is closed by all possible users.
2. Choose Database Utilities from the Tools menu and click Make MDE File.
3. Enter the name of the database you want to save in the Database To Save As MDE dialog box and click Make MDE.
4. Enter a database name and choose the .MDE file location in the Save MDE As dialog box.

Note   The action of creating an MDE file is a one-way street. After the file is created, it's only good for execution. If you need to modify the design or convert to a future version of Access, you will need the original database in non-MDE format. Be sure to save your original database in a safe place.

If you do not use the MDE format to distribute your database, be sure to compact the database before building your distribution disk set.

Using the Add-In Manager

With your USysRegInfo table and database properties set up, you are now ready to use the Add-In Manager to install your add-in. Note that the Add-In Manager can also be used to uninstall your add-in if necessary (but who would want to?).

Choose Add-Ins from the Tools menu and then click Add-In Manager. The Available Add-Ins list in the Add-In Manager dialog box lists add-ins that are currently installed (those with an X next to them) and files in the Office directory with a .MDA or .MDE extension.

You can install one of the add-ins in the list by choosing it and clicking Install, or you can add a new add-in by clicking Add New. After installing the add-ins you want, click the Close button to exit the Add-In Manager dialog box.

The Add-In Manager accesses your USysRegInfo table and enters the keys and values you specified there into the system registry. You can use the Registry Editor to view your add-in entries.

With your add-in installed by the Add-In Manager, you can now run a complete test of the add-in to determine proper installation and functionality before distribution to your end users.

With the information provided in this chapter and the sample add-in in CH42Gold.MDA, you'll be able to develop your own add-ins and libraries, which will substantially enhance the features of your Access 2000 applications and ease the difficulty of your maintenance tasks.

Summary

Add-ins and libraries provide a powerful way to enhance an Access application. By referencing other add-in libraries you can keep your original Access application intact but add new features. In this chapter you learned the following:

✦ The types of add-ins that exist

✦ How to create and reference libraries

✦ How to use some of the Access 2000 add-ins

✦ How to create an add-in

✦   ✦   ✦

Microsoft Access 2000 Specifications

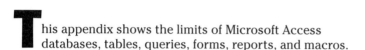his appendix shows the limits of Microsoft Access databases, tables, queries, forms, reports, and macros.

Databases	
Attribute	*Maximum*
MDB file size	2GB (Because your database can include attached tables in multiple files, its total size is limited only by available storage capacity.)
Number of objects in a database	32,768
Number of Modules	1,000
Number of characters in object names	64
Number of characters in a password	14
Number of characters in a user name or group name	20
Number of concurrent users	255

Tables

Attribute	Maximum
Number of characters in a table name	64
Number of characters in a field name	64
Number of fields in a record or table	255
Number of open tables	2048 including tables opened by Microsoft Access internally
Table size	1GB
Number of characters in a Text field	255
Number of characters in a Memo field	65,535 when entering data through the user interface; 1 GB when entering data programatically
Size of OLE object field	1GB
Number of indexes in a record or table	32
Number of fields in an index	10
Number of characters in a validation message	255
Number of characters in a validation rule	2048
Number of characters in a table or field description	255
Number of characters in a record	2,000 (excludes Memo and OLE Object fields)
Number of characters in a field property setting	255

Queries

Attribute	Maximum
Number of tables in a query	32
Number of fields in a dynaset	255
Dynaset size	1GB
Sort limit	255 characters in one or more fields
Number of sorted fields in a query	10
Number of levels of nested queries	50
Number of ANDs in a WHERE or HAVING clause	40
Number of characters in a SQL statement	64,000

Forms and Reports

Attribute	Maximum
Number of characters in a label	2,048
Number of characters in a text box	65,535
Form or report width	22 inches (55.87 cm)
Section height	22 inches (55.87 cm)
Height of all sections plus section headers in design view	200 inches (508 cm)
Number of levels of nested forms or reports	3 (form-subform-subform)
Number of fields/expressions you can sort or group on	10 (reports only)
Number of headers and footers in a report	1 report header/footer; 1 page header/footer; 10 group headers/footers
Number of printed pages in a report	65,536
Number of controls or sections you can add over the lifetime of the form or report	754

Macros

Attribute	Maximum
Number of actions in a macro	999
Number of characters in a condition	255
Number of characters in a comment	255
Number of characters in an action argument	255

Access Projects

Attribute	Maximum
Number of objects in a Microsoft Access project (.adp)	32,768
Modules (including forms and report modules)	1,000
Number of characters in an object name	64

✦   ✦   ✦

Mountain Animal Hospital Tables

The Mountain Animal Hospital Database file is made up of eight tables. There are four main tables and four lookup tables. The main tables are:

- ✦ Customer
- ✦ Pets
- ✦ Visits
- ✦ Visit Details

The four lookup tables are:

- ✦ States
- ✦ Animals
- ✦ Treatments
- ✦ Medications

This appendix displays a database diagram of all eight tables and the relations between them. Figures of each of the tables are shown in the Table Design window.

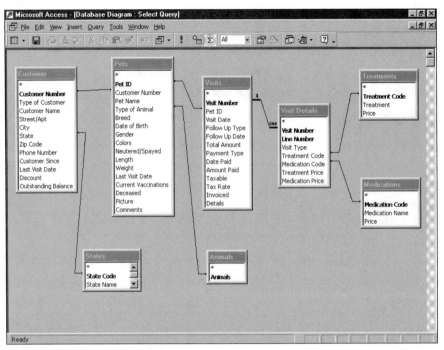

Figure B-1: The database diagram.

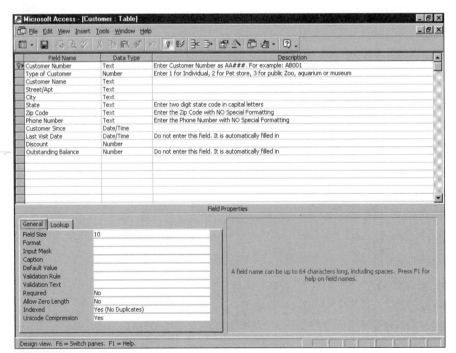

Figure B-2: The Customer table.

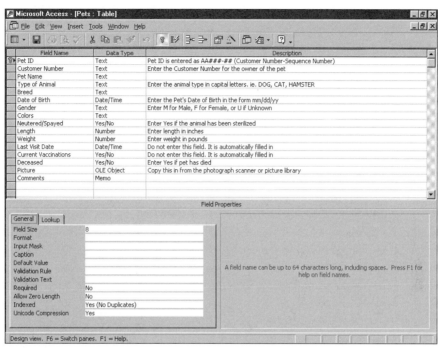

Figure B-3: The Pets table.

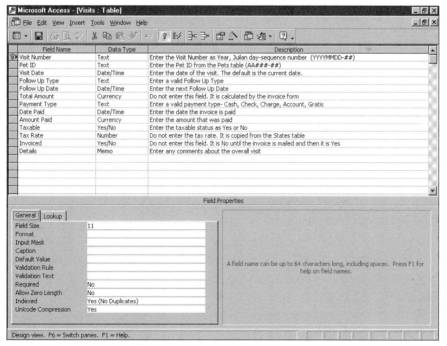

Figure B-4: The Visits table.

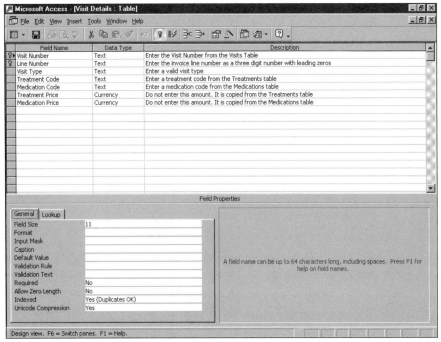

Figure B-5: The Visit Details table.

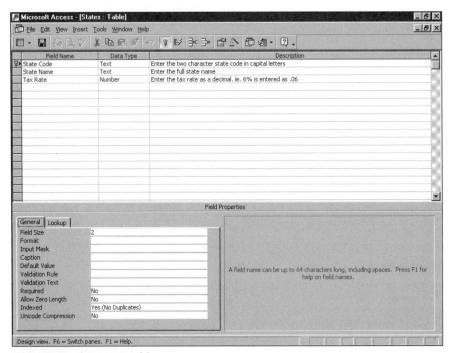

Figure B-6: The States table.

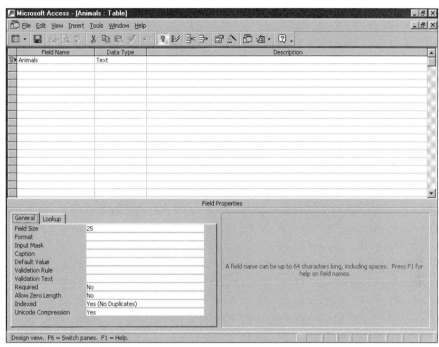

Figure B-7: The Animals table.

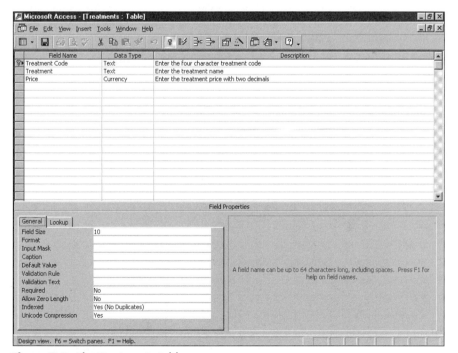

Figure B-8: The Treatments table.

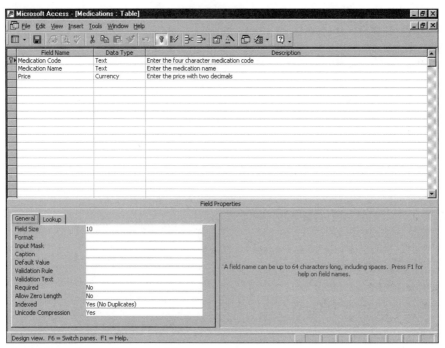

Figure B-9: The Medications table.

What's on the CD-ROM

Your CD-ROM contains all of the example files created or referenced in this book. There are seven main directories on the CD. Some are divided into subdirectories. Most of the directories or subdirectories contain installation files with a .EXE file extension. You can simply display the directories and files using your Windows Explorer, and then double click any .EXE file to launch the install program for the file you want to copy to your hard drive. Each installation file asks you where you want to put the files and sets up a Start menu shortcut for you.

If you have problems with any of the CD files, check out our support Web site at www.databasecreations.com/ access2000bible for any corrections or the latest free downloads.

The seven main directories include

✦ Access 2000 Bible Examples: Used throughout the book to teach Microsoft Access

✦ Access 2000 Product Catalogs: Can be viewed from the CD in full color using Adobe Acrobat

✦ Acrobat Reader from Adobe: The free reader to view Acrobat .PDF files

✦ Demos: Demos from many of the leading add-on software vendors for Microsoft Access

✦ Free Access Software: Real working software — not demos from Database Creations

✦ Other Free Software: Other fun products for Office and Access Users

✦ WinZip95: A free utility to compress data up to 90 percent — great for sending files via e-mail

Figure C-1 shows the full directory structures of all files on the CD.

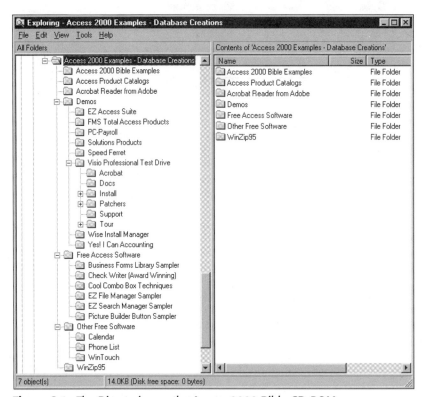

Figure C-1: The Directories on the Access 2000 Bible CD-ROM.

Installing the Files on Your Computer

Each directory on the CD contains a standard setup file that can be selected and run to start the install. While you may be used to seeing the file name SETUP.EXE on your CDs, that convention generally works well when there is one installation file. We have separated all of the files by directory so you can install only the files you want and then give them more readable names such as **Access 2000 Bible Examples.EXE**. Each directory (with the exception of the *Access 2000 Product Catalogs* directory) contains these .EXE files that you can display with your Windows Explorer and then just double-click to run.

You can run the files from the CD by double-clicking them, or you can copy them to your hard drive for later use (again, double-click to run). Remember that the CD is read-only, and you cannot install any of the files on the CD. Each of the installations will ask you for a directory name. Choose a directory on your hard drive or media (Zip or SyQuest drives) which can be written to. None of the files will fit on a floppy when installed.

If you find that any of the files are read-only, display the file in Windows Explorer and then right-click the file name. Select properties and uncheck the read-only property. This will make the file read-write. You should not have to do this under normal conditions.

All the example .MDB files are Microsoft Access 2000 files. They work in Microsoft Access 2000 only and do not work in Microsoft Access 97, 95, 2.0, 1.1, or 1.0.

Installing and using the Access 2000 Example files

When you double-click the file named **Access 2000 Bible Examples.EXE** in the directory **Access 2000 Bible Examples** you will be prompted to install the example files. This process will also create a Start menu entry that you can use to select the example file named *Mountain Animal Hospital*. If you use this Start menu icon to open the example file, it will automatically launch your default version of Microsoft Access. If you get an error message, you either have multiple versions of Microsoft Access on your computer and Access 2000 is not the default or you have never told Windows 95/98/NT to associate .MDB files with the program msaccess.exe (Microsoft Access) Follow the instructions in the next section of this appendix to associate all .MDB files with Microsoft Access 2000.

Associating an .MDB file with Microsoft Access

To change which program starts when you open a file:

1. In My Computer or Windows Explorer, click the View menu and then click Options.

2. Click the File Types tab.

3. In the list of file types, click the one you want to change (Microsoft Access Databases).

4. The settings for that file type are shown in the File Type Details box.

5. Click Edit.

6. In the Actions box, click Open.

7. Click Edit, and then specify the program (msaccess.exe) you want to use to open files that have this extension. Be sure to choose the Access 2000 msaccess.exe program if you have other versions of Microsoft Access on your computer.

Using the Access 2000 Example files

You'll find several main example files throughout this book's first five parts. The last part contains separate example files for each chapter.

Mountain Animal Start.MDB	Contains the tables only, to get you started in Chapters 1–35.
Mountain Animal Hospital.MDB	Contains all of the initial tables, queries, forms, reports, macros, and modules, as well as versions of these items needed at various stages in the chapters, plus a completed version.
ACTIMPEX.MDB	Contains links to various external file formats including dBASE, FoxPro, and Paradox. Used in Chapter 24.
CHAP36.MDB	Main example file for Chapter 36.
CHAP37.MDB	Main example file for Chapter 37.
CHAP38.MDB	Main example file for Chapter 38.
CHAP39.MDB	Main example file for Chapter 39.
CHAP40.MDB	Main example file for Chapter 40.
CHAP41.MDB	Main example file for Chapter 41.
CHAP42.MDA	Main example file for Chapter 42 — this is an .MDA (library) file type.

Figure C-2 shows a list of all of these files and many other peripheral files, while Appendixes D and E show you where each object is referenced in the book.

Name	Size	Type
Asking Price.htm	3KB	Microsoft HTML Document 4.0
Cat.bmp	96KB	Microsoft Imager 1.0 Picture
Chap36.mdb	130KB	Microsoft Access Database
Chap37.mdb	256KB	Microsoft Access Database
Chap38.mdb	228KB	Microsoft Access Database
Chap39.mdb	2,336KB	Microsoft Access Database
Chap40.mdb	704KB	Microsoft Access Database
Chap41.mdb	164KB	Microsoft Access Database
Chap42.mda	576KB	Microsoft Access Add-in
Coffin.bmp	1KB	Microsoft Imager 1.0 Picture
Exit.bmp	3KB	Microsoft Imager 1.0 Picture
Index.hhk	2KB	HHK File
Install.log	2KB	LOG File
Medlimit.txt	2KB	Text Document
Morecust.xls	8KB	Microsoft Excel 5.0 Worksheet
Mountain Animal Hospital.ldb	1KB	Microsoft Access Record-Locking...
Mountain Animal Hospital.mdb	6,500KB	Microsoft Access Database
Mountain Start.mdb	944KB	Microsoft Access Database
Mtn.bmp	51KB	Microsoft Imager 1.0 Picture
mtn.ICO	1KB	Icon
Othrcust.db	4KB	DB File
Petfixed.txt	7KB	Text Document
Pets.xls	12KB	Microsoft Excel 5.0 Worksheet
Petsfox.dbf	9KB	DBF File
Petsfox.fpt	1KB	FPT File
Petsiv.dbf	5KB	DBF File
Petsiv.dbt	1KB	DBT File
Punkin.xls	6KB	Microsoft Excel 5.0 Worksheet
Sale Price.htm	4KB	Microsoft HTML Document 4.0
Table of Contents.hhc	2KB	HHC File
Thanks.dot	30KB	Microsoft Word Template
The Model of the Vehicle.htm	5KB	Microsoft HTML Document 4.0
Treatpdx.db	4KB	DB File
Vehicle Condition.htm	3KB	Microsoft HTML Document 4.0
Vehicle Identification Number.htm	4KB	Microsoft HTML Document 4.0
Vehicle Make.htm	4KB	Microsoft HTML Document 4.0
Vehicle Year.htm	3KB	Microsoft HTML Document 4.0
Vehicle.chm	16KB	Compiled HTML file
vehicle.h	1KB	H File
Vehicle.hhp	1KB	HHP File
VEHICLE.htm	11KB	Microsoft HTML Document 4.0
Visitdtl.dbf	6KB	DBF File
Visitdtl.dbt	1KB	DBT File
Visitdtl.inf	1KB	Setup Information
Visitdtl.ndx	3KB	NDX File

Figure C-2: A list of files included on the CD-ROM.

A Guide to the Expanded Files on the Microsoft Access 2000 Bible CD-ROM

Once you install a file from the CD you may wonder how to use it. Most of the installations will create a Start menu icon for you, while others simply require you to start Microsoft Access 2000 and load the software. The instructions below talk about each directory's files and what to expect when you use them. The best way to learn is to experiment, so don't be afraid to simply install the file on your hard disk and open it — you can always delete it later. This CD holds some very productive tools and demos. All of the vendor's demos have been used by the authors of this book and are all considered worthwhile, or they wouldn't be on the CD. The seven main directories on the CD are described below:

Access 2000 Bible examples

These include all of the files used for the examples as described in Appendixes D and E. Two main example files; Mountain Animal Hospital.mdb and Mountain Animal Hospital Start.mdb, are used for Chapters 1-35. You'll also find many other files, including CHAP36.mdb through CHAP41.mdb and CHAP42.mda, the files used for import and export processing in Chapter 23 named ACTIMPEX.mdb, and many bitmap files

Appendixes D and E provide a cross-reference to each example object, by object name and chapter. Use these appendixes to find the tables, queries, forms, reports, macros, and modules you will use in each chapter. Follow the general instructions to install the examples in the previous few pages.

Access product catalogs

For readers wishing to increase their productivity, we have included the latest catalogs from Database Creations, Inc., the world's largest Microsoft Access and Office mail order Company. The catalogs include both the full 1998 catalog and the 1999 supplement for Microsoft Access and Office as well as a Visual FoxPro and Visual Studio catalog. These catalogs are viewable from the CD using the included Adobe Acrobat viewer. Cary Prague, one of the authors of the Access 2000 Bible, owns this company. Mention the book code BIBCD and receive an additional 10 percent off the prices of any software product in the catalogs. You can also view product updates and new product information at our Web site, www.databasecreations.com, or call us to receive new printed catalogs and product descriptions at (860) 644-5891. E-mail also works well at info@databasecreations.com. The files are in the directory below:

```
Access 2000 Examples - Database Creations\Access Product
Catalogs
```

These files include:

✦ 1998 48 Page Access 97 Product Catalog.pdf

✦ 1999 20 Page Access 2000 Product Catalog.pdf

✦ Visual FoxPro Product Catalog.pdf

Acrobat Reader from Adobe

This free reader from Adobe lets you view and print files stored in Adobe Acrobat .PDF file formats. If you haven't discovered Adobe Acrobat, this is a great opportunity to become a fan. Adobe Acrobat is both a product and a technology. This technology allows someone using virtually any product to create an output file by simply printing it and then allowing anyone else to view the output file without any special software except Adobe Acrobat. You might have had someone e-mail you or send you a .PDF file. This is the output from Adobe Acrobat.

In the future, rather than receive a big catalog in the mail, you might be e-mailed a .PDF file of the catalog. In fact, in the **Access Product Catalogs** directory of the CD, you will find several catalogs with .PDF file extensions. These are also known as Acrobat formats. To view these .PDF files, you must first install the Adobe Acrobat reader. This is a free piece of software available to anyone and is found on your CD in the *Acrobat Reader from Adobe* directory. Double click the installation file and follow the instructions. This file contains just the reader. To create your own .PDF files, you must purchase the full Acrobat program from Adobe.

To run the installation for Adobe Acrobat, run the file **Adobe Acrobat Reader.exe** found on the CD in the directory:

```
Access 2000 Examples - Database Creations\Acrobat Reader from
Adobe
```

Demos

Demonstration databases include locked or timed versions of some of the best commercially available software for Access users. Complete product brochures or reviewer guides in Word or Acrobat format are also included.

To install each of these demos, go to the desired directory and double-click the .EXE file. The instructions will take you through installing the demos. Some of the installations will also create product descriptions in Word 2000 format on your hard drive. Check the CD directories when you are through loading the demos. The vendors and products include:

✦ Database Creations: Yes! I Can Run My Business, EZ Access Developers Suite

✦ PenSoft: PC Payroll

✦ DBI Technologies: Solutions PIM, Solutions Schedule, Components ToolBox

✦ Black Moshannon: Speed Ferret

✦ Visio: Visio Professional

✦ Wise Solutions: Wise Installer (Used to create the CD installs)

EZ Access Developer Suite demo

The EZ Access Developers Suite is a new product specifically designed for Access 2000 and Access 97 developers to help them create great Access applications. The suite consists of eight separate products. Each can be easily integrated into your application to provide new functions in a fraction of the time it would take you to create them yourself. These products are guaranteed to save you hundreds of hours of development time. Think of them as a library of over 100 predesigned, preprogrammed interfaces that you can "legally steal" and use with your application.

Read each of the embedded reviewer's guides in the demo for a complete overview of each product. The entire EZ Access Developer Suite retails for $799.95, and individual products are $199.95. Mention the code, BOOKCD, and purchase the entire suite for just $699.95. View additional samples at www.databasecreations.com.

The eight EZ Access Suite pieces include

✦ EZ Report Manager

✦ EZ Support Manager

✦ EZ Search Manager

✦ EZ Security Manager

✦ EZ File Manager

✦ EZ Extensions

✦ EZ Application Manager

✦ EZ Controls

You can install the EZ Access Developer Suite demo by running:

```
Access 2000 Examples - Database Creations\Demos\EZ Access
Suite\EZ Access Suite Demo.EXE
```

Yes! I Can Run My Business demo

Yes! I Can Run My Business is the most popular accounting software available for Microsoft Access users today. The product is fully customizable and includes all source code. It includes all typical accounting functions, including sales, customers, A/R, purchases, suppliers, A/P, inventory, banking, general ledger, and fixed assets, and features multicompany accounting for any size business. Priced under $1,000 for a LAN version, it is one of the best values for small businesses. For developers, a version is available with royalty-free distribution rights for around $2,000. The full product includes over 1500 pages of professionally written documentation. Yes! I Can Run My Business won the *Microsoft Access Advisor* magazine reader's choice award for best accounting system last year. You can copy the YESICAN.PDF found in the directory referenced below to your hard drive to review the on-line brochure using Adobe Acrobat. The free reader is included on this CD. The entire Yes! I Can Run My Business product retails for $599.95 for the end-user version and just $2,295 for the developer's version. Mention the code, BOOKCD, and purchase the developer version for just $2,095.95. View additional samples at www.databasecreations.com.

You can install the Yes! I Can Run My Business demo by running:

```
Access 2000 Examples - Database Creations\Demos\Yes! I Can
Accounting\Yes4demo.EXE
```

There is also a complete color brochure in Acrobat format you can view from the CD by running:

```
Access 2000 Examples - Database Creations\Demos\Yes! I Can
Accounting\ Yes! I Can Run My Business Brochure.pdf
```

PC-Payroll demo

PC-Payroll from PenSoft is a standalone payroll package for small businesses written in Visual Basic. It interfaces with Yes! I Can Run My Business to provide complete employee, hour, tax, deduction, and benefit processing.

You can install the PC-Payroll demo by running:

```
Access 2000 Examples - Database Creations \Demos\PC-Payroll\PC
Payroll Professional Demo.exe
```

Visio Professional trial run

Visio Professional is an incredible product that lets you diagram anything, including processes or databases. In fact, Access and SQL Server users can diagram a SQL Server or Oracle database and then automatically create a prototype in Access tables. You can also create interactive graphical systems using the embedded VBA. For example, drag-and-drop components of an office (chairs, tables, computers, network cables) into a scale-model floor plan. Visio Professional can be used to cost the floor plan, produce orders to vendors, and even create invoices. The demo includes both a 60-day working version and a complete multimedia guided tour.

You can install the Visio Professional demo by running:

```
Access 2000 Examples - Database Creations\Demos\Visio
Professional Test Drive\Setup.EXE
```

The directory also contains a guided tour:

```
Access 2000 Examples - Database Creations\Demos\Visio
Professional Test Drive\Tour\Setup.EXE
```

Free Access software

The following software extends Access's business uses and provides you with additional productivity tools.

Business Forms Library Sampler

The Access Business Forms Library Sampler is a sample of the Business Forms Library collection of 35 forms and reports. These files contain some innovative techniques that have never been seen elsewhere. The entire library contains tables, forms, reports, and macros for each of the forms and reports. You can integrate them into your own applications, thereby saving you hundreds of hours of work. Microsoft liked these forms so much they distributed this sampler in the Microsoft Access Welcome Kit with Microsoft Access 2.0. These files have been updated for Access 2000 and come with a complete user guide.

You can install the Business Forms Library examples and documentation by running:

```
Access 2000 Examples - Database Creations\Free Access
Software\Business Forms Library Sampler\BusFrm2000.EXE
```

Check Writer 2000 (Microsoft Network Award for Best Access Application)

Check Writer 2000 is a fully functional check writer, including check register and check reconciliation modules. You can pay your bills, print checks, and balance your checkbook by using an incredible Access 2000 application. This application won the Microsoft Network Access product of the year award and is part of the full accounting system, Yes! I Can Run My Business, which won the reader's choice award of *Microsoft Access Advisor* magazine in 1998. A complete user guide is also included in the directory.

You can install the Check Writer 2000 Sampler and documentation by running the file:

```
\Access 2000 Examples - Database Creations\ Free Access
Software\Check Writer (Award Winning)\ Check Writer 2000.exe
```

EZ File Manager Sampler

The EZ File Manager is one of eight products in the new EZ Access Developers Suite. The complete File Utilities tool, which helps you compile, compact, repair, and backup attached data databases, is included along with the entire documentation set from the EZ Access File Manager, to give you a complete overview of the product. To add file management capabilities to your own application, install the sampler and then copy the form and module to your application.

You can install the EZ File Manager Sampler and documentation by running:

```
Access 2000 Examples - Database Creations\ Free Access
Software\EZ File Manager Sampler\EZ File Manager.EXE)
```

EZ Search Manager Sampler

The EZ Search Manager is one of eight products in the new EZ Access Developers Suite. The complete SmartSearch tool is included along with the entire documentation set from the EZ Access Search Manager, to give you a complete overview of the product. Install the sampler and then copy the forms to your own application to add an incredibly flexible search interface to your application.

You can install the EZ Search Manager Sampler and documentation by running:

```
Access 2000 Examples - Database Creations\Free Access
Software\EZ Search Manager Sampler\EZ Search Manager.EXE
```

Cool Combo Box Techniques

This demonstration database includes 25 of the coolest combo and list box techniques. Full documentation is included in the CD directory. This is from a highly acclaimed paper given by Cary Prague at the Microsoft Access conferences.

You can install the Cool Combo Box Techniques examples and paper by running:

```
Access 2000 Examples - Database Creations\Free Access
Software\Cool Combo Box Techniques\ coolcombo.EXE
```

Picture Builder Button Sampler

They can be used on Access 2000 toolbars or on Access 2000 buttons used for switchboards or menus. To use these button faces, simply copy the files onto your hard disk or use the bitmaps as is.

The files named ACTxx.BMP are 32 × 32 pixel .BMPs perfect for Access 2000 command buttons; the files named ACTxx.B24 are 24 × 23 pixel .BMPs perfect for Access 2000 toolbars and any Office-compatible application.

You can install the Picture Builder Button Sampler by running:

```
Access 2000 Examples - Database Creations\ Free Access
Software\ Picture Builder Button Sampler\Picture Builder
Sampler.EXE
```

Other free software

This section includes three programs written by Mike Irwin. These include

+ Calendar: A calendar utility
+ Phone: A phone book utility
+ Wintouch: A utility for updating date/time stamps on files
+ WinZip95: This directory contains WinZip95, a freeware program for compressing data files up to 90 percent — great for making large Access files fit on a floppy disk or for sending e-mail attachments.

Using the Check Writer 2000 database

When the Check Writer starts, just follow the instructions on the screen.

The main Check Writer switchboard contains four basic functions:

+ Check Writer/Register: Add, change, delete, or print checks, deposits, and adjustments, or display the check register.
+ Check Reconciliation: Display the check reconciliation system.
+ Bank Accounts: Add, change, or delete bank account information.
+ Setup: Enter your company information, recurring payees, and default bank account number.

The Check Writer comes with two sample bank accounts and a selection of transactions to get you started. You can practice with those, and then create your own accounts.

You start by creating your own bank account (Bank Accounts icon), and then make that bank account the default bank account (Setup icon). Once you have done that, you can open up the Check Writer and enter transactions.

Use the buttons at the bottom of the form to navigate from record to record or between functions. Click the Register icon to display the check register. In the register, click the Check icon to return to the check writer form to enter or edit checks.

You can change the account being viewed at any time using the combo box at the top of the Check Writer form. You can only change the transaction type for new checks, and you can choose between checks, deposits, and a number of adjustments that you can add to by using the Setup icon.

You can enter the payee for a check or select from the combo box in the payee line of the check. You can add more recurring payees in the Setup screen.

When you mark a check as void, a void stamp will appear on the check and it will not be counted in the check register or check reconciliation.

The area below the check is the voucher stub, and anything you enter is printed when you select certain types of checks.

Press the Find button to display a dialog box showing five ways to find a check, deposit, or adjustment.

Press the Print button to display a dialog box enabling you to print the current check/deposit/adjustment, marked checks, a range of checks by date, or a range of checks by check number. You can modify the reports that print the checks for custom paper.

The Check Writer is normally $179.95. Mention this book and you can buy the full product for only $99.95. To order this product call Database Creations at (860) 644-5891, fax us at (860) 648-0710, or e-mail us at info@databasecreations.com You can also look for our newest products at www.databasecreations.com. If you want to trade up to the full Yes! I Can Run My Business accounting product, we will take up to $200 off the retail product price for the Royalty Free Developers Edition.

Specials from Database Creations, Inc.

You can purchase our fully customizable business accounting product, Yes! I Can Run My Business, at $50 to $200 off of our regular prices:

✦ Single User Edition: $495.95, only $449.95

✦ Unlimited Multiuser: $599.95, only $499.95

✦ Royalty Free Developer: $2,299.95, only $2,095.95

You can purchase our complete EZ Access Developer Suite for $100 off of our regular prices:

✦ Complete EZ Access Developer Suite: $799.95, only $699.95

Contacting Database Creations and the Authors

If you think you have found an example that doesn't work or you have a suggestion, please let us know by e-mail or by visiting our Web site and using the contact information. We get back to our readers who ask questions about the book. While we will answer questions about the material in the Access Bible by e-mail, we are unable to take phone calls from readers other than in the normal course of our consulting and mail-order business. Although there are only 2 of us and 20 people in our company, and there are 300,000 readers of the Access Bible series, Cary Prague or Mike Irwin are very good about responding to e-mails.

All of the products in this book are available from:

✦ Database Creations, Inc.
475 Buckland Rd.
S. Windsor, CT 06074
(860) 648-0710 (24-hour fax)

✦ Sales Web Site: www.databasecreations.com

✦ Access 2000 Bible support Web site:
www.databasecreations.com/access2000bible

✦ Company e-mail: info@databasecreations.com

✦ Cary Prague personal e-mail: dbcreate@aol.com

✦ Mike Irwin personal e-mail: mirwinreg@usa.net

✦   ✦   ✦

Example CD Object Cross-Reference Guide

You will find all objects in Mountain Animal Hospital.mdb. The tables are also located in Mountain Animal Start.mdb.

Tables	
Database Object	*Chapters*
Animals	5, 11, 18
Animations	40
Customer	5, 9-11, 13, 14, 16, 18, 22, 24-28, 31, 32, 33
Customers	36, 40
Medications	5, 11, 22, 26, 27
Pets	4-9, 11, 13-16, 18, 19, 22, 24-27, 31, 33
States	5, 11, 22, 26
tblAccount	39
tblCustomerInfo	36
tblInvoiceInfo	36
Treatments	5, 11, 22, 26, 27
Visit Details	5, 11, 22, 25, 27
Visits	5, 10, 11, 13, 14, 19, 22, 23-25, 27

Queries

Database Object	Chapters
Adding General Pet Visit Info	31
Customer Names	None
Customer Number Lookup	18
Daily Hospital Report	10
Data for Subform Example	27
Database Diagram	11, 13
Hospital Report 8/4/98	10
List Box Examples	15
Mail Merge Report	28
Make: Customer-Pets-Visit	25
Medications Lookup	26, 27
Monthly Invoice Report	10, 22
Monthly Invoice Report -Test Data	22
Pet Lookup	26
Pets and Owners	16, 20
Pets Report	31
Pets, Owners, & Visits	None
Total Amount for Graph	19
Treatment Lookup	26, 27

Forms

Database Object	Chapters
AboutBox	39
Add a Customer and Pets	27
Adding General Pet Visit Info	31
Adding Visit Details	8, 31, 35
Adding Visit Details and Updating Customer	8, 31, 35
Adding Visit Details Updating with DAO	35
Adding Visits for New Pets	35

Database Object	Chapters
Animals	8
Button Wizard VBA Samples	34
Buttons	39
CollectPartialFilter	41
Cust_Pet_Visit	30
Cust_Pet_Visit – Datasheet 2	25
Customer	5, 30, 31
Customer Print Dialog	35
Customer Search Dialog	35
Customer with filter buttons	30
Customer with filter buttons and find button	30
Customers	40
Data for Subform Example	27
FrmReplicationLab	41
FrmSwitchBoard	36, 37
Main Form NO Macros	30
Mountain Switchboard	31-32
Mountain Switchboard – No Buttons	31
Mountain Switchboard – Orig	None
Mountain Switchboard – Picture Buttons	None
Mountain Switchboard Orig - No Buttons	None
Mountain Switchboard Orig – Picture Buttons	None
Multiple Reports Print Dialog	None
OfficeAssistant	40
Orders	40
Percentage Revenue Graph	None
Pet Display Form	30
Pet Picture Creation – Empty	19, 30
Pet Vaccinations List Box Example	None

Continued

Forms *(continued)*

Database Object	Chapters
Pets	4, 5, 8, 19
Pets – Datasheet	7
Pets Data Entry Form	5, 16, 17
Pets Data Entry Form – Without Formatting	16, 17, 18
Pets Data Entry Form With Formatting	16, 17, 18
Pets Data Entry Form With Validation	18
Pets Data Entry With Validation	None
Pets Data Entry Without Validation	18
Pets Original	8
Pets Subform	27
Pets Tabular Example	8
Pets Tabular Form	8, 16
Picture Size Mode Options	19
Pivot Table Example	19
Print Reports Dialog	31
Print Reports Tabbed Dialog	31
Scanned Form	None
Second Form	30
Special Effects Examples	17
SplashScreen	39
Styles	39
Third Form	30
VehicleListings	38
Visit Income History	19
Visit Income History - Without Graph	19

Reports

Database Objects	Chapters
All Customers and Pets	31
Customer Envelope	None

Database Objects	Chapters
Customer Mailing Labels	10, 28
Customer Mailing Labels Original	10, 28
Customer Sale Letter	28
Customers By State (3 Snaking Columns)	28, 32
Daily Hospital Report	10, 20, 31
Daily Hospital Report Original	10
Invoices	22
Mail Merge Report	28
Monthly Invoice Report	5, 22
Monthly Invoice Report – No Cover	22
Monthly Invoice Report – Percentages	22
Monthly Invoice Report – Running Sum	22
Pet Directory	31
Pets and Owners	5, 20, 21
Pets and Owners – Unformatted	20
Sub Report – Complete	None
Sub Report – Top Half	None

Macros

Database Objects	Chapters
AutoKeys	30
ConfirmDelete	30
FindRecord	30
LeaveMsg	None
Menu Builder	None
Menu Builder_File	None
Menu Builder_Forms	None
Menu Builder_Reports	None
Mountain Custom Menu Bar	31

Continued

Macros *(continued)*

Database Objects	Chapters
Mountain File Menu	None
Mountain Forms Menu	None
Mountain Reports Menu	None
Mountain Switchboard	31
Open and Close Forms	28
OpenCust	30, 31
Print Reports	32, 34, 35
PrtLine	30
RequiredEntry	None
Shortcut Menu	31
Shortcut Menu_Shortcut Menu Bar	31
StateFilter	30
Update Form	35
Uppercase	30

Modules

Database Object	Chapters
BeepIt	35
Calendar	35
Converted Macro – Print Reports	35
General Functions	35
IsFocus	None
mdlPerformance	36
mdlSecurity	37
WordIntegration	40

External Files

Database Object	Chapters
CAT.BMP	19
CH16.MDA	41
COFFIN.BMP	18
EXIT.BMP	31
IMEXPORT.MDB	23
MEDLIMIT.TXT	23
MORECUST.XLS	23
MOTORVEHICLES.TXT	38
MTN.BMP	19, 21, 22
OTHERCUST.DB	23
PETFIXED.TXT	23
PETS.XLS	None
PETSFOX.DBF	23
PETSFOX.FPT	23
PETSIV.DBT	23
PUNKIN.XLS	19
THANKS.DOC	40
TOC.DOC	38
TREATPDX.DB	23
VEHICLES.HPJ	38
VEHICLES.TXT	38
VISITDTL.DBF	23
VISITDTL.DBT	23
VISITDTL.INF	23
VISITDTL.NDX	23

✦　　✦　　✦

Chapter Cross-Reference Guide

You will find all objects in Mountain Animal Hospital. mdb. The tables are also located in Mountain Animal Start.mdb.

Part I: First Things First		
Chapter	**Database**	**Objects**
1: What Is Access 2000?	None	
2: Installing and Starting Access 2000	None	
3: A Review of Database Concepts	None	
4: A Hands-On Tour of Access 2000	Hospital	**Tables:** Pets. **Forms:** Pets. Reports: Pets Directory.
5: A Case Study in Database Design	Hospital	**Tables:** Customer, Visits, Visit Details, States, Animals, Treatments, Medications. **Forms:** Customer, Pets, Mountain Switchboard. **Reports:** Pets and Owners, Monthly Invoice Report.

Part II:
Basic Database Usage

Chapter	Database	Objects
6: Creating Database Tables	Hospital	**Tables:** Pets.
7: Entering, Changing, Deleting, and Displaying Data	Hospital	**Tables:** Pets. **Forms:** Pets Datasheet
8: Creating and Using Simple Data-Entry Forms	Hospital	**Tables:** Pets **Forms:** Adding Visit Details, Adding Visit Details and Updating Customer, Animals, Pets Original, Pets Tabular Example, Pets Tabular Form.
9: Understanding and Using Simple Queries	Hospital	**Tables:** Customer, Pets.
10: Creating and Printing Simple Reports	Hospital	**Tables:** Customers, Visits. **Queries:** Daily Hospital Report, Hospital Report 7/7/95, Monthly Invoice Report. **Reports:** Customer Mailing Labels, Customer Mailing Labels Original, Daily Hospital Report, Daily Hospital Report Original.
11: Setting Relationships Between Tables	Hospital, Start	**Tables:** Animals, Customer, Medications, Pets, States, Treatments, Visit Details, Visits. **Queries:** Database Diagram.

Part III:
Using Access in Your Work

Chapter	Database	Objects
12: Using Operators, Functions, and Expressions	None	
13: Creating Relations and Joins in Queries	Hospital	**Tables:** Customer, Pets, Visits. **Queries:** Database Diagram.
14: Creating Select Queries	Hospital	**Tables:** Customer, Pets, Visits.
15: Understanding Controls and Properties	Hospital, Start	**Tables:** Pets. **Queries:** List Box Examples.

Chapter	Database	Objects
16: Creating and Customizing Data-Entry Forms	Start	**Tables:** Customer, Pets. **Queries:** Pets and Owners. **Forms:** Pets Data Entry Form, Pets Data Entry Form – Without Formatting, Pets Data Entry with Formatting, Pets Tabular Form.
17: Creating Great-Looking Forms	Start	**Forms:** Pets Data Entry Form, Pets Data Entry Form – Without Formatting, Pets Data Entry Form with Formatting, Special Effects Examples.
18: Adding Data-Validation Controls to Forms	Hospital, Start	**Tables:** Animals, Customer, Pets. **Queries:** Customer Number Lookup. **Forms:** Pets Data Entry Form – Without Formatting, Pets Data Entry Form with Formatting, Pets Data Entry Form With Validation. **External Files:** COFFIN.BMP
19: Using OLE Objects	Hospital	**Tables:** Pets, Visits. **Queries:** Total Amount for Graph. **Forms:** Pets, Pet Picture Creation – Empty, Picture Size Mode Options, Pivot Table Examples, Visit Income History, Visit Income History – Without Graph. **External Files:** CAT.BMP, PUNKIN.XLS
20: Creating and Customizing Reports	Hospital	**Queries:** Pets and Owners **Reports:** Pets and Owners, Pets and Owners - Unformatted
21: Database Publishing and Printing	Hospital	**Reports:** Pets and Owners. **External Files:** MTN.BMP
22: Creating Calculations and Summaries in Reports	Hospital	**Tables:** Customer, Medications, Pets, States, Treatments, Visit Details, Visits. **Queries:** Monthly Invoice Report, Monthly Invoice Report – Test Data. **Reports:** Invoices, Monthly Invoice Report, Monthly Invoice Report – No Cover, Monthly Invoice Report – Percentages, Monthly Invoice Report – Running Sum. **External Files:** MTN.BMP.

Part IV:
Advanced Database Features

Chapter	Database	Objects
23: Working with External Data	Hospital	**Tables:** Visits. **External Files:** IMEXPORT.MDB, MEDLIMIT.TXT, MORECUST.XLS, OTHERCUST.DB, PETFIXED.TXT, PETSFOX.DBF, PETSFOX.FPT, PETSIV.DBT, TREATPDX.DB, VISITDTL.DBF, VISITDTL.DBT, VISITDTL.INF, VISITDTL.NDX.
24: Advanced Select Queries	Hospital	**Tables:** Customer, Pets, Visits.
25: Creating Action Queries	Hospital	**Tables:** Customer, Pets, Visit Details, Visits. **Queries:** Make: Customer-Pets-Visit. Forms: Cust_Pet_Visit – Datasheet 2
26: Advanced Query Topics	Hospital	**Tables:** Customer, Pets, States, Treatments, Visits. **Queries:** Medications Lookup, Pet Lookup, Treatment Lookup.
27: Creating and Using Subforms	Hospital	**Tables:** Customer, Medications, Pets, Treatments, Visit Details, Visits. **Queries:** Data for Subform Example, Medications Lookup, Treatment Lookup. **Forms:** Add a Customer and Pets, Data for Subform Example, Pets Subform.
28: Creating Mailing Labels and Mail Merge Reports	Hospital	**Tables:** Customers. **Reports:** Customer Mailing Labels, Customer Mailing Labels Original, Customer Sale Letter, Customers By State(3 Snaking Columns), Mail Merge Report. **Macros:** Open and Close Forms.

Part V:
Applications in Access

Chapter	Database	Objects
29: An Introduction to Macros and Events	Hospital	None.
30: Using Macros in Forms and Reports	Hospital	**Forms:** Cust_Pet_Visit, Customer, Customer with filter buttons, Customer with filter buttons and find button, Main Form NO Macros, Pet Display Form, Pet Picture Creation – Empty, Second Form, Third Form. **Macros:** AutoKeys, ConfirmDelete, FindRecord, OpenCust, PrtLine, StateFilter, uppercase.

Chapter	Database	Objects
31: Creating Switchboards, Command Bars, Menus, Toolbars, and Dialog Boxes	Hospital	**Tables:** Customer, Pets. **Queries:** Adding General Pet Visit Info, Pets Report. **Forms:** Adding General Pet Visit Info, Adding Visit Details, Adding Visit Details and Updating Customer, Customer, Mountain Switchboard, Mountain Switchboard – No Buttons, Print Reports Dialog, Print Reports Tabbed Dialog. Reports: All Customers and Pets, Daily Hospital Report, Pet Directory. **Macros:** Mountain Custom Menu Bar, Mountain Switchboard, OpenCust, Shortcut Menu, Shortcut Menu_Shortcut Menu Bar.
32: Using Data Access Pages, Intranets and the Internet	Hospital	**Tables:** Customer Report: Customers by State (3 Snaking Columns)
33: Using the Microsoft Database Engine and SQL Server		**Tables:** Pets, Customer
34: Introduction to Applications with VBA	Hospital	**Forms:** Button Wizard VBA Samples. **Macros:** Print Reports.
35: The Access 2000 Programming Environment	Hospital	**Forms:** Adding Visit Details, Adding Visit Details and Updating Customer, Adding Visit for New Pets, Customer Print Dialog, Customer Search Dialog. **Macros:** Print Reports, Update Form. Modules: BeepIt, Calendar, Converted Macro – Print Reports, General Functions.

Part VI:
Advanced Access Topics

Chapter	Database	Objects
36. Optimizing Performance	CH36	**Tables:** tblCustomerInfo, Customers, tblInvoiceInfo **Forms:** frmSwitchBoard Modules: mdlPerformance
37. Securing an Access Application	CH37	**Forms:** frmSwitchBoard Modules: mdlSecurity

Continued

Part VI *(continued)*		
Chapter	*Database*	*Objects*
38. Creating Help Systems in Access 2000	CH38	**Forms:** VehicleListings External Files: TOC.DCO, VEHICL^.TXT, VEHICL^2.TXT, MOTORV^1.TXT, VEHICL^1.HPJ, VI.HLP
39. Using the Microsoft Office Developer	CH39	**Tables:** tblAccount **Forms:** Styles, SplashScreen, AboutBox, Buttons
40. Integrating with Microsoft Office 2000	CH40	**Tables:** Animations **Queries:** AnimationsSorted **Forms:** Customers, Orders, OfficeAssistant **Modules:** WordIntegration **External Files:** THANKS.DOC
41. Exploring Replication	CH41	**Forms:** frmReplicationLab, CollectPartialFilter
42. Exploring Add-Ins and Libraries	CH42	**External File:** CH16.MDA

Chapters 1–35: All objects are in (Hospital) `Mountain Animal Hospital.MDB`.

Tables are also in (Start) `Mountain Animal Start`.

Chapters 36–42: All objects are in `CHxx.MDB` (where xx is the chapter number — for example, CH36.MDB)

✦   ✦   ✦

Index

SYMBOLS

A

Continued

Continued

Continued

Continued

Continued

Continued

Continued

Continued

Continued

Continued

Continued

P

Continued

Continued

Continued

Continued

IDG Books Worldwide, Inc. End-User License Agreement

<u>READ THIS.</u> You should carefully read these terms and conditions before opening the software packet(s) included with this book ("Book"). This is a license agreement ("Agreement") between you and IDG Books Worldwide, Inc. ("IDGB"). By opening the accompanying software packet(s), you acknowledge that you have read and accept the following terms and conditions. If you do not agree and do not want to be bound by such terms and conditions, promptly return the Book and the unopened software packet(s) to the place you obtained them for a full refund.

1.<u>License Grant.</u> IDGB grants to you (either an individual or entity) a nonexclusive license to use one copy of the enclosed software program(s) (collectively, the "Software") solely for your own personal or business purposes on a single computer (whether a standard computer or a workstation component of a multiuser network). The Software is in use on a computer when it is loaded into temporary memory (RAM) or installed into permanent memory (hard disk, CD-ROM, or other storage device). IDGB reserves all rights not expressly granted herein.

2.<u>Ownership.</u> IDGB is the owner of all right, title, and interest, including copyright, in and to the compilation of the Software recorded on the disk(s) or CD-ROM ("Software Media"). Copyright to the individual programs recorded on the Software Media is owned by the author or other authorized copyright owner of each program. Ownership of the Software and all proprietary rights relating thereto remain with IDGB and its licensers.

3.<u>Restrictions On Use and Transfer.</u>

(a) You may only (i) make one copy of the Software for backup or archival purposes, or (ii) transfer the Software to a single hard disk, provided that you keep the original for backup or archival purposes. You may not (i) rent or lease the Software, (ii) copy or reproduce the Software through a LAN or other network system or through any computer subscriber system or bulletin-board system, or (iii) modify, adapt, or create derivative works based on the Software.

(b) You may not reverse engineer, decompile, or disassemble the Software. You may transfer the Software and user documentation on a permanent basis, provided that the transferee agrees to accept the terms and conditions of this Agreement and you retain no copies. If the Software is an update or has been updated, any transfer must include the most recent update and all prior versions.

4.<u>Restrictions on Use of Individual Programs.</u> You must follow the individual requirements and restrictions detailed for each individual program in Appendix C of this Book. These limitations are also contained in the individual license agreements recorded on the Software Media. These limitations may include a requirement that after using the program for a specified period of time, the user must pay a registration fee or discontinue use. By opening the Software packet(s), you will be agreeing to abide by the licenses and restrictions for these individual programs that are detailed in Appendix C and on the Software Media. None of the material on this Software Media or listed in this Book may ever be redistributed, in original or modified form, for commercial purposes.

5.Limited Warranty.

(a) IDGB warrants that the Software and Software Media are free from defects in materials and workmanship under normal use for a period of sixty (60) days from the date of purchase of this Book. If IDGB receives notification within the warranty period of defects in materials or workmanship, IDGB will replace the defective Software Media.

(b) **IDGB AND THE AUTHORS OF THE BOOK DISCLAIM ALL OTHER WARRANTIES, EXPRESS OR IMPLIED, INCLUDING WITHOUT LIMITATION IMPLIED WARRANTIES OF MERCHANTABILITY AND FITNESS FOR A PARTICULAR PURPOSE, WITH RESPECT TO THE SOFTWARE, THE PROGRAMS, THE SOURCE CODE CONTAINED THEREIN, AND/OR THE TECHNIQUES DESCRIBED IN THIS BOOK. IDGB DOES NOT WARRANT THAT THE FUNCTIONS CONTAINED IN THE SOFTWARE WILL MEET YOUR REQUIREMENTS OR THAT THE OPERATION OF THE SOFTWARE WILL BE ERROR FREE.**

(c) This limited warranty gives you specific legal rights, and you may have other rights that vary from jurisdiction to jurisdiction.

6.Remedies.

(a) IDGB's entire liability and your exclusive remedy for defects in materials and workmanship shall be limited to replacement of the Software Media, which may be returned to IDGB with a copy of your receipt at the following address: Software Media Fulfillment Department, Attn.: *Microsoft Access 2000 Bible, Gold Edition*, IDG Books Worldwide, Inc., 7260 Shadeland Station, Ste. 100, Indianapolis, IN 46256, or call 1-800-762-2974. Please allow three to four weeks for delivery. This Limited Warranty is void if failure of the Software Media has resulted from accident, abuse, or misapplication. Any replacement Software Media will be warranted for the remainder of the original warranty period or thirty (30) days, whichever is longer.

(b) In no event shall IDGB or the authors be liable for any damages whatsoever (including without limitation damages for loss of business profits, business interruption, loss of business information, or any other pecuniary loss) arising from the use of or inability to use the Book or the Software, even if IDGB has been advised of the possibility of such damages.

(c) Because some jurisdictions do not allow the exclusion or limitation of liability for consequential or incidental damages, the above limitation or exclusion may not apply to you.

7. U.S. Government Restricted Rights. Use, duplication, or disclosure of the Software by the U.S. Government is subject to restrictions stated in paragraph (c)(1)(ii) of the Rights in Technical Data and Computer Software clause of DFARS 252.227-7013, and in subparagraphs (a) through (d) of the Commercial Computer — Restricted Rights clause at FAR 52.227-19, and in similar clauses in the NASA FAR supplement, when applicable.

8.General. This Agreement constitutes the entire understanding of the parties and revokes and supersedes all prior agreements, oral or written, between them and may not be modified or amended except in a writing signed by both parties hereto that specifically refers to this Agreement. This Agreement shall take precedence over any other documents that may be in conflict herewith. If any one or more provisions contained in this Agreement are held by any court or tribunal to be invalid, illegal, or otherwise unenforceable, each and every other provision shall remain in full force and effect.

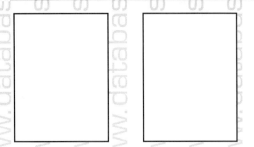

my2cents.idgbooks.com

Register This Book — And Win!

Visit **http://my2cents.idgbooks.com** to register this book and we'll automatically enter you in our fantastic monthly prize giveaway. It's also your opportunity to give us feedback: let us know what you thought of this book and how you would like to see other topics covered.

Discover IDG Books Online!

The IDG Books Online Web site is your online resource for tackling technology — at home and at the office. Frequently updated, the IDG Books Online Web site features exclusive software, insider information, online books, and live events!

10 Productive & Career-Enhancing Things You Can Do at www.idgbooks.com

- Nab source code for your own programming projects.

- Download software.

- Read Web exclusives: special articles and book excerpts by IDG Books Worldwide authors.

- Take advantage of resources to help you advance your career as a Novell or Microsoft professional.

- Buy IDG Books Worldwide titles or find a convenient bookstore that carries them.

- Register your book and win a prize.

- Chat live online with authors.

- Sign up for regular e-mail updates about our latest books.

- Suggest a book you'd like to read or write.

- Give us your 2¢ about our books and about our Web site.

You say you're not on the Web yet? It's easy to get started with IDG Books' *Discover the Internet,* available at local retailers everywhere.

CD-ROM Installation Instructions

The *Microsoft Access 2000 Bible, Gold Edition* CD-ROM contains 2 CD-ROMs. The first CD-ROM contains examples, templates, and code from the book, as well as free software and demo versions of popular Access utilities. The second CD-ROM contains a fully functional 90-day trial version of SQL Server 7.

Most of the directories or subdirectories contain installation files with a .EXE file extension. You can simply display the directories and files using your Windows Explorer and then double-click on any .EXE file to launch the install program for the file you want to copy to your hard drive. Each installation file will ask if you want a Start menu shortcut created for you.

Please read Appendix C for a complete guide to installing and using the CD-ROM.

Microsoft Product Warranty and Support Disclaimer

The Microsoft program on the CD-ROM was reproduced by IDG Books Worldwide, Inc. under a special arrangement with Microsoft Corporation. For this reason, IDG Books Worldwide, Inc. is responsible for the product warranty and for support. If your CD-ROM is defective, please return it to IDG Books Worldwide, Inc. which will arrange for its replacement. PLEASE DO NOT RETURN IT TO MICROSOFT CORPORATION. Any product support will be provided, if at all, by IDG Books Worldwide, Inc. PLEASE DO NOT CONTACT MICROSOFT CORPORATION FOR PRODUCT SUPPORT. End users of this Microsoft program shall not be considered "registered owners" of a Microsoft product and therefore shall not be eligible for upgrades, promotions, or other benefits available to "registered owners" of Microsoft products.